Check out these additional learning tools from SAGE Publications!

SPSS and **Excel** data sets for this textbook are found at: http://www.sagepub.com/smith. Ask your instructor how to use these data sets in your course.

Your purchase of **Fundamentals of Marketing Research** includes a free six-month subscription to **SurveyZ!**, an online survey tool that is widely used by marketing professionals. **SurveyZ!** will help you design, execute, and analyze online surveys in your marketing research course.

To activate your prepaid account:

1. Launch your Web browser and go to: http://www.surveyz.com
2. Click *New User Registration*.
3. Follow the instructions on the screen to register yourself as a new user. Your passkey for SurveyZ.com is:

   VKPQGCKOJANGEMNP

4. During registration, you will choose a personal Login Name and Password that you'll use thereafter to log in to your account.

Once your personal Login Name and Password are confirmed, you can begin building your own online surveys.

Helpful information about building online surveys is found at:
   http://www.surveyz.com/help
   http://www.surveyz.com/tutorial

Contact support@surveyz.com for assistance with your online account.

Note to Student:
If you did not purchase a new textbook, this passkey may not be valid!

To purchase a stand-alone student subscription, please visit: www.surveyz.com or call (801) 374-6682.

Important Information:
- The passkey code can only be used once to establish a subscription.
- The subscription is not transferable.
- Your account is valid for six months from the date of activation.

Fundamentals of Marketing Research

Fundamentals of Marketing Research

Scott M. Smith
Brigham Young University

Gerald S. Albaum
University of New Mexico

SAGE Publications
Thousand Oaks ■ London ■ New Delhi

For information:

Sage Publications, Inc.
2455 Teller Road
Thousand Oaks, California 91320
E-mail: order@sagepub.com

Sage Publications Ltd.
1 Oliver's Yard
55 City Road
London EC1Y 1SP
United Kingdom

Sage Publications India Pvt. Ltd.
B-42, Panchsheel Enclave
Post Box 4109
New Delhi 110 017 India

Printed in the United States of America

Library of Congress Cataloging-in-Publication Data

Albaum, Gerald S. Albaum
Fundamentals of marketing research / Gerald S. Albaum, Scott M. Smith.
    p. cm.
Includes bibliographical references and index.
ISBN 0-7619-8852-1 (cloth: acid-free paper)
   1. Marketing research. I. Albaum, Gerald S. II. Title.
HF5415.2.S567 2005
658.8′3—dc22   2004009992

This book is printed on acid-free paper.

04   05   06   07   10 9 8 7 6 5 4 3 2 1

Acquisitions Editor:	Al Bruckner
Editorial Assistant:	MaryAnn Vail
Production Editor:	Diane S. Foster
Copy Editor:	Publication Services
Typesetter:	C&M Digitals (P) Ltd.
Proofreader:	Libby Larson & Publication Services
Indexer:	Will Ragsdale
Cover Designer:	Michelle Lee Kenny
Graphics Designer:	Janet Fougler

CONTENTS

PREFACE

This book draws its "parentage" from the classic *Research for Marketing Decisions* by Paul E. Green, Donald S. Tull, and Gerald Albaum. But, it is not a revision of that book. Rather, it might best be viewed as a "child" that is targeted to a different audience—primarily senior-level undergraduates, but also MBA students.

Any field subject to systematic inquiry can be characterized by: (a) *content*—what the researcher attempts to study; (b) *method*—the conceptual basis or strategy of inquiry; and (c) *techniques*—the procedures or tactics by which the strategy is implemented. The motivation for this book has arisen from our belief that marketing research is at a stage of development where traditional methods and techniques require synthesis and extension.

We believe this book is "novel" in at least three major respects. First, with respect to *method,* the unifying concept of this book is that marketing research is a cost-incurring activity whose output is information of potential value to managers in making decisions. Second, with respect to *techniques,* this book again departs from tradition in terms of the relatively large coverage of more sophisticated, yet relatively easily implemented, research techniques. We hope that discussion of these techniques—which are at most given limited description in many current marketing research texts—will help close the gap between textbook coverage and the content of professional journals devoted to the advancement of research technique in marketing. For example, there is an entire chapter devoted to online marketing research, and a link is provided to a major Internet survey provider, SurveyZ.com (a division of Qualtrics, Inc.), so that students can design, plan, and implement an online survey of their own at no charge.

Finally, with respect to *analysis,* the book is expansive in its coverage, including relative emphasis on modern analytical tools such as multivariate analysis. In terms of number of chapters, 30 percent of the book is devoted to analysis, but the discussion is at a level that senior-level undergraduates can understand, and the techniques are explained within the context of computer-based analysis using the SPSS package as the primary analysis package.

This book is concerned with *fundamentals* of research. This means that all the basic elements of method, techniques, and analysis are covered, including those at a more sophisticated level. But, the book is *not* a book of only essentials. The methodological scope regarding research design, data collection techniques, and measurement is broad. For example, three chapters are devoted to the critical area of measurement and scaling. The book presents its material from primarily a pragmatic and user-oriented (rather than theoretical research technician) perspective. User-orientation is based on the premise that users need to know method in order to evaluate research presented to them.

At the end of each chapter there are a number of questions for discussion and problems for solution. Cases are placed at the end of each of the major parts of the book. A total of 28 cases are included, with additional cases and data sets available in the Instructor's material. Although each case is designed for use with the material in the preceding part, a case may draw upon the discussions from earlier parts.

Part I of the book is concerned primarily with answering the broad question of what marketing research is. The nature of marketing decision making and who does marketing research are discussed. The nature of the research process, planning for research, and research design are covered in some depth. A major concern in research design is handling potential errors that can arise in conducting a research project.

Part II is directed toward implementation of the research design through collection of data. The various sources of data and techniques for collecting data including secondary sources, respondents, experimentation, qualitative research, and observation are discussed thoroughly. Survey methodologies (mail, telephone, personal interview, and online) and experimental designs are discussed.

Part III deals with measurement and development of questionnaires. These are the instruments by which data are collected and recorded. Of concern at all times is that measurement be reliable and valid.

Part IV discusses in two chapters the sampling of items (people, things, organizations, etc.) from whom information is to be obtained about a larger population of which the sample is representative. Procedures for selecting samples are discussed, as are methods of determining just how large—or small—a sample needs to be in order to provide reliable data.

Part V is concerned with the analysis of the data obtained in a research project. The more widely used, and better-known, techniques of cross-tabulation, chi-square, regression, and the analysis of variance are covered. Also discussed are the more advanced techniques of data analysis—discriminant analysis, factor analysis, cluster analysis, multidimensional scaling techniques, and conjoint analysis. Each procedure is described conceptually, and examples of applications are given. This material is presented at as simple a level as possible consistent with the reader being able to comprehend a higher technical level when it exists.

Part VI consists of a single chapter devoted to the reporting of research results.

There is a Glossary of Terms and an appendix that includes some widely used statistical tables for analysis. These tables will be useful for analyzing appropriate cases.

Many people helped shape the content and style of this book. First, Professors Paul E. Green and the late Donald S. Tull have had a profound influence on the authors' thinking about research, and their book with one of the present authors provided a platform from which the present book was launched.

Our editor at Sage Publications, Al Bruckner, and his assistant, Mary Ann Vail, deserve our appreciation for their encouragement, support, and patience while the manuscript was being prepared. Diane Foster and other production and marketing staff members at Sage cooperated in many ways.

To all these people we are very grateful, and wish to give our thanks.

—Gerald Albaum

—Scott M. Smith

Part I

WHAT IS MARKETING RESEARCH?

Chapter 1

THE NATURE OF MARKETING RESEARCH

Marketing is a restless, changing, and dynamic business activity. The role of marketing itself has changed dramatically due to various crises—material and energy shortages, inflation, economic recessions, high unemployment, dying industries, dying companies, terrorism and war, and effects due to rapid technological changes in certain industries. Such changes (including the Internet) have forced today's marketing executive to assume a wider range of more complex decision-making responsibilities. Companies are becoming more market-driven in their strategic decision-making, requiring a formalized means of acquiring accurate and timely information about the marketplace and the overall environment. The means to help them do this is marketing research.

But, according to Karole Friemann (2003), Director of Products and Services for the marketing services company Market Research Project Management, Inc., a marketing research project will be effective only if the information it provides leads to better business actions, decisions, products, or strategies. In order for this to occur, researchers need to understand the underlying business issues at stake and adjust the information collected and how such information is analyzed. Researchers, therefore, need to spend more time discussing the decisions that need to be made and the results that will help in making them before designing and conducting a study. In effect, this amounts to what has been called "getting a seat at the decision-making table" (James, 2002, p. 1).

In this chapter we describe the nature of marketing research and its relation to decision making. Emphasis is placed on the general problem of rational decision making under conditions of uncertainty and on the informational needs of the marketing executive. We introduce the concept of the value of information in reducing the costs of uncertainty associated with managerial decision making.

In the first section we deal with the nature and content of marketing research. We then examine the characteristics of marketing management from the standpoints of the components of decisions and the generic types of decisions that have to be made. Problem-situation models are introduced and the meaning of the term *information* is examined.

Final topics covered are the role of marketing research in what has come to be known as a marketing information system (MIS) and database mining, the nature of the manager-researcher dialogue, marketing research organizations, and ethical issues in marketing research.

WHAT IS MARKETING RESEARCH?

Definition

Research in general connotes a systematic and objective investigation of a subject or problem in order to discover relevant information or principles. It can be considered to be either primarily fundamental or applied in nature.

Fundamental research, frequently called *basic* or *pure research,* seeks to extend the boundaries of knowledge in a given area with no necessary immediate application to existing problems, for example, the development of a research method that would be able to predict what people will be like *x* years in the future. In contrast, *applied research,* also known as *decisional research,* attempts to use existing knowledge to aid in the solution of some given problem or set of problems. Applied research is solution-oriented, and the quality of the solution will be proportional to the quality of the research process (Cary, 1998). To illustrate, an appliance manufacturer might use applied research to predict consumers' lifestyles five years in the future, so that the planning and development cycle for new products can begin.

Marketing research attempts to provide information to allow executives to make decisions to solve marketing problems. For the purposes of this book, therefore, the following definition is a useful one: *Marketing research is the systematic and objective search for, and analysis of, information relevant to the identification and solution of any problem in the field of marketing.*

There are several important points within this definition. First, marketing research is a systematic search for, and analysis of, information. Careful planning throughout all stages of the research is a necessity. Researchers must start with a clear and concise statement of the problem to be researched. Good research practice requires that the information sought, the methods used to collect the information, and the techniques employed to analyze the information be systematically and carefully laid out in advance. Exhibit 1.1 illustrates the importance of the initiation phase of a research project.

EXHIBIT 1.1   Starting a Project

The support given by the client (user, manager, etc.) of a marketing research project will have a major impact on how effective the project will be. The *initiation phase* starts when the research request is made and ends when the reseach objectives are finalized and agreed upon. According to Karole Friemann (2003), the following six steps during this phase are critical to the project's effectiveness:

1. Educate marketing researchers about why the marketing research is requested. This involves more than simply informing them. A detailed description of the business issues involved, competitors and what they are doing about such issues, and target audiences from which information is to be obtained is included.

2. State the specific actions, decisions, and strategies that managers plan to make based on the research results. Researchers must understand how results are to be used in order to effectively plan the project.

3. Identify the departments, business partners, and individuals who will actually make the decisions about actions and strategies.

4. Project team members need to be recruited.

5. Management (i.e., sponsor, client, etc.) must attend the first meeting of the project team. This will allow for reviewing and revising statements of business issues, and establishment and prioritization of research objectives.

6. Review research alternatives, methodologies, costs, and timeframes (i.e., a preliminary research plan) and finalize research objectives and the scope of the project.

A second point to be emphasized in the given definition of market research is objectivity. Marketing research has sometimes been defined as the application of the scientific method to marketing. At the heart of the scientific method is the objective (rather than subjective) gathering and analysis of information. Research projects that are carried out for the purpose of proving that a prior opinion is correct are, at best, a waste of time and resources; if research is intentionally slanted to arrive at predetermined results, a serious breach of professional ethics is involved. Research based on such an underlying motive is a specific example of what has been called *pseudo-research,* which is research done to satisfy motives other than aiding the making of marketing decisions (Smith, 1974). The motives behind pseudo-research include organizational politics, service promotion, and personal satisfaction.

A similar practice is so-called *advocacy surveys.* These are not real marketing research, but are marketing tools for causes or candidates. Sent by a political or other advocacy group (environmental, etc.), these surveys typically include questions that are worded such that the answers will be the desired ones, and the survey often includes a request for a contribution. Research practitioners must resist efforts to get them to perform research for such purposes.

It will be noted that the definition of market research adopted here contains no reference to a thorough search for and analysis of information. When the nature of the problem requires it, thoroughness is, of course, desirable. For many marketing problems, however, the time and money required for a thorough collection and analysis of the information relevant to their solutions would be completely out of proportion to the benefits gained. The thoroughness with which the research is conducted depends upon the nature of the problem.

The term *problem* is used in the broadest of contexts. That is, there does not have to be something wrong, only a marketing decision to be made. Such a decision, of course, may have arisen in order that a problem can be prevented.

Although the definition given previously is useful, it is by no means the only definition of marketing research, nor is it necessarily the most useful one for all purposes. For example, the American Marketing Association has specified the following definition of marketing research (Bennett, 1988, pp. 117–118):

Marketing Research is the function which links the consumer, customer, and public to the marketer through information—information used to identify and define marketing opportunities and problems; generate, refine, and evaluate marketing actions; monitor marketing performance; and improve understanding of marketing as a process.

Marketing research specifies the information required to address these issues; designs the method for collecting information; manages and implements the data collection process; analyzes the results; and communicates the findings and their implications.

Marketing Research Functions and Tasks

The specific functions of a marketing research department can be summarized by the following statement, which is as valid today as it was when it was put forth many years ago (Cayley, 1968, p. 36):

The task of research is: to provide and maintain for management the research system, to work with management in such a way as to be able to understand its needs, to help define informational requirements, to specify the filter and generate, through application of professional methodology, meaningful information in the most efficient manner. Its role is to broaden managerial decision alternatives and reduce the range of decision error through application of the scientific method to analysis of data and evaluation of information.

In short, marketing research must be viewed as an aid to, not as a substitute for, decision making, and can involve the overall management of market-related information. Exhibit 1.2 presents an interesting comparison between marketing research and geometry.

EXHIBIT 1.2   Marketing Research and Geometry

By borrowing from the field of geometry, marketing research can perhaps become a better aid in solving problems. In particular, geometry is known for solving abstract problems by constructing logical proofs. Marketing and marketing research also can apply a type of proof approach that uses marketing information in a logical, sequential manner, thereby allowing problems to be solved or opportunities identified more quickly.

Although marketing results will never be certain (unlike geometry proofs) and, thus, marketing ideas, strategies, and tactics cannot really be proved before they are implemented, marketing practice may be improved if problems are approached with more discipline and logic (Snyder, 1999). There is a role in this for marketing research. Marketing research, knowledge of past successes and failures, professional market and trade knowledge, internal and external advice, and academic theory can all be used to construct a marketing proof that starts by defining a problem and ends with a solution (or decision). Research provides the facts and information that can be logically and rigorously related to derive the solution to the problem.

The simple act of recording information in a proof format might prevent managers from overlooking key things, which by themselves may not appear to be significant, but which take on more significance when put forth in a logical structure. Snyder (1999) provides an acronym to assist in the construction of a marketing proof, DART: internal *data*, marketing *application* results, trade and consultant *research*, and academic *theory*. By collecting many different types of information, the bigger picture might just appear!

Very broadly, the functions of marketing research today include description and explanation (which are necessary for understanding), prediction, and evaluation. More narrowly, marketing research within a company provides the informational and analytical inputs necessary for effective planning of future marketing activity, control of marketing operations in the present, and evaluation of marketing results.

A variety of organizations conduct marketing research projects on a broad array of topics. Projects are performed by companies for their own internal use, by commercial marketing research firms, and by government and nonprofit institutions (see Exhibit 1.3).

EXHIBIT 1.3   Examples of Doers of Marketing Research

The "doers" of marketing research and examples of projects include the following:

- A company's own *research staff* conducting projects for internal use, for example, Intel doing a customer satisfaction study
- *Commercial marketing research firms* conducting syndicated studies, for example, Mediamark Research, Inc., doing media research that is sold to multiple clients
- *Commercial marketing research firms* doing research for a specific client, for example, M/A/R/C conducting a customer satisfaction study for a corporate client
- *Advertising agencies* doing research for their own use or for a client, for example, Grey Advertising studying consumer brand preferences or media viewing habits for a client
- *Trade associations,* for example, the Direct Selling Association either doing a study itself or having a research company do a study of characteristics of the direct selling industry
- *Government and nonprofit organizations*, for example, the Environmental Protection Agency of the U.S. Government providing reports concerning pollution

---

Despite the widespread use of marketing research, many small companies and nonprofit organizations avoid its use because of certain persistent myths, as shown in Exhibit 1.4.

EXHIBIT 1.4   Some Basic Myths About Marketing Research

Many small companies and nonprofit organizations fail to make the best use of marketing research because of erroneous beliefs held about the research function. These myths are all either untrue or badly misstate the true potential of marketing research.

Myth 1:   *The Big Decision.* Research is used only when a major decision is involved; it has no role in day-to-day operational decision making.

Response: Marketing research potentially has an important role to play in a wide range of decisions, major and minor, made by the small businessperson or the nonprofit marketing manager.

Myth 2:   *Survey Myopia.* Marketing research is synonymous with field survey research using random samples, questionnaires, computer printouts, statistical analysis, and esoteric technology.

Response: In most sophisticated organizations, marketing research is not just survey research but encompasses a diversity of approaches ranging from using secondary sources to systematic observation to elaborate experimental designs.

Myth 3:   *Big Bucks.* Marketing research is very expensive and, thus, can be used only by wealthy organizations.

Response: Marketing research can be carried out with a very modest budget using creative but legitimate research strategies. Some low-cost strategies include secondary research, Internet research tools, focus groups, and collaborating with distributors and other channel members. For new companies, Levenburg and Dandridge (1997) suggest such so-called mini-research techniques as watching competitors, tracking competitors' promotion, setting up a mini test market, and using local direct mail. For existing businesses, they suggest studying in-house sources of information, observing customers in the purchasing process, and using large companies that have complementary products for information and promotional support.

Myth 4:   *Sophisticated Researcher.* Only well-trained experts can and should do marketing research, since it involves use of complex and advanced technology.

Response: Since much research does not necessarily involve complex sampling problems or statistics, minimal familiarity with the kinds of things that could go wrong with various projects is all that the manager needs to know to undertake a careful, low-cost marketing research program. Where expert assistance is necessary, it can be obtained on an ad hoc basis, often at little cost.

Myth 5:   *Most Research is Unread.* A large amount of research is not relevant to managers or confirms what they already know or believe. Other research is so poorly designed or so poorly written up by the experts (or both) that it ends up neglected or in the bottom drawer.

Response: While there are many ways to carry out useless research, there is a limited set of critical guidelines that, if adopted, can assure the manager that virtually all the research he or she carries out will be useful and used. Although research can be poorly designed, this is not inherent in the research function.

SOURCE: Adapted from *Methodological Barriers to the Use of Marketing Research* by Small and Nonprofit Organizations by A. Andreasen. Copyright © 1981. Reprinted with permission.

We know a great deal about the nature of marketing research projects conducted from research carried out in this area (Dunn, Hisinger, & McLaughlin, 1998). A sizable amount of research is done to identify marketing problems and opportunities and to solve problems. A wide range and variety of types of marketing research are done in practice. Types of research conducted include the following:

- Qualitative
- Product/service tests
- Brand/advertising tracking
- New product screening tests
- External market volume/share
- Advertising pretest/copy text
- Marketing strategy/structure
- Customer satisfaction
- Name/package tests

- New product forecasting
- Pricing
- Purchase/usage panels
- Geo/demographics
- Market Information System/DSS
- Database marketing
- Sales/marketing mix models
- Product category management/retail level

The most used research techniques are qualitative, followed by product tracking, new product screening, and market volume/share studies. The least used techniques are product category management at the retail level, sales and market mix models, and database marketing. A good example of product identification research is that done by a company that introduced a new line of women's swimwear. Before creating the new line, the company did research to learn which women buy bathing suits, how many they buy per year, their ages, and their incomes. The company also did some research on fabric and found that many women liked a cotton and spandex blend.

Many of these techniques are used in research projects carried out to help solve marketing problems. For example, Johnson Wax did extensive marketing research prior to the national launch of Agree Shampoo. Research helped identify the market opportunity, define the target user, determine the positioning and strategy, and define the attributes and features the product should have. In addition, the marketing plan was tested.

Examples of the application of these marketing research techniques abound. Amoco Oil has done research involving market share determination, customer satisfaction (Amoco and competitors), credit card handling, tracking of attitudes of dealers and other distributors, and advertising campaigns, among other topics. Saab-Scania AB, the Swedish-based automobile manufacturer, has conducted a great deal of marketing research in the U.S. market using a commercial marketing research firm (Whalen, 1984). Surveys were conducted among current and prospective owners to determine wants and needs, likes and dislikes. Clinics were run in which buyers compared Saab vehicles with competitive makes. Specific customized studies were done to analyze demographic characteristics of buyers of Saab and competitive automobiles. On occasion brand mapping (via multidimensional scaling) was used to forecast within the company's designated market segment. Results of such research were used in product design, advertising, market segmentation, and sales training.

More recent examples come from the high-tech marketplace, where some people believe that conventional marketing research is not adequate to gain insight into technology consumers. Research must go beyond demographics and buying patterns—to assess how people use technology in performing daily tasks, and how they feel about it. Some research firms, such as Odyssey Research and Yankelovich Partners' Cyber Citizen are looking at how consumers use the Internet. Swinyard and Smith (2002) further identified eight psychographic segments, offering insight into the attitudes underlying the behavior of online shoppers and shopping avoiders. SRI Consulting, Inc., is using traditional marketing research methods that combine demographic information with an analysis of consumer emotion to predict behavior of technology buyers (Judge, 1998).

The consumer electronics group of Sony of Canada Ltd. needed a baseline measurement of where the company stood in the marketplace. This included assessing Sony's status with channel members and determining whether it was giving distributors the support they needed and wanted. To find out whether they were doing things that mattered most to channel partners, Sony conducted an extensive survey with key buyers and managers in each channel. Participants were asked to rate the importance of Sony's performance on product features and price, retail promotion, availability of product, profit margins, and ease of doing business (Roche & O'Connell, 1998).

Service and Nontraditional Research

We now move our discussion away from the traditional product-based companies to companies in the service and nontraditional product industries. These companies represent such diverse industries as transportation, hospitality, health care, electric utility, interior home design, real estate development, military recruiting, trade shows, movies, financial institutions such as banks and brokerage houses, and orchestras. For example, a large national brokerage and financial services company uses marketing research techniques to ascertain client needs for a wide range of services, including order-execution, market-monitoring, financial-advising, and information-providing services. The company uses a customer-profiling information system to enhance its market segmentation activities and better match clients and products. Marketing research also played a major role at Citicorp, a global financial services holding company, and its largest operating unit, Citibank (Brock, Lipson, & Levitt, 1989). There, marketers used research information for the following:

- Monitoring customers and markets
- Measuring awareness, attitudes, and image
- Tracking product usage behavior
- Diagnosing immediate business problems
- Supporting strategy development

Finally, today most movie and television producers, an increasing number of record companies, and book publishers employ sophisticated market-research techniques to test the appeal of the creative endeavors that are their products, including film tests of alternative plot twists and endings.

Boston Symphony Orchestra, Inc. (BSO), whose "brands" are the Boston Symphony, the Boston Pops, and Tanglewood Music Center, has used research to help it develop marketing strategies for attracting a younger audience, improving sales and memberships, and driving more revenues through its Web site (Vence, 2003). BSO wanted to research how audiences perceived the orchestra, why they attended concerts, negative and positive attributes of going to concerts, habits associated with charitable contributions in general, and attitudes toward contributing money to the BSO. Quantitative surveys and focus groups were conducted by a commercial research and consulting company.

At the Internet World trade show in 2002 detailed attendee information was sought in the post-show attendee survey. Both quantitative and qualitative questions were asked. Such information is useful to exhibitors who have to convince their management that participation enhances revenues and ultimately return on investment (Jarvis, 2002b).

Another nontraditional use of marketing research is law. If research is designed properly and is relevant to the logic of the litigated issues, survey research results can be used as legal evidence. Major areas of law using marketing research results include trademark protection, intellectual property rights, and advertising claims. In intellectual property rights and trademark litigation, Federal courts are in favor of objective surveys to help determine, for example, if conflicts between names result in what is called "likelihood of confusion," a legal concept meaning that two names are so alike consumers might think they come from the same source. One case in which survey results were used involved a dental company using the name "McDental" for dental services (Rens, 1994). The court granted McDonald's a permanent injunction against the dental company, relying in part on survey results showing that more than 30% of the population surveyed associated McDental with McDonald's.

Surveys used in litigation are required to meet strict standards. All of the following must apply (Gelb, 2001):

1. The population is properly chosen and precisely (but not too broadly or narrowly) defined.

2. The sample represents that population.

3. The data are accurately reported.

4. The data are analyzed against statistical principles.

5. The questions asked are clear and not misleading.

6. Proper interviewing procedures are followed.

7. The process ensures *objectivity;* for example, the interviewers are not aware of the purpose of the survey.

Excellent sources on how to conduct legal surveys and what questions are more likely to be permissible are McCarthy (1996) and Welter (1998).

Even when the results are not brought into court, marketing research methods are used in legal disputes. Green, Krieger, and Wind (2002) report on the use of marketing experiments and psychometric scaling in a legal dispute between two giant pharmaceutical companies, Schering-Plough Corp. and Pfizer, Inc. The dispute involved physicians' perceptions about various antihistamines and sales messages about the products used by sales representatives. The dispute was settled out of court.

Government agencies, trade associations, trade periodicals, and colleges and universities are other organizations that do marketing research. Such agencies of the federal government as the Federal Trade Commission, the Anti-Trust Division of the Department of Justice, the Food and Drug Administration, and the Interstate Commerce Commission carry out studies on specific marketing problems from time to time. Trade associations and trade periodicals often collect and disseminate marketing research data on the industries with which they are concerned. Bureaus of business and economic research at universities also regularly conduct research projects of interest to marketers. Chambers of Commerce, brokerage houses, railroads, airlines, and such reporting services as Standard and Poor's, Moody's, and Dun and Bradstreet also conduct marketing research. For the most part, these agencies provide secondary data, a topic discussed in Chapter 4.

THE CHARACTERISTICS
OF MARKETING MANAGEMENT

A primary characteristic of management is decision making, which permeates the management process. (Since the terms *decision making* and *managing* are so closely interwoven, we shall use them almost interchangeably.) In considering the characteristics of marketing management, it is appropriate that we first examine the types of decisions managers generally make.

Types of Management Decisions

There are six types of management decisions that are important to consider:

1. Deciding what the problems are. This involves recognizing and defining the problems currently faced by the organization.

2. Selecting the immediate problem for solution. Priorities must be determined according to the importance of the problems and the timing of their solution.

3. Solving the problem selected. This includes finding alternative solutions, evaluating the consequences of each, and selecting the most favorable one.

4. Implementing the solution. After a solution is proposed, the decisions necessary to carry out the solution must be found.

5. Modifying the original solution based on observation of results. Management decides whether, when, and how original solutions should be modified after experiencing results.

6. Establishing policy. Policy is established by deciding which problems occur often enough and are sufficiently similar to warrant a policy decision and making the policy decision.

The primary activity of marketing management is making such decisions with regard to marketing problems. This includes identification of problems in the areas of product design, price, distribution, and promotion. A marketing manager must prioritize the more important and pressing problems selected for solution, reach the best possible solution based on the information available, implement the solution, modify the solution when additional information so dictates, and establish policy to act as a ready-made solution for any recurrence of the problem.

Problem-Situation Models and Decision Making

Suppose that a marketing manager is considering increasing the advertising appropriation for one of the company's products. As long as one of the company's objectives is to increase profits, the decision to increase the appropriation will be at least partially dependent on the amount of net additional sales generated. In turn additional sales will depend on factors such as the nature of the campaign, the advertising-sales response relationship, and the actions of competitors.

A necessary part of the process of making this decision—or of any generalized decision process—is the formulation of a problem-situation model. The model may take many forms, ranging from implicit models that the decision maker may not even be aware of using to elaborate mathematical models whose solution requires the aid of a computer. The term

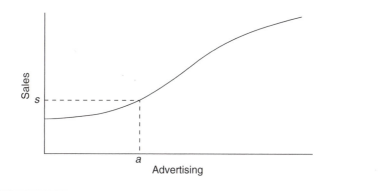

Figure 1.1   Model of the Sales-Advertising Relationship

model refers to a conceptual scheme that specifies a measure of the outcomes to be achieved, the relevant variable or variables, and their functional relationship to the outcomes.

To return to our example of the decision concerning increasing the advertising appropriation, what kind of a problem-situation model might be appropriate? In this case the executive may have a set of intuitive, non-formalized judgments, which might be expressed somewhat as follows: "Assuming that nothing else changes, as advertising for this product is increased, sales will increase in the form of a 'flat S' curve. I think we are on the lower end of the curve."

If pressed further, the executive might agree that his conception of the sales-advertising relationship could be represented by a graph. Some specification of the level of the other controllable variables and of the environmental variables would have to be made; let us assume that they are all held at their present levels. The graph would be of the general nature of Figure 1.1, with present sales and advertising designated as *s* and *a*, respectively.

An analysis of the sales-advertising relationship in the past might indicate that it takes the form of Gompertz-type (S-shaped) curve such that the equation

$$\log Y = \log k + (\log G)B^p$$

where *Y* is sales response, *p* is amount of advertising, and *k*, *G*, and *B* are constants, provides a reasonably good predictive equation over the range of advertising of interest to the decision maker.

Several points concerning this example are worth noting. First, we have been dealing with explicit forms of a model. It should be clearly understood, however, that if the conceptualization of a specific problem by the decision maker remains implicit, it is no less a model. It may be, in fact, that an explicit model is not worth the cost of formalization.

The second point concerns the form in which explicit models may be expressed. In our example, a verbal statement, a graph, and an equation described the same basic explicit model. Models described verbally are known simply as *verbal* models. Those that are expressed as a graph or diagram are known as *schematic* models, and those expressed as a logical sequence of questions are called *logical flow* models. Models represented in equation form are called *symbolic* (*mathematical*) models. All explicit models may be described in one or more of these forms.

Table 1.1   Marketing Program Illustration

Action	S_1: New Marketing Program Superior	S_2: Old Marketing Program Superior
A_1: Adopt new	$U_{11} = 15$	$U_{12} = -7$
A_2: Retain old	$U_{21} = -2$	$U_{22} = 4$

A third point relates to the degree of simplification of models. Models are necessarily simplifications and abstractions, to some degree, of the reality of the problem situation. The decision maker attempts to extract the important elements of the problem situation (not all the variables, as that is not possible) and represent them so that they are simple enough to be understood and manipulated, yet realistic enough to portray the essential constructs and parameters of the situation.

Often, a more efficient way of using a problem-situation model is to structure the problem into a relatively small number of discrete courses of action and states of nature. That is, we designate the courses of action we want to consider by specifying two or more levels of one or more of the controllable subset of variables (A), while holding the others constant. Similarly, we designate the states of nature under which outcomes are to be predicted by specifying two or more levels of one or more of the environmental (S) subset of variables. A functional model that defines the result is then applied to predict the outcome for each action-state pair.

Suppose that a marketing manager is considering changing the marketing program for a product. The change would reallocate a part of the present advertising trade media expenditures to hire an additional salesperson to call upon retailers. To make such an action worthwhile would require that there be a net increase in sales. Additional sales will depend upon the effectiveness of the new salesperson in the following ways: (a) convincing existing retail customers to purchase more; (b) getting new dealers to stock the product; (c) the possible loss of sales from the reduction in advertising expenditures; (d) competitors' actions; and (e) other external factors.

The decision model in Table 1.1 shows the problem structured into a matrix defined by two courses of action and two states of nature. The decision to hire another salesperson or retain the present advertising program is concerned with two controllable variables—the extra salesperson and the amount of advertising expenditure. There is no contemplated change in any of the other controllable variables.

The two states of nature shown in Table 1.1 reflect different environmental conditions. In state S_1, the environment is such that retailer purchases will increase more as a result of the salesperson than they decrease as a result of the reduction in advertising expenditures. The reverse is true in state S_2. There is no expected change in other environmental variables; they may be assumed to be the same between the two states.

Although Table 1.1 illustrates the application of the problem-situation model, it immediately raises another question: How does one go about selecting a course of action without knowing which state of nature is the true state? If the new promotional program in our example is adopted, there is a potential gain of 15 units if S_1 is the true state and a potential loss of seven units if it is not. Similarly, if the old program is retained, a loss of two units will result if S_1 is the true state and a gain of four units will be realized if it is not.

The answer to the question of which alternative to choose, given the conditional payoffs of each, lies in the choice criterion adopted. Choice-criterion models have been developed by decision theorists to illustrate this problem (Green, Tull, & Albaum, 1988, pp. 23–26).

A further comment about models is in order. We have already noted that models may be either implicit or explicit. When the cost of formulating an explicit model is justifiable, it is preferable for several reasons:

1. *Clarification.* Explication usually results in the clarification of relationships and interactions. The need for more rigorous definitions of key variables often becomes apparent.

2. *Objectivity.* Often as a direct result of clarification, the process of explicating the model often discloses rationalizations and unfounded opinions that had not been recognized as such before.

3. *Communication.* When different people hold alternative implicit models of the same problem situation, discussion may not be based on common points of reference, and communication problems arise. Explication reduces these problems.

4. *Improvement of models.* Explicit models can be tested by different persons and in differing situations to see if the results are reproducible. The degree of adaptability and range of applicability can thus be extended.

5. *Guide to research needs.* Formulating models explicitly can better pinpoint information gaps and, thus, aid in determining the nature of research needs.

Having considered problem-situation models, we now specify more completely what is meant by the term *information.*

Information and Decision Making

Information as used here refers to *recorded experience that is useful for decision making.* It consists of that recorded experience which reduces the level of uncertainty in making a decision. Therefore, it is communicated knowledge that changes the state of knowledge of the person who receives it.

This definition makes the existence of information dependent upon the decision maker and the context of the decision. The model that is being used for a specific problem situation defines both the information required for solution and the way in which it will be interpreted. Exhibit 1.5 shows this in a different way.

EXHIBIT 1.5   Applications and Objectives in Research

An often-forgotten fundamental of marketing research is that the research process should start with a clear statement of the decisions that managers have to make. A relatively easy process for making sure that research designs are decision-oriented is *applications and objectives* (Conner, 1996). Applications represent the decisions that will be made on the basis of the research results, whereas objectives (i.e., information objectives) represent the data needed to support the applications. A four-step process is involved:

1. *Applications.* The decisions to be made or the actions to be taken must be clearly listed.

2. *Application options.* For each decision or action, existing options must be specified.

3. *Application criteria.* For each decision or decision option, the criteria on which the decision will be based must be specified.

4. *Information objectives.* The needed information must be determined from the decision criteria.

Most research is conducted to support more than one application, often with less-well-defined options. Also, many times application criteria need to be more complex; different research results may be needed for different options. Nevertheless, this process shows that the information needed for a project follows directly from, and thus supports, the *decision purpose* of the research.

At this point, we can state that from a practical point of view, information must possess certain characteristics if it is to be useful for decision making. That is, information must be all of the following:

Accurate   Accuracy, the degree to which information reflects reality, is a relative criterion in terms of the specific decision at hand.

Current   Information must reflect events in the *relevant* time periods, both past and present.

Sufficient   The degree of completeness and level of detail required to allow a decision to be made varies with the decision.

Available   Information must be available *when a decision is being made.*

Relevant   Relevance, the pertinence and applicability of information to the decision, is *the single most important characteristic.*

Realistically, trade-offs often must be made among the accuracy, timeliness, sufficiency, and availability. For example, sufficiency may be relaxed to increase accuracy. However, relevance of information is the one characteristic that can never be compromised because to do so would make the information useless.

Many companies develop a formal system for obtaining, processing, and disseminating decision information. Such a system is known as a Marketing Information System (MIS). An MIS attempts to ensure that decision information will possess the relevant characteristics for problem solving.

If there were no costs of obtaining information, decision makers might have difficulty limiting the amount of information they require to make decisions. Since obtaining information is a cost-incurring activity, rational decision-making requires consideration of the value of information needed.

The marketing executive usually deals with events that are unique. No two marketing problems are ever precisely the same. When a decision maker possesses partial information about a problem and the environment within which events take place, he or she may elect to collect more information before making a final choice among the courses of action. However, the decision maker will do so only if the value of the additional information is greater than the cost of obtaining it. The value versus the cost of information is a central issue in marketing research.

MARKETING RESEARCH IN MARKETING INFORMATION SYSTEMS

Every marketing-oriented company has a functioning marketing information system. These systems can vary from sales analysis data that tracks the product from the manufacturer through the distribution chain to consumer purchase information and analysis of the effects of marketing variables on consumption of the product to environmental analysis and predictions of changes in the distribution and marketing system.

Elements of an MIS

A marketing information system includes elements other than marketing research. The concept of a marketing information system, illustrated in Figure 1.2, shows that marketing research is one subsystem—the others are concerned with the following:

- Internal records consist of the internal computerized system that reports such items as sales, orders, prices, costs, etc.
- Marketing intelligence is the set of procedures and sources used to provide information about relevant developments in the marketing environment.
- Information analysis consists of advanced techniques for analyzing data and problems, including a statistical bank and a model bank.

The activities performed by an MIS and its subsystems include information discovery, collection, interpretation (which may involve validation and filtering), analysis, and intracompany dissemination (storage, transmission, and/or dumping).

More specifically, the MIS should be tied directly to the decision process. A good MIS provides relevant information in some way to every part of this process. It should have the following capabilities:

- Store and retrieve data easily
- Generate required reports and analyses, both standard and ad hoc
- Provide modeling, what-if scenarios, and other spreadsheet-type analysis
- Create high quality visual aids such as graphics
- Integrate all of these functions easily

Form of an MIS

Often, the MIS is developed as a computer-based system, primarily due to the predominance of personal computers with networking capability and the development of wireless technology. The system must be easily operable by any decision maker (i.e., it must be user-friendly). It must have built-in structure to allow the orderly transfer of information and

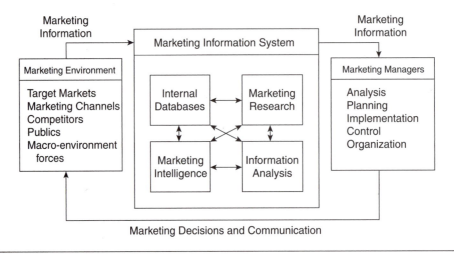

Figure 1.2   Model of a Marketing Information System

SOURCE: From Kotler, P., & Armstrong, G., *Activebook, Principles of Marketing,* 1st edition, Copyright © 2002. Reprinted with permission of Pearson Education, Upper Saddle River, NJ.

flexibility to allow quick response to program changes. Finally, as marketing research becomes increasingly tied to overall corporate strategic planning, the MIS must have the capability to link with corporate information systems. This has led to using the Web for development of intranet systems (Cortese, 1996).

MIS Information

The MIS is concerned with all internal and external information relevant to solving marketing problems and making marketing decisions. Marketing information may be either *planned* or *unsolicited,* depending on the degree of collection effort required and the user's advance knowledge of the need for information. Planned information exists when a manager recognizes a need and he or she makes a request that information be provided. In contrast, unsolicited information is that which may, in fact, exist and be obtainable from within the company, but which potential users do not know is available unless they happen to chance upon it. A manager is dependent upon others in the organization to supply and transmit this type of information. In the MIS framework, marketing research is mainly concerned with planned information.

Decision makers, as a rule, dislike being surprised. The ideal MIS contains a significant proportion of planned decision-making information. This requires that decision makers make their needs known. It also requires a clear dialogue between the information users (e.g., marketing managers) and the information providers (e.g., marketing researchers). We discuss this dialogue in the next section.

The food industry provides many examples of manufacturers who have developed strategic information systems for marketing. Scanner data has become a keystone of such systems, especially from single-source databases (e.g., Nielsen). For example, in the late 1980s the desserts division of General Foods developed a system based on data integration. This system, which looked at the condition of retail shelves, worked as follows (Rubenstein, 1989):

1. Data to be collected and market/sales questions to be answered were downloaded to the salesperson's handheld computer.

2. Stores were visited daily and the salesperson scanned the shelf, collected data, and answered specific questions.

3. The salesperson sent data up to the main computer and reloaded the handheld computer with new questions, if needed.

4. The systems database integrated salespersons' data with other marketing systems.

5. Data were available the next morning to sale managers to determine shelf-problem areas.

Another example concerns a company motivating its channel intermediaries to provide important intelligence. A manufacturer, one of the largest in the industry, asked each of its distributors to send to its marketing research division a copy of all invoices containing sales of its products. The manufacturer analyzed the invoices to learn what other products end users were purchasing in combination with their products. In addition to obtaining valuable information for its own use, the manufacturer provided the distributors with breakdowns by industry, customer size, and business focus.

Marketing Decision Support System (MDSS)

A marketing decision support system is closely related to the MIS and is a "coordinated collection of data, systems, tools, and techniques with supporting software and hardware by which an organization gathers and interprets relevant information from business and environment and turns it into a basis for marketing action" (Little, 1979, p. 11). Components include a data bank, models, statistics, and optimization techniques. The desired end result is the application of computer technology and marketing science toward increasing the productivity of marketing activities.

MANAGER-RESEARCHER DIALOGUE

Problem formulation is probably the single most critical aspect of the research process. Unless the problem is formulated properly, any research, although sound in method, is worthless to the decision maker. Critical to problem formulation is the need for a clear and relevant dialogue between managers and researchers. There must be a minimum of conflict areas.

The Dilemma

Table 1.2 illustrates potential conflicts between managers and researchers. Conflicts may arise in a number of important areas. These conflict areas are as prevalent today as they were when the study was conducted more than 30 years ago. If research is to make a contribution to managerial decision making, it is essential that managers and researchers communicate with each other. There must be a reconciliation of opposing positions on key issues. According to Larry Stanek, vice president of consumer and marketplace knowledge for Minute Maid, Inc., "There is a gap between what research believes it's capable of providing and what top management perceives it can get from research; researchers believe they have answers critical to decision-making, while management views research as having the data but maybe not the insight to drive business" (quoted in James, 2002, p. 19). Studies by Deshpande and Zaltman (1982, 1984) confirmed the importance of research-manager interaction (i.e., communication), attributes of the final report, and technical quality.

Table 1.2   Areas of Top Management (TM)-Marketing Research (MR) Conflict

Top Management Position	Area	Marketing Research Position
• MR lacks sense of accountability • Sole MR function is as an information provider	Research responsibility	• Responsibility should be explicitly defined and consistently followed • Desire decision-making involvement with TM
• Generally poor communicators • Lack enthusiasm, salesmanship, and imagination	Research personnel	• Should be hired, judged, and compensated based on research capabilities • TM is anti-intellectual
• Research costs too much • Since MR contribution is difficult to measure, budget cuts are relatively defensible	Budget	• "You get what you pay for" defense. • There needs to be continuing, long-range TM commitment
• Tend to be over-engineered • Not executed with proper sense of urgency • Exhibit ritualized, staid approach	Assignments	• Too many non-researchable requests • Too many "fire-fighting" requests • Insufficient time and money allocated
• MR best equipped to do this • General direction sufficient . . . MR must appreciate and respond • Can't help changing circumstances	Problem definition	• TM generally unsympathetic to this widespread problem • Not given all the relevant facts • Changed after research is underway
• Characterized as dull, with too much researchese and qualifiers • Not decision-oriented • Too often reported after the fact	Research reporting	• TM treats superficially • Good research demands thorough reporting and documentation • Insufficient lead time given
• Free to use as it pleases . . . MR shouldn't question • Changes in need and timing of research are sometimes unavoidable • MR does not know all the facts	Use of research	• TM use to support a predetermined position represents misuse • Isn't used after requested and conducted . . . wasteful • Uses to confirm or excuse past actions

SOURCE: Reprinted with permission from "Some Observations on Marketing Research in Top Management Decision Making," by J. G. Keane in *Journal of Marketing, 33*, p. 13. October 1969. Published by the American Marketing Association.

The element of surprise is another issue that can cause manager-researcher conflict. Researchers are not as concerned as managers about the level of surprise in research results. The message here should be clear. There must be interaction between the manager and the researcher. Each can contribute a specific type of knowledge and experience to the formulation and solution of the problem. The marketing researcher is seldom asked—or even permitted— to assist in the structuring of a managerial problem. Instead, the researcher may be given the following type of directive: "Find out all you can about the market for tranquilizers." If the researcher can even implement this type of general request, he or she then serves principally as a fact finder, unaware of the use to which the findings are to be put, the scale of effort to be devoted to the inquiry, and the accuracy required in the findings. Better communication between management and researchers allows both to contribute more to the research process.

Further complications may arise when the researchers are not members of the manager's company but, instead, belong to private external research firms and agencies. For these outside researchers effective communication with managers is critical to being able to market the research project. A dialogue will establish for the researchers what the researchable issues are, how they should be addressed, when the client wants results delivered, and so on.

MARKETING RESEARCH ORGANIZATIONS

Marketing research is conducted by many different entities. Included are a firm's own research staff, syndicated research services (e.g., Nielsen, MRCA), general or specialized private marketing research agencies, advertising agencies, interviewing services, management and nonbusiness organizations such as government agencies. A company often may face a so-called "make or buy" decision when it comes to its marketing research. This decision involves choosing between internal research staff (make) or external research organizations (buy). This decision is discussed in Chapter 2.

A company with its own marketing research staff must determine where marketing research should be located in the organization. The location of the department, and the amount of resources allocated to staffing will vary from company to company. Some companies do all their own research, while others rely heavily on external research organizations. Some companies have only a single marketing research department that handles all research projects within the company, whereas others decentralize research activities and assign them by functional departments. For example, where marketing research is decentralized, sales analysis may be done by the sales department, cost analysis by the accounting department, and advertising research by the advertising department. All other marketing research dealing with marketing activities (e.g., price decisions, packaging materials, etc.) can be done by the internal marketing research department.

Other companies may have more than a single marketing research department. Marketing research can also be decentralized down to operating divisions or perhaps SBUs (strategic business units) if the company is so organized. Also, many companies use combinations of various types of organization. Eli Lilly and Co., for example, officially has a marketing research department, but the company is organized into teams by therapeutic area (diabetes, women's health, etc.), and marketing researchers sit on each team (James, 2002, p. 19). There is no one optimum method for organizing marketing research, because organization depends upon company needs, the way marketing and other functions of the company are organized, and the basic orientation of the company. The marketing research organization most appropriate for Intel as a technology-driven company would not be best when it is today a market-driven company.

ETHICAL ISSUES IN MARKETING RESEARCH

By its very nature marketing research involves interaction between the researcher and other people, including other researchers, clients, survey respondents and experimental subjects, and society as a whole. During this interaction relationships emerge, and it is from these relationships that ethical problems arise. Many of the techniques widely used in marketing research practice are inherently sources of potential ethical concern. Still other practices used by researchers give rise to ethical issues that are not inherent in the research process but arise from other sources. This section will examine the major ethical issues facing marketing researchers and methods that can reduce ethical problems, including the developing and implementation of codes of conduct.

Some Problems

What is the major issue or problem facing the marketing research profession? In repeated surveys of marketing professionals during the past 10 to 15 years a frequently mentioned response was "the *image* and *credibility* of marketing research." More specific responses included telemarketing and selling or fundraising under the guise of marketing research; poor quality of data collection, including declining response rates, nonresponse bias, professional respondents, and biased questionnaires; and attempting to prove a predetermined hypothesis with research (what we have called pseudo-research). All those specific things mentioned have a bearing on image and credibility. The extent to which these are problems is supported by the public's reaction to the marketing research industry. A large percentage of the public refuses to participate in surveys conducted by, and for, commercial organizations. In 2001 nearly 45% of U.S. consumers reported refusing to participate in a survey over the past year, up from 40% in 1999; the overall trend is upward (Jarvis, 2002a). At times this may be due to the mode of data collection being used, such as telephone surveys and the Internet.

Misuse of marketing research and excessive use of certain techniques and practices seems to be on the increase. Although some such practices may have legal ramifications, most are either simply bad research or are in the realm of ethical problems and dilemmas not covered by law. Collecting, analyzing, and presenting information from people raises important ethical (and perhaps even legal) questions. How much clients need to know about their market, for example, has to be balanced against an individual's right to privacy. The interpretation and use of data, both secondary and primary, also raise ethical questions. Similarly, nonreactive or unobtrusive methods raise these types of questions and more. Any type of research done in naturalistic settings where there are no volunteer subjects, no informed consent, no option to quit the study, and no briefing or debriefing might involve legally questionable activities such as fraud, invasion of privacy, trespass, harassment, and disorderly conduct.

One area where this may lead to problems is in the use of scanner data by marketing research firms that have purchased the data from retail chains. Is privacy being violated in this instance? After all, a purchaser of a product or products has become a respondent in a study, without knowledge of this and without giving consent. While this has not caused much controversy yet, it is one practice that will be closely monitored by ethicists, legal experts, and privacy advocates.

Another area that has been generating ethical, as well as legal, concerns is electronic-based marketing research, including online research and the use of e-mail. Although the ethical issues are similar to those existing for other modes of data collection, what sets electronic data collection apart from the others is that there is no set legal structure that regulates the use of the Internet, except for those activities that are illegal per se. With technology developing quickly it is difficult to keep up with the potential uses and abuses of the Internet. This will be an evolving situation, one that may take many years to resolve.

Nature of Ethics in Research

Ethics has been defined as moral principles, quality, or practice. Ethical behavior is viewed as conforming to professional standards of conduct, whether or not such standards of conduct are formalized into a code. That is, ethics is what most people in a given society or group view as being moral, good, or right. Ethical problems are relationship problems in the sense that fundamental human relationships are involved.

There is no universally agreed upon, or even widely accepted, ethical standard or model. Some codes of conduct that research industry groups have agreed to follow may be the procedures most widely accepted as ethical. Carroll and Buchholtz (2000) have provided a useful summary of a variety of approaches to ethics that may give helpful insights to research practitioners (and to managers as well). These include the following:

- **Principle of utilitarianism:** The correctness of an action is determined by its results, such as the efficiency of use of resources or overall benefits to society. A weakness of this principle is that it may lead to a failure to consider the morality of the means used.
- **Principle of rights:** Individual or group rights should not be overridden simply because overall benefits to society occur. What is claimed as a right by one individual or group may be validated by law or claimed on some other basis. Various rights may be in conflict (smokers versus nonsmokers).
- **Principle of justice:** Fairness makes actions correct. *Distributive justice* refers to equal distribution of benefits and burden; *compensatory justice* refers to making up for past injustices; and *procedural justice* refers to fair treatment.
- **Additional approaches:** The *principle of caring* focuses on people, *virtue ethics* are concerned with the development of virtuous people, and other approaches include the Golden Rule.

The different approaches will not always lead to the same conclusion or course of action. Thus the individual still must make decisions based upon his or her understanding of the way in which the people involved will view the decisions from the perspective of ethics and morals.

In marketing research, ethical concerns arise from a researcher's relationships with various stakeholders—both within and outside the research process (Akaah and Riordan, 1989, p. 113; Murphy & Laczniak, 1992). Relevant stakeholders include clients (or managers), survey respondents and experimental subjects, the general public, and the research profession itself. In a real sense, ethical standards are a personal matter, something that has been influenced by culture and other learning situations, and which becomes ingrained in a person's value system. Part of this value system is a perceived set of obligations and responsibilities toward other groups of people. For example, a researcher has an obligation to treat human participants fairly, but at the same time the researcher needs to gather accurate and reliable information for the client. To the extent that these responsibilities create conflicts, a research ethics problem arises. The issue of ethics in marketing research all too often revolves around the balancing of a researcher's obligation and responsibilities toward all stakeholders affected by the research process (Hunt, Chonko, & Wilcox, 1984).

Major Considerations

There are a number of considerations that are ethical in nature that arise in conducting marketing research projects. These are summarized in Exhibit 1.6, which lists the major issues involved in three main areas of ethical interest: deceptive and fraudulent practices, invasion of privacy, and lack of consideration for research subjects and respondents.

EXHIBIT 1.6   Ethical Considerations
in Treatment of Subjects and Respondents

Schneider (1977) enumerated three general areas of ethical concern: deceptive practices, invasion of privacy, and lack of consideration. Specific examples of each are listed here.
Deceptive or fraudulent practices include the following:

- Unrealized promise of anonymity
- Use of disguised questionnaires and interviews
- Faked sponsor identification
- Implication of required response
- Lying about research procedure
- Faked testing in experimental research
- Promise of undelivered compensation
- Sales solicitation

The following are examples of invasions of privacy:

- Observation without informed consent
- Questions concerning people other than the subject
- Projective techniques
- Personal classification data
- Full disclosure and use of "optional" participation

All of the following practices exhibit a lack of consideration for subjects or respondents:

- Overuse of public (i.e., research placing an unreasonable demand on the time and energy of respondents)
- Research in subject areas with a depressing effect on respondents

- Subjects of no immediate interest to respondents
- Poor interviewers
- Contacts at inconvenient times
- No mention of procedural aspects
- Failure to debrief
- Failure to present subject with option to discard results upon completion

Of specific concern to many are excessive interviewing, lack of consideration for and abuse of respondents, and the use of marketing research as a sales ploy (McDaniel, Verille, & Madden, 1985).

The scenarios listed in Exhibit 1.7 present a range of ethical dilemmas confronting marketing research practitioners today. As these situations show, ethical difficulties involve technical, managerial, and societal issues.

EXHIBIT 1.7   Selected Ethical Dilemmas for Marketing Researchers

The following scenarios represent a wide range of marketing practices that give rise to ethical concerns. Scenarios 1 through 6, from Murphy and Laczniak (1992), and Scenarios 7 through 10, from Weinberg (1989), pose questions that marketing researchers often encounter.

Scenario 1

The research director of a large corporation is convinced that using the company's name in surveys with consumers produces low response rates and distorted answers. Therefore, the firm routinely conducts surveys using the title Public Opinion Institute. Is this an ethical practice?

Scenario 2

A survey finds that 80 percent of the doctors responding do not recommend any particular brand of margarine to their patients who are concerned about cholesterol. Five percent recommend Brand A, four percent recommend Brand B, and no other brand is recommended by more than two percent of the doctors. The company runs an advertisement that states, "More doctors recommend Brand A margarine for cholesterol control than any other brand." Does this represent a proper usage of marketing research findings?

Scenario 3

A research supplier estimates that a study will cost $10,000 ± 10%. The client agrees that this price is reasonable. However, when the study is completed, the research supplier submits a bill for $15,000, claiming that the cost increased because of changes the client wanted made during the course of the study. The client, though acknowledging that certain unplanned changes were made, argues that such changes should have cost no more than an additional $2,000. How should this problem be resolved?

Scenario 4

"We're conducting a survey," reads the letter from the XYZ Survey Research Company. The survey will be sent to 50 million homes this year. The questionnaire asks for the respondent's preferences on consumer products plus demographic and personal information such as name, address, telephone number, occupation, and family income. To improve respondent cooperation, the sponsoring company offers free samples of various consumer products. What is not said is that the personal information as well as the product choices collected will be compiled onto data tapes and sold to other marketers so they can promote their products. Is this ethical?

Scenario 5

A marketing research firm conducted an attitude study for a client. The data indicate that the product is not being marketed properly. This finding is ill-received by the client's product management team. They request that the damaging data be omitted from the formal report—which will be widely distributed—on the grounds that the verbal presentation is adequate for the client's needs. What should the research firm do?

Scenario 6

Automated polling devices are often placed in malls, airports, and other locations with substantial pedestrian traffic. The hardware includes a computer, monitor, and keyboard. Through graphics, music, and a taped message, passers-by are attracted to these devices, which invite participation in a self-administered survey. The results of these self-selected polls regularly appear in newspaper articles that analyze upcoming elections. Is this a proper use of marketing research?

Scenario 7

The market research director of a pharmaceutical company is given the suggestion by an executive that physicians be telephoned by company interviewers under the name of a fictitious market research agency. The purpose of the survey is to help assess the perceived quality of the company's products, and it is felt that the suggested procedure will result in responses that are more objective. Is this an ethical practice?

Scenario 8

The market research director of a manufacturing company receives a request from a project director to use ultraviolet ink in precoding questionnaires on a mail survey. She points out that the accompanying letter refers to a confidential survey, but she needs to be able to identify respondents to permit adequate cross-tabulation of the data and to save on postage costs if a second mailing is required. Is this an ethical practice?

Scenario 9

A clothing manufacturer has retained a research firm to conduct a study for them. The manufacturer wants to know something about how women choose clothing, such as blouses and sweaters. The manufacturer wants to conduct group interviews, supplemented by a session devoted to observing the women trying on clothing, in order to discover which types of garments are chosen first, how thoroughly they touch and examine the clothing, and whether they look for and read a label or price tag. The client suggests that the observations be performed unobtrusively by female observers at a local department store, via a one-way mirror. One of the research firm associates argues that this would constitute an invasion of privacy. How should this situation be handled?

Scenario 10

A research company is supervising a study of restaurants conducted for a federal government agency. The data, which have already been collected, include specific buying information and prices paid. Respondent organizations have been promised confidentiality. Agency officials demand that all responses be identified by business name. Their rationale is that they plan to repeat the study and wish to limit sampling error by returning to the same procedures. Open bidding requires that the government maintain control of the sample. What should the company do?

Summary

These are but a few of the many abuses in marketing research, which have often generated initiatives for legal action. It is in the best interest of marketing research that these practices do not get out of control. In short, the researcher who acts responsibly does not engage in any of these practices.

A researcher who does not abuse respondents recognizes that such respondents do have certain rights, as shown in Table 1.3. These rights—to choose, to be safe, and to be informed—are fundamental. Moreover, researchers must also acknowledge that respondents have a right to privacy. This is a touchy area as it is difficult to define the meaning of privacy, and to find that delicate balance between the need for research and the privacy interests of individuals. The industry needs to control itself on this issue or the government will, as is the situation in Germany (Bowers, 1989). For many years, there has been a law in Germany that protects data; privacy is defined as being a composite of basic personal data. The gathering and distribution of data is monitored. There are three other provisions of the German law: (1) informed consent is required and the respondent must know the consequences of the interview; (2) respondents must agree in writing for researchers to store data; and (3) data cannot be transferred (even between research companies) without written permission from the respondent. While the German law is an example of extreme regulation, researchers need to be aware that data privacy regulations do exist throughout the world.

Codes of Conduct

In 1974 the Congress of the United States created the National Commission for the Protection of Human Subjects of Biomedical and Behavioral Research. One of the charges to the Commission was to identify the basic ethical principles that should underlie the conduct of biomedical and behavioral research involving human subjects and to develop guidelines that should be followed to ensure that such research is conducted in accordance with those principles. The outcome of this was reported in a document called the Belmont Report

Table 1.3   Ethical Questions Regarding Subjects' Rights

Subjects' Rights	*Possible Results of Violation of Rights*
A. The right to choose 1. Awareness of right 2. Adequate information for an informed choice 3. Opportunity to make a choice	1. Feelings of forced compliance, biased data 2. May violate the client's desire for anonymity, may enable subjects to enact subject role 3. Subjects may avoid environments where this right is violated
B. The right to be safe 1. Protection of anonymity 2. Subjects' right to be free from stress	1. Biased data, refusal to participate in future research 2. Biased data, refusal to participate in future research
C. The right to be informed 1. Debriefing 2. Dissemination of data 3. Right to not be deceived	1. Unrelieved stress, feelings of being used, refusal to participate in future research 2. Subjects may feel that they gain nothing from and are exploited by participating in research and consequently may distort their response and decline to participate in future research 3. Biased data, refusal to participate in future research

SOURCE: Reprinted with permission from "Ethics in Marketing Research: Their Practical Relevance," by Tybout, A.M. & Zaltman, G., in *Journal of Marketing, 11*, p. 359. November, 1974. Published by the American Marketing Association.

(National Commission for the Protection of Human Subjects, 1979). The basic ethical principles that emerged from the work of the Commission are threefold:

- *Respect for humans.* Individuals should be treated as autonomous agents and persons with diminished autonomy are entitled to protection. An autonomous person is an individual capable of deliberation about personal goals and of acting under the direction of such deliberation. Respect for persons demands that subjects enter into the research voluntarily and with adequate information.
- *Beneficence.* Beneficence is viewed as an obligation to make efforts to secure the well being of research subjects. The general rules to be followed are simple: (1) do not harm, and (2) maximize possible benefits and minimize possible harms.
- *Justice.* The concept of justice answers the question of who ought to receive the benefits of research and bear its burdens.

Application of the general principles to the practice of research leads to consideration of the following requirements: (a) informed consent; (b) risk/benefit assessment; and (c) selection of subjects of research.

As mentioned earlier, one way of defining ethics is conforming to professional standards of conduct. If this is so, then in order to evaluate behavior in research there is need for a standard of conduct embodied in a written code. Corporate codes of conduct are relatively common. In addition, there are industry and professional codes of ethics for guiding marketing research behavior. The code used by the American Marketing Association is shown in Exhibit 1.8. One other code is that of the International Chamber of Commerce (ICC) and European Society for Opinion and Marketing Research (ESOMAR), which is summarized in Exhibit 1.9. The New York chapter of the American Marketing Association has its own code.

EXHIBIT 1.8   AMA Marketing Research Code of Ethics

The American Marketing Association, in furtherance of its central objective of the advancement of science in marketing and in recognition of its obligation to the public, has established these principles of ethical practice of marketing research for the guidance of its members. In an increasingly complex society, marketing management is more and more dependent upon marketing information intelligently and systematically obtained. The consumer is the source of much of this information. Seeking the cooperation of the consumer in the development of information, marketing management must acknowledge its obligation to protect the public from misrepresentation and exploitation under the guise of research.

Similarly, the research practitioner has an obligation to the discipline and to those who provide support for it—an obligation to adhere to basic and commonly accepted standards of scientific investigation as they apply to the domain of marketing research.

FOR RESEARCH USERS, PRACTITIONERS, AND INTERVIEWERS

1. No individual or organization will undertake any activity which is directly or indirectly represented to be marketing research, but which has as its real purpose the attempted sales of merchandise or services to some or all of the respondents interviewed in the course of the research.

2. If respondents have been led to believe, directly or indirectly, that they are participating in a marketing research survey and that their anonymity will be protected, their names shall not be made known to any one outside the research organization or research department, or used for other than research purposes.

FOR RESEARCH PRACTITIONERS

1. There will be no intentional or deliberate misrepresentation of research methods or results. An adequate description of methods employed will be made available upon request to the sponsor of the research. Evidence that fieldwork has been completed according to specifications will, upon request, be made available to buyers of the research.

2. The identity of the survey sponsor and/or the ultimate client for whom a survey is being done will be held in confidence at all times, unless this identity is to be revealed as part of the research design. Research information shall be held in confidence by the research organization or department and not used for personal gain or made available to any outside party unless the client specifically authorizes such release.

3. A research organization shall not undertake marketing studies for competitive clients when such studies would jeopardize the confidential nature of client-agency relationships.

FOR USERS OF MARKETING RESEARCH

1. A user of research shall not knowingly disseminate conclusions from a given research project or service that are inconsistent with or not warranted by the data.

2. To the extent that there is involved in a research project a unique design involving techniques, approaches, or concepts not commonly available to research practitioners, the prospective user of research shall not solicit such a design from one practitioner and deliver it to another for execution without the approval of the design originator.

FOR FIELD INTERVIEWERS

1. Research assignments and materials received, as well as information obtained form respondents, shall be held in confidence by the interviewer and revealed to no one except the research organization conducting the marketing study.

2. No information gained through a marketing research activity shall be used, directly or indirectly, for the personal gain or advantage of the interviewer.

3. Interviews shall be conducted in strict accordance with specifications and instructions received.

4. An interviewer shall not carry out two or more interviewing assignments simultaneously, unless authorized by all contractors or employers concerned.

Members of the American Marketing Association will be expected to conduct themselves in accordance with the provisions of this code in all of their marketing research activities.

SOURCE: Reprinted with permission from the American Marketing Association.

EXHIBIT 1.9   Summary of the ICC/ESOMAR Code of Practice

This code of ethics is reprinted with the permission of the European Society for Opinion and Marketing Research.

Marketing and social research depends upon public confidence: confidence that the research is conducted honestly, objectively, without unwelcome intrusion and without disadvantage to informants, and that it is based upon the willing cooperation of the public.

The basic principles of the ICC/ESOMAR International Code of Marketing and Social Research Practice are as follows:

(1) *Any statement made to secure cooperation and all assurances given to an informant, whether oral or written, shall be factually correct and honored.*

(2) *The identity of informants shall remain entirely anonymous* and all records containing references to the identity of an informant shall be securely and confidentially stored. No information which could be used to identify an informant either directly or indirectly, shall be revealed other than to research staff within the Researcher's own organization who may require access to this kind of information for checking interviews or other administrative reasons. The only exceptions to this rule are where an informant has been told the identity of the client, the purposes of the survey and has then given consent in writing to the disclosure; or where the disclosure to a third party (such as a sub-contractor) is essential for a purpose such a follow up interview with the same informant.

(3) *Informants shall be told in advance where observation or recording techniques* are to be used except where the actions or statements of individuals are observed or recorded in a public place in which they could reasonably be expected to be overheard or observed by others.

(4) *The informant's right to withdraw, or to refuse to cooperate at any stage of an interview shall be respected.* Any or all of the information provided by an Informant must be destroyed without delay if the Informant so requests.

(5) *Special care shall be taken when interviewing children.* Before a child is interviewed or asked to complete a questionnaire, the permission of a parent, guardian, or other person responsible for the child at the time (such as a school teacher) shall be obtained. In obtaining this permission the Interviewer shall describe the nature of the interview in sufficient detail to enable the responsible person to reach an informed decision.

(6) *No activity shall be misrepresented as marketing research.* Specifically, the following activities shall in no way be associated with marketing research:
  (a) Enquiries designed to obtain personal information *per se* about private individuals, whether for legal, political, or any other purpose.
  (b) The compilation of lists, registers or data banks which are not for marketing research.

(c) Industrial, commercial, or any other form of espionage.

(d) The acquisition of information for use in credit rating or similar services.

(e) Sales or promotional approaches.

(f) The collection of debts.

(g) Direct or indirect attempts to influence an Informant's opinions or attitudes on any issue.

(7) *The research findings and data from a marketing research project are the property of the Client.* No findings or data shall be disclosed by the Researcher to any third party without the prior written consent of the Client.

I subscribe to the Code of Ethics and will adhere to it.

Signature _____

Date _____

Codes of conduct will not eliminate abuses and questionable practices in marketing research. They are a starting point, however, and cannot but help in the industry's fight to police and regulate itself.

SUMMARY

In this chapter we introduced marketing research as the link between the consumer and industrial buyer and marketer through information. We learned what marketing research can do—for managers, for those pursuing a marketing research career, and for groups within companies. Managers use marketing research to facilitate decision making.

Next we discussed marketing research functions and the description and explanation that accurate prediction and evaluation of market opportunities require.

There are several groups who conduct marketing research. We presented examples of the organizations that perform research projects and then moved to the types of decisions made by marketing managers. After a brief discussion of models, and the necessity for using some problem-solving model, whether implicit or explicit, for decision making, the importance of good information was presented. Information should be accurate, current, sufficient, available, and, most important, relevant to be meaningful to organizations.

In addition to the marketing research system, the internal records, marketing intelligence, and information analysis subsystems make up an MIS. These subsystems are independent from, and interdependent with, each other within the marketing structure.

Next we discussed the types of dialogue and challenges between manager and researcher. This dialogue can encompass objectives, courses of action, and environmental variables affecting decision outcomes.

We then presented a brief discussion of who should do the marketing research for a company. This decision is a "make or buy" decision for a company; options range from the internal research staff to different types of outside agencies.

The chapter concluded with an examination of ethical issues in marketing research. Although there are many concerns among researchers and others, they can be summarized as deceptive/fraudulent practices, invasion of privacy, and lack of consideration for subjects/respondents. Ethical dilemmas arise because of the relationships that exist between a researcher and stakeholders in the research process. Professional codes of conduct of marketing research were presented, which are indicative of an industry that is trying to clean up its own act.

New and exciting developments are occurring within the marketing research industry. One major change is that the set of alternative research techniques has been expanding due to technology developments. For survey research, for example, researchers are no longer limited to the traditional triad of data collection techniques—mail, telephone, and personal interview. Self-administered electronic modes of data collection, from e-mail and the Internet to interactive voice response (IVR) have been developed and are continually being refined. Software developments in word processing, ranging from font changes to the use of icons and colors, have expanded options in measurement instrument (questionnaire) design. Also, the emergence of optical character recognition and imaging technologies have led to increasing opportunities for automating data entry. Clearly, marketing research is *not* static! The integration of customer relationship management (CRM) systems with accounting and marketing databases has expanded access to and understanding of customers and markets, and their use of products and services.

ASSIGNMENT MATERIAL

1. Assume that you are faced with the alternative of changing a package design for a firm marketing frozen peas. Describe the major environmental conditions that could affect sales and cost considerations associated with changing over to the new design.

2. It has been suggested that the distinction between basic and decisional research is that the purpose of the former is to answer a question and the purpose of the latter is to solve a problem. Comment.

3. Give several examples of research projects dealing with human behavior that might be either basic or decisional, depending upon who the client of the project is.

4. Identify the types of management decisions presented in this chapter. For each, give examples of marketing research that might be done for a company manufacturing bicycles.

5. What are the practical characteristics information must have to be useful for making decisions? Can we really say that one is more important than the others?

6. Specify the types of marketing research groups or organizations that might be best to consider using in the following situations and explain your choice:
   a. Determining the size of a market for a new product
   b. Assessing the impact of a change in a marketing mix variable
   c. Determining what features consumers desire in a product

7. Of what value is it to the marketing researcher to explore with a client the actions that would be taken, given alternative research outcomes, before the contemplated research is undertaken?

8. Is it necessary that a company have a formal MIS in order to effectively use marketing research? Explain.

9. A number of areas of manager-researcher conflict have been identified. Discuss what you feel are the best ways to resolve such conflicts.

10. Bobbie Murria is the project director for an outside research company that is doing a project for a regular client. A study she is working on is about to go into the field when the questionnaire sent to the client for final approval comes back drastically modified. The client has rewritten it, introducing leading questions and biased scales. An accompanying letter indicates that the questionnaire must be sent out as revised. She does not believe that valid information can be gathered using the revised instrument. What should Ms. Murria do?

11. A marketing research firm has conducted an attitude study for a client. The data indicate that the product is not being marketed properly. This finding is ill-received by the client's product management team. They request that the researcher omit that data from its formal written report (which will be widely distributed) on the grounds that the verbal presentation was adequate for their needs. What should the researcher do about the formal written report?

12. Exhibit 1.7 presents ten scenarios involving marketing research. If you were the person that had made the decision, what would you do in each case and why?

13. A marketing research project director feels that as long as a practice is legal, it also is ethical. Indicate whether you agree or disagree with this person and defend your position.

REFERENCES

Akaah, I. P., & Riordan, F. A. (1989). Judgments of marketing professionals about ethical issues in marketing research. *Journal of Marketing Research, 26,* 112–120.

Andreasen, A. (1981). *Mythological barriers to the use of marketing research by small and nonprofit organizations.* (Faculty Working Paper No. 70). Urbana: University of Illinois, College of Commerce and Business Administration.

Bennett, P. (1988). *Glossary of marketing terms.* Chicago: American Marketing Association.

Bowers, D.K. (1989, September). Bundesdatenchutzgestz. *Marketing Research, 1,* 73–76.

Brock, S., Lipson, S., & Levitt, R. (1989, December). Trends in marketing research and development at Citicorp/Citibank. *Marketing Research, 1,* 4.

Carroll, A., & Buchholtz, A. (2000). *Business and society: Ethics and stakeholder management* (4th ed.), Chaps. 4–5. Cincinnati, OH: South-Western.

Cary, M. S. (1998, January 5). 7 Steps to obtain practical research. *Marketing News, 32,* 16–17.

Cayley, M. (1968, Autumn). The role of research in marketing. *The Business Quarterly, 33,* 32–40.

Conner, P. (1996, September 23). Defining the "decision-purpose" of research. *Marketing News, 30,* 18.

Cortese, A. (1996, February 26). Here comes the intranet. *BusinessWeek,* pp. 76–84.

Deshpande, R., & Zaltman, G. (1982, February). Factors affecting the use of market research information: A path analysis. *Journal of Marketing Research, 19,* 14–31.

Deshpande, R., & Zaltman, G. (1984, February). A comparison of factors affecting researcher and manager perceptions of market research use. *Journal of Marketing Research, 21,* 32–38.

Dunn, T. F., Hisinger, B., & McLaughlin, T. (1998). *1998 ARF/AMA marketing research industry survey.* Chicago: American Marketing Association.

Friemann, K. (2003, January 20). 6 Steps during initiation critical to efficacy. *Marketing News, 37,* 14.

Gelb, U. (2001, September 24). Litigation surveys have special rules. *Marketing News, 35,* 26–27.

Green, P. E., Tull, D. S., & Albaum, G. (1988). *Research for marketing decisions* (5th ed.). Englewood Cliffs, NJ: Prentice Hall.

Green, P. E., Krieger, A. M., & Wind, Y. (2002, September 16). Survey methods help to clear up legal questions. *Marketing News, 36,* 34–36.

Hunt, S. D., Chonko, L. B., & Wilcox, J. B. (1984, August). Ethical problems of marketing researchers. *Journal of Marketing Research, 21,* 309–324.

James, D. (2002, September 16). Your seat here: Establish your place at the table. *Marketing News, 37,* 1ff.

Jarvis, S. (2002a, February 4). CMOR study finds survey refusal rate still rising. *Marketing News, 36,* 4.

Jarvis, S. (2002b, June 24). MR adds value to shows. *Marketing News, 36,* 11.

Judge, P. C. (1998, January 26). Are tech buyers different? *BusinessWeek,* pp. 64–68.

Keane, J. G. (1969, October). Some observations on marketing research in top management decision making. *Journal of Marketing, 33,* 10–15.

Kotler, P., & Armstrong, U. (2001). *Principles of marketing,* Activebook Version 1.0. Upper Saddle River, NJ: Prentice Hall.

Levenburg, N., & Dandridge, T. (1997, March 31). Can't afford research? Try miniresearch. *Marketing News, 31,* 19.

Little, J. D. C. (1979, Summer). Decision support systems for marketing managers. *Journal of Marketing, 43,* 9–26.

McCarthy, J. T. (1996). *McCarthy on trademarks and unfair competition* (4th ed.). New York: Clark Boardman Callaghan.

McDaniel, S. W., Verille, P., & Madden, C. S. (1985, February). The threats to marketing research: An empirical reappraisal. *Journal of Marketing Research, 22,* 74–80.

Murphy, P. E., & Laczniak, G. R. (1992, March). Traditional ethical issues facing marketing research. *Marketing Research,* pp. 8–21.

National Commission for the Protection of Human Subjects of Biomedical and Behavioral Research. (1979, April 18). The Belmont report: Ethical principles and guidelines for the protection of human subjects of biomedical and behavioral research. Washington, DC: Author.

Rens, M. (1994, May 9). Survey results can be persuasive evidence. *Marketing News, 28,* 26–27.

Roche, K., & O'Connell, B. (1998, November 9). Dig a wider channel for your products. *Marketing News, 32,* 10.

Rubenstein, E. (1989, May 22). Food manufacturers discover value of intelligence systems. *Marketing News, 23,* 11–12.

Schneider, K. C. (1977, Spring). Subjects and respondent abuse in marketing research. *MSU Business Topics,* pp. 13–19.

Smith, S. A. (1974, March/April). Research and pseudo-research in marketing. *Harvard Business Review,* pp. 73–76.

Snyder, M. (1999, October 25). How marketing research is (or should be) like geometry. *Marketing News, 33,* 44–45.

Swinyard, W., & Smith, S. (2001, July 9). Compressed data: Painting some pictures of the online shopper. *New York Times,* Section C, p. 4.

Tybout, A. M., & Zaltman, G. (1974, November). Ethics in marketing research: Their practical relevance. *Journal of Marketing Research, 11,* 357–368.

Vence, D. L. (2003, June 23). Boston Orchestra tunes up new campaign. *Marketing News, 37,* 5–6.

Weinberg, C. B. (1989). Ethical dilemmas in marketing research. In C. H. Lovelock & C. B. Weinberg, *Marketing challenges: Cases and exercises* (2nd ed.). New York: McGraw-Hill.

Welter, P. J. (1998). *Trademark surveys.* Eagen, MN: West Group.

Whalen, B. (1984, March 16). 'Tiny' Saab drives up profits with marketing niche strategy, repositioning. *Marketing News, 18*(Section 1), pp. 14–16.

Chapter 2

PLANNING FOR MARKETING RESEARCH AND THE RESEARCH PROCESS

In Chapter 1, we made a distinction between basic and decisional (applied) research. This distinction is important because information is gathered and used differently. Decisional research gathers information for a pending decision; basic research gathers information to increase the level of knowledge in a given area. No matter what type of research is conducted, there are essentially four broad determinants of how a research project should be conducted: the nature of the problem, the researcher, the survey respondent or experimental subject, and the client.

The factor that determines whether a research project is basic or decisional is the client. Basic and decisional research projects can deal with the same problem, be conducted by the same researcher, and use the same respondents to provide information, but the goals, and therefore the clients, would be different. For example, a consumer motivation study and a voting behavior study could both be conducted using the same researcher and respondents. However, these projects would have different clients, and the difference in clients and their levels of error tolerance would be the source of differences in method and design requirements.

All clients seek information whose errors are small and can be measured or estimated with reasonable, objective accuracy. Information of unknown accuracy may be worse than none at all. The basic-research client is a part of the scientific or managerial community. Scientists historically have insisted upon eliminating as much error as possible and obtaining objectively verifiable measures of the remaining potential error. Ideally, the research will have been conducted with full disclosure of procedures and the researcher will have acted independently. The capability of other investigators to replicate the project from the report is a means of ensuring that these requirements are met.

In contrast, the decisional-research client would seek as little error as possible and objective measurement of the residual potential error if these options were available at no additional cost.

The client may find, however, that beyond some point, added accuracy is not worth the cost of obtaining it. The same conclusion may also be reached about objective measurement of residual error. And because the decisional-research client typically will have been closely associated with the project from its start and may have chosen the principal researcher or researchers involved, he also has an additional means of assessing research information that is not generally available to basic-research clients. Due to such close involvement, he or she will have many opportunities to assess both the general competence of the researchers and the manner in which the project has been conducted. Therefore, there may be less need for objective measurement of error and for investigator independence in procedures.

Finally, there is rarely a need for replication in decisional research projects. Most research projects conducted for decision-making purposes are concerned with problems that are essentially unique and nonrecurring. A new product is to be evaluated before deciding whether to introduce it, or the proportion of the electorate who favor a political candidate is to be determined. Such topics may require decisions at a later date, but the circumstances will inevitably have changed.

OVERVIEW OF THE PLANNING PROCESS

The differences in client requirements often give rise to different requirements in basic and decisional research projects. The value-versus-cost orientation of the decisional research process is an outgrowth of these differences. With these differences in mind, we now turn to a discussion of the broad research process and what a research project entails. In planning a project, the overriding concern facing the researcher is error. Consequently, the practice of marketing research may be viewed as involving the management of total error. The concept of total error is discussed in Chapter 3.

In this chapter we first provide an overview of the research process and then specifically discuss what is involved in planning a research project, namely the following steps:

- Problem formulation
- Method of inquiry
- Research method
- Research design
- Selection of data collection techniques
- Sample design
- Data collection
- Analysis and interpretation of data
- Research reports

This chapter will discuss each step of the process, and then the research plan will be covered.

For purposes of planning, the research process can be viewed as consisting of a number of interrelated steps, as shown in Figure 2.1. Although presented in a hierarchical format, some of the steps may be performed simultaneously, such as selecting data collection techniques and sample design. There are other times when alternatives for "later" decisions influence decisions that are made early in the research planning process. For example, desired analysis

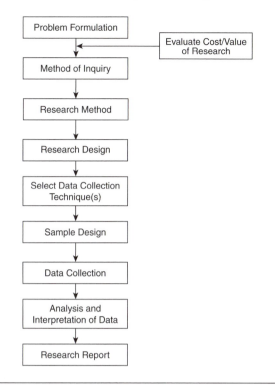

Figure 2.1 The Research Process

techniques often influence the selection of data collection techniques (e.g., measurement) and sample design.

Also, what is to be included in the research report helps determine the research design and data collection procedures (Andreasen, 1988, Chapter 4). Such a "backward" marketing research process actually involves problem formulation based on the needs of the ultimate user—the client—and translates a management problem into a research problem. That is, if the client can clearly articulate the desired outcome or products of the research process, research results should prove to be more meaningful.

STAGE 1: PROBLEM FORMULATION

In a very real sense, problem formulation is the heart of the research process. As such, it represents the single most important step to be performed. From the researcher's point of view, problem formulation means translating the management problem into a research problem (Table 2.1).

In order to formulate an appropriate research problem, the researcher must understand the origin and nature of management's problem and then be able to rephrase it into meaningful terms from an analytical point of view. This involves timely and clear communication

Table 2.1   Examples of Management Problems and Related Research Problems

Management Problems	Research Problems
Allocate advertising budget among media	Estimate awareness generated by each media type
Decide whether to keep office open on Saturday	Evaluate use of services on Saturday and determine on Saturday whether customers will shift usage to weekdays
Introduce a new health service	Design a concept test and assess acceptance and use
Change the marketing program	Design a test-marketing situation such that the effect of the new program can be estimated
Increase the sales of a product	Measure a product's current image

between manager and researcher, as we discussed in Chapter 1. Examples of good and bad communication are presented in Exhibit 2.1.

The end result of problem formulation is a statement of the management problem that is analytically meaningful and that often points the way to alternative solutions. An accurate problem formulation specifies the types of information needed to help solve the management problem. In short, the quality of thinking about an issue (i.e., a problem situation) prior to data collection largely determines the quality of thinking (i.e., analysis and problem solving) after the data have been collected (Barabba & Zaltman, 1991, Chapter 5).

EXHIBIT 2.1   In Support of Good Communication

Case 1: How Communication Went Wrong

Some years ago a manager of an entertainment company decided she knew too little about the consumer segments her company served and, particularly, about those where an opportunity for entry or growth existed (Andreasen, 1988, pp. 61–62). The manager was disappointed by the study done to analyze the company's market because she felt the research provided information she already knew. Primary consumers of the industry previously had been studied numerous times, and the manager felt that the researcher had not, from the outset, understood what she wanted. The researcher assumed his client wanted a behavioral measure of loyalty, but the manager also wanted an attitudinal measure. It is clear that there was not a dialogue between the manager and the researcher.

Case 2: How Communication Worked

More than 20 years ago Joseph E. Seagram & Sons, Inc., was marketing a new wine and the vice-president of marketing requested a survey of the U.S. wine market ("Action-oriented research," 1981). Discussion between management and the research department led to the final decision that the survey objectives should be expanded to include determination of advertising target market groups, measurement of the image of the brand compared with other wines, development of an advertising copy strategy, and determination of the optimal media mix. According to Robert W. Better, vice-president of marketing services:

It's fundamental, but I think we would have not done anybody involved any favor if we had just done a survey when we were asked to do a survey. It is up to the marketing and research people involved to, up front, build Action intentions or objectives into the research. ("Action-oriented research," 1981, page 7)

After combining the research results with other data to develop an advertising campaign, sales of the brand increased 74 percent in two years while category sales increased only 13 percent.

Closely related to problem formulation is the development of a working hypothesis, or an assertion about a state of nature. While hypotheses are crucial for basic research because they tell the researcher what to do, the concept of a hypothesis can also be useful in decisional research to direct the development of the research problem statement. In most cases, the marketing researcher will not explicitly state hypotheses for the research. Exhibit 2.2 lists criteria for research problems and hypotheses.

EXHIBIT 2.2 Problems and Hypotheses

Kerlinger and Lee (2000, Chapter 2) presented criteria of good research problems and problem statements, and of good hypotheses. Good research problems and problem statements meet all of the following criteria:

1. The problem statement expresses a relationship between two or more variables.

2. The problem is stated clearly and unambiguously in question form.

3. The problem statement implies possibilities of empirical testing.

Properties of good hypotheses include the following:

1. The hypothesis is a statement about the relationship between two or more variables in declarative statement form.

2. The hypothesis carries clear implications for testing the stated relationship (i.e., variables must be measurable or potentially measurable).

Problem Components

A problem consists of specific components:

1. The manager(s)/decision maker(s) and his, her, or their objectives

2. The environment or context of the problem

3. The nature of the problem

4. Alternative courses of action

5. A set of consequences that relate to courses of action and to the occurrence of events not under the control of the manager

6. A state of uncertainty as to which course of action is best

We will examine these components and discuss their role in defining the problem.

1. Objectives

The "manager" making a decision may be one individual, a marketing group of two or more people, or an agent acting for a group or other individuals. Moreover, some members of the group may not agree with the choice made because of differences either in objectives (i.e., valued outcomes) or in their appraisal of the effectiveness of means chosen to achieve the objectives.

The objectives of the decision maker provide motivation for the decision. These objectives, or goals, may range from business goals, such as a desire to maintain or increase company profits and market share to personal goals such as maintaining prestige and a desire to advance within the company. However, most of the objectives involve monetary considerations such as net profits, cash flow, and return on investment. And, in the end, this is what managers are most concerned with and what influences the problem formulation the most.

The manager's objectives may also be characterized as hierarchical in nature and as evolving over time. For example, an increase in the firm's profits may result from an increase in the firm's sales, which, in turn, may result from the firm's sales personnel contacting a greater number of new accounts per month. The goal for the salesperson may be to increase sales contacts 10 percent over those made in some base period. This represents a sub-goal and should be consistent with the higher-level objective.

Determining Objectives

Objectives range from the very general, such as profit maximization, to the highly specific, such as obtaining a particular account. They also vary from jointly agreed-upon corporate objectives to the individual objectives of each employee. Suppose that the marketing manager says, "I need to know how effective our last advertising campaign was." Superficially, it may seem that this is an adequate statement of the objective of the research project to be initiated—to determine the effectiveness of the last advertising campaign. However, on reflection this statement does not state an objective at all. Why does the marketing manager want this information? If her purpose is to evaluate the agency's handling of the campaign, an entirely different kind of research may be appropriate than if the purpose is, say, to decide the level and allocation of the advertising budget for the coming period. Knowledge of the specific objectives influences the kind of information desired and the degree of accuracy that is required. The research problem cannot be adequately formulated without knowing the objectives of the client.

It is rare that the objectives are explained fully to the researcher. The researcher will normally need to take the initiative, therefore, in developing a clear statement of objectives. This can frequently turn out to be a difficult task, but is nonetheless a necessary and valuable one. The researchers will usually find it necessary to resort to indirect methods of determining objectives. Two techniques are useful in this indirect approach.

The first of these is the "explosion" method whereby the researcher explores with the manager the meaning of each term in the statement of the problem. For example, in the statement, "I need to know how effective out last advertising campaign was," the researcher must know what the marketing manager means by the word "effective" in order to ensure that the problem statement specifies the kinds of information that the manager needs. Is the manager referring to the extent to which the campaign informed the audience of the content of the advertising? If so, the research project should be designed to measure such variables as audience level, recall, and level of knowledge. If the manager means the degree to which the campaign persuaded the audience of the merits of the product, then the project should measure changes in attitudes and/or preferences and link the changes with exposure to the advertising. Or, if the manager means only the volume of sales resulting from the campaign, project objectives will require other types of information. By raising such questions, noting the answers, and probing where required, the researcher will have a clear formulation of the problem and may also help the manager to more fully understand the possible project objectives and to sort out the important ones.

The researcher can also raise questions with the manager and other personnel regarding the actions they intend to take, given specified outcomes of the study. If research shows that the last advertising campaign was ineffective, will the advertising budget be increased? Will different appeals be used? Will the allocation of the budget among media be changed? Will the account go to a new agency?

Objectives guide the researcher in developing good, useful research, and they help the client evaluate the completed project. Each study should have as few objectives as feasible (Schmalensee, 1982). The fewer the objectives of any study the easier it is to keep track of progress toward the objectives, to ensure that each is properly addressed, and to determine the best methodology. If there are too many objectives separate studies may be more desirable.

Finally, it is critical to note that although objectives change over time, we assume they are relatively stable over the decision period that is relevant in a research project. This is critical for the research process to continue in the active business environment.

2. Environment of the Problem

Every problem exists within the context of the characteristics of the company and of the market, including:

- Consumer tastes and preferences
- Level of income and rate of growth in the market area
- The degree of competition and competitor action and reaction
- Government regulation (both type and extent)

These environmental factors may individually and collectively affect the outcomes of the decision made. Therefore, the researcher must assist the manager in identifying those environmental factors that are relevant to the problem.

Consider the problem of deciding whether to introduce a new consumer product. The following are some of the environmental factors that could affect the decision:

- The types of consumers that comprise the potential market
- The size and location of the market
- The prospects for growth or contraction of the market over the planning period
- The buying habits of consumers
- The current competition of the product
- The likelihood and timing of entry of new competitive products
- The current and prospective competitive position of the company with respect to price, quality, and reputation
- The marketing and manufacturing capabilities of the company
- The situation with respect to patents, trademarks, and royalties
- The situation with respect to codes, trade agreements, taxes, and tariffs

This list is by no means exhaustive; it illustrates some of the more important environmental factors that could influence the outcome of the decision and so must be considered in the problem statement. Each problem has a comparable set of environmental factors that are worthy of consideration.

Although the effects of the environment of the problem—those factors that both affect the outcome and are uncontrollable—cannot be predicted with certainty, for a given problem it may be sufficient to consider only a few of the many possible outcomes for each of the alternatives. For example, in a decision concerning whether or not to introduce a new product, the executive may be interested only in whether the sales volume is likely to exceed some desired level.

One of the jobs of the market researcher is to assemble information concerning the firm's environmental variables to assist in identifying the states of nature that should be considered. The possible states may range from fairly detailed descriptions to broad summaries in which data are condensed into a relatively small number of potential sales levels over a specific time period.

In summary, the marketing researcher, to be effective as an information supplier, must work closely with his or her client in effecting a transformation of the client's problem into a research problem. Since the researcher's and client's interests are both concerned with the potential value of the research findings versus their cost, the researcher must become aware of, and assist in, the identification of objectives, courses of action, and environmental variables, insofar as they affect the design of the research investigation. For that matter, the researcher's efforts should be oriented toward helping the manager decide whether any investigation is justified. If research is undertaken and if the resulting findings are to be utilized (i.e., have an influence on the user's decision making), the user must trust the researcher and users must view user-researcher interactions as being productive (Moorman, Zaltman, & Deshpande, 1992).

3. The Nature of the Problem

Every problem has associated relationships that offer alternative explanations of the problem. Some of these relationships are simple and may be dependent on time or on only one environmental variable; others are very complex and involve the relationships between multiple variables. A thorough preliminary investigation using focus groups of consumers, salespeople, managers, or others close to the problem may produce much needed insight.

Alternatively, in-depth personal interviews using means-end analysis may provide insight into motivations for product usage. Perhaps an investigation of behavioral issues may demand a different course of action for the research, including purchase audits, habit and use studies, purchase diaries, and in-depth analysis of product use experiences.

Each of the many available approaches to preliminary investigation of the problem produces insights into the true nature of the problem. If the problem is incorrectly identified or the objective behind the problem investigation is misunderstood, no amount of research can help produce an optimal course of action around which a marketing plan can be developed. Exhibit 2.3 shows how understanding consumers can aid in assessing the relevance of data to be collected.

EXHIBIT 2.3   Assessing Relevant Data

What data will really help sell more of a product? An answer to this question involves understanding the consumer. A clear understanding of consumer behavior ensures that relevant data are collected. Since consumers are satiable regarding the information they use, purposeful, and comparative, markets are changing all the time and the need for data is ongoing.

Bill Marefka, vice president of marketing and strategic planning for Birmingham, Alabama–based Intermark Group, Inc., suggests that for any firm marketing to its customers, the following types of questions will provide insights into the data's ability to answer strategic questions (Marefka, 2003):

- Do the data reflect who is purchasing the product or service?
- Can the data be related to, and offer insight useful for, solving the immediate problem?
- Do the data include whether a company was in the consumers' consideration set?
- Will the data say why consumers bought from the company or its competitors?
- Will the data say why the products of the company or its competitors were not purchased?
- Can the data speak to the relevance of the target consumer?
- Can the data help position the company in the competitive environment?
- Can the data suggest what kind of consumers the company wants to attract in the future?
- Do the data deal with when and why the company was successful?
- Do the data address the matter of who the target of the marketing is?

Understanding the nature of the problem helps a researcher ensure that the right problem is being investigated and that a marketing plan can be developed to solve the problem.

4. Alternative Courses of Action

A course of action specifies a behavioral sequence, such as the adoption of a new package design, or the introduction of a new product. All courses of action involve, either implicitly or explicitly, the element of time. For example, the course of action "Introduce the new product starting next week" is a different course of action from "Introduce the new product starting next year." "Do nothing new" is just as much a course of action as a change from the status quo.

A decision to stipulate a program of action becomes a commitment, made in the present, to follow some behavioral pattern in the future. The implementation of this course of action may well extend over time. For example, a program involving the construction of a new plant may be executed over the course of several years. The complexity of alternative courses of action may range from a single act requiring immediate implementation to a large set of related acts implemented either in parallel or sequentially over time. The time interval, which is one part of the course of action, may be highly important, since both the costs of implementation and the probabilities of alternative outcomes will typically vary as a function of time. Errors in forecasts usually increase as a function of time. Frequently, however, implementation of some action may be delayed pending the receipt of better information with relatively little cost associated with this delay.

It is possible to specify courses of action to a greater or lesser degree, depending on the problem. For some purposes it may be sufficient merely to state the course of action, for example, "Add two new salespeople in the Chicago district starting next month." Other instances may require a more detailed specification (regarding the type of previous experience, education, product familiarity, etc., of the two salespeople to be hired). Courses of action may include decision rules, that is, various conditional statements in the program of action: "Start designing a new plant; if sales from the existing plant exceed 100,000 units by the end of next year, start construction; if not, reconsider the decision to build a new plant." This course of action is a contingency plan, since its implementation is contingent, or dependent, upon some unknown event at the time of stipulation. Although we have a recipe for reacting to each possible event, we do not know which action will be implemented until one of the possible events occurs.

It is usually desirable to generate as many alternatives as possible during the problem-formulation stage and state them in the form of research hypotheses to be examined. A hypothesis often implies a possible course of action with a prediction of the outcome if that course of action is followed. For example, if a decision is to be made concerning whether or not to adopt a new package, and the immediate objective is to obtain a 15-percent share of the market, a hypothesis may state that adoption of the proposed new package will result in a market share of at least 15 percent. It will then become the task of the researcher to obtain information to test this assertion (for example, by developing hypotheses concerning acceptance on a trial-market basis) and, thus, to assist in the process of deciding whether or not to change to the new package.

How does the researcher recognize relevant alternative courses of action and thus develop hypotheses? This process is at least as much an art as it is a science, as it is dependent to a significant extent on the experience, judgment, and creative capabilities of the individuals concerned. It is also apparent that relevant alternative courses of action should be closely related to the objectives to be achieved.

There is perhaps no better illustration of the relationship between objectives and courses of action than the general problem of diversification of products. The general objective of increasing profits through the addition of new products is almost always primary, but other objectives are usually invariably present, such as utilization of excess capacity in one or more of the functional areas of the business (manufacturing, marketing, etc.), reducing seasonal or cyclical fluctuations in sales, and rounding out the product line. If one major objective is to utilize excess manufacturing capacity, this may greatly limit the number of possible products that should be considered. This would impact the relevant possible courses of action for consideration.

The identification of possible courses of action is closely related to the problem-situation model. Once the objectives have been agreed upon, the formulation of the model consists of the following:

1. Determining which variables affect the solution to the problem

2. Determining which of these variables are controllable and to what extent control can be exercised

3. Determining the functional relationship of the variables; the nature of this relationship will indicate which variables are critical to the solution of the problem.

A notable example of a failure to follow through with these aspects of the problem-situation model is presented in Exhibit 2.4. Another example is CPC International, which met some resistance when it tried to sell its dry Knorr soups in the United States. The company had test-marketed the product by serving passersby a small portion of its already-prepared warm soup. After the taste test, the individuals were questioned about possible sales. The research revealed U.S. consumer interest, but sales were very slow once the packages were placed on the grocery-store shelves. Further investigation indicated that the market tests had overlooked the fact that American consumers have historically avoided most dry soups. During the testing, those interviewed were unaware that the soup they were tasting was a dried soup. Finding the taste quite acceptable, the interviewees indicated they would be will-ing to buy the soup. Had they known the soup was sold in a dry form and that preparation required 15–20 minutes of occasional stirring, they would have shown less interest in the product. In this particular case, the preparation was extremely important, and the failure to test for this unique difference resulted in a sluggish market (Ricks, 1999, p. 141).

EXHIBIT 2.4   "New Coke" Versus Original Coke

In the mid-1980s the Coca Cola Company made a decision to introduce a new beverage product (Hartley, 1995, pp. 129–145). The company had evidence that taste was the single most important cause of Coke's decline in the market share in the late 1970s and early 1980s. A new product dubbed "New Coke" was developed that was sweeter than the original-formula Coke. Almost 200,000 blind product taste tests were conducted in the United States, and more than one-half of the participants favored New Coke over both the original formula and Pepsi. The new product was introduced and the original formula was withdrawn from the market. This turned out to be a big mistake! Eventually, the company reintroduced the original formula as Coke Classic and tried to market the two products. Ultimately, New Coke was withdrawn from the market. What went wrong? Two things stand out. First, there was a flaw in the market research taste tests that were conducted: They assumed that taste was the deciding factor in consumer purchase behavior. Consumers were not told that only one product would be marketed. Thus, they were not asked whether they would give up the original formula for New Coke. Second, no one realized the symbolic value and emotional involvement people had with the original Coke. The bottom line on this is that relevant variables that would affect the problem solution were not included in the research.

---

5. The Consequences of Alternative Courses of Action

One of the manager's primary jobs is to anticipate and communicate the possible outcomes of various courses of action. Outcomes will depend on various environmental factors. For example, suppose that a manufacturer of industrial belting is interested in increasing the tensile strength of this product. Presumably, higher production costs will be incurred for this increase in strength. The decision to modify the product depends on factors such as additional sales anticipated through marketing a stronger product. Additional sales obviously will depend on how customers react to the modification, the actions that competitors take, and other variables.

6. Degrees of Uncertainty

Most marketing problems are characterized by a situation of uncertainty. Experience in dealing with similar problems may allow the decision-making manager to assign various "degrees of belief" to the occurrence of various possible outcomes, given specific courses of action. As we have stated previously, a carefully formulated problem and statement of research purpose is necessary for competently conducted research. In effect, this statement of purpose involves a translation of the decision maker's problem into a research problem and the derivation of a study design from this problem formulation. The research problem provides relevant information concerning recognized (or newly generated) alternative solutions to aid in this choice.

Evaluation of Cost and Value

At some point during the problem formulation process, sometimes only at the end, a decision must be made as to whether a formal investigation is justified. This choice involves communication between the manager and the researcher. Of interest to the decision maker is whether the marketing decision should be made using only experience, judgment, and existing knowledge or whether the decision should be delayed until the proposed project is completed. This discussion situation involves comparing the additional value to the marketing decision that the researcher will provide with the cost of conducting the research. Exhibit 2.5 describes different approaches to this step of the problem formulation process.

EXHIBIT 2.5   Approaches to Determining the Value of Information

There are several methods of establishing the value of marketing research information. Each is applicable primarily to the individual project rather than to the total research effort. Some methods are applied before doing any research, some after. Ideally, value should be established before the research is conducted, but this is not always feasible.

Bayesian Approach

The Bayesian approach (so named for its frequent use of Bayes' theorem) to decision making in situations with uncertainty makes use of personal probabilities rather than the classical relative-frequency probabilities. A personal probability may be viewed as the confidence the decision maker has in the truth of a specific proposition, where the confidence is expressed numerically and where the expressed judgments obey certain rules of consistency. Multiplying each numerical outcome, or payoff, by the appropriate probability and summing the products gives an expected value. The difference between the expected value when research is done and the expected value without research being done is the *expected value of information* (EVI). The net expected payoff of the research is the difference between EVI and the expected cost of obtaining the information.

Simple Savings Method

This method assumes that management can make a single reasonably accurate estimate of the cost of making a wrong decision as well as estimate the chance of making such an incorrect decision. The value of information is determined as follows:

$$\text{Value} = E(\text{Cost})_N - E(\text{Cost})_I$$

where

$E(\text{Cost})_N$ = estimated cost of mistake using no additional information

$E(\text{Cost})_I$ = estimated cost of mistake using additional information

Return on Investment

Another approach views research as an investment and calculates a return on this investment after the research has been completed and acted upon.

Present Value Method

This method also treats research expenditures as an investment. Incremental cash benefits (receipts due to the research minus costs of the research) expected over the life of the research investment are discounted by the marginal cost of the capital. This approach can be applied both to individual projects and to a total marketing research effort by an organization.

Cost-Benefit Approach

This approach determines value using a cost-benefit framework. Evaluation is done by one of the following three methods:

1. Setting a cost figure and maximizing benefits from that cost

2. Establishing a desired level of benefits and minimizing the cost of achieving that level of benefits

3. Maximizing benefits

Generically, this method is non-Bayesian in structure. However, it can be used very effectively with a Bayesian approach; the expected value of perfect information places an upper limit on benefits to be obtained.

Compared with determining the value of information, determining the cost of acquisition is relatively simple. If fact, if the research is to be done by an outside supplier such as an independent research firm, advertising agency, and so forth, there is no problem—the cost is the price asked for by the supplier.

For in-house projects, it is necessary to have accurate internal accounting data and good information about the costs of purchasing required materials, including any subcontracting, for example, use of a field service to collect data for a survey. The research manager must know all the activities that will be performed in the project, from problem formulation to preparation and presentation of the research report. Whether the research manager must present the research plan as a formal proposal depends on the organizational structure of the firm. For example, some companies have centralized research departments from which users in the company "buy" research. This arrangement is similar to purchasing research from an outside supplier and would require that a formal proposal be submitted with a price for doing the project.

The types of costs that may arise in any project are operational and creative. Operational costs are those involved in implementing the project itself including such items as, for example, for a survey, costs of mailing questionnaires, interviewing, and printing of research materials. Creative costs are costs related to planning the project, including such tasks as problem formulation, research and sample design, drawing a sample, and analyzing obtained data.

Operational costs can be more easily determined, since they are direct costs—that is, costs incurred only because the project will be undertaken. In contrast, creative costs involve cost categories that are joint in nature; therefore they require allocation to a specific project. The cost involved in using a piece of apparatus in an experiment is a joint cost if the company uses the equipment for other projects. It would, however, be a direct cost if the equipment had to be purchased for the contemplated project and would have no other use in the research activities of the company.

Which costs are relevant to projects? Certainly, all direct costs must be included in an evaluation of the cost of a research project. Whether to allocate joint costs involves managerial philosophy—total versus contribution costing. For purposes of determining the net expected payoff of research, the total cost of a project should include all the direct and allocated joint costs.

Costs are often used to choose a specific methodology to employ in a study. These costs can vary widely. For example, in a study of alternative contact strategies in mail surveys, the cost per response varied from $6 to $12 (Peterson, Albaum, & Kerin, 1989). Similarly, in a study of corporate reputation conducted for a large multinational company the cost per response was $30 when data were collected by telephone survey and $14 per response for an Internet-based survey (Roster, Rogers, Klein, & Albaum, 2003).

No matter how costs are determined, they must be examined during the problem formulation process at some point to determine if the potential gain of information is worth the costs incurred to obtain the information. If the decision is made that the costs are too high, the problem formulation stage may be redesigned to be more cost-effective or the marketing research may be discontinued all together.

STAGE 2: METHOD OF INQUIRY

In establishing investigative methods, market researchers look to the scientific method. Even though this method is not the only one used, it is the standard against which other investigative methods are measured. The scientific method makes great use of existing knowledge both as a starting point for investigation and as a check on the results of the investigations (i.e., a test of validity). Its most distinctive characteristic is its total lack of subjectivity. The scientific method has evolved objective and rigid procedures for verifying hypotheses or evaluating evidence. It is analytical in its processes and is investigator-independent. Thus, the scientific method is for the most part logical and objective, and frequently makes extensive use of mathematical reasoning and complicated experiments (see Exhibit 2.6). The goal of a scientific methodologist, also called an objectivist, is to run a hypothesis test using publicly stated procedures that are investigator-independent.

Other investigators (the subjectivists) differ in kind or degree of requirement for publicity of procedures or investigator-independence. The Bayesian methodologist also tests hypotheses, using either objectivist or subjectivist methods in addition to his or her prior judgments. Therefore, the Bayesian insists that procedures cannot be either fully publicly available or investigator-independent. The phenomenologist insists that hypotheses not be tested, that the procedures for inquiry need not to be public, and that the process of inquiry cannot be investigator independent.

EXHIBIT 2.6   The Scientific Method

In structure, if not always in application, the scientific method is simple and consists of the following steps:

1. *Observation.* This is the problem-awareness phase, which involves observing a set of significant factors that relate to the problem situation.

2. *Formulation of hypotheses.* In this stage, a hypothesis (i.e., a generalization about reality that permit prediction) is formed that postulates a connection between seemingly unrelated facts. In a sense, the hypothesis suggests an explanation of what has been observed.

3. *Prediction of the future.* After hypotheses are formulated, their logical implications are deduced. This stage uses the hypotheses to predict what will happen.

4. *Testing the hypotheses.* This is the evidence collection and evaluation stage. From a research project perspective this is the design and implementation of the main study. Conclusions are stated based on the data collected and evaluated.

A simple example will show how the scientific method works. Assume a researcher is performing a marketing research project for a manufacturer of men's shirts:

1. Observation: The researcher notices some competitors' sales are increasing and that many competitors have shifted to a new plastic wrapping.

2. Formulation of hypotheses: The researcher assumes his client's products are of similar quality and that the plastic wrapping is the sole cause of increased competitors' sales.

3. Prediction of the future: The hypothesis predicts that sales will increase if the manufacturer shifts to the new wrapping.

4. Testing the hypotheses: The client produces some shirts in the new packaging and market-tests them.

The objectivist, subjectivist, and Bayesian follow the same steps:

- Formulate a problem
- Develop a hypothesis
- Make predictions based on the hypothesis
- Devise a test of the hypothesis
- Conduct the test
- Analyze the results

Even though the terminology used is that associated with basic research, the process described is analogous to that of decision making. Although the steps are the same, there are differences in the way in which the steps are performed and in the underlying assumptions about behavior. For example, the essential difference between the objectivist and the subjectivist is the latter's allowance for use of subjective judgments both when collecting data and when analyzing data (Diesing, 1966). The distinction has very practical meaning, particularly when considering the use of outside research suppliers. There are commercial research firms that tend to specialize in one or the other method of inquiry. Objectivist-based research is often called *quantitative research*, whereas subjectivist-based research is often called *qualitative research*.

The method of inquiry resulting in the greatest degree of investigator-independence is phenomenology (Spiegelbug, 1969). A difference of kind in belief between objectivist-subjectivist-Bayesian on the one side and the phenomenologist on the other is with respect to the role of the explanatory hypothesis. The phenomenologist is opposed to the use of explanatory hypotheses. Hypotheses represent preconceived ideas of the phenomenon and, as such, are viewed as leading to selective perception and distortion of measurement.

STAGE 3: RESEARCH METHOD

Whether a particular method of inquiry is appropriate for a research problem depends in large part on the nature of the problem itself and the extent or level of existing knowledge. In addition to selecting a method of inquiry, the research planner must also select a research method. Two broad methodologies can be used to answer any research question–experimental research and nonexperimental research. The major advantage of experimental research lies in the ability to control extraneous variables and manipulate one or more variables by the intervention of the investigator. In nonexperimental research, there is no intervention beyond that needed for purposes of measurement.

STAGE 4: RESEARCH DESIGN

Research design is defined as the specific methods and procedures for acquiring the information needed. It is a plan or organizational framework for doing the study and collecting the data. Research designs are unique to a methodology. We discuss research design in depth in Chapters 3 and 8.

STAGE 5: DATA COLLECTION TECHNIQUES

Research design begins to take on detailed focus as the researcher selects the particular techniques to be used in solving the problem formulated and in carrying out the method selected. A number of techniques available for collecting data can be used. Some techniques are unique to a method of inquiry. For example, many of the qualitative research techniques, such as projective techniques, are used only in subjectivist-type research.

In general, data collection uses either communication or observation. Communication involves asking questions and receiving responses. This process can be done in person, by mail, by telephone, by e-mail, and over the Internet. In most instances this constitutes the broad research technique known as the survey. In contrast to this process, data may be obtained by observing present or past behavior. Regarding past behavior, data collection techniques include looking at secondary data such as company records, reviewing studies published by external sources, and examining physical traces such as erosion and accretion.

In order to collect data from communication or observation there must be a means of recording responses or behavior. Thus, the process of measurement and the development of measurement instrument are closely connected to the decision of which data collection technique(s) should be used. The relationship is two-way. That is, the structure and content of the measurement instrument can depend on the data collection technique, and measurement considerations often influence technique selection.

STAGE 6: SAMPLE DESIGN

Rarely will a marketing research project involve examining the entire population that is relevant to the problem. For the most part, practical considerations (e.g., absolute resources available, cost vs. value, etc.) dictate that one use a sample, or subset of the relevant population. In other instances the use of a sample is derived from consideration of the relevant systematic and variable errors that might arise in a project.

In designing the sample, the researcher must specify three things:

1. Where the sample is to be selected

2. The process of selection

3. The size of the sample

The sample design must be consistent with the relevant population, which is usually specified in the problem-formulation stage of the research process. This allows the data obtained from the sample to be used in making inferences about the larger population.

The process of sample selection may be done by probability or nonprobability methods. In probability sampling every element in the population has a known nonzero probability (chance) of being selected for inclusion in a study. In contrast, a nonprobability sample is one selected on the basis of the judgment of the investigator, convenience, or by some other means not involving the use of probabilities.

STAGE 7: DATA COLLECTION

Data collection begins after the previous six stages of the research process are complete. Data collection, whether by communication or observation, requires the use of data collection personnel which then raises questions regarding managing these people. Because data collection can be costly, firms often utilize outside limited-service research suppliers, particularly when the extent of in-house research activity does not warrant the cost of having permanent data collection personnel. Also, project design may require specialized data collection, which might best be obtained from an outside supplier.

The working relationship between the data collection agency (a so-called field service) and the research supplier or client is a major factor affecting the quality of fieldwork and data collection. A study of marketing research firms found that the major barriers to the communication of information from clients to research suppliers to field service firms were insufficient information supplied by the client, the research supplier as an intermediary between client and field service firm, and lack of client interest in data collection (Segal & Newberry, 1983). The major suggestion for improving communication is for clients to provide more information to both suppliers and field service firms. Another way to overcome communication barriers is for the field service to be consulted on such major issues as scheduling, costs, and purpose of the study. Finally, it was suggested that two-way communication with suppliers be established or strengthened. Although this study was conducted more than 20 years ago, these are enduring problems that exist today.

STAGE 8: ANALYSIS AND INTERPRETATION

Data that are obtained and presented in the same form as originally collected are seldom useful to anyone. Data must be analyzed. The data must be edited, coded, and tabulated before performing formal analyses such as statistical tests. The types of analyses that can be properly performed depend upon the sampling procedures, measurement instruments, and data collection techniques used. Consequently, it is imperative that the techniques of analysis, associated descriptive or prescriptive recommendation types, and presentation formats be selected prior to data collection.

This is a characteristic of the so-called backward approach to research design that was presented earlier in this chapter.

STAGE 9: THE RESEARCH REPORT

The culmination of the research process is the research report. It includes a clear, accurate, and honest description of everything that has been done and the results, conclusions, and—whenever possible—recommendations for courses of action. Two critical attributes of the report are that it provides all the information readers need using language they understand (completeness) and that it contains selective information chosen by the researcher (conciseness). These attributes are often in conflict with each other.

Two approaches can be taken to ensure that this conflict is not a problem. One approach involves preparing two reports: (1) a technical report that emphasizes the methods used and underlying assumptions, and presents the findings in a detailed manner; and (2) a popular report that minimizes technical details and emphasizes simplicity. The second approach is concerned with how the report is communicated.

Because people vary a great deal in how they are affected by different forms of communication, the ideal reporting process should try to encompass all major forms. Thus, a written report, by itself, may be inadequate and only an invitation to inaction. There are simply a lot of people who, for various reasons, don't respond to the printed word. There are still more that, although they may respond, will often misunderstand the meaning of what is written. For these reasons, it is vitally necessary to get management to sit down with the research manager, or with the researcher and the outside research firm, in a face-to-face reporting situation. The research report is discussed in more detail in Chapter 20.

THE RESEARCH PLAN

It is important to carefully plan the research process and formally recognize the relationship between the stages. The researcher should write a formal plan for the project, including the background information and statement of objectives, which then becomes the master guide for implementing and controlling the research project.

The components of a research plan are outlined in Exhibit 2.7.

EXHIBIT 2.7   Outline of a Research Plan

Objectives

State the primary and secondary objectives of the study, including operational objectives and more general aims.

Problem Analysis

Present a statement of the research problems and questions and the hypothesis or hypotheses relevant to the stated problem (i.e., testable hypotheses). Show the relationship of the objectives to the problem at hand.

Research Design

The design of a research project includes four components:

1. *Research methodology*. Describe how the investigation is to be made in general terms. Justify selection of the methodology to be used.

2. *Research techniques*. Describe the methods and procedures to be used in collecting the data in some depth. Who is to be solicited, how contact is to be made, special techniques to be used, and so on are to be covered. Discuss forms to be used to collect data and, if already developed, include with the plan.

3. *Sample design and selection*. State the size of the total sample and any proposed subsamples. Describe in detail the procedure to be used to ensure a representative (or other appropriate) sample of survey respondents or experimental subjects. Include any technical notes as to how the sample size was determined in an appendix.

4. *Proposed analysis*. Describe general tabulation procedures, any cross-analysis tabulations, and the reasons for such tabulations. Include discussion of proposed methods of statistical analysis together with reasons why such analyses will be used. If possible, show dummy tables with the "stubs" that will be used.

Personnel Requirements

List all personnel who will be involved with the project, the exact assignment of each person, the time to be spent, and the pay for each.

Time and Cost Requirements

Present a budget and time schedule for the major activities involved in conducting the study.

A useful device for showing the time schedule is a graphic work plan, shown in Figure 2.2, which indicates the relevant tasks and the time allotted to each. This graphic plan was used in a study for a state government agency. This work plan is a useful planning device and can also serve as a control mechanism.

The research plan may also be viewed as a research proposal, particularly when the research supplier is an external firm. It becomes a proposal to commit funds either to in-house or external researchers. To a large extent, the contents of a proposal are the same as those of a research plan, although the proposal format contains less technical material and is not as detailed. It is important to include the following topics in every proposal, although not necessarily in the order listed:

- Background
- Statement of the problem
- Statement of research objectives
- Research methods
- Nature of the report
- Timing and costs
- Appropriate special information (e.g., biographies of professional staff)

There is no uniform guideline about how to present a proposal. It depends on the nature of the project and client and can range from a short letter covering the minimum necessities to an extensive document presented in great detail. See Appendix 2–1 for two examples of proposals in condensed form, one for a product company and one for a service provider.

Many research companies are paying increasing attention to what goes into their proposals, in light of the lawsuit (settled out of court) that Beecham Products filed many years ago against the marketing research firm Yankelovich, Clancy, Shulman (YCS). Beecham contracted with YCS to test a new cold-water detergent, Delicare, in a simulated laboratory test market. The test predicted a market share of 45 to 52 percent, if a certain level of advertising expenditure was used to launch the product. The actual share hovered around 20 percent. Beecham sued

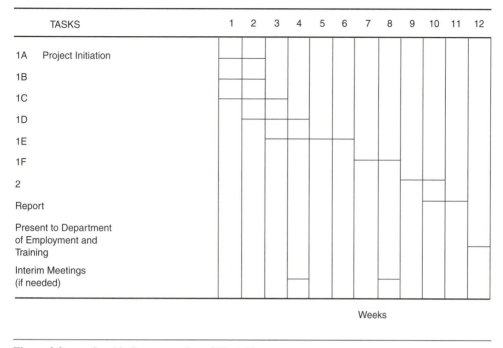

Figure 2.2 Graphic Representation of Work Plan

YCS and accused the company of negligence and professional malpractice. One research supplier company in Ohio has said that the lawsuit affected the way they prepare proposals— no limit of outcomes or results are promised; only the process of research is sold ("Lawsuit prompts some researchers," 1989). To formally schedule a research project, the marketing researcher must isolate the major activities to be performed and determine a sequence of tasks. Some tasks must be performed before others can be started, whereas some activities can be carried out concurrently.

One approach to scheduling research activities is to use an activity flow chart. The work plan presented in Figure 2.2 is an illustration of such a flow chart. A more detailed example is given by Fink (2003, pp. 134–135). This approach describes the tasks to be accomplished, the months in which each task will be performed and completed, the staff members who will perform each task, the number of days that each staff member will spend on each task, and the total number of days needed for all staff to complete each task. Preparing such a chart is essential; it helps in research budget preparation and management as well as in managing the work schedules of staff members.

Another approach uses the *critical path method* (CPM). This is a network approach in which the component activities are diagrammed in sequence of performance and a time estimate for each activity is presented. A modification of the critical path method is the *program evaluation and review technique* (PERT). PERT is a probabilistic scheduling approach using three time estimates: optimistic, most likely, and pessimistic. Whether CPM or PERT is used, the critical path is the sequence of activities resulting in the longest project completion time.

MAKE OR BUY DECISION

A decision facing all companies that want to use marketing research is who should do the research. Alternatives are to have it done in-house, to utilize outside suppliers, or some combination of the two. In short, having marketing research done is a "make or buy" decision regarding the production of marketing research information. For some companies, this decision is automatic—the in-house organization will do all research unless it is beyond their technical expertise. Other companies with in-house capabilities treat the internal units the same as outside suppliers: they must compete with outside suppliers, and prepare proposals and make bids for the business. In short, the user establishes a supplier-client relationship with all potential research suppliers.

Almost all research users will at some time require the services of outside research suppliers. These outside suppliers range from a full-service marketing research agency such as M/A/R/C Research, IMS International, and Maritz Marketing Research, Inc., to a specialized field service company that does nothing but collect data. Even full-service companies may perform only limited services, for example, research design and data collection only, if that is all the client wants. Thus, there are many variations in the way outside suppliers are used.

When might the use of an outside research supplier be appropriate? There are a number of situations that may call for the use of such firms:

1. The capabilities or technical expertise of in-house researchers are not adequate for the needed research.

2. The outside supplier has the needed facilities for doing the research, such as those needed for focus groups or laboratory experiments.

3. A research firm has developed a formula approach for handling a particular need in a specific industry. For example, a research firm in California developed a standardized survey of customer satisfaction for Toyota dealers. This survey addressed issues related to the purchase act, service, and parts.

4. There is no unused capacity in the in-house research organization.

5. There is reason to believe that in-house personnel may become emotionally or politically attached to the project, thereby losing objectivity.

6. The outside research supplier can do the research quicker.

7. The cost of the research may be reduced by having it done out-of-house. At the very least, some aspect such as data collection may be cheaper when done by an outside research supplier. Overall, purchasing data generated by syndicated services such as supermarket-based scanner data may be less costly than attempting to collect the data from scratch.

8. There is a need for anonymity or confidentiality that may be provided best by an outside research firm.

9. The results of the research may be used in legal proceedings. If so, the outside research firm may have more credibility in the eyes of the court or regulatory or legislative body.

Once it is determined that an outside supplier is desirable there remains the job of selecting the specific firm. Important considerations include the supplier's reputation, technical competence, experience, reliability in completion, and other characteristics. It would seem obvious that cost of the project is relevant. The buyer of the research must be aware that cost-cutting can be illusionary—quality must also be considered. Finally, the person who is to be project director can be a determining factor. The research buyer must know who the project director will be and, at the very least, what his or her experience has been. Finally, it has been suggested that clients should seek outside suppliers whose "cultures" complement their own. That is, they should choose a supplier with a way of thinking and an approach to problem solving that is sufficiently different from their own (Zaltman, 1989, p. 28–30).

Not all suppliers can do all types of research equally well. The buyer should develop some type of formal evaluation procedure to compare alternative suppliers, including in-house and outside companies. The approach should be as simple as possible, but still be capable of distinguishing among alternatives (see Exhibit 2.8).

EXHIBIT 2.8   Evaluating Research Suppliers

There are many approaches that can be used to evaluate research suppliers. They can range from a simple checklist rating scale such as the one shown in Example A to a more formal modeling approach involving differential weighting of criteria, as shown in Example B.

Example A*

EVALUATION

ACTIVITY	*Outstanding*	*OK*	*Unsatisfactory**	*Not applicable*
1. Consultation	✓			
2. Sampling	✓			
3. Interviewing	✓			
4. Coding/Tabulating	✓			
5. Validation	✓			
6. Analysis & Report	✓			
7. Meeting Deadlines	✓			
8. Meeting Cost Estimates	✓			
9. Overall Professionalism	✓			
10. Presentation	✓			

* Explain

COMMENTS:

Example B

Criteria	Poor/ Little			Good/ Much		Weight	Scale Value × Weight
Background factors							
Product knowledge	1	2	3	4	5	.XX	.XX
Experience with type of study	1	2	3	4	5	.XX	.XX
Skill of the account person	1	2	3	4	5	.XX	.XX
Technical backup staff	1	2	3	4	5	.XX	.XX
Questionnaire construction							
Proper questions asked	1	2	3	4	5	.XX	.XX
Logical flow/order	1	2	3	4	5	.XX	.XX
Pretest conducted	1	2	3	4	5	.XX	.XX
Sample selection							
Basic design	1	2	3	4	5	.XX	.XX
Nonresponse follow-up procedures	1	2	3	4	5	.XX	.XX
Procedures for checking responses	1	2	3	4	5	.XX	.XX
Supervision of data collection							
Level of personal involvement	1	2	3	4	5	.XX	.XX
Procedures	1	2	3	4	5	.XX	.XX
Data processing							
Procedures for coding	1	2	3	4	5	.XX	.XX
Editing and cleaning of responses	1	2	3	4	5	.XX	.XX
Basic reports	1	2	3	4	5	.XX	.XX
More complex analyses	1	2	3	4	5	.XX	.XX
Interpretation and follow-up							
Interpretation skills	1	2	3	4	5	.XX	.XX
Follow-up work	1	2	3	4	5	.XX	.XX
Overall quality							
Competence	1	2	3	4	5	.XX	.XX
Likely effort level	1	2	3	4	5	.XX	.XX
Specific factors							
Delivery time	1	2	3	4	5	.XX	.XX
Cost	1	2	3	4	5	.XX	.XX
Total							

ADDITIONAL CONSIDERATIONS

Many other considerations must be taken into account when developing the research plan. Occasionally, the research is driven by the desire or need to use a particular research methodology that provides unique analyses and associated perspectives on the data. Likewise, international research brings into play many country-specific issues related to culture, business environment, or even government regulation. Each research project is unique and must be developed with the broader environment and application in mind.

Orientation Toward Technique

Some researchers may become more concerned with finding an application for their techniques and technologies than with supplying information for decision making. The researcher must protect against testing for its own sake using the most sophisticated techniques. A project designed to obtain the most useful information may not allow the researcher to use all the advanced technologies and new statistical techniques, but it is what decision makers want. For example, consumer goods companies that are trying to learn about the behavior and attitudes of consumers toward various products and services or that are trying to determine what drives their brand equity, tend to favor the use of somewhat esoteric techniques as conjoint analysis, choice modeling, and perceptual mapping (Vence, 2003). These techniques are discussed in later chapters.

Although advanced technologies and techniques are favored, research basics must not be overlooked. These basics, presented in Exhibit 2.9, are timeless.

International Research

The internationalization of business today makes marketing research even more important; effective decisions about developing international marketing strategy require even more information than domestic marketing. Managers facing problems in the global marketplace are not likely to be able to draw upon an intimate knowledge of the environment within which they operate because they lack such knowledge. The approach to the international marketing research process does not differ from that already described; however, there are certain unique considerations to keep in mind, as shown in Figure 2.3. A number of conceptual, methodological, and organizational issues may impede data collection and other aspects of research for international marketing decisions (Albaum, Strandskov, & Duerr, 2002, pp. 227–228).

- The complexity of research design, due to operation in a multinational, multicultural, and multilinguistic environment
- The lack of secondary data available for many countries and product markets
- The high costs of collecting primary data, particularly in developing countries
- The problems associated with coordinating research and data collection in different countries

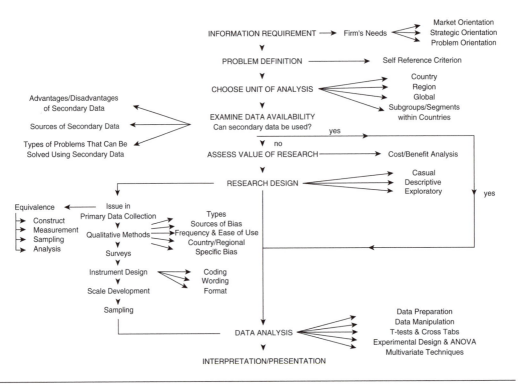

Figure 2.3   International Marketing Research Process

SOURCE: From Kumar, V., *International Marketing Research,* 1st edition, Copyright © 2000. Reprinted by permission of Pearson Education, Inc., Upper Saddle River, NJ.

- The difficulties of establishing the comparability and equivalence of data and research conducted in different contexts
- The intrafunctional character of many international marketing decisions
- The economics of many international investment and marketing decisions

As marketers increase and broaden their participation in foreign markets, the issue of comparability takes on special importance. To an extent, each market may be characterized by a unique pattern of sociocultural behavior patterns and values. Consequently, attitudes and behavior may be expressed differently in different markets. Relevant constructs and their measures will be unique to a particular country.

There may also be similarities. This is the emic (culture-specific) versus etic (culture-free) issue in cross-national research, which has implications for the appropriate research process. The international marketer is most likely to prefer the etic approach in international marketing research, with the primary emphasis on constructs and methods that are comparable across countries and cultures. However, one can never assume equivalence. To illustrate, an American company, assuming that a similar language must indicate similar tastes, tried to sell after-shave lotion in England. The product never got off the ground, and it was discovered (unfortunately after the fact) that the average British male saw no functional value in the use of after-shave lotion (Ricks, 1999, p. 144).

EXHIBIT 2.9   Research Basics

As technology advances, marketing researchers are continually looking for ways to adapt new technology to the practice of research. Both hardware and software are involved in such adaptations. However, researchers must never forget that research basics cannot be overlooked. Rather, what must be done is to adapt the new techniques and technologies to these basics. All studies must address the following basic issues (Anderson, Berdie, & Liestman, 1984):

1. *Ask the right questions.* This is the essence of project design, and the heart of proper planning. The research planner must remember that every project is unique, and as such must be tailored to the user's needs.

2. *Ask the right people.* Sample design should be such that only those people who are of interest to the research user are contacted, and such that those who are contacted are reasonably representative of the group of interest.

3. *Ask questions the right way.* It is not enough to be able to ask the right questions; they must be asked in the right way. This is the essence of questionnaire design. The researcher can use all the aids available from the new technologies, but if the wording of the questions is not clear to the respondents, the results will be useless. One basic that is overlooked all too often is pretesting the questionnaire; this is crucial for ensuring that responses are the ones that are needed to address the problem.

4. *Obtain answers to questions.* The process of data collection is central to all marketing research. Techniques used should be selected for how each bears on nonresponse and response alike.

5. *Relate answers to the needs of the research user/client.* Data seldom speak for themselves. Proper data analysis is needed if a study is to have any value to the user. Here there is a risk of letting advanced techniques become the master of the researcher rather than the opposite. Common sense is a valuable tool for the researcher when considering alternative analysis approaches for any project.

6. *Communicate effectively.* Many good projects are ruined in this stage. The information that is reported to the user should be in a form that is understandable to the user so that he or she can tell that it is relevant to the issues at hand.

In the previous section we discussed some issues relevant to dealing with outside research suppliers. Companies are concerned with similar issues surrounding the potential use of outside international research suppliers. In addition to locating and evaluating qualified foreign suppliers, major problems that have been identified include communicating across language barriers, translating project materials, distance, time zone differences, communicating the goals of the research to suppliers, maintaining quality control over the data collection at such distances, difficulty with different methodologies, and varying professional standards.

Business-to-Business Research

Most of what is studied and written about marketing research methodology concerns business-to-consumer (B2C) marketing situations. It is assumed, and on some occasions even stated explicitly, that these techniques apply equally to business-to-business (B2B) situations. Although there is some merit to this inference on general grounds, it is more accurate to state that the set of techniques, methods, processes, and so forth that are available are available to all. The trick to applying B2C methodology to B2B situations is to determine which standard consumer research approaches will work, which ones will not, and what modifications need to be made.

Some rules of thumb that warrant consideration have been proposed by Schmalensee (2001). For the most part these represent adaptation of more standard techniques and methods to fit a B2B situation. These suggestions are organized around the typical flow of a research project:

1. *Design research to foster customer relationships.* This applies to all stages of a project. The research process should be designed to strengthen relationships with business customers.

2. *Lay the groundwork.* It is suggested that the researcher allow extra time to talk with the staff, especially those with customer contact. In B2B situations there may be many people who have customer contact, and their views may differ enough that it is beneficial to talk with as many as possible.

3. *Select and draw the samples.* There may be a choice of respondents within each business customer organization, including senior executives, contract administrators, and so-called daily interactors. In a typical project it is often difficult to decide which type of respondent to contact. One way to overcome this is to interview all major types identified as having relevant information for the problem at hand, although the questions asked each type of respondent will differ.

4. *Select the research approach and methodology.* Business respondents tend to be busy people, so it is important to be creative in selecting data collection methodologies. The use of fax, e-mail, and the Internet may lead to greater response than telephone calls or sending a questionnaire through the mail. It is helpful if the researcher knows something about how each individual respondent works, as this may be a determining factor in the selection of a data collection methodology. However, it may be unwise in a study to collect data by different means, as a potential for systematic error exists. Consequently, it is prudent to use the method that is best for the majority of the sample.

5. *Design the questions.* Because businesspeople are busy, keep the questionnaire as "short and sweet" as possible. This, of course, applies to all research projects. Business respondents will be more likely to respond if the questions are interesting and allow them to respond in their own words in a conversational way. Exhibit 2.10 addresses word meaning. This is related to the first rule; enjoyable questionnaires can be a relationship-building experience.

6. ***Record and analyze the data.*** Much of the information collected in B2B research is qualitative, making the analysis crucial.

7. ***Report the results.*** A good way to increase credibility and ensure that results lead to action is to personalize results. This includes use of individual respondent anecdotes and other humanizing details.

8. ***Plan, communicate, and act.*** A good way to increase response rates and build relationships with customers is to share with them what has been learned and what is planned. Communicating with customers allows a company to involve them in implementing whatever action the research suggests. This, again, is part of relationship building.

EXHIBIT 2.10   The Meaning of Words

The meaning of a word is not the same for all people, nor even for the same person at different times. Context can enter into the equation, particularly in cultures (and nations) where the language is considered to be high-context. That is, words do not necessarily speak for themselves.

A word in a questionnaire, for example, may be easily understood by some populations but unknown to others. Whether research respondents' understanding of a word is a problem to the researcher or not depends on the purpose of the research. For instance, is the research relevant to a decision regarding the design of a product or service, or is it concerned with communications to the market, like labeling or advertising or sales promotion? According to marketing consultant Thomas Semon (2003), if the research concerns the physical design of a product or service, the words must be translated into the respondents' actual understanding. However, if the research is aimed at communication decisions, the researcher can assume with much confidence (although not 100 percent) that the respondents' understanding of the word or words in an advertisement will be the same as in an interview.

Of course, the researcher has to be told what the purpose of the research is.

A final suggestion is knowing when not to do research (Schiffenbauer, 2001). In short, if a researcher feels that a customer respondent is not sufficiently motivated to tell the truth, do not ask!

Evaluation of Research Information Usage

Our last consideration is the evaluation of the use of the research information. Barabba and Zaltman (1991) propose a procedure for such an evaluation. Their procedure is based on the idea that the quality of thinking about an issue prior to data collection is the major determinant of the quality of thinking after data collection. They argue that technologies for improving research must involve people, as conversion of data into knowledge is necessarily a human (behavioral) process. Exhibit 2.11 describes some of the areas that need to be considered to get the most out of research information.

EXHIBIT 2.11   Some Obstacles to Effective Use of Research Information

There are at least two basic kinds of information managers need to make decisions:

1. *Instrumental.* This information is collected in response to specific needs and therefore has a direct application to decision making. For example, a manager may need to know what product features are most important to consumers.

2. *Conceptual.* This information is needed to provide a background setting and is collected to enhance the general thinking about a matter of concern rather than to provide a specific solution. For example, managers within the packaged foods industry may want to know about trends in food preferences.

The difference between the two types of information, and the determination of how much of each is needed, is a matter of timing, circumstances, and a manager's perceptions.

There are several common and serious obstacles to effective research design and use of the research findings. These obstacles are interrelated, and each may arise around the same event:

1. **Post-survey regret.** After data collection, a manager or researcher may assume that certain questions were not asked or were not asked in a particular way. Some regret is unavoidable. However, post-survey regret generally reveals that information use planning did not occur early enough in the research process.

2. **Data-poor thinking.** There is a tendency to think differently about an issue when it is illustrated with relevant data, including hypothetical or simulated data. Thinking without formal data is poorer than thinking with it.

3. **Pseudo-clairvoyance.** This is also called hindsight bias and may lead to the conclusion that the research was unnecessary or intuitively obvious since it reports "what we know" or "what could have been predicted." Often what managers say after a study and what they, in reality, would have predicted before the study are different. The results of most research are intuitively obvious *after the fact.*

4. **Misunderstanding comfort zones.** Comfort zones are ranges for expected and acceptable research results. A more knowledgeable and experienced manager has wider zones. A researcher should know an information user's comfort zones to help decide how to best present results.

5. **Failure to perform action audits.** When the research results suggest an unusual or new decision or action, but do not provide sufficient information for its evaluation, it may become necessary to do additional work. It is important to identify alternative actions or decisions prior to study design.

6. **Unequal-opportunity methodologies.** Ideally, a research methodology should give negative and positive findings an equal opportunity to emerge. The unequal-opportunity method favors positive results. This situation most often results from not thinking carefully about potential answers, including negative ones. Unequal opportunity in methods is usually unintentional.

7. ***Missing information and uncertainty.*** Research results are often evaluated and translated into action on the basis of assumptions made about variables not examined in the project. It is important to identify differences of opinion about missing data early in a research project in addition to those areas where uncertainty may persist even after reporting the research.

Consideration of these obstacles will improve the research process and help researchers obtain the kinds of information managers need to make decisions and enable them to make more effective use of information.

SOURCE: Reprinted from *Hearing the Voice of the Market: Competitive Advantage Through Creative Use of Market Information,* by Barabba, V. & Zaltman, G. Copyright © 1991. Used with permission of the Harvard Business School.

SUMMARY

This chapter introduced research process planning from the perspective of evaluating research on the basis of how well it has been done (the management of total error). A research project includes nine stages:

- Problem formulation
- Method of inquiry
- Research method
- Research design
- Selection of data collection techniques
- Sample design
- Data collection
- Analysis and interpretation of data
- Research reports

The differences in client requirements give rise to different requirements in basic and decisional research projects. The value-versus-cost orientation of decisional research is an outgrowth of these differences.

APPENDIX 2.1
Illustration of Research Proposals

Proposal 1

Nature of the Problem

Wine produced in South Africa is beginning to appear in stores in various parts of the United States. Although South Africa has produced wine for more than three centuries and its total annual production is equal to that of Germany, relatively few sales have been made to North America. South African producers appear to be planning a campaign that they hope will give them a significant share of the U.S. market.

Yankee Traders (disguised name) is becoming involved in importing South African wines, including table wines, champagne, and liquors (e.g., rum and brandy). Initial targeted markets are New York, Chicago, and Washington, D.C. Of immediate concern is market acceptance of these products, on the part of both distributors and consumers.

The process of gaining market acceptance, and thus a profitable share of the market, is often time-consuming and requires that many hurdles be overcome. In the South African wine situation there is the general problem of consumer and distributor awareness that South Africa is a wine-producing area. Thus, an issue of trust may be involved. Unlike major wineries in the United States, France, Germany, and Italy, specific wineries in South Africa are totally unknown to the American wine-consuming public. This lack of awareness may also exist to a significant extent among wine distributors.

Regarding South Africa, there is another major potential hurdle that does not confront products imported into the United States from most countries. This problem stems from South Africa's historical political and socioeconomic policies toward certain segments of its population. The issues have been exposed widely throughout the United States as being concerned with human rights. The American public's feelings toward the South African government may carry over into prejudices against products from that country. The nature of such prejudices, and the extent to which they exist, will affect market acceptance of South African wines.

Objective of the Study

The proposed study is designed to provide information helpful to Yankee Traders in planning and implementing a marketing approach for South African wines. More specifically, the study will attempt to provide answers to the following research questions:

1. What is the state of awareness among distributors about South African wines, what are their attitudes and beliefs about such wines, and to what extent are they likely to purchase such wines?

2. What general beliefs are held by consumers regarding products made in South Africa, and what are their attitudes about purchasing such products? One concern here is the extent to which general prejudices carry over to products, specifically wine.

3. What is the likelihood that wine drinkers will purchase South African wines, and what factors affect that likelihood?

These three research questions are broadly stated and will serve as a guide to the specific kinds of information to be sought.

Method

The study will be conducted in two parts: (1) the distributor study and (2) a survey of the general public. The geographic areas in which the studies will be conducted are the New York, Chicago, and Washington, D.C., metropolitan areas, including the core city and selected suburbs.

Distributor Study

The study of distributors will be conducted as a telephone survey of a random sample of wine distributors in the three market areas. The specific questionnaire to be used will be constructed once the project is approved. Information will be obtained to answer research question 1. This phase of the study will serve the additional role of situation analysis and informal investigation for the consumer survey. As such, then, more open-ended questions will be asked. It is felt that a sample size of ten in each market area will be sufficient.

Consumer Survey

This phase of the study will be conducted as a mail questionnaire survey. At first thought, it would appear that since prejudice is somewhat fluid and can change rapidly, the use of the telephone to collect data would be most appropriate. However, in this case it is felt that the nature of the prejudice involved is not something that can easily be changed. Also, product and brand images do not change very rapidly unless one has had a bad experience with the product or brand. A third reason for choosing the mail survey approach is that some of the information to be requested can be viewed as sensitive, and anonymity is necessary for good response rates and quality. The mail survey provides the highest degree of anonymity. Finally, cost considerations enter.

The approach to be used can be summarized as follows:

1. An introductory postcard to mention the study and inform the potential respondent that he or she will soon receive a questionnaire will be sent one week before the survey.

2. The initial mailing of the survey includes the questionnaire, a cover letter, a return envelope, and a postcard to be returned independently. This card will inform the researchers that a particular person has responded, so that he or she will not be sent a follow-up questionnaire.

3. A reminder postcard will be sent to the sample members.

4. A second questionnaire (a follow-up) will be sent to those sample members who have not responded.

5. A sample of those potential respondents who have not responded after the follow-up will be contacted by telephone for purposes of nonresponse validation.

Recent studies using this design have realized a response rate of 40 percent or better.

The sample will be developed on an area basis. Within each of the central cities and selected suburbs, sample members will be chosen by random sampling techniques from appropriate sample frames (e.g., telephone directories). The primary sampling element will be the household. Since the population to be sampled is the general public, both drinkers and nondrinkers of wine will be included. This is deliberate, since nondrinkers may be potential drinkers, and they also have an effect on overall attitudes within a community.

Based on normal response rates for surveys of this type, and considering costs, an original sample size of 500 in each market area should provide sufficient returns to produce reliable results. For example, with an original sample of 500 and the expected response rate of 40 percent, 200 responses should be obtained. If we assume a wine consumption incidence of 50 percent, this should provide 100 drinking and 100 nondrinking respondents in each market. The obtained sample of 200 with a .50 proportion will generate no more than a ± 5 percent error with 95 percent confidence. Naturally, if greater accuracy is desired the original sample size can be increased.

The specific questionnaire will be constructed once the project is approved. The questionnaire will be developed in accordance with generally accepted survey research principles and will employ the funnel sequence, which results in ordering questions from the most general to the most specific. Image data will be collected by using a set of semantic differential or Stapel scales; these involve survey respondents describing a particular object. Such scales have been widely used in determining images of, and attitudes toward, products made in foreign countries. Likert scales, which involve respondents indicating the extent of agreement with statements, will also be used. This format will be best for measuring prejudice. Of course there may be a standard scale for measuring prejudice that is appropriate for the study. Although a preliminary search of the literature has not yet revealed such a scale, we will search further.

Direct questions will be used to obtain the usual demographic and socioeconomic information as well as wine consumption and purchase data.

Cost and Time

Following the procedures outlined above, the study should be completed within eight to ten weeks from the date of acceptance of the proposal. The total cost will be $18,500.

Proposal 2

Objective

The objective of the proposed study is to obtain information from a carefully chosen sample of respondents from the counties served by a particular hospital regarding their perceptions of the present health care facilities and providers, the reasons for their present use or nonuse, and the attributes and services desired by the present and potential users of these facilities.

Methodology

The survey itself is intended not only to encompass health care consumers within the hospital's service area, but also to include the hospital staff and medical staff.

In determining the method of data collection, two factors become important: (1) the information to be obtained is to focus on respondents' health care activities, and (2) the officers of the medical staff and several key managers would like to participate in the survey design.

In our judgment, not only is information needed from the hospital and medical staff, but such internal information and attitudinal data should be gathered prior to the design of the instrument (questionnaire) intended to elicit information from the patrons of the hospital. Therefore, we would propose to conduct four focus groups—two each with the hospital and the medical staff. The focus group technique uses a small group setting with selected participants to elicit qualitative (attitudinal and other) information in-depth. Such a focus group is moderated by a knowledgeable and credible individual experienced in eliciting such information. The reason for the use of two focus groups for each category is that one group acts as a validator for the other, to assure that the information gathered is not from an atypical group.

The four focus groups, in our judgment, will not only provide a technique for gathering internal information and attitude about yourselves, but will also provide a basis for the design of the instrument (questionnaire). The information obtained from the focus groups and the consultation with the officers of the medical staff and the key managers will be the basis for finalizing the survey design and the instrument (questionnaire) of data collection.

Survey Method

The literature on surveys conducted regarding health care utilization and related questions reveals that respondents tend to be self-conscious when contacted in person and that the information obtained through a self-administered mail questionnaire tends to be less reliable, as the respondents attempt to portray desirable usage patterns and ideal answers. In addition, the mail survey suffers from a low response rate; respondents seem to be embarrassed because the mail questionnaire requires written answers and knowledge of terms used. Since the area from which the sample will be taken is a small geographic area, and since it is easier to clarify both the questions asked and responses obtained over the telephone, we would recommend the telephone survey method be used to gather information from your patrons.

Sample

Since some of the information to be obtained relates to respondents' attitudes about quality and services, we would like to propose that the total sample consist of both the present users of the facility and potential users. Present users will provide evaluative information, and potential users might contribute information about the type of services needed and the reasons for not utilizing the present providers and facilities.

Sample size, in part, depends on the level of accuracy desired and the dollar amounts available for gathering information. Three different sample sizes and their associated costs are outlined in the "Budget" section.

For obtaining the participants for the focus groups, we can use a list of the hospital and medical staff. The user portion of the sample will be derived from a list (record) of recent users of the hospital and the nonusers will be selected on the basis of characteristics (male/female ratio, for example) and the locations desired.

Incentives

In our view, no monetary incentive is needed if the telephone survey method is utilized. The incentive that is needed to elicit responses in the telephone survey method focuses on prior notification and the involvement of non-hospital-related personnel in asking the questions. Therefore, we would like to provide the "incentive" of sending a letter, signed by the investigator, identifying himself as a professor and the hospital administrator. The letter will inform the respondent that he or she is specially chosen by a scientific method of sample selection and that his or her responses are very important for our understanding of their needs and perceptions. The letter will also state that the respondent will be contacted by one of the interviewers working for the consultants (university professors), and therefore the individual responses will not be provided directly to the hospital and that only the findings will be reported to the hospital.

Since we believe that focus group methodology should be used with the hospital staff and the medical staff, the appropriate incentives for such groups will be based on the time of day and the location (incentives such as lunch, or cocktails and hors d'oeuvres "after hours").

Monetary incentives will be used only with the consumer-patrons and only if the self-administered mail questionnaire is used as the survey instrument. In such an event, either a fresh five-dollar bill will be included with each questionnaire or a coupon redeemable at a local store (for value up to $10) will be mailed out after receipt of the completed questionnaire.

Response Rate

If the telephone survey is chosen as the method, then we would accept a 60 percent rate (with three call-back attempts) as the minimally acceptable rate of return; and if the mail-survey is chosen, with one or two reminders sent, we would accept between 40 and 50 percent as the minimally acceptable rate.

Survey Results

We agree that the participants should have access to the survey results. Survey participants will be told that if they are interested in obtaining the results by mail, we will be glad to mail a copy of our findings. They will also be told that they can pick up a copy of the survey results at the reception desk at the hospital, if they wish, or call the hospital for a copy of the results of the survey.

Timeframe

It is estimated that the entire project will be completed in 90 days' time. Findings will be formally presented in a written report and we will also make an oral presentation of the survey results.

Within 30 days from the date of awarding the research project to us, the focus groups will be scheduled and we will attempt to complete them soon after. Immediately following the completion of focus groups, we expect that the consultation with the "hospital group" will take place and we expect that in about two weeks' time the questionnaire will be ready for pretesting. Since our proposed method of collecting data is through a telephone survey, completion of this data collection phase is expected within 30 days after pretest of the questionnaire. It will take two weeks' time after collection of data to complete our tabulation and analysis and present our findings to you. The written report will be delivered within 10 days after the oral presentation.

We would recommend, if there is any interest at all, that more than one hospital in the county be involved in the survey, as it will not only reduce the costs for the survey, but will also afford an opportunity to share the baseline information. However, a realistic timeframe needs to be established, as more coordination will be involved and sample sizes may need to be revised.

Budget

Total Costs

Option 1 Sample Size: 600 $29,500
User–400
Nonuser–200
Plus Four Focus Groups

Option 2 Sample Size: 500 $28,500
User–300
Nonuser–200
Plus Four Focus Groups

Option 3 Sample Size: 400 $27,500
User–250
Nonuser–150
Plus Four Focus Groups

Breakdown

A. Focus groups (4)	$10,000
B. Survey with 600	$19,500
Survey with 500	$18,500
Survey with 400	$17,500

These costs include pretesting of the questionnaire, training of interviewers, long distance calls, travel, data analysis, and final written report plus oral presentation of findings.

Any sample has some error–that is, the amount the responses from the sample may differ from the true value for the entire population. In this case, this includes all households in the defined hospital service area. In the proposed study, the possible error for the following subgroup sizes at a 50/50 split on a given variable are given in the following table:

Group Size	Sampling Error*
600	±4.1%
500	±4.5%
400	±5.0%

*Ninety-five percent (95%) confidence level. If 100 samples were drawn in the same manner, in 95 out of 100 times one can be sure that answers from the samples are within these sampling errors of the true population.

❖

ASSIGNMENT MATERIAL

1. Four methods of inquiry were discussed in this chapter. Which methods are more appropriate for basic research and which are more suited to decisional research? Explain.

2. For each of the following stated management problems, suggest some likely research questions and research problems:
   a. Decide whether to allow a bank to install an automated teller machine (ATM) outside the premises.
   b. Develop a package for a new product.
   c. Allocate the advertising budget among sales territories.
   d. Expand product distribution to a new area.
   e. Set up a plant in an overseas market area.

3. Why is it difficult to do research on marketing problems?

4. When doing research on international marketing problems there is often need to do cross-national research (i.e., research in a number of countries dealing with essentially the same problem). A problem of comparability may arise, which has implications for the equivalence of various aspects of the research process. Discuss the process of establishing data equivalence within the context of constructs, measures, and sampling.

5. How does a research proposal differ from a research plan?

6. Are B2B situations really so different from B2C that standard research methodologies need to be modified? Explain.

❖

REFERENCES

Action-oriented research spells success for new Seagram wine. (1981, January). *Marketing News, 15,* 7.

Albaum, G., Strandskov, J., & Duerr, E. (2002). *International marketing and export management* (4th ed.). Harlow, UK: Pearson Education Ltd.

Anderson, J. F., Berdie, D. R., & Liestman, R. (1984, January 16). Hi-tech techniques OK, but don't forget research basics. *Marketing News, 18* (Sec. 2), 12.

Andreasen, A. R. (1988). *Cheap but good marketing research.* Homewood, IL: Dow Jones–Irwin.

Barabba, V. P., & Zaltman, G. (1991). *Hearing the voice of the market: Competitive advantage through creative use of market information.* Boston: Harvard Business School Press.

Diesing, P. (1966, March–June). Objectivism vs. subjectivism in the social sciences. *Philosophy of Science, 33,* 124–133.

Fink, A. (2003). *The survey handbook* (2nd ed.). Thousand Oaks, CA: Sage Publications.

Hartley, R. F. (1995). *Marketing mistakes* (6th ed.). New York: Wiley.

Kerlinger, F. N., & Lee, H. (2000) *Foundations of behavioral research* (4th ed.). Belmont, CA: Wadsworth Publishing.

Kumar, V. (2000). *International marketing research.* Upper Saddle River, NJ: Prentice Hall.

Lawsuit prompts some researchers to change operation of practices. (1989, September 11). *Marketing News, 19,* 4.

Marefka, B. (2003, January 20). Selecting relevant data helps sell more stuff. *Marketing News, 37,* 16.

Moorman, C., Zaltman, G., & Deshpande, R. (1992, August). Relationship between providers and users of market research: The dynamics of trust within and between organizations. *Journal of Marketing Research, 29,* 314–328.

Peterson, R. A., Albaum, G., & Kerin, R. (1989). A note on alternate contact strategies in mail surveys. *Journal of the Market Research Society, 31* (3), 409–418.

Ricks, D. A. (1999). *Blunders in international business* (3rd ed.). Oxford, UK: Blackwell Publishers Ltd.

Roster, C., Rogers, R., Klein, D., & Albaum, G. (2003). Application of a paradigm to compare sample data: Web vs. telephone survey results. Paper presented at the annual meeting of the Western Decision Sciences. Kauai, HI, April 15–20.

Schiffenbauer, A. (2001, May 21). Study all of a brand's constituencies. *Marketing News, 35,* 17.

Schmalensee, D. (1982, January 22). Establishing objectives with client is vital to success of research project. *Marketing News, 16,* 2ff.

Schmalensee, D. (2001, November 19). One researcher's rules of thumb for B-to-B arena. *Marketing News, 35,* 17–19.

Segal, M. N., & Newberry, C. (1983, Winter). On the field service agency-supplier/client relationships: Problems and perspectives. *Journal of Data Collection, 23,* 58–59.

Semon, T. T. (2003, January 6). Determine survey's purpose for best results. *Marketing News, 37,* 7.

Spiegelbug, H. (1969). *The phenomenological movement, Vols. 1 and 2.* The Hague, Netherlands: Martinus-Nijhoff.

Vence, D. L. (2003, May 12). Companies look to tools that improve sites, connect goals. *Marketing News, 37,* 4.

Zaltman, G. (1989). *The use of development and evaluative market research.* Report No. 89–107. Cambridge, MA: Marketing Science Institute.

Chapter 3

RESEARCH DESIGN

A research design is the specification of methods and procedures for acquiring the information needed to structure and solve problems. The major purpose of any design is to provide the information needed to answer a specific research question using well-developed principles of scientific inquiry. The overall operational design for the project stipulates what information is to be collected, from what sources, and by what procedures. A good design ensures that the information obtained is relevant to the research problem, and that it was collected by objective and economical procedures. A research design might be described as a series of advance decisions that, taken together, form a specific master plan or model for conducting the investigation.

In this chapter we discuss the problems of research tactics regarding the sources and means available for acquiring marketing information, and the types of research designs appropriate for organizing and analyzing this information. In particular, this chapter covers the following five topics:

- Research design characteristics
- Sources of marketing information
- Types of errors affecting research designs
- Methods for dealing with potential errors
- Choosing a research design

We will examine secondary data sources, surveys of respondents, and controlled experiments in detail in subsequent chapters.

RESEARCH DESIGN CHARACTERISTICS

Another way of looking at research design is as a way of arranging the environment in which a research study takes place (Fink, 2003). The environment includes the individuals or groups of people, places, activities, or objects that are to be studied.

Although research designs may be classified by many criteria, the most useful focuses on the major purpose of the investigation and identifies three broad classes of designs:

- Exploratory
- Descriptive
- Causal

Exploratory Studies

The major purposes of exploratory studies are the identification of problems, the precise formulation of problems (including the identification of relevant variables), and the formulation of new alternative courses of action. An exploratory study is often the first project in a series that culminates in a final project that answers research questions and produces research findings to be used as the basis of management action. That is, an exploratory study is often used as an introductory phase of a larger study, and its results are used to develop specific techniques or focus the scope of the larger study.

The design of an exploratory study is characterized by a great amount of flexibility and ad hoc versatility. By definition, the researcher is investigating an area or subject in which he or she is not sufficiently knowledgeable to have formulated detailed research questions. No clear hypotheses have been developed about the problem. The researcher is seeking information that will enable him or her to formulate specific research questions, or to state hypotheses about the problem. In short, the researcher seeks to gain familiarity or achieve new insights into the problem situation.

For a given problem situation, the results of an exploratory study may indicate that further research can be reduced, or certain aspects of the larger study can be eliminated. This will result from narrowing the problem area. Although rare, it may be that the problem, if clearcut, can be solved by an exploratory study. For example, the researcher may discover that another study exists which provides the needed information.

An example of an exploratory study is one conducted by a major manufacturer of kitchen ranges. The purpose of their research was to investigate the design of their ranges to see if they could be improved functionally. One part of the project design involved setting up a booth in department stores handling the brand. People shopping in the stores were invited to simulate cooking a meal that called for one menu item to be boiled, another fried, another simmered, and so on. They almost invariably used the same burners for the same type of cooking: the left front burner for frying, the left back burner for boiling, and the right back burner for simmering. These exploratory research findings led to a prototype redesign of burners and to additional research on them, along with a habits, usage, and preferences study of baking and the storage of cooking utensils.

Despite the necessity for flexibility in exploratory study design, we can distinguish three separate stages that are usually included in exploratory studies and typically conducted in the sequence listed:

- A search of secondary information sources
- Interviews with persons knowledgeable about the subject area
- The examination of analogous situations

Search of Secondary Sources

Secondary sources of information are the "literature" on the subject. It is the rare research problem for which there is no relevant information to be found by a relatively quick and inexpensive search of the literature. If the question to be answered by the preceding research project is "How might we improve the functional design of our ranges?" it is likely that information answering this question already has been published. Studies performed on this subject by home economists at universities, governmental agencies, or cooking magazines probably have been conducted and published.

Secondary sources for exploratory studies are not limited to external sources. Searches should also be made of company records. For larger firms this may be difficult, since operations may be spread out geographically. A search should be attempted despite such complications, since various operational units within a company often face similar problems, and it may be that one unit has recently done research pertaining to the problem at hand. One large company, for example, frequently used outside consultants for projects relevant to new product decisions. This practice was stopped when it was realized that these consultants obtained much of their information directly from company records. A properly functioning Marketing Information System (MIS) within the company can assist in exploratory studies.

Obtaining Information from Knowledgeable Persons

Having searched secondary sources, it is usually desirable to talk with persons who are well informed in the area being investigated:

- Company executives
- Experts
- Consumers
- Users outside the organization

This type of inquiry is sometimes called an experience survey. Rarely is it structured in the sense of a formal questionnaire being prepared, a probability sample selected, or the sample size specified in advance. Rather, the usual procedure is to look for competent, articulate individuals and talk with them about the problem. They will often suggest others who should be reached; a "referral" sample frequently results. The investigator continues these interviews until he or she feels that the marginal return in information is less than the costs involved.

With respect to the example of the redesign of ranges, knowledgeable persons—housewives—were asked to provide information. A convenience sample was taken of housewives who were shopping in the department stores where booths were installed. Observations were made until it was established that there was a consistent behavior pattern with respect to the use of each burner. Once this finding was established, this phase of the exploratory study was terminated.

A widely used technique in exploratory research is the focus group. In a focus group interview, a group of knowledgeable people participates in a joint interview that does not use a structured question-and-answer methodology. The group, usually consisting of 8 to 12 people (but may have as few as 5 or as many as 20), is selected purposely to include persons who have a common background, or similar buying or use experience, relating to the problem being researched. The interviewer or moderator of the session works with the client to develop a general discussion outline that typically includes such topics as usage experience, problems with use, and how decisions are made. The objective is to foster involvement and interaction among the group members during the interview that will lead to spontaneous discussion and the disclosure of attitudes, opinions, and information on present or prospective buying and use behavior.

Focus groups are used primarily to identify and define problems, provide background information, and generate hypotheses, rather than to provide solutions for problems. Areas of application include detecting trends in lifestyles, examining new product concepts, generating ideas for improving established products, developing creative concepts for advertising, and determining effective means of merchandising products.

If the sole purpose is to create ideas, then individual interviews may be a better alternative than focus groups. Limited research on this issue conducted more than 20 years ago suggests that the number and quality of ideas generated may be greater from such interviews (Fern, 1982).

More specific uses of focus groups include identifying how people perceive a product category (e.g., frozen baked goods), detecting the language consumers use to talk about a product category (e.g., "toilet paper" rather than "bathroom tissue"), determining the wording and structure of an entire questionnaire to be used in quantitative research, and interpreting new questions that have been raised by quantitative research (Arnold, 1988). An example of the latter situation is when focus groups are used to determine the reasons for the decline in a product's overall rating, as reported in a syndicated research report. Exhibit 3.1 shows an example of an application of focus groups in exploratory research.

EXHIBIT 3.1   An Application of Focus Groups in Exploratory Research

The most important function of focus group interviewing is as a device to guide the design and conduct of a subsequent large-scale quantitative survey. In this context, group interviews are used to accomplish several goals:

1. Identify and understand consumer language relating to the product category in question. What terms do they use? What do they mean?

2. Identify the range of consumer concerns. How much variability is there among consumers' perception of the product, and in the considerations leading them to accept or reject the product?

3. Identify the complexity of consumer concerns. Do a few simple attitudes govern consumer reaction toward the product, or is the structure complex, involving many contingencies?

4. Identify specific methodological or logistical problems that are likely to affect either the cost of the subsequent research, or one's ability to generate meaningful, actionable findings.

In the mid-1970s, Volvo of America Corporation commissioned a study to explore the differences between Volvo buyers and Volvo considerers (people who thought about buying a Volvo, but in the end bought some other car) (Dupont, 1976). The company wanted to learn the reasons for, and resistances to, buying a Volvo. The research design called for two phases of research:

1. An exploratory stage, involving four group interviews—two with Volvo buyers and two with Volvo considerers (prior research has shown that buyers and considerers don't mix well).

2. A quantification phase involving telephone interviews with 400 first-time Volvo buyers and 200 Volvo considerers.

A great deal of Volvo's past research generated hypotheses about what makes a considerer become a Volvo buyer. In spite of this, researchers learned important things from the focus groups that led to a quantification study that was both more insightful, and less expensive, than would otherwise have been conducted.

One of the most important things the company learned was that there are a number of different ways in which considerers considered Volvo. Thus, they felt the quantification study should include questions designed to segment considerers according to the degree to which they seriously considered Volvo and the methods used to arrive at their purchase choice. To that end, researchers designed a question to determine which specific actions were taken when considering Volvo, such as talking with current Volvo owners, reading evaluative articles in magazines, paying more attention to Volvo advertising, visiting a Volvo showroom, negotiating over price, and others.

The group interviews strongly suggested that the primary variable differentiating the Volvo buyer from the Volvo considerer was the set of concerns that individuals brought to the car-buying process. Further, it was readily apparent that these concerns varied widely, implying that it would be necessary to measure the importance of a number of a car's characteristics to the consumer, such as safety, exterior styling, anticipated cost of service, and so forth. Consequently, Volvo prepared a list of 26 automobile attributes—some drawing on prior research and new ones based upon the group session findings—to present to consumers in the quantification study.

However, the desirability of this approach led to a methodological dilemma. It was important that not only the importance of these 26 factors to Volvo buyers and considerers be determined, but also how considerers compared Volvo, on the factors they considered important, to the car actually bought. The logical solution, after having respondents rate all 26 factors for importance, was to have them rank the five factors which played the largest role in the automobile selection decision, and then rate Volvo against the competitive car on those top five factors.

This example illustrates the value of conducting exploratory focus-group interviews prior to a larger, quantified study. Such an exploration will not always pay for itself in a more efficient final research design, as this one more than did, but will nearly always lead to a subsequent survey richer in content, more adroit in interpretation, and more actionable to marketing management.

SOURCE: *From Advances in Consumer Research,* 3rd edition, by Dupont, T.D. Copyright © 1976. Reprinted with permission of the Association for Consumer Research.

Technological advances have led to an increasing use of focus groups conducted online through chat sessions. The Internet and the World Wide Web have created new opportunities for companies to market their products and services, so it is natural that companies look to them for research purposes. Online marketing and research are appropriate for certain market segments, even though online users are not representative of the general population; they tend to be better educated, younger, more affluent, and, more often than not, male. Online focus groups often prove effective in getting participation from elusive teen, single, affluent, and well-educated audiences (Murphy, 1997). In short, chat sessions are effective to reach certain hard-to-get segments. Online focus groups offer two distinct advantages over more traditional methods: speed and cost effectiveness. But they are not for everyone! Researchers retain verbal interaction, but lose nonverbal communication such as body language and eye contact, which often provide greater insight into the verbal statements. Focus-group methodology is discussed further in Chapter 7.

Examination of Analogous Situations

It is also logical that a researcher will want to examine analogous situations to determine what else can be learned about the nature of the problem and its variables. Analogous situations include case histories and simulations.

Case histories provide a fruitful area of investigation for an exploratory study when the cases are similar in content and generally available. Examining another actual case will often clarify the nature of the problem, suggest which variables are relevant, and indicate the nature of relationships among the variables. This method of investigation is widely used in the behavioral sciences, where it is called the "case study."

However, the results of the investigation of case histories are always suggestive rather than conclusive, because the examination is being conducted after the fact. It is not possible to manipulate the independent variables, or to randomize treatments and the selection of groups concerned. For these reasons, interpretations reached concerning the relevancy and relationships among variables are judgmental and always subject to error. More detailed discussions of the methodology of case study are presented by Yin (2003a; 2003b) and Gomm, Foster, and Hammersley (2000).

In the example problem of redesigning kitchen ranges, ready-made case histories may well be observed by studying previous design changes made by competitors. One might be able to observe the sales of one or more competitors' ranges following design changes. As always in case studies, one would have to examine the situation(s) carefully to identify and assess the effect of any other independent variable changes (price, advertising, changes in income, etc.) on sales. Tentative conclusions can be reached, however, and a hypothesis stated. This hypothesis can be tested in a subsequent causal study designed for that purpose, if desired.

Simulating the general problem situation may also be useful to provide a better understanding of the problem and its components. Simulation involves the construction of a model representing the situation and, in effect, experimenting with it rather than the actual situation.

Descriptive Studies

Much research is concerned with describing market characteristics or functions. A market-potential study may describe the number, distribution, and socioeconomic characteristics of potential customers of a product. A market-share study finds the share of the market received by both the company and its major competitors. A sales analysis describes sales by territory, type of account, size or model of product, and the like. Descriptive studies are also made in the following areas:

- Product research: a listing and comparison of the functional features and specifications of competitive products
- Promotion research: the demographic characteristics of the audience being reached by the current advertising program

- Distribution research: the number and location of retailers handling the company's products that are supplied by wholesalers versus those supplied by the company's distribution centers
- Pricing research: competitors' prices by geographic area

These examples of descriptive research cover only a few of the possibilities. Descriptive designs, often called observational designs by some researchers, provide information on groups and phenomena that already exist; no new groups are created (Fink, 2003).

Descriptive studies often involve determining the association between two or more variables. A two-way frequency distribution of sales revenue by membership in an organization (e.g., a cross-tabulation) is an example. A proprietary study of business involvement in a small community's Chamber of Commerce reported the data shown in Table 3.1. This type of information may be used to draw inferences concerning the relationship between the variables involved (revenue and membership). It may also be used to predict whether a new company in the area will join the Chamber of Commerce.

Although associations can be used only to infer, and not establish, a causal relationship, they are often useful for predictive purposes. It is not always necessary to understand causal relations in order to make accurate predictive statements. Descriptive information often provides a sound basis for the solution of marketing problems, even though it does not explain the nature of the relationship involved. The basic principle involved is to find desirable behavior correlates to predict that are measurable when the predictive statement is made.

Descriptive research, in contrast to exploratory research, is marked by the prior formulation of specific research questions. The investigator already knows a substantial amount about the research problem, perhaps as a result of an exploratory study, before the project is initiated, and should be able to clearly define what should be measured and how one should set up appropriate and specific means for the measurements.

One example of a descriptive study was performed by a company considering entering the greeting card industry. A previous exploratory study revealed that only two percent of greeting card sales were made through supermarkets. Since the potential of this type of outlet is large, and other outlets were heavily franchised or otherwise dominated by well-entrenched companies in the field, the company performed a descriptive study to answer the specific question, "What are the major problems of selling greeting cards in volume through supermarkets?" The answers obtained resulted in the company's development of a greeting card vending machine that was used successfully in supermarkets.

Another example of a descriptive study is one conducted by a school-employees credit union in order to gain information useful to provide better service to its members. Management knew very little about the members, other than that they were school employees, family members of employees, or former employees. In addition, the credit union knew very little about members' awareness and use of, and attitudes toward individual services available to them. Consequently, investigators undertook a study to answer the following research questions:

1. What are the demographic and socioeconomic characteristics of primary members?

2. How extensively are existing services being used, and what are members' attitudes toward such services?

3. What is the degree of interest in specific new services?

Table 3.1   Companies Reporting Annual Sales Revenue and Membership in the Chamber of Commerce

	Membership in Chamber	
Annual Sales Revenue	*Member*	*Nonmember*
Less than $50,000	10	6
$50,000–$99,999	7	8
$100,000–$249,999	24	8
$250,000–$499,999	19	5
$500,000–$999,999	9	0
$1,000,000 and above	25	2

Management found the answers helpful when evaluating the financial and non-financial services offered and deciding which new services to add.

Descriptive research is also characterized by a preplanned and structured design. Contrasting the flexibility of the exploratory study, the descriptive study should be planned carefully with respect to the sources of information to be consulted and the procedures to be used in collecting information. Since the intent of the study is to provide answers to specific questions, more care is normally exercised against the possibility of systematic (nonrandom) errors than is the case with the exploratory study. The designs used in descriptive research can employ one or more general sources of information. Furthermore, they may be cross-sectional (at a point in time) or longitudinal (over time) in nature.

For descriptive studies (and causal studies as well) proposed data analysis and project output are critical aspects of research planning. One approach to including such output planning into a research design is illustrated in Exhibit 3.2, where a meat packer tests the market potential of a new sport-related hot dog. What was unique about the product concept was that it featured a winter sport—ice hockey—rather than the more usual link with baseball. As illustrated, this aspect of the design should include analysis procedures for each question, an assessment of their information value, and how the information may be used.

EXHIBIT 3.2   Illustration of Proposed Analysis for New Hot Dog Study

Question number(s) and variable name(s): Questions 5.0 and 5.1 ask the number of packages of hot dogs consumed per month by household, usual number of hot dogs per package, plus number of loose links consumed per month. Variable name is USAGE.

Information content of questions: Multiply number of packages per month by dogs per package and add loose links to obtain the total household usage of hot dogs per month.

Reasons for including question(s): These questions provide information needed to segment the population of hot dog users into submarkets based on usage level. Usage volume can serve as an excellent predictor of future purchase patterns, may be related to interest in proposed new hot dog products and may support media selection that will reach high-usage households with the least cost.

Primary Analysis and Information Value:

I. Frequency distribution: This indicates the number of dogs used per month for all respondents. These will be coded into three categories: light, moderate, and heavy users.

II. Relation to demographics: Usage types will be cross-tabulated with size of household; sex, age, and education of shopper; and total household income in order to identify the characteristics of the three user segments. Statistic used will be chi-square.

III. Relation to price: Usage will be systematically related to responses on purchase probability under different pricing conditions. This will express the importance of price for the user segments and help estimate volume of sales at different price points.

Additional Analysis and Information Value:

Relation to importance of product features: User segments will be compared in terms of their mean responses to the ten-point importance-attribute scales, which include package, brand name, quality, contents, taste, texture, smell, shape, and color of the hot dogs. This will provide information on the relative importance of attributes and assist in formulating advertising approaches for the target segments.

SOURCE: Adapted from Sackmary, 1983.

Causal Studies

Although descriptive information is often useful for predictive purposes, where possible we would like to know the causes of what we are predicting—the "reasons why." Further, we would like to know the relationships of these causal factors to the effects that we are predicting. This is, no doubt, in part because we each have an innate desire to understand. Of a more direct and practical consequence, however, is the fact that if we understand the causes of the effects we want to predict, we invariably improve our ability both to predict and to control these effects. Many of the notions of causality are described in depth in Cook and Campbell (1979, pp. 9–36) and Bagozzi (1980, Chapter 1).

Causal Relationships

Suppose that a particular manufacturer of color television sets reduces the wholesale price of his sets by 10 percent, and that this reduction is passed on to the consumer. Further assume that sales to the consumer rose by 15 percent during the succeeding three months, compared to a similar period prior to the price reduction. Did the price cut by itself cause the increase in sales (Figure 3.1A), did it only contribute, along with other marketing actions (Figure 3.1B), or did it have no effect whatsoever (Figure 3.1C)?

Deterministic Causation

Real-world events occur in and are affected by a real-world environment. The nature of this environment determines the rules that describe the relationship between events. The nature of the relationship between price and quantity of a product sold by a state-owned enterprise in the People's Republic of China is quite different from that for an individual producer in the United States.

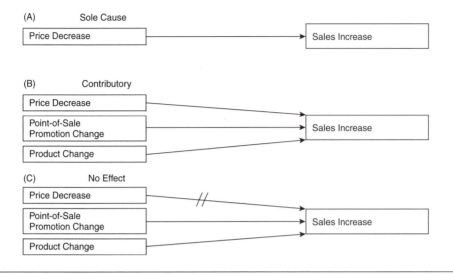

Figure 3.1   Alternative Price Change/Sales Change Causal Relationships

Suppose that we establish a functional relationship between two events, *X* and *Y*, such that *Y* is some function of *X*. This statement may be written

$$Y = f(X)$$

Further suppose we know the environment of these two events well enough to determine the "rule" that relates them, and thus specify *f*. Once we specify *X*, we have completely determined *Y*. In this case we say that *X* is both a necessary and a sufficient condition for *Y*. We must specify *X*, but only *X*, to determine *Y*. We can, therefore, say that *X* is a deterministic cause of *Y*. A deterministic cause is any event that is necessary and sufficient for the subsequent occurrence of another event.

Returning to our color television example, would it be realistic to conclude that the price cut was a deterministic cause of the sales increase? Clearly not. Many factors other than price affect the level of sales; a change in price is, therefore, not a sufficient condition for determining the level of sales. More generally, the multivariate nature of the complex world of marketing indicates that deterministic causes are quite rare. Yet, there are occasions when companies do research that borders on deterministic causation. For example, Wrangler Jeans has sponsored sports such as rodeo and dirt bike racing. In the mid 1980s it measured the impact of its sports marketing dollars as follows:

Consumer interviews were conducted before the company became involved to figure out how many pairs of Wrangler jeans are being purchased by spectators of that sport. After sponsorship is undertaken, follow-up interviews are conducted to measure incremental purchase in Wrangler purchases. The rate of increased purchasing is multiplied by the company's profit margin per pair of jeans to compute the sponsorship's sales contribution to the company. That figure is compared to the cost of sponsorship. (Higgins, 1984, p. 6)

Probabilistic Causation

Relationships in marketing usually involve several variables. As further complications, these relationships are almost invariably complex, subject to change, and difficult to measure. Consider now a multivariable relationship of the form

$$Y = f(X_1, X_2)$$

where X_1 and X_2 are independent. Assuming that we are able to specify f, the variables X_1 and X_2 become jointly necessary and sufficient to determine Y.

Suppose that we know the value of X_1 but do not know the value of X_2. Since X_1 and X_2 are assumed to be independent, no inferences can be drawn about the value of X_2 from the known value of X_1. In this situation, the only statements that can be made about the value of Y must be conditional upon the unknown value of X_2. The effect on Y of a known change in X_1 may be reinforced, counteracted, or left the same, depending upon what happens to X_2. X_1 by itself is not sufficient to determine Y.

Where multivariable relationships exist, we may say that any one of the independent variables X_j is a probabilistic cause of the effect of Y. The term *producer* is sometimes used, and will be used here, as being synonymous with probabilistic cause. When "producer" is used, the resulting effect is referred to as a product.

In the more general case, we may define a probabilistic cause, or producer, as any event (e.g., X_1 or X_2) that is necessary, but not sufficient, for the subsequent occurrence of another event, Y.

Are we to conclude that the price reduction was a producer of the sales increase (product) in our example? Given that we believe that the price level and amount of sales of television sets are inversely and functionally related, we are, in fact, drawing that conclusion.

The reader should be careful not to read more into the last statement than is actually there. It does not say that the price reduction determined the amount of the sales increase, or that it was even a major factor in bringing about any increase in sales. It may have been that a newly redesigned model series prompted a concomitant change in advertising and price, and the other changes were more important producers of the sales increase than the price change.

Bases for Inferring Causal Relationships

There are three types of evidence that can be used for drawing inferences about causal relationships:

1. Associative variation

2. Sequence of events

3. Absence of other possible causal factors

In addition, the cause and effect have to be related. That is, there must be logical implication (or theoretical justification) to imply the specific causal relation.

Associative Variation

Associative variation, or "concomitant variation," as it is often termed, is a measure of the extent to which occurrences of two variables are associated. Two types of associative variation may be distinguished:

1. Association between two variables: A measure of the extent to which the presence of one variable is associated with the presence of the other

2. Association between the changes of two variables: A measure of the extent to which a change in the level of one variable is associated with a change in the level of the other

It has been argued that two other conditions may also exist, particularly for continuous variables: (a) the presence of one variable is associated with a change in the level of other; and (b) a change in the level of one variable is associated with the presence of the other (Feldman, 1975).

As an example, suppose the brand manager of a particular brand of detergent notices that sales have shown an unusually large increase in the third quarter, and suppose he is also aware that a number of detergent sales personnel took a retraining course during the second quarter. How may the brand manager determine if the retraining was a producer of the sales increase?

Two basic approaches, with variations on each, can be followed to obtain evidence concerning this relationship. The first is to start with the hypothesized producer (salesperson retraining) and see if there is an associated variation with the product (large territorial sales increase). This could be done by determining which salespeople had been retrained during the second quarter, and comparing the net changes in sales between the second and third quarters in their territories with the corresponding net changes in sales of those salespeople who were not retrained.

The second approach is to start with the product (large territorial sales increase) and work back to the producer (salesperson retraining). If this approach were used, all territories with large sales increases would be examined to determine whether they were predominantly composed of retrained salespeople.

Suppose that one of these approaches was used to collect information that showed a high degree of association between large territorial sales increases and salesperson retraining. Would this information constitute experimental proof of a causal relationship? The answer to this question is, unfortunately, "No." The reasons why this is the case are discussed in detail in later chapters. It is sufficient to state here that this associated variation might be the result of random variation, or both variables being associated with some extraneous variable, such as a change in the point-of-sale displays provided to the retrained salespeople.

If we have no basis for believing that either of these situations exists, then associated variation can be used as a basis for inferring—but not scientifically testing—that there is a causal relationship.

Sequence of Events

A second characteristic of a causal relationship is the requirement that the causal factor occur first; the producer must precede the product. In order for the salesperson retraining to result in an increase in sales, the retraining must have taken place prior to the sales increase.

The fact that a possible producer precedes a product does not establish that a causal relationship exists between the two, however. It might be simply a coincidence that the retraining took place prior to the sales increase. It might also be that sales training and sales increases are associated but not causally related.

It is not always easy to determine the sequence of events. In such cases where an actual causal relationship does exist, it is difficult to determine which is the producer and which is the product. The relationship between retail store shelf space and sales is an example. Other factors being equal, those brands having larger relative amounts of shelf space tend to have higher sales. And likewise, those brands having the higher sales tend to be allotted larger relative amounts of shelf space.

Absence of Other Possible Causal Factors

A final basis for inferring causation is the absence of any possible causal factors (producers) other than the one(s) being investigated. If it could be demonstrated, for example, that no other factors present could have caused the sales increase in the third quarter, we could then logically conclude that the salesperson training must have been responsible.

Obviously, in an after-the-fact examination of a situation such as the detergent sales increase, it is impossible to clearly rule out all other factors. One could never be completely sure that there were no competitor-, customer-, or company-initiated causal factors that would account for the sales increase.

In experimental designs in which control groups are used, it is possible to control some of the variables that might otherwise obscure or lead to a misinterpretation of the relationship(s) under study. In addition, a soundly designed experiment will include an attempt to balance the effects of the uncontrolled variables on the experimental results in such a way that only random variations resulting from the uncontrolled variables will be measured.

For example, an experiment might be designed in which salespeople who have not yet undergone retraining are matched in pairs with respect to age, past sales history, type of territory, and other variables believed to be possible determinants of sales performance. A control group could then be created by selecting one salesperson from each pair at random to not be retrained during the period of the experiment. The experimental group would then consist of the other salesperson from each of the pairs, who would then be retrained. An analysis of the differences in sales results for the two groups during the period of the experiment could then be made to test the hypothesis that salesperson retraining does result in a significant increase in sales.

Conclusions Concerning Types of Evidence

No one of the three types of evidence, or even all three types combined, can ever conclusively demonstrate that a causal relationship exists. However, we can obtain evidence that makes it highly reasonable to conclude that a particular relationship exists. Exhibit 3.3 shows certain questions that are necessary to answer.

EXHIBIT 3.3   Issues in Determining Causation

Several questions arise when determining whether a variable *X* has causal priority over another variable, *Y:*

1. What is the source of causality—does *X* cause *Y,* or does *Y* cause *X?*

2. What is the direction of causality—does *X* positively influence *Y,* or is the relationship negative?

3. Is *X* a necessary and sufficient cause—or necessary, but not sufficient cause—of *Y?* Is *X*'s causation deterministic or probabilistic?

4. Which value of the believed cause exerts a causal influence—its presence or absence?

5. Are the causes and effects the states themselves or changes in the states? Is the relationship static or dynamic?

In the end, the necessary conditions for causality to exist are a physical basis for causality, a cause that temporally precedes the effect (even for associative variation), and a logical reason to imply the specific causal relation being examined. (Monroe and Petroshius, n.d.).

The accumulation of evidence from various investigations will, if all findings point to the same conclusion, increase our confidence that a causal relationship exists. A diversity of types of evidence is also convincing in this respect. If all three types of evidence discussed above can be obtained, the resulting inference is more convincing than if only one type of evidence is found.

Causal Inference Studies

We have considered the nature and meaning of causation and the types of evidence useful for drawing inferences about causal relationships. We now turn to consider the design of causal studies.

There are two broad classes of designs for causal inference research:

- Natural experiments
- Controlled experiments

The distinguishing feature between the two is the extent of intervention by the investigator in the situation under study. As the name implies, a natural experiment may not require investigator intervention in the situation at all and, at most, involves intervention only to the extent required for measurement. A controlled experiment requires investigator intervention to control and to manipulate variables of interest as well as to measure the response.

The salesperson-retraining example (as originally described) illustrates a natural experiment. In this case no intervention was involved in the situation; the measurements made were conducted as a normal part of doing business. Had the investigator wanted to measure results other than those normally measured—the amount of shelf space in retail stores the company's detergents had in the affected territories before and after the retraining of salespeople, for example—there necessarily would have been investigator intervention to the extent required to perform such measurements.

One possible controlled experiment for assessing the effect of sales retraining on the level of sales has already been described. Investigator intervention was involved in matching the salespeople in pairs and randomly selecting one from each pair for inclusion in the test group. Therefore, the experimental procedures were the determinant of which salespeople were to be retrained. Clearly, intervention of this kind is not always practical, or even possible.

It is apparent from the discussion thus far that causal studies presuppose a considerable amount of knowledge by the investigator about the variables being studied. The design of causal inference studies is also highly formalized. The experiment just described uses a form of "before/after with control group" design. Specific designs of both natural and controlled experiments are discussed in Chapter 8.

SOURCES OF MARKETING INFORMATION

There are five major sources of marketing information:

- Secondary sources
- Respondents
- Natural experiments
- Controlled experiments
- Simulation

In this section we briefly describe each as an introduction to subsequent chapters that describe some of these sources in more depth.

Secondary Sources of Information

Secondary information is information that has been collected by persons or agencies for purposes other than the solution of the problem at hand. If a furniture manufacturer, for example, needs information on the potential market for furniture in the Middle Atlantic states, many secondary sources of information are available. The federal government collects and publishes information on the numbers of families, family formation, income, and the number and sales volume of retail stores, all by geographic area. It also publishes special reports on the furniture industry. Many state and local governments collect similar information for their respective areas. The trade associations in the furniture field collect and publish an extensive amount of information about the industry. Trade journals are also a valuable source of secondary information, as are special studies done by other advertising media. Private research firms collect specialized marketing information on a continuing basis and sell it to companies. These so-called syndicated services, particularly those for packaged consumer goods, are becoming more sophisticated as they are increasingly becoming based on scanner data. Technology advancements have a measurable impact on the availability of secondary data.

These and other sources will yield much information of value to the researcher concerned with this problem. The nature of secondary data and its sources is presented in more depth in Chapter 4.

Information from Respondents

A second major source of information is obtained from respondents. Asking questions and observing behavior are primary means of obtaining information whenever people's actions are being investigated or predicted. The term respondent literally means "one who responds; answers." In this book it is useful to include both verbal and behavioral response in the usage of the term. That is, we shall consider both the information obtained from asking people questions, and that provided by observing behavior (or the results of past behavior) to comprise information from respondents.

Information from Communication with Respondents

The survey is a widely used and well-known method of acquiring marketing information by communicating with a group of respondents. Researchers can obtain information from consumers, industrial users, dealers, and others knowledgeable about the problem at hand. People are asked questions through personal interviews, telephone interviews, mail questionnaires, and, increasingly, e-mail and the Internet. They are asked for information either once, in a self-contained, one-time survey, or repetitively as part of a continuing panel.

Questioning respondents is virtually necessary to obtain information about their level of knowledge, attitudes, opinions, motivations, or intended behavior. If, for example, a bank considered providing a service of direct payment of utility and credit card bills for its depositors, the only practical way of determining how much its depositors knew about this type of service, their attitudes and opinions of it, and whether they intended to use it would be to ask them.

Although questioning respondents is often the most efficient and economical way to obtain information, it requires considerable skill and care in application if the information is to be of maximum value. At best, people will respond with the most honest information they are able to provide. At worst, they may offer misleading and highly biased information.

The kinds of information that may be obtained from respondents, the different means of communicating with respondents, and the errors associated with each are discussed in Chapters 5 through 11.

Information from Observation of Respondents

Relevant information for many marketing problems may be obtained by observing either present behavior or the results of past behavior. The researcher who requires information on the color and style preferences for men's shoes may well find the observation method ideally suited to this purpose.

Observational methods make it possible to record behavior as it occurs, and thus eliminate errors due to reporting past behavior. For example, the researcher who observes the number of units and brands of a product class actually bought in supermarkets by a sample of housewives, rather than questioning the housewives later, will avoid the errors inherent in relying on respondents' memories. However, there still exists the possibility of errors in recording.

Observing people's behavior cannot be used effectively to obtain information about the level of knowledge, opinions, motivations, or intended behavior of respondents. In instances where the behavior is private or impossible to observe, observation cannot be used at all. Observation of respondents is discussed in detail in Chapter 7.

Information from Natural and Controlled Experiments

As described earlier, three types of evidence provide the bases for drawing inferences about causal relationships. Either natural or controlled experimental designs are capable of providing associative variation and sequence of events, but only controlled experiments can provide reasonably conclusive evidence concerning the third type of evidence, the absence of other possible producers.

A natural experiment is one in which the investigator intervenes only to the extent required for measurement. That is, there is no manipulation of an assumed causal variable. The investigator merely looks at what has happened. As such, the natural experiment is a form of ex post facto research. In this type of study, the researcher approaches data collection as if a controlled experimental design were used. The variable of interest has occurred in a natural setting, and the researcher looks for respondents who have been exposed to it and also, if a control group is desired, respondents who have not been exposed. Measurements can then be made on a dependent variable of interest. For example, if the impact of a television commercial on attitudes were desired, the investigator would contact a sample of people after the commercial was shown. Those who saw the commercial would constitute the experimental group, and those who did not see it would be a type of control group. Differences in attitudes could be compared as a crude measure of impact. Unfortunately, one can never be sure whether the obtained relationship is causal or noncausal, since the attitudes may be affected by the presence of other variables. For a brief discussion of natural experiments, see Anderson (1971).

In controlled experiments, investigator intervention is required beyond that needed for measurement purposes. Specifically, two kinds of intervention are required:

1. Manipulation of at least one assumed causal variable

2. Random assignment of subjects to experimental and control groups

Manipulation of at least one variable is required in order to administer the treatment(s) whose effects are desirable to measure. Randomizing the assignment of subjects to groups controls differences arising from extraneous variables.

The nature of experimentation; potential errors affecting experimental designs; and natural experimental, pre-experimental, quasi-experimental, and true experimental designs are treated in Chapter 8.

Simulation

The expense, time involved, or other problems associated with field experimentation may preclude it as a source of information for a particular operational situation. In such cases it may be desirable to construct a model of the operational situation and to experiment with it instead of the real-world situation. The manipulation of such models is called simulation.

This approach to obtaining information has a long history in, and is borrowed from, the physical sciences. An example of using physical analogs for simulative purposes is the use of scaled replicas of aircraft in a wind tunnel. The model's performance can be tested and observed under widely varying simulated conditions of wind velocity, altitude, and speeds. It is far less expensive and time-consuming to use such simulation procedures than to construct and test actual prototype aircraft on test flights.

Physical analogs are seldom used in marketing, but conceptual models are constructed and manipulated to obtain information on the effect of specifically modifying combinations of the variables. The information obtained consists of numerical output from the simulation models. As such, it differs from that provided by secondary sources, respondents, and field experimentation. The latter sources provide information directly from the situation being investigated. Simulation provides information from an imitation of this situation.

Simulation can be defined as a set of techniques for manipulating a model of some real-world process to find numerical solutions useful in the real process being modeled. Models that are environmentally rich (that is, that may contain complex interactions and nonlinear relationships among the variables, probabilistic components, time dependencies, etc.) are usually too difficult to solve by standard analytical methods such as calculus or other mathematical programming techniques. Rather, the analyst views a simulation model as an imitation of the process or system under study and attempts to run the system on a computer to see what would happen if a particular policy were put into effect.

Simulations may be used for research, instruction, decision-making, or some combination of these applications. Their use as an aid in decision-making is our primary concern here. As a historical illustration of a market simulation developed for that purpose in the early 1960s, the Simulmatics Corporation reported on the development of a "marketing microcosm" consisting of almost 3,000 hypothetical persons who, purportedly, were representative of the U.S. population. The analyst could then study the impact of various media schedules on the reading characteristics of this "toy" population and attempt to extrapolate these findings to the total population. The microcosm was stratified by age, gender, educational level, race, and political affiliation. By means of the computer model, alternative media schedules could be "tested" on the microcosm and summary figures prepared on the type of audience and projected size and frequency with which the population is exposed to each media schedule.

During the past 30 – 40 years, simulations have been developed for such marketing decision-making applications as marketing systems, marketing-mix elements (new-product, price advertising, and sales-force decisions), and interviewing costs in marketing surveys.

More recently, simulation has been used in test marketing. A number of research firms offer test-market simulators designed to predict market share and sales for a new product introduced nationally using a specific marketing mix. A related application is the use of simulation with conjoint analysis. When conjoint analysis is used to design optimal product and product lines, or to assess how people value different product attributes, the resulting data can be entered into choice simulators to predict market share and test sensitivity of market share to changes in product attributes. Conjoint analysis is discussed in more detail in Chapter 19.

TYPES OF ERRORS AFFECTING RESEARCH DESIGNS

The marketing research process (and research design) involves the management of error. Potential errors can arise at any point from problem formulation through report preparation. Rarely will a research project be error-free. Consequently, the research designer must adopt a strategy for managing this error. As we shall see in the next section of this chapter, there are alternative strategies one can follow.

The objective underlying any research project is to provide information that is as accurate as possible. Maximizing accuracy requires that total study errors be minimized. Total study error has two components—sampling error and non-sampling error—and can be expressed as follows:

$$\text{Total error} = \text{Sampling error} + \text{Non-sampling error}$$

Total error is usually measured as total error variance, also known as the mean-squared error (Assael & Keon, 1982):

$$(\text{Total error})^2 = (\text{Sampling error})^2 + (\text{Non-sampling error})^2$$

Sampling error refers to the variable error resulting from the chance specification of population from elements according to the sampling plan. Since this introduces random variability into the precision with which a sample statistic is calculated, it is often called random sampling error. Exhibit 3.4 gives an illustration of how total error is assessed.

EXHIBIT 3.4   How Errors Add Up

It is important to know all the sources of error that contribute to inaccuracy, and to assess the impact of each. As an example, consider the figure below, which shows components of error in a personal computer study designed to estimate the size of the market (Lilien, Brown, & Searls, 1991). When estimating the market, adjustments are made for each source of error. The components are then combined mathematically to create the total error. For purposes of simplicity, total error is shown here as the sum of the component errors. In actuality, total error would be smaller, as it is usually based on the square roots of summed squares of component errors. Assessing the individual components of total error is highly judgmental and subjective, but it is worth the effort.

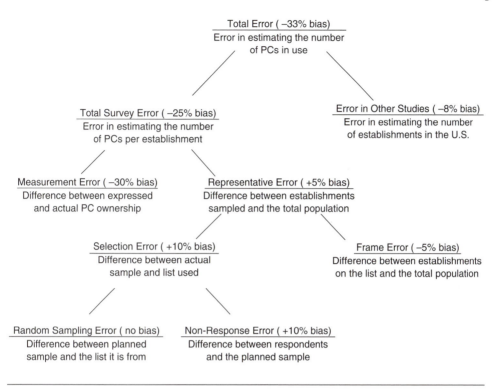

Total Error (−33% bias)
Error in estimating the number
of PCs in use

Total Survey Error (−25% bias)
Error in estimating the number
of PCs per establishment

Error in Other Studies (−8% bias)
Error in estimating the number
of establishments in the U.S.

Measurement Error (−30% bias)
Difference between expressed
and actual PC ownership

Representative Error (+5% bias)
Difference between establishments
sampled and the total population

Selection Error (+10% bias)
Difference between actual
sample and list used

Frame Error (−5% bias)
Difference between establishments
on the list and the total population

Random Sampling Error (no bias)
Difference between planned
sample and the list it is from

Non-Response Error (+10% bias)
Difference between respondents
and the planned sample

SOURCE: Reprinted with permission from "How Errors Add Up," by Lilien, G., Brown, R., & Searls, K. in *Marketing News, 33,* January 7, 1991. Published by the American Marketing Association.

Non-sampling error consists of all other errors associated with a research project. Such errors are diverse in nature. It is often thought of as resulting in some sort of bias, which implies systematic error. Bias can be defined simply as the difference between the true value of that which is being measured and the average value derived from a number of independent measurements of it. However, there can be a random component of non-sampling error. For example, misrecording a response during data collection would represent a random error, whereas using a loaded question would be a systematic error. Non-sampling errors arise from nonresponse and response.

To a large extent these major error components are inversely related. Increasing the sample size to reduce sampling error can increase non-sampling error in that, for example, there are more instances where such things as recording errors can occur, and the impact of loaded (i.e., nonobjective) questions and other systematic errors will be greater. Thus, this inverse relationship lies at the heart of our concern for total error.

Ideally, efforts should be made to minimize each component. Considering time and cost limitations this can rarely be done. The researcher must make a decision that involves a trade-off between sampling and non-sampling errors. Unfortunately, very little is known empirically about the relative size of the two error components, although there is some evidence that non-sampling error tends to be the larger of the two. In a study comparing several research designs and data collection methods, Assael and Keon (1982) concluded that non-sampling error far outweighs random sampling error in contributing to total survey error.

Exhibit 3.5 briefly defines eight major types of errors that can influence research results. Each is discussed in more detail in subsequent chapters.

EXHIBIT 3.5   Types of Errors in the Research Process

Different types of errors can influence research results:

- **Population specification:** noncorrespondence of the required population to the population selected by the researcher
- **Sampling:** noncorrespondence of the sample selected by probability means and the representative sample sought by the researcher
- **Selection:** noncorrespondence of the sample selected by nonprobability means and the sought representative sample
- **Frame:** noncorrespondence of the sought sample to the required sample
- **Nonresponse:** noncorrespondence of the achieved (or obtained) sample to the selected sample
- **Surrogate information:** noncorrespondence of the information being sought by the researcher and that required to solve the problem
- **Measurement:** noncorrespondence of the information obtained by the measurement process and the information sought by the researcher
- **Experimental:** noncorrespondence of the true (or actual) impact of, and the impact attributed to, the independent variable(s)

Population Specification Error

This type of error occurs when the researcher selects an inappropriate population or universe from which to obtain data. For example, if Cessna Aircraft wanted to learn what features should be added to a proposed corporate jet, they might conduct a survey of purchasing agents from major corporations presently owning such aircraft. However, this would be an inappropriate research universe, since pilots most likely play the key role in the purchase decision. Similarly, packaged goods manufacturers often conduct surveys of housewives, because they are easier to contact, and it is assumed they decide what is to be purchased and also do the actual purchasing. In this situation there often is population specification error, for the husband may purchase a significant share of the packaged goods, and have significant direct and indirect influence over what is bought.

Sampling Error

Sampling error occurs when a probability sampling method is used to select a sample, but this sample is not representative of the population concern. For example, a random sample of 500 people composed only of people aged 35 to 55 would not be representative of the general adult population. Sampling error is affected by the homogeneity of the population being studied and sampled from and by the size of the sample. In general, the more homogeneous the population, the smaller the sampling error; as sample size increases, sampling error decreases. If a census were conducted (i.e., all elements of the population were included) there would be no sampling error.

Selection Error

Selection error is the sampling error for a sample selected by a nonprobability method. Consider the case of interviewers conducting a mall intercept study: There is a natural tendency for investigators to select those respondents who are the most accessible and agreeable whenever there is latitude to do so. Such samples often comprise friends and associates who bear some degree of resemblance in characteristics to those of the desired population. Selection error often reflects people who are most easily reached, better dressed, and have better kept homes or more pleasant personalities. Samples of these types rarely are representative of the desired population.

Frame Error

A sampling frame is the source for sampling that accounts for all the elements in the population. It is usually a listing of the elements, but need not be a printed list. The sample frame for a study using intercepts at a shopping mall, for instance, includes all shoppers in the mall during the period of data collection. A perfect frame identifies each population element once, but only once, and does not include elements not in the population. A commonly used frame for consumer research is the telephone directory. This frame introduces error because many elements of the population are not included in the directory (unlisted phone numbers, new arrivals), some elements are listed more than once, and nonpopulation elements are also included (businesses, people who have left the area).

Nonresponse Error

Nonresponse error can exist when an obtained sample differs from the original selected sample. There are two ways in which nonresponse can occur: (a) noncontact (the inability to contact all members of the sample); and (b) refusal (nonresponse to some or all items on the measurement instrument).

Errors arise in virtually every survey from the inability to reach respondents. In telephone surveys, some respondents are inaccessible because they are not at home (NAH) for the initial call or call-backs. Others have moved or are away from home for the period of the survey. Not-at-home respondents are typically younger with no small children, and have a much higher proportion of working wives than households with someone at home. People who have moved or are away for the survey period have a higher geographic mobility than the average of the population. Thus, most surveys can anticipate errors from non-contact of respondents.

Refusals may be by item or for the entire interview. Income, religion, sex, and politics are topics that may elicit item refusals. Some respondents refuse to participate at all because of time requirements, past experiences in which an "interviewer" turned out to be a telemarketer, their own ill health, or other reasons. A kind of refusal specific to the method is the nonresponse to a mail questionnaire. Nonresponse to mail questionnaires sometimes runs as high as 90 percent of the initial mailing, even after several successive mailings.

The amount of effort involved in data collection is another possible way to affect nonresponse error. However, little research has been done to examine the impact of effort. In a national telephone survey, a so-called five-day "standard" survey was compared to a "rigorous" survey conducted over an eight-week period (Keeter, Miller, Kohut, Groves, & Presser, 2000). Response rates were significantly different; the rigorous survey generated about two-thirds greater response. But the two surveys produced similar results. Most of the statistically significant differences were for demographic items. Very few differences were found on substantive variables.

Nonresponse is also a potential problem in business-to-business research situations. Surveys in this type of situation, for example, are often referred to as organizational surveys. Although specific respondents are individuals, organizations are not, as they are differentiated and hierarchical. These characteristics may affect organizational response to survey requests. Tomaskovic-Devey, Leiter, and Thompson (1994) believe the likelihood that an organizational respondent will respond is a function of three characteristics of the respondent:

1. Authority to respond: The degree to which a designated respondent has the formal or informal authority to respond to a survey request

2. Capacity to respond: Organizational practices and divisions of labor and information that affect the assembly of relevant knowledge to reply adequately

3. Motive to respond: Both individual and organizational motivations to provide information about the organization

Surrogate Information Error

In many problem situations in marketing research, it is necessary to obtain information that acts as a surrogate for that which is required. The necessity to accept substitute information arises from either the inability or unwillingness of respondents to provide the information needed.

Decision-oriented behavioral research is always concerned with the prediction of behavior, usually nonverbal behavior. This limits most marketing research projects to using proxy information. Since one cannot observe future behavior, one must use a surrogate. Typically, researchers obtain one or more kinds of information believed to be useful in predicting behavior. One may obtain information on past behavior because it is believed that there is sufficient stability in the underlying behavior pattern to give it reasonably high predictive validity. One may ask about intended behavior as a means of prediction. Or one may obtain information about attitudes, level of knowledge, or socioeconomic characteristics of the respondent in the belief that, individually or collectively, they have a high degree of association with future behavior.

Since the type of information required is identified during the problem-formulation stage of the research process, minimizing this error requires as accurate a problem definition as possible.

Measurement Error

Measurement error is generated by the measurement process itself, and represents the difference between the information generated and the information wanted by the researcher. Such error can potentially arise at any stage of the measurement process, from the development of an instrument through the analysis of the findings. To illustrate, Figure 3.2 depicts the stages at which errors in eliciting information may arise when interviewing respondents for a survey.

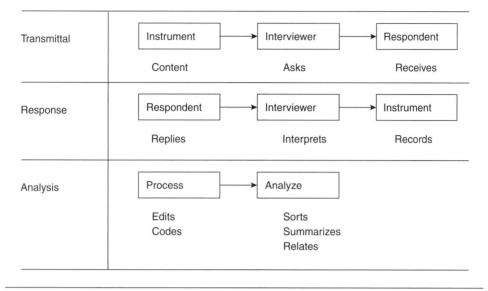

Figure 3.2   Potential Sources of Measurement Error in a Survey

In the transmittal stage, errors may be due to the faulty wording of questions or preparation of nonverbal materials, unintentional interviewer modification of the question's wording, or the way in which a respondent interprets the question. In the response phase, errors may occur because the respondent gives incorrect information, the interviewer interprets it incorrectly, or recording errors occur. One aspect of this regards form; form-related errors concern psychological orientation toward responding to different item formats and include:

1. Leniency: the tendency to rate something too high or too low

2. Central tendency: reluctance to give extreme scores

3. Proximity: giving similar responses to items that occur close to one another (Yu, Albaum, & Swenson, 2003, p. 217)

In the analysis stage, errors of incorrect editing and coding, descriptive summarization, and inference can contribute substantially to measurement error. Measurement error is particularly troublesome for the researcher, since it can arise from many different sources and take on many different forms.

Experimental Error

When an experiment is conducted, the researcher attempts to measure the impact of one or more manipulated independent variables on some dependent variable of interest, while controlling for the influence of all other (i.e., extraneous) variables. Unfortunately, control over all possible extraneous variables is rarely possible. Consequently, what may be measured is not the effect of the independent variables but the effect of the experimental situation itself.

This is the meaning of experimental error, which can arise from many sources. Experimental errors and alternative ways of dealing with them are discussed in Chapter 8.

Another Viewpoint

A useful way of summarizing the types of errors that can influence research results is that they arise from five sources as shown in Table 3.2:

- Researcher
- Sample
- Interviewer
- Instrument
- Respondent

Because each source has a different viewpoint, these differing opinions can introduce errors in to the process. Each of these is discussed, directly or indirectly, at various places in the text.

Table 3.2 A   Classification of Errors

	Source	*Error Type*
I	Researcher	Myopia (wrong question) Inappropriate analysis Misinterpretation Experimenter expectation Communication
II	Sample	Frame (wrong target) Process (wrong method) Response (wrong people)
III	Interviewer	Interviewer bias Interpretation Carelessness
IV	Instrument	
	Scale	Rounding Truncating
	Questionnaire	Positional Confusion Evoked Set Construct—Question Congruence
V	Respondent	Consistency/Inconsistency Ego/Humility Fatigue Lack of Commitment Random

SOURCE: Hulbert and Lehman, 1975, p. 168.

METHODS FOR DEALING WITH POTENTIAL ERRORS

For any research project, recognizing that potential errors exist is one thing, but doing something about them is another matter. There are two basic approaches for handling potential errors:

1. Minimize errors through research design
2. Measure or estimate the error or its impact

Minimize Error

Two different approaches can be taken to minimize total error. The first uses research design to minimize errors that may result from each of the individual error components. Much of the material in Chapters 5 through 13 of this book discusses effective research methods, and as such, involves techniques designed to minimize individual errors. This is consistent with our view that research design innately involves error management. However, this approach is often limited by the budget allotted to a project.

The second approach recognizes that individual error components are not necessarily independent of each other. Thus, attempts to minimize one component may lead to an increase in another. Reducing sampling error by increasing sample size, for example, leads to potentially greater non-sampling error. This means that the research designer must trade off errors when developing a research design that minimizes total error. For a fixed project budget, therefore, it may be prudent for the research designer to choose a smaller sample size (which will increase sampling error) if the cost savings by doing this can develop techniques that will reduce nonresponse and/or improve the measurement process. If the reduction in these non-sampling errors exceeds the increase in sampling error, there will be a reduction in total error.

Estimate or Measure Error

Even though the researcher has designed a project to minimize error, it is almost never completely eliminated. Consequently, the error that exists for every project must be estimated or measured. This is recognized for sampling error when probability samples are used, though non-sampling errors typically are ignored. Although estimating or measuring errors is better than ignoring them, there may be times when ignoring non-sampling error may not be that bad. For example, if non-sampling error is viewed as a multiple of sampling error, ignoring non-sampling errors up to an amount equal to one-half of sampling error reduces a .95 confidence level only to .92 (Tull & Albaum, 1973). However, ignoring a non-sampling error equal in amount to sampling error reduces the .95 level to .83.

Estimating or measuring individual components and total error is not easy, primarily due to the nature of non-sampling errors. There is a body of accepted sampling theory that allows the researcher to estimate sampling error for a probability sample, but nothing comparable exists for non-sampling errors. Consequently, subjective or judgmental estimates must be made.

For individual error components, many diverse procedures can be used to estimate and measure their impact as illustrated in Table 3.3. These are discussed where appropriate in subsequent chapters.

Table 3.3   Selected Methods for Handling Non-Sampling Errors

Type of Error	Design to Avoid	Measure	Estimate
Surrogate information	Strive for realism	No method of direct measurement, as event has not yet occurred	Use track record of studies Use surrogate variables
Measurement			
1. Instrument induced	Pretest, alternative wording, alternative positions, etc.	Experiment by using alternative wording, alternative positioning, etc., in a subsample	Estimate will likely be for no bias but some variable error
2. Interviewing-associated (e.g., bias, recording, cheating)	Select and train interviewer correctly Use same editor for all of interviews by one interviewer Use cheater questions Use computer program to analyze for patterns of responses by interviewer	Re-interview subsample using expert interviewer Analysis of variance Use cheater questions Use computer program to analyze for patterns Use interpenetrating sample	Estimate will be for both bias and variable error
3. Response	Use randomized response technique Ask for verification checks Cross-check questions Use mail-back technique	Compare with known data	Have interviewer evaluate respondent Estimate will be for both bias and variable error
4. Editing	Prepare editing manual Train editors Require daily return of data	Use master editor to edit subsample	Estimate will be for limited bias, some variable error
5. Coding	Pre-code Use coding manual Use computer program to clean data	Use master coder to check subsample	Some bias and variable error
6. Tabulation	Use verification for data entry	Recheck sample of forms	Variable error
7. Analysis	No remedy except competence	Use more competent analyst	
Frame	Use multiple frames	Take subsample of excluded segments	Use compensating weights Use past data
Selection	Make sample element and sample unit the same Use probability sample	Compare with known population	Use compensating weights
Nonresponse	Use callbacks Call at appropriate time Use trained interviewers	Take subsample of nonrespondents	Use Politz-Simmons method Use wave analysis

CHOOSING A RESEARCH DESIGN

The overview of research designs and sources of marketing information just presented should make it apparent that, given a specified problem, many competing designs can provide relevant information. Each design will have an associated expected value of information and incurred cost.

Suppose, for example, that a researcher is assigned to determine the market share of the ten leading brands of cigarettes. There are many possible ways of measuring market share of cigarette brands, including questioning a sample of respondents, observing purchases at a sample of retail outlets, obtaining sales figures from a sample of wholesalers, obtaining sales figures from a sample of retailers and vending machine operators, obtaining tax data, subscribing to a national consumer panel, subscribing to a national panel of retail stores, and, possibly, obtaining data directly from trade association reports or a recent study by some other investigative agency. Though lengthy, this listing is not exhaustive.

The selection of the best design from the alternatives is no different in principle from choosing among the alternatives in making any decision. The associated expected value and cost of information must be determined for each contending design. If the design is such that the project will yield information for solving more than one problem, the expected value should be determined for all applicable problems and summed. The design with the highest, positive, net expected payoff of research should be selected.

SUMMARY

In this chapter we dealt with a subject of central importance to the research project: research design. We described what a research design is, discussed the classes of designs, and examined major sources of marketing information that various designs employ. Finally, we considered the errors that affect research designs.

Treating these topics presented an introduction to, and overview of, the next several chapters. These chapters deal with major sources of marketing information—respondents and experimentation—and the means of obtaining and analyzing information from them.

ASSIGNMENT MATERIAL

1. A consumer durable goods manufacturer makes a public announcement that it will raise the price of its most popular model in 30 days. During this period, sales at the retail level increase 40% above prior forecasted levels.

   a. What kind of evidence is necessary to prove that the announced price change caused the increase in sales?
   b. Is such evidence available?

2. You are a senior analyst in the marketing research department of a major steel producer. You have been requested to make a forecast of domestic automobile production for the forthcoming calendar year and, from this forecast, to make a forecast of the total tonnage of steel that will be used by the automobile manufacturers.

   a. Is this an exploratory, descriptive, or causal study?
   b. What data would be useful for making the forecast of steel tonnage to be used by domestic automobile manufacturers next year?
   c. How would you design the study to obtain these data?

3. Donald Stam is the product manager for Brand M margarine, a nationally distributed brand. Brand M has been declining in absolute level of sales for the past four months. Mr. Stam asks the marketing research department to do a study determining why sales have declined.

   a. Is this an exploratory, descriptive, or causal study?
   b. What data would be useful for determining why sales have declined?
   c. How would you design the study to obtain these data?

4. You are the manager of product planning and marketing research for the personal appliances department of a large and widely diversified corporation. You have under consideration a proposal to produce and market a hearing aid, an appliance line in which your company currently does not have a product. You have assigned one of the analysts to work on this project.

   a. Is this an exploratory, descriptive, or causal study?
   b. What data would be useful for deciding whether or not to develop and introduce a hearing aid?
   c. How would you design a study to obtain these data?

5. Discuss the extent of the surrogate information error present in each of the following research situations:

Information Required	Information Sought
a. Consumer purchases of medium-priced table wines during the next 12 months	Consumer purchase intentions over the next 12 months
b. Purchases of ten-speed bicycles during the next 12 months	Actual purchases during the past 12 months

6. Explain what is meant by the following statement: "The planning and conducting of a marketing research project is essentially an exercise in error management."

7. What is meant by total error in a research project?

8. Is it better to estimate, measure, or minimize error? Explain.

9. An experiment was once conducted in which three matched samples of respondents were asked one of the following three questions:

   1. Do you think anything should be done to make it easier to pay doctor or hospital bills? (Eighty-two percent replied "Yes.")

2. Do you think anything could be done to make it easier to pay doctor or hospital bills? (Seventy-seven percent replied "Yes.")

3. Do you think anything might be done to make it easier to pay doctor or hospital bills? (Sixty-three percent replied "Yes.")

These questions are identical except for the use of the words *should, could,* and *might.* Is this an example of measurement error? Explain.

REFERENCES

Anderson, B. F. (1971). *The psychology experiment: An introduction to the scientific method* (2nd ed.). Belmont, CA: Brooks/Cole.

Arnold, D. T. (1988, August 29). Quantitative or qualitative: That is the research question. *Marketing News, 22,* 46.

Assael, H., & Keon, J. (1982, Spring). Non-sampling vs. sampling errors in survey research. *Journal of Marketing, 46,* 114–123.

Bagozzi, R. P. (1980). *Causal models in marketing.* New York: Wiley.

Cook, T. D., & Campbell, T. D. (1979). *Quasi-experimentation: Design & analysis issues for field settings.* Boston: Houghton Mifflin.

Dupont, T. D. (1976). Exploring group interviews in consumer research: A case example. In B. B. Anderson, Ed., *Advances in Consumer Research.* (Vol. III). Valdosta, GA: Association for Consumer Research.

Feldman, J. (1975). Considerations in the use of causal-correlational technique in applied psychology. *Journal of Applied Psychology, 60,* 663–670.

Fern, E. F. (1982, February). The use of focus groups for idea generation: The effects of group size, acquaintanceship, and moderator on response quantity and quality. *Journal of Marketing Research, 19* (February), 1–13.

Fink, A. (2003). *How to design surveys* (2nd ed.). Thousand Oaks, CA: Sage.

Gomm, R., Foster, P., & Hammersley, M. (2000). *Case study method: Key issues, key texts.* Thousand Oaks, CA: Sage.

Higgins, K. (1984, June 22). Olympics and other sports may be a bonanza—but for whom? *Marketing News, 18,* 6.

Keeter, S., Miller, C., Kohut, A., Groves, R. M., & Presser, S. (2000). Consequences of reducing non-response in a national telephone survey. *Public Opinion Quarterly, 64,* 125–148.

Lilien, G., Brown, R., & Searls, K. (1991, January 7). How errors add up. *Marketing News, 25,* 20–21.

Monroe, K. B., & Petroshius, S. M. (n.d.). Developing causal priorities. Unpublished working paper, College of Business, Virginia Polytechnic Institute and State University.

Murphy, I. P. (1997, January 20). Interactive research. *Marketing News, 31,* 1 ff.

Sackmary, B. D. (1983, January 23). Data analysis and output planning improve value of marketing research. *Marketing News, 17,* 6.

Tomaskovic-Devey, D., Leiter, J., & Thompson, S. (1994). Organizational survey response. *Administrative Science Quarterly, 39,* 439–457.

Tull, D. S., & Albaum, G. S. (1973). *Survey research: A decisional approach.* New York: Intext Educational Publishers.

Yin, R. K. (2003a). *Case study research: Design and methods* (3rd ed.). Thousand Oaks, CA: Sage.

Yin, R. K. (2003b). *Applications of case study research.* Thousand Oaks, CA: Sage.

Yu, J., Albaum, G., & Swenson, M. (2003). Is a central tendency error inherent in the use of semantic differential scales in different cultures? *International Journal of Market Research, 45* (2), 213–228.

Cases for Part I

Case Study I–1

Patterns, Inc.

Patterns, Inc., is a small company whose product line consists of patterns for home sewing. The company has been in operation for two years, and sales are starting to increase as the company's products become better known. Although there have been no profits as yet, it is anticipated that the turning point will soon be reached and that the company will show a profit in its third year.

For two years Patterns, Inc., has been marketing sewing patterns for women's clothing items. All the patterns have been designed by Sue Johnson, who operates the company together with her husband, Colin. There are no other regular employees. All production is handled by a local printer. At certain times the Johnsons hire a part-time employee to help package the patterns into the final product. Distribution is by mail order and through retail outlets that sell fabrics and materials. Prices are competitive with those of other patterns.

Sue Johnson has designed a new set of patterns that she calls "For Kids Only." These patterns have been in development for some time, having started as something for her own family, friends, and neighbors. The availability of patterns for young children's items has been very limited.

Initially, the "For Kids Only" patterns are to include unique, "lovable" creations that are full-size patterns and represent quality for a reasonable price. At the present time, patterns for the following items are being considered: (1) weatherproof backpack, (2) carpenter belt with stuffed tools, (3) soft ball toy that is squeezable, (4) happy counting clock with movable hands, and (5) quilts. There are also a few other sewing patterns for children that Sue is in the process of designing.

All the patterns come with complete instructions and a materials list. The detailed instructions for each item are contained in a three-page insert included with the pattern.

The exhibit shows some information for the carpenter belt.

EXHIBIT I–1.1   Instructions Included With
Carpenter's Belt Pattern

Both useful and easy on the house, this carpenter's belt with stuffed toy tools is just the thing for that little carpenter in your life. Your little one can bang to his heart's content, and can't hurt himself or anyone or anything else. The belt and tools are machine washable and dryable, cute as can be, and sure to be your little one's favorite toy. This is also a good project to use up your fabric scraps.

Materials Needed: Yardage Measured to 45″ Width

Gray: 1/5 yard (or use your scraps)

Plaid: 1/2 yard reversible quilt fabric

Small Fry Nail Belt...

A carpenter belt with stuffed tools for fun and play. Tools are soft and cannot hurt little ones no matter how much they bang. Later on the belt can be used for real tools for that special carpenter.

Stock # 009

OR

1/2 yard plaid

1/2 yard blue } IF YOU QUILT YOURSELF

1/2 yard batting

Red: 1/3 yard or piece 6" × 8"

Yellow: 1/2 yard or piece 6" × 6"

White: piece 2" × 2"

1 piece iron-on denim mending fabric

Notions:

1 small spool yellow thread

1 large spool red thread

1 small spool gray thread

1 small spool black thread

1/2 yard iron-on interfacing

1/3 yard black velvet ribbon 1/4"

1 buckle with 2½″ opening

4 large white snaps

10 yards red double-fold ¼″ bias tape

1/3 package polyester stuffing

You can use the above colors or create your own combinations, use your scraps, etc. . . . In any case you will have fun, and make a beautiful toy at the same time.

Happy Creating,

Sue

QUESTIONS FOR DISCUSSION

1. Does a small company such as Patterns, Inc., have a need for marketing research?

2. If it does have a need, explain how the company can make use of marketing research. If not, explain why marketing research may be of no value to Patterns, Inc.

❖

REFERENCE

Hulburt, J., & Lehman, D. R. (1975). Reducing error in question and scale design: A conceptual framework. *Decision Sciences, 6.*

CASE STUDY I-2

Cougar Business Forms, Inc. (A)

Cougar Business Forms, Inc.,[1] is a large manufacturer of products for business. Its headquarters is located in a large city in the eastern part of the United States.

The company contacted a local marketing research consultant, Pam Menak, for assistance in developing a way to monitor awareness of and preference for Cougar and its major product, business forms. The desire was to have an annual tracking or monitoring of awareness and preference to aid in the measurement of progress in the movement of market awareness and preference for Cougar and its major competitors. These indicators reflect some of the results for the advertising programs, whose goal is to create an awareness of the products that Cougar offers in the market segment that it serves.

After a period of time spent thinking about Cougar's underlying objectives for the study, Ms. Menak proposed to Cougar management that survey research techniques using a self-report questionnaire administered by mail be used to collect the necessary data. She suggested two attempts at data collection, with each mailing including a cover letter, a copy of the questionnaire, and a postage-paid return envelope. Since there was no identification on the questionnaire, the second mailing (i.e., the follow-up) would be sent to each member of the original sample. The follow-up mailing was to be two weeks after the original mailing. The questionnaires were to be returned to an independent company, Cascade Consulting Group, located in the western United States, for processing and data analysis. This was to be done to ensure complete anonymity.

Ms. Menak worked with Cougar's Director of Corporate Communication in developing the questionnaire. The result of this collaborative work is the one-page questionnaire shown in Exhibit I–2.1. The questionnaire was designed to elicit the following information: (1) awareness and familiarity with business form manufacturers; (2) current suppliers of business forms; (3) respondents' first choice when selecting a business forms manufacturer; (4) sources of respondents' information about business forms manufacturers (publications read); (5) number of employees of the company; and (6) the job title of the respondent and their role in the decision process. This questionnaire was pre-tested with a select number of purchasing agents to make sure that the questions were clear and unambiguous and that the length was short enough to induce their responses.

It was determined that information must be obtained from the six market segments that Cougar served at the time: hospitals, financial services, manufacturers, retail, government, and transportation. In addition, subcategories within these broad categories were selected from the list of Standard Industrial Classifications. Since each category involved many hundreds of business firms, it was decided that proportionately more sample survey responses should come from those segments where the number of sampling units were large. The final original sample size for each segment was determined:

Hospitals	1,200
Financial services	1,200
Manufacturing	1,200
Retail	800
Government	800
Transportation	800

Each of the 6,000 sample members was selected from a directory purchased from a commercial mailing list company. The prescribed sample size for each segment was based on preset size or sales volume criteria. For example, financial service firms were required to have assets of at least $5 million, city governments had to be for cities with population greater than 100,000, and retail companies (headquarters unit only) were to have at least $5 million in sales.

EXHIBIT I–2.1   Questionnaire to Be Used in Annual Cougar Study

BUSINESS FORMS SURVEY

I. Please check (X) appropriate box(es) to indicate your response to the questions.

I. What role do you play in the purchase of business forms?

Specify _____   Purchase _____

Recommend _____   None _____

2. There are a number of business forms manufacturers. How familiar are you with each of the business forms manufacturers listed below? Check (X) appropriate box.

	Don't Know	Aware of Name Only	Somewhat Familiar	Very Familiar
a. Ajax	____	____	____	____
b. Bits	____	____	____	____
c. Cougar	____	____	____	____
d. Dot	____	____	____	____
e. Extor	____	____	____	____
f. ____	____	____	____	____
[Other]				

3.

A. Please indicate your current supplier(s) of business forms.

_____

_____

_____

_____

_____

_____

B. Check (X) the one manufacturer that you would consider first when selecting a business forms manufacturer.

a. Ajax _____

b. Bits _____

c. Cougar _____

d. Dot _____

e. Extor _____

f. _____ _____

(Other)

4. List three (3) publications that you read regularly.

1. _____

2. _____

3. _____

II. Background information.

5. How many employees are there in your company or organization?

Over 500   _____   101 to 250   _____

251 to 500   _____   Under 100   _____

6. Your present job title: _____

Thank you very much for completing the questionnaire.

Since the questionnaire did not ask for "industry," and there was no coding used, there needed to be some way to identify market segment. Ms. Menak had decided that this could best be handled by color-coding the questionnaires. Accordingly six different colors were used—green, white, blue, canary, buff, and goldenrod. This had no significant effect upon the cost of conducting the survey.

QUESTIONS FOR DISCUSSION

1. Evaluate the monitoring system that Pam Menak has proposed for Cougar Business Forms.

2. Will the questionnaire provide the data necessary? Why or why not?

3. What changes would you suggest Cougar make in its awareness/preference monitoring?

ENDNOTE

1. Disguised name.

Syd Company (A)

The market for women's hair shampoos has become highly specialized and segmented. In recent years a large number of special-purpose shampoos have appeared on the market, each promising to provide various hair-care benefits to the potential user. The Syd Company[1] is a diversified manufacturer of consumer packaged goods. At this time the firm has no women's shampoo in its product line.

The company's marketing research personnel met recently with a small research firm, FC Associates, and discussed the possibility of a study of young female adults living in a large city in the eastern part of the United States.

The Syd Company had established—through a series of recently completed interviews with small groups of female consumers—that increasing "body" (connoting hair thickness or fullness) was frequently mentioned as a desired characteristic in a hair shampoo. Armed with this still rather sketchy information concerning the desirability of "body" from a shampoo, the firm's laboratory personnel had set to work on developing some prototypical compounds that appeared potentially capable of delivering this result to a greater extent than brands currently on the market.

During the initial conversations between Syd and FC Associates, the following managerial problems came to light:

1. Assuming that laboratory personnel could produce a women's shampoo with superior "body" characteristics, is the market for this product large enough to justify its commercialization?

2. What benefits in addition to improving hair's "body" should be incorporated into the new shampoo?

3. What are the characteristics—product usage, hair type, and demographics—of people who are particularly attracted to a "body"-enhancing shampoo? (Knowledge of these characteristics would be desirable in defining the target segment for the new product.)

4. How should the concept of "body" be communicated; what does the *consumer* mean by "body" in regards to shampoo? (Knowledge of the connotations of "body" would be valuable in the design of promotional messages and point-of-purchase materials.)

Since Syd had no entry in the shampoo market, the company had relatively little to go on in the way of secondary sources of information. While various market statistics could be obtained for existing brands, the firm was primarily interested in characteristics appropriate for a relatively new concept in the marketplace—a shampoo that emphasized "body."

PROBLEM STRUCTURING

Although formal statistical decision analysis was not applied in this case, it became apparent that the firm faced three primary courses of action:

1. Continue technical development of a new shampoo that delivers the consumer benefit: "body."

2. Terminate technical development related to this characteristic and redirect efforts toward some other shampoo benefit.

3. Discontinue all effort in women's shampoo products.

Continuation of technical development on the "body" front, in turn, is based on two considerations:

1. The belief that the new product can be developed successfully from a technical standpoint.

2. The assumption that the new product can be sold in sufficient quantities to justify future development outlays, start-up expense, and ongoing production and marketing costs, earning an appropriate return on invested funds.

Informal analysis indicated a high probability of technical success during the ensuing 12 months with relatively modest additional outlays in technical resources. The major problem appeared to be one of market potential—more specifically, whether a target segment of sufficient size was available to warrant continued technical development and eventual commercialization.

COST AND VALUE OF MARKETING RESEARCH

Current uncertainties about potential demand for the new product suggested the desirability of conducting marketing research beyond the preliminary consumer group interviews that had recently been conducted by the firm. Crude estimates of the cost versus value of additional information (including such aspects as the costs of continuing technical development and start-up, the probability of technical and marketing success, and the likelihood that survey results would correctly identify the appropriate state of nature) clearly indicated the advisability of further marketing research.

The problem was not whether more marketing research could be justified—the quickest and crudest estimates demonstrated its potential value—but rather, what *kind* of research would be most likely to answer management's questions. Indeed, the main purpose of the marketing personnel's visit to FC Associates was to discuss an exploratory study that could be helpful in designing the main study that would eventually be conducted on a national, probability-based sample. What should the main study cover? How could management's questions be translated into a research design? What additional research questions should be raised?

Agreement was reached that FC would do the exploratory study.

RESEARCH DESIGN

Given the exploratory character of the research, questions of adequate sample size and representativeness were not of primary importance. What was germane to the pilot research was the need for FC to translate management's questions into operational terms and, in the process, to develop additional questions relevant to the design of the main study.

The principal focus of the exploratory research was to be on shampoo benefits. In the course of conducting preliminary consumer group interviews the client's marketing research personnel assembled a list of approximately 30 benefits that either had been advertised or were thought by at least some consumers to be relevant in the choice of a hair shampoo. Not surprisingly, many of the benefit descriptions were redundant; hence, the first step was to trim down the list to a smaller set. Sixteen benefits consumers desired from shampoo emerged from the culling process:

- Hair stays clean a long time
- Hair stays free of dandruff or flaking
- Hair that looks and feels natural
- Hair with body
- Manageable hair that goes where you want it
- Hair with sheen or luster
- Hair with no split ends
- Hair with enough protein
- Hair that doesn't get oily fast
- Hair that's not too dry
- Hair with fullness
- Hair that's not frizzy
- Hair that holds a set

- Hair with texture
- Hair that's easy to comb when it dries
- Hair that looks free and casual

The preliminary research seemed to indicate that the first 10 benefits were probably the most important of the 16. Indeed, the preliminary research suggested that the first six benefits probably constituted the "core set"—that is, those benefits of primary importance to consumer choice.

A second matter of importance concerned the nature of respondents to be interviewed. The study's sponsor suggested a purposive sample of young female adults aged 18 through 30, with an approximate 60:40 split between married and single. Only consumers who shampooed their hair at least twice a month, on the average, were to be interviewed. In brief, the sample was to be aimed at a specific age group of relatively active users of shampoo.

KEY RESEARCH QUESTIONS

Given the emphasis placed on product benefit preferences, particularly the benefit of "body," a number of ancillary research questions were developed from the primary ones indicated by the client:

1. How do consumers of hair shampoos perceive various benefits as commonly (or rarely) available in shampoos currently on the market?

2. Given freedom to make up their own ideal shampoo, what combination of benefits do consumers want? Specifically, how often is "body" included in consumers' ideal benefit bundles?

3. Assuming that a consumer desired and could get a shampoo that delivered "body," what other benefits are also desired in the same brand?

4. What is conjured up by the phrase "body" in regards to shampoo, and what are its various connotations—that is, what words are elicited on a free-association basis?

5. How do preferences for "body" in shampoo benefits relate to
   a. Frequency of hair shampooing (i.e., heavy versus light users of shampoos)?
   b. Perceptions of its availability in current shampoos?
   c. Preference for other benefits in addition to "body"?
   d. Hair physiology and wearing style?
   e. Demographics (e.g., age, marital status, education, etc.)?

These questions set the stage for FC Associates to develop the questionnaire.

ADMINISTRATION

The questionnaire was first pretested. Following this, the questionnaire was administered on a personal, in-the-home basis by interviewers. Respondents were drawn from the city on a purposive basis. Interview time averaged about half an hour; all data were collected over the span of one week.

QUESTIONS FOR DISCUSSION

1. Assume that you are the research and development manager for the Syd Company. How would you criticize the study in terms of its usefulness to you?

2. As the research and development manager for the Syd Company, if you had the opportunity to design the pilot project from *your* viewpoint, what questions would you want to include in the questionnaire?

ENDNOTE

1. Disguised name.

CASE STUDY I–4

Fred Meyer Corporation (A)

Fred Meyer, Inc., is a unique regional retailer noted for its unparalleled selection, customer-pleasing service, low prices, and one-stop shopping. Founded in 1923, the company operates stores in six western states: Oregon, Washington, Utah, Idaho, Alaska, and Montana. Stores range in size up to 200,000 square feet and include up to 11 major departments: food, general merchandise, soft goods, home improvement, pharmacy, photo and consumer electronics, garden, shoes, fine jewelry, nutrition, and restaurants or snack bars. Dozens of merchandise sections within these departments together offer customers one-stop shopping convenience for more than 220,000 food and nonfood products. The company operates a dairy, bakery, kitchen, and photo plant in Portland to provide products and services to a number of its stores.

In effect, the company operates a chain of hypermarkets (i.e., supermarkets). The company acquired Smith's, a Rocky Mountain area food chain, and itself was acquired by Kroger, though all companies are operated independently.

Fred Meyer has decided to do a major consumer survey in the Portland, Oregon and Seattle, Washington market areas. These areas are two of its largest market areas. The company has contracted with Cascade Consulting Group, a marketing research and consulting firm in Portland, Oregon, to conduct this consumer study. Cascade has assigned Ms. Jule Yo to be project director. Ms. Yo has several years of experience in the marketing research business, after receiving her MBA from a leading university in the United States.

COMPANY ORGANIZATION

Fred Meyer has a strong vertical organizational structure. The 11 basic departments are each organized into divisions corresponding to departments found at the store level. Each division is divided into two parallel vertical structures, operations and merchandising, both geared to focus primarily on the needs and activities of individual departments and sections within the stores. The most striking characteristic of this system is that Fred Meyer does not have store managers. Rather, the highest authorities at each store are the department managers. These department managers command the company's front lines. The department managers report to district managers who are responsible for the operational aspects of their division's departments at the stores in their respective districts. The district managers, in turn, report to senior operations managers at the corporate office.

On the merchandising side, one or more buyers are assigned to each merchandise classification within each department. They purchase the products to be sold, and develop marketing plans, displays, and advertising for the products and departments they represent. More than 100 buyers and assistant buyers are located at Fred Meyer's main office in Portland. The buyers report to departmental merchandisers, who report to divisional vice presidents where merchandising and operations are brought together to set strategies, tactics, policies, and procedures for the divisions.

Fred Meyer's vertical structure is extraordinarily effective in fostering the company's

Author's Note: This case was prepared with the assistance of Dr. William Swinyard, the Fred G. Meyer Professor of Retailing at Brigham Young University. The introductory materials are based largely on Fred Meyer, Inc., annual reports. The research study was developed with Ben Adams, Wess Chambers, Mike Denison, Arjun Sen, and Mike Zahajko, graduate students at Brigham Young University.

strategy of seeking competitiveness through specialization. It enables each department and each product division to be extremely responsive to local competition and to bring the entire company's marketing and other support capabilities to bear rapidly at various store, regional, or company-wide levels.

THE FRED MEYER PHILOSOPHY

Fred Meyer's basic philosophy is to "think like a customer"—to figure out what customers want and give it to them first at the best possible price. Hailed by the *Wall Street Journal* as one of the retailing industry's true pioneers with "a reputation as an innovative genius" he was a leader in the development of one-stop shopping, self-service, and product diversification. Mr. Meyer led and shaped the company right up to his death at the age of 92. For Fred Meyer, Inc., the development of a statement of philosophy was a broad-based effort involving many levels of management. Every word was carefully considered in order to crystallize Mr. Meyer's key principles into a document that would be practical and not disappear into a corporate policy book as a useless cliché.

Time has proven the effort a success. A corporate philosophy emerged that gained the acceptance of those who had worked the longest and closest with Mr. Meyer. Fred Meyer's corporate philosophy is a modern mission statement that helps keep its founder's spirit of innovation and customer service a guiding force for the company today:

At Fred Meyer we are governed by the beliefs that:
Customers are essential, for without them we would have no business. Customers shop most where they believe their wants and needs will be satisfied best.
Satisfactory profits are essential, for without profits our business can neither grow nor satisfy the wants and needs of our customers,
employees, suppliers, shareholders, and the community.
Skilled, capable, dedicated employees are essential, for the overall success of our business is determined by the combined ideas, work, and effort of all Fred Meyer employees.

Based on these beliefs, we are committed to:
Serving customers so well that after shopping with us they are satisfied and want to shop with us again.
Operating our business efficiently and effectively, so we can earn a satisfactory profit today and in the future.
Providing an environment that encourages employees to develop their abilities, use their full potential, and share ideas that further the success of the business, so they gain a sense of pride in their accomplishments and confidence n their capabilities.

THE STUDY

The purpose of this study was to provide Fred Meyer with information about its customer segments (i.e., profiling its customers), how these segments shop, and how Fred Meyer rates in comparison to other retail stores. In order to fulfill this general purpose, five objectives were formulated to serve as a detailed guide to the research.

1. *Determine Fred Meyer's overall position in the Portland, Oregon and Seattle, Washington markets.* This position is measured by such concepts as awareness, use, share, and competitive evaluation.

2. *Examine how and why customers shop the different Fred Meyer departments.* What are the major shopping factors customers cite for each Fred Meyer department? What is the purchase share of each department in the overall Fred Meyer business? What is the overall usage level of shoppers by department? What do people like and dislike in each department?

3. *Identify Fred Meyer's competitive position against other retail stores on a department-by-department basis.* What is Fred Meyer's market share for each department category? What is the market share for the next closest competitor or the leading competitor for each department category?

4. *Identify and describe the major customer segments currently shopping Fred Meyer stores.* What is the demographic profile of each segment? What are the lifestyle characteristics of each shopping segment? How does each segment rate each Fred Meyer department? What portion of each department's business volume does each segment account for? How does each segment rate the overall customer service at Fred Meyer?

5. *Evaluate the cross-shopping behavior of each Fred Meyer customer segment.* What is each segment's usage level within each department? What are the reasons non-shoppers of each department within each particular customer segment don't shop that Fred Meyer department? What percentage of each segment's shopping in more than one department is planned?

QUESTIONS FOR DISCUSSION

1. Evaluate the plan for research in the Portland and Seattle markets.

2. What changes would you make if you were doing the study? Explain.

CASE STUDY I–5

PCCP Research

Ken is in his second month of employment as a marketing research analyst with PCCP Research. The firm is a large, well-known, highly respected, very successful supplier of marketing research. Its clients include major companies in many different industries throughout the world.

Routine procedure is for Ms. Rogers and Mr. George, co-owners of PCCP Research, to secure business in the form of research projects. Projects are then assigned to one of the 16 research analysts by Susan, the project coordinator, depending on the workloads of the different analysts. Given the volume of projects and the similarity of most projects, different analysts usually work on different parts of a project. For example, different analysts are used to plan the sample, construct the questionnaire, and interpret the data. Data collection and computer processing of data are conducted by separate companies contracted with the PCCP Research Company. Each project ends with an analyst preparing a written report with marketing strategy recommendations based on his or her interpretation of the data. This report is given to Susan, who gives it to Ms. Rogers and Mr. George, who then deliver the written report, along with a verbal presentation, to the client.

Ken's responsibilities are to interpret the data and write a report with marketing strategy recommendations. He has completed about 20 such projects, for which the co-owners have praised his work. On Wednesday afternoon he completed a project. Following regular procedures, he gave the completed report to Susan to give to Ms. Rogers and Mr. George. Thursday morning when Ken arrived at work, he found the original computer data printouts by his office door with many of the numbers in the tables changed with red ink. There was also a note to see Susan.

Susan explained that Mr. George thought the findings should have been different and that the client would probably not agree with the actual findings and related recommendations. He has therefore taken "research licensee" and changed a few numbers in the computer data printouts. Now he wants Ken to rewrite his report accordingly. Susan explained that since clients are provided with a copy of these summary printout sheets, she has called the outside computer firm to send new printouts with the revised numbers.

QUESTIONS FOR DISCUSSION

1. Discuss any ethical issues that arise in this situation. If no such issues exist, explain why.

2. What action(s) should Ken take? Why should he take such action(s)?

CASE STUDY 1-6

Badger Research Associates

Elspeth, associate research specialist for Badger Research Associates, a marketing research firm in a large midwestern city, moderated a very successful focus group for a regional personal injury law firm. This was the first time the law firm had used any type of marketing research.

The purpose of the study was to aid the law firm's partner in charge of marketing in developing a new series of TV commercials. Franklin, the project coordinator and Elspeth's immediate supervisor, along with three senior partners of the law firm, had observed the focus group from a viewing room. Because everyone was so pleased with her performance, Elspeth felt confident that the law firm would hire her company for additional marketing research and that she would be asked to moderate more groups in the future.

During the focus group session, Peggy, one of the participants, mentioned that her husband had used the services of the client firm to handle an insurance claim for a work-related injury. Peggy said that she and her husband were dissatisfied with the handling of the case. The next day, Franklin told Elspeth to give the client Peggy's last name so that the law firm could investigate Peggy's complaint. If Peggy's complaint was justified, the firm would take steps to prevent similar occurrences.

Focus group participants had been told that the study was being conducted for a personal injury law firm, but the name of the company had not been revealed. Participants also knew that the proceedings were to be videotaped and that representatives of the law firm would observe through one-way glass in the wall of the focus group room. Although Elspeth's company had the full name, address, and telephone number of each participant, these were not made available to the client. Only first names were used during the focus group.

As Elspeth was looking up Peggy's last name, she began to think that giving it to the client would be a violation of participant confidentiality. She trusted that the law firm's intentions were sincere and knew that no one had ever told the participants that they would not be identified to the client. Still, it seemed wrong to her. However, marketing research usage was down among traditional research users because of poor economic conditions in the area and her firm was doing everything possible to obtain assignments from nontraditional organizations such as law firms. What would Franklin think if she said it was improper to identify Peggy?

QUESTIONS FOR DISCUSSION

1. Is Elspeth justified in giving the client the information about Peggy? Why or why not?

2. What are the alternatives open to Elspeth and what should she do?

Part II

TECHNIQUES FOR OBTAINING DATA

Chapter 4

SECONDARY DATA AND SOURCES

Secondary data (or secondary information) is information that has been collected by persons or agencies for purposes other than the solution of the marketing research problem at hand. These data may have been collected by the researcher or someone else in the researcher's firm (an internal source) or they may have been collected by some person outside the firm (an external source). The key point is that the data were collected for some other project, or reason, than the current one.

In addition to primary and secondary data, a third category—commercial data—exists, as shown in Table 4.1. Commercial data sold in the form of syndicated services are collected by commercial marketing research firms or industry associations and, as such, have characteristics of both primary and secondary data.

Later in this chapter we discuss syndicated services, which offer marketing information to companies for a fee. Since these data relate to ongoing concerns of a marketer they can be viewed as primary data. However, the commercial agency did not design its service solely to provide information for one company's specific project. Thus, there are elements of secondary data. It should be clear that distinctions between primary and secondary commercial data may be minimal.

IN THIS CHAPTER

In this chapter, we discuss the following:

- Reasons for obtaining secondary information
- Types of secondary information
- Sources of external secondary data
- Syndicated services that provide commercial data

Data, in all their forms, are the heart of marketing research. Secondary research can help provide a clearer picture of a problem so that researchers and marketing managers can make the necessary critical decisions.

Table 4.1   Types of Marketing Research Data

	Purpose of Collection	
Source	*Current project*	*Other project*
Researcher	Primary	Secondary
Other individual	Commercial (Primary)	Secondary

SOURCE: From *Marketing Research* by R.A. Peterson. Copyright © 1988. Reprinted with permission.

REASONS FOR OBTAINING SECONDARY INFORMATION

As a general rule, no research project should be conducted without a search of secondary information sources. This search should be conducted early in the problem investigation and prior to any organized collection of information from primary sources. There are several reasons for this.

Secondary Information May Solve the Problem

If adequate data are available from secondary sources, primary data collection will not be required. For example, Campbell Soup Co. based a long-running advertising campaign on the theme "soup is good food." This theme emerged from federal government data pertaining to eating habits, nutritional health, and related topics collected over a period of 15 years.

Secondary Information Search Costs Substantially Less

A comprehensive search of secondary sources can almost always be made in a fraction of the time and at a fraction of the cost required for the collection of primary information. This is particularly true today because of rapidly changing technology and electronic access to databases via the Internet. This direct, high-speed access to online databases can help companies become more efficient in two basic ways (Elkind & Kassel, 1995, p. 2):

1. By avoiding duplicating primary/original research

2. By helping target primary research expenditures to key information areas that cannot be found elsewhere

Although many marketing problems do not warrant the expenditures involved for primary information collection, it is a rare situation in which obtaining secondary data is not worth the time and cost invested.

Secondary Information Has Important Supplementary Uses

Even when the secondary information obtained is not adequate for solving the problem, it often has valuable supplemental uses. These include the following:

1. *Defining the problem and formulating hypotheses about its solution.* The assembling and analyzing of available secondary data will almost always provide a better understanding of the problem and its context and will frequently suggest solutions not considered previously. Thus, secondary data can represent a major source of information in exploratory research.

2. *Planning the collection of primary data.* An examination of the methods and techniques employed by other investigators in similar studies may be useful in planning the present one. It may also be of value in the establishment of classifications that are compatible with past studies so that trends may be more readily analyzed.

3. *Defining the population and selecting the sample.* Past information and samples may help establish classifications for current primary information collection.

The researcher must be careful when using secondary data, particularly as the only source of data. To be useful, secondary data must be available, relevant to the information needs (which includes being timely), accurate, and sufficient to meet data requirements for the problem at hand. Potential sources of bias have been identified to include selective recording (or deposit), deliberate original distortion, and selective survival (Sechrest & Phillips, 1979, pp. 5–6; Webb, 1966, Chaps. 3–4). Although such types of errors may not exist for a given piece of secondary data, the researcher nevertheless should always be vigilant in detecting or assessing any one or more that may exist. Little is known about the extent to which each error exists for a given type of record. Consequently, it is important that the researcher know something about how the secondary data being considered for use were collected. Despite this warning, if the right techniques are used, creative secondary research can provide at least a partial answer to almost any information question, as illustrated in Exhibit 4.1.

To illustrate selective recording (deposit), consider the company wanting to do segmentation analysis on foreign markets with a particular emphasis on examining demographics (Albaum, Duerr, & Strandskov, 2005, Chap. 5). One major secondary source that is useful is the official government census of the population. However, data are not available from all markets in equal quantity, aggregation, and detail, and the reliability of data is not the same. What one gets from a census depends on what was on the census form in the first place—typically a mixture of traditional questions and new items of interest to public policy makers and civil servants at the time. These same forces also determine what is released in printed and electronic form (perhaps a form of selective survival). Some countries publish information about noncitizens, and others collect data on religion—both of these topics are ignored in U.S. Censuses. Income is one of the major dimensions of U.S. segmentation research, but many highly developed nations ignore the income question in their censuses.

One cannot always expect to find the same range of data topics from one country to the next (or one market to the next). Moreover, many countries do not use the same categories when showing relevant distributions of demographic variables, such as age. In short, comparability and equivalence issues arise, and these can hinder a company's effectiveness in crossnational research of its foreign markets and potential markets.

EXHIBIT 4.1   Creative Approach to Using Secondary Sources

Often, a researcher must be creative when conducting secondary-source–based research. This applies to issues that are drawn from strategic matters as well as those of a more tactical nature. Some guidelines for creative secondary research are provided by Stephen J. Bass, at the time director of Strategic Intelligence Services, Cedar Hills Associates, Inc. in Washington, Ohio ("Right techniques needed to conduct secondary research," 1981). The guidelines are the following:

1. When examining an unfamiliar topic, start by seeing what directories, special reports, and other information are available.

2. Do not overlook basic and obvious reference materials such as telephone and city directories, company annual reports, and so forth.

3. Although secondary research departments cannot identify and keep track of all information sources, a network of external specialists can help locate strategic (and tactical) information. Some examples include trade associations, government agencies, and the trade press.

4. Government-provided data often are not available in published form until out of date, and may be available only as "raw" data. Personal contacts within government agencies often can provide timely unpublished data. Sometimes preliminary data are better than none. To an extent this can be overcome by purchasing census data from a private source. For example, the software developer GeoLytics sells data products based on the U.S. Census that report demographics, psychographics, economic, and other data for the United States (www.GeoLytics.com). The company compresses large amounts of government data, and packages it with easy-to-use software.

5. An "Old-Friends Network" is a valuable, low-cost information source that is worth maintaining.

6. Where uncertain about where to find an information source, ask the following question, "Who wants or has a need for the information as much or more than me or my client?"

7. When dealing with external information sources, gain their cooperation by being upbeat and optimistic, building their ego, and offering to exchange information or other incentives.

In the end, the ultimate positive payoff when doing secondary research in a new area occurs when the person has a creative, inquisitive, research-oriented mind.

TYPES OF SECONDARY INFORMATION

Secondary information falls into two categories, the distinguishing feature being whether it is available within the company (internal) or must be obtained from outside sources (external).

Internal Secondary Information

All companies collect information in the everyday course of conducting business. Orders are received and filled, costs are recorded, warranty cards are returned, salespeople's reports are submitted, engineering reports are made—these are but a few of the many sources of company information, collected for other purposes, that are often useful to the researcher (Andreasen, 1988, pp. 77–89).

A basic source of information, one that is all too often overlooked, is the sales invoice. By simple analyses of this information, details about sales volume and trends can be determined, including:

1. Model and size of product by territory, type of account, and industry

2. Average size of sale by territory, type of account, industry, and sales volume

3. Proportion of sales volume by model, size of product, territory, type of account, size of account, and industry

For example, a retailer selling baby cribs could get some idea of the type of people purchasing baby cribs by using its sales invoices to determine where in the community its customers live. Once this information is known, certain general demographic and socioeconomic characteristics can be estimated by examining government census data (external information) broken down into census tracts, blocks, and so on.

Not all internal secondary information is of this accounting type. Company files are often loaded with special reports, previous marketing research studies, special audits, and other reports purchased from outside suppliers for past problems. Any one of these types of reports may be relevant to current problems. The key, of course, is knowing where they are and how to access them. In order to do this efficiently, the firm must have an effective marketing information system.

For instance, Spectra Physics Retail Systems division (producing laser grocery store scanners) regularly performs customer satisfaction studies. Whereas these studies are primary research to the Retail Systems organization, they are internal secondary information to other divisions in Spectra Physics that may want to look at them. Also, they can be secondary data to Retail Systems should they be used at a much later date for aiding in decision-making or for purposes other than those originally intended when the studies were done.

External Secondary Information

External secondary information is available in staggering assortments and volumes. It also is applicable to all of the major types of marketing research projects and is mainly concerned with the noncontrollable aspects of the problem:

- Total market size
- Market characteristics
- Competitor products, prices, promotional efforts, and distribution methods

The use of external secondary data is illustrated by a company seeking to enter the lodging market or, perhaps, expand or make changes in an existing situation. One source of secondary data would be a trade association, such as the American Hotel & Motel Association. The Association has available numerous publications, such as the following:

- *Economic Impact of Hotels and Motels.* Helps determine the economic impact of lodging on a local community.
- *Lodging Survey: Lodging Services, Facilities and Trends.* An annual survey of the industry.
- *Analysis of Hotel/Motel Usage By and Needs of Travelers with Disabilities.* A study on a specific segment of the travel market.

Exhibit 4.2 (see p. 132) shows an entry from the Association's Web page that gives a profile of the lodging industry for the year 2002 (www.ahla.com). Data such as these are potentially useful to any company directly involved with the lodging industry as a member, supplier, and so forth. In contrast, there may be studies available from individual companies in the industry that study broader questions.

Another example would be a consumer goods company that is considering whether it should establish a direct selling operation. Direct selling is defined as personal contact between a salesperson and a consumer away from a fixed business location such as a retail store. The Direct Selling Association (DSA) provides secondary information in the form of a regular survey of the industry. Some types of information on industry statistics and salesforce demographics are available on a regular basis. Some of the types of industry statistics are the following (Direct Selling Association, 2003):

- Estimated 2002 U.S. sales
- Estimated 2002 U.S. salespeople
- Percent of sales by major product groups
- Location of sales
- Percent of sales by census region
- Sales strategy
- Compensation structure by percent of firms
- Compensation structure by percent of sales dollars
- Compensation structure by percent of salespeople

The following are some of the salesforce demographics available:

- Gender
- Age
- Education
- Independent contractor/employee status
- Hours per week dedicated to direct selling
- Average time spent on direct selling tasks
- Main reasons for becoming a direct sales representative
- Percent of salespeople by distributorship type

Age, education, average time spent on direct selling tasks, and main reason for becoming a direct sales representative data are from DSA's 2002 National Salesforce Survey.

The data in Table 4.2 are selected aggregate data about how direct selling companies operate. In addition to the industry's trade association, a company could benefit by looking at the academic literature. For example, a study of consumers in the United States, the Czech Republic, and Slovakia (Wotruba & Pribova, 1995) sought to determine the following:

- The extent to which consumers buy from direct sales companies
- The characteristics of purchasers
- Perceptions of the advantages and disadvantages of buying from a direct sales company

More recently, a study in Australia and the United States developed a measure of trust in salesperson/customer relationships that can be used by a company to assess the extent to which consumers trust the direct selling salesperson they deal with (Young & Albaum, 2003).

SOURCES OF EXTERNAL SECONDARY DATA

The major original sources of external secondary information are:

1. Government (supranational, federal, state, and local)

2. Trade associations and trade press

3. Periodicals and professional journals

4. Institutions (e.g., universities)

5. Commercial services

The federal government is by far the largest single source of this type of data. Both governmental and trade sources are so important that the experienced and competent researcher will be thoroughly familiar with them in his or her field of specialization. Periodicals and the publications of research projects conducted by universities and research institutes frequently provide valuable information. Commercial services of many types are available that are highly useful for specific research problems.

Market performance studies on consumer products, for example, will normally require such demographic information as the number of consumers (or consuming units) by age group, income class, gender, and geographic area. Such data are usually available on a reasonably recent basis from censuses conducted by federal, state, local, and, when needed, supranational governments.

Often, a good first source to explore is the *Statistical Abstract of the United States,* published annually by the Bureau of the Census. This reference abstracts data from original reports and gives some useful material on social, political, and economic matters. The source is a good reference to the more detailed data in the original sources. *The State and Metropolitan Area Data Book* is a publication of the Bureau of the Census that provides detailed comparative data on states, metropolitan areas and their component counties, and

Table 4.2   Selected Characteristics of the Direct Selling Industry in the United States, 2002

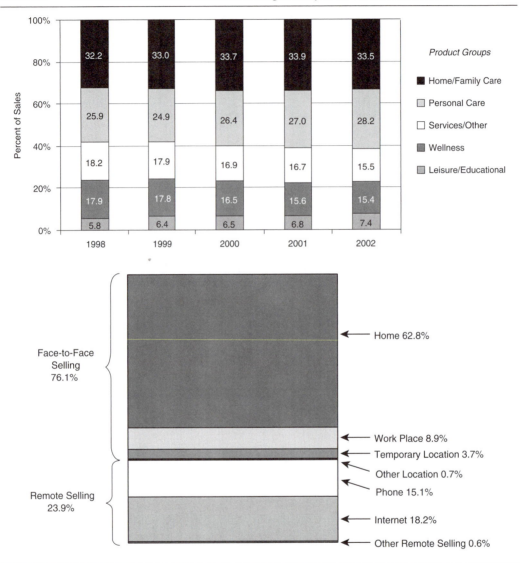

Locus of Sales	Percent of Sales Dollars
In the home	62.8
In the workplace	8.9
Over the phone	15.1
Over the Internet	8.2
Other remote selling	0.6
At a temporary location (fair, exhibition, shopping mall, etc.)	3.7
Other locations	1.3

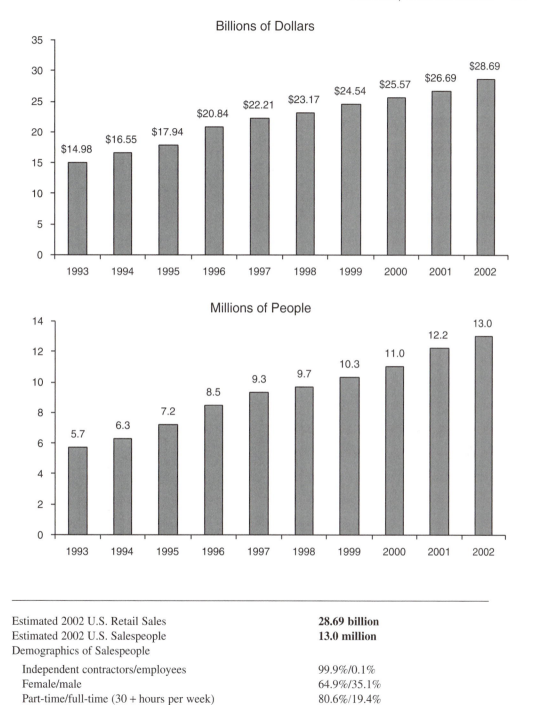

Billions of Dollars

Year	Value
1993	$14.98
1994	$16.55
1995	$17.94
1996	$20.84
1997	$22.21
1998	$23.17
1999	$24.54
2000	$25.57
2001	$26.69
2002	$28.69

Millions of People

Year	Value
1993	5.7
1994	6.3
1995	7.2
1996	8.5
1997	9.3
1998	9.7
1999	10.3
2000	11.0
2001	12.2
2002	13.0

Estimated 2002 U.S. Retail Sales	**28.69 billion**
Estimated 2002 U.S. Salespeople	**13.0 million**
Demographics of Salespeople	
Independent contractors/employees	99.9%/0.1%
Female/male	64.9%/35.1%
Part-time/full-time (30 + hours per week)	80.6%/19.4%

SOURCE: Reprinted with permission from Direct Selling Association.

central cities. It covers information about numerous topics relevant for both B2C and B2B marketing, including population, income, labor force, commercial office space, banking, health care, housing, and so forth. The *Census of Population* and the *Census of Housing* taken by the U.S. Department of Commerce every 10 years are the most comprehensive of such censuses. Updates of various census measurements based on smaller yearly surveys are available in *Current Population Reports* and *Current Housing Reports*. Other up-to-date estimates are made periodically by non–federal government agencies.

Data from the U.S. Census Bureau is available in printed form, on CD-ROM, and for downloading from the Internet. Often these data are in more or less raw form and require the user to make sense of the data structures. There are, however, private companies that make such data available—for a fee—in more processed form, which, in effect, adds value to the Census Bureau data. The company previously mentioned, GeoLytics, markets a line of software data products under the brand name *CensusCD*. The following formats are available:

- Demographic reports (and maps)
  - Custom data sets and reports
  - Area segmentation
  - Area-to-area correspondence files
  - Banking and realtor tract level data and maps

- Services
  - Geocoding
  - Custom-built databases
  - Normalizing data
  - Database compression

Other companies include census data in mapping software that is used for geographic market analysis. This type of software is potentially useful for such applications as retail site analysis, real estate site reports, direct marketing, database creation, and so forth. One supplier is Scan/US, Inc., whose software product *Scan/US Streets and Data U.S.A.* includes maps for the entire United States. These maps include all types of demographics.

EXHIBIT 4.2   The 2003 Lodging Industry Profile

2002 At-A-Glance Statistical Figures

47,040	properties*
4,397,534	guestrooms
$102.6	billion in sales
·$49.41	revenue per available room (RevPAR)
59.1%	average occupancy rate

*Based on properties with 15 or more rooms. All figures are for year-end 2002.

In 2002, the lodging industry grossed $14.2 billion in pretax profits according to Smith Travel Research. Total industry revenue declined in 2002 to $102.6 billion from $103.5 billion in 2001.

The Lodging Industry

The average room rate was $83.54 in 2002—down from $88.27 in 2001. However, throughout the past 10 years this number has increased significantly: $85.89 in 2000, $81.33 in 1999, $78.62 in 1998, $75.31 in 1997, $70.93 in 1996, $66.65 in 1995, $62.86 in 1994, $60.53 in 1993, and $58.91 in 1992.

The Tourism Industry

In the United States, tourism is currently the third largest retail industry, behind automotive and food stores. Travel and tourism is the nation's largest services export industry, the third largest retail sales industry, and one of America's largest employers. In fact, it is the second or third largest employer in 30 states. The tourism industry includes more than 15 interrelated businesses, from lodging establishments, airlines, and restaurants to cruise lines, car rental firms, travel agents, and tour operators.

Tourism Effects on Our Economy

- Resident and international travelers in the United States spend an average $1.4 billion a day, $60 million an hour, $1 million a minute, and $17 thousand a second.
- Tourism generates $525 billion in sales (excluding spending by international travelers on U.S. airlines).
- The tourism industry pays $96 billion in federal, state, and local taxes.

Lodging and Overall Tourism Employment

- The industry employs more than 2 million hotel property workers.
- Tourism directly supports more than 7.8 million travel and tourism jobs.
- One of every seven Americans is employed either directly or indirectly because of people traveling to and within the United States.

Promotional Spending

In 2002, states plan to spend a projected $554.2 million for development and promotion in the travel and tourism industry. Hawaii again edged out the other states with a tourism office spending budget of $56 million for 2002, despite its budget decreasing 21 percent from 2001. Following second is Illinois with a budget of $49.7 million, down nearly 9 percent from last year. Rounding out the top five is Pennsylvania ($35 million, down 9%), Texas ($31 million, down 13%), and Florida ($29 million, down 40%). Texas and Florida plan to spend the most on domestic advertising, each budgeting nearly $12 million for 2002, followed by Illinois ($7.8 million), Pennsylvania ($6.6 million), and Louisiana ($6.4 million). The total collective domestic advertising budget is $145.5 million.

2002 Property/Room Breakdown

By Location	Property*	Rooms†
Airport	3,305 (7.0%)	455,175 (10.4%)
Suburban	17,006 (36.6%)	1,395,378 (31.7%)
Urban	5,502 (11.7%)	712,256 (16.2%)
Highway	18,918 (40.2%)	1,351,073 (30.7%)
Resort	2,309 (4.9%)	483,652 (11%)
By Rate		
Under $30	942 (2%)	61,757 (1.4%)
$30–$44.99	8,040 (17.1%)	526,687 (12%)
$45–$59.99	16,129 (34.3%)	1,077,454 (24.5%)
$60–$85	13,666 (29.1%)	1,318,367 (30%)
Over $85	8,263 (17.6%)	1,413,269 (32.1%)
By Size		
Under 75 rooms	26,840 (57.1%)	1,126,219 (25.6%)
75–149 rooms	14,170 (30.1%)	1,511,729 (34.4%)
150–299 rooms	4,422 (9.4%)	882,765 (20.1%)
300–500 rooms	1,103 (2.3%)	409,779 (9.3%)
Over 500 rooms	505 (1.1%)	467,042 (10.6%)

*Based on a total of 47,040 properties.
†Based on a total of 4,397,534 guestrooms.
Please note: Total percentages may not add up to 100 because of rounding.

The Typical Lodging Customer

29% are transient business travelers

25% are attending a conference/group meeting

24% are on vacation

22% are traveling for other reasons (e.g., personal, family, special event)

The typical business room night is generated by a male (71%), age 35–54 (54%), employed in a professional or managerial position (54%), earning an average yearly household income of $81,600. Typically, these guests travel alone (61%), make reservations (91%), and pay $93 per room night.

The typical leisure room night is generated by two adults (52%), ages 35–54 (43%), earning an average yearly household income of $71,600. The typical leisure traveler also travels by auto (74%), makes reservations (83%), and pays $85 per room night.

For a hotel stay, 42 percent of all business travelers spend one night, 25 percent spend two nights, and 33 percent spend three or more nights.

Of leisure travelers, 46 percent spend one night, 27 percent spend two nights, and 27 percent spend three or more nights.

International Travel**

- According to the Office of Travel and Tourism Industries (OTTI), the top 10 overseas regions in terms of U.S. arrivals for 2002 were Western Europe (8.2 million), United Kingdom (3.8 million), Germany (1.2 million), France (734,260), Italy (406,160), Netherlands (384,367), Spain (269,520), Ireland (259,687), Switzerland (253,940), Sweden (204,156), and Belgium (159,052).
- OTTI says 41.9 million international travelers visited the United States in 2002, a 7 percent decrease in travel from 2001. Overseas*** arrivals decreased by 12 percent to 19.1 million. Canadian arrivals decreased by 7.8 percent to 13.5 million. Mexican arrivals decreased by 4 percent to 13 million. Concurrently, U.S. residents' travel abroad decreased overall by 2 percent to 56.6 million. Overseas departures decreased by 6 percent to 23.7 million. Canadian departures increased 3 percent to 16.0 million. Mexican departures decreased 2 percent to 16.8 million.
- Figures for 2002 reveal that international visitor spending in the United States decreased by 4 percent, resulting in $87.8 million total travel receipts. Simultaneously, American spending followed closely with $80.3 million (3%) spending outside the United States.

**International includes Canada, Mexico, and overseas.

***Overseas excludes Canada and Mexico.

SOURCES: American Economics Group, Inc.; D.K. Shifflet & Associates, Ltd.; Smith Travel Research; the Travel Industry Association of America; and the U.S. Department of Commerce, International Trade Administration, Office of Travel and Tourism Industries.

American Hotel & Lodging Association (www.ahla.com)

Private organizations are another source of demographic information useful to marketers. To illustrate, Standard Rate & Data Service publishes *The Lifestyle Market Analyst.* This annual provides demographic and lifestyle information for 210 Designated Market Areas (DMAs) in the United States. There are different ways that the market, demographic, and lifestyle data can be accessed:

- *Demographic categories for each DMA:* Start with a specific demographic segment, such as dual-income households, and identify lifestyles and geographic locations.
- *Most popular lifestyles for each DMA:* Specify a lifestyle and then identify what other interests frequently appeal to those consumers and what demographic information corresponds to that profile.

Table 4.3 shows demographics and lifestyles for the Seattle-Tacoma, Washington, market area.

Table 4.3   Demographics and Lifestyles, seattle-Tacoma, Washingotn

Seattle-Tacoma, WA

Demographics
Base Index US = 100

Total Adult Population   2,939,296

Occupation	Population	%	Index
Administrative	379,169	12.9	101
Blue Collar	276,294	9.4	93
Clerical	235,144	8.0	93
Homemaker	373,290	12.7	92
Professional/Technical	837,699	28.5	112
Retired	502,619	17.1	92
Sales/Marketing	173,418	5.9	109
Self Employed	88,179	3.0	107
Student	73,482	2.5	104

Education (1990 Census)			
Elementary (0–8 years)	99,748	4.4	42
High School (1–3 years)	226,599	10.0	69
High School (4 years)	621,155	27.4	91
College (1–3 years)	752,641	33.2	133
College (4+ years)	584,481	24.9	123

Race/Ethnicity			
White	2,486,544	84.6	115
Black	114,633	3.9	33
Asian	182,236	6.2	182
Hispanic	111,693	3.8	36
American Indian	41,150	1.4	200
Other	2,939	0.1	100

Total Households   1,539,954

Age of Head of Household	Households	%	Index
18–24 years old	90,858	5.9	111
25–34 years old	318,773	20.7	108
35–44 years old	378,831	24.6	109
45–54 years old	277,194	18.0	101
55–64 years old	167,856	10.9	67
65–74 years old	164,776	10.7	88
75 years and older	140,137	9.1	87
Median Age	44.5 years		

Sex/Marital Status			
Single Male	318,773	20.7	102
Single Female	346,492	22.5	93
Married	876,240	56.9	102

Children At Home			
At Least One Child	491,249	31.9	102
Child Age Under 2	73,918	4.8	112
Child Age 2–4	135,517	8.8	107
Child Age 5–7	127,817	8.3	102
Child Age 8–10	126,277	8.2	101
Child Age 11–12	92,398	6.0	103
Child Age 13–15	129,357	8.4	99
Child Age 16–18	109,337	7.1	92

Home Ownership			
Owner	964,017	62.6	96
Renter	575,947	37.4	107

Stage in Family Lifecycle	Households	%	Index
Single, 18–34, No Children	197,115	12.8	107
Single, 35–44, No Children	100,098	6.5	108
Single, 45–64, No Children	129,357	8.4	93
Single, 65+ No Children	117,037	7.6	84
Married, 18–34, No Children	84,698	5.5	120
Married, 35–44, No Children	61,599	4.0	121
Married, 45–64, No Children	201,735	13.1	96
Married, 65+ No Children	157,076	10.2	93
Single, Any Child at Home	120,117	7.8	94
Married, Child Age Under 13	223,295	14.5	109
Married, Child Age 13–18	147,837	9.6	98

Household Income			
Under $20,000	309,533	20.1	76
$20,000–$29,999	212,515	13.6	95
$30,000–$39,999	195,575	12.7	98
$40,000–$49,999	194,035	12.6	108
$50,000–$74,999	344,952	22.4	117
$75,000–$99,999	158,616	10.3	126
$100,000 and over	124,737	8.1	114
Median Income	$42,738		

Income Earners			
Married, One Income	385,531	25.1	98
Married, Two Incomes	488,169	31.7	106
Single	683,724	43.1	97

Dual Income Households			
Children Age Under 13 years	130,897	8.5	105
Children Age 13–18 years	103,178	6.7	99
No Children	255,634	16.6	111

Age By Income			
18–34, Income under $30,000	184,796	12.0	103
35–44, Income under $30,000	80,078	5.2	85
45–64, Income under $30,000	92,398	6.0	69
65+ Income under $30,000	164,776	10.7	74
18–34, Income $30,000–$49,999	107,797	7.0	108
35–44, Income $30,000–$49,999	101,638	6.6	108
45–64, Income $30,000–$49,999	104,718	6.8	91
65+ Income $30,000–$49,999	76,468	4.9	109
18–34, Income $50,000–$74,999	76,468	4.9	120
35–44, Income $50,000–$74,999	106,258	6.9	121
45–64, Income $50,000–$74,999	123,197	8.0	110
65+ Income $50,000–$74,999	40,039	2.6	124
18–34, Income $75,000 and over	40,039	2.6	118
35–44, Income $75,000 and over	90,858	5.9	128
45–64, Income $75,000 and over	126,277	8.2	119
65+ Income $75,000 and over	26,179	1.7	113

Credit Card Usage			
Travel/Entertainment	183,256	11.9	88
Bank Card	1,233,511	80.1	104
Gas/Department Store	631,288	34.5	108
No Credit Cards	218,675	14.2	87

Lifestyles
Base Index US = 100

Seattle-Tacoma, WA

The Top Ten Lifestyles Ranked by Index

Snow Skiing Frequently	181
Camping/Hiking	159
Boating/Sailing	144
Frequent Flyer	140
Recreational Vehicles	139

Use an Apple/Macintosh	138
Foreign Travel	136
Own a Cat	132
Real Estate Investments	132
Wines	127

Home Life	Households	%	Index	Rank
Avid Book Reading	660,645	42.9	116	5
Bible/Devotional Reading	266,414	17.3	91	159
Flower Gardening	622,145	40.4	119	19
Grandchildren	323,392	21.0	89	184
Home Furnishing/ Decorating	326,472	21.2	95	141
House Plants	489,709	31.8	100	158
Own a Cat	535,907	34.8	132	16
Own a Dog	494,328	32.1	94	183
Shop by Catalog/Mail	445,050	28.9	98	114
Subscribe to Cable Tv	1,030,236	66.9	103	92
Vegetable Gardening	381,911	24.8	109	115

Good Life				
Attend Cultural/ Arts Events	287,973	18.7	119	15
Fashion Clothing	180,176	11.7	85	135
Fine Art/Antiques	192,496	12.5	113	10
Foreign Travel	300,293	19.5	136	12
Frequent Flyer	472,769	30.7	140	8
Gourmet Cooking/ Fine Foods	340,332	22.1	123	10
Own a Vacation Home/ Property	200,195	13.0	124	21
Travel for Business	358,812	23.3	114	17
Travel for Pleasure/ Vacation	640,625	41.6	110	5
Travel in USA	609,826	39.6	108	8
Wines	264,874	17.2	127	11

Investing & Money				
Casino Gambling	201,735	13.1	98	89
Entering Sweepstakes	217,135	14.1	93	177
Moneymaking Opportunities	174,016	11.3	95	138
Real Estate Investments	133,977	8.7	132	11
Stock/Bond Investments	337,252	21.9	116	7

Great Outdoors				
Boating/Sailing	232,535	15.1	144	13
Camping/Hiking	595,966	38.7	159	27
Fishing Frequently	360,352	23.4	95	175
Hunting/Shooting	209,435	13.6	87	177
Motorcycles	129,357	8.4	111	77
Recreational Vehicles	186,336	12.1	139	42
Wildlife/Environmental	281,813	18.3	111	42

Sports, Fitness & Health	Households	%	Index	Rank
Bicycling Frequently	309,533	20.1	111	56
Dieting/Weight Control	309,533	20.1	89	196
Golf	321,852	20.9	105	70
Health/Natural Foods	292,593	19.0	113	23
Improving Your Health	364,971	23.7	100	62
Physical Fitness/Exercise	600,586	39.0	107	23
Running/Jogging	204,815	13.3	114	37
Snow Skiing Frequently	214,055	13.9	181	21
Tennis Frequently	84,698	5.5	93	60
Walking for Health	508,188	33.0	99	133
Watching Sports on TV	569,787	37.0	97	141

Hobbies & Interests				
Automotive Work	234,075	15.2	104	136
Buy Pre-Recorded Videos	304,913	19.8	106	37
Career-Oriented Activities	157,076	10.2	110	30
Coin/Stamp Collecting	103,178	6.7	99	136
Collectibles/Collections	194,035	12.6	101	120
Community/Civic Activities	141,677	9.2	101	117
Crafts	418,870	27.2	100	151
Current Affairs/Politics	277,194	18.0	108	2.5
Home Workshop	428,570	27.7	107	83
Military Veteran in Household	391,151	25.4	109	79
Needlework/Knitting	247,934	16.1	104	126
Our Nation's Heritage	76,998	5.0	100	116
Self-Improvement	295,673	19.2	104	43
Sewing	271,034	17.6	105	129
Supports Health Charities	283,353	18.4	96	95

High Tech Activites				
Electronics	186,336	12.1	104	50
Home Video Games	192,496	12.5	102	110
Listen to Records/ Tapes/CDs	828,501	53.8	106	16
Own a CD Player	1,036,396	67.3	113	11
Photography	317,233	20.6	116	13
Science Fiction	172,476	11.2	124	8
Science/New Technology	177,096	11.5	126	13
Use a Personal Computer	814,641	52.9	124	13
Use an Apple/Macintosh	195,575	12.7	138	16
Use an IBM Compatible	697,604	45.3	121	14
VCR Recording	298,753	19.4	100	104

SOURCE: Reprinted with permission from SRDS.

Market sales (e.g., size in dollars or units) studies often are conducted by trade associations, media, firms in the industry, and private research organizations. These studies are published and made available to interested parties. Industry-type studies may be concerned with such types of information as total market size, market characteristics, market segments and their size and characteristics, and similar types of information. For example, Mediamark Research, Inc. conducts a single-source continuing survey, primarily aimed at the advertising industry, that provides demographics, lifestyles, product usage, and exposure to all advertising media data. One part of this study is a series of studies on specific products/services. An illustration of product purchase data is presented in Table 4.4 for boxed chocolates. Mediamark produces syndicated reports, provides data for electronic access, and conducts custom studies.

As with other secondary sources, these studies may contain bias, and the researcher must know as much as possible, although not necessarily in great detail, about the research process used.

Information on new products and processes is available from such sources as patent disclosures, trade journals, competitors' catalogs, testing agencies, and the reports of governmental agencies, such as the Food and Drug Administration, the Department of Agriculture, and the National Bureau of Standards.

Table 4.4   Purchase Data for Boxed Chocolates

	Thousands	*Percent*	*UNWGT*	*Share of Users*
Total bought in last six months*	39,461	20.0	5,338	
How purchased:				
Bought as gift	23,158	11.7	3,292	
Bought for self	16,465	8.3	2,124	
Boxes in last 30 days				
L none	13,047	6.6	1,805	
L 1	14,721	7.5	1,972	
M 2	5,976	3.0	830	
H 3	1,845	0.9	284	
H 4	1,501	0.8	177	
H 5	797	0.4	75	
H 6	561	0.3	80	
H 7	131	0.1	16	
H 8	170	0.1	29	
H 9 or more	714	0.4	70	
L Total	27,768	14.1	3,777	70.4
M Total	5,976	3.0	830	15.1
H Total	5,718	2.9	731	14.5

*Base: Adults (197,462,000)

SOURCE: Mediamark Research, Inc., Web site, January 9, 2002

An extensive amount of information is available concerning advertising. Through the Publishers Information Bureau, for example, one can obtain a compilation of expenditures by medium for each competitor. The Audit Bureau of Circulation provides data on the numbers of magazine copies sold under specified conditions. The reports of the Standard Rate and Data Service provide complete information on the rates and specifications for buying advertising space and time. Mediamark Research, Inc. publishes data on multiple major local media markets, relating detailed media behavior to demographic characteristics of readers/viewers/listeners. A number of commercial services, such as the Arbitron Radio and Television Market Reports, the Nielsen Radio-Television Index, Hooperating, Trendex, the Starch Advertising Readership Service, and AdTel supply measures of audience exposure to specific advertisements or programs. Exhibit 4.3 briefly summarizes the approach used in the Starch Readership Reports by RoperASW.

There are also a substantial number of sources and amounts of data available for distribution research. The Census of Business provides information on retail and wholesale sales by type of outlet and geographic area. The Census of Manufacturers lists geographical and industry data on manufacturers, including costs of materials and quantities of products produced. County Business Patterns gives the locations of businesses by a large number of classifications. Commercial organizations and trade associations also provide such data.

An earmark of the experienced researcher is his of her knowledge of specific sources and efficient search procedures for other published sources of relevant information. This personal knowledge is indispensable in finding, evaluating, and using information from secondary sources. With the mass of secondary information currently available in print and on the Internet, however, even the experienced researcher will often need to refer to general reference works, bibliographies, indexes, and other guides to ensure that they have obtained all the secondary information relevant to the particular problem on which they are working. A detailed listing of selected additional secondary sources relevant for domestic and international markets and marketing is found in the appendix to this chapter.

EXHIBIT 4.3   Starch Readership Reports

The best way to create print ads for the future, and for the long term, is to get feedback on a constant basis in order to find out what works and what doesn't.

Each year, Starch measures over 25,000 ads in over 400 magazine issues. On the most basic level you get raw readership scores—the percent of readers who saw the ad and read the copy. Then the data are put into a context: The ad is ranked not only against other ads in the issue but also against other ads in its product category over the past two years. These norms are a fast and easy way for you to judge the performance of your ad over time and against the competition.

The Benefits of Starch Ad Readership

In-Depth Analysis

- Campaign analyses inform clients not only about the scores of the ads but also why they performed as they did and what can be done to improve the ads. Moreover Starch also is unique in its ability to tell clients about the best positions in various publications (e.g., whether far-forward positioning is superior to ads in the back of the book).

Extra Questions

- To give you information on advertising likeability, persuasiveness, intent to purchase, and so on.

You Can Often Get Much of This for Free...

- Many times, if you ask a publisher to Starch an issue your ads will appear in, they will assume the cost and pass on the data to you for free.

The Starch Ad Readership Program

Through-the-Book, Recognition Method

- One-to-one in-person interviews
- Generally, 100–200 sample, but can be more if client desires
- Sample approximates readership of publication, but is not representative
- Reports present data on:

  Noted: percent who saw any part of the ad
  Associated: percent who saw advertiser's name
  Read Some: percent who read any of the copy
  Read Most: percent who read more than half the copy

- Most reports also offer indexed scores, based on ads of the same size, color, product category

SOURCE: Adapted from Roper, 2002.

With the increased usage of the personal computer has come the development of commercial electronic databases. Thousands of such databases are available from numerous subscription systems, such as DIALOG, NEXIS, or Dow Jones News/Retrieval. Table 4.5 shows examples. A good discussion of these is provided by Lescher (1995, Chap. 6).

In general, there are five categories of commercial databases:

1. Bibliographic databases that index publications

2. Financial databases with detailed information about companies

3. Statistical databases of demographic, econometric, and other numeric data for forecasting and doing projections

4. Directories and encyclopedias offering factual information about people, companies, and organizations

5. Full-text databases from which an entire document can be printed out

The advantages of such current databases are obvious. All that is needed is a personal computer, a modem, and appropriate software. Some databases are accessible by direct online contact through the Internet, whereas others are based on CD-ROM technology.

In Exhibit 4.4 Elkind and Kassel (1995) provide some guidelines for operating on what they call the information superhighway. As far as cost is concerned, there is an increasing

Table 4.5   Computerized Secondary Databases

Database	Subject and Source
ABI/INFORM	Abstracts of significant articles from approximately 800 publications in business and related fields
EIS nonmanufacturing	Information on location, headquarters, establishment name, percent of industry sales, industry classification, employment size, etc., for nearly 200,000 nonmanufacturing establishments that employ at least 20 people; from Economic Information Systems, Inc.
PAIS (Public Affairs Information Service)	Covers public policy, social issues, political science, public administration, etc.; indexed for journals, books, government documents, and reports
Foods Adlibra	Covers all facets of the food industry with emphasis on new products, management, marketing, research and technology, patents, and government activities; from General Mills
PTS F&S indexes	Domestic and international company, product, and industry information; gives online access to a bibliography of more than 5,000 publications; from Predicasts, Inc.
Magazine Index	Covers popular periodical literature (twice the coverage of Reader's Guide); from Information Access Corp.
Psycinfo	Covers world literature in psychology (psychology-related disciplines in the behavioral abstracts) and sciences; from American Psychological Association
MARS	Abstracts information on the advertising and marketing of consumer goods and services; from Predicasts, Inc.
GEOBASE	Abstracts of material by online access to 4,000 journals and other publications throughout the world covering the major areas of geography (including economic geography, human geography, international development, and regional studies), geology, and ecology; from Geo Abstracts Ltd.
LEXIS	Major source of legal information, including international
NEXUS	Comprehensive full-text news and business information
DIALOG	A catalog of databases covering business, law, news, science, etc.

change from transactional (per unit of time) pricing to the use of a subscription fee, thus allowing the user to become part of a syndicated service. These services are discussed in the next section.

Computerized databases have led to an expanded role in marketing for database marketing. Database marketing has been defined as an extension and refinement of traditional direct marketing, which uses databases to target direct response advertising efforts and tracks response and/or transactions. In database marketing, the marketer identifies behavioral, demographic, psychographic, sociological, attitudinal, and other information on individual consumers/households who are already served or are potential customers. Data may come from secondary and/or primary sources. Placed in a database, this information is used to create database profiles and predictive models. In addition, databases are used to estimate market size, find segments and niches for specialized offerings, and analyze customer use and spending (Morgan, 2001). In short, it helps the marketer develop more specific, effective, and efficient marketing programs. Exhibit 4.5 discusses skills needed for database marketing.

Computerized databases also can be useful in data mining. Data mining involves the use of computers to dig through large volumes of data to discover patterns and relationships involving a company's products and customers. Viewed as a complement to more traditional statistical techniques of analysis, two of the more powerful data mining techniques are neural networks and decision trees (Garver, 2002). Further discussion of data mining techniques is beyond the scope of this text, but good discussions are found in Berry & Linoff (1997, 2002) and Dehmater & Hancock (2001).

EXHIBIT 4.4   Attaining Market Knowledge From Online Sources

Elkind and Kassel (1995) provided essential guidelines for attaining market knowledge from online sources:

- *Develop an online research plan.* The plan will outline all the key areas of inquiry and will provide a systematic pathway to search, retrieve, and arrive at the desired data, information, and knowledge.
- *Clearly define your information needs, knowledge gaps, and issue to be resolved.* One of the best ways is to do a knowledge inventory or review to determine what you already know or have in your possession, both primary and secondary research.
- *Focus the search.* Start by applying the learning from your knowledge inventory and specify the new areas that are critical to your project. The focus can be further enhanced by specifying key hypotheses regarding possible findings, information categories relevant to the issue, and other criteria such as product categories, consumer targets, market areas, time frames, and so on.
- *Search across multiple sources.* Don't expect to find what you need in single pieces of data or sources of information. You only rarely will find what you need in one place.
- *Integrate information from the multiple sources.* Use techniques of trend analysis to identify patterns that emerge when various information elements are combined; for example, content analysis, stakeholder analysis, paradigm shift, trendlines, critical path analysis, sector analysis (technological, social/cultural, occupational, political, economic), or other analytic techniques that facilitate integration of diverse data and information and identification of underlying patterns.
- *Search for databases that contain analyses rather than limiting the search to just data or information.* Many of the professional online database producers and vendors offer thousands of full-text articles and resources that contain analyses. You may be able to find material that already provides some interpretation that may be helpful.
- *Enhance the robustness of your data or information through multiple-source validation.* You can increase confidence in the validity of the findings of your secondary searches by looking for redundant patterns that cut across different sources and studies.

EXHIBIT 4.5   Skills for Database Marketing

Technology is continually evolving and has led to the emergence of marketing professionals who have the following needed skills for successful database marketing (Morgan, 2001):

- *Secondary data acquisition:* including analyzing the value of lists, list subscriptions, and list vendors, and testing list samples before buying to optimize the database budget
- *Database-building:* including understanding computer hardware, software, networking, user interfaces, and database refreshes and contracting for large annual data subscriptions to Dun & Bradstreet and other suppliers
- *Target marketing:* including maximizing database record use by developing effective lists, combining the right sources, and managing the delivery of target lists to marketing groups within program timelines as well as consulting on and managing creative agency relationships
- *One-to-one marketing:* having systems and people in place to track responses to database marketing contacts over time, building that response information back into the database through feedback loops and refining the targeting process to customize contacts for every customer

Technology also has fostered the development of so-called data warehouses and data marts. A data warehouse is a collection of information from many different sources, such as electronic point of sale, billing, sales, and customer services (Houlder, 1995). Data marts contain subsets of information contained in the data warehouse. These data are organized specifically to make it easy to perform online queries. These warehouses make it easier to use various data mining techniques in working with the database.

SYNDICATED SERVICES

Some of the aforementioned commercial services are examples of what are called syndicated services. Research organizations providing such services collect and tabulate specialized types of marketing information on a continuing basis for purposes of sale to a large number of firms. In general, syndicated data are made available to all who wish to subscribe. Reports are made available on a regular basis (for example, weekly, monthly, quarterly). Since these data are not collected for a particular firm for use in a specific research problem situation, they can properly be viewed as secondary data. Syndicated services are widely used in such areas as movement of consumer products through retail outlets, direct measures of consumer purchases, social trends and lifestyles, and media readership, viewing, and listening.

The syndicated Survey of American Consumers (based on surveying more than 25,000 adults) by Mediamark Research, Inc. provides an illustration of syndicated services. This survey provides data useful for detecting a marketer's best prospects by providing answers to such questions as the following:

- How many customers are there for the products or services we market? Is the size of the market growing? Stabilizing? Or shrinking?
- Who are the customers? How old are they? What do they earn? Where do they live?
- How do customers differ in terms of how often and how much they buy? Who are the heaviest purchasers of the product?
- What brands are customers buying? How have shares of the market changed? What differences are there among brand buyers?
- What's the best way of reaching prospects? Which media vehicles and formats are most efficient in delivering the message to the customer?

Mediamark is able to profile American consumers on the basis of more than 60 demographic characteristics and covers usage of some 500 product categories and services and 6,000 brands.

Types of Syndicated Services

Syndicated data may be obtained by personal interviews, direct observation, self-reporting and observation, or use of certain types of mechanical reporting or measuring devices. One of the most widely used approaches is the continuous panel, which refers to a sample of individuals, households, or firms from whom information is obtained at successive time periods. Continuous panels are commonly used for the following purposes:

1. As consumer purchase panels, which record purchases in a consumer diary and submit them periodically.

2. As advertising audience panels, which record programs viewed, programs listened to, and publications read.

3. As dealer panels, which are used to provide information on levels of inventory, sales, and prices.

Of these types of panels, the consumer purchase panel is the most often used and has the widest range of applications. Such panels have been established by many different organizations, including the federal government, various universities, newspapers, manufacturers, and marketing research firms. One of the largest of the consumer panels is maintained by NPD Research, Inc. This panel comprises 13,000 families and is national in coverage. NPD also maintains self-contained panels in 29 local markets. Other well-known national consumer panels are maintained by the Market Research Corporation of America (MRCA), Market Facts, National Family Opinion (NFO), ACNielsen, and IRI.

The typical consumer purchase panel furnishes information at regular intervals on continuing purchases of the products covered. The type of product, brand, weight or quantity of unit, number of units, kind of package or container, price per unit, whether a special promotion was in effect, store name, and date and day of week are reported for each product bought. In the NPD and MRCA panels these data are recorded in diaries, which are mailed in each month.

Advertising audience panels are undoubtedly more widely publicized than other panels. It is from these panels that television and radio program ratings are derived. These panels are operated by independent research agencies rather than the media—both for reasons of economy and to avoid any question of partisanship. Traditionally, audience panels have used the diary method for collecting data. In the late 1980s ACNielsen switched to the use of a metering device that transmits demographic information overnight to measure national television audiences. The meter provides information on what TV shows are being watched, how many households are watching, and which family members are watching. The type of activity is recorded automatically; household members merely have to indicate their presence by pressing a button. The sample is about 5,000 households. In local markets, the sample may be 300 to 400 households.

One problem, of course, is that people may leave the room where the TV set is playing while the commercials are being run. Thus, the commercial audience is not the same as the program audience, both in size and in the nature of the people. Another problem is that viewers may not push the buttons on the meter to indicate their age or gender. Thus, it has been claimed that Nielsen ratings tend to be distorted (Grover, Lesley, & Byrne, 1996). In the local markets meter ratings are supplemented by diaries. Another major firm that provides TV ratings is Statistical Research, now known as Knowledge Networks/Statistical Research, Inc. (KN/SRI). Their measurement system, like Nielsen's based on a meter, is called Systems for Measuring and Reporting Television (SMART). This system is known for its ability to count more viewers than Nielsen's (Fellman, 1994, p. 1). KN/SRI has another audience measurement system for radio. Its system, Radio's All-Dimension Audience Research (RADAR), is the only service available for measurement of national radio audiences. To a large extent a meter provides a way of measuring the extent to which people use methods such as channel switching to skip the commercial. However, the meter does not indicate when a person leaves the room unless they log out.

Dealer panels are sponsored by both individual firms and independent research agencies. Nielsen's Retail Measurement Services is prepared from audits conducted on a fixed national sample of food and drug stores, including hypermarkets and warehouse clubs. Each store in the sample is audited by in-store scanning of product codes and store visits to obtain information on purchases, inventories, sales, special promotions, and prices of each brand of each product class of interest. The resulting data are compiled, analyses are made, and reports are distributed to clients. Data on product movement, market share, distribution, price, and other market-sensitive information is provided for more than 60 countries.

The 1980s saw the widespread emergence of scanner technology and its use in retail stores, particularly grocery stores, for packaged consumer goods. With this development came the ability to collect data on products purchased. As the product is scanned at checkout, the Universal Product Code (UPC) information and unit and price information are recorded electronically. Companies such as National Brand Scanning obtain this information from supermarket chains where it is edited, tabulated, and projected for online delivery (through a service called NABSCAN-ON-LINE) for hard-copy reports.

Various types of data are provided by such sales tracking: product category sales, geographical area sales, new-product sales, new-product activity, competitor action, and so on. In addition to regular weekly sales data, other types of studies possible are trade promotion evaluation, price elasticity research, in-store experimentation, and so on. In addition to general syndicated services, there also are companies that provide scanner-based data using a type of statistically designed continuous panel. For tracking purposes, Nielsen has Scantrack

Services, which provides scanner-based marketing and sales information gathered weekly from a sample of more than 4,800 retailers in 50 major markets.

The growth in use of scanner technology for both consumer research and media research, particularly TV viewing, has led to the development of syndicated services that provide what is known as single-source data. Such data include TV viewing and product purchase information from the same household. Mediamark's national survey and IRI's BehaviorScan are examples of such single-source data. The single-source concept was developed for manufacturers who wanted comprehensive information about brand sales and share, retail prices, consumer and trade promotion activity, TV viewing, and household purchases. Athough there are some real advantages of single-source data to some manufacturers, potential users should be aware that such data-management issues as store sample coverage, quality of store-level data, compensation for missing stores, and variations in reporting schedules have the potential to distort results and should be avoided or at least minimized (Weinberg, 1989).

The information obtained from the types of syndicated services described previously has many applications. The changes in level of sales to consumers may be analyzed directly without the problem of determining changes in inventory levels in the distribution channel. Trends and shifts in market composition may be analyzed both by type of consumer and by geographic areas. A continuing analysis of brand position may be made for all brands of the product class. Analyses of trends of sales by package or container types may be made. The relative importance of types of retail outlets may be determined. Trends in competitor pricing and special promotions and their effects can be analyzed along with the effects of the manufacturer's own price and promotional changes. Heavy purchasers may be identified and their associated characteristics determined. Similarly, innovative buyers may be identified for new products and an analysis of their characteristics made to aid in the prediction of the growth of sales. Brand-switching and brand-loyalty studies may be made on a continuing basis.

It is apparent that panels established for advertising audience measurement and dealer panels that accrue from the collection of data at regular intervals have similar advantages. Audience-measurement panels provide a continuous record of the size and composition of the audience for the medium measured. If television viewing is being measured, for example, a week-by-week measurement of the audience for each program is provided, permitting trends to be spotted quickly. Similarly, in the case of dealer panels, inventory buildups or depletions may be determined and corrective measures taken long before this requirement would have been recognized from factory sales data.

There are many organizations that provide syndicated services using methods other than the continuous panel. Many are done annually. The Gallup Organization, for example, conducts multiclient or syndicated surveys ranging from descriptive studies of the "market for product X" to major analytical investigations. An annual study of changing social values and how they can affect consumer marketing is available from the Yankelovich Monitor, a service of Yankelovich, Skelly and White, Inc. Similarly, SRI Consulting Business Intelligence provides a syndicated segmentation scheme known as Values and Lifestyles Segmentation (VALS). VALS combines demographic, attitudinal, and psychographic data for segmentation, according to VALS-defined segments. One reported use of this syndicated service has been to design products for specific segments.

Obviously, there are many organizations offering a wide range of syndicated services. Our discussion of specific sources and types of data has been illustrative rather than comprehensive.

These are viable alternatives to primary data collection, and a firm is well advised to make sure that the information it requires is not already being gathered by one or more syndicated services. Since there is cost sharing, syndicated data usually is less costly than the same data gathered by a firm as part of a primary marketing research project. Moreover, for certain kinds of information the syndicated method is the only feasible method for data collection. Time may be saved as well—doing an original study takes considerably more time than utilizing an ongoing syndicated service. Another advantage of syndicated market studies is that they tend to be more objective than those commissioned by a specific client. There are some potential limitations of syndicated studies. They may not be as up-to-date as desired. Also, there may be some information gaps. A particular product may be "hidden" within a broader product category. What all this means is that before purchasing syndicated services, a research user should evaluate what is being offered in terms of such characteristics as coverage, orientation, research methods used, types of analyses, writing style, presentation, price, and the track record of the research firm.

The products from syndicated services are continually changing with client needs and new technological opportunities. Competition forces actions to maintain any sustainable competitive advantage a company has. An example of the dynamics of syndicated services is the enhancement IRI has made in BehaviorScan. Household panel members show their ID card at participating stores and are asked to report their purchases from nonparticipating retailers by using a handheld scanner at home. It is necessary to consider the needs of the consumers and others who provide the data such that the burden placed upon them does not become too cumbersome.

An Example of Using Syndicated Data

In this section, we show an example of how marketing and media decisions can be made using syndicated data. The specific case illustration is data from Mediamark and is intended to relate to the process of defining markets and determining the best way(s) to reach prospects (Mediamark Research, 1987). Although this study was done more than 17 years ago, this type of research is still being done by syndicated services today.

A medium-size Midwest pharmaceutical company has been exploring market opportunities in the over-the-counter proprietary drug field and the toiletries field. Its research and development department has developed a formula for a lip balm with exceptional therapeutic properties. The company has no experience marketing products in this category. It needs basic information about the market and, importantly, about the consumer.

Using the Mediamark database, the current market for such products can be evaluated thoroughly. Historical data can be used to examine past trends. Directions can be developed for positioning the new entry. The target audience can be defined, and the most efficient media for reaching that audience can be selected.

Assessing the Market

The penetration of the lip balm category is substantial. Nearly one-half of all adults use the product. The lip balm category is substantially stable, not experiencing wide swings in its consumer base of users.

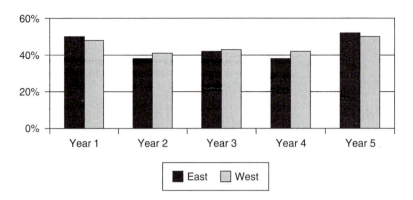

Using Demographics to Determine Who the Customers Are

The profile of the lip balm user reflects the overall stability of the category. Women are somewhat more likely to use the product than men. Young people, particularly those 18 to 24 years old, are more inclined to use lip balm than older adults. Similarly, single people are somewhat more likely to be users than married adults. Household income does not influence usage of the product because users are present at all income levels. Geographically, users are slightly underrepresented in the Northeast region of the country and marginally above average in the West. This profile has not changed significantly in recent years.

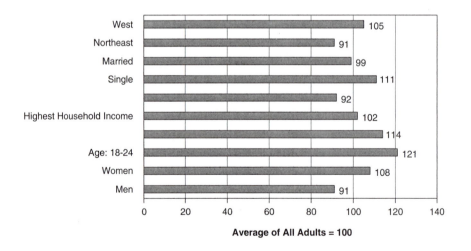

These data suggest that the company can pursue different target groups, depending on its marketing goals:

- If the new entry is to achieve a major share of market, the target audience to aim for is the young, single user.

- If the new entry is intended to gain a modest market share, there may be opportunities to plan a strategy that is a countertrend to the leading brands by appealing to smaller groups of users in the population, such as men, mid-thirties, or married consumers.

How Often and How Much Do Consumers Buy?

While one-half of the adult population uses lip balm, usage is highly concentrated. Some consumers report using the product less than twice a week (classified as light users), whereas at the other extreme, some use it eight or more times a week (the heavy-user segment).

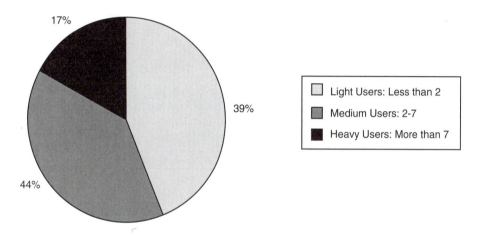

Heavy users represent 16.7 percent of all product category users and tend to be young women and those who have graduated from college. Black consumers are also heavy lip balm users.

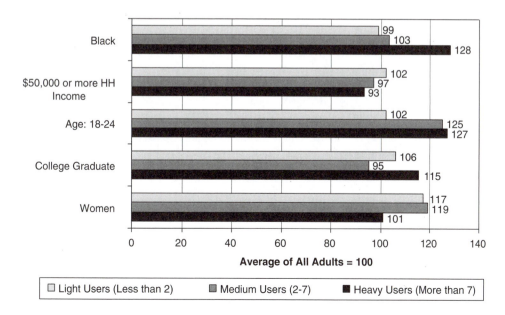

Heavy users account for a disproportionately large volume of consumption, 57.4 percent. Light users, on the other hand, consume only 2.6 percent of the volume, and medium users (two to seven times a week) consume 39.9 percent of the volume.

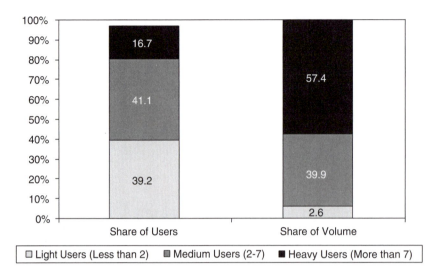

The company can now begin to refine its planning by deciding between a heavy-user strategy or a medium-user strategy. Competitive brand positioning, demographic profiles, and media activities can all be analyzed to determine where the greatest potential opportunity lies.

Brand Analysis: What's Moving and Who's Buying?

In the Mediamark database, the company finds information about a number of competitive brands of lip balm. Share of market figures are developed, and the company attains an overview of the competitors' relative strengths. Even more importantly, Mediamark data can be used to create a sharply etched profile of each of the major brands' consumer franchise.

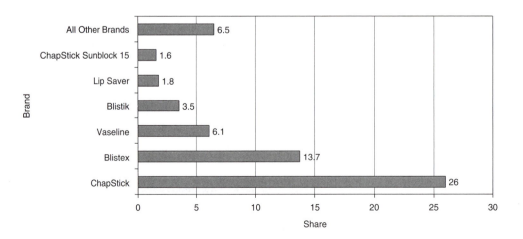

Chap Stick, used by 26 percent of all adults, has a broadly based franchise in terms of being used by a full spectrum of demographic groups. Vaseline usage leans heavily toward young women, ages 18 to 24, to a greater degree than Chap Stick. Vaseline also enjoys a high incidence of heavy users.

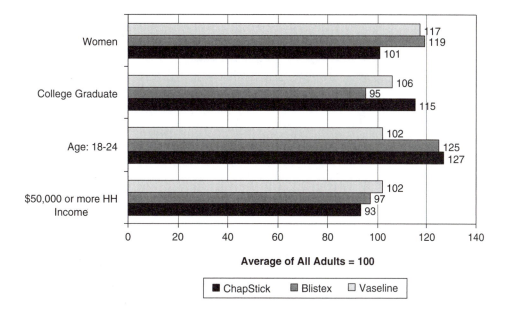

Average of All Adults = 100

■ ChapStick ▦ Blistex □ Vaseline

Through a detailed analysis of the relative strengths and weaknesses of each brand's user base, the company can now determine the potential competitive stance its new entry can take.

In addition to working with syndicated demographic information, the company would probably also want to study competitive aspects of the market on a more specialized basis. The company could then commission a research firm to conduct an independent study, using a questionnaire of its own design and respondents of its own selection. For example, the company may want to study users, triers, and aware nonusers of the major competitive brands to learn about consumer perceptions, experience, and attitudes.

What's the Best Way to Reach Customers?

Heavy and medium users of lip balm have similar media habits. Both user segments tend to be slightly below average in television viewing and above average in reading magazines. In general, the magazine advertising medium reaches both user segments more effectively than TV.

Radio is also a potent medium for communicating with lip balm users. Specific radio program formats are particularly strong among heavy users: Golden Oldies, Black, Urban Contemporary, Jazz, and Classical Programming. News and Talk shows are not effective vehicles for reaching either the heavy or the medium user of lip balm.

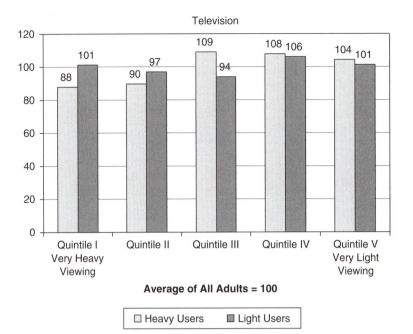

Average of All Adults = 100

□ Heavy Users   ■ Light Users

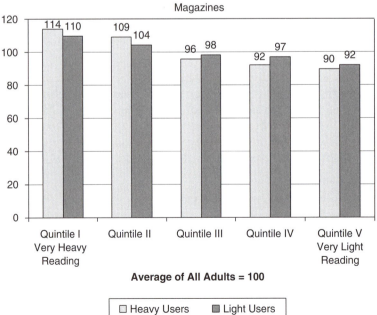

Average of All Adults = 100

□ Heavy Users   ■ Light Users

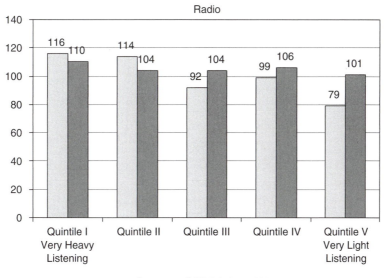

Radio

Average of All Adults = 100

☐ Heavy Users   ■ Light Users

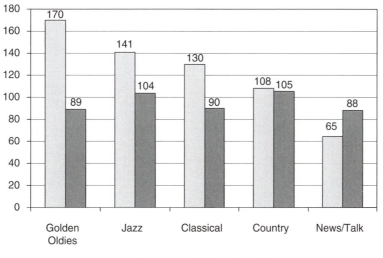

Average of All Adults = 100

☐ Heavy Users   ■ Light Users

The pharmaceutical company is now in a more informed position to make decisions about marketing its new lip balm entry. The information itself does not make decisions, obviously, but it can point the way to preferred alternatives. Utilizing the sound consumer data available through Mediamark Research can help this company, and yours, to make the right choices in brand positioning, audience definition, and media planning.

SUMMARY

This chapter has been concerned with secondary information and sources of such information. We started with some reasons why secondary information is essential to most marketing research projects. Then, various sources and types of secondary information—internal and external—were discussed in some depth. Also given more than cursory treatment was syndicated data, a major type of service provided by commercial agencies. An established concept of syndicated service based largely on scanner-generated data is single-source data. We ended the chapter with a case example of the use of syndicated data.

APPENDIX 4.1
Selected Secondary Sources

Marketing/Advertising

Directories

American Marketing Association. *Green Book: International Directory of Marketing Research Houses and Services.* Annual. www.greenbook.org

The Green Book lists and describes services offered by major marketing firms. Foreign as well as U.S. research firms are entered alphabetically in a single list.

Broadcasting/Cablecasting Yearbook. Annual.

In addition to its radio section, this source includes sections that survey the broadcasting industry, profile television and cable stations, and focus on programming, professional services, technology, advertising and marketing, and satellites.

The Direct Marketing Market Place. Annual. www.dirmktgplace.com

Of possible interest to direct marketers, this directory lists the following: direct marketers of products and services (catalog and retail sales, financial and investment services, fund raising, etc.); service firms and suppliers to direct marketing companies (printers, list brokers and managers, computer services, etc.); creative and consulting services (agencies, artists, copywriters, etc.); and lists of organizations, courses, awards, and so on. For each it includes a description of the firm's product or service, names of key executives, sometimes number of employees, gross sales or billings, advertising budget and expenditures spent in direct marketing media, and countries in which business is conducted.

Rand McNally. *Commercial Atlas and Marketing Guide.* Annual. www.randmcnally.com

Brings together current economic, demographic, and geographic information. In addition to a series of area maps highlighting major military installations, trading areas, retail sales, and manufacturing centers, it includes statistics on business and manufacturers, retail trade, sales, and the largest corporations in the United States.

Standard Directory of Advertising Agencies. Annual.

Also known as the Agency Red Book, this directory contains current information about 4,500 American advertising agencies and their branches, including their names and addresses, specialization, major accounts, and key staff members.

Standard Directory of Advertisers. Annual.

A companion directory to the aforementioned Agency Red Book. It focuses on companies and other organizations that advertise and includes trade names, the types of media used for advertising, the advertising agencies employed, and, frequently, annual advertising budgets.

Indexes

ABI Inform C.D. Rom. Current five years on disc.

Among the fields covered are marketing and advertising. Over 800 journals are indexed and each article is fully annotated. A full list can be printed from the CD-ROM.

Business Index. Monthly.

This is a microfilm index that is a cumulative, three-year index to over 800 business periodicals and newspapers.

Business Periodicals Index. Monthly.

Indexes over 300 business periodicals. Most are general business periodicals; trade journals are not well represented.

Predicasts F & S Index United States. Weekly.

Excellent for the latest news on product and industry developments or for information on specific companies, particularly those that are not well known. Indexes over 750 periodicals, reports, and trade journals.

Public Affairs Information Source Bulletin. Semimonthly.

The index covers periodical articles, books, government documents, conference proceeds, and other publications that touch on topics of interest to public policy. Over 1,400 journals are indexed. Also on CD-ROM.

Consumer Index. Monthly.

Topicator. Monthly.

Other Sources

New York Times Index.

Statistical Indexes

1. *American Statistics Index.* Monthly.

   The ASI is a master guide to statistical publications of the federal government. It is published in two parts, an Index Section and an Abstract Section. It is arranged by subject with references to microfiche reproduction of the publication found there.

2. *Statistical Reference Index.* Monthly.

   Same format as aforementioned ASI except it indexes and abstracts statistics contained in publications not issued by the federal government. It includes statistics published by private organizations, corporations, commercial publishers, and independent and university-affiliated research organizations.

Government Publications

1. *Monthly Catalog of United States Government Publications.*

    Records and indexes documents received by the Government Printing Office from all areas of government, legislative, judicial, and executive branches, and independent and regulatory agencies as well.

2. *Congressional Information Service.* CIS/Index. Monthly.

    This is a comprehensive subject index and abstract to the working papers of Congress comprising committee hearings, reports, and prints, as well as publications of joint committees and subcommittees, executive documents, and special publications.

Bibliographies

1. Special Librarian Association. *What's New in Advertising and Marketing.* Monthly.

    List by subject new books, periodicals, and trade publications in marketing and advertising. It includes many titles that are free, especially summaries of market research.

Special Marketing, Advertising, and Consumer Reference Sources

Editor and Publisher Market Guide. Annual.

Market data for over 1,600 U.S. and Canadian newspaper cities covering facts and figures about location, transportation, population, households, banks, autos, gas and electric meters, disposable income, income per capita and per household, and many others.

Leading National Advertiser. *Ad. $ Summary.* Annual.

Lists brands alphabetically and shows total 9-media expenditures, media used, and parent company. Also included in this report are industry class totals and rankings of the 1,000 leading companies by total 9-media spending.

Sales and Marketing Management. Publishes an annual statistical issue and a loose-leaf data source.

1. *Survey of Buying Power.* Annual

    Contains geographically oriented demographic, income, and retail sales statistics for metropolitan areas and counties. Also lists areas by population, number of households, total retail sales, and much more.

2. *Survey of Buying Power Data Service.* Annual.

    Has more detailed and additional information than the *Survey of Buying Power.*

Simmons Study of Media and Markets.

Forty volumes devoted to the determination of use of various products and services.

Standard Rate and Data Service.

This service offers separate directories giving advertising rates, specifications, and circulation for publications, broadcast stations, and so forth in the following media: business publications (monthly), community publications (semiannual), consumer magazines and agri-media (monthly), newspapers (monthly), print media production (quarterly), spot radio (monthly), spot television (monthly), and weekly newspapers (monthly). This service also publishes an annual *Newspaper Circulation Analysis* covering newspaper circulation and metro area, TV market, and county penetration. Entries include daily and Sunday circulation figures, by county, for each newspaper.

Company and Industry Data

Dun and Bradstreet. *Million Dollar Directory.* Annual.

Lists over 160,000 American companies having an indicated net worth of $500,000 or more.

Standard and Poor's Register of Corporations, Directors and Executives. Annual.

Lists over 45,000 U.S. businesses.

Directory of Corporate Affiliations. (Annual) and *America's Corporate Families: The Billion Dollar Directory* (Annual).

Each directory features lists of divisions and subsidiaries of parent companies.

MOODY's Investor Service. Various call numbers. Seven annual volumes plus twice-a-week supplements.

Includes Bank and Finance, Industrial, Municipal and Government, Over-the-Counter, Public Utility, Transportation, and International.

Standard and Poor's Corporation Records.

Value Line Investment Survey. Weekly.

Walker's Manual of Western Corporations and Services. Annual.

Standard and Poor's Corporation. *Industry Surveys.*

This loose-leaf service includes for 22 industry categories detailed analysis of each category and of the industries that comprise it.

Predicasts Forecasts. Quarterly.

Is useful both as a source of forecasts and projections of industries, products, and services and as a finding aid to other sources.

U.S. Industrial Outlook. Annual.

Contains short-term forecasts for specific industries.

International Business

Many sources listed previously also are relevant to foreign markets and international marketing activities.

Indexes and Guides

Predicasts Funk and Scott Indexes.

1. *F & S Europe.* Monthly.

   Covers articles or data in articles on foreign companies, products and industries.

2. *F & S International Index.* Monthly.

   Covers articles or data in articles on foreign companies, products, and industries.

Economic Trends

Asia Yearbook. Annual.

Contains information on individual countries plus finance, investment, economics, trade, and aid, and so on.

Europa Yearbook. Annual.

Includes history, economic affairs, economic statistics, constitution, government, and so on of individual countries.

Foreign Economic Trends and Their Implications for the United States. Semiannual.

Series of brief reports on more than a hundred countries that are prepared by U.S. embassies and consulates and provide current data on gross national product, foreign trade, unemployment figures, wage and price index, and so on.

Organization for Economic Cooperation and Development Economic Surveys of the O.E.C.D. Annual.

Economic surveys of each of the 24 OECD member countries that contain information on current trends in demand and output, price and wages, foreign trade and payments, economic policies, and future economic prospects.

Overseas Business Reports. Irregular.

Provides current and detailed marketing information for businesses evaluating the export market. Includes trade outlooks, statistics, advertising and market research, distribution and sales channels, regulations, and market profiles.

Price Waterhouse Guide Series. Continual update.

A series of guides on various aspects of doing business where Price Waterhouse has offices or has business contacts. Topics covered include investments, corporate information, business regulations, accounting, taxes, and so on. Over 75 countries are represented in this series.

World Economic Survey. Annual.

A comprehensive picture of the economic situation and prospects for the world as a whole and for major world regions. Analysis of inflation, rates of interest, exchange rates, trade balances, commodity prices, and indebtedness are included.

Directories

Bradford's Directory of Marketing Research Agencies and Management Consultants in the United States and the World.

Directory of American Firms Operating in Foreign Countries.

Gives alphabetical index of U.S. Corporations and international geographic distribution; alphabetized by country, then firm.

Directory of Foreign Firms Operating in the U.S.

Has:

1. Alphabetical listing by country—shows American Company and parent company.

2. Alphabetical listing of foreign parent companies and corresponding American subsidiaries or affiliates.

3. Alphabetical listing of American subsidiaries, branches, or affiliates of foreign companies.

Dun and Bradstreet. *Principal International Businesses.* Annual.

Complete legal name, parent company, address, cable or telex, sales volume, number of employees, SIC number, description of activities, and chief executives are given for over 50,000 businesses.

Foreign Commerce Handbook. Irregular.

Information on all phases of international business is included in this reference source, including foreign-trade services, daily language of foreign commerce, bibliography, and lists of organizations.

International Directory of Corporate Affiliations. Annual.

A comprehensive reference source of foreign companies with U.S. holdings and U.S. companies with foreign holdings.

Worldwide Chamber of Commerce Directory. Annual.

Listing of U.S. Chambers of Commerce, American Chambers of Commerce abroad and chief executive officer, and Foreign Chambers of Commerce in principal cities of the world.

Special Services

African Research Bulletin: Economic, Financial and Technical Series. Monthly.

Asian Recorder. Weekly.

Business International.

1. Business International *Loose-Leaf Services.* Weekly.

   This is a newsletter service that offers short articles on capital sources, economy, industry, exporting, foreign trade, management, and marketing. These newsletters cover the following areas: Asia, China, Eastern Europe, Europe, International, and Latin America.

2. *Financing Foreign Operations.* Irregular.

   Current guide to sources of capital and credit in 34 major markets.

3. *Investing, Licensing and Trading Conditions Abroad.* Annual. ·

   Covers African-Middle East, Europe, Asia, North America, and Latin America. Includes information on state role in industry, rules of competition, price controls, corporate taxes, personal taxes, incentives, labor, and foreign trade.

4. *Research Reports.* Irregular.

   These are in-depth reports prepared by the B.I. service on various subjects and countries. "Marketing in China," "Andean Common Market," and so on.

5. *Worldwide Economic Indicators.* Annual

   Includes key economic indicators for over 130 countries. Includes G.D.P., demographic and labor force data, foreign trade, and production and consumption data.

Commerce Clearing House. *Common Market Reporter.* Weekly.

Ernst and Whinney. *International Business* Series. Irregular.

Very much like Price Waterhouse Guides described previously but not as extensive in coverage.

Federation of International Trade Associations. *Really Useful (Web) Sites for International Trade Professionals.* Bi-weekly (http://fita.org, newsletter@fita.org)

Moody's International Manual. Twice weekly.

Provides financial and business information on more than 5,000 major foreign corporations and national and transnational institutions in 100 countries.

Statistics

Demographic Yearbook. Annual.

Comprehensive collection of international demographic statistics. Includes population, demographic and social characteristics, geographical, educational, and economic information.

U.S. Statistical Office. *Statistical Yearbook.* Annual.

Kept up to date by the *Monthly Bulletin of Statistics.* Comprehensive compendium of international comparable data for the analysis of socioeconomic development at the world, regional, and national levels.

International Labor Office. *Yearbook of Labor Statistics.*

Includes total and economically active population, employment, unemployment, hours of work, wages, and so on.

U.N. Department of Economic and Social Affairs. *International Trade Statistics Yearbook.* Annual.

Kept up to date by Commodity Trade Statistics and Direction of Trade.

U.N. Statistical Office. *National Accounts Statistics.* Annual.

UNESCO. *Statistical Yearbook.* Annual.

Contains tables grouped according to various subjects: population, education, libraries and museums, book production, newspapers and broadcasting, television, and cultural expenditure. Over 200 countries or territories represented.

U.N. Statistical Office. *Yearbook of Industrial Statistics.* Annual.

Covers general industrial statistics data for each country and commodity production data.

The United Nations has separate Economic and Social Commissions for each geographical region. Each publishes an annual report that surveys the economic and social trends of that area, including economic prospects, foreign trade, investments, oil industry, and agricultural. The titles of these annual reports are listed next, followed by the title of the periodical and supplements that update them if one exists.

1. *International Financial Statistics.* Monthly.

    Data on exchange rates, international reserves, money and banking, trade, prices, and production for all IMF member countries.

2. International Monetary Fund. *Balance of Payments Yearbook.* Annual.

    Five-year detailed balance of payments statistics for about 100 countries. Includes statistics for goods, services, capital, SDRs, and so on. Pay special attention to notes that accompany each table.

This appendix was developed from information provided by Rodney Christensen, former reference librarian, Knight Library, University of Oregon.

ASSIGNMENT MATERIAL

1. Explain why secondary information can be useful to a marketer. Is it ever not useful? Explain.

2. Is there such a thing as a best source for secondary information? Explain.

3. In Problem 3 of Chapter 3, Mr. Donald Stam, product manager for brand M margarine, had asked that a study be done to determine why sales have declined.
   a. How would you go about locating sources of secondary data useful for determining why sales have declined?
   b. What external secondary data are, in fact, available that would be useful for this purpose? From what sources can they be obtained?

4. A packaged consumer goods company has decided to explore business opportunities in foreign markets. The newly appointed manager of international operations is Menak Ven. Mr. Ven knows that a number of variables affect the market potential of a foreign market. A useful starting point is to search secondary sources for the most up-to-date information on these variables. Included among the variables are the following:

Demographics

- Population: total, age distribution, sex distribution, relevant geographic distribution
- Income: income distribution, per capita income
- Cultural Factors: languages (relevant distributions), literacy, religions, relevant habits, customs

Geography

- Climate, topography, major regions

Economic

- GNP (or GDP)
- Major industries
- Major exports and major export markets
- Major imports and major import source countries
- Total amount of foreign investment in the country and major country sources; climate for investment
- Currency and its stability

Government

- Restrictions and encouragements affecting international marketing transactions
- Political stability and maturity

Mr. Ven asks that the following foreign market be evaluated using secondary data (country to be assigned by instructor). He asks you to acquire the most recent data available on these variables, using as many secondary sources as necessary and identifying these sources.

5. In problem 4 of Chapter, the manager of product planning and marketing research for a large, diversified company is considering a proposal for adding a new product to the company's product line—a hearing aid. An analyst has been assigned to work on the project.
   a. Identify internal and external sources of secondary data useful for aiding in making the recommendation.
   b. What external data are, in fact, available for making this decision? From what sources can they be obtained?

6. You are an analyst in the research department of a major steel producer. Your immediate supervisor assigns you the task of making a forecast of domestic automobile production for the next calendar year and, from that forecast, to make a forecast of total tonnage of steel that will be used by automobile manufacturers.
   a. How would you go about locating secondary data useful for the forecast?
   b. What external secondary data are, in fact, available that would be useful for this purpose? Explain.

7. What is a syndicated service? What role can such a service play in the marketing research activities of a company? Explain.

REFERENCES

Albaum, G., Duerr, E., & Strandskov, J. (2005). *International marketing and export management* (5th ed.). Harlow, UK: Pearson Education.

Andreasen, A. (1988). *Cheap but good marketing research*. Homewood, IL: Dow-Jones Irwin.

Berry, M., & Linoff, G. (1997). *Data mining techniques: For marketing, sales, and customer support*. New York: Wiley.

Berry, M., & Linoff, G. (2002). *Mining the Web: Transforming customer data*. New York: Wiley.

Dehmater, R., & Hancock, M. (2001). *Data mining explained: A manager's guide to customer centric business intelligence*. Burlington, MA: Digital Press.

Direct Selling Association. (2003). *2003 Direct selling growth & outlook survey*. Washington, DC. http://www.dsa.org/

Elkind, F., & Kassel, A. (1995, July 31). A marketer's guide for navigating the information superhighway. *Marketing News, 29,* 2ff.

Fellman, M. W. (1994, September 14). A smart move. *Marketing News, 32,* 1ff.

Garver, M. S. (2002, September 16). Try new data mining techniques. *Marketing News, 36,* 31–33.

Grover, R., Lesley, E., & Byrne, J. A. (1996, February 12). Nielsen schmielsen. *BusinessWeek,* pp. 38.

Houlder, V. (1995, November 28). Database mining. *Financial Times,* 13.

Lescher, J. F. (1995). *Online market research*. Reading, MA: Addison-Wesley.

Mediamark Research. (1987). *Winning the marketing game: How syndicated consumer research helps improve the odds*. New York: Mediamark Research.

Morgan, M. S. (2001, October 8). Research boosts database's power. *Marketing News, 35,* 16.

Peterson, R. A. (1988). *Marketing research* (2nd ed.). Plano, TX: Business Publications.

Right techniques needed to conduct secondary research. (1981, January 9). *Marketing News, 15,* 30.

RoperASW. (2002). Available at RoperASW.com. Accessed January 9, 2002.

Sechrest, L., & Phillips, M. (1979). Unobtrusive measures: An overview. In L. Sechrest (Ed.), *Unobtrusive measurement today.* San Francisco: Jossey-Bass.

Webb, E., Campbell, D., Schwartz, N., & Sechrest, L. (1966). *Unobtrusive measures: Nonreactive research in the social sciences.* Chicago: Rand McNally.

Weinberg, B. (1989). *Building an information strategy for scanner data.* Cambridge, MA: Marketing Science Institute, Report No. 89–121.

Wotruba, T. R., & Pribova, M. (1995). Direct selling in Central Europe: A comparison with the U.S. In T. R. Wotruba (Ed.), *Direct Selling in Central and Eastern Europe: An International Symposium.* Washington, DC: Direct Selling Education Foundation, 87–103.

Young, L., & Albaum, G. (2003, Summer). Measurement of trust in salesperson/customer relationships in direct selling. *Journal of Personal Selling and Sales Management, 23*(3), 253–269.

Chapter 5

INFORMATION FROM RESPONDENTS

Respondents are a major source of marketing information. As stated in Chapter 3, a respondent is an individual who provides information passively through the observation of his or her behavior, as well as actively through verbal response. Researchers must be concerned with information obtained both by asking questions and by observing behavior or the results of past behavior.

This chapter first examines the types of information that can be obtained from respondents, with a specific emphasis on that information used to predict what actions marketing participants would take to solve a specific marketing problem. The types of information relevant to predicting behavior are categorized as behavioral correlates and nonbehavioral correlates.

Next, the chapter examines means of obtaining information from respondents. Generally, researchers use the same methods as in their everyday, informal association with people. That is, if we want to find out something from someone, we either ask them, observe their behavior (or results of their behavior), or do both. Formal research has simply formalized these methods. To be sure, many techniques, some of them highly ingenious, have been developed and are in use. All of these techniques, however, ultimately reduce to some form of communication, observation, or combination of the two. This chapter discusses communication as a means of obtaining information. Observation is covered in Chapter 7.

Asking straightforward questions and receiving straightforward answers, or observing people's behavior, could be rife with serious problems. The subtleties and complexities of obtaining information from respondents have been the subject of extensive investigation and experimentation for the past 50 years. Moreover, widespread access to computers and the Internet has led to unique interviewing and data collection problems that have never been encountered before. Methodologies are being developed in what might be called "uncharted waters." For example, survey techniques are being developed based on wireless technology and the use of cell phones (Long, Tomak, & Whinston, 2003).

TYPES OF INFORMATION THAT CAN BE OBTAINED FROM RESPONDENTS

To some extent, all marketing decisions involve recognizing alternatives to, and making predictions of, the behavior of market participants. Choose any marketing problem, and the decisions made to solve it will ultimately hinge, in whole or in part, on a prediction of the behavior of consumers, industrial users, marketing intermediaries, competitors, and, at times, the government. Whether deciding to introduce a particular new product, raise the price of an existing product, change distribution channels, or determine an advertising budget, the solution to each of these problems involves forecasting the behavior of one or more groups of market participants.

We now consider the general types of information that can be obtained from these market participants for use in forecasting behavior. The information used to predict behavior is divided into behavioral correlates (information that is correlated with behavior) and nonbehavioral correlates.

Behavioral Correlates

Past Behavior

Past behavior is a type of information widely used as a predictor of future behavior. Each of us relies heavily upon our knowledge of others' past behavior in our everyday relationships with our family, friends, and associates. When we state that we "know" someone well, we are implicitly saying that we believe we are able to predict that person's behavior in a wide range of social situations. This ability to predict stems to a considerable extent from our observations of past behavior. In more formal applications, the use of trend, seasonal, and cyclical data for forecasting is an example of the use of records of past behavior to predict future behavior.

Regardless of the nature of the variable or variables to be forecasted, a basic premise of using past behavior to predict future behavior is that there is a relationship between the two that, to some extent, is stable. Recognizing that the degree of stability is sometimes difficult to determine, and that the extent of our understanding of underlying causal relationships is always imperfect, we nonetheless must believe that there is some continuity and stability in the behavior patterns of people.

Records of past behavior may be obtained from either a natural situation or a controlled experiment. The assumption of a continuing and relatively stable relationship between past and future behavior is basic to, and explicitly recognized in, the use of controlled experiments in marketing. Test marketing operations involve such variables as product variations, differing prices, and varying levels of advertising for one basic purpose: to obtain information on customer and/or competitor response to the differing levels of the variables involved. This recorded response is used to predict future responses, even though in many cases allowances must be made for expected changes in conditions.

Information on the past behavior of respondents, whether obtained via experimental or nonexperimental methods, is frequently sought. The typical consumer brand purchase study, for example, concerns itself in part with determining such facts as what brands have been used, the last brand bought, where and with what frequency purchases are made, what the exposure to company advertising has been, and similar aspects of past behavior. United Way of America obtains such types of information when it collects performance data on local chapters by using survey methods, as shown in Exhibit 5.1.

Information about past behavior toward products may be classified into three categories: acquisition, use, and possession. Within each of these behavioral areas, information in the categories of who, what, when, where, how much, and in what situation becomes useful for understanding consumption patterns of the product. The particular study's requirements will dictate which of these types of information will be most useful. Table 5.1 shows the requirements for a study on tomato juice to determine, among other things, whether a new type of container should be developed. Often, such information comes from secondary sources, as discussed in Chapter 4.

Intended Behavior

Intentions may be defined as presently planned actions to be taken in a specified future period of time. What more logical method of predicting the future behavior of respondents could be used, it might be asked, than determining their intentions? After all, intentions are self-predictions of behavior, and thus, if obtained from people whose behavior we want to predict, would seemingly be the most direct and reliable method of prediction.

Intentions are a relevant and commonly sought type of information. However, consideration of our own experiences in terms of what we have planned to do vis-à-vis what we have actually done later should raise some questions concerning the reliability of intentions as a predictive tool. The question "What will you do?" must always be answered conditionally. The degree of assurance that planned actions will be translated into actual actions varies widely depending on circumstances and future happenings, many of which are outside the respondent's control.

EXHIBIT 5.1 Information Needs
of Selected Nonprofit Organizations

United Way of America is a nonprofit organization consisting of more than 2,000 autonomous local United Way organizations, which are its primary customers. Other customers include national agencies (e.g., American Red Cross), the federal government, national labor organizations, and so forth. Working through these customers, United Way seeks to affect its markets, consisting of donors, volunteers, and people in need. To serve such markets, diverse types of information are needed (Wilkinson, 1989).

At its most general level, United Way of America collects data for what it calls "environmental analysis." Of concern are the social, economic, political, technological, and philanthropic forces of change in the United States. These data are used to identify the broad threats and opportunities facing the organization and its customers as a result of changes in the marketplace. While not directly involving respondents, such information may be related to information that does come directly from respondents.

One type of data from respondents is performance data on local United Way agencies. Several standard surveys are conducted regularly to obtain detailed information on donors, those to whom the raised funds are given, and costs and income sources for United Way operations. To keep track of attitudes and perceptions of donors and volunteers, a variety of surveys are run and focus groups are used.

Less ambitious, but nevertheless as serious, is research undertaken by a community symphony orchestra. The Edgewood Symphony Orchestra, located in a suburb of Pittsburgh, Pennsylvania, used volunteers to conduct a telephone survey to determine how local residents felt about the orchestra's value to the community image, their interest in attending concerts, and the type of classical music they preferred. The targeted group consisted of area residents who had not attended concerts in the past.

Table 5.1   Information on Past Behavior Exploratory Study of Tomato Juice Usage Patterns

	Acquisition	*Use*	*Possession*
Who	Who in your family usually does the shopping?	Who in your family drinks tomato juice?	
What	What brand of tomato juice did you buy last time? What is your regular brand?	What dishes do you cook or prepare with tomato juice?	What brands of tomato juice do you now have on hand?
When	About how long has it been since you last bought tomato juice?		
Where	Do you usually do your food shopping at a particular store or supermarket? (If "Yes") What is the name of the store?		
How much	What size can of tomato juice do you usually buy? About how often do you buy tomato juice? About how many cans do you buy at a time?	About how much juice does your family drink in a week? For which purpose, drinking or cooking, does your family use more juice?	Do you now have any unopened cans of tomato juice on hand? (If "Yes") About how many cans do you now have?
In what usage situation		How does your family use tomato juice? Beverage _____ Cooking _____ Both _____ Beverage with friends _____	How do you store tomato juice after it is opened? Can _____ Bottle _____ Plastic Container _____ Other _____

The results of a hypothetical study of expected and purchase rates of a few products and services are shown in Table 5.2. Researchers collected intentions data from a consumer panel sample using a 0 to 10 scale to measure purchase probabilities. Verbal definitions were assigned to each point on the scale. A 10 was defined as "absolutely certain of buying" and a 0 as "absolutely no chance of buying." The definition of a 5 was given as "five chances out of ten of buying," and the other points between 1 and 9 inclusively were similarly defined.

Table 5.2   Expected and Actual Purchase Rates During a 60-Day Period

Product/Service	Intentions-Based Expected Purchase Rate (%)	Purchase (%)	Difference
Ride local public transportation	22.5	21.7	−0.8
Purchase tax-sheltered investment	11.4	7.2	−4.2
Purchase stereo system	17.6	15.6	−2.0
Trip on cruise ship	4.2	3.7	−0.5
Purchase new automobile	14.3	14.1	−0.2

Expected purchase rates were calculated as the average purchase probability for each item. The actual rate was determined by reinterviewing the panel members 60 days later to find out what purchases they had actually made.

Intentions to buy are often conditioned by judgments and expectations of future events or situations, as well as past experiences. Such variables as expected change in financial status, price expectations, general business forecasts, and predictions of need all contribute to the final intention decision. Since each of these is (to some extent, at least) a random variable, it seems plausible to suppose that the intender views them as such and that his or her stated intention is based on a subjective probability of purchase. This supposition is supported by the fact that intentions data with assigned probabilities have generally proven to be more accurate than those expressed in "either/or" form.

Past experiences can often be inferred from a customer's level of satisfaction. Increasingly, customer satisfaction surveys fill a critical role in many firms' customer relationship management (CRM) systems (James, 2002). Customer satisfaction relates to intentions as it can significantly affect the repurchase decision of consumers.

Verbal attitude scales and variously calibrated probability scales (such as the one used in collecting the data for Table 5.2) have also been used. A commonly used verbal attitude scale consists of five categories: (1) definitely will buy, (2) probably will buy, (3) might buy, (4) will not buy, and (5) don't know. Numerical scales from 1 to 10 or 0 to 100 have also been used. See Exhibit 5.2 for other types of scales.

A major use of intentions data has been to forecast sales. In general, sales forecasts of industrial products using intentions data have been more accurate than those for consumer products. The difference between expected and actual purchase rates of the items in Table 5.2 in terms of forecast error (using actual as the base) range from a low of 1.4 percent for automobiles to a high of 58.3 percent for tax-sheltered investments.

One study sponsored by *Newsweek* magazine involved a telephone survey of households with home systems to determine the early outlook for a new type of personal audio disk player product, and to forecast market growth (Shapiro & Schwartz, 1986). The results of this study suggested certain guidelines to follow when studying consumer purchase intent in such a high technology product class, including the following:

1. Understand the technology and its role.

2. Understand the consumer motivations and the context in which the product will be bought and used.

3. Make sure the survey is of consumer behavioral groups with the greatest purchase potential.

4. Go beyond the simplistic and traditional "intent to purchase" questions.

Regarding this last guideline, a better estimate of intent to buy was obtained by using a series of filters (e.g., varying time frames and cost or replicating the purchase process) to separate "yea-sayers" from true potential buyers. Although 25 percent of the sample indicated intent to buy at a specific low price, this dropped to nine percent when considering a firm commitment to a decision. Further, when purchase actions already taken were considered, the proportion dropped to two percent. It has been suggested that when high technology products are involved, conventional marketing research must go beyond demographics and buying patterns; they must examine how people really use technology on a day-to-day basis, and how they feel about it (Judge, 1998). Only then can intentions information become more precise and accurate.

EXHIBIT 5.2   Measuring Intentions

Measuring intentions takes on various forms. Hotel chains such as Hyatt, Radisson, Marriott, Red Lion, and Rantasipe (Finland) place self-report satisfaction questionnaires in each room. A typical intentions question would be:

Do you plan to return to this hotel on your next visit?

_____ *Yes*   _____ *No*

If not, why? _____

Automobile dealers also conduct customer satisfaction surveys of car owners. The following question was asked on such a survey for a Volvo dealer:

If you had to do it over again, would you still buy a Volvo?

_____ *Yes*

_____ *Not sure, probably would*

_____ *Not sure, probably wouldn't*

_____ *No*

A somewhat different approach would ask consumers about their plans regarding a number of behaviors. A survey of consumers attending a theater activity during a special festival were asked the following question:

What other activities have you done or plan to do while visiting the area? Check all that apply.

Attend other cultural events:

(Please list) _____

Drive up McKenzie River _____

Attend sports event _____

Fish _____

Shop _____

Antiquing _____

Sight-seeing _____

Golf _____

Sailing _____

River running _____

Visit U of O _____

Visit wineries _____

Other: _____

As a final example, consider a study of the demand for newly constructed housing in a community of 110,000 people. This study included the following set of questions:

When would you be most likely to purchase a new home?

[ ] *Immediately*

[ ] *Within 6 months*

[ ] *Within 1 year*

[ ] *Within 2 or 3 years*

[ ] *Within 4 or 5 years*

[ ] *More than 5 years*

[ ] *Would never be interested in purchasing a new home*

How important might each of the following reasons be in perhaps preventing you from purchasing a new home with the next two or three years?

	Very Unimportant		Neither Important nor Unimportant		Very Important
Might move away	1	2	3	4	5
Happy with present home	1	2	3	4	5
Could not afford down payment	1	2	3	4	5
Could not afford higher monthly payment	1	2	3	4	5
Present home is already paid for	1	2	3	4	5
Haven't seen any new homes that I like	1	2	3	4	5
Cheaper to rent	1	2	3	4	5
Will wait until children leave	1	2	3	4	5
Other: _____	1	2	3	4	5

In actuality, how would you assess your chances of buying a newly constructed home in the area during the next two or three years, assuming you found one that met your requirements with regard to quality and price?

[ ] 100% certain to buy   [ ] About 50–50   [ ] Zero – no chance
[ ] Better than 50–50   [ ] Less than 50–50

It will be noted that interest in "new products" is a surrogate for direct intentions.

Nonbehavioral Correlates

So far we have discussed how people's past behaviors and their intentions are correlates of what they will do. We now need to examine the nonbehavioral correlates that are useful for predicting their future behavior.

Socioeconomic Characteristics

How is information on the social and economic characteristics of respondents useful for forecasting what they will do? The answer can be readily suggested by an illustration. The Radio Corporation of America (RCA), when introducing color television in the 1950s, was very much interested in the age, income, educational, and occupational composition of the market. They judged that the initial market for color television sets would be families proportionally higher in income and educational levels and older, on the average, than either the black-and-white set owners or the population as a whole. These judgments were subsequently confirmed by a study of early purchasers of color sets. This information was useful for both pricing and promotional decisions, since certain characteristics were found to be correlates of purchase behavior. That is, an association was found to exist between families with these characteristics and the purchase of color televisions sets.

In studies of consumers where there is a basis for believing that such associations might exist, researchers obtain information on one or more socioeconomic characteristics; those most frequently obtained are income, occupation, level of education, age, sex, marital status, and size of family. While socioeconomic characteristics are by far the most widely used bases for classification of consumers, other bases exist. Among these are preferences, personality traits, perceived risk, and such measures of actual buying behavior as amount purchased and brand loyalty.

In general, the identification of consumer segments is useful in marketing so long as the following three statements apply:

1. There is differential purchase behavior among the segments of the market identified.

2. There are practicable means of differentiating the marketing effort among segments.

3. The value in terms of potentially increased sales makes it worthwhile to do so.

It may be interesting to know, for example, that owners of SUVs show different personality traits than owners of other vehicles; such knowledge will be useful in marketing automobiles, however, only if it can be used to develop and evaluate appeals for each type of buyer. Doing so can enhance segmentation, positioning, and market targeting.

Two commonly used and widely accepted classifications of consumers are by stage of the life cycle and by lifestyle. One classification of the household life-cycle states is the following:

1. Young unmarrieds

2. Young marrieds, no children

3. Young marrieds, with children, youngest child under six

4. Older marrieds, with children, youngest child six or older

5. Older marrieds, with children maintaining separate households

6. Solitary survivors or older single people

Some writers have expanded the number of stages by distinguishing in the last two stages whether a person is in the labor force or retired. See Wells and Gubar (1966) and Wagner and Hanna (1983) for more detailed explanations of the life-cycle concept and marketing research.

The life-cycle stage has obvious implications with respect to purchases associated with family formation (furniture, appliances, household effects, and housing) and addition of children (food, clothing, toys, expanded housing). Other, less obvious relationships exist as well. New-car buying reaches its peak among the older married couples whose children have passed the age of six. A second stage of furniture buying takes place when children begin to date and have parties at home. Dental work, travel, and purchases of insurance are examples of service purchases associated with the life cycle.

Lifestyle has a close association with membership in a social class. It is a basis for segmenting customers by values, attitudes, opinions, and interests, as well as by income. These differences tend to be expressed through the products bought and stores patronized, as well as the area in which one lives, club membership, religious affiliation, and other means. These media are used, either consciously or subconsciously, as symbolic representations of the class to which the person perceives he or she belongs (or would like to belong). When used with personality traits, lifestyle variables form the basis of psychographic classification, as illustrated in Exhibit 5.3. An illustration of psychographic questions is shown in Table 5.3. These questions were used in a study of values and motorcycle use segmentation.

A common designation of social classes is the one originally used by Warner and others (1960) that designates the familiar *upper*, *middle*, and *lower* class designations, each divided into upper and lower segments. Thus, the Warnerian classification results in six classes, ranging from the UU (upper upper) down through the LL (lower lower). Somewhat newer is the value and lifestyles (VALS) schema, which classifies the American public into the following lifestyle groups: survivors, sustainers, belongers, emulators, achievers, I-am-me's, experientials, societally conscious, and integrateds (Mitchell, 1983).

EXHIBIT 5.3   Harley Owners Group Classification by Psychographics

Psychographic research has suggested many different segmentation schemes. Such schemes profile interesting demographic and product markets, and provide much more colorful description of the group as a whole as well as the diversity within.

Research by William Swinyard (1994a, 1994b) suggests that Harley-Davidson owners are a diverse group consisting of six distinct segments with very different motorcycling lifestyles:

- **Tour Glides**. Members of the Tour Glides segment find the appeal of motorcycling in long-distance touring. They like riding long distances, use their bike both for touring and everyday transportation, are more interested in the comfort of their motorcycle than its speed, prefer riding with a passenger, and wear a helmet.

  More than the average HD rider, Tour Glides are traditionally religious, have somewhat old-fashioned tastes and habits, are disciplinarians with their children, like reading, and feel they live a full and interesting life. They are less ambitious than others, and are distinctively unattracted by social gatherings and danger.

- **Vanilla Dream Riders.** The Vanilla Dream Riders are more interested in the dream of motorcycling than in motorcycling itself, and are otherwise just plain vanilla—a relatively undistinguished group.

  This is the largest, oldest, wealthiest, and among the best educated segment of HD owners, who have the newest motorcycles yet ride them least and tie (with the Hog Heaven segment) in spending the least accessorizing them.

  Vanilla Dream Riders like wearing a helmet, tend to have a stock bike, and mainly use it for short trips around town. They are distinctively unaffiliated with the "live to ride" ethic, and receive relatively little psychic satisfaction from riding. Their motorcycle is merely a possession, having no real place as a "family member." They are conservative in their moral values, marital roles, and daily behavior.

- **The Hard Core.** More than other segments, members of the Hard Core are on the fringe of society, and identify with the stereotypical biker subculture.

They are the youngest, next-to-least well-educated, and certainly the poorest, yet spend nearly 50 percent more than any other segment on accessorizing their motorcycles. Virtually all are blue-collar workers. In relative terms, Hard Core members are much more likely than others to feel like an outlaw, and believe people would call them and their friends "dirty bikers." Note, however, that they still only "slightly agree" that these lifestyles describe them well.

More than others, the Hard Core likes to be outrageous, enjoys danger, favors legalizing marijuana, and embraces the ethic of "eat, drink, and be merry, for tomorrow we die."

- **Hog Heaven**. The Hog Heaven segment finds great pscyhic and spiritual satisfaction in owning and riding a Harley-Davidson motorcycle.

  Although their accessories spending on their motorcycle this past year is lowest of any, over the years of owning their bike they spent the second-to-most. More than others, these riders feel like an "old wild west cowboy" and closer to nature when they ride. They have many motorcycle friends, and when group riding they feel the group becomes "one." They do not like helmets, and feel cars are like a "cage."

  This segment is distinctively mechanically inclined, likes to work on their motorcycles, has old-fashioned tastes and habits, reads relatively little, and is less likely than others to believe in a life after death. Hog Heaven members often think about how short life really is.

- **Zen Riders.** As Zen Riders ride, they too find solace and spiritual satisfaction, but find it in motorcyling itself, and escape life's stresses in doing so.

  They include the highest percentage of married riders, but otherwise are typical of HD owners in most demographic characteristics. More than others, Zen Riders find motorcycling fulfilling in many of its dimensions: their motorcycle seems alive, they like dirt bikes and the even the sound of four-cylinder Japanese motorcycles.

  Zen Riders are more impulsive and believe they are more ambitious than other segments, like to party, and have trouble relaxing in everyday life. They are "modern" husbands, are opposed to legalizing marijuana, but are willing to take chances and to run risks.

- **Live to Ride.** The Live to Ride segment "rides to live and lives to ride"; they ride more than any other segment, and motorcycles represent a total lifestyle to them.

  Members of this, the smallest segment, are most likely to have bought their motorcycle new, and ride it the most by a wide margin. They simply love riding; more than other HD owners, they use their bike for everyday transportation, enjoy riding long distances, and use their bike for touring. They find riding to be a magical experience, and motorcycling is a total lifestyle to them.

  If they did not have family, members of this segment would quit their jobs and take off. They agree with an "eat, drink, and be merry" premise, like to create a stir, like danger, and get lots of satisfaction from their hobbies. They care little about their appearance and tend not to believe in a life after death.

According to Swinyard, there are significant implications for marketing and advertising to these groups both in terms of actually reaching the group and in the product configuration and accessories that appeal to each group.

Table 5.3 Examples of Psychographic Measurement Questions for Motorcycle Owners: Most and Least Frequent Motorcycle Lifestyle Descriptors, by Segmenta

	Most Frequently Agreed With	*Least Frequently Agreed With*
T O U R G L I D E R S	I like long-distance touring bikes. I use my bike for touring. My bike is made more for comfort than for speed. I love to ride long distances . . . to me, 500 miles is a short trip. I like bikes with plastic farings and engine covers. I like good bikes no matter where they are made. I usually ride with someone on the back of my bike. I like it best when someone is on my bike with me. When I ride I wear leather boots. I use my bike for everyday transportation.	My bike is really quick. I only wave at other riders on bikes like mine. I like to ride aggressively. I have spent a lot of money modifying my bike. I like to have my bike look really different. I don't pay much attention to what I wear when I ride. Most of the time, my motorcycle is just parked. I have spent lots on speed modifications for my bike. I get excited about motocross or scrambling. I like dirt bikes.
D R E A M R I D E R S	Most of the time, my motorcycle is just parked. I like wearing a helmet when I ride. I don't know many other people that ride motorcycles. My bike is pretty much stock. I mainly use my bike for short trips around town. To me, a motorcycle is just transportation. I don't pay much attention to what I wear when I ride. All things considered, I think Japanese bikes are the best. Hot 4-cylinder bikes sound fantastic. I like to ride alone.	It's true that "I live to ride and ride to live." Riding, to me, is often a magical experience. To me, motorcycles are a symbol of freedom. Motorcycles are a total lifestyle to me. My bike is everything to me. When I am riding in a group, the group almost becomes one. When I'm on my bike it's sometimes a spiritual experience. When I'm on my bike, people seem to be admiring me. I spend most of my free time with my bike buddies. I like to have my bike look really different.
H A R D C O R E	Some people would call me and my friends "outlaws." I have spent lots on speed modifications for my bike. Sometimes I feel like an "outlaw." Some people would call me a "dirty biker." I think it's true that "real men wear black." My bike is everything to me. I have spent a lot of money modifying my bike. I spend most of my free time with my bike buddies. Motorcycles are a total lifestyle to me. I like tattoos.	My bike is pretty much stock. Most of the time, my motorcycle is just parked. I like wearing a helmet when I ride. I don't know many other people that ride motorcycles. I like bikes with plastic farings and engine covers. I like good bikes no matter where they are made. I like the spacecraft look of some bikes today. Hot 4-cylinder bikes sound fantastic. My bike is made more for comfort than for speed. I mainly use my bike for short trips around town.

(Continued)

Table 5.3 (Continued)

	Most Frequently Agreed With	Least Frequently Agreed With
H O G H E A V E N	When I'm on my bike, people seem to be admiring me. I really believe that cars are confining, like a "cage." Women admire my motorcycle. When I ride I feel like an Old Wild West cowboy. I feel close to other motorcyclists I see on the road. When I am riding in a group, the group almost becomes one. When I'm on my bike I feel closer to nature. I like the attention I get when I'm on my bike. To me, motorcycles are a symbol of freedom. It's true that "I live to ride and ride to live."	I like dirt bikes. I like wearing a helmet when I ride. I like bikes with plastic farings and engine covers. I like good bikes no matter where they are made. I like longdistance touring bikes. All of my real friends ride bikes. My bike is pretty much stock. I don't pay much attention to what I wear when I ride. Most of the time, my motorcycle is just parked. Hot 4-cylinder bikes sound fantastic.
Z E N R I D E R S	I like dirt bikes. When I'm on my bike, people seem to be admiring me. I like the attention I get when I'm on my bike. Most of the time, my motorcycle is just parked. I get excited about motocross or scrambling. I think it's true that "real men wear black." Hot 4cylinder bikes sound fantastic. When I'm on my bike it's sometimes a spiritual experience. I like to have my bike look really different. My motorcycle often seems like it's alive.	When I ride I wear leather boots. I use my bike for everyday transportation. I love to ride long distances . . . to me, 500 miles is a short trip. I use my bike for touring. Some people would call me a "dirty biker." I like to ride alone. To me, a motorcycle is just transportation. I usually wear leather chaps when I ride. I like to wear chapter "colors." I really believe that cars are confining, like a "cage."
L I V E T O R I D E	I love to ride long distances . . . to me, 500 miles is a short trip. Motorcycles are a total lifestyle to me. Riding, to me, is often a magical experience. It's true that "I live to ride and ride to live." My bike is everything to me. My bike sometimes seems to have magical power. Sometimes I feel like an "outlaw." I use my bike for touring. When I'm on my bike it's sometimes a spiritual experience. Some people would call me a "dirty biker."	I mainly use my bike for short trips around town. Most of the time, my motorcycle is just parked. My bike is pretty much stock. I don't know many other people that ride motorcycles. I like wearing a helmet when I ride. I like to spend time at my motorcycle dealership. All things considered, I think Japanese bikes are the best. Women should only be passengers on motorcycles. My bike is really quick. Hot 4-cylinder bikes sound fantastic.

ªRank orders based on relative standard scores

SOURCE: Swinyard, 1994b, p. 10.

Another approach to values and lifestyles is the List of Values (LOV). Kahle (1983) suggests the following values that provide the basis for segments using the LOV approach:

- Self-respect
- Security
- Warm relationships with others
- Sense of accomplishment
- Self-fulfillment
- Being well-respected
- Sense of belonging
- Fun and enjoyment in life

Although less direct and more subtle than life-cycle stage in its effect on overt buying behavior, there can be little question that an upper-middle-class household will show more similarity in purchasing and consumption patterns of food, clothing, furniture, and housing to another upper-middle-class household than it will to a blue-collar, upper-lower-class household. The media to which the managerial-professional, upper-middle-class family is exposed, and the appeals to which it responds, are also likely to be closer to those of other managerial-professional families than to those of the blue-collar family. Similarly, on the basis of VALS, a processor and packager of tofu may find that because "experientials" have a greater appreciation for natural things, they are heavier users of tofu. The marketer can then direct the product at this lifestyle group.

Classification of consumers is vital if we are to learn more about consumer behavior and utilize this information to develop more efficient marketing techniques. But caution is needed to ensure that managers do not segment too finely and use categorizations when they should not. Given the new software available that simplifies using such advanced techniques as neural networks, latent-class models, fuzzy or overlapping clustering, and even occasion-based segmentation, there will be a tendency to use a jackhammer when a shovel is more appropriate. The technology in this area is far ahead of other aspects of the marketing process, and ahead of most managers' needs (Freeman, 2001). Such techniques as regression analysis, factor analysis, discriminant analysis, cluster analysis, and canonical analysis are described in later chapters. Examples of the use of these techniques for consumer classification purposes are given in those chapters.

Although the discussion thus far has focused on consumers, similar classification requirements exist and are used in studies of industrial users and marketing intermediaries. Comparable characteristics of these firms include sales volume, number of employees, and the type of products manufactured or handled.

Information on Extent of Knowledge

Prediction of what actions respondents will take is often aided by knowing "how much they know." This is especially so when making advertising budget and media allocation decisions, where consumers' choices are strongly affected by their levels of awareness and extent of knowledge of the product and its attributes. To illustrate questions measuring consumer awareness, a study of homeowners examined their knowledge of conventional and variable-rate mortgages. One question sought knowledge of interest rate differences:

If you were offered both types of mortgages, indicate the difference, if any, between the interest rate for the fixed-rate plan and the initial interest rate for the variable-rate plan.

[ ] *Fixed rate was higher*   [ ] *Cannot recall*

[ ] *Variable rate was higher*   [ ] *Did not inquire*

[ ] *No difference*

Information on Attitudes and Opinions

Investigators in the behavioral science fields of psychology, sociology, and political science have made extensive studies of attitudes and opinions over a wide range of subject areas. The study of people's behavior in business and economic contexts is also a behavioral science. As such, it has been a natural consequence that many techniques employed in these related fields have been adopted, adapted, and applied to business problems. Marketing research has made wide use of opinion-attitude studies to obtain information applicable to the solution of marketing problems.

The terms *attitude* and *opinion* have frequently been differentiated in psychological and sociological investigations. A commonly drawn distinction has been to view an attitude as a predisposition to act in a certain way, and an opinion as a verbalization of an attitude. Thus, a statement by a respondent that he or she prefers viewing HDTV color to standard-format color television programs would be an opinion expressing (one aspect of) the respondent's attitude toward high-definition television.

When used to predict actions that the respondent will take, this distinction between attitude and opinion rapidly becomes blurred. Since the major purpose of attitude-opinion research in marketing is to predict behavior, this differentiation is, at best, of limited usefulness. We shall therefore use the terms interchangeably.

Attitude research in marketing has been conducted with the use of both qualitative and quantitative techniques. In either form, researchers encounter problems that are more severe than those involved in obtaining any other type of descriptive information discussed. Despite these problems, which we will discuss in later chapters in some detail, attitude-opinion research has been widely used to provide information for choosing among alternatives. Its greatest use has been in the areas of product design (including packaging and branding) and advertising. Other uses have been in selecting store locations, developing service policies, and choosing company and trade names. In fact, attitudes and opinions are central in customer-satisfaction studies.

Customer satisfaction has been defined as the state of mind that customers have about a company and its products/services when their expectations have been met or exceeded over the lifetime of the product or service (Cacioppo, 2000, p. 51). Customer satisfaction usually leads to customer loyalty and product repurchase. But measuring satisfaction is not measuring loyalty. The following are typical satisfaction questions asked:

1. Overall, how satisfied are you with (brand name)?

2. Would you recommend (brand name)?

3. Do you intend to repurchase (brand name)?

According to William Neal (2000), these questions are usually measuring the same thing—satisfaction with the product or service. Satisfaction is a necessary, but not sufficient, component of loyalty. Customer satisfaction can be measured by traditional surveys, by using comment cards, and for business-to-business situations by field or call reports, to name just some of the methods (Cochran, 2001). Many companies routinely measure satisfaction in consumer tracking studies.

The attitudes and opinions of prospective buyers clearly affect purchase decisions. Consequently, the marketing manager should be as well informed as possible about both the nature of their relevant attitudes and opinions and the intensity with which they are held. Subaru of America, for example, has a program that includes a Purchase Experience Survey and a Service Experience Survey that goes out to all customers who have purchased a Subaru or had it serviced. Findings from these surveys are reported back to the dealer, who then acts on them. In addition, Subaru sends out a Product Survey to a sample of new Subaru owners every year. This survey examines the quality of the product and whether new owners are satisfied with the performance, fit, and finish of their new vehicle.

FORM OF INTERVIEWS

The interview is central to communication as a means of obtaining information from respondents. We can define an interview as a form of dyadic (person-to-person) communication that involves the asking and answering of questions. There is an interviewer and an interviewee. As we shall see later in the chapter, an interviewer is not always physically present during an interview for some approaches to self-reporting. Nevertheless, two parties are always involved, and there is always the asking and answering of questions (see Exhibit 5.4).

EXHIBIT 5.4   What's in an Interview

Each interview is a relationship with certain universal and underlying dimensions:

- *Inclusion* encompasses the degree to which each party wants to take part in the interview, including the degree of commitment of each to making it a success.
- *Control* refers to the degree of power the interviewer or interviewee has to affect the interview process and its outcome.
- *Affection* is the degree of warmth or friendship between the interview parties.

Each relationship also has a number of basic elements:

1. **Context.** The total situation in which an interview takes place, including location, physical arrangements, the people present, and those absent. This also includes status differences between parties, temperature, privacy, and time.
2. **Content.** What the parties talk about during the interview. It involves topic selection and treatment, arguments, supporting materials, language, and questions and answers.

3. **Structure.** Includes the interviewer's or interviewee's basic organizational patterns, sequences of topics and questions, and the means used to open and close interviews.

4. **Disclosure.** The willingness on the part of both parties to reveal their "true" selves to one another.

5. **Feedback.** The continuous stream of verbal and nonverbal signals (e.g., smiles, puzzled expressions, raised eyebrows, moans) sent between interview parties that reveal feelings, belief or disbelief, approval or disapproval, understanding or misunderstanding, interest or disinterest, and awareness or unawareness.

6. **Cooperation.** The degree to which the interview parties are willing and able to reduce the competition inherent in most interview situations and work together for their mutual benefit.

7. **Conflict.** The potential or actual struggle between parties because of incompatible or opposing needs, desires, demands, and perceptions.

8. **Trust.** Belief in the good, worth, ethics, believability, and reliability of the other party.

Each of the three dimensions has some effect upon each of the elements. These dimensions and elements of relationships are present in each interview but are not of equal importance. Although they are independent of each other, they have strong interdependence as well.

SOURCE: From Stewart, C. J. and Cash, W. B., *Interviewing Principles and Practices, 4/e.* Copyright © 1985 William C. Brown, Publishers. Reprinted with permission of The McGraw-Hill Companies, pp. 9–13.

The dyadic nature of the interview is such that bias and error potentially will be present. The major sources of bias are derived from three factors that relate to both the interviewer and the interviewee: background characteristics, psychological attributes, and behavior in the interview itself. These factors have direct influence when an interviewer is actually present and are implied when a self-report approach (e.g., mail, e-mail) is used for data collection.

A model that links these factors is shown in Figure 5.1. This model is based on the following assumptions:

1. The interview is an interactive process in which the background characteristics, psychological attributes, and behaviors of both principals are important determinants of the product.

2. Interviewer and respondent are perceiving and reacting to the observable background characteristics and specific behaviors of each other.

The background characteristics of interviewer and respondent (A_I, A_R) directly affect the psychological factors (B_I, B_R) of each. The psychological factors directly influence behavior (C_I, C_R) and act as intervening variables for background characteristics. The behavior of each part, in turn, directly affects the psychological factors of the other party. It will be noted that there is no direct linkage between the behavior of interviewer and respondent. Thus, the behavior of one does not occur merely as a physical reaction to the behavior of the other.

Another issue of concern is that style of interviewing can affect the quality of information obtained. Styles can range from socio-emotional (maintaining a warm, sympathetic, and understanding relationship with the respondent) to formal (where the person-oriented actions

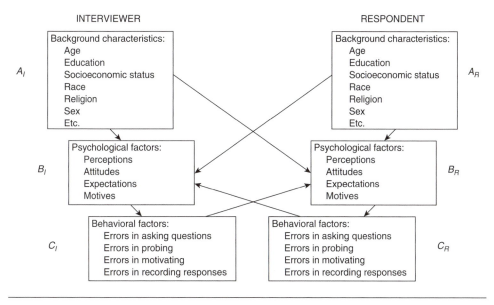

Figure 5.1   A Model of Bias in the Interview

SOURCE: Reprinted from Kahn, R. L., & Cannell, C. F. *The Dynamics of Interviewing: Theory, Techniques and Cases.* Copyright @ 1957, Reprinted by permission of the author.

of the interviewer are held to a socially acceptable minimum). Intervening variables such as respondent's role expectations, the interviewer's task behavior, differences in social desirability of response alternatives, extent of topic threat, and salience of topic affect the desirability of one style over the other in a given situation.

Interviews in marketing research, which typically involve information gathering, are usually classified by two major characteristics. An interview is either structured or unstructured, depending on whether a formal questionnaire has been formulated and the questions asked in a prearranged order. An interview is also categorized as either direct or indirect, reflecting whether the purposes of the questions are intentionally disguised. Cross-classifying these two characteristics provides four different types of interviews. That is, there are four types of interviews: (a) structured and direct; (b) unstructured and direct; (c) structured and indirect; or (d) unstructured and indirect. Types a and b are basically objectivist; types c and d, subjectivist.

We discuss each type of interview in turn (although the discussion of the two indirect types of interviews is combined). We then discuss the media through which interviews may be conducted.

Structured-Direct Interviews

The usual type of interview conducted during a consumer survey to obtain descriptive information uses a formal questionnaire consisting of nondisguised questions designed to "get the facts." If the marketing research manager of a bedroom-furniture manufacturer wants to find out how many and what kinds of people prefer various styles of headboards and dressers, for example, the manager may draw up a set of questions that asks for these facts directly. Assuming that personal interviewing is being used, each interviewer will be instructed to ask the questions in the order given on the questionnaire, and to ask only those questions. The resulting interviews will be structured-direct in nature.

A portion of a questionnaire designed to obtain information on furniture styles owned, bedroom furniture design preferences, and socioeconomic characteristics follows:

Which of the styles of furniture shown in these pictures is most nearly similar to your furniture?
(Show folder with furniture pictures.)

Style A	*Style C*	*Style E*
Style B	*Style D*	*Style F*

Which of the styles of bedroom sets shown in these pictures do you like best?
(Show folder with bedroom set pictures.)

Style H	*Style J*	*Style L*
Style I	*Style K*	*Style M*

What is (your)(your spouse's) occupation?
About how much was the total income of you and (your spouse) last year from salary and other sources?

Less than $20,000	_____	*$60,000 to $99,999* _____
$20,000 to $39,999	_____	*$100,000 to $149,999* _____
$40,000 to $59,999	_____	*$150,000 and over* _____

For a problem of this type, the structured-direct interview has many desirable features. Since the questions are formulated in advance, all the required information can be obtained in an orderly and systematic fashion. The exact wording of the questions can be worked out carefully to reduce the likelihood of misunderstandings or influencing the answer by the phrasing used. Pretests can (and should) be made on the questionnaire to discover any problems in the wording or ordering of questions before the questionnaire is finalized.

The same questions are asked of all respondents in the same order. This provides maximum control of the interviewing process and reduces the variability in results caused by differences in interviewer characteristics. This type of interview is less demanding insofar as the abilities of the interviewer are concerned, permitting the use of less-skilled interviewers and resulting in a lower cost per interview. The standardized, direct questions and uniform recording of answers also facilitates editing, tabulating, and analysis of the information.

The major problems associated with this type of interview involve wording questions properly and the difficulties encountered in getting unbiased and complete answers to questions concerning personal and motivational factors. Despite these problems, the structured-direct interview is by far the most commonly used type of interview in marketing research. An alternative approach is suggested in Exhibit 5.5.

EXHIBIT 5.5   Conversational Interviewing As an Alternative

Despite pretesting, every survey question contains terms that have the potential to be understood differently than the survey designer intends. For example, in a study for an outdoor clothing company the interviewer might ask, "During the past two weeks, did you do any hiking?" A respondent might answer, "Well, that depends. What exactly do you mean by hiking?" The interviewer is now faced with a choice. Should he use his knowledge to answer the respondent's question, or leave the interpretation of "hiking" up to the respondent?

The normal way of handling this situation would be to leave the interpretation of the question up to the respondent—this is the standardization approach. In this approach, interviewers must read exactly the same question and never interpret the question in any way (Fowler, 1991; Fowler & Mangione, 1990). When a respondent asks for help, the interviewer should use so-called neutral probing techniques, like repeating the question, presenting response alternatives, and so forth. The premise is that the only guarantee that respondents are answering the same question comes when the stimulus—the words used by the interviewer—is uniform from one interview to the next.

Another school of thought holds that the interviewer in the example above should help the respondent and define "hiking." This group argues that response validity can be undermined if respondents interpret questions idiosyncratically. An approach suggested is that interviewers be allowed to use conversationally flexible interviewing techniques. This means that interviewers should engage respondents in a manner similar to ordinary conversation, deviating from the standardized script to ensure that respondents interpret questions consistently and correctly.

In two studies comparing the standardized and conversationally flexible methods, Schober and Conrad (1997; Conrad & Schober, 2000) found that each approach might be best under certain circumstances. Both approaches produced high levels of accuracy when respondents have no doubts about the meaning of concepts. However, when respondents are unsure of meanings, flexible interviewing leads to greater accuracy. But this accuracy comes at a cost—an increase in the duration of the interview. Thus, there will be a trade-off involved between accuracy and cost. Ultimately, flexible interviewing is not a panacea. More research needs to be done on this very promising technique of interviewing.

Unstructured-Direct Interviews

In the unstructured-direct method of interviewing, the interviewer is given only general instructions to obtain the type of information desired. He or she is left free to ask the necessary direct questions to obtain this information, using the wording and order that seems most appropriate in the context of each interview.

Unstructured-direct interviews are often used in exploratory studies, and also in qualitative research (see Chapter 7). Many research projects that use a formal questionnaire for the final interviews go through an exploratory phase in which researchers contact respondents and hold unstructured interviews. These interviews are useful for obtaining a clearer understanding of the problem, and determining what areas to investigate. To use the bedroom furniture example again, the company considering entering the field will want to know what consumers' experiences with bedroom furniture have been, their attitudes toward it, suggestions they have for improvement, and so on. Unstructured and direct pilot interviews at the beginning of such a project are often helpful in determining which topics should be included on the final questionnaire.

This type of interview is also often useful for obtaining information on motives. If the owner of a bedroom set is asked the free-answer question, "Why did you buy your bedroom set?" the answer is almost certain to be incomplete and may be worthless. Consider, for example, answers such as "Because we needed a bed," "Our old bed was worn out," or "Because it was on sale." These answers are expressions of proximate causes rather than motivational causes. When motivations are given, such as "We enjoy a comfortable mattress that gives us a good night's sleep," they are rarely complete. The added enjoyment may be because the mattress is firmer, because of the pillow top, because of the prestige the owner attaches to having a carved oak bedroom set, or some combination of these and other factors. In addition, it is probable that motives other than "enjoyment" influenced the purchase.

When used to establish motives, the unstructured-direct interview is known as a *depth interview*. The interviewer will continue to ask probing questions: "What did you mean by that statement?" "Why do you feel this way?" "What other reasons do you have?" The interviewer continues with similar questions until satisfied that all the information that can be obtained has been obtained, considering time limitations, problem requirements, and the willingness and ability of the respondents to verbalize motives.

It should again be noted that there is always the danger that, consciously or unconsciously, people will offer wrong answers to prestige questions or to questions about why they took a particular action. Although a depth interview using direct questions may help the respondent recognize and verbalize motives that otherwise would not have been disclosed, it still does not satisfactorily solve this problem in all cases.

The unstructured interview is free of the restrictions imposed by a formal list of questions. The interview may be conducted in a seemingly casual, informal manner in which the flow of the conversation determines which questions are asked and the order in which they are raised. The level of vocabulary used can be adapted to that of the respondent to ensure that questions are fully understood and rapport is developed and maintained. The flexibility inherent in this type of interview, when coupled with the greater informality that results when it is skillfully used, often results in the disclosure of information that would not be obtained in a structured-direct interview (see Exhibit 5.6).

In the structured-direct interview, the questionnaire is, in effect, the dominant factor in the interview. The interviewer's role is simply to ask questions. In the unstructured interview, the interviewer must both formulate and ask questions. The unstructured interview can therefore be only as effective in obtaining complete, objective, and unbiased information as the interviewer is skilled in formulating and asking questions. Accordingly, the major problem in unstructured-direct interviews is ensuring that competent interviewers are used. Higher per-interview costs result, both as a result of this requirement and the fact that unstructured interviews generally are longer than those that use a questionnaire. In addition, editing and tabulating problems are more complicated as a result of the varied order of asking questions and recording answers.

Structured-Indirect and Unstructured-Indirect Interviews

A number of techniques have been devised to obtain information from respondents by *indirect* means. Both structured and unstructured approaches can be used. Many of these techniques employ the principle of *projection*, in which a respondent is given a nonpersonal, ambiguous situation and asked to describe it. It is assumed that the respondent will tend to interpret the situation in terms of his or her own needs, motives, and values. The description, therefore, involves a projection of personality characteristics to the situation described. These techniques are discussed in more depth in Chapter 7.

EXHIBIT 5.6   Direction of Interviewing

Regardless of interview type or setting, the interviewer may select from two basic interviewing approaches: directive and nondirective. A directive interview is one in which the interviewer establishes the purpose of the interview and, at least at the outset, controls the pacing of the communication situation. Stewart and Cash (1985, pp. 16–18) define the advantages and disadvantages of directive interviewing as follows:

Advantages	Disadvantages
1. Easy to learn	1. Inflexible (especially if a standardized list of questions is used and are scheduled to be asked in a particular order)
2. Takes less time	2. Limited in the variety and depth of subject matter
3. Provides quantifiable data	3. Does not allow the interviewer to use a broad range of techniques
4. Can be used to supplement other methods of data collecting such as questionnaires, interaction analyses, and observations	4. Often used to replace more effective and efficient means of collecting data
5. Can be replicated by controlling variables such as language, voice, sex of interviewer, and appearance	5. Validity of information may be questioned because of variables such as voice, facial expressions, and appearance

In contrast to the directive approach, a nondirective interview is one in which the interviewee, guided by the interviewer, controls the purpose, subject matter to be discussed, and pacing of the interview. The advantages and disadvantages of nondirective interviewing are as follows:

Advantages	Disadvantages
1. Provides an opportunity to deal in depth with a wide range of subjects	1. Time-consuming
2. Allows the interviewer greater flexibility	2. Requires acute psychological insight and personal sensitivity
3. Provides the interviewer with an opportunity to establish an ongoing relationship with the interviewee	3. Usually generates nonquantifiable data
4. Allows for the widest possible means expression on the part of the interviewee	4. May generate more information than is needed or can be processed

In practice, interviewers are required (or find it desirable) to use a combination of the two approaches. For some types of surveys the task of the interviewer is to know when a particular approach is best and when to switch from one to the other during an interview, if given that freedom in the first place.

MODES OF INTERVIEWING

Several alternative media are available for obtaining information from respondents through communication. Respondents may be interviewed in person or by telephone, or they may be mailed a questionnaire. The use of fax, e-mail, and the Internet is similar to mail in that self-reporting is involved.

Response and Nonresponse Bias

A major concern of the research planner when choosing which medium to use is the potential systematic error (i.e., bias) that might arise. In Chapter 3, we discussed total error and looked at its major components. At this point, it is useful to explore error further, but in a slightly different context. Controlling errors related to the sampling process is discussed in Chapter 12. Our concern here is with nonsampling-based potential error. In communication, error may be due to the nature of response given or due to the fact that the sample member has not responded.

Response Bias

Response as a source of error, or response bias, may arise because of carelessness in reporting and recording, measurement error, or when respondents lie. For instance, questions that ask respondents to reconstruct past experiences run a high risk of response bias. More specific is the possibility of a respondent *telescoping,* or misremembering when an event occurred during a short recent time period. *Forward telescoping* occurs when a respondent believes something happened more recently than it did, and *backward telescoping* occurs when the event actually happened later than reported. In a study of durable-goods purchases in the United States, respondents on average displayed forward-telescoping biases, and the magnitude of this reporting increased—while the likelihood of backward-telescoping errors decreased—with the time since purchase (Morwitz, 1997). Overall, the tendency to make forward-telescoping errors was greater for men than for women, and for younger and older adults relative to middle-age adults. In another study conducted in the United Kingdom, the relative likelihood of forward and backward telescoping varied, depending upon the nature of the study (Gaskell, Wright, & O'Muircheartaigh, 2000). In addition, demographic patterns differed from those found in the U.S. study. Thus, the event itself being studied—purchase, reading of an ad, or some other event—will have an effect on the nature of any telescoping errors.

One suggestion for reducing telescoping is to use bounded recall procedures, which involve asking questions about the events of concern in previous time periods as well as the time period of research interest (Sudman, Finn, & Lannam, 1984). Other approaches for reducing effects of telescoping are to ask respondents to use finer time intervals, and to use a well-known or personal time anchor. The latter has been referred to as a landmark event (which may be a date-defined landmark such as New Year's Day or Easter) or an individual-event landmark (for example, if appropriate to the study, the date of a child's wedding).

A complex source of inaccuracy in response stems from the respondents' appraisal of the investigator and the opinions and expectations imputed to him or her. Although much remains to be learned about the nature of the cues from which respondents infer investigators' opinions, there is sufficient evidence to conclude both that such inferences are drawn and that they influence responses.

The investigator's appearance and manner will often influence responses. A classic example is a cosmetics study that showed an unexpectedly high reported usage of luxury cosmetics among women from low-income families. In this case, one woman interviewer had conducted all the interviews in the low-income area. She was an exceptionally well-dressed and carefully groomed person known to be a very competent interviewer. The director of the study hypothesized that the responding women had reported using more expensive cosmetics than they actually used because they thought the interviewer used these kinds of cosmetics. To test this hypothesis, a matronly woman, dressed similarly to the women to be interviewed, was asked to call on the same respondents and use the same questionnaire on the following days. The reported brands of cosmetics used were much less expensive, on the average, in this series of interviews.

So far we have considered only the unwillingness (or lack of ability) of the respondent to provide accurate information. The investigator's willingness should also be considered. The investigator may be unwilling to obtain accurate information, even if the respondent is willing to provide it.

The most common form of this problem is interviewer cheating. The ways in which the interviewer may obtain inaccurate information deliberately, and his or her motives for doing so, are limited only by ingenuity and personality. It may be, for example, that an interviewer finds a particular question too embarrassing to ask. As a result, the interviewer may decide to supply answers or to make an estimate or inference of what the respondent's answer would be if the questions were asked. It is likely that this happens relatively frequently with respect to the age, income, and certain behaviors of respondents. At the other extreme, reports of interviews are occasionally submitted without the interviewer having taken the trouble to contact any respondents. A compromise between these extremes finds investigators interviewing their friends but listing the names of the people that were supposed to be interviewed.

Interviewer cheating can be kept to a low level of incidence but not eliminated completely. Careful selection, training, and supervision of interviewers will eliminate much of the problem. In addition, control procedures can and should be established to reduce it even more.

The simplest control procedure is the *call-back*. If the interviewers are aware that a sub-sample of respondents will be queried after the interviewing reports have been turned in, the fear of being caught will discourage cheating. If the information on an initial interview is found to disagree significantly with that on the call-back interview, additional call-backs may be made on respondents originally interviewed by the same person.

Other control procedures include the analysis of responses obtained by each investigator and the use of "cheater" questions. Analyses of the patterns of responses obtained by each interviewer can be made at very little additional cost. Significant variations from expected norms can then be investigated. In many telephone surveys, for example, this type of analysis is possible. Similarly, mall-intercept and other personal interview approaches involving respondents interacting with a personal computer can use these control procedures.

The use of "cheater" questions in the questionnaire is a less widely used and publicized control device. Questions can be devised that will disclose fabricated answers with a reasonably high probability of success. Understandably, the research directors using this technique have not been interested in publicizing either the fact that they use it or the type of questions they use. Response bias (in the context of inaccuracy related to the asking of questions) is also discussed in Chapter 9.

Nonresponse Error

A nonresponse error occurs when an individual is included in the sample to be taken but, for any of many possible reasons, is not reached. In most consumer surveys this is a source of a potentially sizable error.

Families who, after several attempts, cannot be reached generally have different characteristics than those who can be reached. For example, families in which all members are usually away from home during the day differ from those in which at least one member can usually be found at home with respect to age, number of small children, and the proportion of time in which the wife is employed. Similarly, fathers who are unwed, poor, and live in large cities are difficult to locate and interview. This is an example of a hard-to-reach-population (Teitler, Reichman, & Sprachman, 2003).

The seriousness of nonresponse error is magnified by the fact that the direction of the error is often unknown, and while the maximum error due to the nonresponse can be determined (by assuming that the nonrespondents would all have responded in a given way), it is difficult to estimate the actual magnitude of the error. When considering whether to attempt to increase response rates, the researcher must weigh the costs against the benefits (Teitler et al., 2003). That is, given the real world where budgets are finite, and often not very large, it is necessary to consider whether the benefits of marginal increases in response rates outweigh the costs. This is a critical issue in all decisional research.

A method of estimating both the direction and the magnitude of the nonresponse error is that devised by Politz and Simmons (1949). In addition to the regular questions on the questionnaire, each respondent is asked on how many of k similar periods (evening if the respondent is being interviewed in the evening) he or she would have been home.

For example, one typically sets up seven respondent groups, where the estimated proportion of the time persons in each group are at home is $1/7, 2/7, \ldots, 7/7$ of the time. Having done this, the researcher estimates a total-sample mean by weighting the separate results of each group by the reciprocal of the estimated proportion of time that the group members are at home. In this way, respondents who are not often at home receive more weight than those who are usually at home in the calculation of the weighted mean.

So-called not-at-homes are, of course, only one source of nonresponse bias. The other major source is refusals, which were discussed in Chapter 3. According to the Council for Marketing and Opinion Research (CMOR), a national nonprofit research industry trade group, 44 percent of U.S. respondents in mid-2001 indicated they had refused to participate in a survey during the previous year (Jarvis, 2002). This is almost three times greater than the 15 percent who refused in 1982. This figure may actually be understated, as the CMOR definition of a survey refusal does not include instances in which consumers use caller IDs, answering machines, or blocking devices to avoid telephone calls from researchers. Researchers believe that major reasons for refusal include continual difficulty overcoming the public's concerns for data privacy protection; a negative association with telemarketing efforts of all types; consumers' natural aversion to telephone surveys combined with a lack of survey choices for consumers; low salaries of interviewers; and the fact that financial remuneration is not widely used in surveys to compensate consumers for their time.

The Personal Interview

As the name implies, the personal interview consists of an interviewer asking questions of one or more respondents in a face-to-face situation. The interviewer's role is to get in touch with the respondent(s), ask the desired questions, and record the answers obtained. Recording of the information may be done either during or after the interview. In either case, it is the interviewer's responsibility to ensure that the content of the answers is clear and unambiguous and that it has been recorded correctly.

While it is substantially more expensive on a per-completed-interview basis, the personal interview, as a collection medium, has several advantages relative to telephone interviews and mail questionnaires. It provides the opportunity to obtain a better sample, since virtually all the sample units can be reached and, with proper controls and well-trained interviewers, non-response can be held to a minimum. It also gives the opportunity to obtain more information, as a personal interview can be of substantially greater length than either a telephone interview or mail questionnaire. Finally, it permits greater flexibility. More freedom is provided for adapting and interpreting questions as the situation requires, especially in the case of unstructured personal interviews where visual, auditory, and olfactory aids can be used. When developing a system for interactive home shopping in the late 1980s, Telecton Corporation used one-on-one interviews when they had an interactive prototype system that could be used by the consumer. The same consumers were used as respondents in a longitudinal approach to assess initial reactions, determine the learning curve for the system, and observe respondents' comfort using the system.

The limitations of the personal interview are the time, cost, and response bias that may be induced by poorly trained or improperly selected interviewers. Recalling the discussion of interviewer-induced response bias in the previous section, the problems of the personal interview arise from its very nature in that it is bound up with social interaction and the communication of meaning in language. A personal interview, after all, is an interaction between strangers often (but not always) on the respondent's territory, initiated by the interviewer.

In addition to the home and workplace, many studies conduct consumer interviews in malls, where the so-called mall-intercept method is used. This method involves having interviewers stationed at selected places in a mall who request interviews from people passing by. Presumably the people are chosen on the basis of a predetermined sampling plan. At times, monetary incentives may have positive effects (Wiseman, Schafer, & Schafer, 1983).

The mall-intercept method is a widely used method of data collection in marketing research, as indicated in Exhibit 5.7. Overall quality of data (completeness, depth) appears to be about equal to that of other methods, since mall-intercept respondents are more frequent users of shopping centers, and they may be better able to provide more brand and store-oriented information than respondents contacted by other means.

EXHIBIT 5.7 Mall Intercepts Are Widely Used

Marketing researchers are devoting larger percentages of their research budgets to mall inter-cepts. Indeed, studies have shown the majority of consumer-goods companies spend the major share of their budgets on this approach to data collection. It has been estimated that as many as 90 percent of marketing researchers have used mall intercepts.

Many malls within the United States have permanent research facilities located within them. These facilities may be equipped with videotape equipment, private interviewing compartments, food preparation facilities for taste tests, and a variety of other research equipment.

According to Katherine Smith (1989), mall intercepts have the following advantages:

1. They allow researchers to test visual material, product concepts, and other physical stimuli.

2. They offer an opportunity to obtain immediate response.

3. They have the potential to provide more depth of response than interviews not conducted face-to-face.

4. Researchers can use various types of equipment to analyze responses (for example, voice-pitch analysis).

5. A large number of respondents from a wide geographic area can be interviewed in a limited time.

6. Researchers can control the interviewing environment and supervise the interviewer.

Soundproof rooms free from distractions and equipped with proper lighting and materials can contribute to reliable data collection. Researchers can observe an interviewer's technique and check the completed work immediately.

Another advantage for the mall intercept is that it is less expensive than door-to-door inter-viewing, because travel time and the "not-at-home problem" are eliminated. It is becoming increasingly more difficult to locate people at home, and even then people are hesitant to let strangers inside.

Using the mall intercept, interviewing often takes place where members of the population of interest are doing something related to what is being measured. For studying certain types of products or behaviors, the mall is a more realistic setting when a respondent is being asked to make choices. Finally, using certain sampling methods, the mall-intercept procedure may give a better fit to the distribution being studied than normal household sampling methods.

Despite all these virtues, mall intercepts have limitations:

1. The mall customer may not reflect the general population.

2. The intercept is not well-suited to probability sampling.

3. Shoppers in a hurry may respond carelessly.

4. The interview time constraint is more severe with mall intercepts than with other personal interviewing methods.

Although the mall intercept is not as well suited to probability sampling as other face-to-face interviewing methods, with control for frequency of shopping visit and use of quota sampling the mall-intercept method can be a powerful approach for data collection, as indicated in Exhibit 5.8.

Closely related to the mall intercept for consumer research is data collection at the place of purchase. Such in-store interviewing asks questions about a just-made specific purchase decision and is conducted at the point of purchase. There are obvious advantages of this method:

1. The respondent is usually in a proper state of mind.

2. The recall task is easier.

3. It is easier to contact actual purchasers of a target product category.

4. Response rates are high.

5. The technique seems to be robust in its application.

In more general terms, research should be conducted on site whenever the premises are the subject of the research or when the purchase decision is made on the premises. Consumers tend to react to an entire shopping experience, but may be most influenced by details. Thus, they are most likely to recall and discuss their experiences during the shopping experience, not days later during a survey. David Kay (1997), a partner in Research Dimensions International, suggests there are five types of interviews for on-site research:

1. **Stream of consciousness interview.** This is a conversation with questions designed to elicit what the respondent is experiencing at every moment of shopping.

2. **Spontaneous reaction interview.** This asks for spontaneous, minimally prompted reactions of customers to their environment.

3. **Directed general-response interview.** Useful to assess effectiveness of strategy, this method asks general questions directed to the strategy.

4. **Directed specific-response interview.** This is useful to determine why consumers feel as they do, as indicated by answers to other questions.

5. **Prompted reaction to execution elements.** This is designed to elicit response to specific elements. For example, in a clothing store the question might be "What do you think about the shelf arrangement for sweaters?"

Not all types of interviews need to be conducted in every on-site study.

In-store interviewing, and mall intercepts as well, have been used for interactive interviewing. This is possible whether or not a research company has a fixed office location for interviewing. All that is needed is space set aside to place one or more personal computers where respondents can use them. Laptop computers, increasingly small in size, are ideal for this type of arrangement. One thing is essential, however: The researcher needs the permission of mall management if any interviews are to be conducted in the mall proper. Obviously one cannot do in-store interviewing without the permission of store management.

Another version of the intercept method is to interview people in the parking lot, either before they enter the mall or non-mall-based store or after they exit.

EXHIBIT 5.8   Almost All Types of Surveys Can Be Conducted in Malls

Most marketing researchers realize that shopping-mall research facilities are useful for advertising and product tests. However, many such researchers do not seem to use malls for other kinds of marketing research, especially surveys. Person-to-person, mail, telephone, and, increasingly, Internet surveys are still the favorites of quite a number of researchers.

Shopping malls have become the new "main streets" of North America, visited by a broad cross-section of mobile consumers. If indeed a cross-section of consumers go to malls, it makes sense to use them for almost every type of marketing and social science survey. At the very least, it makes sense to include them among the viable alternatives being considered.

A research firm located in Winnipeg, Canada, did just this (Reid, 1984). This firm first opened its permanent facility in a mall in Winnipeg and interviewed 3,000 shoppers, asking a variety of demographic questions. Upon determining that the shoppers came from all over the area, the wisdom of doing personal interviews in the home, as opposed to the mall, was questioned. The company still uses other forms of data collection when deemed appropriate.

The company's experience has been that with a quota sample by age, sex, and geographic location within a city or other area, and control questions to avoid interviewing the same people twice, the results have been excellent. Doing mall-situated research is faster and less costly than using the telephone. Quality, too, is usually better. Often, many people seem to be more candid in malls than they are in other research environments. It may be that the mall is more anonymous and less threatening to them.

The Winnipeg research firm conducted a telephone survey of about 1,000 people throughout the province and found that 95 percent of adults had visited one or more shopping centers during the year preceding data collection. At the time there were 30 malls in the province. In Winnipeg, where one-half of the province's population lives, 50 percent of the people had visited more than five malls during the year, and 70 percent had been to the one where the company had its facility. Since the company knows where nonusers of the mall in which it usually conducts research are located, it can go to their malls when geographic reliability is needed.

Paying people to participate in surveys, in the form of prepaid incentives, tends to increase overall response rates for personal interviews, as well as for other types of interviews. But, what effect, if any, do such incentives have on the quality of the data collected? In a study that looked at whether using monetary incentives affects the completeness and accuracy of the information collected by personal interview, Davern, Rockwood, Sherrod, and Campbell (2003) experimented with a $10 incentive voucher, a $20 incentive voucher, and no monetary incentive. Measuring data quality by three indicators, these researchers found that incentives did not affect data quality in three areas:

1. The number of responses that are imputed

2. Inconsistency in response

3. Interview breakoffs

These findings are based on a large federal study with high response rates and reports on factual items. The effects on attitudinal studies and smaller sample sizes need to be examined.

The Telephone Interview

Telephone interviews are often used in lieu of personal interviews, especially when information must be collected quickly and inexpensively, and the amount of information required is relatively limited. Compared to the mail survey, telephone interviews often are more costly in terms of total costs of data collection. However, when cost is figured on a per completed questionnaire basis, telephone interviews tend to be less costly. In addition, mail surveys offer no opportunity to probe for clarification or further information.

The telephone interview is well suited to such research problems as determining "coincidental" viewing of television or listening to radio programs. In this type of study, calls are placed to a sample of telephone subscribers during the time the program is on the air. The person receiving the call is simply asked, "Are you now watching television?" and, if so, "What program are you watching?" Other related questions may also be asked: "How often do you watch this program?" and "What sponsors this program?" The result is a rapid and inexpensive measurement of audience level. D'Lites of America, a restaurant chain, used telephone tracking studies to gauge advertising awareness, product trial and retrial, rejection of individual products or restaurants, and to determine how D'Lites compared with its competitors with regard to service and quality. Telephone interviews are also useful for early projections of the success of a new product. Telephone interviews were used for this purpose and to forecast market growth for the CD player.

Technically, telephone interviews may be either structured or unstructured, but since the information sought is usually nonconfidential in nature, well defined, and limited in amount, virtually all telephone interviews are structured. This medium does not lend itself well to indirect interviews and has not been used much for this purpose. However, when the population to be studied is business decision makers, some research practitioners believe that more information may be obtained using the telephone for in-depth interviews than by conducting focus groups (Eisenfeld, 2003). This is especially the case when the population is geographically dispersed, as using the telephone may be more cost-efficient. Current customers, former customers, and prospects all can be contacted relatively easily, if the researcher has a detailed database to use as a sample frame.

The telephone interview has other advantages in addition to speed and economy. It is frequently easier to get the cooperation of people over the telephone than in a personal interview. This is particularly true in business-to-business surveys, where an executive may be busy with appointments and unable to see an interviewer who makes a personal call (if a prior appointment has not been made), but can often be reached readily by telephone. Consumer interviews by telephone may also be successfully conducted during evening hours, a time when many people are reluctant to be interviewed personally. It is generally recognized that for business-to-business marketing research (as well as general marketing research), telephone interviewing is as effective as personal interviewing for scope and depth of information obtained. In addition, a telephone survey can be better supervised than door-to-door, and even mall-intercept, surveys if the interviewing is done from a monitored centralized Computer Aided Telephone Interviewing System (CATI) facility.

When starting a telephone interview, potential respondents may refuse to be interviewed for one or more of many reasons. Unlike mail surveys, where there is no opportunity to respond to a refusal statement, telephone surveys allow the interviewer to respond to the potential respondent and attempt to turn a refusal into a completed interview. In his classic treatise on telephone surveys, Dillman (1978) identifies common reasons people give for refusals and suggests some possible responses the interviewer can give. These are shown in Table 5.4.

Table 5.4   Possible Answers to Reasons for Refusals

Reasons for Refusing	*Possible Responses*
Too busy	This should only take a few minutes. Sorry to have caught you at a bad time, I would be happy to call back. When would be a good time for me to call in the next day or two?
Bad health	I'm sorry to hear that. Have you been sick long? I would be happy to call back in a day or two. Would that be okay? (If lengthy or serious illness, substitute another member of household. If that isn't possible, excuse yourself and indicate they will not be called again.)
Too old	Older people's opinions are just as important in this particular survey as anyone else's. In order for the results to be representative for all residents of the city, we have to be sure that older people have as much chance to give their opinion as anyone else. We really do want your opinion.
Feel inadequate: Don't know enough to answer	The questions are not at all difficult. They mostly concern your attitudes about local recreation areas and activities, rather than how much you know about certain things. Some of the people we have already interviewed had the same concern you have, but once we got started they didn't have any difficulty answering the questions. Maybe I could read just a few questions to you and you can see what they are like.
Not interested	It's awfully important that we get the opinions of everyone in the sample, otherwise the results won't be very useful. So, I'd really like to talk with you.
No one else's business what I think	I can certainly understand, that's why all of our interviews are confidential. Protecting people's privacy is one of our major concerns, and to do it people's names are separated from the answers just as soon as the interview is over. And, all the results are released in a way that no single individual can ever be identified.
Objects to surveys	We think this particular survey is very important because the questions are ones that people in parks and recreation want to know answers to, so they would really like to have your opinion.
Objects to telephone surveys	We have just recently started doing our surveys by telephone, because this way is so much faster and it costs a lot less, especially when the survey is not very long, like this survey.

SOURCE: Reprinted from *Mail and Telephone Surveys: The Total Design Method* by Dillman, D. Copyright © 1978. This material is used by permission of John Wiley & Sons, Inc.

As with all types of surveys, telephone surveys benefit from the use of inducements or incentives—monetary or nonmonetary—to encourage potential respondents to participate. Incentives may be promised or sent in advance with a preliminary letter when the mailing address of the potential respondent is known. They may also be offered when the initial request for participation is a refusal. When used this way it is known as a *refusal conversion incentive*. The main purpose of such incentives is to generate a greater response rate with the effect of reducing nonresponse error. Their use has implications as well. First, total cost will increase, although cost per response may decrease depending on how effective the incentive is. Second, data quality may be affected, leading to a change in response bias, which may be a positive or negative change. Third, sample composition may be affected, again with a positive or negative effect. Fourth, expectations of interviewer and respondent may be changed. Finally, interviewer effort may be affected. In a recent study, Singer, Van Hoewyk, and Maher (2000) examined the effects of using a *monetary* incentive and an advance letter in a telephone survey where the sample was chosen by random-digit-dialing and concluded:

1. Neither promised incentives nor advance letters reliably increase response rates.

2. Prepaid incentives enclosed with advance letters do reliably increase response rates in such surveys, by at least ten percentage points in this study.

3. Prepaid incentives do not reduce the likelihood that respondents will participate in a reinterview later, even if they are not offered an incentive again. That is, they do not create expectations for payment of incentives on subsequent interviews.

4. Neither prepaid incentives nor refusal conversion incentives increase item nonresponse, which is a measure of data quality.

5. Prepaid incentives did not appear to affect the sample composition, although refusal conversion payments did.

The above conclusions can be used as general guidelines, but much is still unknown about incentives in telephone surveys. Before using an incentive, the prudent researcher might test effects in a pilot study. A recent study of political telephone surveys concluded that although advance prenotification letters do not solve the problem of sample nonresponse, they can significantly increase response rates (Goldstein & Jennings, 2002).

The telephone survey may be a good approach to reach specific market segments, particularly when door-to-door interviews are not possible or might lead to serious distortions in response. It is obvious that there must be sufficiently high telephone penetration in the segment for this mode of data collection to be advantageous. For example, the use of surname sorts makes telephone surveys the most efficient way to locate, contact and survey ethnic groups in the United States.

The basic limitations of telephone interviews are the relatively limited amounts of information that can be obtained (at least compared with alternative methods) and the bias that exists in any sample of subscribers. Subscribers have different characteristics than non-subscribers, particularly with respect to income and location. The inability to include non-subscribers in the sample may seriously affect the findings. Perhaps even more sample bias is introduced in the typical telephone survey by the more than 25 percent nationally and more than 50 percent in large cities who are not listed in the directory, either because they have an unlisted number or as a result of moving (www.busreslab.com/articles/article3.htm). A technique for including unlisted telephone numbers in the sample frame is called random-digit dialing (RDD). This, together with other telephone sampling approaches, is discussed in Chapter 12.

Additional problems associated with telephone interviewing are those of sample control and interviewer performance. Often this is manifested by inadequate efforts to complete interviews with some of the harder-to-reach respondents. Adding another sample is no substitute for dealing properly with the original sample. Usual control efforts require large clerical staffs to monitor results. Computerized control techniques that can more easily handle the factors involved are now available, and such control techniques are most essential for computer-assisted telephone interviewing.

Another aspect of interviewer performance that can influence response rates and data quality is actually something beyond any given interviewer's control. This is the interviewer's accent. There is evidence that accent can influence respondents' participation. Linguistic experts have found that listeners form mental impressions of people who speak with an accent different from theirs, impressions that may lead to a refusal or bias the responses. In the United States there are many region-specific accents (New England, the Deep South) and also those that are cultural (Hispanic, Asian). When faced with an unfamiliar accent, people may have trouble communicating. When communication becomes difficult, refusals will increase. Alternatively, some accents increase curiosity (British) and can actually increase response rates. In addition, respondents who identify an interviewer's accent may apply preconceived biases to the interviewer and to the survey. Stereotypes identified with region-specific accents may lead respondents to assume differences in socioeconomic characteristics between themselves and the interviewers. Accent-free interviewing eliminates one potential source of nonresponse and bias. At the very least, if a study is regional in nature, then having interviewers from that region will also reduce nonresponse and bias.

The so-called "answering machine problem" has emerged for telephone surveys as the number of households having answering machines has increased. One way people use answering machines is to screen incoming calls. The second, of course, is to allow those calling to leave a message when members of the household are not at home. One might be tempted to assume that screening and leaving messages would allow potential respondents to choose to not participate—a form of refusal. Interestingly, some research conducted on this issue has found that households with answering machines were more likely to complete the interview and less likely to refuse to participate compared to households where there was no answer on the initial call attempt (Xu, Bates, & Schweitzer, 1993). This suggests that where answering machines are operating, the call can represent a form of prenotification. It is generally believed that prenotification in any type of survey increases participation rates. Since this phenomenon has the potential to generate bias in the sample (Oldendick & Link, 1994), we discuss this further in Chapter 12 in the context of sample representativeness.

A standard aspect of telephone interviewing is the use of CATI. An interviewer having the questionnaire on the computer can proceed through it easily, resulting in less interviewer-induced error. Software that allows this to be handled on personal computers is widely available.

An "advanced" version of CATI is known as either Totally Automated Telephone Interviewing (TATI) or Completely Automated Telephone Systems (CATS), depending upon which research firm is doing the research. These systems use interactive voice-response technology to conduct interviews. The recorded voice of a professional interviewer asks the questions. A typical approach is to mail potential respondents a packet including a unique ID number, stimulus materials (if necessary), an incentive, and instructions to call an 800-number, which is available 24 hours a day, seven days a week. The ID number prevents multiple responses and can be used for a lottery/sweepstakes incentive. Respondents use their telephone keypads to enter responses, and answers to open-ended questions are recorded verbatim for subsequent analysis. A major brewer used this method for a beverage needs gap analysis (Becker, 1995). A packet of materials was sent to potential respondents who were asked to call an 800-number to be interviewed and learn if they had won one of several prizes.

A major advantage of this technique, compared to regular telephone interviewing, is that respondents can be asked to do certain tasks before calling. Accordingly, respondents in this study were asked to rank their occasions for consuming alcoholic beverages. The total interview lasted just 15 minutes. Response rates in studies using these systems have varied widely depending upon the type of study, product, and respondents, and the use of incentives and reminders. Experience indicates that response comes within plus or minus five percentage points of traditional methods, and that merchandise tends to work better than cash as an incentive (Triplett, 1994). When stimulus materials are not used or sent in advance, the initial contact with ID and 800-number can be sent by e-mail, where appropriate. One potential problem with this approach is that the regulatory environment may not be favorable. For example, there are communities with an ordinance where telephone numbers must be dialed by a human (rather than by a computer) in telemarketing situations. This may very well carry over to survey research and may be expanded to where the interview itself must be conducted by a human.

Telephone interviewing is an important methodology for marketing research. It is widely used, but is sometimes abused by use of questionable techniques, particularly for consumer research, as shown in Figure 5.2, which is a schematic diagram of the telephone survey research response decision. Only one of six possible outcomes results in a response. The researcher should strive to maximize the proportion of the original sample that completes the interview.

Among the general population there is increasing confusion between telemarketing and telephone-based marketing research. This is happening throughout the world as each is being used more and more. Of primary concern to the research community is the use by telemarketers of selling-under-the-guise-of-research techniques. This leads to an increase in the number of unsolicited telephone calls, which causes public irritation to grow, thereby reducing willingness to participate in a true research project. Finally, there may be an issue of invasion of privacy involved. Legitimate users of both techniques should be striving to eliminate misuse, as there could be public pressure for restrictions or even a total ban on the use of telephone for both research and selling. The European Society for Opinion and Marketing Research (ESOMAR) has responded by issuing guidelines for distinguishing telephone research from telemarketing (ESOMAR, 1989).

In the United States, major legislation affecting telemarketing went into effect in mid-2003. This was the creation of the National Do Not Call Registry. Research practitioners are exempt from this law. Thus, it may help the telephone survey industry by leading to a reversal in the trend of falling survey cooperation rates. To the potential respondent who has registered for the Do Not Call program, there will be a clear demarcation between teleresearch and telemarketing.

A good overview of telephone surveys is given by Bourque and Fielder (2003a).

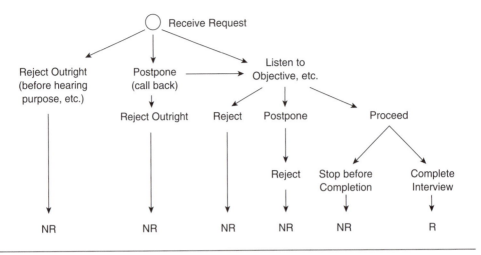

Figure 5.2   Telephone Survey Response Decision Process

The Mail Interview

Mail interviews have been widely used for a variety of purposes. Mail questions provide great versatility at relatively low cost. A questionnaire may be prepared and mailed to people in any location at the same cost per person: the cost of preparing the questionnaire, address-ing the letter or card sent, and the postage involved. Unless a name is requested, the ques-tionnaire is openly coded, or some ethically-questionable practice is employed, respondents remain anonymous and therefore may also answer the questionnaire at their leisure, rather than being forced to reply at the time a personal or telephone call is made. There are times, however, when a researcher states a deadline for return of the questionnaire. If the time given is reasonable, say one or two weeks, this should not adversely affect the response rate. Stating such a deadline may encourage the potential respondent not to postpone the task indefinitely. When used with a reminder notice, a deadline may be very effective in generating responses within the desired time period for data collection.

Serious problems are involved in the use of mail questionnaires, however. Perhaps the most serious is the problem of nonresponse. Typically, people indifferent to the topic being researched will not respond. It is usually necessary to send additional mailings (i.e., follow-ups) to increase response. Even with added mailings, response to mail ques-tionnaires is generally a small percentage of those sent; the modal response rate is often only 20 to 40 percent. Experiments involving preliminary contact by letter or telephone call, cover letters, and monetary inducements have increased response rates dramatically in some cases.

An intriguing dimension of a mail survey—or any survey for that matter—that we know very little about is the use of endorsement. This could be viewed as a way of identifying spon-sorship, or it could be completely independent of sponsorship. Endorsement is defined as "approval and support for a survey from an individual or organization." An endorsement can be included as a separate letter along with a cover letter, or the cover letter itself could be sent from this external source. Endorsement may have a positive, neutral, or negative effect, depending on how the endorser is perceived by a potential respondent. Consequently, the researcher may decide this is a dimension to be tested in a pilot study. It is obvious that the potential respondent should know the endorser, or the organization he or she represents. In a study of a targeted population, Rochford and Venable (1995) found that significantly higher response rates were observed when there was endorsement by an external party associated with the targeted audience than when there was no such endorsement. This result occurred after both the initial mailing and follow-up mailings were done. In addition, endorsements by locally known individuals produced higher response rates than endorsements by highly placed but less well-known individuals from a national headquarters office.

One problem is how response rate is to be measured. For most uses, the relevant rate is the percent of questionnaires delivered. This measure takes into account both undeliverables (from the postal system viewpoint) as well as completed returns. But it does not mean necessarily that each person in the sample actually received the questionnaire; nor does it mean that the original list from which the sample was drawn did not have flaws, such as duplications or wrong addresses. An alternative measure uses the find rate as the basis for calculating response, which also is of particular value in surveys of hard to locate populations (Nieva, 1989). In calculating the find rate, a researcher must differentiate nonresponding sample members who received their mail (and refused to respond) from those who were never located. The total find rate is equal to the sum of completed surveys, ineligibles, actual refusals, and assumed refusals divided by the total sample. The survey completion rate is the percentage of located sample members who returned completed questionnaires.

Other aspects of mail surveys that are of concern to research designers include follow-up, reminder, questionnaire format and length, survey sponsorship, endorsement, type of postage, personalization, type of cover letter, anonymity and confidentiality, deadline date premiums and rewards, and perceived time for task. Reported results of experiments involving these techniques vary, and there appears to be no strong empirical evidence that any one is universally better than the others, except for the follow-up and use of monetary incentives. There is no disagreement that use of a monetary incentive increases response rates significantly. Indeed, nonmonetary incentives (such as a pen) also appear to have such a positive impact. A major concern, however, is how much the incentive should be. Typically, amounts are one dollar. The key issue is whether a larger incentive is cost-effective. That is, does it generate a sufficiently greater response to justify the added cost? For some studies, the use of a follow-up mailing may be an alternative to monetary incentives. That is, an initial mailing and follow-ups without an incentive may be more cost-effective and generate a greater response than one mailing with an incentive.

One potential problem with using any incentive, monetary or nonmonetary, is that it may result in responses from people who otherwise might not respond, and the quality of such responses may be suspect. Table 5.5 shows some alternative versions for some of the dimensions of a mail survey. An example of a cover letter included as the first page of a questionnaire is shown in Exhibit 5.9. This letter could have been a separate page if more space was needed for the questionnaire. There is no evidence that any alternative is universally better than another within each dimension. The best rule of thumb is to use common sense. Further discussion of these will be found in the many review articles and studies published in such sources as the *Journal of Marketing Research* and *Public Opinion Quarterly*, in the book by Bourque and Fielder (2003b), and in the classic works of Dillman (1978, 2000).

Table 5.5   Selected Dimensions of a Mail Survey and Alternatives for Choice

Dimension	Alternatives
Preliminary notification	Letter, postcard, telephone call, e-mail, none
Reminder	Letter, postcard, telephone call, e-mail, none
Follow-up (additional mailing)	Yes (how many?), no
Cover letter	Separate item, included as first page of questionnaire Personalized, nonpersonalized Color of ink in signature (black, blue)
Length of questionnaire	Number of pages
Format of questionnaire	Print front, print front and back, individual stapled pages, booklet
Type of outgoing postage	First-class stamp, first-class metered, bulk, nonprofit (where appropriate)
Return envelope postage	First-class stamp, metered, first-class permit, none
Inducements	Monetary (amount), nonmonetary (pen, silver jewelry, trinkets of all types), contribution to charity, none when given (prepaid, promise to pay)
Coding with a number	Yes (on questionnaire, on return envelope), none
Anonymity/Confidentiality	Yes, no
Endorsement	Yes, no

EXHIBIT 5.9   Example of a Cover Letter

My colleague, Dr. David Boush, and I are engaged in a study of consumers' use of financial services. The broad objective of this study is to gain an understanding of how people use banks and similar financial organizations, and what characteristics influence their behavior with such companies. The Bank of Anytown has agreed to cooperate with us in this endeavor by assisting us in data collection.

The enclosed questionnaire is being sent to a large number of the customers of the Bank of Anytown, each of whom has been selected by a random process. I would greatly appreciate your completing the questionnaire and returning it in the envelope provided. Please note that you do not have to add postage to this envelope.

All individual replies will be kept in strictest confidence. No person associated with The Bank of Anytown will see any questionnaire. Only aggregate results will be shown in our write-up of the results. No person other than Dr. Boush, myself, and our research assistant will ever see a completed questionnaire. If you do not wish to participate in this survey simply discard the questionnaire. Completing and returning the questionnaire constitutes your consent to participate.

The code number at the top of the questionnaire will be used only for identifying those people who have not responded so that he or she will not be burdened by receiving a follow-up mailing. After the second mailing has been made, all records that match a number with a person's name will be destroyed.

The success of this project depends upon the assistance of persons such as yourself. If you have any questions, please call me at 503-346-4423.

Sincerely,

Gerald Albaum
Professor of Marketing

Since people responding to a mail questionnaire tend to do so because they have stronger feelings about the subject than the nonrespondents, biased results are to be expected (see Exhibit 5.10). To measure this bias, it is necessary to contact a sample of the nonrespondents by other means, usually telephone interviews. This is a type of nonresponse validation. The low level of response, when combined with the additional mailings and telephone (or personal) interviews of nonrespondents, results in substantial increases in the per-interview cost. The initial low cost per mailing may therefore be illusory. On the other hand, the nonresponse validation may indicate that populate subgroups have not been omitted and that results may not be biased.

Additional limitations are the length of time required to complete the study and the inability to ensure that questions are fully understood and answers are properly recorded. Proper administration can hold this to a minimum.

EXHIBIT 5.10   Theories of Mail Survey Response

Why do people participate as respondents in a survey? The question is often asked by marketing researchers, perhaps all too often implicitly, and seldom is an answer provided other than in terms of specific techniques (including inducements) that have been used to increase participation. The following theories are among those proposed (and studied to varying degrees) as answers to this question (Evangelista, Albaum, & Poon, 1999).

Exchange

The process of using mail survey techniques to obtain information from potential respondents can be viewed as a special case of *social exchange*. Very simply, social exchange theory asserts that the actions of individuals are motivated by the return (or rewards) these actions are expected to, or usually do, bring from others. Whether a given behavior occurs is a function of the perceived costs of engaging in that activity and the rewards (not necessarily monetary) one expects the other participant to provide at a later date. In order that survey response be maximized by this theory, three conditions must be present:

1. The costs for responding must be minimized.
2. The rewards must be maximized.
3. There must be a belief by potential respondents that such rewards will, in fact, be provided.

Cognitive Dissonance

Cognitive dissonance theory appears to provide a mechanism for integrating, within a single model, much of the empirical research that has been done on inducement techniques for survey response. As used to explain survey response, the theory postulates that reducing dissonance is an important component of the "respond/not respond" decision by potential survey respondents.

The process is triggered by receipt of a questionnaire and cover letter asking for participation. Assuming that failure to respond might be inconsistent with a person's self-perception of being a helpful person, or perhaps at least one who honors reasonable requests, failure to respond will produce a state of dissonance that the potential respondent seeks to reduce by becoming a survey respondent. Since the decision process involves a series of decisions for some people, delaying the ultimate decision may be a way to avoid completing the questionnaire without having to reject the request outright (and thus experience dissonance). Delaying a decision, therefore, may in itself be a dissonance-reducing response.

Self-Perception

Self-perception theory asserts that people infer attitudes and knowledge of themselves through interpretations made about the causes of their behavior. Interpretations are made on the basis of self-observation. To the extent that a person's behavior is attributed to internal causes and is not perceived as due to circumstantial pressures, a positive attitude toward the behavior develops. These attitudes (self-perception) then affect subsequent behavior.

The self-perception paradigm has been extended to the broad issue of mail survey response. To increase the precision of this paradigm, the concepts of *salience* (behaviors one has attended to), *favorability* (the affect or feeling generated by a given behavioral experience), and *availability* (information in memory) are utilized. In addition, to enhance the effects of these on response, researchers should create labels. *Labeling* involves classifying people on the basis of their behavior such that they will later act in a manner consistent with the characterization. Self-perception would predict that labeling one's behavior would cause that person to view himself or herself as the kind of person who engages in such behavior; therefore, the likelihood of later label-consistent behavior is increased.

Commitment and Involvement

Of concern here is the range of allegiance an individual may be said to have for any system of which he or she is a member. Consistent behavior is a central theme, including the following characteristics:

1. Persists over some period of time

2. Leads to the pursuit of at least one common goal

3. Rejects other acts of behavior

Consequently, the major elements of commitment are viewed as including the following:

1. The individual is in a position in which his or her decision regarding particular behavior has consequences for other interests and activities not necessarily related to it.

2. The person is in that position by his or her own prior behavior.

3. The committed person must recognize the interest created by one's prior action, and realize it as being necessary.

A person who is highly committed to some activity is less likely to terminate the activity than one who is uncommitted.

The theory of commitment (or involvement) can be extended to explain survey response behavior. To do this requires recognition that commitment can be attached to many different aspects of a survey, such as the source or the sponsor, the researcher, the topic and issues being studied, and/or the research process itself. To a large extent, commitment is manifested by interest in what is being asked of the potential respondent. The following hypotheses (untested) can be proposed:

1. The less favorable the attitude toward a survey's sponsor, topic, and so forth, the less involvement with, and thus commitment to, anything related to that study.

2. The less the extent of involvement, the more behavior productive of disorder (e.g., nonresponse, deliberate reporting of false information, etc.) is perceived as legitimate.

3. The more behavior productive of disorder is perceived as legitimate, the less favorable the attitude toward the survey.

The overall process of data collection from a mail survey is summarized in Figure 5.3, which illustrates the sequence of contact activities for an optimal mail survey. With minor modifications this general sequence is applicable to personal interview, telephone, and e-mail surveys. When designing a survey, the researcher must consider issues that can affect response rate and data quality, including the following:

- Preliminary notification
- Time required of respondent
- Use of inducements
- Open coding
- Identification of sponsor and source
- Follow-up policy
- Questionnaire (measurement instrument) design
- When to contact respondents
- Type of appeal to use
- Potential respondents' interest and commitment to the topic and/or study
- Others unique to a specific technique of data collection (e.g., type of postage for a mail survey)

Variations on Mail Interview

A frequently used variation of the mail interview is the warranty form. Most consumer durables have a warranty card or other type of form included in the packaging. The buyer is instructed to fill out the card and send it to the manufacturer if he or she wishes to take advantage of the warranty. Information is usually requested on where the item was purchased, what kind of store or outlet sold it, and when it was purchased. If the item is of the type that may be used as a gift (an electric shaver, for example), information on the purpose for the purchase

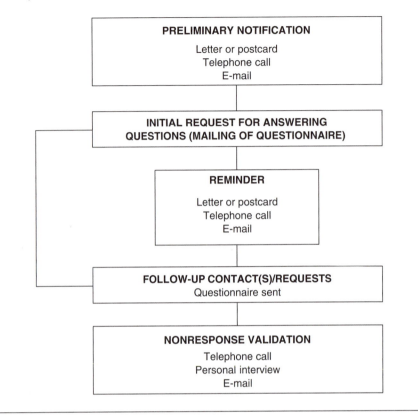

Figure 5.3   Sequence of Contact Activities for Ideal Mail Survey

is also sought. Finally, many warranty forms ask for information about variables constituting lifestyle. Although warranty cards do not provide an extensive amount of information, response rates are substantially higher than for the usual mail questionnaire. They are very useful for creating a database.

Another variation of the mail questionnaire is a questionnaire that is delivered personally and is either returned via a representative of the research organization or by mail. Dealer surveys are often conducted in this manner, with salespeople delivering the questionnaires. This is known as a drop-off/pick-up survey.

A third variation is the questionnaire that is either printed or inserted in a newspaper or magazine. Potential respondents are requested to mail or fax this back to a designated address/fax number. Among the many problems with this approach is the lack of any formalized control over the sample. Yet, despite this major limitation, the approach does have a possibility of better hitting the target population, depending on the match between the readership and the population of interest. An example is drawn in Figure 5.4, which was used by Microsoft in the *South China Morning Post* newspaper in Hong Kong.

A similar method has been used to survey audiences of classical entertainment. Surveys are inserted into the program and the respondent is asked to complete the survey and leave it

WIN MICROSOFT SOFTWARE

COMPUTER
S U R V E Y

South China Morning Post

*Readers who complete the following survey questions
have a chance to win software from Microsoft.*

Take a few minutes of your time to complete this questionnaire, and fax or mail it back to: South China Morning Post, PC Post Survey, 29/F Dorset House, 979 King's Road, Quarry Bay, Hong Kong, Fax: 2811-4804.

Microsoft has kindly consented to provide the following gifts to respondents who fill out and return the questionnaire.

1. First 5 who return the questionnaire will receive a copy of Microsoft Windows 95 and Internet Starter Kit.

2. Following 100 respondents will receive a copy of Microsoft Internet Starter Kit.

3. Following 200 respondents will receive a copy of Microsoft CD Games for Windows 95.

Kindly return this questionnaire to us by May 15, 1996.

1. Rate the following topics according to how interested you would be in reading about it (1=Interested; 2=Somewhat Interested; 3=Not Interested).

Hardware	1	2	3
Software	1	2	3
Internet	1	2	3
Upgrading Hardware and Software	1	2	3
Overcoming Technology Problems	1	2	3
Windows 95 Tips	1	2	3
_____	1	2	3
_____	1	2	3

2. Please check the products you currently own or/and plan to purchase the near future.

	Currently Own	Plan to Purchase
Hardware (please specify)	_____	_____
Software (please specify)	_____	_____
Peripherals (please specify)	_____	_____

3. Which column in this issue of PC post do you like most?
_____
_____
_____

4. What columns would you like us to add in the future?
(If you have other suggestions, please feel free to fax us at 2811-4804)
_____
_____

5. Regarding the usage of Internet, please indicate whether you are interested in the following topics (check Y=Yes or N=No)

Overall Introduction on the Internet	___Yes	___No
How to Get On-Line	___Yes	___No
World Wide Web (WWW)	___Yes	___No
Service Providers List	___Yes	___No
General Tips to Internet Users	___Yes	___No
Business Softwares	___Yes	___No

6. Regarding the web sites, please indicate what topics you are interested in

❑ News   ❑ Business/Finance   ❑ Games
❑ Sports   ❑ Meeting People   ❑ Software download
❑ Other_____

7. Are you currently an Internet user?
___Yes   ___No

8. If you replied NO in question 7, do you plan to subscribe to an Internet service in the near future?
___Yes   ___No

9. If you replied Yes in question 7, which Internet Service Provider (ISP) are you currently using?
_____
_____

10. What browser do you use?

❑ Netscape ❑ Microsoft Internet Explorer ❑ Mosaic ❑ Other_____

11. What is the average time a week you spend surfing on the Internet?
_____

12. What difficulties do you usually encounter when using the Internet? (Please tick)

❑ Busy Line   ❑ Transmission speed limitations
❑ Dropping line while downloading   ❑ Difficult to find interesting site
❑ Technical Problems sometimes occur ❑ Other_____

13. What new services do you hope to see on the Internet?

❑ Internet Phone   ❑ Home banking
❑ Home shopping   ❑ Creating your home page
❑ Other: _____

14. What type of PC do you own?
❑ 386   ❑ 486   ❑ Pentium   ❑ Other_____

15. How much RAM do you have?
❑ 4 MB   ❑ 8MB   ❑ 16 MB   ❑ Other_____

16. Do you own a modem?
❑ Yes   ❑ No

17. What is the speed of your modem?
_____

ABOUT YOU

Name : _____ Title : _____

Name of Company : _____

Address :_____

Tel No.: _____ Fax No.: _____ E-mail Add.: _____

Age Group:
_____ Below 15
_____ 15-25 years
_____ 26-35 years
_____ 36-45 years
_____ 46-55 years
_____ Above 55 years

Highest Level of Education:_____ Primary
_____ Secondary / High School
_____ Post-secondary
_____ University / Post-graduate

Income Group:
(per year)
_____ None
_____ Less than HK$200,000
_____ HK$200,000 - 299,999
_____ HK$300,000 - 499,999
_____ HK$500,000 - 699,999
_____ HK$700,000 - 999,999
_____ HK$1 - 1.5 million
_____ HK$1.5 or more

Sponsored by
Microsoft

Figure 5.4   Reprinted with permission from the *South China Morning Post,* April 28, 1996.

in a designated place. This approach can lower administration and return costs but lead to greater costs in terms of technical quality. This can be minimized by sound control over the research procedure.

Another modification of including a questionnaire in a printed publication asks respondents to return the questionnaire by fax. One advantage of this approach is that those who do respond will be truly committed to the project. But, again there is little control over the sample. A major Airlines routinely printed questionnaires to be returned by fax in its in-flight magazine.

In addition to asking that completed questionnaires be returned by fax, the entire survey can be conducted via fax. In previous research that examined the use of fax, findings indicate that compared to mail, fax responses arrived quicker and at a greater rate (Dickson & MacLachlan, 1992, 1996). Potential advantages of using fax include quick contact, rapid response, retention of the original document format and visual images used, modest cost, and automated faxing that works directly with the computer (Baker, Hozier, & Rogers, 1999). One hybrid approach, used by McDonalds, had employees ask patrons to take a brief survey on a mark sense sheet, as shown in Figure 5.5. When completed, the sheets were faxed for processing using a technique that converted the image directly to data without being printed to paper on the receiving end. The results were then available online in real time. Some potential drawbacks are that the recipient's fax machine will determine the resolution and density—and thus the quality—of the received document, fax machines often jam and/or send multiple pages through as one page because the paper sticks together, and anonymity cannot be guaranteed as the return fax normally shows the respondent's fax number. Despite these limitations, use of the fax for data collection is a viable technique for business-to-business research situations.

Yet another variation, one that combines the monetary incentive and the questionnaire, is the answer check. The questions to be answered are printed on the back of a commercial bank check. The major benefit of this approach is reduced cost. This lower cost is obtained, however, at the expense of the amount of information obtainable and the low response to open-ended questions.

When there is concern in a mail survey for anonymity, and at the same time the researcher desires to know who has already responded so that reminder notification or follow-up mailings will not be made, a useful technique is to enclose with the mailing a postcard that can be returned by the respondent indicating that he or she has responded as requested. An illustration of a simple-structured card is shown in Figure 5.6.

Potential survey respondents are being exposed directly to high technology and the electronic age in surveys. Portable automated polling machines are being used to conduct surveys in retail stores, hotels, casinos, shopping malls, and other places. These are interactive machines whose reliability has proved to be very good.

Another form of interactive interviewing involves using mail to get the questionnaire to the respondent. A computer diskette is mailed to the respondent, who is asked to answer the questionnaire on the diskette. This is known as disk-by-mail. Incentives can be included since mail is the mode of delivery, and a return mailer is necessary. Different operating system versions for PCs and Macs may need to be developed. Experience has shown that the equivalent of a 20–25 page questionnaire can be sent, meaning that a study may be using a questionnaire that takes 25 to 50 minutes complete. Typically, response rates are higher and the cost lower than for regular mail surveys. Potential respondents need to be screened to obtain agreement to participate and the necessary information for mailing the disk. In addition, the potential

Form 0089
© Copyright 1998
Ver 1.00

Please rate this McDonald's:

Date

MM DD YY

FREE Low Fat Ice Cream Cone!

We at McDonald's take pride in providing you with the highest standards of QUALITY, SERVICE, CLEANLINESS and VALUE in the restaurant industry. Your opinion is ***extremely important*** in evaluating our business. Thank you for taking a moment to answer the following questions:

Please completely fill in your selection
Please use dark ink or heavy pencil
Correct Mark ● Incorrect Marks ✗ ✓ ◉

Today's visit was			Inside the Restaurant	Through the Drive-Thru
Today's visit was between..................			6:00 am - 7:00 am	7:00 am - 8:00 am
	8:00 am - 9:00 am	9:00 am - 10:00 am	10:00 am - 11:00 am	11:00 am - 12:00 noon
	12:00 noon - 1:00 pm	1:00 pm - 2:00 pm	2:00 pm - 3:00 pm	3:00 pm - 4:00 pm
	4:00 pm - 5:00 pm	5:00 pm - 6:00 pm	6:00 pm - 7:00 pm	7:00 pm - 8:00 pm
	8:00 pm - 9:00 pm	9:00 pm - 10:00 pm	10:00 pm - 11:00 pm	
Place of residence..............................			Local (St. George, Santa Clara, Washington)	Outside a 100 mile radius
Direction..			Off Northbound Freeway	Off Southbound Freeway

Food Quality	Excellent	Very Good	Average	Needs Improvement	Unsatisfactory
Food served hot and fresh..........................					
Taste and flavor of food..........................					
Variety of menu items..........................					
Overall food quality..........................					
Service					
Order was correct and complete..................					
Responsiveness of service					
When hurried..........................					
When unhurried..........................					
Availability of ketchup, sauces, utensils, straws, napkins, etc					
Clarity of ordering system					
Menu board..........................					
Drive-thru sound system (if applicable).........					
Employee communication..........................					
Friendly and courteous attitude of employees.............					
Responsiveness to special requests or problems........					
Value					
Food quantity appropriate to cost..........................					
Competitive prices					
Restaurant					
Comfort and appearance..........................					
Cleanliness of the restaurant					
Dining area..........................					
Service area..........................					
Restroom..........................					
Drive-thru convenient and easy to use.......................					

Please return survey to any St. George McDonald's Location for a complimentary Ice Cream Cone.

10803
Survey
#0898

Not Valid if returned after Sept. 25, 1998

Figure 5.5 Example of Questionnaire Processed by Fax

Cascade Consulting Group
P.O. Box 1234
Albuquerque. NM 87112

This postcard is to inform you that I have returned my questionnaire for the bank study in
a separate envelope on _____ .
                                        (date)

                                                        _____

                                                        Your name (please print)

Identification Number: 335 *(if coding is used)*

Figure 5.6   Example of Separate Return Card Used to Protect Anonymity

respondent's computer system needs to be known so that the proper version of the question-naire can be sent. Overall, the benefits of CATI are transferred to a self-administered inter-view format. The viability of this method depends upon the incidence of personal computers in the targeted population. Clearly this can be useful in business-to-business research with rigorous surveys that require research for reported data or stopping and restarting the survey. But the Internet-based survey is an alternative.

As computer coverage in home markets increases, the use of electronic surveys, particu-larly by e-mail and Internet, will increase. The use of online surveys is discussed in depth in Chapter 6.

Direct computer interactive data collection is being used increasingly. With the rapid tech-nological advancements in laptop and notebook personal computers, it is not difficult for interviewers to take these with them, especially in mall-intercept approaches. As the public becomes used to personal computers in their everyday lives, it will be an easier transition to more regularly use computers in survey data collection.

These direct computer interactive systems are one form of so-called *electronic research* techniques. Other forms include tuning meters, UPC scanners, people meters, hand-held video cameras for self-taping of behavior, automated data collection networks, wireless keypads, touch screen, preference and perceptions analyzers, and wireless technology (cell phones, PDAs). These techniques can be used in an ad hoc study or as part of a panel study, and may be used in-home or at some other site. The usage of such techniques is expected to grow, par-ticularly as point-of-origin data collection becomes more widespread. Some of these electronic techniques are very useful in generating *single-source data*. In its purest sense, single-source means obtaining all data on product purchases and causal factors (such as media exposure, pro-motional influences, and consumer characteristics) from the same households. Single-source data typically are provided by panels, but this is not inherent for obtaining such data.

Some of the benefits of the various approaches to computer-assisted data collection in surveys are shown in Table 5.6. When comparing these methods to the non-computer-based approaches, tradeoffs must always be considered.

Table 5.6 Benefits of Computer-Assisted Survey Data Collection Methods

Benefits	Personal	On-Site		Telephone		Mail	E-mail	Fax
	Computer-Assisted Personal Interviewing	Computer-Assisted Self-Interviewing	Fully-Automated Self-Interviewing	Computer-Assisted Telephone Interviewing	Fully-Automated Telephone Interviewing	Computer Disks by Mail	Electronic Mail Survey or Web Survey	Computer-Generated Fax Survey
Respondents need not have any computer-related skills	Yes			Yes	Yes		Minimal	Yes
Allows respondent to choose own schedule for completing survey		Yes	Yes			Yes	Yes	Yes
Can easily incorporate complex branching questions into survey	Yes	Yes	Yes	Yes	Yes	Yes	Yes	
Can easily use respondent-generated words in questions throughout the survey	Yes	Yes	Yes	Yes		Yes	Some	
Can accurately measure response times of respondents to key questions	Yes	Yes	Yes	Yes	Yes	Yes	Some	

(Continued)

Table 5.6 (Continued)

Benefits	Personal	On-Site		Telephone		Mail	E-mail	Fax
	Computer-Assisted Personal Interviewing	Computer-Assisted Self-Interviewing	Fully-Automated Self-Interviewing	Computer-Assisted Telephone Interviewing	Fully-Automated Telephone Interviewing	Computer Disks by Mail	Electronic Mail Survey or Web Survey	Computer-Generated Fax Survey
Can easily display a variety of graphics and directly relate them to questions	Yes	Yes	Yes			Yes	Yes	
Eliminates need to encode data from paper surveys	Yes	Yes	Yes	Yes	Yes	Yes	Yes	Some
Errors in data less likely, compared to equivalent manual method	Yes	Yes	Yes	Yes	Yes	Yes	Yes	
Speedier data collection and encoding, compared to equivalent manual method	Yes	Yes	Yes	Yes	Yes	Yes	Yes	Yes

SOURCE: Reprinted with permission from "Data Collection Should Not Be Manual Labor," by Dacko, S. G., in *Marketing News*, 33, January 7, 1991. Published by the American Marketing Association.

One final question that can be asked about electronic-based research is whether the techniques are, in fact, real advances, or just examples of gadgetry? Similarly, as technology continues to advance as rapidly as it has in the past, some of the techniques mentioned above will become obsolete, if not already so.

STRATEGIES OF DATA COLLECTION

When designing a survey, particularly a mail survey, concern should be for the total package of survey procedures rather than any single technique (Dillman, 1978, 2000). While there has been considerable research done on individual methodological techniques, even in combination with others, misleading results can still emerge from these studies. For example, in one study three additional contact variables (preliminary notice, follow-up one, follow-up two) for a mail survey were examined experimentally, each with three alternatives. The results showed that response rate varied from 10 percent to 28 percent and the net cost per response ranged from $6.00 to $12.00. Moreover, as the number of contacts increased, the overall response rate rose about 3.5–4 percentage points for each additional contact made (Peterson, Albaum, & Kerin, 1989). Today the cost per respondent would be much higher, and there would be a wide range differing by contact strategy.

Personal-interview-based surveys and telephone-based surveys also should be designed on the basis of the total package of activities. Each of these may involve multiple contacts, including preliminary notice, follow-ups, and nonresponse validations.

The total package concept underlying survey design strategy goes beyond contacts with respondents. All aspects of a study must be considered when comparing alternative strategies. This is the essence of a total design. Table 5.7 summarizes the characteristics for eight distinct survey-based methods of data collection.

Pretesting and Pilot Survey

A distinction should be made between a pretest and a pilot survey. Pretesting is an activity related to the development of the questionnaire or measurement instrument to be used in a survey or experiment. In contrast, a pilot survey is a small-scale test of what the survey is to be, including all activities that will go into the final survey.

Pretesting a questionnaire answers two broad questions:

1. Are we asking "good" questions?

2. Does the questionnaire flows smoothly, and is the question sequence is logical?

Pretesting does not, however, ensure that the questionnaire (or even the survey) will be valid, particularly in its content. A general rule of thumb for most surveys is that a pretest of about 30 to100 interviews is adequate, provided this covers all subgroups in the main survey population. Ideally, the sample for the pretest should mirror in composition that of the main survey.

The pilot study is designed to ascertain whether all the elements in the survey fit together. Thus, questionnaire pretesting may be part of the pilot study but normally should not be. One

Table 5.7   Comparative Evaluation of Alternative Survey Methods of Data Collection

Criteria	Telephone CATI	In-Home Interviews	Mall-Intercept Interviews	CAPI	Mail Surveys	Mail Panels	Internet/ Web
Flexibility of data collection	Moderate to high	High	High	Moderate to high	Low	Low	Moderate to high
Diversity of questions	Low	High	High	High	Moderate	Moderate	Moderate to high
Use of physical stimuli	Low	Moderate to high	High	High	Moderate	Moderate	Moderate
Sample Control	Moderate to high	Potentially high	Moderate	Moderate	Low	Moderate to high	Low to moderate
Control of data collection environment	Moderate	Moderate to high	High	High	Low	Low	Low
Control of field force	Moderate	Low	Moderate	Moderate	High	High	High
Quantity of data	Low	High	Moderate	Moderate	Moderate	High	Moderate
Response rate	Moderate	High	High	High	Low	Moderate	Very low
Perceived anonymity of respondent	Moderate	Low	Low	Low	High	High	High
Social desirability	Moderate	High	High	Moderate to high	Low	Low	Low
Obtaining sensitive information	High	Low	Low	Low to moderate	High	Moderate to high	High
Potential for interviewer bias	Moderate	High	High	Low	None	None	None
Speed	High	Moderate	Moderate to high	Moderate to high	Low	Low to moderate	Very high
Cost	Moderate	High	Moderate to high	Moderate to high	Low	Low to moderate	Low

SOURCE: From Malhotra, N., *Marketing Research: An Applied Orientation,* 4th edition, Copyright © 2004. Reprinted with permission of Pearson Education, Inc., Upper Saddle River, NJ.

aspect of the pilot survey is that it can help researchers decide the size of the original sample for the main survey. Response to the pilot can be used, together with the desired obtained sample size, to determine the size of the original sample.

Both pretesting and pilot surveys can provide information helpful to manage some of the sources of potential research error. Moreover, in the long run they can both make a survey more efficient and effective.

THE USE OF PANELS

Panels are widely used in marketing research. In the preceding chapter we discussed the continuous panel as used by such syndicated services as Market Research Corporation of America. In this chapter we present some general characteristics of panels. Although the panel concept has been used in business-to-business marketing research, by far its greatest application has been in studying consumer purchase and consumption patterns, as well as other aspects of consumer behavior. For example, panels have been effectively used to develop early forecasts of long-run sales for new products. There are major commercial consumer panel organizations, and a number of consumer product companies maintain their own panels or create short-term ad hoc panels as the need arises to test new products. In addition, several universities maintain consumer panels to obtain research data and generate revenues by providing data to others. Moreover, the application of electronic and communications technology has encouraged new types of panels using advertising delivery via split-cable television and in-store scanner recording of purchases.

The distinguishing feature of a panel is repeated data collection from a sample of respondents on the same topic. The repeated collection of data from panels creates both opportunities and problems. Panel studies appear to offer at least three advantages over one-time surveys:

1. Deeper analysis of the data is possible so that the researcher can, for example, determine whether an overall change is attributable primarily to a unidirectional shift for the whole sample or reflects overlapping changes for subgroups.

2. Additional measurement precision is gained from matching response from one interview/ data collection point to another.

3. Panel studies offer flexibility that allows later inquiries to explain earlier findings.

Because responses are obtained at two or more times, the researcher assumes that an event happens or can happen (i.e., changes may occur) during the time interval of interest. In fact, it is just such changes, analyzed in the form of a turnover table, that provide the heart of panel analyses. Assume that we have changed the package in one market for a brand of tissue called Wipe, and that we run a survey of 200 people purchasing the product two weeks before the change (T_1) and a similar measure for the week after (T_2). The results are shown in Table 5.8. Both (A) and (B) tell us that the gross increase in sales of Wipe over X (this represents all other brands) is 20 units (or 10 percent). However, only the turnover table from the panel in (B) can tell us that 20 former buyers of Wipe switched to X and that 40 former buyers of X switched to Wipe. In those instances where there is experimental manipulation, such as the

Table 5.8   Change in Sales of Wipe Between T_1 and T_2 (Hypothetical Data)

(A) Cross-Sectional

	T_1	T_2
Bought Wipe	100	120
Bought X	100	80
Number of Purchasers	200	200

(B) Panel

		T_1		
		Bought Wipe	Bought X	
At T_2	Bought Wipe	80	40	120
	Bought X	20	60	80
		100	100	N = 200

introduction of a new product or the use of split-cable advertising, the manipulation is presumed to cause changes between time x (when the change is made) and time $x + 1$. We discuss panels and experimental design in Chapter 8.

Panel studies are a special case of longitudinal research, where respondents are typically conscious of their ongoing part in responding to similar questions over a period of time. This consciousness of continuing participation can lead to panel conditioning, which may bias responses relative to what would be obtained through a cross-sectional study. As in any effort at scientific measurement, the researcher should be concerned with threats to internal validity, since internal validity is a precondition for establishing, with some degree of confidence, the causal relationship between variables. Another issue of concern is panel attrition, the extent of nonresponse that occurs in later waves of study interviewing. Some persons who were interviewed at the first time may be unwilling or unable to be interviewed later on.

There are many distinguishing characteristic of panel types. We have already mentioned different types of sponsoring organizations (such as commercial), permanence (continuous or ad hoc), and research design (nonexperiment). Panels can also be characterized by geographic coverage (ranging from national to local), whether a diary is used, data collection method (all types are used), sampling method employed for a given study (probability or not), and type of respondent.

A unique type of panel is the scanning diary panel. This panel involves recruiting shoppers in the target market area to participate in the panel, and each person typically is compensated for participation. An identification card (similar to a credit card) is given to each member of the panel household. At the end of a normal shopping trip in a cooperating store, the card is presented at the start of the checkout process. This identifies the respondent for input of purchases into the computer data bank. The types of information available from this sort of panel are similar to those discussed in the preceding chapter for scanner-based syndicated services. An added advantage here, of course, is that there is a carefully designed sample providing purchase data.

One last comment about panels is that they are often used for a cross-sectional study. When used this way and only one measurement is made, the panel is merely the source of a sample (the sample frame).

SUMMARY

This chapter first examined the various types of information that can be obtained from respondents. It then considered communication as a means to obtain information from respondents. The types of respondent interviews—structured-direct, unstructured-direct, and structured- and unstructured-indirect—were discussed.

The media through which interviews may be conducts were then considered. The personal interview, the telephone interview, the mail interview and online e-mail interview were discussed, including the merits and limitations of each. Variations of these basic methods, including electronic-based variations, were briefly described. Finally, the use of panels was presented in a general context.

ASSIGNMENT MATERIAL

1. Indicate whether you agree or disagree with the following statement and defend your position:

   One of the important reasons to use surveys is that they can obtain sound information on what people's future actions will be.

2. State the conditions under which you believe information on (a) past behavior and (b) intentions can each be a reliable predictor of future behavior.

3. You are a senior analyst in the marketing research department of a major steel producer. You have been requested to make a forecast of domestic automobile production for the forthcoming calendar year and, from this forecast, make a forecast of the total tonnage of steel to be used by the automobile manufacturers.
   a. What information, if any, could be obtained from respondents that would be useful to forecast the steel tonnage to be used by the automobile manufactures? If it is concluded that no useful information could be obtained from respondents, indicate so and do not answer questions (b) though (d).
   b. What techniques are applicable to obtain each item of information?
   c. Design a survey to obtain the information desired. Prepare all instructions, collection forms, and other materials required to obtain such information.
   d. Estimate the cost to conduct the survey you have designed.

4. You are a product manager for Brand M peanut butter, a nationally distributed brand. Brand M has been declining in absolute level of sales for the last four months. What information, if any, could be obtained from respondents that would be useful to determine the cause or causes of this decline?

5. You are the manager of product planning and marketing research for the personal appliances department of a large and widely diversified corporation. You have under consideration a proposal to produce and market a hearing aid, an appliance line in which your company currently does not have a product.

    a. What information, if any, could be obtained from respondents that would be useful to decide whether to develop and introduce a hearing aid? If it is concluded that no useful information could be obtained from respondents, indicate so and do not answer questions (b) through (d).

    b. What techniques are applicable to obtain each type of information?

    c. Design a survey to obtain the information desired. Prepare all instructions, collection forms, and other materials required to obtain such information.

    d. Estimate the cost to conduct the survey you have designed.

    e. How might you incorporate the use of a computer in data collection?

6. "All things considered, and without cost as a determining factor, the most valid and reliable approach to data collection in a survey is a personal interview." Comment.

7. A merchants' association for a relatively small shopping center located in a metropolitan area with a population of 125,000 conducted a survey of shoppers. The survey was conducted with no interviewers present. Instead, copies of the one-page questionnaire (front and back used) were placed on a table in the mall with a sign asking people to participate and then place the completed questionnaire in a box on the table.

    a. Evaluate this survey.

    b. If you had been conducting the survey, how would you have done it?

REFERENCES

Baker, K. G., Hozier, G. C., Jr., & Rogers, R. D. (1999, February). *E-Mail, mail and fax survey research: Response pattern comparisons.* Paper presented at the 6th Annual Meeting of the American Society of Business and Behavioral Sciences, Las Vegas, NV.

Becker, E. E. (1995, January 2). Automated interviewing has advantages. *Marketing News, 29,* 9.

Bourque, L. B., & Fielder, E. P. (2003a). *How to conduct telephone surveys.* Thousand Oaks, CA: Sage.

Bourque, L. B., & Fielder, E. P. (2003b). *How to conduct self-administered and mail surveys.* Thousand Oaks, CA: Sage.

Cacioppo, L. (2000, September). Measuring and managing customer satisfaction. *Quality Digest,* 49–53.

Cochran, C. (2001, November). Customer satisfaction: The elusive quality. *Quality Digest,* 45–50.

Conrad, F. G., & Schober, M. F. (2000). Clarifying question meaning in a household telephone survey. *Public Opinion Quarterly, 64*(1), 1–28.

Dacko, S. G. (1995, August 28). Data collection should not be manual labor. *Marketing News, 29,* 31.

Davern, M., Rockford, T. H., Sherrod, R., & Campbell, S. (2003). Prepaid monetary incentives and data quality in face-to-face interviews. *Public Opinion Quarterly, 67,* 139–147.

Dickson, J. P., & MacLachlan, D. L. (1992, September). Fax surveys? Study finds the time may be right for business research. *Journal of Marketing Research, 29*(3), 26–30.

Dickson, J. P., & MacLachlan, D. L. (1996, February). Fax surveys: Return patterns and comparison with mail surveys. *Journal of Marketing Research, 33,* 108–113.

Dillman, D. A. (1978). *Mail and telephone surveys: The total design method.* New York: Wiley-Interscience.

Dillman, D. A. (2000). *Mail and internet surveys: The tailored design method* (2nd ed.). New York: Wiley.

Eisenfeld, B. (2003, March 3). Phone interviews may garner more data. *Marketing News, 37,* 57.

European Society for Opinion and Marketing Research. (1989). *Distinguishing telephone research from telemarketing: ESOMAR guidelines.* Amsterdam: ESOMAR.

Evangelista, F., Albaum, G., & Poon, P. (1999, April). An empirical test of alternative theories of survey response behavior. *Journal of the Market Research Society, 41,* 2, 227–244.

Fowler, F. J. (1991). Reducing interviewer-related error through interviewer training, supervision, and other means. In P. P. Bremer, R. M. Groves, L. E. Lyberg, N. A. Mathiowetz, & S. Sudman, *Measurement errors in surveys* (pp. 259–278). New York: Wiley.

Fowler, F. J., & Mangione, T. W. (1990). *Standardized survey interviewing: Minimizing interviewer-related errors.* Newbury Park, CA: Sage.

Freeman, L. (2001, September 24). Small, smaller, smallest: New analytical tools can slice markets too thin. *Marketing News, 35,* 1ff.

Gaskell, G. D., Wright, D. B., & O'Muircheartaigh, C. A. (2000, Spring). Telescoping of landmark events. *Public Opinion Quarterly, 64,* 77–89.

Goldstein, K. M., & Jennings, M. K. (2002). The effect of advance letters on cooperation in a list sample telephone survey. *Public Opinion Quarterly, 66,* 608–617.

James, D. (2002, May 13). Better together. *Marketing News, 36,* 15–16.

Jarvis, S. (2002, February 4). CMOR finds survey refusal rate still rising. *Marketing News, 36,* 4.

Judge, P. C. (1998, January 26). Are tech buyers different? *BusinessWeek,* pp. 64–68.

Kahle, L. R. (1983). *Social values and social change: adaptation to life in America.* New York: Praeger.

Kahn, R. L., & Cannell, C. F. (1957). *The dynamics of interviewing: Theory, techniques and cases.* New York: Wiley.

Kay, D. (1997, January 6). Go where the consumers are and talk to them. *Marketing News, 31,* 14.

Long, J., Tomak, K., & Whinston, A. B. (2003, January 20). Calling all customers: Conduct marketing surveys via cell phones. *Marketing News, 37,* 18–22.

Malhotra, N. K. (2004). *Marketing research: An applied orientation* (4th ed.). Upper Saddle River, NJ: Pearson Education.

Mitchell, A. (1983). *The nine American lifestyles.* New York: Warner Books.

Morwitz, V. G. (1997). It seems like only yesterday: The nature and consequences of telescoping errors in marketing research. *Journal of Consumer Psychology, 6*(1), 1–29.

Neal, W. D. (2000, June 5). When measuring loyalty satisfactorily, don't measure CS. *Marketing News, 34,* 19.

Nieva, V. F (1989). Refining response rate calculations for mail surveys: Address verification procedures. Paper presented at the annual meeting of the American Association for Public Opinion Research.

Oldendick, R. W. (1994). The answering machine generation. *Public Opinion Quarterly, 58,* 264–273.

Peterson, R. A., Albaum, G., & Kerin, R. A. (1989, July). A note on alternative contact strategies in mail surveys. *Journal of the Market Research Society, 31*(3), 409–418.

Politz, A., & Simmons, W. (1949, March). An attempt to get the 'not at homes' into the sample without callbacks. *Journal of the American Statistical Association, 44,* 9–31.

Reid, P. M. (1984, January 6). 'Purists' may disagree, but almost all types of surveys can be conducted in malls. *Marketing News, 18*(Sec. 1), 5.

Rochford, L., & Venable, C. F. (1995, Spring). Surveying a targeted population segment: The effects of endorsement on mail questionnaire response rate. *Journal of Marketing Theory and Practice,* pp. 86–97.

Schober, M. F., & Conrad, F. G. (1997). Does conversational interviewing reduce survey measurement error? *Public Opinion Quarterly, 61,* 576–602.

Shapiro, A., & Schwartz, J. (1986, January 3). Research must be as sophisticated as the product it studies. *Marketing News, 20,* 2.

Singer, E., Van Hoewyk, J., & Maher, M. P. (2000, Summer). Experiments with incentives in telephone surveys. *Public Opinion Quarterly, 64* (2), 171–188.

Smith, K. T. (1989, September 11). Most research firms use mall intercepts. *Marketing News, 23,* 16.

Stewart, C. J., & Cash, W. B. (1985). *Interviewing principles and practices* (4th ed.). Dubuque, IA: William C. Brown.

Sudman, S., Finn, A., & Lannam, L. (1984, Summer). The use of bounded recall procedures in single interviews. *Public Opinion Quarterly, 48,* 520–524.

Swinyard, W. (1994a). *The six nations of Harley-Davidson owners.* (Research Report.) Provo, UT: Marriott School of Management, Brigham Young University.

Swinyard, W. (1994b). *The characteristic low rumble: Lifestyles of Harley-Davidson market segments.* (Research Report.) Provo, UT: Marriott School of Management, Brigham Young University.

Teitler, J. D., Reichman, N. E., & Sprachman, S. (2003). Cost and benefits of improving response rates for a hard-to-reach population. *Public Opinion Quarterly, 67,* 126–138.

Triplett, T. (1994, October 24). Survey system has human touch without the human. *Marketing News, 28,* 16.

Wagner, J., & Hanna, S. (1983, December). The effectiveness of family life cycle variables in consumer expenditures research. *Journal of Consumer Research, 10,* 281–291.

Warner, W. L., Meeker, M., & Eells, K. (1960). *Social class in America.* New York: Harper & Row.

Wells, W. D., & Gubar, G. (1966, November). Life cycle concept in marketing research. *Journal of Marketing Research, 3,* 355–363.

Wilkinson, G. W. (1989, September). Getting and using information, the United Way. *Marketing Research, 1,* 5–12.

Wiseman, F., Schafer, M., & Schafer, R. (1983). An experimental test of the effects of a monetary incentive on cooperation rates and data collection costs in central-location interviewing. *Journal of Marketing Research, 20,* 439–442.

Xu, M., Bates, B. J., & Schweitzer, J. C. (1993). The impact of messages on survey participation in answering machine households. *Public Opinion Quarterly, 57,* 232–237.

Chapter 6

ONLINE MARKETING RESEARCH

Web and e-mail surveys promise to be a driving force in marketing research as access to the Internet increases throughout the world. Current projections indicate that by the year 2005, 75 percent of all U.S. households will have Internet access, and by the year 2010, 90 percent of all U.S. households will have Internet access.

The Internet has experienced a growth rate that has exceeded any other modern technology, including the telephone, VCR, or even TV. However, the Internet has diffused from a highly educated, white-collar, upper-income, male dominated core. At the opposite end of the spectrum, the elderly, single mothers, African Americans and Hispanics, and lower-income individuals are less likely to adopt or have access to the Web.

Until the Internet and e-mail are adopted by the entire population, online survey research of the general population may be limited. For some studies, this may be a serious limitation. However even today, special interest groups such as computer users, company employees, students, or association members may have nearly 100 percent Internet access and check e-mail on a daily basis.

Lifestyle and attitude changes are seemingly responsible for changes in the way we buy products. Strong upward trends are observed in the percentage of Internet purchases for airline tickets, CDs, DVDs, books, computer software, hardware and systems. These online customers provide excellent access for research purposes.

Advocates of online surveying quickly point to the elimination of mailing and interviewing costs, elimination of data transcription costs, and reduced turnaround time as the answer to client demand for lower cost, more timely, and more efficient surveys. As a result, online marketing research has become so widely accepted that by the year 2005, online research has been optimistically projected to account for as much as half of all marketing research revenue, topping $3 billion. While these numbers appear to be overly optimistic, it is clear that online research is growing and that researchers operate in a much faster-paced environment than ever before (see Exhibit 6.1). This pace will continue to increase as new modalities for research open: wireless PDAs, Internet-capable mobile phones, Internet TVs, and other Internet-based appliances yet to be announced. Each is an acceptable venue for interacting with the marketplace and conducting online research.

Researchers are experienced in conducting research, but often not in using or implementing online methodologies, assessing the challenges (limitations and demands) associated with the technology, or selecting and managing the respondents to be interviewed.

Jeff Miller (Miller, 2000) of Burke Research described cooperative research with the Gallup organization that was conducted to compare the way people respond to face-to-face, telephone, and online focus groups by stating that results indicate that people use more strong words (positive and negative) online. This may be because there is less social pressure, or they are more honest because they feel anonymous. Respondents to online survey questions about the likelihood of purchasing household consumer products were less likely to use the end points of the scale, "definitely will buy" and "definitely will not buy," than people responding to telephone surveys about the same products. Giving a scale online may be different from listening to scale point descriptions in a telephone interview. When online surveys were compared with paper-and-pencil surveys, the between- and within-subjects components to the experimental design showed comparability of results. Exhibit 6.2 shows the experience of one research firm.

Another study by ACNielsen (Miller, 2001) reported the results of 75 parallel tests comparing online and traditional mall intercept methods. Researchers noted high correlations in aggregate purchase intentions. While online measures may yield somewhat lower score values, recalibration of averages against appropriate norms produced accurate sales forecasts. Wilkie further reported that while responses may be similar, the demographic profiles of online and traditional respondents groups do differ. Given that the current percentage of households online is approximately 60 percent, statistical weighting of cases could be used to adjust demographic differences of online groups to match mall intercept or telephone populations. However, the possibility of weighting actually raises the question of whether to model phone or mall intercept behavior or to attempt to independently model the actual behavior of the respondents.

This chapter addresses some of the issues that must be considered to make effective use of online research and to provide a better value than conventional research approaches, including the following:

- E-mail survey error
- Probability and nonprobability survey approaches
- Internet survey software
- Online survey capabilities and technologies
- Online qualitative research

The majority of online research can be typified as a one-shot mailout, the objective of which is to obtain a sufficient number of completed responses. However there is rarely much thought given to the issues of representativeness of the sample, or validity and accuracy of the results. The question is, then, what is required for effective online research?

EXHIBIT 6.1   Growth of Online Research

Donna Wydra, director of the interactive solutions group for Market Facts, Inc., recently surveyed her clients and found that on average they plan to devote a third of their research budget to online studies in the coming years (James, 2000). John Gilbert, market research manager for Atlanta-based United Parcel Service, Inc., conducts internal research but also uses market research firms and says it's been a no-brainer to use the online medium. "Between 40 percent and 50 percent of our customers are online so it makes sense . . . nearly 40 percent of U.S. households have online access, which makes sample quality less of an issue than in the past" (James, 2000) Clients find no difference in the results of traditional and online studies, and the online studies are considerably cheaper and faster to execute. Companies need more and more data tracking the performance of e-commerce solutions and the behavior of online consumers. "It doesn't make sense to use mall research," says Dennis Gonier, president of Dallas-based Digital Marketing Services (James, 2000).

EXHIBIT 6.2   Gelb Consulting Group

Gabe Gelb is founder and senior consultant with Houston-based Gelb Consulting Group, Inc., a marketing research and consulting firm. For five years, Gelb conducted an annual survey of commercial office building candidates for Hines Property Management, part of the extensive Hines real estate development and management empire also based in Houston. The first four studies were done by mail to more than 1,000 tenants in Hines buildings throughout North America.

This year, the firm offered respondents a choice of going online and being surveyed electronically (they were holding a mailed copy of the survey form as they considered the online invitation). Ultimately 40 percent of the tenants completed the password protected online survey, which resulted in an amazing 71 percent response rate. Because the Hines managers were concerned that electronic data might differ significantly from questionnaires spelled out by hand, Gelb's team tabulated paper and Web responses separately. There was no statistical difference in the two subsets. Each Hines property manager could view the results for his property online and compare them with regional and national averages (Lamons, 2001, 9).

Online research works for more conventional surveys too. Gelb had success with using gift certificates as inducements in e-mail studies where recipients met demographic requirements. The chance to win a $50 or $100 Amazon.com gift certificate is popular, he says. The firm typically budgets $500 for these incentives and builds the cost into the total survey budget (Lamons, 2001).

Speed is another advantage of online surveys. Gelb observed that 75 percent to 80 percent of the surveys using online methodologies targeted response to be generated within 48 hours. Compare that to a telephone survey that recently was involved in a study for one of his clients: It took almost 70 days to obtain 150 interviews (Lamons, 2001). Voicemail in corporate America has created an almost impenetrable barrier to most professional survey candidates.

E-MAIL SURVEY ERROR

Researchers generally recognize four major sources of survey error:

- Coverage error
- Sampling error
- Nonresponse error
- Measurement error

These same sources of error must be addressed regardless of the mode of survey data collection. Fundamental to effective sampling is proper definition of the sampling plan. The sampling plan details the source, nature, and size of the sample. This requires that we specify, in detail, the characteristics of survey respondents and the methodology for finding and contacting these respondents. Sampling procedures are discussed in detail in Chapter 12.

The sample design includes such decisions as how to identify an appropriate sample frame—a means of accounting for the individual elements or members of the target population of interest—and determining the type of sample, whether it be a probability sample or nonprobability (judgment, convenience, or other nonrandom) sample. The objective is to minimize error and control precision and accuracy by properly selecting the sample.

Coverage Error

Coverage error occurs when the sample frame or group from which the sample is drawn does not represent the population as a whole. For example, a random sample of AOL users would be a mismatch for the adult population of the United States.

In more traditional research methods such as mail or telephone methodologies, samples are drawn from sources such as telephone directories, driver's license records, rolls of property owners, credit reports, and so forth. Companies such as Experian provide credit reports based on extensive databases that record the credit and asset acquisition (home and car buying) history of individuals. Experian is judged to be one of the most accurate sources for demographic and geographic sampling frames, but is of limited value for online e-mail surveys in that it is not at present replete with e-mail contact information and tends to ignore those who have not applied for credit.

For the time being, however, e-mail lists for specific sample frames are less than perfect. Internet businesses are regularly offered CDs containing millions of e-mail addresses for $100 or less. These lists are generally heavily loaded with business rather than consumer contacts and are rarely identified or sorted by any usable market or segment characteristic. Furthermore, no demographic information is available, and, if included, is highly suspect.

Firms such as Experian, NetCreations (postmasterdirect.com), sendmoreinfo.com, and surveysampling.com offer e-mail addresses selected by gender, interests (computers, electronics, family, finance, Internet, medical, and travel), and online purchasing. Furthermore these lists consist of what is known as double opt-in, meaning that the users have specifically indicated their agreement to receive surveys or other promotional materials. The more detailed the sample criteria selected by the researcher, the higher the cost of these listings. Targeted specialty lists that reduce coverage error are not inexpensive, often costing 50 cents or more per delivered e-mail address and much more per completed response. E-mail name brokers make a practice of not providing the list, but of sending the survey invitation out, thereby controlling their list and avoiding repeated use of the list.

Because online sampling frames rarely include all elements of the target population, coverage error will continue to be the greatest source of inaccuracy for online surveys for many years to come. While this same problem is often encountered in the use of mail and phone lists, it is not as severe as with online e-mail lists, which are often based on lists from sites that have specialized hobby and interest affiliations. Selecting lists from carefully constructed probability panels or panels having millions of members helps in reducing coverage error.

Sampling Error

Sampling error occurs when a nonrepresentative sample is drawn from the sampling frame. The estimation of sampling error requires that probability sampling methods be used, where every element of the frame population has a known nonzero probability of being selected, which may be made the same (i.e., equal) for all.

Online surveys are subject to certain amounts of sampling error. However, unless the sample is drawn from an online panel or other frame with known size and characteristics, the degree of sampling error is generally unknown. Sampling error is reduced in part by increasing the sample size, a relatively easy task when using online survey methodology. However when the relationship between the sample frame and the target population is unknown, statistical inferences to the target population using confidence intervals may be inaccurate or entirely misleading.

Nonresponse Error

Researchers frequently debate whether the validity and accuracy of online survey methodology is sufficient to justify its adoption. Advocates of online surveying quickly point to the increased number of unlisted telephone numbers as a reason for the change from traditional research methods. The decline in telephone survey response rates has spurred the switch from telephone surveys to online-based research.

Cost issues aside, Internet surveys face the same nonrespondent problems for which telephone survey methodologies are criticized. Online surveys present unique challenges. Not only are spam filters preventing many survey requests from getting reaching the "In Box," but frequent users of the Internet often run in a fast-paced world, resulting in lower response rates and self-selection bias depending on the appeal of the survey topic, survey length, and incentives to complete the survey.

It has been suggested by Shaffer and Dillman (1998) that fundamental to this issue is the assurance of acceptable levels of response quantity and quality. Without adequate survey response, the representativeness of the sample, and consequently validity or accuracy of results, will never be achieved.

As with traditional marketing research, the keys to increasing response rates and reducing nonresponse error are the use of multiple notifications and requests, and the use of personalization in the contact and request to be interviewed. In addition, when the population of interest is not adequately represented online, a mixed-mode survey strategy is appropriate. A combination of e-mail and telephone, mail, or mall intercept should be considered.

The single most important factor contributing to a survey's response rate is the number of attempts to make contact with each prospective respondent. While many studies have confirmed this fact, one of the more rigorous is by Shaffer and Dillman (1998), who conducted a comparative study of response rates for mail and e-mail surveys. In this field study, respondents in the mail and e-mail treatment groups were contacted four times and sent (1) pre-notifications, (2) letters and surveys, (3) thank-you/reminder notes, and (4) replacement surveys. Results showed no statistically significant difference between the 57.5 percent response rate for the mail group, and the 58.0 percent response rate for the e-mail group.

It should be noted that although the response rates for their university faculty population were considerably higher than would be expected for a consumer survey, the similarity across survey modes stands as a solid finding. Perhaps most noteworthy is the finding that when compared with the mail survey, the survey administered by e-mail produced 12.8 percent more respondents who completed 95 percent or more of the questions. Individual item response rates and item completion rates were also higher. For the e-mail based open-ended text responses, the same 12% increase in completion rates was observed, but in addition, responses were longer, averaging 40 words versus 10 words for the paper-and-pencil survey.

It is clear that the use of multiple contacts to secure cooperation, including reminders to complete the survey, increases response rates not only in traditional mail surveys but also in e-mail surveys. Exhibit 6.3 discusses response rate variations.

EXHIBIT 6.3   Response Rate Variations

The variation in response rates for surveys is enormous, especially when interest and incentives are considered. Ryan Smith, director of sales and marketing at SurveyZ.com, relates his experience with three client surveys that differed greatly in their respective response rates (Smith, 2002). These three very different surveys provide insight into the types of variables that influence response rate:

1. The first survey consisted of a short 10-question survey entitled "What Do Women Want . . . For Valentines Day?" This somewhat whimsical survey was sent using a single mailout (with no second communication) to a "random sample" of Internet users using the e-mail list broker Sendmoreinfo.com. Recipients of the survey were offered the chance to win $500 in a random drawing and in addition were promised a copy of the results. This combination of incentives with a short, interesting survey produced a 43 percent response rate.

2. A second e-mail survey, a very long academic survey of more than 100 questions, focused on developing a demographic, psychographic, and technological expertise profile of the online shopper. This survey measuring attitudes and behaviors was sent through the same broker to a random sample of "Internet shoppers." Respondents were promised the chance to win $500 in one of seven random drawings. The university sponsorship of the survey was identified in the cover letter that contained the professor's name, contact information, and link to the survey. The response rate was 11 percent. It is interesting to note that a parallel paper and pencil survey was also conducted for comparison purposes using a national sample provided by Experian, a provider of credit rating reports. This mail survey was implemented using separate mailings for a prior notification, the survey, and a follow-up reminder. The mail version produced a 20 percent response rate. Comparison of the mail and online survey results showed that demographic profiles were very different. Respondents to the mail sample were older, had different family structures and were more financially secure. However, the psychographic profiles related to online shopping were nearly identical.

3. Another academic survey of more than 100 questions that asked for evaluations of business school priorities was sent to a sample through the same e-mail list broker. Interest in this survey was recognizably low to most respondents in that there was little involvement or interest in the topic. Furthermore, the very lengthy cover letter detailed how important this information was to the school, but offered no incentives. In this case the online survey was a complete flop; the response rate was a dismal one-half of one percent.

Smith believes that keys to increasing response rate are to make your survey as short as possible by removing marginal questions, to make your survey interesting to the respondent, to include an offer of incentives, and to use group affiliations whenever possible.

State-of-the-art online survey technology includes survey tracking and address books that use embedded codes to facilitate the identification and tracking of survey respondents and nonrespondents. With this information, follow-up mailouts and reminders can be sent to nonrespondents, further increasing response rates. Additional technologies enable the compilation of statistics on the status of the survey, including the number of surveys e-mailed, the number received by potential respondents, the number of e-mails opened, the number of surveys viewed (link clicked on), and the number of surveys completed.

Online surveys are not only self-administered but are subject to the conditions of the respondents' computers, which may affect response rates and measurement error. Surveys are often affected by the resizing of windows and narrower windows may cause text to wrap onto multiple lines. Depending on the resolution of the screen and the length of the survey, respondents may be required to scroll in order to respond to the entire survey. While scrolling may appear more tedious for the user, there is a psychological impact to being able to see the entire survey and know how much time and effort will be required. Surveys that are broken into pages requiring multiple submissions leave the respondents continually clicking through segments of the survey, wondering when the survey task will be completed. SurveyZ.com, an online research company, has monitored the results of many surveys and has observed that opportunities of disruption are created when the respondent is required to repeatedly click Submit. These disruptions in survey flow provide opportunities for the respondent to quit the survey. The company has observed that noncompletion ratios are as much as 40 percent higher for long surveys requiring multiple use of the submission button (identical surveys were presented to two groups of respondents; one survey appeared in long format, while the other survey was broken into multiple pages that required repeated use of the submit button). Compounded with the effect of the multiple submissions is the fact that the respondent's ISP and the researcher's server are repeatedly contacted as data is submitted and the next portion of the survey is downloaded. When survey participants are using low-speed data lines and unstable equipment (either through the ISPs or the modem), they are sometimes disconnected from the Internet.

It is clear that multiple factors are responsible for nonresponse rates, many of which are not addressable through the administration and handling of the survey.

Measurement Error

Measurement error is a result of the measurement process itself and represents the difference between the information generated on the measurement scale and the true value of the information. Measurement error may be due to such factors as faulty wording of questions, poor preparation of graphical images, respondent misinterpretation of the question, or incorrect answers provided by the respondent. Measurement error is troublesome to the researcher because it can arise from many different sources and can take on many different forms. For telephone and personal interviews, measurement error will often occur when the interviewer misinterprets responses, makes errors recording responses, or makes incorrect inferences in reporting the data.

One fundamental advantage of Web-based surveys over traditional methods is that there are no interviewers involved in the process. Interviewer errors resulting from inadequate training, inability to pronounce many technical terms, or lack of understanding of the survey's purpose, terminology, or meaning reduce the effectiveness of interviewer-based surveys. Interviewers also make mistakes in transcription and interpretation of responses, and may even introduce tiredness, moodiness, prejudice, impatience, or their own opinions. Web surveys are multimedia-based and are being used to introduce audio and video, as well as static images. The introduction of logic checks can identify contradictory or nonsensical answers to reduce the need for editing and cleaning of the data. The order of questions and multiple-choice answers can be randomized to eliminate order bias.

Technical issues may, however, affect measurement error. For example, the size and type of the monitor, monitor resolution, color palette, browser, and operating system (Mac, Microsoft Windows, Linux) all change the appearance of the survey. Similarly, the actual survey's appearance is affected by spacing between questions, the appearance of horizontal lines separating questions or sections, the use of horizontal versus vertical scales, drop-down boxes versus checkboxes or radio buttons, and even font characteristics including size, type-face, the use of boldface and italics, and even spacing between scale items.

Concerning the relative amount of measurement error for various modes of data collection, while differences do exist, online surveys are similar to standard paper-and-pencil or telephone surveys. Measurement patterns for standard surveys more or less follow the same structured questionnaire approach and the change from paper and pencil to the familiar radio button or checkbox formats is of little concern. However, as will be discussed later, the difference between online and in-person qualitative research is far more extreme.

Many of the traditional measurement errors associated with transcription and recording of data are eliminated through electronic real-time entry of the data. With Web-based surveys, the survey as well as the analysis of results can be conducted in real-time and posted to a secure Web site. In one recent survey of programmers and software developers conducted by SurveyPro.com for Microsoft, 6,000 invitations were sent out with the promise of a $20 Amazon.com gift certificate. Nine hundred responses were received within 48 hours, and results were monitored online in real time. Studies completed in four days online may take eight to ten weeks using paper-and-pencil methodologies. Mail surveys must be prepared, printed, mailed, followed up with mail reminders, coded, manually entered or scanned into the database, analyzed and then compiled into a managerial report; Web surveys eliminate some of these steps, and often speed and combine the others. Exhibit 6.4 discusses the experiences of one Internet market research firm.

EXHIBIT 6.4 Harris-Black International

Krauss (1998) reported the experiences and views of Gordon Black, chairman and CEO of Harris-Black International, the Internet market research firm that conducts Harris Poll Online and the Harris/Excite Poll as well as customized studies. Black says, "While its up-front programming costs are more expensive, the cost for Internet data collection can be 90 percent cheaper over traditional telephone random sampling techniques" (p. 18).

Black believes that concern about the Internet population not being representative of the general population is becoming less of an issue. At election time in November, Black ran an 18-state study to verify the effectiveness and projectability of Web-based research techniques versus random telephone techniques. He says in only a few categories, such as financial services and technology products, might the nature of Web-user demographics skew the projectability of results to the broader marketplace.

Today electronic commerce providers routinely poll and research their customers and act on the data. Qualtrics.com provides corporate survey Web sites to companies like Royal Caribbean, Celebrity Cruises, Sabre, Travelocity, and Intel—all of which routinely conduct customer surveys. Dell Computer has an "online user survey" button on its home page. Excite has a "feedback" button to learn users' views. AOL conducts polls.

But the greater opportunity isn't in applying more sophisticated techniques over the Web. Black points out that a typical advertising test, concept assessment, conjoint study, volume forecast, or pricing evaluation done by a packaged goods provider might be scoped to reach 500 or 1,000 respondents with the telephone. On the Web, a research company can economically reach 2,000, 5,000, or even 10,000 respondents.

Telephone surveys make it cumbersome or even impossible to present concisely the alternatives in a conjoint study or pricing test. The Web allows the controlled and rapid display of survey questions that otherwise would have to be read over the phone. That means less respondent fatigue, fewer terminations, and better research outcomes.

Black adds that on a recent study he received 2,000 responses in two to three days where typical telephone techniques would deliver 200 responses in two weeks. The benefits in terms of speed to market for new product developers who repeatedly enhance and refine a prospective product feature would be enormous.

Black sees great opportunity ahead. He predicts (Krauss, 1998, p. 18), "In the next three to five years virtually all advertising copy research will migrate to the Internet. Mail-panel surveys will disappear—the cost of the mail panel is so much greater than the cost of the Internet panel there's no comparison. Half of all customer satisfaction studies will be done over the Internet. Most of product research will be done over the Internet."

PROBABILITY AND NONPROBABILITY SURVEY APPROACHES

A variety of approaches to presentation of surveys and recruitment of respondents are used on the Web. Surveys based on probability samples, if done properly, provide a bias-free method of selecting sample units and permit the measurement of sampling error. Nonprobability samples offer neither of these features. Nonprobability-sample–based surveys, generally for entertainment or to create interest in a Web site, are self-selected by the respondent from survey Web sites either for interest or compensation, or are provided to members of volunteer panels such as in the example of panels for Internet market testing performed by ACNielsen described in Exhibit 6.5.

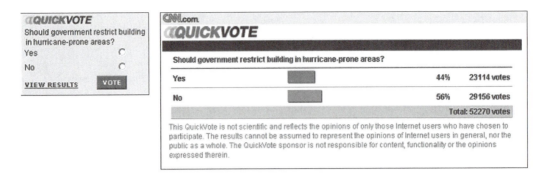

Figure 6.1   Web Site Interest Survey

Online Nonprobability Surveys

As an example of the Web site interest variety of survey, Figure 6.1 shows a CNN.com "Quick Vote" survey, which includes a link to the online results page.

Several Web sites have been popularized through their Web surveys. The National Geographic Society Web site offered surveys that focus on a variety of educational, social and environmental issues at www.nationalgeographic.com/geosurvey/. The surveys include lengthy inventories covering demographics, Internet usage, and attitudes about such topics as geographic literacy, conservation and endangered species, culture, and a variety of other topics (see Figure 6.2). The 2002 Global Geographic Literacy Survey was conducted jointly with Roper Research to assess the geographic knowledge of young adults ages 18 to 24 in nine countries including the United States. An additional sample focused on 25- to 34-year-olds in the United States. Specific questions focused on benchmarking attitudes towards the importance of geography and how aware young adults are of geography in the context of current events.

Respondents were recruited to the survey through a snowball sampling technique implemented through invitations that appeared on the National Geographic Web site, in the National Geographic print magazine, and invitations from other Web sites such as HotWired. The 2000 survey showed 80,012 respondents participating from 178 different countries.

In this example, the use of a sample representative of the U.S. population as a whole cannot be verified because of the nonprobability snowball sampling technique that was employed. Although the large number of respondents may provide data representative of Internet users, the sample certainly is not a random probability sample of the entire population of the United States, from which sampling error could be measured. An excellent review of the methodological merits and sampling issues of this online study has been prepared by Witte, Amoroso, and Howard (1999), and is available online.

Other well-recognized nonprobability surveys include the ACNielsen BASES (see Exhibit 6.5) and Harris-Black panels. Although nonprobability surveys, these panels are continually redefined to match the demographic characteristics of telephone and mall intercept surveys. The parallel telephone and mall intercept studies provide weighting to proportionately adjust online samples to reduce selection bias.

Figure 6.2   National Geographic Web Survey

SOURCE: From Nationalgeographic.com. Copyright © 2001 The National Geographic Society. Used by permission.

EXHIBIT 6.5   ACNielsen BASES

Jim Miller and Sheila Lundy of ACNielsen BASES (2003) describe the evolution of Internet usage for test marketing in the following document, which is available online.

TEST MARKETING PLUGS INTO THE INTERNET

With the advent of the Internet, simulated test marketing has kicked things up another notch—replacing mall intercept and phone feedback with an online respondent community.

Test marketing affords companies the opportunity to prove-up concepts and tweak packaging and advertising presentations while tightening sales and profit forecasts. In addition to acquiring valuable customer feedback, test markets present the chance to observe potential impacts on the entire product line, such as cannibalization, and can be used to assess the reaction of the sales force, retailers, and distributors to the new product.

Taking Their Measure

Within the world of test marketing, an entire portfolio of techniques is available to marketers:

- **Standard test markets.** Actual launches in smaller markets including sell-in to the trade and complete marketing support.

    Rating: best possible read of the market at the highest possible cost with the longest execution time. Open to competitive attack.

- **Controlled test markets.** Comprises a panel of stores with good geographic dispersion that carry new products controlling for facings, displays, POP promotions and pricing. Conducted by companies such as Market Decisions.

    Rating: provides accurate barometer of trade reception. Great for evaluating environmental issues like unusual shelving requirements. Affordable. Minimizes exposure if product fails. Requires sell-in.

- **Simulated test markets.** Consumers use seed money to buy new items in a laboratory store and researchers follow up. Consumers recruited at malls react to product and promotional concepts, then provide feedback via traditional survey methods. Electronic panelists sample products at home, review concepts and promotions online, then provide feedback via traditional survey methods.

    Rating: Lowest execution costs. Fastest feedback. No finished packaging or advertising requirements. Minimal security issues. High degree of accuracy.

Share Versus Sales

There are many classic debates in marketing, and the comparative strength of share vs. unit-based forecasting is one of them. This debate was especially prevalent during the early days of simulated test markets. Share is a powerful metric, but ultimately must be translated into volume estimates for production and pro forma financial statement purposes. One area of vulnerability for share data relates to truly new products or categories.

Take the case of a new product that spans two categories, such as the first combination shampoo/conditioner. Which category multiplier should be applied to convert share into an accurate volumetric prediction? Good question, and in the case of radically new products, there is no definitive answer.

Volumetrics Speak Volumes

This unit vs. share dilemma was one of the reasons that led to the development of the BASES simulated test approach in the late 1970s. BASES yields a two year volume number rather than a market share estimate. Tapping into the average American mindset, BASES recruits respondents at shopping malls, then shows them concept boards and preliminary packaging ideas to gather feedback early in the new product development process.

Underlying it all is a simple premise: ask consumers what they plan to do and they'll tell you. Although people never do exactly what they say, they always do something related to their claim. In a matched comparison of more than 800 cases, BASES volume estimates fell within +/– 20 percent of actual in-market results nine out of ten times.

Worldwide, the BASES model has been applied successfully to more than 28,000 new product concepts from food and beverage to household items, personal care, over-the-counter drugs, pet products and other consumer packaged goods ideas. Today, BASES holds a 60 percent global share of all simulated test marketing for consumer packaged goods.

Seismic Changes

Two concurrent circumstances converged to permanently alter the BASES approach to simulated test marketing. First, mall traffic, the source of consumer input to the BASES models, plummeted from an average of 30 completed questionnaires per location per day in the 1970s to a mere five a day by the 1990s.

Eighty percent of shoppers diligently avoided recruitment and fully one-third of those who did qualify refused to participate, boosting administrative costs and causing timing delays. When queried, it turned out that time-stressed consumers wanted to participate in research, but on their own terms and in their own time.

Second, the Internet gained a foothold in American households, thanks to the proliferation of personal computers and low-cost Internet service providers. Putting the two trends together, BASES explored the idea of operating an electronic panel (e-Panel) that recruited respondents from the virtual society.

Proof of Concept

BASES spent more than $1 million developing and testing the e-Panel concept to ensure forecasting accuracy and equivalency with the mall-based historical archives. There were many questions to resolve: Could a demographically matched panel be assembled? Would cooperation rates differ? Would mall and e-Panelist responses be similar?

As Chart 1 illustrates, the initial investigation showed that wired panelists were virtually indistinguishable from the mall recruits. The panelist profile is practically identical on important criteria such as household size, average age, employment, race, gender, and education levels.

Chart 1
Panel Consumption

	Mall Tests	Internet Tests	Panel Members
Household Size	2.8	2.9	3.0
Average Age	40.5	39.2	37.2
Employed	71%	72%	69%
Caucasian	86%	88%	89%
Male	20%	21%	15%
College Educated	40%	43%	46%

Chart 2
Correlation Coefficients

	Mall/ Internet	Test/ Retest
Purchase Intent	.86	.94
Frequency	.94	.97
Liking	.85	.91
Price/Value	.90	.99
Uniqueness	.91	.99

To validate e-Panel, BASES conducted more than 100 parallel tests over three years, representing a broad spectrum of categories. Clients were so intrigued by the potential of the Internet as a simulated test marketing tool, they volunteered concepts for methodology prove-up tests and anted up dollars to support validation checks. A critical finding emerged from the verification effort: as suspected, the key survey measures for the e-Panel and mall tests were highly correlated and the system showed very strong test/retest reliability (*see Chart 2*).

The Online Community

After screening for issues like employment sensitivities and demographic markers, eligible respondents complete a test questionnaire prior to going live with a study. This allows BASES to sync up results and match with the current panel.

To keep respondents engaged, and build a sense of community, BASES personalized the panel, gave it a name (PineCone Research) and a facilitator who serves as its voice (Karen Scott), and posted interesting editorial content on a dedicated Web site (The Treehouse). The typical panelist gets tapped for a survey once every three to four weeks.

Who Are These People?

As with most longitudinal panels, the diversity of respondent information on the BASES e-Panel is impressive. It includes media usage, shopping habits, pets and appliances. It covers chronic ailments such as allergies and acid indigestion. It tracks promotion, media and shopping habits including coupon use and preferred retail channels.

Every e-Panelist is also Spectra-coded, enabling clients to incorporate lifestage and lifestyle information into their analyses for a holistic view of the marketplace when making tactical decisions about couponing, media, and distribution.

How It Works

Each e-Panel study begins with outbound letters to selected participants containing a log-in password, in parallel with e-mail reminders. Panelists respond to a survey online for a $5 incentive that is mailed prior to the interview. Product samples are delivered directly to the home. While a bevy of incentive opportunities were investigated, a cash incentive won hands down by an overwhelming 65% margin.

The Net Take

Now fully operational, e-Panel has been rated a resounding success by clients for its robust capabilities, equivalent forecasting accuracy, richer open-ended questions and brand claim capability. On average, e-Panel yields savings of 20% per study, lower ancillary costs for concept boards and product shipment, and an accelerated execution time that cuts one full week off the mall production schedule.

An unexpected benefit of the e-Panel was the unfettered honesty of answers. Respondents proved less restrained in expressing dislikes via the impartial computer as opposed to discussing dislikes with an interviewer.

BASES intends to pace technology advancements and continuously enhance its e-Panel offering. Plans are already in the works to introduce video testing in the first quarter of 2002 and to grow the panel to 90,000 participants. As personal digital assistants, RIM devices like Blackberry, and cell phones go mainstream, wireless networks may represent the next simulation frontier.

Online Probability Surveys

Probability-based surveys allow the researcher to estimate the effects of sampling error and thereby provide inferences about the target population through hypothesis testing. Coverage errors, nonresponse errors, and measurement errors still apply and may reduce the generalizability of the data. Online probability samples generally result where e-mail surveys are sent to comprehensive lists that represent the target population. When the target population is large, random samples from the list will be used. For smaller populations such as employees of a company, the survey may be sent to the entire population, thus representing a census.

Where the target population of interest is visitors to a given Web site, pop-up surveys may be presented randomly to visitors when they first enter the site. In this case, the target population is well defined and the sample element has a known nonzero probability. A cookie, a small file used to help identify the respondent, is often placed on the respondent's machine so that ballot box stuffing will not occur.

Prerecruited online panels, when recruited using probability-based sampling methods such as random-digit telephone dialing, also produce probability surveys. In this case, random-digit dialing would be used to contact the prospective panel members who would be qualified as Internet worthy before being recruited for the panel. The initial interview may also include a variety of demographic, lifestyle, and computer usage questions that would help in weighting the panel, thereby reducing selection bias.

Mixed-mode designs provide another alternative for the respondent, presenting them with a choice of responding via online survey or via another mode. Respondents contacted by telephone, mail, or other probability-based sampling mechanism are given the opportunity to respond online. It is not uncommon for businesses or individuals to prefer the online survey format. Wisconsin cheese producers respond annually to an industry group survey that reports production by the type of cheese. This more-than-90-page survey details the desired information for a separate type of cheese product on each page. When asked if they would prefer a paper-and-pencil or online survey, more than 50 percent favored the online mode. While the online methodology may be preferred, access to the survey must be provided to all cheese producers, even those without Internet access. A mixed-mode survey design is the obvious choice.

It is clear that when online samples are used to make inferences about the general population, we must recognize the multiple factors that distinguish online samples from the general population. These factors include nonsampling errors unique to the Internet methodology: for example, fewer households have adopted the Internet than have telephone or mail and researchers lack control of the respondent's computer setup (browser, operating system, fonts, resolution). In addition, refusals, partial completions, measurement, and all other nonsampling factors that bias traditional survey measurement and results still exist in online surveys. (Sources of nonsampling error were discussed in Chapter 3.)

Online survey techniques are also subject to many of the other errors that affect telephone and mail surveys. Marketing researchers, both professional and casual, often neglect to consider the implications that nonprobability sampling and surveys have on the ability to make inferences regarding the target population. While this brief review has done little more than identify the topic areas to be considered, much research on the topic has been completed for both traditional and online surveys. The next section, which focuses on the forms and capabilities of Internet survey software, will build upon this discussion of general survey and sampling methodology.

INTERNET SURVEY SOFTWARE

A variety of approaches to conducting Web and e-mail surveys are available. In general terms, online surveys may be built, distributed, collected, compiled, and analyzed using one of three general forms of online survey technology. These technologies differ in their level of sophistication, the amount of internal information technology (IT) support required, and certainly in cost.

Option 1: E-Mail Submission Form

An e-mail submission form requires the researcher to build an HTML or rich-text survey, distribute it actively to each respondent, and receive the responses as part of e-mail messages directed back to the researcher. Depending on the sophistication of the software package, the responses will either be automatically read from the e-mail and posted to the database, or the researcher may manually cut and paste from each received e-mail into the data file. If the researcher is willing to manually cut and paste information, this no-cost alternative only requires the addition of a few lines of HTML for a submit button that sends the response back to the researcher.

Option 2: Self-Hosted Server Software

A variety of survey-building software is available that requires hosting on the researcher's server. These systems require little more than a PC with the appropriate (generally Microsoft or Linux) operating system. The researcher is able to build the survey and then post it to the server for distribution by e-mail or Web hosting. This technology makes the researcher responsible for purchasing the software and installing it, and then providing IT support for the system. Depending on the software, and the sophistication of the surveys being designed, IT support may play a major role in the survey process and represent a significant cost.

Option 3: Online Application Service Provider (ASP)

The ASP model most often requires what is called thin client technology, meaning that nothing more than a browser is required. ASPs such as SurveyZ.com and Qualtrics.com are accessed through the Internet, where surveys are built online, requiring no user software, no user server, and no user-provided IT support. When the researcher builds a survey, the database is automatically wired, and report generation is automatically enabled. The researcher simply sends out the survey itself, or an invitation with a link to the survey, by e-mail. The respondents complete and submit the survey using a browser, and the ASP automatically receives the results, directs them to the survey database, and provides real-time access to the results. One major advantage of the ASP model is that the researcher always has access to the most current version of the software. A variety of pricing and service plans are available for these services, ranging from a monthly fee to a fee per completed response.

ONLINE SURVEY CAPABILITIES AND TECHNOLOGIES

The power and speed of today's multi-gigahertz servers make it possible to construct a very sophisticated survey that features a broad variety of questions and capabilities. Indeed, online survey systems are even capable, through the use of "software agents," of analyzing responses and developing and presenting dynamic new questions to the respondents as they continue through the survey. Exhibit 6.6 presents a list of questions, capabilities and features that should be considered when evaluating online survey software. While this list does appear somewhat overwhelming, for the professional researcher it represents state-of-the-art development and meets the requirements for most survey applications. Moreover, it provides the capability for advanced analysis and the needed information to evaluate probability samples and estimate the effects of nonresponse.

EXHIBIT 6.6   Survey-Building Software Considerations

SURVEYZ

Professional Survey Software

Survey Delivery Options

- Corporate Enterprise Solutions (qualtrics.com)
- Hosted Solutions (companyname.surveyz.com)
- Hosted Surveys through the Web site (www.surveyz.com)
- E-mail invitation surveys with link
- E-mail invitation surveys with viewable HTML survey
- Portable technology for mobile surveys (mall intercept, business applications)
- Web site entry and exit with quota based Pop-up survey capabilities
- Address book invitations for respondent tracking
- 360 degree respondent tracking (passing of customer number with the survey link). This feature enables tracking of the customer ID from the customer database to the survey, with feedback sent back to the customer database for a reminder mailing.

General Survey Creation Capabilities

Standard Question Types

- Multiple choice single item check
- Multiple choice check all that apply
- Short text answer
- Open-end text answer
- Horizontal rating scales
- Vertical rating scales
- Drop-down list

Advanced Question Types

- Constant sum
- Rank order with validation
- Pick k of n with validation
- Multiple choice matrix
- Multiple open-end numeric text
- Dynamic questions based on answers to previous questions

- Wizard-based survey creation for easy control of all question and answer options
- Insert graphics, audio, and video, including company logos
- Response checking and validation
- Multiple choice with "Other (customizable text message): Specify open ended text"
- Sophisticated multi-level branching capabilities and survey paging
- Randomization of answer choice order
- Randomization of question order
- Text piping: answer to question, answer to answer, question to question, question to answer
- Sample quota checking with termination and branching
- Personal user question and survey libraries
- Multiple-language support (including Chinese, Japanese, Russian)
- No survey posting or IT support required. Your survey is online in real-time while you build.

Survey and Question Editing

- Single click survey copying (duplicate entire survey)
- View, copy and edit from our large online survey library
- Wizard-based question insertion, movement, deletion and copying
- Text search and replace
- Instant survey "preview" (actually test your survey and collect your data)

Survey Appearance and Formatting

- HTML viewable surveys as part of e-mail or Web site survey
- Customizable survey header and footer support for each survey page
- Customizable buttons for submit, continue, and URL redirection
- Complete branding of your survey: insert JPG and GIF files, including your company's logo
- Single click change of background color, question separators
- Font selection and answer category width control
- Customizable "Thank You" page with definable redirection link

Respondent Control and Redirection

- Optional answer validation and question flagging for required questions
- Answer change prevention from previous pages
- Stop/Start feature that allows respondents to "Continue where you left off" feature
- Anti-"Ballot box" stuffing
- Password protection and access control for survey (password or user ID *and* Password)
- Secure data transmission
- Survey activation/deactivation to terminate data collection
- Survey transfer to multiple respondents (stop start with password protection that can be passed to multiple respondents (for example, CEO, CFO, COO each complete separate sections of the same survey)

Analysis and Results

- Completion rate and survey abandonment analysis
- Real-time Web accessibility of analysis tools, report generators and graphics
- Public Access to Results (No Access, Password Protected Access, or World Access options)
- Display and coding of verbatim comments
- Selective removal of respondent from answer set
- Desktop delivery of charts and respondent-level data
- Excel, SPSS, and CSV deliverable data sets (real-time data downloads)
- Automatic delivery of SPSS command file (variable list, variable labels, value labels)
- Full Statistical Analysis and Hypothesis testing with "Select If" filter support Summary Statistics (Mean, Variance, Std. Dev., Median, Range, Min, Max, Q1, n, Q3) Frequency table, Cross-Tabulation (Contingency Table Analysis) One Sample, Two Sample Z statistics, Paired T statistics, Proportions Simple, Multiple Linear Regression, One-way ANOVA, One Sample, Two Sample Inference on variance
- Full Graphical Analysis: Bar Plot, Pie Chart, Histogram, Stem and Leaf Plot, Boxplot, Dotplot, Means Plot, Parallel Coordinates Plot, Scatter Plot, QQ Plot, Index Plot, Pairs Plot, Control Charts (X-bar, R, X-bar - R, np, p, c, u)
- Conjoint and other advanced analysis

Custom Panel, CRM, and Data Integration

- Seamless e-mail integration with company databases
- Transparent support for respondent ID sharing and tracking inbound to survey
- Transparent support for respondent ID tracking and transfer to secondary survey or database
- Customer ID import and export for respondent tracking and for follow-up survey mailout
- Administrator assigned (optional) User ID and Passwords for survey access

Online Address Book for address import, mailout and tracking of respondents

---

SOURCE: www.surveyz.com

ONLINE QUALITATIVE RESEARCH

Web-based qualitative research is bringing marketers closer to the customer. Many Web sites are now introducing survey technology to measure customer satisfaction, motivations, and preferences; to track activities and time spent on the Web site; and to interact more effectively with the customer to meet their needs and wants.

Research companies are increasingly looking to the Internet as an online tool to facilitate qualitative research and discussions with customers. Online bulletin boards and focus groups provide approaches for interviewing respondents in a discussion format and are being adopted more frequently by researchers because it is easier to recruit hard-to-reach individuals like physicians, executives, singles, people with high incomes, the well-educated, and even teens.

In this section, we consider the use of online bulletin boards and focus groups as alternatives to traditional methodologies where participants are assembled in a central location to discuss their views and experiences relevant to the topic of interest.

Bulletin Boards

Bulletin board technology has been available for a number of years, but has been modified in format for more effective use in conducting marketing research. The bulletin boards found on many Web sites allow users to register and then participate in unmoderated discussions of topics of interest to participants of the bulletin board. When bulletin boards are used for marketing research, moderators become involved to direct discussions and to obtain targeted feedback from participants. When properly controlled, the procedure includes recruiting individuals to participate in the bulletin board discussion and then providing them with password information so that they can enter a password-protected Web page. Participants are scheduled for a specific time of day so that they may participate with other individuals recruited for the discussion. Individuals log on, read the information pertaining to the discussion, and respond either to listed questions or to those posed by the moderator. Where a list of questions is prepared, the participants are often free to respond at their convenience.

Bulletin boards may be thought of as appearing midway on a continuum that extends between in-depth personal interviews and group-based focus groups. Discussions can be facilitated by involving all participants and allowing them to interact among themselves, with the moderator posing questions and asking for follow-up responses. Alternatively, most bulletin board software provides the option to conduct interviews where the respondent's replies are masked or hidden from the other participants. Bulletin boards provide for in-depth responses where respondents answer specific questions after reflection on their own experiences. These responses may be the basis for the dynamic synergism that results from interaction with an online group, or the researcher may choose to structure the discussion so that individual responses are not shared with the group.

The major advantages of online bulletin boards lie in the flexibility they offer participants and researchers:

1. Participants can be recruited from a broad geographic area.

2. Participants are able to provide feedback at their own convenience.

3. Participants are able to spend the time that they require to provide thoughtful comments and perspectives.

4. Participants are allowed to start and stop their participation so that they can carry out other activities, including those requested by the bulletin board moderator, such as trying or experimenting with suggested products.

Other advantages are shown in Exhibit 6.7.

EXHIBIT 6.7   Bulletin Board Report

Susan Semack, vice president for Farmington Hills, Michigan–based MORPACE International, Inc., reports that bulletin boards have distinct advantages over real-time and face-to-face groups (James, 2002). One advantage is more detailed responses. Bulletin board participants, with equal chance to voice their opinions and no pressure to talk or type fast, may write responses that run several paragraphs, compared to one or two lines in real-time chat. Bulletin board participants are also more likely to comment on prior postings than in real-time. Researchers report that a single five-day bulletin board group often produces 120 pages of transcripts, or as much information as four focus groups.

Bulletin boards work well when researching topics that are sensitive or controversial, when respondents are anonymous and have time to formulate their responses. Ricardo Lopez, president of Hispanic Research, Inc., conducted a four-day bulletin board group with Hispanic cancer survivors. This methodology was chosen because cancer and death are taboo topics among Hispanics, and participants who have survived such an emotional experience are often unable to provide little more than emotional responses when discussions occur in a traditional face-to-face focus group situation. Lopez reports that because board responses were anonymous and respondents had time to formulate their thoughts, answers were more direct to the questions posed (James, 2002).

When recruiting participants, the researcher should select those with a strong interest in the topic. This is consistent with the practice of inviting knowledgeable and involved individuals to traditional focus groups. The moderators must be actively involved in controlling the pace and flow of the discussion. It is the duty of the moderator to make discussions relevant to the participants and to continually involve them in the discussion. Participants of bulletin boards and online focus groups often spend much more time than the 90 minutes typically required by traditional focus groups. Online, participants are actively involved in sharing their ideas and feelings, but in a setting that allows the moderator to control and drop participants who are either not contributing or contributing adversely to the discussion.

Focus Groups

Focus groups provide qualitative insights into products and concepts through discussions and through interaction that clarifies ambiguity and establishes a dialogue between the participants and the topics to be discussed.

Each focus group has a very distinctive interactive climate since each individual participating in the group brings a personality, a communication style, and a level of involvement that provides direction and intensity to the group. It is the responsibility of the moderator to draw out individuals who are reluctant to participate, who are shy, or who have little desire to participate. This is not always an easy task when focus groups are conducted online. In-person focus groups have the advantage of being able to incorporate taste, smell, sight, sound, and touch into the setting.

However, online focus groups offer several advantages:

- Flexibility of scheduling and format
- Convenience of office or home access
- Geographic dispersal of participants for a more representative or more targeted group of participants
- Availability of technologies such as streaming video for presenting points of discussion and concepts to participants
- Remote and on-demand access for the client from anyplace in the world

Focus groups and their customer interactions can be broadcast so that clients and researchers do not have to physically attend focus group activities. Streaming media provides the flexibility to watch events, jump through specific discussions, and extract segments for use in e-mail attachments or in advertisements and testimonials. Clients may use focus group data to reinforce points of discussion, in decision making, and in marketing.

When moderating online focus groups, moderators do not have the advantage of reading an individual's body language. In online research it is more difficult to pick up on nonverbal components of a respondent's answers. For example, do respondents hesitate? Do they type confused answers? Do they have trouble providing answers? Online moderators must consider comment length, frequency, and relevance, as well as frequency and appropriateness of emoticon use, and whether they dominate, draw in, or alienate other participants.

How is an online focus group constructed and how does one operate? Casey Sweet, principal of Quesst Qualitative Research of Brooklyn, New York, provides an "anatomy" lesson on conducting online focus groups (Sweet, 1998), as shown in Exhibit 6.8.

EXHIBIT 6.8   Anatomy of an Online Focus Group

Online focus groups, also referred to as cyber groups, e-groups, or virtual groups, are gaining popularity as the research marketplace discovers the advantages they offer. In addition to saving time and money, they can easily bring together respondents and observers in far-flung locations in a dimension of qualitative research, aided by customized software, that creates virtual facilities with waiting rooms, client backrooms, and focus group rooms.

Screeners, Recruitment, and Virtual Facilities

Every online group is initiated by contracting with a virtual facility that usually offers recruitment services as well as virtual rooms. Virtual facilities typically recruit respondents electronically from established panels, compiled online lists, targeted Web sites, or client-provided lists. Sometimes, telephone recruiting is used to make the initial recruitment contact or to obtain e-mail addresses.

Recruiting online groups requires specially crafted screening questionnaires that are similar in content and depth to those used for in-person groups. Since these screeners are administered electronically, some questions are worded differently to disguise qualifying and disqualifying answers. A professional online facility, in combination with a well-written screener, will thank and release all disqualified respondents without them knowing why. This, as well as putting a block on their electronic address, discourages them from re-trying to qualify by logging back in or from sharing information about the specific screener questions with friends. Depending upon the target markets, it is not unusual with high-incidence groups to have an excess of qualified respondents to choose from; either the virtual facility or the qualitative researcher will select the best. (A project recently conducted by one company received over 1,000 qualified responses for the required 24 respondent spots.)

Invitations and Preparation

Respondents who are invited to the group receive invitations with passwords and usernames, instructions, dates, and times. The invitation requests that they log on to the site in advance of the group, using the computer they will use during the group, to guarantee technology compatibility. If there are any complications or questions, the respondents can contact tech support in advance to resolve them. They can also contact tech support during the group for online support, as can the moderator and client observers.

The content and structure of the inquiry resembles in-person groups. The major difference is in the actual presentation of questions, which are mostly written in full sentence form, in advance. The main topic questions must be written clearly and completely; otherwise respondents will have to ask for clarification, which uses up valuable time and diverts the attention of the group.

Online groups often meet for a shorter time (typically 60 to 90 minutes) than in-person groups and the ideal number (30 to 45) of prepared questions depends on the complexity of the subject and the extent of follow-up probes required. Whenever desired, follow-up questions and probing can be interjected to either an individual respondent or the entire group. This enriches the inquiry and uncovers deeper insights. Unfortunately, sometimes research sponsors can insist on an excessive amount of prepared questions that minimize the amount of probing time. The result is a missed opportunity to uncover deeper insights.

Preparation for Groups

Fifteen to 30 minutes prior to the group, the moderator and technical assistant log on to watch as respondents enter the virtual waiting room using their usernames and passcodes. Similar to in-person groups, some respondents arrive very early and others arrive at the last minute. As they arrive, some virtual facilities can administer a re-screener to re-profile them and to assure that the attendee is the person who originally qualified. In addition to a few demographic and product usage questions, the re-screener can include a verification question that refers to a piece of unique, personal information, such as the name of their first teacher or pet, that was subtly asked in the original screener.

Show Rates and Selecting Final Respondents

Show rates can vary dramatically based on a number of factors, including: the origination of the respondent (online database, established panel, Web site intercept, etc.), confirmation procedures, respondent comfort and familiarity with the online venue in general, and the typical kinds of personal and business commitments that can inhibit attendance. For eight respondents to show, 10 or 15 may have to be recruited. However, it should be noted that the weather, traffic, and transportation have less of a negative impact on show rates for online focus groups than for in-person groups since the respondents may participate from their home or office, and even if they travel, respondents are typically participating from a variety of locations and not encountering the same delays. Based on the re-screener information and final screener spreadsheet, the moderator and client select the respondents together, similar again to in-person groups.

Moderating

For a moderator, the excitement and pace of moderating an online group can be likened more to a roller-coaster ride than an in-person group. Ideally, the discussion guide is downloaded directly onto the site so the moderator can, with one click, enter a question into the dialogue stream.

To begin a group, the moderator introduces the purpose of the group and lays the ground rules. This includes a personal introduction, timeline, instructions for entering responses, encouragement to be candid and honest, and instructions for signing back on if they accidentally drop off. Respondents are also encouraged to "feel free to agree, disagree, or ask questions of each other that relate to the subjects being discussed" and are told that this interaction will help bring the discussion to life. Online groups demand that a moderator possess strong and fast keyboard skills or be willing to hire an assistant who does. There are no unused moments during a group to accommodate slow typists on the moderator side. Respondents can type slower, but most are keyboard-proficient and save time by cutting corners on spelling and not worrying about sentence construction. It helps to tell them at the beginning that typos and sentences don't matter.

Moderating online groups requires someone who relates to the online venue and recognizes that respondents are adept at developing relationships in this medium. Many respondents participate in chat rooms and feel comfortable relating online. At the same time, it is the responsibility of the moderator to help make the respondents who are not as comfortable or experienced feel valuable.

The strategy of online moderating resembles in-person moderating. That is, the moderator follows the discussion guide to the extent that it continues obtaining the desired information. If a subject that was supposed to be covered later in the group is brought up earlier by the respondents, those questions can be inserted as the moderator sees fit. In addition, if topics not covered in the guide are introduced, the moderator can choose to interject a new line of questioning.

If all is going well, most of the moderating elements will be transparent to the research sponsor and observers. Similar to in-person groups where notes are passed to the moderator, a single client-designated liaison decides what is important to pursue and approves questions given to the moderator.

Transcripts, Analysis, and Reporting

Soon after the completion of the groups, transcripts are available for analysis and reporting. These transcripts may document all interactions from logon to logoff, or they may be slightly edited (by the facility or moderator) to begin with the first question and end with the last question, eliminating the hellos and good-byes. Inappropriate respondent comments can also be easily removed.

Analysis and reporting are similar to in-person groups, with the exception that transcripts are quickly available for every group. The analysis will be very inclusive and reflect the input of most respondents since most of them answer every question. In the absence of visual and verbal cues, analysis of some areas, such as appeal, will be based on an interpretation of respondent statements and the ratings they use to indicate levels of appeal.

Reports are just about the same as other qualitative reports, covering areas such as objectives, methodology, conclusions, and detailed findings. They can be in topline, executive summary, or full-report form. Typically, reports can be turned around more quickly due to the immediate availability of the transcripts.

A Qualitative Caveat

Results from online groups depend on the expertise and qualifications of the professional who is conducting them. The most knowledgeable and qualified professionals to conduct online groups are qualitative researchers who have research and marketing expertise and experience managing group interactions. "Techies" sometimes attempt to do groups because they are comfortable with the technology and mechanics and some even have experience with chat groups. However, they often lack research, analysis, moderating, and marketing expertise and the results can suffer from these deficiencies.

SOURCE: Sweet, 1998.

It is easy to understand that critics of online focus groups might have reservations about holding online rather than face-to-face focus groups. Creativity is the critical element in a successful focus group. To the degree that online participants are able to be realistic and balanced in their views and at the same time visionary in applications and insightful in motivations, the focus group promises to be a success.

The typical screener study for focus groups, including those online, includes questions aimed at identifying expressive and visionary individuals. The following are examples of screener questions with which the respondent is asked to agree or disagree:

1. I like to use my imagination.

2. I always need to know all the facts before I'll consider something.

3. I enjoy puzzles and word games and I like to figure out how to do things.

4. I really don't like new ways of doing things; I think the tried-and-true works best.

5. I am comfortable expressing my thoughts and feelings to others even if we just met.

6. I'm shy and quiet in the company of people I don't know and I tend to let them do most of the talking.

In this example, items 1, 3, and 5 are key indicators of success and would generally mean that prospective participants would be qualified. Agreement with items 2, 4, and 6 will generally disqualify prospective participants.

The final result of the focus group research is not merely the set of transcripts, but an analysis that identifies the themes and insights that have been uncovered. It is a contextual analysis of the transcripts, including language choice, that provides the tone and emotional content of the message. Careful analysis of words in context produces interpretations far more meaningful than simple emotions. One interesting focus group study found that passengers of cruise lines focused on the core ideas of escape and fantasy, wanting to take a vacation that was out of the ordinary. They expressed a desire to escape from the ordinary and try something different, but to accompany that escape with good food and service. Certainly romance is part of this image. Are online focus group participants able to verbalize concepts such as these? Certainly, and they can verbalize them very effectively.

The technology for online focus groups continues to evolve. Their suitability continues to broaden as more and more people become Internet savvy. Hard-to-reach professionals, teens, seniors, and specialty markets such as those who are homebound or otherwise unable to participate in centrally located focus groups all can be enthusiastic participants in online focus groups. Growth in online focus groups, as with all online research methodologies, will mirror growth in Internet adoption rates, e-commerce, and development of graphical interfaces. These qualitative research methods can provide a more holistic and understanding profile of the consumer information than can be obtained through quantitative research.

SUMMARY

Every marketing manager knows that the objective of effective marketing is to create a one-on-one relationship in which offerings are targeted directly to the individual consumers. Ideally, we would never receive online promotional material or sales contacts from companies selling products that do not interest us. The objective of marketing research is to understand the consumer and apply information and knowledge for mutual benefit. Technological advances in online marketing research provide the ability to monitor customer knowledge, perceptions, and decisions to dynamically generate solutions tailored to customer needs. In this chapter we have stressed the advantages as well as the caveats associated with online research. A review of the topic is also provided in Couper (2000). Perhaps the biggest mistake the market researcher could make would be to view online research as simply a time- and cost-saving extension of traditional modes of data collection. New technologies will continue to be developed, tested for applicability in marketing research settings, and refined so that marketers are able to better identify the needs and wants of today's consumers.

ASSIGNMENT MATERIAL

1. Go to www.surveyz.com and do the following:
   a. Design and build a short questionnaire on the topic of attitudes toward the McDonald's "Big Mac" and the Burger King "Whopper."
   b. Use at least three different question formats to gather information related to freshness, taste, service, value, and overall satisfaction. Include other attributes as you see fit.
   c. Test the survey by e-mailing it to friends or other class members.
   d. Summarize the results online.
   e. Evaluate the usefulness of the tool you have used.

Note that some sites, such as SurveyZ.com support academic and class research and allow students and faculty to register and use the service free of charge.

2. Conduct a comparative analysis of at least two different online survey software providers (such as www.surveytime.com, www.surveyz.com, www.zoomerang.com, www.surveymonkey.com).

a. Identify features that would be important for adopting this software if you were conducting a market research project.

b. Provide a comparison of available services and features:
   (1) Is software required on your computer or server?
   (2) Does the service provide database and survey hosting?
   (3) What question types are available?
   (4) Can you track who viewed your survey and who actually took your survey?
   (5) Can you send out a second mailing?
   (6) Are results available in real time?
   (7) What capabilities are available for online data analysis and report generation?
      • Frequency analysis
      • Descriptive statistics
      • Cross tabulations
      • Advanced statistical analysis
      • Specialty analyses (conjoint, etc.)

3. Set up an online chat session related to a topic of interest to college students. Use the insights and material found in Exhibit 6.8 to prepare for the discussion.

a. Develop an outline of topics to be discussed.

b. Register as "Moderator" and moderate the chat group by directing the discussion.

c. Summarize the results.

d. Identify difficulties you experienced in moderating and managing the discussion.

4. Search the Internet for information about increasing response rates for online surveys.

a. Develop a list of what a researcher "Must Do" to increase response rate for surveys.

b. Identify any novel ideas that have produced exceptional results.

c. Identify the types of incentives that are most popular.

5. Develop a list of e-mail list providers and visit their Web sites to determine what they offer, specifically consider the following:

a. What types of demographic and interest groups can they provide for a business-to-consumer survey?

b. What are the sources of these lists (from where do they originate)?

c. What are the cost structures for using these mailing lists?

6. Suppose you are interested in surveying a group of shoppers of home improvement stores such as Home Depot or Lowe's. Using e-mail list providers, how would you identify names of shoppers of these stores so that you could complete your survey? Which e-mail list providers would you recommend for this project?

❖

REFERENCES

Couper, M. P. (2000). Web surveys: A review of issues and approaches. *Public Opinion Quarterly, 64,* 464–494.

James, D. (2000, January 3). The future of online research. *Marketing News, 34,* 2.

James, D. (2002, March 4). This bulletin just in: Online research techniques proving invaluable. *Marketing News, 36,* 45.

Krauss, M. (1998, December 7). Research and the Web: Eyeballs or smiles? *Marketing News, 32,* 18.

Lamons, B. (2001, September 24). Eureka! Future of B-to-B research is online. *Marketing News, 35,* 9–10.

Miller, T. W. (2001, September 24). Make the call: Online results are mixed bag. *Marketing News,* 30.

Miller, J., & Lundy, S. (2003). Test marketing plugs into the Internet. Retrieved May 18, 2004 from http://acnielsen.com/pubs/ci/2002/q1/features/internet.htm

Schaffer, D. R., & Dillman, D. A. (1998). Development of a standard e-mail methodology: Results of an experiment. *Public Opinion Quarterly, 62,* 378–397.

Smith, R. (2002). Personal communication [interview].

Sweet, C. (1998, December). Anatomy of an on-line focus group. *Quirk's Marketing Review,* December, 57–60.

Witte, J. C., Amoroso, L. M., & Howard, P. E. N. (1999). Method and representation in Internet-based survey tools: Mobility, community, and cultural identity in Survey2000. Retrieved May 18, 2004 from http://business.clemson.edu/socio/S2koview.pdf

Chapter 7

QUALITATIVE RESEARCH AND OBSERVATION

In Chapters 5 and 6 we discussed communication as a means of obtaining information from respondents. Respondents provide information by answering questions (via an interview) or by having their behavior observed. It will be recalled that at the extremes an interview will be either structured or unstructured and that it may be either direct or indirect. In this chapter we consider the use of indirect interviews of all kinds, special types of unstructured-direct interviews, and observation as means of obtaining information from respondents. We conclude the chapter with an assessment of direct and indirect research techniques.

INDIRECT INTERVIEWS AND QUALITATIVE RESEARCH

A number of techniques have been devised to obtain information by indirect means. Most of these techniques employ the principle of projection. That is, the subject is given a non-personal, ambiguous situation and asked to describe it, expand on it, or build a structure around it. The person giving the description will tend to interpret the situation in terms of his or her own needs, motives, and values. The description therefore involves a projection of personality characteristics to the situation described. Projection techniques include word association, sentence completion tests, interpretation of pictorial representations, and other devices that have been developed as a means of inducing people to project their feelings (see Table 7.1). These techniques have been most widely used for studies of consumer products that are similar in quality, performance, and price—notably for such products as automobiles, soaps and detergents, gasoline, cigarettes, food products, beverages, and drug sundries. Projection techniques can stimulate a relaxed free flow of associations that tap and identify deep, unacknowledged feelings to a degree not usually possible by other research techniques. Because projective techniques are designed to bypass people's built-in censoring mechanisms, they are useful in eliciting information about sensitive or threatening topics and products.

Table 7.1   Classification of Projective Techniques

Technique	Response Requested of Subjects

Construction
  Item substitution test
  Thematic apperception test (TAT)
	To respond for or to describe a character in a simulated situation

Association
  Word-association test
  Auditory projective techniques
	To reply to a stimulus with the first word, image, or percept that comes to mind

Completion Sentence-completion test	To complete incomplete expressions, images, or situations

Most indirect interviews are at least partially structured in that they are conducted using a predefined set of words, statements, cartoons, pictures, or other representation to which the subject is asked to respond. However, the interviewer is usually allowed considerable freedom in questioning the respondent in order to ensure a full response. Indirect interviews, therefore, are commonly neither fully structured nor fully unstructured; ordinarily they utilize both types of question. Within the marketing research community these techniques constitute qualitative research techniques.

Electronic technology has had an impact on qualitative research. One example of this is Advanced Neurotechnologies, Inc.'s development of a brainwave-to-computer interface that measures direct emotional response to most any communication medium (Shermach, 1995). Known as MindTrack, this system evaluates emotional response and measures emotional dimensions and core emotional states relevant to advertising impact on attitude formation, recall, persuasion, and purchase intent. The basic emotional dimensions of brainwave activity are pleasure/displeasure, arousal/sluggishness, and submission/dominance to the advertising message. Individual emotional response profiles are compiled to attain a group profile for the target group. Individuals that are "average" can be used for one-on-one in-depth interviews to obtain significant qualitative data.

Focus Group Interviews

Perhaps the best-known and most widely used type of indirect interview is that conducted with a focus group. As we mentioned in Chapter 3, a focus group interview is one in which a group of people jointly participate in an interview that does not use a structured question-and-answer method to obtain information from these people. A trained moderator conducts the interview with a group of, ideally, 8 to 12 (but increasingly only 6 to 8) willingly recruited participants. The composition of the group varies according to the needs of the client, especially the problem under study.

Although the technique is widely used in exploratory research, it also is useful in non-exploratory research. Such applications include, broadly, direct exposure to consumers for firsthand knowledge, idea generation for management consideration (e.g., problem, unmet needs, ideas for new products), concept development and screening, tests for comprehension of promotion and communication materials, and establishment of "opinion leader" panels.

An example of the use of focus groups is the Federal Duck Stamp Office of the Department of Interior, U.S. Fish and Wildlife Service (Rydholm, 2000) focus group study. Migratory Bird Hunting and Conservation Stamps, known commonly as duck stamps, are required for hunters of ducks. They are also popular among stamp collectors. Funds from the sale of these stamps are used to help fund the preservation of wetlands in the United States. Because the number of hunters has been declining, there was a need to find a way to reach a new audience and to broaden the market for the stamps. Focus groups were used during the development of a marketing campaign in which a certificate bearing a duck stamp and stating that the recipient has helped preserve one-tenth of an acre of wetlands could be purchased for $30. The objective was to appeal to bird watchers, hikers, and other naturalists. Focus groups showed that the stamp itself was not enough to make the sale. The certificate idea came directly from the research. Focus groups were conducted throughout the country, two groups per city—one with environmentally active people, the other with people who were not predisposed against environmental issues. Once a range of appeals was identified in the groups, the questioning centered on isolating the elements that made people change their minds.

Another example is the Jacksonville, Florida, symphony orchestra's use of focus groups to identify lifestyle marketing issues to explore entertainment alternatives, and to provide some ideas about what future audiences would want and expect from the orchestra (LaFlamme, 1988).

The use of focus groups is not limited to consumer products and services. This technique can provide a relatively easy and cost-effective way to interact with business consumers in industries ranging from pharmaceuticals to computer software. Xerox used focus groups to improve consumer satisfaction by developing a new guarantee on all company products. Within three years of purchase or for the full term of financing, Xerox agreed to replace any product for any reason ("Xerox guarantees," 1990). For the most part, the ways in which focus groups are structured and conducted are similar for consumer-based and business-to-business groups. However, there are some differences, which are identified by Fedder (1990).

Raymond Johnson (1988) has identified four distinctive categories of focus groups on the basis of examining tapes from the project files of several research companies. Johnson, a practitioner, has defined each type of focus group by the adaptation of an interviewing technique to answer one of four basic research questions. The focus group types are as follows:

- *Exploratory studies* of consumer lifestyles and probing to "just find out what's on the consumers' minds these days."
- *Concept testing studies* of how a group, without prompting, interprets a deliberately sketchy idea for a new product or service. Potential users are able to react to a concept still in its formative or experimental stage.
- *Habits and usage studies* deal with the real world of actual consumers. The topic is framed by the moderator's instructions to describe, usually by situation-specific narratives, the details of personal experiences in using a particular product or service.
- *Media testing* in which participants are asked to interpret the message covered in media usually seen in rough form is the fourth type. All types of media may be covered. Group members talk about their understanding of the message and evaluate the extent to which they find it credible, interesting, and emotionally involving.

It seems to be a well-accepted fact that focus groups work, especially (but not limited to) when used with other techniques. Practitioner researchers accept the idea that qualitative (e.g., focus groups) and quantitative methodologies are complements, not substitutes. Quantitative research measures, estimates, and quantifies whereas qualitative research explores, defines, and describes (Wade, 2002). Typically, when both types of methodologies are used in the same study, the qualitative research precedes quantitative research. But, there are situations where a company may already have a substantial amount of existing research data to prepare a quantitative survey questionnaire. In this case, the sequence can be reversed and focus groups, for example, can be used to expound on the meaning of survey findings (Garee & Schori, 1996).

A natural question, of course, is, "Why do focus groups work?" One view is that clients are provided with a gut-level grasp of their customers. This means that a sense of what is unique about customers—their self-perceptions, desires, and needs that affect everything they do—is gained. For more detailed discussions, see Bloor, Frankland, Thomas, and Robson (2001), and Fern (1981).

When conducting a focus group, the session is often videotaped for further in-depth analysis. At the very least the session is audiotaped. In some instances, clients observe the group session firsthand in a type of observation room. When this is done (or the client sees a videotape), the impact can be a powerful emotional force. Seeing and hearing consumers, up close, has an impact that no set of data and no written report alone can have. It makes the abstract real because it is human and individual. Qualitative research offers not just an intellectual comprehension of consumers but a vivid, visceral recognition that affects, on a very deep level, how clients see, feel about, and deal with their customers from then on. Some guidelines and questions for clients who observe groups are discussed briefly in Exhibit 7.1.

EXHIBIT 7.1   Observation of Focus Groups by Clients

As an observer, a client should be cognizant of certain things as he or she observes the dynamics of a focus group in the "back room" from behind a one-way mirror. According to Judith Langer (2001), a client should consider the following:

1. Determine your overall impression of the people in the group by looking at their sophistication level, appearance, and the way they express themselves.

2. Do the respondents' reactions support your assumptions? A way to assess whether the people are atypical or less than fully honest is to have outside data.

3. Are there segments that seem to exist in the focus groups, perhaps based on psychographics?

4. Are there patterns that emerge after several groups? Watch out for making conclusions after just one session. Look for variance! Do not count numbers.

5. A single comment by a respondent may be quite insightful.

6. Look at how people say things, not just what they say. Nonverbal communication can be valuable in interpreting the verbal responses.

7. If a new product or product concept is involved, are the respondents enthusiastic or are they neutral about it?

8. Although certain statements by respondents may appear to be complimentary, they may not really be. This is known as a false positive and is something to be avoided.

9. Be aware of any contradictions that arise between what respondents say and what they report as behavior.

10. Are respondents open to changing their minds, given other information?

11. After the session, talk with the moderator and ask him or her to put the responses in perspective.

The last suggestion may be difficult for a client to accept. Never take what is said as being personal. Forget about ego and company politics.

One practitioner has pointed out that using the one-way mirror puts the focus group into a type of theatrical situation (Chekman, 1990). Viewers are an audience to the "onstage" events going on in the group. Of concern is not the direct effect on participants of the mirror but its indirect consequences. Group members can soon forget the mirror is there. But, the mirror does separate viewers and participants, set up boundaries between them, and perhaps promote a relationship between the parties that neither may be aware exists. Thus, an unintended disturbance may be caused. If viewers realize this possibility, the chance of it happening will be minimized.

More recent technology has allowed clients to view focus groups live without traveling to the geographic areas where they are held. One company has a video system whereby live focus groups are broadcast from a nationwide network of independently-owned focus group facilities to reception centers in a company's own office or that of its ad agency. Clients view all of the action on a large monitor and control two cameras that allow a full group view, close-up, zoom, or pan. They can maintain audio contact with the moderator, videotape highlights or complete sessions, and hold "open-mike" post-group debriefings. Major advantages of this system include saving time and money. Such video-system focus-group facilities have expanded to include global options.

In addition to in-person group interaction, a focus group can be conducted over the telephone by use of a conference call. Respondents are recruited from across the country and are told to call a toll-free number at a certain time to participate. Groups have included doctors, car dealers, accountants, travel agents, and others for projects relating to product development, promotion feedback, reasons why a product was not selling, and similar issues. Simon (1988) listed some of the advantages of this approach:

1. Groups can have tremendous geographic diversity.

2. Travel costs can be virtually eliminated.

3. Recruitment is easier because you do not ask a respondent to spend an evening traveling to, sitting in, and returning from a facility.

4. Mixed groups are no problem.

5. Bad weather generally has no effect on the carrying out of a group session.

6. The information from a telephone group is clean, concise, and to the point.

7. Overbearing respondents can be better handled without disrupting the group.

8. Concept testing is easy.

9. Researchers and clients do not have to go all over the country to put together a sufficient number of representative groups from among the smaller sub-specialties.

One disadvantage of the telephone focus group is that the researcher loses the ability to evaluate verbal response within the context of nonverbal communication.

When conducting focus groups with professionals, however, the practical aspects of focus group use are somewhat unique. Special attention must be given to recruitment, type of compensation or gratuity, convenience of the facility to be used, and the moderator. Unlike other types of focus groups, when professionals are involved the moderator's interaction must be such that he or she is presented as an authority on research in the field of the professional. At least a working knowledge of current technical terminology is necessary.

One critical aspect of a focus group's success is the moderator (Exhibit 7.2). The moderator's job is to focus the group's discussion on the topics of interest. To accomplish this, the moderator needs to explain to the group the operational procedures to be used, the group's purpose, and why the group is being observed and/or taped. Rapport with the group must be established and each topic introduced. The respondents need to feel relaxed early on, and often moderator humor helps this to happen. Once the respondents are comfortable, the moderator needs to keep the discussion on track while not influencing how the discussion proceeds. A moderator has done a good job if, after the topic has been introduced, the discussion proceeds with little direction from the moderator. There must be synergy among the group members. Thus, a critical measure of success is that the group members have talked with each other, not with the moderator.

EXHIBIT 7.2   The Make or Buy Decision for Focus Groups

Focus groups are widely used in industry, either in addition to traditional survey research or as a substitute for surveys. As the costs of doing focus groups increase, some companies are questioning the need to hire an "outsider" to conduct groups. Some marketing managers believe that almost one-half the cost of the research can be saved by having internal marketing research people conduct the groups. In short, the decision surrounding who should be the moderator is a make or buy decision.

In general, managers' argument for having the groups done internally is based on the following:

1. Money can be saved as the cost of the moderator is eliminated.

2. Company personnel are more familiar with the product and will be able to ask the right questions, recognize the nuances, and know when the group is not telling the truth.

3. The groups can be scheduled as the managers' schedules permit.

4. There have been bad experiences with the outside moderators used in the past.

To an extent, these points can be valid for a company and could represent an advantage for doing it internally. However, Thomas Greenbaum (1991) believes that when the total situation is considered, hiring the right outsider to conduct the group is a more preferable decision. He lists the following reasons:

1. An outside moderator can be more objective than an insider, and is less likely to lead the group in a specific direction.

2. Focus group moderation is a learned skill that is developed over time.

3. An outside moderator can be helpful in designing the groups and in developing an effective moderator guide.

4. The lack of detailed product knowledge often is an advantage, not a disadvantage. Since moderators pretend not to know much about the category being discussed, it is possible to ask the seemingly dumb question or seek "help" from the participants that will generate information to achieve the goals of the research.

5. There is less chance that the participants will refrain from showing concern or reacting negatively to ideas when an outside moderator is used.

6. An outsider will be more objective in interpreting results than will an insider.

7. Clients work better by doing what they need to do from the back room, behind the mirror, rather than by conducting the groups themselves.

It seems clear that much of the argument for using outsiders is based on their greater experience and objectivity. Of course, there may be insiders who possess the experience and can, indeed, be objective in doing focus group research.

Greenbaum (1999) presents a practical perspective and a more detailed guide of moderators.

One question that has not been addressed to any great extent regarding moderators is whether interactions between their research philosophies and qualitative information-gathering objectives have effects on the outcomes of focus groups. A study by McDonald (1993) shows that there is indeed an interaction between moderator types, different types of focus group interviewing approaches, and group processes and reporting. The study shows how to best use the two types of moderators identified—everyday moderators and scientific moderators.

Focus group researchers tend to not like to use quantitative techniques for analyzing the qualitative data they obtain from focus groups. Newer techniques, such as neural networks, provide a means whereby quantification of text (excerpts from a focus group) is possible. Figure 7.1 shows the steps involved in quantitative analysis of a focus group interview. First, one must record the focus group discussion. Second, a complete text excerpt of the verbal communication is produced. Third, the input (i.e., the text body) has to be coded (prepared) appropriately. Then, the analysis is done, the findings interpreted, and the report prepared. A wide array of software programs is available for analyzing text (Catterall & Maclaren, 1998). Quantitative analysis should be done only as a supplement to the qualitative report. By itself, it has no justification. An excellent discussion of this issue is the study by Schmidt (2001).

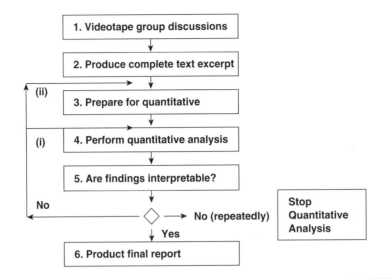

Figure 7.1   Steps in Quantitative Analysis of Focus Group Interviews

SOURCE: Schmidt, 2001, p. 101.

Focus group methodology is not static. Some of the changes that have occurred in the past and that continue to occur are presented in Exhibit 7.3.

EXHIBIT 7.3   Focus Groups Are Changing

During the 1990s, changes occurred in how focus groups were created and used. Many changes were based on technology and newly developed techniques. Some of the changes in how focus groups were run in Canada and the United States are outlined below (Harris, 1995).

Some of the major trends in Canada include:

1. Group size is typically five or six respondents, not the traditional eight to 10.

2. There is less demand for regional representation; groups are usually conducted in one center, such as Montreal or Toronto or Vancouver. It is rare to conduct groups across the country.

3. Fewer groups are being used—four to six instead of eight to 10.

4. Clients demand knowledge and actionable results, thus decreasing the need and demand for exploratory research.

5. Clients go beyond marketing and advertising agency people. More clients are directly observing groups.

6. Groups are tending to become more structured and focused.

7. Business-to-business groups are on the increase, but they still are not widely used.

8. Increasingly, questionnaires are being used in groups.

9. Costs of recruiting and respondent incentives have increased.

10. Clients want shorter and more precise reports more quickly after groups have been conducted.

In the United States, many of the same type of changes have occurred. Group size is more commonly six to eight respondents than the traditional 10 to 12. The overall number of groups being used has risen, but the number of groups at each location has declined, leading to broader geographic coverage. The number of clients attending focus groups is also increasing. Groups are being run throughout the day and the use of Friday evenings and Saturday mornings is becoming more prevalent.

The nature of recruiting respondents has also undergone change. Groups are recruited more quickly and respondents who are not articulate are dropped from the study. Screening questions are becoming more specific. There is growth in the use of ethnic-based groups such as Asian Americans and Hispanics, especially in Southern California.

Technology has had a dramatic impact on focus group structure and method. Videoconferencing is being used to reduce costs. Related to this is conducting focus groups at conventions, which has application for business-to-business situations and to situations where the target market consists of professionals. With the right convention, a large concentration of the target market can be accessed (Greenbaum, 1993). Focus groups conducted in cyberspace can replace face-to-face research. This so-called virtual research has the appeal of groups being run more quickly and at lower cost. But, there is a cost! This cost is that the researcher loses the ability to relate nonverbal communication by respondents to the verbal aspects. That is, body language, voice inflection, facial expression, and interaction between people cannot be observed (Miller, 1994).

Another approach is that developed by Zaltman (2003). His approach uses focus groups to penetrate the human mind by asking subjects to explain their true feelings about objects of concern with images, not just words. This method, labeled ZMET, works with photos (Wieners, 2003).

The Third-Person Technique

The simplest way of obtaining information through indirect questioning of a respondent is to ask for the view of a neighbor, an (unnamed) associate, or some other person whose views on the subject at hand might reasonably be known. This permits the respondent to project his or her own views with no feeling of social pressure to give an "acceptable" answer.

A study of flying that was performed for a commercial airline is a good example of the use of this technique. When respondents were asked, "Are you afraid to fly?" very few people gave any indication of fear. The major reasons given for not flying were cost, the inconvenience of getting to and from the airport, and the uncertainty of airline schedules during the winter due to bad weather. When, in a follow-up study, respondents were asked, "Do you think your neighbor is afraid to fly?" most of the neighbors who traveled by some other method of transportation were said to do so because they were afraid to fly.

An early study using a variation of this technique that has come to be regarded as a classic is the study by Mason Haire (1950) on instant coffee. This study was conducted when instant coffee was first being introduced. The purpose of the study was to determine the motivations of consumers toward instant coffee in general and Nescafe, a brand of instant coffee, in particular. Interviews of consumers had been conducted using a questionnaire employing direct questions. Among the questions asked were "Do you use instant coffee?" and (if "No") "What do you dislike about it?" The majority of the unfavorable responses were of the general content "I don't like the flavor." This answer was suspected to be a stereotype rather than revealing the true reasons. An indirect approach was therefore chosen.

Two shopping lists were prepared that were identical in every respect except that one contained "Nescafe instant coffee" and the other "Maxwell House coffee (drip grind)." These shopping lists were shown alternately to a sample of 100 respondents, each being unaware of the other list. Each subject was given the following instructions:

Read the shopping list below. Try to project yourself into the situation as far as possible until you can more or less characterize the woman who bought the groceries. Then write a brief description of her personality and character. Wherever possible indicate what factors influenced your judgment.

The results were quite revealing. The descriptions given were summarized as follows (Haire, 1950, p. 652):

- Forty-eight percent of the people described the woman who bought Nescafe as lazy; four percent described the woman who bought Maxwell House as lazy.
- Forty-eight percent of the people described the woman who bought Nescafe as failing to plan household purchases and schedules well; 12 percent described the woman who bought Maxwell House this way.
- Four percent described the Nescafe woman as thrifty; 16 percent described the Maxwell House woman as thrifty; 12 percent described the Nescafe woman as spendthrift; 0 percent described the Maxwell House woman this way.
- Sixteen percent described the Nescafe woman as not a good wife; 0 percent described the Maxwell House woman this way; 4 percent described the Nescafe woman as a good wife; 16 percent described the Maxwell House woman as a good wife.

The implications of these findings seem clear. The woman using the instant coffee was characterized as being lazier, less well organized, more of a spendthrift, and not as good a wife as the one using the conventional coffee. These imputed characteristics must have been the result of the respondents' projecting their own feelings toward instant coffee in their descriptions of the woman using it.

This study has been replicated a number of times. The general acceptance of instant coffee and the change in dietary habits since it was done originally have resulted in different findings in the more recent studies. Nevertheless, the original study remains as a classic application of the third-person technique of research.

Word Association Tests

Word association tests have been used for more than 120 years by psychologists and are considered to be the forerunner of more recent projective techniques. The test consists of presenting a series of stimulus words to a respondent who is asked to answer quickly with the first word that comes to mind after hearing each. The respondent, by answering quickly, presumably gives the word that he or she associates most closely with the stimulus word.

A word association test was used by AT&T to choose the name that best communicated the service provided by long distance dialing. Seven names were tested, including "Nationwide Dialing," "Customer Toll Dialing," and "Direct Distance Dialing." Responses to "Nationwide Dialing" were (somewhat surprisingly) weighted in the direction of "worldwide," an apparent interpretation that this new system would permit dialing telephone numbers all over the world. "Customer Toll Dialing" received a high response rate of "money" and "charges," indicating an unfavorably high association with the cost of making long-distance calls. "Direct Distance Dialing" was chosen by AT&T since it seemed to convey the idea of long-distance dialing without the use of an operator and did not have an unfavorable association.

Word association tests are simple and easy to use, and offer powerful insights into the perceptions and associations related to the concepts being tested.

Sentence Completion Tests

Sentence completion tests are similar to word association tests, both in concept and in use. A sentence stem (the beginning phrase of a sentence) is read to the respondent, who is asked to complete the sentence quickly and with the first thought that occurs to him or her. In some applications, participants are asked to fill in the sentence several times rather than once. Recognizing that people may react in more than one way to a sentence stem increases the likelihood of uncovering all major feelings on a topic.

Sentence completion was one of the techniques used in a study of automobile buying. The purpose of the study was to probe the motivations of automobile buyers to provide a sounder basis for advertising. Although this study itself may be dated, the methodology is representative of this technique. The following are examples of the sentence stems used:

People who drive a convertible . . .

Factory workers usually drive . . .

Most of the new cars . . .

When I drive very fast . . .

Analysis of selected responses of men and women to two of the sentence stems illustrates how inferences of motivational influences can be drawn through the use of this technique (Newman, 1957, pp. 227–228).

Sentence stem: *When you first get a car . . .*

Women's responses:
... you can't wait till you drive.
... you would go for a ride.
... you would take rides in it, naturally.
... you would put gas in it and go places.

Men's responses:
... you take good care of it.
... I want to make darn sure it has a good coat of wax.
... check the engine.
... how soon can I start polishing it.

Sentence stem: *A car of your own . . .*

Women's responses:
... is a pleasant convenience.
... is fine to have.
... is nice to have.

Men's responses:
... I would take care of it.
... is a good thing.
... absolutely a necessity.

The interpretation of these results was as follows: The women's responses indicated that for them a car is something to use and that pride of ownership stresses being seen in the car. For men a car was something for which they should be protective and responsible. Their emphasis was on examining the car and doing things to it. Men appeared to feel closer to their car and regarded it as more of a necessity than did women.

Sentence completion tests provide a top-of-mind association between the respondent and the topic/product/subject being investigated. This data is easy to collect, but is difficult to analyze so that an accurate perspective is obtained of the differences between groups and the meanings of the comments.

Thematic Apperception Tests

The Thematic (for themes that are elicited) Apperception (from the perceptual-interpretative use of pictures) Test (TAT) consists of one or more pictures or cartoons that depict a situation relating to the product or topic being studied. Generally, one or more persons are shown in an ambiguous situation and the respondent may be asked to describe or to assume the role of one of these people and explain the scene, tell what is happening, and describe the characters. Sometime respondents are asked to make up a story about what is happening now and what may happen in the future.

Figure 7.2   Cartoons Used in a Thematic Apperception Test

A common form of the TAT as used in marketing research is the cartoon. The cartoons shown in Figure 7.2 were used to study the price-quality association of a sample of women with respect to a beauty cream. Each woman in the sample was shown one of the cartoons (in random order) and asked to describe first the person in the cartoon and then to indicate what she thought the beauty cream shown would be like.

The general nature of the responses for the cartoon showing the $4.95 beauty cream are well summarized by the answers of one of the women:

- "Any female over 18 interested in her appearance who falls for the advertising claims and doesn't have too much money to spend on cosmetics."
- "It's a poor quality product that is probably greasy and oily."

For the cartoon showing the $25.00 cream, the responses given below are generally representative of those of the sample:

- "Someone who cares what she looks like—possibly a businesswoman interested in her appearance."
- "It's a cream that leaves your skin clear and refreshed. It probably would keep your skin young-looking by softening and cleansing the skin."

The reader may draw his or her own conclusions as to the association of price and quality for this product. (Before a sound conclusion can be reached, however, additional information is needed with respect to the size and nature of the sample used.)

The TAT, or a modification of it, is used by marketing researchers to aid in developing advertising, particularly print ads and billboards. Participants are first shown an unbranded visual that is under consideration for the ad and asked to create a story around it. The interviewer encourages participants to go beyond the literal and release some of the more elusive feelings and associations that the imagination stirs up:

- What is happening in this picture?
- What are the characters doing, thinking, and feeling?
- What happens next?
- What will the outcome be?

Participants do not directly address their feelings about a product or brand, but reveal them indirectly through their responses to visuals and changes in the visuals. Even a slight change in presentation—a tilt of the model's head in a photograph, for example—can evoke a significantly different response.

The picture might be shown a second time with a brand name and a tagline. The participant is asked whether he or she sees the same scenario and how well the picture and the brand match. Sometimes an appealing story loses its intrigue when a less-than-popular brand is added. On the other hand, a neutral visual can become more exciting when a well-liked product or tagline is added. The interplay of brand and visual can then be explored.

Because most people view these exercises as fun, they take the opportunity to express themselves more fully and openly. Research that has used this technique has shown that people from different segments of the population tell similar stories about the same photos or images (Exhibit 7.4).

The Depth Interview

There is substantial use of the unstructured informal interview in marketing research to explore the underlying predispositions, needs, desires, feelings, and emotions of the consumer toward products and services. This method of interviewing was discussed in Chapter 5 and referred to as a depth interview.

Insofar as obtaining information on motivations is concerned, the concept of "depth" refers to the level at which underlying motivations are uncovered. Both the method of interviewing and the term *depth interview* were borrowed from clinical psychology, where the method has been used to probe and assess the sources and nature of the problems of patients. In marketing research, the depth of the interviews has been varied, with a general level that is substantially less deep than the level used in the field of psychology. Mariampolski (1988) listed different types of probes that can be used:

1. The silent probe (use eye contact and body language)

2. Request elaboration

   3. Request definition

   4. Request word association

   5. Request context or situation

   6. Shift context or situation

   7. Request clarification

   8. Request comparison

   9. Request classification or typology

   10. Compare and contrast to a previous statement

   11. Challenge veracity

   12. Challenge completeness

   13. Confrontational probe

   14. Echo probe

   15. Interpretive probe

   16. Summary probe

   17. Purposive misunderstanding

   18. Playing naive

   19. Projective probe

These alternative techniques of probing have varied effectiveness. Often, more than one type may be necessary in a given interview.

EXHIBIT 7.4   Images Can Be Guided

Another approach involving a modified TAT is called guided imagery. Instead of asking participants to appraise a product or brand directly, they are asked to concentrate on creating and experiencing an associated image. This technique takes pressure off the respondents because they do not have to come up with a rational or "right" response.

   To illustrate, Solutions Marketing Research in Locust Valley, New York, uses an approach to guided imagery called "The Looking Glass." This technique asks participants to imagine the kind of door that would bear the imprint of a particular brand name. Participants are then asked to walk through their imagined door and experience what's behind it.

According to Sharon Hollander, president of Solutions Marketing Research, people tend to forget themselves in their involvement with the process, allowing them to be more creative in their images and ultimately more honest in revealing their inner thoughts and feelings. Experience shows that common responses often are found. Positive feelings about a brand name usually generate a solid or carved oak door, with a brass lever handle. Negative feelings usually conjure up a plain or shabbier door that lacks a handle and simply pushes open.

The depth interview, or the "one-on-one" as it is sometimes called, in marketing research may consist of direct or indirect questions, or some combination of the two. The skilled interviewer will generally employ both types of questions. A direct, free-answer question such as "What are the major reasons why you bought your cellular telephone?" might well be followed up, for example, with an indirect question such as "Why do you think people who own cellular telephones bought them?" By following leads and cues provided by respondents, phrasing questions to continue the flow and pattern of the conversation and to maintain the rapport established, the competent interviewer can explore and probe the underlying motivations of the respondent.

Many examples of the use of depth interviewing in marketing research could be cited. One study, which relates to coffee, was done for the Pan-American Coffee Bureau many years ago. Exploratory depth interviews were conducted with 36 respondents, and an additional sample of 96 respondents was depth-interviewed later. In each depth interview, a trained interviewer encouraged the respondent to talk freely about his associations and feelings related to coffee. Direct questions seldom were asked. Instead, the interviewer attempted by skillful probing to learn what was important to the respondent and to investigate the emotional facets that often determined apparently rational behavior.

Interviewer instructions for the initial set of 36 interviews are given in Figure 7.3. These instructions are worthy of careful reading, since they illustrate both the major strength—adaptability—and the primary weakness—opportunity for subjective biases in interviewing and interpretation—of the depth interview.

Several recommendations were made as a result of the study. One of these was to change coffee, in psychological terms, from a "sinful and escapist" beverage to a positive, life-accepting product. Although many of the respondents showed a liking for coffee, they were afraid of drinking too much of it and reluctant about letting young people drink it. A second recommendation was to provide a greater variety of coffee flavors. Coffee should not just be "coffee"; restaurants should treat it as more of a specialty by listing four or five varieties of coffee. A third recommendation was that coffee advertising should be more permissive about suggesting how people should make and drink their coffee, since people were proud of having individual tastes and, in some cases, resented authoritarian advertisements that told them the "right" way of making coffee.

The individual depth interview has been used less extensively as the focus-group interview has become more prominent. However, dissatisfaction with the group influence and the high cost of focus groups, together with certain evolving factors in the marketing environment, have led to recent increased use of the individual depth interview. The depth interview is ideal for obtaining from consumers anecdotes of times they used a product or service, and such "stories" provide the marketer with a good view of what products

Sample Note

Of your two respondents, please make sure that you have represented one male, one female; one "dark strong" coffee drinker, one "light weak" coffee drinker; one "heavy drinker" (6–8 cups per day), one "light drinker" (2–3 cups per day).

Just for Your Information

There are five major practical questions that we want to answer in this study:

1. What is the real role of coffee drinking in people's lives today?

2. What people drink coffee more frequently, or less?

3. Why people prefer stronger, or weaker coffee brewing?

4. At what age levels and why is coffee drinking morally possible?

5. Any special feelings about coffee on the part of older people.

To answer these questions, we need to probe for the whole range of people's feelings about coffee and its real role in their lives. Encourage maximum spontaneity and feel free to probe any area that seems likely to be significant.

It would be most helpful for these initial interviews if you could just get people talking freely on all their feelings about coffee for an hour or so.

The areas below are to be probed only after fullest possible rambling free association is exhausted.

Some Suggested Research Areas

Among others, try to probe the following areas that we have found helpful in our preliminary field testing:

- Spontaneous Associations—*First try to encourage maximum free association with coffee, everything that comes into people's minds as they think of coffee . . . Probe in detail for all sensory impressions, smell, taste, appearance, etc.*
- Kinds of Coffee—*All impressions about different types of coffee—strong, weak, black, etc., difficulties in making coffee, how one brews coffee, etc. . . .*
- Coffee Drinking Occasions—*When respondent drinks coffee and attitudes to coffee at all these specific occasions—when it is most wanted, best liked . . .*
- Best Cup—*The best cup of coffee—how it tasted, etc. . . .*
- Childhood—*Impressions about coffee in childhood—when first asked for some—parents' attitude—when he and friends first started drinking coffee—all impressions of that first cup, taste, smell, etc.*
- His Children—*Any comments about or requests for coffee by his children—what he said—at what age allowed, or will be allowed, to drink coffee?*
- Frequency—*Average number of cups per day, ...*
- Health—*All feelings about coffee and health, ...*

Figure 7.3   Pan-American Coffee Bureau Study—Interviewer Instructions

mean to consumers. When used this way, the result of the interview is usually presented verbatim. Telephone interviewing has proved to be effective in obtaining such consumer stories. The depth interview offers insights with depth, whereas focus groups offer information with breadth. Thus, each has its place in the total set of methodologies from which marketing researchers can draw.

There are three distinct research situations where depth interviews can be used (Kates, 2000):

1. Depth interviews in this situation are used to obtain background information to support the development of a quantitative survey instrument. Thus, it is useful in exploratory research.

2. Depth interviews may be the sole research method used. Often, this occurs with hard-to-reach groups, and with groups that are highly internally competitive so a focus group is not feasible. Obviously, results normally cannot be statistically significant, but results can be projected if the size of the sample interviewed is at least 60 percent of the population, indicating, of course, a relatively small population.

3. Depth interviews are used to obtain information on a subject without being biased by the group dynamic that often occurs in a focus group. For instance, in the case of a rollout of a new product the marketer may not want respondents to be influenced by the views of others.

When conducting in-depth interviews these can be done in-person at a home, a place of work, or a central location or by telephone. Oftentimes, use of telephone is best in business-to-business research situations and in situations where respondents are geographically dispersed. In addition, with technology advancing methodology we can expect increased use of interactive in-depth interviewing by computer using Webcam-based techniques and the Internet. Regardless of mode of data collection, the use of an incentive, monetary or otherwise, is often needed. When executives are respondents the incentive is often a contribution to a charity of their choice.

A specific form of in-depth interview involves the use of empathic interviewing. Empathy is understanding and appreciating someone else's beliefs, feelings, and behaviors. Interviews of this type elicit people's feelings, attitudes, and beliefs and identify the social factors that influence their behavior. Many standard qualitative techniques neglect empathy. Specific guidelines for conducting empathic interviews include the following (Lawless, 1999):

1. The researcher needs to imagine himself/herself in the respondent's situation and must listen to the respondent fully.

2. Do not be hindered by the discussion guide; react and improvise as needed.

3. Ask open-ended, non-leading questions that start with how, what, and why.

4. Avoid self-referencing by setting aside thoughts, preconceptions, and interpretations.

5. Challenge generalizations by asking for specific examples.

6. Probe nonjudgmentally to understand the person's beliefs, feelings, and behaviors.

7. Let the respondent reveal himself/herself through personal studies.

Depth interviews, if conducted in sufficient detail, produce accurate and understandable qualitative information about the research problem (exploratory studies), or for concept or habits and uses studies. Depth interviews can however be directed even further. The next section demonstrates a depth interviewing technique called means-end analysis, which focuses on discovering the interviewee's motivation to use the product.

MEANS-END ANALYSIS

Means-end analysis, also known as Laddering and Means-End Chain, is an in-depth, one-on-one interviewing technique that identifies the linkages people make between product attributes (the means), the benefits derived from those attributes (the consequences), and the values that underlie why the consequences are important (the ends). The premise of means-end analysis is that consumers learn which products contain attributes that lead to their desired benefits or consequences and are consistent with their personal values.

As an in-depth interviewing technique, laddering interviews employ structured dialogues that identify the most important attributes, benefits (consequences) derived from those attributes and values linked to the consequences in a given usage situation. The interviewer moves up and down the means-end chain, identifying the hierarchical structure of the components and linkages, usually by asking questions like "Why is that important to you?" Interviews typically last between 45 and 90 minutes and are recorded for analysis and preparation of the resulting laddering maps of the components and linkages.

Laddering focuses on reasons why positive and negative linkages between attributes and consequences are important in choosing a brand. This laddering of the reasons that underlie a decision provides much deeper understanding of the consumer than does a traditional "ratings survey" of product attributes.

The first task of a laddering exercise is to elicit the attributes that are important in distinguishing between brands. Exhibit 7.5 identifies a series of approaches that might be used to elicit the attributes that are most important in distinguishing between brands.

In practice, several different methods may be used to capture a full range of meaningful distinctions between a brand and its competitors. For example, a laddering interview might start with top-of-mind imaging to understand general product-category beliefs, then increase in brand-related specificity by asking about the usage context (contextual environment), and finally about alternative usage occasions. Other tools, such as a worksheet (Exhibit 7.6) might also be used.

One study using the Reynolds and Gutman (1988) approach to analyzing and quantifying the results of laddering exercises, used laddering to understand the development of a new bank credit card. The study found that nine attributes were critical to consumers considering a new card: no annual fee, status, low interest rate, added value features, acceptance, credit limit, ability to carry a balance, location of the sponsoring bank, and availability. These attributes were found to be linked to 12 benefits (consequences) that were perceived as part of card usage: not feeling cheated, independence, convenience, dependability, saving money,

(Text continues on p. 270)

EXHIBIT 7.5   Methods for Eliciting Brand Attitudes

A variety of methods can be used in marketing research to elicit brand attitudes:

- *Top-of-mind imaging.* The respondent gives positive and negative associations for the brand or product category, along with reasons why the characteristic is viewed that way. This line of questions uncovers the attributes and consequences that distinguish the characteristic.
- *Grouping similar brands.* Grouping identifies similar and dissimilar brand groupings within a product category and the reasons for this perceived similarity or dissimilarity. The primary reasons, most important attributes, and most representative brands are identified and attributes and consequences are laddered.
- *Contextual environment.* The usage context for a brand or product can be described either as physical occasions (place, time, people), or need state occasions (relaxing, rejuvenating, building relationships, feeling powerful, reducing stress, and getting organized). A brand or product is associated with a usage context. For example, "You have just completed your workout and arrive home thirsty and go to the refrigerator for a beverage . . . what product or brand would you like to find there?"
- *Preference, usage, similarity and dissimilarity differences.* Comparing brands based on personal preference or usage is commonly used to distinguish between brands. Similarity and dissimilarity groupings also provide a direct method of distinguishing between brands. When compared against each other, questions of why Brand A was grouped differently or ranked higher than Brand B produce elicitations of attributes and consequences.
- *Timing of purchase or consumption.* Timing issues are often related to product or brand choice and usage. For example, a respondent might be asked to identify products used for relief of a stuffy nose into several stages like onset, full-blown, and on-the-mend, or day-time and nighttime. Then the respondent would relate which brands were preferred for each time-related stage.
- *Usage trends.* Dialogues about past and expected future usage of a brand help to elicit attributes and consequences that lead to different usage patterns. For example, respondents may be asked, "Will this brand be used more often, less often, or about the same as you have used it in the past?" Then, reasons for increased, decreased, or unchanged usage are discussed.
- *Product or brand substitution.* Product and brand substitution methods elicit the degree of similarity of perceived attributes and consequences associated with usage. When questions are asked about the degree of substitutability, attributes and consequences are discovered that inhibit or promote substitution (attributes or consequences that need to be added or removed for substitution or trial to occur). For an unfamiliar brand, the respondent first can sample or be given a description of the brand, followed by questions like: how likely would you be to substitute (name of the new brand) for your current brand for this occasion—why is that?
- *Alternative usage occasions.* Alternative uses are presented to the respondent to determine if and why the brand is present or absent from the choice set. Questions might be phrased to ask: why would you consider using Brand A for this occasion, or what is keeping you from using Brand A for this occasion now? Both positive reasons why a brand fits a new occasion and negative reasons why it does not fit can be elicited and laddered.

SOURCE: Adapted from by Reynolds, Dethloff, and Westberg, 2001, and Reynolds and Whitlark, 1995.

EXHIBIT 7.6   Sample Means-End Worksheet

What product or service attributes do you consider when deciding on a bankcard? Please list the attributes and then rate them as a value from 1–10, with 1 being not very important and 10 being very important.

Attributes	Rating	Attributes	Rating

Please list your three most acceptable sources when seeking a banking or credit card (beside the consideration, describe it with one adjective):

First:

Second:

Third:

- Why do you prefer these cards?
- How do they benefit you?
- How are they different from others?
- What is your least favorite banking or credit card and why?
- What specific things did you dislike about this card?
- Have you had negative experiences that affect your current preferences?
- Under what conditions would you consult these rejected sources for a card?
- How does your preferred card affect your life?
- How does this card make you feel as a consumer?
- What does this preferred card do for you that the rejected cards don't?
- During what period of your life are you most likely to need these services?
- During which period has it most benefited you? Why?
- Describe the best personal experience you have ever had concerning credit cards.
- How has that experience changed your life?
- Do you seek out similar experiences today?
- How would you describe a card that could help you achieve this?

financial responsibility, freedom, establishing a credit history, power, security, supporting the community (local card), and confidence. Finally the consequences were linked to four personal values: family concerns, improved self-esteem, improved quality of life, and peace of mind. This analysis is actually mapped to show the hierarchy of attribute relationships. In Figure 7.4, four distinct sub-hierarchies are shown that focus respectively on the four values. Means-end analysis provides a valuable platform upon which media can be developed. In this case, it is easy to imagine four separate commercials, each stressing a different set of attributes and consequences with overall personal value appeals to "Providing for the Family," "Superior Quality of Life," "Peace of Mind," and "Heightened Self-Esteem." Reflection upon the most effective credit card commercials shows that they are well targeted toward these very same appeals.

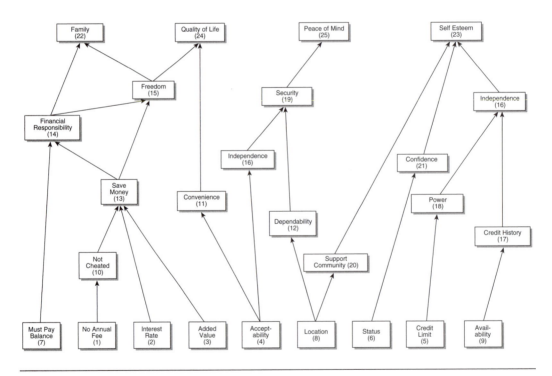

Hierarchical Value Map

Figure 7.4   Hierarchical Value Map

SOURCE: Gibby, Holland, Lee, Lundell, Merrill, and Robison, 1995.

The advantage of the benefit chain is that it is relatively easy to administer without a highly sophisticated interviewer. The only key decision is when to stop probing.

OTHER TECHNIQUES

Other variations of projective techniques have been used that are similar in nature but different in form from those already described. The *repertory grid,* for example, is a partially structured technique that requires the respondent to compare objects along dimensions that he or she selects. The usual procedure is to present the interviewee with a pack of cards on which brand names or other stimuli are printed. The respondent is asked to cull unfamiliar brands (stimuli) from the pack, and three cards with familiar brand names (stimuli) are selected at random. Following this, the respondent is asked to describe a way in which any two of the familiar brands (stimuli) are like each other and different from the third. The respondent is then asked to rate all the brands (stimuli) with respect to this dimension. The response may be in the form of a paired comparison, a ranking, or a numerical rating on a scale. This process is repeated using three different brands (stimuli) until the dimensions of the respondent are exhausted. Additional respondents are interviewed until no new dimensions are given. On the average, 40 interviews are required to identify most of the relevant dimensions.

An example of the use of the repertory grid is a study done for a major producer of frozen foods who was interested in introducing a new type of toaster item that could be made to taste like a variety of freshly baked products. The research director was interested in the attributes of bakery items that consumers use to distinguish one product from another. The stimuli were 20 products as shown in Table 7.2. The study resulted in a list of 22 attributes that were scaled as bipolar scales (see Chapter 11) for further analysis, as shown in Table 7.3. The stimuli and attributes can be set up as a grid whereby respondents can then rate each stimulus (i.e., bakery item) on each attribute.

Exhibit 7.7 discusses the use of *protocols* (Ericsson & Simon, 1984). This technique allows respondents to respond freely without intervention of an interviewer.

Story completion, a logical extension of the sentence completion technique, consists of presenting the beginning of a situational narrative to a respondent, who is asked to complete it. The general underlying principle is that the person will project his or her own psychological interpretation of the situation into the response. For example, the situation could be formulated

Table 7.2   List of Food-Item Stimuli Used in Repertory-Grid Study

Stimulus	*Stimulus*
1. Toast pop-up	11. Cinnamon bun
2. Buttered toast (white)	12. Danish pastry
3. English muffin and margarine	13. Buttered toast (rye)
4. Jelly donut	14. Chocolate chip cookie
5. Cinnamon toast	15. Glazed donut
6. Blueberry muffin and margarine	16. Coffee cake
7. Hard rolls and butter	17. Apple strudel
8. Toast and marmalade	18. Toasted pound cake
9. Buttered toast and jelly	19. Corn muffin and butter
10. Toast and margarine (white)	20. Bagel and cream cheese

SOURCE: Green, Tull, and Albaum, 1988, p. 712.

Table 7.3   Twenty-Two Bipolar Scales Found in Repertory Grid

		1	2	3	4	5	6	7	
1.	Nonfruity flavor	1	2	3	4	5	6	7	Fruity flavor
2.	Easy to prepare	1	2	3	4	5	6	7	Hard to prepare
3.	Low crispness	1	2	3	4	5	6	7	High crispness
4.	Natural flavor	1	2	3	4	5	6	7	Artificial flavor
5.	Dry texture	1	2	3	4	5	6	7	Moist texture
6.	Complex flavor	1	2	3	4	5	6	7	Simple flavor
7.	Complex shape	1	2	3	4	5	6	7	Simple shape
8.	Not very filling	1	2	3	4	5	6	7	Highly filling
9.	Appeals mainly to kids	1	2	3	4	5	6	7	Appeals mainly to adults
10.	Served formally	1	2	3	4	5	6	7	Served informally
11.	Primarily breakfast item	1	2	3	4	5	6	7	Primarily non-breakfast item
12.	Soft texture	1	2	3	4	5	6	7	Hard texture
13.	High perishability	1	2	3	4	5	6	7	Low perishability
14.	Mostly eaten at home	1	2	3	4	5	6	7	Mostly eaten away from home
15.	High calories	1	2	3	4	5	6	7	Low calories
16.	Highly nutritious	1	2	3	4	5	6	7	Low in nutrition
17.	Drab appearance	1	2	3	4	5	6	7	Colorful appearance
18.	Usually eaten alone	1	2	3	4	5	6	7	Usually eaten with other foods
19.	Low general familiarity	1	2	3	4	5	6	7	High general familiarity
20.	Highly liked by men	1	2	3	4	5	6	7	Highly disliked by men
21.	Ordinary-occasion food	1	2	3	4	5	6	7	Special-occasion food
22.	Expensive	1	2	3	4	5	6	7	Inexpensive

SOURCE: Green, Tull, and Albaum, 1988, p. 713.

as follows: "Last weekend my partner and I were deciding which jewelry store to visit for a purchase. When I mentioned XYZ, my partner remembered the last visit there. Now you complete the story."

EXHIBIT 7.7   Protocols for the Qualitative Research Tool Kit

A protocol is a record of a respondent's verbalized thought processes while performing a decision task or while problem solving. This record is obtained by asking the respondent to "think out loud" or talk about anything going through his or her head while performing the task. Protocols can be collected either in a laboratory situation while the respondent is making a simulated purchase or in the field while an actual purchase decision is being made. This approach is the concurrent protocol. Another version is the retrospective protocol in which the verbalizing aloud is done just after the task has been finished.

In contrast to traditional survey methods, protocol methodology allows a person to respond freely in his or her own terms in relation to the actual choice task or decision situation. The form and particular stimuli to which the research subject should respond is not defined or specified by the researcher.

Protocols can be useful in studying brand choice, product categorization, product usage patterns and attitudes, and the impact of shopping environment and situational variables on behavior.

Since data are collected in an unstructured way, there is the problem of interpretation. By its very nature protocol-based data are subjective. Thus, some form of content analysis will be needed. This could lead to incomplete information being provided. Although protocols can provide great detail and breadth of coverage, they are best suited for use with other techniques.

Projection through sketching by the respondent has been used in a study of supermarket layout and design (Krugman, 1960). A sample of 50 housewives was asked to "draw a supermarket" in conjunction with an interview. Some of the findings were:

1. The meat department was omitted in about one out of 10 drawings, produce in one out of five, and dry groceries in one out of four.

2. The produce department was drawn first in about two out of five drawings, meats in one out of five, dairy in one out of six, and dry groceries in one out of six.

3. The meat department was, on the average, about 50 percent larger than the dry groceries department. Actually it is only about one-third as larger as the dry groceries department in a store of the dimensions involved. Produce was drawn 80 percent as large as dry groceries, though it too occupies only about one-third of the space actually allotted to dry groceries.

Although not a projective technique, *ethnography* is a qualitative research approach that is finding use by marketing researchers. Ethnography is the study of human behavior within a cultural context. Implementing an ethnographic study involves observation of behavior and the physical setting, as well as intensive interviews to gain the perspective of participants. Ethnographic methods can be used to generate hypotheses and ideas that can be translated into new product concepts, positioning and promotion strategies, etc. Thus, the methods are useful in exploratory as well as more "confirmative" type research. As a form of qualitative research, ethnography uses the natural language of people for data analysis. Interviews are nondirected or semi-structured and can yield spontaneous attitudes, detailed responses, and unanticipated findings. Visual recording has widespread use in ethnographic studies. Photographs or videotapes of the environment and observed behavior can be linked to expressed attitudes of respondents. Although applications are broad, it has been used extensively in at-home studies of packaging and product use. A treatment of the methodology of qualitative research and cultural studies is given by Alasuutari (1995) and ten Have (2004).

OBSERVATION

The remaining major method of collecting information is through observation. Observation is used to obtain information on both current and past behavior of people. Rather than asking respondents about their current behavior, it is often less costly and/or more accurate if the behavior is observed. We clearly cannot observe past behavior, but the results of such behavior are often observable through an approach known as the case study or customer case research. This exploratory qualitative methodology traces the stories of people, circumstances, decisions and events leading to actual purchase decisions through one-on-one interviews (Berstell & Nitterhouse, 2001). The case study approach allows for determining any underlying patterns and may uncover unforeseen problems and unexpected opportunities. Some key characteristics of this approach are (Berstell, 1992):

- Case studies uncover motivations through demonstrated actions, not through statements of opinions.
- Studies are conducted where a product is bought or used.
- Observation and documentation are used to stimulate questions and corroborate responses.
- Case studies can access multiple decision makers because they are done on site.
- Case studies require researchers who are essentially "market detectives" rather than "census takers." Such detectives must have the skills necessary to continue asking "why" questions until answers emerge that show and explain motivations.

Observation may be used as the sole means of collecting data or, as is frequently the case, it may be used in conjunction with other means. It is a method that should always be considered in designing marketing research investigations that call for information on past or current behavior. In some circumstances, observation is the only means of collecting the data desired. Department managers in Lord and Taylor's department store in New York City will need information on the prices of similar products at Bloomingdale's if they want to ensure their prices remain competitive. The observation of Bloomingdale's prices through "shopping" may be the only means of collecting this information, although "observing" Bloomingdale's prices in local newspaper advertising may also be a viable way of collecting the information. As a matter of practice, all department stores in a locality continuously "shop" each other to determine prices.

In other circumstances, alternative methods of collecting information are available, but observation may be the preferable method from either considerations of cost, improved accuracy, or both. Respondents often cannot and sometimes will not report information accurately. Brands usage reports of well-established brands generally show a "halo effect," an upward bias reflecting the prestige the respondent associates with the use of the brand. Many companies, for example, have found that respondent reports of brand purchases of products vary widely from the actual brand of product that the consumer has on hand.

Other examples include a food retailer who tested a new type of shelving for canned goods by observing shoppers as they used the new shelves, a toy manufacturer who, in a laboratory setting, observes children playing with product prototypes, and a manufacturer of disposable diapers who used the results of watching videotape recordings of diaper changing at a day care center to redesign its product. In all these cases other research techniques could have been used, but observation was preferable.

There are some problems in using observation. One concern is with selective perception. Since human perception is quite selective, what people observe depends upon their backgrounds. Thus, what is observed, and reported as such by an observer, depends upon who is doing the observing. The second potential problem is that the behavior being observed is not representative. It may be that what has been observed is the "exception" rather than the rule. That is, the behavior observed may be a unique incident. Of particular concern is whether those being observed know they are being observed. If a person is being observed, his or her behavior may not be a "true" behavior. Also, the presence of others (e.g., in a crowded retail store) may influence behavior at the time. Thus, the situation and setting are critical to the observation experience.

The major applications of observation as an information-collection method may be classified into the categories of the audit, coincidental recording devices, and a general classification, direct observation. Within this classification schema, observation techniques can be distinguished on the basis of extent of naturalness, disguise, structure, directness, and human involvement, into the following categories:

- *Natural/Contrived:* Natural observation involves observing behavior as it occurs normally in the environment, whereas contrived observation involves observing behavior in an artificial environment.
- *Concealment:* Concealment concerns whether the people to be observed are aware they are being observed (undisguised) or are not so aware (disguised).
- *Structured/Unstructured:* The distinction is whether the approach to be followed is specified in detail including what behaviors are to be observed in the first place.
- *Directness:* Behavior can be observed as it occurs (direct) or in the form of a record of past behavior (indirect).
- *Mode:* The main distinction here is whether a human observer or mechanical device is used.

The Audit

Audits of both distributor inventories and consumer purchases are widely conducted to understand purchase patterns. The distributor audit is the more widely known of the two. The commercially available Nielsen Retail Index, an audit of retail stores performed regularly, was described in Chapter 4. As indicated there, data from this and audits available through other research agencies provide estimates of market size, market share, geographic pattern of the market, seasonal purchasing patterns, and results of promotional and pricing changes.

Manufacturers often perform their own audits of distributors through their salespeople. Although the data collected are not as comprehensive as those described above, information on inventories and prices can usually be obtained and reported. These salesperson audits have the additional advantage of ensuring that the salespeople check inventories and prices as a routine part of their sales calls. Improved sales performance is an important co-product of such an auditing program.

Pantry audits of consumer homes is the second type of audit that is sometimes performed. In this type of audit, the field worker takes an inventory of the brands, quantities, and package sizes that the consumer has on hand. When this type of audit is performed on a recurring basis, inconspicuous labels may be attached to the package showing the date the item was first included in the inventory. When the audit is combined with questioning of the consumer, an estimate of usage may be made. The pantry audit is relatively expensive in terms of data obtained, compared with a self-reporting consumer panel, however. Its use has declined as the use of consumer panels has increased.

Recording Devices

A number of electromechanical devices for "observing" the behavior of respondents are in use in marketing research. Some of these devices are used primarily in laboratory-type investigations and others are used to record behavior in its natural setting. Types of recording instruments used in laboratory studies are the eye camera, the pupilometric camera, and the psychogalvonameter. Three of the devices used in noncontrived situations are the motion-picture camera, the video camera, and the Audimeter.

The "observing" of respondent behavior in a laboratory situation with the aid of recording devices has been largely confined to the pretesting of advertising. Eye cameras, for example, are specially designed cameras that record eye movements in relation to the specific location of material on a page. Subjects may be given an advertisement and, through the use of the photographic record provided by the eye camera, analyses can be made of the pattern in which the advertisement is "read." A determination may be made of which parts of it tend to attract attention initially, the relative amounts of time spent in looking at the illustration versus that used for reading the copy, which portions of the copy are actually read, and so on.

The pupilometric camera photographs eye movements of an entirely different sort and for a different purpose. The dilation and restriction of the pupil of the eye has been found to correlate with the degree of interest aroused by the visual stimulus. Interest-arousing stimuli result in the dilation of the pupil. An advertisement or a product that has a pleasurably toned interest to the subject will be evidenced by dilation of the pupil. Further, there are indications that the extent of pupil dilation will indicate degree of interest. While this technique has not yet been fully validated, it shows some promise as a means of measuring consumer interest.

The psychogalvanometer is used for measuring the extent of the subject's "response" to the advertisement. The principle involved is that the perspiration rate of the body is increased by excitement. The amount of stimulation provided by an advertisement, therefore, can be measured by recording changes in perspiration rate. This is done by measuring the change in electrical resistance in the palms of the subject's hands.

Other devices are also used for "observing" behavior under laboratory conditions. In general, all such devices have the advantage of permitting careful and detailed observations of behavior that could not be made otherwise. They have the added advantage of providing permanent records of the behavior observed. In using these devices, however, one should always keep in mind two important questions:

1. Is the behavior we are observing a valid predictor of the behavior we want to predict?

2. Are the subjects behaving as they would in a natural situation?

The answer to the second question can clearly be in the affirmative if the observation is made outside the laboratory and in the natural situation, such as in ethnographic research. Hidden motion-picture cameras, for example, are used in many situations to record respondent behavior.

One such application was a study performed for a manufacturer of frozen juice concentrates who was considering changing the design and amount of information given on the label. Before this change was made, information was needed on the extent to which consumers actually read information on labels. Hidden cameras were stationed in a sample of supermarkets in front of the frozen food cases, and pictures were taken of consumers selecting frozen juice concentrates. An analysis of these pictures indicated that far more time was spent in the selection and more careful attention given to the label than had previously been believed to be the case. It is not necessary for the camera to be hidden in order for it to be a useful device for recording behavior.

The Audimeter is another device for recording respondent behavior under normal conditions. It is, in effect, an electromechanical equivalent of the consumer "diary" so far as obtaining a record of television viewing is concerned. It is used by the AC Nielsen Company to record automatically the times the television set is turned on and off and the stations to which it is tuned. It is installed in the television sets of a selected panel of families. The tapes on which the recording is made are collected and the National Nielsen TV Ratings is issued regularly. Measurements of total, average, and share of audience are available to clients.

This method of recording the viewing behavior of set owners has some obvious advantages. It permits a complete and accurate record to be obtained of the programs to which each set included in the panel was tuned. Careful analyses can be made of switching during a program to determine the effect of competing programs and of commercial messages. It has the limitation shared by all fixed-sample collection procedures with respect to the inability of obtaining a completely random sample. It also fails to provide information concerning the number of viewers of the program that are tuned in or, indeed, whether the program is actually being watched at any particular time.

Direct Observation

Direct observation of people and how they behave in situations of interest is a commonly used method of collecting information. Many studies have been made of shopping behavior to determine the relative effects of such variables as displays, availability, and reliance on salesperson advice on the brand selected and the quantity purchased. Supermarkets and department store managers continually rely on observation of traffic flows and length of waiting lines to determine the proper location of the various lines of products and the number and location of salespeople and cash registers. An important consideration in the location of banks, retail stores, and entire shopping centers is the amount and pattern of traffic at alternative sites.

Information obtained from direct observation of purchasers can be highly useful in helping to answer such questions as

- Who actually buys the product?
- Do they appear to be influenced by an accompanying person?
- To what extent do brand choices appear to have been made earlier versus at the point of purchase?
- What proportion of shoppers appear to check prices?
- What proportion of shoppers study the package before purchase?

Unobtrusive Measures

Observation is the method of data collection underlying a set of methods known as unobtrusive measures. By their very nature these are nonreactive measures. Included are all the types of data collection mentioned in this section. In addition, other types of unobtrusive measures are traces and archives. Regarding traces, studies of garbage can tell much about consumers. There is the "classic" study of alcoholic beverage purchases in a "dry" community in which types and brands purchased and consumed were determined by examining residents' garbage.

Garbage data can be used to examine many aspects of consumption behavior (Reilly, 1984):

1. Brand and product type switching patterns

2. Market share estimation

3. Lifestyle patterns

4. Ethnic and social group differences

5. Media usage patterns

6. Free samples, deal packs, trial sizes, coupons

In this type of research, there are some biases that can arise. In general, these biases may include the following (as each applies to the subject being considered):

- Missing evidence. Compost piles, pets, garbage disposals, and recycling all affect estimates of product usage and waste and can lead to inaccurate estimates.
- Incomplete evidence. Discard of packaging material may not correspond to usage.

Despite these limitations, it appears they are minor relative to the advantages, particularly when the refuse analysis is part of an accepted project. Reilly (1984, 127–128) listed the following advantages of garbage analysis:

- Unobtrusiveness. Under the current practices used (random sampling of household refuse within selected neighborhoods), individuals are not aware that their refuse is being analyzed.
- Nonreactivity. Because they are not aware that their consumption is being monitored, consumers are unlikely to alter their behavior to appear more rational, more socially acceptable, or more economical.
- Nonresponse. There is no selective bias in participation. Problems in estimating the effects of an imperfect sample are not evident.
- Interviewer effects. Garbage is coded according to objective standards. There is limited possibility for the recorder to consciously or unconsciously bias the outcome of the analysis.
- Response effects. As a result of the unobtrusiveness of the procedure, respondents are not capable of misrepresenting their behavior, either because they can't remember accurately or because they wish to create some type of favorable impression.
- Longitudinal. The behavior of the same household can be observed over time. Patterns of brand/type/product switching can be accurately observed.
- Satisfaction. Refuse provides an accurate measure of the waste of the product, which is a good indicator of the consumer's liking for the product.
- Completeness. Garbage provides information on products that are difficult to monitor through traditional means. Illegal behaviors, purchases from unscanned stores, outlier behaviors (such as beer consumption at parties), and socially sensitive aspects of behavior are all amenable to quantitative analysis using refuse evidence.
- Consumption. Garbage analysis includes accurate measures of when products were used, as opposed to measures of when the products were purchased. This makes measurement of stock-up effects and cross-consumption possible.

Archives, which include published data and internal records, are also a form of observation. In fact, such data are the only way we can observe past behavior. Sales invoices disclose much about how buyers have behaved in the past. We discussed these briefly in Chapter 4.

For a more detailed discussion of unobtrusive methods, we refer the reader to the writings of Webb, Campbell, Schwartz, and Sechrest (1966); Sechrest (1979); and Bouchard (1976). In many cases it is desirable to use these methods in conjunction with other more traditional ones. This is the process known as *triangulation*.

DIRECT VERSUS INDIRECT RESEARCH TECHNIQUES—AN ASSESSMENT

Opinion has been divided among practitioners about the role and relative merits of indirect research techniques in marketing research. This division reflects in marketing research the objectivist-subjectivist debate in the behavioral sciences in general. The controversy has largely centered on three areas:

- The applicability of the techniques
- Sample selection and sizes employed
- Accuracy of utilizing disguised modes of obtaining such information

We will discuss each of these areas.

Applicability of Indirect Research Techniques

The basic premises leading to the use of indirect research techniques are as follows:

1. The criteria employed and the evaluations made in most buying and use decisions have emotional and subconscious content.

2. This emotional and subconscious content is an important determinant of buying and use decisions.

3. Such content is not adequately or accurately verbalized by the respondent through direct communicative techniques.

4. Such content is adequately and accurately verbalized by the respondent through indirect communicative techniques.

How valid are these premises? From the earlier discussion of specific cases, we have already seen that they are valid for some problems. Conversely, it is not difficult to cite cases in which one or more of the premises are not valid. The general answer to the question of whether the premises are valid or not must then be that it "depends on the problem."

As it stands, this is a correct but not a very satisfactory answer. To extend it somewhat and to give it more meaning, it is useful to review the categories of situations in which information might reasonably be sought from respondents and to decide in which of these categories indirect research techniques are the proper ones to apply. Four situational categories can be distinguished in which information might be sought from respondents.

First is the category in which the information desired is known to the respondent and he or she will give it if asked. Direct questioning will therefore provide all of the needed information in this situation. If the reason a consumer does not buy brand X tires is because he believes they do not wear as well as they should, he will willingly say so given the opportunity.

In the second category, the information desired is known to the respondent, but he or she does not want to divulge it. Matters that are considered to be private in nature, that are believed to be prestige- or status-bearing, or that are perceived as presenting a potential respondent-investigator opinion conflict may not be answered accurately. That many people do not fly because they are afraid to do so; that stout people often do not diet because they are afraid that they will not gain the social acceptance they desire anyway; that otherwise quiet and retiring people sometimes buy powerful cars because it gives them a feeling of superiority on the highway are not reasons that will likely be expressed openly and candidly in response to direct questions. When underlying motivations of this general nature are believed to exist, indirect techniques are well suited to elicit such information.

Third, the information desired is obtainable from the respondent, but he or she is unable to verbalize it directly. When respondents have reasons they are unaware of, such as the association of the use of instant coffee with lack of planning and spendthrift purchasing, or the refusal to accept a palatable aspirin because of the association of effectiveness of headache remedies with the requirement that they be taken with water, properly designed and administered indirect techniques can be highly useful for uncovering such motivations.

Fourth, the information desired is obtainable from the respondent only through inference from observation. In some cases motivations of respondents are so deep-seated that neither direct nor indirect methods of questioning will bring them to the surface. An experiment in which the same detergent package in three different-colored boxes resulted in the opinion of housewives using them that the detergent in the blue box left clothes dingy, that the one in the yellow box was too harsh, and that the one in the blue-and-yellow box was both gentle and effective in cleaning is an illustration of color association and its effect on assessment of product quality that very likely would not have been discovered through either direct or indirect questioning. In another experiment, orange-scented nylon hose placed on a counter in a department store next to identical, but unscented, hose were bought by approximately 90% of the women making purchases. Questioning of the women who bought the scented hose as to why they preferred the hose they bought resulted in answers such as "of better quality," "sheerer," and the like.

Of these four informational categories, two of them lend themselves to the use of indirect research techniques. It remains, of course, for the analyst to decide in which one or more of these categories the information he or she requires will fall.

While neither the universally applicable methodology nor the panacea that some proponents have claimed, indirect research techniques can provide information on some types of marketing problems that is not now obtainable by other means.

Sample Selection and Sizes

The subject of sampling is considered in detail in subsequent chapters. However, it is desirable to examine here the typical sampling procedures and practices that have been used in qualitative research studies, as this has been an area of considerable controversy.

Sample selection in qualitative research studies has tended to be done on nonprobabilistic (purposive) bases rather than by probabilistic methods. Typically, selection has been on a judgment or quota basis. As an illustration, the instructions to interviewers in the Pan American Coffee Bureau study asked each interviewer to select two respondents: "one male and one female; one 'dark strong' coffee drinker; one 'light weak' coffee drinker; one 'heavy drinker' (7–8 cups per day); one 'light drinker' (2–3 cups per day)." Although this sample was selected for exploratory purposes, unfortunately it is not an isolated example. There are times, however, when the sample is close enough to the target market population, in terms of characteristics. Although not statistically representative, it is close enough to be used as a basis for judgment.

Serious sampling errors can result from purposive sampling, and, in any case, the extent of the sampling error is unknown. One of the reasons often given for using purposive rather than probability sampling is the high nonresponse rate. To refer again to the coffee study cited above, the statement was made in the instructions to the interviewers, ". . . it would be most helpful . . . if you could just get people talking freely on all their feelings about coffee for an hour or so." One can well imagine that some sample members would be reluctant to spend this much time in an interview, thus creating a bias in the research process.

A second area of controversy over the samples typically taken in qualitative research studies relates to their size. Generally, samples have been small, often ranging from 20 to 50 in size. The use of a small sample in a qualitative research study suggests that the population of psychological attributes and motivations being sampled is sufficiently homogeneous that only a limited sample is required to provide an adequate representation of the population. However, the bulk of the evidence amassed by psychologists suggests that motivations are myriad and varied in their effect on behavior. To assume that the motivations of a very small group of people adequately represent those of the population at large is to ignore the high degree of variability that empirical studies have substantiated.

The Validity of the Findings

What about the validity of indirect research findings? How has their performance in these respects compared with that of the more conventional research methods? The question of validity of findings is, of course, the heart of the issue here, as it is in the general objectivist-subjectivist controversy. Unfortunately, to raise the question is to beg it; no definitive answer can be given. As has already been indicated, the answer is necessarily conditional on the nature of the problem being investigated.

An observation does need to be made, however, about the differences in judging validity by the "clients" of basic research versus those of decisional research projects. The client of the basic research project is the professional in the field. Judgment of the validity of findings of a study is a highly impersonal process and one that is seldom urgent. The purpose of the project is either to make the best estimate of a population parameter or to conduct the best test of a hypothesis within the constraints of available resources. In the absence of data that can be used for direct validation, the basic research project is judged tentatively on the basis of method. The rules of evidence for a basic research study require that the procedures be public, the results investigator-independent, and the project replicable.

Since indirect research methods violate each of these requirements to some extent, there has been reluctance on the part of some basic researchers to give even tentative acceptance to unvalidated findings of studies that employ indirect methods. They tend to look upon indirect research methods as a means of generating hypotheses for testing by objectivist methods rather than as a source of valid findings.

The client for a decisional research project has a different set of requirements. Rather than wanting to be assured that the best estimate of a parameter or the most definitive test of a hypothesis has been made, the client needs information that will assist him or her in making the best decision possible in the circumstances. The procedures of the investigation need not be public, and there is seldom a need for replication. The client works directly with the researcher and is able to raise any questions he or she has about the project. The client usually will have had the opportunity to judge the validity of the findings of past research projects conducted by either the researcher or the organization for which he or she works. An assessment of validity of the findings must be made now; to await the outcome to determine if the findings are valid would obviate the very purpose for which the research was conducted. Judgment of degree of validity therefore turns out to be a much more subjective process in decisional than in basic research.

Indirect techniques serve several useful purposes in marketing research. They can be used to obtain information from respondents unwilling or unable to provide it by direct methods, to check the validity of responses to direct techniques, and to provide supplemental information. Included in the supplemental information that is of value is that which suggests hypotheses that can be tested by direct methods.

SUMMARY

In this chapter we first examined the various types of indirect interviews and qualitative research techniques that can be used to obtain information from respondents. In the indirect types of interviews, we described the more commonly used projective techniques, including the third-person technique ("what does your neighbor think of . . .?"), word association, sentence completion, Thematic Apperception Tests, and depth interviews. Also discussed were focus groups.

We then considered the means of obtaining information through observation of people. The use of audits, recording devices, and direct observation were described and their applications discussed. Of particular interest is the use of refuse (or garbage) analysis to study consumption behavior.

Finally, an assessment was made of direct (discussed in Chapters 5 and 6) versus indirect research techniques from the standpoints of applicability to marketing problems, sample selection and sizes, and validity of findings.

ASSIGNMENT MATERIAL

1. "Projective techniques belong in clinical psychology, not in marketing." Do you agree or disagree? Defend your position.

2. Comment on the following statement: "The proper role of qualitative research is to suggest rather than to test hypotheses."

3. Zilch Marketing Research Associates was hired by the local chamber of commerce to do research that would help the chamber develop a marketing plan to enhance the economic

development of the area. The project was turned over to George Hoser, who was to be project director. Mr. Hoser felt that a useful starting point would be to conduct three focus groups: (a) business leaders; (b) government officials; and (c) the general public.

   a. Do you agree that the three focus groups are the ones to be conducted? If not, what additional groups should be run?

   b. Assuming that the three groups are to be run, develop a research plan for conducting each one. Include in the plan major topic areas to be covered, and a moderator guide.

4. Explain how the third-person technique, sentence completion, Thematic Apperception Test, and a depth interview each can be used to provide information useful in the development of advertising of a packaged food product such as corn chips or crackers.

5. Is it true that observation is a technique that is used more in objective survey research than in subjective survey research? Why?

6. For your household and two additional households (friends) conduct a pantry audit of packaged food products. What can you conclude about this method of data collection?

7. The analysis of traces is a major form of unobtrusive measure. Go to a local museum or art gallery and assess the most popular exhibits, sections, or displays by examining the dirt around them (dirty floors, trash in containers, etc.). What can you conclude from this analysis?

REFERENCES

Alasuutari, P. (1995). *Researching culture: Qualitative method and cultural studies.* London: Sage.

Berstell, G. (1992, January 6). Study what people do, not what they say. *Marketing News, 26,* 15ff.

Berstell, G., & Nitterhouse, D. (2001, February 26). Getting whole story can reveal surprise opportunities. *Marketing News, 35,* 45.

Bloor, M., Frankland, J., Thomas, M., & Robson, K. (2001). *Focus groups in social research.* Thousand Oaks, CA: Sage.

Bouchard, T. J., Jr. (1976, February). Unobtrusive measures: An inventory of uses. *Sociological Methods & Research, 4,* 267–300.

Catterall, M., & Maclaren, P. (1998, August). Using computer software for the analysis of qualitative market research data. *Journal of Marketing Research, 40,* 207–222.

Chekman, D. (1990, December). Focus group research as theater: How it affects the players and their audience. *Marketing Research, 1*(4), 33–40.

Ericsson, K. A., & Simon, H. A. (1984). *Protocol analysis: Verbal reports of data.* Cambridge: MIT Press.

Fedder, C. J. (1990, January 8). Some differences between consumer-based and business-to-business groups require a special touch. *Marketing News, 24,* 46.

Fern, E. (1981). Why do focus groups work? A review and integration of small group process theories. *Proceedings of the Association for Consumer Research Annual Conference,* pp. 441–451.

Garee, M. L., & Schori, T. R. (1996, September 23). Focus groups illuminate quantitative research. *Marketing News, 30,* 41.

Gibby, K., Holland, D., Lee, F., Lundell, C., Merrill, S., & Robison, J. (1995). *Positioning a credit union Visa.* (Field study conducted under the supervision of Professor Scott M. Smith.) Provo, UT: Brigham Young University.

Green, P. E., Tull, D. S., & Albaum, G. (1988). *Research for marketing decisions* (5th ed.). Englewood Cliffs, NJ: Prentice Hall.

Greenbaum, T. (1991, May 27). Doing your own focus group is like doing your own plumbing. *Marketing News, 25,* 8.

Greenbaum, T. (1993, January 4). Convention focus groups are a way to increase geographic representation. *Marketing News, 27,* FG-2.

Greenbaum, T. (1999). *Moderating focus groups: A practical guide for group facilitation.* Thousand Oaks, CA: Sage.

Haire, M. (1950, April). Projective techniques in marketing research. *Journal of Marketing, 14,* 649–656.

Harris, L. M. (1995, February 27). Technology, techniques drive focus group trends. *Marketing News, 29,* 8.

Johnson, R. R. (1988, October 24). Focus groups are divided into 4 distinctive categories. *Marketing News, 22,* 21.

Kates, B. (2000, April). Go in-depth with depth interviews. *Quirk's Marketing Research Review,* pp. 36–40.

Krugman, H. E. (1960, Spring). The 'draw a supermarket' technique. *Public Opinion Quarterly, 24,* 148–149.

LaFlamme, T. A. (1988, August 29). Symphony strikes a note for research as it prepares to launch a new season. *Marketing News, 22,* 12.

Langer, J. (2001, September 24). Get more out of focus group research. *Marketing News, 35,* 19–20.

Lawless, P. (1999, January 4). Empathic interviewing for insightful results. *Marketing News, 33,* 20.

Mariampolski, H. (1988, October 24). Probing correctly uncovers truth behind answers in focus group. *Marketing News, 22,* 22ff.

McDonald, W. (1993). Focus group research dynamics and reporting: An examination of research objectives and moderator influence. *Journal of the Academy of Marketing Science, 21*(2), 161–168.

Miller, C. (1994, July 4). Focus groups go where none has been before. *Marketing News, 28,* 2ff.

Newman, J. W. (1957). *Motivation research and marketing management.* Cambridge, MA: Harvard University Graduate School of Business Administration.

Reilly, M. D. (1984, September/October). Household refuse analysis and market research. *American Behavioral Science, 28,* 115–128.

Reynolds, T. J., & Gutman, J. (1988, February/March). Laddering theory, method, analysis, and interpretation. *Journal of Advertising Research, 28,* 11–31.

Reynolds, T. J., Dethloff, C., & Westberg, S. (2001). Advancements in laddering. In T. J. Reynolds & J. C. Olson, Eds., *Understanding Consumer Decision Making: A Means-End Approach to Marketing and Advertising Strategy.* Mahwah, NJ: Lawrence Erlbaum.

Reynolds, T. J., & Whitlark, D. (1995, July/August). Applying laddering data to communications strategy and advertising practice. *Journal of Advertising Research, 35*(4), 9–17.

Rydholm, J. (2000, March). Preserving the preservationists. *Quirk's Marketing Research Review,* pp. 8–19ff.

Schmidt, M. (2001). Using an ANN approach for analyzing focus groups. *Qualitative Market Research: An International Journal, 4*(2), 100–111.

Sechrest, L., Ed. (1979). *Unobtrusive measurement today.* San Francisco: Jossey-Bass.

Shermach, K. (1995, August 28). Respondents get hooked up and show their emotions. *Marketing News, 29,* 35.

Simon, M. (1988, August 29). Focus groups by phone: Better way to research health care. *Marketing News, 22,* 47–48.

ten Have, P. (2004). *Understanding qualitative research and ethnomethodology.* London: Sage.

Wade, R. K. (2002, March 4). Focus groups' research role is shifting. *Marketing News, 36,* 47.

Webb, E., Campbell, D., Schwartz, R., & Sechrest, L. (1966). *Unobtrusive methods: Nonreactive research in the social sciences.* Chicago: Rand McNally.

Wieners, B. (2003, April). Getting inside—way inside—your customer's head. *Business* 2.0, pp. 54–55.

Xerox guarantees 'total satisfaction'. (1990, October 15). *Marketing News, 24,* 2.

Zaltman, G. (2003). *How consumers think.* Boston: Harvard Business School Press.

Chapter 8

EXPERIMENTATION

Experimentation is widely used in marketing research. Marketing experiments have been conducted in such diverse activities as evaluating new products, selecting advertising copy themes, determining the frequency of salespeople's calls, and evaluating all aspects of a movie—including ending, pacing, music, and even the storyline (Diamond, 1989). For example, as shown in Exhibit 8.1, the ending of the very successful movie *Fatal Attraction* was changed because test audiences did not like the original ending.

This chapter discusses the objectives of experimentation and illustrates techniques for designing and analyzing marketing experiments, including the following:

- The nature of experimentation
- Ingredients of a marketing experiment
- Sources of invalidity
- Models of experimental design
- Panels and experimental design
- Field experimentation in marketing

EXHIBIT 8.1   Test Audiences
Have Profound Effect on Movies

What if E.T. hadn't made it home, or Richard Gere had failed to come back for his pretty woman, Julia Roberts? Believe it or not, in the original versions of these films, E.T. died on American soil and it was Roberts who rejected Gere at the end of *Pretty Woman*.

So who changed these potential misses into hits? It wasn't the producers or the writers who prevailed for change—it was the moviegoers. In what may be Hollywood's last and most closely guarded secret, the test audience is having a profound effect on the movies you watch.

Scientific Findings?

In the original version of the hit *My Best Friend's Wedding,* Rupert Everett had a minor role as Julia Roberts' gay best friend. But test audiences wanted more. So the ending was scrapped, the set rebuilt, and Everett's character came back for one final appearance. That's what can happen if test audiences love you. But what if they loathe you? In the 1987 thriller *Fatal Attraction,* test audiences so despised Glenn Close's character that they became responsible for having her killed off in the end.

Music, endings, even character development can be radically altered as a result of audience research. Audience testing is the movie studios' way of hedging their bets. Although it's been around for a long time, it has never been a completely reliable process. In 1939, test audiences for *The Wizard of Oz* felt that the now-classic scene in which Judy Garland sings "Somewhere Over the Rainbow" slowed down the action. Somehow, the songwriters prevailed, and the song stayed put.

Director Ron Howard and his partner, producer Brian Grazer, are responsible for hits like *Far and Away, Ransom, Apollo 13,* and *A Beautiful Mind.* Howard says, "What I would hate to do is put the movie out there, find out that the audience is confused about something or upset about something that you could have fixed and realize I had no idea they'd respond that way." Grazer and Howard were dealt one surprise when they tested the 1989 film *Parenthood.* "The audience told us there was too much vulgarity in the movie," Grazer says. "We took out a lot of the vulgarity. The scores went up, made us feel better, the movie played better. It didn't offend anybody."

The Process

So how does the process work? First, test audiences are recruited from movie lines. The audience sees the film for free. Afterwards, each participant fills out a survey. It has a lot of questions about what you thought of the film, what five things you liked best, what five things you liked least, which scenes you liked the most, and which characters you identified with. Some members of the audience are asked to join a smaller discussion, known as a focus group. There, the process works the same way.

Robert Kessler, a focus group facilitator, stated that he "basically asked people to comment on whether they liked or disliked certain characters, whether you thought certain things should have been more developed, less developed, et cetera."

"A Huge Amount of Money"

At the end of the process, the studios treat the research as valuable inside information, and they guard it zealously. Studios use some of this information to market their films. But studios also use research as a mandate for creative change. There's a huge amount of money at stake, and more importantly, a lot of careers at stake.

So why do filmmakers like Howard and Grazer feel they get so much out of this controversial process? In part, because they're in the enviable position of having artistic control – they make the final cut on their films. According to Howard, "the whole preview experience is not fun. Even when it's going well, it's not fun. You never want to be proven to be mistaken about anything." But in the end, it is often the audience who makes the judgment.

SOURCE: Adapted from Bay, 1998.

THE NATURE OF EXPERIMENTATION

In Chapter 3, we discussed experimentation as a source of marketing information. Two general types of experimental designs were identified—natural and controlled. A natural experiment is one in which the investigator intervenes only to the extent required for measurement, and there is no deliberate manipulation of an assumed causal variable. "Nature" produces the changes. In contrast, in a controlled experiment two kinds of intervention are needed:

1. Manipulation of at least one assumed causal variable

2. Random assignment of subjects to experimental and control groups

An experiment having both types of intervention is known as a true experiment. When there is manipulation of variables but there is not random assignment of subjects, the design is known as a quasi-experiment.

All true experiments have certain things in common—treatments (i.e., assumed causal variables), an outcome measure, units of assignment, and some comparison from which change can be inferred and, it is hoped, attributed to the treatment. Quasi-experiments, on the other hand, have treatment, outcome measures, and experimental units but do not use random assignment to create the comparisons from which treatment-caused change is inferred. Rather, such comparisons depend on groups that differ from each other in ways other than the presence of a treatment whose effects are being tested (Cook & Campbell, 1990).

Objectives

The term experimentation is used in a variety of ways and for a variety of objectives which, for our purposes, should be distinguished. Some marketing researchers use the term synonymously with market measurement and estimation. In this use of the term, it is assumed that the analyst has already formulated a model of how the phenomenon under study behaves and is interested only in obtaining numerical values for some of the parameters of the model. Considered literally, "experimentation" in this context does not involve a possible rejection of the model itself.

In other cases, experiments may be conducted for the primary objective of determining the functional form that links some criterion variable to a set of input variables. For example, a marketing analyst may postulate that sales response to increasing amounts of advertising is either linear or quadratic over some range of interest. The analyst may conduct an experiment to establish which functional form better fits the data.

In still other cases, the experimenter may not even know what variables are relevant. An experiment may be conducted for the purpose of identifying relevant variables as well as the functional form of the model that links these variables with the criterion variable under study. In the discussion of this chapter we shall use the term "experimentation" in this third context, realizing that the term has been and will probably continue to be used in other ways as well. Perhaps the characteristic that best distinguishes experimentation from observational studies (which are also employed in measurement and estimation) is that experimentation denotes some researcher intervention and control over the factors affecting the response variable of interest to the researcher.

We have already discussed the nature of the term *cause* in Chapter 3. Experimentation permits the establishment of causal relationships. In contrast, correlation analysis (a useful technique in observational studies) permits the analyst to measure the degree to which changes in two or more variables are associated with each other.

Although we cannot infer causality from simple associations alone, correlation techniques are still useful. If association is found, we can use the results of this preliminary analysis to provide possible candidate variables for later experimentation.

As an illustration of tying in correlation analysis with experimentation, a major chemical firm was interested in the relationship of its antifreeze sales to changes in total expenditures for advertising. By using multiple regression analysis, the firm was able to establish an association between its sales and (regional) variations in advertising expenditures. Unfortunately, historical variations in past advertising expenditures by region had been too small to enable the firm to construct a sales-response function over a range of advertising sufficiently broad to be useful for policy purposes. Accordingly, a field experiment was designed that revealed the nature of the response function over a wide enough range to determine the optimal advertising expenditure level. Thus, the regression analysis first served to give insight into the variables that were affecting the sales-response function and later paved the way for direct manipulation of advertising expenditures.

Some Industry Examples

The use of experimental design principles is not uncommon in marketing. To illustrate, a large western petroleum refiner was interested in what type of merchandise catalog to send out to its credit card customers to induce them to purchase various kinds of gift merchandise. An experiment was designed in which three test catalogs were prepared covering the same merchandise at the same prices. The catalogs differed in terms of layout and copy. A set of marketing regions were chosen as experimental blocks, and an equal number of each of the three test catalogs were sent to a random sample of credit card holders in each region. In addition to recording sales response to each test catalog, each merchandise order was analyzed to determine the credit card holder's extent of past purchases of the firm's catalog merchandise over the previous year. A randomized block design (described later in the chapter) with past purchases serving as a covariate was used to analyze the data. After statistically adjusting for the effect of past purchases on current sales response, it turned out that one of the test catalogs resulted in 50 percent more purchases than the second catalog and almost 80 percent more purchases than the third. Needless to say, the company adopted the winning catalog for national distribution.

As a second example, a national producer of packaged candies was interested in children's preference for various formulations of one of its well-known candy bars. Type of chocolate, quantity of peanuts, and amount of caramel were independently varied in a factorial design (described later in the chapter) of two types of chocolate by three quantities of peanuts by three amounts of caramel. Paired combinations (i.e., two combinations at a time) comparisons involving the 18 combinations were made up and evaluated by various schoolchildren between eight and 12 years of age. Interestingly enough, the company found that preferences for type of chocolate varied with the amount of caramel. In addition, while children preferred more peanuts to fewer peanuts, the intermediate level of caramel was the most preferred. The company modified its formulation to match the most preferred test combination.

Another example is provided by Johnson Wax's use of different types of experiments prior to the introduction nationally of Agree Shampoo. For the product itself, the test design used a blind-paired comparison among members of a mail panel. Two products, identified only by some code letters, were sent to 400 women and each was to be used for two weeks. At the end of the use period a telephone interview determined overall preferences and ratings for key performance attributes. Next, Johnson Wax used a lab test-market. This technique simulates the awareness, trial, and repurchase sequences by using a finished advertisement and final label product and by providing a shopping situation in a simulated store, actual use, and simulated repurchase. The lab test-market was conducted in Fresno, California, and in South Bend, Indiana. The model predicted a market share that met the objectives of the marketing plan. Finally, the product was test-marketed in Fresno and South Bend by using controlled store tests. The test-market was used not only for measuring sales and market share but also for testing elements of the marketing plan. On the basis of test-market results, the product was then launched nationally.

Other examples of the use of experimentation in industry involve the use of scanners in supermarkets and cable television. Using two cities as test markets, Information Resources, Inc., of Chicago developed a service based on monitoring purchases by 2,000 households in each market at selected supermarkets and a type of split-cable capability that allows cable television stations to selectively send commercials to participants on a house-by-house basis. In one test, the objective was to determine the cost-effectiveness of a product sample as either an alternative or an accompaniment to television commercials to sell a children's food product. The household panelists were split into four groups of 1,000 and various combinations of samples and advertising were used. Sales doubled in all the groups receiving samples, but the group also exposed to advertising was more brand loyal over time. Another test looked at whether a switch to television advertising would benefit household products marketed chiefly through price promotions.

Many other experiments have been carried out involving taste testing, package design, advertising type and quality, price sensitivity, and other marketing variables.

INGREDIENTS OF A MARKETING EXPERIMENT

In Chapter 2, the research process in general was discussed in the context of a series of interrelated steps. In a similar manner, an experiment involves interrelated steps, as shown in Figure 8.1 (note the similarity to Figure 2.1). Our concern in this chapter is primarily with defining variables, designing the experimental procedure, and conducting the experiment. The other steps are discussed elsewhere in this book, and for experimentation general concepts provide similar information.

All experiments involve three types of variables. First, there is the variable whose effect upon some other variable the experiment is designed to measure. In a causal study this variable is the presumed cause. Since this is the variable that is manipulated, it is known as the treatment, although it is often referred to as the independent variable. Marketing experiments often involve more than one treatment variable. When this is the case, the researcher may be interested in observing the effects of combinations of treatment variables, in addition to the effect of each one individually. In short, there may be interaction effects. Interaction refers to the situation where the response to changes in the levels of one treatment variable is

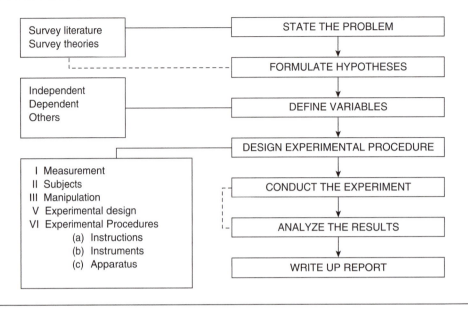

Figure 8.1   Components of an Experiment

dependent on the level of some other treatment variable(s) in the experiment. For example, suppose we design an experiment to measure the effects of price and advertising on the sales of a product. Not only will each of these two marketing variables, independent of the other, have an effect on sales, but the combination of the two may also have a separate effect.

The second broad type of variable in an experiment is the effect of interest. This is the outcome or dependent variable. In the preceding price and advertising example, the dependent variable was product sales.

The last category of variables consists of those that could influence the observed effects (i.e., dependent variable), other than the manipulated independent variables. These are known as extraneous variables, and unless controlled adequately they are the source of errors in an experiment. These will be discussed in a later section of this chapter.

Measurement, Manipulation, and Experimental Procedures

A critical aspect of all experiments, indeed of all marketing research, is measurement. Our concern at this point is with the operational problems of measurement. The concepts, levels, and techniques of measurement, and scaling are covered in Chapters 9 and 10.

In a marketing experiment, it is the outcome or dependent variable that is measured. Generally, the operational measures used can be classified into verbal, electromechanical, and direct measures. Verbal measures include spoken and written responses, including responses provided interactively with a personal computer. Electromechanical measures include those obtained from devices that measure such things as eye movements during advertising readership, pupil dilation, and responses to sensory stimuli obtained from using a psychogalvanometer or tachistoscope. Such devices are used in laboratory experiments. Direct measures are illustrated by dollar amount of sales or profit, units of a product that are sold or consumed, and actual behavior (or assumed actual behavior) of people under the conditions of the experiment. Direct measures are obtained by communication, self-report, observation, or mechanical or electronic means.

Turning now to manipulation, an experimental treatment must be capable of variation. There are at least three ways in which variation in the independent variable can be achieved. First, there is the presence versus absence technique. This approach requires that the treatment be given to one group of subjects while another group does not receive the treatment. For instance, one group of people could be shown a new advertisement and their responses to an attitude measurement could be compared with the response from a group that did not see the advertisement. Second, the amount of a variable can be manipulated; different amounts are administered to different groups. This technique is used in such experiments as those where different prices for a product are tested and the outcome "units sold" is measured. Finally, the type of variable can be manipulated. For example, a company interested in the effect of image on some outcome measure could conduct an experiment by running a series of advertisements, each of which was designed to convey a different image of its product. Regardless of whether the dependent variable was attitude or sales, variation was generated in the type of image conveyed.

In all of the situations described above, there could be other variables having an effect upon the outcome in addition to the one(s) deliberately manipulated. These are the extraneous variables. Ways to handle extraneous variables are shown in Figure 8.2.

As with any approach to marketing research, all phases of an experiment should be carefully planned in advance. After decisions have been made concerning measurement, research subjects, experimental design, control techniques, and manipulation, there is the need to plan everything that will take place in the actual experiment itself through to the end of data collection. This includes the setting of the experiment, physical arrangements, apparatus that will be used, data collection forms, instructions, recording of the dependent variable, and so forth.

Classical Versus Statistically Designed Experiments

We are all familiar with the image of the laboratory scientist who carefully fixes all factors (or treatment variables) assumed to affect the outcome of the experiment except the one whose effect he or she is trying to measure. If several factors are under study, the scientist then proceeds to fix all factors except the second one under study, and so on, until the effect of each factor is measured.

There are two things wrong with the "varying one factor at a time" approach (Anderson & Kraber, 1999, p. 34). First, this procedure is inefficient in the sense that other experimental designs (to be described) yield more information per observation. Second, the procedure does not enable the researcher to measure any interactions that may exist among the experimental factors. For example, suppose that a laboratory scientist (working in the field of electrolytic chemistry) is attempting to study the effect of temperature and reagent concentration on the amount of copper deposited (per unit of time) on a steel bar. If the scientist holds the temperature constant, we assume that so many additional milligrams of copper are deposited with each increase of five percentage points in the electrolytic concentration. Similarly, holding the concentration of the electrolytic solution constant while varying the temperature results in so

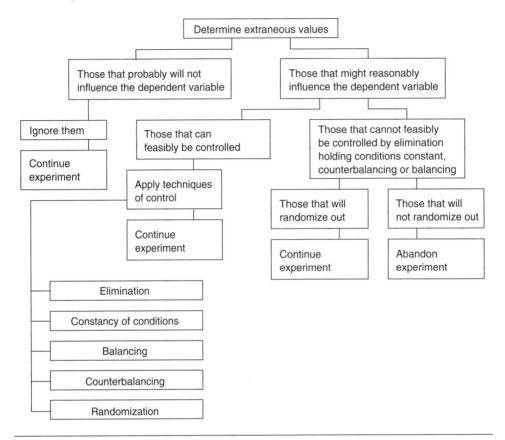

Figure 8.2   Ways to Handle Extraneous Variables

many milligrams of copper being deposited per unit of time. If, however, the mass of copper deposited per unit change in temperature differs among levels of electrolytic concentration, the "varying one factor at a time" approach will not reveal this tendency.

These difficulties are even more pronounced when conducting experiments in a field research situation where many factors vary and influence the results. Both classical and statistically controlled experimental designs are discussed later in this chapter.

Difficulty of Control

In any experiment, as previously mentioned extraneous factors could potentially affect the response. Those factors that probably would not influence the dependent variable can be ignored. On the other hand, those extraneous variables that might be reasonably expected to influence the dependent variable must be controlled in some way in order that error, and thus threats to valid inference, can be minimized (see Figure 8.2).

The concept of control has different meanings (Cook & Campbell, 1990). First, it may refer to the ability to control the situation in which an experiment is being conducted so as to keep out extraneous forces. Used in this way, control is much easier to achieve in a laboratory environment than in a field setting. A second meaning of control refers to the ability to determine which subjects or test units receive a particular treatment at a particular time. Control over the treatment variable helps separate out the effects attributable to irrelevancies that are correlated with a treatment. The third meaning of control relates to a particular identified extraneous factor that the researcher has attempted to eliminate with the design of the experimental procedures or by measuring the factor and then in some manner using the measure in data analysis to remove its influence. The researcher working in the marketplace can more readily use control in our last two meanings than in the first one.

In general, then, control can be achieved by:

1. Designing the experiment appropriately

2. Making statistical adjustments through the use of such techniques as covariance analysis

3. Incorporating one or more of the available control techniques into the design of the experiment

A problem in deciding how best to achieve control is that in a given experimental situation some extraneous factors will be known, but others will be unknown.

In any experiment, control over all possible variables affecting the response is rarely possible. Even in the laboratory it is not possible to control all variables that could conceivably affect the outcome. But compared with the laboratory situation, the researcher who is working in the marketplace has a really difficult control job to do. In real-world market experimentation, it is not possible to come even close to holding other factors constant. Rather, the marketing researcher must try to design the experiment so that the effects of uncontrolled variables do not obscure and bias the nature of the response to the treatment variables that are being controlled.

An illustration should make this point clearer. Suppose that a marketing researcher is interested in conducting a series of taste-testing experiments for a new soft drink. Subjective interpretations of, say, "sweetness" may well vary from subject to subject. If half the subjects were asked to taste only the new brand, the average sweetness rating could mainly reflect the inherent perceptual differences between each group of subjects. A preferable procedure might be to have each subject taste each of two drinks on the assumption that intrasubject expressions of sweetness will affect each response approximately equally; that is, ratings will be expressed in terms of differences in sweetness perceived by each subject. To avoid "ordering" effects on responses, the new drink and the control drink would be presented in randomized order, that is, one-half of the group would follow the sequence "established-new" while the other half would use the sequence "new-established." To reduce carryover tendencies, the subject would be asked to take a sip of water between testing trials. This is the control technique known as counterbalancing.

Such attempts to control confounding, or the tangling effects of two or more levels of a treatment variable (or two or more treatment variables), are commonly used in experimentation. Ideally, the researcher would like to be able to show that the manipulated variables are related to direct measure of the underlying variables they have been designed to change and that such manipulations did not produce changes in measures of related but different constructs. The first situation is a widely used form of manipulation check, whereas the second condition refers to a confounding check. If either check fails, confidence in the researchers' causal explanation of the experimental results is reduced significantly because the construct validity of the operational measures of the supposed independent variables would be highly questionable. This would suggest the need to perform manipulation and confounding checks for every experiment. Since the major issue is one of construct validity, concern is for assessing convergent, discriminant, and nomological validity. These are discussed in Chapter 9. These two types of checks appear to have their greatest value during the pretest and/or pilot testing phases of an experiment. After all, they are of little use if the manipulation cannot be changed when a problem is identified (Perdue & Summers, 1986).

The fact remains, however, that confounding can never be entirely eliminated. Replicating (repeating) an experiment on a new test object (a company, other test object, or human subject) or applying a second treatment to the same test object (after a suitable length of time) always leads to some confounding, since obviously no two test objects will ever be exactly alike, and the conditions of the environment will usually be different over the time lapse required to apply the second treatment, even if one assumed that a "treated" object could return to its original state after the first treatment.

Statisticians have made a major contribution to experimental design in the development of statistical models that feature randomization over uncontrolled variables so as to reduce the effect of these variables on comparative measures of response to the variables under the experimenter's control. In general, the use of "matched groups" (where subjects possess similar characteristics) and "before and after" experiments (where measurements are made before and after the treatments are applied) reduces variation in response due to variables that are not of direct interest to the experimenter. Randomization is a useful device for ensuring, at least on the average, that uncontrolled variables do not favor one treatment over others. Randomization is also useful for experiments using more classical designs. The purpose of randomization is to provide assurance that known and unknown extraneous factors will not cause systematic bias. Consequently, it is assumed that the effects of the extraneous variables will affect all groups in an experiment to the same extent. In theory, randomization is supposed to accomplish the conversion of all irrelevant sources of possibly systematic variability into unsystematic variability, that is, into random error (Brown & Melamed, 1990).

A third major control technique is that of matching, which is sometimes called balancing. Matching is perhaps the best technique for increasing the sensitivity of the experiment, allowing a researcher to detect the influence of the independent variable regardless of how small its influence may be. To increase sensitivity, the error variance must be reduced, and the best way to achieve this is to engage in some form of matching. For the marketing researcher, perhaps the most valuable types of matching are equating subjects and holding variables constant. In the former, subjects are equated on the variable or variables to be controlled. Thus, the composition of each group is essentially the same with respect to all variables except the treatment variable. In the taste-testing illustration, if it were felt that gender and age of subject would influence results, each group should have the same proportions of gender-and-age combinations. Matching by holding variables constant involves constancy of conditions for all groups. Again referring to the taste-testing experiment, the gender variable could be controlled by using only all males or all females as subjects. If time of day is an important extraneous variable that could affect one's taste buds, then subjects should be introduced into the experiment at approximately the same time on successive days. Or, if time of day affects subjects' purchasing behavior in that purchase occurs after a certain time, then the experiment should not be conducted before that time; this was used by McDonald's in their testing of pizza for the dinner hour in that the product being tested was not available until after 4:00 P.M. Similarly, if it were deemed desirable to control for experimenter effects, the same person might be used in all administrations of the taste experiment.

Test Objects

In the preceding discussion we have used the terms test units, test objects, and subjects frequently and interchangeably. All are used to refer to the units whose responses to the experimental treatment are being studied. In marketing research the experimenter has a choice of three possible universes of test units—people, stores, and market areas. Which is most appropriate depends on the problem forming the basis of the experiment (Banks, 1965).

The experimenter must contend with differences among the inherent properties of the test objects. For example, if a researcher is interested in the effect of shelf height on the sales of a packaged consumer product, it is to be expected that stores will vary in their amount of shopping traffic, placement of shelving units, and the like. If the experimenter is interested in the effect of various shelf heights on product sales over a variety of store sizes, several stores will have to be used in the analysis. If so, he or she may use the technique of covariance analysis, in which responses to the controlled variables (shelf height) are adjusted for inherent differences in the test objects (stores) through measurement of these characteristics before or during the experiment.

In summary, the experimenter can use randomization, control groups, covariance analysis, and similar devices to reduce the impact of uncontrolled variations resulting from other environmental variables affecting response and inherent differences among the test objects receiving treatments so long as the interest is in comparative effects among the responses to variables under his or her control. In practice, however, the experimenter can never be sure that all uncontrolled sources of distortion have been guarded against or that even the very process of measurement does not distort the response of the test object being measured. The latter point is particularly true when the test object is a human being. It is not at all unusual to find distorted behavioral patterns when people know that they are participating in an experiment.

Our comments regarding the control of extraneous variables and the techniques used to achieve control are not exhaustive. We have, however, discussed some of the critical issues faced with such variables and we have covered the more widely used techniques for achieving control. A more in-depth discussion is given in Christensen (2004, Chaps. 7 and 8). We now discuss the major extraneous variables that need to be controlled, as each poses a threat to the internal and/or external validity of an experiment.

SOURCES OF INVALIDITY

In Chapter 3, we briefly introduced experimental errors as the extraneous forces that can affect the outcome of an experiment. Each extraneous force potentially has a bearing on the validity of an experiment and, consequently, may threaten the validity of the results.

In the context of experimentation, the term *validity* refers to the extent to which we really observe from an experiment what we say we observe. Four distinct types of validity have been identified (Cook & Campbell, 1990, Chap. 2):

- Statistical conclusion
- Internal
- Construct
- External

A necessary condition for inferring causation is that there be covariation between the independent and dependent variables. Statistical conclusion validity involves the specific question as to whether the presumed independent variable, X, and the presumed dependent variable, Y, are indeed related (Rosenthal & Rosnow, 1991, Chap. 3). This aspect of validity appears to be more closely related to tests of statistical significance used than magnitude estimates. After it has been determined that the variables covary, the question arises as to whether they are causally related. This is the essence of internal validity. A given experiment is internally valid when the observed effect is due solely to the experimental treatments and not due to some extraneous variables. In short, internal validity is concerned with how good the experiment is, as an experiment. The third type of validity, construct validity, is essentially a measurement issue. The issue revolves around the extent to which generalizations can be made about higher-order constructs from research operations and is applicable to causes and effects. Because construct validity is concerned with generalization, it is a special aspect of external validity. External validity, however, refers more broadly to the generalizability of a relationship beyond the circumstances under which it is observed. That is, external validity is concerned with how good an experiment is in terms of the extent to which the conclusions can be applied to and across populations of persons, settings, times, and so on.

To a large extent, the four kinds of validity are not independent of each other. That is, ways of increasing one kind may decrease another kind. Consequently, in planning an experiment it is essential that validity types be prioritized, and this varies with the kind of research being done. For applied research, our primary concern in marketing research, it has been observed that the priority ordering is internal, external, construct of the effect, statistical conclusion, and construct of the cause (Cook & Campbell, 1990). Accordingly, we now examine those extraneous factors that affect internal and external validity. Construct validity is discussed in Chapter 9, and factors affecting statistical conclusion validity are covered throughout the later sections of this book.

Internal Validity

Internal validity is concerned with whether the observed effect is due solely to the experimental treatments or due to some other extraneous variables.

The kind of evidence that is required to support the inference that independent variables other than the one(s) used in an experiment could have caused the observed effect(s) varies, depending on the independent variable(s) being investigated. However, there are some general classes of variables affecting designs that deserve mention. The following factors affect internal validity:

1. *History.* An extraneous event that takes place between the pre-measurement and post-measurement of the dependent variable has an impact on the results.

2. *Maturation.* The results of an experiment are contaminated by changes within the participants with the passage of time.

3. *Testing.* A prior measurement can have an effect on a later measurement.

4. *Instrumentation.* Changes in the measuring instrument or process, including interviewers' instructions, over time, affects the results.

5. *Selection.* Different kinds of research subjects have been selected for at least one experimental group than have been selected for other groups.

6. *Mortality.* Different types of persons drop out from experimental groups during the course of an experiment.

7. *Statistical regression.* This error may arise when experimental groups have been selected on the basis of extreme pretest scores or correlates of pretest scores.

8. *Interactions with selection.* Independent effects of the interaction of selection with history and maturation have an impact on experimental results.

To illustrate each of these factors, suppose that the salesperson-retraining situation described in Chapter 3 had been set up as a controlled experiment. That is, one group of salespeople had taken a retraining course during a three-month time period, while another group had not been retrained. The brand manager of a particular brand of detergent wanted to determine if the retraining was a producer (i.e., a cause) of sales performance. During the three-month period after retraining, sales of the detergent showed an unusually large increase.

History deals with events outside the design that affect the dependent variable. History is therefore comprised of the producers that are extraneous to the design. In the salesperson-retraining example, the level of competitive promotion and advertising, the overall level of demand, or any one of many other producers may have changed substantially in some territories. Clearly, the longer the time period involved, the greater the probability that history will significantly affect the results.

Maturation is concerned with the changes that occur with the passage of time in the people involved in the design. For example, as time passes, salespeople gain more experience in selling and hence know their customers better, and the customers become better acquainted with the product. Again, the effect of maturation on the results is a direct function of the time period involved. Similarly, some biological and psychological changes within salespeople and customers over time can affect the performance of either.

Testing effect has to do with the effect of a first measurement on the scores of a second measurement. In particular, familiarity with a measurement (i.e., a test) can sometimes enhance performance because items and error responses are more likely to be remembered at later measurement sessions. Suppose that in both groups the attitudes of the salespeople toward their job, performance, the company, and so on, had been measured prior to and after the retraining program. There is the possibility that some responses obtained after the retraining program were due to the salespeople remembering responses given on the first measurement rather than being independent responses at the time of the later measurement.

Instrument effect refers to the changes in the measuring instrument or process that may affect the measurements obtained. If total dollar sales volume per territory on a "before and after" basis were being used to determine the effect of retraining, a price change in the interim could clearly make a substantial difference. This is an obvious change in the measuring instrument, but many other and more subtle changes can occur. The learning process on the part of the investigators, a change in investigators, or simply boredom or fatigue may affect the measurements and thus the interpretation of results. A related issue arises when self-report instruments are used. When such instruments are used, it is the research subjects themselves who serve as recorders. Since subjects in the treatment group have had different experiences than control subjects (i.e., they have received the experimental treatment), there exists the possibility of a confounding of the instrument with the experimental treatment. This potential is strengthened when the purpose of the treatment is to change the subjects' understanding or awareness of the variable being measured. The salesperson-retraining program is of this type, as is an experiment designed to measure advertising's impact on attitude. An alternative to the pretest-posttest design is the retrospective pretest-posttest design. In this design, the pretest is given retrospectively after the treatment has been given. Not much is known about this technique, so we cannot generalize about its value in improving internal validity. Some ideas are given in Howard et al. (1979).

Selection is concerned with the effect of the selection procedure for the test and control groups on the results of the study. If the selection procedure is randomized, the effect will be a measurable random variation. However, if the selection is by the investigator, self-selection, or some other nonrandom (purposive) procedure, the results will be affected in a nonmeasurable manner. Sizable systematic errors may well result. The concern, of course, is that the resulting groups may differ in important characteristics, and these differences may influence the dependent variable.

Statistical regression may have an impact when experimental subjects are chosen on the basis of pretest scores. In this situation and when measures are unreliable, high pretest scorers will score relatively lower at the posttest and low pretest scorers will score higher. There is a tendency with repeated measures for scores to regress to the population mean of the group (Cook & Campbell, 1990). This could be operating in the retraining example if the group receiving retraining consisted of salespeople who had high and low attitude scores on the pretest. Similarly, it could be a factor if this group consisted of salespeople with the highest and lowest sales of the detergent.

Some of the foregoing error sources affecting internal validity can interact with selection to produce forces that might appear to be treatment effects. Selection-maturation interaction results when experimental groups mature at different speeds. Selection-history can occur when the experimental groups come from different settings. For example, the salespeople receiving the retraining all come from one region of the country, whereas those not retrained come from some other region. In this situation, each group may have a unique local history that might affect outcome variables.

External Validity

External validity is concerned with whether or not conclusions are externally valid, that is, whether conclusions apply to and across populations of persons, settings, times, and so on. The following are sources of error in external validity:

1. *Reactive effect of testing (interaction).* Pre-measurement may have an impact on the experimental subject's sensitivity or responsiveness to the treatment variable.

2. *Reactive effects of experimental situation.* Experimental subjects react to the experimental situation (such as setting, arrangements, and experimenter).

3. *Interaction of history and treatment.* Measuring the dependent variable at a point in time that does not reflect the actual effect of the independent variables can skew results.

4. *Interaction of selection and treatment.* The method of selection affects the extent to which the measured effect can be generalized to the population of interest.

Reactive effect of testing refers to the learning or conditioning of the persons involved in the design as a result of knowing that their behavior is being observed or that the results are being measured. If salespersons know that they are being retrained as a part of a study to determine how effective retraining is, they may act differently than they would have otherwise. A frequent problem in research design is that a "before" measurement is desired, but it is recognized that making such a measurement may alert the subjects that they are participating in a study. If they surmise that an "after" measurement will be taken, they may become sensitized to the variables involved and behave differently as a result (see Exhibit 8.2). Similarly, if an experiment is being conducted on the impact of advertising, a pre-measurement may sensitize an experimental subject to pay particular attention to a company's advertising, product(s), or both. Although this potential source of error may seem the same as that from testing, it is distinctly different in that it is an interaction of testing and treatment.

EXHIBIT 8.2   Bias in Posttest Scores

In many marketing experiments, particularly the nonfield ones, the subjects take one or more attitude measures both before and after the experimental treatment. Because of a sensitization effect of the pretest, this pretest-treatment-posttest design may confound the treatment effect (Hoogstraten, 1979). Previous research suggests several sources of such bias in the posttest scores:

1. The pretest may raise the curiosity of subjects and thus have a motivational effect.

2. Pretesting may orient the subject's attention selectively toward certain aspects of the treatment. For example, subjects in an educational experiment may learn what to concentrate on during their study of the instructional materials.

3. Taking a pretest engages the subject in a form of public commitment and may therefore have an inhibitory influence on subsequent attitude change.

4. The pretest items may alert the subject to the intent of the investigator and may subsequently facilitate or inhibit opinion change depending on the subject's willingness to comply with the experimental demands.

5. The information contained in the pretest may induce the subject to consider the position implied by this information. This advertising or priming effect may facilitate attitude change.

Despite the plausibility of these explanations, the empirical evidence of a pretest treatment interaction bearing on attitude change research is, in general, meager.

Experimental situation reactive effects concern those effects that may arise from experimental subjects' reacting to the situation surrounding the conduct of an experiment rather than to the treatment variables. By situation surrounding an experiment we mean such things as the setting within which the experiment is conducted, the arrangements made for the experiment such as the apparatus used, and the presence and behavior of an experimenter. These reactive effects involve both experimenter and subject effects (Christensen, 2004, Chap. 7). An important consideration is the presence of demand characteristics (artifacts), which are defined as including "all aspects of the experiment which cause the subject to perceive, interpret, and act upon what he believes is expected or desired of him by the experimenter" (Sawyer, 1975, p. 20). Included among experimenter effects, particularly in laboratory experiments, are the following:

1. **Experimenter expectancies** are biasing effects attributed to the expectancies of the experimenter regarding the outcome of the experiment; these are linked to the hypothesis as a self-fulfilling prophecy, as illustrated in Exhibit 8.3 (Rosenthal & Rosnow, 1991, Chap. 6).

2. **Early data returns bias** describes the effect of early data obtained on subsequent data obtained.

3. **Experimenter modeling** is the extent to which an experimenter's own performance of an experimental task determines his or her subjects' performance of that task.

4. **Experimenter attributes** include effects that result from biosocial (e.g., sex, age, and race of the experimenter), psychosocial (e.g., personality of the experimenter), and situational (e.g., experience in performing a given type of experiment) factors (Barnes & Rosenthal, 1985).

To a large extent, the effects of demand characteristics depend on the roles adopted by subjects, particularly when subjects become aware of, or believe they know, the experimental hypothesis. There are several alternative subject roles:

Good: tries to confirm what is believed to be the experimental hypothesis

Faithful: has no intention to bias and is concerned only with following instructions

Negative: tries to disconfirm a suspected hypothesis by behaving in a contrary or intentionally random or neutral manner

Apprehensive: effects are ambiguous and unpredictable because these types of subjects often worry about how their performance will be judged by others

Ideally, the investigator would seek subjects who are faithful or naïve (i.e., do not know the hypothesis).

Unfortunately, you can never be absolutely certain that demand characteristics will not be present in the chosen experimental procedures. Research design, measurement of dependent variables, and use of procedures (e.g., deception and natural environments) will reduce such demand characteristics (Sawyer, 1975). In addition, manipulation and confounding checks can be used to investigate the plausibility of demand characteristics (Perdue & Summers, 1986).

History-treatment interaction can affect external validity when the dependent variable is measured at a point in time that is not representative of the timing of the effect of the treatment variable on the dependent variable. Time periods to which a particular causal relationship can be generalized are of concern. Returning to the retraining program example, if the retraining had been run during the winter or early spring and detergent sales measured during the quarter following, results may have been misleading because sales would normally be expected to increase greatly during late spring or summer as outdoor activities increase. Similarly, if an experiment were conducted on the effectiveness of advertising and this experiment were run at a time close to any holiday, then a question would remain as to whether the same cause-effect relationship would exist at some other point in time. Moreover, the effects of some independent variables may be long-run in nature, but dependent variable measurement typically occurs at one point in time.

Selection-treatment interaction refers to the categories of people to which a cause-effect relationship can be generalized. That is, can the observed effects be generalized beyond the groups used to establish the relationships? Even when research subjects belong to the target group of interest, the recruitment approach used may limit any generalizations to only those who participated in a given experiment. Experiments, particularly laboratory experiments, rely heavily upon volunteers, paid or otherwise. There is some evidence that volunteer experimental subjects differ from nonvolunteer subjects in more or less systematic ways, as shown in Exhibit 8.4. Although almost 30 years old, these findings are as true today as they were then. In the salesperson-retraining example, this potential threat to external validity would arise if the company attempted to generalize the results to other types of salespeople, such as those who sell food items or small appliances.

EXHIBIT 8.3   Reducing Experimenter Expectancy Effects

Different strategies are available for the reduction of experimenter expectancy effects. These techniques are based on the premise that the mediation of such effects depends to some extent on various nonverbal communication processes that can be controlled or bypassed. The following strategies are listed in Rosenthal and Rosnow (1991, pp. 113–114):

1. Increasing the number of experimenters
   - Decreases learning of influence techniques
   - Helps to maintain "blindness"
   - Minimizes effects of early data returns
   - Increases generality of results
   - Randomizes expectancies
   - Permits the method of collaborative disagreement
   - Permits statistical correction of expectancy effects

2. Observing the behavior of experimenters
   - Sometimes reduces expectancy effects
   - Permits correction for unprogrammed behavior
   - Facilitates greater standardization of experimenter behavior

3. Analyzing experiments for order effects permits inference about changes in experimenter behavior.

4. Developing training procedures permits prediction of expectancy efforts.

5. Maintaining "blind contact" minimizes expectancy effects.

6. Minimizing experimenter-subject contact minimizes expectancy effects.

7. Employing expectancy control groups permits assessment of expectancy effects.

SOURCE: From Rosenthal, R. *Essentials of Behavioral Research: Methods and Data Analysis,* copyright © 1991. Reprinted with permission of the McGraw-Hill Companies.

EXHIBIT 8.4   Characteristics of the Volunteer Subject*

Conclusions Warranting Maximum Confidence

1. Volunteers tend to be better educated than nonvolunteers, especially when personal contact between investigator and respondent is not required.

2. Volunteers tend to have higher social-class status than nonvolunteers, especially when social class is defined by respondents' own status rather than by parental status.

3. Volunteers tend to be more intelligent than nonvolunteers when volunteering is for research in general, but not when volunteering is for somewhat less typical types of research such as hypnosis, sensory isolation, sex research, and small-group and personality research.

4. Volunteers tend to be higher in need for social approval than nonvolunteers.

5. Volunteers tend to be more sociable than nonvolunteers.

Conclusions Warranting Considerable Confidence

1. Volunteers tend to be more arousal-seeking than nonvolunteers, especially when volunteering is for studies of stress, sensory isolation, and hypnosis.

2. Volunteers tend to be more unconventional than nonvolunteers, especially when volunteering is for studies of sex behavior.

3. Females are more likely than males to volunteer for research in general, but less likely than males to volunteer for physically and emotionally stressful research (e.g., electric shock, high temperature, sensory deprivation, interviews about sex behavior).

4. Volunteers tend to be less authoritarian than nonvolunteers.

5. Jews are more likely to volunteer than Protestants, and Protestants are more likely to volunteer than Catholics.

6. Volunteers tend to be less conforming than nonvolunteers when volunteering is for research in general, but not when subjects are female and the task is relatively "clinical" (e.g., hypnosis, sleep, or counseling research).

Conclusions Warranting Some Confidence

1. Volunteers tend to be from smaller towns than nonvolunteers, especially when volunteering is for questionnaire studies.

2. Volunteers tend to be more interested in religion than nonvolunteers, especially when volunteering is for questionnaire studies.

3. Volunteers tend to be more altruistic than nonvolunteers.

4. Volunteers tend to be more self-disclosing than nonvolunteers.

5. Volunteers tend to be more maladjusted than nonvolunteers especially when volunteering is for potentially unusual situations (e.g., drugs, hypnosis, high temperature, or vaguely described experiments) or for medical research employing clinical, rather than psychometric, definitions of psychopathology.

6. Volunteers tend to be younger than nonvolunteers, especially when volunteering is for laboratory research and especially if they are female.

Conclusions Warranting Minimum Confidence

1. Volunteers tend to be higher in need for achievement than nonvolunteers, especially among American samples.

2. Volunteers are more likely to be married than nonvolunteers, especially when volunteering is for studies requiring no personal contact between investigator and respondent.

3. Firstborns are more likely than laterborns to volunteer, especially when recruitment is personal and when the research requires group interaction and a low level of stress.

4. Volunteers tend to be more anxious than nonvolunteers, especially when volunteering is for standard, nonstressful tasks and especially if they are college students.

5. Volunteers tend to be more extroverted than nonvolunteers when interaction with others is required by the nature of the research.

---

*Derived from content analysis of published research. The extent of confidence about a conclusion refers to confidence in the relationship stated.

SOURCE: From Rosenthal, R., & Rosnaw, R., *The Volunteer Subject,* copyright © 1975. This material is used by permission of John Wiley & Sons, Inc.

MODELS OF EXPERIMENTAL DESIGN

A number of experimental designs have been developed to overcome and reduce the various sources of invalidity. Experimental designs can be categorized into two broad groups—classical and statistical. Classical designs consider the impact of only one dependent variable at a time, whereas statistical designs allow for examining the impact of two or more independent variables.

Classical Designs

The major types of classical designs fall into three groups:

- Pre-experiment
- Quasi-experiment
- True experiment

Pre-experimental designs are so called because there is such a total absence of control that they are of minimal value in establishing causality. Quasi-experimental designs involve control but lack random assignment of subjects, as required for true experiments. Where any given design fits in this categorization spectrum will depend on whether the treatment variable has been deliberately manipulated, the nature of control, and whether there has been random assignment of subjects to experimental groups.

The following notational system will be used in the discussion of classical experimental designs:

- X represents the exposure of test groups to an experimental treatment of a producer or event whose effect is to be observed and/or measured.
- O refers to the measurement or observation taken.
- R indicates that individuals have been selected at random to differing treatments.
- Movement from left to right indicates a sequence of events. When O's and X's are found in a given row, they are to be interpreted as having occurred in sequence to the same specific individual or group. Vertical arrangement of symbols is to be interpreted as the simultaneous occurrence of the events that they denote.

Three classes of designs apply to pre- and quasi-experiments:

- Time-series and trend designs
- Cross-sectional designs
- Combinations of the two previous classes

Time-Series and Trend Designs

Time-series and trend designs are similar in concept, yet their differences in implementation and analytic procedures warrant a brief discussion. A time-series design involves obtaining data from the same sample (or population) for successive points in time. The common method of gathering primary data of this kind is to collect current data at successive intervals through the use of a continuous panel. One may, however, collect current and retrospective data from respondents during a single interview. If the latter technique is used, respondent recall must be relied on to reconstruct quasi-historical data. An alternative method of obtaining data for past periods is to use secondary sources, when available.

Trend data differ from time-series data in that they are obtained from statistically matched samples drawn from the same population over time. Current data are gathered from each successive sample.

Both time-series and trend data are used to investigate the existence and nature of causal relationships based on associative-variation and sequence-of-events types of evidence. While individuals or households are the most commonly used sample units, data are also obtained from retail stores, wholesalers, manufacturers, and other units.

Since trend designs provide no continuity in the sample units from which data are obtained, there is no opportunity to observe changes over time in individual sample units. Trend data, therefore, can only be analyzed in the aggregated form in which they are collected. Time-series data generated from continuous panels and, to a lesser extent, from retrospective interviews permit analysis of effects by individual sample units. Microanalyses of this type can provide valuable information on buyer behavior, including purchase rates, brand switching, and brand loyalty. The analysis of microeffects is called longitudinal analysis.

Time-series and trend designs involve at least one treatment and a subsequent measurement and can involve a large number of measurements with several interspersed treatments over a long period of time. We now describe and discuss four types of time-series and trend designs.

After-Only Without Control Group

This design is often termed a "tryout" or "one-shot case study." It is the simplest of all designs, as it involves only one nonrandomly selected group, one treatment, and one measurement. Symbolically, it may be diagrammed as follows:

$$X \quad O \tag{1}$$

The many weaknesses of this design may be illustrated by applying it to the salesperson-retraining problem. Assume that no prior measurement of sales volume of the salespeople to be retrained had been made. A group of salespeople are selected by a nonrandom method and retrained (X); a measurement (O) is made after the retraining.

Since no prior measurement of sales volume of each of the retrained salespeople was made, there is no method, short of making assumptions as to what would have happened in the absence of retraining, of estimating what the effect of retraining was. The effects of history, maturation, and selection are all potentially substantial and nonmeasurable. Because of these limitations the use of this design is to be avoided if at all possible.

Before-After Without Control Group

This design is the same as (1) with the addition of a "before" measurement. In its simplest form it is shown as

$$O_1 \quad X \quad O_2 \tag{2}$$

and in extended form as

$$O_1 \quad O_2 \quad O_3 \quad O_4 \quad X \quad O_5 \quad O_6 \quad O_7 \quad O_8 \tag{3}$$

Although design (2) is relatively weak, it is frequently used. It is a decided improvement over (1) in that the apparent effect of the treatment, $O_2 - O_1$, is measured. In terms of the salesperson-retraining illustration, a measurement (O_1) of sales volume of the salesperson is made for the quarter of the year preceding retraining.

Design (3) is an improvement over design (2) in that data for a larger number of periods are available. The apparent results of the treatment (X) can be analyzed as either the difference of averages

$$\left(\frac{O_5 + O_6 + O_7 + O_8}{4} - \frac{O_1 + O_2 + O_3 + O_4}{4} \right)$$

or the difference in trends of "before" and "after" measurements. This type of design is implicit in many of the aggregate analyses made of consumer-panel data.

The weaknesses of both designs (2) and (3) include neglect of the effects of history, maturation, testing effect, instrument effect, and selection. History can play a large role in determining the level of difference in the before and after measurements, as can maturation. Since measurements are made both before and after the treatment, both testing effect and instrument effects can be present. The testing effect can be particularly important in design (3). The effect of nonrandom selection is also potentially present in both designs. Careful investigation and close scrutiny are necessary to estimate the effect of each of these uncontrolled and unmeasured sources of variation.

Multiple Time Series

In using a time-series design, the possibility of establishing a control group should always be investigated. It may be possible to find a comparable, if not equivalent, group to serve as a control against which to compare the results of the group that underwent the treatment involved. This design may be diagrammed as

$$
\begin{array}{ccccccccc}
O_1 & O_2 & O_3 & O_4 & X & O_5 & O_6 & O_7 & O_8 \\
O_1' & O_2' & O_3' & O_4' & & O_5' & O_6' & O_7' & O_8'
\end{array}
\tag{4}
$$

where the primed O's represent measurement of the control group. Note that the individuals constituting the groups were not selected at random. It may be possible, however, to select at random the group that will receive the treatment.

This design can easily be adapted to the sales-retraining evaluation problem. If it is assumed that the sales volume of each of the salespeople is measured during each period as a matter of course anyway, a group could be selected for retraining after period 4. Either a comparable group or all the rest of the salespeople could be selected as the control group. After the sales of both groups in the periods after the training had been measured, the apparent effect of the training would be shown by comparing the differences in average sales volume for the two groups before and after treatment.

This design is a substantial improvement over design (3) in that the control group, even though purposively selected, provides a basis for allowing for history, maturation, and testing effect. To the extent that the groups are similar, the effects of each of these factors will tend to affect both groups in the same manner. The nonrandom selection of the test and control groups, although less than ideal, may provide a practical and workable substitute for use in situations where random selection is not possible.

Cross-Sectional Designs

Cross-sectional designs involve measuring the product (i.e., dependent variable) of interest for several groups at the same time, the groups having been exposed to different levels of treatments of the producer whose effect is being studied. Cross-sectional designs may be viewed diagrammatically as follows:

$$
\begin{array}{ll}
X_1 & O_1 \\
X_2 & O_2 \\
X_3 & O_3 \\
 & \\
\cdot & \\
\cdot & \\
\cdot & \\
X_n & O_n
\end{array}
\tag{5}
$$

Examples of frequent applications of this design are studies of the effect of such variables as price, package design, or level of advertising in different geographic areas. This design can be used when direct manipulation of the producer involved is not possible or practical. When this is the case, the design is being used in a natural experiment. The effect of the different levels of treatment is measured by determining the degree of association between producer and product. The techniques that can be employed are discussed in later chapters.

A variation of this design is the static-group comparison. This is a design in which a group exposed to a treatment is compared with one that was not:

$$
\begin{array}{ll}
X & O_1 \\
& O_2
\end{array}
\tag{5a}
$$

History may play a critically important role in cross-sectional designs. There may be a sizable differential effect of extraneous producers between the groups being measured. The effects of maturation and testing tend to be reduced to a minimal level, and the instrumentation effect is certainly no greater than in any other design.

Combination Cross-Sectional, Time-Series Designs

A number of designs employing a combination of time-series and cross-sectional treatment and measurement may be used in observational studies. The multiple-time-series design (4) could be considered a combination of the two types, as it involves measurements of a product for different groups at the same time as well as for the same group over time.

Combination designs are well adapted for use with consumer-panel data. One commonly used design is the ex post facto test-control group. In this design the test and control group are not known until after the treatment has been administered. This design is illustrated as follows:

$$O_1 \quad X \quad O_3$$
$$O_2 \qquad O_4 \qquad\qquad (6)$$

This design is widely used in connection with testing the sales effectiveness of price changes, "deals," and advertising. Data on the sales of the brand of interest are reported regularly by the members of a continuous consumer panel. After a given advertisement is run (X), panel members may be questioned to determine whether or not they saw it. Those who saw it are part of the test group, since they have had exposure to the treatment involved. Those who did not see the advertisement become a part of the control group. The apparent effect is determined by comparing the difference in test and control-group purchases before with that after the advertising was run.

The ex post facto determination of test and control group members is another selection method used as a substitute for random selection. Self-selection is involved; the individuals determine by their actions whether or not they will be included in the test or the control group. The self-selection feature of this design can be an important source of systematic error. It has been demonstrated in many studies of advertising, for example, that the individual who has seen the advertising for a particular brand is more likely to have purchased the brand before he or she saw the advertising than is the individual who did not see it.

A variation of the same general design is the nonequivalent control group. This involves purposive selection in advance of the treatment, and measurements are made on the test and control groups. The selection of the two groups must of necessity be determined entirely by the problem environment. An example of the use of this type of design occurred in the early stage of the development of network television. Advertising of a hand soap on network television was initiated at a time when only about one-half of the present number of cities were covered by stations. An analysis was made of sales in network versus nonnetwork cities and compared with sales in the same cities for a comparable period before television advertising was initiated. In this case it was evident that the test and control cities were not equivalent, since a larger amount was spent on advertising in other media in nonnetwork cities than in network cities.

In addition to the error induced by the method of selection, testing effect may be a substantial contributor of error in this design. Despite these error sources, the design is a useful one. It can be adapted to a variety of situations to provide information relatively quickly and inexpensively, particularly when panel data are already available.

True Experimental Designs

As previously mentioned, for true experiments two kinds of investigator intervention are required:

- Manipulation of at least one assumed causal variable
- Random assignment of subjects to experimental and control groups

Through use of a random selection procedure, systematic errors due to selection are eliminated and the effects of the many extraneous variables tend to be equalized between the experimental and the control groups as the size of these groups increases. Random selection permits the use of inferential statistical techniques for analyzing the experimental results. The most fundamental technique for this purpose is analysis of variance. The rationale and some applications of analysis of variance are treated in Chapter 16.

Three single-variable experimental designs are described below.

After-Only With Control Group

The simplest of all experimental designs is the after-only with control group. It requires only one treatment and an "after" measurement of both the experimental group and the control group. Yet it has the essential requirements of the true experiment: manipulation of at least one variable and randomly selected test and control groups. It is illustrated as follows:

$$R \quad X \quad O_1$$
$$R \quad\quad\quad O_2 \tag{7}$$

The absence of a "before" measurement (or pretest) is a feature that concerns many researchers about this design. Such a measure is not actually essential to true experimental designs. In marketing research, it seems difficult to give up the notion that the experimental and the control groups might have been unequal before differential experimental treatment and to rely upon randomization to reassure us that there will be a lack of initial biases between groups.

This design, by avoiding the "before" measurement, provides control over testing and instrument effects. It is of major interest, therefore, when "before" measurements are impractical or impossible to obtain and/or when the testing and instrument effects are likely to be serious.

A common application of this design is in the testing of direct-mail advertising. Random-sampling procedures are used to select an experimental and a control group. Direct-mail pieces are sent to the experimental group and withheld from the control group. "After" measurements of sales to each group are made and the differential is determined ($O_1 - O_2$).

A variation of this design is the so-called simulated before-and-after design. Separate samples are used for the before and after measurements:

$$R \quad O \quad (X)$$
$$R \quad\quad X \quad O \tag{7a}$$

Although there is random assignment, this design is perhaps more properly classified as a quasi-experimental design. Weaknesses of this design are that history and maturation are not controlled. However, this design lends itself to modification by adding features to control specific factors. For example, if this design were repeated in different settings at different times, history would be controlled (Campbell & Stanley, 1966).

Before-After With One Control Group

If "before" measurements are added to design (7), we arrive at the following configuration:

$$
\begin{array}{ccccc}
R & O_1 & X & O_2 & \\
R & O_3 & & O_4 & \quad (8)
\end{array}
$$

This design is very similar to that of (6) but with an important difference: the experimental and control groups are randomly selected, rather than self-selected. Most of the sources of systematic error are controlled in this design. Maturation is controlled in the sense that it is present in both the experimental and control groups. The same observation applies to the testing effect, although it should be noted that no measurement of the testing effect is possible in this design. (Such a measurement is possible in the next design to be discussed.) History is controlled so long as the two "before" measurements (O_1 and O_3) and the two "after" measurements (O_2 and O_4) are made at the same time. A potential instrument effect is established, as is always the case when sequential measurements are made on the same subjects and the same measuring instruments are used.

This design offers three ways to evaluate the effect of the treatments: $O_2 - O_1$, $O_2 - O_4$, and $(O_2 - O_1) - (O_4 - O_3)$. If the results of each of these evaluations are consistent, the strength of our inferences about the effect of the experimental treatment is substantially increased.

An example of the use of this design is in advertising tests that use a dual cable television system with two consumer purchase panels (one from the subscribers to each cable). "Before" measurements can be made on both the test and control panels, an experimental advertising treatment introduced on the test cable, and "after" measurements made for both panels.

Four-Group, Six-Study Design

By combining (7) and (8) we arrive at the following design:

$$
\begin{array}{ccccc}
R & O_1 & X & O_2 & \\
R & O_3 & & O_4 & \\
R & & X & O_5 & \\
R & & & O_6 & \quad (9)
\end{array}
$$

This design provides the opportunity for not only testing the effect of the experimental variable but also testing the effect and the combined effects of maturation and history. This design is also known as the Solomon Four-Group Design.

The effect of the treatment can be evaluated in a number of ways, the usual ones being to determine the differentials $O_2 - O_1$, $O_2 - O_4$, $O_5 - O_6$, $O_4 - O_3$, and $(O_2 - O_1) - (O_4 - O_3)$.

The "after" measurements provide a useful basis for drawing inferences about the testing effects as well as that of the treatment. They can be placed into a 2×2 table as follows:

	No X	*X*
"Before" measurements taken	O_4	O_2
No "before" measurements taken	O_6	O_5

The effect of the treatment can be estimated from the difference in the column means. The difference in row means provides the basis for estimating testing effect. The differences in the individual cell means can be used for testing the interaction of testing and treatment. Analysis-of-variance procedures are useful for analyzing these results.

There are many classical designs. In this section, we have discussed the more common designs. A useful way to summarize what we have discussed is to look at each in terms of sources of potential error and whether such sources are controlled for, as shown in Table 8.1. More detailed discussions are found in Cook and Campbell (1990), Campbell and Stanley (1966), and Shadish, Cook, and Campbell (2002).

Statistical Designs

For the most part, statistical designs are "after-only" designs (7) in which there are at least two treatment levels. In addition, such designs can examine the effects of more than one independent variable. Two principal aspects of statistical designs are the following:

- The experimental layouts by which treatment levels are assigned to test objects
- The techniques that are used to analyze the results of the experiment

We will now briefly discuss the major types of layouts used to obtain data. These are discussed in more depth in Brown and Melamed (1990) and other specialized experimental design texts such as Field and Hole (2003) and Shadish, Cook, and Campbell (2002). Analysis techniques, known generically as analysis of variance and covariance, are discussed in Chapter 16.

Completely Randomized Design

The completely randomized design is the simplest type of statistical design. In this design, the experimental treatments are assigned to test units on a random basis. Any number of treatments can be assigned by a random process to any number of test units.

As an illustration, suppose that a marketer is interested in the effect of shelf height on supermarket sales of canned fruit. The marketer has been able to obtain the cooperation of a store manager to run an experiment involving three levels of shelf height ("knee" level, "waist" level, and "eye" level) on sales of a single brand of fruit, which we will call Sunshine. Assume further that our experiment must be conducted in a single supermarket and that our response variable will be sales, in cans, of Sunshine fruit within some appropriate unit of time. But what shall we use for our unit of time? Sales of canned fruit in a single store may exhibit week-to-week variation, day-to-day variation, and even hour-to-hour variation. In addition, sales of this particular brand may be affected by the price or special promotion of competitive brands, the store management's knowledge that an experiment is going on, and other variables that we cannot control at all or would find too costly to control.

Table 8.1   Sources of Invalidity and Selected Experimental Designs

Sources of Invalidity	Internal								External		
	History	Maturation	Testing	Instrument	Regression	Selection	Mortality	Interaction of selection and others	Interaction of testing and X	Interaction of selection and X	Reactive arrangements
One-Shot Case Study X O	−	−				−	−			−	
One-Group Pretest-Posttest Design O X O	−	−	−	−	?	+	+	−	−	−	?
Time Series O O O X O O O	−	+	+	?	+	+	+	+	−	?	?
Multiple Time-Series O O O X O O O O O O O O O	+	+	+	+	+	+	+	+	−	−	?
Static-Group Comparison X O O	+	?	+	+	+	−	−	−		−	
Nonequivalent Control Group Design O X O O O	+	+	+	+	?	+	+	−	−	?	?
Posttest-Only Control Group Design R X O R O	+	+	+	+	+	+	+	+	+	?	?
Separate-Sample Pretest-Posttest Design R O (X) R X O	−	−	+	?	+	+	−	−	+	+	+
Pretest-Posttest Control Group Design R O X O R O O	+	+	+	+	+	+	+	+	−	?	?
Solomon Four-Group Design R O X O R O O R X O R O	+	+	+	+	+	+	+	+	+	?	?

Note: In the tables, a minus (–) indicates that the factor is not controlled, a plus (+) indicates that the factor is controlled, a question mark (?) indicates a possible source of concern, and a blank indicates that the factor is not relevant.

SOURCE: From Campell, D. T., & Stanley, J. C., *Experimental and Quasi-Experimental Designs for Research*. Copyright © 1963 by Houghton Mifflin Company. Adapted by permission.

Table 8.2   Completely Randomized Design—Sunshine Fruit Experiment

	Shelf Height		
	Knee Level	*Waist Level*	*Eye Level*
Day 1	X_{11}	X_{12}	X_{13}
Day 2	X_{21}	X_{22}	X_{23}
Day 3	X_{31}	X_{32}	X_{33}
Day 4	X_{41}	X_{42}	X_{43}
Day 5	X_{51}	X_{52}	X_{53}
Day 6	X_{61}	X_{62}	X_{63}
Day 7	X_{71}	X_{72}	X_{73}
Day 8	X_{81}	X_{82}	X_{83}

We will address some of these questions shortly, but for the time being, assume that we have agreed to change the shelf-height position of Sunshine three times per day and run the experiment over eight days. We will fill the remaining sections of the particular gondola that houses our brand with a "filler" brand that is not familiar to customers in the geographical area in which the test is being conducted. We will assign the shelf heights at random over the three time periods per day and not deal explicitly with within-day and among-day differences. Our experimental design might look like that shown in Table 8.2. Here we let X_{ij} denote unit sales of Sunshine during the *i*th day under the *j*th treatment level.

The preceding example dealt with the simplest of statistical designs—classification by a single factor. This design is most applicable when it is believed that extraneous variables will have about the same effect on all test units, and when the marketer is interested in only one independent variable. Moreover, there is no absolute guarantee that randomization will keep extraneous influences in check. Suppose that our marketing researcher were interested in the effect of other point-of-purchase variables such as shelf facings (width of display) and shelf fullness on sales. Or, suppose that the researcher would like to generalize the results of the experiment to other sizes of stores in other marketing regions. It may be preferable to ask many rather than few questions if the researcher would like to establish the most general conditions under which the findings are expected to hold. That is, not only may single-factor manipulation be difficult to do in practice, but it may be inefficient as well. We now discuss somewhat more specialized experimental designs, all of which are characterized by two or more variables of classification.

Factorial Designs

A factorial experiment is one in which an equal number of observations is made of all combinations involving at least two levels of at least two variables. In essence, the factorial design is one that has combined two or more completely randomized designs into a single experiment. This type of experiment enables the researcher to study possible interactions among the variables of interest. Suppose we return to our canned fruit illustration, but now

Table 8.3   Factorial Design—Sunshine Fruit Experiment

	Shelf Height		
Facings	*Knee Level*	*Waist Level*	*Eye Level*
Level 1 (half width)	$F_1 H_1$	$F_1 H_2$	$F_1 H_3$
Level 2 (full width)	$F_2 H_1$	$F_2 H_2$	$F_2 H_3$

assume that the researcher is interested in studying the effects of two variables of interest: shelf height (still at three levels) and shelf facings (at two levels, that is, at half the width of the gondola and at the full width of the gondola). The design is shown in Table 8.3. Note that each combination of $F_i H_j$ occurs only once in the design. While the plan still is to use a single store for the experiment, the researcher intends to replicate each combination three times, leading to $3 \times 2 \times 3 = 18$ observations.

In the factorial experiment we can test for all main effects (i.e., facing, height), and in this case, where we have replicated each combination, for the interaction of the variables as well. If the interaction term is significant, ordinarily the calculation of main effects is superfluous, since the experimenter will customarily be interested in the best combination of variables. That is, in market experimentation the researcher is typically interested in the combination of controlled variables that leads to the best payoff in terms of sales, market share, cash flow, or some other measure of effectiveness.

Latin Square

Latin-square designs are multivariable designs that are used to reduce the number of observations that would be required in a full factorial design. In using Latin-square designs, the researcher is usually assuming that interaction effects are negligible; in so doing, all main effects can be estimated by this procedure.

As an illustration of a Latin-square design, suppose that the researcher were interested in three variables (each at four levels) on store sales. For example, in the canned fruit illustration the researcher may be interested in the following:

1. Shelf height—four levels: knee level, waist level, eye level, and reach level

2. Shelf facings—four levels: 25%, 50%, 75%, and 100% of total width of gondola

3. Shelf fullness—four levels: 25%, 50%, 75%, and 100% of total height of gondola section

If the researcher were to run a full factorial experiment, with one replication only, there would be $4 \times 4 \times 4 = 64$ observations required. By using a Latin-square design, only 16 observations are required (with estimation of main effects only).

Table 8.4 shows one possible Latin-square design for the Sunshine fruit experiment. Notice in Table 8.4 that each level of treatment C (shelf fullness) appears once in each row and once in each column. Also the number of levels (four) is the same for each treatment. Exhibit 8.5 shows procedures for randomization of a Latin-square design (Edwards, 1968, pp. 175–177).

Latin-square designs can also be used to control for two so-called nuisance variables (sources of uncontrolled variation) when there is a single treatment of interest. When there are three such variables, a Greco-Latin square design is used.

Cross-Over Design

Cross-over design is the name given to a type of design in which different treatments are applied to the same test in different time periods. This design can be viewed as a type of repeated-measures design as subjects are measured more than once on a dependent variable. Although use of this type of design can reduce the effect of variation among test units, the experimenter must consider another problem: the possibility that successive observations may not be independent. That is, the experimenter may have to contend with a carry-over effect. If the researcher can assume that no carry-over effect exists, then a Latin-square design could be used, as shown in Table 8.5.

In this design each test unit receives each treatment in randomized order over the three time periods, each treatment appearing once in each row and column.

In the case where carry-over effects are assumed to exist, the experimenter must make some assumptions about the nature of this carry-over effect. A particularly simple set of assumptions is that the effect obtained on a single test object in a specific time period is made up of three parts:

1. A quantity reflecting only the test object-time period combination

2. A quantity reflecting only the treatment applied in that time period

3. A quantity reflecting only the treatment applied in the preceding period

In the case described above, the experimenter would design the experiment so that (a) each treatment follows each other treatment the same number of times, and (b) each treatment occurs in each period and on each test unit. A design that meets these conditions is shown in

Table 8.4   Latin-Square Design—Sunshine Fruit Experiment

	Variable B—Shelf Facing			
Variable A—Shelf Height	B_1	B_2	B_3	B_4
A_1	C_1	C_2	C_3	C_4
A_2	C_4	C_1	C_2	C_3
A_3	C_3	C_4	C_1	C_2
A_4	C_2	C_3	C_4	C_1

NOTE: Variable C is shelf fullness.

EXHIBIT 8.5 Randomization of Latin-Square Design

To illustrate the procedures for randomization of a Latin-square design, assume that we have four treatment variables. Also assume that we have the following four 4 × 4 Latin-square designs:

(a)	(b)	(c)	(d)
A B C D	A B C D	A B C D	A B C D
B A D C	B C D A	B D A C	B A D C
C D B A	C D A B	C A D B	C D A B
D C A B	D A B C	D C B A	D C B A

In general, the procedure involves selecting at random one of the 4 × 4 squares, randomizing the rows and columns of the square, and assigning the treatments at random to the letters A–D.

Assume we have randomly selected square (a). Using a table of random numbers we can write down three random permutations of the numbers 1–4:

(1) 1, 3, 4, 2
(2) 4, 1, 2, 3
(3) 2, 4, 3, 1

Using permutation (1), we rearrange the rows of square (a) in the order 1, 3, 4, 2, which gives us

A B C D
C D B A
D C A B
B A D C

We now rearrange the columns of this square in accordance with (2) above:

D A B C
A C D B
B D C A
C B A D

Finally, if the treatments have been numbered 1–4, we rearrange them in accordance with (3). This results in:

Permutation   2 4 3 1
Treatment   A B C D

Thus treatment 2 is assigned to A, etc., in the Latin square.

Table 8.6. Notice that in Table 8.6 each treatment is followed by each other treatment the same number of times. This design, also known as double change-over design, consists of reversing the sequence of treatments in two orthogonal (independent) Latin squares.

Table 8.5   Latin-Square Design—No Carry-Over Effect

	Time Period		
Test Unit	*1*	*2*	*3*
1	A	C	B
2	C	B	A
3	B	A	C

Table 8.6   Latin-Square Design—Carry-Over Effect

	Time Period		
Test Unit	*1*	*2*	*3*
1	A	B	C
2	B	C	A
3	C	A	B
4	C	B	A
5	A	C	B
6	B	A	C

Randomized Block Design

Randomized-block designs, also known as treatments by blocks designs, represent a frequently used experimental framework for dealing with multivariable classifications. These designs are typically used when the experimenter desires to eliminate a possible source of uncontrolled variation (a nuisance variable) from the error term in order that the effects due to treatments will not be masked by a larger-than-necessary error term. For example, suppose that our researcher were interested only in the effect of shelf height on sales of canned fruit but had designed the experiment so that more than a single store was used in the study. The effect of store type could influence sales, and the experimenter might wish to remove this effect from the error term by "blocking" on store types. That is, each store would be considered a test unit and each level of shelf height would be tested in each store. To illustrate, if the researcher were interested in examining three levels of shelf height in each of four stores, results could be summarized in the form shown in Table 8.7. Table 8.7 indicates that we are dealing with a two-variable classification and can, accordingly, separate the block effect from the error term. Thus, if genuine treatment effects are present, this type of design will be more likely to detect them than a single-variable classification in which the block effect would become part of the error term.

Covariance Design

Covariance designs are appropriate in situations where some variable affects response but is not subject to control during the experiment. For example, if test units consist of human

Table 8.7   Randomized-Block Design—Sunshine Fruit Experiment

	Treatments—Shelf Height		
Blocks—Stores	*Level 1*	*Level 2*	*Level 3*
1	X_{11}	X_{12}	X_{13}
2	X_{21}	X_{22}	X_{23}
3	X_{31}	X_{32}	X_{33}
4	X_{41}	X_{42}	X_{43}

subjects and the response variable is the number of correct identifications of trademarks that are shown on a projection screen (where such factors as length of exposure and clarity of focus are varied), it may be that response is affected by the general intelligence level of the viewing subject. Suppose that it is too costly to screen subjects, and only those with approximately the same intelligence quotient are selected. We shall assume that the researcher is able to measure each subject's IQ.

In this type of situation, the researcher may use covariance analysis. Roughly speaking, the computational procedure is similar to a regression problem. The researcher, in effect, determines the effect on response resulting from differences (e.g., in IQ) among test units and removes this influence so that the effect of the controlled variables on response can be determined independent of the effect of test differences.

Recapitulation

As noted earlier, the study of experimental design is basically the study of two things:

1. Various experimental layouts, such as single factor, factorial, Latin-square, and randomized block designs.

2. Analysis of variance and covariance techniques for testing whether the various treatment effects are significant.

Many other kinds of design layouts, including fractional factorial designs, balanced incomplete blocks, hierarchical designs, split-plot designs, and partially balanced incomplete blocks are available. More information on these designs and the ones discussed above can be found in more specialized works on experimentation, including Brown and Melamed (1990), Edwards (1968), Field and Hole (2003), Christensen (2004), and Shadish, Cook, and Campbell (2002). We have only described briefly the characteristics of some of the many specialized statistical designs.

We have not covered the issue of how to select an experimental design. The design chosen must be congruent with the research question and capable of implementation with resources that are available. Such issues as the number of independent variables, the sources and number of extraneous variables, the nature of the dependent variable, the number of subjects available for participation in the experiment, and other methodological issues will have a bearing on the choice of an appropriate design, as will cost and budget availability concerns.

Increasingly, marketing researchers use personal computer software to aid in this selection. These software programs range from a type of expert system wherein a design can be selected based on answers to questions about a proposed experiment to programs that actually design the experiment itself by providing values for the relevant design elements.

PANELS AND EXPERIMENTAL DESIGN

In Chapter 4 we discussed the use of the continuous panel by syndicated services. Continuous panels also may be used for data collection in either a natural or a controlled experimental design.

The Panel as a Natural Experimental Design

The normal course of operation of a consumer panel generates a continuing set of natural experimental data. Buyer responses to changes in any of the controllable or environmental variables affecting purchase decisions are recorded in the normal process of conducting the panel. Audience and deal panels provide similar response measurements.

Time-series, cross-sectional, and combination cross-sectional, time-series designs are all inherent in panel data. To illustrate their application, suppose that we have increased the price of a particular product in selected territories. We can analyze the price-increase effect, at either the aggregated or individual household level, using the data from those territories in which price was increased and either the after-only without control group or the before-after without control group designs [classical designs (1) through (3)]. A cross-sectional analysis may be made by comparing, for a given period after the increase, the purchase data for the territories in which the price was raised with those in which no change was made [classical design (5)]. A preferable approach here would be to use a combination cross-sectional, time-series design and compare the change in purchases before and after the price increase in the territories in which price was not changed (control group) with the change in territories in which the price was changed. Such a study could employ either classical design (4) or (6).

The limitations of each of these designs discussed earlier still apply when they are used with panel data. A major difficulty, of course, is in sorting out the effect of the price increase form the extraneous producers affecting purchases over time and among territories. In this illustration selective price increases by territory would only have been made in response to differing conditions among the sales territories (a price increase by competitors, higher levels of demand, etc.). History variables must therefore be analyzed carefully in using panel data.

Controlled Experimental Designs Using Panels

The controlled experimental design in conjunction with a panel is most often applied to market tests of prospective new products, different levels of promotion, new campaign themes, price changes, and combinations of two or more of these variables. Consider, for example, a market test of a general price increase. The requirement of random selection of test and control groups can be met by selecting territories at random in which to raise prices. The remaining territories automatically constitute the control group. Depending on the kinds of information desired, an after-only with control group [classical design (7)], a before-after with one control group [classical design (8)], or a four-group, six-study [classical design (9)] design may be used.

The general advantages and limitations of these designs were discussed earlier. We must, however, consider the limitations that arise from the use of the panel for measurement, applicable to both natural and controlled experimental designs.

The Limitations of Continuous Panels

Although panels can provide highly useful marketing information that is difficult to obtain by alternative research methods, there are some important limitations. The first of these limitations involves selection and stems from the difficulty of obtaining cooperation from the families or firms selected in the sample and the resulting effect on the degree of representativeness of the panel. To be most useful for drawing inferences about the population being studied, the sample should be drawn by a random process. The sample of families to compose a consumer purchase panel may be chosen randomly, but the typical panel has experienced a high refusal rate during the period of establishment and a high attrition rate once in operation.

Evidence indicates that the characteristics of both those families who refuse to participate and those who later drop from the panel are different from those who agree to participate and remain. In one major panel, for example, it was found that a significantly higher percentage of nonurban households agreed to participate than did urban households. In another consumer panel, it was found that a larger proportion of nonusers than users of the products about which purchase data were being reported dropped out after the first interview. To reduce the bias introduced by such nonrandom attrition, replacements are typically chosen from families with the same demographic and usage characteristics as those lost from refusals and dropouts.

An additional source of bias is in the testing effect arising from continued participation on the panel. Since the individual is undoubtedly conditioned to some extent by the fact that data on purchases are reported, panel members may become atypical in their purchase behavior as a result of being a part of a panel. In short, being a panel member may influence what products and brands are purchased as the panel member is sensitized.

Panel data may also be systematically biased through instrument effects. The majority of panels use diaries for reporting. These are self-administered, structured questionnaires. An attempt is made to have panelists record each purchase in the diary at the time it is made to avoid having to rely on the purchaser's memory. To the extent that this is not done, the accuracy of the data suffers. If properly filled out and submitted on schedule, the information is relatively inexpensive to obtain. However, in those cases where there are omissions or the diary is not mailed on time, either a follow-up personal or telephone interview must be made or the data must be omitted from the tabulation. If the follow-up interview is made, the cost of obtaining the data is increased considerably. If it is not made, possible biases are introduced and the total amount of data is decreased.

Despite these limitations, the use of data from panels has become widespread. If the panel is administered carefully, the resulting data are important additions to the information required for making sound marketing decisions.

FIELD EXPERIMENTATION IN MARKETING

Field experimental methods are not always the methods of choice in the study of marketing phenomena for several reasons:

1. Field experiments may be quite expensive.

2. Field experiments are subject to large amounts of uncontrolled variation.

3. Field experiments may produce results that are difficult to generalize to other products, market areas, or time periods.

There is little question that field experimentation in marketing is a costly undertaking. Consider the case of a sales manager who wishes to determine the effects of varying amounts of sales effort on product sales of a nationally distributed brand. Sales in a given time period could be affected by point-of-purchase advertising, personal sales effort, broadcast promotion, competitors' sales efforts, relative prices, seasonal effects, past promotional expenditures, and so on.

Suppose that the manager wished to consider only three levels of each of three variables: the firm's point-of-purchase promotion, personal sales effort, and broadcast promotion. A full factorial experiment would require 27 market areas that, in turn, should be measured to account for differences in initial sales potential, competitive activity, and so on. Aside from the fact that regional managers may not like to see some of their market areas receive "low doses" of each of the variables, the process of measuring response, adjusting response for different levels of various uncontrolled variables, and so on, is both time-consuming and expensive.

There are alternatives to the traditional somewhat lengthy market test (Power, 1992):

- *Pretesting*. Show a few consumers samples of new products along with advertisements, for example, to gauge probable response.

- *Computer modeling*. Use historical data on similar products to turn small samples of data into projections of sales.

- *Rolling the dice*. Introduce a new product region by region, fixing advertisements and promotions along the way to going national. This is one way to have a national rollout.

- *Foreign venture*. Try a product first in a foreign market, then roll it out in the national home market. This is a version of the lead country concept.

- *Simulated test markets*. Ask respondents, typically recruited from a high-traffic location such as a shopping mall, to react to a new-product concept in a real-life or laboratory environment. They then have the opportunity to buy the product. Those who buy the new product are then interviewed further about repeat purchase intentions. Mathematical estimates of market share are derived from this procedure (Malhotra, 1999, pp. 237–238).

Suppose, however, that the initial cost of such an experiment could be justified and that the experiment yields a set of values for the three control variables that is deemed optimal. Can the manager assume that if this combination is introduced in all territories optimal profits will result? Not at all. First, some of the uncontrolled variables may be changing in some way to produce an environment different from that which existed at the time the experiment was conducted; that is, the environment may not be stable in terms of consumer tastes, consumer incomes, seasonal factors, and the like. Second, other producers may willfully change the competitive environment by changing the price or characteristics of their products. Third, the manager may find it impossible to implement the "best strategy," since promotional expenditures cannot be altered quickly enough to ensure that essentially the same environmental conditions prevailing during the experiment are still in effect.

Earlier in the chapter we pointed out that the test units of marketing experiments can be broadly classified as involving people, stores, and market areas. Each class of units presents its own set of problems for the experimenter. In cases where people are the test units (e.g., product usage, advertising copy themes, package tests), the researcher must contend with such things as interview bias, subject conditioning, and subject dropouts. In experiments in which the test units are stores (e.g., pricing, couponing, point-of-purchase displays), the researcher must contend with the possible reluctance of store managers to implement the design, competitors' activities, contamination of the data of control stores by test-store influences, and so on. In experiments emphasizing market areas, the problems of measurement and control became the most difficult of all. Seldom can market territories be partitioned without sales-response overlap and stimulus (sales promotion, pricing) overlap. Furthermore, there is a danger that an experiment may be conducted for too short a period of time, so that the carry-over effect of such treatments as advertising and sales promotion is not appropriately measured. It has been reported that most test-market research programs do not collect enough information to provide a reliable basis for management decisions. What appears to be missing most are monitoring of competitive and other marketing activities and (often) control markets to serve as benchmarks for evaluation (e.g., when testing advertising campaigns).

Although this suggests a rather bleak picture of the value of field experimentation in marketing, the fact remains that experimentation and measurement provide the only sound basis for model validation in marketing and the establishment of causal relationships. It is to be hoped that as our technology advances, our knowledge of techniques improves, and superior means are developed for measuring sales (e.g., via consumer panels, store audits, home audits, etc.), market experimentation will provide a significant tool for the development of information for decision-making purposes. A couple of examples illustrates this.

Ameritech, the midwestern U.S telecommunications company, felt that market tests were worthwhile. As part of what the company called "human factors" techniques, in the mid-1990s the company used both laboratory tests and field tests that were incorporated into their advertising (Murphy, 1996). Ameritech brought prospective users into the lab for design and testing focus groups. In addition, prototypes were taken on the road to a test town. Specific test-town locations were chosen by identifying demographic potential for the product or service to be tested. At any given time, approximately 20 field locations were used for testing products. Towns used for this purpose include Wheaton, Naperville, and Springfield, Illinois, and Kalamazoo and Detroit, Michigan. Products that have been marketed based on testing include cellular modems, flip telephones, pagers, home-security systems, and videoconferencing phones.

Sometimes a laboratory-type experiment may serve the needs of the marketer. For example, Entenmann's, Inc., a baker of cakes, pastries, and cookies, entered the California market in 1984, launching first in San Diego. Prior to the San Diego launch, studies were conducted in a lab environment. About 20 consumers at a time were brought into the labs. Demographic and background information was recorded before respondents were exposed to the range of bakery goods available in their local supermarkets. Subjects were given seed money that could be used to buy any product. Consumers were asked why they chose as they did. This line of research indicated that the company's product would be successful in California. In a sense, San Diego was being viewed as a test market to test the marketing mix;

Los Angeles was to be the second market area. This use of a lab experiment confirmed the receptivity of the market to Entenmann's products and provided a low-cost view of consumer purchase behavior before products were introduced into the market.

The Cost Versus Value of Market Experimentation

Market experimentation represents a cost-incurring activity, just as any other form of information gathering. The manager (and researcher) must weigh the potential value of the information against this cost. One point of interest, however, is that, given a reasonably stable marketing environment, a field experiment can yield information that is useful for a series of future decisions. If so, the value of the research should be appropriately estimated over a time horizon involving a series of future decision choices. This value will, of course, depend on how cleverly the researcher can design the experiment along lines that are expected to remain reasonably stable over time.

SUMMARY

In this chapter our primary objectives were twofold:

1. To introduce the conceptual bases underlying marketing experimentation
2. To discuss the various models of experimental design

The statistical machinery used to analyze experimental data will be discussed in Chapter 16.

The first section of the chapter covered the nature of experimentation. The critical aspects of this discussion were the various ingredients of an experiment. We next turned to the potential sources of invalidity, internal and external, associated with an experiment. These are the experimental errors that relate to extraneous factors that can affect an experimental outcome.

We next described some of the major classical and statistical experimental designs. Some of these designs—single-factor, factorial, randomized blocks, and Latin-square—were illustrated. We concluded the chapter with a discussion of some of the problems involved in marketing experimentation and the relationship of this means of data collection to the cost and value of information.

ASSIGNMENT MATERIAL

1. Which of the following questions can be tested experimentally and which cannot? Where a test is possible, briefly suggest an approach. Where a test is not possible, explain why.
    a. Do children from the urban inner cities drink less milk than those from the suburbs?
    b. Would frequent shoppers' reactions to a retailer changing its store layout differ from the reactions of infrequent shoppers?

    c. How will purchase behavior change if a manufacturer of greeting cards changes the package?

    d. Why do clothing fashions change?

    e. Should a gasoline company add a covering over the gasoline pumps at its retail outlets?

    f. How detailed should a manufacturer of microwave ovens make the instruction booklet provided with the oven?

2. A mail-order marketer wanted to determine the effect that special promotional material pertaining to its products had on purchases by selected families. The procedure was to analyze changes in purchases for groups of families. Each group received a different number and kind of promotional material. What control problems are likely to emerge in such an experiment and how should they be handled?

3. Suppose that you are the manager of a supermarket and want to determine the sales effectiveness of the announcement of items over the public-address system in the store.

    a. Describe how you would design an experiment to test the sales effectiveness of an announcement of frozen orange juice, using the before-after with one control group design.

    b. Describe how you would design the same type of experiment using a statistically controlled design.

    c. What sources of invalidity would be of major concern in each of the experiments in items a and b?

4. Users of credit cards not only benefit from the convenience of their use but can delay payment from the time of purchase through the billing and payment dates. If the customer is not charged for the use of the credit card, the seller must finance the purchase until payment is made. Such costs inevitably get reflected in prices, and so the customer who pays cash actually pays a part of the cost of financing credit card purchases as well.

    An oil company decided to test the effects of a 5% discount for cash on cash and credit gasoline sales by conducting a market test. The test was to be conducted at the company's stations in Austin, Texas, and Orlando, Florida. It was planned to run the test for six months, after which a survey of dealers and customers would be conducted and the sales results analyzed. If the results were favorable, the cash discounts were to be introduced nationwide.

    a. Was this an appropriate research design to test the use of the cash discount? Explain.

    b. In your judgment, what would constitute sufficiently favorable results from the test using this design to warrant use of the cash discount at all their stations?

5. What major difficulties are encountered in attempting to use field experimentation in marketing contexts?

6. You are general manager of a hotel with 300 rooms. All rooms are of the same size and are furnished with two queen-sized beds. Rates vary by number of people occupying a room and by the floor level. On a typical weekend (Friday, Saturday, and Sunday evenings) you have no more than 50 percent of your rooms rented. The average rate received on a weekend is $95 per night. You are convinced that appropriate pricing

could increase occupancy on the weekend nights to at least 75 to 80 percent, and that profits would be increased as well.

a. Design an experiment that would help you determine what price(s) you should charge. Describe all instruments you would use.

b. What problems and extraneous factors are you likely to encounter with this design and how should they be handled?

REFERENCES

Anderson, M. J., & Kraber, S. L. (1999, July). Eight keys to successful DOE. *Quality Digest,* 39–43.

Banks, S. (1965). *Experimentation in marketing.* New York: McGraw-Hill.

Barnes, M. L., & Rosenthal, R. (1985). Interpersonal effects of experimenter attractiveness, attire, and gender. *Journal of Personality and Social Psychology, 48,* 435–446.

Bay, W. (1998, September 28). *NewsStand: CNN & Entertainment Weekly Report.* Retrieved May 15, 2004 from www.cnn.com

Brown, S. R., & Melamed, L. E. (1990). *Experimental design and analysis.* Newbury Park, CA: Sage.

Campbell, D. T., & Stanley, J. C. (1966). *Experimental and quasi-experimental designs for research.* Chicago: Rand McNally.

Christensen, L. B. (2004). *Experimental methodology* (9th ed.). Boston: Allyn & Bacon.

Cook, T. D., & Campbell, D. T. (1990). *Quasi-experimentation: Design and analysis issues for field settings.* Boston: Houghton Mifflin.

Diamond, H. (1989, September 11). Lights, camera . . . research! *Marketing News, 23,* 10–12.

Edwards, A. E. (1968). *Experimental design in psychological research* (3rd ed.). New York: Holt, Rinehart & Winston.

Field, A., & Hole, G. (2003). *How to design and report experiments.* Thousand Oaks, CA: Sage.

Hoogstraten, J. (1979, Winter). Pretesting as determinant of attitude change in evaluation research. *Applied Psychological Measurement, 3,* 25–30.

Howard, G. S., Ralph, K. M., Gulanick, N. A., Maxwell, S. E., Nance, S. W., & Gerber, S. K. (1979, Winter). Internal validity in pretest-posttest self-report evaluations and a re-evaluation of retrospective pretests. *Applied Psychological Measurement, 3,* 1–23.

Malhotra, N. K. (1999). *Marketing research: An applied orientation.* Upper Saddle River, NJ: Prentice Hall.

Murphy, I. P. (1996, November 18). Ameritech test towns market innovation. *Marketing News, 30,* 2ff.

Perdue, B. C., & Summers, J. O. (1986, November). Checking the success of manipulations in marketing experiments. *Journal of Marketing Research, 23,* 317–326.

Power, C. (1992, August 10). Will it sell in Podunk? Hard to say. *BusinessWeek,* pp. 46–47.

Rosenthal, R., & Rosnow, R. L. (1975). *The volunteer subject.* New York: Wiley.

Rosenthal, R., & Rosnow, R. L. (1991). *Essentials of behavioral research: Methods and data analysis* (2nd ed.). New York; McGraw-Hill.

Sawyer, A. G. (1975, March). Demand artifacts in laboratory experiments in consumer research. *Journal of Consumer Research, 1,* 20–30.

Shadish, W., Cook, T. D., & Campbell, D. T. (2002). *Experimental and quasi-experimental designs for causal inference.* Boston: Houghton Mifflin.

Cases for Part II

CASE STUDY II–1

SAN A/S

SAN A/S,[1] a company incorporated in Denmark, manufactures electric heating products for the industrial market. The company was founded in 1950 and was involved in a limited way in the production of heating elements. Its primary activity originally consisted of acting as a trading company handling products for other manufacturers. This relationship has gradually shifted, and the company now generates the greatest part of its sales volume from its own production, handling only a few products of other manufacturers that complement its own production. Production, sales, and profitability have grown steadily, and by the early 1970s the company had a dominating share of the Danish market for its products.

Growth since this time has been achieved mainly by an increase in export sales, which at present account for one-third of the company's sales. It is anticipated that exports will increase to about one-half of corporate sales by the year 2005. The company's recent export expansion is the result of increasing involvement in larger-scale projects. Production of small products will remain unchanged in the coming years (although share of company sales is expected to decrease from two-thirds to one-half), and the company has not actively sought to export these small products due to intense competition in overseas markets.

COMPANY OBJECTIVES

The company's stated primary function is the coverage of industrial needs for electric heating products in Denmark and abroad. The company seeks to compete primarily on the basis of its know-how, product development, and service. Expansion is sought through export, as the Danish market no longer offers expansion possibilities. The company aims to increase its sales by at least 15 percent per year, and this expansion is not to occur through competition with mass-producers.

THE COMPANY'S PRODUCTS, RESOURCES, AND ORGANIZATION

SAN A/S develops and produces custom-made load resistors and electric heating systems, and standard heating elements and cables. The company describes this as a narrow, deep, and consistent product mix. Heating systems are designed to customer specifications and include heaters for water, fluid, chemical, plastic, and oil heating; industrial ovens; air duct heaters; unit and battery heaters; defrosting elements; space heating systems; and tunnel ovens. The know-how acquired through the development of heating systems to customer specifications enables the company to develop new standard heating elements and cables that have a technological lead over similar products. The products are consistent in that they have similar production requirements, distribution channels, and, with the exception of load resistors, the same market.

The company is economically sound, and its steady expansion has not caused profit or financing problems. Sales were approximately 120 million Danish kroner in 2003 and are expected to increase to 130 million kroner in 2004 due in large part to growth in exports. The company now operates at its full production capacity and is in the process of expanding its production facilities. In spite of this capacity expansion, the company anticipates that its continuing sales growth will result in a continued full utilization of capacity. This high capacity utilization has led to delivery delays in the past, and the company has now decided that delivery time for its standard products must not exceed six weeks.

The company is a 100-percent privately owned Danish company, with its own production facilities located near Copenhagen. At present there are 70 employees, of whom eight are civil engineers and 12 are technicians. Product development is typically organized in project groups. The company sells directly to customers in Denmark, and both directly and through import agents overseas.

MARKET

The company's customers are mainly industrial processors. Heat processes have almost countless applications. The petrochemical industry and industries with a drying process are of particular importance in SAN's market. The company concentrates solely on electric heating processes. These can be divided into those in which heating requirements can be covered by standard and mass-produced products, and those in which requirements demand the development of tailor-made products or systems.

The market for standard and mass-produced heating elements and cables is well developed; there are established producers in all industrialized countries and competition is intense. The buyer is seeking a product that can fulfill specifications that can be met by many suppliers. The market demands high quality, quick delivery, good parts availability, and a competitive price. The buying decision is typically made by an engineer seeking to reduce operating costs. Competition in the market for special products

and systems is less intense, as there are fewer suppliers. Here the buyer is seeking a supplier whose know-how will help to develop a product or system that can fulfill new specifications—for example, higher heating temperatures, better heat-to-energy ratios, resistance to corrosion—that are not available with existing products. The buyer still demands high quality and good back-up (parts availability and service) but is not seeking quick "off-the-shelf" delivery. Price is also of less importance, as the product or system is required to pay for itself through either reduced operating costs or increased productivity. Again the buying decision is typically made by an engineer. Direct contact between the buyer and the supplier is important in the buying process, as the product development is a new task for both parties.

Export Markets

SAN is a niche marketing company and has had a typical export history. As the home market became saturated, the company started exploiting the possibilities in geographically and culturally close markets through import agents. Exports started with the Scandinavian countries and have since expanded by agents to most of western Europe (except Germany and the United Kingdom), Poland, Greece, and North America. At the present time the company has no international investments in the form of sales or production companies or joint ventures. As export now accounts for a rapidly increasing share of sales, management is becoming increasingly interested in being able to control its international marketing efforts. The company's expansion strategy, therefore, is to establish sales companies wherever economically possible, and agents are seen as a second-best solution.

The growing share of sales accounted for by project-export has also led to a changing emphasis in marketing strategy. While import agents have fulfilled a useful role in establishing SAN's export of products, their use in project-export is much more limited, as direct information exchanges between the supplier and the buyer are very important. For the company this means that increased expansion will lead to increased direct involvement in foreign markets. In some foreign markets there is a dual-distribution system in which SAN is responsible for projects and special products and agents are responsible for small and standard products.

Expansion to Australia

As part of its long-term expansion strategy, SAN is considering entering markets in other parts of the world. One such market is Australia, where SAN has had no export experience. Due to the company's present expansion in Scandinavia and western Europe, it has limited resources to devote to the Australian market. The company is somewhat cautious and is not anxious to expand too quickly. In the short term, therefore, if the company were to enter the Australian market its goals would be twofold: (a) to establish the company's reputation in Australia, with a view to more intensive market development at a later stage when resources permit; and (b) to obtain a quick return on its investment in order to avoid delays in its expansion in other markets as a result of a financial overextension in Australia.

Management has authorized a comprehensive market study with the following objectives: (a) analyze the Australian market and determine the sales potential for the company's products; (b) evaluate the different marketing strategies and policies that might be used; and (c) choose the strategy and policies that harmonize best with the company's expansion strategy and current resource availability.

QUESTIONS FOR DISCUSSION

1. Explain how secondary information can be used to meet the objectives of the market study.

2. What kind(s) of data and sources of such data would be useful?

3. Should SAN A/S enter the Australian market? Defend your answer.

ENDNOTE

1. Disguised name.

Quiet Inn (A)

The Quiet Inn[1] is a medium-sized motel located in the western United States in a metropolitan area having a population of about 150,000. The owners of the motel are concerned that occupancy has not been growing as they think it should. In order to explore why occupancy has not grown, the owners decided that a study of two potential target markets—bus tourism and general tourism—be conducted. The metropolitan area is located on Interstate Highway 5 and many bus tours pass through the area on their travel north and south to Seattle, Portland, San Francisco, Los Angeles, and Vancouver, Canada.

Quiet Inn management contracted with CA Associates, a local marketing research firm, to conduct the study. The project director assigned to the Quiet Inn study, Joan Carol, determined that the purpose of the study is to provide information useful to the management of the Quiet Inn in their decision about what actions to take that will lead to an increased occupancy rate. This was to be approached by examining the overnight lodging preferences and perceptions of two identified target markets: (a) general tourism; and (b) bus tours.

The major objective was to distinguish among these target markets in such a way that unique marketing strategies could be oriented toward each market. The following research actions were needed:

1. Identify competitors and people's perceptions of them.
2. Identify operating features needed to meet market needs and preferences.
3. Develop a user profile of each segment.
4. Determine travel patterns and behavior.

This list is not all-inclusive. Rather, these goals served as the focal point around which the study would be developed.

In order to achieve the objectives stated above and to delineate the needs of the two target markets, the researchers decided to use two different research methods. All measurement instruments used were pretested to identify any problems that respondents might have in responding to them.

BUS TOURS

Two separate sample groups are to be contacted for this aspect of the study: (a) tour operators; and (b) consumers. Regarding tour operators, a mail survey will be conducted using a sample of travel agencies and bus tour lines located in the cities of Vancouver, Seattle, Portland, San Francisco, and Los Angeles. The purpose of this survey is to determine what criteria these organizations use when booking a bus tour into a one-night stop at a motel. The following procedure will be used:

1. Preliminary notification letter.
2. First mailing of questionnaire with cover letter.
3. Second mailing of questionnaire to nonrespondents.

All questionnaires are to be openly coded. A sample of 15 companies will be selected from telephone directories using judgment sampling methods. Information from consumers of bus tours will be obtained by using a focus group. The purpose of the focus group is to help identify the needs and preferences of bus tourists, and to establish an awareness of traveling problems. The composition of the focus group will include seven residents of a senior center in the local area. All participants will have previous experience with bus tours. The focus group will last for about one hour, and the two broad topics to be discussed are bus tours in general and motel lodgings on bus tours.

GENERAL TOURISM

General tourism is defined to include both business and vacation travel. In order to examine this market segment, it is proposed that a mail survey be conducted using a sample of past users of the Quiet Inn. The sample will be selected from motel records of those people who used the motel during the past 24 months.

In order to ensure that sampling error would be no more than five percent with 90 percent confidence, a sample size of 900 will be used. The sample is to be stratified proportionately by month during the two-year period. Thus, the number of sample members selected for each of the 24 months will be proportionate to the number of customers who stayed at the motel for each month.

The overall data collection procedure is as follows:

1. Introductory postcard.

2. First mailing of questionnaire and cover letter.

3. Second mailing of questionnaire and cover letter to nonrespondents 11 days after the first mailing.

The questionnaire, which is to be openly coded, is designed to provide information about the travel behavior of sample members, criteria that influence choice of lodging, perceptions of selected lodging facilities in the area where the motel is located, and specific attitudes and perceptions of the Quiet Inn itself.

QUESTIONS FOR DISCUSSION

1. Can a service facility like Quiet Inn make use of marketing research? Explain.

2. Evaluate the study design proposed by CA Associates.

3. Can CA Associates use the Internet for data collection? If so, explain how this might be done, what potential problems might arise, and how these problems should be handled? If not, why not?

ENDNOTE

1. Disguised name.

CASE STUDY II–3

Vacation Traveler

Vacation Traveler is a consumer magazine devoted to consumer travel and the travel industry. The magazine is published, bimonthly and contains extensive advertising in addition to articles about vacation travel destinations throughout the world.

The magazine often utilizes marketing research to aid in article preparation as well as in selling advertising. For example, the company has used full-service marketing research agencies to conduct surveys. The purpose of such surveys has been to bring readership and demographic data up-to-date. One approach has been to survey subscribers. A typical survey of this type involves a data collection procedure consisting of a preliminary notification postcard, the questionnaire mailing (with a monetary incentive), and a follow-up letter. A study using this approach generates, on the average, a total response rate of 55 percent to 65 percent.

The research department at *Vacation Traveler* decided to try another approach to obtain information about travelers and travel behavior. The questionnaire shown below was run in the early pages of a Spring issue of the magazine. Potential respondents could either mail the completed questionnaire to the magazine or return it by fax.

QUESTIONS FOR DISCUSSION

1. Will the research being done by *Vacation Traveler* provide the information necessary for selling advertising and deciding upon articles for publication?

2. Evaluate the use of media for conducting surveys.

3. How might studies of this type be conducted through use of the Internet? Explain whether this would be better than use of a mail survey.

VACATION TRAVELER

HOW DO YOU TRAVEL?

What kind of traveler are you? When you fly off to Paris, is it for the weekend or for a week? On business or pleasure—or both? Do you fly coach, business or first class? What do you look for in your hotel accommodations? These are the kinds of questions we'd like you to answer. Please take a minute to check the boxes on this and the backing page, and then tear out and return to us—see address at the end. We will share the results with all readers in a future issue. Thank you in advance for your time.

—The Editors

ABOUT VACATION PLANNING & TRAVEL

1. When planning a vacation trip, which of the following do you generally do? (Please check all that apply.)
   Consult a travel agent . . . . □–1   5.
   Seek friends' advice . . . . □–2
   Plan independently . . . . □–3
   Refer to magazine/
   newspaper articles . . . . □–4
   Let someone else
   handle all arrangements . . . . □–5

2. Who in your family actually decides where to go on vacation? (Please check only *one*.)
   You alone . . . .   □–1   Children . . . . □–3   6.
   Spouse or
   companion . . . .   □–2   Joint decision . . . . □–4

3. How long does your typical vacation trip usually last?
   Weekend . . . .   □–1   2 weeks . . . . □–3   7.
   I week . . . .   □–2   3 weeks or more . . . . □–4

4. Who makes most of the specific arrangements for your vacation? (Please check only *one*.)
   You alone . . . .   □–1   Travel agent . . . . □–3   8.
   Spouse or
   companion . . . .   □–2   Secretary . . . . □–4

5a. On a vacation trip, where do you prefer to stay overnight when youre in an American city?
   At the first comfortable
   motel on the way into town . . . . □–1   9.
   At the last motel on
   the other side of town . . . . □–2
   In the center of the city . . . . □–3
   In a landmark hotel . . . . □–4
   Bed and breakfast inn . . . . □–5

   b. Do you usually make advance reservations?
   Yes . . . .   □–1   No . . . . □–2   10.

6. How far ahead do you plan a vacation of a week or more?
   Spontaneously . . □–1   2–3 months . . .□–3   A year . . . . . □–5   11.
   A month . . . .□–2   6 months . . . .□–4

7. How do you usually pay for these five aspects of travel?

	Car				
	Plane	Rental	Hotel	Meals	Shopping
Cash	□12–1	.□13–1	.□14–1	.□15–1	.□16–1
Personal check	□–2	. . .□–2	. . .□–2	. . .□–2	. . .□–2
Charge card	□–3	. . .□–3	. . .□–3	. . .□–3	. . .□–3
Travelers cheques . .	□–4	. . .□–4	. . .□–4	. . .□–4	. . .□–4
Money order	□–5	. . .□–5	. . .□–5	. . .□–5	. . .□–5

8. For a long-weekend getaway, which of the following destinations appeals to you most?
   Full-service resort hotel . . . . .□–1   Driving/Sightseeing . . .□–3   17.
   City weekend in a hotel . . . . .□–2   Secluded motel/hotel . . □–4

9. If time and money were no consideration, how would you prefer to spend a 2-week vacation?
   Driving in the U.S./ . . . .   At a spa . . . . □–5   18.
   Sightseeing . . . .□–1   Staying in *one* big city
   Driving in a foreign country . .□–2   —London, Rome,
   Being active—skiing, etc. . . .□–3   New York, etc . . . . . □–6
   In a resort . . . .□–4   Off-the-beaten-track . . □–7

10. Are your vacation plans most influenced by: (Please check all that apply.)
   Work/Office schedules . . .□–1   Season . . . . □–4   19.
   Family obligations . . . .□–2   Holiday periods (Christmas,
   Personal preferences . . .□–3   July 4th, etc.) . . . . . . □–5

11. How do you choose a new destination for a vacation?
   Magazines/   Trends . . . . □–3   20.
   Newspapers . . . .□–1   Travel agents . . . . □–4
   Word of mouth . . . .□–2   Movies/TV . . . . □–5
                                        Internet . . . . □–6

12. When you travel, do you prefer to:
   Have a detailed itinerary . . . . □–1   21.
   Have a moderately structured itinerary . . . . □–2
   Have no itinerary . . . . □–3

13. Which of the following problems, if any, do you worry about when you plan a foreign trip? (Check all that apply.)
   Forgetting or losing   Getting to and from
   your passport . . . .□–1   the airport . . . . □–6 22.
   Dealing with . . . .   Luggage problems . . . . □–7
   foreign currency . . . . .□–2   Language problems . . . . . . □–8
   Tipping . . . .□–3   Protecting money
   Flight delays . . . .□–4   and valuables . . . . □–9
   Settling into a new . . . . .   Jet lag . . . . □–10
   environment . . . .□–5   Security . . . . □–11
                                        Terrorism . . . . □–12

14a. How much vacation time do you usually have? (employed or self-employed)?
   1 week . . . .□–1   4 weeks . . . .□–4 23.
   2 weeks . . . .□–2   4–6 weeks . . . .□–5
   3 weeks . . . .□–3   Over 6 weeks . . . .□–6

   b. Do you generally take all of your vacation time?
   Yes . . . .□–1   No . . . . □–2 24.

15. When you travel on vacation, what grade or class do you usually use in planes, in hotels, and in restaurants?
   Flights: Economy . . . . □–3 25.
   First class . . .□–1   Promotional (APEX,
   Business class . . .□–2   Super saver,
                                        Internet, etc.) . . . . □–4
   Hotels:
   Deluxe . . . . . .□–1   First class . .□–2   Economy . . . .□–3 26.
   Restaurants:
   Expensive . . .□–1   Moderate . . .□–2   Economical . .□–4 27.

16. If you have ever had a poor or bad experience while on a vacation, which of the following has particularly bothered you? (Please check all that apply.)

   Hotel . . . .   *Transportation*
   Rude Staff . . . . □ 28–1   Rude airline personnel .□ 29–1
   Room not available . . . .   Cancellation of flight/
   on arrival . . . . □–2   transportation . . . . . □–2
   No record of reservation . . . . □–3   Missed connection . . . □–3
   Room too small or noisy . . . . □–4   Overbooked flight . . . . □–4
   Room not clean . . . . □–5   Excessive delays . . . . □–5
   Poor room service . . . . □–6   Smoking . . . . □–6
   Room overpriced . . . . □–7   Taxi rip-offs . . . . □–7
   Security . . . . □–8   Security . . . . □–8

(Continued)

ABOUT TRANSPORTATION

1. Given a choice, what means of long-distance vacation travel do you prefer? (Please check only *one*.)
   Air ...... □–1   Train .... □–3   Rental car ... □–5   30.
   Ship........ □–2   Personal car ... □–4   Tour bus ..... □–6

2. How many times have you or other members of your household flown on a commercial airline either for business, pleasure or both during the past 12 months?
   (Count each round trip as two.)

	U.S. Travel	Foreign Travel
Business trip	_____ 31.	_____ 37.
Pleasure trip	_____ 33.	_____ 39.
Business/pleasure combined	_____ 35.	_____ 41.

3. How did you feel about the following during your *last* flight?

	(1.) Very Satisfied	(2.) Somewhat Satisfied	(3.) Somewhat Dissatisfied	(4.) Very Dissatisfied	
Service	□	□	□	□	43.
Comfort	□	□	□	□	
Food/Drink	□	□	□	□	
Convenient flying time ...	□	□	□	□	
Luggage retrievel	□	□	□	□	
Delays in takeoff/landing .	□	□	□	□	
Airport Security	□	□	□	□	48.

4. Have you rented a car for vacation purposes in the past 12 months?
   Yes .... □–1   No .... □–2   49.

ABOUT HOTELS

1. How many trips have you made in the past 12 months where you stayed at a hotel or resort for business, pleasure, or both?

	Number of Trips
Business	_____ 50.
Pleasure	_____ 52.
Business/pleasure combined	_____ 54.

2. On vacation, how important are each of the following when you choose a resort hotel, big-city hotel, or country inn?

Resort Hotel	(1.) Very Important	(2.) Slightly Important	(3.) Not At All Important	
Location	□	□	□	56.
Health/Sports facilities	□	□	□	
Beach/Pool	□	□	□	
Air conditioning	□	□	□	59.
Part of a package	□	□	□	
Good food on premises	□	□	□	
Gambling	□	□	□	
Nightlife	□	□	□	63.

Big-City Hotel	(1.) Very Important	(2.) Slightly Important	(3.) Not At All Important	
Location	□	□	□	64.
Sleek/Modern	□	□	□	
Old/Charming	□	□	□	
Good restaurants	□	□	□	
Health/Sports facilities	□	□	□	
24-hour room service	□	□	□	69.

Country Inn	(1.) Very Important	(2.) Slightly Important	(3.) Not At All Important	
Location	□	□	□	70.
Private bath	□	□	□	
Food other than breakfast	□	□	□	
Takes credit cards	□	□	□	
Surrounding sights	□	□	□	
Charm	□	□	□	75.

   80–1.

3. How important is each of the following in making your stay in a hotel pleasant?

	(1.) Very Important	(2.) Slightly Important	(3.) Not At All Important	
Courteous staff	□	□	□	5.
Comfortable/Spacious/ Attractive room	□	□	□	
Comfortable bed	□	□	□	
Quiet	□	□	□	
Well-equipped bathroom	□	□	□	9.
Internet access	□	□	□	10.
Prompt room service	□	□	□	
High-tech phone systems	□	□	□	
Cable Tv	□	□	□	13.
In-house movies	□	□	□	
Alarm clocks/radios	□	□	□	
Minibars	□	□	□	16.

4. What safety features, if any, do you look for in a hotel?   17.
   Sophisticated door locks ... □–1   Wall safes .... □–4
   In-room sprinklers .... □–2   Fire exit directions .... □–5
   In-room smoke alarms ..... □–3   None of the above ... □–6

5a. Do you use hotel concierge services?
   Yes. .... □–1   No .... □–2   18.

b. If "Yes," for what do you use them? (Check all that apply.)
   Theater tickets .... □–1   Tour information ..... □–3   19.
   Restaurant reservations ... □–1   General information ... □–4

ABOUT YOU AND YOUR FAMILY

(Confidential information for the statistical analysis of previous data.)

1. Your gender:
   Male .... □–1   Female .. □–2   20.

2. What is your marital status?
   Married .... □–1   Single ... □–2   21.
   Widowed/Separated/Divorced ...... □–3

3. Your age:
   Under 25 ...... □–1   40–44 .... □–5   60–64 .... □–9   22.
   25–29 .... □–2   45–49 .... □–6   65 and over .. □–0
   30–34 .... □–3   50–54 .... □–7
   35–39 .... □–4   55–59 .... □–8

4. Please check the highest level of education you completed.
   Postgraduate degree .. □–1   1–3 years college .... □–4   23.
   Some postgraduate   High school graduate .□–5
     schooling .... □–2   Some high school
   College graduate ..... □–3   or less .... □–6

5a. Are you employed (or self-employed)?
   Full-time .... □–1   Not at all .... □–3   24.
   Part-time .... □–2   Retired .... □–4

b. What is your occupation? (Please check only *one*)
   Professional .... □–1   Sales/Clerical .... □–4   25.
   Business executive/   Homemaker....... □–5
     managerial ...... □–2
   Owner/Proprietor .... □–3   Other:_____   26.
                                (Please Specify)

5. What was your total family income before taxes last year? (Please include income from all household members and from all sources, such as salaries or wages, bonuses dividends, etc.)
   Under $20,000 .... □–1 $75,000 – $99,999 ....□–6   27.
   $20,000 – $24,999 ..□–2 $100,000 – $149,999 ....□–7
   $25,000 – $34,999 ..□–3 $150,000 – $199,999 ....□–8
   $35,000 – $49,999 ..□–4 $200,000 or over ...... □–9
   $50,000 – $74,999 ..□–5

   CITY: _____   STATE: _____   28.
   ZIP CODE: _____   80-2.

PLEASE TEAR OUT PAGE AND MAIL TO:
Research Department
Vacation Traveler Magazine
123 Any Street
Chicago, IL 12345
or
FAX: 123-555-0000

CASE STUDY II–4

RAP Food Stores

RAP Food Stores[1] is a chain of large food stores in the United States that operate as supermarkets. The management of the chain has decided to expand to a new market area. At present, the company has stores located throughout the Midwest. The area targeted for expansion includes the northwestern states of Washington, Oregon, and Idaho.

One member of the management group has suggested that the company take a thorough look at the store design. This manager feels that the store design and layout that have been appropriate for the Midwest may not be so for the Northwest. The marketing research group at the corporate level has been asked to look at this issue for the stores that are to be opened in the new market area.

Ms. Panda Beaver has been appointed as the project director. Ms. Beaver has been with the company for about two years, having joined RAP upon receiving an M.B.A. degree from a leading Midwestern university. In thinking about the problem posed by management, Ms. Beaver came to the conclusion that some form of qualitative research would be most appropriate. She also believed that whatever research was conducted should be done directly with potential consumers in the targeted market area.

Remembering what she learned in graduate school, Ms. Beaver is considering using focus groups and/or some form of projective technique. If focus groups are to be used, several questions arise: who should conduct the focus groups, how many should be used, where they should be done, and similar methodological issues. Ms. Beaver has had experience with

focus groups, having moderated some for one of her instructors in graduate school.

Selecting an appropriate projective technique would be difficult because of the many alternatives available. For example, Ms. Beaver believes that such techniques as the TAT, story completion, third-person approach, and others might be appropriate.

Using something like the "picture" shown in Figure II–4.1 is a possibility. A series of such drawings could be used. In addition, Ms. Beaver remembers an unusual technique mentioned by a speaker in one of her marketing research courses. This speaker discussed an approach developed in clinical psychology—the "draw a supermarket" technique. Although the technique is mentioned in several marketing research texts, it has seen only limited application.

The "draw a supermarket" technique involves having a sample of people draw a picture of the interior of a supermarket in a simple rectangle on a blank piece of paper. These drawings are then analyzed with regard to the departments omitted, the order in which the departments were drawn, and the space allocated to each department. In addition to sketches, Ms. Beaver thought it would be helpful to get additional information from the members of the sample. Thus, sample members would be asked to indicate (a) the supermarket where most of the family groceries were purchased, (b) the supermarket department considered most important, and (c) the supermarket department considered least important. Another option for additional information is the series of questions shown in Exhibit II–4.1.

Joan, when I first enter a
grocery store I go to the
meat department, then the
dairy, and so on. How do
you do it?

Figure II–4.1   Projective Technique

EXHIBIT II–4.1   Additional Questions

1. Upon entering my favorite supermarket the first products I place in my basket are _____
   _____

2. The nonfood items that I usually purchase at my favorite supermarket are _____
   _____

3. The last product I want to place in my basket before check-out is _____
   _____

4. If my favorite supermarket does not have my preferred brands in stock on the day I shop, I purchase
   them at _____
   _____

5. My favorite supermarket is _____

QUESTIONS
FOR DISCUSSION

1. Evaluate the potential use of qualitative techniques by RAP Food Stores in providing information to aid in the design and layout of supermarkets in the targeted market area.

2. Which techniques(s) should Ms. Panda Beaver use, and why?

ENDNOTE

1. Fictitious company.

Product H-2 is a variation of a common canned food item that is used regularly in over 80 percent of the households in the United States.[1] The product can be used as a cooking ingredient or eaten by itself. The normal retail price is between $0.70 and $0.75.

The category of products into which product H-2 falls is dominated by three major brands. These three manufacturers share over 70 percent of the market, with the remainder split among many small canners and private-label brands. The total retail value of all brands sold in the product category is over $825 million per year. This is considerably greater than the retail value of such categories as peanut butter, jams and jellies, canned beans, canned peas, or packaged desserts.

Hanson Foods, Inc., is one of the fastest growing, most aggressive companies in the industry. In the past year, sales of its regular item in this category (product H-1) had grown at a rate three times faster than either of its major competitors, but the brand was still third in market share. Brand K had been the historical market leader and was regarded by most consumers as the best-quality item in the product category. The retail price for brand K had been $0.75 per can for many years. This was normally 8 to 15 cents higher than either brand V or brand H-1. A large part of the total volume of brand H-1 was sold at specially reduced prices.

The popularity of brand K varied considerably in different regions of the country, as shown in Table II–5.1. In many eastern areas, its market share was over 50 percent, whereas in the West and South the brand was in third position.

The development of product H-2 may be described as the result of an attempt to differentiate an existing product. Two years earlier, the management of Hanson and its advertising agency were faced with a problem common to many companies in the food industry. They were attempting to develop an advertising campaign that would differentiate brand H-1 from its competition, but the three major brands had essentially the same formulation. It was decided that product differentiation was needed, and, in order to accomplish this, the research and development people within the company were instructed to reformulate the product to incorporate some new and exotic spices. The copy strategy would emphasize the taste difference resulting from the new spices.

In the course of this development work, some interesting things began to happen. As various new spices were added to product H-1 and different flavor-intensity levels were evaluated by employee taste panels, it became apparent that some of these changes were perceived as completely new products.

It was quickly recognized that the introduction of a new product such as this could expand Hanson's share of the market considerably and increase sales for the whole product category. The possibility of cannibalization existed because a new product might derive a major part of its sales from former users of Hanson's current brand. But this strategy of fragmentation had been utilized in the soap industry with great success. New products were continually introduced for specialized uses, with resulting volume increases for the whole category. There was another danger that was not generally recognized by the company management. This new-product idea had originated in the research and development laboratories rather than having evolved from a discovered consumer need. This is a common cause of failure of many new consumer products by many manufacturers.

---

[1] Product H-2 is not identified because to do so would have almost certainly identified the company that developed it. The company preferred to remain anonymous. A fictitious company name has also been used.

Table II-5.1　　Share of Market

Region	Brand K (%)	Brand V (%)	Brand H-1 (%)	All others (%)
New England	37.0	10.1	12.5	40.4
New York	42.6	14.2	27.7	15.5
Middle Atlantic	37.6	11.7	13.6	37.1
East Central	27.2	17.4	17.3	38.1
West Central	25.6	24.7	14.6	35.1
Southeast	13.0	22.1	22.7	42.2
Southwest	11.6	35.4	25.6	27.4
Pacific	19.8	27.7	29.4	23.1
Total	25.3	21.4	20.1	33.2

Further work by the research and development department resulted in three variations of product H-2, with distinctly different tastes resulting from different spices used. These products were retested by the employee taste panels, and the most popular formulation of the three was packed in limited quantities for consumer and market tests.

The next step was to find out if the idea made any sense to consumers. A small pilot study was conducted in which 24 respondents were asked for their reaction to the product idea. They were then given a sample can to use and the interviewer returned a week later to question them. The concept of product H-2 appeared to be well received by over three-fourths of the consumers contacted. The product seemed to live up to their prior expectations and there were no appreciable complaints about the flavor. The participants in the test were given a three-months' supply of the product and a further interview was conducted after eight weeks had elapsed. At this time, 64 percent of the respondents said, "If this were available, I would go out and buy some right away."

Further research was then conducted on a national basis to determine consumer acceptance of the concept and formulation. Depth interviews were used to probe top-of-mind meanings and associations generated by the concept. Then the respondent was given a can of the product and the interviewer returned a week later to measure the response to the product itself. Approximately 450 interviews were conducted in Los Angeles, Minneapolis, Atlanta, Philadelphia, Tacoma, Topeka, Columbus, and Bridgeport. The reaction to the product in this study is summarized in Table II–5.2.

With this apparent consumer satisfaction with the product concept and formulation, the next step was to determine whether they would *purchase* the product with satisfactory regularity over a period of time. In order to measure this without going into an actual test market, an extended in-home usage test was conducted. Consumers in four cities—Sacramento, Baltimore, Milwaukee, and Jacksonville—were given the product to try for two weeks. If they had an interest in participating in the study, all competitive products were removed from their homes, and from then on they purchased their requirements from survey representatives. They were allowed to purchase product H-2 or any of the three major brands K, V, or H-1, as well as the strongest local brand in the area. Each family was contacted once a week for orders. The product was delivered to the participants' homes and a 10 percent discount on the normal retail price was given for all items purchased.

The response to product H-2 in this test was much better than had been anticipated, and the demand for it did not diminish appreciably in a 16-week test period. The management of

Table II-5.2   Respondent Study Results

	Respondents (%)
Would use	34
Probably would use	15
Might use	6
Probably would not use	15
Would not use	30

Table II-5.3   Finance Department Projections

Distribution level	Year 1	Year 2	Year 3
35%	($1,800,000)	($700,000)	($700,000)
45%	($ 700,000)	$950,000	$1,200,000
55%	($ 200,000)	$1,650,000	$2,000,000

Hanson had not previously been exposed to tests of this type, but representatives from the advertising agency who had observed the experience of other products in such tests were surprised to find a very high level of product usage and a negligible drop-off in demand.

On the basis of their previous experience with this type of extended-use testing of new grocery products, the advertising agency projected first-year sales and market-share estimates for product H-2. The forecasts were based on different levels of distribution that might be achieved by the product in its first year:

- At 35 percent distribution, sales were estimated at 847,000 cases, or 8 percent of the market.
- At 45 percent distribution, sales were estimated at 1,220,000 cases, or 12 percent of the market.
- At 55 percent distribution, sales were estimated at 1,500,000 cases, or 15 percent of the market.

Distribution of 35 percent would mean that the product would be available for sale in stores doing 35 percent of the total grocery business in the United States. The agency believed that a distribution level of 45 percent was the most likely of the three if the product were introduced. Hanson management concurred in this judgment.

The finance department at Hanson was asked to make projections of profit (or loss) for the first three years after H-2's introduction, conditional on the distribution level achieved. Assuming that the distribution level achieved in the first year would be maintained over the full three-year period, their estimates were as shown in Table II–5.3.

These estimates were discussed by Hanson's management with the account executive from the agency. He recommended that they run a market test for H-2. He thought that the test should be conducted in four or five cities for a period long enough to determine trial and repeat-purchase rates. He estimated that such a test would cost $400,000 to $450,000.

QUESTIONS FOR DISCUSSION

1. Evaluate the concept and the use tests conducted on the product.

2. What action should the Hanson management have taken?

Dellan Video Concepts

Dellan Video Concepts[1] is a producer of video games. It is a relatively small company when compared to companies such as Nintendo.

In retail outlets, video games are typically stocked in a locked area such that the customer has to go to a window, or find a sales clerk to assist them, and request the game desired. Some retail store managers have argued that this mode of display is inconvenient for the customers, and may be having a negative effect upon sales of the product. The primary customers of video games are boys aged 6 to 15 years.

The marketing director for Dellan has decided that a study is needed to answer the question whether the current method of display was having an adverse effect upon the sales of video games. Since Dellan does not have an in-house marketing research capability they contacted Omi Research and asked them to submit a proposal. In broad terms, the purpose of the study is to determine if changing the displays for video games as well as increasing the number of retail outlets will increase sales of the games while at the same time encouraging a new segment of consumers to buy games.

Omi Research submitted the following plan.

VIDEO GAME RESEARCH PLAN

Background

Preliminary studies have suggested that increasing convenience may increase impulse buying by customers. Convenience can be served by both changing the point-of-sale displays and increasing the number of sales outlets. A primary consideration in video game displays is theft protection. Therefore, we propose to study two types of secure displays and one unlocked display, stocked with games in large packaging, in order to monitor sales and detect theft.

Industry data show that the months of April, May, and June have shown steady sales trends over the past five years. Sales in these months have shown a three percent sales increase trend each year. We therefore propose to conduct the study during these months to better control for seasonal fluctuations.

Objectives

The proposed research will involve a field experiment testing the relative sales ability of locked, unlocked, and vending machine displays of video games in four types of stores. The study will indicate the viability of using convenience stores and computer software stores as sales outlets in addition to toy and discount department stores. A postcard survey will be included with the video game package for consumers to complete and return.

The survey will generate information on customer demographics, which can be grouped by display type and store type, as well as elicit customer feedback on the product, place of purchase, and display of purchase.

Problem Analysis

Prior research has suggested that sales could be positively affected by more convenient sales displays and availability. Customers do not like going to a locked area and ordering games through a window. This inconvenience may be limiting the customer base to boys aged 6 to 15 years. Further, customers have to go to specific stores in order to purchase games. There has been some indication that consumers would buy more frequently if the games could be bought in a wider variety of stores. There is also some indication that computer owners may be a viable market for video games.

The proposed research will test the ability of three different types of point-of-purchase displays in four different types of outlets to monitor sales and consumer demographics. The return mail surveys will provide information on consumer demographics. We will be able to determine if display and type of retail store have an influence on who buys the product. We will also be able to analyze the effect of the new displays on increasing the market for video games. The survey cards will be precoded for display type and store of purchase.

Research Methodology

The research project will be conducted in two parts: store experiment and a limited survey of video game customers. The store experiment will be conducted in the Phoenix, Arizona, metropolitan area with four different types of retail outlets. The survey of consumers will consist of a customer response/warranty card.

Research Techniques

The store experiment will be conducted using a randomized block design. It will take place in four different types of stores: toy, discount department, convenience, and computer software. In each store, three different types of displays will be rotated on a monthly basis. The first display type is the locked display where a customer must ask a sales clerk for a certain video game. This display, currently used in most stores, will serve as a control for the display type variable. The second type of display is an unlocked display rack where video games are packaged in a container designed to prevent shoplifting. The display itself will be a revolving stand holding a variety of video games from which the customer may make a selection after viewing the displayed games at his or her convenience. The last display to be used is a vending machine that holds a variety of games. To purchase a video game, the customer inserts his or her credit card (VISA or MasterCard) into the machine, similar to an automatic teller machine. Once a selection has been made, a receipt is printed for the customer and the desired game is ejected from the vending machine. Easy to follow instructions on the proper use of the machine are placed on the vending machine.

While the experiment is underway, a weekly physical inventory will be made at each store.

Three different chains of each store type will be targeted for the experiment, with the exception of convenience stores, where only two chains will be used. The store locations will be chosen randomly so that all of the stores, collectively, cover a broad range of consumer demographic characteristics. Store locations should include both urban and suburban settings throughout the entire Phoenix metropolitan area.

Once the specific store locations have been selected, a letter describing the experiment and the goals of the experiment will be mailed to all of the store managers. The letter will advise the store manager that a representative from our company will contact them within a few days to further explain the nature of the experiment in an attempt to persuade the store to participate in the experiment. If necessary, authorization will be requested from the store's headquarters or regional manager. This field experiment including the use of a questionnaire survey was chosen because it is an effective method of obtaining the necessary data. While the experiment is scheduled to be run for a period of three months, the results of the data collection should be worth the time invested. The analysis of the data from the store experiment will allow us to prove or disprove the hypotheses stated earlier.

The survey of video game customers will take the form of a combination customer response card and warranty registration form. The customer response card is shown in Exhibit II–6.1. The information sought from customers is their preference of store type and display type for purchasing video games. Preferences may vary according to the demographic characteristics of the customer.

EXHIBIT II–6.1   Questionnaire

Age of person for whom video game was purchased:

_____ under 6   _____ 6–15   _____ 16–19

_____ 20–26   _____ 26–32   _____ over 32

Gender of person for whom video game was purchased:

_____ Female   _____ Male

Relationship of person who purchased the video game to user of the game:

_____ self   _____ mother   _____ father   _____ other relative

_____ brother   _____ sister   _____ grandparent   _____ friend

Reason for purchase:

_____ gift   _____ personal use

How well did you like the way the video game was displayed in the store?
(1 = not at all, 3 = neither liked nor disliked, 5 = liked very much)

1   2   3   4   5

How many video games have you purchased and/or received in the past 12 months?

_____ 1   _____ 2   _____ 3   _____ 4–6   _____ 7–9   _____ 10–12   _____ more than 12

Where do you prefer to buy video games?

_____ Toy store

_____ Convenience grocery store (such as 7-Eleven and Plaid Pantry)

_____ Discount department store (such as Kmart and Fred Meyer)

_____ Computer software store

If purchaser is under age 20, please answer the following:

_____ I bought the video game with my allowance money.

_____ I bought the video game with money from my job

_____ I bought the video game with money given to me

Selection of Sample

The sample size for the store experiment will be 24 stores, consisting of six stores for each store type. Each store will be randomly selected in an attempt to obtain representative samples from the sample frame.

For each store, the three different types of displays will be rotated on a monthly basis. An example using 7-Eleven stores is shown below.

	7-Eleven Store		
Month	*1*	*2*	*3*
1	Locked	Unlocked	Vending
2	Unlocked	Vending	Locked
3	Vending	Locked	Unlocked

The goal in randomly selecting the stores is to obtain data that is representative of the total population, including economic factors, demographics, and store size.

Another factor that will influence sales of video games is demographics, including teenager population of the area. Boys between the ages of 6 and 15 are the primary consumers of video games. Also, store size will vary with the type of store and its location. Selecting stores at random should allow these and other factors to be considered representative of the population.

A sample size of 24 stores has been chosen in order to obtain data representative of the entire population. Two to three stores of a particular chain for each store type will be chosen so that variance analysis can be conducted on the three types of displays in every store.

The second part of the research proposal is a survey of the video game buyers. This will be a short questionnaire form to be completed in conjunction with their warranty registration. A higher than average response rate is anticipated with combining the questionnaire with the warranty registration for the video game purchased. The sample size of this survey will depend upon the number of customers buying the video games while the store experiment is under way and returning a completed questionnaire.

Proposed Analysis

The first test is to determine whether there is a difference in sales between stores located in urban and suburban areas. If there is no difference in sales, the data will be treated as one population. However, if there is a difference in sales, the data will be analyzed separately for urban and suburban areas. A cross-tabulation test will be used to determine whether there is a significant difference in sales depending on location.

A two-factor ANOVA test will also be used to determine whether there is a difference between each store type and the different kinds of displays used.

To analyze the questionnaires for preferences among different types of displays and different types of stores, we will make use of a frequency distribution, cross tabulation, and graphic illustrations. Descriptive analysis from this customer survey is needed to support the analysis of the store experiment.

QUESTIONS
FOR DISCUSSION

1. Evaluate the Omi Research plan for Dellan Video Concepts.

2. Make the changes you feel should be made in the plan. Defend the changes you make.

ENDNOTE

1. Disguised name.

Part III

MEASUREMENT

Chapter 9

GENERAL CONCEPTS OF MEASUREMENT

As indicated in Chapter 5, survey procedures for obtaining respondent data represent one of the most prevalent sources of marketing research information. In many cases of practical interest—concept testing for new products, corporate image measurement, ad copy evaluation, purchase intentions, and so forth—the researcher is seeking information of a psychological nature. Such information can include how consumers evaluate the new-product concept or the firm's image. To obtain useful data, the researcher must exercise care in certain areas of procedural definition:

1. Defining what is to be measured

2. Deciding how to make the measurements

3. Deciding how to conduct the measuring operations

4. Planning how to analyze the resulting data

Definitions play a significant role in scientific inquiry, especially in marketing research and behavioral sciences.

In the first section of this chapter, we focus on conceptual and operational definitions and their use in research. Increasingly, behavioral scientists are paying greater attention to refining the concepts measured in their specific disciplines. Operational definitions must specify how to measure and quantify the variables that define a concept. The process of measurement is integrated with the definition of constructs and variables.

In the next section we discuss various types of measurements and the relationship of measurement scales to the interpretation of statistical techniques. This section serves as useful background for the discussion of psychological scaling methods in Chapter 10, and for multivariate statistical techniques covered in later chapters.

The overall quality of a research project depends not only on the appropriateness and adequacy of its research design and sampling techniques, but also on the measurement procedures used. The third section of this chapter looks at measurement error and how we may control the sources of variation in measurement. We discuss also reliability and validity in these measurements.

Throughout this chapter we emphasize procedures for developing unidimensional scales, in which stimulus objects or people are scaled along a single continuum. Later chapters extend these procedures to analyses in which stimulus objects or people may be represented as points (or vectors) in a multidimensional space.

DEFINITIONS IN MARKETING MEASUREMENT

An important part of surveys and other marketing research applications is deciding what variables to measure and how to measure them. For example, marketers typically spend time and money tracking their brands' performance. So-called metrics that reflect how successful a marketing program is at reaching its target market can include brand awareness, ad awareness, ratings of brand likeability and uniqueness, new product concept ratings and purchase intent, and customer satisfaction (Morgan, 2003). Researchers often develop models to assist them in depicting, examining, specifying, and operationalizing variables and their relationships.

Models are intended to represent reality; therefore, a fundamental issue is the convergence between a model and the reality it is designed to represent. Hopefully a model would confidently represent reality on all significant issues. Researchers should measure the quality of their models against the criteria of *validity* and *utility*. Validity refers to a model's accuracy in describing and predicting reality, whereas utility refers to the value it adds to the making of decisions. A sales forecasting model that does not forecast sales with reasonable accuracy is probably worse than no sales forecasting model at all.

A major obstacle to many marketing models is not that they are incomplete, but that they are too complete. In achieving validity, model builders sometimes include so many variables (with correspondingly difficult data-collection problems) that the basic structure of the model is buried, input data costs escalate, and confidence in them is lost. The models may be reasonably valid, but they have little utility because they slow down the decision-making process and increase its cost.

The completeness and validity required in a model depends on the accuracy required in the results. Managers should not expect a model to make decisions for them. The output from a model should typically be taken as one additional piece of information to help the managers make their own decisions.

Given this perspective, models can be excused from not representing reality perfectly and, in fact, will probably benefit from it if they are simple enough for the managers to understand and deal with. Clearly, though, models used to help make multimillion-dollar decisions should be more complete than those used to make hundred-dollar decisions. Also, the type of model to be used depends on the model's purpose. A simplified model does not preclude its user from considering other factors not included in it. We measure the value of a model on the basis of its efficiency in helping us arrive at a decision. If we more easily arrive at better decisions without the model, then the model is inefficient. In fact, models should be used only if they can help us arrive at results faster, with less expense, or with more validity.

Building Blocks for Models

We cannot measure an attitude, a market share, or even sales, without first having defined the concept and how it is formed or related to other marketing variables. The building blocks of a model are concepts, constructs, variables, operational definitions, and propositions. (For a more detailed explanation of models and modeling, see Smith and Swinyard, 2001.) Let us take a brief look at each of these.

Concepts and Constructs

A *concept* is an abstraction formed by a generalization about particulars. "Mass," "strength," and "love" are all concepts, as are "advertising effectiveness," "consumer attitude," and "price elasticity." Constructs are also concepts, but they are conscious inventions of researchers and should be used for a special research purpose. When we refer to "consumer attitude" as a construct, we are suggesting not only that it exists as a concept, but that it can be observed and measured, and is related to other constructs. In fact, a constitutive or conceptual definition is one that defines a construct in terms of other constructs. For example, the construct "attitude" may be defined as "a learned tendency to respond in a consistent manner with respect to a given object of orientation," or as "latent dispositions toward objects."

Variables

Market researchers loosely call the constructs that they study *variables*. Variables are constructs that can be measured and quantified. A variable can take on different values (i.e., it can vary). Treated as a variable, "consumer attitudes" suggests that some form of measurement may be used to produce data that represents consumer attitudes.

Operational Definitions

We can talk about "consumer attitudes" as if we know what it means, but the term makes no sense at all until we define it in a specific, measurable way. An *operational definition* assigns meaning to a variable by specifying what is to be measured and how it is to be measured. It is a set of instructions defining how we are going to treat a variable. For example, the variable "height" could be operationally defined in a number of different ways:

- Measured in inches with a precision ruler with the person wearing shoes
- Measured in inches with a precision ruler without the person wearing shoes
- Measured by an altimeter or barometer
- Measured by the number of "hands"

As another example, suppose a marketer is interested in measuring "purchase intentions" for Brand X window cleaner. The variable might be operationally defined as the answer to the following question:

Please indicate your intention to purchase Brand X window cleaner the next time you purchase a window-cleaning product:

I definitely will purchase Brand X   _____

I probably will purchase Brand X   _____

I probably will not purchase Brand X   _____

I definitely will not purchase Brand X   _____

The marketer could have chosen to operationally define a score measuring "purchase intention" in other ways. For example, the concepts of "attitudes" and "beliefs," which have been shown to predict purchase intention, could have been used and related with a simple mathematical model summing the multiplicative product of a series of attributes like cleaning ability, fresh smell, and so forth:

$$ P = \qquad PI = \qquad Ai \quad \times \quad Bi $$

| Purchase behavior toward Brand X | Purchase intention for Brand X | Attitudes about window cleaners | Beliefs about Brand X |

Propositions

A *proposition* is a statement of the relationships between variables. Propositions require an explicit statement of the relationship between variables, including both the variables influencing the relationship and the form of the relationship. It is not enough to simply state that the concept "sales" is a function of the concept "advertising," such that $S = f(Ad)$. More appropriately, any intervening variables must be specified, along with the relevant ranges for the effect, including saturation effects, threshold effects, and the symbolic form of the relationship.

A proposition is quite close to a *model*. A model is produced by linking propositions together in a way that gives us a meaningful explanation for a system or a process.

The marketing research project provides the means for implementing the key components of this building process. The process itself is helpful to managers and researchers because it sensitizes them to variables that are important in explaining a process. Rigorous development of a research plan forces managers and researchers to scrutinize and select appropriate variables, and to consider the relationships between them.

Conceptually, we ask the following questions of a research plan:

- Are concepts and propositions specified in the model?
- Are the concepts relevant to solving the problem at hand?
- Are the principal parts of the concept clearly defined?
- Is there consensus as to which concepts are relevant in explaining the problem?
- Are the concepts properly defined and labeled?
- Is the concept specific enough to be operationally reliable and valid?
- Are clear assumptions made in the model that links the concepts?
- Are the limitations of the model stated?

- Can the model predict?
- Can the model explain?
- Can the model provide results for managerial decision making?
- Can the model be readily quantified?
- Are the outcomes of the model supported by common sense?

If the model does not meet the relevant criteria, it probably should be revised. Concept definitions may be made more precise; variables may be redefined, added, or deleted; operational definitions and measurements may be tested for validity; and/or mathematical forms revised.

Cause and Effect

Relationships between variables usually involve cause and effect. For example, if we turn up the heat under a pan of water, the water will boil. We conclude that the heat caused the water to boil. Alternatively, if we increase our advertising expenditures, we might see our sales increase. We could conclude that the advertising caused the sales to increase.

As we discussed in Chapter 3, to establish a cause-effect relationship, three conditions must be met:

1. Concomitant variation
2. A proper time order of effects in that the "cause" should occur first
3. An absence of competing explanations

Based on this conceptual development, we specify what is to be observed and how the observations are to be made. Generally this involves specifying five things:

1. The class of persons, objects, events, or states to be observed
2. The environmental conditions under which the observation takes place
3. The operations to be performed in making the observations
4. The instruments to be used to perform the operations
5. The observations to be made

For example, an attitude of consumers toward a specific brand can be operationally defined as the results obtained from consumers of the brand at a given time, and in a given geographic area, personally interviewed using a specified attitudinal scale to obtain response information provided by the attitude scale.

In marketing research, the conceptual and operational developments often become synonymous with the measurements. Attitudes toward products may be defined operationally as numerical ratings on a "like-dislike" measurement scale. Various aspects of advertisement recall are often defined by having magazine readers go through an unmarked copy of the magazine and note those ads that they remember seeing and those they remember reading, at least in part. In other recall procedures, the respondents are presented with cards showing the names of all products advertised in a particular issue of a magazine. Respondents are then asked to pick out those products for which they remember seeing an advertisement. This is followed by their (unaided) description of the ads, the copy points remembered, what information they got out of the ad, and so on.

In still other situations (such as theater tests), measurements extend beyond mere recall to test the effectiveness of a television commercial. Effectiveness is defined in terms of the difference in the proportion of audience members who pick a particular brand that they would like to receive (if they should turn out to be winners in a studio lottery). The comparative measures are taken before and after watching a series of commercials about one or more of the brands of interest. The effectiveness of direct-mail ads is often defined operationally in terms of the percentage of recipients who respond to the ad's offer. These have been only a few of the many examples that could be mentioned.

MEASUREMENT CONCEPTS

Consider the following set of incomplete statements:

- "The mean amount of shelf facing our brand currently receives is . . ."
- "The Consumer Price Index for the first quarter of this year was . . ."
- "The preferred brand of this product class, as determined from a survey of consumers, is . . ."
- "The number of supermarkets carrying one or more of our brands in April was . . ."

What process is required to supply the missing information in each? The answer to this question is "measurement." Yet the reason why may not be immediately apparent. The first statement requires a determination of lengths to complete it, the second requires an observation of prices, the third requires questioning consumers, and the fourth requires complete enumeration. Not only is there a difference in what is measured in each case, but there is also a different metric for each measurement process. The first involves the universal standard of computing an average. The second involves an arbitrary standard. The third involves a ranking. And the fourth involves a categorization. These are examples of the use of different scales of measurement.

Measurement Defined

Conceptually, *measurement* can be defined as a way of assigning symbols to represent the properties of persons, objects, events, or states, in which the symbols have the same relevant relationship to each other as do the things represented. Another way of looking at this is that measurement is "the assignment of numbers to objects to represent amounts or degrees of a property possessed by all of the objects" (Torgerson, 1958, p. 19). If a characteristic, property, or behavioral act is to be represented by numbers, a one-to-one correspondence between the number system used and the relations between various quantities (degrees) of that being measured must exist. There are three important characteristics or features of the real number series:

1. **Order:** Numbers are ordered.

2. **Distance:** Differences exist between the ordered numbers.

3. **Origin:** The series has a unique origin indicated by the number zero.

In measurement, then, numbers are assigned to objects (e.g., people) in such a way that the relations between the numbers reflect the relations between the objects (people) with respect to the characteristic involved. The end result establishes a scale of measurement that allows the investigator to make comparisons of amounts and changes in the variable being measured. It is important to remember that it is the attributes or characteristics of objects we measure, not the objects themselves.

Primary Types of Scales

To many people, the term *scale* suggests such devices as yardsticks, pan balances, gasoline gauges, measuring cups, and similar instruments for finding length, weight, volume, and the like. We ordinarily tend to think about measurement in the sense of well-defined scales possessing a natural zero and constant unit of measurement. In the behavioral sciences (including marketing research), however, the researcher must frequently settle for less-informative scales.

Scales can be classified into four major categories:

- Nominal
- Ordinal
- Interval
- Ratio

Each scale possesses its own set of underlying assumptions about the characteristics of order, distance and origin, and how well the numbers correspond with real-world entities. As our rigor in conceptualizing these ideas increases, we can upgrade our measurement scale. One example is the measurement of color. We may simply categorize (nominal scale) elements into colors, or measure the frequency of light waves (ratio scale). The specification of scale is extremely important in all research, because each level of scale is associated with specified analytical (statistical) techniques that are most appropriate to use in analyzing the obtained data.

Nominal Scale

Nominal scales are the least restrictive and, thus, the simplest of scales. The nominal scale does not possess order, distance, or origin. In this type of scale, the numbers serve only as labels or tags to identify objects, properties, or events. For example, we can assign numbers to baseball players or telephone subscribers. In the first case, each player receives a different number (any convenient number will do) and we have a simple list that attaches a number label to player's name. That is, we have a one-to-one correspondence between number and player and are careful to make sure that no two (or more) players receive the same number (or that a single player is assigned two or more numbers). Telephone numbers are another illustration of nominal scales, as are classifications into categories. The classification of supermarkets that "carry our brand" versus those that "do not carry our brand" is further illustration of the nominal scale.

It should be clear that nominal scales permit only the most rudimentary of mathematical operations. We can count the number of stores that carry each brand in a product class and find the modal (highest number of mentions) brand carried. Also, we may cross-tabulate variables and make various contingency tests having to do with the likelihood that a member of one category is also a member of another category, but the usual statistical operations (calculations of means, standard deviations, etc.) are not appropriate or meaningful.

Ordinal Scale

Ordinal scales are ranking scales and possess only the characteristic of order. These scales require the ability to distinguish between elements according to a single attribute and direction. For example, a respondent may be asked in a survey to rank a group of floor polish brands according to "cleaning ability." If we assign the number 1 to the highest-ranking polish, 2 to the second-highest ranking polish, and so on, an ordinal scale results. Note, however, that the mere ranking of brands does not permit us to say anything about the differences separating brands with regard to cleaning ability. We do not know if the difference in cleaning ability between the brands ranked 1 and 2 is larger, less than, or equal to the difference between the brands ranked 2 and 3. The absence of an equal interval constraint permits us to conclude that any series of numbers preserving the ordering relationship (say 2, 4, 9, etc.) is as good as our original number assignment involving successive integers. Ordinal scales are thus unique up to a strictly *increasing* transformation (which is a function preserving order).

An ordinal scale possesses all the information of a nominal scale in the sense that equivalent entities receive the same rank. Notice, however, that in dealing with ordinal scales, statistical description can employ positional measures such as the median, quartile, and percentile, or other summary statistics that deal with order among entities. Like the nominal scale, arithmetic averaging cannot be meaningfully interpreted with ranked data. Similarly, the practice of calculating an overall index ranking (a weighted ranking of a set of brands according to several properties) is often suspect from an interpretative point of view. As an illustration, note the data summarized in Table 9.1.

From Table 9.1 we see that brands A, B, and C are first ranked with respect to attribute X (cleaning ability) and then with respect to attribute Y (ease of application), where the number 3 denotes the highest ranked item. Numerical weights of 0.2 and 0.8 are then assigned to attributes X and Y, respectively, to reflect the assumed relative importance of each attribute in contributing to overall evaluation. An overall index rank of each brand is then determined. Notice, however, that by making two arbitrary order-preserving transformations in the lower half of the table, a different set of weighted indexes results, but, more importantly, this set does not have even the same ordering as the first set.

Interval Scale

Interval scales approach the person-on-the-street's conception of measurement in that an interval scale possesses a constant unit of measurement. Interval scales permit one to make meaningful statements about differences separating two objects. This type of scale possesses the properties of order and distance, but the zero point of the scale is arbitrary. Among the most common examples of interval scaling are the Fahrenheit and centigrade scales used to measure temperature and various types of indexes like the Consumer Price Index. While an arbitrary zero is assigned to each temperature scale, equal temperature differences are found by scaling equal volumes of expansion in the liquid used in the thermometer. Interval scales

Table 9.1   Illustration of the Misuse of Ranked Data

Brand	Rank on Cleaning Ability X	Rank on Ease of Application Y	Importance Weights w(X)	w(Y)	Weighted- Index Rank
A	1	2	0.2	0.8	1.8
B	2	3	0.2	0.8	2.8
C	3	1	0.2	0.8	1.4
A	2	11	0.2	0.8	9.2
B	20	100	0.2	0.8	84.0
C	50	10	0.2	0.8	18.0

permit inferences to be made about the differences between the entities to be measured (say, warmth), but we cannot meaningfully state that any value on a specific interval scale is a multiple of another.

An example should make this point clearer. It is not empirically correct to say that an object with a temperature of 50°F is twice as hot as one measuring 25°F. Remembering the conversion formula from Fahrenheit to centigrade,

$$T_C = 5/9 \ (T_F - 32)$$

we can find that the corresponding temperatures on the centigrade scale are 10°C and –3.9°C, which are not in the ratio 2:1. We can say, however, that differences between values on different temperature scales are multiples of each other. That is, the difference of 50°F–0°F is twice the difference of 25°F–0°F. Corresponding differences on the centigrade scale are 10°C – (–17.7°C) = 27.7°C and –3.9°C – (–17.7°C) = 13.8°C, which, aside from rounding error, are in the same ratio of 2:1. Another example is shown in Exhibit 9.1.

EXHIBIT 9.1   The Elusive Interval Scale

Our familiarity with everyday ratio indices, such as miles per gallon for a characteristic of an automobile, often causes us to use similar ratio indices on scales where comparisons should be made in terms of differences, rather than proportions. By doing this, the measure is being used in a way that is not consistent with the way the scale actually works.

Consider the measurement of a product attribute, "performance," on a 5-point scale and a 10-point scale. The comparison between a scale rating of 4 and 1 (a difference of 3, but a ratio of 4) is the same as the comparison between ratings of 8 and 2 (also a ratio of 4, but a difference of 6). Respondents using such a scale tend to think in terms of distance and not ratio, and regard the difference between 4 and 1 as equivalent to that between 8 and 5, not 8 and 2. When people respond to a self-administered questionnaire by marking the positions of their ratings on a linear scale, the scale is always a simple equal-interval diagram, like a ruler or thermometer, not a logarithmic scale (Semon, 1996). In short, visual perception follows an arithmetic series rather than a series that is geometric, and you cannot make ratio statements that one value is x times as large as y.

Interval scales are unique up to a transformation of the form $y = a + bx$; $b > 0$. This means that interval scales can be transformed from one to another by adding or multiplying a constant.

Most ordinary statistical measures to be discussed in later chapters (such as arithmetic mean, standard deviation, and correlation coefficient) require only interval scales for their computation.

Ratio Scale

Ratio scales represent the elite of scales, in that all arithmetic operations are permissible on ratio-scale measurements. These scales possess a unique zero point, in addition to equal intervals, and are scales usually found in the physical sciences (such as length and weight). As the name suggests, the scale values correspond to equal ratios among the entities being measured.

An example of ratio-scale properties is that 3 yards is three times 1 yard. If transformed to feet, then 9 feet and 3 feet are in the same 3:1 ratio. It is easy to move from one scale to another merely by applying an appropriate positive multiplicative constant; this is the practice followed when changing from grams to pounds or from feet to inches. As would be surmised, a ratio scale contains all the information (class, order, equality of differences) of lower-order scales and more besides. All types of statistical operations can be performed on ratio scales.

A Measurement Instrument Can Include All Four Types

Often, a single measurement instrument, or questionnaire, will include questions involving all four types of scales. Exhibit 9.2 shows an example of questions taken from a corporate reputation study conducted in a local area by a large high-technology company.

Sometimes it is difficult to assess whether a question involves one type of scale or another. This happens often with ordinal and interval scales. Questions 5 and 6 in Exhibit 9.2 are such scales. There are times when ordinal scales are treated in analysis as if they were interval because the statistical tests being used are robust, meaning that the assumptions do not always have to be strictly met.

Relationships Among Scales

To provide some idea of the relationships among nominal, ordinal, interval, and ratio scales, consult Table 9.2 (Stevens, 1946, p. 678; 1968). From the standpoint of the marketing researcher interested in analyzing data from sample surveys and the like, it is appropriate to note from the table that most commonly used descriptive statistics (arithmetic mean, standard deviation) and tests of significance (*t*-test, F-test) assume that the data are (at least) interval-scaled.

From a purely mathematical point of view, you can obviously do arithmetic with any set of numbers—integer ranks, numbers used to label classes, and so on. Certainly the computation of a *t*-statistic is no different, if the numbers are ranks as opposed to interval-scaled measurements. What is at issue here is the interpretation of the results. As our ability to make meaningful empirical analyses decreases, so does our ability to predict, explain, and otherwise make common sense evaluations. Exhibit 9.3 (see p. 359) shows one way to adjust when the researcher does not really know how respondents use scales.

EXHIBIT 9.2 Examples of Types of
Scales Used in a Study of Corporate Reputation

Nominal Scale

1. What do you think are the main causes of health problems in the community? (check all that apply)
   _____ Air pollution   _____ Alcoholism
   _____ Water pollution   _____ Drug usage
   _____ Cigarettes   _____ Overweight
   _____ Lack of healthy lifestyle

2. What is your ethnic descent?
   _____ Anglo   _____ Native American
   _____ Hispanic   _____ Other
   _____ African-American

Ordinal Scale

3. How serious a problem is our current supply of water?
   ___ A very serious   ___ A somewhat serious   ___ A minor   ___ Not a
       problem (4)   problem (3)   problem (2)   problem (1)

4. What is the highest level of education you have attained?
   ___ Some high school   ___ College graduate (4 years)
   ___ High school graduate   ___ Graduate work or degree
   ___ Some college

Interval Scale

5. Following is a set of statements regarding the XYZ Corporation. Please indicate whether you strongly agree, somewhat agree, neither agree nor disagree, somewhat disagree, or strongly disagree with each statement.

XYZ Corporation:	Strongly Agree	Somewhat Agree	Neither Agree nor Disagree	Somewhat Disagree	Strongly Disagree
Conserves and recycles	5	4	3	2	1
Supports the advancement of minorities	5	4	3	2	1
Is a trustworthy neighbor	5	4	3	2	1

6. Indicate the importance to you in deciding whether the promotion by XYZ Corporation of the advancement of minorities is good for the community by circling a number from 1 to 5. 1 = not important and 5 = very important.)

   Not Important   1   2   3   4   5   Very Important

Ratio Scale

7. What is your age?   _____ years

8. How many times in the past month have you driven by the XYZ Corporation's facilities?

Table 9.2   Scales of Measurement

Scale	Mathematical Group Structure	Permissible Statistics	Typical Examples
Nominal	Permutation group $y = f(x)$ [$f(x)$ means any one-to-one correspondence]	Mode Contingency coefficient	Numbering of football players Assignment of type or model numbers to classes
Ordinal	Isotonic group $y = f(x)$ [$f(x)$ means any strictly increasing function]	Median Percentile Order correlation Sign test; run test	Hardness of minerals Quality of leather, lumber, wool, etc. Pleasantness of odors
Interval	General linear group $y = a + bx$ $b > 0$	Mean Average deviation Standard deviation Product-moment correlation t-test F-test	Temperature (Fahrenheit and centigrade) Energy Calendar dates
Ratio	Similarity group $y = cx$ $c > 0$	Geometric mean Harmonic mean Coefficient of variation	Length, weight, density, resistance Pitch scale Loudness scale

SOURCES OF VARIATION IN MEASUREMENT

Variations in a set of measurements arise from a variety of sources or factors. These sources may affect both the characteristic or property of concern and the measurement process itself. In any measurement, a major problem arises when distinguishing between true differences and error. A portion of the variation among individual scores can be considered to represent true differences in what is being measured. A portion of variation represents error in measurement. Although many possible sources can cause variations in respondent scores (such as in a survey), they can be categorized in a number of ways:

- True differences in the characteristic or property
- Other relatively stable characteristics of individuals that affect scores (intelligence, extent of education, information processed)
- Transient personal factors (health, fatigue, motivation, emotional strain)
- Situational factors (rapport established, distractions that arise)
- Variations in administration of measuring instrument, such as interviewers
- Sampling of items included in instrument
- Lack of clarity of measuring instrument (ambiguity, complexity, interpretation)
- Mechanical factors (lack of space to record response, appearance of instrument)
- Factors in the analysis (scoring, tabulation, statistical compilation)
- Variations not otherwise accounted for (chance), such as guessing an answer

For any given research project, not all will necessarily be operative.

In the first place, variation within a set of measurements can represent only true differences in the characteristic being measured. This, of course, is the ideal situation. For instance, a company wanting to measure attitudes toward a possible new brand name and trademark would like to feel confident that measurement differences concerning the proposed names represent the individuals' differences in this attitude, and that none of the differences are a reflection of chance variations or other attitudes, such as the individuals' attitudes toward the company itself.

EXHIBIT 9.3   How Do Respondents Use Scales?

By themselves, scale ratings are ordinal. But researchers do not know whether they are equal-interval as well. In many instances it is assumed that they are so that certain statistical manipulations can be used. And it is clear that researchers do not really know how survey respondents or experimental subjects use a rating scale presented to them. Do they select a value in terms of how far it is below the top or above the bottom of the scale's anchors, or relative to the midpoint, which may be misidentified in an even-numbered scale like 1 to 10? For example, if you double a 5-point scale (with a midpoint of 3) to a 10-point scale, the midpoint is 5.5, not 6!

Respondents may have trouble choosing a scale value on the high end, but not so at the low end. One person's rating of 9 or 10 may be equal in meaning to another's 7 or 8. Semon (1999) suggests that one way to find the real difference in perception or attitude is to ask each respondent three questions at the start of an interview:

1. On this scale, how do you rate the brand you now use or that you know best?

2. How do you rate the best brand you know about?

3. What rating represents the minimum acceptable level?

Questions such as these are often asked in product and brand studies, but are only examined in terms of the substantive content they possess. In the case of trying to interpret ratings, answers to these questions provide anchor points for a respondent's ratings.

A respondent's actual ratings can be translated into responses relative to one or more of these anchors to produce real-meaning relative ratings that can be reliably aggregated and analyzed without depending upon assumptions that may be questionable.

Obviously the ideal situation seldom, if ever, exists. Measurements often are affected by characteristics of individual respondents such as intelligence, education level, and personality attributes. Therefore, the results of a study will reflect not only differences among individuals in the characteristic of interest but also differences in other characteristics of the individuals. Unfortunately, this type of situation cannot be easily controlled unless the investigator knows all relevant characteristics of the population members such that control can be introduced through the sampling process.

Differences in measurement scores may also arise when personal factors such as health, mood, and state of fatigue vary among the respondents. These transient personal characteristics of people do not necessarily affect different measurement instruments in the same way. Closely related to these personal factors is the setting in which measurement occurs. For instance, if measurement is desired from married women, individual responses may vary depending on whether the husband or any other person is present at the time and place of measurement. Not only is this source of variation potentially present in cross-sectional marketing studies, it is often an even greater danger in longitudinal studies. The real danger lies in the investigator's being unaware that this source of variation is operative. In a study conducted many years ago, it was shown that when measuring attitudes of school-age children about non-school activities, the place of measurement (in school or at home) affected responses (Albaum, 1976).

Other sources of variation in measurement scores come from the instrument itself. Any measuring instrument includes only a sample of items relevant to the characteristic or property of concern. For example, if we attempt to analyze variations in an attitude by using different measurement instruments, we must recognize that the measures are not entirely comparable even though the same construct was supposedly measured. The effect of this source should decrease as the number of relevant items included in the instrument increases.

Still other sources of variation in responses are the clarity and bias of the measuring instrument itself. Ambiguity, complexity, and bias result from choice of words and context and may mean that respondents have to interpret meaning. People tend to interpret statements differently and will respond accordingly.

The more mechanical aspects of measurement can also have an effect. These arise from both the construction of the instrument and the recording and analysis of responses. Researchers must be extremely careful when performing tasks such as scoring, tabulation, and statistical manipulation to prevent errors.

Finally, there may be some variation that is not otherwise accounted for. This may arise because respondents simply guess at answers. Consequently, responses are a result of chance.

There are many influences in a measurement other than the true characteristic of concern—that is, there are many sources of potential error in measurement. Measurement error has a constant (systematic) dimension and a random (variable) dimension. If the error is truly random, it is just as likely to be greater than the true value as less, and the expected value of the sum of all errors for any single variable will be zero. Because measurement errors are assumed to be unrelated to true scores, random measurement error is considered less worrisome than nonrandom measurement error (Davis, 1997). Systematic error is present because of a flaw in the measurement instrument or the research or sampling design. Unless the flaw is corrected, there is nothing the researcher can do to get valid results after the data are collected. These two subtypes of measurement error affect the validity and reliability of measurement, to which we now turn.

VALIDITY AND RELIABILITY OF MEASUREMENT

The measurement of psychological constructs such as perceptions, preferences, and motivations is complex. Some questions are representative of this problem:

1. Do the scales really measure what we are trying to measure?

2. Do subjects' responses remain stable over time?

3. If we have a variety of scaling procedures, are respondents consistent in their scoring over those scales that purport to be measuring the same thing?

By solving these problems, we establish the validity and reliability of scaling techniques.

Our focus is the general concepts and measures of validity and reliability that are used in cross-sectional studies. There is little documented research on issues of measure reliability and validity for time-series analysis. Presumably, this is so because typical marketing time-series research involves nonpersonal variables like sales, advertising expenditures, and market share, and such variables are assumed not to be subject to the kinds of human-based variability that can affect measurement. Yet for all types of research, unless there is prior evidence that a measure does what it is supposed to and does it well, steps should be taken to develop and assess the best measure possible. A procedure for developing and assessing measures of constructs in time-series research is presented by Didow and Franke (1984).

Validity

Validity simply means that we are measuring what we believe we are measuring. The data must be unbiased and relevant to the characteristic being measured. The validity of a measuring instrument can be judged in terms of its freedom from systematic error. Does it reflect true differences, either among individuals at a point in time or within a single individual over time? Systematic error may arise from the instrument itself, the user of the instrument, the subject, or the environment in which the scaling procedure is being administered. Since in practice we rarely know true scores, we usually have to judge a scaling procedure's validity by its relationship to other relevant standards.

The validity of a measuring instrument hinges on the availability of an external criterion that is thought to be correct. Unfortunately the availability of such outside criteria is often low. What makes the problem even more difficult is that the researcher often is not interested in the scales themselves, but the underlying theoretical construct that the scale purports to measure. It is one thing to define IQ as a score on a set of tests; it is quite another to infer from test results that a certain construct, or intelligence, is being measured.

In testing the validity of a scale, the researcher must be aware that many forms of validity exist:

1. Content validity

2. Criterion validity

3. Construct validity

Content Validation

The content of a measurement instrument concerns the subject, theme, and topics included as they relate to the characteristic being measured. Since a measuring instrument includes only a sample of the possible items that could have been included, *content validation* concerns how the scale or instrument represents the universe of the property or characteristic being measured. For example, a bank contemplating a new automatic overdraft plan might be interested in estimating the need for such a plan. The bank may attempt to measure certain individuals' need to borrow money. If the measurement instrument includes items concerned with annual income, age, size of family, education level, occupation, number of times money was borrowed during some previous time period, home ownership, and so on, the instrument's level of content validity depends on how representative these surrogates are of the need to borrow money. The question, then, is how to assure representativeness.

Content validation is essentially judgmental. The marketing researcher ordinarily attempts to measure content validity by the personal judgments of experts in the field. That is, several content experts may be asked to judge whether the items being used in the instrument are representative of the field being investigated. The results of this procedure reflect the informed judgments of experts in the content field. Closely related to this approach for assessing content validation is a method involving known groups. For instance, if a scale were being constructed to measure attitudes toward a brand of a product, the questions could be tested by administering it to a group known to be regular buyers of the product (which presupposes a favorable attitude). The results would be compared with those from a group of former buyers or other nonbuyers (who presumably have a negative attitude). If the scale does not discriminate between the two groups, then its validity with respect to measuring attitude is highly questionable. When using this method there is danger that other differences between relevant groups besides their known behavior might exist, which might account for the differences in measurement. Therefore, this approach should be used cautiously.

Another approach to content validity is *face validity*. Indeed it might even be viewed as a preliminary or exploratory form of content validity. Face validity is based on a cursory review of items by nonexperts such as one's wife, mother, tennis partner, and so forth. A simple approach is to show the measurement instrument to a convenient group of untrained people and ask them whether they think the items look okay (Litwin, 2003).

A final approach to content validation is known as *logical validation*. This refers simply to an intuitive, or commonsense, evaluation. This type of validation is derived from the careful definition of the continuum of a scale and the selection of items to be scaled. Thus, in an extreme case, the investigator reasons that everything that is included is done so because it is obvious that it should be that way. Because things often do not turn out to be as obvious as believed, it is wise for the marketing researcher not to rely on logical validation alone.

An example of research lacking content validity is the Coca-Cola Company's introduction many years ago of New Coke. Because the product represented a major change in taste, thousands of consumers were asked to taste New Coke. Overwhelmingly, people said they liked the new flavor. With such a favorable reaction, why did the decision to introduce the product turn out to be a mistake? Executives of the company acknowledge that the consumer survey conducted omitted a crucial question. People were asked if they like the new flavor, but they were not asked if they were willing to give up the old Coke. In short, they were not asked if they would buy the new product in place of the old one.

Criterion Validation

In pursuing the objective of *criterion validity*, the researcher attempts to develop or obtain an external criterion against which the scaling results can be matched. From a decision-making perspective, criterion validity is known as *pragmatic validity*, and its two basic dimensions are *predictive validity* and *concurrent validity*. Decision makers are interested simply in whether the instrument works so that better decisions can be made with it than without it.

The New Coke example also illustrates a case of poor predictive validity. The measures of liking, and so on, were not very good predictors of purchase, which was the real measure of managerial interest.

In concurrent validity, a secondary criterion, such as another scale, is used to compare results. Concurrent validity can be assessed by correlating the set of scaling results with some other set, developed from another instrument administered at the same time. Often product researchers will ask a question like, "Overall, how much do you prefer Brand A soft drink?" and then follow with another question such as, "Given the following four brands, indicate the percentage of your total soft drink purchases that you would make for each brand."

Alternatively, the correlation may be carried out with the results of the same question asked again later in the survey or on another testing occasion.

Construct Validation

In *construct validation* the researcher is interested not only in the question, "Does it work?" (i.e., predict), but also in developing criteria that permit answering theoretical questions of why it works and what deductions can be made concerning the theory underlying the instrument. Construct validity involves three subcases: convergent, discriminant, and nomological validity.

In *convergent validity* we are interested in the correspondence in results between attempts to measure the same construct by two or more independent methods. These methods need not all be scaling techniques.

Discriminant validation refers to properties of scaling procedures that do differ when they are supposed to—that is, in cases where they measure different characteristics of stimuli and/or subjects. As Campbell and Fiske (1959) indicate, since characteristics of the subject and measuring instrument can each contribute variation to the scaling results, more than one instrument and more than one subject characteristic should be used in convergent-discriminant validation work (Exhibit 9.4). Discriminant validity concerns the extent to which a measure is unique (and not simply a reflection of other variables), and as such it provides the primary test for the presence of method variance.

Nomological validity comes closest to what is generally meant by "understanding" a concept (or construct). In nomological validity the researcher attempts to relate measurements to a theoretical model that leads to further deductions, interpretations, and tests, gradually building toward a nomological net, in which several constructs are systematically interrelated. Since nomological validity is concerned with whether a measure behaves as expected, it is sometimes called "lawlike validity." Overall, it involves studying "both the theoretical relationship between different constructs and the empirical relationship between different measures of those different constructs" (Peter & Churchill, 1986, p. 5).

EXHIBIT 9.4   Multitrait-Multimethod Matrix (Correlations)

The multitrait-multimethod matrix is a generalized approach to establish the validity and reliability of a set of measurements (traits). From this matrix, reliability (in form of repeatability), convergent validity, and discriminant validity can be assessed. This matrix consists of a set of correlation coefficients, usually shown as the upper-half matrix, illustrated in the table below:

		M_A $I_1 I_2 I_3$	M_B $I_1 I_2 I_3$	M_C $I_1 I_2 I_3$
Method A	Trait 1	R M M	C H H	C H H
	Trait 2	R M	H C H	H C H
	Trait 3			
Method B	Trait 1		R M M	C H H
	Trait 2		R M	H C H
	Trait 3		R	H H C
Method C	Trait 1			R M M
	Trait 2			R M
	Trait 3			R

Convergence validity = C

Discriminant validity = difference between C and M correlations; size of H relative to C (ideally H should be approximately zero if traits and methods each are independent)

Reliability = R

Method variance = M

Hetero-trait hetero-method correlations = H

SOURCE: Adapted from Campbell and Fiske, 1959.

Ideally, the marketing researcher would like to attain construct validity, thus achieving not only the ability to make predictive statements but understanding as well. Frequently the researcher must settle for only content validity or, at best, criterion validity. It should be evident, however, that the quest for construct validity may be well justified, particularly if the instrument is to be used in new situations with new groups of individuals. That is, generalization of a scale's validity over groups, situations, and times is most readily accomplished by establishing construct validity. Peter and Churchill (1986) conducted a meta-analysis of the relationships among research design variables, the psychometric measures of reliability, and the three subclasses of construct validity as these relate to rating scales. These researchers concluded that there are important differences between the conceptual and empirical relationships among variables involved. They believe that marketing researchers are overly concerned with the magnitude of the empirical estimates of these psychometric properties, which can hide the importance of judgments about nonempirical issues. Specifically, more emphasis should be placed on the theories, the processes used to develop the measures, and the judgments of content validity.

Reliability

Reliability is concerned with the consistency of test results over groups of individuals or over the same individual at different times. A scale may be reliable but not valid. Reliability, however, establishes an upper bound on validity. An unreliable scale cannot be a valid one. Reuman (1982, p. 1099) states that "according to classical test theory, highly reliable measures are necessary, but not sufficient, for demonstrating high construct validity or high criterion validity."

The achievement of scale reliability is, of course, dependent on how consistent the characteristic being measured is from individual to individual (homogeneity over individuals) and how stable the characteristic remains over time. Just how reliable a scaling procedure turns out to be will depend on the dispersion of the characteristic in the population, the length of the testing procedure, and its internal consistency. Churchill and Peter (1984) concluded that rating scale estimates were largely determined by measuring characteristics such as number of items in a scale, type of scale, and number of scale points. They further concluded that sampling characteristics and measurement development processes had little impact.

In general, a measurement of the reliability of a scale (or measurement instrument) may be obtained by one of three methods:

1. Test-retest

2. Alternative forms

3. Internal consistency

The basics of reliability in a marketing context are reviewed by Peter (1979).

Test-Retest

When measuring the reliability of a scale, our interest may sometimes center on the extent to which repeated applications of the instrument achieve consistent results, assuming that the relevant characteristics of the subjects are stable over trials. The *test-retest method* examines the stability of response. One potential problem, of course, is that the first measurement may have an effect on the second one. For example, there may be a testing effect and/or a reactive effect of testing as defined in Chapter 8. Such effects can be reduced when there is a sufficient time interval between measurements. If at all possible, the researcher should allow a minimum of two weeks to elapse between measurements. Reliability may be estimated by any appropriate statistical technique for examining differences between measures.

Alternative Forms

The *alternative forms method* attempts to overcome the shortcomings of the test-retest method by successively administering equivalent forms of the measure to the same sample. Equivalent forms can be thought of as instruments built in the same way to accomplish the same thing, but consisting of different samples of items in the defined area of interest. The same types and structures of questions should be included on each form, but the specific questions should differ. The forms of the measurement device may be given one after the other or after a specified time interval, depending upon the investigator's interest in stability over time. Reliability is estimated by correlating the results of the two equivalent forms.

Internal Consistency

Internal consistency refers to estimates of reliability within single testing occasions. In a sense it is a modification of the alternative form approach, but differs in that alternatives are formed by grouping variables. The basic form of this method is split-half reliability, in which items are divided into equivalent groups (say, odd- versus even-numbered questions, or even a random split) and the item responses are correlated. In practice, any split can be made. To correct for the situation that a full-length scale will be more reliable than a split (such as any ratio of altered test length to the original length), the generalized Spearman-Brown formula is applied:

$$r_n = \frac{n_r}{1 + (n - 1)r}$$

where r_n is the estimated reliability of the entire instrument, r is the correlation between the half-length measurements, and n is the ratio of the number of items in the changed instrument to the number in the original.

When the length is doubled, as in the split-half method, the formula becomes

$$r_n = \frac{2r}{1 + r}$$

Thus, if the correlation between the two forms in a split-half test is .50, the estimated reliability of the entire instrument is

$$r_n = \frac{2(0.50)}{1 + 0.50} = 0.667$$

Where many items are measured, each split scale must contain enough items to be reliable itself. For a split-half scale this is often considered to be 8 to 10 items, which means that the entire scale should consist of at least 16 to 20 items.

A potential problem arises for split-half in that results may vary depending on how the items are split in half. A way of overcoming this is to use coefficient alpha, known also as Cronbach's alpha, which is a type of mean reliability coefficient for all possible ways of splitting a set of items in half (Cronbach, 1951). Whenever possible, alpha should be used as a measure of the internal consistency of multi-item scales. Alpha is perhaps the most widely used measure of internal consistency for multiple-item measures within marketing research. One caution, however, is that there should be a sufficient number of items in the measure so that alpha becomes meaningful. Alpha has been used for as few as two items, and this essentially amounts to a simple correlation between the two. Although there is no generally acceptable heuristic covering the number of items, common sense would indicate that the minimum number of items should be four or perhaps even six. What is clear, however, is that alpha is a function of the number of items in a scale (i.e., the more items, the greater alpha will tend to be), and also a function of the intercorrelation of the items themselves (Cortina, 1993; Voss, Stem, & Fotopoulos, 2000). Consequently, when interpreting an obtained alpha, the number of items must always be kept in mind.

The usual application of coefficient alpha is to calculate it using SPSS or other statistical packages, report it, and assess whether the value obtained exceeds some rule-of-thumb minimum value, typically 0.70. There now exist methods to make inferential tests about the size of alpha, and to attach confidence intervals to the measure (Iacobucci & Duhachek, 2003).

In many projects, measurements or evaluations are made by more than a single evaluator. Sometimes this is done when coding answers to open-ended questions. In these situations, the researcher is interested in the reliability of these evaluations. This is known as *interrater* or *interobserver reliability*. The most common measure used is a correlation (Litwin, 2003). For yet another approach to measuring reliability see Exhibit 9.5, which is based on the discussion by Kerlinger (1973).

A Concluding Comment

Although it is not our objective to pursue in detail the methods by which reliability or validity can be tested, we hope that at least an appreciation of the difficulties encountered in designing and analyzing psychological measure has been conveyed to the reader. One question that has not been answered is, "What is a satisfactory level of reliability, or what minimum level is acceptable?" There is no simple definitive answer to this question. Much depends on the investigator's or decision maker's primary purpose in measurement and on the approach used to estimate reliability. In trying to arrive at what constitutes satisfactory reliability, the investigator must at all times remember that reliability can affect certain qualities of a study:

1. Validity

2. The ability to show relationships between variables

3. The making of precise distinctions among individuals and groups.

EXHIBIT 9.5   Reliability as Measured by Variance

Another approach to measuring internal consistency utilizes estimation of variances. In this case, reliability is defined as the proportion of the true variance to the total variance of the data obtained from a measurement instrument, or

$$r_n = \frac{V_t - V_e}{V_t}$$

where r_n is the coefficient of reliability, V_e is the error variance, and V_t is the total variance. If the measuring instrument is split into sub-samples, such as a split-half, this formula gives results approximately the same as the Spearman-Brown correction.

To illustrate this approach, suppose we have obtained data using two different measurement instruments. Each instrument consists of four items administered to six individuals. The items are six-point scales, relevant to determining attitude toward an extra reserve plan. To estimate variance we use a two-way analysis of variance (see Chapter 15). The summary ANOVA table is shown at the end of this exhibit, and serves as the basis of the following calculations:

$$\text{Test I } r_{tt} = \frac{V_{ind} - V_e}{V_{ind}} = \frac{9.06 - .96}{9.06} = .89$$

$$\text{Test II } r_{tt} = \frac{5.12 - 2.27}{5.12} = .56$$

Test I is an example of high reliability, while Test II exemplifies low reliability. It will be noted that the equation has been rewritten to take into account that the variance due to items has been removed from the total variance. Our interest is in the individual variances. Actually, the total variance is an index of differences between individuals. Thus, we write V_{ind}, instead of V_t, to mean the variance resulting from individual differences.

The following table shows hypothetical analysis of variance for computation of coefficient of reliability:

Test I	ANOVA			
Source	Degrees of Freedom	Sum of Squares	Mean Square	F
Items	3	7.20	2.40	2.50
Individuals	5	45.30	9.06	9.44
Residual	15	14.40	.96	
Total	23	66.90		

Test II	ANOVA			
Source	Degrees of Freedom	Sum of Squares	Mean Square	F
Items	3	7.20	2.40	1.06
Individuals	5	25.60	5.12	2.26
Residual	15	34.10	2.27	
Total	23	66.90		

SUMMARY

This chapter focused on general concepts of measurement. We discussed the role of definitions and defined concepts, constructs, variables, operational definitions, and propositions. We then turned to measurement and examined what it is and how measurement relates to development of scales. Also discussed, but rather briefly, were alternative sources that cause variations within a set of measurements derived from a single instrument. This was followed by a description of measurement validity and reliability, and the various types of each that are of concern to an investigator.

ASSIGNMENT MATERIAL

1. Categorize each of the following measurements by the type of scale it represents:
   a. Determination of whether a sample of respondents have used instant coffee within the past four weeks
   b. The number of ounces of instant coffee a respondent has bought within the past four weeks

   c. Establishing preference among instant coffee brands A, B, C, and D

   d. A respondent's answer of "probably buy" to a question of purchase intention

   e. The use of the number 4 (from a scale of 1 to 5) by a respondent to indicate the importance of good service by marketers

2. For each of the following, indicate the ones where interval or ratio data are required, ordinal data are sufficient, and nominal data adequate:

   a. Measurement of price elasticity of demand for a new product

   b. Determination of preference of three levels of "sweetness" for a new product

   c. Measurement of change of attitude toward a political candidate as the campaign progresses

   d. Measurement of proportion of voters who will vote for Candidate X rather than Candidate Y

   e. Determination of which respondents have tried a particular brand of product

   f. Measurement of which of three advertisements has the greater readership

   g. Measurement of which stores stock one or more brands of a product class

   h. Measurement of the proportion of "triers" who make repeat purchases of a new product

3. The number series, 1, 2, 3, 4, 5 and 1, 6, 14, 16, 28 could each be used equally well to denote the rank order assigned to a set of five objects. Explain why statistics like the arithmetic mean and the standard deviation should not be calculated from such a series.

4. It has been asserted that for decisional research purposes, the investigator is interested in predictive validity to the exclusion of reliability or any other kind of validity. Do you agree? Explain.

5. Evaluate the following statements:

   a. The reliability of my creativity test is .85. I can therefore be reasonably sure that I am measuring creativity.

   b. My creativity test really measures creativity, because I had an expert on creativity carefully screen all the items on the test.

   c. Since reliability of a test is only .40, its validity is negligible.

6. Does each of the following refer to reliability, validity, or both?

   a. The test was given twice to the same group. The coefficient of correlation between the scores of the two administrations was .90.

   b. Four teachers studied the items of the test for their relevance to the objectives of the curriculum.

   c. The items seem to be a good sample of the item universe.

   d. Between a test of academic aptitude and grade-point average, $r = .55$

   e. The mean difference between Republicans and Democrats on the conservatism instrument was highly significant.

7. Suppose that properly gathered and tabulated data show the same results over many replications. Are the results valid? Are they reliable? Explain.

8. If you could use only one measure of validity and one measure of reliability which would you use? Is there one most important measure? Explain.

❖

REFERENCES

Albaum, G. (1976). Measuring attitudes of school-age children: A note on effects of place of measurement on validity of outcomes. *Educational and Psychological Measurement, 36*, 515–519.

Campbell, D. T., & Fiske, D. W. (1959). Convergent and discriminant validation by the multitrait-multimethod matrix. *Psychological Bulletin, 56*, 81–105.

Churchill, G. A., Jr., & Peter, J. P. (1984, November). Research design effects on the reliability of rating scales: A meta-analysis. *Journal of Marketing Research, 21*, 360–375.

Cortina, J. (1993). What is coefficient alpha? An examination of theory and applications. *Journal of Applied Psychology, 78*(1), 98–104.

Cronbach, L. J. (1951, September). Coefficient alpha and the internal structure of tests. *Psychometrika, 16*, 297–334.

Davis, D. W. (1997). Nonrandom measurement error and race of interviewer effects among African-Americans. *Public Opinion Quarterly, 61*, 183–207.

Didow, N. M., Jr., & Franke, G. R. (1984, February). Measurement issues in time-series research: Reliability and validity assessment in modeling the macroeconomic effects of advertising. *Journal of Marketing Research, 21*, 12–19.

Iacobucci, D., & Duhachek, A. (2003). *Applying confidence intervals to coefficient alpha.* Unpublished working paper, Kellogg School of Management, Northwestern University, Evanston, IL.

Kerlinger, F. N. (1973). *Foundations of behavioral research* (2nd ed.). New York: Holt, Rinehart, and Winston.

Litwin, M. S. (2003). *How to assess and interpret survey psychometric* (2nd ed.). Thousand Oaks, CA: Sage.

Morgan, M. (2003, March 31). Be careful with survey data. *Marketing News, 37,* 26.

Peter, J. P. (1979, February). Reliability: A review of psychometric bases and recent marketing practices. *Journal of Marketing Research, 16*, 6–17.

Peter, J. P., & Churchill, G. A., Jr. (1986, February). Relationships among research design choices and psychometric properties of rating scales. *Journal of Marketing Research, 23*, 1–10.

Reuman, D. A. (1982). Ipsative behavioral variability and the quality of thematic apperceptive measurement of the achievement motive. *Journal of Personality and Social Psychology, 43*(5), 1098–1110.

Semon, T. T. (1996, May 20). Is a rating of 10 twice as good as a rating of 5? *Marketing News, 30,* 16.

Semon, T. T. (1999, August 30). Scale ratings always betrayed by arithmetic. *Marketing News, 33,* 7.

Smith, S. M., & Swinyard, W. R. (2001). *Marketing models. Internet edition.* Retrieved June 15, 2004, from http://marketing.byu.edu

Stevens, S. S. (1946). On the theory of scales of measurement. *Science, 103,* 677–680.

Torgerson, W. S. (1958). *Theory and methods of scaling.* New York: Wiley.

Voss, K. E., Stem, D. E, Jr., and Fotopoulos, S. (2000). A comment on the relationship between coefficient alpha and scale characteristics. *Marketing Letters, 11*(2), 177—191.

Chapter 10

Measurement and Scaling in Marketing Research

Scaling is the generation of a broadly defined continuum on which measured objects are located (Peterson, 2000, p. 62). In Chapter 9, we established that some sort of scale—nominal, ordinal, interval, ratio—is necessarily involved every time a measurement is made.

This chapter continues our discussion of how scales are developed and how some of the more common scaling techniques and models can be used. The chapter focuses on broad concepts of attitude scaling—the study of scaling for the measurement of managerial and consumer or buyer perception, preference, and motivation. All attitude (and other psychological) measurement procedures are concerned with having people—consumers, purchasing agents, marketing managers, or whomever—respond to certain stimuli according to specified sets of instructions. The stimuli may be alternative products or services, advertising copy themes, package designs, brand names, sales presentations, and so on. The response may involve which copy theme is more pleasing than another, which package design is more appealing than another, what do each of the brand names mean, which adjectives best describe each salesperson, and so on.

Scaling procedures can be classified in terms of the measurement properties of the final scale (nominal, ordinal, interval, or ratio), the task that the subject is asked to perform, or in still other ways, such as whether the emphasis is to be placed on subject, stimuli, or both (Torgerson, 1958).

This chapter begins with a discussion of various methods for collecting ordinal-scaled data (paired comparisons, rankings, ratings, etc.) in terms of their mechanics and assumptions regarding their scale properties. Then specific procedures for developing the actual scales that measure stimuli and/or respondents are discussed. Techniques such as Thurstone Case V scaling, semantic differential, the Likert summated scale, and the Thurstone differential scale are illustrated. The chapter concludes with some issues and limitations of scaling.

DATA COLLECTION METHODS

Scaling methods may be classified by the level of scaling used to collect the data. In ordinal measurement methods, it is assumed that the basic data are only ordinal-scaled. Often, however, some type of model is then applied to transform the ordinal data into an interval scale. For example, ordinal-scaled data with a given mean and standard deviation can be converted into a standard-score scale, with a mean of zero and a standard deviation of 1.0. A more general procedure allows researchers to convert to a common scale with any specified mean and standard deviation, say a mean of 50 and a standard deviation of 10 (Guilford & Fruchter, 1973). The form of distribution will not change. This procedure does not normalize the distribution; there are other procedures to do this.

In *metric measurement* methods, the respondent makes direct numerical judgments and it is assumed that the data are either interval- or ratio-scaled. In this method, models are also used at times to further refine the data. Models are typically directed toward finding the scale values most consistent with the input data. (Often the model will involve nothing more than a simple averaging of the original numerical responses.)

Ordinal Measurement Methods

The variety of ordinal measurement methods includes a number of techniques:

- Paired comparisons
- Ranking procedures
- Ordered-category sorting
- Rating techniques

We discuss each of these data collection procedures in turn.

Paired Comparisons

As the name suggests, paired comparisons require the respondent to choose one of a pair of stimuli that "has more of," "dominates," "precedes," "wins over," or "exceeds" the other with respect to some designated property of interest. If, for example, six laundry detergent brands are to be compared for "sudsiness", a full set of paired comparisons (if order of presentation is not considered) would involve (6 × 5) / 2, or 15, paired comparisons. Respondents are asked which one of each pair has the most sudsiness. Obviously each respondent would have to have used each brand, perhaps set up using an experiment design. A question format for paired comparisons is shown in Table 10.1. The order of presentation of the pairs and which item of a pair is shown first typically are determined randomly. The following are the brand names (and numbers): Arrow (1), Zip (2), Dept (3), Advance (4), Crown (5), and Mountain (6).

The upper panel of Figure 10.1 illustrates how paired-comparison responses may be recorded for a single respondent. As noted from the figure, Brand 2 (Zip) dominates all the other five brands. This is shown by the fact that all of its paired comparisons with the remaining stimuli involve 1s (arbitrarily letting row dominate column) in the table of original data. In the lower panel of Figure 10.1, rows and columns of the original table have been permutated to yield the stimulus rank over: 2, 1, 5, 6, 4, 3, from most suds to least suds. The total number of votes received by each brand appears in the last column.

These hypothetical data are characterized by the fact that the respondent was transitive in making judgments, leading (after row and column permutation) to the triangular response pattern of 1s shown in the lower panel of the figure.

Table 10.1   Example of Paired Comparisons Question

For each of the pairs of laundry detergent brands shown below, indicate which one has the most sudsiness:

a. Arrow ____   Zip   ____
b. Arrow ____   Advance ____
c. Dept ____   Arrow   ____
d. Crown ____   Arrow   ____
e. Arrow ____   Mountain ____

       .
       .
       .

o. Crown ____   Mountain ____

Brand

	1	2	3	4	5	6	
1	X	0	1	1	1	1	
2	1	X	1	1	1	1	Original Data
3	0	0	X	0	0	0	
4	0	0	1	X	0	0	
5	0	0	1	1	X	1	
6	0	0	1	1	0	X	

(Brand — left label)

Brand

	2	1	5	6	4	3	Sum	
2	X	1	1	1	1	1	5	
1	0	X	1	1	1	1	4	(Permutated
5	0	0	X	1	1	1	3	Rows and
6	0	0	0	X	1	1	2	Columns)
4	0	0	0	0	X	1	1	
3	0	0	0	0	0	X	0	

(Brand — left label)

* A cell value of 1 implies that the row brand exceeds the column brand, "0," otherwise

Figure 10.1   Paired-Comparison Responses for a Single Subject*

But what if the judgments are not transitive? For example, the respondent may say that Brand 2 exceeds Brand 1, Brand 1 exceeds Brand 5, and Brand 5 exceeds Brand 2, leading to what is called a circular triad. The presence of circular triads in a subject's data requires the researcher to examine two questions: (a) how serious are the subject's violations of transitivity; and (b) if not too serious, how can the data be made transitive with the fewest number of alterations in the original paired-comparisons table?

Kendall (1962) has developed summary measures and statistical tests regarding the incidence of tolerable levels of intransitivity. One may compute a coefficient of consistency and test this measure against the null hypothesis that the respondent is responding randomly. Slater (1961) and Phillips (1967) have described ways of finding the best rank order (one that least disturbs the original paired-comparison judgments) in the presence of intransitive data. Of course, the motivation for using paired comparisons in the first place stems from the researcher's interest in the consistency of respondents' choices; otherwise, the researcher might just as well have the respondent rank the six brands, thereby reducing labor (but forcing consistency within that set of choices). Obviously, from such a direct ranking, paired-preferences can be developed.

Other than the transitivity issue for more than two alternatives, there is a possibility that respondents' judgments are not consistent or stable in that they prefer Brand A to B on one trial but Brand B to A on another. In this situation there exists an underlying preference probability distribution and multiple judgments are needed (Gottlieb, n.d.)

Implicit in the preceding discussion has been the assumption that the respondent must force a choice between each pair of brands. Variations in the method of paired comparisons allow the subject to express indifference between members of the pair (i.e., to "tie" the stimuli with respect to the property level of interest) or, after having chosen between members of the pair, to indicate on an intensity scale how much the chosen member of the pair exceeds the other with regard to some designated property, such as sudsiness.

For another approach to paired comparison data collection see Exhibit 10.1.

EXHIBIT 10.1   Method of Choices

This method provides a procedure for indirectly arriving at paired-comparison proportions of the form $p(B>A)$. Each respondent is presented with a set of n stimuli and is asked to indicate which one appears greatest or largest on, or has the most of, the attribute or characteristic being studied. The resulting data are the frequency with which each stimulus was the first choice. For any two stimuli X and Y, the sum of the two frequencies gives the total number or observations in which we know the result of comparing the two stimuli. The proportions of times that X appeared greater than Y is given by

$$p(X > Y) = \frac{f(x)}{f(x) + f(y)}$$

where $f(x)$ is the number of times X was first choice and $f(y)$ is the number of times Y was first choice.

For example, if stimulus X was the first choice of 10 respondents and stimulus Y the favored choice of 15 respondents.

$$p(X > Y) = \frac{10}{10 + 15} = .40$$

All pairs of the stimuli can be analyzed in this manner to arrive at the matrix of preference proportions.

This method has some deficiencies. In the first place, full use is not made of the ranked data that may be available—only top rankings are considered. Second, each proportion is based on different subsets of respondents. In addition, the number of observations upon which each proportion is based will differ. Third, those stimuli that never receive a first choice cannot be scaled. Finally, this method does not provide for appropriate goodness-of-fit tests (Torgerson, 1958).

Ranking Procedures

Ranking procedures require the respondent to order stimuli with respect to some designated property of interest. For example, instead of using the paired-comparison technique for determining the perceived order of six laundry detergents with respect to sudsiness, each respondent might have been asked to directly rank the detergents with respect to that property. Similarly, ranking can be used to determine key attributes for services.

In a survey conducted during the 1990s, Subaru of America asked new Subaru car purchasers questions regarding the purchase and delivery processes. One question required a ranking procedure:

From the following list, please choose the three most important factors (other than price or deal) that attracted you to shop at this Subaru dealership. Please rank these three factors in order of importance to you by writing the number 1 in the box which was most important, followed by numbers 2 and 3 in the appropriate boxes. Rank three boxes only.

a) Location ____

b) Previous experience ____

c) Experiences of others ____

d) Dealer's reputation ____

e) Had specific model you wanted ____

f) Financing ____

g) Advertising reputation ____

h) Service ____

Subaru could just as easily have asked respondents to rank all eight items. One major concern in asking a ranking question is whether the number of items is too many for a person to be able to make distinctions. If it is desired that a respondent rank all items, and there are many to rank, one procedure would be to have the respondents first sort the items into a number of piles (each of which has a relatively small and equal number of items, that go from high to low. Then, the request is made to rank within each pile. Unfortunately, there is no set number of items that constitutes a maximum that people can easily handle. This will vary depending upon the stimuli (items) to be ranked, and where groupings (piles), or other aid is used.

A variety of ordering methods may be used to order k items from a full set of n items. These procedures, denoted by Coombs (1964) as "order k/n" (k out of n), expand the repertory of ordering methods quite markedly. At the extremes, "order 1/2" involves a paired comparison, while "order $(n-1)/n$" involves a full rank order. The various ordering methods may pre-specify the value of k ("order the top three out of six brands with respect to sudsiness") as illustrated by the Subaru study, or allow k to be chosen by the respondent ("select those of the six brands that seem to exhibit the most sudsiness, and rank them").

Ordered-Category Sorting

Various data collection procedures are available that have as their purpose the assignment of a set of stimuli to a set of ordered categories. For example, if 15 varieties of laundry detergents represented the stimulus set, the respondent might be asked to complete the following task:

Please sort the 15 detergents into three sudsiness categories: (1) high suds, (2) moderate suds, and (3) low suds. Next, order the brands within each category from most suds to least suds.

Sorting procedures vary with regard to the following characteristics:

- The free versus forced assignment of stimuli to each category
- The assumption of equal intervals between category boundaries versus the weaker assumption of category boundaries that are merely ordered with regard to the attribute of interest

In ordinal measurement methods one assumes only an ordering of category boundaries. The assumption of equal intervals separating boundaries is part of the interval/ratio measurement set of methods. Ordered-category sorting appears especially useful when the researcher is dealing with a relatively large number of stimuli (over 15 or so) and it is believed that a subject's discrimination abilities do not justify a strict (no ties allowed) ranking of the stimulus objects. If the equal-intervals assumption is not made, it then becomes the job of the researcher to scale these responses (by application of various models) to achieve stronger scales, if so desired.

Rating Techniques

Some data collection methods, most notably rating scales, are ambiguous. In some cases, the responses are considered by the researcher to be only ordinal, while in other cases, the researcher treats them as interval- or ratio-scaled. The flexibility of rating procedures makes them appropriate for either the ordinal or interval/ratio measurement data collection methods.

Rating measurement methods represent one of the most popular and easily applied data collection methods in marketing research (Peterson, 2000). The task typically involves having a respondent place that which is being rated (a person, object, or concept) along a continuum or in one of an ordered set of categories. Ratings allow the respondent to register a degree or an amount of a characteristic or attribute directly on a scale. The task of rating is used in a variety of scaling approaches, such as the semantic differential and the Likert summated scale.

Rating scales can be either monadic or comparative. In monadic scaling, each object is measured (rated) by itself, independently of any other objects being rated. In contrast, comparative scaling objects are evaluated in comparison with other objects. For example, an in-flight survey conducted by a major airline asked the following questions:

Please rate the service you received from the airline reservations agent.

	Among the Best	Better Than Most	About the Same as Most	Not as Good as Most	Among the Worst
Courtesy/friendliness	_____	_____	_____	_____	_____
Knowledge/helpfulness	_____	_____	_____	_____	_____
Efficiency on completing transaction	_____	_____	_____	_____	_____

The rating is monadic. The airlines then asked respondents another question:

Please rate today's fight attendants compared to flight attendants on other airlines on each of the following items.
- Courtesy/friendliness
- Assistance in cabin before departure
- Responsiveness to your needs
- Availability throughout flight
- Professional appearance
- Tray pick up after meal

Ratings would again be completed using the same five response alternatives shown above—among the best, better than most, about the same as most, not as good as most, among the worst. In this application, the rating is comparative.

Ratings are used very widely because they are easier and faster to administer and yield data that are amenable to being analyzed as if they are interval-scaled. But there is a risk that when the particular attributes are worded positively or are positive constructs, such as values, respondents will end-pile their ratings toward the positive end of the scale—this leads to little differentiation among the scores. Such lack of differentiation may potentially affect the statistical properties of the items being rated and the ability to detect relationships with other variables. McCarty and Shrum (2000) offer an alternative to simple rating. They compared two approaches to assessing personal values using rating scales. Simple ratings were compared to an approach where respondents first picked their most and least important values (or attributes or factors), and then rated them (most to least). The remainder of the values was then rated. Their results indicate that, compared with a simple rating of values, the most-least procedure reduces the level of end-piling and increases the differentiation of values ratings, both in terms of dispersion and the number of different rating points used.

Rating methods can take several forms:

1. Numerical

2. Graphic

3. Verbal

Often two or more of these formats appear together, as illustrated in Figure 10.2. As shown in Panel (a) of the figure, the respondent is given both a series of integers (1 through 7) and verbal descriptions of the degree of "gentleness/harshness." The respondent would then be asked to circle the number associated with the descriptive statement that comes closest to his or her feelings about the gentleness/harshness of the brand(s) of say, dishwasher detergent, being rated. In Panel (b) of Figure 10.2, the need is only to check the appropriate category that best expresses feelings about some attitude statement regarding dishwashing detergents, whereas in Panel (e) the category checked represents the importance of characteristics of a retail store.

In Panel (c), the figure represents a graduated thermometer scale with both numerical assignments and a (limited) set of descriptive statements. This illustrates another type of rating device. A so-called "feelings thermometer" is illustrated in Exhibit 10.2 (see p. 380) and is a type of pure numerical scale. A pure numerical version would ask respondents to rate objects on some characteristic using a scale of, say, 1 to 10, (or 1 to 100), where the number 10 (100) represents the most favorable (or most unfavorable) position. It is assumed that this numerical scale has more than ordinal properties. This scale may properly be viewed as a metric measurement (quantitative judgment) method. Panel (d) attempts to anchor the scale using a comparison with the "average" brands. Many other types of rating methods are in use (Haley & Case, 1979).

One type of itemized rating scale that has merit in cases where leniency error may be troublesome is the behaviorally-anchored rating scale, or BARS (see Exhibit 10.3 on p. 381). This scale uses behavioral incidents to define each position on the rating scale rather than verbal, graphic, or numeric labels. The underlying premise is that response biases may emerge since scale positions on most graphic rating scales are vague and undefined. Thus, providing specific behavioral anchors can reduce leniency errors and increase discriminability. Developing scales such as these requires a great amount of testing and refinement to find the right anchors for the situation under examination.

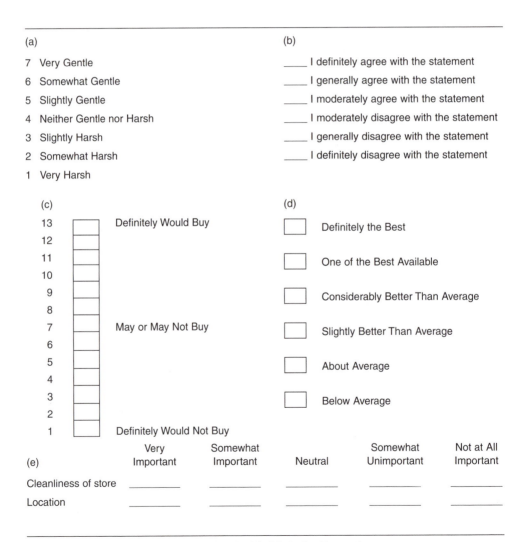

Figure 10.2   Examples of Rating Scales Used in Marketing Research

The basic process of BARS scale development consists of four steps:

1. Construct definition—the construct being measured must be explicitly defined and the key dimensions identified.

2. Item generation—statements must be generated describing actual behaviors that would illustrate specific levels of the construct for each dimension identified.

3. Item testing—items must be tested; the purpose is to be able to unambiguously fit behavioral statements to dimensions.

4. Scale construction—the process of laying out the scale with behavioral statements as anchors follows item testing.

In following this process, sets of judges are used. It should be clear that developing BARS is a time-consuming and costly task. Thus, they should be reserved for those applied settings where they can minimize the errors they are designed to curtail, especially leniency error. As an example, families with elderly members were surveyed to determine their need for in home health-care services. BARS was used for one critical measure of how well elderly members of the household were able to perform everyday living activities:

Now about your ability to perform everyday living activities. Which of the following best describes your everyday living capacities:

- You can perform all physical activities of daily living without assistance. (Excellent capacity)
- You can perform all physical activities without assistance, but may need some help with the heavy work (such as laundry and housekeeping). (Good capacity)
- You regularly require help with certain physical activities or heavy work, but can get through any single day without help. (Moderate capacity)
- You need help each day, but not necessarily throughout the day or night. (Severely impaired capacity)
- You need help throughout the day and night to carry out the activities of daily living. (Completely impaired capacity)

In many instances where rating scales are used, the researcher assumes not only that the items are capable of being ranked, but also that the descriptive levels of progress are in equal-interval steps psychologically. That is, the numerical correspondences shown in Panels (a) and (c) of Figure 10.2 may be treated—sometimes erroneously—as interval- or ratio-scaled data. Even in cases represented by Panels (b), (d), and (e), it is not unusual to find that the researcher assigns successive integer values to the various category descriptions and subsequently works with the data as though the responses *were* interval-scaled.

Treating rating scales as interval or even ratio measurements is a practice that is well documented and widespread. Research shows that there is little error in treating the data as being of a higher level of measurement than it is. Research evidence supports this practice, in that often when ordinal data are treated as interval and parametric analysis are used, the conclusions reached are the same as when the data are treated as ordinal and tested using non-parametric analyses.

EXHIBIT 10.2   A Rating Thermometer

Sudman and Bradburn (1983, p. 159) present the following rating thermometer, with an introductory statement, "We'd also like to get your feelings about some groups in American society. When I read the name of a group, we'd like you to rate it with what we call a feeling thermometer. It is on Page 19 of your booklet. Ratings between 50° and 100° mean that you feel

A	Big Business				S	Labor unions			
B	Poor people				T	Young people			
C	Liberals				U	Conservatives			
D	Southerners				V	Women's liberation movement			
E	Hispanics/Mexican Americans				W	People who use marijuana			
F	Catholics				X	Black militants			
G	Radical students				Y	Jews			
H	Policemen				Z	Civil rights leaders			
J	Older people				AA	Protestants			
K	Women				BB	Workingmen			
M	The military				CC	Whites			
N	Blacks				DD	Men			
P	Democrats				EE	Middle-class people			
Q	People on welfare				FF	Businessmen			
R	Republicans								

100° Very warm or favorable feeling

85° Quite warm or favorable feeling

70° Fairly warm or favorable feeling

60° A bit more warm or favorable than cold feeling

50° No feeling at all

40° A bit more cold or unfavorable than warm feeling

30° Fairly cold or unfavorable feeling

15° Quite cold or unfavorable feeling

0° Very cold or unfavorable feeling

favorably and warm toward the group; ratings between 0° and 50° mean that you don't feel favorably and warm toward the group and that you don't care too much for that group. If you don't feel particularly warm or cold toward a group, you would rate them a 50°. If we come to a group you don't know much about, just tell me and we'll move on to the next one. Our first group is Big Business—how warm would you say you feel toward them? (Write number of degrees or DK (don't know) in boxes provided below.)"

Research on use of the feeling thermometer tends to validate its use, even though must of the variance is left unexplained (Wilcox, Sigelman, & Cook, 1989). This may be due to random noise, idiosyncratic factors hard to measure by the survey method, and a type of response set that parallels some respondents' habitual tendency to answer "yes" regardless of question type. The primary effects observed were shown to be substantively interpretable.

Since the scale has been shown to be valid for evaluating social and other types of groups, it should be of usefulness to marketing researchers. Oftentimes, target groups, segments, and so forth, are evaluated along different dimensions of interest to the marketing manager.

EXHIBIT 10.3   Measuring Preferences of Young Children Calls for Creativity

The children's market is a multibillion dollar market in direct purchasing power and an even greater market in purchasing influence. Thus, it is important that companies wishing to gain a competitive advantage in understanding and responding to children's preferences be able to measure such preferences. In a fairly recent study of companies marketing to children, the development of better measurement technique was identified as a major priority for future research by a majority of responding companies.

Among the areas of most concern are better scaling techniques for measuring children's product preferences. Widely used approaches for assessing children's preferences are itemized rating scales using a series of stars (a scale from 1 to 5 stars) or a series of facial expressions (a scale anchored at one end with a happy face and at the other end with a sad face), as illustrated below:

A. Facial Scale

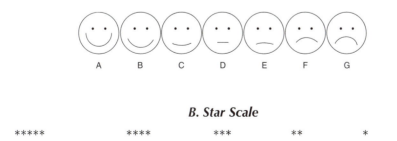

B. Star Scale

*****   ****   ***   **   *

Children are asked to indicate how much they like a product, or how much they like a particular feature of a product, by pointing to one of the visual anchors on the scale. These responses are then analyzed to determine which products children like best and which features they prefer in particular products.

Although these scales have done well in varied research applications, there are some problems that emerge, particularly when used with young children under the age of eight. A major potential problem is leniency error. This error emerges when young children consistently use the extreme positions (usually on the positive side) with relatively little use of intermediate scale positions. If this is done for all products tested, the overall sensitivity of existing (traditional) rating scales is lowered, resulting in inconclusive findings about children's preferences. Regardless of the reasons for this bias—and there are some alternative explanations—it is important that its potential for existence be acknowledged and reduced.

One type of scale that has been introduced to reduce leniency error in young children's ratings is an itemized rating scale based on the concept of behaviorally-anchored rating scales (BARS).

A.   "SHOPPING" SCALE (BARS1)

B.   "SHARING" SCALE (BARS2)

Behaviorally-anchored rating scales use critical behavioral incidents to define various positions on the rating scale, instead of the more usual verbal labels or graphic devices such as stars or faces. The use of behavioral anchors would appear to be useful in studying children's markets since they provide a familiar and concrete way of expressing preferences and can be readily displayed in a visual format for young children.

One illustration of behaviorally-anchored scales is a study of children's preferences for cereals in which the scale used pictures depicting sharing and shopping behavior, rather than verbal descriptions of behavior. The children studied were less than eight years of age. These two BARS were effective in lowering leniency bias when tested against the more usual facial and star scales.

The extent to which creative researchers can develop such scales for use in children's markets is almost limitless. When older children are of concern, the more traditional type of BARS (with verbalized descriptions of behavior for each scale position) can be used (Karsten & John, 1991).

In Chapter 9 we illustrated some of the problems associated with treating ordinal data as interval- or ratio-scaled data. Although methods are available for scaling the stimuli under weaker assumptions about the intervals that separate category labels (as mentioned earlier under ordered-category sorting), in practice these methods are often cumbersome to use and, accordingly, may not justify the time and effort associated with their application. However, this should not negate the importance of being aware of the implicit assumptions that one

Table 10.2   Issues in Constructing a Scale

1. Should negative numbers be used?
2. How many categories should be included?
3. Related to the number of categories is: Should there be an odd number or an even number?
    That is, should a neutral alternative be provided?
4. Should the scale be balanced or unbalanced?
5. Is it desirable to not force a substantive response by giving an opportunity to indicate
    "don't know," "no opinion," or something similar?
6. What does one do about halo effects—that is, the tendency of raters to ascribe favorable property
    levels to all attributes of a stimulus object if they happen to like a particular object in general?
7. How does one examine raters' biases—for example, the tendency to use extreme values or,
    perhaps, only the middle range of the response scale, or to overestimate the desirable
    features of the things they like (i.e., the generosity error)?
8. How should descriptive adjectives for rating categories be selected?
9. How anchoring phrases for the scale's origin should be chosen?

makes about the scale properties of rating instruments when certain statistical techniques are used to summarize and interrelate the response data.

Table 10.2 identifies nine questions that must be identified and answered when a scale is constructed.

These questions may be related. For example, questions 2 and 3 are obviously related. Similarly questions 2 and 7 also appear to be related. A series of experiments involving the middle response alternative in general—neutral scale item, middle position of the scale, and so forth—showed that (a) people are more likely to select it when it is part of the scale than they are to volunteer it; (b) the order in which it is presented in the scale question and response set can make a difference in results; and (c) people who choose the middle alternative when available would not necessarily answer the question in the same way that others do if forced to choose sides on the matter of concern (Bishop, 1987).

More recent research on the neutral option is inconclusive (Nowlis, Kahn, & Dhar, 2002). A conclusion is reached that consumer responses can be significantly altered by excluding a neutral position when respondents are ambivalent. Further, the study showed that scales excluding this option produce a different response from scales that include it. The question to be answered is which of the two scales—neutral-included or neutral-excluded—is likely to best reflect the underlying attitudes. Unfortunately, the researchers were reluctant to state which would most accurately reflect the truth. Since it has not been shown that there are errors made when a neutral option is provided, our suggestion is that it always be included, unless the researcher has a compelling reason to not do so (e.g., the problem situation/sample mix is such that each sample member can be expected to have a non-neutral attitude). Expected voting in a survey of voters is an example.

Question 4 deals with an interesting issue. *Balance* refers to having an equal number of negative response alternatives as positive ones. Or the alternatives may just be in opposite directions from some mid-point. When using importance scales for attributes, the alternatives provided may be "very important," "important," "neither important nor unimportant," "unimportant," and "very unimportant," or additional categories may be included. Thomas Semon (2001) has questioned the use of balance (or symmetry, as he calls it) in importance scales. He argues that importance is not a bipolar concept. Importance ranges from some positive amount to none, not a negative amount. Although this appears to have conceptual appeal, researchers continue to successfully use importance scales from some mid-point—specified or implied. There would seem to be three keys to successful importance scale use:

1. Isolating any findings of unimportance

2. Recognizing that importance is ordinally scaled

3. Accurately interpreting the relative nature of importance findings

Answers to questions such as these will vary by the researcher's approach, and by the problem being studied. For example, there are many alternative response categories that can be used to measure satisfaction. Table 10.3 shows just a few. The effects of research design on reliability and validity of rating scales are discussed in two excellent review papers (Churchill and Peter, 1984; Peter and Churchill, 1986).

In summary, rating methods—depending on the assumptions of the researcher—can be considered to lead to ordinal-, interval-, or even ratio-scaled responses. The latter two scales are taken up next. We shall see that rating methods figure prominently in the development of quantitative-judgment scales.

Ratio/Interval Procedures

Direct-judgment estimates, fractionation, constant sum, and rating methods (if the researcher wishes to assume more than ordinal properties about respondents' judgments) are all variants of ratio/interval procedures or metric measurement methods.

Direct-Judgment Methods

In direct-judgment methods, the respondent is asked to give a numerical rating to each stimulus with respect to some designated attribute. In the unlimited-response category sub-case, the respondent is free to choose his or her own number or, in graphical methods, to insert a tick mark along some line that represents his or her judgment about the magnitude of the

Table 10.3   Alternative Scales for Measuring Satisfaction

1. A numerical scale from 1 to 7 where 1 = completely satisfied and 7 = completely dissatisfied
2. A percentage scale using the following categories: 91–100, 81–90, 71–80, 61–70, 51–60
3. A verbal scale using the following choices: very satisfied, somewhat satisfied, somewhat dissatisfied, very dissatisfied, uncertain
4. A verbal scale using the following: very satisfied, somewhat satisfied, unsatisfied, very unsatisfied
5. A verbal scale using the following: completely satisfied, very satisfied, fairly satisfied, somewhat dissatisfied, very dissatisfied
6. A verbal scale using the following: very satisfied, quite satisfied, not very satisfied, not at all satisfied
7. A verbal scale using the following: very satisfied, somewhat satisfied, not at all satisfied

stimulus relative to some reference points. This is illustrated in Panel (a) of Figure 10.3 for the rating of Brand A.

This is a simplified version of a magnitude scale, which is based on psychological scaling (Lodge, 1981). It is an alternative to category scaling. This method has been studied for use in a semantic differential context (to be discussed later in this chapter) and was found to have advantages in individual measurement without affecting aggregate properties of the measurement (Albaum, Best, & Hawkins, 1981). Another study showed that these unlimited response scales, also known as continuous-rating scales, appear to be insensitive to fluctuations in the length of the line used (Hubbard, Little, & Allen, 1989).

The limited-response category subcase is illustrated by Panel (b) in Figure 10.3. Here the respondent is limited to choosing one of seven categories. We note that in this instance the direct-judgment method is nothing more than a straight rating procedure, with the important addition that the ratings are now treated as either interval- or ratio-scaled data (depending on the application) rather than as simple ratings.

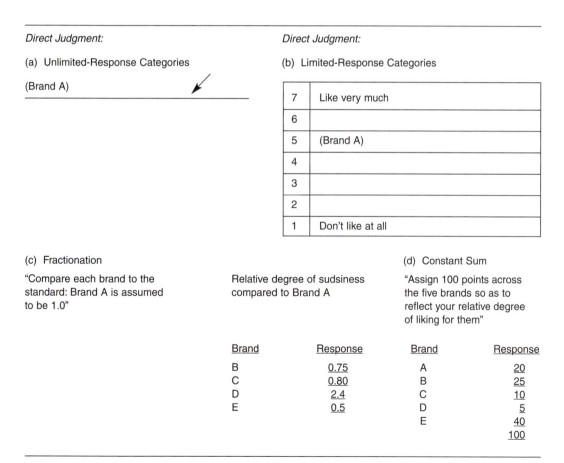

Figure 10.3   Some illustrations of Interval-Ratio Scale

If the respondent has several items to rate, either the unlimited- or limited-response category procedures can be employed. In the former case, the respondent arranges the stimuli (usually described on small cards) along a sort board, provided by the researcher, so that each is separated according to a subjective distance relative to the others. In the latter case, one assigns cards to the designated category on the sort board that best matches one's evaluation of the stimulus.

Fractionation

Fractionation is a procedure in which the respondent is given two stimuli at a time (e.g., a standard laundry detergent and a test brand) and asked to give some numerical estimate of the ratio between them, with respect to some attribute, such as sudsiness.

The respondent may answer that the test brand, in his or her judgment, is three-fourths as sudsy as the standard. After this is done, a new test brand is compared with the same standard, and so on, until all test items are judged. Panel (c) in Figure 10.3 illustrates this procedure.

In other cases where the test item can be more or less continuously varied by the respondent, the respondent is asked to vary the test item so that it represents some designated ratio of the standard. For example, if the attribute is sweetness of lemonade, the respondent may be asked to add more sweetener until the test item is "twice as sweet" as the standard.

Constant Sum

Constant-sum methods have become quite popular in marketing research, primarily because of their simplicity and ease of instructions. In constant-sum methods the respondent is given some number of points—typically 10 or 100—and asked to distribute them over the alternatives in a way that reflects their relative magnitude of some attitudinal characteristic. Panel (d) of Figure 10.3 shows an illustration of the constant-sum procedure. Constant sum forces the respondent to allocate his or her evaluations and effectively standardizes each scale across persons, since all scores must add to the same constant. As such, the constant-sum procedure requires the respondent to make a comparative evaluation of the stimuli. Generally, it is assumed that a subjective ratio scale is obtained by this method.

In a study of its customers and noncustomers, a local bank asked the following question:

Please divide 100 points among the characteristics listed below to indicate how important each is to you in doing business with a financial institution. The more important a trait is to you, the more points you should give it. You may give as many or as few points as you like.

	Number of Points
The bank is locally owned	_____
Friendly, helpful personnel	_____
Conveniently located	_____
Offers a full range of financial services	_____
Price of its services	_____
Decisions are made locally	_____
Must total to	100

To sum it up, unlike ordinal measurement methods, the major assumption underlying ratio/interval measurement methods is that a unit of measurement can be constructed directly from respondents' estimates about scale values associated with a set of stimuli. The respondent's report is taken at face value and any variation in repeated estimates (over test occasions within respondent or over respondents) is treated as error; repeated estimates are usually averaged over persons and/or occasions.

The problems associated with interval-ratio scaling methods include the following:

1. Respondents' subjective scale units may differ across each other, across testing occasions, or both.

2. Respondents' subjective origins (zero points) may differ across each other, across occasions, or both.

3. Unit and origin may shift over stimulus items within a single occasion.

These problems should not be treated lightly, particularly when data for several subjects are being averaged.

In addition, researchers should be aware of the constraints placed on the respondent's response format. For example, if asked to rate laundry detergents on a five-point scale, ranging from 1 ("least sudsy"), to 3 ("moderate sudsy"), to 5 ("sudsiest"), the respondent may not be capable of accurately carrying out the task. That is, one's subjective distance between the sudsiest detergent and the moderate detergent(s) may not equal one's perception of the distance between the moderate detergent(s) and the least sudsy detergent.

Most ratings measurement methods have the virtue of being easy to apply. Moreover, little additional work beyond averaging is required to obtain the unit of measurement directly. Indeed, if a unique origin can be established (e.g., a zero level of the property), then the researcher obtains both an absolute origin and a measurement unit. As such, a subjective ratio scale is obtained.

TECHNIQUES FOR SCALING STIMULI

Any of the data collection methods just described—whether for the measurement of ranking or ratings data—produce a set of raw-data responses. In the case of ranking methods, the raw data, describing ordinal-scaled judgments, usually undergo a further transformation (via a scaling model) to produce set of scale values that are interval-scaled. Technically speaking, the raw data obtained from ratings methods also require an intervening model. However, in this case the model may be no more elaborate than averaging the raw data across respondents and/or response occasions.

Thurstone's Case V method is a popular model for dealing with ordinal data obtained from ranking methods. Osgood's semantic differential is an illustration of a procedure for dealing with raw data obtained from interval-ratio scale ratings methods. We consider each of these techniques in turn.

Case V Scaling

Thurstone's Case V Scaling model, based on his law of comparative judgment, permits the construction of a unidimensional interval scale using responses from ordinal measurement methods, such as paired comparisons (Thurstone, 1959). This model can also be used to scale ranked data or ordered-category sorts. Several subcases of Thurstone's model have been developed. We shall first describe the general case and then concentrate on Case V, a special version particularly amenable to application in marketing situations.

Essentially, Thurstone's procedure involves deriving an interval scale from comparative judgments of the type "A is fancier than B," "A is more prestigious than B," "A is preferred to B," and so on. Scale values may be estimated from data in which one individual makes many repeated judgments on each pair of a set of stimuli or from data obtained from a group of individuals with few or no replications per person.

The concept that underlies the model of comparative judgment on which Case V scaling is based is simple to describe. Suppose that we have a group of respondents, almost all of whom prefer A to B. Then the proportion of total comparisons (no ties allowed) in which A is preferred to B will be close to 100 percent. Suppose, however, that when B is compared with C, only 55 percent of the group prefers B to C. Intuitively, we might think that the difference between the scale values associated with A and B should be much larger than the difference between the scale values associated with B and C. Under certain assumptions, Thurstone's model of comparative judgment provides a means to develop an interval scale from these stimulus-comparison proportions.

An example should make the Case V procedure easier to follow. Assume that 100 homemakers were asked to compare five brands of canned tomato juice with respect to "overall goodness of flavor." The homemakers sipped a sample of each brand paired with a sample of every other brand (a total of 10 pairs) from paper cups that were marked merely with identifying numbers. Table 10.4 shows the empirically observed proportion for each comparison.

From this table we see that 69 percent of the respondents preferred Juice C to Juice A and the remainder, 31 percent preferred Juice A to Juice C (if we arbitrarily let column dominate row). It is customary to set self-comparisons (the main-diagonal entries of Table 10.4) to 0.5; this has no effect on the resulting scale values (Edwards, 1957). From the data of this table we next prepare Table 10.5, which summarizes the Z-values appropriate for each proportion. These Z-values were obtained from Table A.1 in Appendix A at the end of this book. If the proportion is less than 0.5, the Z-value carries a negative sign; if the proportion is greater than 0.5, the Z-value carries a positive sign. The Z-values are standard unit variates associated with a given proportion of total area under the normal curve. The Thurstonian model assumes normally distributed scale differences in mean = 0 and standard deviation = 1.0.

For example, from Table 10.4 we note that the proportion of respondents preferring Juice B over Juice A is 0.82. We wish to know the Z-value appropriate thereto. This value labeled Z in the standard unit normal table of Table A.1 is 0.92. That is, 82 percent of the total area under the normal curve is between $Z = -\infty$ and $Z = 0.92$. All remaining entries in Table 10.5 are obtained in a similar manner, a minus sign being prefixed to the Z-value when the proportion is *less* than 0.5.

Column totals are next found for the entries in Table 10.5. Scale values are obtained from the column sums by taking a simple average of each column's Z-values. For example, from Table 10.5, we note that the sum of the Zs for the first column (Juice A) is -0.36. The average Z for column A is simply:

$$Z = -\frac{0.36}{5} = -0.072$$

Table 10.4 Observed Proportions Preferring Brand *X* (Top of Table) to Brand Y (Side of Table)

| | Preferred Brand | | | | |
Brand	A	B	C	D	E
A	0.50	0.82	0.69	0.25	0.35
B	0.18	0.50	0.27	0.07	0.15
C	0.31	0.73	0.50	0.16	0.25
D	0.75	0.93	0.84	0.50	0.59
E	0.65	0.85	0.75	0.41	0.50

Table 10.5 Z-Values Related to Preference Proportions in Table 10.4

| | Brand | | | | |
Brand	A	B	C	D	E
A	0	0.92	0.50	−0.67	−0.39
B	−0.92	0	−0.61	−1.48	−1.04
C	−0.50	0.61	0	−0.99	−0.67
D	0.67	1.48	0.99	0	0.23
E	0.39	1.04	0.67	−0.23	0
Total	−0.36	4.05	1.55	−3.37	−1.87
Mean (Z)	−0.072	0.810	0.310	−0.674	−0.374
R	0.602	1.484	0.984	0	0.300

This scale value expresses Juice A as a deviation from the mean of all five scale values. The mean of the five values, as computed from the full row of Zs, will always be zero under this procedure. Similarly, we find the average Z-value for each of the remaining four columns of Table 10.5.

Next, since the zero point of an interval scale is arbitrary, we can transform the minimum scale so that it becomes zero. We will let Juice D ($R_D = Z_D = -0.674$) be the reference point (or origin) of zero by adding .674. We then simply add 0.674 to each of the other Z-values to obtain the Case V scale values of the other four brands. These are denoted by R and appear in the last row of Table 10.5.

The scale values of Juices A through E indicate the preference ordering

$$B > C > A > E > D$$

Moreover, assuming that an interval scale exists, we can say, for example, that the difference in "goodness of flavor" between Juices B and A is 2.3 times the difference in "goodness of flavor" between Juices C and A, since

$B - A = 2.3 (C - A)$

$1.484 - 0.602 = 2.3 (0.984 - 0.602)$

$0.882 = 2.3 (0.382)$

(within rounding error).

The test of this model is how well scale values can be used to work backward—that is, to predict the original proportions. The Case V model appears to fit the data in the example quite well. For any specific brand, the highest mean absolute proportion discrepancy is 0.025 (Juice A). Moreover, the overall mean absolute discrepancy is only .02 (rounded). Even the simplest version (Case V) of the Thurstonian model leads to fairly accurate predictions. The $R*$ scale values of the Case V model preserve the original rank ordering of the original proportions data.

Another approach to obtain numerical scores from rankings is shown in Exhibit 10.4.

EXHIBIT 10.4   Converting Ranks into Scale Values

Another approach to convert ranks into numerical scores is based on the assumption that true differences between adjacent objects ranked near the extremes tend to be larger than differences between objects falling near the middle of the rank. Specifically, we can view relative differences among ranked objects as being similar to differences between the standardized or Z-values falling at the boundary points of N–1 equally probable intervals falling in the midrange of a normal distribution. We would like the interval between each adjacent pair of ranks (e.g., 1 and 2, 7 and 8) to define an interval corresponding to $100/N$ of cases in a normal distribution. Finally, we arbitrarily set $100/2N$ as the percentage of cases in a normal distribution to be cut below the value of the object ranked I and above the value of the object ranked N.

We can proceed as follows. For any stimulus object (such as a brand of soap) that has been ranked j, we find from the normal tables the Z-score cutting off the lower proportion of the area under the normal curve. Using this procedure we determine the Z-values for 10 brands of soap (A–J) as follow:

Brand	Rank	Percentile	Z-Value
C	1	5	−1.65
E	2	15	−1.04
A	3	25	−.67
D	4	35	−.39
F	5	45	−.13
H	6	55	.13
G	7	65	.39
J	8	75	.67
I	9	85	1.04
B	10	95	1.65

For Brand E, for example, we find that the lower $(2 − 5)/10$ or .15 proportion of the area under the normal curve corresponds to a Z-value of −1.04. The end result is that the original ranks have been transformed into scale values, which can then be treated as if they were intervally-scaled.

This exposition has assumed a single evaluator. More realistically, a sample of people will do the rankings, thus creating for each brand a distribution of ranks. Each brand's scale value will then be an average Z-value, as shown below:

Rankings Given to Ten Objects by Fifty Judges

Brand Rank	A	B	C	D	E	F	G	H	I	J	z
1	20	6	2	12	0	0	0	10	0	0	−1.65
2	6	5	27	10	2	0	0	0	0	0	−1.04
3	2	27	15	6	0	0	0	0	0	0	−.67
4	12	10	6	7	15	0	0	0	0	0	−.39
5	10	0	0	15	17	8	0	0	0	0	−.13
6	0	0	0	0	10	17	21	2	0	0	.13
7	0	0	0	0	0	10	7	33	0	0	.39
8	0	0	0	0	6	0	10	5	27	2	.67
9	0	0	0	0	0	15	12	0	23	0	1.04
10	0	2	0	0	0	0	0	0	0	48	1.65
	−.931		−.875		−.096		.493		.840		
		−.676		−.778		.413		−.0004		1.61	
										scale=	average
										value	Z-Value

Although perhaps not as refined as the Thurstone law of comparative judgment, this technique is computationally simpler and gives results comparable with paired-comparison methods. The objects judged by this method can be viewed as being intervally-scaled where the unit is one standard deviation in the distribution of true values over all possible objects on this scale.

SOURCE: Adapted from Hays, 1967, pp. 35–39.

The Semantic Differential

The semantic differential (Osgood, Suci, & Tannenbaum, 1957) is a ratings procedure that results in (assumed interval) scales that are often further analyzed by such techniques as factor analysis (see Chapter 19). Unlike the Case V model, the semantic differential provides no way to test the adequacy of the scaling model itself. It is simply assumed that the raw data are interval-scaled; the intent of the semantic differential is to obtain these raw data for later processing by various multivariate models.

The semantic differential procedure permits the researcher to measure both the direction and the intensity of respondents' attitudes (i.e., measure psychological meaning) toward such

Extremely								Extremely
Powerful	X	___	___	___	___	___	___	Weak
Reliable	___	___	X	___	___	___	___	Unreliable
Modern	___	___	X	___	___	___	___	Old-fashioned
Warm	___	___	___	___	X	___	___	Cold
Careful	___	X	___	___	___	___	___	Careless

Figure 10.4   Corporate Profile Obtained by Means of the Semantic Differential

concepts as corporate image, advertising image, brand or service image, and country image. One way this is done is to ask the respondent to describe the concept by means of ratings on a set of bipolar adjectives, as illustrated in Figure 10.4.

As shown in Figure 10.4, the respondent may be given a set of pairs of antonyms, the extremes of each pair being separated by seven intervals that are assumed to be equal. For each pair of adjectives (e.g., powerful/weak), the respondent is asked to judge the concept along the seven-point scale with descriptive phrases:

- *Extremely* powerful
- *Very* powerful
- *Slightly* powerful
- *Neither* powerful nor weak
- *Slightly* weak
- *Very* weak
- *Extremely* weak

This is repeated for the other pairs of terms.

In Figure 10.4, a subject evaluated a corporation and scored the company on each scale:

- Extremely powerful
- Slightly reliable
- Slightly modern
- Slightly cold
- Very careful

In practice, however, profiles would be built up for a large sample of respondents, with many more bipolar adjectives being used than given here.

By assigning a set of integer values, such as +3, +2, +1, 0, –1, –2, –3, to the seven gradations of each bipolar scale in Figure 10.5, the responses can be quantified under the assumption of equal-appearing intervals. These scale values, in turn, can be averaged across respondents to develop semantic differential profiles. For example, Figure 10.5 shows a profile comparing evaluations of Companies X and Y. The average score for the respondents show that the Company X is perceived as very weak, unreliable, old-fashioned, and careless,

Extremely	+3	+2	+1	0	−1	−2	−3	Extremely
Powerful								Weak
Reliable								Unreliable
Modern								Old-fashioned
Warm								Cold
Careful								Careless

Figure 10.5   Average-Respondent Profile Comparisons of Companies X and Y via the Semantic Differential

NOTE: Company X = _____
         Company Y = _____

but rather warm. Company Y is perceived as powerful, reliable, and careful, but rather cold as well; it is almost neutral with respect to the modern/old-fashioned scale.

In marketing research applications, the semantic differential often uses bipolar descriptive phrases rather than simple adjectives, or a combination of both types. These scales are developed for particular context areas, so the scales have more meaning to respondents, thus leading usually to a high degree of reliability.

To illustrate, a supermarket chain was interested in knowing how the general public perceived it and one of its major competitors. Table 10.6 lists the semantic differential scale items used in this study. Both descriptive terms and so-called phrases were used. One thing to note about these scales is that polarity is mixed; for some items the negative term is on the left, while for others it is on the right (and vice-versa for the positive item). This is a form of reversed polarity and is done to reduce the effects of, or even to eliminate, acquiescence bias or yea-saying, and halo effects. The idea is to force respondents to read each item and make independent judgments about each item.

The same type of questions presented in Table 10.2 as being applicable to rating scale use also apply to the semantic differential. In addition, the researcher must select an overall format for presentation of the scales. Figure 10.6 illustrates (in the context of evaluating national retailers in the United States) the four major approaches, from which there are many specific variations.

The traditional approach is shown in Panel (a) of Figure 10.6. The object of concern, Kmart, is rated on all attribute dimensions before the next object, Wal-Mart, is rated on these dimensions. Panel (b) illustrates a modified traditional format, in that Kmart and Wal-Mart, and Sears are evaluated on a single attribute (dull/exciting) before the next attribute (high quality/low quality) is introduced into the measurement process. Panel (c) illustrates what is called the graphic positioning scale (Narayana, 1977) in which all objects (i.e., Sears, Kmart and Ward's) are evaluated on the same scale by some graphical means (usually letters) to reflect relative perceptual placement. Finally, Panel (d) illustrates the numerical comparative scale (Golden, Brockett, Albaum, & Zatarain, 1992). Respondents make their judgments for Kmart, Wal-Mart, and Sears on one attribute before moving to the next one.

The number and type of stimuli to evaluate and the method of administration (personal interview, mail, telephone) should determine at least which format the researcher should

Table 10.6   Scale Items Used in Comparative Study of Supermarkets

Inconvenient location	___	___	___	___	___	___	___	Convenient location
Low prices	___	___	___	___	___	___	___	High prices
Pleasant atmosphere	___	___	___	___	___	___	___	Unpleasant atmosphere
Low quality products	___	___	___	___	___	___	___	High quality atmosphere
Modern	___	___	___	___	___	___	___	Old-fashioned
Unfriendly clerks	___	___	___	___	___	___	___	Friendly clerks
Sophisticated customers	___	___	___	___	___	___	___	Unsophisticated customers
Cluttered	___	___	___	___	___	___	___	Spacious
Fast check-out	___	___	___	___	___	___	___	Slow check-out
Unorganized layout	___	___	___	___	___	___	___	Well organized layout
Enjoyable shopping experience	___	___	___	___	___	___	___	Unenjoyable shopping experience
Bad reputation	___	___	___	___	___	___	___	Good reputation
Good service	___	___	___	___	___	___	___	Bad service
Unhelpful clerks	___	___	___	___	___	___	___	Helpful clerks
Dull	___	___	___	___	___	___	___	Exciting
Good selection of products	___	___	___	___	___	___	___	Bad selection of products
Dirty	___	___	___	___	___	___	___	Clean
Like	___	___	___	___	___	___	___	Dislike

use. Comparative studies of these formats are inconclusive and seem to indicate small differences in the content provided in the quality, including reliability, of the data obtained. Therefore, choice of a format may be appropriately made on the basis of other considerations, such as ease of subject understanding, ease of coding and interpretation for the researcher, ease of production and display, and cost. If a large number of stimuli are to be evaluated, this would tend to favor use of the graphic positioning or numerical comparative scales.

A recent study raises a question of whether the semantic differential, as used in a single-stage format asking for both direction and strength (amount), leads to a central tendency error (Yu, Albaum, & Swenson, 2003). This error is one in which there is reluctance on the part of respondents to give extreme responses. A two-stage approach is suggested in which respondents are first asked to indicate one of the adjectives or phrases from a pair and then they are asked to

(a)

                Kmart

Friendly   X _____   Unfriendly

Modern   _____X_____   Old-fashioned

(b)

                    Dull   Exciting

            Kmart   1   2   3   4   5   6   7
            Wal-Mart 1   2   3   4   5   6   7
            Sears   1   2   3   4   5   6   7

(c)

Friendly   S   W   K _____   Unfriendly

Modern   __K__W_____S_____   Old-fashioned

(d)

                                                                Kmart   Wal-Mart   Sears

High Quality   1   2   3   4   5   6   7   Low Quality   3   5   4

Dull   1   2   3   4   5   6   7   Exciting   6   4   2

Figure 10.6   Formats of the Semantic Differential

---

indicate "how much." For example, in a study of shoppers at supermarkets, this format of the semantic differential can be used as follows:

> For each of the descriptors shown below please tick the term which best describes
>
> ABC Food Stores.
>
> _____ Inconvenient location   _____ Convenient location   _____ Neither

> If you ticked one of the two terms or phrases (i.e., you did NOT tick "neither"),
>
> Indicate whether it is *very*, *somewhat*, or *slightly* descriptive of ABC.
>
> _____ Very   _____ Somewhat   _____ Slightly

This study reported that the two-stage format generated a greater proportion of responses in the extreme (i.e., the *very*) categories than did the regular one-stage format. If a researcher is interested primarily in people with extreme views, then the two-stage approach provides better data quality. But if interest is in central tendencies and/or overall distributions such as group means, then the one-stage format is adequate.

Stapel Scale

A modification of the semantic differential is the Stapel scale (Crespi, 1961). This scale is an even-numbered nonverbal rating scale used in conjunction with single adjectives or phrases, rather than bipolar opposites, to rate an object, concept or person. Figure 10.7 shows the format of this scale, although it is not necessary that the scale have 10 points. Both intensity and direction are measured at the same time. It cannot be assumed that the intervals are equal and that ratings for a respondent are additive. Research has shown no differences in reliability and validity between this scale and the semantic differential (Hawkins, Albaum & Best, 1974; Menzes & Elbert, 1979).

A Concluding Remark

Currently the semantic differential technique is being used in diverse applications:

- Comparing corporate images, both among suppliers of particular products and against an ideal image of what respondents think a company should be
- Comparing brands and services of competing suppliers
- Determining the attitudinal characteristics of purchasers of particular product classes or brands within a product class, including perceptions of the country of origin for imported products
- Analyzing the effectiveness of advertising and other promotional stimuli toward changing attitudes

The comparatively widespread use of the semantic differential by marketing researchers suggests that this method provides a convenient and reasonably reliable way for developing consumer/buyer attitudes on a wide variety of topics.

TECHNIQUES FOR SCALING RESPONDENTS

Thurstone's Case V model and Osgood's semantic differential are primarily designed for scaling stimuli—tomato juices, brands of toothpaste, corporate images, retailing services, and the like. Researchers also have available techniques whose primary purpose is to scale respondents along some attitude continuum of interest. There are three better-known procedures for doing this:

1. The summated scale

2. The Q-sort technique

3. The differential scale

Each of these is described in turn.

High Quality

( )   +5
( )   +4
( )   +3
( )   +2
( )   +1
( )   −1
( )   −2
( )   −3
( )   −4
( )   −5

Figure 10.7   A Stapel Scale

The Summated Scale

The summated scale was originally proposed by Rensis Likert, a psychologist (Likert, 1967; Kerlinger, 1973). To illustrate, assume that the researcher wishes to scale some characteristic, such as the public's attitude toward travel and vacations. In applying the Likert summated-scale technique, the steps shown in Table 10.7 are typically carried out.

Many researchers using the final Likert summated scale (the one developed after the pretest) assume only ordinal properties regarding the placement of respondents along the attitude continuum of interest. Nonetheless, two respondents could have the same total score even though their response patterns to individual items were quite different. That is, the process of obtaining a single (summated) score ignores the details of just which items were agreed with and which ones were not. Moreover, the total score is sensitive to how the respondent reacts to the descriptive intensity scale.

Respondents' reactions to the items may be affected by the polarity of the items. That is, when developing a set of items for use, the researcher needs to consider the possibility of acquiescence bias, or agreement, arising. Polarity refers to the positiveness or negativeness of the statement used in a scale. Often, a researcher will reverse the polarity of some items in the set (i.e., word items negatively) as a way to overcome this bias. Having positively and negatively worded statements hopefully forces respondents with strong positive or negative attitudes to use both ends of a scale, but the cost may be losing unidimensonality of the scale (Herche & Engelland, 1996). This suggests a trade-off is necessary: unidimensional measurement with acquiescence bias versus nonbiased measurement tainted by suspect unidimensionality. The latter is preferred in most cases. Thus, a researcher should reverse the polarity of some items and adjust the scoring, as appropriate. That is, a "strongly agree" response to a positive statement and a "strongly disagree" to a negative statement should be scored the same, and so forth.

A recent study of five cultures questions the issue of reverse-worded items, ultimately preferring a mixed-worded Likert format, especially in cross-cultural research on consumers (Wong, Rindfleisch, & Burroughs, 2003). These researchers studied the mixed-worded format for a particular scale—the Material Values Scale (MVS) (Richins & Dawson, 1992). When applied cross-culturally, the mixed-worded format of MVS tended to confound the

Table 10.7   Steps in Constructing a Likert Scale

1. The researcher assembles a large number (e.g., 75 to 100) of statements concerning the public's sentiments toward travel and vacations.

2. Each of the test items is classified by the researcher as generally "favorable" or "unfavorable" with regard to the attitude under study. No attempt is made to scale the items; however, a pretest is conducted that involves the full set of statements and a limited sample of respondents. Ideally, the initial classification should be checked across several judges.

3. In the pretest the respondent indicates approval (or not) with *every* item, checking one of the following direction-intensity descriptors:
   a. Strongly approve or agree
   b. Approve or agree
   c. Undecided or neither agree nor disagree
   d. Disapprove or disagree
   e. Strongly disapprove or disagree

4. Each response is given a numerical weight (e.g., +2, +1, 0, −1, −2). It could be +1 to +5.

5. The individual's *total-attitude score* is represented by the algebraic summation of weights associated with the items checked. In the scoring process, weights are assigned such that the direction of attitude—favorable to unfavorable—is consistent over items. For example, if a + 2 were assigned to "strongly approve/agree" for favorable items, a + 2 should be assigned to "strongly disapprove/disagree" for unfavorable items.

6. On the basis of the results of the pretest, the analyst selects only those items that appear to discriminate well between high and low *total* scorers. This may be done by first finding the highest and lowest quartiles of subjects on the basis of *total* score. Then, the mean differences on each *specific* item are compared between these high and low groups (excluding the middle 50 percent of subjects).

7. The 20 to 25 items finally selected are those that have discriminated "best" (i.e., exhibited the greatest differences in mean values) between high versus low total scorers in the pretest.

8. Steps 3 through 5 are then repeated in the main study.

scale's applicability. Translation errors, variable response biases, and substantive cultural differences all can lead to confounding. To correct for this, adapting the statements into a set of nondirectional questions will lead to largely alleviating the problems associated with mixed-wording scales (Wong, Rindfleisch, & Burroughs, 2003). As an illustration, a nondirectional format for one item of MVS would be

"How much pleasure do you get from buying things? [Very little . . . A great deal]"

In contrast, the normal Likert format for this item is

"Buying things gives me a lot of pleasure [strongly agree, agree, neither agree nor disagree, disagree, strongly disagree]"

To further illustrate the use of the Likert scale, a set of seven statements regarding travel and vacations used in a study by a travel company are shown in Figure 10.8. Assume now that each of the seven test items has been classified as "favorable" (items 1, 3, and 7) or

In this part of the questionnaire we are interested in your opinions about vacations. There are no right or wrong answers to any of these statements. What we would like you to do is simply read each statement as it appears. Then indicate the extent of your agreement or disagreement by circling the number that best describes your reaction to the statement: strongly agree (5), agree (4), neither agree nor disagree (3), disagree (2), strongly disagree (1).

	Please circle the number that best describes your reaction				
	Strongly Agree	Agree	Neither Agree nor Disagree	Disagree	Strongly Disagree
1. In the winter I need to go south to the sun.	5	4	3	2	1
2. When you take trips with the children you're not really on vacation.	5	4	3	2	1
3. I look for travel bargains.	5	4	3	2	1
4. I "hate" to spend money.	5	4	3	2	1
5. I do not like the fresh air and out-of-doors.	5	4	3	2	1
6. I would feel lost if I were alone in a foreign country	5	4	3	2	1
7. A good vacation shortens the year and makes life longer.	5	4	3	2	1

Figure 10.8   A Direction-Intensity Scale for Measuring Attitudes Toward Travel and Vacations

"unfavorable" (items 2, 4, 5, and 6). Each subject would be asked to circle the number that most represents his or her agreement with the statement. We may use the weights +2 for "strongly agree," +1 for "agree," 0 for "neither," −1 for "disagree," and −2 for "strongly-disagree." Since, by previous classification, items 1, 3, 7 are "favorable" statements, we would use the preceding weights with no modification. However, on items 2, 4, 5, and 6 ("unfavorable" statements), we would reverse the order of the weights so as to maintain a consistent direction. Thus, in these items, +2 would stand for "strongly disagree," and so on.

Suppose that a subject evaluated the seven items in the following way:

Item	Response	
1	Strongly agree	+2
2	Disagree	+1
3	Agree	+1
4	Strongly disagree	+2
5	Disagree	+1
6	Strongly disagree	+2
7	Strongly agree	+2

The respondent would receive a total score of

$$+ 2 + 1 + 1 + 2 + 1 + 2 + 2 = 11$$

Suppose that another respondent responded to the seven items by marking (1) strongly disagree, (2) neither, (3) disagree, (4) strongly agree, (5) strongly disagree, (6) strongly agree, and (7) neither. This person's score would be

$$- 2 + 0 - 1 - 2 - 2 - 2 + 0 = -9$$

This listing indicates that the second respondent would be ranked "lower" than the first—that is, as having a less-favorable attitude regarding travel and vacations. However, as indicated earlier, a given total score may have different meanings.

Some final comments are in order. When using this format, Likert (1967) stated that a key criterion for statement preparation and selection should be that all statements be expressions of desired behavior and not statements of fact. In practice this has not always been done. The problem seems to be that two persons with decidedly different attitudes may agree on fact. Thus, their reaction to a statement of fact is no indication of fact. Pragmatically, a researcher may use this approach for fact so long as it is recognized that direction is the only meaningful measure obtained.

The second concern is that the traditional presentation of a Likert scale is one-stage, with both intensity and direction combined; this may lead to an underreporting of extreme positions. This is a type of form-related error known as a *central tendency error*. As stated earlier, a central tendency error represents reluctance on the part of respondents to either give extreme scores or use the extreme position on an individual scale item. To compensate for this situation, a two-stage format, whereby direction and intensity are separate evaluations, can be used. Respondents are first asked to indicate agree, disagree, or neither. Then they are asked how strongly they feel about their response. The limited research on this phenomenon showed that in three separate studies, the two-stage format generated a greater proportion of extreme responses (on both ends) in all cases but four single scales and did a better job in predicting preferences (Albaum, 1997).

One impact of using a two-stage format is that the length of the measuring instrument will be increased, perhaps leading to greater time and money costs in implementing research projects. The mode of data collection—mail, Internet, telephone, personal—may have an effect on the advisability of using a two-stage format. Two-stage formats are used quite often in studies where telephone interviewing is used for data collection. Perhaps the main justification for using this format is that for researchers interested primarily in respondents holding the most intense (i.e., extreme position) views, the two-stage seems to provide higher data quality. Typically, mean values of a group are not affected that much.

Earlier in this chapter we discussed central tendency errors related to the semantic differential. It is fair to speculate that central tendency errors probably exist for all types of rating scales, and that an appropriate two-stage format would minimize the error. Figure 10.9

gives an example of the one-stage and two-stage formats for satisfaction questions. But, as for the Likert scale and the semantic differential, use should probably be limited to those situations where one wants to know about people with extreme views or those situations where respondents can more easily answer the questions.

The Q-Sort Technique

The Q-sort technique has aspects in common with the summated scale. Very simply, the task required of a respondent is to sort a number of statements (usually on individual cards) into a predetermined number of categories (usually 11) with a specified number having to be placed in each category.

In illustrating the Q-sort technique, assume that four respondents evaluate the test items dealing with travel and vacations. For purposes of illustration, only three piles will be used. The respondents are asked to sort items into:

MOST AGREED WITH (TWO ITEMS) +1	NEUTRAL ABOUT (THREE ITEMS) 0	LEAST AGREED WITH (TWO ITEMS) −1

The numbers represent the number of items that the respondents must place into piles 1, 2, and 3, respectively. That is, they may first select the two items that they most agree with; these go in pile 1. Next, they select the two statements that they least agree with; these go in pile 3. The remaining three items are placed in pile 2. The numbers below the line represent scale values. Suppose that the responses of the four respondents, A, B, C, and D, result in the following scale values:

| Item | *Respondent* | | | |
	A	*B*	*C*	*D*
1	+1	+1	−1	−1
2	0	0	0	0
3	+1	0	0	−1
4	−1	−1	+1	+1
5	0	0	0	0
6	−1	−1	+1	+1
7	0	+1	−1	−1

As can be noted, the respondent pairs A & B and C & D seem "most alike" of the six distinct pairs that could be considered. We could, of course, actually correlate each respondent's scores with every other respondent and, similar to semantic differential applications, conduct factor or cluster analyses (see Chapter 19) to group the respondents or items. Typically, these additional steps *are* undertaken in Q-sort studies.

ONE-STAGE: Now I'll ask you to give me a number between one and seven that describes how you feel about your health. . . . "One" stands for completely dissatisfied, and "seven" stands for completely satisfied. If you are right in the middle, answer "four." So, the low numbers indicate that you are dissatisfied; the high numbers that you are satisfied.

First, what number comes closest to how satisfied or dissatisfied you are with your health and physical condition in general?

_____ Number

| 8. Never thought; No feelings |

TWO-STAGE: Now, thinking about your health and physical condition in general, would you say you are satisfied, dissatisfied, or somewhere in the middle?

| 7. Satisfied | | 1. Dissatisfied |

How satisfied are you with your health and physical condition—completely satisfied, mostly, or somewhat?

How dissatisfied are your with your health and physical condition—completely dissatisfied, mostly, or somewhat?

7. Completely		1. Completely
6. Mostly		2. Mostly
5. Somewhat		3. Somewhat

| 4. In the middle. |

If you had to choose, would you say that you are closer to being satisfied or dissatisfied with your health and physical condition, or are you right in the middle?

| 5. Satisfied |
| 3. Dissatisfied |
| 4. In the middle |

Figure 10.9   Examples of One- and Two-Stage Satisfaction Questions

SOURCE: From Miller, P. V., "Alternate Question Forms for Attitude Scale Questions in Telephone Interviews, *Public Opinion Quarterly, 48,* copyright © 1984. Reprinted with permission of The University of Chicago Press.

The Differential Scale

When using a differential scale, it is assumed that a respondent will agree with only a subset, say one or two, of the items statements about an object, a concept, a person, and so forth. The items agreed with correspond to the respondent's position on the dimension being measured, while the items disagreed with are on either side of those selected. This means that the respondent localizes his or her position.

Each of the items or statements used to construct a differential scale has attached to it a score (that is, a position on the scale) determined by outside judges. Judgments of scale position can be made by one of the following methods: paired-comparisons, equal-appearing intervals, or successive intervals. The most commonly used method is equal-appearing intervals.

To develop this type of scale, the researcher starts with a large number of statements related to the attitude under study. These are given to a number of judges, who are asked to independently sort each statement into one of a specified number of piles (often 11), ranging from most strongly positive or favorable to most strongly negative (i.e., least favorable). The scale value for each statement is assigned by the judges and is usually computed as the median pile, although in some cases the mean is used. A final list of statements consists of statements that have a relatively small dispersion across judges and that cover the range of attitude values. A respondent's attitude score (i.e., scale value) is the mean (or median) of the scale values of the statements with which he or she agrees. By using this procedure, respondents can be rank-ordered according to positiveness of attitude.

Developing differential scales can be time-consuming. In addition, respondents with different attitudes on specific dimensions may end up being classified as similar on an aggregate basis. This is so because of the averaging process used. To illustrate, assume that seven statements about advertising were scaled as follows:

Statement	Scale Value
1	2.8
2	7.9
3	4.3
4	1.4
5	9.2
6	6.1
7	5.0

We assume that the lower the value the more negative a respondent is. Also, we have two respondents who are asked to indicate the two statements they most agree with. If Respondent A agrees with statements 2 and 4, the score assigned that person is $7.9 + 1.4 / 2 = 4.65$. Suppose Respondent B agrees with statements 3 and 7. This person's score would be the same—$4.3 + 5.0 / 2 = 4.65$. A and B would both be classified as near-neutral (on, say, an 11-point scale). But Respondent A has a greater variance, as he or she is quite negative on one aspect but positive on another. B, on the other hand, is relatively neutral on both. This example illustrates that a researcher must be careful when interpreting the score of differential scales. Although aggregates may be of interest, the researcher—and the manager as well—should not ignore the individual items themselves.

SCALING BOTH STIMULI AND RESPONDENTS

When both stimuli and respondents can be scaled, this is called the response approach to scaling. One approach to this involves cumulative scales. Cumulative scales are constructed of a set of items with which the respondent indicates agreement or disagreement. If a cumulative scale exists, the items included are unidimensional. This means that they are related to each other such that (in the ideal case) a respondent who responds favorably to Item 2 also responds favorably to Item 1; one who responds favorably to Item 4 also responds favorably to Items 1, 2, and 3, and so on. This scale is based on the cumulative relation between items and the total scores of individuals. An individual's score is calculated by counting the number of items answered favorably. The basic idea is that if individuals can be ranked along a uni-dimensional continuum, then if A is more favorably inclined than B, he or she should endorse all the items that B does plus at least one other item. There is a pattern of item responses that is related to total score. If the scale is truly cumulative, when we know a person's total score we can predict his or her pattern.

In addition, if we know responses to "harder" items, we can predict the response to the easier items. For instance, suppose we gave a respondent three mathematical problems to solve, each of differing difficulty. If he correctly answered the most difficult one, he is likely to answer the other two correctly. On the other hand, a respondent who incorrectly solves the most difficult problem but correctly solves the next most difficult one will most likely answer the least difficult one correctly. In a similar manner, people can be asked attitudinal-oriented questions, and if the patterns of response arrange themselves similarly to the mathematical problem situation, then the questions are unidimensional. Consequently, people can be ranked on the basis of their scale responses. The resulting scale is ordinal.

One of the best-known approaches to cumulative scaling is *scalogram analysis,* developed by Louis Guttman (1985; Manfield, 1971). The technique is designed to determine whether the items used to measure an attitude form a unidimensional scale. That is, if we know a person's rank order on a set of questions, can we predict his or her response to each question in some area of content? Both items and people can be scaled. A so-called universe of content is unidimensional, using the Guttman approach, if it yields a perfect or almost perfect cumulative scale. Unfortunately, scalogram analysis is useful *ex post* and does not help in selecting items that are likely to form a cumulative scale.

To illustrate this approach, assume our interest is in obtaining a measurement of an advertisement's ability to stimulate a consumer to some kind of action. We select four items representing actions that might occur, and we transform these actions into questions that call for a yes/no answer:

- Would you go out of your way to look at this product in a store? (2)
- Would you stop to look at this ad in a magazine? (4)
- Would you buy this product after reading this ad? (1)
- Would you want to show the ad to a friend or a neighbor? (3)

We present this set of questions to a group of respondents, whose task is to indicate "Yes" or "No" to each one. Their responses indicate the relative difficulty of answering "Yes." Assume the ranking of difficulty from most to least is shown by the numbers in parentheses. To determine whether the questions form a cumulative scale, we look at whether a pattern exists such that a respondent who answers "Yes" to a difficult question also answers "Yes" to the less-difficult ones. If a scale exists, then a respondent can be classified into one of five types of respondents depending on his or her response pattern. Table 10.8 shows the response patterns for an ideal cumulative scale. In practice this perfect pattern will not exist.

Table 10.8   Ideal Pattern From Scaleogram Analysis

Type of Respondent	"Yes" Answers				"No" Answers				Scale Score
	3	*1*	*4*	*2*	*3*	*1*	*4*	*2*	
1	X	X	X	X					(4)
2		X	X	X	X				(3)
3			X	X	X	X			(2)
4				X	X	X	X		(1)
5					X	X	X	X	(0)

Experience has shown that a cumulative scale will exist if no more than 10 percent of the answers vary from this geometric pattern. We have discussed only the content component of the Guttman scale. There are also components concerned with intensity and location of origin, which are discussed in detail in Guttman (1985), Manfield (1971) and Torgerson (1958).

Our discussion so far has been concerned with unidimensional scales in which stimuli and respondents can be placed along a linear continuum. In multidimensional scaling models, discussed in Chapter 19, the existence of an underlying multidimensional space is assumed. The stimuli in such models are represented by points in a space of several dimensions. Both stimuli and respondents can be scaled. The dimensions of this space represent attributes that are perceived to characterize the stimuli or respondents.

MULTI-ITEM SCALES

Each of the types of scales discussed in this chapter can be used either alone or part of a multi-item scale used to measure some construct. A multi-item scale consists of a number of closely related individual rating scales whose responses are combined into a single index, composite score, or value (Peterson, 2000). Often the scores are summed to arrive at a total score. Multi-item scales are used when measuring complex psychological constructs that are not easily defined by just one rating scale or captured by just one question.

Figure 10.10 (Spector, 1992) outlines the major steps in constructing a multi-item scale. The first, and perhaps most critical, step is to clearly and precisely define the construct of interest. A scale cannot be developed until it is clear just what the scale is intended to measure. This is followed by design and evaluation of the scale. A pool of items is developed and then subject to analysis to arrive at the initial scale. Along the way, a pilot study is conducted to further refine the scale and move toward the final version. Validation studies are conducted to arrive at the final scale. Of concern is construct validation, in which an assessment is made that the scale measures what it is supposed to measure. At the same time that validity data are collected, normative data can also be collected. Norms describe the distributional characteristics of a given population on the scale. Individual scores on the scale then can be interpreted in relation to the distribution of scores in the population (Spector, 1992, p. 9).

A good multi-item scale is both reliable and valid. Reliability is assessed by the scale's stability (test-retest reliability) and internal consistency reliability (coefficient alpha). These measures have been discussed in Chapter 9. According to Spector (1992), there are several other characteristics of a good multi-item scale:

- The items should be clear, well-written, and contain a single idea.
- The scale must be appropriate to the population of people who use it, such as having an appropriate reading level.
- The items should be kept short and the language simple.
- Consider possible biasing factors and sensitive items.

Table 10.9 gives an example of a multi-item scale developed to measure consumer ethnocentrism within a nation, the CETSCALE (Shimp & Sharma, 1987). This scale is formatted in the Likert scale format. A compilation of multi-item scales frequently used in consumer behavior and marketing research is provided by Bearden and Netemeyer (1999).

Multi-item scales come in all sizes and shapes with varied numbers of items. Often, researchers want to use shorter versions of the scale. For example, the CETSCALE shown in Table 10.9 has a 10-item shorter form as well as the 17-item full version. Richins (in press) has studied short versions of the Material Values Scale, some of which have acceptable psychometric properties when used to measure materialism at a general level. Researchers must be careful when attempting to shorten scales, as psychometric properties and any effects on construct validity of shorter versions must first be assessed.

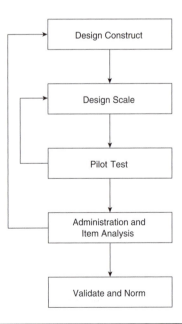

Figure 10.10   Steps in Developing a Multi-Item Scale

Table 10.9   Example of Multi-Item Scale: Consumer Ethnocentrism (CETSCALE)

1. American people should always buy American-made products instead of imports.
2. Only those products that are unavailable in the United States should be imported.
3. Buy American-made products. Keep America working.
4. American products first, last and foremost.
5. Purchasing foreign-made products is un-American.
6. It is not right to purchase foreign products.
7. A real American should always buy American-made products.
8. We should purchase products in America instead of letting other countries get rich off us.
9. It is always best to purchase American products.
10. There should be very little trading or purchasing of goods from other countries unless out of necessity.
11. Americans should not buy foreign products, because this hurts American business and causes unemployment.
12. Curbs should be put on all imports.
13. It may cost me in the long run, but I prefer to support American products.
14. Foreigners should not be allowed to put their products on our markets.
15. Foreign products should be taxed heavily to reduce their entry into the United States.
16. We should buy from foreign countries only those products that we cannot obtain within our own country.
17. American consumers who purchase products made in other countries are responsible for putting their fellow Americans out of work.

NOTE: Items composing the 10-item reduced version are items 2, 4 through 8, 11, 13, 16, and 17.

LIMITATIONS OF SCALING PROCEDURES

Although psychological measurement offers an interesting and potentially rewarding area of study by the marketing researcher, there are some limitations of current scaling techniques in their applicability to marketing problems.

First, it is apparent that more progress has been made in the construction of scales for measuring attitudes along a single dimension than in dealing with the more complex cases of multidimensional attitudes. However, a person's decision to purchase a particular brand usually reflects a response to a variety of stimuli, such as the brand's functional features, package design, advertising messages, corporate image, and so on. Much work still remains to be done on the development of scales to measure multidimensional stimuli.

Second, relatively little development has been done of anything like a general theory of individual buyer behavior that is testable in terms of empirical findings from psychological and sociological studies. In addition to consumer perception and preference studies, we still need to know much more about the influence of other persons (peers, superiors, subordinates) on the buyer decision process, consumer habit formation, and so on. The development of anything close to a general, operationally-based theory will require—at the least—validation of scaling techniques by behavioral-type measures under experimentally controlled conditions.

Finally, predictions from attitude scales, preference ratings, and the like still need to be transformed into measures (sales, market share) of more direct interest to the marketer. We still do not know, in many cases, how to effectively translate verbalized product ratings, attitudes about corporations, and so on into the behavioral and financial measures required to evaluate the effectiveness of alternative marketing actions.

SUMMARY

In this chapter, the major objective has been to discuss some of the fundamental concepts of measurement and psychological scaling and their relationship to the gathering and analysis of behavioral data. The chapter first covered variability (ordinal) and quantitative-judgment (ratio/interval) methods of data collection.

Scaling procedures were next commented upon within the framework of stimulus-centered and subject-centered methods. As examples of stimulus-centered techniques, Thurstone's Case V model and Osgood's semantic differential were described in a marketing research context. Subject-centered scaling techniques—the Likert summated scale, Stephenson's Q-sort technique, and Thurstone's differential scale—were also described and illustrated by numerical examples. Next we covered techniques for scaling both stimuli and respondents. Guttman's scalogram analysis and an introduction to the multidimensional nature of attitudes were presented. The chapter concluded with a discussion of multi-item scales and some of the difficult problems associated with testing the validity and reliability of psychological scales.

ASSIGNMENT MATERIAL

1. Take an article from a current marketing journal and do the following:
   a. Define key terms from an operational standpoint.
   b. Examine the author's justification for the type of measurement scale(s) used.
   c. Criticize the article from the standpoint of its operational usefulness to marketing management.

2. Design and administer a short questionnaire on the topic of student attitudes toward the teaching competence of your university's faculty members. Include questions dealing with paired comparisons, agree-disagree responses, and rating-type scales.
   a. Apply Thurstone's Case V procedure to the paired-comparisons data. Apply also the method of Exhibit 10.4. What can you conclude about these approaches?
   b. Summarize the rating-scale patterns in terms of a semantic differential profile.
   c. Evaluate the usefulness of these procedures in the context of your problem.

3. The Grandma's Own Soup Company was considering the possibility of changing the consistency of its famous tomato soup. Five test soups were prepared, ranging from "very light" to "very heavy consistency". A consumer clinic was held in which 15 housewives ranked each soup (no ties allowed) from 1 (liked best) to 5 (liked least).

The data for this test are as follows:

Soup	1	2	3	4	5	6	7	8	9	10	11	12	13	14	15
A	2	4	3	2	2	1	2	2	2	2	3	1	2	3	2
B	1	2	1	1	1	2	1	3	1	1	1	2	1	2	4
C	4	1	4	5	4	5	3	1	5	3	4	4	5	4	5
D	3	3	2	3	3	3	5	4	3	4	2	3	3	1	3
E	5	5	5	4	5	4	4	5	4	5	5	5	4	5	1

a. On the basis of a composite (sum of the ranks), what is the rank order of the soups—from best- to least-liked?
b. What, if anything, can be said about how much better Soup B is than Soup E?
c. By going across rows of the above table one can count the number of times one soup of each possible pair is ranked higher than the other soup in the pair. Prepare a table of paired comparisons as derived from the ranked data, express the table entries in terms of proportions, and construct an interval scale, using Thurstone's Case V scaling.
d. What major assumption are we making about the sample of subjects when we construct the interval scale above? Criticize this type of application of the Thurstone comparative judgment technique.
e. Apply the method described in Exhibit 10.4 to the rankings above. What can you conclude about this approach and that of Thurstone Case V?

4. Using the method of choices, construct an interval scale using Thurstone Case V scaling of the data shown in question 3 above. Evaluate the scale you have just derived from the standpoint of efficient use of data.

5. Assume that two groups—a group of housewives and a group of small businessmen—are asked to rate the Mighty Electric Company on the basis of three bipolar adjective pairs:
   - Powerful/weak
   - Reliable/nonreliable
   - Modern/old-fashioned

The frequencies of each group of 100 respondents are shown below (numbers above the horizontal lines refer to housewives' responses; numbers below refer to businessmen's responses):

Powerful	20 —: 40	42 —: 30	10 —: 15	5 —: 5	5 —: 5	12 —: 5	7 —: 0	Weak
Reliable	52 —: 20	12 —: 25	8 —: 12	10 —: 22	8 —: 35	5 —: 6	5 —: 0	Nonreliable
Modern	5 —: 6	14 —: 20	21 —: 25	25 —: 20	20 —: 12	10 —: 9	5 —: 8	Old-Fashioned

a. Using a 7-point scale (where, for example, 7 = extremely powerful and 1 = extremely weak), find a summary rating index for each group of raters for each set of adjective pairs.

b. What assumptions are made by using the integer weights, 7, 6, . . . , 1?

c. In which adjective pairs are the rating indexes between the groups most similar? Most dissimilar?

d. How would your answer to part (a) change if the weights +3, +2, +1, 0, –1, –2, and –3 were used instead of the weights, 7, 6, ... , 1? Would rank order between pairs of summary indexes (for each adjective pair) be affected, and if so, how?

6. Select the scaling technique you would recommend be used to obtain measurements for the situations described below. Explain why you chose each.

a. Measurement of price elasticity of demand for a new product.

b. Determination of preference of three levels of sweetness for a new product.

c. Measurement of change of attitude toward a product as the package is changed.

d. Determination of which respondents have tried a particular brand of product.

e. Measurement of which of three advertisements has the greatest readership.

f. Comparison of three retail stores on 15 attributes.

g. Measurement of the proportion of "triers" who make repeat purchases of a new product.

7. Construct a multi-item scale to measure public satisfaction with local government services. Include at least five items in your scale. Also, develop a single-item measure of public satisfaction with local government services. Administer each of these scales to a group of 25 residents in your local area, including demographic variables of gender, marital status, and age. What can you conclude about any differences that emerge in your findings?

REFERENCES

Albaum, G. (1997, April). The Likert scale revisited: An alternate version. *Journal of the Market Research Society, 39* (2), 331–348.

Albaum, G., Best, R., & Hawkins, D. (1981). Continuous vs. discrete semantic differential scales. *Psychological Reports, 49,* 83–86.

Bearden, W. O., & Netemeyer, R. G. (1999). *Handbook of marketing scales* (2nd ed.). Thousand Oaks, CA: Sage.

Bishop, G. F. (1987). Experiments with the middle response alternative in survey questions. *Public Opinion Quarterly, 51,* 220–232.

Churchill, G. A., Jr., & Peter, J. P. (1984, November). Research design effects on the reliability of rating scales: A meta analysis. *Journal of Marketing Research, 21,* 360–375.

Coombs, C. H. (1964). *A theory of data.* New York: Wiley.

Crespi, I. (1961, July). Use of a scaling technique in surveys. *Journal of Marketing, 25,* 69–72.

Edwards, A. L. (1957). *Techniques of attitude scale construction.* New York: Appleton-Century-Crofts.

Golden, L., Brockett, P., Albaum, G., & Zatarain, J. (1992). The golden numerical comparative scale format for economical multi-object/multi-attribute comparison questionnaires. *Journal of Official Statistics, 8* (1), 77–86.

Gottlieb, M. J. (n.d.). *A modern marketing approach in measuring consumer preference*. New York: Audits and Surveys, Inc.

Guilford, J. P., & Fruchter, B. (1973). *Fundamental statistics in psychology and education* (5th ed.). New York: McGraw-Hill.

Guttman, L. (1985). Measuring the true-state of opinion. In R. Ferber & H. Wales (Eds.), *Motivation and market behavior*. Homewood, IL: Richard D. Irwin, 393–415.

Haley, R., & Case, P. (1979, Fall). Testing thirteen attitude scales for agreement and brand determination. *Journal of Marketing, 43,* 20–32.

Hawkins, D. I., Albaum, G., & Best, R. (1974, August). Stapel scale or semantic differential in marketing research? *Journal of Marketing Research, 11,* 318–322.

Hays, W. L. (1967). *Quantification in psychology*. Belmont, CA: Brooks/Cole.

Herche, J., & Engelland, B. (1996). Reversed-polarity items and scale unidimensionality. *Journal of the Academy of Marketing Science, 24* (4), 366–374.

Hubbard, R., Little, E. L., & Allen, S. J. (1989). Are responses measured with graphic rating scales subject to perceptual distortion? *Psychological Reports, 69,* 1203–1207.

Karsten, Y. G., & John, D. R. (1991). Measuring children's preferences: The use of behaviorally anchored rating scales. Paper presented at the 1991 Attitude Research Conference.

Kendall, M. G. (1962). *Rank correlation methods*. New York: Hafner.

Kerlinger, F. (1973). *Foundation of behavioral research* (2nd ed.). New York: Holt, Rinehart & Winston.

Likert, R. (1967). The method of constructing an attitude scale. In M. Fishbein (Ed.), *Readings in attitude theory and measurement*. New York: Wiley, pp. 90–95.

Lodge, M. (1981). *Magnitude scaling: Quantitative measurement of opinions*. Beverly Hills, CA: Sage.

Manfield, M. N. (1971). The Guttman scale. In G. Albaum & M. Venkatesan (Eds.), *Scientific marketing research*. New York: The Free Press.

McCarty, J. A., & Shrum, L. J. (2000). The measurement of personal values in survey research: A test of alternative rating procedures. *Public Opinion Quarterly, 64,* 271–298.

Menzes, D., & Elbert, N. F. (1979, February). Alternative semantic differential scaling formats for measuring store image: An evaluation. *Journal of Marketing Research, 16,* 80–87.

Miller, P. V. (1984). Alternative question forms for attitude scale questions in telephone interviews. *Public Opinion Quarterly, 48,* 766–778.

Narayana, C. (1977, February). Graphic positioning scale: An economical instrument for surveys. *Journal of Marketing Research, 14,* 118–122.

Nowlis, S. M., Kahn, B. E., & Dhar, R. (2002). Coping with ambivalence: The effect of removing a neutral option on consumer attitude and preference judgments. *Journal of Consumer Research, 29,* 319–334.

Osgood, C. E., Suci, G. J., & Tannenbaum, P. H. (1957). *The measurement of meaning*. Urbana: University of Illinois Press.

Peter, J. P., & Churchill, G. A., Jr. (1986, February). Relationships among research design choices and psychometric properties of rating scales: A meta-analysis. *Journal of Marketing Research, 23,* 1–10.

Peterson, R. A. (2000). *Creating effective questionnaires*. Thousand Oaks, CA: Sage.

Phillips, J. P. N. (1967). A procedure for determining Slater's *i* and all nearest adjoining orders. *British Journal of Mathematical and Statistical Psychology, 20,* 217–223.

Richins, M. (in press). The material values scale: Measurement properties and development of a short form. *Journal of Consumer Research*.

Richins, M., & Dawson, S. (1992, December). A consumer values orientation for materialism and its measurement: Scale development and validation. *Journal of Consumer Research, 19,* 303–316.

Semon, T. T. (2001, October 8). Symmetry shouldn't be goal for scales. *Marketing News, 35,* 9.

Shimp, T. A., & Sharma, S. (1987, August). Consumer ethnocentrism: Construction and validation of the CETSCALE. *Journal of Marketing Research, 24,* 280–289.

Slater, P. (1961). Inconsistencies in a schedule of paired comparisons. *Biometrica, 48,* 303–312.

Spector, P. E. (1992). *Summated rating scale construction: An introduction*. Newbury Park, CA: Sage.

Sudman, S., & Bradburn, N. (1983). *Asking questions*. San Francisco: Jossey-Bass.

Thurstone, L. L (1959). *The measurement of values*. Chicago: University of Chicago Press.

Torgerson, W. S. (1958). *Theory and methods of scaling*. New York: Wiley.

Wilcox, C., Sigelman, L., and Cook, E. (1989). Some like it hot: Individual differences in responses to group feeling thermometers. *Public Opinion Quarterly, 53*, 246–257.

Wong, N., Rindfleisch, A., & Burroughs, J. E. (2003, June). Do reverse-worded items confound measures in cross-cultural research? The case of the material values scale. *Journal of Consumer Research, 30*, 72–91.

Yu, J., Albaum, G., & Swenson, M. (2003). Is a central tendency error inherent in the use of semantic differential scales in different cultures. *International Journal of Market Research, 45* (2), 213–228.

Chapter 11

DESIGNING QUESTIONNAIRES

Throughout this book, we have discussed methodological issues in the context of error and ways to manage such error. At this point, we turn to the questions asked of respondents and consider the sources of error due to the nature of the questions themselves, such as question selection, structure, wording, order of presentation, and so on.

We begin by considering the dimensions of the questionnaire design process, focusing on explaining the steps involved in designing a quality data collection instrument. Very simply, a quality instrument does two things: It accurately portrays to the respondent what is desired by the researcher, and it accurately reports to the researcher information about the respondent. Many years ago, a practitioner stated that a questionnaire should be viewed as "spoken questions that are put down on paper. A questionnaire is not a document—it's a conversation." This task, though simple in concept, is sometimes monumental in application. Proper procedures for developing a questionnaire are required, and these are based on several key questions and concerns:

1. What information do we need?

2. What type of data is required?

3. What questionnaire type is used to collect this data?

4. Develop question content, format, and phrasing.

5. Develop response format.

6. Sequence and layout the questionnaire.

7. Pretest the questionnaire.

8. Revise the questionnaire (Repeat 1–7).

Peterson (2000, p. 14) summarizes the steps in questionnaire construction as shown in Figure 11.1.

ASKING QUESTIONS

The major source of error for questionnaires and individual questions is response error. However, nonresponse error also may be relevant if such factors as the complexity, length, or subject matter of the instrument or individual questions are the cause of the respondent's refusal to participate. How the quality of the questionnaire can affect response rate in a survey has not been given due attention (Carroll, 1994). For more information, see Exhibit 11.1. Response error occurs if the reported value differs from the actual value of the variable concerned. Strictly speaking, response error can also be due to the interviewer or investigator. This aspect of response error was discussed in Chapter 5.

As discussed previously, a respondent is a person who either provides information actively (through communication) or passively (by his or her behavior being observed). Response error, therefore, includes errors arising through communication, observation, or both. To discover the source of the response error, a researcher must consider the stages involved in providing information. The information must first be formulated; that is, it must be assimilated and made accessible for transmission. This may be a case of simply remembering and reporting, or may involve something as detailed as researching company records to find the requested information. Once this has been accomplished, it must be transmitted. Errors can arise in either stage or in both. The term *inaccuracy* denotes errors arising in the formulation stage; the term *ambiguity* regards errors arising in the transmission stage.

Since the purpose of making this distinction in types of response errors is to help understand and control this important source of error, this chapter examines each type of error in some detail.

---

1. Review information requirements of problem, opportunity, decision to be made, and so on.

2. Develop and prioritize a list of potential research questions to provide required information.

3. Evaluate each potential research question:
   - Can potential study participants understand the question?
   - Can potential study participants answer the question?
   - Will potential study participants answer the question?

4. Determine types of question to be asked?
   - Open-end questions
   - Closed-end questions

5. Decide on specific wording of each question to be asked.

6. Determine questionnaire structure.

7. Evaluate questionnaire.

Figure 11.1 Steps in Constructing a Questionnaire

SOURCE: From Peterson, R., *Constructing Effective Questionnaires*, copyright © 2000. Reprinted by permission of Sage Publications, Inc.

EXHIBIT 11.1   How to Affect Survey Response Rate Through Questionnaire Design

There are a few relatively simple things that can be done to a questionnaire to help stimulate response rates beyond the normal industry average.

First, at times, use nontraditional ways to structure questions on the questionnaire. Keep the questions simple in appearance, but sophisticated. For example, if a researcher is interested in the importance a respondent attaches to six factors that may have influenced a decision, instead of using a traditional rating scale for each factor, a constant sum scale can be used and the respondent asked to allocate, say, 100 points among the six factors to reflect importance.

Second, mix up response formats on the items you are asking respondents to complete. A questionnaire that repeats the same response format over and over again can appear boring to a respondent. As we indicated in an earlier chapter, interest in a study can have a huge positive impact on response rates.

Third, never assume that respondents know what you want them to do with any question. Specific directions should be given for each group or section of items included in the questionnaire.

Fourth, pay particular attention to visual aspects of the questionnaire. Such issues as layout, typeface, shadings, using boxes where appropriate, and color of paper can affect whether a particular respondent participates. Visual dimensions may vary by mode of data collection. Visual effects are a form of nonverbal communication. Not only may response rates be affected, but the quality of collected data may also be affected (Sanchez, 1992).

Fifth, all items should be numbered. This can be done within each section, or, if the questionnaire is relatively short, within the entire questionnaire itself. Doing this assists the respondent in self-report questionnaires and helps the interviewer in non–self-report questionnaires.

INACCURACY

Inaccuracy refers to errors made in the formulation of information. There are two types of inaccuracies: predictive and concurrent inaccuracies. Predictive inaccuracy, as a source of response error, is a special case caused by inaccurate intentions. Concurrent inaccuracy occurs when the respondent intentionally does not provide accurate information. Concurrent inaccuracies are a major concern for many kinds of information obtained from respondents (information on past behavior, socioeconomic characteristics, level of knowledge, and opinion-attitude).

To explain predictive inaccuracy, suppose that a male respondent is asked, "Do you intend to buy a new automobile within the next six months?" His answers are limited to "Yes," "No," or "Uncertain." A brief examination of possible answers and subsequent actions indicates that there are two different kinds of inaccuracies. If the respondent answers "Yes," but really has no intention of buying a car within this period or, conversely, answers "No," but does intend to buy a car, then we may say that there is concurrent inaccuracy in his statement. Suppose, however, that his present intention is to buy a new car; he so indicates in his answer, and then he does not, in fact, buy one within six months. Or, alternatively, he does not now intend to buy, he answers "No" to the question, and then buys a car within the six-month period. There is no concurrent inaccuracy in either case; the response has reflected the actual intention of the person. The intention, however, was not followed. This situation is a predictive inaccuracy.

A similar type of predictive inaccuracy can occur when marketing researchers try to predict actual market response to a price by asking consumers, "How much are you willing to pay for Product X?" Differences between predicted and actual purchases may occur because the true range of prices acceptable to the consumer may change between the time of data collection and the point of purchase for a number of reasons, such as budget constraints or windfalls, the price of substitutes at point of purchase, search costs, and purchase urgency.

Now, let's focus on concurrent inaccuracies and their sources. Both our everyday experiences and empirical evidence suggest that there are two basic sources from which inaccurate information may result:

- The inability of the respondent to provide the desired information
- The unwillingness of the respondent to provide the desired information

In those instances where observation is used, this statement may also be applied to the observer; the observer may be unable or unwilling to provide the desired information.

Inability to Respond

Even such a simple and straightforward question as "What is the model year of your family car?" may result in an information-formulation problem, particularly if the car is several years old. If the additional question were asked, "What brand or brands of tires do you now have on your car?" most respondents would have even more difficulty in providing an accurate answer without looking at the tires. Finally, if respondents were asked, "What reasons did you have for buying Brand A tires instead of some other brand?" most respondents would have even more difficulty in providing an accurate answer.

In addition to the two basic sources of inaccuracies, Semon (2000a, 2000b) reports that there are three major types of inaccuracies:

- Memory error: A respondent gives the wrong factual information because he or she simply does not remember an event asked about. It may be due to underestimating or overestimating the time that had elapsed since an event occurred. Better questionnaire and survey design can help reduce this error, but many proven techniques are not used because they add to the length of the survey. For instance, in a personal or telephone interview survey a follow-up call can be made to confirm the answers given.

- Ignorance error: This is due to research design in terms of question content and sampling. A question (or even an entire questionnaire) may be unrealistic, deficient, or directed to the wrong persons. If a potential respondent perceives the questionnaire, or individual questions, to be irrelevant, it probably is.

- Misunderstanding: This can be a matter of careless question design. Poorly defined terms and words with different meanings can lead to inaccurate, or even deliberately falsified responses. Proper question design would avoid words with multiple meanings and definitions, or would clearly define the context in which the word is being used in the questionnaire.

Respondents must be able to determine what is expected of them. Also, problems can arise when respondents are unfamiliar with the expected patterns of interaction involved in any interview situations. This can be especially important in international and multicultural research. Exhibit 11.2 gives additional information.

EXHIBIT 11.2   Response Error and Questionnaire Design

One of the keys to minimizing concurrent errors is for researchers to better translate the clients' information needs into a set of practical questions that respondents can and will answer to the best of their ability. When serving as senior vice-president of marketing at PepsiCo Restaurants International, Dwight Riskey suggested that any marketing research question can be charted in a two-by-two matrix by plotting the urgency and importance of the question (Murphy, 1997). This matrix breaks down into four categories:

- Important/urgent
- Unimportant/urgent
- Important/nonurgent
- Unimportant/nonurgent

Questions falling in the first and last categories are easy to identify. It is the other two categories that can cause most of the problems. Often, the urgent/unimportant questions are best answered by a judgment-call than by extensive research. In contrast, the important/nonurgent questions are the ones that often need to be addressed. In the short run, a company will carry on without answers to these questions. But these answers may be essential to the long-term future direction of the company.

Unwillingness to Respond

When we move to the problem of unwillingness of respondents to provide accurate information, the topic is more complex. Here we are dealing with the motivations of people: why they are not willing to accurately provide the information desired. No fully accepted general theory of motivation has yet emerged from the behavioral sciences to explain this behavior, other than general theoretical concepts that attempt to explain survey response behavior. As discussed in Chapter 5, any or none of these might be applicable in any given situation. There is no conclusive evidence favoring one theory to the exclusion of the others. However, by again applying everyday experiences to this problem, and adding some research findings and the accumulated experiences of practitioners, several reasons are suggested why people may not be willing to make accurate information accessible.

Except in those instances where the respondent provides information by being observed in a natural situation, there are always costs (negative utilities) attached to his or her formulating information. The time required is one such cost that is always present. Others include perceived losses of prestige and some degree of invasion of privacy.

When possible to do so, a respondent will tend to act in a manner that will reduce these costs. Such behavior will sometimes result in inaccurate information being provided.

Time Costs

Perhaps the most common reason for respondent unwillingness to provide accurate information, or any information for that matter, is the result of the time required to make the information available. A person may simply be busy and wish to complete the interview as quickly as possible. In this circumstance it is not unusual for the respondent to decide that abrupt answers are the easiest and quickest way of terminating the interview. Rather than reflecting on or verifying the information provided, the respondent gives hasty, ill-considered answers and resists probing if attempted, leading to inaccurate information. In addition, time pressures may lead respondents to not answer all questions, thus providing incomplete data.

Another aspect of the time dimension is that this potential respondent may not be in a "comfortable" position to provide the information at the time requested (he or she may have just come home, sat down to a meal, have a child doing something, etc.). This arises for data collection in telephone and personal interviews. Rather than asking "May I ask you some questions?" as an introductory comment, it would seem preferable to ask, "Do you have time now to answer questions, or would you rather set a time when I could contact you again?" Experience has shown this latter technique only slightly lowers response rates.

Perceived Losses of Prestige

When information involving the prestige of the respondent is sought, there is always a tendency toward inaccurate formulation in the direction of the higher-prestige responses. Although all experienced researchers recognize this tendency, two problems remain:

1. Recognizing the items of information that the respondent will interpret as having prestige content

2. Measuring the resulting amount of inaccuracy

Information that affects prestige is often sensitive information.

Some information items have prestige content associated with them by virtually all respondents. Among these are such socioeconomic characteristics as age, income, educational level, and occupation. Other informational items, such as place of birth or residence, are more difficult to identify as having prestige content. People who live in rural areas or in suburbs are prone to give the nearest city in answer to questions concerning where they live. In part, this no doubt reflects a belief that the investigator would not otherwise recognize the location given; it may also reflect a higher level of prestige associated with being born or living in a large and well-known city.

An example of a still more subtle prestige association that resulted in a sizable error in information obtained is the experience of a marketing research firm that conducted a study on nationally known brands of beer. One of the questions asked was, "Do you prefer light or regular beer?" The response was overwhelmingly in favor of light beer. Since sales data indicated a strong preference for regular beer, it was evident that the information was inaccurate. Subsequent investigation revealed that the respondents viewed people who drank light beer as being more discriminating in taste. They had, therefore, given answers that, in their view, were associated with a higher level of prestige.

Measuring the amount of inaccuracy is a difficult task. In the ideal case, it requires that information be available on the item from sources external to the sample, and further, that these external data be more accurate than those obtained from the respondents. Clearly, in most cases such data are not available; if there were, the information would not have been collected from the respondents.

One solution to this problem is to ask for the information in two different ways. When one is obtaining information on respondents' ages, for example, it is a common practice to ask early in the interview, "What is your present age?" and later "In what year were you born?" or "In what year did you enter high school?" or "In what year did you graduate from high school?" In one study, when respondents were asked, "Are you afraid to fly?" very few people indicated any fear of flying. In a follow-up study, when they were asked, "Do you think your neighbor is afraid to fly?" (a technique known as the *third-person technique*), most of the neighbors turned out to have severe anxieties about flying.

A method used to obtain information about sensitive matters is the randomized-response technique (Campbell & Joiner, 1973; Fox & Tracy, 1986; Reinmuth & Geurts, 1975). When using this technique the investigator presents two questions, either of which can be answered by a "Yes" or a "No," one innocuous ("Were you born in May?") and the other sensitive ("Did you shoplift any items from the Downtown Mall during the month of December?"). The respondent is asked to flip a coin or use a randomizing device (provided with the survey) to select the question to answer. The respondent is instructed not to in any way communicate to the interviewer which question was answered. Only the answer "Yes" or "No" is given.

The proportion of respondents who answered "Yes" to the sensitive question can be estimated from the formula

$$P(\text{yes}|\text{sensitive question}) = \frac{P(\text{yes}) - P(\text{innocent question})\ P(\text{yes}|\text{innocent question})}{P(\text{sensitive question})}$$

In the example, if the proportion of respondents who answered "Yes" is .06, the proportion born in May (determined from the Census of Population) is .08, and the probability of answering each question is .5, the estimated proportion who answered "Yes" to the shoplifting question would be

$$P(\text{yes}|\text{shoplifting question}) = \frac{.06 - (.5)(.08)}{.5} = .04$$

This is a point estimate of the (hypothetical) proportion of the population from which the sample was drawn who shoplifted at the place during the period specified.

This example of the randomized technique is simplified. There are approaches that can use a single question, but the mathematical and statistical properties tend to be more complex. For most marketing applications, the two-question structure will work nicely. All that is needed is a suitable randomizing device (for which the investigator knows the relevant distributions) and knowledge of the distribution of responses to the innocuous question. Although this technique is perhaps most easily administered in person, there have been approaches suitable for telephone and mail administration, as shown in Exhibit 11.3 (Stem & Steinhorst, 1984). Umesh and Peterson (1991) provide an evaluation of this technique.

Invasion of Privacy

Clearly, some topics on which information is sought are considered to be private matters. When such is the case, both nonresponse and inaccuracy in the responses obtained can be anticipated. Matters about which respondents resent questions include money matters or finance, family, life, personal hygiene, political beliefs, religious beliefs, and even job or occupation. Either indirect questions or the randomized-response technique can sometimes be used to avoid intrusion. If direct questions are used concerning such matters, they should be placed as near the end of the questionnaire as other considerations permit.

It should be recognized, however, that invasion of privacy is an individual matter. Thus, what one person considers to be sensitive information may not be viewed that way by others. In fact, it has been suggested that researchers often view topics as sensitive that a majority of respondents would not view as sensitive. Because the response to the way in which questions are asked and the order in which they are asked will be affected by the "sensitivity" of the requested information, the investigator should attempt to determine sensitivity if it is suspected to be a problem. One way of handling this is adding questions in the pretest stage that ask about the extent of sensitivity to topics and specific questions. A comprehensive treatment of sensitive information and how to ask questions about it is given by Bradburn and Sudman (1979).

EXHIBIT 11.3   Randomized Response

One approach to administrating the randomized response approach to obtain sensitive information by mail and/or telephone involves the use of a spinner (the randomizing device) and questionnaire. A cover (I) fits over a base (II) with instructions on the bottom (III) to form the device. This device may then be used with a questionnaire (IV).

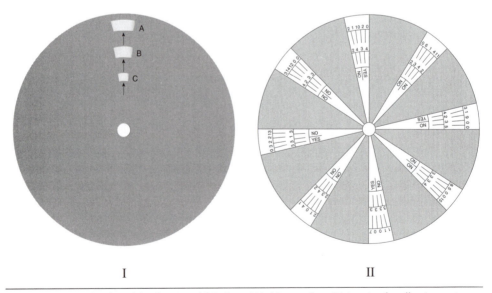

I   II

SOURCE: We are deeply indebted to Donald E. Stem, Washington State University, for allowing us to use illustrations of his spinner randomizing device. Reprinted with permission of Donald E. Stern, Jr.

III
INSTRUCTIONS
1. Place the spinner in front of you on a flat surface such as a table.

2. With one hand holding down the spinner, flip the disk with the other hand hard enough so that it spins rapidly.

3. Each question on the questionnaire will indicate which window to use for that particular question. When the disk stops, look in the window assigned for that question.
   - If the arrow lands on a shaded area, enter your actual answer to the question on the questionnaire.
   - If the arrow lands on a lettered or numbered area, enter the randomly assigned answer. (YES, NO, 1, 2, 3, etc.)
   - If the answer lands on a line, answer according to the numbered, lettered, or shaded area to the left of the line.

4. When you repeat the process for the next question, always start from the last stopping point. (Do not spin from the same starting point each time.)

IV

For Questions 1 through 20 use <u>Window C</u> on the spinner
1. Do you currently maintain a 'prospect locator' or 'bird dog'? That is, someone you will pay a fee to if that person sends you a customer that results in a sale?

   WINDOW C   _____ Yes   _____ No

2. Do you regularly use direct mail as a reminder to past customers that you would like their business again?

   WINDOW C   _____ Yes   _____ No

For Questions 21 through 29 use <u>Window A</u> on the spinner

21. How many times within the past year have you knowingly misrepresented a vehicle's warranty in order to close a sale?

    WINDOW A   _____ Times

22. How many times in the last year have you 'low balled' a customer?

    · WINDOW A   _____ Times

For Questions 30 through 34, use <u>Window B</u> on the spinner. If the arrow lands on 1, mark the answer labeled one (1); If it lands on 2, mark the answer labeled two (2); and so on. If the arrow lands on the <u>shaded area</u>, please answer the question truthfully by checking the <u>best</u> space provided.

30. Do you agree that the average automobile salesperson <u>is trusted</u> by the buying public?

Window	____ Strongly Agree	____ Agree	____ Neither Agree nor Disagree	____ Disagree	____ Strongly Disagree
B	(1)	(2)	(3)	(4)	(5)

(Continued)

Another approach to randomized response by mail is to have the randomizing device built-in the questionnaire itself. The following questionnaire illustrates this approval:

Do you have a telephone in your family unit? _____ Yes _____ No

1. Your telephone number is of the form 7 _ _ - W X Y Z. If the digit in the W position is 0, 1, or 2, check Agree; if it's 3, 4, 5, 6, 7 or 8, respond to the statement; if it's 9, check Disagree.

   Manufacturers should be doing more to encourage the recycling of containers and materials that would otherwise be tossed onto the trash pile, even if this means an increase in the price of their products.

   _____ Agree   _____ Disagree   _____ No response

2. Your telephone number is of the form 7 _ _ - W X Y Z. If the digit in the X-position is 0 or 1, check True; if it's 2, 3, 4, 5, 6, 7 or 8, respond to the statement; if it's 9, check False.

   I deposit recyclable materials such as newspapers, aluminum containers, glass containers, etc. on a regular basis at an appropriate recycling center.

   _____ True   _____ False   _____ No response

3. Your telephone number is of the form 7 _ _ - W X Y Z. If the digit in the Y position is 0 or 1, check True; if it's 2, 3, 4, 5, 6, 7 or 8, respond to the statement; if it's 9, check False.

   I make a conscious effort at conserving fuel by a cutback in my home thermostat setting and/or a reduction in my use of automobile gasoline.

   _____ True   _____ False   _____ No response

4. Your telephone number is of the form 7 _ _ - W X Y Z. If the digit in the Z position is 0 or 1, check Agree; if it's 2, 3, 4, 5, 6, 7 or 8, respond to the statement; if it's 9, check Disagree.

   The current welfare program plays an important as well as beneficial role in our society.

   _____ Agree   _____ Disagree   _____ No response

AMBIGUITY

Ambiguity may be defined as the errors made in interpreting spoken or written words or behavior. Ambiguity, therefore, occurs in the transmission of information, through either communication or observation.

Ambiguity in Communication

Ambiguity is present in all languages. Unambiguous communication in research requires that the question asked and the answers given each mean the same thing to the questioner and the respondent. A two-step process is therefore involved:

1. Question as understood by respondent is same as question as understood by questioner

2. Answer as understood by questioner is same as answer as understood by respondent

The first step in this process is the controlling one. If the question is not clearly understood by the respondent, frequently the answer will not be clearly understood by the questioner. To illustrate this point, in an actual research project on tomato juice, the question

Do you like tomato juice?

Yes   No   Neither like nor dislike

was changed, after pretesting, to

Do you like the taste of tomato juice?

Yes   No   Neither like nor dislike

Even a careful reading of these two questions may not disclose any real difference in their meaning. The analyst who drew up the question assumed that "like" refers to taste. In pretesting, however, it was discovered that some housewives answered "Yes" with other referent in mind. They "like" the amount of Vitamin C their children get when they drink tomato juice, they "liked" the tenderizing effect that tomato juice has when used in cooking of meat dishes, and so on. If the wording of the question had not been changed, there would have been a complete misunderstanding in some cases of the simple, one-word answer "Yes."

A related issue is one where *implicatures* are added to questions by respondents (Barnes, Jr. & Dotson, 1989). A receiver of a message in any communication is expected to take what is said, along with what is inferred, and derive what is implicated. One source of implicatures is the use of elliptical sentence structure. An elliptical sentence is a shortened form of other sentences. When such a sentence is used, something that is sought is left out. Examples are, "How come?," "What?," and "How?" The respondent of a questionnaire, after reading an elliptical sentence, first considers the context of the sentence and then adds the missing parts. When the mental process of transformational rule is the same in both researcher and respondent, communication occurs unambiguously. If the process differs, communication is lost and interpretation of a person's response is faulty and ambiguity exists.

The understanding of questions is an issue that goes beyond ambiguity. All too often a respondent may not understand a question, but may have no opportunity to request clarification. In mail and online surveys, the extreme response is to not respond at all. In telephone or personal interview settings, the more captive individual might participate even though specific questions or topics are not fully understood. The quality of such data, of course, would be highly questionable. However, the mode of interviewing might be used to mitigate this potential problem. Most personal and telephone interviewing uses *standardized interviewing,* in which the interpretation of questions is left up to the respondent. The interviewer is not permitted to answer any query raised. In contrast, in conversational interviewing the interviewer should answer the respondent's query with whatever words it takes to help the respondent understand the question from the survey designer's perspective, without unduly influencing the response. One interesting approach taken in online surveys by www.surveypro.com, www.surveyz.com, and www.perfectsurveys.com is to use context-sensitive help. The respondent can click on it to receive further clarification or instruction for a given question. In a recent study of households using telephone interviewing, Conrad and Schober (2000) found that compared to strictly standardized interviewing, conversational interviewing improved respondents' comprehension of questions, but at a cost; the time to complete an interview was lengthened. Depending upon the particular questionnaire, this may be a small price to pay for better understanding.

How serious a problem ambiguity represents is subjective. A study conducted more than 20 years ago using telephone interviews reported a 74.9 percent incidence of question understanding, and this understanding varied systematically with the socioeconomic characteristics of respondents (Peterson, Kerin, & Sabertehrani, 1982). The danger, of course, lies in having a "significant" incidence of question misunderstanding but not knowing it. Thus, examining question understanding should be a part of every survey whenever possible. Used in this manner it can help interpret and gain further insights into the data (Exhibit 11.4).

The question both initiates and gives direction to the communication process in research. In addition, the form and wording of the question, unlike that of the answer, can be completely controlled by the researcher. It is not surprising, therefore, that a large number of investigations have been carried out on both the form and wording of questions. It is appropriate that we consider both question form and question wording and their relationships to ambiguity.

EXHIBIT 11.4   Using "Question Understanding" for Explanation

Consider the data below, which are raw responses to the question "Government regulation is necessary to protect and improve the quality of life."

Question Understanding	Response			
	Agree	*Uncertain*	*Disagree*	*Total*
MALE RESPONDENTS:				
Good	447	10	332	839
Fair/poor	128	11	33	172
FEMALE RESPONDENTS:				
Good	453	17	215	685
Fair/poor	248	20	72	340
TOTAL	1326	58	652	2036

From these data, several percentages can be calculated. For example, while 65.1 percent of the total sample agreed with the statement, 61.8 percent of the males and 68.4 percent of the females agreed. But the data reveals more specific interpretations:

- Of the males whose question understanding was "good," 59.2 percent agreed.
- Of the males whose question understanding was "fair/poor," 74.4 percent agreed.
- Of the females whose question understanding was "good," 66.1 percent agreed.
- Of the females whose question understanding was "fair/poor," 72.9 percent agreed.

Generally, of the survey participants whose question understanding was "good," 62.3 percent agreed with the statement. Hence, in certain instances question understanding can be used to enhance the interpretation of, and even, to a limited extent, "explain" item responses.

(Peterson, Kerin, & Sabertehrani, 1982)

Forms of Questions and Answers

Underlying every question is a basic reason for asking it. If the reason for it is clear when constructing a question, there is a higher probability that the desired response will be obtained. Table 11.1 shows nine different types of questions (based on the nature of content), the broad reason underlying asking each type of question, and some examples of each type. Based on this structure, and the information in Table 11.2, which deals with standard answer formats, we are able to distinguish four basic question/answer types:

1. Free-answer (open-ended text)

2. Dichotomous and multiple choice answers (select k of n)

3. Rank order answers

4. Constant sum answers

Free Answer or Open-Ended Text Answers

The free answer (or open-ended text question) is, as the name implies, a question that has no fixed alternatives to which the answer must conform. The respondent answers in his or her own words and at the length he or she chooses, subject of course to any limitations imposed by the questionnaire itself. Interviewers are usually instructed to make a verbatim record of the answer.

An example of a free-answer question in the tomato-juice study already referred to is

What suggestions could you make for improving tomato juice?

The suggestions made included packaging it in glass containers, finding some way to keep it from separating, and improving the flavor by adding lemon juice, salt, or hot spices.

Free-answer questions are usually shorter than multiple-choice and dichotomous questions. A corollary characteristic is that free-answer questions are also invariably less complex in sentence structure than multiple-choice questions on the same issue, and are usually less complex than dichotomous questions.

Common sense suggests, and reading tests have confirmed, that short and simply structured sentences are more easily understood than long and complex ones. The tendency toward ambiguity of the long and complex sentence is accentuated, if anything, by listening to it rather than reading it. Further, there would seem to be no reason to believe that the findings would be any different for question than for declarative statements. Based on these premises, we should be on reasonably sound grounds for drawing inferences about the relative probability of ambiguity in questions and answers based on length and complexity of structure.

Free-answer questions place greater demands on the ability of the respondents to express themselves. As such, this form of question provides the opportunity for greater ambiguity in interpreting answers. To illustrate, consider the following verbatim transcript of one female respondent's reply to the question

What suggestions could you make for improving tomato juice?

"I really don't know. I never thought much about it. I suppose that it would be nice if you could buy it in bottles because the can turns black where you pour the juice out after it has been opened a day or two. Bottles break, though."

Table 11.1   Basic Question Types

Type of Question	Goal of Question	Positioning of Question
Factual or behavioral	To get information.	Questions beginning with what, where, when, why, who and how.
Explanatory	To get additional information or to broaden discussion.	How would that help? How would you go about doing that? What other things should be considered?
Attitudinal	To get perceptions, motivations, feelings, etc., about an object or topic.	What do you believe to be the best? How strongly do you feel about XYZ?
Justifying	To get proof to challenge old ideas and to get new ones.	How do you know? What makes you say that?
Leading	To introduce a thought of your own.	Would this be a possible solution? What do you think of this plan?
Hypothetical	To use assumptions or suppositions.	What would happen if we did it this way? If it came in blue would you buy it today?
Alternative	To get a decision or agreement.	Which of these plans do you think is best? Is one or two o'clock best for you?
Coordinative	To develop common agreement. To take action.	Do we all agree that this is our next step?
Comparative	To compare alternatives or to get a judgment anchored by another item.	Is baseball more or less exciting to watch on TV than soccer?

Should the conclusion be drawn that she had "no suggestion," "suggested packaging in a glass container," or "suggested that some way be found to prevent the can from turning black around the opening?" Note that she seems to have made the implicit assumption that the bottle would not turn black around the opening.

One way to overcome some of these problems, at least in personal and telephone surveys, is to have interviewers probe respondents. When this is done, primary concern should be for probing for clarity rather than additional information. One practitioner has gone so far as to suggest that questionnaires should clearly instruct interviewers to probe only once for additional information, and to continue to probe for clarity until the interviewer understands a respondent's reply.

From the criteria previously stated, we may tentatively conclude that the free-answer question provides the lowest probability of the questions being ambiguous, but the highest probability of the answers being ambiguous, compared with the other two question forms (see Exhibit 11.5).

Table 11.2   Standard Answer Formats Based on Task

Select 1/*n*—*pick-1*: The respondent is given a list of *n* options and is required to choose one option only.

Select *k*/*n*—*pick-k*: The respondent gets a set of *n* options to select from but this time chooses up to *k* options (*k* = *n*).

Select *k*1/*n* and Rank *k*2/*k*1—*pick and rank*: This question type is similar to pick-*k*, but in addition to selecting *k*1 options from a list of *n* options, the respondent is then asked to rank *k*2 of those options selected.

Select *k*1/*k*2/*n*—*pick-and-pick*: Respondent is asked to select *k*1 options in Category 1 and *k*2 options in Category 2. Each option can be selected in only one of the two categories.

Rank *k*/*n*—*rank*: In this question the respondent gets *n* options and is asked to rank the top *k* (*k* = *n*).

Integer Rating: The respondent is asked to rate on a linear scale of 1 to *n* the description on the screen or accompanying prop card (for example, 1 for completely disagree to 5 for completely agree). Only integer responses are accepted.

Continuous Rating: This is similar to integer rating, except that the response can be any number (not necessarily an integer number) within the range (for example, 5.2 on a scale of 0 to 10).

Constant Sum: The respondent is provided with a set of attributes (5, 10, etc.) and is asked to distribute a total of *p* points across those attributes.

Yes/No: This type of question entails a yes/no answer.

Integer—*integer-#*: The respondent is asked for a fact that can be expressed in integer number form. A valid range can be provided for error checking. Example: Age.

Real—*real-#*: Similar to integer-# except that the answer expected is in the form of a real (not necessarily an integer) number. Example: Income. A valid range can be provided for error checking.

Character: The respondent types in a string of characters as a response. Example: Name. No error checking is done on this type of input.

Multiple Integer Ratings: This question type is identical to integer-scale except that multiple questions (classified as "options") can appear on a single screen. Each question is answered and recorded separately.

Multiple Real Number Ratings: This question type is identical to real-scale except that multiple questions (classified as "options") can appear on a single screen. Each question is answered and recorded separately.

Dichotomous and Multiple-Choice Answers

The select *k* of *n* format is the workhorse of survey building and provides the general form for both dichotomous and multiple-choice answer types. Three general forms of questions are frequently used:

Select Exactly 1 of n Answers:

When *k* = 1, the type of answer scale is dependent on *n*, the number of answers. A dichotomous question has two fixed answer alternatives of the type "Yes/No," "In favor/Not in favor," "Use/Do not use," and so on. The question quoted earlier,

Do you like the taste of tomato juice?

is an example of a dichotomous question. Multiple-choice questions are simply an extension of the dichotomous question that have more answer points and often take the form of an ordered or interval measurement scale.

EXHIBIT 11.5 Open-Ended Questions and Answers

The advantages of the open-ended format are considerable, but so are its disadvantages (Sudman and Bradburn, 1982). In the hands of a good interviewer, the open format allows and encourages respondents to give their opinions fully and with as much nuance as they are capable of. It also allows respondents to make distinctions that are not usually possible with the fixed alternative formats, and to express themselves in language that is comfortable for them and congenial to their views. In many instances it produces vignettes of considerable richness and quotable material that will enliven research reports.

The richness of the material can also be a disadvantage if there is need to summarize the data in concise form. One example is the need to reduce the complexity of the data to fewer or simpler categories and in order to place the data into categories that can be counted. Coding of free-response material is not only time consuming and costly, but also introduces some amount of coding error. This is known as *content analysis*.

Open-ended questions also take somewhat more time to answer than closed questions. They also require greater interviewer skill to recognize ambiguities of response and to probe and draw respondents out, particularly those who are reticent and not highly verbal, to make sure that they give answers that can be coded. Open-ended response formats may work better with telephone interviews, where a close supervision of interview quality can be maintained, although there is a tendency for shorter answers to be given on the telephone. No matter how well controlled the interviewers may be, however, factors such as carelessness and verbal facility will generate greater individual variance among respondents than would be the case with fixed alternative response formats.

In general, the free-response format requires more psychological work on the part of respondents; that is, respondents must think harder about the question and pay more attention to what is being asked and marshal their thoughts in order to respond to the interviewers' questions. If the question comes more or less out of the blue, the respondent's thoughts will not be organized and may emerge somewhat haphazardly and in a confused fashion. What is reported first, however, may be important to the investigator as an indicator of the saliency of issues or the importance of things to the respondents.

SOURCE: From Sudman, S. & Bradburn, N., *Asking Questions: A Practical Guide to Questionnaire Design*, copyright © 1982. This material is used by permission of John Wiley & Sons, Inc.

Traditional multiple–choice questions also are of the select k of n answer form, but have more than two possible answers. For example, an agreement scale could have three, five, or seven possible answers.

Three answers:	Agree/Neutral/Disagree
Five answers:	Strongly Agree/Agree/Neither/Disagree/Strongly Disagree
Seven answers:	Very Strongly Agree/SA/A/N/D/SD/Very Strongly Disagree

As with all select *k* of *n* answers, the specific text associated with the answer options is variable and could measure many different constructs such as affect (liking), satisfaction, loyalty, purchase likelihood, and so forth.

Select Exactly k of n Answers

When questions are developed that accept or require multiple responses within a set of answers, the form "exactly *k* of *n*" or "as many as *k* of *n*" can be used. This general form asks the respondent to indicate that several answers meet the requirements of the question. In the "exactly" case, questions can be formatted to require "exactly" *k* answers, (where *k* is greater than 1), as when the respondent is asked to "select the best three of the 10 possible answers" (in other words, select exactly three of 10). This type of question might be

Please identify the three (3) of the following service activities that are most likely to be outsourced in the next 12 months.

☐ *Retirement benefits*   ☐ *Recruitment*

☐ *Medical benefits*   ☐ *Security services*

☐ *Health services/medical*   ☐ *Training, education*

☐ *Management/Executive selection* ☐ *Travel services*

☐ *Organization development*   ☐ *Work/Life programs*

Select as Many as k of n Answers

A variable number of answers may also be appropriate, particularly where long lists of attributes or features are given. In these cases, the respondent is asked to select as many as *k* of the *n* possible answers, where *k* can be any number from 2 to *n*. For example, in the previous question, the respondent could select as many as three (one, two, or three) of 10 possible answers. The question might be reworded to read something like

Please identify which service activities are most likely to be outsourced in the next 12 months (check all that apply).

Rank-Order Questions/Answers

As discussed in Chapter 9, rank-order questions increase the power of the measurement scale by including the characteristic of order to the data. Whereas the categorical data associated with many dichotomous or multiple-choice items does not permit us to say that one item is greater than another, rank-order data allows for the analysis of differences. Rank-order questions use an answer format that requires the respondent to assign a rank position for the first, second, and so forth up to the *n*th item to be ordered. This format of assigning position numbers can be very versatile, resulting in different types of questions that can be asked. Respondents may be asked to rank a specified subset from the list (such as their first, second, and third choices from a list), or to rank all items in the list. Typical questions might include identifying preference rankings, attribute association strength, first to last, most recent to least recent or relative position (most, next most, and so forth, until either a set number of items is ordered or all items may be ordered).

When this type of question is administered online or using a CATI system, additional options for administration may exist, including randomization and acceptance/validation of ties in the ranking. Randomization of the answer order helps to control for presentation order bias. It is well established that in elections, being the first on the list increases chances of receiving the voter's election. Similar bias occurs in questions where the same answer appears at the top of the list for each respondent, and is controlled by presenting the choice options in a different random order for each respondent.

Tied rankings are another issue to be considered when a rank-order question is constructed. When ties are permitted, several items may be evaluated as having the same rank. In general, this is not a good idea because it weakens the data. However, if ties truly exist, then the ranking should reflect this. Rank-order questions are generally a difficult type of question for respondents to answer, especially if the number of items to be ranked goes beyond five or seven.

Constant Sum Questions/Answers

A constant sum question is a powerful question type that permits collection of ratio data, meaning that the data is able to express the relative value or importance of the options (option A is twice as important as option B). This type of question is used when you are relatively sure of the reasons for purchase, or you want to evaluate a limited number of reasons that you believe are important. An example of a constant sum question follows:

The following question asks you to divide 100 points between a set of options to show the importance you place on each option. Distribute the 100 points giving the more important reasons a greater number of points. The computer will prompt you if your total does not equal exactly 100 points.

When thinking about the reasons you purchased our TargetFind data mining software, please allocate 100 points to the following reasons according to their relative importance.

Seamless integration with other software	_____
User friendliness of software	_____
Ability to manipulate algorithms	_____
Level of pre- and post-purchase service	_____
Level of value for the price	_____
Convenience of purchase/quick delivery	_____
Total	**100 points**

Question Ambiguity

Ambiguity is critical in both the respondent's understanding and proper consideration of the question, and in the researcher's understanding of the answer's meaning. In this section we discuss issues in question structure and form that can greatly influence and improve the quality of your questionnaire.

Neutrality and Don't Know or No Opinion

When a third alternative "Neither like nor dislike" is added to the example dichotomous question discussed previously, it becomes multiple choice and allows for those people who do not have a definite liking or disliking for tomato juice.

> *Do you like the taste of tomato juice?*
>
> ○ *Yes*   ○ *No*   ○ *Neither*

It is usually desirable to provide a category of this type to avoid forcing the respondent to make a definite stand when he or she may really be neutral. Similarly, it may be desirable to add other types of categories such as "don't know," "no opinion," or "not applicable," as the nature of the question and question format dictates. For example, "don't know" would apply to a question dealing with fact, whereas "no opinion" would apply to an attitude. Unfortunately there is a tendency to treat neutral, no opinion and don't know responses as indicating the same thing, something they obviously do not.

One potential problem with offering a "don't know" or "no opinion" option is that a false negative error may arise. This type of error occurs when a respondent reports not having an attitude when he or she really does have one. Quite often people who appear on first glance to have no attitude turn out to take a position if they are asked other questions on the same topic (Gilljam & Granberg, 1993). Attitudes that turn up only on the follow-up questions may be used to predict behavior to a significant degree. It is possible, however, that people who appear to have attitudes because of what they say on the follow-up questions may be guilty of creating a false positive error—this is created by the researcher's persistence. A false positive error occurs when a person appears to have an attitude when he or she really does not. So, offering a "don't know" option can lead to a reduced incidence of false positives. In addition, use of filter questions and easy-out alternatives also can lower the number of false positives. Filter questions are used to sort out respondents for whom detailed follow-up questions may not apply and therefore should not be asked (Knauper, 1998). A risk with using a filter question is that there will be an underreporting of events in which the researcher is interested; for example, more respondents are filtered out than intended as a more extreme question meaning has been conveyed. It is clear that protecting against false positives and false negatives seem to be counter to each other. There is no evidence that one of these errors is generally more serious than the other.

There is some evidence that offering a "no-opinion" response in attitudinal studies does not improve the quality of the data obtained (Krosnick et al., 2002). The over-time consistency of attitudes does not increase, nor does the statistical predictability of obtained responses. The idea that "no opinion" options discourage respondents from providing meaningless answers to survey questions is highly questionable. Many, and perhaps most, respondents who choose an explicitly offered "no opinion" response option may have meaningful attitudes, but the possibility that some people do so because they truly do not have attitudes cannot be dismissed (Krosnick et al.). Where does this leave us? It appears that offering a "no opinion" (or "don't know" where applicable) option does not improve things, but it also does not appear to make things worse. One impact is that the probably effective sample size will be decreased, leading to reduced statistical power. But for researchers who prefer to offer a "no opinion" option, two things can be done to compensate for this. First, the original sample size can be increased. Second, respondents who say they have no opinion can then be asked if they lean toward one of the substantive response options (Krosnick et al.). Use of the "no opinion" and "don't know" options appears to be a matter of researcher preference.

Dichotomous Questions

In terms of length and complexity of structure, the dichotomous question falls between the free-answer questions (shortest and least complex) and the multiple-choice questions (longest and most complex). The dichotomous question places the least demands on the respondent in terms of formulating and expressing an answer. With respect to ambiguity in dichotomous questions, therefore, we may tentatively conclude that this form of question provides roughly an average probability of the question's being ambiguous, but the lowest probability of the answer's being ambiguous, compared with the other two forms.

Multiple-Choice Questions

The multiple-choice question provides several set alternatives for the answer to it. In this respect it is in the middle ground between the free-answer and the dichotomous question.

Below is an example of the multiple-choice type of question from the tomato juice study:

Why do you use the brand you do?

- ○ *It is reasonably priced*
- ○ *I like the taste*
- ○ *The brand I'm used to and rely on*
- ○ *Other reason*

It should be noted that this question could have been asked as a free-answer question, and as a series of dichotomous questions. The choice between the free-answer and the multiple-choice forms of asking a question must always be made if the same question is not asked in both forms.

The multiple-choice question must be longer and more complex than either the free-answer or dichotomous questions in order to state the several alternatives. The statement of the alternatives is provided to assist the respondent in recalling and in formulating his or her answer. In giving this assistance, however, added opportunities to misunderstand the question are also provided.

A common source of ambiguity in the multiple-choice question is the difficulty of making the alternatives mutually exclusive. In the above example this requirement was met reasonably well. (It might be argued, however, that one would have to be "used to" and be able to "rely on" the taste's being consistently the same in order to give the "taste" alternative as the answer.) Another common source of ambiguity in multiple-choice questions is the implied restriction on alternatives. The example strongly implies that the respondent should have a single, most important reason for using the brand. This may very well not be the case.

In attempting to reduce the burden of respondents, self-report questionnaires often use the technique of asking respondents to examine a list of items and mark, circle, or check all that apply. This is useful in asking about alternative behaviors, attitudes, influencing factors, and so forth. For example, in a study done by *Money* magazine in the mid-1990s, one question asked used the technique described above:

Where would you place the greatest blame for escalating health-care costs?
(Circle as many as you wish.)
    a. Rising doctors' fees
    b. Rising cost of medications
    c. Inefficiency and waste at hospitals
    d. Rising insurance premiums
    e. Frivolous malpractice lawsuits
    f. Fraud in Medicare, Medicaid or private insurance programs
    g. Too much government bureaucracy
    h. Other

A question has been raised whether respondents really do mark "all that apply" as requested (Rasinski, Mingay, & Bradburn, 1994). The alternative is to ask about each of the items in a yes/no format. For example, the *Money* magazine question shown above could be worded:

Please indicate whether you think each of the following factors adds to escalating health-care costs by checking "Yes" or "No."

a. *Rising doctors' fees*	*Yes* ☐	*No* ☐
b. *Rising cost of medications*	*Yes* ☐	*No* ☐
c. *Inefficiency and waste at hospitals*	*Yes* ☐	*No* ☐
d. *Rising insurance premiums*	*Yes* ☐	*No* ☐
e. *Frivolous malpractice lawsuits*	*Yes* ☐	*No* ☐
f. *Fraud in Medicare, Medicaid, or private insurance programs*	*Yes* ☐	*No* ☐
g. *Too much government bureaucracy*	*Yes* ☐	*No* ☐

These all-that-apply instructions and the explicit yes/no instructions are considered to be functionally equivalent. The limited research on this matter suggests that respondents tend to give more answers when explicit yes/no instructions are given. Unfortunately, it is unknown whether this also means that more accurate reporting has occurred.

Whitlark and Smith (forthcoming) do report that there is an optimal number of k of n that should be picked. That number is approximately one-third. A value of k greater or less than that reduces the ability to discriminate or accurately profile the issue being investigated.

At the same time, there is no evidence that the mark-all-that-apply approach provides less accurate reporting. So the researcher should use common sense when deciding which approach to use. Let the nature of the question itself dictate and decide which would be less burdensome for the respondent. If the number of items is small, it would seem reasonable to use the yes/no format.

There is a tendency for the alternatives appearing first and last in a multiple-choice question to be used as answers more frequently than those in other positions. This systematic error, often called position bias or order bias, may be indicative of ambiguity in the question. In a "classic" experiment reported by Payne (1951), in which several alternatives were presented in different positions to matched samples of respondents results were that the top position, on the average, out-drew the middle position by six percentage points. The bottom position out-drew the middle position by two percentage points. In no instance did the middle position out-draw the top or bottom position.

This problem can be solved satisfactorily in most cases by rotating the order of the alternatives. This may be done by printing cards for each of the desired different orders of alternatives and instructing the interviewers to use the cards in a prescribed sequence. For mail or other self-report instruments, rotation means that different questionnaires must be prepared. Practical and economic considerations will limit the extent to which this can be done. Response order effects are discussed in more depth by Sudman, Bradburn, and Schwarz (1996).

With respect to ambiguity in multiple-choice questions, we may tentatively conclude that this form of question provides the highest probability of the question's being ambiguous, and an average probability of the answer's being ambiguous, compared with the other two forms.

Table 11.3 summarizes our tentative conclusions concerning the form of question and the probability of ambiguity. These conclusions should not be used as the final arbiter on the choice of question form. Some question forms are suited better to eliciting certain kinds of information than others. In "reason why" questions, for example, one would normally use free-answer or multiple-choice questions rather than dichotomous ones.

Each question form has been used extensively and has its proponents. There is no one "best" form of question for obtaining all types of information from respondents. Figure 11.2 (see p. 436) shows examples of different types of question taken from two questionnaires, a simple customer satisfaction questionnaire used by Sizzler Restaurants and a product usage questionnaire for a toothpaste brand. Figure 11.3 (see p. 438) reproduces a questionnaire that is totally open-ended. One broad question is asked, and the respondent is free to say anything he or she wants.

Question Wording

The wording of questions is a critical consideration when obtaining information from respondents. Consider the following three questions and the percentage of affirmative responses to each from three matched samples of respondents (Payne, 1951, pp. 8–9).

- Do you think anything should be done to make it easier for people to pay doctor or hospital bills? (82 percent replied "Yes.")
- Do you think anything could be done to make it easier for people to pay doctor or hospital bills? (77 percent replied "Yes.")
- Do you think anything might be done to make it easier for people to pay doctor or hospital bills? (63 percent replied "Yes.")

These questions differ only in the use of the words should, could, and might. Although these three words have different connotations, they are sometimes used as synonyms. Yet the responses, at the extreme, are 19 percentage points apart.

Table 11.3   Form of Question and Relative Probability of Ambiguity

	Relative Probability of Ambiguity	
Form of Question	Question	Answer
Free-answer	Lowest	Highest
Dichotomous	Average	Lowest
Multiple-choice	Highest	Average

Designing Questionnaires   435

As another example consider the following questions, posed by Rasinski (1989), for which labels for the issues of concern were changed:

- Are we spending too much, too little, or about the right amount on welfare (23.1 percent replied "too little"); assistance to the poor (62.8 percent replied "too little")
- Are we spending too much, too little, or about the right amount on halting the rising crime rate (66.8 percent replied "too little"); law enforcement (52.9 percent replied "too little")

In these questions, a more descriptive and more positive explanation is used and there is as much as 39.3 percent difference in evaluation.

Framing Questions

This last example is related to what is known as *framing* in communication. Information framing effects reflect the difference in response to objectively equivalent information depending upon the manner in which the information is labeled or framed. Levin, Schneider, and Gaeth (1998) and Levin et al. (2001) identify three distinct types of framing effects:

- Attribute framing effects. Occur when evaluations of an object or product are more favorable when a key attribute is framed in positive rather than negative terms.
- Goal framing effects. Occur when a persuasive message has different appeal depending on whether it stresses the positive consequences of performing an act to achieve a particular goal or the negative consequences of not performing the act.
- Risky choice framing effects. Occur when willingness to take a risk depends upon whether potential outcomes are positively framed (in terms of success rate) or negatively framed (in terms of failure rate).

Which type of potential framing effect should be of concern to the research designer depends upon the nature of the information being sought in a questionnaire. At the simplest level, if intended purchase behavior of ground beef was being sought, the question could be framed as "80 percent lean" or "20 percent fat." This is an example of attribute framing. It should be obvious that this is potentially a pervasive effect in question design, and is something that needs to be addressed whenever it arises. More detailed discussion of these effects are given by Hogarth (1982).

The ability to construct clear, unambiguous questions is an art rather than a science. It has remained so despite the extensive investigations and accumulated experience of practitioners over the past four decades. Although principles of question wording have evolved, they are more indicative than imperative.

According to Oppenheim (1992, pp. 128–130), these principles can be summarized by asserting that ambiguity in question wording arises from one or more of the following sources:

1. Question length
2. Respondent unfamiliarity with one or more words
3. Ambiguity of one or more words in context
4. Two questions combined in one
5. Lack of specificity

A brief discussion on each of these sources of ambiguity in question wording is in order.

(Text continues on page 439)

A. Sizzler

We would like you to rate some specific characteristics about your visit to Sizzler today.

A. Taste of the food
(1.) ☐ Excellent
(2.) ☐ Above Average
(3.) ☐ Average
(4.) ☐ Below Average
(5.) ☐ Poor

C. Value for the money
(1.) ☐ Excellent
(2.) ☐ Above Average
(3.) ☐ Average
(4.) ☐ Below Average
(5.) ☐ Poor

E. Efficiency of service
(1.) ☐ Excellent
(2.) ☐ Above Average
(3.) ☐ Average
(4.) ☐ Below Average
(5.) ☐ Poor

Multiple-Choice

B. Size of the portion
(1.) ☐ Excellent
(2.) ☐ Above Average
(3.) ☐ Average
(4.) ☐ Below Average
(5.) ☐ Poor

D. Employee attitude
(1.) ☐ Excellent
(2.) ☐ Above Average
(3.) ☐ Average
(4.) ☐ Below Average
(5.) ☐ Poor

F. Cleanliness
(1.) ☐ Excellent
(2.) ☐ Above Average
(3.) ☐ Average
(4.) ☐ Below Average
(5.) ☐ Poor

Was the food cooked as ordered?
☐ Yes   ☐ No

Dichotomous

Was the food served at the proper temperature?
☐ Yes   ☐ No

Menu item ordered_____

Open-end

Please rate some specific characteristics about the Buffet Court (if ordered).

A. Quality
(1.) ☐ Excellent
(2.) ☐ Above Average
(3.) ☐ Average
(4.) ☐ Below Average
(5.) ☐ Poor

B. Cleanliness
(1.) ☐ Excellent
(2.) ☐ Above Average
(3.) ☐ Average
(4.) ☐ Below Average
(5.) ☐ Poor

C. Variety
(1.) ☐ Excellent
(2.) ☐ Above Average
(3.) ☐ Average
(4.) ☐ Below Average
(5.) ☐ Poor

Multiple-Choice

What additional items would you like for the Buffet Court? _____
_____

What did you like best about your visit today? _____
_____

Open-end

What did you like least about your visit today? _____
_____

Overall, how would you rate your eating experience at Sizzler today? Was it:
(1.) ☐ Excellent (2.) ☐ Above Average (3.) ☐ Average (4.) ☐ Below Average (5.) ☐ Poor

Multiple-Choice

Name _____

Address _____

City _____

Date _____ Time _____

Figure 11.2   Illustration of Question Types

B. Sensodyne Toothpaste

BEFORE MAILING, MOISTEN THIS AREA, FOLD IN HALF AND SEAL

☐ Miss.

☐ Ms.

☐ Mrs.

☐ Mr. | | | | | | | | | | | | | | | | | | | | | | | | | | | | | | | | | | | | | | | | | | | | |

Last Name   First Name

| | | | | | | | | | | | | | | | | | | | | | | | | | | | | | | | | | | | | | | | | |

Street Address   Apt. #

| | | | | | | | | | | | | | | | | | | | | | | | | | | | | | | | | | | | | | | | | |

City   State   Zip Code

Home Telephone | | | | | | | | | | | | | | Your Sex: Male 1. ☐ Your Age | | |

(area code)   Female 2. ☐

---

1. How many tubes of Fresh Mint Sensodyne® have you used?
   1. ☐ One   2. ☐ Two
   3. ☐ Three or More

2. What is your overall opinion of Fresh Mint Sensodyne®?
   1. ☐ Excellent   2. ☐ Very Good
   3. ☐ Good   4. ☐ Fair   5. ☐ Poor

3. What do you like about Fresh Mint Sensodyne®?

   _____

   _____

4. What do you dislike about Fresh Mint Sensodyne®?

   _____

   _____

5. How do you feel about buying Fresh Mint Sensodyne® again?
   1. ☐ I will buy it again
   2. ☐ I will not buy it again
   3. ☐ I don't know

   Dichotomous
   Open-end

6. How did you first learn about Fresh Mint Sensodyne®?
   1. Recommended by dentist
   2. Tried various brands
   3. ☐ Television
   4. ☐ Friend/Relative/Druggist
   5. ☐ Saw in store
   6. ☐ Coupon/Newspaper Insert/Magazine
   7. ☐ On sale
   8. ☐ Received sample
   9. ☐ Other _____

   Dichotomous

   Multiple-Choice

7. If recommended by a Dentist, did you receive a sample of Fresh Mint Sensodyne®?
   1. ☐ Yes
   2. ☐ No

   Open-end

Figure 11.2 (Continued)

8. If you were given a sample of French Mint Sensodyne®, how many samples did you receive?

⎵⎵

9. How many times a week do you use Fresh Mint Sensodyne®?

⎵⎵

10. Just before you started to use Fresh Mint Sensodyne®, what product, if any, were you using for your teeth sensitivity problem?
    1. ☐ Original Sensodyne®
    2. ☐ Cool Gel Sensodyne®
    3. ☐ Denquel®
    4. ☐ Promise®

5. ☐ Aquafresh Sensitive®   Open-end
6. ☐ Other _____
7. ☐ Sensitivity Protection Crest®

11. What other toothpaste(s) do you use in addition to Fresh Mint Sensodyne®?
    1. None - Use Fresh Mint Sensodyne® exclusively   Multiple-
    2. ☐ Sensodyne® Cool Gel   Choice
    3. ☐ Original Formula Sensodyne®-SC
    4. ☐ Sensodyne® w/Baking Soda
    5. ☐ Any regular toothpaste
    6. ☐ Any tartar control toothpaste
    7. ☐ Any baking soda toothpaste   Multiple-
    8. ☐ Any baking soda peroxide   Choice
          toothpaste
    9. ☐ Any other desensitizing toothpaste

Horizon Air	Please give us your thoughts.

| The Horizon people serving you today would like to hear from you, and so would I. How well did we meet your expectations? Was there anyone in particular who served you exceptionally well? We'd like to thank and recognize them on your behalf. Was there anything that we could have done better? Is there anything that we're not currently doing that you would like to see us do? We love new ideas! Anything that is important to you is important to us. If you need more room, you can write to me at the address on this card or fax me your comments at (206) 248-6200.
   Thanks for flying with us today and for sharing your thoughts.
     Jeff Pinneo
     Vice President, Customer Services | Name: ☐ Mr. ☐ Mrs. _____
Flight # _____
Flight Date _____
From _____
To _____
Your Company Name _____
Daytime Phone ( ) _____
Purpose of trip? ☐ Business
☐ Pleasure ☐ Other
Number of Horizon roundtrips in last
12 months _____
(Complete return address information
on other side if you would like a reply) |

Dear Horizon: _____

_____

_____

_____

_____

_____

_____

_____

Figure 11.3   Completely Open-Ended Questionnaire

SOURCE: Reprinted with permission from Horizon Air.

1. Questions that are too long. There is a class of questions known as "flabbergasters" that are long, complex, and verge on being incomprehensible. A classic example is a reported 13-line question asking farm managers whether they used mostly inductive or deductive logic. Each word in a question is a potential source of ambiguity. The greater the number of words, the more complex the structure of the question must become. For both these reasons, brevity in question construction is a virtue. As a general rule-of-thumb, questions should be held to no more than 20 words if at all possible.

The following question has been paraphrased from one actually used on a survey in a different field:

Do you think of new-car dealers as being independent business people like appliance dealers and furniture merchants who own their own stores, or as being employees of the automobile companies?

Suppose, if you will, that this question is being read to you rather than your reading it. It refers to three different types of businesses, as well as to owning one's business versus being employed by a manufacturer. The researcher who constructed this question went to the trouble of using at least 10 extra words, which add opportunities for having the question misunderstood. Do you think that you would be more likely to understand the question above or this revised and shortened version?

Do you think of new-car dealers as owning their business, or as being employees of the automobile companies?

2. Questions that use one or more words that are unfamiliar to the respondent. The vocabulary used in questions should match that normally used by the respondents as closely as possible. For example, the wording of the question

Do you think that the processing of dehydrated soups reduces the caloric content?

might well be appropriate if it is to be asked of a group of food chemists. It would require a heroically optimistic researcher, however, to seriously consider asking this question of a sample of consumers. There are at least four words that individually, and in some cases collectively, would be unfamiliar to some consumers.

The principle of matching question vocabulary and respondent vocabulary is not always easy to follow. In the case of a group of food chemists, there is a similarity of training and a common usage of terms. It is probable that their individual vocabulary levels are uniformly high. For this group, question vocabulary and respondent vocabulary can be matched reasonably well. In the case of consumers, however, vocabulary levels vary widely.

When the sample of respondents is large and nonhomogeneous in background, it is desirable to word the question at the lowest vocabulary level represented in the sample. The researcher must guard against the use of more difficult synonyms for their simpler equivalents such as "observe" instead of "see," "obtain" instead of "get," and "purchase" instead of "buy."

The question should be worded to be understood by the respondent—not to impress him or her with the researcher's vocabulary.

3. Questions that use one or more words that are ambiguous in context. A common source of ambiguity of words in context is the way in which the question is constructed. Some illustrations of ambiguities arising from poor sentence structure are given below.

If Security Bank were to install an automatic teller machine and discontinue Saturday teller assisted hours, would you change your banking practice? (Would you use the machine, change banking hours, or change banks?)

A more serious and less easily corrected source of ambiguity of words in context is words that have two or more meanings. Most words have several meanings out of context, and we rely on the topic being discussed to indicate the intended meaning. In these questions the meaning intended should be clear. In many cases, however, the intended meaning of a word is not clear from the context in which it is used. Consider the following question:

Have you been satisfied with the service provided by the Sight and Sound Company?

In this question, both the words "you" and "service" are subject to misinterpretation. Does "you" mean the person being addressed only, or does it include this person's family? Does "service" refer to the assistance and consideration given the customer in making purchases, or does it refer to the repair of equipment done by the company?

Contextual effects are especially troublesome in research involving foreign markets, or any multicultural market. Some countries are what are known as linguistic high-context countries (Asian countries, for example), whereas others (like the United States and Canada) are low-context countries. In a high-context country, words by themselves carry little meaning. How the words are used, or their context, provides the meaning. Consequently, ambiguity in context may be quite significant in international marketing research.

4. Combined Questions. Careless question wording sometimes results in two questions being asked as one. A question asked of commuters is illustrative of such questions:

Which would you say is the more convenient and economical way to commute, by car or by train?

It is obvious that the respondent who believed that one method was more convenient and the other more economical could not logically answer the question as it was asked. Combined questions should be avoided. The above question should have been broken into two separate questions, one dealing with "convenience" and the other with "economy."

5. Questions that lack specificity. Ambiguity often arises because of the vagueness of questions. A question such as

Do you listen to FM radio stations regularly?

will involve ambiguity because it is by no means clear whether "regularly" means three times a day, twice a week, once a month, or some other frequency of listening. If the question is to be understood correctly, the desired information must be clearly specified.

Procedures for Recognizing and Reducing Ambiguity in Communication

Every research design that uses communication to obtain information should have as many safeguards against ambiguity as possible. Procedures should be employed to recognize where ambiguity may be present and to reduce it to the lowest practicable level.

Three procedural steps are useful for these purposes and should be considered in every project:

1. Alternative question wording

2. Pretesting

3. Verification by observation

1. Alternative question wording. We have already seen that the present state-of-the-art question formulation cannot guarantee unambiguous questions. In questions where there is reason to suspect that ambiguity may exist, it is advisable to consider alternative wordings and forms of questions to be asked of sub-samples of respondents.

The simplest application of this procedure applies to dichotomous questions. If it is believed that the order in which the alternatives are stated may influence the responses, the question can be asked of half the sample of respondents with the alternatives in one order, and of the other half with the order reversed. For example, the question

Which make of car would you say is more powerful, Ford or Chevrolet?

can be asked of half the respondents, and the question

Which make of car would you say is more powerful, Chevrolet or Ford?

of the other half. If the order of the alternatives does, in fact, affect the responses, this will become apparent and can be allowed for when interpreting the results.

The use of this simple experimental technique costs little more than having an extra set of questionnaires printed. In personal and telephone interviewing situations, the interviewers can be instructed to change the order for one-half the interviews, and the cost will be nil. For electronic modes of data collection, again two sets of questionnaires are constructed at little or no cost. It may reveal no significant differences in response. If so, it will usually be worth the cost involved simply to know that this is the case. Where significant differences in response are discovered, it will be even more worthwhile as a warning in interpreting the information.

2. Pretesting. Pretesting of questionnaires is a virtual necessity (Converse & Presser, 1986, pp. 51–75). The only way to gain real assurance that questions are unambiguous is to try them. Pretesting is usually done initially by asking proposed questions of associates. To be truly effective, however, pretesting of questions should be conducted by asking them of a group of respondents who are similar to those to be interviewed in the final sample.

A typical way to assess problems with individual questions included in the questionnaire is to ask those participating whether they had any trouble with each of the questions. For a self-report survey (nonelectronic or electronic), a simple way is to add a sheet that asks about each question and requests a response on some type of scale—understanding, difficulty in responding, and so forth. This may indicate if there are "problems" but may not indicate the exact nature of the problem.

If the pretest is done by an interviewer, each respondent can be asked about each question and probing can get more depth in the response. Another method, one which requires that pretest be done by personal interview, has been suggested by Bolton and Bronkhorst (1995) and Bolton (1993). This method was developed for GTE's use to pretest its customer satisfaction questionnaires, and involves the use of concurrent verbal protocols and an automatic coding scheme, designed to measure respondents' cognitive difficulties answering questions about low-involvement, low-frequency events. As respondents go through and respond to a questionnaire during a pretest interview, they concurrently verbalize aloud their thoughts. While this occurs, there is automatic coding of the verbal reports, which would then be content analyzed. Obviously, this procedure requires much more time and effort than is usually devoted to design and evaluation of pretests, and may not be appropriate for many studies.

It is the rule, rather than the exception, that questions will be revised as a result of pretesting. Several versions of a question may need to be considered as a result of pretesting before the final version is decided upon.

3. Verification by observation. Whenever cost, time, and the type of information desired permit, information obtained through communication should be verified by observation. The housewife may state that the only brand of toothpaste she buys for her children is Crest. Where possible, it is desirable to verify this statement partially by observing whether this is the only brand of toothpaste she now has on hand.

Clearly, verification by observation is not always possible or practical. In the above example, the housewife may object to a pantry audit. Even greater difficulties would be involved in attempting to verify via observation her statement that her children brush before going to bed.

Ambiguity in Observation

Although it has been suggested that, where practical to do so, information obtained by communication should be verified by observation, the implication should not be drawn that observation is free of ambiguity. If we conduct an in-home audit and find that Crest is the only brand on hand, this in itself does not disclose whether it was purchased or received as a gift, whether it is used or not, or, if used, for what purpose.

In making observations, we each select, organize, and interpret visual stimuli into a picture that is as meaningful and as coherent to us as we can make it. Which stimuli are selected and how they are organized and interpreted are highly dependent on both the backgrounds and frames of reference of the observer. If a customer, a floorwalker, and the department manager are each standing side by side on the mezzanine overlooking the jewelry department, what each "sees" will very likely differ markedly from the others.

The trained observer will invariably "see" more that relates to his or her specialty in an ambiguous situation than the untrained observer. As an illustration, many years ago a cereal manufacturer ran a promotional campaign involving a drawing contest for children. Each child who entered was required to submit (along with a box top) a picture he or she had drawn that depicted Brand X cereal being eaten. The contest was run, the prizes awarded on the basis of artistic merit, and the brand manager turned his attention to other matters. A short time later a psychologist who worked for the company happened to see the pictures. He asked to be permitted to study them. He found that a sizable proportion of them showed a child eating cereal alone, often with no other dishes on the table. This suggested to him that cereal is often eaten by children as a between-meal snack. Later studies by the company's marketing research department showed that cereals are eaten between meals by children in greater amounts than are eaten for breakfast. The advertising program of the company was subsequently changed to stress the benefits of its cereals as between-meal snacks.

SOME CONCLUDING COMMENTS

We have not discussed broader issues of overall questionnaire design, question sequencing, and so forth (see Table 11.4). This is not to say that these are not important issues. To the contrary, they are. For example, research has shown that questions appearing early in a questionnaire and early within their respective groups (when the questionnaire is so organized) are more likely to be answered and may influence responses to later questions than are questions placed elsewhere. This is the question-order effect issue. Question-order effects can occur along two different dimensions (Moore, 2002): (a) the relative judgments that respondents make about each of the items being evaluated (the item dimension); and (b) the judgments made about the larger framework within which the evaluations are being made (the framework dimension). As in the case of response order, rotation of questions may help reduce any such effects. But the researcher has to be careful not to destroy any logical sequencing of questions within a topic area.

Similarly, a well-known principle is that questionnaire design should follow a *funnel approach* with respect to where variable kinds of questions should be placed (e.g., sensitive, important, hard to answer, demographic). There are two ways to look at the funnel technique. First, it is a sequencing of questions where one proceeds from the general to the specific (or from easier questions to answer to those more difficult), keeping in mind that there must be topic consistency. A second view is that a set of funnel questions exists in a form of a "contingency tree" in that each succeeding question is contingent on a respondent's answer to the preceding question, as shown in Figure 11.4 (Peterson, 2000, page 110). One advantage of this approach is that it minimizes the chance that respondents are asked irrelevant questions or questions to which they do not know the answers. These issues are covered rather thoroughly in books that are more narrowly focused (Peterson, 2000; Dillman, 2000; Bourque & Fiddler, 2003a, 2003b; Labaw, 1988; Converse & Presser, 1986; Payne, 1951).

What is clear, however, is that there is no such thing as a "pure" optimum length of questionnaire, as usually understood by marketing researchers. There may be an *operational* optimum length. Such an optimum would be determined by interest value of the topic(s) covered, their importance, the motivation of the respondent, the quality of the interviewer where one is used, and a myriad of other considerations.

One issue is that of comparability across different populations when doing cross-cultural/national research. An area of great concern to marketing researchers is the differences that have existed among countries in demographic variation and categorizations. The European Society for Opinion and Research (ESOMAR) worked on the development of a common questionnaire that can be used for Pan-European and multicountry surveys. Figure 11.5 shows one English language version (ESOMAR, 1990, p. 4).

Another issue that arises in cross-cultural/national research is the question of whether or not to translate a questionnaire. A typical cross-national study has the questionnaire developed by someone in one country, and it is then to be administered in another country. In a few rare cases and for certain "populations," the questionnaire can be administered in the language of the country in which it was developed, even if the languages differ. For example, an English language questionnaire may be able to be used in Denmark and The Netherlands

(Text continues on p. 447)

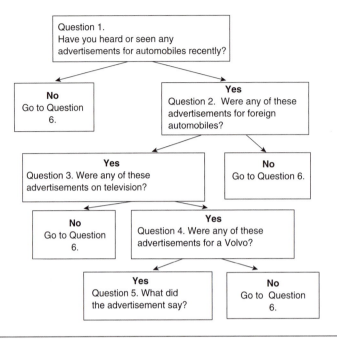

Figure 11.4   Funnel Questions

SOURCE: From Peterson, R., *Constructing Effective Questionnaires,* copyright © 2000. Reprinted by permission of Sage Publications, Inc.

Table 11.4   Major Aspects of Questionnaire Design

Researcher Question	Audit Questions	Possibilities
What information is to be sought?	What is the purpose of the study?	Descriptive: Awareness, attitudes, importance, acceptabilities, preference, past behavior, trial, use, market position
What information is to be presented at the end of the research project?	What am I trying to describe, segment, or predict?	Segment the market: Attitude, benefit, demographic, psychographic, usage
	How do I identify or classify results by market segment?	Estimate/predict: Market share, elasticity
	Can I picture the tables and graphs to be presented when the final data is analyzed?	
What type of data is required?	Are we conducting exploratory research or can Structured Direct methods be used?	How is the data to be collected?
What type of questionnaire is appropriate to collect this data?	Are respondents willing to provide the requested info?	Focus groups, mail questionnaire, phone interview, personal interview, combination, Internet/e-mail

(Continued)

Table 11.4 *(Continued)*

Researcher Question	Audit Questions	Possibilities
How is the questionnaire to be administered?	Do we need special considerations? Disguise needed? In-depth interviews? Projective methods?	

Question content, question format, question phrasing	Does the question answer the study objective(s)?
	
	Do respondents have the ability to answer the question?
	
	Does the statement communicate?
	
	Does the question purpose match the question?
	
	Can the result be interpreted?
		Consider:
		  Able to answer, time required, prestige, privacy, etc.
		Question types:
		  Open-ended, dichotomous, multiple-choice, measurement scale, etc.
		Question wording:
		  Biased wording, length, unfamiliar words, ambiguous content, combined quest., specificity, etc.
		Some question types
		  Demographics, attribute strength, attribute importance, satisfaction, preference, future behavior, trade-offs, psychographics, etc.

Response format of the individual questions.	Is there a better way to measure this response?
	
	Does the question purpose match the response format?
	
	How is the data analyzed?
	
	Can the result be interpreted?
		Measurement level:
		  Nominal, ordinal, interval, ratio?
		
		Scaling objective:
		  Scale stimuli, scale respondents
		
		Scale type:
		  Paired comparison, ranking methods, rating methods, etc.

Sequencing and layout of the questionnaire	How many questions should be added or deleted? Do questions flow building on previous questions? Are similar response formats grouped together?	Funnel approach: General—Warm-up Specific—In-depth General—Wind-down **Funnel Approach** **General Warm-Up** → **Specific In-Depth** → **General Wind-Down**
Re-examine, rethink and revise	Review questionnaire re-examine steps 1–4	
Pretest and revise	Formal pretest of survey	

I	II	III
(1) Sex: M □ F □	(10) At present, are you . . .? self-employed □ ▶ q.11A□	(12) How many hours per week do you normally work? □ □
(2) What is your age? □ □	• in a paid employment □ ▶ q.11B□	(13) Do you, or anyone else in your household, own . . .?
(3) How many people live in your household, including yourself? □ □	• temporarily not working □ ▶B	• a color TV set Y □ N □
(4) How many children under 15 are there? □ □	• retired □ ▶B	• a video recorder Y □ N □
(5) Are you, in your household . . .	• not working/responsible for ordinary shopping and looking after the home (E13) □▶ q.13	• a radio-clock Y □ N □

(1) Sex: M □ F □

(2) What is your age? □ □

(3) How many people live in your household, including yourself? □ □

(4) How many children under 15 are there? □ □

(5) Are you, in your household . . .
- The person who contributes most to the household income?
YES □ NO □
- The person mainly responsible for ordinary shopping and looking after the home?
YES □ NO □

(6) Are you . . .?
- Married/living together □
- Single □
- Separated/divorced/ widowed □

(7) At what age did you finish full-time education? □ □
Still studying (E10)▶ q.13

(8) Any time after that, did you . . .
- Resume general education at a later stage in your life?
YES □▶ q.9 NO □ ▼
- Take any apprenticeship/ professional training for your job?
YES □ ▶ q.9 NO □▶ q.10

(9) How many months did your . . . (further education/prof. training) last in total? □ □

II

(10) At present, are you . . .?
self-employed □ ▶ q.11A□
- in a paid employment □ ▶ q.11B□
- temporarily not working □ ▶B
- retired □ ▶B
- not working/responsible for ordinary shopping and looking after the home (E13) □▶ q.13
- And formerly, have you been . . .?

(11) What kind of work do you do? (What position do you hold?)

A – Self-Employed

- PROFESSIONAL (Doctor, Lawyer, Accountant, Architect)(E2) □▶ q.12 (in actual profession)
- GENERAL MANAGEMENT □ (Exec./Manag. Dir., Officer, Mgr)
- MIDDLE MANAGEMENT □ (Dmt/Branch Head, Junior Mgr)
  - How many employees are you responsible (or heading)?
  GM MM
0–5: (E4) (E6) □▶ q.12
6 or +:(E1) (E5) □▶ q.12
- OTHER EMPLOYMENT □ ▶ Do you work mainly in an office? YES (E8) □▶ q.12 NO □
  – In your job, do you spend much of your time writing or working with figures?
YES (E11) □ NO (E14) □

III

(12) How many hours per week do you normally work? □ □

(13) Do you, or anyone else in your household, own . . .?
- a color TV set Y □ N □
- a video recorder Y □ N □
- a radio-clock Y □ N □
- a video camera/ camcorder Y □ N □
- a PC/home computer Y □ N □
- an electric deep fryer Y □ N □
- an electric drill Y □ N □
- a still camera Y □ N □
- at least 2 cars Y □ N □
- a second home or a vacation house/flat Y□ N□

(14) Your main home: do you . . .?
- rent it □
- own it □

(15) Which foreign languages do you understand well enough to read a newspaper or listen to radio news?

Danish □	Greek □
Dutch □	Italian □
English □	Portuguese □
French □	Spanish □
German □	Swedish □
	Other □

FULL ADDRESS

(16) • REGION
(17) • SIZE OF TOWN
USING THE LOCAL, USUAL CATEGORIES
(As documented in available statistics on universe)

Figure 11.5 A Sample Questionnaire for Demographics

as the incidence of English-speaking is very high in these two countries. The issue often is one of cultural comfort versus loss in meaning. Any time a questionnaire is translated, there will be some loss in meaning. A normal procedure for translation is to follow a translation/back-translation process. The extent to which a questionnaire can be successfully translated depends upon (a) the lack of semantic equivalence across languages; (b) the lack of conceptual equivalence across cultures; and (c) the lack of normative equivalence across societies. This is a specialized topic and is covered in depth by Behling and Law (2000).

SUMMARY

This chapter looked at issues involved in asking questions of respondents. The exposition was in the context of response error and what might be done to control and, it is hoped, eliminate as much of this error as possible. Some general principles of question formation were presented.

It is often difficult to separate the questionnaire and questions asked in a marketing research study from the mode of data collection used. This is especially so for surveys or when a survey method (communication) is used in an experiment. The interview (telephone or personal) can be a key element in errors of inaccuracy and ambiguity arising. This is especially so for surveys designed to produce quantitative data about some population—a common type of marketing research project—and for cross-cultural/national studies as well.

ASSIGNMENT MATERIAL

1. The manufacturer of a certain brand of nationally advertised and distributed frozen fruit juices has retained you as a consultant to advise on a questionnaire that is being prepared. The purpose of the survey is to determine consumer opinion and attitudes about frozen versus fresh fruit juices. Personal interviews are to be conducted on a randomly selected sample of families.

    a. The questions listed below are being considered for the questionnaire. Comment on each, indicating whether you would leave the question as it is or change it. If you think if should be changed, rewrite it as you believe it should be asked.

    (1) *Do you or any of your family drink fruit juices?*
    Yes _____ No _____
    If yes:

    (2) *Is the juice drunk at a meal or between meals or both*
    At meal _____ Between meals _____ Both _____

    (3) *Do you prefer frozen or fresh juices?*
    Frozen _____ Fresh _____

    (4) *What advantages, if any, do you believe using fresh juice has over using frozen juice?*

    (5) *What advantages, if any, do you believe using frozen juice has over using fresh juice?*

(6)   *What brand or brands of juice do you regularly buy?*
       Don't know

(7)   *On this card is a list of fruit juices. Tell me which are your family's first, second, and third choices.*

> *grape* _____
> *tomato* _____
> *lime* _____
> *lemonade* _____
> *orange* _____
> *V-8* ___
> *other* _____

(8)   *What is the last brand of juice bought by your family?* _____
       Don't know

b.   Classify each of the above questions by type (free-answer, multiple-choice, or dichotomous).

2.   The No-Fault Insurance Company, a relatively small company specializing in insuring automobiles, was interested in learning in what proportion of automobile accidents, in which the police were not called, an insuree was involved who had been driving under the influence of alcohol or some form of drugs. A member of the company's marketing research department took a simple random sample of 100 accidents by their insurees over the past 12 months in which there was no police investigation. The insuree was interviewed personally and, after a suitable introduction, handed a card with the following instructions printed on it:

PLEASE READ THIS CARD ALL THE WAY
THROUGH BEFORE DOING ANY OF THE THINGS REQUESTED

1.   The interviewer will hand you a penny after you have finished reading the card and have asked any questions you may have.

  Please flip the penny and determine whether it came up HEADS or TAILS without letting the interviewer know which it was.

2.   The side of the coin that came up will determine which of the two questions given below you will answer. Please answer the question with "YES" or "NO" only and do not say anything else as we do not want the interviewer to know which question you answer.

3.   If the penny came up HEADS, answer "YES" or "NO" (only) to the question:

  "Was your mother born in August?"

4.   If the penny came up TAILS, answer "YES" or "NO" (only) to the question:

  "Before your last automobile accident had you been drinking alcohol or taken any drugs (including tranquilizers) that might have caused you to be unable to drive as well as you usually do?"

5.   If you have any questions about any of these instructions, please ask the interviewer for an explanation before you flip the penny. If the instructions are followed properly, ONLY YOU SHOULD KNOW WHICH QUESTION YOU ANSWERED.

Responses were obtained from 91 persons (four had died or otherwise could not be contacted and five refused to answer). Twenty-four (24) of the respondents answered "Yes."

    a. What is the estimated proportion of respondents who answered "Yes" to the question concerning driving after drinking alcohol or taking drugs?

    b. What are the nonsampling errors that are actually or potentially present in this estimate?

    c. Should these nonsampling errors be reflected in the estimate? If so, how?

3. A U.S. senator sent the questionnaire reproduced below to a mailing list of his constituents. Comment on the questionnaire indicating
    a. Your evaluation of each question
    b. Your appraisal of the questionnaire as a device for informing the senator of his constituents' opinions

---

QUESTIONNAIRE

1. Under present law, families who run small businesses and farms are often forced to sell their holdings rather than pass them on to the next generation owing to the burden of estate taxes. Would you favor legislation to ease this burden?

   Yes _____   No _____

2. Of the following areas of federal spending, choose one in which you would prefer to make a budget cut:
   a. Public welfare payments   _____
   b. Public works projects   _____
   c. Defense spending   _____
   d. Foreign assistance programs   _____
   e. Food stamps   _____
   f. Education   _____
   g. Other   _____

3. Do you believe that charitable organization, such as churches and nonprofit hospitals should remain tax-exempt?

   Yes _____   No _____

4. Which one of the following would you choose as the most important in solving the energy shortage over the next 20 years?
   a. Solar/geothermal power development   _____
   b. Nuclear power development   _____
   c. Conservation of present sources
      of energy   _____
   d. Expansion of domestic oil reserves   _____
   e. Increased use of coal   _____

5. Which one of the following would you say is the most important effort Congress could make to prevent crime?
   a. Enact harsher penalties to deter crimes   _____

---

b. Reenact the death penalty for certain crimes _____

c. Enact restrictions on violence on television _____

d. Increase funding for the courts _____

e. Increase funding for law enforcement agencies _____

f. Reform the country's prison system _____

6. Most of the economic indicators for the nation show positive signs of a recovery. Unemployment is down to 7.6 percent, personal incomes are up, and the prime lending rate is down.

a. Do you feel that we are in a recovery?   Yes _____   No _____

b. Do you feel that the economy has stabilized?   Yes _____   No _____

c. Do you expect inflation to increase?   Yes _____   No _____

d. Do you believe that unemployment will stabilize   Yes _____   No _____

Should Congress finance more jobs producing programs with tax revenues?

Yes _____   No _____

7. In each of the following areas do you feel that Congress' efforts should be increased?

a. Energy research and development   Yes _____   No _____

b. Health care and insurance   Yes _____   No _____

c. Crime control   Yes _____   No _____

d. Tax reform   Yes _____   No _____

e. Preservation of the environment   Yes _____   No _____

f. Other   Yes _____   No _____

❖

REFERENCES

Barnes, J. H., Jr., & Dotson, M. J. (1989, November). The effect of mixed grammar chains in response to survey questions. *Journal of Marketing Research, 26*(4), 468–472.

Behling, O., & Law, K. S. (2000). *Translating questionnaires and other research instruments: Problems and solutions.* Thousand Oaks, CA: Sage.

Bolton, R. N. (1993). Pretesting questionnaires: Content analysis of respondents' concurrent verbal protocols. *Management Science, 12*(3), 280–303.

Bolton, R. N., & Bronkhorst, T. M. (1995). Questionnaire pretesting: Computer assisted coding of concurrent protocols. In N. Schwarz and S. Sudman (Eds.), *Answering questions: Methodology for determining cognitive and communiciative processes in survey research.* San Francisco: Jossey-Bass.

Bourque, L. B., & Fielder, E. P. (2003a). *How to conduct self-administered and mail surveys* (2nd ed.). Thousand Oaks, CA: Sage.

Bourque, L. B., & Fielder, E. P. (2003b). *How to conduct telephone surveys* (2nd ed.). Thousand Oaks, CA: Sage.

Bradburn, N., & Sudman, S. (1979). *Improving interview method and questionnaire design.* San Francisco: Jossey-Bass.

Campbell, C., & Joiner, B. L (1973, December). How to get the answer without being sure you've asked the question. *American Statistician, 27,* 229–231.

Carroll, S. (1994, January 3). Questionnaire design affects response rate. *Marketing News, 28,* 14ff.

Conrad, F. G., & Schober, M. F. (2000). Clarifying question meaning in a household survey. *Public Opinion Quarterly, 64,* 1–28.

Converse, J. M., & Presser, S. (1986). *Survey questions: Handcrafting the standardized questionnaire*. Beverly Hills, CA: Sage.

Dillman, D. A. (2000). *Mail and internet surveys: The tailored design method* (2nd ed.). New York: Wiley.

ESOMAR Working Party on Harmonization of Demographics. (1990). *Getting ready for single European sample surveys*. Amsterdam: ESOMAR.

Fox, J. A., & Tracy, P. E. (1986). *Randomized response: A method for sensitive surveys*. Beverly Hills, CA: Sage.

Gilljam, M., & Granberg, D. (1993). Should we take 'don't know' for an answer? *Public Opinion Quarterly, 57,* 348–357.

Hausknecht, D. R. (1990). Measurement scales in consumer satisfaction/dissatisfaction. *Journal of Consumer Satisfaction, Dissatisfaction and Complaining Behavior, 3,* 1–11.

Hogarth, R. M. (Ed.) (1982). *Question framing and response consistency*. San Francisco: Jossey-Bass.

Knauper, B. (1998). Filter questions and question interpretation: Presuppositions at work. *Public Opinion Quarterly, 62,* 70–78.

Krosnick, J. A., Holbrook, A. L., Berent, M. K., Carson, R. T., Hanemann, W. M., Kopp, R. J., et al. (2002). The impact of 'no opinion' response options on data quality: Non-attitude reduction or an invitation to satisfice? *Public Opinion Quarterly, 66,* 371–403.

Labaw, P. (1980). *Advanced questionnaire design*. Cambridge, MA: Abt Books.

Levin, I. P., Gaeth, G. J, Evangelista, F., Albaum, G., & Schreiber, J. (2001). How positive and negative frames influence the decisions of persons in the United States and Australia. *Asia Pacific Journal of Marketing and Logistics, 13*(2), 64–71.

Levin, I. P., Schneider, S. L., & Gaeth, G. J. (1998, November). All frames are not created equal: A typology of framing effects. *Organizational Behavior and Human Decision Processes, 76*(2), 149–188.

Moore, D. W. (2002). Measuring new types of question-order effects. *Public Opinion Quarterly, 66,* 80–91.

Murphy, I. P. (1997, January 6). Keynote speaker emphasizes urgency of strategic research. *Marketing News, 31,* 6.

Oppenheim, A. N. (1992). *Questionnaire design, interviewing and attitude measurement*. London: Pinter Publishers.

Payne, S. L. (1951). *The art of asking questions*. Princeton, NJ: Princeton University Press.

Peterson, R. A. (2000). *Constructing effective questionnaires*. Thousand Oaks, CA: Sage.

Peterson, R. A., Kerin, R. A., & Sabertehrani, M. (1982). Question understanding in self-report data. In B. J. Walker, et al. (Eds.), *An assessment of marketing thought and practice* (pp. 426–429). Chicago: American Marketing Association.

Rasinski, K. A. (1989). The effect of question wording on public support for government spending. *Public Opinion Quarterly, 53,* 388–394.

Rasinski, K. A., Mingay, D., & Bradburn, N. (1994). Do respondents really "mark all that apply" on questionnaires? *Public Opinion Quarterly, 58,* 400–408.

Reinmuth, J. E., & Geurts, M. D. (1975, November). The collection of sensitive information using a two-stage randomized response model. *Journal of Marketing Research, XII,* 402–407.

Sanchez, M. E. (1992). Effects of questionnaire design on the quality of survey data. *Public Opinion Quarterly, 56,* 206–217.

Semon, T. T. (2000a, August 14). Better questions means more honesty. *Marketing News, 34,* 10.

Semon, T. T. (2000b, January 17). If you think a question is stupid—it is. *Marketing News, 34,* 7.

Stem, D.F., Jr., & Steinhorst, R. K. (1984). Telephone and mail questionnaire applications of the randomized response model. *Journal of the American Statistical Association, 79,* 555–564.

Sudman, S., & Bradburn, N. (1982). *Asking questions*. San Francisco: Jossey-Bass.

Sudman, S., Bradburn, N., & Schwarz, N. (1996). *Thinking about answers: The application of cognitive processes to survey methodology*. San Francisco: Jossey-Bass.

Umesh, U. N., & Peterson, R. A. (1991). A critical evaluation of the randomized response method: Applications, validation, and research agenda. *Sociological Methods and Research, 20,* 104–138.

Whitlark, D., & Smith, S. (forthcoming). Using pick data to measure brand performance: Advantages and issues for outline questionnaires. *Marketing Research.*

APPENDIX 11.1
Applied Measurement and Scaling

Chapters 9 and 10 introduced the basic concepts of measurement and scale development. These concepts are the building blocks from which most questionnaires are constructed. The progression from a blank sheet of paper to a completed questionnaire can be a long and difficult process, especially when the researcher has little previous experience from which to draw. In this appendix we attempt to extend the discussion of questionnaire construction by illustrating actual questions that may help when constructing a questionnaire.

The combination of question purpose, approach, and format for question and response creates an endless set of options to be considered when designing a questionnaire. Fortunately, most market studies are directed at market segmentation and use variants of standard market analysis questions. By focusing on the segmentation of markets, we will pinpoint some of these "standard market analysis questions" that lead to a descriptive analysis of market segments. These standard questions may be used for purposes other than segmentation (see Table 11.5).

Table 11.5   Segmentation Measures

Questions About Segments	Possible Measures
What are the external characteristics of the segment? Are they identifiable; do they have the ability to buy?	Demographic Geographic Socioeconomic Family Life Cycle Culture Personality Self-concept
What do the segments like and dislike? What product or service attributes made a difference in their purchase?	Awareness Attitudes Interests Opinions Beliefs Motivation Involvement Values Satisfaction Activities
How do members of each segment make decisions? How do members of the segment intend to behave? How have they acted in specific situations in the past?	Situational decision making Decision making style Information processing style Intention to purchase Past purchases Brand loyalty Information search and evaluation Decision attribute tradeoffs

A variety of concepts, such as demographics, are commonly measured in many market studies. If you were to examine some of the questionnaires to which you have been asked to respond, you would find that many contain the same concepts. You would also observe that these measures have minor variations in the response scales used.

One important key to maximizing the effectiveness of survey research and measurement is to establish and maintain comparable response scales. This comparability, if present, is useful in linking the current study to previous research, be it of primary or secondary source. For example, in the United States, researchers often match demographic scales with those of the Census of Population. Other applications may require standards that are industry or company based. The point being that comparability between data sources and study results is much easier when scales are similar.

In the following sections, sample questions and scales can be found that are useful to measure demographic characteristics, attitudes, product/service attributes, psychographics, and consumer satisfaction.

I. Demographics

Example 1. General Demographics

Example 1. General Demographics

---

1. What is your occupation?

O Executive/ Managerial	O Government/ Military	O Homemaker
O Professional/ Technical	O Craftsman/ Laborer	O Not Employed
O Teacher/ Professor	O Airline Employee/ Travel Agent	O Student
O Salesperson/ Buyer	O Self-Employed	O Retired
O Secretary/Clerk/ Office Worker		O Other

1a. What is the approximate annual income, before taxes, for yourself and for your entire household?

	Your- self	Total Household
No Income	O	O
Under – $10,000	O	O
10,000 – 19,999	O	O
20,000 – 29,999	O	O
30,000 – 39,999	O	O
40,000 – 49,999	O	O
50,000 – 59,999	O	O
60,000 – 74,999	O	O
75,000 – 100,000	O	O
Over $ 100,00	O	O

1b. How many wage earners (or employed persons) are in your household?

O   None
O   1
O   2
O   3
O   4 or more

2. What is the highest level of education you have completed?

O Less than high school graduate	O Some college
O High school graduate	O College graduate
O Vocational/Trade school	O Post graduate degree

3. What age group are you in?

O 12–17	O 30–39	O 60–64
O 18–21	O 40–49	O 65 & over
O 22–29	O 50–59	

3a. Are you
O Male
O Female

b. Are you:
O White
O Black
O Hispanic
O Asian/ Oriental

c. Are you:
O Married
O Single
O Other

4a. Where do you live?
O USA
O Canada
O Mexico
O Europe
O Orient
O South America
O Other

b. If USA, what is ZIP Code

Fill matching circles below

O	O	O	O	O
O	O	O	O	O
O	O	O	O	O
O	O	O	O	O
O	O	O	O	O
O	O	O	O	O
O	O	O	O	O
O	O	O	O	O
O	O	O	O	O
O	O	O	O	O
O	O	O	O	O

Example 2. Socio-Economic Status	Respondent	Respondent's spouse

EDUCATION:

	Respondent	Respondent's spouse
Grammar school (8 years or less)	−1	−1
Some high school (9 to 11 years)	−2	−2
Graduated high school (12 years)	−3	−3
Some post high school (business, nursing, technical, 1 year college)	−4	−4
Two, three years of college: possible Associate of Arts degree	−5	−5
Graduated four-year college (B.A./B.S.)	−7	−7
Master's or five-year professional degree	−8	−8
Ph.D. or six/seven-year professional degree	−9	−9

OCCUPATION PRESTIGE LEVEL OF HOUSEHOLD HEAD:
Interviewer's judgment of how head-of-household rates in occupational status.

(Respondent's description—ask for previous occupation if retired, or if R is widow, ask husband's: _____)

Chronically unemployed: "day" laborers, unskilled; on welfare	−0
Steadily employed but in marginal semiskilled jobs: custodians, minimum pay factory help, service workers (gas attendants, etc.)	−1
Average-skill assembly line workers, bus or truck drivers, police and firefighters, route deliverymen, carpenters, brick masons	−2
Skilled craftsmen (electricians), small contractors, factory foremen, low-pay salesclerks, office workers, postal employees	−3
Owners of very small firms (2 to 4 employees), technicians, salespeople, office workers, civil servants with average level salaries	−4
Middle management: teachers, social workers, lesser professionals)	−5
Lesser corporate officials, owners of middle-sized businesses (10 to 20 employees), moderate-success professionals (dentists, engineers, etc.)	−7
Top corporate executives, "big successes" in the professional world (leading doctors and lawyers), "rich" business owners	−9

AREA OF RESIDENCE: *Interviewer's impression of the immediate
neighborhood in terms of its reputation in the eyes of the community.*

Slum area: people on relief, common laborers	−1
Strictly working class; not slummy, but some very poor housing	−2
Predominantly blue-collar with some office workers	−3
Predominantly white-collar with some well-paid blue collar	−4
Better white-collar area; not many executives, but hardly any blue-collar either	−5
Excellent area; professionals and well-paid managers	−7
"Wealthy" or "society"–type neighborhood	−9

TOTAL FAMILY INCOME PER YEAR: TOTAL

				SCORE ____
Under $20,000	−1	$80,000–99,999	−5	
$20,000–39,999	−2	$100,000–139,999	−6	
$40,000–59,999	−3	$140,000–199,999	−7	
$60,000–79,999	−4	$200,000 +	−8	*Estimated*

Status ____

(Interviewer's estimate: _____ and explanation:_____)

R's MARITAL STATUS: Married ___ Divorced/Separated ___ Widowed ___ Single ___ (CODE:__)

II. Attitude Measurement

Example 1. Multi-Attribute Measurement

Attribute measurement in marketing has been used to predict behaviors, such as intention to purchase a specific brand or product. The most common attitude measurement models define the relationship between behavior and attitude as:

$$B = BI = w_1 \sum_{i=1}^{k} a_i * b_i + w_2 \left(\sum_{i=1}^{k} nb_i * mc_i \right)$$

where

w_1, w_2 = weights that indicate the relative influence of the overall attitude toward the object and the normative influence to purchase the product

$\Sigma a_i * b_i$ = the overall attitude toward the object. The overall attitude is formed by the multiplicative product of a_i (the person's evaluation of attribute i), and b_i (here defined as the importance of attribute i in the purchase decision). The sum is taken over the k attributes that are defined as salient in the purchase decision. For example:

Please consider the Toyota Corolla, and evaluate the following characteristics:

Importance				Performance			
Not at all Important	Somewhat Unimportant	Somewhat Important	Very Important	Poor	Good	Very Good	Excellent
Gets 35 miles per galion.							
○	○	○	○	○	○	○	○
Has a five-year/50,000-mile drive train warranty.							
○	○	○	○	○	○	○	○

$\Sigma nb_i * mc_i$ = The overall normative component of the decision process. This is computed as the multiplicative product of nb_i (the norms governing attitude i), and mc_i (the motivation of the respondent to comply with those norms). For example:

The normative component is often considered to be absorbed in the overall attitude component and depending on the application, is often ignored.

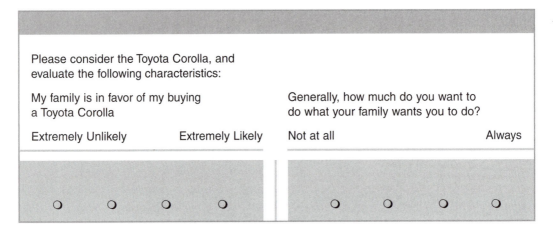

Please consider the Toyota Corolla, and evaluate the following characteristics:

My family is in favor of my buying a Toyota Corolla	Generally, how much do you want to do what your family wants you to do?
Extremely Unlikely Extremely Likely	Not at all Always

The Multi-Attribute Attitude Model

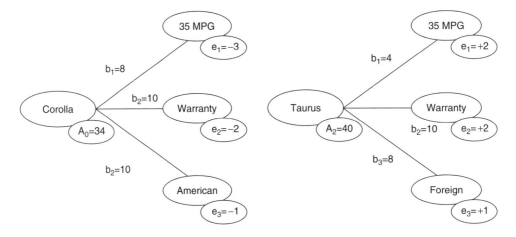

$$Attitude_{Corolla} = \sum_{i=1}^{3} b_i e_i$$

$$A_e = (8)(3) + (10)(2) + (10)(-1)$$

$$A_e = 24 + 20 - 10$$

$$A_e = 34$$

$$Attitude_{Taurus} = \sum_{i=1}^{3} b_i e_i$$

$$A_e = (4)(3) + (10)(2) = (8)(1)$$

$$A_e = 12 + 20 + 8$$

$$A_e = 40$$

III. Product/Service Attributes

Example 1. Attribute Importance

*A. How important are the following product characteristics to you in the selection of new **desktop publishing software packages?***

		Not Important			Moderately Important			Extremely Important		
		1	2	3	4	5	6	7	8	9
Please rate each product characteristic on a scale of 1 to 9, where 1 equals not important, 5 equals moderately important, and 9 equals extremely important.	Completeness & Organization of Documentation	☐	☐	☐	☐	☐	☐	☐	☐	☐
	Clarity of Documentation	☐	☐	☐	☐	☐	☐	☐	☐	☐
	Ease of Training/Ease of Use	☐	☐	☐	☐	☐	☐	☐	☐	☐
	Input/Output Driver Support	☐	☐	☐	☐	☐	☐	☐	☐	☐
	PostScript Printer Compatibility	☐	☐	☐	☐	☐	☐	☐	☐	☐
	Accuracy of On-Screen Representation	☐	☐	☐	☐	☐	☐	☐	☐	☐
	Overall Quality of Output	☐	☐	☐	☐	☐	☐	☐	☐	☐
	Accessibility of Product Support	☐	☐	☐	☐	☐	☐	☐	☐	☐
	Quality of Product Support	☐	☐	☐	☐	☐	☐	☐	☐	☐
	Value Relative to Cost	☐	☐	☐	☐	☐	☐	☐	☐	☐
	Overall Reliability	☐	☐	☐	☐	☐	☐	☐	☐	☐
	Overall Performance	☐	☐	☐	☐	☐	☐	☐	☐	☐

B. Please divide 10 points among the four items listed below to indicate how important each of these was to you in selecting today's flight. The more important one of these items was to you in selecting your flight, the more points you should give it. You may give any statement all or none of the 10 points, or as many or as few as you like, but please remember, THE TOTAL NUMBER OF POINTS YOU GIVE MUST ADD TO 10.

	NUMBER OF POINTS	Fill in the circle that matches the points you assign to each item. If no points are assigned to an item, fill in the zero.										
		0	1	2	3	4	5	6	7	8	9	10
Schedule Convenience.............												
Price of the Ticket..............		○	○	○	○	○	○	○	○	○	○	○
Frequent Flyer Mileage Program...		○	○	○	○	○	○	○	○	○	○	○
Airline Preference...............		○	○	○	○	○	○	○	○	○	○	○
<u>Must add to</u>	10											

(Continued)

C. Please tell us how important each of the following was in making your decision to choose Caren for today's flight.

	Very Important	Somewhat Important	Not at all Important
Carent's departure and/or arrival time was more convenient.	☐	☐	☐
Carent's flight had fewer stops or better connections	☐	☐	☐
Carent's air fare was better	☐	☐	☐
Carent's Mileage program	☐	☐	☐
Carent's in-flight services are better (meals, movies, flight attendants, etc.)	☐	☐	☐
Carent's ground services are better (ticketing, baggage handling, check-in, etc.)	☐	☐	☐
Personal preference for Caren Airlines	☐	☐	☐
Caren was the only airline with seats available	☐	☐	☐
Travel agent/Company travel department recommendation of Caren Airlines	☐	☐	☐
Aircraft preference	☐	☐	☐

Example 2. Attribute Evaluation

A. Below are several pairs or words that can be used to describe department stores. Place a check in the one box in each row (i.e. good selection-poor selection) that best indicates the way you would describe each store. Example: For the pair of words, good location-poor location, box three has been checked to indicate that the store has a somewhat poor location.

	Very 1	Somewhat 2	Somewhat 3	Very 4	
Good location	☐	☐	☒	☐	Poor location

SAKS FIFTH AVENUE
(Place one check in each row)

	Very		**Somewhat**		**Somewhat**		**Very**		
Good selection	1	☐	2	☐	3	☐	4	☐	Poor selection
High prices	1	☐	2	☐	3	☐	4	☐	Low prices
High quality	1	☐	2	☐	3	☐	4	☐	Low quality
High fashion	1	☐	2	☐	3	☐	4	☐	Low fashion
Good service	1	☐	2	☐	3	☐	4	☐	Poor service
Easy to shop in	1	☐	2	☐	3	☐	4	☐	Difficult to shop in
Friendly	1	☐	2	☐	3	☐	4	☐	Cold
Good sales and promotions	1	☐	2	☐	3	☐	4	☐	Poor sales and promotions

IV. Psychographics

Example 1. Clothing Purchases

	Definitely Agree	Somewhat Agree	Neither Agree nor Disagree	Somewhat Agree	Definitely Disagree
I buy clothes I like, regardless of current fashion.	O	O	O	O	O
I buy new fashion looks only when they are well accepted.	O	O	O	O	O
I am not as concerned about fashion as I am about modest prices and wearability.	O	O	O	O	O
I prefer to buy well-known designer labels rather than take a chance on something new.	O	O	O	O	O
My friends regard me as a good source of advice on fashion selection.	O	O	O	O	O
I am confident of my own good taste in clothing.	O	O	O	O	O
I am not afraid to be the first to wear something different in fashion looks.	O	O	O	O	O
I like to buy clothes.	O	O	O	O	O
I feel good when I buy something new.	O	O	O	O	O
I like clothes that make the most of my figure.	O	O	O	O	O
I am the first to try new fashions, therefore many people regard me as being a fashion pacesetter.	O	O	O	O	O
In this period of rising prices, spending excessive amounts of money on clothes is ridiculous.	O	O	O	O	O
What you think of yourself is reflected by what you wear.	O	O	O	O	O
I plan my shopping trips carefully.	O	O	O	O	O

Example 2. Attribute Evaluation

A. Below are several pairs or words that can be used to describe department stores. Place a check in the one box in each row (i.e., good selection/poor selection) that best indicates the way you would describe each store. Example: For the pair of words "good location/poor location," box three has been checked to indicate that the store has a somewhat poor location.

Good location ○	○	○	○	Poor location ○
Good selection ○	○	○	○	Poor selection ○
High prices ○	○	○	○	Low prices ○
High quality ○	○	○	○	Low quality ○
High fashion ○	○	○	○	Low fashion ○
Good service ○	○	○	○	Poor service ○
Easy to shop in ○	○	○	○	Difficult to shop in ○
Friendly ○	○	○	○	Cold ○
Good sales and promotions ○	○	○	○	Poor sales and promotions ○
Sophisticated ○	○	○	○	Down-to-earth ○
Traditional ○	○	○	○	Modern ○
Different ○	○	○	○	Conventional ○
Take chances ○	○	○	○	Play it safe ○
Confident ○	○	○	○	Uncertain ○
Creative ○	○	○	○	Stable ○
Sociable ○	○	○	○	Reserved ○
Stands out in the crowd ○	○	○	○	Blends into the crowd ○
Simplified lifestyle ○	○	○	○	Complicated lifestyle ○

B. How would you evaluate the Center for Women's Health on the following:

Not convenient				Very convenient
○	○	○	○	○
Low-cost hospital				High-cost hospital
○	○	○	○	○
Poor-quality medical care				High-quality medical care
○	○	○	○	○
Does not understand women's total needs				Good understanding of woman's total needs
○	○	○	○	○
Inferior physicians on staff				Superior Physicians on staff
○	○	○	○	○
Patients have no options or control over their hospital experience				Patients have many options/control
○	○	○	○	○
Not at all caring, responsive, and restful				Very caring, responsive and restful
○	○	○	○	○
Provides little education and information				Provides much education and information
○	○	○	○	○
Not very sophisticated				Very sophisticated
○	○	○	○	○

V. Consumer Satisfaction Research

(a) Evaluative/Cognitive Measures in Consumer Satisfaction

Verbal

Disconfirmation measures

1. My expectations were:

   Too high: Accurate: Too low:
   It was poorer than I thought   It was just as I had expected   It was better than I thought

   _____ :   _____ :   _____ :   _____ :   _____ :   _____ :   _____ :

2. _____ was much better (worse) than I expected.

   Yes   Strong   Yes   ?   No   Strong   Very
   Strong   Yes   No   Strong
   Yes   No
   No

   _____ :   _____ :   _____ :   _____ :   _____ :   _____ :   _____ :

   Degree of satisfaction measure

3. Overall, how satisfied have you been with this _____?

100%	90	80	70	60	50	40	30	20	10	0%
Completely					(Half & Half)					Not at all
Satisfied										Satisfied

4. How satisfied were you with _____?

Very Dissatisfied	Somewhat Dissatisfied	Slightly Dissatisfied	Neither	Slightly Satisfied	Somewhat Satisfied	Very Satisfied
_____	_____	_____	_____	_____	_____	_____

5. I am always or   I am sometimes   I am sometimes   I am always or almost
   almost always   satisfied with . . .   dissatisfied with . . . always dissatisfied with . . .
   satisfied with . . .

   _____   _____   _____   _____

6. Now that you've actually used the product, how satisfied with it are you?

   Dissatisfied   Satisfied

   ____ ____ ____ ____ ____ ____ ____ ____ ____ ____ ____

7. I am satisfied with _____.

   Agree _____ :   _____ :   _____ :   _____ :   _____ :   _____ :   _____ :   _____ :   _____ Disagree

Other evaluations

8. To what extent does this _____ meet your needs at this time?

   Extremely Well ____ : ____ : ____ : ____ : ____ : ____ : ____ : ____ : ____ : ____ Extremely Poorly

Graphic

9. Imagine that the following circles represent the satisfaction of different people with _____. Circle 0 has minuses in it, to represent a person who is completely dissatisfied with _____. Circle 8 has all pluses in it, to represent a person who is completely satisfied with _____. Other circles are in between.

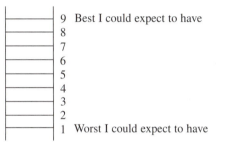

Which circle do you think comes closest to matching your satisfaction with _____? Write the circle number here: _____.

10. Here is a picture of a ladder. At the bottom of the ladder is the worst _____ you might reasonably expect to have. At the top is the best _____ you might expect to have. On which rung would you put _____?

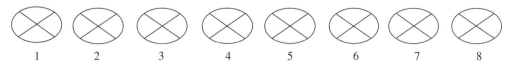

9 Best I could expect to have
8
7
6
5
4
3
2
1 Worst I could expect to have

(b) Emotional/Affective Measures in Consumer Satisfaction

Verbal

11. Likert scales

   a. I am satisfied with _____.

   b. If I had it to do all over again, I would _____.

   c. My choice to _____ was a good one.

   d. I feel bad about my decision concerning _____.

   e. I think that I did the right think when I decided _____.

   f. I am not happy that I did what I did about _____.

   Agree...(9)...(7)...(5) Disagree

   Strongly Agree..........Sometimes Disagree

12. Mark on one of the nine blanks below the position that most closely reflects your satisfaction with _____.

Delighted	Pleased Satisfied	Mostly	Mixed Dissatisfied	Mostly	Unhappy	Terrible	Neutral Thought	Never

(Continued)

Graphic

13. How satisfied are you with your dining experience?
    I feel . . .

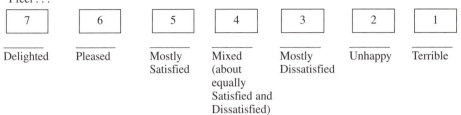

7	6	5	4	3	2	1
Delighted	Pleased	Mostly Satisfied	Mixed (about equally Satisfied and Dissatisfied)	Mostly Dissatisfied	Unhappy	Terrible

14. "Feeling" Thermometer
    Where would you put _____ on the feeling thermometer?

    WARM 100° — Very warm or favorable feeling
    | 85° — Good warm or favorable feeling
    | 70° — Fairly warm or favorable feeling
    | 60° — A bit more warm or favorable than cold feeling
    _____   50° — No feeling at all
    _____
               40° — A bit more cold or unfavorable feeling
    | 30° — Fairly cold or unfavorable feeling
    | 15° — Quite cold or unfavorable feeling
    COLD   0° — Very cold or unfavorable feeling

15. Smiling Faces scale

    The following faces express various feelings. Find the face that best shows your feeling about Miss Jeannie's Montessori School?

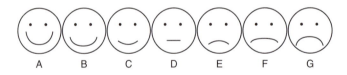

Verbal

Behavioral intentions

16. Frank's Bikes provides an excellent service and I would have my bike repaired here again.

Very Strong Yes	Strong Yes	Yes	?	No	Strong No	Very Strong No
_____	_____	_____	_____	_____	_____	_____

17. How likely are you to purchase Brand X in the future?

Very Likely	Unlikely	Likely	Very Likely
−2	−1	+1	+2

SOURCE: Adapted from Hausknecht, 1990.

Cases for Part III

CASE STUDY III–1

Intra-State Bank

Jim Hawkins, the new CEO of Intra-State Bank needs an image study to determine how his customers perceive the bank. He wants to know what banking services are desired by his customers and how to inform customers of the services that are available.

The bank, which is located in a western state, operates six branches:

1. Big Mountain
2. City Center
3. Lake View
4. Stadium Square
5. Crossroads Mall
6. University Center

Mr. Hawkins contracted with a local market research firm, MBA Associates, to conduct a study that would find the following information:

- Demographic description of current customers
- Customer perception of the current services provided
- Services desired by the customers
- Customers' views and use of Automated Teller Machines (ATMs)
- Customers' knowledge of and attitudes toward current advertising of the bank

MBA Associates assigned Mr. Mike Swoonson to be project director. Mr. Swoonson knew that he must develop a data collection and sampling plan and a questionnaire for data collection, and then he must implement these plans to obtain the needed data from the members of the selected sample. You have been assigned to assist Mr. Swoonson.

QUESTIONS FOR DISCUSSION

1. Develop a questionnaire that can be used by Intra-State Bank to obtain the information needed.

2. How would this questionnaire differ by mode of data collection—mail, telephone, personal interview, or Internet?

3. What types of scaling would you include? Explain your choices.

CASE STUDY III–2

Merchant's Association Shopper Survey

A merchant's association for a relatively small shopping center located in a metropolitan area of 150,000 population conducted a survey of shoppers. The survey used a self-report questionnaire and there were no interviewers present. Rather, the questionnaires were placed on a table in the mall with a sign asking people to participate. The following questionnaire was used.

MARTIN MALL–QUICK ROAD MERCHANT'S ASSOCIATION SHOPPER'S SURVEY

In an attempt to serve you better, the Martin Mall–Quick Road Merchant's Association requests that you complete this questionnaire and deposit it in the special container marked *"Deposit Shopper's Survey Here"* located in the Mall. All information is strictly confidential and *you need not sign the Survey.* Your cooperation will be sincerely appreciated.

Check one: Male _____   Female _____

1. Name of city or town in which you live _____

2. How long have you lived there? _____

3. Are you buying or renting a home? _____

4. How many automobiles in your household? _____

5. Husband's occupation? _____

6. Wife's occupation? _____

7. What is your annual income? (If both husband and wife work, please indicate total.) _____

8. What is your age? _____

9. Number of children in your family? _____

10. What are the ages of your children? _____

11. What radio station do you listen to most? _____

12. How often do you shop the Martin-Quick area? (Check one.)

    Weekly _____   Once or twice a month _____

    1–6 times a year _____   Only during special sales or events _____

13. Do you enjoy shopping the Martin-Quick area? Yes _____   No _____

14. In general, how would you rate the people who work the Martin-Quick shopping area on courtesy?

    Excellent _____   Good _____   Fair _____   Poor _____   Very Poor _____

15. In general, are you able to find what you are shopping for in the Martin-Quick area? _____
    _____

16. How much time per shopping trip do you spend in the Martin Mall–Quick Road shopping area?
    _____

QUESTIONS FOR DISCUSSION

1. What response errors are likely to arise? Explain.

2. Evaluate this survey and the questionnaire used as decisional research.

3. Revise the questionnaire to better obtain the information being sought.

CASES STUDY III–3

Caren Airlines

Caren Airlines (disguised name) conducts periodic in-flight passenger surveys. Caren views these surveys as providing information, current and trends, relevant to three major areas:

1. Attitudes toward ground and in-flight services

2. Behavior associated with air travel

3. Characteristics of Caren Airlines passengers

A preferred approach to data collection is to prepare a questionnaire such that responses to the questions can be machine read directly from the form. For convenience in administration, questionnaires are limited in size to four letter-size pages ($8\frac{1}{2} \times 11$ inches). One oversized sheet of paper (11×17 inches) is folded to give four pages.

Often, the needs of a particular survey require a series of questions that exceed the four-page format. Alternative data collection methods for this situation are to expand the length of the questionnaire or use a split-ballot approach. When a split-ballot is used, flight attendants randomly distribute the forms to passengers in-flight and passengers self-report. The split-ballot approach can be administered either by using separate flights for each version or by administering all versions on each flight. Caren uses the latter approach.

As an example of the split-ballot approach, Caren recently sought information regarding descriptive aspects of the trip being taken, how arrangements were made and how the airline was chosen, service at check-in and during the boarding process, in-flight service, and demographic information. When the project director completed the questionnaire it included 64 questions, a few of which were multi-part. Some of the attitudinal questions were multi-item rating scales with as many as 10 items. Because of the length of the questionnaire the decision was made to use a split ballot, and three versions were developed. Ten substantive and 6 demographic questions were common to all three versions. Each version also included 16 unique substantive questions that covered arrangements, check-in service, or in-flight service.

All versions were administered by the flight attendants on each flight on the same date.

QUESTION FOR DISCUSSION

1. Should Caren Airlines use the split-ballot approach for collecting data? What alternatives might have been used?

CASE STUDY III–4

Syd Company (B)

FC Associates agreed to do an exploratory study for the Syd Company, a large packaged consumer goods company. The project related to whether Syd should enter the women's shampoo market, a market for which it did not at present have a product. The study was to be concentrated among young female adults aged 18 through 30.

The concerns of Syd management and the overall design selected by FC Associates were discussed in the Syd Company (A) case at the end of Part I. For clarification, primary research questions are repeated here:

1. How do consumers of hair shampoos perceive various benefits as commonly (or rarely) available in shampoos currently on the market?

2. Given freedom to make up their own ideal shampoo, what combination of benefits do consumers want? Specifically, how often is "body" included in consumers' ideal benefit bundles?

3. Assuming that a consumer desired and could get a shampoo that delivered "body," what other benefits are also desired in the same brand?

4. What is conjured up by the term "body" in regards to shampoo, and what are its various connotations—that is, what words are elicited on a free-association basis?

5. How do preferences for "body" in shampoo benefits relate to
   a. Frequency of hair shampooing (i.e., heavy versus light users of shampoos)?
   b. Perceptions of its availability in current shampoos?
   c. Preference for other benefits in addition to "body"?
   d. Hair physiology and wearing style?
   e. Demographics (e.g., age, marital status, education, etc.)?

With these questions in mind, FC Associates designed the questionnaire shown in Figure III–4.1. The personal interview was selected as the mode of data collection because the types of questions raised meant that various interviewer props would be needed.

Note that the first two questions serve as screening criteria; in other words, to qualify for inclusion the respondent must both shampoo her hair at home at least twice a month on the average and be between 18 and 30 years of age.

Part A of the questionnaire first attempts to measure respondents' perceptions of the prevalence of each shampoo benefit in brands currently on the market. Then, respondents are allowed to choose from the total set of 16 benefits [see the Syd (A) case] those four benefits that they would most like to have in an ideal shampoo. Part B—using the first 10 benefits in Table 1 of the Syd (A) case—examines respondents' benefit preferences in a conditional sense, assuming that they could obtain a shampoo that delivered "body."

Part C deals with free-association data, whereas Part D requests information on hairstyle and hair problems. Part E is devoted to more or less standard questions dealing with demographic variables.

Time Interview Started _____
Ended _____

Respondent Name _____   Respondent No. _____

Address _____

City _____   State _____   Zip Code _____

Telephone No. _____

Interviewer Name _____

Interview Date _____

Screening Questions (Part S)

Hello, I'm _____ of FC Associates. We're conducting a survey on women's attitudes and opinions about hair care products.

1. On the average, how often do you shampoo your hair at home?
   More than twice a week _____
   Once or twice a week _____
   Once or twice every two weeks _____
   Once or twice every three weeks _____
   Twice a month _____
   Less than twice a month _____
   IF LESS THAN TWICE A MONTH, TERMINATE INTERVIEW

2. What is your age? _____
   IF UNDER 18 OR OVER 30 TERMINATE INTERVIEW

PART A

First I'm going to show you a set of 16 cards. Each card contains the name of a benefit that a hair shampoo might provide. (PLACE SET OF WHITE CARDS ON TABLE IN FRONT OF RESPONDENT.) Please take a few moments to look over these benefits. (ALLOW TIME FOR RESPONDENT TO STUDY THE CARDS.)

Now, thinking about various brands of hair shampoo that you have tried or heard about, pick out those benefits that you think are most likely to be found in almost any hair shampoo that one could buy today. (RECORD CARD NUMBERS IN FIRST COLUMN OF RESPONSE FORM A AND TURN SELECTED CARDS FACE DOWN.)

Next, select all of those remaining benefits that you think are available in at least some hair shampoo—but not necessarily all in a single brand—that's currently on the market. (RECORD CARD NUMBERS IN SECOND COLUMN OF RESPONSE FORM A. RECORD REMAINING CARD NUMBERS IN THIRD COLUMN. THEN RETURN ALL CARDS TO TABLE.)

Next, imagine that you could make up an ideal type of shampoo—one that might not be available on today's market. Suppose, however, that you were restricted to only four of the sixteen benefits shown on the cards in front of you. Which four of the sixteen benefits would you most like to have? (RECORD CARD NUMBERS IN FOURTH COLUMN OF RESPONSE FORM A.)

RESPONSE FORM A			
(1)	(2)	(3)	(4)
Benefits Most Likely to be Found in Almost Any Hair Shampoo— Card Numbers	Benefits Available in Some Shampoos— Card Numbers	Remaining Benefits—Card Numbers	Four-Benefit Ideal Set—Card Numbers

Figure III-4.1   Interviewer Questionnaire Used in Hair Shampoo Study

PART B

Now, let's again return to some of the shampoo benefits you have already dealt with. (SELECT WHITE CARD NUMBERS 1 THROUGH 10; PULL OUT CARD 4 AND PLACE IT IN FRONT OF RESPONDENT.)

Suppose a shampoo were on the market that primarily stressed this benefit," Produces Hair That Has Body." If you could get a shampoo that made good on this claim, which one of the remaining nine benefits would you most like to have as well? (RECORD NUMBER IN RESPONSE FORM B.) Which next most? (RECORD.) Please continue until all of the 9 benefits have been ranked.

RESPONSE FORM B

(Enter Card Numbers 1 Through 10 Excluding Card #4)

( ) Most Like to Have   ( )   ( )
( ) Next Most   ( )   ( )
( )   ( )   ( ) Least Most

PART C

Now, I am going to read to you some short phrases about hair. Listen to each phrase carefully and then tell me what single words first come to your mind when you hear each phrase? (RECORD UP TO THE FIRST THREE "ASSOCIATIVE-TYPE" WORDS THE RESPONDENT SAYS AFTER EACH PHRASE IN RESPONSE FORM C.)

RESPONSE FORM C

(a) Hair that has body   _____   _____   _____

(b) Hair with fullness   _____   _____   _____

(c) Hair that holds a set   _____   _____   _____

(d) Bouncy hair   _____   _____   _____

(e) Hair that's not limp   _____   _____   _____

(f) Manageable hair   _____   _____   _____

(g) Zesty hair   _____   _____   _____

(h) Natural hair   _____   _____   _____

PART D

At this point I would like to ask you a few questions about your hair.

1. Does your hair have enough body?   Yes _____   No _____

2. Do you have any special problems with your hair?   Yes _____   No _____

   If yes, what types of problems? _____

_____

How would you describe your hair?

3. My hair type is: Dry _____   Normal _____   Oily _____

4. The texture of my hair is: Fine _____   Normal _____   Coarse _____

5. My hair style (the way I wear my hair) is: Straight _____   Slightly wavy or curly _____

                                           Very wavy or curly_____

(Continued)

6. The length of my hair is: Short (to ear lobes) _____

   Medium (ear lobes to shoulder) _____   Long (below shoulder) _____

7. How would you describe the thickness of your hair?   Thick _____   Medium _____

                                            Thin _____

PART E

Now I would like to ask you a few background questions.

1. Are you working (at least twenty hours per week, for compensation)?   Yes _____   No _____

2. Are you married?   Yes _____   No _____

3. What is your level of education?

   Some high school _____   Completed high schoo _____

   Some college _____   Completed college _____

4. (HAND RESPONDENT INCOME CARD.) Which letter on this card comes closest to describing your total annual <u>family</u> income before taxes? (CIRCLE APPROPRIATE LETTER.)

   A. Under $10,000

   B. $10,000 – $20,000

   C. $20,001 – $30,000

   D. $30,001 – $50,000

   E. $50,001 – $75,000

   F. $75,001 – $100,000

   G. Over $100,000

(THANKS VERY MUCH FOR YOUR HELP)

QUESTIONS FOR DISCUSSION

1. Critically evaluate this questionnaire in the context of proper questionnaire design.

2. How would you approach the same (shampoo-benefits) problem if you were
   a. developing a mail questionnaire?
   b. developing a telephone questionnaire?
   c. developing an Internet questionnaire?

3. Suppose that you wished to add a section to the questionnaire that dealt with general attitudes toward hair and personal grooming.

   a. Prepare a set of sample statements that ask for the respondent's degree of agreement/disagreement.
   b. What other aspects of lifestyle might be worthwhile to include?

4. What kinds of questions should be added regarding
   a. Other types of hair-grooming products, such as rinses and setting gels?
   b. Current brand usage and preference?

Case Study III–5

Day Airlines (A)

Day Airlines is a large United States–based commercial airline that specializes in passenger flights to Mexico, the Caribbean, Central America, and South America. Recently its president, Rafael Falcon, approached his marketing research manager, Kurt Abba, to inquire if a study could be undertaken that would help prospective vacationers select a location that suited their interests and background.

Kurt, a former pilot, was new at the job of marketing research. Accordingly, he sought the services of several consultants, each of whom was a specialist in one of the areas Kurt thought would be relevant to this study:

- Psychographics
- Motivation research
- Preference analysis

The result of their deliberation was the questionnaire shown in Exhibit III–5.1. Kurt, however, was still somewhat apprehensive of the group's resulting "product."

As noted from the questionnaire, the survey deals primarily with four major aspects of a vacation:

1. Psychographics are contained in Question 1 of the questionnaire.

2. Preferences for a variety of interests and activities associated with taking a vacation.

3. Characteristics of respondent's next vacation, such as time of year, anticipated duration, and so forth are asked in Questions 20 through 23.

4. Places already visited and, if visited, liked or not liked are listed in Question 26.

Kurt has data available on the attractions and general characteristics of each of the 22 foreign countries that Day Airlines serves.

EXHIBIT III–5.1 Questionnaire

Questions	Column A Statement	Column B – Phrase				
		Strongly Agree (1)	Tend to Agree (2)	Hard to Decide (3)	Tend to Disagree (4)	Strongly Disagree (5)
1. To the right is a list of statements under *Column A*. Please put a check mark in a box under *Column B* for the phrase which most expresses how you feel about each statement.	1. I usually have one or more outfits of the very latest styles.	☐	☐	☐	☐	☐
	2. Work is a drag.	☐	☐	☐	☐	☐
	3. Most people respect what I say.	☐	☐	☐	☐	☐
	4. I hate days that are very humid.	☐	☐	☐	☐	☐
	5. Ben Franklin was a bore.	☐	☐	☐	☐	☐
	6. There is no excuse for poor planning.	☐	☐	☐	☐	☐
	7. Too much sunshine makes me ill.	☐	☐	☐	☐	☐
	8. I wish most days were longer.	☐	☐	☐	☐	☐
	9. Parents should spend a lot of time educating their children themselves.	☐	☐	☐	☐	☐
	10. I often take the long route home from work, even if I am in a hurry.	☐	☐	☐	☐	☐
	11. I love seafood and eat it whenever I can.	☐	☐	☐	☐	☐
	12. I phone a physician whenever I am feeling ill.	☐	☐	☐	☐	☐
	13. I enjoy hot weather.	☐	☐	☐	☐	☐
	14. I am very interested in nature and wildlife.	☐	☐	☐	☐	☐
	15. I hate to follow the crowds and do what the masses do.	☐	☐	☐	☐	☐
	16. I hate to have my plans interrupted by the weather.	☐	☐	☐	☐	☐

(Continued)

Questions	Column A Statement	Column B – Phrase				
		Strongly Agree (1)	Tend to Agree (2)	Hard to Decide (3)	Tend to Disagree (4)	Strongly Disagree (5)
	17. Skydiving is a sport I would enjoy.	☐	☐	☐	☐	☐
	18. I usually donate to local community agencies.	☐	☐	☐	☐	☐
	19. Driving alone at night scares the hell out of me.	☐	☐	☐	☐	☐
	20. Happiness is a double martini at the end of the day.	☐	☐	☐	☐	☐
	21. Even though I enjoy good food, I am quite conscious of my weight.	☐	☐	☐	☐	☐
	22. I believe in giving children lots of help and advice.	☐	☐	☐	☐	☐
	23. I admire big spenders.	☐	☐	☐	☐	☐
	24. I have never been on a diet.	☐	☐	☐	☐	☐
	25. I usually make decisions on my own.	☐	☐	☐	☐	☐
	26. I am almost never late for an appointment.	☐	☐	☐	☐	☐
	27. I am quite active in the PTA.	☐	☐	☐	☐	☐
	28. I like my house to look spotless when people visit.	☐	☐	☐	☐	☐
	29. When I was young, I learned the value of money.	☐	☐	☐	☐	☐
	30. I"d like to try living in a commune.	☐	☐	☐	☐	☐
	31. Children should never be spanked.	☐	☐	☐	☐	☐
	32. I would like to be a fashion model.	☐	☐	☐	☐	☐
	33. Blue jeans are all the clothes I want.	☐	☐	☐	☐	☐
	34. I like to walk around in strange cities.	☐	☐	☐	☐	☐

(Continued)

2. What sounds like you? Please put a check mark underneath the one you pick.	3. Which one would you like to be? Please put a check mark underneath the one you pick.

4. Which, if any, of the following 8 people would you like to meet on your vacation? Please make a *first, second,* and *third* choice only.	First Choice (1)	Second Choice (2)	Third Choice (3)
1. A fire-walker to lead you through a live volcano.	☐	☐	☐
2. A guide to take you through a delicious-smelling rum distillery.	☐	☐	☐
3. A mountain climber to show you the way to the summit.	☐	☐	☐
4. A grower to take you around a plantation so you can learn all about sugar cane.	☐	☐	☐
5. A pan man to play a tune for you on a steel drum.	☐	☐	☐
6. A naturalist to name the tropical birds and plants for you.	☐	☐	☐
7. A drummer to evoke the ancient sounds of Africa.	☐	☐	☐
8. A marvelous cook to teach you a little West Indian food magic.	☐	☐	☐
Would not care to meet any.	☐	☐	☐

Questions	Activities	Column A 5 Most Like	Column B				
			Prefer Most (1)	Second (2)	Third (3)	Fourth (4)	Fifth (5)
5. To the right is a list of 23 different activities. From the list, we would like you to *pick only 5 activities* that you would most like to do on your next vacation. *Please put your answers in Column A.*	1. Swim at best beaches	☐	☐	☐	☐	☐	☐
	2. Water Ski	☐	☐	☐	☐	☐	☐
	3. Snorkel/ Scuba dive/ Underwater photography	☐	☐	☐	☐	☐	☐
	4. Go sailing for a day	☐	☐	☐	☐	☐	☐

(Continued)

Questions	Activities	Column A 5 Most Like	Column B				
			Prefer Most (1)	Second (2)	Third (3)	Fourth (4)	Fifth (5)
a. Now, would you *rank these 5 activities* you just checked in terms of preference. That is, which one would you prefer the *most*, then prefer *second*, prefer *third, fourth*, and then *fifth*. *Please* put your answers in *Column B*.	5. Charter a yacht for a week or more to sail through the islands	☐	☐	☐	☐	☐	☐
	6. Play golf	☐	☐	☐	☐	☐	☐
	7. Play tennis	☐	☐	☐	☐	☐	☐
	8. Collect shells	☐	☐	☐	☐	☐	☐
	9. Go hiking	☐	☐	☐	☐	☐	☐
	10. Go horseback riding	☐	☐	☐	☐	☐	☐
	11. Go on a picnic	☐	☐	☐	☐	☐	☐
	12. Go cycling	☐	☐	☐	☐	☐	☐
	13. Go rafting on a river	☐	☐	☐	☐	☐	☐
	14. Go camping with tents	☐	☐	☐	☐	☐	☐
	15. Rent a camper	☐	☐	☐	☐	☐	☐
	16. Go sightseeing	☐	☐	☐	☐	☐	☐
	17. Go deep sea fishing for marlin or tuna	☐	☐	☐	☐	☐	☐
	18. Go big game fishing for wahoo, bonito, dolphin, sailfish, kingfish, amberjack or swordfish	☐	☐	☐	☐	☐	☐
	19. Fish the flats for bonefish or permit	☐	☐	☐	☐	☐	☐

(Continued)

Questions	Activities	Column A 5 Most Like	Column B				
			Prefer Most (1)	Second (2)	Third (3)	Fourth (4)	Fifth (5)
	20. Fish with light tackle for barracuda, tarpon	☐	☐	☐	☐	☐	☐
	21. Go reef or bottom fishing for snapper, grouper, queen trigggerfish, or yellow tail	☐	☐	☐	☐	☐	☐
	22. Go fresh water fishing for bass, bream, or catfish	☐	☐	☐	☐	☐	☐
	23. Go shopping at "duty free" shops where you find merchandise from all over the world at low prices	☐	☐	☐	☐	☐	☐

	History/Historical Sites	First Choice (1)	Second Choice (2)	Third Choice (3)
6. Next please rate your interest, if any, in respect to History/Historical sites. That is, which of the following items to the right do you have an interest in and would like to explore on your next vacation? Please give your *first, second,* and *third* choices only from the list of seven.	1. Arawak/Carib	☐	☐	☐
	2. Pre-Columbian	☐	☐	☐
	3. Spanish, 17th, 18th Century	☐	☐	☐
	4. British, 18th, 19th Century	☐	☐	☐
	5. Dutch, 18th, 19th Century	☐	☐	☐
	6. Danish, 19th Century	☐	☐	☐
	7. French, 18th, 19th Century	☐	☐	☐
	No interest in any.			☐

(Continued)

7. Now please give *first, second,* and *third* choices only on the following 11 items to the right related to your interest, if any, in Nature and Natural Scenery.	*Nature/Natural Scenery*	First Choice (1)	Second Choice (2)	Third Choice (3)
	1. National/State Parks	☐	☐	☐
	2. Rain Forests	☐	☐	☐
	3. Tropical Birds	☐	☐	☐
	4. Marine Life	☐	☐	☐
	5. Wildlife Refuges	☐	☐	☐
	6. Mountains	☐	☐	☐
	7. Everglades	☐	☐	☐
	8. Plantations	☐	☐	☐
	9. Volcanoes	☐	☐	☐
	10. Tropical Flora	☐	☐	☐
	11. Waterfalls	☐	☐	☐
	No interest in any.			☐
8. And your *first, second,* and *third* choices from the list of 6 items, concerning your interest in seeing exhibits of Native Arts and Crafts.	*Native Arts and Crafts*			
	1. Painting and Sculpture	☐	☐	☐
	2. Pottery and Ceramics	☐	☐	☐
	3. Silver Jewelry	☐	☐	☐
	4. Woodcarvings	☐	☐	☐
	5. Straw, Sisal and Hemp Crafts	☐	☐	☐
	6. Religious Art/Wood Figurines	☐	☐	☐
	No interest in any.			☐
9. Now your *first, second,* and *third* choices from the list of 9 items, related to your interest, if any, in Architecture.	*Architecture*			
	1. Spanish Colonial	☐	☐	☐
	2. Plantation Greathouses	☐	☐	☐
	3. Georgian	☐	☐	☐
	4. Danish Colonial	☐	☐	☐
	5. Victorian	☐	☐	☐
	6. Dutch Colonial	☐	☐	☐
	7. Pre-Columbian	☐	☐	☐
	8. French Colonial	☐	☐	☐
	9. British 18th, 19th Century	☐	☐	☐
	No interest in any.			☐

(Continued)

10. And your *first, second,* and third choices only from the following 6 items listed to the right related to your interest, if any, in Spectacles.	*Spectacles*	First Choice (1)	Second Choice (2)	Third Choice (3)
	1. Fiestas/Carnivals	☐	☐	☐
	2. Jai Alai Matches	☐	☐	☐
	3. Horse Races	☐	☐	☐
	4. Bull Fights	☐	☐	☐
	5. Soccer Matches	☐	☐	☐
	6. Polo	☐	☐	☐
	No interest in any.			☐
11. Now from the list of 7 items to the right, pick the kind of Evening Entertainment, if any, you would enjoy at your next vacation. Please give your *first, second,* and *third* choices only.	*Evening Entertainment*			
	1. Gambling/Casinos	☐	☐	☐
	2. Top Name Entertainment	☐	☐	☐
	3. Native Music and Shows	☐	☐	☐
	4. Theater	☐	☐	☐
	5. Discotheque/Music for dancing	☐	☐	☐
	6. Folklore	☐	☐	☐
	7. Flamenco Dancing	☐	☐	☐
	No interest in any.			☐

12. Which design looks best? Please answer with a check mark on the one you pick.	

13. It's now possible to fly to Florida or Puerto Rico and spend your vacation aboard a luxurious cruise ship sailing the Caribbean for a week or more. Would this kind of air/sea vacation appeal to you? Please put your answer in a box to the right.	Yes (1) ☐	No (1) ☐

14. Would you like to spend your vacation on board a luxurious 60-foot yacht sailing the Caribbean? (The minimum charter is a week.)	Yes (1) ☐	No (1) ☐

15. Are you interested in the Food of another country— trying different kinds of foods that you usually don't have at home? If so, from the list of 10 items to the right please check your *first, second* and *third* choices only.	FOOD	First Choice (1)	Second Choice (2)	Third Choice (3)
	1. French/Creole	☐	☐	☐
	2. Spanish/Basque	☐	☐	☐
	3. Cuban	☐	☐	☐
	4. Puerto Rican	☐	☐	☐
	5. West Indian	☐	☐	☐
	6. Mexican	☐	☐	☐
	7. East Indian/Dutch	☐	☐	☐
	8. Bahamian	☐	☐	☐
	9. International	☐	☐	☐
	10. Fresh caught seafood	☐	☐	☐
	No interest in any.			☐

16. During which time of the year were you born? Please put a check mark in the appropriate space.	Jan 21-Feb 19	Mar 21-Apr 19	May 21-Jun 21	Jul 22-Aug 21	Sep 23-Oct 22	Nov 22-Dec 21
	(1)	(3)	(5)	(7)	(9)	(11)
	Feb 20-Mar 20	Apr 20-May 20	Jun 22-Jul 21	Aug 22-Sep 22	Oct 23-Nov 21	Dec 22-Jan 20
	(1)	(4)	(6)	(8)	(10)	(12)

	CHILDREN'S SECTION		*First Choice* (1)	*Second Choice* (2)	*Third Choice* (3)
NOTE: Please complete the following section, questions 17 and 18, only if you plan to take your children with you on this vacation and if you want your children to influence where you go on your vacation . . . if not, then skip to Q. 19.	17. Please check which of the following 11 places to stay you would be most comfortable in. Give *first, second,* and *third* choices only.	1. See Animals from Foreign Lands	☐	☐	☐
		2. Collect Seashells	☐	☐	☐
		3. Visit Museums	☐	☐	☐
		4. Ride Bicycles	☐	☐	☐
		5. Go on Picnics	☐	☐	☐
		6. See and Feed Tropical Birds	☐	☐	☐
		7. Go to the World's Biggest Amusement Park	☐	☐	☐
		8. Learn to Sail	☐	☐	☐
		9. Go Sightseeing	☐	☐	☐

(Continued)

CHILDREN'S SECTION		First Choice (1)	Second Choice (2)	Third Choice (3)
	10. Learn to Play Tennis or Golf	☐	☐	☐
	11. Go Fishing	☐	☐	☐
	No interest in any.			☐

18. Would you like a place that offers child-sitting services?	Yes (1) ☐		No (2) ☐

19. What route would you take to get from A to B? Please answer with a check mark underneath the one you pick.	
	1. _____ 2. _____ 3. _____ 4. _____

20. Which month of the year do you plan to take your next vacation? Check the box to the right.	Jan Feb Mar Apr May June July Aug Sept Oct Nov Dec 1 2 3 4 5 6 7 8 9 10 11 12

21. How many days do you plan to stay on your vacation? Check the box to the right.	Three to five days 1. _____	Seven days 2. _____	Ten days 3. _____	Fourteen days 4. _____	Longer 5. _____

22. Who else will be accompanying you on your vacation? Check as many boxes to the right as appropriate.	No one 1. _____	Wife 2. _____	Husband 3. _____	Adults other than spouse 4. _____	Children 5. _____

23. What price range of accommodations would you prefer? Check a box to the right.	Luxury 1. _____	Moderate 2. _____	Economy 3. _____

24. Please check which of the following 11 places to stay you would be most comfortable in		First Choice (1)	Second Choice (2)	Third Choice (3)
	12. A large hotel	☐	☐	☐
	13. A medium sized hotel	☐	☐	☐

Give *first, second,* and *third* choices only		First Choice (1)	Second Choice (2)	Third Choice (3)
	14. A small hotel	☐	☐	☐
	15. A motel	☐	☐	☐
	16. Your own private villa	☐	☐	☐
	17. An efficiency (housekeeping) apartment	☐	☐	☐
	18. Your own cottage	☐	☐	☐
	19. A guest house or inn	☐	☐	☐
	20. A stateroom aboard a cruise ship	☐	☐	☐
	21. A cabin on a chartered yacht	☐	☐	☐
	22. A camping tent	☐	☐	☐

25. Which window would you like to look through? Please check one underneath the picture.	
	1. _____ 2. _____ 3. _____ 4. _____ 5. _____

26. To the right is a list of 15 vacation places. In column A, please check any place on the list that you have been to. Then in Column B, please check any of those places that you would *not* care to go back to.	Places	HAVE BEEN TO	WOULD *NOT* CARE TO GO BACK TO
	1. The mountains	☐	☐
	2. Nearby sea shore	☐	☐
	3. A lake	☐	☐
	4. On a cruise	☐	☐
	5. Miami	☐	☐
	6. Other vacation places in Florida	☐	☐
	7. Bahamas	☐	☐
	8. Europe	☐	☐
	9. Puerto Rico	☐	☐
	10. The Virgin Islands	☐	☐
	11. Jamaica	☐	☐
	12. Other islands in West Indies	☐	☐
	13. Mexico	☐	☐
	14. Bermuda	☐	☐
	15. On a Chartered Yacht	☐	☐

Please write your own zip code number in the space provided below. This is very important for our processing.

ZIP CODE# ☐ ☐ ☐ ☐ ☐

Please print or type your name and address clearly. Thank you.

Mr.
Mrs.
Ms.
Miss

| Your First Name | Last Name |

Street Address

| City | State |

Telephone #

If you obtained this questionnaire from a Travel Agent whose imprint appears below, he will notify you as soon as your personal vacation analysis is ready.

If you did not obtain this questionnaire from a Travel Agent but would like a copy of your vacation analysis to be sent to one, please list his/her name and address below.

Travel Agent Name and Agency

Address

City/State

QUESTIONS FOR DISCUSSION

1. Assuming that you would be able to obtain any data you need on each country's tourist attractions, accommodations, land costs, and other factors related to tourism, how could the questionnaire responses be used to help prospective vacationers select a location that is consistent with their likes and dislikes?

2. What parts of the present questionnaire can be deleted? What new questions would you like to see added? (Please list them by the four major aspects of a vacation described above.)

3. Evaluate the use of scaling techniques in this questionnaire.

4. Is this too complicated a questionnaire to be administered over the Internet? Explain. What changes would have to be made?

CASE STUDY III–6

Subaru of America, Inc.

A Subaru automobile owner's experience at a Subaru dealership's sales and service departments helps define his or her opinion of the dealership and its employees, products, and practices. Subaru is extremely interested in not only meeting but also exceeding all of its customers' expectations, and in continuously fine-tuning its products and services. The company regularly gauges all facets of its customers' relationship with Subaru through its Owner Loyalty Program (OLP) customer surveys.

"The purpose of the program," says George Dubinsky, Owner Information Manager for Subaru of America, Inc., "is to provide our dealers with information that they can use for operational improvement. It's really to gauge the customer's experience and help make his or her next experience—or the experiences of the customers who follow them—better."

The surveys, which typically are mail surveys, are designed to be quick and easy to complete, and can even be completed via the Internet. There are three types of surveys: (1) the Purchase Experience Survey; (2) the Service Experience Survey; and (3) the Owner Experience Survey.

PURCHASE EXPERIENCE SURVEY

Subaru owners are introduced to the company's survey program through the Purchase Experience Survey, which is scheduled to arrive shortly after delivery of a new vehicle to the customer. In it, the customer is asked to rate several key aspects of his or her purchasing experience, from the time of arrival at the dealership through when the customer took delivery of the vehicle.

The findings of the program are reported back to the dealer and reviewed by the company's field management team. The dealers can use the survey results to make operational adjustments if they need to, whether it has to do with their negotiation methods, their hours of operation, their facilities, or even how they greet customers. The results really help the dealers make their customers' experiences better.

SERVICE EXPERIENCE SURVEY

When a customer returns to the dealership to have his or her vehicle serviced, the customer may receive a Service Experience Survey. It's sent to owners of new and used Subaru vehicles after warranty work is completed at a Subaru dealership. Even years after a customer drives his or her new vehicle off the lot, Subaru wants to make sure the customer is satisfied with the service provided by the dealership. Exhibit III–6.1 shows an example of a cover letter and questionnaire used in a Service Experience Survey sent by mail that provides customers an option to complete the survey online.

OWNER EXPERIENCE SURVEY

One version of the Owner Experience Survey is a Product Survey sent to a sampling of new Subaru owners every year. Unlike the company's other surveys, the Product Survey is intended to measure the quality of the owner's new Subaru vehicle. The survey helps ensure that new owners are satisfied with the performance, fit, and finish of their new vehicle. It also includes a section where owners can suggest improvements or changes they would like to see on future models. The company's designers and engineers look very closely at that survey for customer input and quality perception and direction on features and attributes.

A second type is a general Owner Experience Survey. The example shown in Exhibit III–6.2 was sent to an owner more than two years after the purchase of his vehicle. The Ownership Experience survey tracks the same subset of owners over six years of ownership experience, starting with the Purchase Experience Survey and then following up with the general survey two, four, and six years later. It ends with an approaching repurchase decision.

QUESTIONS FOR DISCUSSION

1. Evaluate Subaru's use of customer satisfaction research. Is it of any real value to the company? Explain.

2. If you were the project director for this research program, which mode of data collection would you prefer, mail or Internet?

3. When two methods of data collection are used in a research project, such as in Subaru's ongoing surveys, can the responses be combined into a simple sample? What conditions have to be met for this to be a useful approach?

EXHIBIT III–6.1   Service Experience Survey

SUBARU

April 11, 2003

NEW
Internet survey
option
(see information below)

Mr. Gerald S Albaum
6109 Paper Flower Pl. NE
Albuquerque, NM 87111-8233

Dear Mr. Albaum:

Thank you for your recent visit to Prestige Subaru for service on your 2001 Subaru Legacy Outback.

We set very high performance standards for the Service Department at each of our dealerships. The enclosed *Service Experience* survey is one way we measure the quality of service you received during your recent dealership visit. It also helps us determine if your service experience satisfied your needs and expectations. Your valuable opinions will help us serve you and other Subaru owners and lessees in the best possible way. Please take a few minutes to complete this important survey and return it in the enclosed postage-paid envelope as soon as possible.

As an added convenience, we are pleased to offer the option of completing this survey via the Internet! The web address for the survey is:

www.survey.subaru.com

Your personalized ID number to log onto the web site for completing the internet survey is

XXXYYZZX7

Again, thank you for your assistance. We are eager to hear about your service experience.

Sincerely,

James C. Sinclair
Vice President, Service

Introducing My. Subaru

The on-line resource exclusively for Subaru Owners.

Imagine logging on to your own personal Subaru Web site, a site with features and tools designed to aid you in managing and caring for your vehicle. It's your own personal resource which stays with you throughout the ownership of your Subaru. Thanks to an innovative new program, Subaru of America, Inc. is bringing this image to life!

Introducing My.Subaru, exclusively for Subaru Owners. My. Subaru allows owners to create a web site designed specifically for you and your Subaru. With the click of a mouse, My.Subaru provides you with:

- Automated warranty history
- Personal service history
- Email maintenance reminders
- Notice of recalls and service programs
- On-going Subaru news

My.Subaru can link you directly to your preferred Subaru dealer to request a service appointment or parts and accessory information. You can even connect to popular sites such as Kelley Blue Book, or access an on-line Owner's Manual. Its great features help you manage your Subaru while maintaining all your vehicle records in one place. And have no worries, My.Subaru is password protected to keep all your owner information confidential.

To set up your personal account, simply go to the Internet and type www.My.Subaru.com. Once there, select "Create An Account" and enter your VIN and PIN, which appear below. Then follow the on-screen prompts. Or, if you have already created a site, simply use your own information to log back in. It's that easy.

We hope you enjoy My.Subaru and find its features useful. Once you've established your site, you can visit as often as you like. After all, My.Subaru is your personal site.

www.My.Subaru.com personal log on information for new users:

VIN: 1X3XX787667701361

PIN: 3779

014987478

SERVICE EXPERIENCE SURVEY

MARKING DIRECTIONS: Please use a BLUE or BLACK Ink pen.
Right ☒   Wrong ☑ ◯ ⊙

If we have made a mistake and you did not have service performed, or you no longer have this vehicle, please mark one of the boxes, and return this survey in the postage-paid envelope provided.

NO LONGER HAVE THIS SUBARU	☒
DID NOT HAVE SERVICE PERFORMED	☒
DID NOT HAVE SERVICE PERFORMED AT PRESTIGE SUBARU	☒

1. **Overall, how satisfied are you with your Service Department experience specifically at . . .**

Prestige Subaru?

- ☒ Very satisfied
- ☒ Satisfied
- ☒ Somewhat satisfied
- ☒ Neither satisfied nor dissatisfied
- ☒ Somewhat dissatisfied
- ☒ Dissatisfied
- ☒ Very dissatisfied

2. **Please rate the extent to which you agree with the following statements:**

Completely Disagree
Disagree
Somewhat Disagree
Neither Agree nor Disagree
Somewhat Agree
Agree
Completely Agree

☺ ☹ ☹

a. When phoning, I was promptly connected to someone who could help me schedule an appointment. . . . . ☒ ☒ ☒ ☒ ☒ ☒ ☒

b. My repairs were scheduled to occur within a reasonable amount of time. . . ☒ ☒ ☒ ☒ ☒ ☒ ☒

c. I was promptly greeted upon my arrival at the service department . . . . ☒ ☒ ☒ ☒ ☒ ☒ ☒

d. The service representative thoroughly inquired about my service concerns. . . . . ☒ ☒ ☒ ☒ ☒ ☒ ☒

e. The service representative was knowledgeable about my car . . . . ☒ ☒ ☒ ☒ ☒ ☒ ☒

f. The service department had a comfortable waiting room. . . . . ☒ ☒ ☒ ☒ ☒ ☒ ☒

g. Convenient arrangements for transportation were offered while my car was being serviced. . . . . ☒ ☒ ☒ ☒ ☒ ☒ ☒

2. **Cont.**

Completely Disagree
Disagree
Somewhat Disagree
Neither Agree nor Disagree
Somewhat Agree
Agree
Completely Agree

☺ ☺ ☺

h. The time it took to complete the service was acceptable . . ☒ ☒ ☒ ☒ ☒ ☒ ☒

i. My car was ready when promised . . . . ☒ ☒ ☒ ☒ ☒ ☒ ☒

j. My car was fixed right the first time. . . . . ☒ ☒ ☒ ☒ ☒ ☒ ☒

k. The service representative demonstrated a commitment to seeing that the job was done right . . . . . . ☒ ☒ ☒ ☒ ☒ ☒ ☒

l. My paperwork was ready when I walked in to pick up my car . . . . ☒ ☒ ☒ ☒ ☒ ☒ ☒

m. The repair work was clearly explained to me . . . . ☒ ☒ ☒ ☒ ☒ ☒ ☒

n. I was completely satisfied with the condition of my car when it was returned to me . . ☒ ☒ ☒ ☒ ☒ ☒ ☒

o. The service department demonstrated a willingness to take extra steps to satisfy me . . . . ☒ ☒ ☒ ☒ ☒ ☒ ☒

p. The service department followed up to make sure the repairs were completed to my satisfaction. . . . . ☒ ☒ ☒ ☒ ☒ ☒ ☒

3. **Overall, please rate . . .**

Prestige Subaru compared to other automotive service providers you have visited.
- ☒ Much better
- ☒ Better
- ☒ Somewhat better
- ☒ About the same
- ☒ Somewhat worse
- ☒ Worse
- ☒ Much worse

4. Please rate this dealership's service department compared to other automotive service providers you have used in the following areas:

Much Worse
Worse
Somewhat Worse
About the Same
Somewhat Better
Better
Much Better

a. Reputation in the marketplace. . . . . ☒ ☒ ☒ ☒ ☒ ☒ ☒
b. Convenience of location. . . . . . ☒ ☒ ☒ ☒ ☒ ☒ ☒
c. Hours of operation. . . . . ☒ ☒ ☒ ☒ ☒ ☒ ☒
d. Cleanliness of the service department. . . . . ☒ ☒ ☒ ☒ ☒ ☒ ☒
e. Size of service department . . . ☒ ☒ ☒ ☒ ☒ ☒ ☒
f. Reputation of repair staff. . . . . ☒ ☒ ☒ ☒ ☒ ☒ ☒
g. Ease of scheduling an appointment. . . . . ☒ ☒ ☒ ☒ ☒ ☒ ☒
h. Availability of courtesy transportation . . . . ☒ ☒ ☒ ☒ ☒ ☒ ☒
i. Time it took to complete repair(s). . . . . ☒ ☒ ☒ ☒ ☒ ☒ ☒
j. Notifying you when your car is due for routine maintenance. . . . . ☒ ☒ ☒ ☒ ☒ ☒ ☒

Definitely Would Not
Most Likely Would Not
Might Not
Unsure
Might
Most Likely Would
Definitely Would

Based on your experience to date . . .

5. Would you consider using this dealership for service again?. . . . . ☒ ☒ ☒ ☒ ☒ ☒ ☒

6. Would you recommend this dealership for service to your family/friends? . . . . . . ☒ ☒ ☒ ☒ ☒ ☒ ☒

Use the space below if you have additional comments about your service experience. (Please Print)

_____
_____
_____

7. Dealership service departments can provide a variety of customer services. Please indicate all items below that are important to you:

☒ Service reminders   ☒ Accessory specials
☒ Service discounts   ☒ Free service clinics
☒ Service follow-up calls   ☒ New owner orientations
☒ Parts promotions   ☒ Dealer news

8. Are you: ☒ Female   ☒ Male

9. Do you have children aged 18 or younger living at home?

☒ Yes   ☒ No

10. Are you: ☒ Married   ☒ Single

11. Please mark the range that includes your age:

☒ Under 25   ☒ 55-64
☒ 25-34   ☒ 65-74
☒ 35-44   ☒ 75 or over
☒ 45-54

12. Please mark if your current profession or the profession of other household members is listed below.

	You	Others
a. Health Care	☒	☒
b. Education	☒	☒
c. Technical/Communications . .	☒	☒
d. Retired	☒	☒

13. What is your household income level?

☒ $29,999 or less   ☒ $60,000 to 79,999
☒ $30,000 to 39,999   ☒ $80,000 to 99,999
☒ $40,000 to 49,999   ☒ $100,000 to 149,999
☒ $50,000 to 59,999   ☒ $150,000 or more

14. Before acquiring your vehicle, had you or other household members ever owned/leased a Subaru?

☒ Yes   ☒ No

If yes, how many?

15. Do you regularly use this Subaru dealership for routine maintenance?

☒ Yes   ☒ No

16. Approximately how many miles are currently on the odometer?

✎ *Please enter your e-mail address.*

EXHIBIT III-6.2   Owner Experience Survey

SUBARU

September 30, 2003

Mr. Gerald S Albaum
6109 PAPER FLOWER PL NE
ALBUQUERQUE, NM 87111-8233
║┃ɪ┃ɪ┃ɪɪ┃┃ɪɪɪ┃┃ɪɪɪ┃┃┃ɪɪ┃ɪɪɪ┃┃ɪɪɪ┃┃ɪ┃ɪ┃ɪɪɪ┃ɪɪɪ┃ɪɪɪ┃┃

Dear Mr. Albaum:

At Subaru of America, Inc., we value your decision to purchase your 2001 Subaru LEGACY
OUTBACK from Lee Galles Subaru in June 2001. The enclosed Subaru Owner Experience Survey
is part of our continuing commitment to understand and improve owner satisfaction in three key
areas: our products, dealerships and company overall.

We are asking a group of Subaru owners, like yourself, who completed a survey shortly after their
purchase to again assist us with their feedback. The purpose of the enclosed survey is to gather
your perspective based on your ownership experience during the years that followed your vehicle
purchase.

Please take a few minutes to complete this important survey and return it in the enclosed postage-
paid envelope as soon as possible. As an added convenience, we are pleased to offer the option of
completing this survey via the Internet! The web address to the survey is:

www.survey.subaru.com

Your personalized ID number to log onto the web site for completing the Internet survey is

LYDA6LE5

Thank you for your help.

Sincerely,

Keith Tilton
Vice President - Customer Relationship and Loyalty
Subaru of America, Inc.

You can help make a difference.

When you return this survey, you help to shape how Subaru continues to improve in the future!
Thank you for helping us become a premium brand automobile company.

SUBARU OWNER EXPERIENCE SURVEY

102485402

MARKING DIRECTIONS: Please use a BLUE or BLACK ink pen.   Right ☒   Wrong ☑ (□) ⊙

ABOUT YOUR SUBARU

1. **Do you still own this Subaru?**
2001 LEGACY OUTBACK purchased on
06/04/01 from Lee Galles Subaru

☒ No   ☒ Yes ⟶ Please skip to **question 2**

If no, please mark all that apply, and continue based on your experiences with this vehicle.

I no longer own this Subaru because . . .

☒ Lease expired
☒ Dissatisfied with vehicle
☒ Dissatisfied with Subaru as a company
☒ Dissatisfied with dealership where car was purchased
☒ Dissatisfied with dealership where car was serviced
☒ Cost too high to maintain
☒ Needed more cargo capacity
☒ Car totaled (major accident), or stolen
☒ Needed more passenger carrying capacity
☒ Bought another Subaru
☒ Bought a different make of car

2. **Overall, how satisfied are you with this Subaru?**
☒ Very satisfied
☒ Satisfied
☒ Somewhat satisfied
☒ Neither satisfied nor dissatisfied
☒ Somewhat dissatisfied
☒ Dissatisfied
☒ Very dissatisfied

3. **Overall, how does this Subaru compare to vehicles from other manufacturers?**
☒ Much better
☒ Better
☒ Somewhat better
☒ About the same
☒ Somewhat worse
☒ Worse
☒ Much worse

		Definitely Would Not		
		Most Likely Would Not		
		Might Not		
		Unsure		
		Might		
		Most Likely Would		
		Definitely Would		

Based on your experience to date . . .   ☺   ☺   ☹

4. Would you consider buying/leasing this Subaru model again? ..... ☒ ☒ ☒ ☒ ☒ ☒ ☒

5. Would you consider buying/leasing another Subaru? .... ☒ ☒ ☒ ☒ ☒ ☒ ☒

6. Take a minute to think about your ownership experience with this Subaru. Considering the age and mileage of this Subaru, please rate the durability/reliability of the following:

	Far Worse Than Expected				
	Worse Than Expected				
	Met Expectation				
	Better Than Expected				
	Far Better Than Expected				
a. Ride, handling and braking (e.g., pulling, noise, vibration, steering response, wheel alignment)	☒	☒	☒	☒	☒
b. Features and controls (e.g., wipers, signals, sunroof, lights, locks, mirrors)	☒	☒	☒	☒	☒
c. Seats (e.g., adjustment, support, belts, comfort, material)	☒	☒	☒	☒	☒
d. Sound system (e.g., reception, speakers, cassette, CD player)	☒	☒	☒	☒	☒
e. Heating, ventilation and cooling (e.g., defrost, AC, heater, fan/blower)	☒	☒	☒	☒	☒
f. Vehicle exterior (e.g., tailgate/trunk, wind noise, water leaks, paint, doors)	☒	☒	☒	☒	☒
g. Vehicle interior (e.g., dashboard, carpeting, console, lights, glove box)	☒	☒	☒	☒	☒
h. Transmission (e.g., shifting, clutch, gears, all wheel drive)	☒	☒	☒	☒	☒
i. Engine (e.g., acceleration, power, oil usage, idle)	☒	☒	☒	☒	☒
j. Tires (e.g., wear and performance)	☒	☒	☒	☒	☒
k. Overall, please rate your vehicle	☒	☒	☒	☒	☒

7. Based on your ownership to date, please rate your satisfaction with the following:

	Very Dissatisfied				
	Dissatisfied				
	Neither Satisfied nor Dissatisfied				
	Satisfied				
	Very Satisfied				
a. Overall value for the money	☒	☒	☒	☒	☒
b. Reliability	☒	☒	☒	☒	☒
c. Quality	☒	☒	☒	☒	☒
d. Purchase price/lease rate	☒	☒	☒	☒	☒
e. Warranty coverage	☒	☒	☒	☒	☒
f. All Wheel Drive	☒	☒	☒	☒	☒
g. Product style/image	☒	☒	☒	☒	☒

8. Approximately how many miles are currently on the odometer of this Subaru? (No tenths)

					0

9. Did you use the Internet to help you shop for this vehicle?
☒ Yes   ☒ No

ABOUT SUBARU DEALER SERVICE

10. Have you used a Subaru dealer for at least <u>some</u> routine maintenance, warranty service or repair work on this Subaru?

☒ Yes   ☒ No ➤ Please skip to **question 24**

11. Please indicate the Subaru Dealer you frequent the <u>most</u> for service and will evaluate below:

☒ Dealer where I purchased the vehicle ➤ Please skip to **question 13**

☒ Other Subaru dealership. **Please write in name of dealership and state where located:**

12. If you have <u>switched</u> from the dealer where you purchased this Subaru (selling dealer), please indicate <u>why</u> you switched. (Mark all that apply)

☒ I relocated
☒ Too far to drive to selling dealer
☒ Service costs too high at selling dealer
☒ Too difficult to get appointment at selling dealer
☒ Unfavorable purchase experience at selling dealer
☒ Unfavorable service experience at selling dealer
☒ Quality of maintenance or repairs
☒ Other:

13. Please indicate the <u>primary</u> type of service you have had performed at this dealership.

☒ Primarily repair
☒ Primarily maintenance
☒ All repair <u>and</u> maintenance

14. Overall, how satisfied are you with your service department experience at this Subaru dealership?

☒ Very satisfied
☒ Satisfied
☒ Somewhat satisfied
☒ Neither satisfied nor dissatisfied
☒ Somewhat dissatisfied
☒ Dissatisfied
☒ Very dissatisfied

	Yes	No
15. Have you ever had a disagreement/ dispute with this Subaru dealership?	☒	☒
a. If yes, did you tell anyone about it at the dealership?	☒	☒
b. If yes, was it resolved to your satisfaction?	☒	☒

16. Please rate this Subaru dealership compared to other automotive service providers you have visited.

☒ Much better
☒ Better
☒ Somewhat better
☒ About the same
☒ Somewhat worse
☒ Worse
☒ Much worse

17. To what type of automotive service provider were you primarily comparing this Subaru dealership? **(Mark <u>only</u> one)**

☒ Luxury (e.g., Lexus, Mercedes, Cadillac)
☒ Sport/performance (e.g., Audi, Porsche)
☒ Moderately priced import vehicles (e.g., Honda, Nissan, Toyota)
☒ Moderately priced American vehicles (e.g., Ford, GM, Daimler-Chrysler)
☒ Economy vehicles (e.g., Kia, Suzuki, Hyundai)
☒ Subaru (other Subaru dealerships)
☒ Chain store (e.g., Jiffy Lube, Pep Boys, Midas)
☒ Department store (e.g., Sears, Walmart)
☒ Independent garage

18. Based on your experience to date, would you consider using this dealership for service again?

☒ Definitely would
☒ Most likely would
☒ Might
☒ Unsure
☒ Might not
☒ Most likely would not
☒ Definitely would not

19. Please rate this Subaru dealership in the following areas:

This dealership has . . .	Strongly Agree	Agree	Somewhat Agree	Neither Agree nor Disagree	Somewhat Disagree	Disagree	Strongly Disagree
a. Clearly identifiable signage as a Subaru dealership	☒	☒	☒	☒	☒	☒	☒
b. A clean and inviting <u>exterior</u> building appearance	☒	☒	☒	☒	☒	☒	☒
c. Clearly identifiable <u>exterior</u> signage for the location of sales, service, and parts departments and customer parking . .	☒	☒	☒	☒	☒	☒	☒
d. A clean and inviting <u>interior</u>	☒	☒	☒	☒	☒	☒	☒
e. Clearly identifiable <u>interior</u> signage for the location of departments, waiting area and restrooms	☒	☒	☒	☒	☒	☒	☒
f. Clean restrooms . . .	☒	☒	☒	☒	☒	☒	☒
g. A <u>comfortable</u> service waiting area	☒	☒	☒	☒	☒	☒	☒
h. A service waiting area that allows me to make good use of my time	☒	☒	☒	☒	☒	☒	☒
i. A clean, comfortanle and organized showroom	☒	☒	☒	☒	☒	☒	☒
j. An adequate number of Subaru display vehicles in the showroom	☒	☒	☒	☒	☒	☒	☒

20. Considering <u>all</u> the service you have had at this dealer, please rate the extent to which you agree with the following:

	Completely Agree ☺	Agree	Somewhat Agree	Neither Agree nor Disagree ☺	Somewhat Disagree	Disagree	Completely Disagree ☹
a. When phoning, I was promptly connected to someone who could help me schedule appointments	⊠	⊠	⊠	⊠	⊠	⊠	⊠
b. My repairs were scheduled to occur within a reasonable amount of time	⊠	⊠	⊠	⊠	⊠	⊠	⊠
c. I was promptly greeted upon my arrival at the service department	⊠	⊠	⊠	⊠	⊠	⊠	⊠
d. The service representative thoroughly inquired about my service concerns	⊠	⊠	⊠	⊠	⊠	⊠	⊠
e. The service representative was knowledgeable about my car	⊠	⊠	⊠	⊠	⊠	⊠	⊠
f. Convenient arrangements for transportation were offered while my car was being serviced .	⊠	⊠	⊠	⊠	⊠	⊠	⊠
g. The time it took to complete the service was acceptable ...	⊠	⊠	⊠	⊠	⊠	⊠	⊠
h. My car was ready when promised. ...	⊠	⊠	⊠	⊠	⊠	⊠	⊠
i. Parts were readily available	⊠	⊠	⊠	⊠	⊠	⊠	⊠
j. My car was fixed right the first time ..	⊠	⊠	⊠	⊠	⊠	⊠	⊠
k. The service representative demonstrated a commitment to seeing that the job was done right.	⊠	⊠	⊠	⊠	⊠	⊠	⊠
l. The repair work was clearly explained to me	⊠	⊠	⊠	⊠	⊠	⊠	⊠
m. I was completely satisfied with the condition of my car when it was returned to me	⊠	⊠	⊠	⊠	⊠	⊠	⊠
n. The service department was willing to take extra steps to satisfy me .	⊠	⊠	⊠	⊠	⊠	⊠	⊠

21. Did you feel free to respond to previous surveys from Subaru with your true opinions?

	Yes	No
a. That is, did you feel pressure from this <u>**servicing**</u> dealer to answer in a specific way?	⊠	⊠
b. That is, did you feel pressure from your <u>**selling**</u> dealer to answer in a specific way?	⊠	⊠

22. Do you typically receive a follow-up phone call after each service visit?

⊠ Yes   ⊠ No   ⊠ Not sure

23. How far do you travel to have your vehicle serviced?

⊠ 0–10 miles   ⊠ 26–50 miles
⊠ 11–25 miles   ⊠ 51 or more miles

24. If you do not use a Subaru dealer for routine maintenance or repair, where do you go? (Mark all that apply)

⊠ Chain store (e.g., Jiffy Lube, Pep Boys, Midas)
⊠ Department store (e.g., Sears, Walmart)
⊠ Non-Subaru dealership (e.g., Ford, Nissan, VW)
⊠ Independent garage
⊠ Service own car
⊠ Other:

25. If you do <u>not</u> use a Subaru dealer for routine maintenance or repair work on your vehicle please indicate why. (Mark all that apply)

⊠ Service own car
⊠ Too far to drive to a dealer
⊠ Too difficult to get an appointment
⊠ Takes too long to complete service
⊠ Dissatisfied with quality of repairs
⊠ Service costs too high
⊠ Unfavorable purchase experience with dealer
⊠ Unfavorable service experience with dealer
⊠ Uncomfortable waiting area/facilities
⊠ Other:

ABOUT SUBARU AS A COMPANY

26. Overall, how satisfied are you with Subaru of America as a company?

⊠ Very satisfied
⊠ Satisfied
⊠ Somewhat satisfied
⊠ Neither satisfied nor dissatisfied
⊠ Somewhat dissatisfied
⊠ Dissatisfied
⊠ Very dissatisfied

27. Overall, how do you feel Subaru compares to other car companies?

⊠ Much better
⊠ Better
⊠ Somewhat better
⊠ About the same
⊠ Somewhat worse
⊠ Worse
⊠ Much worse

28. Because vehicles are lasting longer, we are interested in determining how far ahead Subaru owners plan for and conduct their search for a new vehicle.

a. When do you anticipate you will be buying your next car?

⊠ 1–5 months   ⊠ 1–2 years
⊠ 6–11 months   ⊠ 3–5 years   ⊠ 6 or more years

b. About how far ahead of your next car purchase will you begin searching for your next car?

⊠ Less than 1 month   ⊠ 3–5 months   ⊠ 1–2 months
⊠ More than 1 year   ⊠ 6 months to a year

29. Please respond to the following statements about Subaru as <u>a car company</u>, separate from your feelings or experiences with a dealership:

	Strongly Agree	Agree	Neither Agree nor Disagree	Disagree	Strongly Disagree
	☺		☺		☹
a. Subaru as a company really cares about Subaru owners ...	☒	☒	☒	☒	☒
b. Subaru advertising connects with me personally	☒	☒	☒	☒	☒
c. Subaru as a company is concerned about the environment	☒	☒	☒	☒	☒
d. Subaru is an innovative company	☒	☒	☒	☒	☒
e. Subaru has models that consider to be performance cars	☒	☒	☒	☒	☒

30. Please mark <u>any</u> of the following factors which may prevent you from purchasing a Subaru in the future.

- ☒ Price/Lease Rate
- ☒ Environmental concerns (better mileage, etc.)
- ☒ A downturn in the economy
- ☒ Other manufacturers offering all wheel drive
- ☒ Need more cargo capacity
- ☒ Styling/features
- ☒ Dealership experience
- ☒ Reliability/dependability of vehicle
- ☒ Cost of operation too high
- ☒ Need more passenger carrying capacity
- ☒ Other:

31. Please indicate which of the following actions you would take when searching for a new car:

	Very Likely	Likely	Neither Likely nor Unlikely	Unlikely	Very Unlikely
	☺		☺		☹
a. Browse car-related sites on Internet (e.g., cars.com, edmunds.com, carpoint.com, kellybluebook.com)	☒	☒	☒	☒	☒
b. Browse Subaru.com	☒	☒	☒	☒	☒
c. Read Subaru promotional materials (e.g., sales brochures, Drive magazine)	☒	☒	☒	☒	☒
d. Visit Subaru dealerships	☒	☒	☒	☒	☒
e. Visit non-Subaru dealerships ..	☒	☒	☒	☒	☒
f. Read car ads in magazines ...	☒	☒	☒	☒	☒
g. Read car ads in newspapers ..	☒	☒	☒	☒	☒
h. Read consumer rating publications (Consumer Reports, Consumer Digest) ...	☒	☒	☒	☒	☒
i. Consider J. D. Power reports ..	☒	☒	☒	☒	☒

32. Your expectations about repairs and recalls

	Far More Than Expected	More Than Expected	Met Expectations	Fewer Than Expected	Far Fewer Than Expected
	☺		☺		☹
a. How does the number of **repairs** you experienced on this Subaru compare to your expectations	☒	☒	☒	☒	☒
b. How does the number of **recalls** you experienced on this Subaru compare to your expectations	☒	☒	☒	☒	☒

ABOUT YOU

33. Is this your primary vehicle? That is, is it driven at least 5 times a week?
☒ Yes ☒ No ☒ Unsure

34. Do you have children aged 18 or younger living at home?
☒ Yes ☒ No

35. Are you: ☒ Married ☒ Single

36. Please mark the range that includes your age:
- ☒ Under 25
- ☒ 25–34
- ☒ 35–44
- ☒ 45–54
- ☒ 55–64
- ☒ 65–74
- ☒ 75 or over

37. What is your household income level?
- ☒ $29,999 or less
- ☒ $30,000 to 39,999
- ☒ $40,000 to $49,999
- ☒ $50,000 to $59,999
- ☒ $60,000 to $79,999
- ☒ $80,000 to $99,999
- ☒ $100,000 to $149,999
- ☒ $150,000 or more

38. Please provide any additional comments below.

Thank you for taking the time to give us your opinions! Your feedback will be considered solely to help improve the Subaru ownership experience. Please call your dealer directly if you need any repair work. If you currently have any concerns with your Subaru vehicle, please contact us directly at 1-800-SUBARU-3 or write us at Subaru of America, Inc., Subaru Plaza, P.O. Box 6000, Cherry Hill, NJ 08034-6000 or e-mail us by going to the Web address www.subaru.com.

Part IV

SAMPLING

Chapter 12

SAMPLING PROCEDURES IN MARKETING RESEARCH

Marketing researchers must answer many questions when developing a project to collect information about a population of interest. Consider the following questions involving sampling:

- Should we take a census (complete canvass) or a sample?
- What kind of sample should be taken?
- What size should the sample be?

Answering these questions depends upon the application of statistical inference. This chapter first considers the selection of sample types and the process of sample planning. It then describes different kinds of samples. The final section concerns telephone sampling plans. Chapter 13 covers the issue of sample size.

PLANNING THE SAMPLE

Two broad objectives are fundamental to the use of samples in research projects:

- Estimation
- Testing of hypotheses

Each involves making inferences about a population on the basis of information from a sample. We discuss these inferences within the context of sample size in Chapter 13. The precision and accuracy of project results are affected by the manner in which the sample has been chosen. However, as Exhibit 12.1 illustrates, precision is a reflection of sampling error and confidence limits. These things have nothing to do with accuracy.

EXHIBIT 12.1   Precision Versus Accuracy in Sampling

There often is confusion between precision and accuracy in marketing research. When a researcher speaks of sampling error and the size of the confidence limits placed on an estimate, that researcher is speaking of precision. Accuracy is not affected by sample size, but rather by nonresponse bias, memory error, misunderstanding of questions, problematic definition of terms, and processing errors (Semon, 2000). The formulas used to estimate error that sampling may cause are based on probability theory. Statistical inference does not deal with the major sources of inaccuracy:

1. Have we asked the right questions?

2. Have we measured what we want to measure properly and correctly?

In general, the quality of a sample depends upon the quality of design and execution of a research project at every stage of the process.

The difference between precision and accuracy is analogous to the difference between errors of degree and errors of kind. The latter are clearly more serious. If a researcher has made the correct measurements, precision will show the degree of error; but if the right measurements have not been taken, precision is probably meaningless (Semon, 2000).

Consequently, strict attention must be paid to the planning of the sample. It must also be recognized that sample planning is part of the total planning of the research project, regardless of the type of project conducted. The process of selecting a sample follows a well-defined progression, the major steps of which are shown in Figure 12.1.

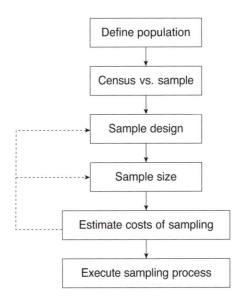

Figure 12.1   Steps in Sample Planning

Defining the Population

The first thing the sample plan must accomplish is to define the population to be investigated. A population, also known as a universe, is defined as the totality of all units or elements (individuals, households, organizations, etc.) possessing one or more particular relevant features or characteristics in common, to which one desires to generalize study results. While seemingly an easy task, defining the population often is one of the most difficult things to do in sampling. The greatest difficulty is due to imprecise research problem definition. Imprecision of problem definition, in turn, often results when the purpose or objectives of the study, based on the decision problem of concern, are not clearly transmitted from the decision maker to the investigator.

Specifying a population involves identifying which elements (in terms of kind) are included, as well as where and when. For example, a group medical practice that is considering expanding into sports medicine might acquire information from any or all of the groups listed in Table 12.1.

Table 12.1   Possible Population Choices for a Research Study by a Medical Practice

Group Members	Where	When
All patients	Designated group practice	Last 12 months
Patients who have had orthopedic work	Designated group practices	Last 12 months
All people	Specified geographic area	Last 12 months
All people who have had orthopedic work	Specified geographic area	Last 12 months

From a research point of view, each group represents a distinct population with corresponding implications for the interpretation of any information obtained. The population element is the unit of analysis, and may be defined as an individual, a household, an institution, a patient visit, and so on.

The second and third columns of Table 12.1 represent dimensions designed to more precisely define the population in terms of its location and timeframe. As such, these dimensions also define which units are to be excluded. Clearly, the population should be defined as precisely as possible. One useful approach is to first define the ideal population to meet study objectives. Practical constraints then ultimately define the study population. The advantage of starting with an ideal population is that exclusions are made explicit. At the same time, however, overdefining the population should be avoided unless it is absolutely necessary. Overdefining can limit the extent to which findings can be generalized, and greatly increase the operational cost and difficulty of finding population elements (Sudman, 1976). Also, overdefinition means that certain unnecessary elements will be included, possibly leading to a situation where the elements of interest become obscured.

Census or Sample?

Once the population has been defined, the investigator must decide whether to conduct the survey among all members of the population, or only a subset of the population. That is, a choice must be made between census and sample. Obviously, this cannot be done before the population is specified, since the choice depends largely upon the size of the population, which is determined by the precise boundaries of the population. In practice, this is often done in advance, as the investigator usually has some concept of the population and its approximate size.

Although ideal conditions (all needed information collected with little cost) might indicate that a census would be preferable, such ideal conditions rarely exist in the real world. Sometimes, a census may just not be feasible. In most instances, samples are used. The desirability and advantages of using a sample rather than a census depend on the absolute size of the population as well as on the relative proportion of the population that will be used as the sample, so as to provide results sufficiently accurate and precise for the required purposes. Another factor may be the location of the population elements. Although relatively small, the population may be so geographically dispersed that a census would not be practical for the desired mode of data collection.

Two major advantages of using a sample rather than a census are speed and timeliness. A survey based on a sample takes much less time to complete than one based on a census. Moreover, in certain instances a complete count may require such a long time that, because of changes in conditions, it becomes a historical record by the time it is completed and available for use.

Another consideration when deciding whether or not to use sampling is the relative cost and effort involved. The amount of effort and expense required to collect information is always greater per unit for a sample than for a complete census, but if the size of the sample needed to give the required accuracy represents only a small fraction of the whole population, the total effort and expense required to collect the information by sampling methods will be much less than for a census of the whole population (Yates, 1971). For example, a census of all U.S. automobile owners regarding the type of wheels on their cars, even if possible, would hardly be economically practical for a manufacturer of magnesium wheels.

Administrative considerations often dictate that sampling be used, particularly when a census would necessitate hiring, training, and supervising many people. Frequently, therefore, the use of a sample results in a notable economy of effort. This is particularly true when experimental methods will be used.

In other situations, a sample is necessary because of the destructive nature of the measurement, such as quality testing of matches or paint. There is a related serious problem in surveys of human populations when many different surveys need to be conducted on the same population within a relatively short period of time. In such a case, if a census is used, there is a great risk that many individual members of the population will react negatively to being asked to participate in more than one study during a given time period. The chance that this can occur when sampling techniques are used is low, if the sample is a small proportion of the total population and probability techniques are used for selecting the individual sample elements. When nonprobability techniques are used for selection, the problem can be protected against explicitly.

In still other situations, a sample may be desirable for controlling nonsampling errors. The smaller-scale aspects of taking a sample may permit tighter control of the measuring operations (better interviewing, less nonresponse through more call-back, and so forth) to a point where the total amount of sampling and nonsampling error is actually less for the sample than the nonsampling error alone would be for a census. In Chapter 3, we emphasized the importance of minimizing total error.

A sample enables one to concentrate attention on individual cases. For example, in-depth studies of why a product is bought and how it is consumed may not be feasible to carry out on a census basis. Closely related to this is the possibility to obtain more detailed information from a sample. The reason is that the individuals concerned may be more willing to provide detailed information if they know they represent only a small proportion of the population.

Finally, a sample may be necessary simply because the only other alternative would be to collect no information at all. The entire population may not be available for measurement at the time of the study.

However, under certain conditions a census may be preferable to a sample. When the population is small, the variance in the characteristic being measured is high, the cost of error is high, or the fixed costs of sampling are high, sampling may not be useful. If one were doing a study to determine the acceptability to U.S. original equipment manufacturers of a new drive mechanism for snowmobiles, one might be well advised to conduct a census of the small number of manufacturers involved. In addition, if the characteristic or attribute of interest occurs rarely in the population, then a census might be desirable, since a relatively large sample would be necessary to provide statistically reliable information. Obviously, the practicality of this depends upon the absolute size of the population. Other alternatives would be to use snowball or multiplicity types of sampling, particularly when of the population size is large.

Sample Design

Operationally, sample design is the heart of sample planning. It is "the theoretical basis and the practical means by which data are collected so that the characteristics of a population can be inferred with known estimates of error" (Survey Sampling, Inc., 1992, p. 16). A sample design specification, including the method of selecting individual sample members, involves both theoretical and practical (such as cost, time, labor involved, organization) considerations. The following checklist has been suggested to obtain a sample that represents the target population (Fink, 2003, pp. 3–10):

1. Are the survey objectives stated precisely?

2. Are the eligibility criteria clear and definite? The criteria for inclusion into a research project refer to the characteristics of survey respondents or experimental subjects who are eligible for participation in the study; exclusion criteria rule out certain people.

3. Are rigorous sampling methods chosen? This involves selecting an appropriate probability or nonprobability sampling method.

4. Further questions to be answered in this section:
   - What type of sample should be used?
   - What is the appropriate sampling unit?
   - What frame (that is, list of sampling units from which the sample is to be drawn) is available for the population and what problems might arise in using it for the particular design and unit decided upon?
   - How are refusals and nonresponse to be handled? (See Table 5.2 in Chapter 5)

Type of Sample

Much of the sampling in marketing research, by its nature, concerns nonprobability. That is, samples are selected by the judgment of the investigator, convenience, or other nonrandom (or nonprobabilistic) processes, rather than by the use of a table of random numbers or another randomizing device.

If done properly, probability sampling provides for bias-free selection of sample units and permits the measurement of sampling error. Nonprobability samples offer neither of these features. In nonprobability sampling, one must rely on the expertise of the person taking the sample, whereas in probability sampling the results are independent of the investigator.

One should not conclude that probability sampling always yields results superior to nonprobability sampling, nor that the samples obtained by nonprobability methods are necessarily less representative of the populations under study. For example, a marketing researcher for a drug firm may develop an index of salespeople's performance by measuring such items as doctor calls completed per week, number of new drugs promoted during call, and length of call. A particular item is included in the index because the marketing researcher feels that it is representative of a factor labeled "performance." And the researcher's nonprobability sampling may be a better way to achieve a representation of the population than dropping a bunch of cards (on which are written possible characteristics of sales performance) in a hat and, blindfolded, selecting five or six of the cards. A further indication that otherwise well-conducted nonprobability sampling studies can be representative and reliable enough is that such studies have been accepted in court cases involving trademark infringement and unfair competition (Jacoby and Handlin, 1990). In addition, nonprobability sample designs can be representative and reliable enough for use in pretesting measurement instruments and pilot studies. In these situations, the researcher is not trying to estimate any parameters or do any generalizing per se, but is interested in planning a further research activity. If a probability sampling process is to be used in the final study, then the pilot study should use a similar process if it is designed to show what will happen in the final study.

On the other hand, a dog food manufacturer may test consumer reactions to a new dog food by giving product samples to employees who own dogs and eliciting their responses about a week later. In both cases, the samples are "biased" in the sense that they have been deliberately chosen to conform to the selector's idea of what the population does, or perhaps should, look like. In the first case, we might argue that the marketing researcher's choice of characteristics is reasonable, in view of the purposes for preparing the index. In the second case, assuming that the dog food manufacturer is attempting to infer typical pet liking of the new dog food, we might question the relevance of the reactions, independent of the small sample size. In this second case, the employees' dogs liked the food and the pet food manufacturer actually introduced the new dog food product. However, when it hit the market, the product was a flop . . . dogs simply would not eat it. As managers scrambled to find out what went wrong, research showed that employees were so loyal to the company's products that their dogs would eat anything for a change. In the broader market, dogs were used to a greater variety of dog foods and just did not like the taste of the new dog food.

A researcher choosing between probability and nonprobability sampling ultimately judges the probability sample's relative size of sampling error against the nonprobability sample's combined sampling error and selection bias. For a given cost, one can normally select a larger nonprobability sample than probability sample. This means that the sampling error should be lower in the nonprobability sample. However, the nonrandom process used for selecting the sample will have introduced a selection bias.

Sampling Unit

The sampling unit is the basis of the actual sampling procedure. It is that segment of the population actually chosen by the sampling process. The sampling unit may contain one or more population elements. That is, these units may be individual elements or aggregates of individual elements. For instance, in the new medical service problem the group medical practice may be interested in past patient behavior of the male wage earner *or* his entire household. In either case, it may be preferable to select a sample of households as sampling units.

Sample Frame

In Chapter 3, a sampling (or sample) frame was defined as a means of accounting for the elements in the population. The sampled elements are selected from the frame. In some cases, however, the frame consists of sampling units that are aggregates because the individual elements are not known. The sampling frame usually is a physical listing of the population elements. In those instances where such a listing is not available, the frame is a procedure producing a result equivalent to a physical listing. For instance, in a consumer survey where personal interviews are conducted with a sample of people "on-the-street" who pass by the interviewer, the frame might be defined as a "listing" of those people who might reasonably be expected to pass by the interviewer during a specified time period. Similarly, when the mall intercept method is used to obtain data, the sample frame includes all those people who enter the mall during the study period.

Ideally, the sample frame should identify each population element once, but only once, and not include elements not in the defined population. Such a perfect frame is seldom available for marketing research purposes. As shown in Figure 12.2, a sampling frame may be incomplete, too comprehensive, or a combination of both. In addition, the frame may

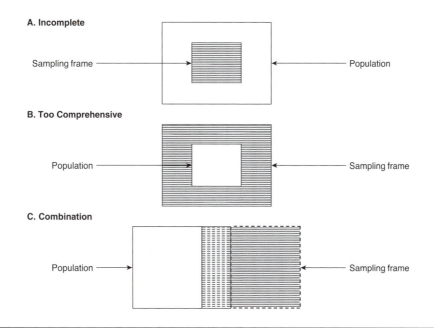

Figure 12.2   Sampling Frame–Population Relationships

include individual population elements more than once. Any of these situations can lead to coverage error. Interestingly, coverage error also may arise from survey definitions; for example, the definition of a housing unit (See Hogan, Garrett, and Pautler, 1986).

Perhaps the most widely used frame in survey research for sampling human populations is the telephone directory. Use of such a frame, however, may lead to frame error from the exclusion of nonsubscribers, voluntarily unlisted subscribers, and involuntarily unlisted subscribers. For example, within the top 25 unlisted markets in the United States the proportion of subscribing households unlisted in 1994 ranged from 68 percent in the Sacramento, California, PMSA to 36 percent in the Houston, Texas, PMSA. Ten years earlier this same group ranged from 59 percent in Las Vegas, Nevada, to 25 percent in Seattle-Bellevue-Everett, Washington ("Sacramento is Top," 1995). Similar frame errors can arise from such other sampling frames as city directories, maps, trade association membership lists, or any other incomplete or dated listing or representation of a population. The National Do Not Call Registry provisions do not cover calls from political organizations, charities, telephone surveyors, or companies with which a consumer has an existing business relationship, nonetheless, resident push back leads to further frame error.

Researchers who regularly do studies may compile their own lists to reduce coverage error. Technology makes compiling and maintaining such lists easier than in the past. For researchers doing many studies using self-report mail and electronic means to obtain data, having a readily available list as a frame for sampling is very helpful. The list is effectively a type of database which, because of legal and ethical concerns, may not contain all types of information desired by the researcher. Since sampling is probably the single most important problem in e-mail and Internet-based surveys, a company that can compile a list of addresses is ahead of the game! Dillman (2000) suggests asking the following five questions about any potential sampling list:

- Does the list contain everyone in the survey population?
- Does the list include names of people who are not in the study population?
- How is the list maintained and updated?
- Are the same sample units included on the list more than once?
- Does the list contain other information that can be used to improve the survey?

The answers to these questions have obvious meaning. Even if a researcher does not compile his or her own lists, many lists can be purchased from commercial services, to which the questions asked above are equally applicable.

Refusals and Nonresponse

The sample plan must include provisions for how to handle refusals and nonresponse. Of concern is whether to choose additional sampling units as replacements and, if so, how to select these.

Sample Size

Somewhat related to sample design, but in many ways a separate decision area for the investigator, is the determination of the sample size. In general, size of sample is directly related to precision. Four traditional approaches can determine the sample size to be used in any given research project. The first three are:

1. Arbitrarily or judgmentally determined

2. Minimum cell size needed for analysis

3. Budget-based

After compiling the results of the study, the precision could then be measured by applying the appropriate standard error formula or formulas if a probability design is being used. The fourth approach involves the opposite procedure. That is, by specifying a desired precision in advance, and by applying the appropriate standard error formula, sample size can be determined. Determining sample size will be discussed in depth in Chapter 13.

Costs of Sampling

The sample plan must account for the estimated costs of sampling. Such costs are of two types:

1. Overhead costs, which are relatively fixed for a sampling procedure

2. Variable costs, which depend on the scope of the study

In reality, it is difficult, and perhaps not even reasonable, to separate sampling costs from overall study costs. Consequently, costs from all aspects of a typical study are usually considered together. Note that there is a dashed line shown in Figure 12.1 that relates this aspect of the plan to sample design and sample size. This means that the estimated costs may be so great that the investigator may want to consider using other sample designs and/or smaller-sized samples.

Execution of the Sampling Process

The last step in sample planning is to execute the sampling process. In short, the sample is actually chosen. There are two basic requirements for the sampling procedure to fulfill: A sample must be both representative and adequate. A representative sample will be a relatively small piece of the population that mirrors the various patterns and subclasses of the population (Exhibit 12.2). An adequate sample is of sufficient size to provide confidence in the stability of its characteristics. This, in turn, requires a measure of precision, which necessitates using probability-based design. From this discussion, one might conclude that an ideal sample is obtained with a probability process. In general, this is preferable. However, recognize that it is more important to avoid distorted samples than to be able to measure sampling error. There may be a tendency to ignore the existence of potential bias when using probability designs.

This chapter is primarily concerned with probability sampling. However, before discussing this topic, it is useful to describe some of the procedures by which nonprobability samples are taken in marketing research.

EXHIBIT 12.2   Samples Are Not Always an Exact Match

Many researchers feel that the best way to assess the validity of a sample is to compare its demographic profile (i.e., distributions of the key demographic characteristics) with a national or otherwise known profile. This alone does not necessarily guarantee a good sample. At the same time, a poor fit does not necessarily mean that the obtained sample is bad.

When the fit is not good, some researchers tend to develop a weighting scheme. According to Thomas Semon (1990), this is not always necessary. What appear to be large differences in demographic characteristics may translate into a very small difference in the variable of interest, whether it is a behavior or an attitudes, interests, or opinions (AIO) measure.

To illustrate, suppose survey results in a sample were as follows: 48 percent of the respondents are under age 50, and 52 percent are 50 and above. Assume that the respondents' stated preference for a test product is 50 percent in the older group and 35 percent among the younger ones. Overall, the preference would be 42.8 percent. Now, if the population proportions are 60 percent under age 50 and 40 percent above, the overall preference would be reduced to 41.0 percent. Thus, a 12-percentage-point mismatch on age, together with a 15-percentage-point difference in stated preference, leads to a difference of only 1.8 percentage-points for the entire group.

The point is that large differences between sample and population demographic characteristics may have a minor distortion effect on an overall measure. Of course, there could be serious distortion if specific segments are of concern. But the differences generally have to be much greater than we would think for a significant effect.

NONPROBABILITY SAMPLING PROCEDURES

Nonprobability sampling is distinguished from probability sampling on the basis that in nonprobability sampling, the sample elements do not have a known, nonzero chance of being selected for the sample. Although widely used in exploratory research, this type of sampling also is valuable for nonexploratory research.

Quota Sampling

Perhaps the most commonly employed nonprobability sampling procedure in marketing research is the quota sample. Roughly described, in quota sampling the sizes of various subclasses (or strata) of the population are first estimated from some outside source, such as from Bureau of the Census data. For example, census data shows the proportion of the adult population who fall into various age-by-sex-by-education groupings.

Next, if an interviewer has a total number of, say, 100 interviews to obtain, the age-gender-education proportions in the population are applied to the 100 total interviews to determine the appropriate quotas. This could lead, for example, to a quota of four interviews of respondents between 18 and 30 years of age, female, with some college (or above) and nine interviews of respondents over 30 years of age, male, with high school (or below) education. Exhibit 12.3 presents another illustration.

So far, this approach to stratification is statistically quite sound. Indeed, as will be discussed later, this same initial step is employed in proportionate stratified random sampling.

However, in quota sampling the interviewer is *not* required to select the respondents necessary to fill each quota on a random basis. This is the major distinction between quota sampling and stratified random sampling.

EXHIBIT 12.3   Instructions for a Quota Sample

A recent consumer study of fast-food restaurants gave the following instructions for the sample:
There are to be 200 completed interviews. To the extent possible, the sample should be as follows:

Area
25–30% from Springfield
70–75% from Greater Eugene
Gender
60% males
40% females

Age
40% between 16 and 24
40% between 25 and 50
20% to be under 16 and over 50

Occupation
20% university students
80% non-students

The interviews should be conducted in the following areas:

(a) Valley River Shopping Center
(b) Downtown Springfield
(c) ©Big M-Marks Shopping Center
(d) Willamette Plaza
(e) Downtown Eugene
(f) University campus

The number of people to contact will depend upon the incidence or rate of occurrence of persons eligible to fill each of the 24 cells. Obviously, low incidence rates can lead to a greater number of needed contacts, which then leads to greater costs.

Since the interviewer's judgment is relied upon to select actual respondents within each quota, many sources of selection bias are potentially present. For example, the interviewer may not bother to call back if the first call results in a "not-at-home." Interviewers may go to selected areas where the chances are good that a particular type of respondent is available. Certain houses may be skipped because the interviewer does not like the appearance of the property, and certain people may be allowed to pass in a mall-intercept approach because they do not "look right." Still other ways exist in which the habits and biases of interviewers can influence their selection of respondents within quota.

The advantages of quota sampling are, of course, the lower costs and greater convenience provided to the interviewer when selecting respondents to fill each quota. Recently, tighter controls have been established on the permissible travel patterns of interviewers, thus tending to reduce this potential source of selection bias. In fact, it has been shown that quota sampling is quite close to traditional probability sampling under certain conditions (Sudman, 1976).

Quota sampling is discussed rather extensively in Stephan and McCarthy (1958). A critique of the method is offered by Deming (1960). A comparison of quota and probability sampling was the subject of a seminar held in 1994 at the Survey Methods Centre in the United Kingdom (Survey Methods Centre, 1995).

Judgment Sampling

A somewhat representative sample may be provided through the use of purposive, or judgment, sampling. The key assumption underlying this type of sampling is that, with sound judgment or expertise and an appropriate strategy, one can carefully and consciously choose the elements so as to develop suitable samples. The intent is to select elements typical or representative of the population in such a way that errors of judgment in the selection will cancel each other out. One weakness of this approach is that without an external check or objective basis for making the judgments, there is no way of knowing whether the so-called typical cases are, in fact, typical.

The relative advantages of judgment sampling are that it is inexpensive, convenient to use, less time-consuming, and provides results as good as probability sampling. However, its value depends entirely upon the expert judgment of the researcher. An example of the use of this type of sampling is a company, wanting to know why its new products failed, conducting surveys on competitors for products similar or related to those it produced. Another example is the choice of specific international banking personnel and government trade specialists as a sample to provide information to a company assessing whether it should begin marketing in a foreign market.

Convenience Sampling

Convenience sampling is a generic term that covers a wide variety of ad hoc procedures for selecting respondents. For example, some cities, such as Fort Worth, Texas, and Syracuse, New York, are viewed as "typical" cities whose demographic make-ups are close to the national average. In market tests of new products, it is not unusual to select such cities to obtain consumer evaluations believed to reflect national tastes. As in any other nonprobability procedure, however, there is no sound basis for estimating statistical confidence intervals around the sample statistics of interest. Interestingly, the cities with demographic characteristics closest to the national average are not the most surveyed, at least by researchers using telephone interviewing methods. The most popular markets are not necessarily the largest Metropolitan Statistical Areas (MSAs); during the mid-1990s they were small and medium-sized areas. For example, in 1995 the most popular area for telephone surveys was Portland, Maine, followed by Fort Collins–Loveland, Colorado ("Portland, Maine," 1996). These two areas had an average household income, but that was it! For example, both of these areas were racially imbalanced, having 97.8 percent and 94.1 percent Caucasian residents, respectively and each about 0.7 percent African-American residents. At the time, the national averages for these races were 79.4 percent and 12.2 percent, respectively. Unfortunately, no one seems to report exactly why these cities are surveyed so much.

Other forms of convenience sampling are prevalent. Many firms conduct "intercept" interviews among shopping-mall customers or in other areas where large numbers of consumers may congregate. It is possible to use other types of sampling, including probability sampling similar to a multistage area probability sample (see Reid, 1984, and Sudman, 1980). But the researcher needs to do so with care. For example, people stay in malls different lengths of time, which leads to a biasing effect if a probability sample is attempted. A sample is said to be *length biased* if the probability of observing an individual at a particular site is dependent on the individual's length of stay at the site. Clearly, the chance of interviewing an individual at a shopping center or other site with no clearly defined entrances and exits (such as a strip mall or street site) increases as the individual spends more time there. If people who spend more time at shopping centers differ in demographic characteristics from those who spend less time there, data obtained will be biased. Nowell and Stanley (1991) provide correction techniques applicable when the total length-of-stay is known or estimated, and when the recurrence time is accurately known. When necessary, mall intercept data should be adjusted not only by frequency of visit, but also by length of stay at the mall.

Not all intercept methods will result in proportionally length-biased data. If the interception occurs at entrances or if the site is such that all individuals simply walk from one fixed point to another, passing an interviewing station on the way, there will be no length bias (Nowell and Stanley, 1991). Firms may also authorize samples to be taken from such intact groups as Parent-Teacher Associations, church groups, philanthropic organizations, and so on. Again, the purpose is to obtain a relatively large number of interviews quickly from a cooperating group of respondents. Usually the sponsoring organization receives a donation from the interviewing firm for the help and cooperation of its members.

Surveys based on convenience sampling are also carried out by magazines and newspapers (using subscriber lists and/or a pull-out or tear-out questionnaire included in the publication), department stores (using charge account lists), or gasoline companies (using credit card lists). An example is the questionnaire shown in Figure 12.3, which appeared in the in-flight magazine of a major airlines during the 1990s. It is clear that this questionnaire is for business people, who are asked to fax it back. Since large numbers of business people fly, this is a convenient way to request information. In this example, the researcher knows nothing about the obtained sample. Again, many potential sources of selection bias are present, assuming that the population under study is larger than the members of the various lists. For instance, past research has shown that newspaper and magazine surveys suffer from sampling bias in that less than 10 percent of readers return the questionnaires, and respondents tend to be disproportionately white, educated, and affluent (Shaver and Rubenstein, 1983).

Convenience sampling means that the sampling units are accessible, convenient and easy to measure, cooperative, or articulate. An illustration of convenience sampling is the in-flight surveys conducted periodically by the airlines. These surveys use convenience samples, although one might also call them judgment samples, in that the sample is representative of the population defined as the flying public, or the potential flying public. Often, such surveys are designed to provide information that will enable an airline to better attract nonregular customers and perhaps even nonfliers. Certain flights on specific days are selected and everyone on the airplane is asked to participate. Not all say that they will participate, nor do all those who initially say they will participate actually complete the questionnaire.

INVESTING IN THE PACIFIC RIM

Beginning on page 33, you will find an article on doing business in the Pacific Rim. To help us plan future issues, we would like to know about your experiences and opinions in regard to this topic. Please take a minute to fill out this questionnaire, then tear it out and fax it (anonymously) to us at (222) 900–0000.

1. Do you currently do business in any of the Pacific Rim countries?

   yes _____   no _____

   If yes, which countries? _____
   _____

2. How many times a year do you usually visit the Pacific Rim region? _____

   What is the average length of these visits? _____ days

3. What kind of business is your company in? (check all that apply)

   Advertising _____   Manufacturing _____
   Construction _____   Media _____
   Entertainment _____   Publishing _____
   Fashion/consumer goods _____   Real estate _____
   Financial services _____   Retailing _____
   Import/export _____   Tourism _____
   Legal services _____   Transportation _____
   Management consulting _____   Other _____

4. Does your company have any business arrangements in the Pacific Rim? Is your company considering some kind of arrangement? (check all that apply)

	OPERATING	CONSIDERING
Subsidiary	_____	_____
Licensing	_____	_____
Branch office	_____	_____
Joint venture	_____	_____
Manufacturing facility	_____	_____
Financial investment	_____	_____
Management contract	_____	_____
Sales representative/ distributor/agent	_____	_____
Supplier	_____	_____
Home office	_____	_____

5. On a scale of 1 to 10 (10 is tops), rate the importance of the following reasons for doing business in the Pacific Rim:

   Source of raw   Consumer buying
     materials _____   patterns _____
   Lower operating   Investment capital _____
     costs _____
   Skilled labor _____   Technology _____
   Other _____

6. Rate the impact of social and cultural differences and language barriers on doing business in the following Pacific Rim countries: (check all that apply)

	SIGNIFICANT	MODERATE	LITTLE OR NONE
Australia	_____	_____	_____
China	_____	_____	_____
Hong Kong	_____	_____	_____
Indonesia	_____	_____	_____
Japan	_____	_____	_____
Korea	_____	_____	_____
Malaysia	_____	_____	_____
New Zealand	_____	_____	_____
Philippines	_____	_____	_____
Singapore	_____	_____	_____
Taiwan	_____	_____	_____
Thailand	_____	_____	_____

7. Do you take part in trade missions or attend trade shows in order to learn about doing business in the Pacific Rim?

   Trade shows: yes _____   no _____
   Trade missions: yes _____   no _____

8. Do you use the facilities of the commercial sections at U.S. embassies or consulates when abroad?

   Frequently _____   Sometimes _____
           Never _____

9. Do you use your local U.S. Department of Commerce district office to research markets, customers or agents, and distributors in Pacific Rim countries?

   Frequently _____   Sometimes _____
           Never _____

10. Which Pacific Rim countries do you think have the most potential for exporting, joint ventures/licensing, single direct investment or other business ventures by U.S. companies? (please list)

    _____
    _____

11. Do you currently have personal investments in any Pacific Rim countries (please list)

    _____
    _____

12. Are you a business owner? _____
    Senior management? _____
    Middle management? _____
    Other _____

Figure 12.3   Instrument Used With a Convenience Sample

New product testing provides another illustration of the use of this type of sampling. A toy manufacturer invited a number of parents to "lend" them their children for a few hours of play with new toys. Based on observations through one-way mirrors, redesigns for some toys were made. Wheels were added to a particular toy when it was observed that the children pulled it around.

Snowball Sampling

Snowball sampling (also known as multiplicity sampling) is the rather colorful name given to a procedure in which initial respondents are selected randomly, but where additional respondents are then obtained from referrals or other information provided by the initial respondents. One major purpose of snowball sampling is to estimate various characteristics that are rare in the total population. A more complete discussion of this technique is given by Zinkhan, Burton, and Wallendorf (1983).

For example, in a study of international tourism, the researchers were required to interview respondents in the United Kingdom, France, and Germany who visited the United States in its bicentennial year. As might be expected, in most areas of these three countries, the likelihood of finding a qualified adult respondent was less than two percent. Accordingly, stratified probability methods were used to select initial respondents. Then a referral procedure (up to two referrals per qualified respondent) was used to obtain a second group of qualified respondents. (However, this particular study did not obtain subsequent referrals from this second group of respondents.)

Another example is the research company who uses the telephone to obtain referrals. Random telephone calls are made, and regardless of whether the person answering the telephone is a qualified respondent, they are asked if someone else they know meets the study's respondent qualifications. If so, the interviewer tries to get that person's name.

In other types of snowball sampling, referrals from referrals are obtained, and so on, thus leading to the "snowballing" effect. Even though a probability-based procedure may be used to select the initial group of respondents, the overall sample is a nonprobability sample. For example, referrals tend to exhibit demographic profiles more similar to the persons referring them than would be expected by chance.

In general, the sampling of rare characteristics is often aided by short and inexpensive screening interviews (usually by telephone), whose major purpose is to locate the subpopulation of interest for a subsequent, more extensive personal interview. For a rare population, screening costs may be large when working with special populations for which no complete list exists. There are, however, vigorous methods for obtaining careful probability samples, although screening costs still may be significant (Sudman, 1985). Finally, it should be mentioned that in the case of rare characteristics, it is not unusual to over-sample some subgroups so as to obtain a sample size with an adequate actual number of respondents to produce reasonably stable estimates. That is, in sampling various rare characteristics, the allocation of interviews may *not* be in direct proportion to the relative size of the strata if this leads to too few respondents in the smaller strata.

Major advantages of this type of sampling over conventional methods are the substantially increased probability of finding the desired characteristic in the population, and lower sampling variance and costs.

PROBABILITY SAMPLING DESIGNS

The best-known type of probability sample is no doubt the simple random sample. However, many occasions in marketing research require more specialized sampling procedures than those of simple random-sampling methods. Statisticians have developed a variety of specialized probability-sampling designs that, although derived from simple random-sampling principles, can be used to gain either lower sampling error for a given cost or equal sampling error for a lower cost. Five major modifications can be made to the basic selection process, as shown in Table 12.2. Conceptually, these five dimensions allow for a total of 32 possible probability samples. However, some designs are used more widely and are of greater interest than others. Designs of particular interest to the marketing researcher are systematic sampling, stratified sampling, cluster sampling, area sampling, and multistage sampling.

These techniques are discussed in turn, following a review of simple random sampling. Our purpose is to describe the major characteristics of each technique, rather than to present a detailed mathematical exposition of its procedures. Many excellent statistics and research books review the mathematical aspects of these sampling techniques.

Table 12.2   Selection Methods for Probability Samples

Probability samples	*Nonprobability samples*
I. *Equal probability* for all elements	*Unequal probabilities* for different elements; ordinarily compensated with inverse weights
Equal probabilities at all stages	Caused by irregularities in selection frames and procedures
Equal overall probabilities for all elements obtained through compensating unequal probabilities at several stages	Disproportionate allocation designed for optimum allocation
II. *Element Sampling*: single stage, sampling unit contains only one element	*Cluster Sampling*: sampling units are clusters of elements
	One-stage cluster sampling
	Sub-sampling or multistage sampling
	Equal clusters
	Unequal clusters
III. *Unstratified Selection*: sampling units selected from entire population	*Stratified Sampling*: separated selections from partitions, or strata, of population
IV. *Random Selection* of individual sampling units from entire stratum or population	*Systematic Selection* of sampling units with selection interval applied to list
V. *One-Phase Sampling*: final sample selected directly from entire population	*Two-Phase (or Double) Sampling*: final sample selected from first-phase sample, which obtains information for stratification or estimation

SOURCE: Adapted from Kish, 1965, p. 20.

Simple Random Sampling

In a simple random sample, each sample element has a known and equal probability of selection, and each possible sample of *n* elements has a known and equal probability of being the sample actually selected. It is drawn by a random procedure from a sample frame—a list containing an exclusive and exhaustive enumeration of all sample elements. This random procedure could be as simple as a coin toss or drawing names or numbers from a container. A widely used process is to number the elements in the frame and then use a spreadsheet's random-number generator to select the sample members.

Simple random samples are not widely used in marketing research, and especially so in consumer research, for two reasons. First, it is often difficult to obtain a sampling frame that will permit a simple random sample to be drawn. Consumer research usually requires either people, households, stores, or areas be the basic sampling units. While a complete representation of areas is available through maps, there normally is no complete listing of persons, the households in which they live, or the stores available. When persons, households, or stores are to be sampled, therefore, some other sample design must be used.

However, in business-to-business (B2B) marketing research, there is a greater opportunity to apply simple random sampling. In this case, purchasing agents, companies, or areas are the usual sampling units. Since the population under study is often relatively small, one is in a better position to develop a complete respondent list or sample frame.

B2B marketing research, however, provides a second reason for not using simple random sampling: One may not want to have an equal probability of selecting all sample units. Most industries are characterized by a wide variation in the size of the comprising firms. One is likely to design the sample so that larger firms have a considerably greater chance of being selected than smaller firms.

Systematic Sampling

Systematic sampling involves only a slight variation from simple random sampling. In a systematic sample, each sample element has a known and equal probability of selection. The permissible samples of size *n* possible to draw have a known and equal probability of selection, while the remaining samples of size *n* have zero probability of being selected.

The mechanics of taking a systematic sample are rather simple. If the population contains *N* ordered elements and a sample size *n* is desired, one merely finds the ratio of N/n and rounds to the nearest integer to obtain the sampling interval. For example, if there are 600 members of the population and one desires a sample of 60, the sampling interval is 10. A random number is then selected between 1 and 10, inclusively; suppose the number turns out to be 4. The analyst then takes as the sample elements 4, 14, 24, and so on.

Essentially, systematic sampling assumes that population elements are ordered in some fashion—names in a telephone directory, a card index file, or the like. Some types of ordering, such as an alphabetical listing, will usually be uncorrelated with the characteristic (say, income level) being investigated. In other instances, the ordering of the elements may be directly related to the characteristic under study, such as a customer list arranged in decreasing order of annual purchase volume.

If the arrangement of the elements of the sample is itself random with regard to the characteristic under study, systematic sampling will tend to give results close to those provided by simple random sampling. We say "close" because in systematic sampling, all combinations of the characteristic do not have the same chance of being included. For example, it is clear that in the preceding example, the fifth, sixth, and so on items have zero chance of being chosen in the particular sample after the first item has been determined.

Systematic sampling may, however, increase the sample's representativeness when items are ordered with regard to the characteristic of interest. For example, if the analyst is sampling a customer group ordered by decreasing purchase volume, a systematic sample will be sure to contain both high- and low-volume customers. On the other hand, the simple random sample may yield, say, only low-volume customers, and may thus be unrepresentative of the population being sampled if the characteristic of interest is related to purchase volume.

It is also possible that systematic sampling may decrease the representativeness of the sample in instances where the items are ordered to produce a cyclical pattern. For example, if a marketing researcher were to use systematic sampling of daily retail-store sales volume, and were to choose a sampling interval of seven days, his or her choice of day would result in a sample that would not reflect day-of-the-week variations in sales.

Although systematic sampling can lead to greater reliability (lower sampling error) than simple random sampling, the major difficulty of this technique is estimating the variance of the universe from the variance of the sample. For example, if in the preceding example we happened to sample all "Tuesdays," we would probably find that we have seriously underestimated the variance across all seven days in the week. If we have prior knowledge about the characteristics of the groups making up the population, however, we may use this information to select our sample to increase its reliability over that which would be obtained by simple random-sampling methods.

Stratified Sampling

It is sometimes desirable to break the population into different strata based on one or more characteristics, such as the frequency of purchase of a product, type of customer (e.g., credit card versus noncredit card), or the industry in which a company competes. In such cases, a separate sample is then taken from each stratum. Technically, a stratified random sample is one in which a simple random sample is taken from each stratum of interest in the population. In practice, however, systematic and other types of random samples are sometimes taken from each of the strata and the resulting design is still referred to as a stratified sample.

Stratified samples are generally determined by the following steps:

- The entire population is first divided into an exclusive and exhaustive set of strata, using some external source, such as census data, to form the strata.
- A separate random sample is selected within each stratum.
- From each separate sample, some statistic (such as a mean) is computed and properly weighted to form an overall estimated mean for the whole population.
- Sample variances are also computed within each separate stratum and appropriately weighted to yield a combined estimate for the whole population.

The two basic varieties of stratified samples are proportionate and disproportionate. In proportionate stratified sampling, the sample drawn from each stratum is made proportionate in size to the relative size of that stratum in the total population. In disproportionate stratified sampling, one departs from the preceding proportionality by taking other circumstances, such as the relative size of stratum variances, into account.

The decision whether to use proportionate or disproportionate stratified sampling among strata rests on whether or not the variances among the strata are (approximately) equal. Suppose a marketing researcher is interested in estimating the average purchases of consumers of hot cereal. The researcher may be willing to assume that, although average consumption would vary markedly by family size, the variances around the means of the strata would be more or less equal among family sizes. If so, the researcher would make use of proportionate stratified sampling.

More generally, however, both means and variances will differ among strata. If this is the case, the researcher would make use of disproportionate stratified sampling. In this instance, the number of families included in each stratum would be proportionate to (the product of) the relative size of the different family-sized strata in the population and the standard deviation of each family class. This requires, of course, that the researcher be able to estimate (from past studies) the within-group standard deviation around the average purchase quantity of each purchasing stratum. Formulas for computing sampling errors in stratified samples are briefly discussed in Chapter 13 and can be found in standard texts on sampling.

As intuition would suggest, the increased efficiency of stratified sampling over simple random sampling depends on how different the means (or some other statistic) really are among strata, relative to the within-stratum variability. Desired are strata whose within-stratum variation is small, but whose among-strata differences are large. That is, the greater the within-stratum homogeneity and among-stratum heterogeneity, the more efficient stratified sampling is relative to simple random sampling.

Two final considerations need to be addressed regarding stratified sampling. First, a sample size needs to be calculated for each stratum or subgroup. Second, the process of sample selection can be time-consuming and costly to carry out if many subgroups are to be used. Nevertheless, this method continues to be widely used due to the segmentation of markets that companies routinely engage in.

Cluster Sampling

Although the researcher will ordinarily be interested in the characteristics of some elementary element in the population (such as individual family attitudes toward a new product), he may wish to select primary sampling units on a larger basis than individual family. The researcher may choose to sample city blocks and interview all the individual families residing therein. The blocks, not the individual families, would be selected at random. Each block consists of a cluster of respondents. Formally, a cluster sample is one in which a simple random or stratified random sample is selected of all primary sample units, each containing more than one sample element. Then, all elements within the selected primary units are sampled.

The main advantage of a cluster sample relative to simple random sampling is in lower interviewing costs rather than in greater reliability. To illustrate, a large drug firm ran a survey of salespeople's attitudes toward management policies of the firm, in which sales districts were the primary units sampled and all salespeople of the sampled districts were interviewed. As might be surmised, the attitudes of a given district's salespeople tended to be positively correlated among salespeople, resulting in greater sampling variance than would have been attained if random sampling (with the same sample size) had been performed at the individual salesperson level.

On the other hand, the expense of transporting interviewers to various parts of the firm's overall marketing territory would have added substantially to the costs of the study.

Area Sampling: Single Stage and Multistage

As the name suggests, area sampling pertains to primary sampling of geographical areas—for example, counties, townships, blocks and other area descriptions. If only one level of sampling takes place (such as a sampling of blocks) before the basic elements are sampled (the households), it is a single-stage area sample. If one or more successive samples within the larger area are taken before settling on the final clusters, the resulting design is usually referred to as a multistage area sample.

An example of multistage sampling is the sample design used by the Gallup Organization, Inc., for taking a nationwide poll. Gallup draws a random sample of locations as the first stage of the sampling process. Blocks or geographic segments are then randomly sampled from each of these locations in a second stage, followed by a systematic sampling of households within the blocks or segments. A total of about 1,500 persons are usually interviewed in the typical Gallup poll. Another example is provided by Opinion Research Corporation's (ORC) sampling for studies of the general public, or defined segments of it. The ORC master sample consists of hundreds of communities arranged in blocks. Each block is a random sample of communities, selected with probability proportioned to population. The communities within each block are distributed further into national probability replications, each of a specified number of communities. For any given study, therefore, one or more blocks provide a national probability sample.

SAMPLING FOR TELEPHONE SURVEYS

Our discussion above of probability sampling designs has been general, and is applicable to all methods of data collection. In some ways, sampling for telephone surveys is unique. A description of techniques specifically applicable to telephone surveys now follows.

Creating probability samples for telephone surveys is not an easy task. Although the general approaches to sample design can be used (such as simple random, systematic, stratified, cluster, etc.), there are some unique differences. The most commonly used methods are summarized in Table 12.3.

Methods for telephone sampling can be categorized as either directory-based or random-digit dialing (RDD). In all cases the result is a probability sample, although the actual probability of inclusion, and even the extent of knowing this probability, varies among the methods. In general, all directory-based approaches are limited by the related high frame error due to exclusion of nonsubscribers and generation of many unproductive telephone numbers (non-population elements and nonworking numbers). In contrast, costs are relatively low. Random-digit dialing, on the other hand, tends to have lower frame error but higher costs. But, RDD has coverage limitations as well. The average working telephone rate (WPR) in the United States for random-digit samples was 61.4 percent in 1997 ("Lower Working Phone Rate," 1997). This means that almost 40 percent of possible telephone numbers were not valid. The WPR varied between states, ranging from a high of 72.8 percent in West Virginia to a low of 46.3 percent in Washington, DC, as shown in Table 12.4. In addition to WPR considerations, working numbers are often associated with fax or dedicated computer lines.

Table 12.3   Telephone Sampling Methods

Method	Synopsis of procedure
Directory-Assisted	
Selection of listings	Systematic or simple random selection procedures are used to select a sample of directory lines. In some cases the selected line is used as a starting point for a cluster of k lines.
Add-a-digit	Numbers are selected from the directory, and an integer (between 0 and 9) is added to the number.
Randomization of the r last digits	Numbers are selected from the directory. The r last digits (2, 3, or 4) are replaced by random selection of numbers.
Sudman's method	This is a two-stage procedure. Numbers are selected from the directory. The last three digits are removed, leaving the central office code and thousands digit. A group of three-place random digits is selected and added to the directory.
Random-digit dialing (RDD)	
Pure RDD	All numbers are generated at random and with equal probability.
Two-Stage RDD	This procedure uses known working prefixes (first three digits of the seven-digit number). After these are chosen, there are different ways to select the four-digit number to be attached.
Mitofsky-Waksberg Procedure	This is a two-stage method. All working three-digit prefixes in an area are identified. To each of these, all possible two digits are added. This process defines all banks of 100 numbers in the area. One of the five-digit numbers is selected at random (forming a primary sampling unit), and a randomly selected two-digit number is added. This number is called and if it is a residence, the bank of 100 that was selected is retained, and other numbers formed by adding sets of last two digits. If it is not a residence, the primary sampling unit is rejected. This procedure can be expanded to a national sample by defining the primary sampling unit as area code + prefix + first two digits.

SOURCE: From Kish, L., *Survey Sampling,* copyright © 1965. This material is used by permission of John Wiley & Sons, Inc.

These types of lines are more frequently found among higher socioeconomic status individuals: 23.5 percent hold college degrees and 40.1 percent have household income over $75,000 Tuckel, 2002). Primarily because of frame error, major criticisms of directory-based samples have tended to be statistical in nature. Random-digit dialing methods are designed to overcome these statistical problems.

Some researchers believe that directory-based samples are just as representative and proportionate as those derived from random-digit dialing. Exhibit 12.4 discusses a method for combining RDD with the use of a list. Yet another alternative is disproportionate stratified sampling (DSS). The objective of DSS, like that of Mitofsky-Waksberg designs, is to make

Table 12.4   Working Phone Rates

States With Highest Rates		*States With Lowest Rates*	
1. West Virginia	72.8%	1. Washington, DC	46.3%
2. Mississippi	71.1%	2. Alaska	50.5%
3. Arkansas	69.0%	3. Maine	54.0%
4. Alabama	68.6%	4. Vermont	54.0%
5. Oklahoma	66.3%	5. Hawaii	54.7%
6. Kentucky	66.2%	6. Delaware	55.4%
7. Louisiana	65.3%	7. Nebraska	56.6%
8. Kansas	64.8%	8. New Jersey	57.0%
9. Tennessee	64.8%	9. New Hampshire	57.7%
10. Rhode Island	64.7%	10. Illinois	58.8%

SOURCE: Reprinted with permission from Survey Sampling, Inc.

telephone sampling more efficient by increasing the proportion of target telephone numbers among all numbers called, relative to the proportion obtained by simple random sampling. A Mitofsky-Waksberg design tries to increase the expected "hit rate" by first dividing telephone numbers into blocks—typically 100 numbers per block. Then one number from the block is called. If the number is a target number (e.g., a household), the remainder of the block is accepted for further sampling. By contrast, a DSS design attempts to differentiate, before actual sampling starts, between blocks of telephone numbers containing many target numbers and those containing few target numbers. Sampling is done disproportionately from the high-density blocks (Mariolis, 1992).

EXHIBIT 12.4   List-Assisted Telephone Samples

Probably the best-known method of selecting random samples of telephone households is the Mitofsky-Waksberg method of random digit dialing. It is a two-stage sample in which the first stage—for a national or other non-local sample—consists of clusters of telephone numbers defined as sets of numbers with the first eight digits (area code plus five digits) of the ten-digit telephone number. If a randomly sampled number in a cluster is residential, then the cluster is retained in the sample; otherwise, the cluster is rejected (Waksberg, 1978).

Some have suggested that the sequential nature of the second stage sampling is problematic. To overcome the potential problems associated with making a great number of calls to nonworking and nonresidential numbers, as well as the disadvantages of a straight Mitofsky-Waksberg approach, the researcher can use a method known as list-assisted sampling. A variety of procedures fall under this heading and are described by Lepkowski (1988) and Casady and Lepkowski (1993). This approach combines the use of a list (a sampling frame) with the Mitofsky-Waksberg procedure. A study by Brick, Waksberg, Kulp, and Starer (1995) concludes that the list-assisted

RDD sampling method is efficient, and that although it excludes some households from the sample, estimates from the design are not subject to important coverage bias. This study indicates that only three to four percent of all residential households are excluded when the list-assisted design is used. This design clearly is appropriate for large-scale national surveys.

Due to changes in the technology and operation of telephone systems in the United States and elsewhere during the past 10 years, it has been increasingly difficult to identify residential telephone numbers. This means that list-assisted approaches have also had to change. Such changes are discussed by Tucker, Lepkowski, and Piekarski (2002).

A large-scale study by Survey Sampling, Inc., in 1989 tends to support the differences between directory-listed and unlisted households (Piekarski, 1989). Over 60,000 interviews were completed. Most were conducted in 80 of the largest MSAs in the United States; additional interviews were conducted in the remaining MSAs and nonmetropolitan areas. The incidence of unlisted numbers was 39 percent in the 80 larger MSAs, 34 percent in the other MSAs, and 29.5 percent in the rural areas. This was not an unexpected finding. Overall, the study concluded that when compared to listed households, unlisted households are significantly younger, more mobile, more likely to be rental and multifamily units, more likely to be employed and not married, have a lower income and education level, and belong to a minority group. This study refuted two myths—high-income people are not more likely to be unlisted, and unlisted households are not more likely to refuse to cooperate with a research study.

There are some concerns that affect telephone surveys. First is the trend to have an unlisted directory number. This is tied to a desire for privacy. There also is evidence of declining contact and cooperation rates. These can be dealt with to some extent by sound planning. But, firms should maintain historical databases on these to better weigh and estimate costs. Another impact comes from technology: the growing use of answering machines in households. Many people today use their answering machines to screen incoming telephone calls. When an initial call to conduct an interview is screened, this poses a potential threat to the representativeness of obtained samples in telephone surveys. One study determined that two-thirds of households have answering machines, and 42.9 percent use answering machines or caller ID to screen calls. Such screening is more likely to occur in such demographic groups as those aged 18–29, Hispanics, African Americans, never-marrieds, homemakers, those with $15,000 to $30,000 annual income, one-adult households, and households with young children Tuckel, 2002).

Two major questions arise: (a) What are the chances that additional calls to a household known to use an answering machine will result in a completed interview; and (b) When is the best time to call, in order to minimize an encounter with an answering machine? There are no ready answers to these questions. However, households with answering machines were more likely to be contacted, more likely to complete the interview, and less likely to refuse to participate, compared to households where there was no answer on the initial call attempt (Xu, Bates, and Schweitzer, 1993). Leaving a message on the answering machine when no one answered the phone did result in higher participation rates.

Answering machines undoubtedly cause problems for telephone surveys. But these problems appear to be more of an inconvenience and are not insurmountable. Users of answering machines are more difficult to reach, but once contacted they are just as likely as others to complete an interview (Piazza, 1993). That is, answering machine contact rates parallel overall contact rates.

Another technological development potentially affecting contact rates in telephone surveys is caller ID. Households with caller ID often use it to screen calls. We might surmise that the impact of this technology will parallel that of answering machines. Another technological feature that could possibly have a negative effect is call forwarding. If a person is away from home and has activated call forwarding, it is unlikely that they would want to receive a call from a telephone survey company. There is no way for the researcher to know in advance when this feature has been activated, so we might conclude that this is another risk of the telephone survey business.

Regardless of the method used to draw the sample, consumer studies utilize samples drawn from households. Thus, there still remains the problem of selecting a respondent. One option, of course, is to use the person answering the telephone if that person meets the eligibility requirements, such as minimum age. Technically speaking, this approach may essentially produce a nonprobability sample. A probability-based approach in general use was developed by Kish (1949). This method requires all eligible respondents within a household to be listed by sex, and within sex groupings by age from oldest to youngest. After all eligible respondents are identified, the respondent to be interviewed is selected by using a random number table.

The Kish technique requires much time at the beginning of the interview. To overcome this, Troldahl and Carter (1964) developed a method that requires identifying only two details:

1. The number of people 18 years of age or older in the household

2. The number of men in the household

Using previously developed selection matrices rotated randomly over the sample, the proper selection can easily be made (see Table 12.5). A modification of this technique would be to ask for the number of women. Another technique, even simpler than Troldahl-Carter, is the "birthday" method (Salmon & Nichols, 1983). The interviewer asks to speak to the adult with the most recent birthday, or the one who has the next birthday. There is no evidence that any one of these methods is universally better than the others. In fact, in a study comparing the Kish and Troldahl-Carter methods to a modification of Troldahl-Carter, few differences were found in the cooperation rates and demographic characteristics of the respondents (Czaja, Blair, & Sebsestik, 1982).

In some instances the researcher may find it beneficial to use a crisscross or cross-reference directory. These directories, published by private companies, typically list phone numbers numerically, also listing subscribers geographically, alphabetically, and by numerical street address within each zip code. One use of this type of directory is a study conducted in a medium-sized community to ascertain residents' attitudes and behavior regarding parks and recreation. The client specified a telephone survey due to budget constraints, and also wanted representation from the five park districts within the community. Since telephone exchanges were not area-based, random-digit dialing would have been too cumbersome and time-consuming. Other methods would also have required sequential sampling. Fortunately, a cross-reference directory was available, and once the park districts were outlined on a map, the sample was selected using systematic random sampling.

Table 12.5   Versions of Selection Matrices

Total number of men in household	Total number of adults in household			
	1	*2*	*3*	*4 or more*
Version I				
0	Woman	Oldest woman	Youngest woman	Youngest woman
1	Man	Man	Man	Oldest woman
2		Oldest man	Youngest man	Youngest man
3			Youngest man	Oldest man
4+				Oldest man
Version II				
0	Woman	Youngest woman	Youngest woman	Oldest woman
1	Man	Man	Oldest woman	Man
2		Oldest man	Woman	Oldest woman
3			Youngest man	Woman or oldest woman
4+				Oldest man
Version III				
0	Woman	Youngest woman	Oldest woman	Oldest woman
1	Man	Woman	Man	Youngest woman
2		Youngest man	Oldest man	Oldest man
3			Oldest man	Youngest man
4+				Youngest man
Version IV				
0	Woman	Oldest woman	Oldest woman	Youngest woman
1	Man	Woman	Youngest woman	Man
2		Youngest man	Woman	Youngest woman
3			Oldest man	Woman or youngest woman
4+				Youngest man

SOURCE: From Troldahl, V. C. & Carter, R. E. "Random Selection of Respondents within Households in Phone Surveys," in *Journal of Marketing Research, 1,* copyright © 1964. Reprinted with permission of the American Marketing Association.

INTERNATIONAL RESEARCH

All of the sampling concerns raised throughout this chapter exist for international marketing as well. Some issues are more complex when foreign markets are involved. Another issue arising in the case of international sampling involves the need to balance within-country representativeness with cross-national comparability. Well-defined sample frames are not in existance in all foreign markets. One criticism of sampling methods in international research is that too much reliance has been placed on nonprobability samples. But as we have seen, this type of sampling is used as well in marketing research within domestic markets. As Table 12.6 shows, there are two types of international research where nonprobability sampling is acceptable. A discussion of the theoretical bases for international sampling choices in relation to the objectives of the research study is provided by Reynolds, Simintiras, and Diamantopoulos (2003). A detailed discussion of sampling procedures that can be used in international marketing research is found in Kumar (2000).

Table 12.6   Sampling Choices in International Marketing Research

Type of International Research	Research Objective	Sampling Objective	Desired Sample Attributes	Preferred Sampling Method
Descriptive	Examine attitudes and behavior within specific countries	Within-country representativeness	Ability to estimate sampling error	Probability within each country
Contextual	Examine attributes of a cross-national group	Representativeness of specific population of interest	Ability to estimate sampling error	Probability sampling of population of interest
Comparative	Examine differences or similarities between countries	Cross-national comparability	Homogeneous samples to control extraneous factors	Nonprobability acceptable
Theoretical	Examine the cross-national generalizability of a theory or model	Cross-national comparability	Homogeneous, or deliberately sampled for heterogeneity	Nonprobability acceptable

SOURCE: Reynolds, Simintiras, and Diamantopoulos, 2003, p. 82.

SUMMARY

This chapter has concerned the questions of whether to take a census or a sample and, when sampling, what type of sample to take. We first considered the question of when a sample, rather than a census, should be taken, then followed this with a discussion of sample planning. Next, the major kinds of samples and criteria for choosing among them were discussed. We then presented a discussion of sampling for telephone surveys. Alternative methods were presented, issues raised by technology were discussed, and methods for choosing the specific respondent from a household were presented. The chapter ended with a short discussion of sampling for international marketing research.

ASSIGNMENT MATERIAL

1. The founder of a well-known consulting firm specializing in consumer research once stated that the way he would select a sample of housewives to obtain information for redesigning a line of refrigerators would be to "start talking to housewives I happen to know, ask them to refer me to others they know, and keep talking to additional ones until I found one *who really knows how a refrigerator should be designed.*"

    a. What kind of sampling procedure has the consultant described?

    b. What are its advantages? Disadvantages?

2. Explain the trade-offs that may be necessary between reliability and costs for the various probability sampling designs.

3. Discuss how one might modify quota sampling to make it more closely approximate stratified random sampling.

4. For your local area, compare alternative sample frames for a study of consumer purchases of durable goods on the basis of fit between the frame and the population, as illustrated in Figure 12.2. (Hint: remember the telephone directory, city directory, list of registered voters, patrons of a shopping mall, etc.)

5. The Hoosier Food Products Company is undecided about whether to use a cents-off coupon in a direct consumer promotion or increase its cooperative advertising allowances for food retailers in a particular market area. The marketing research director, Ken Bloker, wants to undertake a study, but is undecided on the sampling plan.

    a. Describe how convenience, judgment and quota sampling can be used for this project.

    b. Develop plans for a simple random sample, a systematic sample, a stratified sample, and an area sample.

    c. Is any one plan better than the others? If so, why? If not, why not?

6. Which method is "best" for choosing which individual in a household to be interviewed in a telephone survey? Defend your choice.

REFERENCES

Brick, J. M., Waksberg, J., Kulp, D., & Starer, A. (1995). Bias in list-assisted telephone surveys. *Public Opinion Quarterly, 59,* 218–235.

Casady, R. J., & Lepkowski, J. M. (1993). Stratified telephone survey designs. *Survey Methodology, 19,* 103–113.

Czaja, R., Blair, J., & Sebsestik, J. P. (1982, August). Respondent selection in a telephone survey: A comparison of three techniques. *Journal of Marketing Research, 19,* 381–385.

Deming, W. E. (1960). *Sample designs in business research.* New York: Wiley.

Dillman, D. A. (2000). *Mail and internet surveys: The tailored design method* (2nd ed.). New York: Wiley.

Fink, A. (2003). *How to sample in surveys* (2nd ed.). Thousand Oaks, CA: Sage.

Hogan, H. R., Garrett, P. K., & Pautler, C. P. (1986, March 23–26). *Coverage concepts and issues in data collection and data presentations.* Paper presented at the Bureau of the Census Second Annual Research Conference.

Jacoby, J., & Handlin, A. H. (1990). *Sampling in the social sciences: Implications for evaluating litigation survey evidence.* (Working Paper Mark-90–14.) Stern School of Business, New York University.

Kish, L. (1949, September). A procedure for objective respondent selection within the household. *American Statistical Association Journal,* 380–387.

Kish, L. (1965). *Survey sampling.* New York: Wiley.

Kumar, V. (2000). *International marketing research.* Upper Saddle River, NJ: Prentice Hall.

Lepkowski, J. (1988). Telephone survey methods in the United States. In R.M. Groves, et al. (Eds.), *Telephone survey methodology.* New York: Wiley.

Lower working phone rate in areas. (1997, November 1). *The Frame,* Retrieved June 4, 2004, from http://www.worldopinion.com/newsstand.taf?f=a&id=1360

Mariolis, P. (1992, Spring). Disproportionate stratified sampling: An emerging standard for RDD surveys. *CATI News, 5*(1), 1ff.

Nowell, C., & Stanley, L. R. (1991, November). Length-biased sampling in mall intercept surveys. *Journal of Marketing Research, 28,* 475–479.

Piazza, T. (1993). Meeting the challenge of answering machines. *Public Opinion Quarterly, 57,* 219–231.

Piekarski, L. B. (1989). *Choosing between directory listed and random digit sampling in light of new demographic findings.* Paper presented at 1989 AAPOR Conference.

Portland, Maine is nation's most surveyed market. (1996, September 3). *The Frame,* Retrieved June 4, 2004, from http://www.worldopinion.com/newsstand.taf?f=a&id=1140

Reid, P. M. (1984, January). Purists may disagree, but almost all types of surveys can be conducted in malls. *Marketing News, 18,* 5.

Reynolds, N. L., Simintiras, A. C., & Diamantopoulos, A. (2003). Theoretical justification of sampling choices in international marketing research: Key issues and guidelines for researchers. *Journal of International Business Studies, 34,* 80–89.

Sacramento is top unlisted market. (1995, February 1). *The Frame,* Retrieved June 4, 2004, from http://www.worldopinion.com/newsstand.taf?f=a&id=1026

Salmon, C. T., & Nichols, J. S. (1983). The next-birthday method of respondent selection. *Public Opinion Quarterly, 47,* 270–276.

Semon, T. T. (1990, January 8). Don't panic when sample isn't quite what you expected. *Marketing News, 24,* 31.

Semon, T. T. (2000, June 9). Quality sampling, research means avoiding sloppiness. *Marketing News, 34,* 11.

Shaver, P., & Rubenstein, C. (1983). Research potential of newspaper and magazine surveys. In H. T. Reis (Ed.), *Naturalistic approaches to studying social interaction* (pp. 75–91). San Francisco: Jossey-Bass.

Stephan, F. J., & McCarthy, P. J. (1958). *Sampling opinions.* New York: Wiley.

Sudman, S. (1976). *Applied sampling.* New York: Academic Press.

Sudman, S. (1980, November). Improving the quality of shopping center sampling. *Journal of Marketing Research, 17,* 423–431.

Sudman, S. (1985, February). Efficient screening methods for the sampling of geographically clustered special populations. *Journal of Marketing Research, 22,* 20–29.

Survey Methods Centre (1995). Quota versus probability sampling. *Survey Methods Centre Newsletter, 15*(1).

Survey Sampling International. (1992). *Glossary handbook.* Fairfield, CT: Author.

Troldahl, V. C., & Carter, R. E., Jr. (1964, May). Random selection of respondents within households in phone surveys. *Journal of Marketing Research, 1,* 71–76.

Tuckel, P., O'Neill, H. (2002, September/October). The vanishing respondent in telephone surveys. *Journal of Advertising Research, 42*(5), 26–30.

Tucker, C., Lepkowski, J. M., & Piekarski, L. (2002). The current efficiency of list-assisted telephone sampling plans. *Public Opinion Quarterly, 66,* 321–338.

Waksberg, J. (1978). Sampling methods in random digit dialing. *Journal of the American Statistical Association, 73*(361), 40–46.

Xu, M., Bates, B. J., & Schweitzer, J. C. (1993). The impact on survey participation in answering machine households. *Public Opinion Quarterly, 57,* 232–237.

Yates, F. (1971). *Sampling methods for censuses and surveys.* London: Charles Griffin & Co., Ltd.

Zinkhan, G., Burton, S., & Wallendorf, M. (1983). Marketing applications for snowball sampling. In W.R. Darden et al. (Eds.), *Research methods and causal models in marketing.* Chicago: American Marketing Association.

Chapter 13

SAMPLE SIZE

The last chapter was concerned with the overall process of sampling and with sample design. Related to design, but a unique decision area in its own right, is the determination of the size of the sample.

There are several ways to classify techniques for determining sample size. Two that are of primary importance are the following:

- Whether the technique deals with fixed or sequential sampling
- Whether its logic is based on traditional or Bayesian inferential methods

Other than the brief discussion of sequential sampling that follows, this chapter is concerned with the determination of a fixed sample size with emphasis on traditional inference, such as Neyman-Pearson, rather than Bayesian inference.[1]

Although the discussion will focus on the statistical aspects of setting sample size, it should be recognized that nonstatistical dimensions can affect the value of a research project. Such things as the length of a questionnaire, budget, and time schedule, as well as attitudes, opinions, and expectations, all have a direct effect on sample size decisions. Exhibit 13.1 outlines some of the nonstatistical considerations affecting sample size decisions.

EXHIBIT 13.1 Sample Size Affected By Practical Issues

Statistical precision requirements are one of many considerations a researcher faces when choosing sample size. Whatever the choice, the researcher should fully understand the consequence of the precision gain or loss due to the choice made. According to Susie Sangren, president of Clearview Data Strategy of Ithaca, New York, there are practical constraints, beyond any precision requirement, affecting sample size (2000, pp. 66–67):

- *Time pressure.* Far too often results are needed almost immediately.
- *Cost constraint.* Unlimited funds are never available for a study.

- *Study objective*. What is the purpose of the study? A decision that does not need great precision can make do with a very small sample size.
- *Data analysis procedures*. The sample size needed for single-variable analysis typically can be smaller than that needed for two or more variable analyses. For example, with cross-tabulation analyses the number of cells in the analysis may be so large that sample sizes within cells may become quite small. Precision estimates then become suspect.

FIXED VERSUS SEQUENTIAL SAMPLING

As the name implies, in fixed-size sampling the number of items is decided in advance. The size of the sample is chosen in such a way as to achieve some type of balance between sample reliability and sample cost. In general, all observations are taken before the data are analyzed.

In sequential sampling, however, the number of items is not preselected. Rather, the analyst sets up in advance a decision rule that includes not only the alternative of stopping the sampling process (and taking appropriate action, based on the sample evidence already in hand) but also the possibility of collecting more information before making a final decision. Observations may be taken either singly or in groups, the chief novelty being that the data are analyzed as they are assembled and sample size is not predetermined.

In general, sequential sampling will lead to smaller sample sizes, on average, than those associated with fixed-size samples of a given reliability. The mathematics underlying sequential sampling are, however, more complex and time consuming. In addition, the problem may be such that it is less expensive to select and analyze a sample of many items at one time than to draw items one at a time (or in small groups) and analyze each item before selecting the next.

What may appear to be sequential sampling is used occasionally—and unwisely—to offset nonresponse. That is, additional sample members are selected to replace nonrespondents. Not only is this not sequential sampling, as there is no decision rule being applied as to whether to sample additional elements, it does not overcome the problem of nonresponse. Nonrespondents still are not represented—and those willing to cooperate are increased in number (Dutka, Frankel, & Roshwalb, 1982, p. 78).

SAMPLING DISTRIBUTIONS AND STANDARD ERRORS

Intuitively we might expect that when we increase the size of the sample, our estimate of the population parameter should get closer to the true value. Also, we might expect that the less dispersed the population's characteristics are, the closer our sample estimates should be to the true parameter. After all, the reason why we sample in the first place is to make some inference about the population. These inferences should be more reliable the larger the sample on which they are based and the less variable the items of the population are to begin with.

The reader will recall from elementary statistics the concept of a sampling distribution. A sampling distribution is the probability distribution of a specified sample statistic (e.g., the sample mean) for all possible random samples of a given size n drawn from the specified population. The standard error of the statistic is the standard deviation of the specified sampling distribution. We shall use the following symbols in our brief review of the elementary formulas for calculating the standard error of the mean and proportion (under simple random sampling):

μ = population mean

π = population proportion regarding some attribute

σ = standard deviation of the population

s = standard deviation of the sample, adjusted to serve as an estimate of the standard deviation of the population

$\overline{X}$ = arithmetic mean of a sample

p = sample proportion

n = number of items in the sample

There are some important properties associated with sampling distributions:

1. The arithmetic mean of the sampling distribution of the mean ($\overline{X}$) or of the proportion (p) for any given size sample equals the corresponding parameter values μ and π, respectively.

2. The sampling distribution of the means of random samples will tend toward the *normal distribution* as sample size n increases, regardless of the original form of the population being sampled.

3. For large samples (e.g., $n \geq 100$ and for π fairly close to 0.5) the normal distribution also represents a reasonable approximation of the binomial distribution for sample proportions.

4. In the case of finite universes, where the sample size n is some appreciable fraction of the total number, N, of items in the universe, the standard error formulas should be adjusted by multiplication by the following *finite multiplier*:

$$\sqrt{\frac{N-n}{N-1}}$$

For practical purposes, however, use of the finite multiplier is not required unless the sample contains an appreciable fraction, say 10 percent or more, of the population being sampled. At a 10-percent sampling fraction, taking it into account will reduce the random sampling error by 5 percent. If the sampling fraction is 5, 2, or 1 percent, not ignoring it will reduce error very slightly—2.5, 1.0, and 0.5 percent, respectively.

5. Probabilities of normally distributed variates depend on the distance (expressed in multiples of the standard deviation) of the value of the variable from the distribution's mean. If we subtract a given population mean μ from a normally distributed variate X_i and divide this result by the original standard deviation σ, we get a standardized variate Z_i that is also normally distributed but with zero mean and unit standard deviation. In symbols this is as follows:

$$Z_i = \frac{X_i - \mu}{\sigma}$$

Table A.1 in Appendix A at the end of this book presents the standardized normal distribution in tabular form. Note further that the original variate may be a sample mean, $\bar{X}$. If so, the denominator is the *standard error* (i.e., standard deviation of the sampling distribution). We can then define Z as some number of standard errors away from the mean of the sampling distribution

$$Z = \frac{\bar{X} - \mu}{\sigma_{\bar{X}}}$$

where $\sigma_{\bar{x}}$ denotes the standard error of the mean. (A similar idea is involved in the case of the standard error of the proportion.)

6. The formulas for the standard error of the mean and proportion of simple random samples are, respectively, the following:

Mean

$$\sigma_{\bar{X}} = \frac{\sigma}{\sqrt{n}}$$

Proportion

$$\sigma_{\bar{p}} = \sqrt{\frac{\pi(1 - \pi)}{n}}$$

7. If the population standard deviation σ is not known, which is often the case, we can estimate it from the sample observations by use ofthe following formula:

$$s = \sqrt{\frac{\sum\limits_{i=1}^{n}(X_1 - \bar{X})^2}{n - 1}}$$

We can consider s to be an *estimator* of the population standard deviation σ. In small samples (e.g., less than 30), the t distribution of Table A.2 in Appendix A is appropriate for finding probability points. However, if the sample size exceeds 30 or so, the standardized normal distribution of Table A.1 is a good approximation of the t distribution. In cases where σ is estimated by s, the standard error of the mean becomes

$$est.\sigma_{\bar{X}} = \frac{s}{\sqrt{n}}$$

where $est.\sigma_{\bar{x}}$ denotes the fact that σ is estimated from s, as defined in the preceding equation.

8. Analogously, in the case of the standard error of the proportion, we can use the sample proportion p as an estimate of π to obtain

$$est.\sigma_{\bar{p}} = \sqrt{\frac{p(1-p)}{n}}$$

as an estimated standard error of the proportion. Strictly speaking, $n{-}1$ should appear in the denominator. However, if n exceeds about 100 (which is typical of the samples obtained in marketing research), this adjustment makes little difference in the results.

METHODS OF ESTIMATING SAMPLE SIZE

In our discussion of sample planning we pointed out that there are four traditional approaches to determining sample size.

First, the analyst can simply select a size either arbitrarily or on the basis of some judgmentally based criterion. Similarly, there may be instances where the size of sample represents all that was available at the time—such as when a sample is composed of members of some organization and data collection occurs during a meeting of the organization. Second, analysis considerations may be involved and the sample size is determined from the minimum cell size needed. For example, if the critical aspect of the analysis required a breakdown (e.g., for a cross-tabulation) on three variables that created 12 cells, and it was felt that there should be at least 30 observations in a cell, then the absolute minimum sample size needed would be 360. Third, the budget may determine the sample size. If, for example, the research design for a survey called for personal interviews, the cost of each interview was estimated to be $50, and the budget allotted to data collection was $10,000, then the sample size would be 200.

It may appear that these methods are for nonprobability samples. While this certainly is true, these methods are also applicable to probability samples and have occasionally been used for such samples. For probability samples, the precision must be determined after the fact.

The fourth approach to sample size determination is based on specifying the desired precision in advance and then applying the appropriate standard error formula to calculate the sample size. This is the approach of traditional inference. Two major classes of procedures are available for estimating sample sizes within the context of traditional (Neyman-Pearson) inference. The first, and better known, of these is based on the idea of constructing confidence intervals around sample means or proportions. This can be called the confidence-interval approach. The second approach makes use of both type I (rejecting the true null hypothesis) and type II (accepting a false null hypothesis) error risks and can be called the hypothesis-testing approach. We discuss each of these approaches in turn.

Before doing this, however, two points must be made. First, as with the other approaches, the analyst must still calculate the standard error after data collection in order to know what it is for the actual sample that provided data. Second, the size of sample that results from traditional inference refers to the obtained (or resultant) sample. Depending on the data collection method used, the original sample may have to be much larger. For example, suppose that the size of the desired sample was 582. A mail survey is used for data collection and past experience has shown that the response rate would be around 25 percent. The original sample size in this case would have to be 2,328 so that 582 responses would be obtained.

The Confidence Interval Approach

It is not unusual to construct a confidence interval around some sample-based mean or proportion. The standard error formulas are employed for this purpose. For example, a researcher may have taken a sample of 100 student consumers and noted that their average per capita consumption of specialty fruit/energy drinks was 2.6 pints per week. Past studies indicate that the population standard deviation σ can be assumed to be 0.3 pint.

With this information, we can find a range around the sample mean level of 2.6 pints for which some prespecified probability statement can be made about the process underlying the construction of such confidence intervals.

For example, suppose that we wished to set up a 95 percent confidence interval around the sample mean of 2.6 pints. We would proceed by first computing the standard error of the mean:

$$\sigma_{\bar{X}} = \frac{\sigma}{\sqrt{n}} = \frac{0.3}{\sqrt{100}} = 0.03$$

From Table A.1 in Appendix A we find that the central 95 percent of the normal distribution lies within ± 1.96 Z variates (2.5 percent of the total area is in each tail of the normal curve).

With this information we can then set up the 95-percent confidence interval as

$$\bar{X} \pm 1.96\,\sigma_{\bar{x}} = 2.6 \pm 1.96(0.03)$$

and we note that the 95-percent confidence interval ranges from 2.54 to 2.66 pints.

Thus, the preassigned chance of finding the true population mean to be within 2.54 and 2.66 pints is 95 percent.

This basic idea can be adapted for finding the appropriate sample size that will lead to a certain desired confidence interval. To illustrate, let us now suppose that a researcher is interested in estimating annual per capita consumption of specialty fruit/energy drinks for adults living in a particular area of the United States. The researcher knows that it is possible to take a random sample of respondents in the area and compute a sample mean. However, what the researcher really wants to do is be able to state with, say, 95 percent confidence that the population mean falls within some allowable interval computed about the sample mean. The researcher wants to find a sample size that will permit this kind of statement.

The Case of the Sample Mean

Let us first assume that the allowable error is 0.5 gallon of energy drinks per capita and the level of confidence is 95 percent. With this in mind, we go through the following checklist:

1. *Specify the amount of error (E) that can be allowed.* This is the maximum allowable difference between the sample mean and the population mean. $\bar{X} \pm E$, therefore, defines the interval within which μ will lie with some prespecified level of confidence. In our example, the allowable error is set at E, or 0.5 gallon per year.

2. *Specify the desired level of confidence.* In our illustrative problem involving specialty fruit/energy drink consumption, the confidence level is set at 95 percent.

3. *Determine the number of standard errors (Z) associated with the confidence level.* This is accomplished by use of a table of probabilities for a normal distribution. For a 95 percent confidence level, reference to Table A.1 indicates that the Z value that allows a 0.025 probability that the population mean will fall outside *one* end of the interval is $Z = 1.96$. Since we can allow a *total* probability of 0.05 that the population mean will lie outside *either* end of the interval, $Z = 1.96$ is the correct value for a 95 percent confidence level.

4. *Estimate the standard deviation of the population.* The standard deviation can be estimated by (a) judgment; (b) reference to other studies; or (c) by the use of a pilot sample. Suppose that the standard deviation of the area's population for specialty fruit/energy drink consumption is assumed to be 4.0 gallons per capita per year.

5. *Calculate the sample size using the formula for the standard error of the mean.* One standard error of the mean is to be set equal to the allowable error ($E = 0.5$) divided by the appropriate Z value of 1.96.

$$\sigma_{\bar{X}} = \frac{E}{Z} = \frac{0.5}{1.96} = 0.255$$

This will assure us that the interval to be computed around the to-be-found sample mean will have a 95 percent preassigned chance of being ± 0.5 gallon away from the population mean.

6. Neglecting the finite multiplier, we then solve for n in the formula

$$\sigma_{\bar{X}} = \frac{E}{Z} = \frac{\sigma}{\sqrt{n}}$$

or

$$\sigma_{\bar{X}} = 0.255 = \frac{4.0}{\sqrt{n}}$$

Hence,

$$n \cong 246 \text{ (rounded)}$$

7. In general, we can find n directly from the following formula:

$$n = \frac{\sigma^2 Z^2}{E^2} = \frac{16(1.96)^2}{(0.5)^2} \cong 246$$

If the resulting sample size represents a significant proportion of the population, say 10 percent or more, the finite population multiplier is required and the sample size must be recalculated using the following formula:

$$n = \frac{N(\sigma^2 Z^2)}{NE^2 + \sigma^2 Z^2}$$

where N is the size of the population.

The relationship between sample size and variability in the population may not be clear. Consider the problem of estimating the mean (i.e., average) salary earned by educators where salary level is a function only of years teaching. For one group of teachers (A) the range in years is very narrow (e.g., 5 years). For another group (B) the range is wide (e.g., 25 years). Both groups have the same population mean. A smaller sample size would be needed for Group A than for Group B. The reason for this is simply that the variance around the mean is less in Group A than in Group B.

The Case of the Sample Proportion

Suppose that, in addition to estimating the mean number of gallons of specialty fruit/energy drinks consumed per capita per year, the researcher is also concerned with estimating the proportion of respondents using one or more specialty fruit/energy drinks in the past year. How should the sample size be determined in this case?

The procedures for determining sample size for interval estimates of proportions are very similar to those for interval estimates of means. In this case the following checklist would be used:

1. *Specify the amount of error that can be allowed.* Suppose that the desired reliability is such that an allowable interval of $p - \pi = \pm 0.05$ is set; that is, the allowable error E is 0.05, or 5 percentage points.

2. *Specify the desired level of confidence.* Suppose that the level of confidence here, as in the preceding problem, is set at 95 percent.

3. *Determine the number of standard errors Z associated with the confidence level.* This will be the same as for the preceding estimation; $Z = 1.96$.

4. *Estimate the population proportion (π).* The population proportion can again be estimated by *judgment*, by *reference to other studies*, or by *the results of a pilot sample*. Suppose that π is assumed to be 0.4 in this case; that is, the researcher assumes that 40 percent of the population used one or more specialty fruit/energy drinks last year.

5. *Calculate the sample size using the formula for the standard error of the proportion.* One standard error of the proportion is to be set equal to the allowable error ($E = 0.05$) divided by the appropriate Z value of 1.96.

$$\sigma_{\bar{p}} = \frac{E}{Z} = \frac{0.05}{1.96} = 0.0255$$

6. Neglecting the finite multiplier, we then solve for n in the following formula:

$$\sigma_{\overline{P}} = \frac{E}{Z} = \sqrt{\frac{\pi(1-\pi)}{n}} = 0.0255 = \sqrt{\frac{0.4(0.6)}{n}}$$

Hence,

$$n \cong 369 \text{ (rounded)}$$

7. In general, we can find n directly from the formula

$$n = \frac{\pi(1-\pi)Z^2}{E^2} = \frac{0.4(1-0.4)(1.96)^2}{(0.05)^2} \cong 369$$

Once again, if the resulting n is 10 percent or more of the population size, the finite population multiplier is required and the sample size can be computed from the following:

$$n = \frac{N\pi(1-\pi)Z^2}{NE^2 + \pi(1-\pi)Z^2}$$

Determining Sample Size When More Than One Interval Estimate Is to Be Made From the Same Sample

The usual case when collecting sample data for estimation of various parameters is that more than one estimate is to be made. The sample size for each of the estimates will usually be different. Since only one sample is to be chosen, what size should it be?

A strict adherence to the allowable error and the confidence levels specified in the calculation of the sample sizes for the individual estimation problems leaves no choice but to take the largest sample size calculated. This will give more precision for the other estimates than was specified but will meet the specification for the estimate for which the size of sample was calculated. In the specialty fruit/energy drink consumption problem, for example, the sample size would be 369 (the sample size calculated for estimating the proportion of users) rather than 246 (the sample size calculated for estimating the mean amount used). Remember, the sample sizes determined in this manner are for obtained samples. In order to determine the size of the original sample the researcher must estimate the rate of response expected. For example, if a mail survey was to be conducted and it was believed that only a 20 percent response would be obtained, a desired obtained sample of 250 would need an original sample of 1,250.

Devices for Calculating Sample Size

In practice, some devices can be used as shortcuts to determine a sample size that will provide sufficient accuracy, which is helpful in rough-guide situations where the researcher is not sure of either allowable error levels or population standard deviations. One such device is the nomograph, which is a graphic instrument relating allowable error, confidence level, mean or proportion, and standard deviation (see Exhibit 13.2). In addition, there are numerous sample-size calculators available, which are similar to slide rules. All of these are based, however, on the preceding formulas or some modification of the formulas. Many marketing research firms use these kinds of devices on a routine basis. Similarly, many sources have tabled sample size values, as shown in Table 13.1.

EXHIBIT 13.2   Using a
Nomogram to Calculate Sample Size*

The specification of sample size depends on two pieces of information:

a. The variability in the universe under study, which can be characterized as the coefficient of variation, C, where

$$C = \sigma / \mu$$

b. The desired precision of the estimate, σ, which is the ratio of the absolute error to μ.

Using the formula the nomogram shown at the end is calculated for 95 percent and 99 percent significance levels.

$$n = \frac{Z^2 C^2}{\sigma^2}$$

The nomogram is very simple to use:

1. Connect the appropriate values of C and σ using a straight-edge

2. Read the appropriate n on the center scale

Unlike the regular formula for sample size involving the mean, using the nomogram requires that a mean be known or estimated. Both C and σ are based on the mean. Another limitation is that precise sample sizes cannot be determined from the figure. Thus, a nomogram may be best used for an approximate sample size, particularly since the error has to be estimated on the basis of the obtained sample anyway.

Calculation of Sample Size

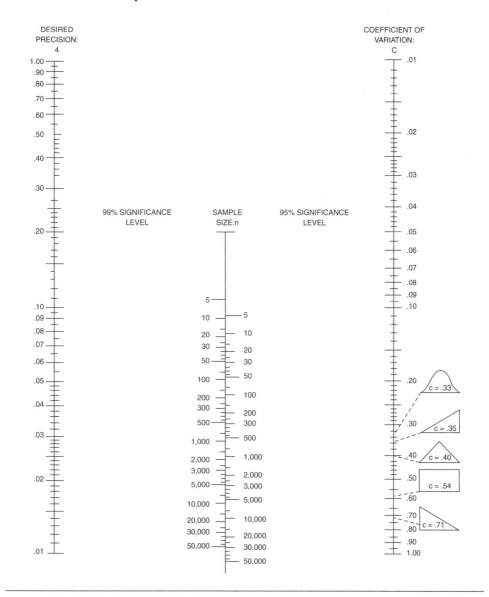

*Adapted from Dutka, Frankel, & Roshwalb, 1982, pp. 72–74.

The Hypothesis-Testing Approach

As indicated earlier, sample sizes can also be determined (within the apparatus of traditional statistical inference) by the hypothesis-testing approach. In this case the procedures are

Table 13.1 Sample Size When Estimating Population Mean or Proportion (Selected Samples)

A. Mean

Population size, N	Reliability, r	Z-value, Z	Standard deviation, s	Precision, d	Sample size, n
400	95%	1.96	1.0	±.25	53
400	90%	1.645	1.0	±.25	39
400	90%	1.645	s	±.25s	39
400	95%	1.96	s	±1/3s	32
400	95%	1.96	1.0	±.33	32
400	99.7%	3.0	s	±1/3s	67
200	95%	1.96	s	±1/3s	30
1600	95%	1.96	s	±1/3s	34
$N \rightarrow \infty$	95%	1.96	s	±1/3s	35
$N \rightarrow \infty$	90%	1.645	s	±.25s	43

B. Proportion

Population Size N	Reliability r	Z-value Z	Standard Deviation s	Precision d	Sample Size n
500	95%	1.96	0.5	±10%	81
500	95%	1.96	.3 or .7	±10%	69
$N \rightarrow \infty$	95%	1.96	0.5	±10%	96
$N \rightarrow \infty$	95%	1.96	0.5	±5%	384
$N \rightarrow \infty$	90%	1.645	0.5	±10%	68
$N \rightarrow \infty$	99%	2.58	0.5	±5%	666
$N \rightarrow \infty$	99.7%	3.00	0.5	±5%	900
$N \rightarrow \infty$	99%	2.58	0.5	±1%	16,641
$N \rightarrow \infty$	99.7%	3.00	0.5	±1%	22,500
400	90%	1.645	.2 or .8*	±10%	39
200	90%	1.645	.2 or .8*	±10%	36

*As the difference between p and 0.5 increases, the sampling distribution for p becomes more skewed and may deviate from the normal approximation. Thus, the data should be interpreted with care for small samples as p approaches either 0.0 or 1.0. (The corresponding percentage would be 0.0 or 100.0.)

SOURCE: Tatham, 1979, p. b.

more elaborate. We shall need both an assumed probability of making a type I error—called the alpha risk—and an assumed probability of making a type II error—called the beta risk. These risks are, in turn, based on two hypotheses:

$$H_0: \text{the null hypothesis}$$

$$H_1: \text{the alternate hypothesis}$$

In hypothesis testing the sample results sometimes lead us to reject H_0 when it is true. This is a Type I error. On other occasions the sample findings may lead us to accept H_0 when it is false. This is a Type II error. The nature of these errors is shown in Table 13.2.

Table 13.2   Types of Error in Making a Wrong Decision

Action	H_0 is true	H_0 is false
Accept H_0	No error	Type II error (β)
Reject H_0	Type I error (α)	No error

A numerical example should make this approach clearer. We first consider the case for means and then the case for proportions. Before doing this, however, a few words on the relationship between the Type I and Type II errors are in order. The relationship between these two errors is inverse. The ability of a sample to protect against the Type II error is called statistical power. When the hypothesis is one of difference, a Type II error occurs when what is really chance variation is accepted as a real difference. Taking statistical power into account often indicates that larger (and, thus, more costly) samples are needed. Sample size is affected by the effect size—the needed or expected difference. When it is large, say more than 15 percentage points, statistical power is usually not a problem. Very small effect sizes (e.g., two percentage points) require such large sample sizes as to be impractical; surveys cannot really reliably measure such small differences or changes. As an illustration, if a researcher wants to discern an effect size of, say, 10 points at a 95 percent confidence level and a desired power to detect the superiority of one alternative over another of 80 percent, the approximate sample size needed would be 310. If the desired power is raised to 95 percent, the sample size needed would be about 540 (Semon, 1994). The researcher, and the manager as well, must consider the relative business risks when setting appropriate levels of protection against the two types of errors (Semon, 1990).

The Case Involving Means

As an illustrative example, let us assume that a store test of a new bleaching agent is to be conducted. It has been determined earlier that if the (population) sales per store average only seven cases per week, the new product should not be marketed. On the other hand, a mean sales level of 10 cases per week would justify marketing the new product nationally. Using methods of traditional inference, how should the number of sample stores for the market test be determined?

The procedures are similar to those for interval estimation problems but are somewhat more complicated. Specifically, we go through the following checklist:

1. Specify the values for the null (H_0) and the alternate (H_1) hypotheses to be tested in terms of population means μ_0 and μ_1, respectively. (By convention, the null hypothesis is the one that would result in no change being made, if accepted.) In the bleach market-introduction problem, the values are set at H_0: $\mu_0 = 7$ cases per week, and H_1: $\mu_1 = 10$ cases per week.

2. Specify the allowable probabilities (α and β, respectively) of Type I and Type II errors. The Type I error is the error of rejecting a true null hypothesis. The Type II error is

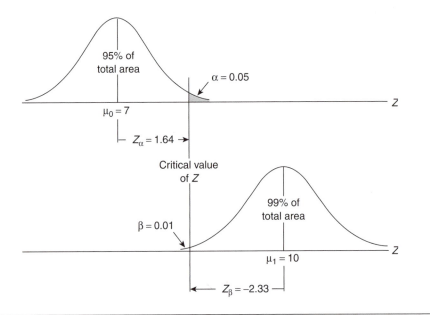

Figure 13.1   Alpha and Beta Risks in the Hypothesis-Testing Approach

made when the alternate hypothesis is rejected when it is true. α and β are the allow-able probabilities of making those two types of errors, respectively. They are shown graphically in Figure 13.1, where we assume that in the bleach-introduction problem the allowable probabilities of error are assigned as $\alpha = 0.05$ and $\beta = 0.01$.

3. Determine the number of standard errors associated with each of the error probabilities α and β. For a one-tailed test the Z values for the 0.05 and 0.01 risks, respectively, are found from Table A.1 in Appendix A to be $Z_\alpha = 1.64$ and $Z_\beta = 2.33$. These are shown in Figure 13.1. Note that in the figure we affix a minus sign to the value of Z_β since the critical values lies to the left of $\mu_1 = 10$.

4. Estimate the population standard deviation σ. In the case of the new bleach, the stan-dard deviation of cases sold per store per week is assumed to be five cases.

5. *Calculate the sample size that will meet the α and β error requirements.* Because *two* sampling distributions are involved, a simultaneous solution of two equations is required to determine the sample size and critical value that will satisfy both equations. These equations are the following:

$$\text{critical value} = \mu_0 + Z_\alpha \frac{\sigma}{\sqrt{n}}$$

$$\text{critical value} = \mu_1 - Z_\beta \frac{\sigma}{\sqrt{n}}$$

6. Setting the right-hand side of these two equations equal and solving for *n* gives

$$n = \frac{(Z_\alpha + Z_\beta)^2 \sigma^2}{(\mu_1 - \mu_0)^2}$$

In the bleach problem the desired sample size is

$$n = \frac{(1.64 + 2.33)^2 5^2}{(10 - 7)^2} \cong 44 \text{ stores (rounded)}$$

Having solved for *n*, the sample size, we can then go on to solve for the critical value for the mean number of cases by means of the following substitution:

$$\text{critical value} = \mu_1 - Z_\beta \frac{\sigma}{\sqrt{n}}$$
$$= 10 - (2.33) \frac{5}{\sqrt{44}}$$
$$= 8.24 \text{ cases}$$

Alternatively, we could find the critical value from the first of the two equations:

$$\text{critical value} = 7 + (1.64) \frac{5}{\sqrt{44}} = 8.24$$

The decision rule then becomes the following: Take a sample of 44 stores for the controlled store test. If the mean number of cases of the new bleach sold per week in the sample stores is less than or equal to 8.24 cases, do not introduce the product. If the mean number of cases of bleach sold per week is greater than 8.24 cases, introduce the product.

The Case Involving Proportions

For sample-size determination involving proportions, the following analogous steps are required:

1. Specify the values of the null (H_0) and the alternate (H_1) hypotheses to be tested in terms of population proportions π_0 and π_1, respectively.

2. Specify the allowable probabilities (α and β, respectively) of type I and type II errors.

3. Determine the number of standard errors associated with each of these error probabilities (Z_α and Z_β).

4. Calculate the desired sample size n from the formula:

$$n = \left[\frac{Z_\alpha \sqrt{\pi_0(1 - \pi_0)} + Z_\beta \sqrt{\pi_1(1 - \pi_1)}}{\pi_1 - \pi_0} \right]^2$$

This formula is appropriate for relatively large samples ($n \geq 100$), where the normal distribution is a good approximation to the binomial. To illustrate its application, suppose that a researcher is interested in the true proportion of residents in a large city who would be willing to pay over \$400 for a portable refrigerator-bar combination if it were commercialized.

Assume that the marketing researcher would recommend commercialization of the firm's refrigerator-bar combination if the true proportion of consumers who would pay over \$400 for this class of goods is 70 percent. If the proportion is only 60 percent, the researcher would not recommend commercialization. The researcher then sets up the hypotheses:

$$H_0 : \pi_0 = 0.6$$
$$H_1 : \pi_1 = 0.7$$

The alpha risk associated with the null (status quo) hypothesis is selected by the researcher to be 0.05 if the true proportion π is equal to 0.6. Moreover, the researcher is willing to assume a beta risk of 0.1 if the true proportion is equal to 0.7. With these assumptions it is possible to obtain the approximate sample size by using the preceding formula:

$$n = \left[\frac{Z_\alpha \sqrt{\pi_0(1 - \pi_0)} + Z_\beta \sqrt{\pi_1(1 - \pi_1)}}{\pi_1 - \pi_0} \right]^2$$

where $Z_\alpha = Z_{0.05} = 1.64$, $Z_\beta = Z_{0.1} = 1.28$, $\pi_0 = 0.6$, and $\pi_1 = 0.7$. The solution follows:

$$n = \left[\frac{1.64\sqrt{0.6(0.4)} + 1.28\sqrt{0.7(0.3)}}{0.7 - 0.6} \right]^2 \cong 193 \text{(rounded)}$$

Accordingly, in this example the sample size to take is 193. The critical value can be found analogously as follows:

$$\text{critical value} = \pi_1 - Z_\beta \sqrt{\frac{\pi_1(1 - \pi_1)}{n}}$$
$$= 0.7 - (1.28)\sqrt{\frac{0.7(0.3)}{193}}$$
$$= 0.658$$

In this case the decision rule is the following: Take a sample of 193 residents. If the sample proportion who would pay over $400 is less than or equal to 0.658, do not commercialize the refrigerator-bar combination. If the sample proportion exceeds 0.658, commercialize the product.

DETERMINING SAMPLE SIZE
FOR OTHER PROBABILITY–SAMPLE DESIGNS

Thus far we have discussed only the determination of *simple* random-sample sizes using the methods of traditional statistical inference. How are the sizes for other types of random-sample designs—systematic, stratified, cluster, area, and multistage—determined?

The answer to this question is that the same *general* procedures are used to determine the overall sample size, but the formulas for the standard errors differ. The formulas become more complex and difficult to estimate as one considers stratified sampling, cluster sampling, or the other more elaborate designs. This is because the standard error for these designs is partially a function of the standard deviation (or proportion) of each stratum or cluster included in the design. For a multistage sample consisting of several strata in one stage followed by clusters in another and systematic sampling in a third, the standard error formula can become very complex indeed. And once the overall sample size is determined, it must be apportioned among the strata and clusters, which also adds to the complexity.

EXHIBIT 13.3   The Standard Error for a Stratified Sample

The formulas for determining sample size for a stratified sample are basically the same as those used for a simple random sample. What is different, however, is the formula for the standard error.

General Stratified Sampling. The standard error of the mean for this type of sample is

$$\sigma_{\bar{X}.5} = \sqrt{\sum_{i=1}^{m} W_i^2 \frac{\sigma_i^2}{n_i}}$$

where

$$W_i = \frac{N_i}{N}, \quad \sum_{i=1}^{m} N_i = N, \quad \sum_{i=1}^{m} W_i = 1$$

and

$$N_i = \text{size of } i\text{th stratum}$$
$$N = \text{population size}$$
$$\sigma_i^2 = \text{variance of the } i\text{th stratum}$$
$$n_i = \text{sample size of the } i\text{th stratum}$$

The standard error of a proportion is

$$\sigma_{p.5} = \sqrt{\sum_{i=1}^{m} W_i^2 \, \frac{\pi_i(1-\pi_1)}{n_1}}$$

where π_i = proportion in the ith stratum

Disproportionate Stratified Sampling. In disproportionate stratified sampling, both the relative size of each stratum and the within-stratum variance is taken into account. Thus, the rule for sample allocation is the following:

$$n_i = \frac{W_i \sigma_i n}{\sum\limits_{i=1}^{m} W_i \sigma_i}$$

The formula for the standard error of the mean of a disproportionate stratified sample becomes as follows:

$$\sigma_{p.5} = \sqrt{\frac{\left(\sum\limits_{i=1}^{m} W_i \sigma_i\right)^2}{\sum\limits_{i=1}^{k} n_i}}$$

When the cost of selecting sample members from one stratum is not necessarily the same as that from another stratum, the allocation rule must be modified:

$$n_i = \frac{W_i \sigma_i n / C_i}{\sum\limits_{i=1}^{m} (W_i \sigma_i / C_i)}$$

C_i is the cost of selecting an individual from the ith stratum.

Proportionate Stratified Sampling. In contrast to disproportionate sampling, in proportionate stratified sampling the same sampling fraction is used throughout all population strata and

$$\frac{n_i}{n} = \frac{N_i}{N}$$

In this type of stratified sampling, only the size of the stratum is used as the guide for determining allocation of the total sample. Thus,

$$n_i = \frac{W_i n}{\sum\limits_{i=1}^{m} W_i}$$

The standard error of the mean for a proportionate stratified sample is

$$\sigma_{\overline{X}.5} = \sqrt{\frac{\sum\limits_{i=1}^{m} W_i \sigma_i^2}{\sum\limits_{i=1}^{m} n_i}}$$

Appropriate formulas for estimating standard errors and sample sizes for other random-sample designs are available elsewhere (Sudman, 1976; Kish, 1965). In general, as compared with the size of simple random samples, systematic samples may be the same (for purposes of calculating the standard error, the assumption is typically made that the systematic sample is a simple random sample). Stratified samples are usually smaller, and cluster samples will usually be larger in size to provide the same reliability as a simple random sample. The approach used for a stratified sample is illustrated in Exhibit 13.3. If used properly, stratification usually results in a smaller sampling error than is given by a comparable-size simple random sample. Consequently, the advantages of a stratified sample design over a simple random sampling design are as follows (Sangren, 2000, p. 67):

- For the same level of precision, one would need a smaller sample size in total, and this leads to a *lower cost*
- For the same total sample size, one would gain a greater precision for any estimates that are to be made

EVALUATION OF THE TRADITIONAL APPROACH

If one were to devise the ideal method of determining sample size, at a minimum one would want it to meet the criteria of being:

1. Logically complete

2. Adaptable to a wide range of sampling situations

3. Simple to use

If the traditional (Neyman-Pearson) approach to sample-size determination were to be rated on these criteria, the rating would be low for logical completeness and high for both adaptability and simplicity.

The traditional approach is logically incomplete because sample size is specified as being a function only of the conditional probabilities of making errors. Consideration of the conditional costs of wrong decisions, prior probabilities, nonsampling errors, and the cost of sampling are not included in the model. More advanced texts, however, do consider traditional sample-size determination by means of formulas that include the costs of sampling (see Cochran, 1963, Chap 4).

The fact that these variables are excluded implies that somehow they must be taken into account outside the model. However, the only way that accommodation can be made is through adjustment of either the specified confidence level or the assigned alpha and beta risks.

SUMMARY

One of the most difficult problems in research design is the one concerned with the size of sample to take. We discussed the determination of sample size from the standpoint of traditional inferential methods and all aspects of sample size determination were covered. Estimation and hypothesis-testing applications were discussed. We concluded the chapter with an evaluation of this traditional approach to determining sample size.

❖

ASSIGNMENT MATERIAL

1. Annual incomes of 900 part-time temporary salespeople employed by the Stem Cosmetics Company (a direct selling company) are known to be approximately normally distributed. Last year the mean income of the group was $8,000, and the standard deviation of incomes was $1,000. Using Table A.1 in Appendix A:

   a. This year (based on nine months experience extrapolated to a one-year basis) a random sample of 49 of Stem's part-time salespeople was selected. What is the probability that the sample arithmetic mean would differ from last year's population mean by more than $150 (assuming no change in parameter values and neglecting the finite multiplier)?

   b. Now assume that the sample mean indicated $8,100 with a sample standard deviation (computed with $n - 1$ in the denominator) of $900. What is the probability of getting at least this large a sample mean given no change in last year's population mean of $8,000?

   c. If the company wants to be 95 percent confident that the true mean of this year's salespeople's income does not differ by more than 2 percent of last year's mean of $8,000, what size of sample would be required (assuming a population standard deviation of $1,000 and neglecting the finite multiplier)?

2. Past information about the proportion of shoppers in a large city who would be receptive to redeeming store coupons indicates a figure of somewhere around 80 percent. Suppose that a supermarket chain would adopt a store coupon plan if the true proportion were 80 percent; if the true proportion were only 70 percent, it would not. The null and alternative hypotheses are as follows:

$$H_0 : \pi_0 = 0.7$$
$$H_1 : \pi_1 = 0.8$$

Assuming an alpha risk of 0.1 if $\pi_0 = 0.7$ and a beta risk of 0.2 if the true proportion were 0.8, what is the appropriate sample size (using traditional methods)?

3. The Schaff Power and Light Company has recently launched a public relations campaign to persuade its subscribers to reduce the wasteful use of electricity. The firm's marketing research director Frank Carmine believes that about 40 percent of the subscribers are aware of the campaign. They wish to find out how large a sample would be needed to be 95 percent confident that the true proportion is within ±3 percent of the sample proportion.

   a. Solve the problem analytically via the confidence-interval approach.

   b. If one sets up the hypotheses

$$H_0 : \pi_0 = 0.4$$
$$H_1 : \pi_1 = 0.5$$

   with an alpha risk of 0.1 and a beta risk of 0.05 if $\pi_1 = 0.5$, what is the appropriate sample size under the hypothesis-testing approach?

4. An international airline is considering adding a super economy plan on its Chicago-Frankfurt-Stockholm flights. All passengers who travel on this plan must buy a round-trip fare, which will be 40 percent less than the regular fare, and fly on a space-available basis. The company's new research director, Charles Shoe, and his assistant, Karen Smyth, decide to conduct an in-flight survey of passengers traveling under the existing fares. Among the informational items they will seek from this survey are the mean number of flights taken per year and the proportion originating in Chicago. They estimate the standard deviation of the number of flights per year at $\sigma = 2.0$. They decide they need a 95.4 percent level of confidence and can allow a difference of sample mean and population mean of ±.10 flight.

   Shoe and Smyth estimate the proportion originating in Chicago at .10. They require that the sample proportion be within ±.02 of the population proportion, and they would like a confidence level of 95.4 percent for the proportion estimate.

   What sample size should they take if it is to be a simple random sample and the traditional method of determining sample size is used?

5. If $n = 100$ and $N = 10,000$ and it is assumed that $\sigma = 2$, compute the standard error of the mean, first with the finite multiplier and then without. How large would the sample size n have to be (given $N = 10,000$) to make the standard error of the mean equal to 0.05?

ENDNOTE

1. Despite the fact that the Bayesian approach is a logically complete model for determining sample size in a decisional situation, it lacks adaptability and is complex in use. Thus, there has been only limited application and the technique is not discussed here. For a more detailed exposition of the underlying theory and specific procedures, see Sudman (1976, Chap. 5), Brown (1967), and Mayer (1970).

REFERENCES

Brown, R. V. (1967, May). Evaluation of total survey error. *Journal of Marketing Research, 4,* 117–127.

Cochran, W. G. (1963). *Sampling techniques* (2nd ed.). New York: Wiley.

Dutka, S., Frankel, L. R., & Roshwalb, I. (1982). *How to conduct surveys.* New York: Audits & Surveys.

Kish, L. (1965). *Survey sampling.* New York: Wiley.

Mayer, C. (1970, August). Assessing the accuracy of marketing research. *Journal of Marketing Research, 7,* 285–291.

Sangren, S. (2000, April). Survey and sampling in an imperfect world: More second-best solutions. *Quirk's Marketing Research Review,* pp. 16ff.

Semon, T. T. (1994, January 3). Save a few bucks on sample size, risk millions in opportunity loss. *Marketing News, 28,* 19.

Semon, T. T. (1990, September 3). Keep ignoring statistical power at your own risk. *Marketing News, 24,* 21.

Sudman, S. (1976). *Applied sampling.* New York: Academic Press.

Tatham, E. (1979). *A report on sample size selection.* Shawnee Mission, KS: Customer Satisfaction Institute.

Cases for Part IV

CASE STUDY IV–1

Fred Meyer Corporation (B)

Fred Meyer is a large regional retailer with a product assortment that ranges from food to soft goods to consumer electronics to building materials. In effect, the company operates a chain of hypermarkets. The company acquired Smith's, a Rocky Mountain area chain, and itself was acquired by Kroger. All companies are operated independently.

Fred Meyer has decided to do a major consumer survey in two of its largest market areas: the Portland, Oregon, area and the Seattle, Washington, area.

The purpose of the study is to compare its customer segments with respect to profiling its customers, determining how these segments shop, and assessing how Fred Meyer rates in comparison with other retail stores. The specific objectives were outlined in the Fred Meyer (A) case at the end of Part I.

The company has contracted with Cascade Consulting Group, a marketing research and consulting firm in Portland, Oregon, to conduct this consumer study. Cascade assigned Ms. Jule Yo to be project director. Ms. Yo has several years of experience in the marketing research business, after receiving her MBA degree from a leading university in the United States.

Ms. Yo has turned her attention to the question of sampling. She knows that the target population is residents of the greater Portland and Seattle areas within prespecified zip codes provided by Fred Meyer Corporation. There is concern about sampling error, so sample size is important.

QUESTIONS FOR DISCUSSION

1. What type of sampling plan should Ms. Yo use if the survey is to be a mail survey? A telephone survey? A personal interview survey?

2. What method should be used to select a sample size? Explain how this might vary depending upon the mode of data collection.

3. What size sample should Ms. Yo use for a mail survey, a telephone survey, and a personal interview survey? Explain differences between original sample size and desired (or obtained) sample size.

4. From a sampling perspective, is it reasonable to consider data collection via the Internet? Explain.

CASE STUDY IV–2

Green Pipe, Inc.

Green Pipe, Inc. is a major producer of polyvinyl chloride (PVC) pipe in 13 states in the western United States. A major segment of their market consists of use in the water sector of the pipe industry. Other major pipe grades (i.e., materials used in making pipe) for use in water pipe are metal and polyethylene (PE). Major customers are public utility water companies.

The company decided that a market study was needed to determine the perceptions of PVC pipe in the water segment of the industry. These perceptions are to be assessed with respect to metal and PE pipe, and to an "ideal" pipe. Of further interest to Green Pipe, Inc., is to determine the extent to which perceptions change with usage. That is, it is expected that heavy users of metal pipe will have different perceptions of PVC pipe than heavy users of plastic pipe. The company's aim in this research is to be able to better position its products in the marketplace.

The company's management agreed that the study should be conducted by an outside, independent research organization, and decided on the Prosurvey Company. Prosurvey assigned Ms. Karen Smyth as project director.

After some checking of secondary data, Ms. Smyth determined that there were about 700 water utility districts in the 13 western states. These districts comprised the population of research interest. The information to be obtained would include semantic differential ratings of PVC, PE, and metal pipes on a number of dimensions such as durability, leakage, ease of handling, and so forth. Respondents would be asked to rank these dimensions in terms of their importance, and to also provide absolute importance ratings. Consequently, self-explicated measures would be obtained. The proposal was to use mail survey techniques for data collection. However, another possibility would be to use the Internet.

Ms. Smyth was concerned about sampling. The area of study included the following 13 states: Alaska, Arizona, California, Colorado, Hawaii, Idaho, Montana, New Mexico, Nevada, Oregon, Utah, Washington, and Wyoming. Since the size of the population of interest (i.e., water utility districts) was believed to be about 700, Ms. Smyth decided that a census of the population should be undertaken, rather than a sample. She believed that the small size together with the relative ease of contact by mail were factors favoring a census. In addition, the cost should not be excessive.

In an ideal situation, using a census would mean that there would be no sampling error. However, a trade-off is that there could be an increase in nonsampling error due to inaccurate responses, selection bias, etc. Thus, a census might increase total error even when it eliminates sampling error. Obviously, the trade-off between sampling and nonsampling errors depends upon which can be most easily controlled and measured, and on how effectively adjustments can be made to obtained data.

QUESTIONS FOR DISCUSSION

1. Evaluate Ms. Smyth's use of a census to obtain data from the water utility districts.

2. Assuming that a sample, rather than a census, is to be used, what type of sample do you believe should be used? Explain.

3. What should the sample size be and how did you decide on this number?

Part V

ANALYZING DATA

Chapter 14

THE ANALYSIS PROCESS—BASIC CONCEPTS OF EDITING, CODING, AND DESCRIPTIVE ANALYSIS

From a managerial perspective, data can be viewed as recorded information useful for making decisions. Completed questionnaires or other measurement instruments must be edited, coded, entered into a data set for processing by computer, and carefully analyzed before their complete meanings and implications can be understood.

Analysis can be viewed as the categorization, the aggregation into constituent parts, and the manipulation of data to obtain answers to the research question or questions underlying the research project. A special aspect of analysis is interpretation. The process of interpretation involves taking the results of analysis, making inferences relevant to the research relationships studied, and drawing managerially useful conclusions about these relationships. The analysis of obtained data represents the end of the research process, and everything done prior to this stage has been done so that the proper analysis can be completed and the research questions can be answered. When planning for a research project, it is important to recognize that all conclusions, recommendations, and decisions are based on the appropriate analysis of the raw data obtained for the research project. This points to the necessity of considering the potential analyses to be conducted and the desired report structure when planning and designing the project.

This chapter examines the major basic processes and concepts pertaining to how the descriptive meanings and interpretations of research data can best be extracted. After a brief discussion of the overall analysis process, the fundamental steps in data coding are presented. The last section of the chapter considers some of the techniques for a descriptive analysis of the data.

AN OVERVIEW OF THE ANALYSIS PROCESS

The overall process of analyzing and making inferences from sample data can be viewed as a process of refinement (see Figure 14.1). This refinement involves a number of separate and sequential steps that may be identified as part of three broad stages:

1. *Tabulation*: identifying appropriate categories for the information desired, sorting the data into them, making the initial counts of responses, and using summarizing measures to provide economy of description and so facilitate understanding.

2. *Formulating additional hypotheses*: using the inductions derived from the data concerning the relevant variables, their parameters, their differences, and their relationships to suggest working hypotheses not originally considered.

3. *Making inferences*: reaching conclusions about the variables that are important, their parameters, their differences, and the relationships among them.

In the tabulation process, appropriate categories are defined for coding the information desired, making the initial counts of responses, and preparing a descriptive summary of the data. In situations where telephone interviews, personal interviews, or Internet-based interviews are conducted using computers, the tabulation process is greatly simplified because the appropriate categories are defined when constructing the complete questionnaire. Although these categories may be modified during the pretest to accommodate unanticipated responses, most computer-based interviewing programs automatically enter responses into a data file with no transcription errors and greatly reduced data entry errors.

Often, additional hypotheses are derived from so-called qualitative exploration of quantitative data (Livingston, 1994). These are analyses and tests that may be conducted in addition to those designed initially to solve the study's particular research problem. For example, in one study a company was concerned with the length of employment, education, position in the company, and other employment demographics of people who made purchase decisions on high-ticket items. However, the survey also asked who the vendor of choice was. Given this information it was possible to do a more in-depth "fishing expedition" to determine factors that would allow a prediction of vendor preference. But these findings should be reported with qualitative validity only, like the results of a focus group, because of the potential for introducing error based on too many statistical tests being run, violations of some statistical assumptions, and findings from small sample sizes (Livingston, 1994).

General Comments on Data Tabulation

Seven steps are involved in the process of data tabulation:

1. *Categorize.* Define appropriate categories for coding the information collected.

2. *Code.* Assign codes to the respondent's answers.

3. *Create Data File.* Enter the data into the computer and create a data file.

4. *Error Checking.* Check the data file for errors by performing a simple tabulation analysis to identify errors in coding or data entry. Once errors are identified, data may be recoded to collapse categories or combine or delete responses.

5. *Generate New Variables.* New variables may be computed by data manipulations that multiply, sum, or otherwise transform variables.

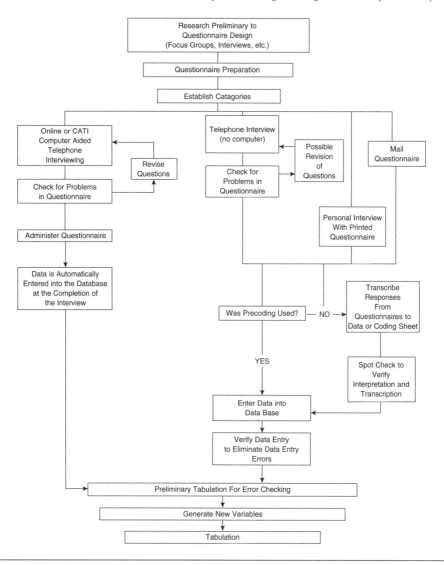

Figure 14.1   The Analysis Process

6. *Weight Data Subclasses.* Weights are often used to adjust the representation of sample subgroups so that they match the proportions found in the population.

7. *Tabulate.* Summarize the responses to each variable included in the analysis.

Our discussion here will be comparatively brief. We consider only the core aspects of the task:

1. Defining of response categories

2. Editing and coding

3. Tabulation

As simple as these three steps are from a technical standpoint, they are most important in assuming a quality analysis and thereby merit introductory discussion. A discussion of survey-based data management, which is another name for this process, is provided by Fink (2003, Chap.1).

Defining Categories

Analysis of any sizable array of data often requires that responses be grouped into categories or classes. The identification of response categories early in the study has several advantages. Ideally, it forces the analyst to consider all possible interpretations and responses to the questionnaire. It often leads to improvements in the questionnaire or observation forms. It permits more detailed instruction of interviewers and results in higher consistency in interpreting responses. Editing problems are also reduced.

For printed questionnaires, the definition of categories allows collection forms to be precoded if necessary to identify the database columns assigned to each question or variable and to indicate the values assigned to each response alternative. Data files typically are free-format, meaning that each variable appears in the same relative position for each respondent with some delimiter between variables, typically a space, comma, or tab. The major data analysis software programs read data files and then display them in a spreadsheet-like database (see Table 14.1). Precoded printed questionnaires have the advantage of eliminating transcription and thereby decreasing both processing errors and costs. Still, they are not as widely used as in the past. Most of today's computer-based software for telephone (CATI) or online (Surveyz.com, Qualtrics.com) surveys automate this entire process. They not only define the question categories in the database but also automatically build the database and record the completed responses as they are submitted. The data may then be either analyzed online, or exported to Microsoft Excel or another data analysis program.

As desirable as the early definition of categories is, it can sometimes only be done after the data have been collected. This is usually the case when free-answer or open-end questions, unstructured interviews, and projective techniques are used. The varieties of responses to a question such as "Why do you watch *Wheel of Fortune*"? have startled many a researcher. Some of the classes of responses to questions such as these are unlikely to be anticipated, even by the experienced analyst.

The selection of categories is controlled by both the purposes of the study and the nature of the responses. Useful classifications meet the following conditions:

1. *Similarity of response within the category*. Each category should contain responses that, for purposes of the study, are sufficiently similar that they can be considered homogenous.

2. *Differences of responses between categories*. Differences in category descriptions should be great enough to disclose any important distinctions in the characteristic being examined.

3. *Mutually exclusive categories*. There should be an unambiguous description of categories, defined so that any response can be placed in only one category.

4. *Categories should be exhaustive*. The classification schema should provide categories for all responses.

The use of extensive open-end questions is a practice often associated with fledgling researchers. Open-end questions, of course, have their place in marketing research. However, the researcher should be aware of the inherent difficulties in questionnaire coding and tabulation, not to mention their tendency to be more burdensome to the respondent. All of this is by way of saying that any open-end question should be carefully checked to see if a closed-end question (i.e., check the appropriate box) can be substituted without doing violence to the intent of the question. Obviously, sometimes this substitution should not be made.

Editing and Coding

Editing

Editing is the process of reviewing the data to ensure maximum accuracy and clarity. Editing should be conducted as the data is being collected. This applies to the editing of the collection forms used for pretesting as well as those for the full-scale project. Careful editing early in the collection process will often catch misunderstandings of instructions, errors in recording, and other problems at a stage when it is still possible to eliminate them for the later stages of the study. Early editing has the additional advantage of permitting the questioning of interviewers while the material is still relatively fresh in their minds. Obviously, this has limited application where data collection is by mail, e-mail, or the Internet, though online surveys can be edited even when data is being collected.

Editing is normally centralized so as to ensure consistency and uniformity in treatment of the data. If the sample is not large, a single editor usually edits all the data to reduce variation in interpretation. In those cases where the size of the project makes the use of more than one editor mandatory, it is usually best to assign each editor a different portion of the collection form to edit. In this way the same editor edits the same items on all forms, an arrangement that tends to improve both consistency and productivity.

Each collection form should be edited to ensure that data quality requirements are fulfilled. Regarding data obtained by an interviewer (and to an extent self-report) the following should be specifically evaluated:

1. *Legibility of entries*. Obviously the data must be legible in order to be used. If an entry cannot be deciphered, and clarification of it cannot be obtained from the interviewer, it is sometimes possible to infer the response from other data collected. In cases where any real doubt exists about the meaning of the data, however, it should not be used.

2. *Completeness of entries*. On a fully structured collection form, the absence of an entry is ambiguous. It may mean either that the interviewer failed to ask the question, that the respondent could not or would not provide the answer, or that there was a failure to record collected data. If the omission was the result of the interviewer's not recoding the data, prompt questioning of the interviewer may provide the missing entry. If the

omission was the result of either of the first two possible causes, it is still desirable to know which was the case and why the question was not asked or answered.

3. *Consistency of entries.* As is the case with two watches that show different times, an entry that is inconsistent with another raises the question of which is correct. (If a respondent family is indicated as being a nonwatcher of game shows, for example, and a later entry indicates that they watched *Wheel of Fortune* twice during the past week, an obvious question arises as to which is correct.) Again, such discrepancies may be cleared up by questioning the interviewer. When discrepancies cannot be resolved, discarding both entries is usually the wisest course of action.

4. *Accuracy of entries.* An editor should keep an eye out for any indication of inaccuracy in the data. Of particular importance is the detection of any repetitive response patterns in the reports of individual interviews. Such patterns may well be indicative of systematic interviewer bias or dishonesty.

Coding

Coding is the process by which responses are assigned to data categories and symbols (usually numbers) are assigned to identify them with the categories. *Precoding* refers to the practice of assigning codes to categories and sometimes printing this information on structured questionnaires and observation forms before the data are collected. The interviewer is able to code the responses when interpreting the response and marking the category into which it should be placed.

Postcoding refers to the assignment of codes to responses after the data are collected. Postcoding is most often required when responses are reported in an unstructured format (open-ended text or numeric input). Careful interpretation and good judgment are required to ensure that the meaning of the response and the meaning of the category are consistently and uniformly matched.

Once a complete code has been established, after postcoding, a formal coding manual or codebook should be created and made available to those who will be entering the data into a data file. This codebook will also be of use to the analyst who will be doing the analysis, although its major function may be that of providing backup. If the data file is created properly, all variables will be defined and appropriate labels included for the variables and the values of each variable. The codebook used for a study of noncustomers of a bank in the United States is shown in Figure 14.2.

An example of a simple and prevalent response that is often miscoded is the familiar "Don't Know" (DK). A respondent may give this reply for a variety of reasons: It may mean that the answer to the question is not known, that the respondent is confused as to the meaning of the question, or that the respondent wants to avoid giving an explicit answer. Good question construction and interviewing can do much to reduce the ambiguity of "Don't Know" answers. Careful coding can also assist in reducing this mismatching of response and category meaning.

Good coding requires training and supervision. The editor-coder should be provided with written instructions, including examples. He or she should be exposed to the interviewing of respondents and become acquainted with the process and problems of collecting the data, thus providing aid in its interpretation. The coder also should be aware of the computer routines that are expected to be applied, insofar as they may require certain kinds of data formats.

Question			Variable
	Sample Group		1
	1 = Astoria	4 = Toledo	
	2 = Seaside	5 = Yachats	
	3 = Tillamook	6 = Florence	
	Type of Customer		2
	1 = personal		
	2 = business		
	Identification		3
	xxx = actual number		
1.	Length in Community		4
	xx = actual number		
	Length on Coast		5
	xx = actual number		
2.	Primary Bank		6
	1 = Bank of Astoria		
	2 = Western Bank		
	3 = Bank of Newport		
	4 = Bank of America		
	5 = Other		
3.	Main Use of Primary Bank		7
	1 = Checking		
	2 = Borrowing		
	3 = Savings		
4.	Travel to Bank		8
	x = actual number		
	9 = 9 or more		
5.	How Often Visit		9
	1 = More than once a week		
	2 = Once a week		
	3 = One to three times a month		
	4 = Less than once a month		
6.	Services Used and Importance of Each		10-49
	Use: 1 = not used		
	2 = used		
	Importance: x = actual number		

	Use	Importance
Automatic Teller Machine	10	11
Deposit After Hours	12	13
Annuities	14	15
Home Equity Loan	16	17
Checking Account	18	19
Certificate of Deposit	20	21
Youth Account	22	23
Individual Retirement Account (IRA)	24	25
Automobile Purchase Loan	26	27
Stock/Bond Transactions	28	29

Figure 14.2   Codebook for Bank Study

(Continued)

		Bank #1	Bank #2	
	Safe Deposit Box	30	31	
	Loans for Other Than Home & Auto	32	33	
	Library of Consumer Information	34	35	
	Financial Counseling	36	37	
	Automatic Bill Paying	38	39	
	Bank by Mail	40	41	
	Savings Account	42	43	
	Drive-up Teller Window	44	45	
	Home Mortgage	46	47	
	Bank Credit Card	48	49	
7.	How Satisfied			50
	x = number			
8.	Use Other Financial Institutions			51-60
	1 = no			
	2 = yes			
	Checking Account			51
	Savings Account			52
	Certificate of Deposit			53
	Home Mortgage			54
	Automobile Purchase Loan			55
	Home Equity Loan			56
	Individual Retirement Account (IRA)			57
	Loans for Other than Auto & Home			58
	Safe Deposit Box			59
	Bank Credit Card			60
9.	Importance of Characteristics			61-66
	xx = actual number			
	Decisions Are Made Locally			61
	Friendly, Helpful Personnel			62
	Conveniently Located			63
	Offers a Full Range of Financial Services			64
	Price of Its Services			65
	The Bank Is Locally Owned			66
10.	Attitudes Toward Banks			67-94
	x = actual number			

	Bank of Newport	Bank #2
Low Prices for Its Services	67	81
Is a Locally Owned Bank	68	82
Offers a Full Range of Banking Services	69	83
Has Friendly, Helpful Personnel	70	84
Is the Same as Most Other Banks	71	85
Has Timely, Accurate Service	72	86
Has Competent Knowledgeable Employees	73	87
Is Innovative	74	88
Is Customer Oriented	75	89
Caters Mainly to Business Customers	76	90
Is Not Conveniently Located	77	91
Major decisions Are Not Made Locally	78	92
Outside Architecture Fits With Environment	79	93
Is Trustworthy	80	94

Note: Bank #2 is either Western, National Security or Oregon Pacific Bank.

11.	Gender of Respondent	95
	1 = male	
	2 = female	

12.	Marital Status	96
	1 = married 3 = widowed	
	2 = divorced 4 = never married	

13.	Age of Respondent	97
	xx = actual	

14.	Who Visits Bank	98
	1 = male	
	2 = female	

15.	Education of Respondent and Spouse	99-100
	Respondent	99
	Spouse	100
	1 = junior high or less	
	2 = some high school	
	3 = graduated from high school	
	4 = some college or technical school	
	5 = graduated from community/junior college or technical school	
	6 = graduated from "four year" college	
	7 = some graduate or professional school	
	8 = a graduate or professional degree	

16.	Household Income	101
	1 = $15,000 or less	
	2 = $15,001 — $25,000	
	3 = $25,001 — $35,000	
	4 = $35,001 — $50,000	
	5 = $50,001 — $75,000	
	6 = $75,001 — $100,000	
	7 = more than $100,000	

17.	Employment Status of Respondent and Spouse	102-103
	Respondent	102
	Spouse	103
	1 = employed full time	
	2 = operate own business	
	3 = temporarily unemployed	
	4 = employed part time	
	5 = retired	
	6 = not employed	

Coding is an activity that should not be taken lightly. Improper coding leads to poor analyses. Whenever possible (and when cost allows) more than one person should do the coding, specifically the postcoding. By comparing the results of the various coders, a process known as determining intercoder reliability, any inconsistencies can be brought out into the open.

In addition to the obvious purpose of eliminating them, inconsistencies sometimes point to the need for additional categories for data classification and may sometimes mean that there is a need to combine some of the categories.

Tabulation for Purposes of Cleaning the Data

The raw input to most data analyses consists of the basic data matrix, as shown in Table 14.1. In most data matrices, each row contains the data for a respondent's records and the columns identify the variables or data fields collected for the respondents. This rectangular array of entries contains information that is to be summarized and portrayed in some way. For example, the analyses of a column of data might include a tabulation of categories or the computation of the mean and standard deviation. This summary analysis is often done simply because we are unable to comprehend the meaning of the entire column of values. In so doing we often (willingly) forgo the full information provided by the data in order to understand some of its basic characteristics, such as central tendency, dispersion, or categories of responses. Because we summarize the data and make inferences from it, it is doubly important that the data be accurate.

The purpose of the initial data cleaning tabulation is to identify data, coding, transcription, or entry errors. The tabulation of responses will invariably reveal codes that are out of range or otherwise invalid. For example, one tabulation might reveal 46 males (category 1), 54 females (category 2), and one category 5 response, which is obviously an error. Some errors, such as the preceding one, represent entry of values that are out-of-range or wild codes (Lewis-Beck, 1995, p. 7). That is, the value is not one that has been assigned to a possible response to a question. A miscoding error that is more difficult to detect is one where this is an erroneous recording of a response category using a number that is assigned to a response. That is, in the coding shown in Figure 14.2 a response of self to question number 3 (code = 1) might have been coded as spouse (code = 2). Hopefully, not too many errors of this type occur.

An aspect of cleaning the data is dealing with missing data. That is, some respondents may not provide responses for all the questions. One way of handling this is to use statistical

Table 14.1   Illustration of Data Matrix

| Object | Variable | | | | | | |
	1	2	3	...	j	...	m
1	X_{11}	X_{12}	X_{13}	...	X_{1j}	...	X_{1m}
2	X_{21}	X_{22}	X_{23}	...	X_{2j}	...	X_{2m}
3	X_{31}	X_{32}	X_{33}	...	X_{3j}	...	X_{3m}
$\vdots$	$\vdots$	$\vdots$	$\vdots$		$\vdots$		$\vdots$
i	X_{i1}	X_{i2}	X_{i3}	...	X_{ij}	...	X_{im}
$\vdots$	$\vdots$	$\vdots$	$\vdots$		$\vdots$		$\vdots$
n	X_{n1}	X_{n2}	X_{n3}	...	X_{nj}	...	X_{nm}

imputation. This involves estimating how respondents who did not answer particular questions would have answered if they had chosen to. Researchers are mixed in their views about this process. A much safer way to handle a nonresponse situation is to treat the nonresponse as missing data in the analysis. Statistical packages such as SPSS can handle this either question-by-question or by deleting the respondent with a missing value from all analyses. Also, the researcher can choose to eliminate a respondent from the data set if there is too much missing data.

Another issue that can arise is how to deal with outliers (Fink, 2003, pp. 22–23). Outliers are respondents whose answers appear to be inconsistent with the rest of the data set. An easy way to check for outliers is by running frequency analyses, or counts, of responses to questions. Outliers can be discarded from the analysis, but one must be careful to not throw out important and useful information.

Short of having two or more coders create the data file independently of each other and then assessing intercoder reliability, there is not much that can be done to prevent coder error except to impress upon coders the necessity of accurate data entry. Multiple coders can be very time-consuming and costly, particularly for large data files. Each error that is identified should be traced back to the questionnaire to determine the proper code. The cleaning process is complete when either the data file has been edited to correct the errors or the corrections have been made in the analysis program.

Weighting the Sample Data

Weighting procedures are often required to adjust the final sample so that specific respondent subgroups of the sample are found in identical proportions to those found in the population. The use of weighting procedures may be required because certain groups are over- or undersampled, or because of nonresponse by certain groups. Exhibit 14.1 addresses one aspect of this problem.

EXHIBIT 14.1   Weighting After Data Collection

So-called poststratification weights can be used to correct for known or expected discrepancies between the sample and the population. One way of handling this is to compute the weights as the proportion of the population for a category from the census divided by the proportion of survey respondents in that category. A special case of this occurs when households are sampled at random, and then a single individual is sampled from each sampled household. In this type of sampling individuals in larger households have a smaller probability of being selected. For a simple random sample of households, where individuals are selected with equal probability and there is no nonresponse, the probability of an individual being included in the survey is inversely proportional to the size of the household. But, nonresponse affects the composition of the obtained sample. In a study dealing with this issue, Gelman and Little (1998, p. 404) conclude that "using weights proportional to the number of adults in the household leads to predictable biases due to nonavailability/nonresponse that can be corrected using poststratification, yielding final weights that are less variable and that more accurately fit the target population."

Basic Tabulation Analysis

Tabulation may be thought of as the final step in the data collection process and the first step in the analytical process. Tabulation is simply the counting of the number of responses in each data category (often a single column of the data matrix contains the responses to all categories).

The most basic is the simple tabulation, often called the marginal tabulation and familiar to all students of elementary statistics as the frequency distribution. A simple tabulation or distribution consists of a count of the number of responses that occur in each of the data categories that comprise a variable. An example is given in Table 14.2.

A cross-tabulation is one of the more commonly employed and useful forms of tabulation for analytical purposes. A cross-tabulation involves the simultaneous counting of the number of observations that occur in each of the data categories of two or more variables. An example is given in Table 14.3. We shall examine the use of cross-tabulations in detail later in the chapter.

Once a data file has been created, tabulation can be done by computers. The choice of the method of tabulation to be used in a particular case is a function of the number of categories of data, the size of the sample, and the amount and kind of analyses to be performed. The researcher has available all types of computer software ranging from broad analytical packages, such as SPSS, to more specialized cross-tabulation packages, such as E-Tabs and

Table 14.2   Simple Tabulation: Olive Oil Purchased in Past Three Months*

Number of liters	Number of respondents
0	350
1	75
2	50
3 or more	25
Total	500

*Hypothetical data

Microtab, to accounting-based spreadsheet programs, such as Microsoft Excel. Every year the American Marketing Association publishes in *Marketing News* an advertising supplement entitled *Directory of Marketing Analysis/Software Suppliers* (see American Marketing Association, 2003).

Tabulation requires that the data be entered into a database that may be accessed for the analyses. Although data editing, coding, and entry is an expensive and time-consuming task, once the data is prepared, tabulations and other more advanced analyses may be done quickly.

Although computer analysis provides the advantages of flexibility and ease when manipulating data, these very advantages increase the importance of planning the tabulation analysis. There is a common tendency for the researcher to decide that, because cross-tabulations (and correlations) are so easily obtained, large numbers of tabulations should be run. Not only is this methodologically unsound, but in commercial applications it is often costly in computer time and the time of the analyst as well. For 50 variables, for example, there are 1,225 different two-variable cross-tabulations that can be made. Only a few of these are potentially of interest in a typical study.

Table 14.3   Cross-Tabulation: Olive Oil Purchased in Past Three Months by Income Classes of Respondents*

| | *Number of liters purchased* | | | | |
Income class	Zero	One	Two	Three or more	Total
Less than $15,000	160	25	15	0	200
$15,000–$24,999	120	15	10	5	150
$25,000–$34,999	60	20	15	5	100
$35,000–$49,999	5	10	5	5	25
$50,000 and over	5	5	5	10	25
Total	350	75	50	25	500

* Hypothetical data

Summarizing Data

Summarization so as to facilitate the understanding and analysis of data is only partly accomplished by the tabulation of frequency distributions. It is also desirable to summarize data by computing descriptive measures; relative measures, such as the percentage of people who have purchased Tropicana orange juice; averages, such as the mean amount of orange juice purchased; and the amount of variation in the distribution, such as the range or standard deviation of the amount of orange juice purchased.

Descriptive measures may be used for drawing inferences and making decisions. That is, in many instances they are crucial for testing hypotheses. For example, the next chapter discusses techniques for analyzing differences in means and proportions. In a more general context, about 20 years ago it was pointed out that the "major results of any empirical study, regardless of whether the prime purpose is description, prediction, or explanation, are the descriptive statistics that indicate the nature and size of any obtained effects" (Sawyer & Peter, 1983, p. 125). This observation is as true today as it was when reported.

When used properly, descriptive statistical measures reduce the data set into simple, precise, and meaningful figures. Similarly, it is often possible to reduce a distribution of data into summary measures (i.e., the mean, standard deviation, etc.) that, for purposes of decisionmaking, can be substituted for the entire distribution (see Lewis-Beck, 1995, pp. 8–18; Pyrczak, 1995, pp. 23–48). Various summary measures and the minimum level of measurement needed for proper use of each are described in the following:

Measures of central tendency

Arithmetic Mean. The point on a scale around which the values of a distribution balance. For a probability distribution, the arithmetic mean is called the expected value of the distribution. The level of measurement must be at least interval.

Median. The midpoint of the data in the distribution. The minimum level of measurement is ordinal.

Mode. The typical or most frequently occurring value in the distribution. Nominal measurement is all that is necessary.

Measures of dispersion

Range. The extreme values of the distribution. Measurement must be at least ordinal.

Semi-interquartile Range. Calculated as one-half of the difference between the extreme values of the middle 50 percent of the values in the distribution. Measurement must be at least ordinal.

Variance. The mean of the squared deviations of the individual measurements from the arithmetic mean of the distribution. Measurements must be at least intervally scaled.

Standard Deviation. A measure that is useful because it is one of the terms included in the equation of the normal distribution. It is calculated as the square root of the variance, and thus, requires at least interval measurement.

Coefficient of Variation. An abstract measure without a base unit; it is the ratio of the standard deviation to the arithmetic mean (σ/μ). Interval measurement is a minimum requirement.

Exhibit 14.2 discusses another aspect of a distribution—its shape.

EXHIBIT 14.2   The "Forgotten" Dimension of a Distribution—Its Shape

Key indicators relating to data analysis are the measures used to indicate the shape of a distribution—skewness and kurtosis. Kurtosis refers to the shape of a distribution in terms of height, or flatness. A given distribution's height is interpreted in relationship to the height of a distribution of the observations if they were distributed as a normal distribution (Urdan, 2001, p. 20).

Skewness is a statistic that gives information about the tails of a distribution. It is the measure of a given distribution's asymmetry (Cleary, 2002). If the skewness is positive, the tail of the distribution goes out to the right, meaning that there are a relatively few observations at the higher end of the distribution. If skewness is negative, the tail of the distribution goes out to the left and there are relatively few observations at those lower-end values. A normal distribution that is symmetrical has a skewness of 0. The figure illustrates positive and negative skewness.

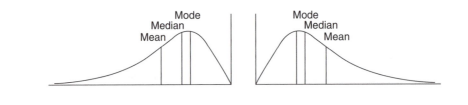

BASIC CONCEPTS OF ANALYZING ASSOCIATIVE DATA

Our brief discussion of cross-tabulations marked the beginning of a major topic of this book—the analysis of associative data. Although we shall continue to be interested in the study of variation in a single variable (or a composite of variables), a large part of the rest of the book will focus on methods for analyzing how the variation of one variable is associated with variation in other variables.

The computation of row or column percentages in the presentation of cross-tabulations is taken up first. We then show how various insights can be obtained as one goes beyond two variables in a cross-tabulation to three (or more) variables. In particular, examples are presented of how the introduction of a third variable can often refine or explain the observed association between the first two variables.

MORE ON CROSS-TABULATION

Cross-tabulation represents the simplest form of associative data analysis. At the minimum we can start out with only two variables, such as occupation and education, each of which has a discrete set of exclusive and exhaustive categories. Data of this type is called qualitative or categorical, since each variable is assumed to be nominal-scaled. This cross-tabulation analysis is known as bivariate cross-tabulation. Bivariate cross-tabulation is widely used in marketing applications to analyze variables at all levels of measurement. In fact, it is the single most widely used bivariate technique in applied settings. Reasons for the continued popularity of bivariate cross-tabulation include the following (Feick, 1984, p. 376):

1. It provides a means of data display and analysis that is clearly interpretable even to the less statistically inclined researcher or manager.

2. A series of bivariate tabulations provides clear insights into complex marketing phenomena that might be lost in an analysis with many variables.

3. The clarity of interpretation affords a more readily constructed link between market research and market action.

4. Bivariate cross-tabulations may lessen the problems of sparse cell values that often plague the interpretation of discrete multivariate analyses (bivariate cross-tabulations require that the expected number of respondents in any table cell be 5).

The entities being cross-classified are often called units of association; usually people, objects, or events. The cross-tabulation, at its simplest, consists of a simple count of the number of entities that fall into each of the possible categories of the cross-classification. Excellent discussions of ways to analyze cross-tabulations can be found in Hellevik (1984) and Zeisel (1957).

However, we usually want to do more than show the raw frequency data. At the very least, row or column percentages (or both) are usually computed.

Percentages

The simple mechanics of calculating percentages are known to all of us. We are also aware that the general purpose of percentages is to serve as a relative measure; that is, they are used to indicate more clearly the relative size of two or more numbers.

The ease and simplicity of calculation, the general understanding of its purpose, and the near universal applicability have made the percent statistic, or its counterpart the proportion, the most widely used statistical tool in marketing research. Yet its simplicity of calculation is sometimes deceptive, and the understanding of its purpose is frequently insufficient to ensure sound application and interpretation. The result is that the percent statistic is often the source of misrepresentations, either inadvertent or intentional.

The sources of problems in using percentages are largely the following:

- Identifying the direction in which percentages should be computed
- Knowing how to interpret percentage of change

Both these problems can be illustrated by a small numerical example. Let us assume that KEN's Original, a small regional manufacturer of salad dressings, is interested in testing the effectiveness of spot TV ads in increasing consumer awareness of a new brand—called Gala. Two geographic areas are chosen for the test: (1) test area A and (2) control area B. The test area receives a media weight of five 15-second television spots per week over an eight-week period, whereas the control area receives no spot TV ads at all. (Other forms of advertising were equal in each area.)

Assume that telephone interviews were conducted before and after the test in each of the areas. Respondents were asked to state all the brands of salad dressing they could think of, on an aided basis. If Gala was mentioned, it was assumed that this constituted consumer awareness of the brand. However, as it turned out, sample sizes differed across all four sets of interviews. This common fact of survey life (i.e., variation in sample sizes) increases the value of computing percentages.

Table 14.4 shows a set of frequency tables that were compiled before and after a TV ad for Gala Salad Dressing was aired. (All four samples were independent samples.) Interpretation of Table 14.4 would be hampered if the data were expressed as raw frequencies and different percentage bases were reported. Accordingly, Table 14.4 shows the data, with percentages based on column and row totals. Which of these percentages is more useful for analytical purposes?

Direction in Which to Compute Percentages

In examining the relationship between two variables, it is often clear from the context that one variable is more or less the independent or control variable and the other is the dependent or criterion variable. In cases where this distinction is clear, the rule is to compare percentages within levels of the dependent variable.

In Table 14.4, the control variable is the experimental area (test versus control) and the dependent variable is awareness. When comparing awareness in the test and control areas, row percentages are preferred. We note that before the spot TV campaign the percentage of

Table 14.4 Aware of Gala Salad Dressing—Before and After Spot TV

	Before Spot TV			*Area*	*After Spot TV*		
	Aware	*Not Aware*	*Total Area*		*Aware*	*Not Aware*	*Total Area*
Test Area							
Freq.	250	350	600		330	170	550
Col %	61%	59%	60%		67%	44%	57%
Row %	42%	58%			66%	34%	
Control Area							
Freq.	160	240	400		160	220	380
Col %	39%	41%	40%		33%	56%	43%
Row %	40%	60%			42%	58%	
Total	410	590	1000	Total	490	390	880
Before TV spot	41%	59%	100%	After	56%	44%	100%

respondents who are aware of Gala is almost the same between test and control areas: 42 percent and 40 percent, respectively.

However, after the campaign the test-area awareness level moves up to 66 percent, whereas the control-area awareness (42 percent) stays almost the same. The small increase of 2 percentage points reflects either sampling variability or the effect of other factors that might be serving to increase awareness of Gala in the control area.

On the other hand, computing percentages across the independent variable (column percent) makes little sense. We note that 61 percent of the aware group (before the spot TV campaign) originates from the test area; however, this is mainly a reflection of the differences in total sample sizes between test and control areas.

After the campaign we note that the percentage of aware respondents in the control area is only 33 percent, versus 39 percent before the campaign. This may be erroneously interpreted as indicating that spot TV in the test area depressed awareness in the control area. But we know this to be false from our earlier examination of raw percentages.

It is not always the case that one variable is clearly the independent or control variable and the other is the dependent or criterion variable. This should pose no particular problem as long as we agree, for analysis purposes, which variable is to be considered the control variable. Indeed, cases often arise in which each of the variables in turn serves as the independent and dependent variable.

Interpretation of the Percentage Change

A second problem that arises in the use of percentages in cross-tabulations is the choice of which method to use in measuring differences in percentages. There are three principal ways to portray percentage change:

1. The absolute difference in percentages

2. The relative difference in percentages

3. The percentage of possible change in percentages

The same example can be used to illustrate the three methods.

Absolute Percentage Increase

Table 14.5 shows the percentage of respondents who are aware of Gala before and after the spot TV campaign in the test and control areas. First, we note that the test-area respondents displayed a greater absolute increase in awareness. The increase for the test-area respondents was 24 percentage points, whereas the control-area awareness increased by only 2 percentage points.

Table 14.5	Aware of Gala—Percentages Before and After the Spot TV Campaign	
	Before the Campaign	*After the Campaign*
Test area	42%	66%
Control area	40%	42%

Relative Percentage Increase

The relative increase in percentage is $[(66 - 42)]/42] \times 100 = 57$ percent and $[(42 - 40)/40] \times 100 = 5$ percent, respectively, for test- and control-area respondents.

Percentage Possible Increase

The percentage of possible increase for the test area is computed by first noting that the maximum percentage-point increase that could have occurred is $100 - 42 = 58$ points. The increase actually registered is 24 percentage points, or $100(24/58) = 41$ percent of the maximum possible. That of the control area is $100(2/60) = 3$ percent of the maximum possible.

In terms of the illustrative problem, all three methods give consistent results in the sense that the awareness level in the test area undergoes greater change than that in the control area. However, in other situations conflicts among the measures may arise.

The absolute-difference method is simple to use and requires only that the distinction between percentage and percentage points be understood. The relative-difference method can be misleading, particularly if the base for computing the percentage change is small. The percentage-of-possible-difference method takes cognizance of the greater difficulty associated with obtaining increases in awareness as the difference between potential-level and realized-level decreases. In some studies all three measures are used, inasmuch as they emphasize different aspects of the relationship.

Introducing a Third Variable Into the Analysis

Cross-tabulation analysis to investigate relationships need not stop with two variables. Often much can be learned about the original two-variable association through the introduction of a third variable. As we shall illustrate, the third variable may refine or explain the original relationship. In some cases, it may show that the two variables are related even though no apparent relationship exists before the third variable is introduced. These ideas are most easily explained by example.

Consider the situation facing MCX, a company that specializes in telecommunications equipment for the residential market. The company has recently test-marketed a new device for the automatic recording of home telephone messages without an answering machine. Several months after the introduction, a telephone survey was taken in which respondents in the test area were asked whether they had adopted the innovation. The total number of respondents interviewed was 600.

One of the variables of major interest in this study was the age of the respondent. Based on earlier studies of the residential market, it appeared that adopters of the firm's new products tended to be less than 35 years old. Accordingly, the market analyst decides to cross-tabulate adoption and respondent age. Respondents are classified into the categories "under 35 years" (<35) and "equal to or greater than 35 years" (=35) and then cross-classified by adoption or not. Table 14.6 shows the full three-variable cross-tabulation. It seems that the total sample of 600 is split evenly between those who are under 35 years of age and those who are 35 years of age or older. Younger respondents display a higher percentage of adoption (37 percent = 100 + 11)/300) than older respondents (23 percent = (60 + 9)/300).

Analysis and Interpretation

The researcher is primarily interested in whether this finding differs when gender of the respondent is introduced into the analysis. As it turned out, 400 respondents in the total sample were men, whereas 200 were women.

Table 14.6 shows the results of introducing gender as a third classificatory variable. In the case of men, 50 percent of the younger men adopt compared with only 30 percent of the older men. In the case of women, the percentages of adoption are much closer. Even here, however, younger women show a slightly higher percentage of adoption (11 percent) than older women (9 percent).

The effect of gender on the original association between adoption and age is to refine that association without changing its basic character; younger respondents show a higher incidence of adoption than older respondents. However, what can now be said is the following: If the respondent is a man, the differential effect of age on adoption is much more pronounced than if the respondent is a woman.

Table 14.6   Adoption—Percentage by Gender and Age

Frequency	Men			Women		
	<35 Yrs	≥35 Yrs	Total %	<35 Yrs	≥35 Yrs	Total%
Adopters						
Number of Cases	100	60	160	11	9	20
Column %	50%	30%	40%	11%	9%	10%
Row %	62.5%	37.5%		55%	45%	
Nonadopters						
Number of Cases	100	140	240	89	91	180
Column %	50%	70%	60%	89%	91%	90%
Row %	41.7%	58.3%		49.4%	50.6%	
Total	200	200	400	100	100	200
Percentage	50%	50%		50%	50%	

Figure 14.3 shows this information graphically. The height of the bars within each rectangle represents the percentage of respondents who are adopters. The relative width of the bars denotes the relative size of the categories—men versus women—representing the third variable, gender. The shaded portions of the bars denote the percentage adopting by gender, the dashed line represents the weighted average percentage adopting by gender, and the dashed line represents the weighted average percentage across the genders. It is easy to see from the figure that adoption differs by age group (37 percent versus 23 percent). Furthermore, the size of the difference depends on the gender of the respondent: Men display a relatively higher rate of adoption, compared with women, in the younger age category.

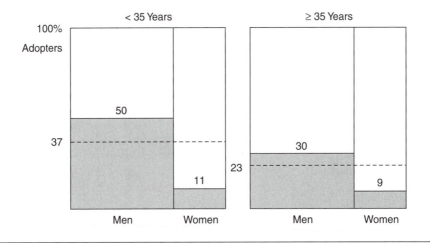

Figure 14.3   Adoption—Percentage by Age and Gender

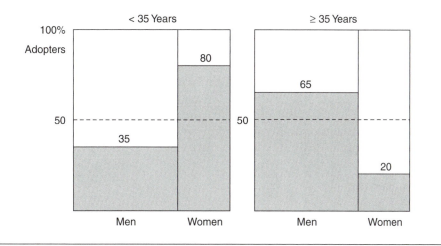

Figure 14.4   Adoption—Percentage by Age and Gender

Other Possible Relationships in Cross-Tabulation Data

The relationships shown in Table 14.6 were consistent for men and women and for age categories. Often, the relationships portray other forms. For example, suppose the introduction of gender as a third variable shows that there is a strong association between adoption and age but that this association runs in opposite directions for men versus women. The overall effect is to suggest that adoption and age are not associated (when the effect of gender is not held constant).

This is often called a suppressor effect. That is, failure to control on gender differences suppresses the relationship between adoption and age to the point where there appears to be no association at all. However, once we tabulate adoption by age within the level of gender, the association becomes evident, as shown in Figure 14.4.

As an additional illustration of what might happen when a third variable (gender) is introduced, consider an example where the association between adoption and age is not affected at all by the introduction of gender.

In this case gender is independent of the association between adoption and age. Although a figure is not shown for this simple case, it should be clear that the bars for the separate men and women classes will look exactly the same.

Our discussion so far about the various ways the original relationship can be modified has assumed that gender was not related to the initial independent variable, age. However, a fourth possibility exists in which the original relationship disappears upon the introduction of a third variable. Behavioral scientists often use the term *explanation* for this case. In order for the original association to vanish, it is necessary that the third variable, gender, be *associated* with the original independent variable, age.

To illustrate the idea of third-variable explanation, consider the new association between adoption and age, where a higher percentage of adopters is drawn from the younger age

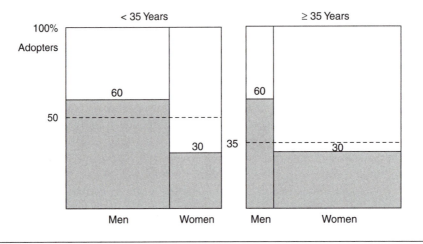

Figure 14.5   Adoption—Percentage by Age and Gender

group. However, within each separate category of gender, there is an equal percentage of adopters. The apparent relationship between adoption and gender is due solely to the difference in the relative size of the subsamples of men versus women within the two age categories.

Figure 14.5 shows an example of this effect graphically. In the case of the under-35 age group there are twice as many men as women. However, in the 35-and-over age group, there are five times as many women as men. These differences in subsample size affect the weighted-average percentages that are shown as dashed lines in the rectangles.

In the present case the gender variable is said to explain the (apparent) relationship between adoption and age. As observed from Figure 14.5, the percentage of adopters is *not* associated with age, once the data are examined separately for men and women.

Recapitulation

Representatives of three-variable association can involve many possibilities that could be illustrated by the preceding adoption-age-gender example:

1. In the example presented, adoption and age exhibit initial association; this association is still maintained in the aggregate but is refined by the introduction of the third variable, gender.

2. Adoption and age do not appear to be associated. However, adding and controlling on the third variable, gender, reveals suppressed association between the first two variables within the separate categories of men and women. In the two-variable cases, men and women exhibit opposite patterns, canceling each other out.

3. Adoption and age are not associated to begin with; furthermore, introducing a third independent variable, gender, does not change the situation.

4. Adoption and age exhibit initial association, which then disappears upon the introduction of the explanatory variable, gender.

Although the preceding examples were contrived to illustrate the concepts, the results are not unusual in practice. It goes almost without saying that the introduction of a third variable can often be useful in the interpretation of two-variable cross-tabulations.

However, the reader should be aware of the fact that we have deliberately used the phrase *associated with* rather than *caused by*. Association of two or more variables does not imply causation, and this statement is true regardless of our preceding efforts to refine some observed two-variable association through the introduction of a third variable.

In principle, of course, we could cross-tabulate four or even more variables with the possibility of obtaining further insight into lower-order (e.g., two-variable) associations. However, somewhere along the line, a problem arises in maintaining an adequate cell size for all categories. Unless sample sizes are extremely large in the aggregate and the number of categories per variable is relatively small, cross-tabulations rarely can deal with more than three variables at a time. A further problem, independent of sample size, concerns the high degree of complexity of interpretation that is introduced by cross-tabulations involving four or more variables. In practice, most routine applications of cross-tabulation involve only two variables at a time.

As noted in Table 14.6, there are definite advantages associated with having a two-category criterion variable, such as adoption versus nonadoption. In many applications, however, the criterion variable will have more than two categories. Cross-tabulations can still be prepared in the usual manner, although they become somewhat more tedious to examine.

PRESENTATION OF DESCRIPTIVE ANALYSES

Throughout this chapter we have presented a series of tables and figures representing simple tabulations, cross-tabulations, and percentage charts (stacked bar charts). These are but a few of the techniques that are readily available to display and provide visual meaning to tabulation analyses.

Visual representations are a critical (and almost mandatory) part of professional presentations (Jacoby, 1997). Today's personal computer programs offer a broad range of these tools. Spreadsheet programs, such as Microsoft Excel, directly translate summary data to graphics format. Specialty graphics programs, such as Microsoft PowerPoint, and Harvard Graphics, similarly offer pie, bar, and other chart capabilities, often with enhancements such as custom editing and slide show capabilities. Finally, data analysis packages, such as SPSS, provide links between analysis and graphics programs. These programs offer more sophisticated plotting and smoothing techniques as well as the ability to link data to geographic area maps. This latter capability is extremely valuable in market segmentation analyses.

SUMMARY

We began Chapter 14 by stating that data can be viewed as recorded information useful in making decisions. In the initial sections of this chapter, we introduced the basic concepts of transforming raw data into data of quality. The introduction was followed by a discussion of elementary descriptive analyses through tabulation and cross-tabulation. The focus of this discussion was heavily oriented toward how to read the data and how to interpret the results.

The competent analysis of research-obtained data requires a blending of art and science, of intuition and informal insight, and of judgment and statistical treatment, combined with a thorough knowledge of the context of the problem being investigated. Some of these qualities can only be acquired through experience, whereas others are heavily dependent on the native abilities of the analyst. Still others can be acquired through education and training. Irrespective of these sources of knowledge, all analysis begins with careful preparation of the data for initial descriptive analysis.

ASSIGNMENT MATERIAL

1. The marketing research department of a prominent advertising agency decides to measure the sales response to the magazine advertising of brand S hand soap. The product is to be advertised initially in the July 4 issue of Magazine M, a magazine issued every two weeks. The agency selects a simple random sample of 200 subscribing families to Magazine M and interviews each of these sample families on July 19. The interview is designed to determine (1) whether the family shopper read the soap advertisement, and (2) whether brand S soap was purchased within the period July 5 through July 18. The results are summarized in the accompanying table.

Reading of Brand S Advertisement in Magazine M Versus Purchase of Brand S During Following Two Weeks

	Number Purchasing Brand S July 5–July 18	Number Not Purchasing Brand S July 5–July 18	Total
Subscribers who read the brand S advertisement in Magazine M issue of July 4	6	54	60
Subscribers who did not read the brand S advertisement in Magazine M issue of July 4	11	129	140
Total	17	183	200

    a. Calculate the percentage of difference between those subscribers who read the advertisement and purchased and those who did not read the advertisement and purchased by each of the following methods: (1) Absolute difference in percentages; (2) Relative difference in percentages.

    b. Which method(s) would you recommend that the agency use in preparing a report to the client?

2. Explain the possible effects that the introduction of a third variable could have on a two-variable cross-tabulation.

3. Why is it important that data collection forms be edited?

4. What is the best way to handle missing data? Explain.

5. Under what conditions should outliers be retained, and when should they be dropped from the analysis? Explain.

6. What is the meaning of intercoder reliability? Should all coding efforts be assessed by this measure? Explain.

7. Which measure of central tendency is the best measure for a researcher to report as a finding—mean, mode, or median? Explain.

8. Decide which measure or measures of central tendency is/are appropriate in each of the following situations.

    a. You have made a study of family incomes in a market area and have found that the range is $22,850 to $423,690 for one year.

    b. A company planning to market only one size of a product makes a study of the distribution of sales for the industry by size of the product.

9. Since our data entry computer programs are so powerful, why is it useful for a researcher to prepare a codebook before data entry?

REFERENCES

American Marketing Association (2003, March 31). Directory of marketing analysis/software suppliers. *Marketing News, 37*, 14–21.

Cleary, M. J. (2002, February). Bring out the barbecue? Discovering the meaning of skewness. *Quality Digest*, 20ff.

Feick, L. F. (1984, November). Analyzing marketing research data with associated models. *Journal of Marketing Research, 21*, 376–386.

Fink, A. (2003). *How to manage, analyze, and interpret survey data*. Thousand Oaks, CA: Sage.

Gelman, A., & Little, T. C. (1998). Improving on probability weighting for household size. *Public Opinion Quarterly, 62*, 398–404.

Hellevik, O. (1984). *Introduction to causal analysis: Exploring survey data*. Beverly Hills, CA: Sage.

Jacoby, W. G. (1997). *Statistical graphics for univariate and bivariate data*. Thousand Oaks, CA: Sage.

Lewis-Beck, M. S. (1995). *Data analysis: An introduction*. Thousand Oaks, CA: Sage.

Livingston, G. (1994, January 3). Fishing the quantitative pool yields qualitative insights. *Marketing News, 28,* 7.

Pyrczak, F. (1995). *Making sense of statistics: A conceptual overview*. Los Angeles: Pyrczak Publishing.

Sawyer, A. G., & Peter, J. P. (1983, May). The significance of statistical significance tests in marketing research. *Journal of Marketing Research, 20,* 125.

Urdan, T. C. (2001). *Statistics in plain English*. Mahwah, NJ: Lawrence Erlbaum.

Zeisel, H. (1957). *Say it with figures* (4th ed.). New York: Harper & Row.

Chapter 15

HYPOTHESIS TESTING AND UNIVARIATE ANALYSIS

Scientific research is directed at the inquiry and testing of alternative explanations of what appears to be fact. For market researchers, this scientific inquiry translates into a desire to ask questions about the nature of relationships that affect behavior within markets. It is the willingness to formulate hypotheses capable of being tested to determine (1) what relationships exists, and (2) when and where these relationships hold.

In Chapter 14, the first stage in the analysis process was identified to include editing, coding, and making initial counts of responses (tabulation and cross-tabulation). In the current chapter, we now extend this process to include the testing of relationships, the formulation of hypotheses, and the making of inferences.

In *formulating hypotheses,* the researcher uses "interesting" variables, and their relationships to each other, to find suggestions for working hypotheses that may or may not have been originally considered. In *making inferences,* conclusions are reached about the variables that are important, their parameters, their differences, and the relationships among them. A *parameter* is a summarizing property of a collectivity—such as a population—when that collectivity is not considered to be a sample (Mohr, 1990, p. 12).

Although the sequence of procedures, (a) formulating hypotheses, (b) making inferences, and (c) estimating parameters is logical, in practice the three steps tend to merge and do not always follow in order. For example, the initial results of the data analysis may suggest additional hypotheses that in turn require more and different sorting and analysis of the data. Similarly, not all of the steps are always required in a particular project; the study may be exploratory in nature, which means that it is designed to formulate the hypotheses to be examined in a more extensive project.

FORMULATING HYPOTHESES

The objectives of the study, with associated hypotheses, should be stated as clearly as possible and agreed upon at the outset. Objectives and hypotheses shape and mold the study; they determine the kinds of questions to be asked, the measurement scales for the data to be collected, and the kinds of analyses that will be necessary. However, a project will usually turn up new hypotheses, regardless of the rigor with which it was planned and developed. New hypotheses are continually suggested as the project progresses from data collection through the final interpretation of the findings.

In Chapter 2 it was pointed out that when the scientific method is strictly followed, hypothesis formulation must precede the collection of data. This means that according to the rules for proper scientific inquiry, data suggesting a new hypothesis should *not* be used to test it. New data must be collected prior to testing a new hypothesis.

In contrast to the strict procedures of the scientific method, actual research projects almost always formulate and test new hypotheses *during* the project. It is both acceptable and desirable to expand the analysis to examine new hypotheses to the extent that the data permit. At one extreme, it may be possible to show that the new hypothesis is not supported by the data and that no further investigation should be considered. At the other extreme, a hypothesis may be supported by both the specific variables tested and by other relationships that give similar interpretation. The converging results from these separate parts of the analysis strengthen the case that the hypothesized relationship is correct. Between these extremes of nonsupport and support are outcomes of indeterminacy: The new hypothesis is neither supported nor rejected by the data. Even this result may indicate the need for an additional collection of information.

In a position even more divergent from scientific method, Selvin and Stuart (1966) convincingly argue that in survey research, it is rarely possible to formulate precise hypotheses independent of the data. This means that most survey research is essentially exploratory in nature. Rather than having a single predesignated hypothesis in mind, the analyst often works with many diffuse variables that provide a slightly different approach and perspective on the situation and problem. The added cost of an extra question is so low that the same survey can be used to investigate many problems without significantly increasing the total cost. However, researchers must resist the syndrome of "just one more question." Often, that "one more" question escalates into many more questions of the it-would-be-nice-to-know variety, which can be unrelated to the research objectives.

In a typical survey project, the analyst may alternate between searching the data (analyzing) and formulating hypotheses. Obviously, there are exceptions to all general rules and phenomena. Selvin and Stuart (1966), therefore, designate three practices of survey analysts:

1. *Snooping* is the process of searching through a body of data and looking at many relations in order to find those worth testing (that is, conducting research with no predesignated hypotheses).

2. *Fishing* is the process of using the data to choose which of a number of predesignated variables to include in an explanatory model.

3. *Hunting* is the process of testing each of a predesignated set of hypotheses with the data.

This investigative approach is reasonable for basic research but may not be practical for decisional research. Time and resource pressures often require that directed problem solving be the focus of decisional research. Rarely can the decision maker afford the luxury of dredging through the data to find all of the relationships that are present. Again, it simply reduces to the question of cost versus value.

As a beginning point in the discussion of hypothesis testing, we ask, "What is a hypothesis"? A hypothesis is an assertion that variables (measured concepts) are related in a specific way such that this relationship explains certain facts or phenomena. From a practical standpoint, hypotheses may be developed to solve a problem, answer a question , or imply a possible course of action. Outcomes are predicted if a specific course of action is followed. Hypotheses must be empirically testable. Hypotheses are often stated as research questions when reporting either the purpose of the investigation or the findings. Hypotheses may be stated informally as research questions, or more formally as a set of alternative hypotheses, or in a testable form known as a null hypothesis, which states that there is no relationship between the variables to be examined (see Pyrczak, 1995, pp. 75–84).

Research questions state in layman's terms the purpose of the research, the variables of interest, and the relationships to be examined. Research questions are not empirically testable, but aid in the important task of directing and focusing the research effort. To illustrate, a sample research question is developed in the scenario described in Exhibit 15.1.

EXHIBIT 15.1   Development of a Research Question for Mingles

Mingles is an exclusive restaurant specializing in seafood prepared with a light Italian flair. Barbara C., the owner and manager, has attempted to create an airy contemporary atmosphere that is conducive to conversation and dining enjoyment. In the first three months, business has grown to about 70 percent of capacity during dinner hours.

Barbara wants to track customer satisfaction with the Mingles concept, the quality of the service, and the value of the food for the price paid. To implement the survey, a questionnaire was developed using a five-point bipolar scale of much worse than expected, a little worse than expected, about average, a little better than expected, or much better than expected. The items were scaled using a –2 to +2 scale.

The owner of Mingles developed a questionnaire that asked, among other things, "How would you rate the value of Mingles food for the price paid"? The response form provided five answers with boxes for the respondent to check:

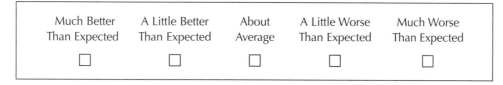

Much Better Than Expected	A Little Better Than Expected	About Average	A Little Worse Than Expected	Much Worse Than Expected
☐	☐	☐	☐	☐

Customers responses were coded using a scale of +2, +1, 0, –1, and –2.

When tabulated, the average response was found to be +0.89 with a sample standard deviation of 1.43. The research question asks if Mingles is perceived as being better than average when considering the price and value of the food.

The research question that Barbara C. has developed is "How satisfied are Mingles customers with the concept, service, food, and value"?

Null hypotheses (H_0) are statements identifying relationships that are statistically testable and can be shown not to hold (nullified). The logic of the null hypothesis is that we hypothesize no difference, and we reject the hypotheses if a difference is found. If, however we confirm that no difference exists we tentatively accept the null hypothesis. We may only accept the null on a tentative basis because another testing of the null hypothesis using a new sample may reveal that sampling error was present and that the null hypothesis should be rejected.

For example, to compare the population and the sample, the null hypothesis might be, "There is no difference between the perceived price-value of Mingles food and what is expected on average." In this example, the difference between the population average, which is assumed to be the middle scale value of 0 = "about average" and the sample's mean evaluation of Mingles can be tested using the z statistic.

A null hypothesis may also be used to specify other types of relationships that are being tested, such as the difference between two groups, or the ability of a specific variable to predict a phenomenon such as sales or repeat business. The following are two examples:

1. *Comparing two sample groups:* H_0: There is no difference in the value of the food for the price paid as perceived by first-time patrons and repeat patrons. This is tested by a t-test of the difference in means between two patron groups.

2. *Predicting intention to return to Mingles:* H_0: The perceived quality of service is not related to the likelihood of returning to Mingles. This is a regression analysis problem that uses the customer rating of quality of service to predict likelihood of returning to Mingles.

Alternative hypotheses may be considered to be the opposite of the null hypotheses. The alternative hypothesis makes a formal statement of expected difference, and may state simply that a difference exists or that a directional difference exists, depending upon how the null hypothesis is stated. Because population differences may exist, even if not verified by the current sample data, the alternative form is considered to be empirically nontestable.

The relationship between hypotheses and research questions is summarized in Table 15.1.

MAKING INFERENCES

Once the data have been tabulated and summary measures calculated, we often will make inferences about the nature of the population and ask a multitude of questions, such as, "Does the sample's mean satisfaction differ from the mean of the population of all restaurant patrons"? and "Does the magnitude of the observed differences between categories indicate that actual differences exist, or are they the result of random variations in the sample"?

In some studies, it may be sufficient to simply estimate the value of certain parameters of the population, such as the amount of a product used per household, or the proportion of stores carrying a brand, or the preferences of housewives concerning alternative styles or package designs of a new product. Even in these cases, however, we would want to know about the underlying associated variables that influence preference, purchase, or use (such as

Table 15.1   Hypotheses and Research Questions

	Purpose	*Example*	*Decision*
Research question	Express the purpose of the research.	What is the perception of Mingles customers regarding the price and value of the food?	None used.
Alternative hypothesis	The alternative hypothesis states the specific nature of the hypothesized relationship, or simply that there is a difference. The alternative hypothesis is the opposite of the null hypothesis. The alternative hypothesis cannot be falsified because a relationship hypothesized to exist, though not verified, may in truth exist in another sample. (You can never reject an alternative hypothesis unless you test the population on all possible samples.)	Mingles is perceived as having superior food value for the price when compared to the average evaluation.	Not tested because we cannot reject. We may only accept that a relationship exists.
Null hypothesis	The null hypothesis is testable in the sense that the hypothesized lack of relationship can be tested. If a relationship is found, the null hypothesis is rejected. The null hypothesis states that there is no difference between groups (with respect to some variable) or that a given variable does not predict or otherwise explain an observed phenomenon, effect, or trend.	There is no difference in perceived food value for the price for Mingles and the average evaluation.	We may reject a null hypothesis (find a relationship). We may only tentatively accept that no relationship exists.

color, ease of opening, accuracy in dispensing the desired quantity, comfort in handling, etc.), if not for purposes of the immediate problem, then for solving later problems. In yet other case studies, it might be necessary to analyze the relationships between the enabling or situational variables that facilitate or cause behavior. Knowledge of these relationships will enhance the ability to make reliable predictions, when decisions involve changes in controllable variables.

The broad objective of *testing hypotheses* underlies all decisional research. Sometimes the population as a whole can be measured and profiled in its entirety. Often, however, we cannot measure everyone in the population but instead must estimate the population using a sample of respondents drawn from the population. In this case we estimate the population parameters using the sample statistics. Thus, in both estimation and hypothesis testing, *inferences* are made about the population of interest on the basis of information from a sample.

The Relationship Between a Population, a Sampling Distribution, and a Sample

In order to simplify the example, suppose there are seven persons who form a population. On a specific topic, they have a range of opinions that are measured on a seven-point scale ranging from very strongly agree to very strongly disagree. The frequency distribution of the population is shown in Figure 15.1.

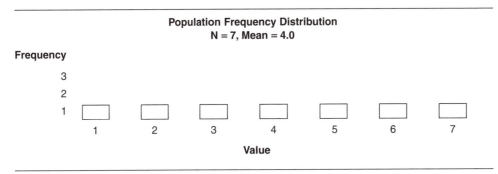

Figure 15.1   Population Frequency Distribution

The population has a mean $\mu = 4$ and standard deviation

$$\sigma_x = \sqrt{\dfrac{\sum\limits_{i=1}^{N}(x_i - \mu)^2}{N}} = 2$$

Now that we know the parameters of the population, we turn to the *sampling distribution*. Assume that we are not able to measure all seven persons in this population, but must rely instead on a sample of size $n = 2$. The sampling distribution (distribution of all possible sample means from samples of size $n = 2$) and the standard error for each sample are shown in Table 15.2.

The mean of all possible two-member sample means is

$$\mu_{\bar{x}} = \frac{84}{21} = 4$$

Table 15.2   Computation of Sampling Distribution, Mean, and Standard Error

All possible sample distributions	Sample mean, $(\bar{x}_i)$	(Error, $(\bar{x}_i - \mu)$	Standard Error $(\bar{x}_i - \mu)^2$
1,2	1.5	−2.5	6.25
1,3	2	−2	4
1,4	2.5	−1.5	2.25
1,5	3	−1	1
1,6	3.5	−0.5	0.25
1,7	4	0	0
2,3	2.5	−1.5	2.25
2,4	3	−1	1
2,5	3.5	−0.5	0.25
2,6	4	0	0
2,7	4.5	0.5	0.25
3,4	3.5	−0.5	0.25
3,5	4	0	0
3,6	4.5	0.5	0.25
3,7	5	1	1
4,5	4.5	0.5	0.25
4,6	5	1	1
4,7	5.5	1.5	2.25
5,6	5.5	1.5	2.25
5,7	6	2	4
6,7	6.5	2.5	6.25

and summing the standard errors gives

$$\sum (\bar{x}_i - \mu_{\bar{x}})^2 = 35.00$$

which gives a standard deviation of

$$\sigma_{\bar{x}} = \frac{\sqrt{\sum (\bar{x}_i - \mu_{\bar{x}})^2}}{N} = \frac{\sqrt{35.00}}{21} = 1.29$$

We know that the sampling distribution becomes more normal as the sample size increases and even in this simple case we observe a somewhat normal shape. We also note that the population mean $\mu = 4$ is equal to the mean $\mu_{\bar{x}} = 4$ of all possible sample means.

The Relationship Between the Sample and the Sampling Distribution

When we draw a sample, we rarely know anything about the population, including its shape, μ, or σ. We must, therefore compute statistics from the sample ($\bar{X}$ and s) and make inferences about the population μ and σ using the sample information.

Suppose we were to repeatedly draw samples of $n = 2$ (without replacement). The relevant statistics for the first of these samples having the values of (1,2) are

$$\text{Sample mean} = \sum x_i/n = (1 + 2)/2 = 1.5$$

$$\text{Sample std. dev.} = s = \sqrt{\frac{\sum(x_i - \bar{x})^2}{n - 1}} = \sqrt{\frac{(1 - 1.5)^2 + (2 - 1.5)^2}{(2 - 1)}} = .71$$

$$\text{Est. std. error} = S_{\bar{x}} = \frac{s}{\sqrt{n}} = \frac{.71}{\sqrt{2}} = .5$$

Given this $\bar{X}$ and $S_{\bar{x}}$, we can now estimate with given probability the intervals that give a range of possible values that could include μ, the population mean. For this single sample, they are

$$68\% = 1.5 \pm 6.31(.5) \text{ or } -1.655 \text{ to } 4.655$$
$$95\% = 1.5 \pm 12.71(.5) \text{ or } -4.855 \text{ to } 7.855$$
$$99\% = 1.5 \pm 31.82(.5) \text{ or } -14.41 \text{ to } 17.41$$

We could state that we are 99-percent confident that the population mean would fall within the interval -14.41 to 17.41. We note that this range is very wide and does include population mean of 4.0. The size of the range is large because the small sample size ($n = 2$) produces a t-statistic with one degree of freedom (df $= n - 1 = 2 - 1 = 1$), and has a large value (31.82). As the sample size increases, the numbers become larger, and gradually approximate a standard normal distribution.

In situations where the population mean is not included in the confidence interval, we have made what is called a Type I error: We have rejected a true null hypothesis. If we hypothesize that the sample mean is from a population with a mean of 4.0, we must reject this null hypothesis. We discuss Type I and Type II errors in the next section.

The above discussion is summarized graphically in Exhibit 15.2. Part I of Exhibit 15.2 shows the relationship between the population, the sample, and the sampling distribution, and Part II illustrates the impact of sample on the shape of the sampling distribution for different population distribution.

EXHIBIT 15.2   Population,
Sample, and Sampling Distribution

Part I

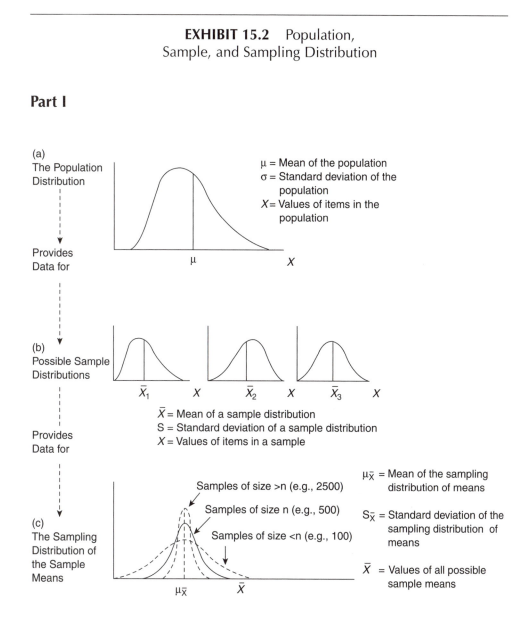

(a)
The Population
Distribution

Provides
Data for

μ = Mean of the population
σ = Standard deviation of the
     population
X = Values of items in the
     population

(b)
Possible Sample
Distributions

Provides
Data for

$\bar{X}$ = Mean of a sample distribution
S = Standard deviation of a sample distribution
X = Values of items in a sample

(c)
The Sampling
Distribution of
the Sample
Means

Samples of size >n (e.g., 2500)
Samples of size n (e.g., 500)
Samples of size <n (e.g., 100)

$\mu_{\bar{X}}$ = Mean of the sampling
     distribution of means

$S_{\bar{X}}$ = Standard deviation of the
     sampling distribution of
     means

$\bar{X}$ = Values of all possible
     sample means

Part II

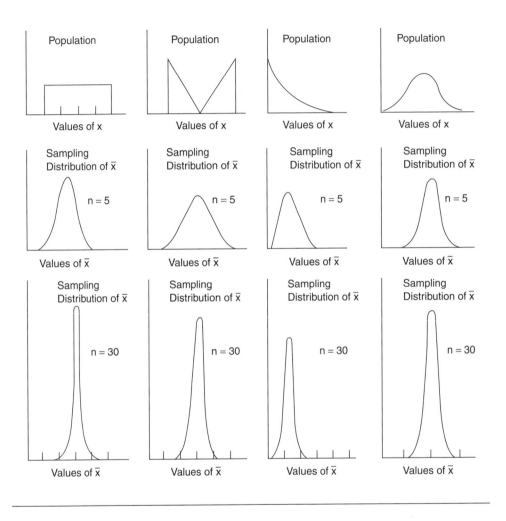

Acceptable Error in Hypothesis Testing

A question that continually plagues analysts is, "What significance level should be used in hypothesis testing"? The significance level refers to the amount of error we are willing to accept in our decisions that are based on the hypothesis test. Hypotheses testing involves specifying the value of α, which is the allowable amount of Type I error.

In hypothesis testing the sample results sometimes lead us to reject H_0 when it is true. This is a Type I error. On other occasions the sample findings may lead us to accept H_0 when it is false. This is a Type II error. The nature of these errors is shown in Exhibit 15.3.

EXHIBIT 15.3   Types of Error in Making a Wrong Decision

There are two types of error that result from a mismatch between the conclusion of a reseach study and reality. In the null-hypothesis format, there are two possible reseach conclusions: to retain H_0 and to reject H_0. There are also two possibilities for the true situation: H_0 is true or H_0 is false. The four possible combinations are shown in the following diagram:

	True Situation	
	H_0 is True	H_0 is False
Retain H_0:	No Error Prob. $= 1 - \alpha$ Confidence Level	Type II Error Prob. $= \beta$
Reject H_0:	Type I Error Prob. $= \alpha$ Significance Level	No Error Prob. $= 1 - \beta$ Power of Test

(Conclusion of Research)

These outcomes provide the definitions of Type I and Type II errors and the significance level and power of the test:

1. A Type I error occurs when we incorrectly conclude that a difference exists. The probability of this is expressed as α, the probability that we will incorrectly reject H_0, the null hypothesis, or hypothesis of no difference.

2. A Type II error occurs when we accept a null hypothesis when it is in reality false (we find no difference when a difference really does exist).

3. We correctly retain the null hypothesis (we could also say we tentatively accept or that it could not be rejected). This is equal to the area under the normal curve less the area occupied by α, the significance level.

4. The power of the test is the ability to reject the null hypothesis when it should be rejected (when false). Because power increases as α becomes larger, researchers may choose an α of .10 or even .20 to increase power. Alternatively, sample size may be increased to increase power. Increasing sample size is the preferred option for most market researchers.

The amount of Type I error, α, we are willing to accept should be set after considering two factors: (a) the costs that result from making such an error and (b) the decision rule used.

A classic paper dealing with criteria relevant for this question is Labovitz (1968). There are substantial differences in costs of errors in research conducted for exploratory purposes and research conducted to make a decision involving large financial investments. The acceptable levels of significance (error) used in a basic research project may be entirely inappropriate for a managerial decision dealing with the same problem, but where millions of dollars or a company's market strategy is involved. Managerial decisions are rarely simple or based on a single piece of research.

A tradition of conservatism exists in basic research and has resulted in the practice of keeping the Type I error at a low level. The Type I error has been traditionally considered to be more important than the Type II error and, correspondingly, that it is more important to have a low α than a low β. The basic researcher typically assigns higher costs to a Type I than to a Type II error.

In decisional research, the costs of an error are a direct result of the consequences of the errors. The cost of missing a market entry by not producing a product and forgoing gain (Type II error) may be even greater than the loss from producing a product when we should not (Type I error). The cost depends on the situation and the decision rule being used. Of course not all decision situations have errors leading to such consequences. In some situations, making a Type I error may lead to an opportunity cost (for example, a forgone gain) and a Type II error may create a direct loss.

In decisional research, the acceptable level of significance (i.e., the specification of a significance level or α) should be made by the client or the manager for whom the study has been conducted. This allows the assessment of risk by the person who will use the results as a basis for decisions (Semon, 2000). This means that the researcher should merely *report the level at which significance occurs*, letting the manager decide what this means. For basic research situations, a typical finding is often reported as significant or not as tested against a specified level, often .05. Again, it would seem sensible that the researcher reports for each finding, the level at which significance occurs, letting the reader of a study decide the meaning of the alpha level.

Power of a Test

The power of a hypothesis test, which we introduced in Chapter 13, is defined as $1 - \beta$, or one minus the probability of a Type II error. This means that the power of a test is its ability to reject the null hypothesis when it is false (or to find a difference when one is present).

The power of a statistical test is determined by several factors. The main factor is the acceptable amount of discrepancy between the tested hypothesis and the true situation. This can be controlled by increasing α. Power is also increased by increasing the sample size (which decreases the confidence interval).

In Figure 15.2, we observe two sampling distributions, the first having a mean μ_0 and the second having a mean $\mu_0 + 1\sigma$. In testing the equality of the two distributions, we first identify α, which is here set to .05. (The one-tail probably is .95 for 1.65σ). In Figure 15.2, we observe that for the second sampling distribution, power is the area to the right of $\mu_0 + 1.65\sigma$, that is, the area in which a difference between means from the two sampling distributions exists and was found to exist.

If α were decreased to, say, $\mu_0 + 1.5\sigma$, the right edge of the shaded area would move to the left, and the area defining power for curve II would increase.

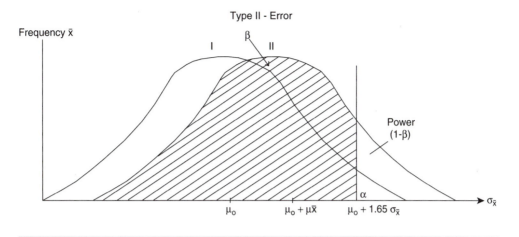

Figure 15.2   Two Sampling Distributions

The second method of increasing power is to increase sample size. Because a sample size increase directly reduces the standard error ($\sigma = \sigma/\sqrt{2}$), any increase in N decreases the absolute width of the confidence interval and narrows sampling distribution I.

In decisions that imply a greater cost for a Type II error (missing a difference that does in fact exist), the analyst may want to consider expanding the probability of a Type I error (α) to .10, .15, or even .20, especially when sample sizes are small. Exhibit 15.4 discusses some ramifications of ignoring statistical power.

SELECTING TESTS OF STATISTICAL SIGNIFICANCE

Up to this point, we have considered data analysis at a descriptive level. It is now time to introduce ways to test whether the association observed is *statistically significant*. In many cases this involves testing hypotheses concerning tests of group means. These types of tests are performed on interval or ratio data using what is known as parametric tests and include such techniques as the F, t, and z tests. Often however, we have only nominal or loosely ordinal data and we are not able to meet the rigid assumptions of a parametric test. Cross-tabulation analysis with the χ^2 test is often used for hypothesis testing in these situations. The χ^2 statistic is from the family of nonparametric methods.

Nonparametric methods are often called *distribution-free* methods because the inferences are based on a test statistic whose sampling distribution does not depend upon the specific distribution of the population from which the sample is drawn (Gibbons, 1993, p. 2). Thus, the methods of hypothesis testing and estimation are valid under much less restrictive assumptions than classical parametric techniques—such as independent random samples drawn from normal distributions with equal variances, or interval level measurement. These techniques are appropriate for many marketing applications where measurement is often at an ordinal or nominal level.

There are many parametric and nonparametric tests. Which one is appropriate for analyzing a particular set of data depends on: (1) the level of measurement of the data, (2) the number of variables that are involved, and (3) for multiple variables, how they are assumed to be related.

As scales move from nominal to ordinal and to interval levels of measurement, the amount of information and power to extract that information from the scale increases. This is illustrated in Figure 15.3. Corresponding to this spectrum of available information is an array of nonparametric and parametric statistical techniques that focus on *describing* (i.e., with measures of central tendency and dispersion) and *making inferences* about the variables contained in the analysis (i.e., using tests of statistical significance), as shown in Exhibit 15.4. Although dated, a useful reference for selecting an appropriate statistical technique is the guide published by the Institute for Social Research at the University of Michigan (Andrews et al., 1981) and its corresponding software, *Statistical Consultant*. Fink (2003, pp. 78–80) presents a summary table of which technique to use under which conditions.

EXHIBIT 15.4   Ignoring Statistical Power

Much has been written about product failure, and about the failure of advertising campaigns. But, except in rare instances, very little has been said about research failure, or research that leads to incorrect conclusions.

Yet research failure can occur even when a study is based on an expertly designed questionnaire, good field work, and sophisticated analysis. The flaw may be inadequate statistical power.

Mistaking chance variation for a real difference is one risk, called Type I error, and the 95-percent criterion largely eliminates it. By doing so, we automatically incur a high risk of Type II error—mistaking a real difference for chance variation. The ability of a sample to guard against Type II error is called statistical power.

Power was hot stuff in the 1980s. According to Semon (1990), however, we continued to ignore statistical power, for three reasons:

1. **Statistical power** is more complicated than statistical significance or confidence limits.

2. **Consideration** of statistical power would often indicate that we need larger (more costly) samples than we are now using.

3. **Numerical** objectives must be specified by management before a research budget is fixed.

The last reason may be the worst of all. Management, even if it has a target in mind, is often unwilling to do so.

The issue really is one of the degree of sensitivity required, the answer to the question, "What is the smallest change or difference we need to measure, with a specified degree of confidence"?

Suppose we have a pricing or a package test using two monadic samples for determining which of two options to use. Suppose also that (unknown to us) Option X is superior to Y by 10 percentage points, say 30 percent strong buying interest versus 20 percent interest.

If we use two samples of 200 each, how likely is it that our study will identify X as being significantly superior, using a 95 percent significance criterion? The likelihood of that correct result is only 68 percent, just a shade better than 2:1, in effect a 32 percent risk of research failure. If we want to reduce that risk to 10 percent (that is, 90 percent statistical power), we need samples of 400 each.

Setting the desired levels of protection against the two types of error should not be a rote process. It should take into consideration the relative business risks and, therefore, requires management participation since researchers usually do not have access to enough information to make these decisions.

Another way of looking at statistical power is to suggest that the researcher look at statistical *insignificance* rather than statistical significance. In testing for statistical insignificance one asks, "Is this result so likely to occur by chance that we should ignore it? Is statistical insignificance high enough to dismiss the finding?"

But, as pointed out by one observer, there is no scientific, objective way to determine what is high enough (Semon, 1999). For example, if the significance level associated with the difference in preference for two packages is 75 percent, the insignificance level is 25 percent. That's the same as saying the likelihood of a difference as large as that observed occurring by chance is one in three. Is that "too high"? Clearly, 1:3 odds deserve some consideration. But the level that such odds should have is a matter of personal preference and reflects one's risk-taking philosophy.

Perhaps we should review the specs. Why do we need 95 percent protection against Type I error? If we lower our significance criterion to 90 percent, the sample size requirement drops to 300.

Table 15.3   Selected Parametric and Nonparametric Univariate Analyses

What type of analysis do you want?	Level of Measurement		
	Nominal	*Ordinal*	*Parametric interval*
Measure of central tendency	Mode	Median	Mean
Measure of dispersion	None	Percentile	Standard deviation
One-sample test of statistical significance	Binomial test	Kolmogorov-Smirnov one-sample test	*t*-test
	$\prod^2$ one-sample test	One-sample runs test	Z-test

PARAMETRIC AND NONPARAMETRIC ANALYSIS

Our discussion of statistical inference has emphasized that analytical procedures require assumptions about the distribution of the population of interest. For example, for normally distributed variables, we assume normality and homogeneity of variances. When a variable to be analyzed conforms to the assumptions of a given distribution, the distribution of the variable can be expressed in terms of its parameters (μ and σ). This process of making inferences from the sample to the population's parameters is called parametric analysis.

Sometimes, however, problems occur: What if we cannot assume normality, or we must question the measurement scale used. Parametric methods rely almost exclusively on either

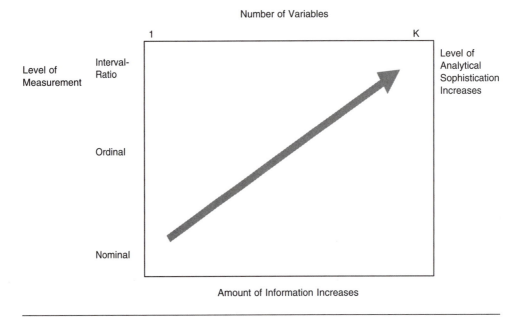

Figure 15.3   Level of Measurement and Amount of Information

interval or ratio scaled data. In cases where data can be obtained only using ordinal or categorical scales the interpretation of the results may be questionable especially if the ordinal categories are not of equal interval. When data do not meet the rigorous assumptions of the parametric method, we must rely on nonparametric methods, which free us of the assumptions about the distribution.

Whereas parametric methods make inferences about parameters of the population (μ and s), nonparametric methods may be used to compare entire distributions that are based on nominal data. Other nonparametric methods use an ordinal measurement scale test for the ordering of observations in the data set.

Problems that may be solved with parametric methods may often be solved by a nonparametric method designed to address a similar question. Oftentimes, the researcher will find that the same conclusion regarding significance is made when data are analyzed by a parametric method and by its "corresponding" nonparametric method. We will now discuss univariate parametric and nonparametric analyses. In the next chapter bivariate parametric and nonparametric analyses are presented. Additional nonparametric analyses are presented in the appendix to Chapter 16.

Univariate Analyses of Parametric Data

Marketing researchers are often concerned with estimating parameters of a population. In addition, many studies go beyond estimation and compare population parameters by testing hypotheses about differences between them. Very often, the means, proportions, and variances are the summary measures of concern. Our concern at this point is with differences between the means and proportions of the sample and those of the population as a whole. These comparisons involve a single variable. In the following sections, we will demonstrate three important concepts: (1) how to construct and interpret a confidence interval; (2) how to perform a hypothesis test; and (3) how to determine the power of a hypothesis test. These issues are discussed in more depth by Mohr (1990).

The Confidence Interval

The concept of a confidence interval is central to all parametric hypothesis testing. The confidence interval is a range of values with a given probability (.95, .99, etc.) of including the true population parameter.

For example, assume we have a normally distributed population with population mean μ and a known population variance σ^2. Suppose we sample one item from the population, X. This single item is an estimate of μ, the population mean. Further, because the single item has been drawn randomly from a normally distributed population, the possible distribution of X values is the same as the population. This normal distribution permits us to estimate the probability associated with various intervals of values of X. For example, $P(-1.96 \leq Z \geq +1.96) = .95$. Or, about 95 percent of the area under the normal probability curve is within this range. The confidence interval shows both the Z values and the values that are included in the confidence interval. We compute this range for the sample problem that follows.

Suppose that it is a well-known fact that the average supermarket expenditure on laundry and paper products is normally distributed, with a mean of $\mu = \$32.00$ per month, and the known population standard deviation is $\sigma = 10.00$. The 95-percent confidence interval about the population mean is given by the following equation:

$$\text{Lower limit} \leq \text{population mean} \leq \text{upper limit}$$
$$\mu - 1.96\,\sigma \leq \mu \leq \mu + 1.96\,\sigma$$
$$32 - (1.96)(10) \leq 32 \leq 32 + (1.96)(10)$$
$$32 - 19.6 \leq 32 \leq 32 + 19.6$$
$$12.4 \leq 32 \leq 51.6$$

Thus, we expect that 95 percent of all household expenditures will fall within this range, as shown in Figure 15.4.

If we expand this analysis to construct a confidence interval around the mean of a sample rather than the mean of a population, we must rely on a sampling distribution to define our normal distribution. The sampling distribution is defined by the means of all possible samples of size n. Recall that the population mean μ is also the mean of the normally distributed sampling distribution, whereas $\mu \pm Z\sigma$ describes the confidence interval for a population, the value $(\pm\,\alpha\,s/\sqrt{n})$ describes the confidence interval for the sampling distribution. This is the probability that this specified area around the sample mean covers the population mean. It is interesting to note that because n, the sample size, is included in the computation of the standard error, we may estimate the population mean with any desired degree of precision simply by having a large enough sample size.

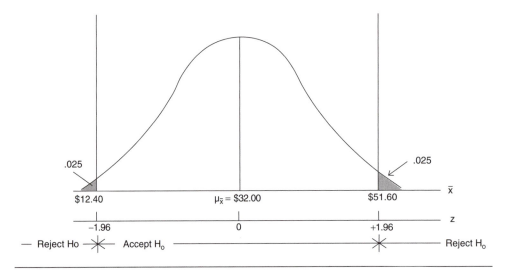

Figure 15.4   Sampling Distribution of the Mean ($\mu_{\bar{x}}$)

Univariate Hypothesis Testing of Means

Population Variance Is Known

Researchers often desire to test a sample mean to determine if it is the same as the population mean. The *Z* value describes probabilities of the normal distribution and is the appropriate tool to test the difference between μ, the mean of the sampling distribution, and $\bar{X}$, the sample mean when the population variance is known. The *Z* statistic may, however, be used only when the following conditions are met:

1. Individual items in the sample must be drawn in a random manner.
2. The population must be normally distributed. If this is not the case, the sample must be large (> 30), so that the sampling distribution is normally distributed.
3. The data must be at least interval scaled.
4. The variance of the population must be known.

When these conditions are met, or can at least be reasonably assumed to exist, the traditional hypothesis testing approach is as follows:

1. The null hypothesis (H$_0$) is specified that there is no difference between μ and $\bar{x}$. Any observed difference is due solely to sample variation.
2. The alpha risk (Type I error) is established (usually .05).
3. The *z* value is calculated by the appropriate *z* formula:

$$Z = \frac{\bar{x} - \mu}{\sigma / \sqrt{n}}$$

4. The probability of the observed difference having occurred by chance is determined from a table of the normal distribution (Appendix A, Table A.1).

5. If the probability of the observed differences having occurred by chance is greater than the alpha used, then H_0 cannot be rejected and it is concluded that the sample mean is drawn from a sampling distribution of the population having mean μ.

Returning to our supermarket example, suppose now that a random sample of 225 respondents was collected. The sample has a mean of $30.80 and the population standard deviation is known to be $10.00. We want to know if the population mean $\mu = \$32.00$ equals the sample mean of $30.80, given sample variation.
Steps:

1. All assumptions are met
2. $H_0 : \mu = \bar{x}$
3. $z = \dfrac{\bar{x} - \mu}{\sigma/\sqrt{n}} = \dfrac{30.80 - 32.00}{10/\sqrt{225}} = -1.20/0.667 = -1.80$
4. $P(z = 1.80) = .928$
   $1 - P(z = 1.80) = .072$
5. Decision: Do not reject

The results are shown in Figure 15.5.

Population Variance Is Unknown

Researchers rarely know the true variance of the population, and must therefore rely on an estimate of σ^2, namely, the sample variance s^2. With this variance estimate, we may compute the t statistic.

$$t = \frac{\bar{x} - \mu}{s/\sqrt{n}}$$

Let's assume that for the supermarket example, we do not know the population values, but we again want to test if the average monthly purchase of laundry and paper goods equals $32.00, when the sample of 225 shoppers shows a mean, $\bar{x}$ of $30.80 and a standard deviation, s, of $9.00. The t statistic is computed as

$$t = \frac{30.80 - 32.00}{9/\sqrt{225}} = \frac{-1.20}{9/15} = -2.00$$

Probability:

$P(t = 2.00, \mathrm{df} = n - 1 = 224) = .951$ (two-tailed test)

$1 - P(t = 2.00) = .049$

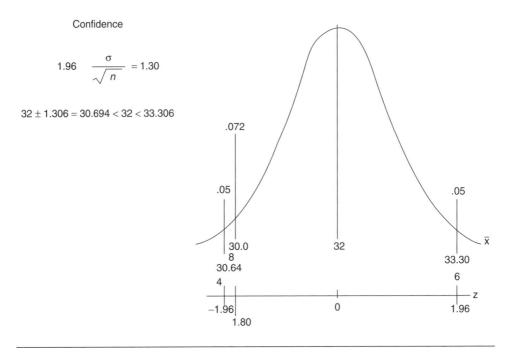

Confidence

$$1.96 \quad \frac{\sigma}{\sqrt{n}} = 1.30$$

$32 \pm 1.306 = 30.694 < 32 < 33.306$

Figure 15.5   Hypothesis Test, Variance Known

Confidence Interval:

$1.96 \ s/\sqrt{n} = 1.176$

$32 \pm 1.176 = 30.824 + 32 + 33.176$

We therefore reject the null hypothesis. Figure 15.6 shows these results.

A question may arise why we reject the null hypothesis for the *t* test but do not reject it for the *z* test. The answer is relatively simple. In the *z* test, the numerator is a known constant $\sigma/\sqrt{n}$. It is the same regardless of the sample that is drawn, as long as the sample is of size *n*. The denominator of the *t* test varies with the sample variance. Because the variance of the sample was less than the variance of the population (9 vs. 10), the size of the confidence interval was reduced, allowing us to reject the null hypothesis.

Unlike the *z* distribution, the *t* is actually a family of distributions, each having a different shape, depending on the number of degrees of freedom (see Figure 15.7). The probability for a given value of *t* varies across distributions.

The appropriate *t* distribution to use in an analysis is determined by the available degrees of freedom. Unfortunately, the concept of degrees of freedom is inadequately defined. Many statisticians use the term to describe the number of values that are free to vary. A second

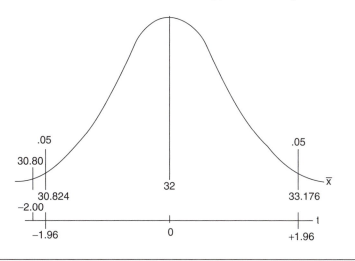

Figure 15.6   Hypothesis Test, Variance Unknown

definition is that "degrees of freedom" is a measure of how much precision an estimate of variation has. A general rule is that the degrees of freedom decrease when more parameters have to be estimated. This concept seems to be something that falls into the category of "we all know what it is, but cannot precisely define it." It seems reasonable to accept the meaning in terms of "values that vary" by specifying that degrees of freedom refers to a mathematical property of a distribution related to the number of values in a sample that can be *freely specified* once one knows something about the sample.

In univariate analyses, the available degrees of freedom are $n - 1$. We lose one degree of freedom for each population parameter that we estimate (μ). To explain further, suppose we have a sample with size $n = 5$ in which the mean value of some measure is calculated to be zero. If we select at random any four numbers from this sample—say –6, –4, 4, and 9—we know that the last number is completely determined and must be –3. Each time we estimate a parameter we lose one degree of freedom, while $n - 1$ are free to estimate that parameter.

As n becomes large (≥ 30) the curve is approximately normal, with true normality reached at the limit ($n = 4$). The t statistic is widely used in both univariate and bivariate market research analyses, due to the relaxed assumptions over the z statistic, as follows:

1. Individual items in the sample are drawn at random.

2. The population must be normally distributed. If not, the sample must be large (> 30).

3. The data must be at least interval scaled.

4. The population variance is not known exactly, but is estimated by the variance of the sample.

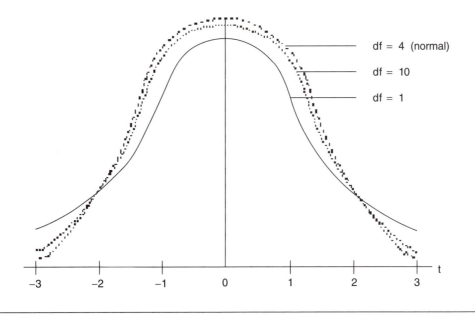

Figure 15.7   The *t*-distributions for df = 1, df = 10, and df = 4

Univariate Analysis of Categorical Data: The Chi-Square Goodness of Fit Test

Chi-square analysis (χ^2) can be used when the data identifies the number of times or frequency that each category of a tabulation or cross-tabulation appears. Chi-square is a useful technique for testing the following:

1. Determining the significance of sample deviations from an assumed theoretical distribution; that is, determining whether a certain model fits the data. This is typically called a goodness-of-fit test.

2. Determining the significance of the observed associations found in the cross-tabulation of two or more variables. This is typically called a test of independence. (This is discussed in Chapter 16.)

The procedure involved in chi-square analysis is quite simple. We compare the observed (frequency) data with another set of theoretical data based on a set of theoretical frequencies. These theoretical frequencies may result from application of some specific model of the phenomenon being investigated—relationship 1 above. Or we might specify that the frequency of occurrence of two or more characteristics is mutually independent—relationship 2 above.

In either case we compute a measure (chi-square) of the variation between actual and theoretical frequencies, under the null hypothesis that there is no difference between the model and the observed frequencies. We may say that the model fits the facts. If the measure of variation is "high," we reject the null hypothesis at some specified alpha risk. If the measure is "low," we accept the null hypothesis that the model's output is in agreement with the actual frequencies.

Single Classification

Suppose that we are interested in how frequently a sample of respondents selects each of two test packages. Test package A contains an attached coupon involving so many cents off on a subsequent purchase of the brand by the respondent. Test package B is the same package but, rather than an attached coupon, it contains an attached premium (a ballpoint pen) that the respondent may keep. The packages are presented simultaneously to a sample of 100 respondents and each respondent is asked to choose one of the two packages.

The frequency of choice is presented in the first column (labeled Observed) of Table 15.4. We see that 63 respondents out of 100 select package A. Suppose that the marketing researcher believes the true probability of selecting A versus B to be 50-50 and that the observed 63-37 split reflects sampling fluctuations. The researcher's model, then, would predict an estimated frequency of 50-50. Are the observed frequencies compatible with this theoretical prediction? In chi-square analysis we put forth the null hypothesis that the observed (sample) frequencies are consistent with those expected under application of the model.

We use the following notation. Assume that there are k categories and a random sample of n observations; each observation must fall into one and only one category. The observed frequencies are

$$f_i = (i = 1, 2, \ldots, k); \sum_{i=1}^{k} f_i = n$$

The theoretical frequencies are

$$F_i = (i = 1, 2, \ldots, k); \sum_{i=1}^{k} F_i = n$$

In the problem above,

$$f_1 = 63, f_2 = 37, F_1 = 50, F_2 = 50, n = 100$$

We compute the chi-square statistic:

$$X^2 = \sum_{i=1}^{k} \frac{(f_i - F_i)^2}{F_i}$$

In the one-way classification of the problem, the statistic above is approximately distributed as chi-square with $k - 1$ degrees of freedom. In our problem we have only two categories and, hence, one degree of freedom. Table A.3 in the Appendix at the end of this book shows the appropriate distribution.

In Table A.3, the tabular chi-square value for $\alpha = 0.05$ and $k - 1 = 1$ is 3.84. If the null hypothesis is true, the probability of getting a chi-square value greater then 3.84 is 0.05. Since our computed chi-square value is 6.76 (see Table 15.4), we reject the null hypothesis that the output of the theoretical model corresponds with the observed frequencies (see Figure 15.8). In using the chi-square table we note that only k, the number of categories, is pertinent, rather than the sample size n. Sample size is important to the quality of the approximation and the power of the test. A good rule of thumb, however, is that chi-square analysis should be used only when the theoretical frequencies in each cell exceed five; otherwise, the distribution in Table A.3 will not be a good approximation. Pragmatically, the "risk" is that with a theoretical frequency less than five, a single cell's chi-square value may be unusually high and, thus, unduly influence the overall value.

Table 15.4   Observed Versus Theoretical Frequencies (Test-Package Illustration)

Package	f_i Observed	F_i Predicted	$f_i - F_i$	$(f_i - F_i)^2 / F_i$
A	63	50	13	169/50 = 3.38
B	37	50	−13	169/50 = 3.38
Total	100	100		6.76

Univariate Analysis: Test of a Proportion

The standard normal distribution may be used to test not only means, as explained above, but also differences in proportions. The univariate test of proportions, like the univariate test of means, compares the population proportion to the proportion observed in the sample. For a sample proportion, p,

$$Z = \frac{p - \pi}{S_p}$$

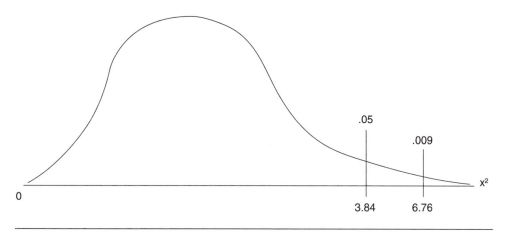

Figure 15.8   Chi-Square Distribution

where s_p, the estimated standard error of the proportion, is given by

$$S_p = \sqrt{pq/n} = \sqrt{\frac{p(1-p)}{n}}$$

and

z = standard normal value

p = the sample proportion of successes

$q = (1 - p)$ = the sample proportion of failures

n = sample size

In a simple example, suppose the marketing manager of a snack food company is evaluating a new snack. Two hundred twenty-five respondents are surveyed at a local shopping mall. The survey indicates that 87 percent are favorable toward the snack. The manager needs a 90-percent favorability rate. Is it safe to say that this is simply sampling variation?

$$Z = 1.338 = \frac{.87 - .90}{.022} \quad \text{where} \quad S_p = \sqrt{\frac{(.87)(.13)}{225}} = .022$$

given $\alpha = .05$ with $Z = 1.96$, we cannot reject the null hypothesis.

CI = $.90 - 1.96(.022) < 90 < 90 + 1.96(.022)$

CI = $.856 < .90 < .944$

In this example the manager could (in a statistical sense) claim that 87-percent approval is no different than 90-percent approval with sampling variation. In terms of corporate policy, however, set cut points may be more rigidly held.

A more detailed explanation of this topic is given by Green, Tull, and Albaum (1988, pp. 418–422).

SUMMARY

Chapter 15 has introduced the basic concepts of formulating hypotheses, hypothesis testing, and making statistical inferences in the context of univariate analysis. In actual research, the analyst may alternate between analyzing the data and formulating hypotheses.

A hypothesis is a statement that variables (measured constructs) are related in a specific way. The null hypothesis, H_0, is a statement that no relationship exists between the variables tested or that there is no difference.

Statistics are based on making inferences from the sample of respondents to the population of all respondents by means of a sampling distribution. The sampling distribution is a distribution of the parameter values (means or variances) that are estimated when all possible samples are collected.

When testing hypotheses, the analyst may correctly identify a relationship as present or absent, or may commit one of two types of errors. A Type I error occurs when a true H_0 is rejected (there is no difference, but we find there is). A Type II error occurs when we accept a false H_0 (there is a difference, but we find that none exists). The power of a test was explained as the ability to reject H_0 when it should be rejected.

Selecting the appropriate statistical technique for investigating a given relationship depends on the level of measurement (nominal, ordinal, or interval) and the number of variables to be analyzed. The choice of parametric versus nonparametric analyses depends on the analyst's willingness to accept the distributional assumptions of normality and homogeneity of variances.

Finally, univariate hypothesis testing was demonstrated using the standard normal distribution statistic (z) to compare a mean and proportion to the population values. The t-test was demonstrated as a parametric test for populations of unknown variance and samples of small size. The chi-square goodness-of-fit test was demonstrated as a nonparametric test of nominal data that make no distributional assumptions. The observed frequencies were compared to an expected distribution.

In this chapter, we focused on *univariate analyses*. Chapter 16 expands this discussion to include nonparametric and parametric analyses involving two variables. In Chapter 17, we focus on bivariate analyses involving measures of association. Finally, in Chapters 18 and 19, we focus on multivariate analyses, involving dependence and interdependence of associative data.

In each chapter we will observe that the appropriate statistical technique is selected in part based on the number of variables and their interrelationships, when included in the analysis. However, without the ability to investigate central tendency, dispersion, and rates of change, the ability to investigate these more complex relationships is not possible.

ASSIGNMENT MATERIAL

1. A marketing researcher interested in the business-publication reading habits of purchasing agents has assembled the following data:

Business-Publication Preferences (First-Choice Mentions)	
Business publication	*Frequency of first choice*
W	35
X	30
Y	45
Z	<u>55</u>
Total	165

   a. Test the null hypothesis ($\alpha = 0.05$) that there are no differences among frequencies of choice for publications W, X, Y, and Z.

   b. Suppose that the researcher had aggregated responses for the publication pairs W-Y and X-Z. Test the null hypothesis ($\alpha = 0.05$) that there are no differences among frequencies of choice for the two publication pairs.

2. What is a hypothesis? How does it differ from a research question and how is it the same? Explain.

3. Distinguish between a null hypothesis and an alternative hypothesis.

4. Explain the types of error that can arise in hypothesis testing. Is there one most important type? Explain.

5. "All sampling distributions of a statistic, such as a mean, are the same." Discuss.

6. What is statistical power? What role does it play in hypothesis testing?

7. How do nonparametric tests differ from parametric tests?

REFERENCES

Andrews, F. M., Klem, L., Davidson, T. N., O'Malley, P. M., & Rodgers, W. L. (1981). *A guide for selecting statistical techniques for analyzing social science data* (2nd ed.). Ann Arbor: Institute for Social Research, University of Michigan.

Fink, A. (2003). *How to manage, analyze, and interpret survey data* (2nd ed.). Thousand Oaks, CA: Sage.

Gibbons, J. D. (1993). *Nonparametric statistics: An introduction.* Newbury Park, CA: Sage.

Green, P. E., Toll, O. S., & Albaum, G. (1988). *Research for marketing decisions* (5th ed.). Englewood Clifts, NJ: Prentice Hall.

Labovitz, S. (1968, August). Criteria for selecting a significance level: A note on the sacredness of .05. *The American Sociologist, 3,* 220–222.

Mohr, L. B. (1990). *Understanding significance testing.* Newbury Park, CA: Sage Publications.

Pyrczak, F. (1995). *Making sense of statistics: A conceptual overview.* Los Angeles: Pyrczak Publishing.

Selvin, H., & Stuart, A. (1966, June). Data-dredging procedures in survey analysis. *The American Statistician,* 20–23.

Semon, T. T. (1990, September 30). Keep ignoring statistical power at your own risk. *Marketing News, 24,* 21.

Semon, T. T. (1999, February 1). Consider a statistical insignificance test. *Marketing News, 33,* 9.

Semon, T. T. (2000, October 9). When determining significance, let clients decide the risks. *Marketing News, 34,* 15.

Chapter 16

BIVARIATE ANALYSIS: DIFFERENCES BETWEEN SAMPLE GROUPS

Marketing activities largely focus on the identification and description of *market segments*. These segments may be defined demographically, attitudinally, by the quantity of the product used, by activities participated in or interests, by opinions, or by a multitude of other measures. The key component of each of these variables is the ability to group respondents into market segments. Often this segmentation analysis involves the identification of differences and the asking of questions about the marketing implications of those differences: Do differences in satisfaction exist for the two or more groups that are defined by age categories?

Bivariate statistical analysis refers to the analysis of relationships between two variables. These analyses are often differences between respondent groups. In Chapter 16, we explore bivariate statistical analysis. This chapter, which focuses on the two-variable case, has been prepared as a bridge between the comparatively simple analyses already discussed and the more sophisticated techniques that will command our attention in later chapters. We begin with what is perhaps the most used test of market researchers: cross-tabulation. As stated in Chapter 15, cross-tabulation is the analysis of frequency counts for nominal variables. Next, we consider analysis of differences in group means. First, we discuss the *t*-test of differences in means of two independent samples, and then we look at one-way analysis of variance (ANOVA) for *k* groups. We conclude this chapter with a brief discussion of two-way ANOVA, which extends the analysis of means to the analysis of differences between two variables and within the *k* groups that define each of the variables. We observe from Table 16.1 that these are but a few of the possible parametric and nonparametric analyses that could be discussed in this chapter. Appendix 16.1 provides a more detailed discussion of the nonparametric techniques.

BIVARIATE CROSS-TABULATION

The discussion of simple cross-tabulation in the previous chapter marked the beginning of a major topic of this book—the analysis of differences between groups. Although we shall

Table 16.1   Selected Nonparametric Statistical Tests for Two-Sample Cases

Sample Cases	Level of Measurement		
	Nominal	Ordinal	Interval/Ratio
Two-sample related samples	McNemar test for the significance of changes	Sign test Wilcoxon matched-pairs signed-ranks test	
Independent samples	Fischer exact probability test	Median test Mann-Whitney U test Kolmogorov-Smirnov two-sample test Wald-Wolfowitz runs test	t-test One-way ANOVA
	χ^2 test for two independent samples		

continue to be interested in the study of variation in a single variable (or a composite of variables), a large part of the discussion of analysis will focus on methods for explaining this variation through the association of two or more variables.

The chi-square statistic in a contingency table analysis is used to answer the following question: Is the observed association between the variables in the cross-tabulation statistically significant? Often called *chi-square analysis,* this technique is used when the data consist of counts or frequencies within categories of a tabulation or cross-tabulation table. In conjunction with the cross-tabulation we will introduce the chi-square statistic, χ^2, to determine the significance of observed association in cross-tabulations involving two or more variables. This is typically called a test of independence.

Cross-tabulation represents the simplest form of associative data analysis. At the minimum we can start out with a bivariate cross-tabulation of two variables, such as occupation and education, each of which identifies a set of exclusive and exhaustive categories. We know that such data are called *qualitative* or *categorical* because each variable is assumed to be only nominal-scaled. Bivariate cross-tabulation is widely used in marketing applications to analyze variables at all levels of measurement. In fact, it is the single most widely used bivariate technique in applied settings.

In marketing research, observations may be cross-classified, such as, for example, when we are interested in testing whether occupational status is associated with brand loyalty. Suppose, for illustrative purposes, that a marketing researcher has assembled data on brand loyalty and occupational status—white collar, blue collar, and unemployed or retired—that describes consumers of a particular product class. The data for our hypothetical problem appear in Table 16.2.

In a study of 230 customers, we are interested in determining if occupational status may be associated with the characteristic loyalty status. The data suggests that a relationship exists, but is the observed association a reflection of sampling variation, or is the variation great enough that we can conclude that a true relationship exists? Expressed in probability terms, we may ask, "Are the conditional probabilities of being highly loyal, moderately loyal, and brand switcher, given the type of occupational status, equal to their respective marginal probabilities?"

Table 16.2   Contingency Table of Observed versus Theoretical Frequencies for Brand-Loyalty Illustration

N, Expected n χ^2 *Contribution* *Occupational* *Status*	*Highly Loyal*	*Moderately Loyal*	*Brand Switchers*	*Total Number* *(percent* *distribution)*
White-collar	30 (30.5) .01	42 (34.1) 1.86	18 (25.4) 2.17	90 (39.1%)
Blue-collar	14 (22.1) 2.93	20 (24.5) .86	31 (18.4) 8.68	65 (28.3%)
Unemployed/retired	34 (25.4) 2.88	25 (28.4) .40	16 (21.2) 1.27	75 (32.6%)
Total	78 (33.9%)	87 (37.8%)	65 (28.3%)	230 χ^2=21.08

In analyzing the problem by means of chi-square, we make use of the marginal totals (column and row totals) in computing theoretical frequencies given that we hypothesize independence (no relationship) between the attributes loyalty status and occupational status. For example, we note from Table 16.2 that 33.9 percent (78/320) respondents are highly loyal. If possession of this characteristic is independent of occupational status, we would expect that 33.9 percent (78/320) of the 90 respondents classified as white-collar workers (i.e., 30.5) would be highly loyal. Similarly, 37.8 percent (87/320) of the 90 (34.1) would be moderately loyal, and 28.3 percent (65/320) of the 90 (25.4) would be brand switchers. In a similar fashion we can compute theoretical frequencies for each cell on the null hypothesis that loyalty status is statistically independent of occupational status. (It should be noted that the frequencies are the same, whether we start with the percentage of the row or the percentage of the column.)

The theoretical frequencies (under the null hypothesis) are computed and appear in parentheses in Table 16.2. The chi-square statistic is then calculated (and shown in the table) for each of the data cells in the table using the observed and theoretical frequencies:

$$\chi^2 = \sum_{i=1}^{k} \frac{(f_i - F_i)^2}{F_i}$$

where f_i = actual observed frequency, F_i = theoretical expected frequency, and k = number of cells ($r \times c$).

The appropriate number of degrees of freedom to use in this example is four. In general, if we have R rows and C columns, the degrees of freedom associated with the chi-square statistic are equal to the product

$$(R - 1)(C - 1)$$

If we use a significance level of 0.05, the tabular value of chi-square (Table A.3) is 9.488. Hence, we reject the null hypothesis of independence between the characteristics loyalty status and occupational status because the computed χ^2 of 21.08 is greater than the table value of 9.488.

When the number of observations in a cell is less than 10 (or where a 2×2 contingency table is involved), a correction factor must be applied to the formula for chi-square. The numerator within the summation sign becomes $(|f_i - F_i| - 1/2)^2$ where the value 1/2 is the *Yates continuity correction*. This correction factor adjusts for the use of a continuous distribution to estimate probability in a discrete distribution.

Chi-square analysis can be extended to deal with more than two variables. No new principles are involved, but the procedure naturally becomes more tedious. Three characteristics of the technique should be borne in mind, however. First, chi-square analysis deals with counts (frequencies) of data. If the data are expressed in percentage form, they should be converted to absolute frequencies. Second, the technique assumes that the observations are drawn independently. Third, the chi-square statistic cannot describe the relationship; it only gauges its statistical significance, regardless of logic or sense (Semon, 1999). To assess the nature of the relationship, the researcher must look at the table and indicate how the variables appear to be related—a type of eyeball approach. This may involve examining any of the following combinations: (a) the variable combinations that produce large χ^2 values in the cells; (b) those with a large difference between the observed and expected frequencies; or (c) those where the cell frequency count, expressed as a percentage of the row total, is most different from the total column percentage (marginal column %). When variables are ordered or loosely ordered, a pattern can sometimes be observed by marking cells with higher than expected observed frequencies with a (+) and those with lower than expected observed frequencies with a (−).

COMPUTER PROGRAMS FOR CROSS-TABULATION

Virtually any general-purpose statistical package has at least one program for constructing and analyzing cross-tabulations from raw categorical data. This is true not only for mainframe and minicomputer installation but also for personal computers.

In addition, there are programs that are designed primarily for cross-tabulation and will present as output report-ready tables. In general, all of these programs will include chi-square for significance-testing purposes. However, the extent to which indexes of agreement are included varies widely. Since there are many software programs available and most of them are somewhat similar in type of output, it is difficult to state which one is best for a marketing researcher's needs. Most programs provide a complete approach to all the topics considered in this chapter and in Chapter 14:

- Computation of row and column percentages
- Introduction of a third variable in describing association between some other pair of variables
- Determination of the statistical significance of the association observed in any cross-tabulation of interest
- Measurement of the strength of that association by means of some type of agreement index

At the very least, selection of specialty cross-tabulation software will depend on the hardware setup and the nature and size of the database to be analyzed.

Table 16.3   Sample Cross-Tabulation Output

PLEASE SELECT ONE OF THE FIVE WORTHY CHARITIES TO WHICH YOU WOULD LIKE A TWO DOLLAR CONTRIBUTION MADE.

		EMPLOYEES IN COMPANY			
	TOTAL	UNDER 100	100-999	1,000 9,999	10.000 PLUS
	(A)	(B)	(C)	(D)	(E)
BASE: ALL RESPONDENTS	492	112	160	118	88
	100.0	100.0	100.0	100.0	100.0
AMERICAN RED CROSS	120	22	43	29	20
	24.4	19.6	26.9	24.6	22.7
WORLD WILDLIFE FEDERATION	80	22	22	12	22
	16.3	19.6	13.8	10.2	25.0
AMERICAN CANCER SOCIETY	198	47	63	54	30
	40.2	42.0	39.4	45.8	34.1
DOCTORS WITHOUT BORDERS	70	16	25	17	11
	14.2	14.3	15.6	14.4	12.5
UNICEF INDIA EARTHQUAKE RELIEF FUND	16	4	6	2	4
	3.3	3.6	3.8	1.7	4.5
NO ANSWER	8	1	1	4	1
	1.6	0.9	0.6	3.4	1.1

SOURCE: Adapted from Wilson Research Group

An example of the output from one program is presented in Table 16.3. This is representative of the output from many other software packages. It will be noted that the output shows one variable, "selection of a charity," cross-tabulated by another, "number of company employees." A total of five columns, known as *banner points,* are shown. Professional cross-tabulation software will output tables that join multiple variables on the column banner points.

BIVARIATE ANALYSIS: DIFFERENCES IN MEANS AND PROPORTIONS

A great amount of marketing research is concerned with estimating parameters of one or more populations. In addition, many studies go beyond estimation and compare such population parameters by testing hypotheses about differences between them. Means, proportions, and variances are often the summary measures of concern. Our concern at this point is with differences in means and proportions. Direct comparisons of variances are a special case of the more general technique of analysis of variance, which is covered later in this chapter.

Standard Error of Differences

In Chapter 15 we briefly discussed sampling distributions and standard errors as they apply to a single statistic. Appropriate formulas were presented. Here we extend this discussion to cover differences in statistics and show a traditional hypothesis for differences.

Standard Error of Difference of Means

The starting point is the standard error of the difference. For two samples, A and B, that are independent and randomly selected, the standard error of the differences in means is calculated by

$$\sigma_{\bar{x}_A - \bar{x}_B} = \sqrt{\frac{\sigma_A{}^2}{n_A} + \frac{\sigma_B{}^2}{n_B}}$$

This estimate of the standard error is appropriate for use in the denominator of the z test formula.

If the population standard deviations, σ_i, are not known, then we must estimate them in the manner shown in Chapter 15. The estimated standard error becomes

$$est.S_{\bar{x}_A - \bar{x}_B} = \sqrt{\frac{S_A{}^2}{n_A} + \frac{S_B{}^2}{n_B}}$$

For relatively small samples the correction factor N_i/n_i-1 is used and the resulting formula for the estimated standard error is

$$est.S_{\bar{x}_A - \bar{x}_B} = \sqrt{\frac{S_A{}^2}{n_A - 1} + \frac{S_B{}^2}{n_B - 1}}$$

Of course, these formulas would be appropriate for use in the denominator of the t-test.

Standard Error of Differences of Proportions

Turning now to proportions, the derivation of the standard error of the differences is somewhat similar. Specifically, for large samples,

$$est.\sigma_{pA - pB} = \sqrt{\frac{p_A(1 - p_A)}{n_A} + \frac{p_B(1 - p_B)}{n_B}}$$

For small samples, the correction factor is applied, resulting in

$$est.\sigma_{pA-pB} = \sqrt{\frac{p_A(1 - p_A)}{n_A - 1} + \frac{p_B(1 - p_B)}{n_B - 1}}$$

This estimate would again be appropriate for use in the denominator of the Z-test of proportions.

Testing of Hypotheses

When applying the standard error formulas for hypotheses testing concerning parameters, the following conditions must be met:

1. Samples must be independent.

2. Individual items in samples must be drawn in a random manner.

3. The population being sampled must be normally distributed (or the sample must be of sufficiently large size).

4. For small samples, the population variances must be equal.

5. The data must be at least intervally scaled.

When these five conditions are met, or can at least be reasonably assumed to exist, the traditional approach is as follows.

1. The null hypothesis (H$_0$) is specified such that there is no difference between the parameters of interest in the two populations (e.g., H$_0$: $\mu_A - \mu_B = 0$); any observed difference is assumed to occur solely because of sampling variation.

2. The alpha risk is established ($\alpha = .05$ or other value).

3. A Z value is calculated by the appropriate adaptation of the Z formula. For testing the difference between two means, Z is calculated in the following way:

$$Z = \frac{(\bar{X}_A - \bar{X}_B) - (\mu_A - \mu_B)}{\sigma_{\bar{x}_A - \bar{x}_B}} = \frac{(\bar{X}_A - \bar{X}_B) - 0}{\sigma_{\bar{x}_A - \bar{x}_B}}$$

and for proportions

$$Z = \frac{(p_A - p_B) - (\pi_A - \pi_B)}{\sigma_{pA-pB}} = \frac{(p_A - p_B) - 0}{\sigma_{pA-pB}}$$

For unknown population variance and small samples, the student t distribution must be used, and for means, t is calculated from

$$t = \frac{(\bar{X}_A - \bar{X}_B) - (\mu_A - \mu_B)}{S_{\bar{x}_A - \bar{x}_B}} = \frac{(\bar{X}_A - \bar{X}_B) - 0}{S_{\bar{x}_A - \bar{x}_B}}$$

4. The probability of the observed difference of the two sample statistics having occurred by chance is determined from a table of the normal distribution (Appendix A, Table A.1) (or the t distribution from Appendix A, Table A.2, interpreted with $[n_A + n_B - 2]$ degrees of freedom).

5. If the probability of the observed difference having occurred by chance is *greater* than the alpha risk, the null hypothesis is accepted; it is concluded that the parameters of the two universes are not significantly different. If the probability of the observed difference having occurred by chance is *less* than the alpha risk, the null hypothesis is rejected; it is concluded that the parameters of the two populations differ significantly. In an applied setting, there are times when the level at which significance occurs (the alpha level) is reported and management decides whether to accept or reject.

An example will illustrate the application of this procedure. Let us assume we have conducted a survey of detergent and paper goods purchases from supermarkets among urban (population A) and rural (population B) families (see Table 16.4).

Table 16.4   Sample Group and Average Expenditure

Family Type	Sample	Average Amount Spent	Standard Deviation
Urban (Sample A)	$n_A = 400$	$\bar{X}_A = \$32.00$	$s_A = \$10.00$
Rural (Sample B)	$n_B = 225$	$\bar{X}_B = \$30.80$	$s_B = \$9.00$

The question facing the researcher is the following: "Do urban families spend more on these items, or is the $1.20 difference in means caused by sampling variations?"

We proceed as follows. The hypothesis of no difference in means is established. We assume the alpha risk is set at .05. Since a large sample test is called for, the Z value is calculated using the separate variances estimate of the standard error of differences in means:

$$S_{\bar{x}_A - \bar{x}_B} = \sqrt{\frac{(10.0)^2}{400} + \frac{(9.0)^2}{225}} = \$0.78$$

The Z value is then determined to be

$$Z = \frac{(32.0 - 30.8) - 0}{0.78} = +1.54$$

The probability of the observed difference in the sample means having been due to sampling is specified by finding the area under the normal curve that falls to the right of the point $Z = +1.54$. Consulting Table A.1 in Appendix A, we find this area to be $1.0 - .9382 = 0.0618$. Since this probability associated with the observed difference ($p = 0.06$) is greater than the preset alpha, a strict interpretation would be that there is no difference between the two types of families concerning the average expenditure on nonfood items. In a decision setting, however, the manager would have to determine whether this probability (0.06) is low enough to conclude, on pragmatic grounds, that the families do not differ in their behavior. As stated previously, and discussed in the previous chapter, often there is no preset alpha and decisional considerations require that the manager determines the meaning of the reported alpha.

To illustrate the small sample case, let us assume that we obtain the same mean values and get values for s_A and s_B such that $s_{xA} - s_{xB} = \$0.78$ from samples $n_A = 15$ and $n_B = 12$. With these data we calculate t as follows:

$$t = \frac{(32.0 - 30.8) - 0}{0.78} = 1.54$$

The critical value of t is obtained from Table A.2 of the Appendix of this book. For, say, $\sigma = .05$, we determine the critical value of t for $(n_A + n_B - 2) = 25$ degrees of freedom to be 1.708 (one-tailed test).

Since the calculated t of $1.54 < 1.708$, we cannot reject the hypothesis of no difference in average amount spent by the two types of families. This result is shown in Figure 16.1.

When samples are not independent, the same general procedure is followed. The formulas for calculating the test statistics differ, however.

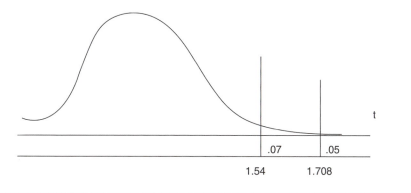

Figure 16.1 *t*-Distribution

Testing the Means of Two Groups:
The Independent Samples *t*-Test

The *t*-distribution revolutionized statistics and the ability to work with small samples. Prior statistical work was based largely on the value of Z, which was used to designate a point on the normal distribution where population parameters were known. For most market research applications, the Z-test's assumed knowledge of μ and σ is difficult to justify. The *t*-test relaxes the rigid assumptions of the Z-test by focusing on sample means and variances (X and s). The *t*-test is a widely used market research statistic to test for differences between two groups of respondents.

In the previous section, the *t* statistic was described. Most computer programs recognize two versions of this statistic. In the previous section, we presented what is called the separate variance estimate formula:

$$t = \frac{\bar{x}_1 - \bar{x}_2}{\sqrt{\frac{s_1^2}{n_1} + \frac{s_2^2}{n_2}}}$$

This formula is appropriate where differences in large samples are tested.

The second method, called the pooled variance estimate, computes an average for the samples that is used in the denominator of the statistic:

$$t = \frac{\bar{X}_1 - \bar{X}_2}{\sqrt{\left(\frac{1}{n_1} + \frac{1}{n_2}\right) S_1^2(n_1 - 1) + S_2^2(n_2 - 1)/n_1 - 1 + n_2 - 1}}$$

The pooling of variances is a simple averaging of variances that is required when (1) testing for the same population proportion in two populations or (2) testing the difference in means between two small samples.

Table 16.5 shows a sample output of *t*-tests from SPSS. Two respondent groups were identified for the supermarket study:

1. Respondents who were males

2. Respondents who were females

The analysis by gender is shown in Part A of the output for the attitudinal dimensions, friendliness of clerks and helpfulness of clerks. It will be noted that the sample sizes are approximately equal. To show a contrast we have included in Part B of the output a *t*-test from another study where the number of males and females varies widely. In all three examples, the differences between separate-variance and pooled-variance analysis are very small. Table 16.5 also shows an *F* statistic. This is *Levene's test for equality of variances*. Using this test the researcher knows which *t*-test output to use—equal variances assumed or equal variances not assumed.

Table 16.5 Selected Output From SPSS *t*-Test

	Mean	*n*	*F*	*Sig*	Equal Variances Not Not Assumed (Separate)			Equal Variances Assumed (Pooled)		
					t	*df*	*Sig (2-tailed)*	*t*	*df*	*Sig (2-tailed)*
Part A										
"Friendliness of clerks"			2713	.102	1.301	126.213	.19	1.298	128	.197
Male	4.55	64								
Female	4.82	66								
"Helpfulness of clerks"			15,401	.000	.308	105.177	.758	.308	126	.758
Male	4.50	64								
Female	4.56	64								
Part B										
"Shopping Experience"										
Male	1.977	44	.089	.765	.569	66,993	.571	.590	189	.556
Female	1.857	147								

TESTING OF GROUP MEANS: ANALYSIS OF VARIANCE

Analysis of variance (ANOVA) is a logical extension of the independent groups *t*-test methodology. Rather than test differences between two group means, we test the overall difference in *k* group means, where the *k* groups are thought of as levels of a treatment or control variable(s) or factor(s). ANOVA is a general set of methodologies that handle many different types of research and experimental designs. Traditional use of analysis of variance has been to isolate the effects of experimental variables that are related in various experimental situations. The respondent receives a combination of the treatment levels from the different factors and the response is measured. More specifically, ANOVA is used to test the statistical significance of differences in mean responses given the introduction of one or more treatment effects. Exhibit 16.1 gives an illustration of the different ways in which means differ.

Much experimental work has been conducted in medicine and agriculture. In pharmaceutical drug testing, positive and negative effects of dosage and formulation are measured over time and for different types of ailments and patient illness levels. The variables influencing the results are called *experimental factors*. In agriculture, crop yields are measured for plots of land, each of which receives a different treatment level that is defined by a factor or control variable. Control variables in this application might include seed type, fertilizer type, fertilizer dosage, temperature, moisture, and many other variables thought to influence production. In each of these plots, the average yield is measured and analyzed to determine the effect of the specific measured levels of the factors being evaluated. Marketing research experiments have control variables that are certainly different from agricultural experiments, but the principles are the same.

EXHIBIT 16.1   Determining When Means Are Significantly Different

As an illustration let us assume that we have measured the purchase of a new brand of ice cream at two food stores—a supermarket (SM) and a convenience store (CV). Observations have been made for five days at each store. This study could have been run as a rigorous controlled experiment or as a more loosely run observational study.

We are interested in determining whether the mean number of quarts sold at the two stores (Y_i) differed significantly. Graph I below shows that the means are numerically different, but we cannot tell whether they are significantly different.

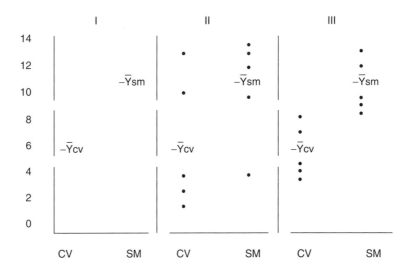

In Graph II the difference between the means is the same it was in I, but the difference is suspect because the individual observations are spread out. Within each group the variance is so great that the difference in the means is not convincing.

The situation differs considerably in Graph III, where the difference between means is the same as in the two previous situations. However, the observations are clustered around the means for each store. This clustering now allows us to conclude that there is a statistically significant difference between the two means.

The problem is how to decide what means are different enough, relative to the spread of the observations (i.e., the variance) in each group, to conclude that there is a statistically significant difference between the means. Analysis of variance helps us answer the questions.

SOURCE: From Iversen, G. R., & Norpoth, H., *Analysis of Variance, 2nd Edition*, copyright © 1987. Reprinted by permission of Sage Publications, Inc.

The proper planning and design of the relationships between the experimental factors results in methodologies having such unfamiliar names as completely randomized, randomized block, Latin square, and factorial designs, as discussed previously in Chapter 8. In this chapter we discuss the two most basic forms of the methodology: the one-way ANOVA and the two-factor ANOVA designs (see Exhibit 16.2).

EXHIBIT 16.2   ANOVA Designs

Example: It is well known that interest ratings for TV ads are related to the advertising message. A simple one-way ANOVA to investigate this relationship might compare three messages:

Advertising message A	Advertising message B	Advertising message C

Two-factor ANOVA includes a second factor, possibly the type of advertisement (magazine or TV):

	Message A	Message B	Message C
Magazine Ad			
TV Ad			

Each of the cells in this matrix would contain an average interest rating for the measures taken for the particular combination of message and media.

This brief introduction to the idea behind an ANOVA will hopefully reduce the impression that the technique is used to test for significant differences among the variances of two or more sample universes. This is not strictly the case. ANOVA is used to test the statistical significance of differences in mean responses given the introduction of one or more treatments effects.

The ANOVA Methodology

The appropriateness of the label analysis of variance comes from explaining the variation in responses to the various treatment combinations. The methodology for explaining this variation is explained in Exhibit 16.3, which presents an example regarding responses to messages.

EXHIBIT 16.3 ANOVA Designs

Using the single-factor ANOVA design for the problem described in Exhibit 16.2, the actual data for 12 respondents appears in tabular and graphical format as follows:

Obs #	Msg. A	Msg. B	Msg. C
1	6	8	0
2	4	11	2
3	3	4	1
4	3	5	1
Mean	4	7	1

It is apparent that the messages differ in terms of their distribution, but how do we perform ANOVA to explain these differences? There are three values that must be computed in order to analyze this pattern of values.

1. Total sum of squares: The grand mean of the 12 observations is computed, followed by the variance of the individual observations from this mean.

$$(\chi_{ij} - \bar{\chi})^2 : (6 - 4)^2 + (4 - 4)^2 + ... + (1 - 4)^2 = 110$$

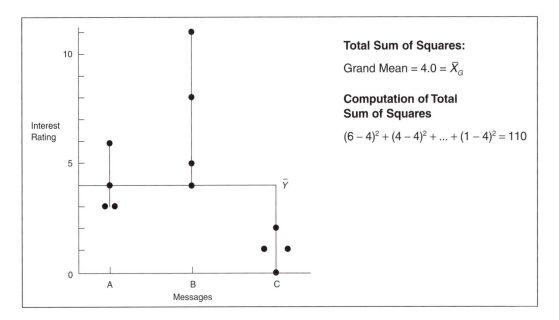

Total Sum of Squares:

Grand Mean = $4.0 = \bar{X}_G$

Computation of Total Sum of Squares

$(6 - 4)^2 + (4 - 4)^2 + ... + (1 - 4)^2 = 110$

2. Between-treatment sum of squares: The means of the factor levels (messages A, B, and C) are computed, followed by the deviation of the factor level means from the overall mean, weighted by the number of observations $\left[n(\bar{x}_j - \bar{x})^2 \right]$.

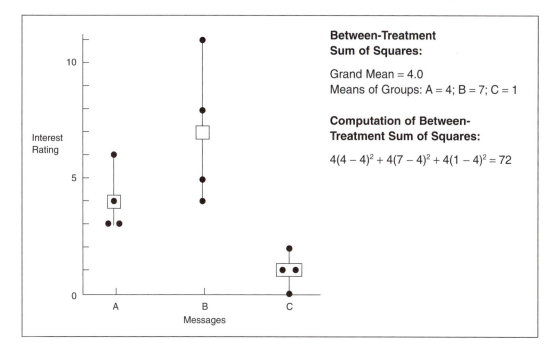

Between-Treatment Sum of Squares:

Grand Mean = 4.0
Means of Groups: A = 4; B = 7; C = 1

Computation of Between-Treatment Sum of Squares:

$$4(4-4)^2 + 4(7-4)^2 + 4(1-4)^2 = 72$$

3. Within-treatment sum of squares: The means of the factor levels are computed, followed by the deviation of the observations within each factor level from that factor level mean.

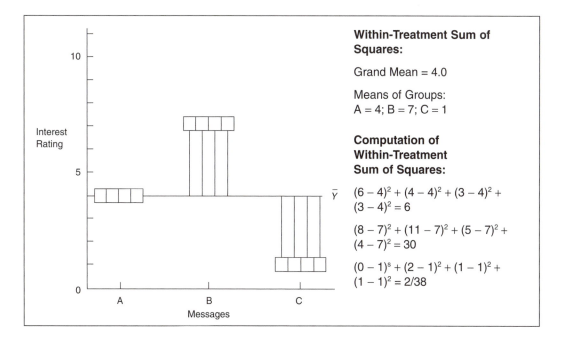

Within-Treatment Sum of Squares:

Grand Mean = 4.0

Means of Groups:
A = 4; B = 7; C = 1

Computation of Within-Treatment Sum of Squares:

$\bar{y}$ $(6-4)^2 + (4-4)^2 + (3-4)^2 + (3-4)^2 = 6$

$(8-7)^2 + (11-7)^2 + (5-7)^2 + (4-7)^2 = 30$

$(0-1)^s + (2-1)^2 + (1-1)^2 + (1-1)^2 = 2/38$

Thus, an observation may be decomposed into three terms that are additive, and each explains a particular type of variance:

> Observation = Overall mean + Deviation of the group mean from the overall mean
> + Deviation of the observation from the group mean

The overall mean is constant and common to all observations: The deviation of a group mean from the overall mean represents the effect on each observation of belonging to that particular group; the deviation of an observation from its group mean represents the effect on that observation of all variables other than the group variable.

The basic idea of ANOVA is to compare the between-treatment-groups sum of squares (after dividing by degrees of freedom to get a mean square) with the within-treatment-group sum of squares (also divided by the appropriate number of degrees of freedom). This is the F statistic that indicates the strength of the grouping factor. Conceptually,

$$F = \frac{\text{Sampling variance} + \text{Variance due to effect of treatment}}{\text{Sampling variance}}$$

The larger the ratio of between to within, the more we are inclined to reject the null hypothesis that the group mean $\mu_1 = \mu_2 = \mu_3$. Conversely, if the three sample means were very close to each other, the between-samples sum of squares would be close to zero and we would conclude that the population means are the same, once we consider the variability of individual cases within each sample group.

However, to make this comparison, it is necessary to assume that the error-term distribution has constant variance over all observations. This is exactly the same assumption as was made for the t-test.

In the next section we shall (a) use more efficient computational techniques, (b) consider the adjustment for degrees of freedom to obtain mean squares, and (c) show the case of the F ratio in testing significance. Still, the foregoing remarks represent the basic ANOVA idea for comparing between- with within-sample variability.

One-Way (Single Factor) Analysis of Variance

One-way ANOVA is analysis of variance in its simplest (single-factor) form. Suppose a new product manager for the hypothetical Friskie Corp. is interested in the effect of shelf height on supermarket sales of canned dog food. The product manager has been able to secure the cooperation of a store manager to run an experiment involving three levels of shelf height (knee level, waist level, and eye level) on sales of a single brand of dog food, which we shall call Snoopy. Assume further that our experiment must be conducted in a single supermarket

Table 16.6   Sales of Snoopy Dog Food (in Units) by Level of Shelf Height

Knee Level		*Shelf Height* Waist Level		Eye Level		Grand Total
X_{11}	77	X_{12}	88	X_{13}	85	
X_{21}	82	X_{22}	94	X_{23}	85	
X_{31}	86	X_{32}	93	X_{33}	87	
X_{41}	78	X_{42}	90	X_{43}	81	
X_{51}	81	X_{52}	91	X_{53}	80	
X_{61}	86	X_{62}	94	X_{63}	79	
X_{71}	77	X_{72}	90	X_{73}	87	
X_{81}	81	X_{82}	87	X_{83}	93	
$X_T 1 = 648$		$X_T 2 = 727$		$X_T 3 = 677$		$X_{TT} = 2,052$
$\bar{X}_1 = 81.0$		$\bar{X}_2 = 90.9$		$\bar{X}_3 = 84.6$		$\bar{X}_{TT} = 85.5$

and that our response variable will be sales, in cans, of Snoopy dog food for some appropriate unit of time. But what shall we use for our unit of time? Sales of dog food in a single store may exhibit week-to-week variation, day-to-day variation, and even hour-to-hour variation. In addition, sales of this particular brand may be influenced by the price or special promotions of competitive brands, the store management's knowledge that an experiment is going on, and other variables that we cannot control at all or would find too costly to control.

Assume that we have agreed to change the shelf-height position of Snoopy three times per day and run the experiment over eight days. We shall fill the remaining sections of our gondola with a filler brand, which is not familiar to customers in the geographical area in which the test is being conducted. Furthermore, since our primary emphasis is on explaining the technique of analysis of variance in its simplest form (analysis of one factor: shelf-height), we shall assign the shelf heights at random over the three time periods per day and not design an experiment to explicitly control and test for within-day and between-day differences. Our experimental results are shown in Table 16.6. Here, we let X_{ij} denote the sales (in units) of Snoopy during the ith day under the jth treatment level. If we look at mean sales by each level of shelf height, it appears as though the waist-level treatment, the average response to which is $X_2 = 90.9$, results in the highest mean sales over the experimental period. However, we note that the last observation (93) under the eye-level treatment exceeds the waist-level treatment mean. Is this a fluke observation? We know that these means are, after all, *sample* means, and our interest lies in whether the three population means from which the samples are drawn are equal or not.

Now we shall show what happens when one goes through a typical one-way analysis-of-variance computation for this problem. These calculations are shown in Table 16.7.

Table 16.7 shows the mechanics of developing the among-treatments, within-treatments, and total sums of squares, the mean squares, and the F ratio. Had the experimenter used an alpha risk of 0.01, the null hypothesis of no differences among treatment levels would have been rejected. A table of F ratios is found in Table B.4, Appendix B.

Table 16.7   Analysis of Variance—Snoopy Dog Food Experiment

Source of Variation	Degrees of freedom	Sum of squares	Mean square	F Ratio
Among treatments	$t - 1 = 2$	399.3	199.7	14.6 ($p < 0.01$)
Within treatments	$n - t = 21$	288.7	13.7	
Total	$n - 1 = 23$	688.0	$MS_T = SSt / df_T$	MS_T
			$MS_W = SSw / df_W$	$F = \text{--------}$
				MS_W

Correction factor

$$C = \frac{(X_{TT})^2}{n} = \frac{(2,052)^2}{24} = 175,446.0$$

Total sum of squares

$$\sum X_{ij}^2 - C = (77)^2 + (82)^2 + \cdots + (87)^2 + (93)^2 - 175,466.0 = 688.0$$

Treatment sum of squares

$$\frac{\sum X_{ij}^2}{n_j} - C = \frac{(648)^2 + (727)^2 + (677)^2}{8} - 175,466.0 = 399.3$$

Within treatment sum of squares

$$\sum X_y^2 \frac{\sum X_{Tj}^2}{n_j} = (77)^2 + (82)^2 + \cdots + (87)^2 + (93)^2 - \frac{(648)^2 + (727)^2 + (677)^2}{8} = 288.7$$

Note that Table 16.7 shows shortcut procedures for finding each sum of squares. For example, the total sum of squares is given by

$$\sum X_{ij}^2 - \frac{(X_{TT})^2}{n} = 688.0$$

This is the same quantity that would be obtained by subtracting the grand mean of 85.5 from each original observation, squaring the result, and adding up the 24 squared deviations. This mean-corrected sum of squares is equivalent to the type of formula used earlier in this chapter.

The interpretation of this analysis is, like the *t*-test, a process of comparing the *F* value of 14.6 (2, 21 df) with the table value of 4.32 ($p = .05$). Because (14.6 > 4.32), we reject the null hypothesis that treatments 1, 2, and 3 have equivalent appeals.

The important consideration to remember is that, aside from the statistical assumptions underlying the analysis of variance, the *variance of the error distribution* will markedly influence the significance of the results. That is, if the variance is *large* relative to differences among treatments, then the true effects may be swamped, leading to an acceptance of the null hypothesis when it is false. As we know, an increase in sample size can reduce this experimental error. Though beyond the scope of this text, *specialized* experimental designs are available, the objectives of which are to increase the efficiency of the experiment by reducing the error variance.

Follow-up Tests of Treatment Differences

The question that now must be answered is the following: Which treatments differ? The *F*-ratio only provides information that differences exist. The question of where differences exist is answered by follow-up analysis, usually a series of independent sample *t*-tests, to compare the treatment level combinations ((1,2), (1,3), and (2,3)). Because of our previous discussion of the *t*-test, we will not discuss these tests in detail. We will only allude to the fact that there are various forms of the *t*-statistic that may be used when conducting a series of two group tests. These test statistics (which include techniques known as the least significant difference, Bonnferoni's test, Duncan's multiple range tests, Scheffe's test, and others) control the probability that a Type I error will occur when a *series* of statistical tests are conducted. Recall that if in a series of statistical tests, each test has a .05 probability of a Type I error, then in a series of 20 such tests we would expect one (20 * .05 = 1) of these tests would report a significant difference that did not exist (Type I error). These tests typically are options provided by the standard statistical packages, such as the SPSS program *Oneway*.

N-Way (Factorial) Analysis of Variance Designs

The preceding example dealt with the simplest of ANOVA designs—classifications by a single factor. Suppose that our marketing researcher is now interested in the effect of other point-of-purchase variables such as shelf facings (width of display) and shelf fullness on sales. Or, suppose that the researcher would like to generalize the results of the experiment to other sizes of stores in other marketing regions. It may be preferable to ask many questions if the researcher would like to measure variables that influence the most general conditions under which the findings are expected to hold. In this section we discuss more specialized experimental design that is characterized by two or more variables of classification.

A *factorial experiment* is one in which an equal number of observations is made of all combinations involving at least two levels of at least two variables. This type of experiment enables the researcher to study possible *interactions* among the variables of interest. Suppose we return to our canned dog food illustration but now assume that the researcher is interested in studying the effects of *two* variables of interest: shelf height (still at three levels) and shelf facing (at two levels—that is, at half the width of the gondola and at full width of the gondola). While the plan still is to use a single store for the experiment, the researcher intends to replicate each combination three times, leading to $3 \times 2 \times 3 = 18$ observations. Assume that the experiment results in the data shown in Table 16.8. Note that for each combination of shelf height and shelf facing we have three observations.

As in Table 16.7 we need to compute the various sums of squares. Each mean square is compared, in turn, with the error mean square via the *F* ratio. The analysis-of-variance summary is shown in Table 16.9.

Looking at the *F* ratios of Table 16.9, we note that the *AB* interaction is insignificant at the 0.05 alpha level (but is significant at the 0.1 alpha level). Still, if the researcher were interested in the single combination of shelf height and shelf facings that would produce the highest sales, it would seem as though the combination full-width, waist-level is best (though a waist-level, half-width display may cost less and produce similar results).

One of the easiest ways to understand the nature of interaction is to plot the average response for levels of one of the treatment variables and different levels of a second treatment

Table 16.8   Factorial Display—Snoopy Dog Food Experiment

Facings	Knee Level	Waist Level	Eye Level
Level 1 (half width)	(70, 75, 79) 224 ($\bar{x} = 74.7$)	(85, 88, 93) 266 ($\bar{x} = 88.7$)	(77, 81, 78) 236 ($\bar{x} = 78.7$)
Level 2 (full width)	(91, 90, 87) 268 ($\bar{x} = 89.3$)	(94, 97, 93) 284 ($\bar{x} = 94.7$)	(87, 90, 90) 267 ($\bar{x} = 89$)
Total	492	550	503

Table 16.9   Analysis of Variance, Factorial Display—Snoopy Dog Food Experiment

Source of Variation	Degrees of Freedom	Sum of Squares	Mean Square	F Ratio
Treatments				
A (facings)	1	480.5	480.5	54.6 ($p < 0.01$)
B (height)	2	316.3	158.2	18.0 ($p < 0.01$)
A × B	2	56.4	28.2	3.2 ($0.1 < p < 0.05$)
Error	12	105.3	8.8	
Total	17	958.5		

variable. This is done for the averaged cell responses in Table 16.8 and the results are shown in Figure 16.2. The vertical axis of the chart shows average unit sales, whereas the horizontal axis shows levels of the shelf-height variable. Connecting lines between effects are shown strictly for visual purposes, only discrete levels of A and B are involved.

For example, averaged unit sales when shelf height is at knee level and facings are at half width is 74.7 units, as shown on the chart. As can be seen, average sales increase (to 88.7) at waist level and then decline (to 78.7) at eye level. However, when we examine the average sales unit response to changes in shelf height when facings are full width, we see that the response *increments* differ; that is, the line segments are not parallel. That is, the response to changes in shelf height differs across the two levels of facings.

Another way of saying this is to note that the *differential effect* of moving from knee level to waist level depends on what the level of facings is. For facings at half width the difference is 88.7 − 74.7 = 14.0. When facings are at full width, the difference is 94.7 − 89.3 = 5.4; that is, the incremental effect is less pronounced. If the *observed* departures from parallelism in each of the line segment pairs cannot be ascribed to sampling fluctuations, then we say that a significant interaction exists.

Technically, what is shown here is an *ordinal* interaction. By this is meant that sales response to waist level is still higher than sales response to knee level, independent of facings level—it is the *incremental* difference that varies. Had average sales response to the combination of waist-level and full-width facings been, say, only 72 units, then the lines would have

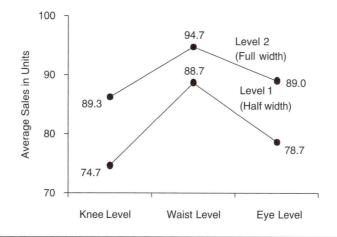

Figure 16.2   Plot of the A × B (Shelf Height by Facings) Interaction

crossed and a *disordinal* interaction would be involved. The latter case is much more serious because before we can specify what level of shelf height to consider from a marketing strategy standpoint, we must know what level of facings is involved. On the other hand, under ordinal interactions (assuming equal implementation costs for each alternative), waist level leads to highest sales at each level of facings.

In summary, factorial experimentation permits the researcher to study the effect on response of several variables in combination. Not only may main effects be estimated but, more importantly, the researcher may study interaction effects as well. This latter advantage is particularly important in market experimentation where the researcher is typically interested in the combination of controlled variables that leads to the best payoff in terms of sales, cash flow, or some other measure of effectiveness. A more detailed discussion of interaction effects is given by Jaccard (1998).

SUMMARY

In this chapter, our primary concern has been to develop the necessary statistical machinery to analyze differences between groups: *t*-test, and one-factor and two-factor analysis of variance. These techniques are useful for both experimental and nonexperimentally obtained data. The first section of the chapter dealt with cross-tabulation and chi-square analysis. This was followed by discussing bivariate analysis of differences in means and proportions. We then looked at the process of analysis of variance. A simple numerical example was used to demonstrate the partitioning of variance into among- and within-components.

The assumptions underlying various models were pointed out and a hypothetical data experiment was analyzed to show how the ANOVA models operate. The topic of interaction plotting was introduced to aid the researcher in interpreting the results of his or her analysis.

APPENDIX 16.1
Nonparametric Analysis

Other Tests

One reason for the widespread use of chi-square in cross-tabulation analysis is that most computer computational routines show the statistic as part of the output, or at least it is an option that the analyst can choose. Sometimes the data available are stronger than simple nominal measurement and are ordinal. In this situation other tests are more powerful than chi-square. Three regularly used tests are the *Wilcoxon Rank Sum* (T), the *Mann-Whitney U*, and the *Kolmogorov-Smirnov* test. Siegel (1956) and Gibbons (1993) provide more detailed discussions of these techniques.

The Wilcoxon T test is used for dependent samples in which the data are collected in matched pairs. This test takes into account both the direction of differences within pairs of observations and the relative magnitude of the differences. The Wilcox matched-pairs signed-ranks test gives more weight to pairs showing large differences between the two measurements than to a pair showing a small difference. To use this test, measurements must at least be ordinally scaled within pairs. In addition, ordinal measurement must hold for the differences between pairs.

This test has many practical applications in marketing research. For instance, it may be used to test whether a promotional campaign has had an effect on attitudes. An ordinal scaling device, such as a semantic differential, can be used to measure attitudes toward, say, a bank. Then, after a special promotional campaign, the same sample would be given the same scaling device. Changes in values of each scale could be analyzed by this Wilcoxon test.

With ordinal measurement and two independent samples, the Mann-Whitney U test may be used to test whether the two groups are from the same population. This is a relatively powerful nonparametric test, and it is an alternative to the Student *t* test when the analyst cannot meet the assumptions of the *t* test or when measurement is at best ordinal. Both one- and two-tailed tests can be conducted. As indicated earlier, results of U and I tests often are similar, leading to the same conclusion.

The Kolmogorov-Smirnov two-sample test is a test of whether two independent samples come from the same population or from populations with the same distribution. This test is sensitive to any kind of difference in the distributions from which the two samples were drawn—differences in location (central tendency), dispersion, skewness, and so on. This characteristic of the test makes it a very versatile test. Unfortunately, the test does not by itself show what kind of difference exists. There is a Kolmogorov-Smirnov one-sample test that is concerned with the agreement between an observed distribution of a set of sample values and some specified theoretical distribution. In this case it is a goodness-of-fit test similar to single-classification chi-square analysis.

Indexes of Agreement

Chi-square is appropriate for making statistical tests of independence in cross-tabulations. Usually, however, we are interested in the *strength* of association as well as the statistical significance of association. This concern is for what is known as *substantive* or *practical* significance. An association is substantively significant when it is statistically significant and of sufficient strength. Unlike statistical significance, however, there is no simple numerical value to compare with and considerable research judgment is necessary. Although such judgment is subjective, it need not be completely arbitrary. The nature of the problem can offer some basis for judgment, and common sense can indicate that the degree of association is too low in some cases and high enough in others (Gold, 1969, p. 44).

Statisticians have devised a plethora of indexes—often called *indexes of agreement*—for measuring the strength of association between two variables in a cross-tabulation. The main descriptors for classifying the various indexes are

1. Whether the table is 2×2 or larger, $R \times C$

2. Whether one, both, or neither of the variables has categories that obey some natural order (e.g., age, income level, family size)

3. Whether association is to be treated symmetrically or whether we want to predict membership in one variable's categories from (assumed known) membership in the other variable's categories

Space does not permit coverage of even an appreciable fraction of the dozens of agreement indexes that have been proposed. Rather, we shall illustrate one commonly used index for 2×2 tables and two indexes that deal with different aspects of the larger $R \times C$ (row-by-column) tables.

The 2 × 2 Case

The *phi correlation coefficient* is a useful agreement index for the special case of 2×2 tables in which both variables are dichotomous. Moreover, an added bonus is the fact that phi equals the product-moment correlation—a cornerstone of multivariate methods—that one would obtain if he or she correlated the two variables expressed in coded $0 - 1$ form.

To illustrate, consider the 2×2 cross-tabulation in Table 16.10, taken from a study relating to shampoos. We wish to see if inclusion of the shampoo benefit of "body" in the respondent's ideal set is associated with the respondent's indication that her hair lacks natural "body." We first note from the table that high frequencies appear in the cells: (a) "body" included in ideal set and "no" to the question of whether her hair has enough (natural) body; and (b) "body" excluded from the ideal set and "yes" to the same question.

Table 16.10   Does Hair Have Enough Body Versus Body Inclusion in Ideal Set

	Hair Have Enough Body?		
	No	*Yes*	*Total*
Body included in ideal set	26 (A)	8 (B)	34
Body excluded from ideal set	17 (C)	33 (D)	50
Total	43	41	84

Before computing the phi coefficient, first note the labels, A, B, C, and D assigned to the four cells in Table 16.10. The phi coefficient is defined as

$$\phi = \frac{AD - BC}{\sqrt{(A + B)(C + D)(A + C)(B + D)}}$$
$$= \frac{26(33) - 8(17)}{\sqrt{(26 + 8)(17 + 33)(26 + 17)(8 + 33)}}$$
$$= 0.417$$

The value 0.417 is also what would be found if an ordinary product-moment correlation, to be described in Chapter 17, is computed across the 84 pairs of numbers where the following code values are used to identify the responses:

- Body included in ideal set $\Rightarrow 1$
- Body excluded from ideal set $\Rightarrow 0$
- Hair have enough body?   No $\Rightarrow 1$
                            Yes $\Rightarrow 0$

This is a nice feature of phi in the sense that standard computer programs for calculating product-moment correlations can be used for dichotomous variables.

The phi coefficient can vary from -1 to 1 (just like the ordinary product-moment correlation). However, in any given problem the upper limit of phi depends on the relationships among the marginals. Specifically, a phi coefficient of -1 (perfect negative association) or 1 (perfect positive association) assumes that the marginal totals of the first variable are identical to those of the second. Looking at the letters (A, B, C, D) of Table 16.10, assume that the row marginals equaled the column marginals: then, $\phi = 1$ if $B = C = 0$; similarly, $\phi = -1$ if $A = D = 0$. The more different the marginals, the lower the upper limit that the (absolute) value of phi can assume.

The phi coefficient assumes the value of zero if the two variables are statistically independent (as would be shown by a chi-square value that is also zero). Indeed, the absolute value of phi is related to chi-square by the expression

$$\phi = \sqrt{\frac{\chi^2}{n}}$$

where n is the total frequency (sample size). This is a nice feature of phi, in the sense that it can be computed quite easily after chi-square has been computed. Note, however, that phi, unlike chi-square, is *not* affected by total sample size because we have the divisor n in the above formula to adjust for differences in sample size.

The R × C Case

One of the most popular agreement indexes for summarizing the degree of association between two variables in a cross-tabulation of R rows and C columns is the *contingency coefficient*. This index is also related to chi-square and is defined as

$$C = \sqrt{\frac{\chi^2}{\chi^2 + n}} \ 2$$

where n is again the total sample size. From Table 16.10 we can first determine that chi-square is equal to 14.61, which, with 1 degree of freedom, is significant beyond the 0.01 level.

We can then find the contingency coefficient C as the following:

$$C = \sqrt{\frac{14.61}{14.61 + 84}}$$
$$= 0.385$$

As may be surmised, the contingency coefficient lies between zero and 1, with zero reserved for the case of statistical independence (a chi-square value of zero). However, unlike the phi coefficient, the contingency can never attain a maximum value of unity. For example, in a 2 × 2 table, C cannot exceed 0.707. As might be noticed by the reader, there is an algebraic relationship between phi and the contingency coefficient (if the latter is applied to the 2 × 2 table):

$$\phi^2 = \frac{C^2}{1 - C^2}$$

In a 4 × 4 table its upper limit is 0.87. Therefore, contingency coefficients computed from different-sized tables are not easily comparable.

However, like phi, the contingency coefficient is easy to compute from chi-square; moreover, like phi, its significance has already been tested in the course of running the chi-square test.

Both phi and the contingency coefficient are symmetric measures of association. Occasions often arise in the analysis of $R \times C$ tables (or the special case of 2 × 2 tables) where we desire to compute an *asymmetric* measure of the extent to which we can reduce errors in predicting categories of one variable from knowledge of the categories of some other variable. Goodman and Kruskal's *lambda-asymmetric coefficient* can be used for this purpose (Goodman & Kruskal, 1954).

To illustrate the lambda-asymmetric coefficient, let us return to the cross-tabulation of Table 16.10. Suppose that we wished to predict what category—no versus yes—a randomly-selected person would fall in when asked the question, "Does your hair have enough body?" If we had no knowledge of the row variable (whether that person included "body" in her ideal set or not), we would have only the *column* marginal frequencies to rely on.

Our best bet, given no knowledge of the row variable, is always to predict "no," the *higher* of the column marginal frequencies. As a consequence, we shall be wrong in 41 of the 84 cases, a probability error of 41/84 = 0.49. Can we do better, in the sense of lower prediction errors, if we utilize information provided by the row variable?

If we know that "body" is included in the ideal set, we shall predict "no" and be wrong in only 8 cases. If we know that "body" is not included in the ideal set, we shall predict "yes" and be wrong in 17 cases. Therefore, we have reduced our number of prediction errors from 41 to 8 + 17 = 25, a decrease of 16 errors. We can consider this error reduction relatively:

$$\lambda_{C|R} = \frac{(\text{number of errors in first case}) - (\text{number of errors in second case})}{\text{numbers of errors in first case}}$$

$$= \frac{41 - 25}{41} = 0.39$$

In other words, 39 percent of the errors in predicting the column variable are eliminated by knowing the individual's row variable.

A less cumbersome (but also less transparent) formula for lambda-asymmetric is

$$\lambda_{C|R} = \frac{\sum_{k=1}^{K} f_{k_R^*} - F_c^*}{n - F_c^*} = \frac{(26 + 33) - 43}{84 - 43} = 0.39$$

where f_R is the *maximum* frequency found within each subclass of the row variable, F is the *maximum* frequency among the marginal totals of the column variable, and n is the total number of cases.

Lambda-asymmetric varies between zero, indicating no ability at all to eliminate errors in predicting the column variable on the basis of the row variable, and 1, indicating an ability to eliminate all errors in the column variable predictions, given knowledge of the row variable.

Not surprisingly, we could reverse the role of criterion and predictor variables and find lambda-asymmetric for the row variable, given the column variable. In the case of Table 16.10, this is

$$\lambda_{C|R} = \frac{\sum_{l=1}^{L} f_{i_c^*} - F_R^*}{n - F_R^*} = \frac{(26 + 33) - 50}{84 - 50} = 0.26$$

Note that in this case we simply reverse the roles of row and column variables.

Finally, if desired, we could find a *lambda-symmetric index* via a weighted averaging of $\lambda_{C|R}$ and $\lambda_{R|C}$. However, in the authors' opinion, lambda-asymmetric is of particular usefulness to the analysis of cross-tabulations because we often want to consider one variable as a predictor and the other as a criterion. Furthermore, lambda-asymmetric h is a natural and useful interpretation as the percentage of total prediction errors that are eliminated in predicting one variable (e.g., the column variable) from another (e.g., the row variable).

A Concluding Comment

The indices discussed previously are optional choices when using SPSS's *Crosstabs*, which is within the Descriptive Statistics module. That is, the researcher indicates which one(s) to include in the analysis.

ASSIGNMENT MATERIAL

1. The marketing research department of the Gamma Adhesive Company is attempting to find some attribute of their gummed labels that can be merchandised as being superior to competitive products. The manager of the department, Mr. Beckwith, feels that the strength of their adhesive represents a good promotional point. Accordingly, samples of the company's adhesive and three other brands are tested by an independent research company. The strength indexes of the four products are as follows:

| | | Competitive Adhesive | | |
Trial	*Gamma Adhesive*	*X*	*Y*	*Z*
1	35	32	22	24
2	11	29	18	19
3	28	17	23	26
4	26	24	17	19
5	32	15	19	22

Assume that trials are merely replications of the same experiment (that is, that a one-way classification is appropriate) and a common error variance exists for all four treatments.

   a. Test the null hypothesis that the means of all treatments are equal (use an alpha risk of 0.05).
   b. Assume now that the trials can be treated as blocks and perform a two-way analysis of variance. Compare your answer with part (a).
   c. What additional statistical assumptions (other than equality of variance) are you making in using analysis of variance procedures in this problem?

2. Consider the following factorial layout:

| | Personal Selling Effort | | |
Direct Mail	*Level 1*	*Level 2*	*Level 3*
Level 1	40; 33	49; 47	56; 60
Level 2	37; 40	47; 51	62; 56
Level 3	51; 47	51; 60	73; 76

As noted, two replications of personal selling effort and direct mail, each at three levels, are made. This leads to 18 observations or sales responses.

   a. Test the null hypothesis (alpha risk at 0.05) of no difference in sales due to personal selling effort versus direct mail.

   b. Does a significant interaction exist (alpha risk at 0.05) between personal selling effort and direct-mail advertising?

   c. If, as a researcher, you had to recommend one particular combination of personal selling effort and direct-mail advertising, what kinds of additional information would you need before presenting your recommendation?

3. A manufacturer wants to determine whether his improved product appeals more to women than to men. A survey is conducted of a group of women and a group of men and each person is asked how many units she or he might purchase during a one-month time period. The samples are randomly selected. The following data are obtained:

	Men	Women
Sample Size	25	25
Total number of units expected to be bought	50	61
Sample standard deviation	0.6	0.8

   a. Is there a significant difference in the mean number of expected purchases between men and women?

   b. Construct an interval estimate around the difference in means between the two groups.

4. A manufacturer of a household cleaner (CLEAN) conducted a survey in two cities, using a randomly-selected sample of 600 households in each city. The following data were obtained:

	City 1	City 2
Had CLEAN in the house:		
Regular size	20%	24%
Large size	16	28
Tried CLEAN in past 4 weeks for:		
Painted woodwork	23%	24%
Painted walls	19	17
Linoleum floors	12	25
Attitude toward CLEAN for cleaning floors (users only):		
Housewives made:		
Favorable comments only	40%	37%
Unfavorable comments only	9	13
Both favorable and unfavorable comments	47	42
No specific comment	4	8
	100%	100%

What inferences can you make based on these data? Explain.

5. In analyzing its sales records for a metropolitan area, a company derives the following information concerning the size distribution of its customers, by locality:

Customer Size (Sales volume)	Number of Central City Customers	Number of Suburban Customers
Under $250,000	20	30
$250,000 to $1,000,000	18	40
Over $1,000,000	40	52

To what extent are size and location related? Is this significant?

6. Since the real world consists of more than two variables operating at a time, of what real value is bivariate analysis to a marketing manager?

REFERENCES

Gibbons, J. D. (1993). *Nonparametric statistics: An introduction*. Newbury Park, CA: Sage.

Gold, D. (1969, February). Statistical tests and substantive significance. *American Sociologist, 4,* 44.

Goodman, L. A., & Kruskal, W. H. (1954, December). Measures of association for cross classification. *Journal of the American Statistical Association, 49,* 732–764.

Iverson, G. R., & Norpoth, H. (1987). *Analysis of variance* (2nd ed.). Newbury Park, CA: Sage.

Jaccard, J. (1998). *Interaction effects in factorial analysis*. Thousand Oaks, CA: Sage.

Semon, T. T. (1999, August 2). Use your brain when using a chi-square. *Marketing News, 33,* 6.

Siegel, S. (1956). *Nonparametric statistics for the behavioral sciences*. New York: McGraw-Hill.

Chapter 17

BIVARIATE ANALYSIS: MEASURES OF ASSOCIATION

In Chapters 14 through 16, we introduced the basic concepts of statistical hypothesis testing and discussed both descriptive analysis and the making of inferences about groups of respondents. Consistent with our focus on market segmentation, we have concerned ourselves with the question of differences between groups. A variety of statistical techniques have been discussed, and we have shown that the choice of which technique is most appropriate depends on the number of dependent and independent variables and the level of measurement of the variables (Andrews, Klein, Davidson, O'Malley, & Rodgers, 1981).

In this chapter, we consider the two-variable case in which both variables are interval or ratio scaled. Our concern is with the nature of the associations between the two variables and the use of these associations in making predictions.

CORRELATION ANALYSIS

When referring to a simple two-variable correlation, we refer to the strength and direction of the relationship between the two variables. As an initial step in studying the relationship between the X and Y variables, it is often helpful to graph this relationship in a *scatter diagram* (also known as an *X-Y* plot). Each point on the graph represents the appropriate combination of scale values for the associated X and Y variables, as shown in Figure 17.1. The values of the correlation coefficient may range from +1 to –1. These extreme values indicate perfect positive and negative linear correlations. Other relationships may appear to be curvilinear or even random plots and have coefficients between zero and the extreme values.

The objective of correlation analysis, then, is to obtain a measure of the degree of linear association (correlation) that exists between the two variables. The Pearson correlation coefficient is commonly used for this purpose and is defined by the formula

$$\rho_{XY} = \frac{1}{n} \sum_{i=1}^{n} \frac{Y_i - \bar{Y}}{S_Y} \frac{X_i - \bar{X}}{S_X} = \sum_{i=1}^{n} \frac{Z_X Z_Y}{n}$$

where n pairs of (X_i, Y_i) values provide a sample size n, and X, Y, s_x, and s_y represent the sample means and sample standard deviations of the X and Y variables.

The alternate formulation shows the correlation coefficient to be the product of the Z scores for the X and Y variables. In this method of computing the correlation coefficient, the first step is to convert the raw data to a Z score by finding the deviation from the respective sample mean. The Z scores will be centered as a normally distributed variable (mean of zero and standard deviation of one).

The transformation of the X and Y variables to Z scores means that the scale measuring the original variable is no longer relevant, as a Z-score variable originally measured in dollars can be correlated with another Z-score variable originally measured on a satisfaction scale. The original metric scales are replaced by a new abstract scale (called correlation) that is the product of the two Z distributions.

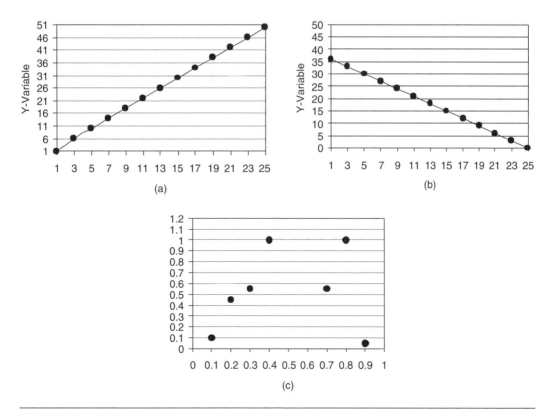

Figure 17.1   Scatter Diagrams

By continuing our digression one step further, we can show how the correlation coefficient becomes positive or negative.

$$\rho_{XY} = \frac{\sum\limits_{i=1}^{n} Z_X Z_Y}{n}$$

where

$$Z_Y = \frac{Y_i - \bar{Y}}{S_Y} \quad Z_X = \frac{X_i - \bar{X}_1}{S_X}$$

We know that the Z_X and Z_Y values will generally fall in the range -3 to $+3$. When both Z_X and Z_Y are positive or both are negative, r_{XY} is positive, as shown in Figure 17.2. When Z_X is positive and Z_Y negative (or the opposite), a negative correlation will exist. Of course, we are talking of individual pairs of the Z_X and Z_Y variables, which when summed produce the overall correlation coefficient.

To summarize, the sign ($+$ or $-$) indicates the direction of the correlation and the absolute value of the coefficient indicates the degree of correlation (from 0 to 1). Thus, correlations of $+ .7$ and $- .7$ are of exactly the same strength, but the relationships are in opposite directions.

We are cautioned that near-perfect positive or negative linear correlations do not mean causality. Often, other factors underlie and are even responsible for the relationship between the variables. For example, at one time Kraft Foods reported that sales of its macaroni and cheese product were highly correlated (negatively) with national indices of the health of the economy. We may not imply that Kraft sales directly caused fluctuations in the national economy, or vice versa. Consumer expectations and possibly personal income vary as a function

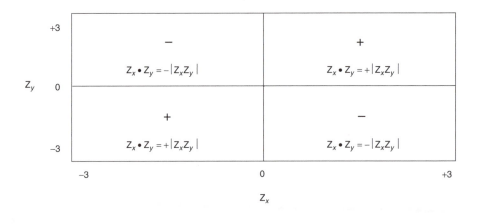

Figure 17.2   Bivariate Products of Standard Z-Scores

X	39	43	21	64	57	47	28	75	34	52
Y	68	82	56	86	97	94	77	103	59	79

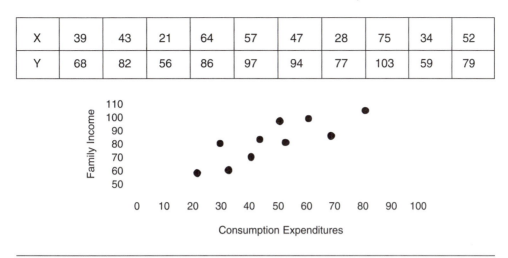

Figure 17.3   Consumption Expenditure and Income Data

of the national economy. In times of reduced family income, macaroni and cheese is a low-price dietary substitute for more expensive meals.

To demonstrate, we will consider a brief example of a correlation analysis that examines the relationships between (1) family income and (2) family consumption expenditures. The data and plot appear in Figure 17.3.

In order to calculate the correlation coefficient, we will reduce the previous formula to the basic computation consisting of sums for the X and Y variables. This equation looks formidable but allows for easy computation by simply entering the appropriate summation values from the bottom of Table 17.1.

$$\rho_{XY} = \frac{n \sum_{i=1}^{} x_i y_i - \sum_{i=1}^{} x_i \sum_{i=1}^{} y_i}{\sqrt{n \sum_{i=1}^{} x_i^2 - \left(\sum_{} x_i\right)^2} \sqrt{n \sum_{i=1}^{} y_i^2 - \left(\sum_{} y_i\right)^2}}$$

$$r_{KY} = .8329 = \frac{(10)(38,800) - (460)(801)}{\sqrt{(10)(23,634) - (460)^2}\sqrt{(10)(66,385) - (801)^2}}$$

Needless to say, computations such as this are rarely done today. Researchers routinely perform their analyses by using Excel spreadsheets or computer packages such as SPSS. However, our brief discussion is included to provide understanding of underlying processes.

Table 17.1   Family Income and Family Consumption Expenditures

Resp.	Y	X	XY	Y^2	X^2
1	68	39	2652	4624	1521
2	82	43	3526	6724	1849
3	56	21	1176	3136	441
4	86	64	5504	7396	4096
5	97	57	5529	9409	3249
6	94	47	4418	8836	2209
7	77	28	2156	15929	784
8	103	75	7725	0609	5625
9	59	34	2006	3481	1156
10	79	52	4108	6241	2704
Sum	801	460	38800	66385	23634
Avg.	80.1	46	3880	6638.5	2363.4

BIVARIATE REGRESSION ANALYSIS

In the analysis of associative data the marketing researcher is almost always interested in problems of predictions:

- Can we predict a person's weekly fast food and restaurant food purchases from that person's gender, age, income, or education level?
- Can we predict the dollar volume of purchase of our new product by industrial purchasing agents as a function of our relative price, delivery schedules, product quality, and technical service?

The list of such problems is almost endless. Not surprisingly, the linear regression model—as applied in either the bivariate (single predictor) or multivariate form (multiple predictors)—is one of the most popular methods in the marketing researcher's tool kit. The bivariate form is also known as *simple regression*.

Some Industry Examples

The regression model has been applied to problems ranging from estimating sales quotas to predicting demand for new shopping centers.

As an illustration, one of the leading ski resorts in the United States used a regression model to predict the weekend ticket sales, based on variables including the following:

- Highway driving conditions
- Average temperature in the three-day period preceding the weekend
- Local weather forecast for the weekend

- Amount of newspaper space devoted to the resort's advertisements in the surrounding city newspapers
- A moving average of the three preceding weekends' ticket sales

The model's accuracy was within ± 6 percent of actual attendance throughout the season. One firm used a regression model to predict physicians' readership of various medical journals, based on physician ratings of several attributes of each journal:

- Writing style
- Quality of illustrations
- Informativeness of advertisements
- Relevance to physician needs
- Authoritativeness in the medical profession
- Frequency of issue

The model predicted actual readership in future time periods quite well. Moreover, it provided diagnostic information as to how various journals' editorial policy and advertising could be improved.

A bakery explored the use of a regression model to predict sales of hamburger buns as a guide to production policy. The following factors were included as independent variables:

- The weather
- The day of month
- The proximity to a holiday

The model was able to predict well enough to reduce the average returned goods by four percentage points (from 10.4 percent to 6.4 percent).

A Numerical Example of Simple Regression

Regression analysis in its simplest bivariate form involves a single dependent (criterion) and a single independent (predictor) variable. In its more advanced multiple-regression form, a set of predictors are used to form an additive linear combination that predicts the single dependent variable. Although we focus only on bivariate regression in this chapter, the principle assumptions and interpretations apply to the multiple regression case.

In each of these examples, the researcher is interested in four main questions:

1. Can we find a predictor variable (a linear composite of the predictor variables in the multiple case) that will compactly express the relationship between a criterion variable and the predictor (set of predictors)?

2. If we can, how strong is the relationship; that is, how well can we predict values of the criterion variable from values of the predictor (linear composite)?

3. Is the overall relationship statistically significant?

4. Which predictor is most important in accounting for variation in the criterion variable? (Can the original model be reduced to fewer variables, but still provide adequate prediction of the criterion?)

The basic ideas of bivariate regression are most easily explained by a numerical example. We proceed one step at a time.

Suppose that a marketing researcher is interested in consumers' attitudes toward nutritional additives in ready-to-eat cereals. Specifically, a set of written concept descriptions of a children's cereal is prepared that varies on

X_1: the amount of protein (in grams) per 2-ounce serving

The researcher obtains consumers' interval-scaled evaluations of 10 concept descriptions using a preference rating scale that ranges from 1, dislike extremely, up to 9, like extremely well.

The (hypothetical) data appear in Table 17.2. We wish to see if we can predict values of Y from values of X.

One of the first things that is usually done in examining two-variable relationships is to prepare a *scatter diagram* in which the values of Y are plotted against their X_1 counterparts. Figure 17.4 shows this plot for our example. It appears that there is a direct relationship between Y and X_1. Moreover, it would seem that a linear or straight-line relationship might be an appropriate model for describing the functional form. A scatter diagram is a useful tool for aiding in *model specification*. The value of using a scatter diagram is illustrated in Exhibit 17.1.

Table 17.2   Consumer Preference Ratings of Ten Cereal Concepts Varying in Protein

(1)	(2)	(3)	(4)	(5)	(6)
Rater	Preference Rating, Y	Protein, X_1	Y^2	X	YX_1
1	3	4	9	16	12
2	7	9	49	81	63
3	2	3	4	9	6
4	1	1	1	1	1
5	6	3	36	9	18
6	2	4	4	16	8
7	8	7	64	49	56
8	3	3	9	9	9
9	9	8	81	64	72
10	2	1	4	1	2
Total	43	43	261	255	247
Mean	4.3	4.3			
Std. Dev.	2.908	2.791			

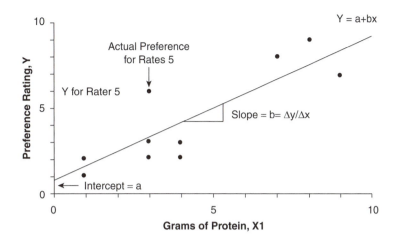

Figure 17.4   Scatter Diagram and Least-Squares Regression Line—Preference Rating versus Grams of Protein

EXHIBIT 17.1   Look at Your Data Before Analysis

In deciding which type of regression approach to use, it is important that the researcher know the *shape* of the interrelationship. The shape of the interrelationship is easy to see on a scatter diagram. Looking at this visually helps decide whether the relationship is, or approximates being, linear or whether it has some other shape that would require a transformation of the data—such as converting to square roots or logarithms—or treatment as nonlinear regression (Semon, 1993).

Examination of the data by scatter diagrams also allows the researcher to see if there are any outliers—cases where the relationship is unusual or extreme as compared to the majority of the data points. A decision has to be made whether to retain such outliers in the data set for analysis.

When the regression line itself is included on the scatter diagram, comparisons between actual values and the values estimated by the regression formula can be compared and used to assess the estimating error. Of course, what the analyst is seeking is a regression function that has the *best fit* for the data, and this is typically based on minimizing the squares of the distances between the actual and estimated values—the so-called *least-squares* criterion.

The equation for a linear model can be written

$$\hat{Y} = a + bX$$

where $\hat{Y}$ denotes values of the criterion that are predicted by the linear model; a denotes the intercept, or value of $\hat{Y}$ when X is zero; and b denotes the slope of the line, or change in $\hat{Y}$ per unit change in X.

But how do we find the numerical values of a and b? The method used in this chapter is known as *least squares*, as discussed in Exhibit 17.1. As the reader will recall from introductory statistics, the method of least squares finds the line whose sum of squared differences between the observed values Y_i and their estimated counterparts $\hat{Y}_i$ (on the regression line) is a minimum.

Parameter Estimation

To compute the estimated parameters (a and b) of the linear model, we return to the data of Table 17.2. In the two-variable case, the formulas are relatively simple:

$$
\begin{aligned}
b &= \frac{\sum YX - n\overline{Y}\,\overline{X}}{\sum X^2 - n\overline{X}^2} \\
&= \frac{247 - 10(4.3)(4.3)}{255 - 10(4.3)^2} \\
&= 0.886
\end{aligned}
$$

where n is the sample size and $\overline{Y}$ and $\overline{X}$ denote the means of Y and X, respectively. Having found the slope b, the intercept a is found from

$$
\begin{aligned}
a &= \overline{Y} - b\overline{X} \\
&= 4.3 - 0.886(4.3) \\
&= 0.491
\end{aligned}
$$

leading to the linear function

$$
\hat{Y} = 0.491 + 0.886X
$$

This function is drawn with the scatter plot of points in Figure 17.4. It appears to fit the plotted points rather well, and the model seems to be well specified (a linear rather than curve line or other form seems to fit).

Assumptions of the Model

Underlying least-squares computations is a set of assumptions. Although least-squares regression models do not need to assume normality in the (conditional) distributions of the criterion variable, this assumption is made when we test the statistical significance of the contribution of the predictor variable in explaining the variance in the criterion (does it differ from zero?). With this in mind the assumptions of the regression model are as follows (the symbols α and β are used to denote population counterparts of a and b):

1. For each fixed value of X we assume a normal distribution of Y values exists. In our particular sample we assume that each Y value is drawn independently of all others. What is being described is the classical regression model. Modern versions of the model permit the predictors to be random variables, but their distribution is not allowed to depend on the parameters of the regression equation.

2. The means of all of these normal distributions of Y lie on a straight line with slope β.

3. The normal distributions of Y all have equal variances. This (common) variance does not depend on values assumed by the variable X.

Because all values rarely fall on the regression line (this only happens when the correlation is 1.0), there is unexplained error in predicting Y. This error is shown in Figure 17.4 as the difference between the values Y_i and the regression line $\hat{Y}$. For the population, our model is expressed algebraically as

$$Y = \alpha + \beta X_1 + \varepsilon$$

where α = mean of Y population when $X_1 = 0$

   β = change in Y population mean per unit change in X_1

   ε = error term drawn independently from a normally distributed universe with mean $\mu(\varepsilon)$; the error term is independent of X_1

The nature of these assumptions is apparent in Figure 17.5. The reader should note that each value of X_1 has associated with it a normal curve for Y (assumption 1). The means of all these normal distributions lie on the straight line shown in the figure (assumption 2).

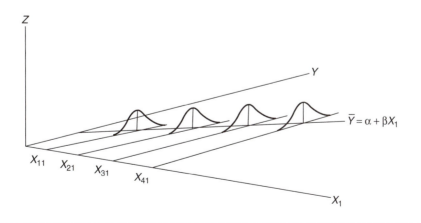

Figure 17.5   Two-Variable Regression Model—Theoretical

What if the dependent variable is not continuous? Exhibit 17.2 gives an alternative when the dependent variable can be viewed as a categorical dichotomous variable—use *logistic regression* (also known as *logit*). The analysis proceeds generally as we are discussing it—the major change is that a transformation has been applied to the dependent-variable values.

EXHIBIT 17.2   When to Use Logistic Regression

Data collected for customer satisfaction research provides a good illustration of when the researcher should consider transformation of data. Typically multipoint rating scales are used to obtain customer satisfaction data. Many believe that customer satisfaction ratings obtained on rating scales are not normally distributed but are skewed toward higher scale values (Dispensa, 1997). Thus, in practice customers do not really view customer satisfaction ratings as continuous.

Ultimately, a customer is either satisfied or not satisfied. This creates a dichotomous dependent variable. Typically those customers who rate at the upper end of the scale, say 9 or 10 on a 10-point scale, are considered satisfied, whereas all others are considered to be not satisfied. If this is so, normal regression analysis is not the proper technique to use as the dependent variable is binary, not continuous.

A binary overall customer satisfaction variable follows the *logistic distribution*, thus allowing for the use of logistic regression. With one or more independent variables, this technique allows a researcher to determine the extent to which an independent variable affects the prediction of a satisfied customer through the logistic regression coefficients and their associated *log-odds* (Dispensa, 1997). Log-odds specify the direct association between the independent variable and the dependent variable. In addition, logistic regression calculates the probability of each customer being satisfied or not.

Typically, logistic regression is used for multiple regression situations where there are two or more independent variables. But, it is suitable for bivariate situations as well. The key to its being of value is the nature of the dependent variable, not the independent variable(s).

In constructing the estimating equation by least squares we have computed a regression line for a sample and not for the population:

$$\hat{Y} = a + bX_1$$

where $\hat{Y}$ is the estimated mean of Y, given X, and a and b are the sample estimates of α and β in the theoretical model. As already noted, this line appears in Figure 17.4 for the specific bivariate problem of Table 17.2.

However, functional forms other than linear may be suggested by the preliminary scatter plot. Figure 17.6 shows various types of scatter diagrams and regression lines for the two-variable case. Panel I shows the ideal case in which *all* the variation in Y is accounted for by variation in X_1. We note that the regression line passes through the mean of each variable and that the slope b happens to be positive. The intercept a represents the predicted value of when $X_1 = 0$. In Panel II we note that there is residual variation in Y and, furthermore, that the slope b is negative.

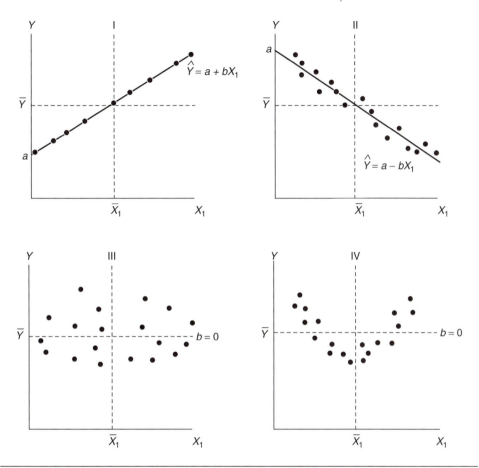

Figure 17.6   Illustrative Scatter Diagrams and Regression Lines

Panel III demonstrates the case in which no association between Y and X_1 is found. In this case the mean of Y is as good a predictor as the variable X_1 (the slope b is zero). Panel IV emphasizes that a linear model is being fitted. That is, no *linear* association is found ($b = 0$), even though a curvilinear relationship is apparent from the scatter diagram. Figure 17.6 illustrates the desirability of plotting one's data *before* proceeding to formulate a specific regression model.

Strength of Association

It is one thing to find the regression equation (as shown in Figure 17.4), but at this point we still do not know the strength of the association. Does the regression line $\hat{Y} = a + bX$ (which uses X as a predictor) explain the variation in Y (predict Y)? To answer this question, consider that the total variation in the Y variable may be divided into two component parts: (1) variance that is explained by the regression line and (2) unexplained variation (residual). This may be expressed as

$$\sum(Y_i - \bar{Y})^2 =$$

Total variation or
Total Sum of
Squares Deviation
from the Mean

$$\sum(\hat{Y}_i - \bar{Y})^2 +$$

Variation Explained
by the Regression or
Sum of Squares Due to
Regression

$$\sum(Y_i - \hat{Y})^2$$

Variation
Unexplained by
the Regression or
Sum of Squares
Deviation from
Regression
(Error)

and is viewed graphically in Figure 17.7.

The measure of strength of association in bivariate regression is denoted by r^2 and is called the *coefficient of determination*. This coefficient varies between 0 and 1 and represents *the proportion of total variation in Y (as measured about its own mean $\bar{Y}$) that is accounted for by variation in X_1*. For regression analyses it can also be interpreted as a measure of substantive significance, as we have previously defined this concept.

If we were to use the average of the Y values ($\bar{Y}$) to estimate each separate value of Y, then a measure of our *inability* to predict Y would be given by the sum of the squared deviations $\sum_{i=1}^{n}(Y_i - \bar{Y})^2$. On the other hand, if we tried to predict Y by employing a linear regression based on X, we could use each $\hat{Y}_i$ to predict its counterpart Y_i. In this case a measure of our *inability* to predict Y_i is given by $\sum_{i=1}^{n}(Y_i - \hat{Y}_i)^2$. We can define r^2 as a function of these two qualities:

$$r^2 = 1 - \frac{\sum_{i=1}^{n}(Y_i - \hat{Y}_i)^2}{\sum_{i=1}^{n}(Y_i - \bar{Y}_i)^2}$$

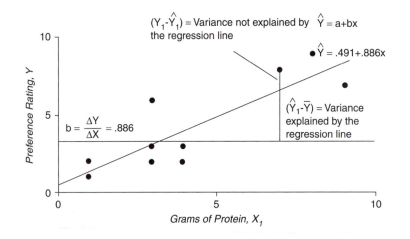

Figure 17.7   Scatter Diagram and Regression Line for Cereal Problem

Table 17.3   Actual Y_i, Predicted $\hat{Y}_i$, and Residuals $Y_i - \hat{Y}_i$

Rater	Actual, Y_i	Predicted,* $\hat{Y}_i$	Residuals $Y_i - \hat{Y}_i$
1	3	4.034	−1.034
2	7	8.464	−1.464
3	2	3.148	−1.148
4	1	1.377	−0.377
5	6	3.148	2.852
6	2	4.034	−2.034
7	8	6.692	1.308
8	3	3.148	−0.148
9	9	7.579	1.422
10	2	1.377	0.623
Mean	4.3	4.3	0

*From the equation $\hat{Y}_i = 0.491 + 0.886X_{i1}$.

If each $\hat{Y}_i$ predicts its counterpart Y_i perfectly, then $r^2 = 1$, since the numerator of the variance unaccounted for is zero. However, if using the regression equation does no better than $\overline{Y}$ alone, then the total variance equals the variance unaccounted for and $r^2 = 0$, indicating no ability to predict Y_i (beyond the use of $\overline{Y}$ itself). The use of X_1 in a linear regression can do no worse than $\overline{Y}$. Even if b turns out to be zero, the predictions are $\hat{Y}_i = a = Y$, which are the same as using the mean of criterion values in the first place.

Table 17.3 shows the residuals obtained after using the regression equation to predict each value of Y_i via its counterpart $\hat{Y}_i$. We then find r^2_{yxi} (where we now show the explicit subscripts) by computing from the table:

$$\sum_{i=1}^{n}(Y_i - \hat{Y}_i)^2 = (-1.034)^2 + (-1.464)^2 + \cdots + (0.623)^2 = 21.09$$

This is the sum of squared errors in predicting Y_i from $\hat{Y}_i$. Next, we find

$$\sum_{i=1}^{n}(Y_i - \overline{Y})^2 = (3 - 4.3)^2 + (7 - 4.3)^2 + \cdots + (2 - 4.3)^2 = 76.10$$

This is the sum of squared errors in predicting Y_i from $\overline{Y}$. Hence

$$r^2_{yx_1} = 1 - \frac{21.09}{76.10}$$
$$= 0.723$$

and we say that 72 percent of the variation in Y has been accounted for by variation in X_1. As might also be surmised, there is one more quantity of interest:

$$\sum_{i=1}^{n}(\hat{Y}-\bar{Y})^2 = (4.034 - 4.3)^2 + (8.464 - 4.3)^2 + \cdots + (1.377 - 4.3)^2 = 55.01$$

which is the accounted-for sum of squares due to the regression of Y on X_1.

Figure 17.8 (and Figure 17.7 as well) put all these quantities in perspective by first show-ing deviation of $Y_i - \bar{Y}$. As previously noted, the sum of these squared deviations is 76.10. Panel II shows the counterpart deviations of Y_i from $\hat{Y}_i$; the sum of these squared deviations is 21.09. Panel III shows the deviations of $\hat{Y}_i$ from $\bar{Y}$; the sum of these squared deviations is 55.01. We note that the results are additive: $21.09 + 55.01 = 76.10$.

Interpretation of Bivariate Regression

The sample data of Table 17.2 were analyzed using the standard linear regression analysis routine from SPSS. Table 17.4 shows the output provided. The coefficients shown earlier appear here, along with some other measures as well. Overall, the linear regression equation is

$$\hat{Y} = 0.491 + 0.886\ X_1$$

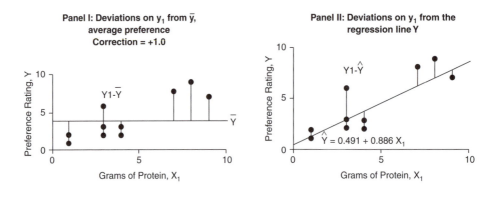

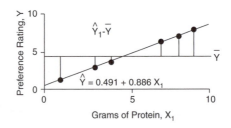

Figure 17.8   Breakdown of Deviations $(Y_i - Y)$ Into Two Additive Parts

The standardized coefficient for the independent variable (beta or β) is more meaningful for multiple regression as it is a measure of the change in Y due to a unit change in X_1 when all independent variables have been transformed to the same units. The F ratio is the appropriate test for the hypotheses that the regression coefficient $b = 0$ and $r^2 = 0$. This test was discussed in more detail in Chapter 16 in the context of analysis of variance. However, as recalled from basic statistics, the F distribution is the distribution followed by the ratio of two independent, unbiased estimates of the normal population variance σ^2. If r^2 is zero, then the sample r^2 reflects only sampling error and the F ratio will tend to be equal to 1.0. We first obtain the mean squares, 55.013 and 2.636, by dividing the corresponding sums of squares by their respective degrees of freedom. Then we find the F ratio of 20.871. This value, with one degree of freedom for the numerator and eight degrees of freedom for the denominator, is compared with a tabular F (see Table A.4 in Appendix A) of 3.46 with an (illustrative) significance level of 0.1. We reject the preceding null hypotheses and conclude that the overall regression equation is statistically significant.

RANK CORRELATION

Our discussion in this chapter is based on the premise that the dependent variable is at least intervally scaled or can be treated as such with little error. There are marketing problems, however, where the dependent and independent variables are rank orders or are best transformed into such rankings. In this situation *rank correlation* techniques can be used to estimate the association between sets of data.

Table 17.4   Summary Output of Regression Analysis of Sample Data From Table 17.2

Variables Entered/Removed[b]

Model	Variables Entered	Variables Removed	Method
1	PROTEIN[aa]		Enter

   a. All requested variables entered.
   b. Dependent Variable: PREFERENCE

Model Summary

Model	r	r^2	Adjusted r^2	Std. Error of the Estimate
1	.850[a]	.723	.688	1.62354

   c. Predictors: (Constant), PROTEIN

(Continued)

Table 17.4 (Continued)

ANOVA[b]

Model		Sum of Squares	df	Mean Square	F	Sig.
1	Regression	55.013	1	55.013	20.871	.002[a]
	Residual	21.087	8	2.636		
	Total	76.100	9			

d. Predictors: (Constant), PROTEIN
e. Dependent Variable: PREFERENCE

Coefficients[a]

Model		Unstandardized Coefficients		Standardized Coefficients	t	Sig.
		b	Std. Error			
1	(Constant)	.491	.979		.501	.630
	PROTEIN	.886	.194	.850	4.568	.002

f. Dependent Variable: PREFERENCE

For two variables the best-known and easiest technique is that involving use of the Spearman rank correlation coefficient, r_s. We show the use of this measure by an example. Suppose a sales manager evaluates salespersons by two different methods (performance index and a new method). Since the new method is easier to use, the manager wants to know if it will yield the same relative results as the proven existing method. The scores have been transformed into rankings so that each salesperson has two rankings. Table 17.5 shows the rankings.

Table 17.5   Ranks on Two Methods of Salesperson Evaluation

	Rank			
Salesperson	Performance Index (X)	New Method (Y)	d_i	d
A	8	6	2	4
B	4	7	−3	9
C	1	2	−1	1
D	6	3	3	9
E	2	1	1	1
F	10	8	2	4
G	5	5	0	0
H	3	9	−6	36
I	7	4	3	9
J	9	10	1	1
			$\sum d_i^2 =$	74

To measure the extent of rank correlation we use the statistic

$$r_s = 1 - \frac{6 \sum\limits_{i=1}^{N} d^2}{N(N^2 - 1)}$$

where N is the number of pairs of ranks and d is the difference between the two rankings for an individual (that is, $X - Y$). Applying this formula to our example, we get

$$r_s = 1 - \frac{6(74)}{10(100 - 1)} = .55$$

If the subjects whose scores were used in computing r_s were randomly drawn from a population, we can test the significance of the obtained value. The null hypothesis is that the two variables are not associated, and thus the true value of ρ is zero. Under H_0 any observed value would be due to chance. When $N \geq 10$, significance can be tested using the statistic

$$t = r_s \sqrt{\frac{N - 2}{1 - r_s^2}}$$

which is interpreted from Table A.3 of Appendix A with $(N - 2)$ degrees of freedom. For our example, we calculate

$$t = .55 \sqrt{\frac{10 - 2}{1 - (.55)^2}} = 1.870$$

Looking at the table of critical values of t, we find that $p > .10$ (two-tailed test) for $(10 - 2 = 8)$ degrees of freedom. Thus, if a strict α level is to be adhered to (.10 or less), we tentatively accept H_0 and conclude that it is unlikely that a correlation exists between the scores from the two evaluation methods.

One final point concerning the use of the Spearman rank correlation coefficient is warranted. At times, tied observations will exist. When this happens, each of them is assigned the average of the ranks that would have been assigned in the absence of ties. If the proportion of ties is small, the effect on r_s is minute. If large, however, a correlation factor must be applied (see Siegel, 1956, pp. 206–10).

Another measure that gives comparable results is the Kendall rank correlation coefficient, (tau). The value of tau ranges between −1 and +1. It measures association in a different way from the Spearman rank correlation. Tau measures the association between X and Y as the proportion of concordant pairs minus the proportion of discordant pairs in the samples. Two bivariate observations, (X_i, Y_i) and (X_j, Y_j), are called concordant whenever the product of the difference between each pair of observations $(X_i - X_j)(Y_i - Y_j)$ is positive, and a pair is called discordant when this product is negative (Gibbons, 1993, p. 11).

In general, the Spearman measure is used more widely than the Kendall measure. It is an easier measure to use. In addition, the Spearman rank correlation coefficient is equivalent to the Pearson product-moment correlation coefficient with ranks substituted for the measurement observations, X and Y. Both the Spearman and Kendall measures are discussed more fully by Siegel (1956, Chapter 9) and Gibbons (1993). These two measures are used when there are two sets of rankings to be analyzed. When there are three or more sets of rankings the measure Kendall's coefficient of concordance should be used (Gibbons, 1993; Siegel, 1956, Chap. 9).

Finally, when the variables are nominally scaled, ordinal measures such as tau and r_s are not appropriate measures. Nominal variables lack the ordering property. One measure that can be used is Goodman and Kruskal's lambda (λ). Lambda is a measure of association whose calculation and interpretation are straightforward. Lambda tells us how much we can reduce our error in predicting Y once we know X, and is shown as

$$\lambda = \frac{\text{reduction in prediction errors knowing } X}{\text{prediction errors in not knowing}}$$

This measure, and others as well, are discussed by Lewis-Beck (1995, Chap. 4). Lambda is an option provided by the SPSS *Crosstab* program.

SUMMARY

In Chapter 17, we have considered bivariate analyses of associations for interval- or ratio-scaled data. The concept of associations between two variables was introduced through simple two-variable correlation. We examined the strength and direction of relationships using the scatter diagram and Pearson correlation coefficient. Several alternative (but equivalent) mathematical expressions were presented and a correlation coefficient was computed for a sample data set.

Investigations of the relationships between variables almost always involve the making of predictions. Bivariate (two-variable) regression was presented in a simple prediction problem. Total variation in the dependent (Y) variable was shown to consist of variance that was explained by the regression line (SS due to regression) and unexplained variance (SS about the regression line). The slope of the regression line, b, was computed along with α, the intercept of the line on the Y axis.

Finally regression diagnostics were presented including r^2, the coefficient expressing the amount of variance explained by the regression line. The F ratio (the ratio of mean square regression to mean square about the regression line) was explained as a statistical test of whether the regression line explains a significant amount of variance.

We ended the chapter with a discussion of the Spearman rank correlation and Kendall tau as alternatives to the Pearson correlation coefficient when the data is of ordinal measurement and does not meet the assumptions of parametric methods. Also, the Goodman and Kruskal lambda measure for nominal measurement was briefly introduced.

❖

ASSIGNMENT MATERIAL

1. A sample survey of home swimming pool owners in southern California has yielded the following information regarding pool costs versus annual income.
   a. Using least squares, compute a linear regression of Y on X. How do you interpret the formula?
   b. Compute the coefficient of determination and the variance of the estimate. Interpret these measures.
   c. What applications would you suggest for the regression formula if you were employed by a California swimming pool builder?

Respondent	Pool Cost, Y (Thousands of Dollars)	Annual Income, X (Thousands of Dollars)
1	34.4	87.2
2	39.2	90.8
3	29.6	88.8
4	48.8	96.0
5	47.6	98.0
6	53.6	106.8
7	62.8	124.4
8	64.8	163.6
9	44.4	102.8
10	51.6	93.2
11	58.0	140.8
12	41.6	99.2

2. Assume next that the survey of swimming pool owners also yielded information on total size of the pool owner's lot. The data (expressed in thousands of square feet) appear as follows:

Respondent	1	2	3	4	5	6	7	8	9	10	11	12
Lot Size, Z	30.2	40.1	35.3	45.1	38.0	50.1	60.2	100.4	25.1	40.7	68.4	60.3

   a. Using the data of the preceding problem, compute, by least squares, a linear regression of Y on Z. How would you interpret this formula?
   b. If you were told that a pool owner had an income of $100,000 annually and a lot size of 40,000 square feet, what pool cost would you predict?
   c. Compute the coefficient of multiple determination r^2. What effect does knowledge of both annual income *and* lot size have on the explanatory power of the regression in contrast to knowledge only about annual income?
   d. What are the assumptions underlying the least-squares regression model?

3. In which ways are regression analysis and correlation analysis related to each other? In which ways are they independent of each other? Explain.

4. Parametric and nonparametric measures of correlation use data in different forms. Under what conditions might the problem represented by the data in Table 17.5 be treated as a parametric correlation problem? Explain.

REFERENCES

Andrews, F. M., Klem, L., Davidson, T. N., O'Malley, P. M., & Rodgers, W. L. (1981). *A guide for selecting statistical techniques for analyzing social science cata* (2nd ed.). Ann Arbor: Institute for Social Research, University of Michigan.

Dispensa, G. S. (1997, January 6). Use logistic regression with customer satisfaction. *Marketing News, 31,* 13.

Gibbons, J. D. (1993). *Nonparametric measures of association.* Newbury Park, CA: Sage.

Lewis-Beck, M. S. (1995). *Data analysis: An introduction.* Thousand Oaks, CA: Sage.

Semon, T. T. (1993, April 26). Look at the data before using statistical analysis programs. *Marketing News, 27,* 12.

Siegel, S. (1956). *Nonparametric statistics for the behavioral sciences.* New York: McGraw-Hill.

Chapter 18

MULTIVARIATE STATISTICAL ANALYSIS

Analyzing Criterion-Predictor Association

In the previous chapters that discussed analysis of differences and association for two variables, we determined that selecting the appropriate method of analysis requires evaluating the number of dependent and independent variables and their level of measurement. The same process applies to multivariate analysis, as is illustrated in Figure 18.1.

Association implies only that two or more variables tend to change together to a greater or lesser degree, depending upon the degree of association involved. If we measure the amount of mutual change and find it to be persistent in both direction and degree, we may *not* conclude that there is necessarily a *causal* relationship, such that one variable is dependent (the effect) and the other variable (or variables) is independent (the deterministic or probabilistic cause). It should be understood, then, that *association does not imply causation*. However, if a set of variables are causally related, they will be associated in some way. Causal-path analysis and structural equation models have been developed to aid in examining possible causal relations in correlational data. These are discussed in depth by Blalock (1962), Bagozzi (1980), and Monroe and Petroshius (n.d.).

In this and the next chapter, we present a series of brief discussions that focus on individual multivariate techniques. Multivariate analyses arise when more than two variables are to be analyzed at the same time. We begin by extending simple regression with the introducion of a second predictor variable. This use of multiple predictors results in both multiple and partial regression.

We next focus on two-group discriminant analysis. Like multiple regression, discriminant analysis is a predictor model. However, the dependent variable is categorical in measurement and defines the groups. In discriminant analysis, the variable's membership in categories or groups is predicted using the multiple independent variables.

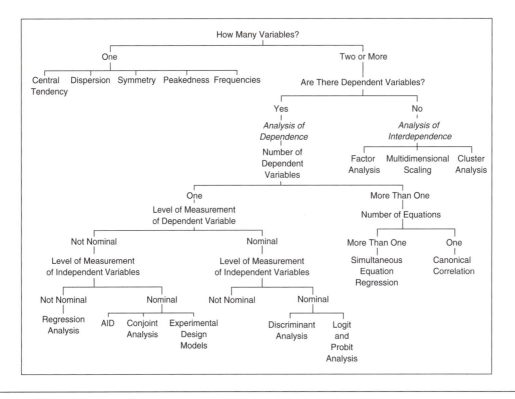

Figure 18.1   Process for Selecting Appropriate Method of Analysis

Finally, a brief conceptual introduction is given to a diverse group of techniques, including canonical correlation, correspondence analysis, Chi-Square Automatic Interaction Detection (CHAID), and probit and logit analyses.

We start with a broad overview of multivariate procedures.

AN OVERVIEW OF MULTIVARIATE PROCEDURES

The Data Matrix

The raw input to any analysis of associative data consists of the *data matrix*, as described in Chapter 14. This is a rectangular array of entries whose informational content is to be summarized and portrayed in some way. For example, the computation of the mean and standard deviation of a single column of numbers is often done simply because we are unable to comprehend the meaning of the entire column of values. In so doing, we choose to forgo the full information provided by the data in order to understand some of its basic characteristics, such as central tendency and dispersion.

In virtually all marketing research studies we are concerned with variation in some characteristic, be it per capita consumption of soft drinks, TV viewing frequency, or customer intention to repurchase. Our objective now, however, is to concentrate on explaining the variation in one variable or group of variables in terms of *covariation* with other variables. When we analyze associative data, we hope to explain variation according to one or more of the following points of view:

1. Determination of the overall strength of association between the *criterion* and *predictor* variables (often called *dependent* and *independent* variables, respectively)

2. Determination of a function or formula by which we can estimate values of the criterion variable(s) from values of the predictor variable(s)

3. Determination of the statistical confidence in either or both of the above

In some cases of interest, however, we may have no criterion (dependent) variable. We may still be interested in the *interdependence* of variables as a whole and the possibility of summarizing information provided by this interdependence in terms of other variables, often taken to be linear combinations of the original ones.

A Classification of Techniques for Analyzing Associative Data

The field of associative data analysis is vast; hence, it seems useful to enumerate various descriptors by which the field can be classified. The key notion underlying our classification is the data matrix. A conceptual illustration is shown in Table 18.1. We note that the table consists of a set of objects (the *n* rows) and a set of measurements on those objects (the *m* columns). The objects may be people, things, concepts, or events. The variables are characteristics of the objects. The cell values represent the state of object *i* with respect to variable *j*. Cell values may consist of nominal-, ordinal-, interval-, or ratio-scaled measurements, or various combinations of these as we go across columns. When using SPSS, the data file created is structured exactly like the basic data matrix, which is, in effect, a type of spreadsheet.

Table 18.1   Illustrative Basic Data Matrix

Object	*Variable*						
	1	*2*	*3*	. . .	*j*	. . .	*m*
1	X_{11}	X_{12}	X_{12}	. . .	X_{1j}	. . .	X_{1m}
2	X_{21}	X_{22}	X_{23}	. . .	X_{2j}	. . .	X_{2m}
3	X_{31}	X_{32}	X_{33}	. . .	X_{3j}	. . .	X_{3m}
.	.	.	.		.		.
.	.	.	.		.		.
.	.	.	.		.		.
i	X_{i1}	X_{i2}	X_{i3}	. . .	X_{ij}	. . .	X_{im}
.	.	.	.		.		.
.	.	.	.		.		.
.	.	.	.		.		.
n	X_{n1}	X_{n2}	X_{n3}	. . .	X_{nj}	. . .	X_{nm}

There are many descriptors by which we can characterize methods for analyzing associative data. Although not exhaustive (or exclusive), the following represent the more common bases by which this activity can be classified:

1. Purpose of the study and types of assertions desired by the researcher: What kinds of statements—descriptive or inferential—does the researcher wish to make?

2. Focus of research: Is the emphasis on the objects (the whole profile or "bundle" of variables), the variables, or both?

3. Nature of the researcher's assumed prior judgments as to how the data matrix should be partitioned (subdivided) in terms of number of subsets of variables.

4. Number of variables in each of the partitioned subsets: How many criterion versus predictor variables?

5. Type of association under study: Is the association linear, transformable to linear, or nonlinear?

6. Scales by which variables are measured: Are the scales nominal, ordinal, interval, ratio, or mixed?

All of these descriptors require certain decisions of the researcher. Suppose there is interest in studying descriptive interrelationships among variables. If so, the researcher must make decisions about how to partition the set of columns (i.e., the variables) into subsets. He or she must also decide on the number of variables to include in each subset and what type of relationship (linear, transformation to linear, or nonlinear) is asserted to hold among the variables.

Most decisions about associative data analysis are based on the researcher's private model of how the data are interrelated and what features are useful for study. The choice of various public models for analysis (multiple regression, discriminant analysis, etc.) is predicated on prior knowledge of both the characteristics of the statistical universe from which the data were obtained and the assumption structure and objectives of each statistical technique.

Fortunately, we can make a few simplifications of the preceding descriptors. First, concerning types of scales, all the multivariate techniques of this book require no stronger measurement than interval scaling. Second, except for the ordinal scaling methods of multidimensional scaling and conjoint analysis (to be discussed in Chapter 19), we shall assume that (a) the variables are either nominal-scaled or interval-scaled, and (b) the functional form is linear in the parameters. While the original data may have been transformed by some nonlinear transformation (e.g., logarithmic), *linear in the parameters* means that all computed parameters *after* the transformation are of the first degree. For example, the function $Y = b_0 + b_1X_1 + b_2X_2 + \ldots + b_mX_m$ is linear in the parameters. Note that b_0 is a constant, while the other parameters, $b_1, b_2, \ldots, b_m$ are all of the first degree. Moreover, none of the b_j's depends on the value of either its own X_j or any other X_k ($k \neq j$). Even with these simplifying assumptions, we shall be able to describe a wide variety of possible techniques, and these may vary from being relatively simple, as shown in Exhibit 18.1, to complex.

Three principal descriptors are now of interest:

1. Whether the matrix is partitioned into subsets or kept intact

2. If the matrix is partitioned into subsets of criterion and predictor variables, the number of variables in each subset

3. Whether the variables are nominal-scaled or interval-scaled

Analysis of Dependence

If we elect to partition the data matrix into criterion and predictor variables, the problem becomes one of analyzing *dependence structures*. This, in turn, can be broken down into subcategories:

1. Single criterion/multiple predictor association

2. Multiple criterion/multiple predictor association

Multivariate techniques that deal with single criterion/multiple predictor association include multiple regression, analysis of variance and covariance, two-group discriminant analysis, and CHAID (chi-square automatic interaction detection).

Multivariate techniques that deal with multiple criterion/multiple predictor association include canonical correlation, multivariate analysis of variance and covariance, and multiple discriminant analysis.

Analysis of Interdependence

In some cases, we may not wish to partition the data matrix into criterion and predictor subsets. If so, we refer to this case as the analysis of *interdependence structures*. Techniques such as factor analysis are used if the focus of interest is on the variables of the (intact) data matrix. Cluster analysis is relevant if we wish to focus on the grouping of objects in the data matrix, as based on their profile similarities.

Selecting a Technique

How does a researcher select the multivariate technique to use in a given situation? In addition to the research question underlying the analysis, we suggested in Figure 18.1 that the number of dependent and independent variables and their levels of measurement are two of the major criteria. Four major sets of factors influence the choice of an appropriate statistical technique:

- Research parameters
- Known characteristics of the data
- Properties of the statistical technique
- Researcher characteristics

Research parameters include the purpose of analysis and the kind of analysis required. Characteristics of the data that are known before analysis, including the level of measurement, distribution of the data, and the nature and size of the sample, may be matched with the properties of a particular statistical technique (robustness, assumptions required, and design purpose). Finally, a researcher's individual philosophy, expertise, and experience will influence the choice of statistical technique.

Operationally, the researcher can be assisted by any of numerous printed or online guides, such as that provided by SPSS (2002), or at www.surveyz.com/tutorials. Another option is to use expert systems, such as The Idea Works' *Statistical Navigator*. Certain research firms have developed—partly for actual use value and partly for promotional purposes—a type of slide rule that relates the number of variables and level of measurement to appropriate tests. To illustrate, Figure 18.2 is a device from SDR, Inc., showing the tests when the level of measurement is metric.

EXHIBIT 18.1   Multivariate Analysis Can Be Simple

Not all multivariate analyses need to involve complex and sophisticated statistical techniques. A relatively simple analysis is importance-performance analysis. In the B2B area, for example, this could be done by asking customers to rate a supplier's performance on a set of attributes and characteristics, and then asking those customers how important each is to them. A central tendency measure would be calculated for each attribute's importance and performance measure and then plotted in two-dimensional space, as illustrated in the following figure, which shows a hypothetical grid for 14 attributes/characteristics.

Importance-Performance Grid With Attribute and Characteristic Ratings

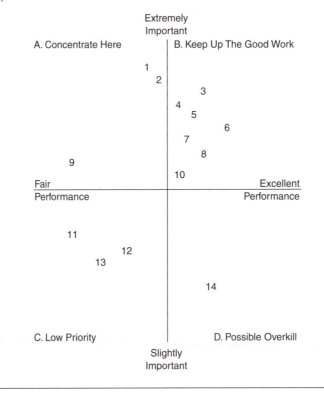

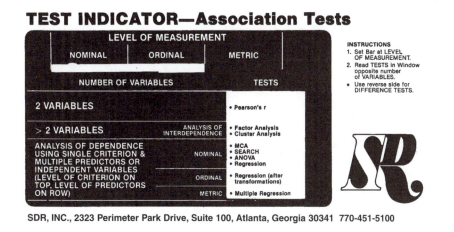

Figure 18.2   Illustration of Slide Rule

SOURCE: Reprinted with permission of SDR, Inc. 2323 Perimeter Park Drive, Suite 100, Atlanta, Georgia 30341.

MULTIPLE AND PARTIAL REGRESSION

Multiple regression extends the concepts of bivariate regression by simply adding multiple predictor (independent) variables. To illustrate this extension, we will introduce the second predictor X_2. Table 18.2 presents a set of example data with two predictor variables. The theoretical model now becomes

$$Y = \alpha + \beta_1 X_1 + \beta_2 X_2 + \varepsilon$$

with parameters estimated by

$$\hat{Y} = a + b_1 X_1 + b_2 X_2$$

All assumptions previously discussed for the bivariate regression model continue to hold in the present case. However, it is important to remember that, in general, the current b_1— now called a *partial* regression coefficient with respect to X_1—will *not* equal its counterpart coefficient (b) obtained from the bivariate regression. This is because X_1 itself will usually be correlated with X_2. In the bivariate case, X_2 was not entered into the analysis and any variation in Y that was shared by X_1 and X_2 was credited solely to X_1. Such will no longer be the case.

When there are only two predictors, X_1 and X_2, it is still possible to prepare a scatter plot. However, now the plot appears in terms of a three-dimensional space. In this space we fit a plane whose sum of squared deviations of the Y_i from their $\hat{Y}_i$ counterparts (on the plane) is a minimum. Figure 18.3 shows the original scatter plot and the fitted plane for the sample problem of Table 18.2. Using the SPSS program *Regression*, the estimated (least-squares) equation is

$$\hat{Y} = 0.247 + 0.493 X_1 + 0.484 X_2$$

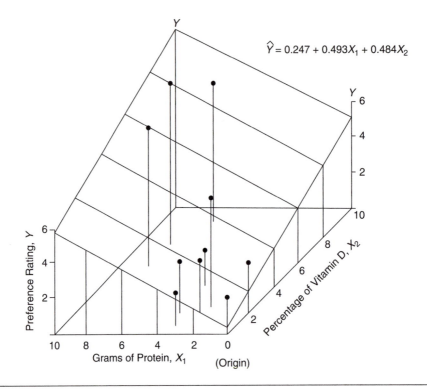

$$\hat{Y} = 0.247 + 0.493X_1 + 0.484X_2$$

Figure 18.3   Scatter Plot and Fitted Regression Plane

Table 18.2   Consumer Preference Ratings of Ten Cereals Varying in Nutritional Level

Rater	Preference	Protein, X_1	Vitamin D, X_2
1	3	4	2
2	7	9	7
3	2	3	1
4	1	1	2
5	6	3	3
6	2	4	4
7	8	7	9
8	3	3	2
9	9	8	7
10	2	1	3
Total	43	43	40
Mean	4.3	4.3	4.0
Standard deviation	2.908	2.791	2.708

Table 18.3   Single Correlation Between X_1 (Protein) and X_2 (Vitamin)

		Protein	*Vitamin*
Protein	Pearson Correlation	1	.838***
	Sig. (2-tailed)	.	.002
	N	10	10
Vitamin	Pearson Correlation	.838**	1
	Sig. (2-tailed)	.002	.
	N	10	10

**Correlation is significant at the 0.01 level (two-tailed).

The first slope coefficient of 0.493 denotes the change in $\hat{Y}$ per unit change in X_1 when X_2 is held constant. Similarly, 0.484 denotes the change in $\hat{Y}$ per unit change in X_2 when X_1 is held constant. We note that $0.493 \neq 0.886$, the slope obtained earlier in the bivariate case discussed in Chapter 17. This is because X_1 and X_2 are themselves correlated, and X_1 is now forced to share some of its Y-variable association with the second predictor, X_2.

Parameter Estimation

Finding the partial regression coefficients $b_1 = 0.493$ and $b_2 = 0.484$ and the intercept $a = 0.247$ is considerably more complicated than finding a single regression coefficient in bivariate regression. Exhibit 18.2 shows summary output from the SPSS program *Regression*. In addition to other statistical packages, a multiple regression function is available in Microsoft Excel.

EXHIBIT 18.2   Summary Output of SPSS Regression
Analysis (All Variables) of Sample Data

Variables Entered/Removed

Model	*Variables Entered*	*Variables Removed*	*Method*
1	VITAMIN, PROTEIN[a]	.	Enter

All requested variables entered.

Dependent Variable: PREFERENCE

Model Summary

Model	R	R Square	Adjusted R Square	Std. Error of the Estimate
1	.885[a]	.783	.721	1.53482

Model Summary

Model	Change Statistics				
	R Square Change	F Change	df1	df2	Sig. F Change
1	.783	12.652	2	7	.005

Predictors: (Constant), VITAMIN, PROTEIN

ANOVA

Model		Sum of Squares	df	Mean Square	F	Sig.
1	Regression	59.610	2	29.805	12.652	.005[a]
	Residual	16.490	7	2.356		
	Total	76.100	9			

Predictors: (Constant), VITAMIN, PROTEIN
Dependent Variable: PREFERENCE

Coefficients

		Unstandardized Coefficients		Standardized Coefficients		
Model		B	Std. Error	Beta	t	Sig.
1	(Constant)	.247	.942		.262	.801
	PROTEIN	.493	.336	.473	1.466	.186
	VITAMIN	.484	.346	.450	1.397	.205

A. Dependent Variable: PREFERENCE

SOURCE: From Curtis, M. E., "Avoid Hazard of Stepwise," in *Marketing News,* September 3, 1990. Reprinted with permission from the American Marketing Association.

Coefficient of Multiple Determination

Finding the *coefficient of multiple determination* proceeds in the same way as the bivariate case. However, there are computational shortcuts available. Exhibit 18.2 shows that using one such shortcut leads to: $R^2_{y,x_1 x_2} = 0.783$.

We note that the multiple regression equation does quite well at prediction, since 78 percent of the variation in Y is accounted for by variation in X_1 and X_2 ($R^2_{y,x_1 x_2} = .783$). However, we recall from Chapter 17 that if only X_1 is employed, the (simple) coefficient of determination is 72 percent. Apparently, X_2 (vitamin) and X_1 (protein) are so highly correlated—their simple correlation is 0.838 (see Table 18.3)—that once X_1 is in the regression equation there is little need for X_2 as well.

What about the *square root* of $R^2_{y,x_1 x_2}$? This is called the *coefficient of multiple correlation:*

$$R^2_{Y,X_1,X_2} = \sqrt{.783} = .885$$

and is interpreted as the *simple correlation* (i.e., bivariate correlation) between Y_i and $\hat{Y}_i$ where, as we know, the $\hat{Y}_i$ are the *predicted* values obtained by the best linear composite of X_1 and X_2 in the least-squares sense; this composite is given by the multiple regression equation.

Standard Errors and *t*-Tests

While the *F*-test indicates that the overall regression model is significant, it does not follow that *both* b_1 and b_2 contribute significantly to overall accounted-for variance. It may be the case that a simpler model involving only X_1 (or only X_2) would be sufficient. The standard error of each individual regression coefficient provides the basis for a *t*-test of this simpler model.

The standard error is a measure of dispersion about the average partial regression coefficient over repeated samplings of Y for a fixed set of values on each of the predictors. The larger the standard error is, the less reliable our estimate of b_1 is (across repeated samplings from the same universe).

Conceptually, this statement means that the standard error of b_1 increases as X_1 becomes more completely accounted for by the remaining predictor variables.

The *t*-value of 1.466 in Exhibit 18.2 is simply the ratio of b_1 to its own standard error, SE(b_1). The test of significance of t_1 is carried out by finding the tabular value of the *t*-distribution (Table A.2 in the Appendix of this book) for seven degrees of freedom. If we continue to use a significance level of 0.1, then the tabular value of t is 1.415 and b_1 is significant. However, b_2 (whose *t*-value is 1.397) is *not* significant at the 0.1 level. Note that in Exhibit 18.2, the two variable (protein and vitamin) regression analysis reports protein to be nonsignificant with a probability of .186. This is due to the degrees of freedom issue used in the two variable regression. When considered alone, the *t*-test for protein is significant at the .1 level.

The *t*-test for each individual partial regression coefficient tests whether the increment in R^2 produced by the predictor in question is significant when a model including the predictor (and all other predictors) is compared with a model including all predictors but the one being tested.

Contribution to Accounted-for Variation

The coefficient of multiple determination in this example indicates that the variation of both independent variables accounted for 78.3 percent of the variation in the dependent variable. Since b_2 is not significant, we can presume that X_2 contributes little to the dependent variable's variation. In fact, this is the case. When a stepwise procedure was used for the regression analysis, X_1 was the only variable included and $R^2 = 0.723$. Thus X_2's contribution to the coefficient of multiple determination is only 0.06 (0.783–0.723).

In summary, Exhibit 18.2 shows the major output measures of interest in applied multiple regression studies:

1. The regression equation
2. R^2—both the sample-determined and the population-adjusted values
3. An F-test for testing the significance of the overall regression (involving both X_1 and X_2)
4. Individual t-tests and standard errors for testing each specific partial regression coefficient
5. Partial correlation coefficients
6. The accounted-for variance contributed by each predictor, where any shared variance of each predictor (beyond the first) is credited to the predictors that precede it, based on the researcher's order for including the predictor variables

In the sample problem R^2 was highly significant, but only the first variable X_1 was needed to account for most of the variance in Y. That is, the addition of X_2 accounted for an incremental variance of only six percentage points; moreover, the t-test for b_2 was not significant at the 0.1 level. Therefore, in practice we would employ a simple regression of Y on X_1 alone. This has already been computed in Chapter 17 as $\hat{Y} = 0.491 + 0.886X_1$.

Other Forms of Regression

With the large variety of computer programs available, the computation of multiple regression analysis is both fast and easy for the user. However, decisions must still be made by the user. Within a package, individual programs may differ with respect to the criterion for including the independent variables in the regression, the ability to repeat the analysis on subgroups of respondents and compare the subgroups, the types of residual analysis available, and the linearity assumption used in the analysis.

The two most widely used approaches are all-variable regression (demonstrated above) and stepwise regression, as shown in Exhibit 18.3 and described further in Exhibit 18.4. Many items shown in an output are common to both procedures, though not necessarily in the same format or sequence. Similarly, the results of the regression analyses are often similar for a small number of variables, becoming increasingly disparate as more variables are introduced. This disparity is explained by the fact that the rationale for including variables differs greatly. For more detail contrasting the difference between the all-variable and stepwise regression methodologies, see Green, Tull, and Albaum (1988, pp. 443–55).

Multicollinearity

Put simply, *multicollinearity* refers to the problem in applied regression studies in which the predictor variables exhibit very high correlation among themselves. This condition distorts the value of the estimated regression coefficients, inflates the standard error of beta, and thereby makes it more difficult to determine which predictor variable is having an effect.

Unless one is dealing with experimental design data, it is almost always the case that predictor variables in multiple regression will be correlated to some degree. The question is, How much multicollinearity can be tolerated without seriously affecting the results? Unfortunately, there is no simple answer to this question.

EXHIBIT 18.3 Summary Output of SPSS Regression Analysis
(Stepwise) of Sample Data from Table 18.2

Variables Entered/Removed

Model	Variables Entered	Variables Removed	Method
1	**VAR00002**		Stepwise (Criteria: Probability of F to enter < =.050, Probability of *F* to remove > =.100).

Dependent Variable:VAR00001

Model Summary

Model	R	R Square	Adjusted R Square	Std. Error of the Estimate
1	.850[a]	.723	.688	1.62354

Model Summary

Model	Change Statistics				
	R Square Change	F Change	df1	df2	Sig. F Change
1	.723	20.871	1	8	.002

Predictors: (Constant), VAR00002

ANOVA

Model		Sum of Squares	df	Mean Square	F	Sig.
1	Regression	55.013	1	55.013	20.871	.002[a]
	Residual	21.087	8	2.636		
	Total	76.100	9			

Predictors: (Constant), VAR00002
Dependent Variable: VAR00001

(Continued)

EXHIBIT 18.3   (Continued)

Coefficients

| | Unstandardized Coefficients | | Standardized Coefficients | | |
Model	B	Std. Error	Beta	t	Sig.
1	(Constant)	.491	.979	.501	.630
VAR00002	.886	.194	.850	4.568	.002

Dependent Variable: VAR00001

Excluded Variables

| | | | | | Collinearity Statistics |
Model	Beta In	t	Sig.	Partial Correlation	Tolerance
1 VAR00003	.450[a]	1.397	.205	.467	.298

Predictors in the Model: (Constant), VAR00002
Dependent Variable: VAR00001

The study of multicollinearity in data analysis evolves around two major problems: (a) How can it be detected; and (b) what can be done about it? These problems are particularly relevant to marketing research, where one often faces the dilemma of needing a large number of variables to achieve accuracy of predictors, and yet finds that as more predictors are added to the model, their intercorrelations become larger.

As indicated above, what constitutes serious multicollinearity is ambiguous. Some researchers have adopted various rules-of-thumb: For example, any pair of predictor variables must not correlate more than 0.9; if so, one of the predictors is discarded. While looking at simple correlations between pairs of predictors has merit, it can miss more subtle relationships involving three or more predictors. The above rule can be extended, of course, to the examination of *multiple* correlations between each predictor and all other predictors. Usually one would want to guard against having any of these multiple correlations exceed the multiple correlation of the criterion variable with the predictor set.

Essentially there are three procedures for dealing with multicollinearity:

1. Ignore it.
2. Delete one or more of the offending predictors.
3. Transform the set of predictor variables into a new set of predictor-variable combinations that are mutually uncorrelated.

Ignoring multicollinearity need not be as cavalier as it might sound. First, one can have multicollinearity in the predictor variables and still have strong enough effects that the estimating coefficients remain reasonably stable. Second, multicollinearity may be prominent in only a subset of the predictors, a subset that may not contribute much to accounted-for variance anyway. A prudent procedure in checking one's predictor set for multicollinearity is to examine the standard errors of the regression coefficients (which will tend to be large in the case of high multicollinearity). Second, one may randomly drop some subset of the cases (perhaps 20 percent or so), rerun the regression, and then check to see if the signs and relative sizes of the regression coefficients are stable. Third, a number of computer regression routines incorporate checks for serious multicollinearity (see SPSS Linear Regression Analysis Statistics Help for a list of diagnostic analyses); if the program does not indicate this condition, the researcher can generally assume that the problem is not acute.

If multicollinearity is severe, one rather simple procedure is to drop one or more predictor variables that represent the major offenders. Usually, because of their high intercorrelations with the retained predictors, the overall fit will not change markedly. Pragmatically, if a particular pair of predictors are highly collinear, one would retain that member of the pair whose measurement reliability or theoretical importance is higher in the substantive problem under study.

Methods also exist for transforming the original set of predictors to a mutually uncorrelated set of linear composites—for example, principal components analysis (which is discussed in Chapter 19). If these components (linear composites) are interpretable in themselves, the researcher may use these in the regression analysis rather than the original variables. If *all* components are retained, the predictive accuracy will be precisely the same as that obtained from the original set of predictors. However, the problem here is that the components may *not* be interpretable in their own right. Another possibility, of course, is to use only one of the variables for each component to represent that component in the regression analysis.

Cross-validation

Probably the safest procedure for dealing with the variety of problems in multiple regression, including multicollinearity, is to use *cross-validation*. We have commented in this chapter on the tendency of regression models (and the same is true of other multivariate techniques) to capitalize on chance variation in the sample data. Since these techniques are optimization methods, they find the best possible fit of the model to the *specific* data, though one can also almost invariably find a poorer fit.

Cross-validation is a simple procedure for examining whether the regression equation holds up beyond the data on which its parameters are based. The researcher simply takes part of the data (perhaps a quarter to a third) and puts it aside. The regression equation is then computed from the remaining data. Following this, the researcher takes the "hold-out" data and computes a set of Y_i using the earlier-computed regression equation and the predictor-variable values of the hold-out sample. The researcher then finds the simple coefficient of determination between the Y_i in the hold-out sample and their predicted Y_i counterparts. This coefficient is compared with the R^2 obtained from the original analysis to find the degree of shrinkage. Doing this requires a larger sample size.

An even better procedure is to *doubly cross-validate*. This is carried out by the following steps:

1. Split the cases randomly into halves.
2. Compute *separate* regression equations for each half.
3. Use the first-half equation to predict the second-half Y_i values.
4. Use the second-half equation to predict the first-half Y_i values.
5. Examine each partial regression coefficient across split halves to see if agreement is obtained in both directions (algebraic sign) and in magnitude.
6. Compute a regression equation for the entire sample, using only those variables that show stability in the preceding step.

Since high multicollinearity will make sample-to-sample regression coefficients unstable, double cross-validation can help the researcher determine which coefficients exhibit stability across split halves.

Depending on the sample size, of course, one could split the sample into thirds, quarters, and so on. Usually, however, there are sufficient constraints on sample size, relative to the number of predictors, that split-half testing is about all that gets done. Even so, single and double cross-validation are extremely useful undertakings, and, with a few clicks of a mouse, are easy to implement.

Steckel and Vanhonacker (1991) developed a formal test for the cross-validation of regression models under the simple random splitting framework. Their results indicated that splitting the data into halves is suboptimal. They recommend that more observations should be used for estimation than validation.

EXHIBIT 18.4   Stepwise Regression Can Be Hazardous

Avoid using stepwise regression whenever possible, particularly when dealing with sample data. The theoretical and statistical shortcomings are inherent in the process and difficult to overcome (Curtis, 1990).

If you do use a stepwise approach, however, certain precautions should be taken:

1. Limit the number of variables initially included in the predictor pool, eliminating some with high intercorrelations.

2. Use as large a sample as possible, ideally with 40–50 cases for each variable in the pool.

3. Validate the model through a follow-up sample or by splitting the original sample.

4. When multicollinearity is a problem, consider using factor analysis as a data reduction technique.

Stepwise regression is a computer-driven statistical procedure in which a subset of independent variables is selected from a larger pool of variables through a series of repetitive steps to arrive at the best-fitting model for the data. "Best" typically refers to maximizing the explained variance (R^2) of the dependent variable.

Stepwise regression begins with a dependent variable and a pool of independent variables. It starts building a model by selecting the variable most highly correlated with the dependent variable. The program then looks for the next variable in the pool that offers the largest increment in R^2 when added to the model. As new variables are added, others may be dropped in a repetitive process until the best-fitting model is produced.

But the method has serious implications. First, from a *substantive* perspective, the best-fitting model may not be the best—or even good. There are other variable selection techniques in the stepwise family, such as forward entry and backward elimination, which also are designed to obtain the best-fitting model. It would not be unusual to obtain three completely different best-fitting models from the same data set using these methods. The only time this is unlikely to happen is in the unusual situation when all predictor variables are uncorrelated with one another.

Another problem occurs when high levels of multicollinearity exist in the pool of independent variables. A single variable may be included, while two or more others that combine to make a more accurate predictive model may be excluded. The greater the multicollinearity, the more likely that an unreasonable and unstable best-fitting model will be selected.

Stepwise methods also may cause a problem when used for explanatory model building, which focuses on the causal relationships between the dependent and independent variables.

The problem is that stepwise methods are purely data-driven, after-the-fact techniques not based on a prior theoretical model. Because data are typically nothing more than a snapshot of reality at any given time, and subject to significant fluctuation, theory is ultimately important to understand the true, underlying relationships at work.

TWO-GROUP DISCRIMINANT ANALYSIS

When dealing with associative data, the marketing researcher may encounter cases where the criterion variable is categorical, but where the predictor variables involve interval-scaled data. For example, one may wish to predict whether sales potential in a given marketing territory will be good or bad, based on certain measurements regarding the territory's personal disposable income, population density, number of retail outlets, and the like.

Other potential applications also come to mind:

- How do consumers who are heavy users of my brand differ in their demographic profiles from those who are nonusers?
- How do respondents who show high interest in a new set of concept descriptions differ in their readership levels of certain magazines from those who show low interest?
- How do homeowners who select a variable rate mortgage differ in their demographic profiles, mortgage shopping behavior and attitudes, and preferences for mortgage features from homeowners selecting a conventional fixed-rate mortgage?

The classification need not be limited to two groups:

- Are significant demographic differences observed among purchasers of Sears, Goodyear, Goodrich, and Michelin tires?
- How do doctors, lawyers, and bankers differ in terms of their preference ratings of eight different luxury automobiles?
- Do long-distance, local, and quasi-local and long-distance geographically-mobile people differ in individual household demographic and economic characteristics?
- How can loyal shoppers of Lord & Taylor, Marshall Field's, and Neiman-Marcus be distinguished on the basis of their attitudes about each retailer?

Many other such problems could be added to the list. However, each one has a common structure in which we assume that some test object (usually a person) falls into one of a set of categories. It is also assumed we know that person's profile on a set of (assumed or otherwise) interval-scaled predictor variables, such as age, income, years of education, or other background variables.

The problem is to predict a person's category from some function of the predictor variables. Here we shall assume that the function is linear. If only two categories are involved, the problem is a *two-group* discriminant case; if three or more categories are involved, we are dealing with *multiple* (group) discriminant analysis.

Objectives of Two-Group Discriminant Analysis

Two-group discriminant analysis (and classification) involves four main objectives:

1. Finding linear composites of the predictor variables that enable the analyst to separate the groups by maximizing among-groups (relative to within-groups) variation

2. Establishing procedures for assigning new individuals, whose profiles (but not group identity) are known, to one of the two groups

3. Testing whether significant differences exist between the mean predictor-variable profiles of the two groups

4. Determining which variables account most for intergroup differences in mean profiles

These objectives are the bases for the existence of the two major, and very distinct, purposes and procedures for conducting discriminant analysis (Smith, 2004). The first procedure, *discriminant predictive* (or *explanatory*) *analysis*, is used to optimize the predictive functions. The second procedure, *discriminant classification analysis*, uses the predictive functions derived in the first procedure to either classify fresh sets of data of known group membership, thereby validating the predictive function, or if the function has previously been validated, to classify new sets of observations of unknown group membership. The differences in the application and requirements for each are summarized in Table 18.4.

Geometric Representation

If we have *n* persons measured on *m* variables, the profile of each person can be portrayed as a point in *m* dimensions. If we *also* know the group to which each person belongs, and the groups differ in terms of average profiles (often called *centroids*), we might expect to find different groups occupying different regions of the space. The less overlap noted among intergroup profiles in that space, the more likely it is that discriminant analysis can help us separate the groups.

The scatter diagram and projection in Figure 18.4 provides one way to show what happens when a two-group discriminant function is computed. Suppose that we had two groups, A and B, and two measures, X_1 and X_2, on each member of the two groups. We could plot in the scatter diagram the association of variable X_2 with X_1 for each group, maintaining group identity by the use of filled-in dots or open circles. The resultant ellipses enclose some specified proportion of the points, say 95 percent, in each group. If a straight line is drawn through the two points where the ellipses intersect and is then projected to a new axis Z, we can say that the overlap between the *univariate* distributions A' and B' (represented by the shaded area) is smaller than would be obtained by any other line drawn through the ellipses representing the scatter plots. The shaded region under the curves can also be interpreted as representing the probabilities of mistakes when classification is done on the basis of likelihoods only.

The important thing to note about Figure 18.4 is that the Z-axis expresses the two-variable profiles of groups A and B as *single* numbers. That is, by finding a linear composite of the original profile scores we can portray each profile as a point on a line. Thus, the axis Z

Table 18.4   Stages of Discriminant Analysis

		Stages		
	Predictive Discriminant Analysis	*Classification Analysis of Initial Data Set of Known Groupings*	*Classification Analysis of New Data Set of Known Groupings*	*Classification Analysis of New Data Set of Unknown Groupings*
Purpose	Derive discriminant function using initial data set. No classification involved	Determine how well discriminant function classifies (biased)	(1) Classify data using classification rule derived from predictive function (2) May be part of validation analysis of initial predictive function	(1) Classify data using classification rule derived from predictive function (2) May be part of validation analysis of initial predictive function
Requirements	Assumptions of linear discriminant model. No validation required	No validation required	Validation required	Initial predictive function must have been previously validated

SOURCE: Smith, 2004.

condenses the information about group separability (shown in the bivariate plot) into a set of points on a single axis. Here, Z is the *discriminant* axis.

In most problems of realistic size, we have more than two predictor variables. If so, each predictor can represent a *separate* dimension (although we would be limited to three predictor variables if we wished to plot the data). In any case, the basic objective is still to find one axis in the m-dimensional space that maximally separates the centroids of the two groups after the points are projected onto this new axis.

In our discussion of multiple regression analysis we noted that one finds a linear composite that maximizes the coefficient of multiple determination, R^2. Analogously, in two-group discriminant analysis we try to find a linear composite of the original variables that maximizes the *ratio* of among-to-within groups variability. It should be noted that if m, the number of predictor variables, is quite large, we shall be parsimonious by portraying among-to-within-groups variation in many fewer dimensions (actually a *single dimension* in the two-group case) than found originally.

A Numerical Example

Let us return to the example involving ready-to-eat cereals that was first presented in Table 18.2 in the context of multiple regression. As recalled, we wished to see if amount of protein and vitamin D influenced consumers' evaluations of the cereals.

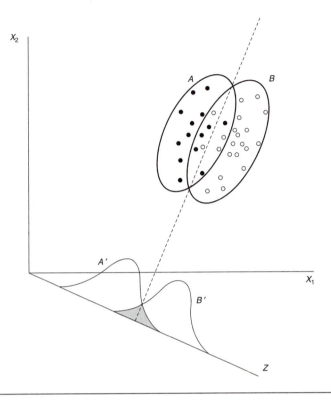

Figure 18.4   Graphical Illustration of Two-Group Discriminant Analysis

---

In the present case we shall assume that each of the ten consumer raters is simply asked to classify the cereal into one of two categories: *like* or *dislike*. The (hypothetical) data appear in Table 18.5, which has two predictor variables(again):

X_1: the amount of protein (in grams) per two-ounce serving

X_2: the percentage of minimum daily requirements of vitamin D per two-ounce serving

We first note in the table that the two groups are much more widely separated on X_1 (protein) than they are on X_2 (vitamin D). If we were forced to choose just one of the axes, it would seem that X_1 is a better bet than X_2. However, there is information provided by the group separation on X_2, so we wonder if some linear composite of both X_1 and X_2 could do better than X_1 alone.

Figure 18.5 shows a scatter plot of the X_1 and X_2 data of Table 18.5. We note that perfect discrimination can be achieved with X_1 if we erect a line perpendicular to the horizontal axis between the scale values of 6 and 7. On the other hand, there is no way that the use of X_2 alone would enable us to separate the groups. Given this picture, we would not be surprised if the best linear composite places a considerably larger weight on X_1 than on X_2.

Why not use X_1 alone, rather than a composite of X_1 and X_2? First, the data of Table 18.5 represent only a *sample*; it is quite possible that additional observations would show that X_1 alone would *not* effect perfect discrimination between the two groups. Second, we have not

Table 18.5   Consumer Evaluations (Like Versus Dislike) of Ten Cereals Varying in Nutritional Content

Person	Evaluation	Protein, X_1	Vitamin D, X_2
1	Dislike	2	4
2	Dislike	3	2
3	Dislike	4	5
4	Dislike	5	4
5	Dislike	6	7
	Mean	4	4.4
6	Like	7	6
7	Like	8	4
8	Like	9	7
9	Like	10	6
10	Like	11	9
	Mean	9	6.4
	Grand Mean	6.5	5.4
	Standard Deviation	3.028	2.011

explicitly taken into consideration either the variability of X_1 versus X_2 or their correlation. One of the nice features of discriminant analysis is that all three aspects of the data— centroid, variance, and correlation—are considered when developing the linear composite that maximally separates the groups.

As noted earlier, the key problem of two-group discriminant analysis is to find a new axis so that projections of the points onto that axis exhibit the property of maximizing the separation between group means relative to their within-groups variability on the composite.

This discriminant axis can be defined in terms of a set of weights—one for each predictor-variable axis—so that we have the following linear function:

$$Z = d_1 X_1 + d_2 X_2$$

where d_1 and d_2 are the weights that we seek.

Using the SPSS program *Discriminant,* we solve for the discriminant weights d_1 and d_2 that maximize the separation between the groups. This involves a procedure where two simultaneous equations are solved, leading to the desired discriminant function:

$$Z = 0.368X_1 - 0.147X_2$$

The weights d_1 and d_2 are known and labeled on computer output from SPSS or other packages as *unstandardized discriminant function coefficients*. The general form for a linear discriminant function is $Z + d_0 + d_1 X_1 + d_2 X_2$, where d_0 is the intercept or constant term in the function. Since the example used deviations to calculate the weights d_1 and d_2, the function goes through

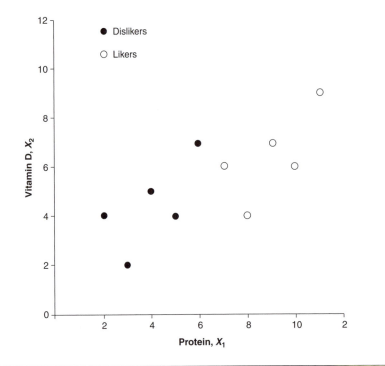

Figure 18.5   Scatter Plot of Two-Group Sample Data of Table

the origin and $d_0 = 0$. Having found the discriminant function, it is a straightforward procedure to find discriminant scores for the centroids of the two groups and the grand mean:

$$\bar{Z}(\text{dislikers}) = 0.368(4) - 0.147(4.4) = 0.824$$

$$\bar{Z}(\text{likers}) = 0.368(9) - 0.147(6.4) = 2.368$$

$$\bar{Z}(\text{grand mean}) = 0.368(6.5) - 0.147(5.4) = 1.596$$

We may also apply this procedure to each of the 10 pairs of X_1, X_2 values in Table 18.5 to get the linear composite. For example, the discriminant score for the first case in the disliker group is

$$Z = 0.368(2) - 0.147(4) = 0.148$$

Plotting the Discriminant Function

The original scatter plot of the ten observations is reproduced in Figure 18.6. However, this time we also show the discriminant axis (linear composite) by passing a straight line through the point $(0.368, -0.147)$ and the intersection of the original axes (i.e., the origin).

Alternatively, one could use any point with coordinates proportional to $(0.368, -.147)$. However, it should be noted that the *scale unit* on the discriminant axis in Figure 18.6 differs from the original unit in which X_1 and X_2 are expressed. To maintain the original unit, d_1 and d_2 would have to be normalized. The original points can then be projected onto this new axis.

To illustrate, we show projections of the grand centroid and the centroids of the dislikers and likers, respectively. (Similarly, all ten original points could be projected onto the discriminant axis as well.) We note that the discriminant axis favors X_1 (as we guessed it would) by giving about 2.5 times the (absolute-value) weight ($d_1 = 0.368$ versus $d_2 = -0.147$ to X_1) as is given to X_2.

The output from an SPSS analysis is shown in Exhibit 18.5. Note that the discriminant function coefficients are different from those shown earlier, meaning that the discriminant scores for each person also will differ. This is because the discriminant axis is *not run through the origin*, but rather there is an intercept term. The unstandardized discriminant function coefficients evaluated at group means sum to zero. The analysis is not affected by this, and all conclusions to be made will not differ whether or not the axis is through the origin.

Classifying the Persons

It is well and good to find the discriminant function, but we are still interested in how well the function classifies the ten cases. The classification problem, in turn, involves two additional questions: (a) how well does the function assign the known cases in the sample; and (b) how well does it assign new cases *not* used in computing the function in the first place?

To answer these questions we need an *assignment rule*. One rule that seems intuitively plausible is based on Figure 18.6. A *classification boundary* between the two groups, Z_{crit}, can be identified as being midway between the means of the function for each of the two groups. To classify an individual, if $Z_i > Z_{crit}$ then the individual belongs in one group, while if $Z_i < Z_{crit}$ then the individual goes into the other group. As can be seen from Figure 18.6, no misassignments will be made if we adopt the rule:

- Assign all cases with discriminant scores that are on the left of the midpoint (1.596) to the *disliker* group.
- Assign all cases with discriminant scores that are on the right of the midpoint (1.596) to the *liker* group.

That is, all true dislikers will be correctly classified as such, as will all true likers. This can be shown by a 2×2 table, known as a classification or *confusion matrix*, as shown later in Table 18.6.

We see that all entries fall along the main diagonal. For example, had any of the five true dislikers been called likers, the first row and second column would contain not a zero but, rather, the number of such misassignments.

The application of this rule can be stated in equivalent terms:

- Substitute the centroid of each group in the discriminant function and find the respective group scores (in our case, 0.824 for dislikers and 2.368 for likers).
- For any new case, compute the discriminant score and assign the case to that group whose group score is closer.

This rule makes two specific assumptions: (a) the prior probability of a new case falling into each of the groups is equal across groups; and (b) the cost of misclassification is equal across groups.

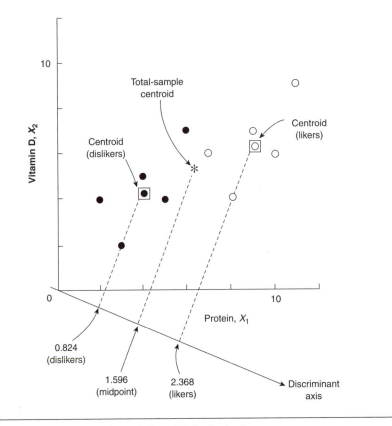

Figure 18.6 Plot of the Discriminant Axis and Point Projections

---

EXHIBIT 18.5 Discriminant Analysis for Cereal Evaluations

Analysis Case Processing Summary

Unweighted Cases	N	Percent
Valid	10	100.0
Excluded		
Missing or out-of-range group codes	0	.0
At least one missing discriminating variable	0	.0
Both missing or out-of-range group codes and at least one missing discriminating variable	0	.0
Total	0	.0
Total	10	100.0

Group Statistics

| EVALUATE | Mean | Std. Deviation | Valid N (listwise) | |
			Unweighted	Weighted
PROTEIN	4.0000	1.58114	5	5.000
VITAMIN	4.4000	1.81659	5	5.000
2.00 PROTEIN	9.0000	1.58114	5	5.000
VITAMIN	6.4000	1.81759	5	5.000
Total PROTEIN	6.5000	3.02765	10	10.000
VITAMIN	5.4000	2.01108	10	10.000

Tests of Equality of Group Means

	Wilks' Lambda	F	df1	df2	Sig.
PROTEIN	.242	25.000	1	8	.001
VITAMIN	.725	3.030	1	8	.120

Summary of Canonical Discriminant Functions

Eigenvalues

Function	Eigenvalue	% of Variance	Cumulative %	Canonical Correlation
1	3.860[a]	100.0	100.0	.891

First 1 canonical discriminant functions were used in the analysis.

Wilks' Lambda

Test of Function(s)	Wilks' Lambda	Chi-Square	df	Sig.
1	.206	11.068	2	.004

Standardized Canonical Discriminant Function Coefficients

| | Function |
	1
PROTEIN	1.323
VITAMIN	−.608

Structure Matrix

	Function
	1
PROTEIN	.900
VITAMIN	.313

Pooled within-groups correlations between discriminating variables and standardized canonical discriminant functions.

Variables ordered by absolute size of correlation within function.

Canonical Discriminant Function Coefficients

	Function
	1
PROTEIN	.837
VITAMIN	−.335
(Constant)	−3.632

Unstandardized coefficients

Functions at Group Centroids

	Function
EVALUATE	1
1.00	−1.757
2.00	1.757

Unstandardized canonical discriminant functions evaluated at group means

Classification Statistics

Classification Processing Summary

Processed		10
Excluded	Missing or out-of-range group codes	0
	At least one missing discriminating variable	0
Used in Output		10

Prior Probabilities for Groups

EVALUATE	Prior	Cases Used in Analysis	
		Unweighted	Weighted
1.00	.500	5	5.000
2.00	.500	5	5.000
Total	1.000	10	10.000

Classification Function Coefficients

	EVALUATE	
	1.00	2.00
PROTEIN	1.035	3.976
VITAMIN	.706	−.471
(Constant)	−4.317	−17.081

Fisher's linear discriminant functions

Classification Tables[b,c]

EVALUATE			Predicted Group Membership		Total
			1.00	2.00	
Original	Count	1.00	5	0	5
		2.00	0	5	5
	%	1.00	100.0	.0	100.0
		2.00	.0	100.0	100.0
Cross-validated[a]	Court	1.00	5	0	5
		2.00	0	5	5
	%	1.00	100.0	.0	100.0
		2.00	.0	100.0	100.0

[a]Cross validation is done only for those cases in the analysis. In cross validation, each case is classified by the functions derived from all cases other than that case.

[b]100.0% of original grouped cases correctly classified.

[c]100.0% of cross-validated grouped cases correctly classified.

If a higher probability existed for likers, we could reduce the expected probability of misclassification by moving the cutting point of 1.596 to the left (closer to 0.824, the mean score for dislikers) so as to give a wider interval for the larger (likers) group. Similarly, if the cost of misclassifying a liker is higher than that for misclassifying a disliker, the cutting point would also be moved closer to 0.824.

A second point of interest concerns the tendency for classification tables (i.e., the confusion matrix) based on the sample used to develop the classification function to show better results than would be found upon cross-validation with new cases. That is, some capitalization on chance takes place in discriminant analysis, and one needs a way to measure this bias of an inflated percentage of correctly classified observations, just as cross-validation should be employed in multiple regression.

Procedures are available to develop a truer summary of the degree of correct assignments than would be obtained from fresh data (Lachenbruch, 1975; Klecka, 1980; Frank, Massy, & Morrison, 1965).

The most frequently suggested validation approach is the *holdout* method, in which the data set is randomly split into two subsamples. One subsample is used to develop the discriminant function and the other subsample is used as "fresh data" to test the function. It is suggested that this split-sample validation be replicated by using a different convention for the random assignment of the observations. Whether a researcher uses only one validation sample or replications, there may be problems associated with the sampling procedures used to arrive at the analysis and validation subsamples. These problems relate to the number of variables included in the discriminant function (when a stepwise procedure is used) and to inferences that the researcher might make concerning the classificatory power of resulting discriminant functions.

There may be differing numbers of variables included on any given replication. Also, there can be a wide range in the correct classification performance of the validation replications, although the analysis functions are quite stable.

There is another dimension to the validation process discussed above. For the analysis and validation samples there is a measure of the percentage of cases that would have been correctly classified based on *chance* alone. Obviously, the researcher is interested in whether the discriminant function is a significant improvement over chance classification.

Because our "Cereal Data" achieved 100 percent correct classification, we will now switch to another example to demonstrate these measures of chance classification. The classification or "confusion" matrix shown in Table 18.6 was derived from a discriminant analysis where accident insurance purchasers and non-purchasers were predicted using demographic variables.

Overall, 74.16 percent of all subjects surveyed were correctly classified as purchasers and non-purchasers of accident insurance. This observed classification was found to be significant at the .001 level ($\chi^2 = 24.59$, df = 1) and ($Q = 69.58$, df = 1). Thus, observed classification is significantly different from expected chance classification.

Tests of Group Differences

Morrison (1969) considered the question of how well variables discriminate by formulating a likelihood ratio to estimate chance classification. This likelihood analysis provides a criterion that may be used to compare the proportion of correctly classified observations with the proportion expected by chance. This proportion, designated the proportional chance criteria, or C_{pro} (Morrison, 1969), is expressed as

$$C_{pro} = p\alpha + (1 - p)(1 - \alpha) = (.295)(.111) + (.705)(.889) = .6594$$

where

α = the proportion of customers in the sample categorized as purchasers

p = the true proportion of purchasers in the sample

$(1 - \alpha)$ = the proportion of the sample classified as non-purchasers

$(1 - p)$ = the true proportion of non-purchasers in the sample

This likelihood analysis states that 65.94 percent of the overall sample is expected to receive correct classification by chance alone. The proportional chance criterion, C_{pro}, has been used mainly as a point of reference for subjective evaluation (Morrison, 1969), rather than the basis of a statistical test to determine if the expected proportion differs from the observed proportion that is correctly classified.

This relationship between chance and observed proportions can be tested using a Z statistic of the form

$$\frac{P_{cc} - C_{pro}}{\sqrt{\dfrac{(C_{pro}) - (1 - C_{pro})}{n}}} = \frac{.7416 - .6594}{\sqrt{\dfrac{(.6594)(.3406)}{298}}} = 2.99$$

where P_{cc} is the percent of observations correctly classified, $C_{pro} = p\alpha + (1 - p)(1 - \alpha)$.

Thus for the example problem, the difference between expected and actual overall correct classification is significantly different at the .01 level. This overall test of significance suggests that further analysis should be conducted to determine the source of the deviation from chance expectations.

Table 18.6 Classification Table for Accident Insurance Purchasers

Fequency, Row % *Chi-Square Contrib.*	*Predicted* *Purchase*	*Predicted* *Non-Purchase*	*Row Total* *Row Percentage*
Actual Purchase	$n = 22$ 66.7% 15.41	$n = 11$ 33.3% 6.46	$n = 33$ 11.1%
Actual Non-Purchase	$n = 66$ 24.9% 1.92	$n = 199$ 75.1% .80	$n = 265$ 88.9%
Column Totals Column Percentage	$n = 88$ 29.5%	$n = 21.0$ 70.5%	$n = 298$ 100%

Percent of Cases Correctly Classified = 221/298 = 74.16%

Chi-Square = 24.599 df = 1, Significance < .001

Divergence may be present in any of the classification matrix cells (i.e., purchasers or non-purchasers, that are either correctly or incorrectly categorized), and thus each may be tested to determine whether its proportion differs from chance.

Classification and Misclassification Within Groups

The analysis to determine the source of deviation is conducted using the maximum chance criterion, designated C_{max} (Morrison, 1969). C_{max} is the maximum expected correct classification for a selected group of interest. The computation of C_{max} is based on the assumption that all observations are categorized as coming from that group: for example, given that all 298 purchasers and non-purchasers were classified as purchasers, then the maximum correct classification, C_{max}, would be expressed

$$C_{max} = \frac{\text{Total purchasers}}{\text{Total customers}} = \frac{33}{298}$$

Because we are interested in the correct classification of insurance purchasers, the test of classification involves asking if the 66.67-correct insurance purchaser classification differs significantly from the 11.1-percent maximum expected chance classification. A Z statistic is used to test this relationship as shown for the example analysis.

$$Z_{11} = \frac{\text{Observed Correct Classification} - C_{max}}{\sqrt{\dfrac{(C_{max}) - (1 - C_{max})}{n}}} = \frac{.667 - .111}{\sqrt{\dfrac{(.111)(.889)}{33}}} = 10.17^*$$

* Significant at the .001 level.

This test may also be conducted for the other cells in the classification matrix:

$$Z_{12} = \frac{.333 - .111}{\sqrt{\dfrac{(.111)(.889)}{33}}} = 4.06$$

$$Z_{21} = \frac{.249 - .889}{\sqrt{\dfrac{(.889)(.111)}{265}}} = -33.16$$

$$Z_{22} = \frac{.751 - .889}{\sqrt{\dfrac{(.889)(.111)}{265}}} = -7.15$$

Thus cell Z_{11} shows that observed classification is significantly greater than is expected to occur by chance classification alone. The analysis of cells (1,2) and (2,1) shows that observed and expected misclassification results differ in that purchasers are misclassified into cell (1,2) less often than expected by chance, and non-purchasers are misclassified into cell (2,2) more often than expected bv chance. Thus the discriminant functions appear to shift the classification of subjects toward the purchaser categories, as demonstrated by significantly greater than expected classification in the upper and left portions of the classification matrix.

At the most basic level, the validity of discriminant function analysis lies in the stability of the coefficients derived. These coefficients are the basis of classifying, profiling, and evaluating the underlying discriminant dimensions. It would be valuable to have a validation procedure that uses all the sample data for evaluating the stability of parameter estimates while allowing unbiased estimation of error rates. The *jackknife statistic* and the *U-method* have been proposed as such procedures. It is beyond the scope of this book to discuss these specialized techniques, and the reader is referred to the excellent references already cited.

When a discriminant analysis is run using a computer program such as SPSS, there is another option for validation, especially when a small sample is involved. The *leave-one-out* procedure operates by having each case (or observation) classified into a group according to classification functions computed from all the data except the case being classified (SPSS, 2002).

While we do not deal specifically with the classification of cases other than those from which the discriminant function is developed, it should be recognized that once the discriminant function is developed and validated for the population it may be used to classify other groups within the population.

Testing Statistical Significance

While the discriminant function perfectly classifies the ten cases of the calibration sample in our cereal likes and dislikes illustration, we still have not tested whether the group centroids differ significantly. This is analogous to testing for the significance of R^2 in multiple regression. Tests of the equality of group centroids can also proceed on the basis of an F-ratio that, in turn, is calculated from a variability measure known as *Mahalanobis squared distance*. We do not delve into the technical details of Mahalanobis squared distance, other than to say that it is like ordinary (Euclidian) squared distance that is computed between two centroids in a space with correlated axes and different measurement units.

Two other measures are widely used for testing overall statistical significance related to a discriminant function. The *canonical correlation coefficient* is a measure of the association that summarizes how related the discriminant function is to the groups. We discuss canonical correlation analysis later in this chapter. An indirect, and most widely used, approach to test for the statistical significance of the discriminant function examines the ability of the variables to discriminate among the group beyond the information that has been extracted by the previously computed functions. This is known as *residual discrimination,* and is measured by the statistic *Wilks' lambda* (also called the *U*-statistic). Wilks' lambda is a multivariate measure of group differences over discriminating variables and can be calculated in several ways. In general, it is calculated such that values of lambda near zero indicate high discrimination, and when it equals its maximum value of 1.0 the group centroids are equal and there is no discrimination (Klecka, 1980).

The statistical significance of a discriminant analysis merely provides answers to assorted questions:

- Is there a relationship?
- Do the predictor variables discriminate among the groups?
- Does this particular discriminant function contribute to the relationship?

Statistical significance says nothing about *how strong* a relationship is, *how much* difference exists between the groups, or to *what extent* a function contributes to overall discrimination. Moreover, tests of statistical significance are sensitive to sample size. For example, with a large sample size it is not difficult to get a significant *F*-ratio, even though classification accuracy is poor. Finally, there is a need to go beyond statistical significance and test for the *practical* (or substantive) significance. There is no single index of practical significance that is widely accepted.

Relative Importance of Predictor Variables

Because the original variables X_1 and X_2 were expressed in different units and display different standard deviations as well, the analyst generally *standardizes* the discriminant weights before examining their relative importance. A simple standardization procedure multiplies each discriminant weight (unstandardized) by the *total sample standard deviation* of that variable:

$$dj^{s(\omega)} = d_j \sigma_j$$

Standardized coefficients allow only an ordinal interpretation of variable importance. These coefficients are not appropriate to assess the relative discriminatory power of the variables included in the analysis. Mosteller and Wallace (1963) offer an appropriate measure of relative discriminating power:

$$I_j = \left| d_j (\bar{X}_{j1} - \bar{X}_{j2}) \right|$$

where

I_j = the importance value of the *j*th variable

d_j = unstandardized discriminant coefficient for the *j*th variable

X_{jk} = mean of the *j*th variable for the *k*th group

The relative importance weights may be interpreted as the portion of the discriminant score separation between the groups that is attributable to the *j*th variable. Since a relative importance value shows the value of a particular variable relative to the sum of the importance values of all variables, the relative importance of a variable (*Rj*) is given by Aw and Waters (1974):

$$R_j = \frac{I_j}{\sum_{j=1}^{n} I_j}$$

The end result of using this procedure is shown in Table 18.7, which is taken from a study of teenage smoking designed to see if consumption values (as represented by underlying

Table 18.7   Relative Importance of Consumption Values for Teenage Smokers and Nonsmokers

Variables (Factors)	Standardized Coefficients	Unstandardized Coefficients (k_j)	Have Smoked Mean (X_1)	Never Smoked Mean (X_2)	$[k_j(X_{ji}-X_{j2})]$ (I_j)	Relative Importance Weight (R_j)
1	−0.298	−0.299	−0.0989	0.0908	0.0567	7.9%
2	−0.091	0.091	0.0301	0.0277	0.0053	0.7%
3	0.832	0.864	0.2861	0.2627	0.4741	66.4%
4	0.344	0.345	0.1144	−0.1050	0.0757	10.6%
5	0.364	0.366	0.1211	−0.1112	0.0850	11.9%
6	−0.018	−0.018	−0.0061	0.0056	0.0002	0.0%
7	−0.004	−0.004	−0.0014	0.0013	0.0000	0.0%
8	−0.007	−0.007	−0.0023	0.0021	0.0000	0.0%
9	0.161	0.161	0.0533	−0.0490	0.0165	2.3%
					0.7135	100.0%

Correctly Classified 60.2% (cross-validated grouped cases); C_{pro} − 51.8%
Wilk's Lambda − .886 (prob. < .01)
Canonical Correlation − .337

SOURCE: Albaum, Baker, Hozier, and Rogers, 2002, p. 68.

factors from a factor analysis) could discriminate between those who had smoked and those who had never smoked (Albaum, Baker, Hozier, & Rogers, 2002).

As these data show, although nine variables were included in the discriminant function, slightly more than 88 percent of the total discrimination was accounted for by only three variables.

Determining relative importance of the predictor variables in discriminant analysis becomes increasingly difficult when more than two groups are involved. Although various coefficients and indices can be determined, interpretation becomes critical since more than one discriminant function may be involved.

Multiple Discriminant Analysis

All of the preceding discussion regarding objectives and assumption structure applies to multiple discriminant analysis as well. Accordingly, discussion of this section will be comparatively brief. What primarily distinguishes *multiple discriminant analysis* from the two-group case is that *more than one* discriminant function may be computed. For example, if we have three groups we can compute, in general, two nonredundant discriminant functions (as long as we also have at least two predictor variables). In general, with G groups and m predictors we can find up to the lesser of $G − 1$, or m, discriminant functions.

Not all the discriminant functions may be statistically significant, however. Moreover, it turns out to be a characteristic of multiple discriminant analysis that the first function accounts for the highest proportion of the among-to within-groups variability; the second function, the next highest; and so on. Accordingly, we may want to consider only the first few functions, particularly when the input data are rather noisy or unreliable to begin with. There remains the problem of interpretation of the functions.

Multiple discriminant analysis is considerably more detailed than might be surmised by this brief overview. Interested readers should consult more extensive and advanced discussions of the topic such as Johnson and Wichen (2002), Hair, Tatham, Anderson, and Black (1998), and Stevens (1996).

OTHER CRITERION-PREDICTOR ASSOCIATION MULTIVARIATE TECHNIQUES

Chi-Square Automatic Interaction Detection (CHAID)

One of today's key tools in database management and data mining is CHAID. This tool allows the researcher to explore relationships where both the number of respondents and the number of variables is very large. Inherent in these relationships, and in the resulting predictive models, is the phenomenon of interaction in which the response to changes in the level of one predictor variable depends on the level of some other predictor (or predictors). When interaction effects exist, the simple additive property of individual predictor-variable contributions to changes in the criterion no longer holds.

The major problem is that when mining data using exploratory analyses of observational and survey data, one does not ordinarily know *which* predictors are interactive (and how they interact). CHAID is insensitive to various forms of interaction.

CHAID is a sequential merging routine that merges nonsignificant predictor variable categories by analyzing a series of two-way cross-tabulations of the predictor and dependent variable.

While the predictor variables might originally be (a) nominal-, (b) ordinal-, or (c) interval-scaled, these predictors are *all* recorded into categorical (nominal-scaled) variables with one of two characteristics:

1. Order across classes can be disregarded

2. Order across classes can be retained

For example, if one of the original predictors is employment status (white-collar, blue-collar, unemployed) one may wish to treat this variable as an unordered polytomy. Some other variable such as age may be recorded into 18–20; 21–23; 24–26 years, and so forth. In this case one would probably wish to maintain order across classes. Each predictor variable can be designated by the researcher as unordered or ordered, independently of the rest.

It has been suggested that the primary goals of CHAID are segmentation analysis and an exploration of the relationships between variables. CHAID is often an appropriate technique in the following circumstances:

- We do not want to make strong assumptions about relationships.
- There are more than just a few potential explanatory variables.
- There are a large number of observations.

CHAID also offers a variety of uses:

- Identification of demographic variables that discriminate and predict the dependent variable category, such as heavy users
- Identification of interaction effects for further analysis, such as logistic regression
- Data mining to find significance among the hundreds of possible crosstabulation combinations
- Identification of predictor variables that contribute little to explaining the dependent variable

Basically, CHAID performs a series of contingency table analyses of the data (similar in spirit to the bivariate cross-tabulation analyses discussed in Chapter 16). After splitting the initial sample on the basis of the "best" predictor, the process is repeated on each of the two subsamples, and so on. At each step of the sequential splitting and merging process, CHAID looks for the best *available* split, not the best set of some number of final groups. The main result of this is a tree structure that shows three statistics at each stage:

1. The predictor variable leading to the best binary split and how that predictor *is* split
2. The number of persons assigned to each of the two subgroups
3. The criterion-variable splits on each of the two subgroups

An Example of CHAID

Advertising executives have conducted research to identify profitable segments for a sweepstakes promotion.

Profit levels associated with responses are found to be $35 when the respondent pays for a subscription; −$7 when a respondent does not subscribe, but receives an introductory issue and follow-up sales materials; −$.15 for nonrespondents for mailing costs.

Of particular interest is the extent to which a respondent is profitable. That is, when asked to consider the subscription to magazines through the associated sweepstakes plan, which market segments are most likely to subscribe?

A large database ($n = 81{,}040$) was available that contained information about their response to the sweepstakes offer and known information about eight different demographic and credit card ownership predictors. All respondents had recently received a sweepstakes offer and had a known response that was recorded in the criterion variable to indicate that he or she was a subscriber (coded "Paid Respondent"), respondent-nonsubscriber (coded "Unpaid Respondent"), or a "nonrespondent."

CHAID was applied to this large data bank, and the results are shown in the tree diagram of Figure 18.7. At the top of the diagram we note that the total-sample probability of being a subscriber is 0.0059. That is, 478 out of the total of 81,040 recipients of the sweepstakes offer paid for a subscription. The first variable on which the total sample is split involves the size of the respondent's household, followed by age, income, and presence of a bankcard in the household.

Figure 18.8 shows a summary map of the CHAID tree that is numbered by the split order. These splits are detailed in Table 18.8, the gain summary, that shows the key segments for sweepstakes profitability based on the measure of profitability gain.

We observe that Node 8 provides the most gain (profitability) and is defined by the predictor variables as a two-person household, headed by an individual aged 55–64 with

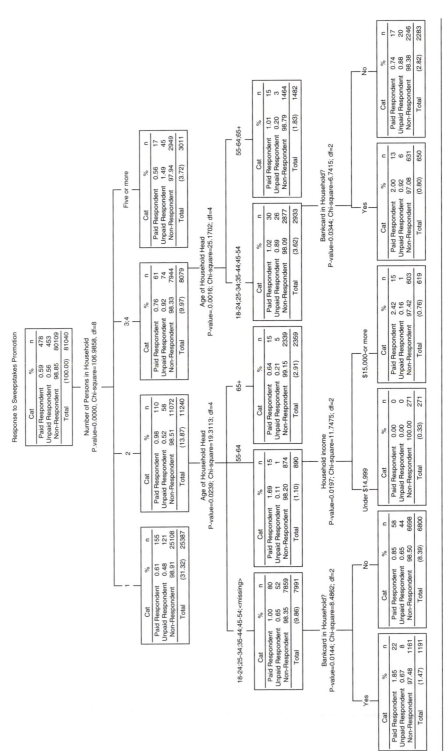

Figure 18.7 CHAID Sweepstakes Tree

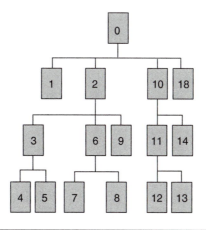

Figure 18.8   CHAID Tree Summary Map

Table 18.8   CHAID Gain

Gain Summary

Target variable: Response to Sweepstakes Promotion

	Node-by-Node				Cumulative			
Node	Node: n	Node: %	Gain	Index (%)	Node: n	Node: %	Gain	Index (%)
8	619	0.76	0.69	3628.50972	619	0.76	0.69	3628.50972
12	650	0.80	0.49	2572.90367	1269	1.57	0.59	3087.81316
4	1191	1.47	0.45	2381.18629	2460	3.04	0.52	2745.70235
14	1482	1.83	0.19	1008.12275	3942	4.86	0.40	2092.45705
5	6800	8.390	0.11	554.14567	10742	13.26	0.21	1118.66098
9	2359	2.91	0.06	309.87554	13101	16.17	0.19	973.02898
13	2283	2.82	0.05	271.75404	15384	18.98	0.17	868.95912
1	25384	31.32	0.03	168.00454	40768	50.31	0.08	432.51311
18	3011	3.72	−0.05	−283.25238	79938	98.64	0.02	115.27446
7	271	0.33	−0.15	−787.99468	80209	98.97	0.02	112.22261

income of $15,000 or more. If we were to label this profile, it is the classic "empty-nester" whose children are no longer at home and now has a little extra money and time for their own pursuits, one of which is reading.

Node 12 is a 3–4 person household with a young to middle-age head of household who holds a bankcard.

The process of identifying profitable segments continues until we observe that Nodes 18 and 7 offer a negative gain (meaning they are unprofitable). We conclude that we should not target the large family segment having five or more family members (Node 18), or the poor empty-nester segment that is identical to our most profitable segment (Node 8), except without the income base.

The upshot of all of this is that by data mining with CHAID, we can identify 50.31 percent of our database that promises to be profitable and another 49.69 percent (39,441 individuals) that may be unprofitable. We further observe that the average gain (profit) drops from 0.17 to 0.08 with the inclusion of Node 1, which has an average gain of 0.03 per person for that segment. The successive targeting of the next most profitable segment can do much to maximize profits, as can eliminating the negative gain segments. Simply refining the database by deleting nonconforming profiles often does much to improve profitability of the marketing effort.

In short, this kind of information underscores the importance of certain types of demographic variables in this case, and leads to a more detailed understanding of the kinds of segments that responded by subscribing to this sweepstakes magazine offer.

While other summary statistics (e.g., probabilities, chi-square) can also be shown, the above outputs represent the principal ones. It should be emphasized that a basic assumption underlying the application of CHAID is that variables useful in explaining one part of the database are not necessarily those most effective for explaining another part.

A few other key considerations, in the nature of restrictions or criteria for the stopping of the splitting sequence, enter into the actual application of CHAID:

1. All partitionings of the sample may be subject to a requirement that the proportionate reduction in the criterion-variable probability exceed some level (specified by the researcher). This is to guard against partitionings that do not appreciably reduce variation in the criterion variable.

2. To qualify for further splitting, a group must have a probability greater than some level (again specified by the researcher). This is to guard against splits that, pragmatically speaking, are not worth the effort (for example, where the group is already quite homogeneous).

3. In addition to the control parameters above, the researcher may place an upper limit on the total number of groups formed and/or the minimum number of persons (or objects) in each group.

A few caveats regarding the application of CHAID should be mentioned at this point. First, CHAID is generally designed for really large samples, on the order of 1,000 or more. Since many versions of CHAID will take many predictors, the program has ample opportunity to capitalize on chance variation in the data. Moreover, no statistical inferential apparatus is associated with the approach. This suggests the value of cross-validating results on new data or, possibly, double cross-validating by applying CHAID to separate halves of the sample.

Second, CHAID, being a sequential search procedure, does not specify an explicit model in the way, for example, that Discriminant Analysis does. In this regard it is often useful to use CHAID as an initial screening device to find those predictors that appear to be most prominent in accounting for criterion dependence. This can then be followed by the formulation of an explicit logit regression model that includes main effect and interaction terms of specific interest to the research. The joint use of CHAID with other statistical techniques, such as CART models (classification and regression trees), provides additional useful features for exploratory data analysis.

Third, despite the explicit concern for interaction, CHAID is found to be insensitive to various forms of interaction. Since CHAID only examines the immediate effect of a predictor as a two-way table and not future possible splits, any interactions that are not one-stage will not be identified.

One of the nice characteristics of CHAID is its simplicity of output, which facilitates an ease of understanding by researchers and managers alike. The output takes the form of a tree diagram, in which one can follow the result of each split as it takes place. This is illustrated in the brief case study analyzed using the SPSS program *AnswerTree,* a suite of programs that includes CHAID and CART models. The data is that supplied by Magidson (1993) in the original SPSS CHAID 6.0 program. *AnswerTree* is compatible with SPSS and all current Windows operating systems.

Canonical Correlation

Canonical correlation is a generalization of multiple correlation to two or more criterion variables.

To illustrate the technique of canonical correlation, let us consider a radial tire study which has three main predictor variables:

X_1: General interest in the product class of steel-belted radials

X_2: Whether the firm's old brand was chosen as the respondent's last purchase of replacement tires

X_3: Pre-exposure (before seeing the commercials) interest in the firms' new brand of steel-belted radials

Now let us assume that *two* criterion variables are involved:

Y_1: Believability of the claims made in the firm's new TV commercial;

Y_2: Post-exposure interest in the claims made in the firm's new brand (as before).

What we would like to find out is how highly correlated the *battery* of two criterion variables is with the *battery* of three predictors. Moreover, we would like to find a linear composite of the *Y*-variable set and a (different) linear composite of the *X*-variable set that will produce a maximal correlation.

This is what canonical correlation is all about. Canonical correlation deals with (a) both description and statistical inference of (b) a data matrix partitioned into at least two predictors where (c) all variables are interval-scaled and (d) the relationships are assumed to be linear. Thompson (1984, p. 10) notes that, in more general terms, canonical correlation analysis can be used to investigate the following research questions:

- To what extent can one set of two or more variables be predicted or explained by another set of two or more variables?
- What contribution does a single variable make to the explanatory power of the set of variables to which the variable belongs?
- To what extent does a single variable contribute to predicting or explaining the composite of the variables in the variable set to which the variable does not belong?
- What different dynamics are involved in the ability of one variable set to explain, in different ways, different portions of the other variable set?
- What relative power do different canonical functions have to predict or explain relationships?
- How stable are canonical results across samples or sample subgroups?
- How closely do obtained canonical result conform to expected canonical results?

Table 18.9 shows the results of the radial tire problem. In general, with p criteria and q predictors, one can obtain more than a single pair of linear composites—up to a maximum of the smaller of p and q. Thus, in our case we would obtain two pairs of linear composites, uncorrelated across pairs, with the first pair exhibiting maximum correlation. In general, the canonical correlation of successive pairs decreases; that is, the first pair displays the highest correlation, the second pair the next highest, and so on. All composites are mutually uncorrelated *across* pairs. However, as it turned out, only the first pair of linear composites was statistically significant at the 0.05 alpha level; hence, only this pair of weights is shown.

Table 18.9 shows that the canonical correlation between the two batteries is 0.582. As is the case with multiple correlations, this measure varies between zero (no correlation) and one (perfect correlation). Since *mutual* association between the pair of batteries is involved, we can say that the pair of linear composites account for $(0.582)^2$, or 34 percent of the shared variation between the two batteries.

The canonical weights for the criterion set show that Y_2 (post-exposure interest) is the dominant variable in the criterion set; its canonical weight is 1.069. The dominant variable in the predictor set is X_3; its weight is 0.817. Since all variables are standardized to zero mean and unit standard deviation *before* the analysis, the weights are already in standardized form.

Table 18.9 really says that if we formed a linear composite of the criterion variables using the canonical weights:

$$T_c = -0.110Y_{s1} + 1.069Y_{s2}$$

and another linear composite of the predictors, using the canonical weights:

$$T_p = 0.346X_{s1} + 0.141X_{s2} + 0.817X_{s3}$$

and took these two columns of numbers (the canonical scores) and correlated them, the result would be a simple correlation of 0.582 (the canonical correlation).

Table 18.9   Result of Canonical Correlation

	Canonical weights	*Structure correlations*
Criterion set		
Y_1	−0.110	0.594
Y_2	1.069	0.997
Predictor set		
X_1	0.346	0.539
X_2	0.141	0.382
X_3	0.817	0.930
Canonical correlation	0.582	

Input Correlations for Canonical Analysis

	Y_1	Y_2	X_1	X_2	X_3
Y_1	1.000				
Y_2	0.659	1.000			
X_1	0.202	0.315	1.000		
X_2	0.097	0.218	0.086	1.000	
X_3	0.321	0.539	0.226	0.258	1.000

The structure correlations are also shown in Table 18.9. These are the simple correlations of each original variable with the canonical scores of its own battery's linear composite. Again we note that Y_2 is the most important variable (structure correlation of 0.997) in the criterion set and X_3 the most important variable (structure correlation of 0.930) in the predictor set. Indeed, as noted in the input correlation matrix, the *simple* correlation between Y_2 and X_3 is 0.539, almost as high as the correlation between the full batteries.

Since this is a rather sophisticated technique, we refer the reader to other sources for further discussion of the procedure, such as Thompson (1984) and Levine (1977).

Correspondence Analysis

Correspondence analysis can be viewed as a special case of canonical correlation analysis that is analogous to a principal components factor analysis (discussed in Chapter 19) for nominal data. Canonical correlation, as we have just seen, examines the relations between two sets of continuous variables; correspondence analysis examines the relations between the *categories of two discrete variables*. Correspondence analysis can be applied to many forms of contingency table data, including frequency counts, associative data (pick k of n), or dummy variables. This analysis develops ratio-scaled interpoint distances between the row and column categories that depict accurate and useful positioning maps.

Correspondence analysis is often used in positioning and image studies where the researcher wants to explore the relationships between brands, between attributes, and between brands and attributes. In strategic terms, the marketing researcher may want to identify (a) closely competitive brands, (b) important attributes, (c) how attributes cluster together, (d) a brand's competitive strengths, and most importantly (e) ideas for improving a brand's competitive position (Whitlark & Smith, 2001).

According to Clausen (1998, p. 1), the main purpose of correspondence analysis is twofold:

1. Reveal the relationships in a complex set of variables by replacing the data with a simpler data matrix without losing essential information.

2. Visually display the points in space. This helps interpretation.

Correspondence analysis analyzes the association between two or more categorical variables and represents the categories of the categorical marketing research data with a two- or three-dimensional map.

This amounts to a special type of cross-tabulation analysis of contingency tables. Categories with similar distributions will be placed in close proximity to each other, while those with dissimilar distributions will be farther apart. The technique is capable of handling large contingency tables.

An example from Whitlark and Smith (2004) will be used to illustrate this technique. When administering long and complicated surveys, sometimes it is impractical to collect attribute ratings for all brands and products. In this situation, researchers will often give respondents a list of attributes and ask them to check off the ones they feel best describe a particular brand. This type of question produces "pick k of n" associative data, where k represents the number of attributes a respondent associates with a brand and n represents the total number of descriptive attributes included in the survey.

The correspondence analysis map shown in Figure 18.9 describes 12 companies providing communications, logistics consulting, and software support to a group of international freight handlers and shippers. Three well-known companies in the United States—Oracle, Nokia, and FedEx—are labeled using their names, and a series of less-familiar companies are labeled using letters of the alphabet. The 12 companies were evaluated by nearly 800 freight handlers, who indicated which attributes (pick k of n) best described the companies. The two-dimensional map of the companies accounts for nearly 90 percent of the variance in the data.

The results of this analysis show that Oracle and Nokia are perceived as being the most innovative and as industry leaders, while FedEx offers a relevant and total solution.

A more detailed explanation of this technique will be found in the excellent works by Clausen (1998), Greenacre (1993), and Carroll, Green, and Schaffer (1986; 1987).

Probit and Logit

At the beginning of this chapter we emphasized that multiple regression is a useful technique for estimating a dependent variable from a set of independent variables. A major assumption of standard regression analysis is that the dependent variable is continuous and at least interval-scaled. When the dependent variable is dichotomous, binary regression can be used.

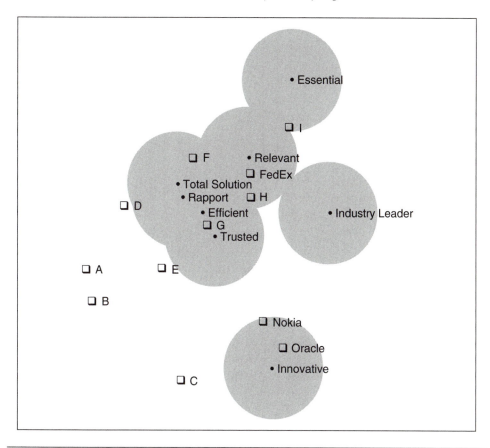

Figure 18.9 Correspondence Analysis of Providers of Logistical Services

What can the researcher do when the problem requires estimating relationships where the dependent variables that are nonmetric (i.e., nominal- or ordinal-scaled)? When regression analysis is misapplied, we often see results with an unnecessarily high proportion of unexplained variance (i.e., a lower R^2), misleading estimates of the effects of the predictor variables, and an inability to make statements about the probability of given responses. To overcome these problems, *probit* and *logit* have been developed.

Probit and logit deal with the same type of problem as regression, the problem of predicting a dependent variable that is nominal- or ordinal-scaled. They differ solely in the assumption made about the frequency distribution of the response:

- In probit, the response is assumed to be normally distributed.
- In logit, a logistic distribution is assumed.

Reported research about marketing applications seems to indicate that logit is the favored technique of the two (Malhotra, 1984).

Explanations of how these techniques work and the underlying theories behind them tend to be technical. For a more detailed explanation we refer the reader to the references already cited and to the excellent works of Aldrich and Nelson (1984), Liao (1994), and Menard (2001).

Path Analysis/Causal Modeling

In recent years, marketing researchers have become increasingly interested in the useful application of path analysis and structural equation modeling as an approach to *causal modeling*. Causal modeling provides the researcher with a systematic methodology for developing and testing theories in marketing. From all this interest has emerged the development of *structural equation modeling procedures*. These procedures blend two basic techniques:

- Factor analysis
- Simultaneous equation regression

Both of these techniques use multiple measures and simultaneous equation models to estimate the path of causation.

The essence of what happens with this type of analysis can be seen from a simple illustration. In Figure 18.10 we show a system with four unobservable constructs, each of which has more than one observable measure. In some situations the measures themselves may be correlated, which precludes finding a strong reliability from either simple indices or regressions that relate the indices themselves as means of showing relations between the unobserved constructs.

To overcome this problem and better estimate the relevant parameters, some rather complicated procedures have been developed which estimate both between the constructs (b_{ij}) and

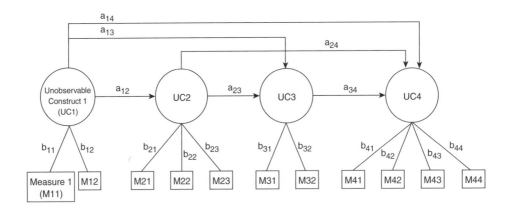

Figure 18.10 Hypothetical Causal Structure

SOURCE: From Albaum, G., Baker, K., Hozier, G., and Rogers, R., "Smoking Behavior, Information Sources, and Other Intervention Activities," in *Journal of Consumer Affairs*, 36/1:68. Copyright © 2002. Reprinted by permission of the University of Wisconsin Press.

their measures and the links between the constructs themselves (a_{ij}) simultaneously. One widely used technique to estimate these parameters is LISREL (structural equation software). Another technique is PLS (partial least squares). A third technique, from SPSS, is AMOS (structural equation and path analysis software). These techniques, and structural equation modeling in general, are highly technical methods of analyses and are recommended only for experienced users.

SUMMARY

Chapter 18 focused on a number of multivariate techniques. Our discussions of multiple regression and discriminant analysis have been more detailed than the descriptions of other techniques. We have deliberately focused on those techniques that are most often used in market research.

We started the chapter with a discussion of multiple regression and described such measures as regression coefficients, the coefficient of determination, and the product-moment coefficient.

Next we discussed discriminant analysis, one of the most widely used criterion-predictor methods. We described a sample problem and solved it numerically. Discriminant analysis was also discussed as a tool for prediction and classification.

This chapter concluded with a brief introduction to some less well-known techniques for analyzing between-set dependence: CHAID, canonical analysis, correspondence analysis, and probit and logit analysis. At this point, it might appear that an almost bewildering array of techniques has been paraded before the reader.

We have tried to discuss the principal assumption structure of each technique, appropriate problems for applying it, and sufficient numerical applications to give the reader a feel for the kind of output generated by each program. Further discussion of the use of multivariate analysis in marketing can be found in Aaker (1981).

Our coverage of so vast and complex a set of methods is limited in depth as well as breadth. The fact remains, however, that marketing researchers of the future will have to seek grounding in multivariate methodology, if current research trends are any indication. This grounding will probably embrace three facets: (a) theoretical understanding of the techniques; (b) knowledge of the details of appropriate computer algorithms to implement the techniques; and (c) a grasp of the characteristics of substantive problems in marketing that are relevant for each of the methods. Fortunately, analysis packages such as SPSS have programs for using these techniques.

ASSIGNMENT MATERIAL

1. A sample survey by the crane Pool Company of home swimming pool owners in southeastern Pennsylvania yielded the following information regarding pool costs versus annual income.

Respondent	Pool Cost, Y (thousands of dollars)	Size of lot, X_1 (thousands of square feet)	Annual income, X_2 (thousands of dollars)
1	3.6	30.2	9.3
2	4.8	40.1	10.2
3	2.4	35.3	9.7
4	7.2	45.1	11.5
5	6.9	38.0	12.0
6	8.4	50.1	14.2
7	10.7	60.2	18.6
8	11.2	100.4	28.4
9	6.1	25.1	13.2
10	7.9	40.7	10.8
11	9.5	68.4	22.7
12	5.4	60.3	12.3

    a. Using least squares, compute a linear regression of Y on X_1 and X_2. How do you interpret the formula?

    b. If you were told that a pool owner had an income of $37, 500 annually and a lot size of 40,000 square feet, what pool cost would you predict?

    c. Compute the coefficient of multiple determination R^2. Interpret this measure.

    d. What applications would you suggest for the regression formula if you were employed by a Pennsylvania swimming pool builder?

2. Apply a stepwise regression program to a data set of your choice:

    a. Using the program's default values on variable inclusion and retention, run the analysis on the whole data set.

    b. Next, split the data into halves by taking odd-numbered and even-numbered cases. Perform separate regression. How do these split-half results compare with those obtained form the full sample?

3. Using the same data set as in Question 2 above, do the same types of analyses but use and all-variable program. what can you conclude about the results from stepwise and all-variables programs?

4. In what ways can multiple regression be use to forecast an industry's sales? A specific company's sales?

5. Assume that the Crane Pool Company has assembled income and lot size data on a group of pool and nonpool owners living in southeastern Pennsylvania. In addition, data are available for each group on attitudes toward sun bathing, scaled from 0— "detest sun bathing," to 10— "extremely fond of sun bathing." The data are summarized below.

Pool Owner	Annual Income (Thousands of Dollars)	Lot Size (Thousands of Square Feet)	Attitudinal Measure
1	45	30.2	8
2	50	40.1	10
3	50	35.3	6
4	60	45.1	4
5	60	38.0	5
6	70	50.1	9
7	95	60.2	10
8	140	100.4	3
9	65	25.1	2
10	55	40.7	7
11	115	68.4	9
12	60	60.3	8

Non-Pool Owner	Annual Income (Thousands of Dollars)	Lot Size (Thousands of Square Feet)	Attitudinal Measure
1	40	30.2	2
2	40	40.2	0
3	55	44.8	1
4	80	50.6	4
5	60	42.5	8
6	60	60.3	0
7	35	39.7	6
8	50	35.4	4
9	70	42.6	3
10	60	38.4	2
11	40	30.2	4
12	45	25.7	5

a. Compute a two-group linear discriminant function using annual income, lot size, and attitude toward sun bathing as predictor variables.

b. How might the pool builder use the results of the function computed in part (a)?

c. Using the function computed in part (a), assign each of the 24 respondents to the class "pool owner" or "non-pool owner." Compare your answer with the known assignment. What is the percentage of correct classifications?

d. The marketing researcher has received the following information about a new respondent not included in the original sample:
   1) Annual income: $60,000
   2) Lot size: 42,000 square feet
   3) Attitude toward sun bathing: "8"
   4) Using the discriminant function, to what class would the respondent be assigned?

6. The credit firm of Schifer and Carmane has expressed interest in the possible use of discriminant analysis in the preliminary screening of credit applications. From past records the company has assembled information on three classes of married credit grantees: (a) poor risks, (b) equivocal risks, and (c) good risks. Additional information about a sample of credit grantees has also been obtained:

Poor Risk	Annual Income (Thousands of Dollars)	Number of Credit Cards	Age	Number of Children
1	45	2	27	3
2	55	3	24	0
3	45	1	32	2
4	55	1	29	4
5	50	2	31	3
6	55	4	29	1
7	45	3	28	1
8	45	0	31	5
9	50	5	26	2
10	55	4	30	3

Equivocal Risk	Annual Income (Thousands of Dollars)	Number of Credit Cards	Age	Number of Children
1	70	4	34	4
2	75	7	33	2
3	70	3	41	1
4	50	1	37	1
5	75	6	39	0
6	80	5	37	3
7	80	4	36	5
8	55	2	35	3
9	65	8	36	2
10	75	3	29	4

Good Risk	Annual Income (Thousands of Dollars)	Number of Credit Cards	Age	Number of Children
1	95	7	42	3
2	90	6	47	5
3	115	4	41	1
4	120	5	39	0
5	95	1	42	2

(Continued)

6	70	12	46	3
7	65	8	42	4
8	110	7	48	2
9	130	5	37	3
10	95	9	51	1

    a. Compute linear discriminant functions for a three-way analysis.

    b. Which variables appear to discriminate best among the three groups?

    c. Criticize the manner in which data were obtained for the three-way discriminant analysis.

7. Describe how a researcher might use automatic interaction detection to single out the best prospects for a firm specializing in selling classical records by mail.

    a. What criterion variable would you use?

    b. What predictor variables appear to be good candidates?

    c. How could the CHAID results be used as a preliminary approach to either multiple regression or two-group discriminant analysis.

8. Search the marketing research literature for individual applications of *canonical correlation, correspondence analysis, probit,* and *logit.*

    a. Why did each author use one of these techniques rather than multiple regression or analysis of variance and covariance?

    b. Describe other ways that the problem could have been handled.

9. Discuss the similarities and differences among multiple regression, discriminant analysis, and canonical correlation in terms of (a) assumption structure and (b) objectives of the techniques.

REFERENCES

Aaker, D. A. (1981). Multivariate analysis in marketing. In *Multivariate analysis in marketing* (2nd ed.). Palo Alto, CA: Scientific Press.

Albaum, G., Baker, K. G., Hozier, G. C., Jr., & Rogers, R. D. (2002). Smoking behavior, information sources, and consumption values of teenagers: Implications for public policy and other invention failures. *Journal of Consumer Affairs, 36*(1), 50–76.

Aldrich, J. H., & Nelson, F. D. (1984). *Linear probability, logit, and probit models.* Beverly Hills, CA: Sage.

Aw, R. W., & Waters, D. (1974). A discriminant analysis of economic, demographic, and attitudinal characteristics of bank charge-card customers. *Journal of Finance, 29,* 973–980.

Bagozzi, R. (1980). *Causal models in marketing.* New York: Wiley.

Berk, K. N., & Carey, P. (2000). *Data analysis with Microsoft Excel.* Pacific Grove, CA: Duxbury Press.

Blalock, H. M., Jr. (1962). *Causal inferences in nonexperimental research.* Chapel Hill: University of North Carolina Press.

Carroll, J. D., Green, P. E., & Schaffer, C. M. (1987). Comparing interpoint distances in correspondence analysis. *Journal of Marketing Research, 24,* 445–450.

Carroll, J. D., Green, P. E., & Schaffer, C. M. (1986). Interpoint distance comparisons in correspondence analysis. *Journal of Marketing Research, 23,* 271–280.

Clausen, S. E. (1998). *Applied correspondence analysis: An introduction.* Thousand Oaks, CA: Sage.

Crask, M. R., & Perrault, W. D., Jr. (1979, February). Validation of discriminant analysis in marketing research. *Journal of Marketing Research, 14,* 60–68.

Curtis, M. E. (1990, September 3). Avoid hazards of stepwise regression. *Marketing News, 24,* 26.

Frank, R. E., Massy, W. F., & Morrison, D. G. (1965, August). Bias in multiple discriminant analysis. *Journal of Marketing Research, 2,* 250–258.

Green, P. E., Tull, D. S., & Albaum, G. (1988). *Research for marketing decisions* (5th ed.). Englewood Cliffs, NJ: Prentice Hall.

Greenacre, M. J. (1993). *Correspondence analysis in practice.* London: Academic Press.

Hair, J. F., Tatham, R. L., Anderson, R. E., & Black, W. (1998). *Multivariate data analysis* (5th ed.). Upper Saddle River, NJ: Prentice Hall.

Johnson, R. A., & Wichen, D. W. (2002). *Applied multivariate statistical analysis* (5th ed.). Upper Saddle River, NJ: Prentice Hall.

Klecka, W. R. (1980). *Discriminant analysis.* Beverly Hills, CA: Sage.

Lachenbruch, P. A. (1975). *Discriminant analysis.* New York: Hafner Press.

Levine, M. S. (1977). *Canonical analysis and factor comparison.* Beverly Hills, CA: Sage.

Liao, T. F. (1994). *Interpreting probability models: Logit, probit, and other generalized linear models.* Thousand Oaks, CA: Sage.

Magidson, J., & SPSS, Inc. (1993). *SPSS for Windows CHAID Release 6.0.* Chicago: SPSS, Inc.

Malhotra, N. K. (1984, February). The use of linear logit models in marketing. *Journal of Marketing Research, 21,* 20–31.

Menard, S. (2001). *Applied logistic regression analysis* (2nd ed.). Thousand Oaks, CA: Sage.

Monroe, K. B., & Petroshius, S. M. (n.d.). *Developing causal priorities in marketing.* Working Paper, Virginia Polytechnic Institute and State University, Blacksburg, VA.

Morrison, D. G. (1969, May). On the interpretation of discriminant analysis. *Journal of Marketing Research, 6,* 156–163.

Mosteller, F., & Wallace, D. L. (1963, June). Influence in an authorship problem. *Journal of the American Statistical Association, 55,* 275–309.

Smith, S. M. (2004). *A note on the interpretation and analysis of the linear discriminant model for prediction and classification.* Retrieved May 18, 2004, from http://marketing.byu.edu/htmlpages/tutorials/discriminant.htm

SPSS. (2002). *Base 11.0 Application Guide.* Chicago: SPSS, Inc.

Steckel, J. H., & Vanhonacker, W. R. (1991). Cross-validating regression models in marketing research. (Working Paper # MARK-91-18.) Stern School of Business, New York University.

Stevens, J. (1996). *Applied multivariate statistics for the social sciences.* Mahwah, NJ: Lawrence Erlbaum.

Thompson, B. (1984). *Canonical correlation analysis: Uses and interpretations.* Beverly Hills, CA: Sage.

Whitlark, D., & Smith, S. (2001, Summer). Using correspondence analysis to map relationships: It's time to think strategically about positioning and image data. *Marketing Research, 2,* 23–27.

Whitlark, D., & Smith, S. (2004). *Measuring brand performance using online questionnaires: Advantages and issues with "pick any" data.* (Research Paper.) Provo, UT: Graduate School of Management, Brigham Young University.

Chapter 19

MULTIVARIATE ANALYSIS: FACTOR ANALYSIS, CLUSTERING METHODS, MULTIDIMENSIONAL SCALING, AND CONJOINT ANALYSIS

In this chapter we discuss two techniques that do not require data to be partitioned into criterion and predictor variables. Rather, it is the entire set of interdependent relationships that are of interest. We discuss factor analysis as a methodology that identifies the commonality existing in sets of variables. This methodology is useful to identify consumer lifestyle and personality types.

Continuing with analyses that do not partition the data, a second set of methods is effective in clustering respondents to identify market segments. The fundamentals of cluster analysis are described using examples of respondents and objects grouped because they have similar variable scores.

Third, we discuss two sets of multivariate techniques, multidimensional scaling and conjoint analysis, that are particularly well suited (and were originally developed) for measuring human perceptions and preferences. Multidimensional scaling methodology is closely related to factor analysis, conjoint analysis uses a variety of techniques (including analysis of variance designs and regression analysis) to estimate parameters, and both techniques are related to psychological scaling (discussed in Chapter 10). The use of both multidimensional scaling and conjoint analysis in marketing is widespread.

AN INTRODUCTION TO THE
BASIC CONCEPTS OF FACTOR ANALYSIS

Factor analysis is a generic name given to a class of techniques whose purpose often consists of data reduction and summarization. Used in this way, the objective is to represent a set of observed variables (or persons or occasions) in terms of a smaller number of hypothetical, underlying, and unknown dimensions called *factors*.

Factor analysis operates on the data matrix, the form of which can be modified to produce different types, or *modes*, of factor analysis. The most widely used modes of factor analysis by marketing researchers are the *R*-technique (relationships among items or variables are examined) and the *Q*-technique (persons or observations are examined). These, together with other modes, are identified in Exhibit 19.1. "Creative" marketing researchers may find *S*- and *T*-techniques helpful when analyzing purchasing behavior or advertising recall data. The *P*- and *O*-techniques might be appropriate for looking at the life cycle of a product class, or perhaps even changes in demographic characteristics of identified market segments.

EXHIBIT 19.1   Modes of Factor Analysis

Six distinct modes of factor analysis have been identified. Stewart (1981, p. 53) summarizes these in the following table:

Technique	Factors Are Loaded by	Indices of Association Are Computed Across	Data are Collected on
R	Variables	Persons	One occasion
Q	Persons	Variables	One occasion
S	Persons	Occasions	One variable
T	Occasions	Persons	One variable
P	Variables	Occasions	One person
O	Occasions	Variables	One person

The alternative modes of factor analysis can be portrayed graphically. The original data set is viewed as a *variables/persons/occasions* matrix (a). *R*-type and *Q*-type techniques deal with the variables/persons dichotomy (b). In contrast, *P*-type and *O*-type analyses are used for the occasions/variables situation and *S*-type and *T*-type are used when the occasions/persons relationship is of interest (c).

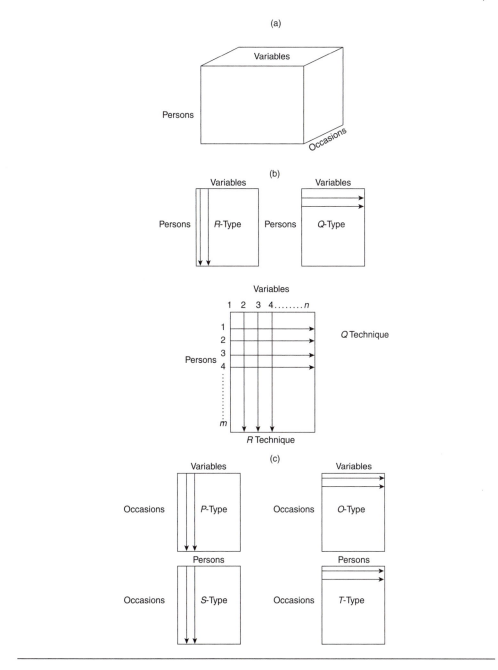

Factor analysis does *not* entail making predictions using criterion and predictor variables; rather, interest is centered on summarizing the relationships involving the *whole* set of variables. Factor analysis has three main qualities:

1. The analyst is interested in examining the strength of the overall association among variables, in the sense that a smaller set of factors (linear composites of the original variable) may be able to preserve most of the information in the full data set. Often one's interest will stress description of the data rather than statistical inference.

2. No attempt is made to divide the variables into criterion versus predictor sets.

3. The models typically assume that the data are interval-scaled.

The major substantive purpose of factor analysis is to search for (and sometimes test) structure in the form of constructs, or *dimensions,* assumed to underlie the measured variables. This search for structure is accomplished by literally partitioning the total variance associated with each variable into two components: (a) common factors and (b) unique factors. *Common factors* are the underlying structure that contributes to explaining two or more variables. In addition, however, each variable is usually influenced by unique individual characteristics not shared with other variables, and by external forces that are systematic (non-random) and not measured (possibly business environment variables). This non-common factor variance is called a *unique factor* and is specific to an individual variable. Graphically, this may appear as diagrammed in Figure 19.1, in which four variables are reduced to two factors that summarize the majority of the underlying structure, and four unique factors containing information unique to each variable alone.

The structure of the factors identified by the analysis will, of course, differ for each data set analyzed. In some applications the researcher may find that the variables are so highly correlated that a single factor results. In other applications the variables may exhibit low correlations and result in weak or ill-defined factors. In response to these eventualities, the researcher may measure and add additional variables to the factor analysis. The process of adding and eliminating variables is common in factor analysis when the objective of the analysis is to identify those variables most central to the construct and to produce results that are both valid and reliable. Behavioral and consumer researchers have employed these methods to develop measurement instruments such as personality profiles, lifestyle indexes, or measures of consumer shopping involvement. Thus, in addition to its role as a data reduction tool, factor analysis may be used for to develop behavioral measurement scales.

We use a numerical example to illustrate the basic ideas of factor analysis. A grocery chain was interested in the attitudes (in the form of images) that customers and potential customers had of their stores. A survey of 169 customers was conducted to assess images. Among the

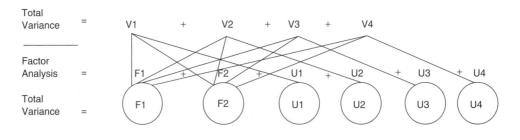

Figure 19.1   The Concept of Factor Analysis

Table 19.1   Bipolar Dimensions Used in Semantic Differential Scales for Grocery Chain Study

Inconvenient location—Convenient location
Low-quality products—High-quality products
Modern—Old-fashioned
Unfriendly clerks—Friendly clerks
Sophisticated customers—Unsophisticated customers
Cluttered—Spacious
Fast check-out—Slow check-out
Unorganized layout—Organized layout
Enjoyable shopping experience—Unenjoyable shopping experience
Bad reputation—Good reputation
Good service—Bad service
Unhelpful clerks—Helpful clerks
Good selection of products—Bad selection of products
Dull—Exciting

information obtained were ratings on 14 items that were scaled as seven-category semantic differential scales. These items are shown in Table 19.1. Thus, the resulting data set is a matrix of 169 rows (respondents) by 14 columns (semantic differential scales). These data will be analyzed as *R*-type factor analysis.

EXHIBIT 19.2   Some Concepts and Definitions of *R*-Type Factor Analysis

Factor Analysis:	A set of techniques for finding the number and characteristics of variables underlying a large number of measurements made on individuals or objects.
Factor:	A variable or construct that is not directly observable, but is developed as a linear combination of observed variables.
Factor Loading:	The correlation between a variable and a factor. It is computed by correlating factor scores with observed manifest variable scores.
Factor Score:	A value for each factor that is assigned to each person. It is derived from a summation of the derived weights applied to the original data variables.
Communality (h^2):	The common variance of each variable summarized by the factors, or the amount (percent) of each variable that is explained by the factors. The uniqueness component of a variable's variance is $1 - h^2$.
Eigenvalue:	The sum of squares of loadings of each factor. It is a measure of the variance of each factor, and if divided by the number of variables (i.e., the total variance), it is the percent of variance summarized by the factor.

IDENTIFYING THE FACTORS

If we now input the raw data into a factor analysis program (e.g., SPSS), correlations between the variables are computed, as is the analysis. Some relevant concepts and definitions for this type of analysis are presented in Exhibit 19.2.

A factor analysis of the 14 grocery-chain observed variables produces a smaller number of underlying dimensions (factors) that account for most of the variance. It may be helpful to characterize each of the 14 original variables as having an equal single unit of variance that is redistributed to 14 underlying dimensions or factors. In every factor analysis solution, the number of input variables equals the number of common and unique factors to which the variance is redistributed. Our task is first to determine how many of the 14 underlying dimensions or factors are common factors, and then to interpret the common factors.

Table 19.2 identifies the proportion of variance associated with the 14 factors produced by the analysis where the factors were extracted by Principal Component analysis. *Principal Components,* one of the alternative methods of factor analysis, is a method of factoring which results in a linear combination of observed variables possessing such properties as being orthogonal to each other (i.e., are independent of each other), and the first principal component represents the largest amount of variance in the data, the second representing the second largest, and so on. It is the most conservative method. For a more detailed discussion of the alternative methods, see Kim and Mueller (1978a, 1978b). In column two, the eigenvalues are reported. Computed as the sum of the squared correlations between the variables and a factor, the eigenvalues are a measure of the variance associated with the factor. The eigenvalues reported in Table 19.2 are a measure of the redistribution of the 14 units of variance from the 14 original variables to the 14 factors. We observe that factors 1, 2, 3, and 4 account for the major portion (66.5 percent) of the variance in the original variables. In Figure 19.2, a *scree plot* depicts the rapid decline in

Table 19.2   Factor Eigenvalues and Variance Explained for Grocery Chain Study

	Initial eigenvalues		
Factor	*Total*	*% of Variance*	*Cumulative %*
1	5.448	38.917	38.917
2	1.523	10.882	49.799
3	1.245	8.890	58.689
4	1.096	7.827	66.516
5	.875	6.247	72.763
6	.717	5.120	77.883
7	.620	4.429	82.312
8	.525	3.747	86.059
9	.478	3.413	89.472
10	.438	3.131	92.603
11	.326	2.329	94.932
12	.278	1.985	96.917
13	.242	1.729	98.646
14	.190	1.354	100.000

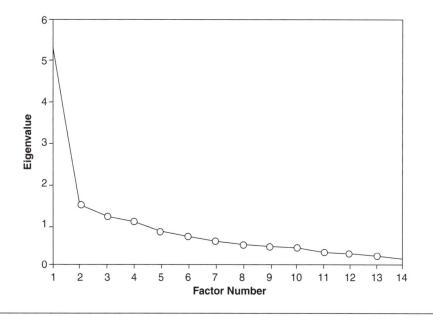

Figure 19.2   Scree Plot for Grocery Chain Data Factors

variance accounted for as the number of factors increase. This chart graphs the eigenvalues for each factor. It is a useful visual tool for determining the number of significant factors to retain. The shape of this curve suggests that little is added by recognizing more than four factors in the solution (the additional factors will be unique to a single variable).

An accepted rule-of-thumb states that if a factor has an associated eigenvalue greater than or equal to 1.0, then the factor is "common" and a part of the solution. This rule-of-thumb is closely aligned with the intuitive decision rules associated with the scree chart. When we observe an eigenvalue less than 1.0, the factor accounts for less variance than was input by a single input variable.

Table 19.3 shows the matrix of factor loadings, or correlations of the variables with the factors. If each factor loading in each column were squared, the sum would equal the eigenvalue shown in Table 19.2. Squaring the loadings (h_2) and summing across the columns results in the amount of variance in the variables that is to be explained by the factors. These values are known as *communalities*.

Interpreting the Factors

The interpretation of the factors is subjectively based on the pattern of correlations between the variables and the factors. The factor loadings provide the basis for interpreting the factors; those variables having the highest loading contribute most to the factor and thereby should receive the most weight in interpreting of the factor.

In factor analysis two solutions typically are obtained. The *initial* solution is based on certain restrictions: (a) there are k common factors; (b) underlying factors are orthogonal

Table 19.3   Rotated Factor Loadings for Grocery Chain Data

| Variable | Factor | | | | Communalities (h²) |
	1	2	3	4	
Location	1.255E-02	.218	1.075E-02	.735	.587
Quality of products	.789	3.318E-02	.237	−8.115E-02	.687
Modern	−.665	.216	−7.144E-02	−.221	.543
Friendliness of clerks	.199	−.298	.606	.433	.683
Customers	−.235	.781	−.139	6.850E-02	.689
Cluttered	7.027E-02	−.162	.894	5.166E-02	.834
Check-out	.170	.720	−3.992E-02	−.326	.655
Layout	.323	−5.814E-02	.742	.150	.681
Shopping experience	−.353	.448	−.183	−.552	.664
Reputation	.724	−.283	9.555E-02	.296	.702
Service	−.257	.339	−.393	−.588	.680
Helpfulness of clerks	.281	−.338	.290	.597	.634
Selection of products	.799	−6.586E-02	.184	.126	.692
Dull	−.284	.668	−.227	4.610E-02	.581

Extraction Method: Principal Component Analysis.
Rotation Method: Varimax with Kaiser Normalization.

(i.e., uncorrelated or independent) to each other; and (c) the first factor accounts for as much variance as possible, the second factor for as much of the residual variance left unexplained by the first factor, and so on (Kim & Mueller, 1978a). This is accomplished through rotation aimed at getting loadings for the variables that are either near one or near zero for each factor. The most widely used rotation is called *varimax*, a method of rotation which leaves the factors uncorrelated. This rotation maximizes the variance of a column of the pattern matrix, thus simplifying the factor structure.

In Table 19.3, Factor 1 is identified by four variables. The major contributions are made by the variables "Quality of products," "Reputation," Selection of products," and "Modernism." We might interpret this factor as the construct *up-to-date quality products*.

Factor 2 is identified by three variables: "Sophistication of customers," "Speed of check-out," and "Dull/Exciting." This factor might be interpreted as the *fast and exciting for sophisticated customers*. Factor 3 is explained by the variables "Friendliness of clerks," Cluttered/Spacious," and "Layout." One interpretation of this factor is that it represents the construct of *friendliness of store*. Finally, the last factor is defined by five variables. These all might be a reflection of *satisfaction with the shopping experience*.

The example of Table 19.3 depicts a set of factors with loadings that are generally high or low. However, the loadings are often in the .4 to .8 range, questioning at what level the variables make significant enough input to warrant interpretation in the factor solution. A definitive answer to this question cannot be given; it depends on sample size. If the sample size is small, correlations should be high (generally .6 and above) before the loadings are meaningful. But as the sample size increases, the meaning of correlations of lower value may be considered (generally .4 and above).

Overall, it should be obvious that *more than one interpretation may be possible for any given factor.* Moreover, it may be that a factor may not be interpretable in any substantive sense. This may or may not be a problem, depending upon the objective of the factor analysis. If done for data-reduction purposes, and the results will be used in a further analysis (such as multiple regression or discriminant analysis), being unable to interpret substantively may not be critical. One use of factor analysis is to identify those variables that reflect underlying dimensions or constructs. Once identified, the researcher can select one or more original variables for each underlying dimension to include in a subsequent multivariate analysis. This ensures that all underlying or latent dimensions are included in the analysis.

Factor Scores

Once the underlying factors are identified, the resulting factors or constructs are often interpreted with respect to the individual respondents. Simply stated, we would like to know how each respondent scores on each factor. Does the respondent have high scores on the *up-to-date-quality products* and *friendliness of store* constructs? In general, since a factor is a linear combination (or linear composite) of the original scores (variable values), it can be shown as

$$F_i = a_1 X_1 + a_2 X_2 + \cdots + a_n X_n$$

where the a_i are weights.

Although the derivation of these scores is beyond the scope of this text, most factor-analysis computer programs produce factor scores and merge them with the original data file. Augmenting the data set with factor scores enables the analyst to easily prepare descriptive or predictive analyses that segment respondents scoring high on a given factor. In short, factor scores (rather than original data values) can be used in subsequent analysis.

BASIC CONCEPTS OF CLUSTER ANALYSIS

Like factor analysis, clustering methods are most often applied to object × variable matrices. The usual objective of *cluster analysis* is to separate objects (or people) into groups such that we maximize the similarity of objects within each group, while maximizing the differences between groups. Cluster analysis is thus concerned ultimately with classification, and its techniques are part of the field of *numerical taxonomy* (Sokal & Sneath, 1963; Sneath & Sokal, 1973). In addition, cluster analysis can be used to (a) investigate useful conceptual schemes derived from grouping entities; (b) generate a hypothesis through data exploration; and (c) attempt to determine if types defined through other procedures are present in a data set (Aldenderfer & Blashfield, 1984). Thus, cluster analysis can be viewed as *a set of techniques designed to identify objects, people, or variables that are similar with respect to some criteria or characteristics.* As such, it seeks to describe so-called *natural groupings.* Another use is illustrated in Exhibit 19.3.

EXHIBIT 19.3   Clustering for Segmentation

From a marketing perspective, it should be clear that a major application of cluster analysis is for *segmentation*. To illustrate, in the 1990s a financial services company wanted to do a segmentation study among its sales force of dealers/agents (Swint, 1994/1995). It was desired to identify the characteristics of "high producers" and "mediocre producers" where "production" indicated revenue generation. The desire was to *profile* the dealers/agents and segment them with respect to motivations, needs, work styles, beliefs, and behaviors. The data were analyzed by a commercially available computer package from Sawtooth Software, *Convergent Cluster Analysis* (CCA). Multiple cluster solutions emerged. The most viable solutions were then subject to the discriminant analysis program of SPSS to see how well the clustering attributes actually discriminated between the segments. The end result of all these analyses defined six clusters as segments.

The typical clustering procedure that we shall discuss assigns each object to one and only one class. Objects within a class are usually assumed to be indistinguishable from one another. Thus, we assume here that the underlying structure of the data involves an unordered set of discrete classes. In some cases we may also view these classes as hierarchical in nature, where some classes are divided into subclasses.

Primary Questions

Clustering procedures can be viewed as preclassificatory in the sense that the analyst has *not* used prior information to partition the objects (rows of the data matrix) into groups. We note that partitioning is performed in terms of the objects rather than the variables; thus, cluster analysis deals with intact data (in terms of the variables). Moreover, the partitioning is not performed *a priori* but is based on the object similarities themselves. The analyst *is* assuming that clusters exist. This type of presupposition is different from the case in discriminant analysis (discussed in Chapter 18), where groups of objects are predefined by a variable:

- Most cluster-analysis methods are relatively simple procedures that are usually not supported by an extensive body of statistical reasoning.
- Cluster-analysis methods have evolved from many disciplines, and the inbred biases of these disciplines can differ dramatically.
- Different clustering methods can (and do) generate different solutions from the same data set.
- The strategy of cluster analysis is structure-seeking, although its operation is structure-imposing.

Given no information on group definition in advance, the major problems of cluster analysis can be stated in four ways:

1. What measure of interobject similarity is to be used, and how is each variable to be weighted in the construction of such a summary measure?

2. After interobject similarities are obtained, how are the classes of objects to be formed?

3. After the classes have been formed, what summary measures of each cluster are appropriate in a descriptive sense—that is, how are the clusters to be defined?

4. Assuming that adequate descriptions of the clusters can be obtained, what inferences can be drawn regarding their statistical reliability?

Choice of Proximity Measure

The choice of a *proximity, similarity,* or *resemblance measure* (all three terms will be used synonymously here) is an interesting problem in cluster analysis. The concept of similarity always raises the question: Similarity with respect to what? Proximity measures are viewed in relative terms—two objects are similar, relative to the group, if their profiles across variables are close or they share many aspects in common, relative to those which other pairs share in common.

Most clustering procedures use pairwise measures of proximity. The choice of which objects and variables should be included in the analysis, and how they should be scaled, is largely a matter of the researcher's judgment. While these (prior) choices are important ones, they are beyond our scope here. Even assuming that such choices have been made, however, the possible measures of pairwise proximity are many. Generally speaking, these measures fall into two classes: (a) distance-type measures (Euclidean distance); and (b) matching-type measures. A simple application illustrating the nature of cluster analysis using a distance measure is shown in Exhibit 19.4.

EXHIBIT 19.4   A Simple Example of Cluster Analysis

We can illustrate cluster analysis by a simple example. The problem is to group a set of twelve branches of a bank into three clusters of four branches each. Groups will be formed based on two variables, the number of men who have borrowed money (X_1) and the number of women who have borrowed money (X_2). The branches are plotted in two dimensions in the figure.

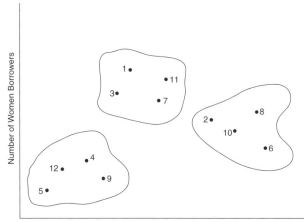

We use a distance measure of proximity, based on Euclidean distances in space,

$$d_{jk} = \sqrt{(X_{1j} - X_{1k})^2 + (X_{2j} - X_{2k})^2}$$

where j and k are any two branches. Branches 2 and 10 appear to be the closest together. The first cluster is formed by finding the midpoint between branches 2 and 10 and computing the distance of each branch from this midpoint (this is known as applying the *nearest-neighbor algorithm*). The two closest branches (6 and 8) are then added to give the desired-size cluster. The other clusters are formed in a similar manner. When more than two dimensions (that is, characteristics) are involved, a computer program must be used for measuring distances and the clustering process.

Clustering Methods

Once the analyst has settled on a pairwise measure of profile similarity, some type of computational routine must be used to cluster the profiles. A large variety of such computer programs already exist, and more are being developed as interest in this field increases. Each clustering program tends to maintain a certain individuality, although some common characteristics can be drawn out. The following categories of clustering methods are based, in part, on the classification of Ball and Hall (1964):

1. *Dimensionalizing the association matrix.* These approaches use principal-components or other factor-analytic methods to find a dimensional representation of points from *interobject* association measures. Clusters are then developed visually or on the basis of grouping objects according to their pattern of component scores.

2. *Nonhierarchical methods.* The methods start right from the proximity matrix and can be characterized in three ways:
   a. *Sequential threshold.* In this case a cluster center is selected and all objects within a prespecified threshold value are grouped. Then a new cluster center is selected and the process is repeated for the unclustered points, and so on. (Once points enter a cluster, they are removed from further processing.)
   b. *Parallel threshold.* This method is similar to the preceding method, except that several cluster centers are selected simultaneously and points within threshold level are assigned to the nearest center; threshold levels can then be adjusted to admit fewer or more points to clusters.
   c. *Optimizing partitioning.* This method modifies categories (a) or (b) in that points can later be reassigned to clusters on the basis of optimizing some overall criterion measure, such as average within-cluster distance for a given number of clusters.

3. *Hierarchical methods.* These procedures are characterized by the construction of a hierarchy or tree-like structure. In some methods each point starts out as a unit (single-point) cluster. At the next level the two closest points are placed in a cluster. At the following level a third point joins the first two, or else a second two-point cluster is formed based on various criterion functions for assignment. Eventually all points are grouped into one larger cluster. Variations on this procedure involve the development

of a hierarchy from the top down. At the beginning the points are partitioned into two subsets based on some criterion measure related to average within-cluster distance. The subset with the highest average within-cluster distance is next partitioned into two subsets, and so on, until all points eventually become unit clusters.

While the above classes of programs are not exhaustive of the field, most of the more widely used clustering routines can be classified as falling into one (or a combination) of the above categories. Criteria for grouping include such measures as average within-cluster distance and threshold cutoff values. The fact remains, however, that even the optimizing approaches achieve only conditional optima, since an unsettled question in this field is *how many* clusters to form in the first place.

Product-Positioning Application

Cluster analysis can be used in a variety of marketing research applications. For example, companies are often interested in determining how their products are positioned in terms of competitive offerings and consumers' views about the types of people most likely to own the product.

For illustrative purposes, Figure 19.3 shows the results of a hypothetical study conducted in which interobject-distance data were developed for seven sport cars, six types of stereotyped owners, and 13 attributes often used to describe cars. The distance data were based on respondents' degree-of-belief ratings about which attributes and owners described which cars. In this case, a complete-linkage algorithm was also used to cluster the objects (Johnson, 1967). The complete linkage algorithm starts by finding the two points with the minimum Euclidean distance. However, joining points to clusters is accomplished by maximizing the distance from a point in the first cluster to a point in the second cluster.

Looking first at the four large clusters, we note the *car* groupings:

- Mazda Miata, Mitsubishi Eclipse
- VW Golf
- Mercedes 600 SL, Lexus SC, Infinity G35
- Porsche Carrera

In this example, the Porsche Carrera is seen as being in a class by itself, with the attributes *high acceleration* and *high top speed*. Its perceived (stereotyped) owners are *rally enthusiast* and *amateur racer.*

Studies of this type enable the marketing researcher to observe the interrelationships among several types of entities—cars, attributes, and owners. The approach displays several advantages. For example, it can be applied to alternative advertisements, package designs, or other kinds of communications stimuli. That is, the respondent could be shown blocks of advertising copy (brand unidentified) and asked to provide degree-of-belief ratings that the brand described in the copy possesses each of the *n* features.

Similarly, in the case of consumer packaged goods, the respondent could be shown alternative package designs and asked for degree-of-belief ratings that the contents of the package possess various features. In either case one would be adding an additional set (or sets) of

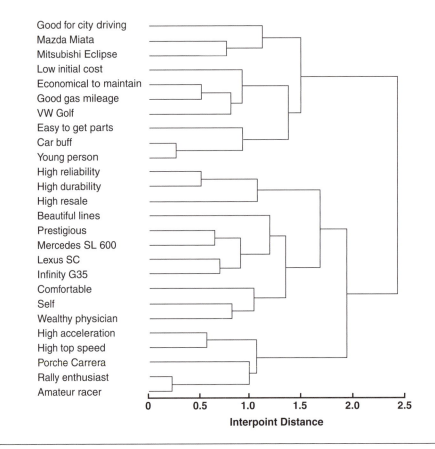

Figure 19.3   Complete-Linkage Analysis of Product-Positioning Data

ratings to the response sets described earlier. Hence, four (or more) classes of items could be represented as points in the cluster analysis.

Foreign Market Analysis

Companies considering entering foreign markets for the first time, as well as those considering expanding from existing to new foreign markets, have to do formal market analysis. Often a useful starting point is to work from a categorization schema of potential foreign markets. Cluster analysis can be useful in this process.

To illustrate, we use the study by Green and Larsen (1985). In this study, 71 nations were clustered on the basis of selected economic characteristics and economic change. The specific variables used were (a) growth in Gross Domestic Product; (b) literacy rate; (c) energy consumption per capita; (d) oil imports; and (e) international debt. Variables a, d, and e were operationalized as change during a specified time period.

Clustering was accomplished by use of a *K*-means clustering routine. This routine is a nonhierarchical method that allocates countries to the group whose centroid is closest, using

Table 19.4   Composition of Foreign Market Clusters

Cluster 1		*Cluster 3*	*Cluster 5*	
Belgium	Finland	Ethiopia	Colombia	Venezuela
Canada	Norway	Ghana	Costa Rica	Yugoslavia
Denmark	Switzerland	India	Ecuador	El Salvador
Sweden	New Zealand	Liberia	Greece	Iran
USA	France	Libya	Hong Kong	Tunisia
Germany	Ireland	Madagascar	Jordan	Indonesia
Netherlands	Italy	Mali	Mexico	Nigeria
UK	Austria	Senegal	Paraguay	Malawi
Australia			Portugal	

Cluster 2		*Cluster 4*		
Cameroon	Honduras	Brazil	Spain	
Central African Republic	Nicaragua	Chile	Sri Lanka	
Egypt	Morocco	Israel	Thailand	
Somalia	Ivory Coast	Japan	Turkey	
Togo	Tanzania	Korea	Argentina	
Zaire	Pakistan	Peru	Guatemala	
Zambia		Philippines	Kenya	
		Singapore	Uruguay	

SOURCE: From Green, R. T. & Larsen, T., *Export Markets and Economic Change,* 1985 (working paper). Reprinted with permission.

a Euclidean distance measure. A total of five clusters was derived based on the distance between countries and the centers of the clusters across the five predictor variables. The number of clusters selected was based on the criteria of total within-cluster distance and interpretability. A smaller number of clusters led to a substantial increase of within-cluster variability, while an increase in the number of clusters resulted in group splitting with a minimal reduction in distance. The composition of the clusters is shown in Table 19.4.

Computer Analyses

There are many computer programs available for conducting cluster analysis. The major packages (such as SPSS and SAS) have one or more routines. Smaller, more specialized packages (such as PC-MDS) have included cluster routines as an addition to their major programs, which are for other purposes. Finally, some academicians have developed their own cluster routines that they typically make available to other academicians for no charge.

MULTIDIMENSIONAL SCALING FUNDAMENTALS

In this section we start with an intuitive introduction to multidimensional scaling that uses a geographical example involving a set of intercity distances. In particular, we show how MDS takes a set of distance data and tries to find a spatial configuration or pattern of points in some number of dimensions whose distances best match the input data.

Let us start by looking at Panel I of Figure 19.4. Here we see a configuration of ten U.S. cities, whose locations have been taken from an airline map (Kruskal & Wish, 1978). The actual intercity distances are shown in Panel II. The Euclidean distance between a pair of points i and j, in any number of r dimensions, is given by

$$d_{ij} = \left[\sum_{k=1}^{r} (x_{ik} - x_{jk})^2 \right]^{1/2}$$

In the present case, $r = 2$, since only two dimensions are involved. For example, we could use the map to find the distance between Atlanta and Chicago by (a) projecting their points on axis 1 (East-West), finding the difference, and squaring it; (b) projecting their points on axis 2 (North-South) and doing the same; and then (c) taking the square root of the sum of the two squared differences.

In short, it is a relatively simple matter to go from the map in Panel I to the set of numerical distances in Panel II. However, the converse is *not* so easy. And that is what MDS is all about.

Suppose that we are shown Panel II of Figure 19.4 without the labels so that we do not even know that the objects are cities. The task is to work backward. That is, we wish to find, simultaneously, the number of dimensions and the configuration (or pattern) of points in that dimensionality so that their computed interpoint distances most closely match the input data of Panel II. This is the problem of *metric* MDS.

Next, suppose that instead of the ratio air mileage data, we had only rank order data. We can build such a data matrix by taking some order-preserving transformation in Panel II. For example, we could take the smallest distance (205 miles between New York and Washington) and call it 1. Then we could apply the same rules and rank order the remaining 44 distances up to rank 45 for the distance (2,734 miles) between Miami and Seattle. We could use a nonmetric MDS program to find the following:

- Number of dimensions
- Configuration of points in that dimensionality

Then the ranks of their computed interpoint distances most closely match the ranks of the input data.

In this example where the actual distance data is considered, it turns out that metric MDS methods can find, for all practical purposes, an exact solution (Panel I). However, what is rather surprising is that, even after downgrading the numerical data to ranks, nonmetric methods can also achieve a virtually perfect recovery as well.

Panel III shows the results of applying a nonmetric algorithm to the ranks of the 45 numbers in Panel II. Thus, even with only rank-order input information, the recovery of the original locations is almost perfect.

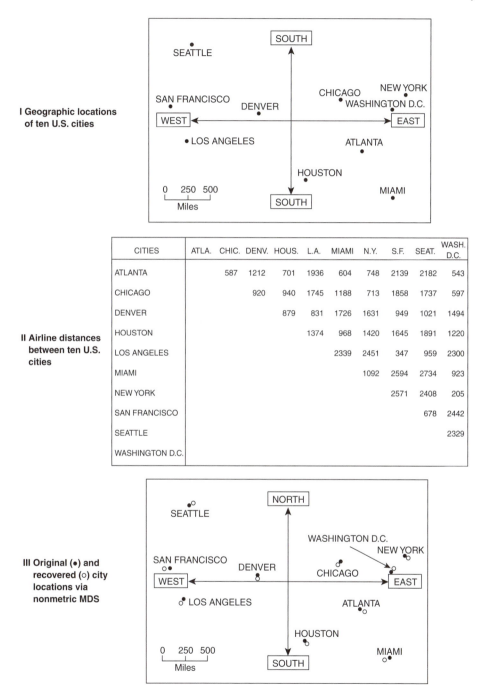

Figure 19.4 Nonmetric MDS of 10 U.S. Cities

We should quickly add, however, that neither the metric nor nonmetric MDS procedures will necessarily line up the configuration of points in a North-South direction; all that the methods try to preserve are *relative* distances. The configuration can be arbitrarily rotated, translated, reflected, or uniformly stretched or shrunk by so-called configuration congruence or matching programs, so as to best match the target configuration of Panel I. None of these operations will change the *relative* distances of the points.

Psychological Versus Physical Distance

The virtues of MDS methods are not in the scaling of physical distances but rather in their scaling of *psychological distances*, often called *dissimilarities*. In MDS we assume that individuals act as though they have a type of "mental map", (not necessarily visualized or verbalized), so that they view pairs of entities near each other as similar and those far from each other as dissimilar. Depending on the relative distances among pairs of points, varying *degrees* of dissimilarity could be imagined.

We assume that the respondent is able to provide either numerical measures of his or her perceived degree of dissimilarity for all pairs of entities, or, less stringently, ordinal measures of dissimilarity. If so, we can use the methodology of MDS to construct a *physical* map in one or more dimensions whose interpoint distances (or ranks of distances, as the case may be) are most consistent with the input data.

This model does not explain perception. Quite the contrary, it provides a useful *representation* of a set of subjective judgments about the extent to which a respondent views various pairs of entities as dissimilar. Thus, MDS models are representations of data rather than theories of perceptual processes.

Classifying MDS Techniques

Multidimensional scaling is concerned with portraying psychological relations among stimuli—either empirically-obtained similarities, preferences, or other kinds of matchings or orderings—as geometric relationships among points in a multidimensional space. In this approach one attempts to represent *psychological dissimilarity as geometric distance*. The axes of the geometric space, or some transformation of them, are often (but not necessarily) assumed to represent the psychological bases or attributes along which the judge compares stimuli (represented as points or vectors in his or her psychological space).

Many different kinds of MDS procedures exist. Accordingly, it seems useful to provide a set of descriptors by which the methodology can be classified. These descriptors are only a subset of those described by Carroll and Arabie (1980):

1. *Mode.* A mode is a class of entities, such as respondents, brands, use occasions, or attributes of a multiattribute object.

2. *Data array.* The number of ways that modes are arranged. For example, in a two-way array of single mode dissimilarities, the entities could be brand-brand relationships, such as a respondent's rating of the *ij*th brand pair on a 1–9 point scale, ranging from

1 (very similar) to 9 (very different). Hence, in this case, we have one mode, two-way data on judged dissimilarities of pairs of brands.

3. *Type of geometric model.* Either a distance model or a vector or projection model (the latter represented by a combination of points and vectors).

4. *Number of different sets of plotted points (or vectors).* One, two, or more than two.

5. *Scale type.* Nominal-, ordinal-, interval-, or ratio-scaled input data.

Data Mode/Way

In marketing research most applications of MDS entail either single mode, two-way data, or two-mode, two-way data. Single mode, two-way data are illustrated by input matrices that are square and symmetric, in which all distinct pairs of entities (e.g., brands) in a $I \times I$ matrix are judged in terms of their relative similarity/dissimilarity on some type of rating scale. The instructions can refer to pairwise similarity, association, substitutability, closeness to, affinity for, congruence with, co-occurrence with, and so on. Typically, only a lower- or upper-half matrix consisting of $I(I - 1)/2$ pairs are evaluated, since all self-similarities are assumed to be equal to each other and dissimilarity itself is assumed to be a symmetric relationship between members of a pair of entities.

MDS solutions based on single mode, two-way input data lead to what are often called *simple spaces*—that is, a configuration of only one set of I points. Pairs of points close together in this geometric space are presumed to exhibit high subjective similarity in the eyes of the respondent.

Another popular form of marketing research data entails input matrices that represent two-mode, two-way relationships, such as the following six examples:

1. A set of judges provide preference ratings of J brands

2. Average scores (across respondents) of J brands rated on I attributes

3. The frequency (across respondents) with which J attributes are assumed to be associated with I brands

4. The frequency (across respondents) with which respondents in each of I brand-favorite groups pick each of J attributes as important to their brand choice

5. The frequency (across respondents) with which each of J use occasions is perceived to be appropriate for each of I brands

6. The frequency (across respondents) with which each of J problems is perceived to be associated with using each of I brands.

These geometric spaces are often called *joint spaces* in that two different sets of points (e.g., brands and attributes) are represented. (In some cases three or more sets of entities may be scaled.)

Type of Geometric Model

In applications of single-mode, two-way data the entities being scaled are almost always represented as points (as opposed to vectors). However, in the case of two-mode, two-way data, the two sets of entities might each be represented as points or, alternatively, one set may be represented as points while the other set is represented as vector directions. In the latter case the termini of the vectors are often normalized to lie on a common circumference around the origin of the configuration.

The point-point type of two-mode, two-way data representation is often referred to as an *unfolding* model (Coombs, 1964). If the original matrix consists of *I* respondents' preference evaluations of *J* brands, then the resulting joint-space map has *I* respondents' ideal points and *J* brand points. Brand points that are near a respondent's ideal point are assumed to be *highly preferred* by that respondent. Although the original input data may be based on between-set relationships, if the simple unfolding model holds, one can also infer respondent-to-respondent similarities in terms of the closeness of their ideal points to each other. Brand-to-brand similarities may be analogously inferred, based on the relative closeness of pairs of brand points.

The point-vector model of two-mode, two-way data is a *projection* model in which one obtains respondent *i*'s preference scale by projecting the *J* brand points onto respondent *i*'s vector. Point-vector models also show ideal points or points of "ideal preference". This ideal point is located at the terminus or end of the vector. Projections are made by drawing a line so that it intersects the vector at a 90-degree angle. The farther out (toward vector *i*'s terminus) the *projection* is, the more preferred the brand is for that respondent.

MARKETING APPLICATIONS OF MDS

MDS studies have been used in a variety of situations to help marketing managers see how their brand is positioned in the minds of consumers, vis-à-vis competing brands. Illustrations include (a) choosing a slogan for advertising a soft drink, (b) the relationship between physical characteristics of computers and perceptions of users and potential users, (c) effectiveness of a new advertising campaign for a high-nutrition brand of cereal, (d) positioning in physicians' minds of medical magazines and journals, and (e) positioning of new products and product concepts. There is no shortage of applications in real-world marketing situations.

Current research activity in MDS methods, including the increasing use of correspondence analyses for representing nominal data (Hoffman & Franke, 1986; Carroll, Green, & Schaffer, 1986; Whitlark & Smith, 2003), shows few signs of slowing down. In contrast, industry applications for the methods still seem to be emphasizing the graphical display and diagnostic roles that characterized the motivation for developing these techniques in the first place. The gap between theory and practice appears to be widening. A comprehensive overview of the developments in MDS is provided by Carroll and Arabie (1998).

COLLECTING DATA FOR MDS

The content side of MDS—dimension interpretation, relating physical changes in products to psychological changes in perceptual maps—poses the most difficult problems for researchers. However, methodologists are developing MDS models that provide more flexibility than a straight dimensional application. For example, recent models have coupled the ideas of cluster analysis and MDS into hybrid models of categorical-dimensional structure. Furthermore, conjoint analysis, to be discussed next, offers high promise for relating changes in the physical (or otherwise controlled) aspects of products to changes in their psychological imagery and evaluation. Typically, conjoint analysis deals with preference (and other dominance-type) judgments rather than similarities. However, more recent research has extended the methodology to similarities judgments.

On the input side, there are issues that arise concerning data collection methods. In MDS studies, there are four most commonly used methods of data collection:

- *Sorting task.* Subjects are asked to sort the stimuli into a number of groups, according to similarity. The number of groups is determined by the subject during the judgment task.
- *Paired comparison task.* Stimuli are presented to subjects in all possible pairs of two stimuli. Each subject has to rate each pair on an ordinal scale (the number of points can vary) where the extreme values of the scale represent maximum dissimilarity and maximum similarity.
- *Conditional ranking task.* Subjects order stimuli on the basis of their similarity with an anchor stimulus. Each of the stimuli is in turn presented as the anchor.
- *Triadic combinations task.* Subjects indicate which two stimuli of combinations of three stimuli form the most similar pair, and which two stimuli form the least similar pair.

When subjects perform a similarity (or dissimilarity) judgment they may experience increases in fatigue, boredom, stimulus knowledge, and task insight. Bijmolt and Wedel (1995, p. 364) have defined these conditions:

1. *Fatigue* is a subjective mental condition caused by the continuation of a mental activity in which the ability to perform a mental or related activity is diminished.

2. *Boredom* is a subjective mental condition caused by the monotony of a mental activity, in which the motivation to continue that activity is diminished.

3. *Stimulus knowledge* refers to the amount of information directly available to a person while performing a task.

4. *Task insight* is the extent to which a person understands what is required in a specific task; it enables that person to perform that task successfully.

In a study of automobile and beer brands, Bijmolt and Wedel examined the effect of the alternative data collection methods on these four mental conditions. Other variables

Table 19.5   Effects on MDS Data Collection Methods

	Data collection methods[a]			
Effects	*ST*	*PC*	*CR*	*TC*
Subject-related variables				
Fatigue	++	+	−	−
Boredom	+	+	−	−
Stimulus knowledge	+	+	+	+
Task insight	+	+	+	+
Similarity judgments				
Completion time	++	+	±	−
Missing values	+	++	+	−
Data quality		+	+	+
MDS solution				
Recovery of known distances	−	+	+	+
Fit of the data	+	+	+	+
Dimensionality	+	+	+	+
Error variance	+	±	−	−
Perceptual map	X	x	x	X

ST = sorting, PC = paired comparisons, CR = conditional
rankings, and TC = triadic combinations.
++ = very good, + = good, ± = medium, studied but no ordering possible.

SOURCE: Reprinted from Bijmolt, T. H. A. and Wedel, M., "The Effects of Alternative Methods of Collecting
Similarity Data for Multidimensional Scaling," *International Journal of Research in Marketing, 12,* 363-371,
copyright ©1995, with permission from Elsevier.

examined were issues surrounding similarity judgments themselves and the MDS solution.
The results of this study, summarized in Table 19.5, show that for each method, subjects
responding to the task became fatigued and bored, but stimulus knowledge and task
insight did not occur. The amount of fatigue and boredom differed between data collection
methods. These researchers draw conclusions and make recommendations about what data
collection method to use under what conditions. For example, conditional rankings and triadic combinations should be used only if the stimulus set is relatively small, and in situations where the maximum amount of information is to be extracted from the respondents.
If the stimulus set is relatively large, sorting and paired comparisons are better suited for
collecting similarity data. Which of these two to use will depend on characteristics of
the application, such as number of stimuli and whether or not individual-level perceptual
maps are desired.

FUNDAMENTALS OF CONJOINT ANALYSIS

Conjoint analysis is one of the most widely used advanced techniques in marketing research.
It is a powerful tool that allows the researcher to predict choice share for evaluated stimuli
such as competitive brands. When using this technique the researcher is concerned with the

identification of *utilities*—values used by people making tradeoffs and choosing among objects having many attributes and/or characteristics.

There are many methodologies for conducting conjoint analysis, including two-factor-at-a-time tradeoff, full profile, Adaptive Conjoint Analysis (ACA), choice-based conjoint, self-explicated conjoint, hybrid conjoint, and Hierarchical Bayes (HB). In this chapter, two of the most popular methodologies are discussed: the full-profile and self-explicated models.

Conjoint analysis, like MDS, concerns the measurement of psychological judgments, such as consumer preferences. The stimuli to be presented to the respondent are often designed beforehand according to some type of factorial structure. In full-profile conjoint analysis, the objective is to decompose a set of overall responses to a set of stimuli (product or service) so that the utility of each attribute describing the stimulus can be inferred from the respondent's *overall evaluations* of the stimuli. In a layman's example, a respondent might be presented with a set of alternative product descriptions (automobiles). The automobiles are described by their stimulus attributes (level of gas mileage, size of engine, type of transmission, etc.). When choice alternatives are presented, choice or preference evaluations are made. From this information, the researcher is able to determine the respondent's utility for each stimulus attribute (i.e., what is the relative value of an automatic versus a five-speed manual transmission). Once the utilities are determined for all respondents, simulations are run to determine the relative choice share of a competing set of new or existing products.

Conjoint analysis models are constrained by the amount of data required in the data collection task. Managers demand models that define products with increasingly more stimulus attributes and levels within each attribute. Because more detail increases the size, complexity, and time of the evaluation task, new data collection methodologies and analysis models are continually being developed.

One early conjoint data collection method presented a series of attribute-by-attribute (two attributes at a time) tradeoff tables where respondents ranked their preferences of the different combinations of the attribute levels. For example, if each attribute had three levels, the table would have nine cells and the respondents would rank their tradeoff preferences from 1 to 9. The two-factor-at-a-time approach makes few cognitive demands of the respondent and is simple to follow . . . but it is both time-consuming and tedious. Moreover, respondents often lose their place in the table or develop some stylized pattern just to get the job done. Most importantly, however, the task is unrealistic in that real alternatives do not present themselves for evaluation two attributes at a time.

For the last 20 years, full-profile conjoint analysis has been a popular approach to measure attribute utilities. In the full-profile conjoint task, different product descriptions (or even different actual products) are developed and presented to the respondent for acceptability or preference evaluations. Each product profile is designed as part of a *fractional factorial experimental design* that evenly matches the occurrence of each attribute with all other attributes. By controlling the attribute pairings, the researcher can estimate the respondent's utility for each level of each attribute tested.

A third approach, Adaptive Conjoint Analysis, was developed to handle larger problems that required more descriptive attributes and levels. ACA uses computer-based interviews to adapt each respondent's interview to the evaluations provided by each respondent. Early in the interview, the respondent is asked to eliminate attributes and levels that would not be considered in an acceptable product under any conditions. ACA next presents attributes for evaluation and finally full profiles, two at a time, for evaluation. The choice pairs are presented in an order that increasingly focuses on determining the utility associated with each attribute.

A fourth methodology, choice-based conjoint, requires the respondent to choose a preferred full-profile concept from repeated sets of 3–5 concepts. This choice activity simulates an actual buying situation, thereby giving the respondents a familiar task that mimics actual shopping behavior.

The self-explicated approach to conjoint analysis offers a simple but robust approach that does not require the development or testing of full-profile concepts. Rather, the conjoint factors and levels are presented to respondents for elimination if not acceptable in products under any condition. The levels of the attributes are then evaluated for desirability. Finally, the relative importance of attributes is derived by dividing 100 points between the most desirable levels of each attribute. The respondent's reported attribute level desirabilities are weighted by the attribute importances to provide utility values for each attribute level. This is done without the regression analysis or aggregated solution required in many other conjoint approaches. This approach has been shown to provide results equal or superior to full-profile approaches, and requires less rigorous evaluations from respondents.

Most recently, academic researchers have focused on an approach called Hierarchical Bayes (HB) to estimate attribute level utilities from choice data. HB uses information about the distribution of utilities from all respondents as part of the procedure to estimate attribute level utilities for each individual. This approach again allows more attributes and levels to be estimated with smaller amounts of data collected from each individual respondent.

An Example of Full-Profile Conjoint Analysis

In *metric conjoint analysis*, the solution algorithm involves a dummy variable regression analysis in which the respondent's preference ratings of the product profile (service or other item) being evaluated serve as the dependent (criterion) variable, and the independent (predictor) variables are represented by the various factorial levels making up each stimulus. In the *nonmetric* version of conjoint analysis, the dependent (criterion) variable represents a ranking of the alternative profiles and is only ordinal-scaled. The full-profile methods for collecting conjoint analysis data will be illustrated to show how conjoint data are obtained.

The *multiple-factor approach* illustrated in Figure 19.5 consists of sixteen cards, each made up according to a special type of factorial design. The details of each card are shown on the left side of Figure 19.5. All card descriptions differ in one or more attribute level(s).[1] The respondent is then asked to group the 16 cards (Figure 19.6) into three piles (with no need to place an equal number in each pile) described in one of three ways:

- Definitely like
- Neither definitely like nor dislike
- Definitely dislike

The criterion variable is usually some kind of preference or purchase likelihood rating. Following this, the respondent takes the first pile and ranks the cards in it from most to least liked, and similarly so for the second and third piles. By means of this two-step procedure, the full set of 16 cards is eventually ranked from most liked to least liked.

Advertising Appeal Study for Allergy Medication	
4^4 Fractional Factorial Design: (4 Levels^4 ^{Factors})	
0, 0, 0, 0	Column 1: "Efficacy", 4 Levels
1, 0, 1, 2	0 = "No med more effective"
2, 0, 2, 3	1 = "No med works faster"
3, 0, 3, 1	2 = "Relief all day"
0, 1, 1, 1	3 = "Right Formula"
1, 1, 0, 3	
2, 1, 3, 2	Column 2: "Endorsements", 4 Levels
3, 1, 2, 0	0 = "Most recommended by allergists"
0, 2, 2, 2	1 = "Most recommended by pharmacist"
1, 2, 3, 0	2 = "National Gardening Association"
2, 2, 0, 1	3 = "Professional Gardeners (Horticulture)"
3, 2, 1, 3	
0, 3, 3, 3	Column 3: "Superiority",4 Levels
1, 3, 2, 1	0 = "Less sedating than Benadryl"
2, 3, 1, 0	1 = "Rec. 2:1 over Benadryl"
3, 3, 0, 2	2 = "Relief 2 × longer than Benadryl"
	3 = "Leading long-acting over-the-counter"
Legend:	
Profile 1 has levels 0,0,0,0:	Column 4: "Gardening",4 Levels
No Medication is More Effective	0 = "Won't quit on you"
Most Recommended by Allergists	1 = "Enjoy relief while garden"
Less Sedating than Benadryl	2 = "Brand used by millions"
Won't Quit on You	3 = "Relieves allergy symptoms"

Figure 19.5   Multiple-Factor Evaluations (Sample Profiles)

Again, the analytical objective is to find a set of part-worths or utility values for the separate attribute (factor) levels so that, when these are appropriately added, one can find a total utility for each combination or profile. The part-worths are chosen so as to produce the highest possible correspondence between the derived ranking and the original ranking of the 16 cards. While the two-factor-at-a-time and the multiple-factor approaches, as just described, assume only ranking-type data, one could just as readily ask the respondent to state his or her preferences on (say), an 11-point equal-interval ratings scale, ranging from like most to like least. Moreover, in the multiple-factor approach, a 0-to-100 rating scale, representing likelihood of purchase, also could be used.

As may be surmised, the multiple-factor evaluative approach makes greater cognitive demands on the respondent, since the full set of factors appears each time. In practice, if more than six or seven factors are involved, this approach is often modified to handle specific *subsets* of interlinked factors across two or more evaluation tasks.

Consider the situation in which a manufacturer of over-the-counter allergy medication is interested in measuring consumers' tradeoffs among the four attributes identified in Figure 19.5. Allergy sufferers are recruited and presented with the 16 alternatives shown in Figure 19.6. Each

Card 1	**Card 2**	**Card 3**	**Card 4**
Efficacy No med more effective	*Efficacy* No med works faster	*Efficacy* Relief all day	*Efficacy* Right Formula
Endorsements Most recom. by allergists	*Endorsements* Most recom. by allergists	*Endorsements* Most recom. by allergists	*Endorsements* Most recom. by allergists
Superiority Less sedating than Benadryl	*Superiority* Rec. 2:1 over Benadryl	*Superiority* Relief 2 × longer than Benadryl	*Superiority* Leading long acting OTC
Gardening Won't quit on you	*Gardening* Brand used by millions	*Gardening* Relieves allergy symptoms	*Gardening* Enjoy relief while gardening
Card 5	**Card 6**	**Card 7**	**Card 8**
Efficacy No med more effective	*Efficacy* No med works faster	*Efficacy* Relief all day	*Efficacy* Right Formula
Endorsements Most recom. by pharmacist	*Endorsements* Most recom. by pharmacist	*Endorsements* Most recom. by pharmacist	*Endorsements* Most recom. by pharmacist
Superiority Rec. 2:1 over Benadryl	*Superiority* Less sedating than Benadryl	*Superiority* Leading long acting OTC	*Superiority* Relief 2 × longer than Benadryl
Gardening Enjoy relief while gardening	*Gardening* Relieves allergy symptoms	*Gardening* Brand used by millions	*Gardening* Won't quit on you
Card 9	**Card 10**	**Card 11**	**Card 12**
Efficacy No med more effective	*Efficacy* No med works faster	*Efficacy* Relief all day	*Efficacy* Right Formula
Endorsements Nat. Gardening Assoc.	*Endorsements* Nat. Gardening Assoc.	*Endorsements* Nat. Gardening Assoc.	*Endorsements* Nat. Gardening Assoc.
Superiority Relief 2 × longer than Benadryl	*Superiority* Leading long acting OTC	*Superiority* Less sedating than Benadryl	*Superiority* Rec. 2:1 over Benadryl
Gardening Brand used by millions	*Gardening* Won't quit on you	*Gardening* Enjoy relief while gardening	*Gardening* Relieves allergy symptoms
Card 13	**Card 14**	**Card 15**	**Card 16**
Efficacy No med more effective	*Efficacy* No med works faster	*Efficacy* Relief all day	*Efficacy* Right Formula
Endorsements Prof. Gardeners (Hortic.)	*Endorsements* Prof. Gardeners (Hortic.)	*Endorsements* Prof. Gardeners (Hortic.)	*Endorsements* Prof. Gardeners (Hortic.)
Superiority Leading long acting OTC	*Superiority* Relief 2 × longer than Benadryl	*Superiority* Rec. 2:1 over Benadryl	*Superiority* Less sedating than Benadryl
Gardening Relieves allergy symptoms	*Gardening* Enjoy relief while gardening	*Gardening* Won't quit on you	*Gardening* Brand used by millions

Figure 19.6   Product Descriptions for Conjoint Analysis (Allergy Medication)

respondent is asked to rate each of the alternatives on a 0–10 scale, where 0 indicates absolutely no interest in purchasing and 10 indicates extremely high interest in purchasing.

Illustratively, Figure 19.6 shows the 16 items to be evaluated by each one respondent. Although a total of $4 \times 4 \times 4 \times 4 = 256$ combinations of attribute levels could be made up, the respondent needs to evaluate only 16 of these. However, this specific set of 16 should be selected in a particular way, as will be noted later.

Figure 19.7 shows a table of the resulting utility values for each of the attribute levels derived for one respondent. These values can be obtained from an ordinary multiple regression program using dummy-variable coding. All one needs to do to estimate the respondent's utility score for a given concept profile is to add each separate value (the regression coefficient) for each component of the described combination. (The regression's intercept term may be added in later if there is interest in estimating the absolute level of purchase interest.) For example, to obtain the respondent's estimated evaluation of card 1, one sums the part-worths:

Value for:	<u>Efficacy</u> "No med more effective"	= 0.00
Value for:	<u>Endorsements</u> "Most recom. by allergists"	= 3.00
Value for:	<u>Superiority</u> "Less sedating than Benedryl"	= 0.00
Value for:	<u>Gardening</u> "Won't quit on you"	= <u>6.00</u>
	Total	= 9.00

In this instance we obtain an almost perfect prediction of a person's overall response to card 1. Similarly, we can find the estimated total evaluations for the other 15 options and compare

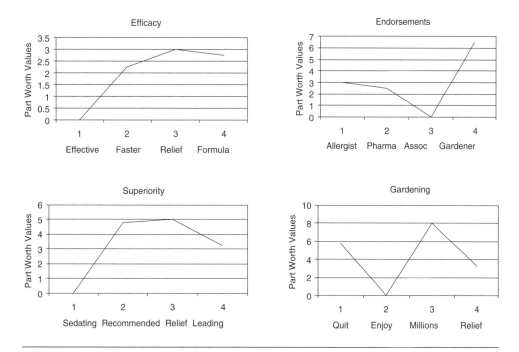

Figure 19.7   Part-Worth Functions Obtained From Conjoint Analysis of One Respondent

Table 19.6   Average Utilities of All Respondents

LEVEL	1	2	3	4
Efficacy IMPORT.%:14.63	Effective 2.48	Faster 2.37	Relief 2.10	Formula 2.18
Endorsements IMPORT.%:54.24	Allergist 3.83	Pharma 3.18	Nat. Ga 2.57	Prof. G 2.41
Superiority IMPORT.%:17.76	Less se 2.78	Recomm 2.63	Relief 2.71	Leading 2.31
Gardening IMPORT.%:13.37	Quit 2.39	Enjoy 2.74	Millions 2.58	Relief 2.54

them with the respondent's original evaluations. The regression technique guarantees that the (squared) prediction error between estimated and actual response will be minimized.

The information in Figure 19.7 also permits the researcher to find estimated evaluations for *all* combinations, including the 256 – 16 = 240 options never shown to the respondent. Moreover, all respondents' separate part-worth functions (as illustrated for the average of all respondents in Table 19.6) can be compared in order to see if various types of respondents (e.g., high-income versus low-income respondents) differ in their separate attribute evaluations.

In short, while the respondent evaluates complete bundles of attributes, the technique solves for a set of part-worths—one for each attribute level—that are imputed from the *overall* trade-offs. These part-worths can then be combined in various ways to estimate the evaluation that a respondent would give to *any* combination of interest. It is this high leverage between options that are actually evaluated and those that can be evaluated (after the analysis) that makes con-joint analysis a useful tool. It is clear that the full-profile approach requires much sophistica-tion in developing the profiles and performing the regression analyses to determine the utilities. We will now consider the self-explicated model as an approach that provides results of equal quality, but does so with a much easier design and data collection task.

Self-Explicated Conjoint Analysis

The development of fractional factorial designs and required dummy regression for each respondent places a burden on the researcher and respondent alike, especially when the number of factors and levels require that a large number of profiles be presented to the respondent.

The self-explicated model provides a simple alternative producing utility score estimates equal to or superior to that of the ACA or full-profile regression models. The self-explicated model is based theoretically on the multi-attribute attitude models that combine attribute impor-tance with attribute desirability to estimate overall preference. This model is expressed as

$$E_o = \sum_{j=1}^{m} \sum_{k=1}^{n} I_j D_{jk}$$

where I_j is the importance of attribute j and D_{jk} is the desirability of level k of attribute j. In this model, E_o, the evaluation of profile for product or service o, is formed by summing the importance weighted desirabilities of the attributes and attribute levels that make up the profile.

The Self-Explicated Data Collection Task

Initially, all attribute levels are presented to respondents for evaluation to eliminate any levels that would not be acceptable in a product under any conditions. Next, the list of attribute levels is presented and each level is evaluated for desirability (0–10 scale). Finally, based on these evaluations, the most desirable levels of all attributes are presented in a constant sum question where the relative importances of the attributes are evaluated. Using this information, the attribute importance scores are used to weight the standardized attribute level scores, thereby producing self-explicated utility values for each attribute level. This is done for each respondent and does not require a fractional factorial designs or regression analysis. As with the full-profile model, these scores can be summed and simulations run to obtain a score for any profile of interest. This simple self-reporting approach is easier for the respondent to complete and straightforward in terms of determining the importance or desirability of attributes and attribute levels (Srinivasan, 1997). An easy to use online implementation of the self-explicated model is found at www.surveyz.com. For this implementation, the conjoint analysis is automatically developed after the attribute level descriptors are entered into the question builder.

Reliability and Validity Checks

Irrespective of the method used to carry out a conjoint analysis, it is useful to include the following ancillary analyses: (a) test-retest reliability; (b) a comparison of actual utilities with those of random respondents; and (c) an internal validity check on model-based utilities.

The test-retest reliability can be conducted by including a few replicate judgments (drawn from the original set of 16) at a later stage in the interview. The purpose here is to see if the judgments are highly enough correlated, on a test-retest basis, to justify the analysis of the respondent's data.

An internal validity check can be carried out by collecting a few new evaluations (drawn randomly from the 240 stimulus combinations not utilized in Figure 19.6). These constitute a hold-out sample. Their rank order is to be predicted by the part-worths developed from the calibration sample of 16 combinations.

Other Models

So far our discussion has centered on the most widely applied conjoint models—a main-effects model using rankings or ratings. Other models are available that permit some or all two-factor interactions to be measured (as well as main effects). Interactions occur when attribute levels combine to provide a differential effect. This often happens in food products where combinations of attribute levels seemingly produce more acceptable combinations than would be predicted by the individual attribute levels when considered alone (oatmeal-raisin cookies vs. oatmeal or raisin). These models again make use of various types of fractional factorial designs or combine attributes. Specialized computer programs have been designed to implement them. In short, the users of conjoint analysis currently have a highly flexible set of models and data collection procedures at their disposal.

OTHER ASPECTS OF CONJOINT ANALYSIS

The typical sequence that one goes through to implement a conjoint study involves four steps:

1. Using one of a variety of data collection procedures just described such that sufficient data are obtained at the individual respondent level to estimate the part-worths of each person's utility function.

2. The matrix of respondent by attribute-level part-worths may then be related to other subject background data in an effort to identify possible market segments based on similarities in part-worth functions.

3. The researcher's client then proposes a set of product configurations that represent feasible competitive offerings. These product profiles are entered into a consumer choice simulator, along with the earlier computed individual utility functions.

4. While choice simulators differ, in the simplest case each respondent's individual part-worth function is used to compute the utility for each of the competing profiles. The respondent is then assumed to choose that profile with the highest utility (i.e., the choice process is deterministic).

Use of Visual Aids

Another problem in the application of conjoint measurement is the pragmatic one of getting fairly complex concepts across to the respondent. Verbal descriptions of the type covered in Figure 19.6 are not only difficult for the respondent to assimilate, but also permit unwanted perceptual differences to intrude. In another example, if conjoint analysis was used to test designs for automobiles, two respondents may have quite different perceptions of the car-length and car-roominess verbalizations.

Wherever possible, *visual props* can help to transmit complex information more easily and uniformly than verbal description. As an illustration of the value of visual props, mention can be made of a study involving styling designs for future compact cars. In the course of preparing the questionnaire, rather complex experimental factors such as overall size and interior layout, trunk size and fuel-tank capacity, exterior and interior width, and interior spaciousness and visibility had to be considered. To provide quick and uniform treatment of these style factors, visual props were prepared, as illustrated for two of the attributes in Figure 19.8. (These can be projected on screens in full view of the respondents during the interview or made part of the questionnaire itself.)

Visual props work particularly well for the multiple-factor approach, since a relatively large amount of information can be communicated realistically and quickly by this means.

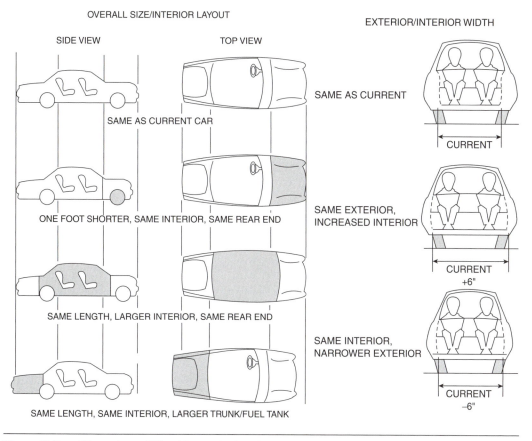

Figure 19.8   Illustrations of Visual Props Used on Conjoint Analysis

Strategic Aspects

The output of conjoint analysis is frequently employed in additional analyses. Since most studies collect full sets of data at the individual respondent level, *individual utility functions and importance weights* can be computed. This fosters two additional types of analyses: (1) market segmentation and (2) strategic simulation of new factor-level combinations. Frequently, both kinds of analyses are carried out in the same study.

In segmentation studies, the respondents are usually clustered in terms of either their commonality of utility functions or their commonality of importance weights. Having formed the segments in one of these ways, the analyst can then determine how the segments differ with regard to other background data—product-class usage, brand-selection behavior, demographics, and so on.

Strategic simulations are also relatively easy to construct from conjoint analysis data by simply including each individual respondent's utility function in a computerized-choice

Table 19.7   Sample List of Conjoint Applications

Consumer Durables	*Other Products*
1. Automotive styling	1. Bar soaps
2. Automobile and truck tires	2. Hair shampoos
3. Car batteries	3. Carpet cleaners
4. Ethical drugs	4. Clothing: sweatshirts, bras
5. Toaster ovens	5. Gasoline pricing
6. Cameras	6. Panty hose
7. Apartment design	7. Lawn chemicals

Financial Services	*Other Services*
1. Branch bank services	1. Car rental agencies
2. Auto insurance policies	2. Telephone services and pricing
3. Health insurance policies	3. Employment agencies
4. Credit card features	4. Information-retrieval services
5. Consumer discount cards	5. Medical laboratories
6. Auto retailing facilities	6. Hotel design
7. High-tech maintenance service	7. Toll collection on tollways
	8. Online auction services
	9. Online corporate logo design

Industrial Goods	*Transportation*
1. Copying machines	1. Domestic airlines
2. Printing equipment	2. Transcontinental airlines
3. Facsimile transmission	3. Passenger train operations
4. Data transmission	4. Freight train operations
5. Portable computer terminals	5. International Air Transportation Association
6. Personal computer design	6. Electric car design

model. Various combinations of factor levels can then be tried out to see what their share of choices would be under different assumptions regarding competitive offerings and total-market demand.

The simulators can employ a variety of consumer-choice procedures, ranging from having each consumer simply select the alternative with the highest utility to more elaborate probability-of-choice rules, where probability is related to utility differences in the set of alternatives under evaluation.

Applications of Conjoint Analysis

Despite its recent development, conjoint analysis has already been applied to a wide variety of problems in product design, price elasticity of demand, transportation service design, and the like. Table 19.7 shows a representative list of applications. As can be noted, areas of application cover the gamut—products and services, as well as consumer, industrial, and institutional markets.

The applications areas most conducive to conjoint analysis are those in which the product or service involves a relatively high resource commitment and tends to be "analyzable" by the purchaser (e.g., banking or insurance services, industrial products). Some idea of the range of possibilities may be gained from the capsule applications that follow.

Recent Developments

Conjoint analysis has become a highly popular technique in a relatively short time. Researchers estimate that business firms' use of conjoint analysis entails several thousand studies since its introduction to marketing. With software packages for the personal computer, as well as conjoint models built into online survey tools (SurveyZ.com, Qualtrics.com), conjoint methodology is accessible to any interested user.

Developments in data collection and analysis and computer programs for easily finding orthogonal main effects plans have been introduced. Conjoint methodology has also been extended to encompass use occasion and situation dependence in a series of dual-conjoint designs, called componential segmentation.

Perhaps the most interesting extension of the methodology, however, is the recent application of conjoint to the design of "optimal" products and product lines. Thus, it is feasible to extend conjoint beyond the simulation stage (where one finds the best of a limited set of options) to encompass the identification of the best product (or line) over the full set of possibilities. These may number in the hundreds of thousands or even the millions. In sum, conjoint methodology, like MDS, appears to be moving into the product-design-optimization arena, a most useful approach from a pragmatic managerial viewpoint.

Still, conjoint analysis, like MDS, has a number of limitations. For example, the approach assumes that the important attributes of a product or service can all be identified and that consumers behave as though tradeoffs are being considered. In some products where imagery is quite important, consumers may not evaluate a product analytically, or, even if they do, the tradeoff model may be only a gross approximation to the actual decision rules that are employed.

In short, MDS and conjoint are still maturing—both as techniques that provide intellectual stimulation and as practical tools for product positioning, segmentation, and strategic planning.

SUMMARY

Chapter 19 has focused on four multivariate techniques: factor analysis, cluster analysis, multidimensional scaling, and conjoint analysis.

The factor-analytic method stressed in this chapter was principal-components analysis. This procedure has the property of selecting sets of weights to form linear combinations of the original variables such that the variance of the obtained component scores is (sequentially) maximal, subject to each linear combination's being orthogonal to previously obtained ones.

The principal-components model was illustrated on a set of data from a study conducted by a grocery chain.

Cluster analysis was described in terms of three general questions: (a) selecting a proximity measure; (b) algorithms for grouping objects; and (c) describing the clusters. In addition, an application of clustering was briefly described.

MDS methods are designed to portray subjective similarities or preferences as points (or vectors) in some multidimensional space. Psychological distance is given a physical distance representation. We discussed metric and nonmetric MDS methods, and ideal-point and vector preference models. A variety of applications were described to give the reader some idea of the scope of the methodology.

Conjoint analysis was described along similar lines. We first discussed the primary ways of collecting tradeoff data and then showed how such data are analyzed via multiple regression with dummy predictor variables. The importance of fractional factorial designs was discussed, as well as other practical problems in the implementation of conjoint analysis.

We next turned to some illustrative applications of conjoint analysis, including the design of new products and services. We then presented a brief description of future developments that could serve to increase the flexibility of conjoint methodology.

This chapter, together with Chapter 18, has covered the major multivariate analysis techniques and has included brief discussions of lesser-used techniques. We have not discussed such extensions as canonical correlation of three or more sets of variables or tests for the equality of sums of squares and cross-products matrices. In addition, other related procedures, such as moderated regression, multiple-partial correlation, discriminant analysis with covariate adjustment, factorial discriminant analysis, to name a few, have been omitted from discussion.

We have discussed the principal assumption structure of each technique, appropriate problems for applying it, and sufficient numerical applications to give the reader a feel for the kind of output generated by each program.

Our coverage of so vast and complex a set of methods is limited in depth as well as breadth. The fact remains, however, that marketing researchers of the future will have to seek grounding in multivariate methodology, if current research trends are any indication. This grounding will probably embrace three facets: (a) theoretical understanding of the techniques; (b) knowledge of the details of appropriate computer algorithms for implementing the techniques; and (c) a grasp of the characteristics of substantive problems in marketing that are relevant for each of the methods.

❖

ASSIGNMENT MATERIAL

1. Examine the marketing literature for three applications of cluster analysis.
   a. What were the purposes of using cluster analysis by each of the authors?
   b. What alternative multivariate methods can you propose to analyze the data of these studies?

2. a. Use the data set given in Problem 5 of Chapter 18 and conduct a cluster analysis of the people using the four variables shown. Pool ownership is to be a predictor variable and should be coded as follows: 1 = nonowner; 2 = owner. How would you interpret the resulting clusters?

   b. Do a factor analysis of these same data and interpret the results.

3. a. Use the data set given in Problem 6 of Chapter 18; do a factor analysis of each risk group and interpret the results.

   b. Do a cluster analysis of the five variables (risk is to be coded as 1 = poor, 2 = equivocal, 3 = good). How would you interpret the resulting clusters?

4. For each of the following situations, indicate the multivariate techniques that would be most helpful to an analyst. Also, explain how you would conduct the analysis.

   a. A manufacturer wishes to develop a profile of his customers so that he can predict whether a potential customer may, in fact, become an actual customer.

   b. A company desires to know which of its 20 salesmen are similar to each other, and which ones differ.

   c. An analyst wants to know which of 18 possible independent variables should be included in a multiple regression model.

5. Collect similarities data from people you know regarding a stimulus set of your choice—for example, toothpaste brands, professors, automobiles, actors, or vacation places.

   a. Using an MDS program of your choice, scale the data.

   b. Randomly divide your sample of respondents (make sure you have enough to do this) and scale the two subgroups' data separately. How do these subgroup scalings compare with the total group?

   c. Cluster-analyze the respondents by treating the similarities as profile data. Then separately scale the cluster averages. How do your configurations compare across clusters?

6. Describe three problems in marketing research (not mentioned in the chapter) that you feel night be amenable to MDS, and discuss how you would use MDS in each situation.

7. Describe three problems in marketing research (not mentioned in the chapter) that you feel might be amenable to conjoint analysis, and discuss how you would use conjoint analysis in each situation.

8. What types of consumer products do you think would *not* be amenable to conjoint analysis?

9. Suppose you were asked to develop a set of factors for a prospective conjoint analysis of home mortgage types. What factors, and levels within each factor, can you suggest? Which approach—tradeoff (two-at-a-time) or full profile—would you use? Defend your choice.

10. For the use of conjoint analysis, what conditions and situations dictate when tradeoff is the preferred approach and when full profile is preferred? Are there conditions in which only one approach can be used, since the other simply will not work?

ENDNOTE

1. Experimental Design

    As mentioned earlier, if multiple-factor evaluations are used, highly fractionated factorial designs are pretty much a necessity if the researcher wishes to keep the stimulus set down to some reasonable number. *Orthogonal arrays* represent a special type of fractional factorial design that allows orthogonal estimation of all main effects (the type of model assumed in additive utility formulations) with the smallest possible number of combinations.

Orthogonal arrays are available for virtually any number of factors and levels within factor that the marketing researcher might need. As long as two-factor and higher-order interactions can be assumed to be negligible, orthogonal arrays represent the most efficient class of fractional factorial design available. Introduction to orthogonal arrays, and to other useful designs in the context of conjoint analysis, can be found elsewhere.

REFERENCES

Aldenderfer, M. S., & Blashfield, R. K. (1984). *Cluster analysis.* Beverly Hills, CA: Sage.

Ball, G. H., & Hall, D. J. (1964, July). *Background information on clustering techniques.* (Working paper.) Menlo Park, CA: Stanford Research Institute.

Bijmolt, T. H. A., & Wedel, M. (1995). The effects of alternative methods of collecting similarity data for multidimensional scaling. *International Journal of Research in Marketing, 12,* 363–371.

Carroll, J. D., & Arabie, P. (1998). Multidimensional scaling. In M. H. Birnbaum (Ed.), *Handbook of perception and cognition. Volume 3: Measurement, judgment and decision-making* (pp. 179–250). San Diego, CA: Academic Press.

Carroll, J. D., & Arabie, P. (1980). Multidimensional scaling. In M. R. Rosenzweig & L. W. Porter (Eds.), *Annual review of psychology.* Palo Alto, CA: Annual Reviews.

Carroll, J. D., Green, P. E., & Schaffer, C. M. (1986, August). Interpoint distance comparisons in correspondence analysis. *Journal of Marketing Research, 23,* 271–280.

Coombs, C. H. (1964). *A theory of data.* New York: Wiley.

Green, P. E. (1975). On the robustness of multidimensional scaling. *Journal of Marketing Research, 12,* 73–81.

Green, P. E., & Rao, V. R. (1972). *Applied multidimensional scaling: A comparison of approaches and algorithms.* New York: Holt, Rinehart and Winston.

Green, R. T., & Larsen, T. L. (1985, May). *Export markets and economic change.* (Working paper 84/85-5-2). Austin: Department of Marketing Administration, University of Texas at Austin.

Hoffman, D. L., & Franke, G. R. (1986, August). Correspondence analysis: Graphical representation of categorical data in marketing research. *Journal of Marketing Research, 23,* 213–217.

Johnson, S. C. (1967, September). Hierarchical clustering schemes. *Psychometrika, 32,* 241–154.

Kim, J.-O., & Mueller, C. W. (1978a). *Introduction to factor analysis: What it is and how to do it.* Beverly Hills, CA: Sage.

Kim, J.-O., & Mueller, C. W. (1978b). *Factor analysis: Statistical methods and practical issues.* Beverly Hills, CA: Sage.

Kruskal, J. B., & Wish, M. (1978). *Multidimensional scaling.* Beverly Hills, CA: Sage.

Sneath, P. H. A., & Sokal, R. R. (1973). *Numerical taxonomy.* San Francisco: W.H. Freeman.

Sokal, R. R., & Sneath, P. H. A. (1963). *Principles of numerical taxonomy.* San Francisco: W.H. Freeman.

Srinivasan, V. (1997, May). Surprising robustness of the self-explicated approach to customer preference structure measurement. *Journal of Marketing Research, 34,* 286–291.

Stewart, D. W. (1981). The application and misapplication of factor analysis in marketing research. *Journal of Marketing Research, 18,* 56.

Swint, A. (1994/1995, Winter). Using cluster analysis for segmentation. *Sawtooth News, 10*(2), 6–7.

Whitlark, D., & Smith, S. M. (2003). *How many attributes does it take to describe a brand? What is the right question when collecting associate data?* Unpublished Paper, Graduate School of Management, Brigham Young University, Provo, UT.

Cases for Part V

CASE STUDY V–1

Quiet Inn (B)

CA Associates, a local marketing research firm, conducted a survey for Quiet Inn[1]. The overall objectives and research design were discussed in the Quiet Inn (A) case following Part II.

Two target markets were identified for study—bus tours and general tourism. The results of the bus tour study were disappointing; only one company responded to the request for information. This response represented a response rate of 8.5 percent of companies receiving the questionnaire. Accordingly, it was decided to drop this aspect of the study.

In contrast, a much better response was received from the general tourism target market, which had an overall response rate of 34.4 percent of questionnaires delivered distributed as shown in Table V–1.1.

The questionnaire used for this target market is shown in Exhibit V–1.1.

QUESTIONS FOR DISCUSSION

- Will this questionnaire provide the information needed by Quiet Inn to develop a marketing program to improve occupancy? Why or why not?
- Prepare a coding manual so that the data can be analyzed.

ENDNOTE

1. Disguised name.

Table V-1.1   Survey Respondents, by Place of Residence

	Place of Residence					
	Oregon	Washington	California	Canada	Other	All respondents
Total number of questionnaires mailed	432	145	189	78	58	902
Number undeliverable	3	104	4	8	3	122
Number delivered	429	41	185	70	55	780
Usable number returned by respondents	136	38	64	10	20	268
Usable responses as a percent of questionnaires delivered	31.7%	92.7%	34.6%	14.3%	36.4%	34.4%

EXHIBIT V-1.1   Questionnaire for General Tourism

Travel Motel Survey

1. Have you stayed in any of these motels within the last two years? Please put a number indicating the number of times you have stayed at that particular motel beside the appropriate names.

_____ Travelodge   _____ Holiday Inn   _____ VIP's Motor Inn
_____ Country Squire   _____ Ramada Inn   _____ Rodeway Inn (presently the Red Lion)
_____ New Oregon   _____ Motel 66
_____ Quiet Inn   _____ Greentree Hotel

2. How often do you take overnight trips that require lodging?

_____ 1 per year   _____ 2–5 per year   _____ 5–10 per year
_____ 10–15 per year   _____ Other (please
                                 specify amount)

3. How long do you usually stay?

_____ one night   _____ more than one night plus one day
_____ one night plus one day _____ two nights plus two days
_____ more than two
      nights and days

4. What time of year and how many overnight lodging trips do you take per year? Please place a number representing the number of trips beside the time of year in the blank space provided.

_____ Fall (Sept.–Nov.)   _____ Spring (Mar.–May)
_____ Winter (Dec.–Feb.)   _____ Summer (June–Aug.)

5. What is your reason for taking overnight trips that require motel lodging?

_____ Business   _____ Via another destination for business
_____ Vacation   _____ Via another destination for vacation
_____ Visiting friends
      or relatives

6a. Who booked your stay for you?

_____ Travel agent   _____ Yourself
_____ Company you work for _____ Your spouse
_____ Someone at that
      destination point

6b. If you checked "Someone at that destination point," indicate their relation to you.

_____ Friend   _____ Relative   _____ Employer
_____ Travel agent   _____ University institution

7. What mode of transportation do you use when you take these trips?

_____ Car   _____ Bus   _____ Train   _____ Airline

(Continued)

EXHIBIT V-1.1 (Continued)

8. Please evaluate how important each of the following variables is to you when choosing a motel for overnight lodging. Check the level of importance of each variable on the following scale.

	Not Important	Fairly Important	Very Important	No Opinion
I. Restaurant	_____	_____	_____	_____
Gift Shop	_____	_____	_____	_____
Lounge/Bar	_____	_____	_____	_____
Night Time Entertainment	_____	_____	_____	_____
Jacuzzi/Sauna	_____	_____	_____	_____
II. Jogging/Bike Trail	_____	_____	_____	_____
Swimming Pool	_____	_____	_____	_____
Racquetball Facilities	_____	_____	_____	_____
Various Room Sizes	_____	_____	_____	_____
HBO TV	_____	_____	_____	_____
III. Room Service	_____	_____	_____	_____
Employees	_____	_____	_____	_____
Parking Availability	_____	_____	_____	_____
Covered Parking	_____	_____	_____	_____
Friendly Service	_____	_____	_____	_____
IV. Non-Smoker Option	_____	_____	_____	_____
Room Rates	_____	_____	_____	_____
Exterior Appearance	_____	_____	_____	_____
Advertised Rates	_____	_____	_____	_____
Room Service	_____	_____	_____	_____

9. Please evaluate each of the motels that you checked in Question #1 on the criteria listed below. Use a numbering scale that ranges from 1 to 5. 1 = poor, 5 = excellent, and 0 means that the criteria does not apply to that motel.

Motel: Criteria	Travelodge	Country Squire	New Oregon	Holiday Inn	Ramada Inn	Quiet Inn	Red Lion (Rodeway)	VIP's Motor Inn	Motel 66	Greentree Motel
1. Restaurant	__	__	__	__	__	__	__	__	__	__
2. Gift Shop	__	__	__	__	__	__	__	__	__	__
3. Lounge/Bar	__	__	__	__	__	__	__	__	__	__
4. Night Entertainment	__	__	__	__	__	__	__	__	__	__
5. Jacuzzi/Sauna	__	__	__	__	__	__	__	__	__	__

(Continued)

EXHIBIT V-1.1 (Continued)

Criteria	Motel:	Travelodge	Country Squire	New Oregon	Holiday Inn	Ramada Inn	Quiet Inn	Red Lion (Rodeway)	VIP/s Motor Inn	Motel 66	Greentree Motel
6. Jogging/Bike Trail		——	——	——	——	——	——	——	——	——	——
7. Swimming Pool		——	——	——	——	——	——	——	——	——	——
8. Racquetball Courts		——	——	——	——	——	——	——	——	——	——
9. Room Comfort		——	——	——	——	——	——	——	——	——	——
10. Employees		——	——	——	——	——	——	——	——	——	——
11. Parking		——	——	——	——	——	——	——	——	——	——
12. Friendly Services		——	——	——	——	——	——	——	——	——	——
13. Room Service		——	——	——	——	——	——	——	——	——	——
14. Rates of Rooms		——	——	——	——	——	——	——	——	——	——

10. What are the three most important criteria that you use when choosing a motel for overnight lodging? You may refer to the above-mentioned criteria or use your own ideas. Consider #1 of your list most important.

    1. _____

    2. _____

    3. _____

11. Are there any other characteristics that are important to you in a motel? If so, please mention them in the space provided below.

12. How many times within the last two years have you driven through via another destination?

    _____ 1 time   _____ 2–5 times   _____ 5–10 times

    _____ 10–15 times   _____ Other (please specify amount)

13. What is your usual destination? Please name city or cities in space provided below.

    1. _____

    2. _____

    3. _____

14. Did you check Quiet Inn in Question #1? If not, please skip to Question #24.

    _____ Yes   _____ No

EXHIBIT V-1.1   (Continued)

15. What made you decide to stay at the Quiet Inn?

    _____ General Appearances   _____ Room Rates

    _____ Referral   _____ Location

    _____ My company booked me there

    _____ Other (please indicate reason in space below)

    _____

16. How many times within the last two years have you stayed in the Quiet Inn?

    _____ 1 time   _____ 2–5 times   _____ 5–10 times

    _____ 10–15 times _____ Other (please specify number)

17a. Please name five positive features of the Quiet Inn.

    1. _____

    2. _____

    3. _____

    4. _____

    5. _____

17b. Please name five negative features of the Quiet Inn.

    1. _____

    2. _____

    3. _____

    4. _____

    5. _____

18. How would you rate the employees at the Quiet Inn on each of the following criteria?

	Excellent	Satisfactory	Unsatisfactory	No Opinion
1. Friendliness	_____	_____	_____	_____
2. Efficiency	_____	_____	_____	_____
3. Promptness	_____	_____	_____	_____
4. Appearance	_____	_____	_____	_____

(Continued)

EXHIBIT V-1.1   (Continued)

19. Please rate your room that you stayed in at the Quiet Inn on your last visit. Check the appropriate column for the given criteria on the left.

	Excellent	Average	Below Average	No Opinion
1. Attractiveness	_____	_____	_____	_____
2. Comfort	_____	_____	_____	_____
3. Cleanliness	_____	_____	_____	_____
4. Complete with all room necessities	_____	_____	_____	_____
5. TV	_____	_____	_____	_____

20. Did you eat at any of the following restaurants during your stay at the Quiet Inn? If so, please check which one(s).

_____ Lyon's   _____ Wendy's   _____ Hoot's

_____ Ye Old Pancake House   _____ Sambo's   _____ Mr. Steak

_____ Louie's   _____ Fancy Q   _____ Treehouse Restaurant

21. If you checked the Fancy Q Restaurant, please comment on the food, service, etc. that you received. If not, go on to the next question.

_____

22. What other motels that you have lodged in are comparable (similar) to the Quiet Inn? Please list them below.

1. _____

2. _____

3. _____

23a. Would you recommend the Quiet Inn to a friend?   _____ Yes   _____ No

23b. Why or why not?

_____

DEMOGRAPHICS: We would appreciate your sharing some information about yourself in the next section. This information will be used only to categorize you with other respondents and will be completely confidential. Thank you.

(Continued)

EXHIBIT V-1.1   (Continued)

24. What is your sex? _____ Male _____ Female

25. What is your age?

_____ under 25 _____ 25–34 _____ 34–44 _____ 45–54 _____ 55 or over

26. What is your marital status?

_____ Married _____ Single _____ Widowed _____ Divorced (Separated)

27a. Do you have children? _____ Yes _____ No

If no, go to Question #28

27b. How many children are there in your household?

_____ One _____ Two _____ Three _____ Four _____ Five _____ Over Five

27c. What are the ages of the children? Please list below.

_____

28. What is your occupation? _____

29. What is the last grade of school you've completed?

_____ High school graduate or less

_____ Some college

_____ College graduate of a four-year college

_____ Postgraduate education

30. Please indicate your approximate income level.

_____ Under $20,000   _____ Between $70,000 and 99,999

_____ Between $20,000 and 39,999   _____ $100,000 or more

_____ Between $40,000 and 69,999

THANK YOU FOR YOUR ASSISTANCE WITH OUR SURVEY.

CASE STUDY V–2

Oerlikon Watch Company

The Oerlikon Watch Company recently introduced a new type of wristwatch. Named the Synchromatic, it operates on the principle of establishing a constant frequency in a tuning fork that is actuated by a piezoelectric generator within the watch. Wrist movement activates the generator and produces current sufficient to power the watch. The stored power vibrates the tuning fork at a frequency of 360 cycles per second. The watch has very few moving parts and is highly accurate. It is housed in a titanium case and is shockproof, waterproof, and antimagnetic. The watch does not require winding or a battery and has a life expectancy of approximately 10 years.

Before the watch was introduced, a consumer use test was held in which a judgment sample of 25 men was selected to wear the watch. These men collectively represented a wide range of occupational and age groups. They each agreed to wear the watch at all times and under the same conditions they would normally wear a wristwatch. They also agreed to be interviewed at the end of a three-month period.

Two of the questions that each man was asked during the interview after having worn the watch were, "What did you find that you liked about the watch?" and "What did you find that you disliked about the watch?" The responses to these questions for each of the 25 respondents are given in Exhibit V–2.1.

1. a. Establish categories and tabulate the responses to the question, "What did you find that you liked about the watch?"

   b. What conclusions could be drawn from the responses about the features that appealed to the wearers? Are these features the ones that should have been used in the appeals and copy of an introductory advertising campaign?

2. a. Establish categories and tabulate the responses to the question, "What did you find that you disliked about the watch?"

   b. What conclusions could be drawn from the responses about the undesirable features or attributes of the watch? Which of these, in your judgment, should have been changed before the product was introduced?

750

EXHIBIT V-2.1 Question: "What did you find that you liked about the watch?"

Respondent Number	*Response*
1	"Most accurate watch I have ever worn." "Everyone at the plant was impressed."
2	"I like not having to worry about the battery."
3	"Kept very good time." "I could see the dial at night."
4	"I have never had to worry about whether my watch was off and I would be late for an appointment."
5	"I didn't miss a single train to work because my watch was wrong."
6	"I work with a group of engineers, and they were all impressed with the watch."
7	"I always forget to wind my watch, and since I am on the road driving a lot, this causes me a lot of trouble. I like this one because I didn't have to maintain it."
8	"I like to try new things. I don't understand how this watch works but I was talking to my doctor about it, and he said he would like to get one too."
9	"I always like to know how things work. I got so interested in how a tuning fork could be used to keep time that I read all the company literature they would send me. I think the design is very clever."
10	"I work around a lot of equipment that generates electrical fields. I found that the watch kept perfect time while my present watch, which is supposed to be antimagnetic, is pretty erratic."
11	"I like a watch with a little heft to it that you don't have to worry about banging it up. This one I dropped at least three times on a hardwood floor, and it didn't affect it at all."
12	"I don't know whether you have other doctors trying the watch or not, but we need watches that are accurate and dependable. I found this watch to be both highly accurate and always running." "Since I have to wash my hands a lot, I have to have a watch that is waterproof. This one seemed completely waterproof." "I need a watch that has a clean design that will not catch and hold dust and dirt. I like the design of this one, since it doesn't have a stem."
13	"All my friends never heard of a watch like this before. The other guys kept asking me who I knew to get to wear a watch like this. This is the kind of a watch a man can be proud of."
14	"This is the most accurate watch I have ever worn. It is even better than my pocket watch and I thought it was good."

(Continued)

EXHIBIT V-2.1 (Continued)

Respondent Number	Response
15	"Everything is electronic these days. A piezo-electric watch is something that not very many people have, however."
16	"We get time signals from the Naval Observatory at the radio station at which I work. I didn't believe that you could get a watch that was this accurate until I had tried it."
17	"I skin-dive a lot and need a watch I can depend on so that I will know how long I have been down. This one worked well. I also need a watch that has a large luminous dial that I can read under water. I could read the time easily with this watch."
18	"I sometimes have trouble getting to sleep and always wear my watch. The view at night feature is great. "
19	"All the guys in the fraternity were pretty impressed. Even my physics prof thought it was a good watch. We checked out the frequency one day in class on a scope."
20	"Riding in a cab over a diesel engine all day I get a lot of vibration. If this watch continues to keep as good time for the next year as it has for the last three months I would say you have a good product on your hands."
21	"I always take off my watch at work and leave it on my desk. The self-winding watch I now have sometimes stops. I didn't have any trouble with this one."
22	"I never placed much stock in this 'taste-maker' concept you read about, but I found that I enjoyed showing and telling people about this watch."
23	"This is a watch that I would like to give my son for graduation, as I think he would be proud to own one."
	"I found I became more time-conscious as a result of wearing such an accurate watch."
24	"The boss heard about me wearing this new kind of watch and called me in one day. We must have spent half an hour talking about it. It was the first time I ever knew he knew I even worked for him."
25	"When are you going to start selling this watch? Everybody I talked with about it seemed very impressed."

(Continued)

EXHIBIT V-2.1 (Continued)

Respondent Number	Response
1	"The watch is too big. My sleeve is always getting hung on it."
2	"The humming bothered me at night. When I put my arm under the pillow, it seemed to come right through."
3	"I was annoyed that it tended to fray the cuff on the left sleeve on my shirts. You ought to do something about the sharp edges on the case."
4	"I would imagine this is going to be a high-priced watch. I didn't like the styling at all. It looked like an inexpensive watch."
5	"The watch is far too large."
6	"I think the watch is too thick and big around even for a man's watch. I don't see how you ever sell a watch of this size to women."
7	"It's a funny thing, but the humming bothered me when I was trying to get to sleep. I never noticed sounds on my regular watch, but the humming noise kept me awake. I don't understand it, as I couldn't even hear the humming during the day."
8	"It wore out the cuff on my sleeve."
9	"I think you ought to make it look more expensive."
	"Something ought to be done about making it smaller. I suppose you have technology problems getting it smaller, but the watch is too big in my opinion."
10	"I am a physicist and I noticed that the headboard of my bed tended to act as a sounding board for the humming. However, since I don't suppose many people tend to wear their watches at night, this wouldn't pose much of a problem generally."
11	"I don't like the styling of the watch."
12	"I prefer a thin case on a watch and one that has a contemporary design. This one looks like the old Ingersoll dollar pocket watch to me."
	"I had a problem with this watch wearing the cuff on my shirt sleeve. I always wear starched cuffs and the watch tended to catch and pull threads in the cuff."
13	"You should reduce the size of the watch."
14	"This watch doesn't look like one an executive should be wearing."
15	"I was bothered somewhat by the humming of the watch while I was trying to get to sleep."
16	"The dial is apparently made out of plastic which scratches easily. This gives a very poor appearance to the watch."

(Continued)

EXHIBIT V-2.1 (Continued)

Respondent Number	Response
17	"I recognize some of the problems of miniaturizing a watch of this kind, but I think you are going to have to get it down to the size of a conventional watch before it will sell very well."
18	"I don't know whether I happened to get a lemon or not, but it kept stopping on me. I notified the people you told me to and they adjusted it several times but it never did work right."
19	"It got to the point where I began to roll back my shirt cuff at work because the edge of the case was wearing it out."
20	"This watch isn't styled very well in my opinion. It looks like it was designed for installation in the instrument panel of a locomotive."
21	"This watch is definitely too large." "I don't like the styling at all. It looks cheap."
22	"The crystal scratches awfully easily." "I think you could improve on the way the watch looks."
23	"You ought to do something about the crystal. It got so scratched that sometimes when the light was from a certain angle I couldn't see the hands."
24	"The watch did a pretty good job on my shirt cuffs. It seemed as if every time I pulled the cuff up to see what time it was it would catch on the watch."
25	"I didn't find anything I disliked about the watch."

CASE STUDY V–3

Mount Rushmore Insurance Company (A)

The management of the Mount Rushmore Insurance Company, a company specializing in automobile insurance, asked the marketing research manager to conduct a survey to determine consumer interest in a new auto insurance concept then under consideration.

The concept involved coverage for costs incurred as a result of a car breaking down while on a trip.

The marketing research manager designed and conducted a small telephone survey involving a sample of 60 respondents. Half of the sample was drawn randomly from the company's present customer list, and half was drawn by means of random-digit dialing. In each interview the following statement describing the proposed insurance coverage was read to the respondent over the telephone:

An insurance company is considering providing a policy that would pay toward expenses incurred when your car breaks down while you are driving more than 150 miles from home. It pays up to $500 toward such items as towing, repair costs, other transportation, rooms, and meals. Payments are subject to a $50 deductible amount. The policy will cost $15 a year.

Following the reading of this statement the respondent was asked to state his or her degree of interest in the policy on a five-point scale ranging from 1 (definitely not interested) to 5 (very much interested).

The respondent was then asked to supply a small amount of background data:

- Age
- Marital status
- Number of cars owned
- Average age of car(s)
- Number of trips taken by automobile (for any purpose whatsoever) over the past year that exceeded 300 miles on a round-trip basis

The data obtained from the survey are shown in Table 1.

QUESTIONS FOR DISCUSSION

1. Divide the sample into two groups:
   a. Those showing high interest—4 or 5 ratings
   b. Those showing lower interest—1, 2, or 3 ratings

   Cross-tabulate high versus low interest in Rushmore customers versus customers of other companies. How strong is the association between interest in the policy and current insurance supplier, and at what levels is it statistically significant?

2. What happens to the association observed in the preceding cross-tabulation when older (40 years and over) versus younger respondents is introduced as a third two-category variable?

3. We can consider the concept rating as a criterion variable and the remaining six variables as predictor variables in a multiple regression. In the case of current insurance supplier, we can use the dummy-variable coding:

   Rushmore customer $\Rightarrow 1$

   Other company customer $\Rightarrow 0$

Similarly, in the case of marital status, we can use the dummy-variable coding:

$$Single \Rightarrow 1$$

$$Married \Rightarrow 0$$

Having done this, regress the column of concept ratings (criterion variable) on the six predictor variables:

a. Interpret the regression equation, and indicate the extent to which the variations in the predictor variables explain the variation in the criterion variable.

b. Is each separate predictor statistically significant at the 0.05 level?

c. Can a simpler model (involving fewer predictor variables) be developed? If so, how do the predictors enter such a simpler model?

4. Divide the sample into four groups: Rushmore, single; Rushmore, married; other company, single; and other company, married.

a. If we consider these four groups in a single-factor analysis of variance with the concept rating serving as a criterion variable, do we accept the null hypothesis that the four mean concept ratings are equal (at the 0.05 level)? If not, which group has the highest rating?

b. What are the assumptions about the error term in the single-factor ANOVA model?

c. Using the concept rating as a criterion variable, examine the significance of current insurance supplier and number of cars (one versus more than one) on ratings in a two-factor ANOVA.

Table V-3.1   Telephone Survey Data*

Respondent	Concept Rating	Current Insurance Supplier	Age	Marital Status	Number of Cars	Average Age of Car(s)	Number of Trips
1	4	Rushmore	42	M	1	0.5	3
2	3	R	39	M	1	1.5	1
3	5	R	47	M	1	1	4
4	2	R	24	S	3	1	2
5	4	R	43	M	2	1.5	4
6	5	R	62	M	1	0.5	6
7	1	R	27	M	1	2	3
8	5	R	55	M	2	0.5	4
9	4	R	42	S	1	2	2
10	3	R	36	M	2	2.5	1
11	4	R	39	M	3	1.5	5
12	2	R	24	S	4	2	0
13	5	R	58	M	1	2	6
14	4	R	43	M	1	0.4	2
15	1	R	23	S	2	2.5	0
16	5	R	59	M	1	0.5	7
17	4	R	43	M	3	1.5	3
18	3	R	36	S	1	2	0
19	3	R	47	M	1	2	1
20	4	R	42	M	1	1.5	4
21	4	R	47	M	4	1.5	4
22	4	R	38	M	2	1	3
23	5	R	37	M	2	0.8	8
24	3	R	39	S	1	2	0
25	4	R	51	M	1	1	2
26	4	R	47	M	2	1.5	1
27	5	R	51	M	1	2	6
28	1	R	30	S	1	2	0
29	1	R	28	S	2	4.5	2
30	3	R	42	M	2	3.5	1
31	2	Other	32	M	3	3	0
32	4	O	29	M	1	2	3
33	2	O	32	M	1	1	0
34	1	O	37	M	1	1	0
35	3	O	24	S	4	2.5	1
36	2	O	41	M	1	2	3
37	3	O	23	M	1	2	0
38	1	O	34	M	5	3	1
39	2	O	38	M	2	2	0
40	4	O	47	M	2	1	5
41	5	O	24	M	1	0.5	9
42	3	O	32	M	1	1.5	0
43	1	O	22	S	1	3	1
44	2	O	27	S	1	2.5	0

(Continued)

Table V-3.1 (Continued)

Respondent	Concept Rating	Current Insurance Supplier	Age	Marital Status	Number of Cars	Average Age of Car(s)	Number of Trips
45	2	O	29	M	3	2.5	0
46	4	O	43	M	2	1	2
47	5	O	48	S	1	0.5	3
48	3	O	36	M	1	1.5	0
49	4	O	42	M	3	1.5	2
50	2	O	26	S	2	2	2
51	2	O	29	S	1	2.5	1
52	1	O	23	S	1	3	0
53	3	O	34	M	1	1.5	0
54	4	O	37	S	1	1.5	2
55	2	O	24	S	2	3	0
56	3	O	32	M	2	2	1
57	5	O	44	M	1	0.5	7
58	1	O	28	M	1	2.5	0
59	1	O	22	S	2	3	1
60	2	O	26	S	1	2	1

* These data are contrived.

CASE STUDY V–4

Cougar Business Forms, Inc. (B)

Cougar Business Forms has started an annual awareness and preference measuring system. The rationale underlying such monitoring, the questionnaire used, and overall methodology were presented in the Case Study Cougar Business Forms, Inc. (A).

Cougar has decided to conduct the survey every February. The most recent survey of 6,000 companies was conducted with the following response:

	Original Sample Size	Number Usable Returns
Hospitals	1200	259
Financial services	1200	164
Manufacturing	1200	205
Retail	800	52
Government	800	213
Transportation	800	109

There were 286 questionnaires returned as undeliverable and 13 responses were unusable. Thus, the 1,002 usable responses represented a response rate of slightly more than 17 percent of questionnaires delivered.

Now that the data have been collected, it must be analyzed. Before that can be done the data had to be entered into a data file. The coding manual developed by the consultant Pam Menak is shown in Figure V–4.1. The resulting data file is labeled "cougar.sav."

QUESTIONS FOR DISCUSSION

1. Is the coding manual sufficient to allow analyses that would achieve the objectives of the annual study? How would you change this coding manual?

2. The data file cougar.sav is based on the coding manual shown in Figure V–4.1. Use the data file to show if there are significant differences among the market segments in awareness of and preference for business forms manufacturers.

3. Regress number of business forms manufacturers used on awareness of individual companies, role played in the purchase of business forms, number of publications read, size of company, and market segment represented.
   a. Interpret the regression equation, and indicate the extent to which the variations in the predictor variables explain the variation in the criterion variable.
   b. Is each separate predictor statistically significant?
   c. Can a simpler model (with fewer predictor variables) be developed? Explain.

4. Do everything requested in Question 3, this time for each individual market segment. What differences are there among the segments?

Variable	Code		
V1	Type (Industry) of Respondent		
	1 = Hospital	4 =	Retailing
	2 = Financial	5 =	Government
	3 = Manufacturing	6 =	Transportation
	Role in Purchase		
	1 = not checked		
	2 = checked		
	V2 Specify		
	V3 Recommend		
	V4 Purchase		
	V5 None		
	Familiarity With Forms Manufacturer		
	1 = aware of name only		
	2 = somewhat familiar		
	3 = very familiar		
	4 = don't know		
	V6 Ajax	V9	Dot
	V7 Bits	V10	Extor
	V8 Cougar	V11	Other
Famsum	Number of Suppliers "Somewhat Familiar" or "Very Familiar" With		
	Current Supplier		
	1 = not checked		
	2 = checked		
	V12 Ajax	V15	Dot
	V13 Bits	V16	Extor
	V14 Cougar	V17	Other
V18	*Number of Companies Used*		
	x = actual number (count from Q. #3a)		
	9 = none (if specified in Q. #3a, otherwise leave blank)		
V19	Manufacturer First Considered		
	1 Ajax	4	Dot
	2 Bits	5	Extor
	3 Cougar	6	Other
	Publications Read		
	1 = not listed		
	2 = listed		
	V20 Bar Code News		
	V21 Packaging Digest		
	V22 Hospitals		
	V23 Health Care Financial Management		
	V24 Modern Health Care		
	V25 Dun's Business Month		
	V26 ABA Banking Journal		

Figure V-4.1 Coding Manual for Business Forms Survey*

*Data file is labeled Cougar.sav

(Continued)

V27 Business Week
V28 Business Computer Systems
V29 Others

V30   <u>Number of Publications Read</u>
                  x = actual number (count from Q. #4)
                  9 = none

V31   <u>Number of Employees</u>
                  1 = Under 100   3 = 251-500
                  2 = 101-250   4 = over 500

V32   <u>Zip Code</u>
                  xxxxx = number

V33   <u>Job Title</u>
                  1 = purchasing manager or agent, buyer materials management
                  2 = data processing
                  3 = office manager
                  4 = administrator, president, vice-president, owner
                  5 = other

---

5. Form two more groups of respondent companies based on number of employees (Group 1 = 250 or less, Group 2 = more than 250). Do a discriminant analysis using manufacturer first considered, number of companies used or suppliers, number of publications read, and familiarity with forms manufacturers as independent or production variables. Interpret.

CASE STUDY V–5

The Diamond Company

The Diamond Company is a Midwestern-based corporation that has concentrated most of its efforts over the past few years in the production and national distribution of global positioning system equipment. However, with the onslaught of foreign competitors, as well as increased domestic competition, Diamond is turning to developing partnerships with mobile telephone manufacturers, as a means for overcoming its recent drop in earnings.

Over the past decade Diamond has developed and leased corporate GPS systems to businesses and private individuals, such as trucking firms and local and federal government organizations. Recent technological breakthroughs involving more sophisticated microcircuitry indicate that it will be possible to integrate GPS systems into telephone units and provide the following advantages over current systems:

- A reliability and accessibility equal to residential phones (instead of the delays that current subscribers face during peak business hours)
- Greater coverage and precision in pin-pointing location
- Improved features, such as one-touch GPS position reporting, optimal routing to destination, and emergency notification
- Leasing and monthly usage charges as low as $9.95 per month

Since the technological breakthrough promises both higher quality, more flexible features, and reduced costs, it is not surprising that many others—including AT&T and Motorola—are also working on new GPS products for their mobile telephone products, and are expected to introduce these features in the next three years or so.

Mr. Peters, president of Diamond, thinks that a new market niche might exist for his company's product line in the residential (upscale professional), as opposed to business, market (where the bigger firms will probably concentrate). In particular, Peters believes that the firm's previous success in designing attractive, easy-to-use systems can be used to advantage in the product/market planning of the new equipment. Possibilities could even exist for incorporating new kinds of equipment into a single package, a kind of phone/GPS/XM radio entertainment/communications center that could at some point even include the ability to store and play MP3 files.

For the present, however, Peters would like to find out what the market reaction would be to an inexpensive, but higher quality, mobile telephone than those now in service that offers the GPS features. Accordingly, Peters called on his old friend, Webster Baker, of Baker Associates, Inc., a marketing research firm specializing in new concept testing.

THE STUDY

Baker designed a pilot study for respondents in the Pittsburgh, Pennsylvania, area, entailing the following steps:

- An initial telephone screening call—handled by random digit dialing—to find out whether the respondent already has a mobile telephone and, if or if not, whether he or she has interest in the new product concept. For those expressing interest in the concept, a follow-up mail questionnaire describing the system in further detail designed to obtain data on degree of interest and selected respondent demographics, was sent.

Approximately six percent of those contacted during the telephone screening call expressed interest in the concept:

A major manufacturer of cellular phones has partnered with a leading manufacturer of GPS (global positioning systems), and has designed a new mobile telephone system. This system will provide one-button GPS positioning information, routes to destinations, and emergency location notification.

The service, including the telephone unit, unlimited calls, and unlimited use of the GPS features could ultimately cost as little as $39.95 per month. Or, if you purchase your own equipment (which may cost as little as $500), the service alone may cost as little as $9.95 per month.

Of the six percent indicating interest during the screening interview, 12 percent currently had a mobile telephone. After receiving the detailed information by e-mail, 80 percent of the respondents returned the questionnaire.

THE DATA

Given the relatively low interest (six percent) in the concept during the initial telephone screening stage, total responses to the follow-up mail questionnaire were limited to 50 respondents who indicated a continued interest (a subjective probability of acquiring that was greater than zero). The remaining four respondents who returned the questionnaire indicated a zero probability of acquisition, now that they had seen the more detailed information on the service. Telephone follow-ups of those who did not return the questionnaire indicated that there was no appreciable response bias insofar as acquisition probability or background data were concerned.

The main responses of interest to Baker were as follows:

1. Likelihood of acquiring the service when it becomes commercially available—a

percentage that ranged from 1% to 100%

2. Preference for purchase versus leasing of the mobile telephone unit:
   Purchase = 1 ; Leasing = 0

3. Respondent's sex:
   Male = 1 ; Female = 0

4. Does respondent have a GPS system in the car that he or she currently drives?

   Yes = 1 ; No = 0

5. Respondent's annual income, in thousands of dollars.

6. Respondent's anticipated use of the service:
   Primarily for   Primarily
   business = 1   ;   for pleasure = 0

7. Respondent's age in years.

Exhibit V–5.1 shows the data for each of the 50 respondents for each of the seven variables. These data are available in a spreadsheet (Diamond.xls) and a SPSS file (Diamond.sav).

QUESTIONS FOR DISCUSSION

1. Using a statistical analysis computer package of your choice, carry out the following analyses.
   a. Find summary statistics for the continuous variables 1, 5, and 7.
   b. Generate scatterplots of variable 1 versus variable 5 and variable 1 versus variable 7.
   c. Create contingency tables between variable 1 (recorded into three classes: 1–39%, low; 40–59%, medium; and 60–100%, high) and variables 2,3, and 6. Also, compute contingency table statistics.

d. Repeat the contingency table analysis for variable 1 versus variable 2, variable 2 versus variable 4, and variable 1 versus variable 6, while holding constant variable 3.

2. Next, examine the results. What can you conclude about how each of the variables, 2 through 7, is associated with variable 1?
   a. Using the stepwise option, regress variable 1 on the other six variables. Interpret your results in terms of the problem. Criticize the use of a linear regression in this example.
   b. Selecting variable 2 as the dependent variable, conduct a two-group discriminant analysis with variables 3 through 7 serving as predictors. Interpret the results substantively.
   c. Apply factor analysis to variables 2 through 7 and compute rotated factor scores for the 50 respondents.

EXHIBIT V-5.1 Response Data for the Baker Research Study

				Variables			
Respondent	*1*	*2*	*3*	*4*	*5*	*6*	*7*
1	18	0	0	0	27.3	0	55
2	24	0	0	1	22.6	0	27
3	30	1	0	1	26.9	0	60
4	90	1	1	0	45.4	1	45
5	1	0	0	0	27.2	0	22
6	85	1	1	1	33.6	1	52
7	12	0	1	0	21.7	0	24
8	20	0	0	1	24.4	0	23
9	35	1	0	0	30.6	1	64
10	55	0	1	0	27.3	1	28
11	80	1	1	1	37.2	1	54
12	75	1	1	1	28.3	1	39
13	95	0	1	0	26.6	0	38
14	100	1	0	1	54.5	1	42
15	18	0	1	0	28.4	1	57
16	15	0	0	1	37.6	0	63
17	90	1	1	1	45.4	1	40
18	85	0	1	1	36.6	1	36
19	95	1	0	0	60.8	1	29
20	70	0	0	1	37.6	0	32
21	60	1	1	0	27.4	1	28
22	55	1	1	1	40.3	0	23
23	40	1	0	1	28.8	0	19
24	45	0	0	0	25.4	0	24
25	35	1	1	1	27.6	0	22
26	22	0	0	0	19.4	1	28
27	90	1	0	1	60.2	1	34
28	100	1	1	1	66.6	1	28
29	18	0	0	1	28.4	0	56
30	5	0	0	0	18.3	0	60
31	100	1	1	1	45.3	1	29
32	80	1	1	0	42.4	0	34
33	95	0	1	0	40.6	1	42
34	70	1	0	0	37.4	1	44
35	30	0	0	0	43.6	0	54
36	75	1	1	1	45.7	1	49
37	85	0	0	0	48.6	1	38
38	18	0	0	0	36.3	1	50
39	75	1	1	0	33.7	0	46
40	95	1	1	0	60.1	1	42
41	92	1	0	1	54.5	1	38
42	20	0	0	0	46.8	0	28
43	25	1	1	0	47.3	0	23
44	85	1	0	1	63.6	0	31
45	95	1	1	1	82.8	1	42
46	15	0	1	0	18.5	0	55
47	100	0	0	0	98.4	1	36
48	85	0	0	1	36.2	1	48
49	18	0	1	0	25.3	0	24
50	60	0	0	1	27.5	1	32

CASE STUDY V–6

Day Airlines (B)

Mr. Kurt Abba, marketing research manager for Day Airlines, had developed and implemented a survey of prospective vacationers to the company's market areas in the Caribbean and Latin America. A rather comprehensive questionnaire had been administered. This questionnaire sought information about preferences for activities while on vacation, characteristics of planned next vacation, places visited and reaction to them, and psychographic characteristics.

Mr. Abba now had to determine how best to analyze the data obtained from the questionnaire. The questionnaire is shown in the (A) case.

QUESTIONS FOR DISCUSSION

1. How could discriminant analysis be usefully employed to help Mr. Abba answer the question of which variables discriminate well between "likers" and "non-likers" of a particular country?

2. What other multivariate tools would you suggest, and how would you use them to implement your analysis?

3. How would you deal with the problem that, in most cases, complete preference rankings are not given (e.g., Question 4)?

4. How could Day Airlines use the results of the analysis in:
   a. Flight scheduling?
   b. Planning new vacation tour packages?
   c. Corporate image promotion?

CASE STUDY V–7

Mount Rushmore Insurance Company (B)

As discussed in the previous case study Mount Rushmore Insurance Company (A), the company conducted a survey of customers and non-customers to determine reaction to a new concept of insurance. Data were obtained by telephone interviews. The marketing research manager has suggested that further insight into whether or not the new policy should be offered; its potential target market and marketing strategy could be obtained by multivariate analysis. The data set in Mount Rushmore Insurance Company (A) is to be used for such analysis.

QUESTIONS FOR DISCUSSION

1. Divide the sample into two groups: one group including respondents rating the concept 4 or 5; the other group including those rating it 1, 2, or 3.
   a. Run a two-group discriminant analysis with the predictor variables of respondent age, number of cars owned, and number of trips.
   b. Interpret the discriminant function.
   c. How well does the function classify the known membership of the sample?

   d. What changes, if any, occur when all six predictor variables are used for the discriminant analysis?
2. Factor-analyze the full 60×7 data matrix by principal components followed by Varimax rotation on those factors whose variance accounted-for values exceed unity.
   a. How would you interpret each set of rotated factor loadings?
   b. What other variables are associated with that factor showing high loadings for the concept-rating variable?
   c. Cluster-analyze the Varimax-rotated factor scores (after first finding inter-point distances in rotated factor space). Find three clusters of respondents.
   d. How would you interpret these clusters with regard to average concept ratings and Rushmore versus other company customers?

3. Having completed the various analyses, what should the marketing research manager recommend regarding (a) the wisdom of offering the policy, (b) its target market, and (c) future research needed before actual introduction of the policy?

CASE STUDY V–8

Popular Food Stores

Popular Food Stores is a regional chain of smaller grocery supermarkets. The company has no megastores. Popular has been in business for more than 35 years. At present it has more than 100 stores located in several states in the Western United States.

As part of its expansion plan, Popular has decided to open its first store in a Southwestern state. A prime location is available at a reasonable price near the campus of the state university located in the city. The university has close to 25,000 students. The company has taken an option on the property. The company naturally is concerned about its competition and how competitors are viewed by consumers in the market area. Very strong positive attitudes may cause the company to delay its entry or to change its mode of operation.

Popular has contracted with Oxford Associates, a marketing research and consulting firm, to do a study in the proposed market area. Oxford has assigned Donald Stom, one of its principals, as project director.

Since the proposed location is close to the university campus, Mr. Stom reasoned that a major segment of the market will be university students. He suggested an image and behavioral study of students be done. The major objects of the image study would be the two major competitors in the market, Albertson's and Smith's. Other major chain food retailers are Raley's and Wal-Mart. Popular's management approved the university student study.

Oxford Associates conducted a survey of 440 students using a self-administered questionnaire. An intercept method was used with students being "interviewed" at various places on campus. The interviews were conducted during a two-week period on Tuesday and Wednesday of the first week and Monday and Thursday of the second week. Different times of the day were used for data collection.

Measurement of attitudes toward (i.e., image of) Albertson's and Smith's was done by use of a traditional seven-category semantic differential scale. The scale items used were drawn from those typically used in studies of retail stores. In order to minimize the amount of time needed to participate in the study, a version of the split-ballot or split-sample technique was used to measure the attitudes. Each respondent evaluated either Albertson's or Smith's. A total of 222 respondents evaluated Albertson's and 218 evaluated Smith's. In addition to the usual demographic variables, questions regarding purchase behavior at food stores and store preference were also included. Finally, Mr. Stom strongly believed that one's personal values would affect attitudes toward food stores so he included a widely used measure known as the List of Values (LOV). The questionnaire used in the study is shown in Figure V–8.1. In Question 6, each respondent answered for either Smith's or Albertson's.

The data obtained for the 440 respondents were entered into a data file (Popular.sav). The codebook for the study is shown in Table V–8.1. Mr. Stom now must decide how to analyze the data.

QUESTIONS FOR DISCUSSION

1. Do respondents have different attitudes toward Albertson's and Smith's? Are the underlying factor structures the same? Explain. How can Popular use these attitudes in deciding whether to enter the market?

2. What differences, if any, exist in attitudes toward Albertson's and Smith's on the basis of demographic characteristics of

Figure V–8.1   Questionnaire

---

1. Which residential district do you live in? _____SE   _____SW   _____NW   _____NE

2. How often do you shop at the following stores to purchase at least one grocery (food or nonfood) item?

    Albertson's   _____ times per month
    Raley's   _____ times per month
    Wal-Mart   _____ times per month
    Smith's   _____ times per month

3. Who is the primary grocery shopper in your family/household?

    _____ self   _____ parent(s)

    _____ spouse   _____ other (please specify): _____

4. A. At which supermarket are you most likely to shop for groceries?

    _____ Albertson's   _____ Wal-Mart
    _____ Raley's   _____ Smith's
    _____ Other (please specify): _____

   B. How long does it usually take you to get to this supermarket from your home?
    _____ minutes

   C. On your last visit to this supermarket how did you get there?
    _____ car/taxi
    _____ bus
    _____ walked

5. Please indicate the average amount of money per month that is spent by your household for groceries at each of the following supermarkets.

    $_____ Albertson's
    $_____ Raley's
    $_____ Wal-Mart
    $_____ Smith's

6. For each pair of descriptors shown below please check the category which best indicates the extent to which you feel either one describes Smith's **(Albertson's)** supermarkets.

Inconvenient location	:___:___:___:___:___:___:	Convenient location
Low prices	:___:___:___:___:___:___:	High prices
Pleasant atmosphere	:___:___:___:___:___:___:	Unpleasant atmosphere
Low quality products	:___:___:___:___:___:___:	High quality products
Modern	:___:___:___:___:___:___:	Old-fashioned
Unfriendly clerks	:___:___:___:___:___:___:	Friendly clerks
Sophisticated customers	:___:___:___:___:___:___:	Unsophisticated customers
Cluttered	:___:___:___:___:___:___:	Spacious
Fast check-out	:___:___:___:___:___:___:	Slow check-out
Unorganized customers	:___:___:___:___:___:___:	Well organized customers
Layout	:___:___:___:___:___:___:	Layout

Enjoyable		Unenjoyable
shopping experience	:___:___:___:___:___:___:	shopping experience
Bad reputation	:___:___:___:___:___:___:	Good reputation
Good service	:___:___:___:___:___:___:	Bad service
Unhelpful clerks	:___:___:___:___:___:___:	Helpful clerks
Dull	:___:___:___:___:___:___:	Exciting
Good selection of		Bad selection of
products	:___:___:___:___:___:___:	products
Dirty	:___:___:___:___:___:___:	Clean
Like	:___:___:___:___:___:___:	Dislike

7. The following is a list of things that some people look for or want out of life. Please study the list carefully and then rate each thing on how important it is in your daily life, where 1=very unimportant and 9=very important.

	Very Unimportant							**Very Important**	
a. Sense of belonging	1	2	3	4	5	6	7	8	9
b. Excitement	1	2	3	4	5	6	7	8	9
c. Warm relationships with others	1	2	3	4	5	6	7	8	9
d. Self-fulfillment	1	2	3	4	5	6	7	8	9
e. Being well-respected	1	2	3	4	5	6	7	8	9
f. Fun and enjoyment in life	1	2	3	4	5	6	7	8	9
g. Security	1	2	3	4	5	6	7	8	9
h. Self-respect	1	2	3	4	5	6	7	8	9
i. A sense of accomplishment	1	2	3	4	5	6	7	8	9

Now reread the items and circle the one thing that is **most important** in your daily life.

Finally, we would like to know something about yourself to help us classify our results. The information will be held in strict confidence.

8. Gender: _____ Female _____ Male

9. What is your marital status? _____ Single _____ Divorced/separated/widowed

_____ Married _____ Other

10. Please indicate your age: _____ years

11. What is your employment status?

_____ Full time _____ Part time _____ Not employed

12. What year are you in university?

_____ Sophomore _____ Junior _____ Senior _____ Graduate student

13. Student status: _____ Resident _____ Non-resident _____ Foreign student

THANK YOU FOR YOUR ASSISTANCE

Table V-8.1   Codebook for Semantic Differential Study

Question Number	Variable	Variable Description
	01	Respondent ID number xxx = actual number
1	03	Residential district 1 = SW 2 = SE 3 = NE 4 = NW
2	04	How often shop at Albertson's xx = actual number
2	05	How often shop at Raley's xx = actual number
2	06	How often shop at Wal-Mart xx = actual number
2	07	How often shop at Smith's xx = actual number
3	08	Primary shopper 1 = self 3 = parent(s) 2 = spouse 4 = other
4A	09	Store most likely to shop at 1 = Albertson's 4 = Smith's 2 = Raley's 5 = other 3 = Wal-Mart
4B	10	Time to get to store xxx = actual number
4C	11	How got there 1 = car/taxi 2 = bus 3 = walked
5	12	Amount spent at Albertson's xxxxx = actual number
5	13	Amount spent at Raley's xxxxx = actual amount
5	14	Amount spent at Wal-Mart xxxxx = actual number
5	15	Amount spent at Smith's xxxxx = actual number

(Continued)

Table V-8.1 (Continued)

Question Number	Variable	Variable Description
6	17	Supermarket evaluated 1 = Albertson's 2 = Smith's
6	18–35	Semantic scales for Albertson's, Smith's x = 1 to 7, starting from the left-side of scale location (18) layout (27) prices (19) shopping experience (28) atmosphere (20) reputation (29) quality of products (21) service (30) modern (22) helpfulness of clerks (31) friendliness of clerks (23) dull (32) customers (24) selection of products (33) cluttered (25) dirty (34) check-out (26) like (35)
7	36	Sense of belonging x = actual number (1 to 9)
7	37	Excitement x = actual number (1 to 9)
7	38	Warm relationships x = actual number (1 to 9)
7	39	Self-fulfillment x = actual number (1 to 9)
7	40	Being well-respected x = actual number (1 to 9)
7	41	Fun x = actual number (1 to 9)
7	42	Security x = actual number (1 to 9)
7	43	Self-respect x = actual number (1 to 9)
7	44	Sense of accomplishment x = actual number (1 to 9)
7	45	Most important in daily life 1 = a 6 = f 2 = b 7 = g 3 = c 8 = h 4 = d 9 = i 5 = e

Table V-8.1 (Continued)

Question Number	Variable	Variable Description
8	46	Gender 1 = female 2 = male
9	47	Marital status 1 = single 2 = married 3 = divorced/separated/widowed 4 = other
10	48	Age xx = actual number
11	49	Employment status 1 = full time 2 = part time 3 = not employed
12	50	Year in university 1 = sophomore 3 = senior 2 = junior 4 = graduate student
13	51	Student status 1 = Resident 2 = Non-resident 3 = Foreign student

respondents, frequency of shopping, and amount of time from home to Albertson's or Smith's?

3. To what extent are attitudes toward either store predictive of amount of money spent for groceries?

4. Do a respondent's values affect his or her attitude toward Albertson's or Smith's? Explain.

5. Using gender as the dependent (criterion) variable, which other variables best distinguish between males and females?

6. Compute an overall attitude score for each respondent by summing responses to the semantic differential scales. Some of the items need to be reverse-scored (i.e., recoded) so that all will be scored so as to have positive and negative directions established. For Albertson's and Smith's separately, form two groups by splitting each subsample at the median attitude score. Which variables best discriminate between the two groups of respondents? Interpret the results of the discriminant analysis.

7. Use attitude score and demographic variables to cluster respondents. Interpret the resulting clusters for Albertson's and Smith's evaluators.

Part VI

THE RESEARCH REPORT

Chapter 20

REPORTING RESEARCH RESULTS

Chapter 2 identified the research report as the culmination of the research process. Whatever is to be included in the report—the study's purpose, methodology, results, conclusions, or recommendations for management—should be presented clearly, accurately, and honestly. We identified the key attributes of a report as being complete and concise. We can go further and state that, when managing a research project by *objectives*, the researcher should start with the last step—*the research report* (Semon, 1998). Managing by objectives focuses on the information needs of the user or client. The report should be designed and outlined in detail at the outset. Since the report needs to focus on information needs, this outline can be an invaluable aid in planning the other stages, such as the plans for analysis, measurement, and so forth.

This chapter examines issues relevant in preparing and presenting reports, both written and oral. All too often the research report is the only aspect of the project that others will ever see. Consequently, if the project is not effectively presented, everything done up to that point will be wasted. A research report must be read (or heard), and its results, conclusions, and recommendations evaluated, if the resources devoted to the project are to have been well spent.

COMMUNICATION

The importance of the research report derives from its role as the major vehicle by which researchers communicate what they have done and found out to others in the organization or to an outside organization. Effective communication has certain characteristics (Rockey, 1984; Vardaman, 1981).

First, the communication is *purposive*. Second, it is an *interchange of symbols*—verbal and graphic representations of a sender's ideas—between people. Third, it seeks workable *understanding and agreement* between the parties. This means that the sender of a report (the researcher) and the receiver (the client) have enough common understanding about, and willingness to accept or at least evaluate, the ideas presented in the report to use them in whatever manner is best. Finally, there is implicit recognition of the *need for feedback*. In order to realize satisfaction, there needs to be a means to confirm response. In short, communication is like playing catch with a baseball: it's not how many are thrown, but how many are caught. To be effective, communication must ultimately be two-way.

One view of the communication process involved in presenting a research report to management or an outside client is illustrated in Figure 20.1, where five basic steps of the communication process are identified:

- Define the context of the report
- Determine the formality of the report
- Select and organize the required information
- Determine the message to be given
- Evaluate feedback for continued success

Following the process when determining how to best communicate your results will help you avoid a minefield of obstacles. Research reports are often laden with multiple objectives, political agendas, and special interests. Further, reports are presented to groups with unique dynamics and individuals with personalities that guide, direct, and even dominate the project, process, or presentation. Each of these factors must be considered when determining how to best communicate the results of your research. Without considering these factors, your research report's effectiveness will be limited.

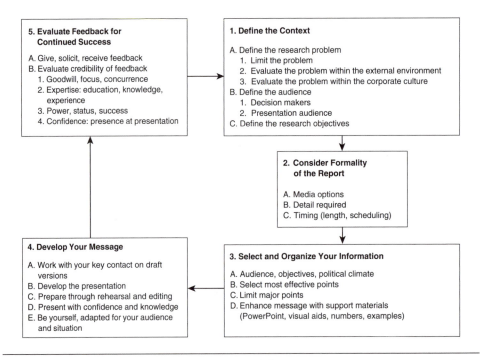

Figure 20.1   Preparing to Communicate the Research Process

SOURCE: From Bienvenu, S., & Timm, P. R., *Business Communications: Discovering Strategy, Developing Skills, 1st edition,* copyright © 2002. Reprinted by permission of Pearson Education, Inc., Upper Saddle River, NJ.

THE RESEARCH REPORT

A research report may encompass a written statement, an oral presentation or both. The purpose of such a report is to communicate research results, recommendations for strategic and tactical action, and other conclusions to management (in-house or outside clients) or other interested parties. Our concern in this chapter is with the final written report. We do, however, make some comments about oral presentations.

Written and oral reports can come in all sizes, shapes, and lengths. The nature of the problem studied, how it was studied, and the client's identity will influence the type of report to be prepared. The length of a report on qualitative research, for example, which can run from as short as eight pages to more than 100 pages, will be influenced by learning garnered, client requirements, writing style, and formatting (Greenberg, 1999). Also, it is important to remember that for many projects two reports are prepared. There is always need for a report to management. This so-called *popular* report minimizes technical details and emphasizes simplicity. Frequently, the simpler reports written in the marketer's language are most understood, read, and, thus, acted upon. However, there also may be need for a more detailed *technical* report. Such a report emphasizes the methods used and underlying assumptions, and presents findings in a detailed manner. This type of report can be a valuable resource for researchers, as well as managers, for future studies.

There are two key dimensions to the report-writing process: (a) analysis of the data; and (b) the actual writing. Analysis is the interpretation of the data obtained to provide useful and meaningful insights into the problem at hand. Writing takes the learning and expresses it in a coherent, logical, and succinct way (Greenberg, 1999). For both analysis and writing, the use of graphical statistical methods can be very beneficial. There are many ways in which data can be presented visually. According to Jacoby (1997, pp. 2–4), graphical statistical methods are used to achieve four broad and mutually supportive objectives:

- Exploring the contents of a data set
- Finding structure in data
- Checking assumptions in statistical models
- Communicating the results of an analysis

A single person may not have the abilities to both effectively analyze data and write a report. Thus, someone other than the analyst often does the report writing.

Criteria for a Good Report

Before turning to what should be included in the report and what the format for presentation should be, we turn to a brief discussion of the criteria for a good report. This most basic criterion is how well the report communicates with the reader. Was the communication effective, in the way defined previously? Practitioners believe that reports written with clarity, brevity, and concreteness get action commitment. The major concerns are that a research report be *complete*, *concise*, *accurate*, and *clear* in what is being said. All these are a reflection of writing style. These topics are discussed in more detail in Rehart (1994), Fink (2003), and Bailey (1990).

Completeness

A report is complete when it gives all the needed information in a language understood by the intended audience. The writing must be done on the level of the reader's understanding; this is fundamental! A report may be incomplete because it is too long *or* too short. Not all information obtained is significant or relevant enough to be reported. In the end, completeness is always defined by the person(s) who will be reading the report and asked to act upon it.

Accuracy

Obviously, accuracy is related to completeness. But it goes further. A report may not be completely accurate because the data (or the information in general) upon which it is based are not accurate. There may have been flaws in research design, measurement and scaling, sampling, and analysis that led to inaccurate results being presented. In addition, carelessness in handling data, interpretation of analyses, or writing style may also lead to inaccuracy. The preparation of a research report calls for attention to detail, including the meaning of every word used, punctuation, and so forth.

Conciseness

Being concise means being selective. Thus, as we said above, not all information obtained needs to be reported. When writing a report, one should write not only so the reader can understand, but can also do so as quickly and easily as possible. Conciseness refers to what is included and how it is included. Sentences should be kept as short as possible. A concise report is not the same as a brief report. A brief report usually contains only the highlights or base essentials of what the researcher has to report. In contrast, a concise report may contain any amount of detail and be very long. A concise report may be very complete. But it is efficient; that is, it conveys all the researcher wants to present in the shortest, most direct way.

Clarity

Clarity may be the most misunderstood criterion for evaluating a research report. Clarity derives from clear and logical thinking and organization. Coherence is important; it involves connections between words, sentences, paragraphs, topics, or ideas. There is always some logical connection between, say, a topic or idea and the one that preceded it. For example, there are different structural ways to organize material in a logical framework, as illustrated in the list below:

1. **Time order.** Ideas are presented in chronological time, either forward or backward.

2. **Space order.** The relationship among places and locations determines organization.

3. **Cause and effect.** Cause may precede effect or the opposite may hold. A report may stress one or the other.

4. **Increasing difficulty.** Structure involves going from the simple to the complex or from the familiar to the unfamiliar, useful when the audience lacks expertise in the topic.

5. **Established category.** When a basic framework is understood, content can be organized in recognized categories. In a market segmentation report, using accepted categories for any of the demographic bases is useful.

6. **Comparison or contrast.** Readers grasp differences or similarities more easily when this structural organization is used.

7. **Pro and con order.** Presenting arguments for and against something, usually without favoring one or the other is another common structure.

A most important rule is that the report be well organized. At the same time, it must be written clearly. This means that researchers who prepare reports should develop a writing style conducive to clarity in presentation. Many different sets of rules for clear writing are available. Most say the same things, but perhaps in different ways. One such set is shown in Exhibit 20.1.

EXHIBIT 20.1   Some Rules for Developing a Writing Style

1. **Use concrete words.** Such words are clear and specific. Be willing to specify, itemize, give details or examples, define, and illustrate.

2. **Keep sentences short.** Shorter sentences usually are more readable, all other things being equal. Lengthy sentences are more likely to cause confusion or complexity.

3. **Vary sentence types and structures.** Use declarative (assertion), interrogative (question), imperative (command), and exclamatory sentences. Do not limit a report, but use all types where appropriate. Also, vary structure among simple, compound, complex, and compound- complex sentences. Varying sentence types and structure increases interest and reduces monotony.

4. **Maintain unity.** Try to build each paragraph around one idea or topic.

5. **Use active verbs.** Active sentences tend to be more forceful and more direct. This does not mean that the passive voice should never be used. Use it sparingly, however.

6. **Avoid wordiness.** Say what is to be said in as few words as possible.

7. **Use varying means of emphasis.** There are different ways to emphasize certain points made in the report: space, repetition, position, and mechanical means (e.g., arrows, color, or underscoring).

8. **Write and speak naturally.** Often it is difficult to identify what is natural. A helpful guide is to use conversational language, but this is only a guide.

9. **Write on the level of reader's understanding.** Do not overestimate the reader's understanding and confuse him or her with highly specialized technical jargon. Also, do not underestimate the reader by using overly simplistic and childish terms.

10. **Watch the pace.** Avoid trying to say too much in too few words. In the same light, it is bad to stretch out an idea by using too many words.

11. **Keep the tone appropriate.** The way in which words are put together says a great deal about the writer. Thus, tone of writing implies something about the personality of the writer and of the writer's organization or company. While it is rare for a person to have complete control of the tone of his or her writing, it is important to acknowledge that it has many shades: positive or negative, helpful or indifferent, courteous or impertinent, humble or arrogant, and so forth.

SOURCE: Rockey, 1984, pp. 101–106.

Practitioners' Views

Many of the ideas presented in the last few pages are widely shared by research practitioners. Some representative thoughts are presented in Exhibit 20.2.

EXHIBIT 20.2   What the Research Practitioner Has to Say

Different researchers have different philosophies regarding what is important in report preparation. All agree that poorly communicated research is useless. All too often, the written report ends up as a second-class citizen to the demonstration of a new or repositioned statistical technique.

In order to strengthen written communication, Teresa Wrobel (1990), Vice-President of Research 100 in Princeton, New Jersey, suggests six things:

1. **Do the readers' work for them.** Presume that a reader feels uncomfortable manipulating or interpreting numbers. The text relates the major issues, while the numerical data serve as supporting information. Numbers should not interrupt the flow of the text, and the reader should not be forced to perform mental calculations in mid-sentence. Calculations should already be completed and presented in an easily discernable form.

2. **You don't have to analyze everything.** Not every attitude or behavior that has been quantified is worthy of discussion. Even statistically significant results do not always merit discussion. Select only those findings that illustrate elements intrinsic to the main issues and problems being explored.

3. **Write in plain English (or whatever language is being used).** Avoid industry jargon. Jargon tends to conceal the main ideas being conveyed and may be incomprehensible to the intended readers, who are often not researchers. The use of jargon can alienate or confuse the reader.

4. **Convey the main ideas quickly.** Most decision-makers don't have time to plow through pages of text to unearth the main findings. The front section of a research document should reduce the findings to their skeletal elements. This section should include the conclusions and recommendations supported by key findings.

5. **Did you answer the question at hand?** Conclusions should address the initial objectives with clarity and precision.

6. **Keep the report interesting.** Take advantage of the richness and breadth of language available. Keep searching for new ways of expressing points that convey ideas most effectively. While it is easiest to rely on language that is familiar and tested, expanding one's use of language can encourage idea generation and provide a more enjoyable document for the reader.

7. **Some format limitations must be followed.** In addition, using esoteric language for its own sake may lose the reader's attention. However, such limitations should not stifle creativity. Diversity in communication styles should be accepted and encouraged.

A slightly different view is that of Howard Gordon (1998), a principal of George R. Frerichs & Associates of Chicago. Mr. Gordon feels the following seven points can contribute to preparing more readable, usable, and action-oriented reports:

1. **Present tense works better**. Use present tense. Results and observations expressed in "now" terms sound better and are easier to read. Don't say: "The test panel liked the taste of the juice." Say: "People like the taste of the juice." We do studies for clients to help them make decisions today and tomorrow—not yesterday. Clients want to know what people think now.

2. **Use active voice**. Use active voice where possible, which is in most cases. There is nothing wrong with saying: "We believe . . ." rather than: "It is believed that . . . ." Passive voice is stilted. Use first person plural, not third person singular. Present tense and active voice make reports sound action oriented and businesslike. And active is easy to read. Passive voice makes the reader work harder.

3. **Findings—don't use the word findings**. This word makes your report sound as if some archaeologist just came across some old bones from the Paleolithic age. Marketers should use results, conclusions, or observations—not findings. Conclusions is the take-away section. What is it you want the reader to take away from your report? If somebody could spend only five minutes with your report, what should that person know?

4. **Use informative headlines, not label headlines**. Your reader will welcome this headline: "Convenience is the packaging's major benefit." Your reader will not generally welcome this headline: "Analysis of packaging." Nor this: "How people feel about packaging."

5. **Let your tables and charts work**. Help them with words when needed. Don't take a paragraph or a page to describe what a table already says. If there is nothing to say about a table or a chart, don't say it. The purpose of a table or a chart is to simplify. Use your words to point out significant items in the table—something that is not readily clear. Or use your words to offer interpretive comments. Use verbatims from sample respondents to support a point.

6. **Use the double-sided presentation whenever possible**. This format will reduce the verbiage in your report. It simply presents the table on the left side of the open report. Your informative headline and interpretive comments are on the right-hand page. The double-sided presentation is one of the most readable report formats. And it is much easier to write a report that uses it. The double-sided system also allows you to use white space effectively. White space helps readers get through your report—especially those readers in executive suites.

7. **Make liberal use of verbatims**. Great nuggets of marketing wisdom have come from people's comments. Use verbatims if you have them. Sprinkle the verbatims throughout your report in appropriate places as they make research reports interesting and readable

Yet another approach views things differently. James Nelems (1997), President of The Marketing Workshop in Norcross, Georgia, cautioned us more than 20 years ago on what should be avoided. He believed that research reports have more faults beyond improper analysis!

1. **The longer the report, the better.** Research isn't bought or sold by the pound. Any research report—regardless of sample size, multivariate techniques, or number of questions—should be reducible to a one-page executive overview. The report itself also should be clearly written and easy to read, including marketing conclusions and implications—the indications for future action—drawn from the data. It's such reports that management has both the time and desire to read—and the confidence to accept.

2. **Indiscriminate use of fancy tools.** Some, particularly the multivariate ones, may confuse rather than enlighten.

3. **Letting questions do all the work.** Research is more than asking questions. How simple it is in a package test to ask if people like the package. Or if someone doesn't use a product, just ask him why he doesn't use it. Even though these are the wrong questions, they are often asked, and, of course, when questions are asked, answers are received. But wrong answers to wrong questions hardly constitute analysis.

4. **Reporting what happened, rather than what it means.** Too much research text simply repeats numbers in the accompanying table. What is the significance of the numbers? How are we better off by knowing the answers?

5. **The fallacy of "single-number research."** This refers to any kind of research, the outcome of which is a "single number" that purports to provide an easy decision, such as an on-air recall score, a positive buying intention, or the overall preference in a product test.

6. **Failure to relate findings to objectives or reality.** Low brand awareness should be improved, of course, but what is unaided brand awareness per $1,000 of advertising spent vs. competition? In a product test, preferences can vary between current users and nonusers. Yet the brand objectives—gain new users or hold current ones—can produce opposite results with the exact same preference data.

7. **Spurious accuracy.** This includes summary statistics to one decimal place. More than likely, they're only accurate within 10 percentage points. Yet we've actually seen in print a comment on "20% of the sample of five respondents . . . ."

A final example of the thinking of practitioners is provided by Lynn Greenberg (1999, pp. 39–41), a principal of Lynn Greenberg Associates, a Scarsdale, New York, research consulting company. She suggests the following 11 tips for qualitative research reports, particularly focus groups:

1. **Capture your initial thoughts** as soon as possible after the groups. Some of your best insights may come at this time.

2. **Have a flexible plan**, one that initially has been developed before starting the writing.

3. **Break the task into small pieces and start with the easiest ones.** Once the basic sections have been written, it is easier to deal with the more challenging areas.

4. **Be succinct.** The reader should be able to clearly and quickly come away with two or three key points after reading the report.

5. **Provide overviews** to promote understanding of the learning. The first statement of a section should be an interpretation of what was learned, followed by more details.

6. **Turns negatives into constructive learning** and be clear about their meaning.

7. **Integrate information** from other sources where appropriate to provide more relevant meaning.

8. **Feature action-oriented conclusions** and implications that address all of the study's objectives, plus any important ancillary issues.

9. **Use a visually appealing format** that allows the readers to skim relevant issues. Use italics, boldface, underlining, bullet points, and so forth, wherever possible.

10. **Edit, edit, and re-edit** with *independent proofing* for clarity, grammar, and typos.

11. **Do it your way!** Write with your natural style.

REPORT FORMAT AND ORGANIZATION

Since every research project is more or less custom-made, each report prepared for a project also is unique and custom-made. And although reports can be customized, there also is a degree of standardization to report format and organization.

Many techniques people use to organize research reports are based on the factor of *place* as a means of emphasis. The underlying idea is that the location where information appears in a report has an effect upon a reader's reaction to that information. If a piece of information appears at the beginning—of a report itself, a section in a report, or perhaps even a paragraph in a section—that information tends to get a disproportionate share of the reader's attention. Thus, something desired to emphasize should be presented at the beginning of the message. In a similar manner, the end of a message also can be used as a point of strong emphasis, while the middle of a message is a point of minimum emphasis. The principle of place is illustrated in a complete report by placing the executive (or management) summary at the front of the report and the conclusions/recommendations at the end of the report.

Parts of a Formal Report

A formal report consists of a number of components that can be organized into three major parts. Exhibit 20.3 shows all the components that would be included in a complete formal report. Research reports, however, vary in formality; not all components will always be included. Figure 20.2 illustrates how the components are affected by a decreased need for formality. Typically, marketing research project reports would follow formats II or III. There are many instances where another version of format IV may be used, in which an executive (management) summary will be substituted for the table of contents.

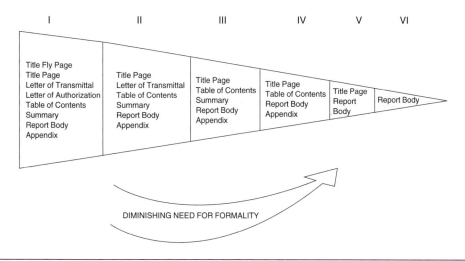

Figure 20.2   Components of a Report and Formality

SOURCE: Robinson, 1969, p. 295.

EXHIBIT 20.3   Components of a Research Report

A formal report consists of the prefatory section, the report body, and the appended materials. Within these sections, a number of components that can be organized and presented. This rather complete outline provides a general framework for organizing your research report.

PREFATORY PAGES

   I. Title Page
      (a) Title
      (b) Author's name
      (c) Documentation numbers and project identification numbers
      (d) Classification
      (e) Circulation test
      (f) Issue date and destroy date

  II. Table of Contents
      (a) Section subtitles and pages
      (b) Illustration titles and pages
      (c) Graph titles and pages
      (d) Figure titles and pages

 III. Letter of Transmittal and Letter of Authorization

 IV. Summary of Report
      (a) Problem definition and date
      (b) What was researched
      (c) When
      (d) Where
      (e) How and with what techniques
      (f) Major findings
      (g) Recommendations

REPORT BODY

   V. Introduction
      (a) What prompted the undertaking of the project
      (b) Who prompted the project
      (c) How the problem was defined

 VI. Statement of Objectives
      (a) How the problem definition was resolved
      (b) What was the research objective

VII. Research Methods
      (a) Research design
      (b) Data instruments (questionnaire, customer records, etc.)
      (c) Data collection methods
      (d) Sampling technique
      (e) Field work

VIII. Methodological Limitations
    (a) Weaknesses in research design
    (b) External events that may have influenced findings
    (c) Errors in research methods
    (d) Alternative causes for findings

IX. Analysis of Findings
    (a) Discussion of items of significance
    (b) Discussion of items of insignificance
    (c) Interpretations of findings

X. Conclusions and Recommendations
    (a) What research findings show
    (b) What actions should be taken (or not taken)

APPENDED PARTS

XI. Technical Appendix
    (a) Informational tables, graphs, illustrations
    (b) Technical discussion of research methodology and sample
    (c) Sample validation (if relevant)

XII. General Appendix
    (a) Selected portions of preliminary interviews
    (b) Project diary: dates, places, names, events
    (c) Copies of forms, questionnaires, records, and data instruments

XIII. Acknowledgments
    (a) Names, titles, and affiliations of contributors
    (b) Contribution of each contributor

XIV. References and Bibliography
    (a) Names, titles, and source-related research

Prefatory Pages

Every research report must have a title page, and may have a title fly page preceding it (only the title appears on a fly page). Any report longer than a couple of pages should have a table of contents. The table of contents can be as thin as having only the major sections of the report listed, or as detailed as including all headings and subheadings. Lists of tables, charts, figures, and so forth, will be included.

Some research reports may include letters of transmittal and authorization. A letter of transmittal is the means by which a report is released to a particular person or group. Often, such a letter contains material usually found in a preface or a foreword. If there is no formal summary included, then a synopsis of the findings should be included in the letter of transmittal. Other times, the letter of transmittal is relatively short. A letter of authorization is a letter to the researcher approving the project and specifying some of the details. Except in the most formal of marketing research projects, a letter of authorization need not be included in the report. An illustration of letters of authorization and transmittal used for a project awarded to an outside firm is given in Figure 20.3.

A. Letter of Authorization

Lane County / Private Industry Council

May 13, 2004

JVJ Research Associates
554 Pinto Way
Eugene, OR 97401

Dear Sirs:

Thank you for your response to our recent solicitation for proposals to conduct public opinion research for the Lane County Private Industry Council and Department of Employment & Training. I am pleased to inform you that your firm has been chosen as the contractor for this study, pending contract negotiation and discussion of certain aspects of your proposal.

Per recent discussions with Dan Cudaback of my staff, we will be meeting with XXX on Monday, May 18, at 4:00 p.m. in our offices to discuss your proposal further. Please call Mr. Cudaback with any questions between now and then.

I am looking forward to working with you.

Sincerely,

Steven J. Ickes, Director
EMPLOYMENT & TRAINING DEPARTMENT
PRIVATE INDUSTRY COUNCIL

B. Letter of Transmittal

JVJ Research Associates
554 Pinto Way
Eugene, Oregon 97401

August 21, 2004

Mr. Steven J. Ickes, Director
Lane County Department of Employment
 and Training
Eugene, Oregon 97401

Dear Mr. Ickes:

This letter accompanies our final report for the Lane County Public Opinion Study.

The findings contained in this report provide an insightful view of the opinions and desires of the residents of Lane County. We trust that this report will provide meaningful direction to the community as a whole and policy makers within Lane County.

Very truly yours,

JVJ Research Associates
John Researcher
Senior Research Associate

Figure 20.3   Illustration of Letters of Authorization and Transmittal

From a manager's (or client's) perspective, the most important component of the research report is the executive (management) summary. This summary reduces the essence of the study—the why, what, how, conclusions, and recommendations—to one or two pages. Often, this is the only part of a project report that the manager reads. Exhibit 20.4 shows examples of management summaries.

Body of the Report

This is the main component of the marketing research project report from the point of view of size or bulk. Included in the body is the introduction, which deals with why the project was undertaken and just what the problem was. Also included are research methods used, their strengths and limitations, and all definitions, results, and analyses. The main body of the report usually ends with the conclusions and any recommendations to be made.

Appended Materials

Several types of materials may be appended to the marketing research report. These may include detailed tables that provide more depth than the data presented in the body of the report, and all forms and measurement instruments used in data collection. If appropriate to the project, a bibliography and list of relevant references should be added to the end of the report.

EXHIBIT 20.4   Project Summaries Come in All Sizes and Shapes

There is no set process for writing a management (executive) summary for a marketing research project report. In many ways, a summary is an abstract. One thing is certain, however: The summary should be the last section of the report prepared. Typically, it will be a one- or two-page exposition. Example A is a one-page report summary of a study done for a pipe manufacturer that examined market potential for epoxy-coated pipe. Example B is drawn from a study of market needs and potential for a local motel. Example C is a two-page summary of a study done for a supplier of janitorial supplies.

A. Epoxy-Coated Pipe Study

The focus of this report is the market potential for epoxy-coated pipe. A survey of three separate samples was conducted to explore the market penetration potential of the product. These samples were: irrigators, municipalities, and industries.

On the basis of data collected from the irrigator sample, it was concluded that the demand for pipe in 2005 would not be greater than that purchased in 2004. Respondents would not be willing to pay more for ECP than for PVC. There is some indication that a higher price would be paid for ECP relative to CTP. The irrigation market appears to be tightly controlled by PVC, decreasing the opportunity for market penetration by ECP.

On the basis of data collected from the municipality sample, it was concluded that the demand for pipe in 2005 would decrease from levels demanded in 2004. This expectation is moderated by the fact that demand in this market fluctuates yearly. The respondents would not be willing to pay more for ECP than for other types of pipe. The municipality market also appears to be tightly controlled by PVC, decreasing the opportunity for market penetration by ECP.

On the basis of data collected from the industry sample, it was concluded that demand for pipe in 2005 would increase relative to demand in 2004. Respondents would be willing to pay more for ECP than for other types of pipe. The industrial market is not tightly controlled by PVC. While other types of pipe dominate, however, ECP does not appear to be perceived as a viable substitute for types of pipe already in use.

Research was conducted on the future price levels of steel and oil to enable a comparison between plastic pipe (PVC) and steel pipe (ECP). Steel prices are extremely difficult to forecast. In general, they are expected to increase. Forecasts for oil prices (in order to predict prices) are also expected to show increase over time.

In general, it is recommended that ECP not be introduced into any of the markets at this time.

B. Motel

The focus of this report is the potential for increase in the occupancy at the Duck Inn Motel. To determine this, three different potential target markets were defined and examined. These markets include bus tourism, university departments, and general tourism. Three separate methodological tools were used and were assigned to the target markets as follows:

TARGET MARKET   METHODOLOGICAL TOOL

BUS TOURISM . . . . FOCUS GROUP/MAIL SURVEY
UNIVERSITY DEPARTMENTS . . . . .PERSONAL INTERVIEWS
GENERAL TOURISM . . . . MAIL SURVEY

On the basis of data collected for the bus tourism market group, it was found that the most important thing to this segment was the attitude of the motel staff towards those traveling in a large group.

According to the results gathered for the university departments group, it was found that the Duck Inn has many qualities attractive to campus departments, but the motel needs to increase its exposure to increase potential customer awareness.

And finally, on the basis of data collected for the general tourism target market, it has been calculated that the target market is generally happy with the Duck Inn on most of the important choice criteria, but improvements can be made in advertising, appearance, and cohesion with the on-site restaurant to increase occupancy rates further.

C. Janitorial Supplies

Objectives

This study attempts to achieve several objectives. There are two primary concerns the research design intends to determine:

1. The need for a distribution center in Eugene

2. The need for a product showroom, if a distribution outlet is established

Also included are four support questions:

1. Current market share of leading competitors

2. Degree of satisfaction with current suppliers

3. Degree of loyalty to current suppliers

4. Customer base and trends, including demand for Saturday access to supplies and the potential for telemarketing

Findings

The study showed that there exists a substantial lack of confidence in the current suppliers operating in the Eugene/Springfield metropolitan area. Common complaints include poor credibility, insufficient product knowledge, and high-pressure sales tactics. Paulsen & Roles Laboratories (P&R) exhibited none of these traits. Quite to the contrary, genuine compliments for P&R's business tactics flowed freely from respondents associated with P&R.

Conclusions

The Eugene/Springfield metropolitan area is the second-largest statistical metropolitan area in Oregon. For this reason alone, it is critically important that Paulsen & Roles actively participate in this market. The foundation is in place. This is exhibited by both current market share and current consumer awareness of Paulsen & Roles in the Eugene/Springfield area.

In order to further penetrate this market, it is necessary to increase local representation. P&R's current lack of sufficient local representation was the only significant complaint lodged against Paulsen & Roles during the entire interviewing process.

Recommendations

Survey respondents offered recommendations to Paulsen & Roles Laboratories:

- Aggressively pursue service as your primary competitive advantage. Develop a "full service" image.
- Continue with competitive pricing. Fully pursue the advantages of P&R's current level of vertical integration (i.e., both the manufacturer and distributor).
- Establish a distribution center in Eugene with a showroom, thus enabling a more complete utilization of P&R's competitive advantage of complete service to the consumer.
- Maintain Saturday business hours.
- Develop a seminar program for end-users in the Eugene/Springfield metropolitan area.
- Incorporate telemarketing techniques enabling (a) a reduction in the cost per sales call, and (b) expansion of coverage per sales representative.
- Establish a direct-mail campaign aimed primarily toward the janitorial contractor segment. The intent will be to minimize the cost associated with informing this market segment of Paulsen & Roles's new services in the Eugene area.
- Attempt to acquire the Johnson Wax franchise from Scot Supply.

USE OF GRAPHICS

Graphical methods and principles are tools for showing the structure of data. They are relevant for data analysis and the communication of data to others. When used properly, graphic material can enhance a research report by emphasizing the important points and more clearly showing complex relationships. However, when used improperly or hastily put together, graphical material can be distracting, misleading, incomplete, confusing. and erroneous (Wainer, 1984).

Many types of graphic aids can be used in a marketing research report, including tables, charts, figures, maps, diagrams (e.g., a flow diagram), and other devices. Our brief discussion will concentrate mainly on tables and charts. Statistical packages and online survey research tools, such as

SPSS and SurveyZ.com, can prepare report-ready tables and charts directly from the data file. More complete discussion is given by Jacoby (1997, 1998) and Witzling and Greenstreet (1989).

Tables

There are many different ways to show numerical information in tabular form. Creating a good table of numerical data is an art as well as a science, and it goes far beyond simply putting data in columns, rows, or both. Using tables allows the researcher to minimize the amount of narrative material in the report. Only relatively short, perhaps even only summary, tables should be included in the report's body. More detailed and comprehensive tables should be placed in an appendix.

Each table should include a number of items:

1. **Table number**
2. **Title.** This should indicate by itself the contents of the table.
3. **Bannerhead and stubhead.** These are the headings for the columns and rows.
4. **Footnotes.** Explanations for particular items are placed here.
5. **Source note.** This acknowledges the source(s) of material used not generated by the project.

Figure 20.4 is taken from a study done for a chamber of commerce to examine involvement by business firms with that chamber and is useful to illustrate the various parts of a table.

Table Number ⟶ Table 5

Title ⟶ Extent of Agreement with Attitude Statement about the Chamber of Commerce[a]

	Member			Non-member			General Public			⟵ Boxhead
Attitude Statement	Percent Agree	Percent Disagree	Mean Value[c]	Percent Agree	Percent Disagree	Mean Value[c]	Percent Agree	Percent Disagree	Mean Value[c]	
Offers business contacts	58.3	10.8	2.5	23.8	57.1	3.5	(b)	(b)	(b)	
Enhance sales	41.2	23.6	2.8	10.0	50.0	3.6	(b)	(b)	(b)	
Achievement is noticeable	42.5	23.0	2.9	34.8	30.4	3.0	62.9	14.3	2.5	
Costs too much to be a member	32.6	39.3	3.1	83.3	5.6	1.9	(b)	(b)	(b)	
Unwilling to aid small businessman	17.3	55.6	3.5	22.7	27.2	3.0	(b)	(b)	(b)	
Benefits community	75.6	8.9	2.2	60.8	13.0	2.5	65.1	9.3	2.3	
Is socially attractive to be a member	29.5	31.8	3.0	9.1	45.4	3.4	(b)	(b)	(b)	
Membership is prestigious	12.6	35.6	3.3	12.5	50.0	3.4	40.5	8.1	2.6	
Enhance image of member firm	24.4	26.8	3.1	13.0	52.1	3.4	48.8	12.8	2.6	

Stubhead ⟶ (Offers business contacts row)

Footnotes ⟶ [a]Responses were either "strongly agree," "agree," "neutral," "disagree," or "strongly disagree."
[b]Not available.
[c]Scoring ranges from 1 for "strongly agree" to 5 for "strongly disagree." Thus, the lower the mean value the greater the tendency to agree with the statement.

Figure 20.4   Example of a Table

Table 20.1   Presenting Survey Response Data

"What role do you play in the purchase of business forms?"

	Role played				
Market segments	*Specify*	*Recommend*	*Purchase*	*None*	*Total sample size*
Hospital	25%	44%	59%	17%	259
Finance	29%	32%	62%	11%	164
Manufacturing	18%	27%	81%	3%	205
Retail	10%	10%	52%	37%	52
Government	39%	48%	54%	8%	213
Transportation	28%	28%	74%	6%	109

Not only are there different ways to show numerical data in a table, there also are different ways to present these data. Table 20.1 shows a typical way to present survey response data. These data were generated in a study for a manufacturer of business forms. Multiple responses from a respondent were possible. It is not always necessary to show the specific question asked in a table. If the title cannot be short, and descriptive as well, then it may be necessary to show the question asked.

When doing statistical analysis of data obtained in a marketing research project, a researcher may use PC software that generates report-ready tables. This is quite common for the many specialized cross-tabulation packages, but is not limited to such packages. An example of such a report-ready table was shown in Table 16.3 of Chapter 16. This table shows one dependent variable cross-tabulated by three demographic variables. Such a table is known as a *stub-and-banner* table, as there are 15 banner points (columns) and four stubs (rows). There is software that will output as many as 99 banner points against one dependent variable.

Charts and Graphs

Charts and graphs are a popular way to present numerical data. In one way or another the information contained in a table can be presented with the help of a chart. The overall advantages are that relationships and structure can be more easily seen and the narrative can be minimized. Indeed, charts and graphs are often constructed with the premise "a picture is worth a thousand words," and as such make results more easily understandable (Gutsche, 2001).

There are many different kinds of charts. These include line charts, bar charts, pie charts, and dot charts. At times, some combinations may be used. Other types of charts have been developed, but these are used sparingly in marketing research projects.

Line Chart

Also known as a line graph, the *line chart* is useful to show the relationship between variables. A *simple line chart* relates two variables, a *multiple line chart* shows the relationship between the independent variable and more than one dependent variable, and a *stratum line chart* (or *stacked line chart*) consists of a set of line charts whose quantities are grouped together. Figures 20.5a–d illustrate horizontal and vertical line charts using categorical and ratio scales, as well as in combination with vertical and horizontal bar charts. It is not necessary that the independent variable be continuous or ordered (The Faneuil Group, Inc. [formerly Faneuil Research], 1999).

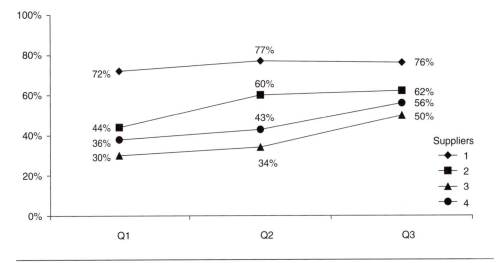

Figure 20.5a   Multiple Horizontal Line Chart: Percentage Change Over Time

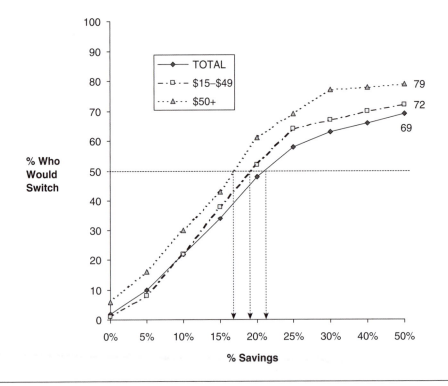

Figure 20.5b   Multiple Horizontal Line Chart: Switching Percent × Percent Savings

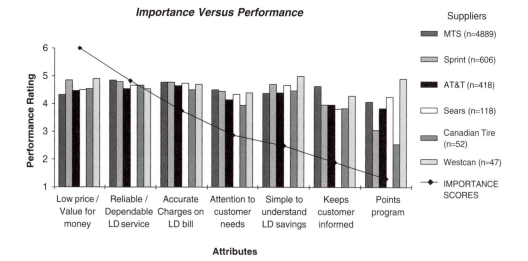

Figure 20.5c   Single Horizontal Line Chart: Attributes × Performance Rating

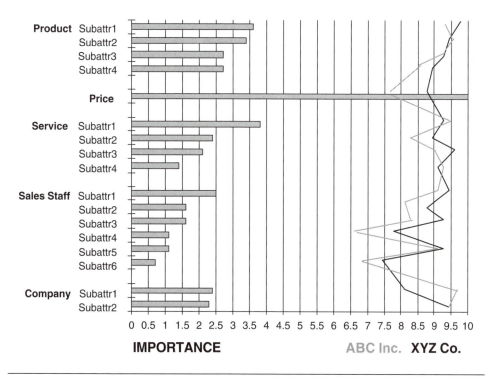

Figure 20.5d   Multiple Vertical Line Chart with Horizontal Bars

Bar Chart

A *bar chart* is another useful type of graph. Such a chart shows the relationship between a dependent variable and some independent variable at discrete levels. The stacked vertical bar chart shown in Figure 20.6a is used to show the relative satisfaction given on-time performance (*x*-axis). Figure 20.6b shows percentages associated with frequency counts of three different market segments by age categories.

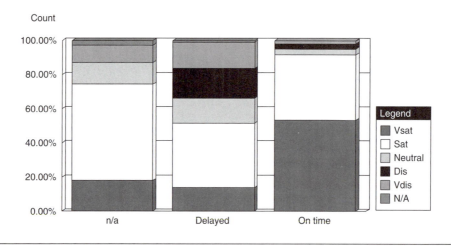

Figure 20.6a   Stacked Vertical Bar Chart

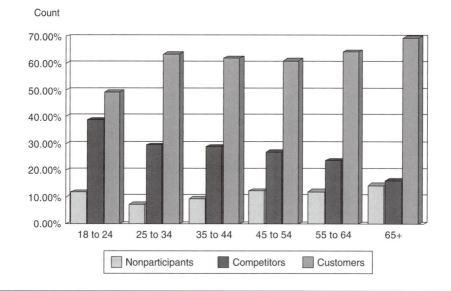

Figure 20.6b   Vertical Bar Chart: Competitive Market Share by Customer Age Segment

There are times when a researcher may feel the need to draw special attention to a particular result and so may add multiple variables with demarcation lines or special cables. When using this type of notation, the researcher should make sure that he or she has not added too much information that confuses the reader. See Figures 20.6c and 20.6d for more detail (The Faneuil Group, Inc. [formerly Faneuil Research], 1999).

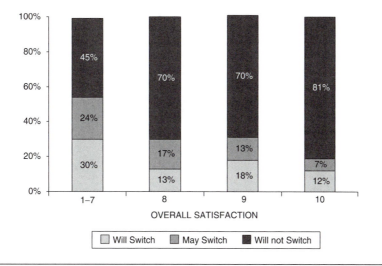

Figure 20.6c   Stacked Vertical Bar Chart: Loyalty × Satisfaction

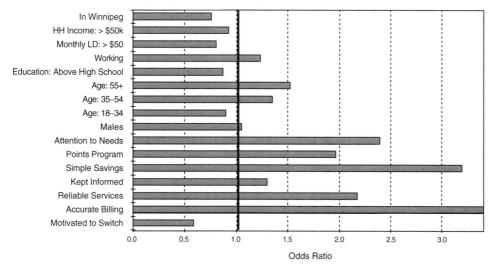

Figure 20.6d   Multivariable Horizontal Bar Chart With Threshold Line

Specialty Charts

Other widely used chart formats include the quadrant, high-low, hierarchical tree, and surface charts (see Figures 20.7–20.10). These charts are particularly useful to display a quantity that is subdivided into parts. When more categories are analyzed, tree diagrams may be used. Care should be exercised when too many subdivisions are shown and some portions are so small and narrow it is difficult to see them.

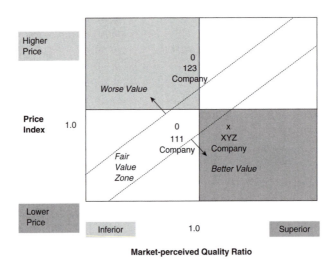

Figure 20.7   Quadrant Chart With Threshold Lines

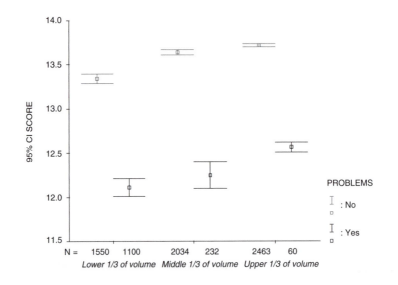

Figure 20.8   High-Low Chart: Satisfaction by Channel

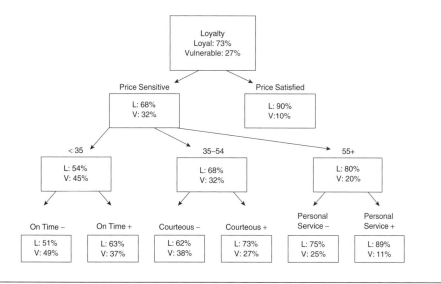

Figure 20.9   Hierarchical Tree Chart: Analysis of Loyalty

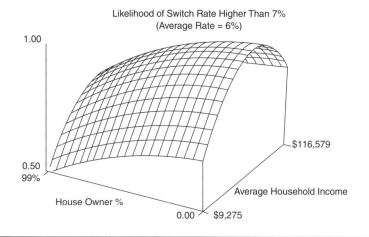

Figure 20.10   Surface Map of Neural Network Analysis

Dot Charts

A simple, yet powerful, type of chart is the *dot chart*. This is a way to display measurements of one or more quantitative variables in which each value may have a label associated with it. We have already shown such charts by the scatter plots (diagrams) in Figures 17.3 and 17.6 of Chapter 17.

Dot charts are used as output from multidimensional scaling (MDS) analyses (see Chapter 19). Figure 20.11 shows a MDS result for a computer manufacturer where attributes of computer manufacturers are plotted as dots. A dot chart may be used in a similar manner; Figure 20.12 presents utility functions obtained from business travelers on long-haul airline flights using conjoint analysis (see Chapter 19). When they appear, the solid lines (they could be dotted as well) should be made light so that they do not detract from the dots themselves.

Although a literal use of this type of chart would show only dots in the body of graph, this need not be the case. Either letters or numbers also can be used, as illustrated by the Importance/Performance analysis of Figure 20.13 (reproduced from Exhibit 18.1 done for a vendor of janitorial supplies and equipment. The numbers are a result of plotting both mean ratings of importance and performance.

Another useful modification of the dot chart is one that essentially uses tick marks, each of which is labeled. A beer company was interested in knowing something about preferences for its beer and a number of competitive brands. Preference rankings for 12 brands were obtained and analyzed by Thurstonian Case V scaling (see Chapter 10). Prior to applying this procedure, each respondent was classified in one of three ways:

1. *Sponsor brand-loyal*—had been drinking the sponsor's brand regularly for at least a year

2. *Other brand-loyal*—had been drinking a particular (competitive) brand regularly for at least one year

3. *Switcher*—others not meeting either of the above conditions

Thurstonian scale of preferences were then developed for each of the preceding segments and appear in Figure 20.14.

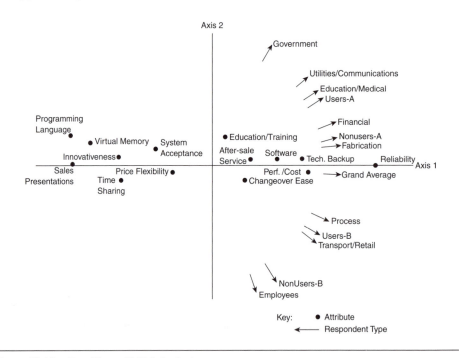

Figure 20.11   Dot Chart of MDS Analysis

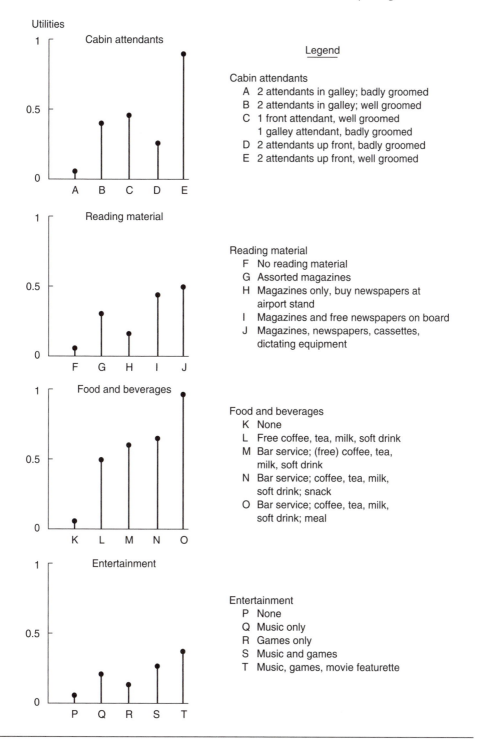

Figure 20.12   Dot Chart for Conjoint-Analysis Derived Utility Functions

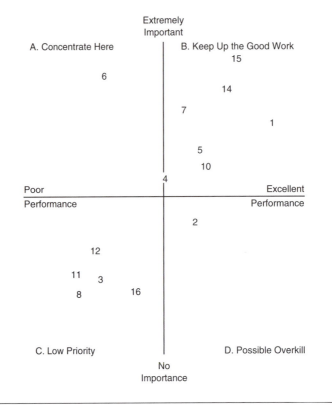

Extremely
Important

A. Concentrate Here   B. Keep Up the Good Work
                                               15

                    6
                                          14

                                    7
                                                    1

                                5
                                    10

                              4
Poor   Excellent
Performance   Performance

                                    2

                    12

        11   3
            8   16

C. Low Priority   D. Possible Overkill

                    No
                Importance

Importance/Performance Ratings for Other: Primary and Secondary Combined

Attribute Number	Attribute Description	Mean Import. Rating	Mean Perform. Rating
1	Credit availability	6.79	8.22
2	Offers nationally advertised products	4.36	6.19
3	Open Saturday for will-call	3.00	3.92
4	Personal contact by sales rep.	5.43	5.55
5	Safety-related products	6.15	6.38
6	Prompt parts and repair service	8.14	4.17
7	Convenient distributor location	7.14	5.98
8	Distributor product showroom	2.65	3.32
9	Comparative prices	7.79	7.52
10	Lowest price	5.72	6.55
11	Distributor puts on seminars	3.15	3.29
12	Telephone contact by sales rep.	3.72	3.77
13	Seldom have backorders	7.79	7.57
14	Complete product line	7.65	7.07
15	Orders delivered timely	8.36	7.31
16	Distributor manufactures own chemicals	2.72	4.79

Figure 20.13   Dot Chart Using Numbers

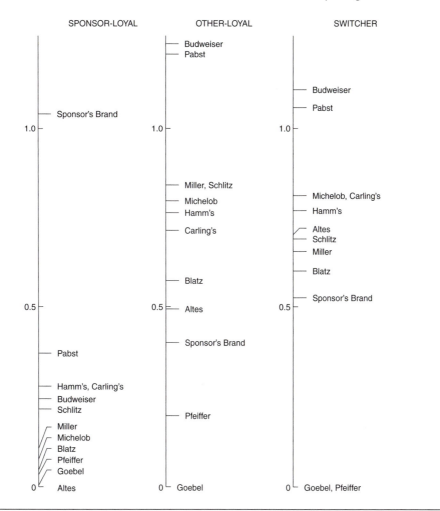

Figure 20.14   Thurstonian Scales by Beer-Drinker Class (Overall Preferences)

Other Graphic Aids

Sometimes key results from a study can be presented by use of maps. Often we see a map of the United States or another political entity used to display census data. Maps are used to enhance the meaning of data. For example, the situation facing the plastic irrigation pipe manufacturer regarding PIP in different selling areas of the country is shown in Figure 20.15a, which shows the geographic boundaries of selling areas. Figure 20.15b shows a map of the eight western states and reports the percent of respondent pipe sellers who sell PIP in each area. This type of map gives some life to the data beyond listing market area and showing percentages.

Another device that can enhance the presentation is a pictorial chart or pictogram. A *pictogram* depicts data with the help of symbols, which can be anything—stars, stacks of coins, trees, castles, facial expressions, money, caricatures of people, and so forth. Each symbol represents a specific and uniform amount or value. An example is shown in Figure 20.16a. There are situations where the size of the pictorial symbol is made proportional to the values that are to be shown, as illustrated in Figure 20.16b. One must be careful when doing this so as to not confuse the reader by distorting symbols. For example when doubling the size of a three-dimensional symbol, if each dimension is doubled the volume is increased eight times.

Pictures or drawings themselves may be useful to show what something looks like. A manufacturer of carpet cleaning agents developed a new type of foam cleaner called *Lift Away*, made especially for spot cleaning. A study was done to test four alternative aerosol packages, which used a sample of 220 housewives. Figure 20.17 shows sketches of the four package designs and frequencies of choice. It would have been difficult to describe the packages in words only. The sketches greatly aid understanding of the differences between the test items.

Selling Area	Percentage of All PIP Respondents Selling in the Area	Percentage of PIP Sellers With More Than 5% Sales in the Area
Area 1	78%	43%
Area 2	71%	71%
Area 3	57%	57%
Area 4	14%	0
Area 5	57%	57%
Area 6	43%	29%

Figure 20.15a Use of Maps in Plastic Irrigation Pipe Study: Selling Areas of PIP Manufacturers

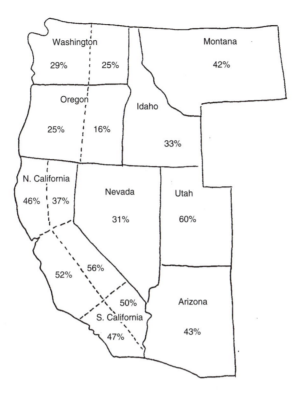

Figure 20.15b Use of Maps in Plastic Irrigation Pipe Study: PIP Respondent Selling Areas as a Percentage of All Respondents Reporting Sales in Area

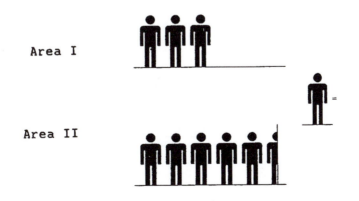

Figure 20.16a Pictogram Illustration of Number of Customers by Sales Area

Figure 20.16b   Pictogram Illustration: Symbol Proportional to Value

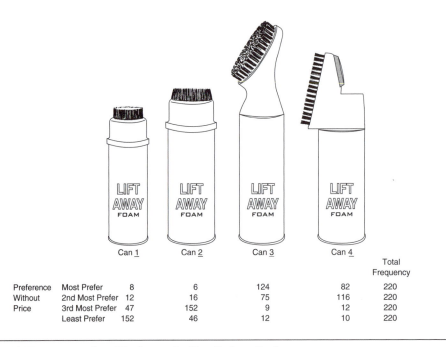

		Can 1	Can 2	Can 3	Can 4	Total Frequency
Preference	Most Prefer	8	6	124	82	220
Without	2nd Most Prefer	12	16	75	116	220
Price	3rd Most Prefer	47	152	9	12	220
	Least Prefer	152	46	12	10	220

Figure 20.17   Frequencies of Preference for New Package Designs

A Warning

When developing graphical material one must be very careful. It is not too difficult to get different impressions from graphs of identical data, each of which is technically correct. Figure 20.18 illustrates this point.

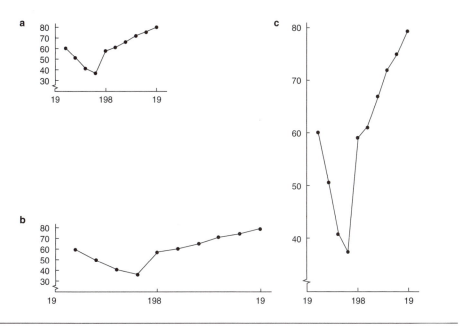

Figure 20.18   Effects of Changing an Axis

By stretching or compressing the horizontal or vertical axis, as the case may be, one can convey different meanings (see Figure 20.18).

A researcher needs to follow sound principles when constructing graphical material. One such set of principles is summarized in Exhibit 20.5. These principles are based on providing clear vision, clear understanding, sound scales, and sound overall strategy for presentation.

EXHIBIT 20.5   A Set of Principles for Graph Construction

Clear Vision

- Make the data stand out. Avoid superfluity.
- Use visually prominent graphical elements to show the data.
- Use a pair of scale lines for each variable. Make the data region the interior of the rectangle formed by the scale lines. Put tick marks outside the data region.
- Do not overdo the number of tick marks.
- Use a reference line when an important value must be seen across the entire graph, but do not let the line interfere with the data.
- Do not allow data labels in the data region to interfere with the quantitative data or to clutter the graph.
- Avoid putting notes, keys, and markers in the data region. Put keys and markers just outside the data region and put notes in the legend or in the text.
- Overlapping plotting symbols must be visually distinguishable.
- Superposed data sets must be readily visually discriminated.
- Visual clarity must be preserved under reduction and reproduction.

Clear Understanding

- Put major conclusions into graphical form. Make legends comprehensive and informative.
- Error bars should be clearly explained.
- When logarithms of a variable are graphed, the scale label should correspond to the tick mark labels.
- Proofread graphs.
- Strive for clarity.

Scales

- Choose the range of the tick marks to include or nearly include the range of data.
- Subject to the constraints that scales have, choose the scales so that the data fill up as much of the data region as possible.
- It is sometimes helpful to use the pair of scale lines for a variable to show two different scales.
- Choose appropriate scales when graphs are compared.
- Do not insist that zero always be included on a scale showing magnitude.
- Use a logarithmic scale when it is important to understand the percent change or multiplicative factors.
- Showing data on a logarithmic scale can improve resolution.
- Use a scale break only when necessary. If a break cannot be avoided, use a full scale break. Do not connect numerical value on two sides of a break.

General Strategy

- A large amount of quantitative information can be packed into a small region.
- Graphing data should be an iterative, experimental process.
- Graph data two or more times when it is needed.
- Many useful graphs require careful, detailed study.

SOURCE: Cleveland, 1985, pp. 100–101. Reprinted with kind permission of Kleuwér Publications.

THE ORAL REPORT

In general, the written report will be supplemented by an oral presentation. The objective behind this oral report is to identify and emphasize the major findings of the study and to allow the client or manager to ask questions about matters not clear to him or her. In some instances, however, the oral presentation may be more important than the written report. When this is the case, the written report consists of an extended management summary (3–4 pages) and copies of all overhead projector transparencies, photocopies, slides, or PowerPoint slides presented in the oral report.

When planning for the oral presentation, the researcher should consider the basic ingredients of such a presentation: (a) the *target* (purpose of the report); (b) the *receiver* of the report (the willingness and capacity of the listeners to understand and accept the report); (c) the *impact* needed; and (d) the *methods* that must be used to achieve the desired impact, given the receiver and target. The presenter must adapt to the audience, and this may require having to defend the results being presented. This is not the same as being in an adversarial position. It does mean, however, that a presenter should be prepared to deal with any and all questions in a professional, expert, and competent manner.

Audiovisual aids tend to make oral presentations graphic and vivid. Each graphic or other visual aid needs to be interpreted for the audience. For some presentations, audio-visuals are supplementary to the oral presentation; for others, the oral presentation supplements the audio-visuals used. When the researcher wants to use visual aids, it is important to keep in mind the difference between type of visual aid and medium of presentation. Any one of the types of visual aids (or graphics) available from graphics programs can be adapted and presented through many of the media available. In addition, actual actions and behaviors can be shown via motion pictures, videos, DVDs, and personal computers.

The personal computer can also be used to show data in table or graphic form. Programs such as PowerPoint exist for developing computer-controlled presentations of marketing research project results. The availability of packages that incorporate text, graphics, and statistical data in the same report helps in the development of effective presentation formats.

Exhibit 20.6 presents some rules-of-thumb for using graphics presentation programs to create oral presentation "shows."

EXHIBIT 20.6   Rules-of-Thumb for Presentation Graphics

The developer of oral presentations, and the presenter as well, must know the limitations and capabilities of the medium to be used. Following certain rules will allow the creation of powerful and effective presentations:

1. **How will you present? Choose the appropriate medium.** The key factor in choosing between computer projection, photographic slides, overhead transparencies, and so forth, is how large is your audience. Will the material project on a screen and be easy to view. Large groups sit in large rooms and are farther from the screen.

2. **Do you need pass along information?** Handouts containing slide miniatures or key points are great, especially for key visuals.

3. **Is it simple enough?** Keep it simple is a rule for *all* presentations.

4. **Is your art effective?** Cluttered slides or cheap-looking clip art may make the presentation less effective, or difficult for the audience to understand or identify with.

5. **Coordinate the presentation visually.** Consistency of colors and type fonts make presentations easier to follow. Select two informal typefaces (one for titles and one for subtitles and text) and use the same background and color (again one or two colors) across all slides.

6. **Use an appealing color scheme.** Look at the color schemes from Microsoft PowerPoint. These professionally developed schemes provide good models from which to build.

7. **Is your text readable in bright rooms?** Text is most readable when displayed against a contrasting background. Use either a light color for text against a dark background or set dark text against a light background for optimum visibility.

8. **Unconventional text is difficult to read.** Avoid rotated, vertical, or curved text.

9. **Don't overdo color.** Use a limited color palette.

10. **Proofread, Proofread, Proofread!** Always check the presentation before finalizing it. Make sure everything looks and works as you intend it.

SUMMARY

This chapter has covered preparing the research report. In order to plan properly for the report, the researcher must understand some basic concepts of communications.

We discussed the components of a formal research report in some depth. Reports need to be complete, accurate, concise, and clear in presentation. There is no one correct way to prepare a marketing research report, although we do discuss some general guidelines or rules for report preparation. The intended audience must be kept in mind at all times. There are many degrees of formality that may be used. Increasingly, marketing research reports seem to be written less formally, with a major emphasis being placed on the oral presentation.

We discussed in some depth the use of graphics to show the structure of data. Tables, charts, figures, maps, and other devices were presented. Numerous examples drawn from real-world marketing research projects were given to illustrate the various graphic aids.

Next we turned to the oral report. In many situations, the oral report is used to supplement a formal written report. This allows the potential user of the study results to ask questions and seek clarification of aspects that may be confusing. In other situations, the oral report is the major vehicle for the presentation of data and information. The written report then consists of an extended management summary and copies of all overhead transparencies used in the presentation.

ASSIGNMENT MATERIAL

1. Is it not inconsistent for a research report to be both complete and concise? Explain this apparent dilemma.

2. What should be included in the executive (management) summary of a report? Why is this considered to be the single most important component of a report?

3. Can a marketing research report be too formal? Can it be too informal? Explain your positions.

4. Can a marketing research report be too long? Can it be too short? Explain your answers.

5. What do you think of a written report that consists of an extended management summary and copies of all the overhead transparencies, PowerPoint slides, and so forth, shown in the oral presentation? Is this really all a client needs in a report?

6. Are some types of charts better than others for graphic presentation? Evaluate the use of bar, pie, and line charts.

REFERENCES

Bailey, E. P., Jr. (1990). *The plain English approach to business report writing*. New York: Oxford University Press.

Cleveland, W. S. (1985). *The elements of graphing data*. Monterey, CA: Wadsworth Advanced Books and Software.

Faneuil Group, Inc., [formerly Faneuil Research]. (1999). *Training Manual*. Boston.

Fink, A. (2003). *How to report on surveys*. Thousand Oaks, CA: Sage.

Gordon, H. (1994, December), in S. J. Levy, G. R. Frerichs, & H. L. Gordon (Eds.) *The Dartnell marketing manager's handbook*. Chicago, IL: Dartnell Corporations.

Greenberg, L. (1999, December). The challenge of qualitative report writing. *Quirk's Marketing Research Review*, 36–41.

Gutsche, A. (2001, September 24). Visuals make the case. *Marketing News*, 21–23.

Jacoby, W. G. (1997). *Statistical graphics for univariate and bivariate data*. Thousand Oaks, CA: Sage.

Jacoby, W. G. (1998). *Statistical graphics for visualizing multivariate data*. Thousand Oaks, CA: Sage.

Nelems, J. H. (1979, January 12). Report results implications, not just pounds of data. *Marketing News*, *12*, 7.

Rehart, M. J. V. (1994). *Writing business research reports: A guide to scientific writing*. Los Angeles: Pyrczak Publishing.

Robinson, D. M. (1969). *Writing reports for management decisions*. Columbus, OH: Charles E. Merrill.

Rockey, E. H. (1984). *Communicating in organizations*. Lanham, MD: University Press of America, Inc.

Semon, T. T. (1998, November 23). To make research effective, start by drafting the report. *Marketing News*, *32*, 24, 17.

Timm, P. R., & Bienvenu, S. (2001). *Business communications: Discovering strategy, developing skills*. Upper Saddle, NJ: Prentice Hall.

Vardaman, G. T. (1981). *Making successful presentations*. New York: AMACOM.

Wainer, H. (1984, May). How to display data badly. *The American Statistician*, *38*, 137–147.

Witzling, L. P., & Greenstreet, R. C. (1989). *Presenting statistics: A manager's guide to the persuasive use of statistics*. New York: John Wiley & Sons.

Wrobel, T. K. (1990, September 3). Research is useless if it's poorly communicated. *Marketing News*, *24*, 18, 41ff.

APPENDIX A

Statistical Tables

Table A.1   Cumulative Normal Distribution—Values of Probability

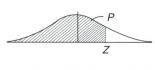

Values of P corresponding to Z for the normal curve. Z is the standard normal variable. The value of P for $-Z$ equals 1 minus the value of P for $+Z$, e.g., the P for -1.62 equals $1 - .9474 = .0526$.

Z	.00	.01	.02	.03	.04	.05	.06	.07	.08	.09
.0	.5000	.5040	.5080	.5120	.5160	.5199	.5239	.5279	.5319	.5359
.1	.5398	.5438	.5478	.5517	.5557	.5596	.5636	.5675	.5714	.5753
.2	.5793	.5832	.5871	.5910	.5948	.5987	.6026	.6064	.6103	.6141
.3	.6179	.6217	.6255	.6293	.6331	.6368	.6406	.6443	.6480	.6517
.4	.6554	.6591	.6628	.6664	.6700	.6736	.6772	.6808	.6844	.6879
.5	.6915	.6950	.6985	.7019	.7054	.7088	.7123	.7157	.7190	.7224
.6	.7257	.7291	.7324	.7357	.7389	.7422	.7454	.7486	.7517	.7549
.7	.7580	.7611	.7642	.7673	.7704	.7734	.7764	.7794	.7823	.7852
.8	.7881	.7910	.7939	.7967	.7995	.8023	.8051	.8078	.8106	.8133
.9	.8159	.8186	.8212	.8238	.8264	.8289	.8315	.8340	.836	.8389
1.0	.8413	.8438	.8461	.8485	.8508	.8531	.8554	.8577	.8599	.8621
1.1	.8643	.8665	.8686	.8708	.8729	.8749	.8770	.8790	.8810	.8830
1.2	.8849	.8869	.8888	.8907	.8925	.8944	.8962	.8980	.8997	.9015
1.3	.9032	.9049	.9066	.9082	.9099	.9115	.9131	.9147	:9162	.9177
1.4	.9192	.9207	.9222	.9236	.9251	.9265	.9279	.9292	.9306	.9319
1.5	.9332	.9345	.9357	.9370	.9382	.9394	.9406	.9418	.9429	.9441
1.6	.9452	.9463	.9474	.9484	.9495	.9505	.9515	.9525	.9535	.9545
1.7	.9554	.9564	.9573	.9582	.9591	.9599	.9608	.9616	.9625	.9633
1.8	.9641	.9649	.9656	.9664	.9671	.9678	.9686	.9693	.9699	.9706
1.9	.9713	.9719	.9726	.9732	.9738	.9744	.9750	.9756	.9761	.9767

(Continued)

Table A.1 (Continued)

Z	.00	.01	.02	.03	.04	.05	.06	.07	.08	.09
2.0	.9772	.9778	.9783	.9788	.9793	.9798	.9803	.9808	.9812	.9817
2.1	.9821	.9826	.9830	.9834	.9838	.9842	.9846	.9850	.9854	.9857
2.2	.9861	.9864	.9868	.9871	.9875	.9878	.9881	.9884	.9887	.9890
2.3	.9893	.9896	.9898	.9901	.9904	.9906	.9909	.9911	.9913	.9916
2.4	.9918	.9920	.9922	.9925	.9927	.9929	.9931	.9932	.9934	.9936
2.5	.9938	.9940	.9941	.9943	.9945	.9946	.9948	.9949	.9951	.9952
2.6	.9953	.9955	.9956	.9957	.9959	.9960	.9961	.9962	.9963	.9964
2.7	.9965	.9966	.9967	.9968	.9969	.9970	.9971	.9972	.9973	.9974
2.8	.9974	.9975	.9976	.9977	.9977	.9978	.9979	.9979	.9980	.9981
2.9	.9981	.9982	.9982	.9983	.9984	.9984	.9985	.9985	.9986	.9986
3.0	.9987	.9987	.9987	.9988	.9988	.9989	.9989	.9989	.9990	.9990
3.1	.9990	.9991	.9991	.9991	.9992	.9992	.9992	.9992	.9993	.9993
3.2	.9993	.9993	.9994	.9994	.9994	.9994	.9994	.9995	.9995	.9995
3.3	.9995	.9995	.9995	.9996	.9996	.9996	.9996	.9996	.9996	.9997
3.4	.9997	.9997	.9997	.9997	.9997	.9997	.9997	.9997	.9997	.9998

Table A.2   Upper Percentiles of the *t* Distribution

df \ 1 − α	.75	.90	.95	.975	.99	.995	.9995
1	1.000	3.078	6.314	12.706	31.821	63.657	636.619
2	.816	1.886	2.920	4.303	6.965	9.925	31.598
3	.765	1.638	2.353	3.182	4.541	5.841	12.941
4	.741	1.533	2.132	2.776	3.747	4.604	8.610
5	.727	1.476	2.015	2.571	3.365	4.032	6.859
6	.718	1.440	1.943	2.447	3.143	3.707	5.959
7	.711	1.415	1.895	2.365	2.998	3.499	5.405
8	.706	1.397	1.860	2.306	2.896	3.355	5.041
9	.703	1.383	1.833	2.262	2.821	3.250	4.781
10	.700	1.372	1.812	2.228	2.764	3.169	4.587
11	.697	1.363	1.796	2.201	2.718	3.106	4.437
12	.695	1.356	1.782	2.179	2.681	3.055	4.318
13	.694	1.350	1.771	2.160	2.650	3.012	4.221
14	.692	1.345	1.761	2.145	2.624	2.977	4.140
15	.691	1.341	1.753	2.131	2.602	2.947	4.073
16	.690	1.337	1.746	2.120	2.583	2.921	4.015
17	.689	1.333	1.740	2.110	2.567	2.898	3.965
18	.688	1.330	1.734	2.101	2.552	2.878	3.922
19	.688	1.328	1.729	2.093	2.339	2.861	3.883
20	.687	1.325	1.725	2.086	2.528	2.845	3.850
21	.686	1.323	1.721	2.080	2.518	2.831	3.819
22	.686	1.321	1.717	2.074	2.508	2.819	3.792
23	.685	1.319	1.714	2.069	2.500	2.807	3.767
24	.685	1.318	1.711	2.064	2.492	2.797	3.745
25	.684	1.316	1.708	2.060	2.485	2.787	3.725
26	.684	1.315	1.706	2.056	2.479	2.779	3.707
27	.684	1.314	1.703	2.052	2.473	2.771	3.690
28	.683	1.313	1.701	2.048	2.467	2.763	3.674
29	.683	1.311	1.699	2.045	2.462	2.756	3.659
30	.683	1.310	1.697	2.042	2.457	2.750	3.646
40	.681	1.303	1.684	2.021	2.423	2.704	3.551
60	.679	1.296	1.671	2.000	2.390	2.660	3.460
120	.677	1.289	1.658	1.980	2.358	2.617	3.373
∞	.674	1.282	1.645	1.960	2.326	2.576	3.291

df = degrees of freedom

SOURCE: From Fisher, R. A., & Yates, F., *Statistical Tables for Biological, Agricultural, and Medical Research, 6/e,* copyright © 1963. Reprinted with permission from Pearson Education, Ltd.

Table A.3   Percentiles of the χ^2 Distribution

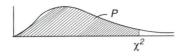

df	$\chi^2_{.005}$	$\chi^2_{.01}$	$\chi^2_{.025}$	$\chi^2_{.05}$	$\chi^2_{.10}$	$\chi^2_{.90}$	$\chi^2_{.95}$	$\chi^2_{.975}$	$\chi^2_{.99}$	$\chi^2_{.995}$
1	.000039	.00016	.00098	.0039	.0158	2.71	3.84	5.02	6.63	7.88
2	.0100	.0201	.0506	.1026	.2107	4.61	5.99	7.38	9.21	10.60
3	.0717	.115	.216	.352	.584	6.25	7.81	9.35	11.34	12.84
4	.207	.297	.484	.711	1.064	7.78	9.49	11.14	13.28	14.86
5	.412	.554	.831	1.15	1.61	9.24	11.07	12.83	15.09	16.75
6	.676	.872	1.24	1.64	2.20	10.64	12.59	14.45	16.81	18.55
7	.989	1.24	1.69	2.17	2.83	12.02	14.07	16.01	18.48	20.28
8	1.34	1.65	2.18	2.73	3.49	13.36	15.51	17.53	20.09	21.96
9	1.73	2.09	2.70	3.33	4.17	14.68	16.92	19.02	21.67	23.59
10	2.16	2.56	3.25	3.94	4.87	15.99	18.31	20.48	23.21	25.19
11	2.60	3.05	3.82	4.57	5.58	17.28	19.68	21.92	24.73	26.76
12	3.07	3.57	4.40	5.23	6.30	18.55	21.03	23.34	26.22	28.30
13	3.57	4.11	5.01	5.89	7.04	19.81	22.36	24.74	27.69	29.82
14	4.07	4.66	5.63	6.57	7.79	21.06	23.68	26.12	29.14	31.32
15	4.60	5.23	6.26	7.26	8.55	22.31	25.00	27.49	30.58	32.80
16	5.14	5.81	6.91	7.96	9.31	23.54	26.30	28.85	32.00	34.27
18	6.26	7.01	8.23	9.39	10.86	25.99	28.87	31.53	34.81	37.16
20	7.43	8.26	9.59	10.85	12.44	28.41	31.41	34.17	37.57	40.00
24	9.89	10.86	12.40	13.85	15.66	33.20	36.42	39.36	42.98	45.56
30	13.79	14.95	16.79	18.49	20.60	40.26	43.77	46.98	50.89	53.67
40	20.71	22.16	24.43	26.51	29.05	51.81	55.76	59.34	63.69	66.77
60	35.53	37.48	40.48	43.19	46.46	74.40	79.08	83.30	88.38	91.95
120	83.85	86.92	91.58	95.70	100.62	140.23	146.57	152.21	158.95	163.64

df = degrees of freedom

For large degrees of freedom. $\chi^2 = \frac{1}{2}(Z + \sqrt{2v - 1})^2$ (approximately) where v = degrees of freedom and Z is given in Table A.1.

SOURCE: Adapted from *Introduction to Statistical Analysis*, 2nd ed., by W. J. Dixon and F. J. Massey, Jr., Copyright 1957, McGraw-Hill Book Company.

Table A.4   Percentiles of the F Distribution

n_1 = degrees of freedom for numerator

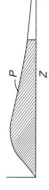

$F_{0.50}(n_1, n_2)$ $\alpha = 0.1$

n_2 \ n_1	1	2	3	4	5	6	7	8	9	10	12	15	20	24	30	40	60	120	x
1	39.86	49.50	53.59	55.83	57.24	58.20	58.91	59.44	59.86	60.19	60.71	61.22	61.74	62.00	62.26	62.53	62.79	63.06	63.33
2	8.53	9.00	9.16	9.24	9.29	9.33	9.35	9.37	9.38	9.39	9.41	9.42	9.44	9.45	9.46	9.47	9.47	9.48	9.49
3	5.54	5.46	5.39	5.34	5.31	5.28	5.27	5.25	5.24	5.23	5.22	5.20	5.18	5.18	5.17	5.16	5.15	5.14	5.13
4	4.54	4.32	4.19	4.11	4.05	4.01	3.98	3.95	3.94	3.92	3.90	3.87	3.84	3.83	3.82	3.80	3.79	3.78	3.76
5	4.06	3.78	3.62	3.52	3.45	3.40	3.37	3.34	3.32	3.30	3.27	3.24	3.21	3.19	3.17	3.16	3.14	3.12	3.10
6	3.78	3.46	3.29	3.18	3.11	3.05	3.01	2.98	2.96	2.94	2.90	2.87	2.84	2.82	2.80	2.78	2.76	2.74	2.72
7	3.59	3.26	3.07	2.96	2.88	2.83	2.78	2.75	2.72	2.70	2.67	2.63	2.59	2.58	2.56	2.54	2.51	2.49	2.47
8	3.46	3.11	2.92	2.81	2.73	2.67	2.62	2.59	2.56	2.50	2.50	2.46	2.42	2.40	2.38	2.36	2.34	2.32	2.29
9	3.36	3.01	2.81	2.69	2.61	2.55	2.51	2.47	2.44	2.42	2.38	2.34	2.30	2.28	2.25	2.23	2.21	2.18	2.16
10	3.29	2.92	2.73	2.61	2.52	2.46	2.41	2.38	2.35	2.32	2.28	2.24	2.20	2.18	2.16	2.13	2.11	2.08	2.06
11	3.23	2.86	2.66	2.54	2.45	2.39	2.34	2.30	2.27	2.25	2.21	2.17	2.12	2.10	2.08	2.05	2.01	2.00	1.97
12	3.18	2.81	2.61	2.48	2.39	2.33	2.28	2.24	2.21	2.19	2.15	2.10	2.06	2.04	2.01	1.99	1.96	1.93	1.90
13	3.14	2.76	2.56	2.43	2.35	2.28	2.23	2.20	2.16	2.14	2.10	2.05	2.01	1.98	1.96	1.93	1.90	1.88	1.85
14	3.10	2.73	2.52	2.39	2.31	2.24	2.19	2.15	2.12	2.10	2.05	2.01	1.96	1.94	1.91	1.89	1.86	1.83	1.80
15	3.07	2.70	2.49	2.36	2.27	2.21	2.16	2.12	2.09	2.06	2.02	1.97	1.92	1.90	1.87	1.85	1.82	1.79	1.76
16	3.05	2.67	2.46	2.33	2.24	2.18	2.13	2.09	2.06	2.03	1.99	1.94	1.89	1.87	1.84	1.81	1.78	1.75	1.72
17	3.03	2.64	2.44	2.31	2.22	2.15	2.10	2.06	2.03	2.00	1.96	1.91	1.86	1.84	1.81	1.78	1.75	1.72	1.69
18	3.01	2.62	2.42	2.29	2.20	2.13	2.08	2.04	2.00	1.98	1.93	1.89	1.84	1.81	1.78	1.75	1.72	1.69	1.66
19	2.99	2.61	2.40	2.27	2.18	2.11	2.06	2.02	1.98	1.96	1.91	1.86	1.81	1.79	1.76	1.73	1.70	1.67	1.63

(Continued)

n_2 = degrees of freedom for denominator

Table A.4 (Continued)

n_1 = degrees of freedom for numerator

$F_{0.50}(n_1, n_2)$ $\alpha = 0.1$

n_2 \ n_1	1	2	3	4	5	6	7	8	9	10	12	15	20	24	30	40	60	120	x
20	2.97	2.59	2.38	2.25	2.16	2.09	2.04	2.00	1.96	1.94	1.89	1.84	1.79	1.77	1.74	1.71	1.68	1.64	1.61
21	2.96	2.57	2.36	2.23	2.14	2.08	2.02	1.98	1.95	1.92	1.87	1.83	1.78	1.75	1.72	1.69	1.66	1.62	1.59
22	2.95	2.56	2.35	2.22	2.13	2.06	2.01	1.97	1.93	1.90	1.86	1.81	1.76	1.73	1.70	1.67	1.64	1.60	1.57
23	2.94	2.55	2.34	2.21	2.11	2.05	1.99	1.95	1.92	1.89	1.84	1.80	1.74	1.72	1.69	1.66	1.62	1.59	1.55
24	2.93	2.54	2.33	2.19	2.10	2.04	1.98	1.94	1.91	1.88	1.83	1.78	1.73	1.70	1.67	1.64	1.61	1.57	1.53
25	2.92	2.53	2.32	2.18	2.09	2.02	1.97	1.93	1.89	1.87	1.82	1.77	1.72	1.69	1.66	1.63	1.59	1.56	1.52
26	2.91	2.52	2.31	2.17	2.08	2.01	1.96	1.92	1.88	1.86	1.81	1.76	1.71	1.68	1.65	1.61	1.58	1.54	1.50
27	2.90	2.51	2.30	2.17	2.07	2.00	1.95	1.91	1.87	1.85	1.80	1.75	1.70	1.67	1.64	1.60	1.57	1.53	1.49
28	2.89	2.50	2.29	2.16	2.06	2.00	1.94	1.90	1.87	1.84	1.79	1.74	1.69	1.66	1.63	1.59	1.56	1.52	1.48
29	2.89	2.50	2.28	2.15	2.06	1.99	1.93	1.89	1.86	1.83	1.78	1.73	1.68	1.65	1.62	1.58	1.55	1.51	1.47
30	2.88	2.49	2.28	2.14	2.05	1.98	1.93	1.88	1.85	1.82	1.77	1.72	1.67	1.64	1.61	1.57	1.54	1.50	1.46
40	2.84	2.44	2.23	2.09	2.00	1.93	1.87	1.83	1.79	1.76	1.71	1.66	1.61	1.57	1.54	1.51	1.47	1.42	1.38
60	2.79	2.39	2.18	2.04	1.95	1.87	1.82	1.77	1.74	1.71	1.66	1.60	1.54	1.51	1.48	1.44	1.40	1.35	1.29
120	2.75	2.35	2.13	1.99	1.90	1.82	1.77	1.72	1.68	1.65	1.60	1.55	1.48	1.45	1.41	1.37	1.32	1.26	1.19
∞	2.71	2.30	2.08	1.94	1.85	1.77	1.72	1.67	1.63	1.60	1.55	1.49	1.42	1.38	1.34	1.30	1.24	1.17	1.00

n_2 = degrees of freedom for denominator

(Continued)

Table A.4 (Continued)

$F_{0.95}(n_1, n_2)$ $\alpha = 0.05$

n_1 = degrees of freedom for numerator

n_2 = degrees of freedom for denominator

n_2 \ n_1	1	2	3	4	5	6	7	8	9	10	12	15	20	24	30	40	60	120	x
1	161.4	199.5	215.7	224.6	230.2	234.0	236.8	238.9	240.5	241.9	243.9	245.9	248.0	249.1	250.1	251.1	252.2	253.3	254.3
2	18.51	19.00	19.16	19.25	19.30	19.33	19.35	19.37	19.38	19.40	19.41	19.43	19.45	19.45	19.46	19.47	19.48	19.49	19.50
3	10.13	9.55	9.28	9.12	9.01	8.94	8.89	8.85	8.81	8.79	8.74	8.70	8.66	8.64	8.62	8.59	8.57	8.55	8.53
4	7.71	6.94	6.59	6.39	6.26	6.16	6.09	6.04	6.00	5.96	5.91	5.86	5.80	5.77	5.75	5.72	5.69	5.66	5.63
5	6.61	5.79	5.41	5.19	5.05	4.95	4.88	4.82	4.77	4.74	4.68	4.62	4.56	4.53	4.50	4.46	4.43	4.40	4.36
6	5.99	5.14	4.76	4.53	4.39	4.28	4.21	4.15	4.10	4.06	4.00	3.94	3.87	3.84	3.81	3.77	3.74	3.70	3.67
7	5.59	4.74	4.35	4.12	3.97	3.87	3.79	3.73	3.68	3.64	3.57	3.51	3.44	3.41	3.38	3.34	3.30	3.27	3.23
8	5.32	4.46	4.07	3.84	3.69	3.58	3.50	3.44	3.39	3.35	3.28	3.22	3.15	3.12	3.08	3.04	3.01	2.97	2.93
9	5.12	4.26	3.86	3.63	3.48	3.37	3.29	3.23	3.18	3.14	3.07	3.01	2.94	2.90	2.86	2.83	2.79	2.75	2.71
10	4.96	4.10	3.71	3.48	3.33	3.22	3.14	3.07	3.02	2.98	2.91	2.85	2.77	2.74	2.70	2.66	2.62	2.58	2.54
11	4.84	3.98	3.59	3.36	3.20	3.09	3.01	2.95	2.90	2.85	2.79	2.72	2.65	2.61	2.57	2.53	2.49	2.45	2.40
12	4.75	3.89	3.49	3.26	3.11	3.00	2.91	2.85	2.80	2.75	2.69	2.62	2.54	2.51	2.47	2.43	2.38	2.34	2.30
13	4.67	3.81	3.41	3.18	3.03	2.92	2.83	2.77	2.71	2.67	2.60	2.53	2.46	2.42	2.38	2.34	2.30	2.25	2.21
14	4.60	3.74	3.34	3.11	2.96	2.85	2.76	2.70	2.65	2.60	2.53	2.46	2.39	2.35	2.31	2.27	2.22	2.18	2.13
15	4.54	3.68	3.29	3.06	2.90	2.79	2.71	2.64	2.59	2.54	2.48	2.40	2.33	2.29	2.25	2.20	2.16	2.11	2.07
16	4.49	3.63	3.24	3.01	2.85	2.74	2.66	2.59	2.54	2.49	2.42	2.35	2.28	2.24	2.19	2.15	2.11	2.06	2.01
17	4.45	3.59	3.20	2.96	2.81	2.70	2.61	2.55	2.49	2.45	2.38	2.31	2.23	2.19	2.15	2.10	2.06	2.01	1.96
18	4.41	3.55	3.16	2.93	2.77	2.66	2.58	2.51	2.46	2.41	2.34	2.27	2.19	2.15	2.11	2.06	2.02	1.97	1.92
19	4.38	3.52	3.13	2.90	2.74	2.63	2.54	2.48	2.42	2.38	2.31	2.23	2.16	2.11	2.07	2.03	1.98	1.93	1.88
20	4.35	3.49	3.10	2.87	2.71	2.60	2.51	2.45	2.39	2.35	2.28	2.20	2.12	2.08	2.04	1.99	1.95	1.90	1.84
21	4.32	3.47	3.07	2.84	2.68	2.57	2.49	2.42	2.37	2.32	2.25	2.18	2.10	2.05	2.01	1.96	1.92	1.87	1.81
22	4.30	3.44	3.05	2.82	2.66	2.55	2.46	2.40	2.34	2.30	2.23	2.15	2.07	2.03	1.98	1.94	1.89	1.84	1.78
23	4.28	3.42	3.03	2.80	2.64	2.53	2.44	2.37	2.32	2.27	2.20	2.13	2.05	2.01	1.96	1.91	1.86	1.81	1.76
24	4.26	3.40	3.01	2.78	2.62	2.51	2.42	2.36	2.30	2.25	2.18	2.11	2.03	1.98	1.94	1.89	1.84	1.79	1.73

(Continued)

Table A.4 (Continued)

n_1 = degrees of freedom for numerator

$F_{0.95}(n_1, n_2)\ \alpha = 0.05$

n_2 \ n_1	1	2	3	4	5	6	7	8	9	10	12	15	20	24	30	40	60	120	x
25	4.24	3.39	2.99	2.76	2.60	2.49	2.40	2.34	2.28	2.24	2.16	2.09	2.01	1.96	1.92	1.87	1.82	1.77	1.71
26	4.23	3.37	2.98	2.74	2.59	2.47	2.39	2.32	2.27	2.22	2.15	2.07	1.99	1.95	1.90	1.85	1.80	1.75	1.69
27	4.21	3.35	2.96	2.73	2.57	2.46	2.37	2.31	2.25	2.20	2.13	2.06	1.97	1.93	1.88	1.84	1.79	1.73	1.67
28	4.20	3.34	2.95	2.71	2.56	2.45	2.36	2.29	2.24	2.19	2.12	2.04	1.96	1.91	1.87	1.82	1.77	1.71	1.65
29	4.18	3.33	2.93	2.70	2.55	2.43	2.35	2.28	2.22	2.18	2.10	2.03	1.94	1.90	1.85	1.81	1.75	1.70	1.64
30	4.17	3.31	2.92	2.69	2.53	2.42	2.33	2.27	2.21	21.6	2.09	2.01	1.93	1.19	1.84	1.79	1.74	1.68	1.62
40	4.08	3.23	2.84	2.61	2.45	2.34	2.25	2.18	2.12	2.08	2.00	1.92	1.84	1.79	1.74	1.69	1.64	1.58	1.51
60	4.00	3.15	2.76	2.53	2.37	2.25	2.17	2.10	2.04	1.99	1.92	1.84	1.75	1.70	1.65	1.59	1.53	1.47	1.39
120	3.92	3.07	2.68	2.45	2.29	2.17	2.09	2.02	1.96	1.91	1.83	1.75	1.66	1.61	1.55	1.50	1.43	1.35	1.25
∞	3.84	3.00	2.60	2.37	2.21	2.10	2.01	1.94	1.88	1.83	1.75	1.67	1.57	1.52	1.46	1.39	1.32	1.22	1.00

n_2 = degrees of freedom for denominator

(Continued)

Table A.4 (Continued)

n_1 = degrees of freedom for numerator

$F_{0.99}(n_1, n_2)$ $\alpha = 0.01$

n_2 \ n_1	1	2	3	4	5	6	7	8	9	10	12	15	20	24	30	40	60	120	x
1	4052	4999.5	5403	5625	5764	5859	5928	5982	6022	6056	6106	6157	6209	6235	6261	6287	6313	6339	63.66
2	98.50	99.00	99.17	99.25	99.30	98.33	99.36	99.37	99.39	99.40	99.42	99.43	99.45	99.46	99.47	99.47	99.48	99.49	99.50
3	34.12	30.82	29.46	28.71	28.24	27.91	27.67	27.49	27.35	27.23	27.05	26.87	26.69	26.60	26.50	26.41	26.32	26.22	26.13
4	21.20	18.00	16.69	15.98	15.52	15.21	14.98	14.80	14.66	14.55	14.37	14.20	14.02	13.93	13.84	13.75	13.65	13.56	13.46
5	16.26	13.27	12.06	11.39	10.97	10.67	10.46	10.29	10.16	10.05	9.89	9.72	9.55	9.47	9.38	9.29	9.20	9.11	9.02
6	13.75	10.92	9.78	9.15	8.75	8.47	8.26	8.10	7.98	7.87	7.72	7.56	7.40	7.31	7.23	7.14	7.06	6.97	6.88
7	12.25	9.55	8.45	7.85	7.46	7.19	6.99	6.84	6.72	6.62	6.47	6.31	6.16	6.07	5.99	5.91	5.82	5.74	5.65
8	11.26	8.65	7.59	7.01	6.63	6.37	6.18	6.03	5.91	5.81	5.67	5.52	5.36	5.28	5.20	5.12	5.03	4.95	4.86
9	10.56	8.02	6.99	6.42	6.06	5.80	5.61	5.47	5.35	5.26	5.11	4.96	4.81	4.73	4.65	4.57	4.48	4.40	4.31
10	10.04	7.56	6.55	5.99	5.64	5.39	5.20	5.06	4.94	4.85	4.71	4.56	4.41	4.33	4.25	4.17	4.08	4.00	3.91
11	9.65	7.21	6.22	5.67	5.32	5.07	4.89	4.74	4.63	4.54	4.40	4.25	4.10	4.02	3.94	3.86	3.78	3.69	3.60
12	9.33	6.93	5.95	5.41	5.06	4.82	4.64	4.50	4.39	4.30	4.16	4.01	3.86	3.78	3.70	3.62	3.54	3.45	3.36
13	9.07	6.70	5.74	5.21	4.86	4.62	4.44	4.30	4.19	4.10	3.96	3.82	3.66	3.59	3.51	3.43	3.34	3.25	3.17
14	8.86	6.51	5.56	5.04	4.69	4.46	4.28	4.14	4.03	3.94	3.80	3.66	3.51	3.43	3.35	3.27	3.18	3.09	3.00
15	8.68	6.36	5.42	4.89	4.56	4.32	4.14	4.00	3.89	3.80	3.67	3.52	3.37	3.29	3.21	3.13	3.05	2.96	2.87
16	8.53	6.23	5.29	4.77	4.44	4.20	4.03	3.89	3.78	3.69	3.55	3.41	3.26	3.18	3.10	3.02	2.93	2.84	2.75
17	8.40	6.11	5.18	4.67	4.34	4.10	3.39	3.79	3.68	3.59	3.46	3.31	3.16	3.08	3.00	2.92	2.83	2.75	2.65
18	8.29	6.01	5.09	4.58	4.25	4.01	3.84	3.71	3.60	3.51	3.37	3.23	3.08	3.00	2.92	2.84	2.75	2.66	2.57
19	8.18	5.93	5.01	4.50	4.17	3.94	3.77	3.63	3.52	3.43	3.30	3.15	3.00	2.92	2.84	2.76	2.67	2.58	2.49
20	8.10	5.85	4.94	4.43	4.10	3.87	3.70	3.56	3.46	3.37	3.23	3.09	2.94	2.86	2.78	2.69	2.61	2.52	2.42
21	8.02	5.78	4.87	4.37	4.04	3.81	3.64	3.51	3.40	3.31	3.17	3.03	2.88	2.80	2.72	2.64	2.55	2.46	2.36
22	7.95	5.72	4.82	4.31	3.99	3.76	3.59	3.45	3.35	3.26	3.12	2.98	2.83	2.75	2.67	2.58	2.50	2.40	2.31
23	7.88	5.66	4.76	4.26	3.94	3.71	3.54	3.41	3.30	3.21	3.07	2.93	2.78	2.70	2.62	2.54	2.45	2.35	2.26
24	7.82	5.61	4.72	4.22	3.90	3.67	3.50	3.36	3.26	3.17	3.03	2.89	2.74	2.66	2.58	2.49	2.40	2.31	2.21

(Continued)

n_2 = degrees of freedom for denominator

Table A.4 (Continued)

n_1 = degrees of freedom for numerator

$F_{0.99}(n_1, n_2)$ $\alpha = 0.01$

n_2 \ n_1	1	2	3	4	5	6	7	8	9	10	12	15	20	24	30	40	60	120	x
25	7.77	5.57	4.68	4.18	3.85	3.63	3.46	3.32	3.22	3.13	2.99	2.85	2.70	2.62	2.54	2.45	2.36	2.27	2.17
26	7.72	5.53	4.64	4.14	3.82	3.59	3.42	3.29	3.18	3.09	2.96	2.81	2.66	2.58	2.50	2.42	2.33	2.23	2.13
27	7.68	5.49	4.60	4.11	3.78	3.56	3.39	3.26	3.15	3.06	2.93	2.78	2.63	2.55	2.47	2.38	2.29	2.20	2.10
28	7.64	5.45	4.57	4.07	3.75	3.53	3.36	3.23	3.12	3.03	2.90	2.75	2.60	2.52	2.44	2.35	2.26	2.17	2.06
29	7.60	5.42	4.54	4.04	3.73	3.50	3.33	3.20	3.09	3.00	2.87	2.73	2.57	2.49	2.41	2.33	2.23	2.14	2.03
30	7.56	5.39	4.51	4.02	3.70	3.47	3.30	3.17	3.07	2.98	2.84	2.70	2.55	2.47	2.39	2.30	2.21	2.11	2.01
40	7.31	5.18	4.31	3.83	3.51	3.29	3.12	2.99	2.89	2.80	2.66	2.52	2.37	2.29	2.20	2.11	2.02	1.92	1.80
60	7.08	4.89	4.13	3.65	3.34	3.12	2.95	2.82	2.72	2.63	2.50	2.35	2.20	2.12	2.03	1.94	1.84	1.73	1.60
120	6.85	4.79	3.95	3.48	3.17	2.96	2.79	2.66	2.56	2.47	2.34	2.19	2.03	1.95	1.86	1.76	1.66	1.53	1.38
∞	6.63	4.61	3.78	3.32	3.02	2.80	2.64	2.51	2.41	2.32	2.18	2.04	1.88	1.79	1.70	1.59	1.47	1.32	1.00

n_2 = degrees of freedom for denominator

SOURCE: Adapted from *Biometrika Tables for Statisticians*, Vol. 1, 2nd ed., edited by E. S. Pearson and H. O. Hartley, Cambridge University, Press. Copyright 1958.

Table A.5   Short Table of Random Digits

9 2 2 1	3 4 5 2	9 7 5 4	8 8 1 3	6 6 7 9	3 0 8 1	3 9 4 5	9 9 8 2	1 5 1 0	8 2 7
8 1 2 7	9 4 2 2	6 6 6 5	2 1 5 4	5 4 5 0	7 0 4 2	1 4 8 1	8 0 1 4	0 9 7 8	8 6 5
4 9 2 7	7 8 8 3	9 2 0 5	7 5 9 0	3 6 2 7	1 8 8 8	1 6 4 1	8 7 8 1	4 1 4 4	5 0 8
6 2 1 3	5 4 4 6	3 7 1 7	0 5 5 2	9 6 2 3	0 0 8 8	9 8 4 3	0 6 3 4	6 8 3 1	8 3 2
5 3 3 4	7 7 5 7	4 7 8 1	5 3 9 5	3 2 5 8	0 2 9 6	7 3 1 8	2 3 2 3	2 4 8 5	4 7 1
3 7 1 6	5 3 7 3	2 9 0 7	9 4 8 8	1 1 6 6	1 2 4 7	4 4 5 1	6 5 5 3	0 1 8 3	3 9 4
5 1 4 5	3 7 6 5	9 4 2 7	6 7 2 5	4 4 6 1	1 2 2 2	8 4 5 7	8 5 1 7	5 3 5 0	8 6 8
9 8 5 1	0 1 7 8	9 6 2 8	7 1 8 3	4 5 9 7	7 0 3 4	6 4 4 4	4 2 6 9	3 5 6 7	5 4 6
3 0 7 4	1 2 2 4	2 6 5 7	6 2 5 5	2 1 5 1	2 3 1 3	6 8 3 4	6 5 2 2	7 5 5 4	6 3 9
1 5 8 8	1 2 7 2	6 5 1 1	3 3 4 9	2 9 6 6	8 1 3 1	6 8 4 5	8 5 8 7	1 9 6 7	6 4 6
6 6 8 7	3 0 2 5	2 3 7 7	8 3 6 5	8 0 4 4	1 7 8 2	0 4 2 2	6 6 6 4	3 6 3 6	8 3 4
0 6 3 7	9 9 0 7	1 3 2 5	1 0 3 3	6 8 2 1	3 4 8 1	5 7 4 9	6 1 7 3	1 4 9 4	5 4 6
7 2 3 1	7 6 4 7	3 7 7 2	5 0 5 7	0 1 2 1	6 3 6 9	2 4 2 6	2 6 1 8	2 5 6 9	8 1 1
7 4 8 4	4 8 4 4	5 4 5 1	1 5 6 1	4 1 0 1	5 4 8 2	5 3 1 5	5 8 7 7	6 4 7 3	7 8 6
7 6 4 2	6 8 2 2	8 2 6 8	5 6 7 1	6 7 3 4	5 7 7 3	6 1 0 3	5 1 3 8	2 6 2 6	0 5 3
3 3 7 1	6 5 7 8	6 1 7 5	6 3 9 7	8 7 4 8	0 4 4 2	4 0 8 4	6 0 5 7	6 8 6 5	6 9 5
2 1 4 7	2 4 0 6	3 4 8 4	4 8 5 2	3 8 2 4	3 3 8 2	4 8 4 4	6 7 8 5	9 8 3 6	1 7 3
8 5 9 9	7 3 7 3	4 1 6 8	6 7 7 7	5 9 0 2	3 2 3 5	0 7 8 4	0 6 8 6	2 1 0 8	8 4 1
0 1 6 5	0 7 8 3	5 4 1 4	6 6 0 5	8 7 8 1	4 3 6 7	4 4 2 2	9 0 7 3	1 1 8 6	8 5 2
6 8 3 8	7 2 3 6	7 3 2 1	7 4 4 5	2 4 9 3	4 5 7 9	8 2 6 7	1 1 1 6	5 1 6 5	7 2 6
6 2 3 9	7 1 2 1	3 2 9 3	3 5 2 3	8 5 8 6	1 7 4 8	6 8 3 7	2 3 2 9	6 1 5 0	1 0 1
8 6 3 0	9 4 6 5	1 7 4 3	7 5 7 6	8 7 3 5	7 7 1 9	8 0 4 1	4 5 4 7	4 3 7 6	6 7 4
8 1 3 6	9 7 6 8	0 1 1 4	3 0 8 9	7 5 2 3	1 7 2 4	3 1 6 6	6 3 7 6	8 2 6 9	6 3 6
6 4 5 7	8 3 4 5	2 0 8 3	1 3 3 3	6 1 4 7	8 1 1 3	5 4 5 8	2 7 1 8	9 5 4 0	3 6 0
4 9 1 1	0 9 8 4	1 2 9 0	0 0 1 1	7 4 8 8	7 1 2 6	8 4 7 5	6 0 7 6	7 1 3 1	7 8 2
8 3 2 6	4 2 2 0	5 6 4 6	2 3 8 6	6 4 5 3	8 4 7 2	3 7 8 4	5 7 8 1	6 1 2 7	3 4 6
7 8 3 1	5 6 8 7	6 4 4 9	3 5 7 6	9 7 3 3	1 5 1 9	7 2 7 5	2 3 3 2	5 8 4 5	6 7 7
9 5 9 9	9 3 8 2	3 1 4 7	0 7 6 3	4 6 6 3	7 0 1 7	0 6 1 1	4 0 0 3	7 5 5 6	2 6 1
1 7 7 4	1 3 3 1	7 4 8 2	1 8 4 3	7 6 3 8	4 4 2 7	6 1 1 7	2 7 9 4	2 1 5 3	6 2 4
0 7 1 5	6 6 2 1	5 7 8 1	3 1 6 5	8 4 6 5	2 1 7 7	1 9 7 5	3 2 2 4	0 2 5 6	9 9 3
3 2 0 8	8 4 1 4	9 2 6 3	0 7 5 3	1 8 8 6	8 8 8 3	8 5 9 3	6 5 2 7	8 2 0 7	7 6 2
4 7 3 0	3 3 6 2	4 4 4 9	4 9 5 6	6 7 2 8	5 5 1 8	1 6 4 2	4 7 1 7	6 2 5 2	3 6 6
7 8 2 7	3 3 1 2	2 7 6 5	4 9 8 1	7 2 6 1	3 0 8 3	9 7 5 6	2 4 0 6	5 7 7 0	1 4 6
4 1 3 7	1 8 7 7	1 3 3 9	1 0 4 7	1 2 4 3	6 2 1 7	6 4 5 2	2 9 1 5	9 8 8 8	5 8 2
6 5 1 4	1 1 2 2	3 1 5 6	6 2 3 9	3 7 0 2	7 0 1 1	7 9 7 9	4 7 1 1	5 8 7 5	6 4 8
8 3 9 4	5 1 4 8	6 2 0 9	8 0 6 3	2 3 8 9	1 8 9 3	9 1 2 5	6 0 2 4	6 3 3 7	8 4 5
5 5 3 1	8 8 8 6	8 8 1 4	2 2 0 2	2 3 4 5	2 2 1 2	3 7 2 2	3 6 0 6	5 2 6 7	1 1 2
6 2 7 1	8 5 8 7	2 6 1 7	8 6 1 9	5 0 7 3	3 8 2 5	8 2 4 6	5 5 2 8	2 5 1 7	7 7 0
2 8 4 6	0 8 5 3	9 4 4 2	5 2 6 7	4 9 0 0	6 4 5 1	1 6 3 3	1 3 5 9	4 8 9 5	2 3 3
1 9 9 6	0 4 1 4	6 7 4 8	2 1 8 5	4 9 7 7	3 2 7 1	9 4 1 1	4 1 8 9	4 2 5 7	0 8 7
8 0 9 3	6 7 2 4	3 8 2 2	4 7 6 1	9 4 7 5	1 2 4 5	3 6 9 4	3 4 5 3	1 1 8 8	6 3 7
8 6 8 8	7 8 3 1	9 8 7 7	4 5 2 2	1 4 2 3	1 9 2 2	3 8 5 2	1 5 4 3	8 4 1 9	0 8 1
1 7 5 6	7 1 5 4	3 6 7 5	7 7 0 2	0 8 5 2	3 8 5 9	5 6 4 1	0 6 5 1	9 3 4 5	0 5 8
8 1 1 2	8 4 3 4	8 8 0 7	0 3 6 2	7 8 2 9	1 9 4 4	4 6 4 4	5 1 0 4	5 3 4 8	4 2 2
1 4 2 1	2 5 3 8	3 2 8 4	9 8 2 6	9 6 3 4	7 7 8 2	8 5 4 1	2 3 8 1	6 3 2 7	3 1 6
7 2 9 8	6 8 0 3	2 6 3 4	8 5 3 5	0 6 0 4	7 5 4 6	1 4 6 8	5 3 5 1	7 7 9 4	2 0 6
2 7 8 2	3 5 1 5	8 3 3 4	5 1 2 7	4 2 8 2	7 8 3 2	2 7 7 9	5 8 3 7	3 1 7 6	4 6 7

(Continued)

Table A.5 (Continued)

3 2 0 9	9 1 2 4	7 1 7 7	1 7 3 9	6 8 7 1	7 1 2 4	8 8 4 5	8 9 2 8	8 4 3 4	9 0 0
9 5 7 2	2 1 6 6	0 2 5 2	0 5 7 1	2 9 8 2	2 3 1 9	3 9 1 3	8 9 7 6	2 4 8 2	5 7 9
1 8 7 7	3 4 0 0	4 8 2 2	3 1 4 3	6 2 1 1	3 1 3 8	0 2 5 3	4 5 4 2	7 5 7 5	5 3 0
0 6 3 5	8 7 2 8	9 4 7 1	6 7 8 2	8 2 6 5	1 0 6 5	7 2 3 9	6 2 7 3	6 4 5 5	2 0 1
2 2 8 2	4 4 6 1	1 4 8 5	2 3 2 3	1 5 5 6	2 2 4 8	8 2 1 6	7 7 7 6	3 5 5 4	6 5 5
3 6 3 8	1 4 8 4	5 6 4 8	2 6 7 3	5 6 4 2	6 0 4 8	9 7 7 7	6 0 3 5	6 9 1 8	2 3 5
6 9 3 8	4 5 8 9	4 8 2 1	5 4 4 3	5 5 1 5	3 4 7 6	5 8 8 5	2 4 6 2	6 3 9 3	9 4 3
7 3 3 7	3 2 6 1	6 4 5 1	8 6 9 8	0 8 1 3	0 2 4 9	5 3 2 8	4 8 6 6	1 4 1 0	6 1 7
8 7 8 2	5 2 2 8	8 3 8 7	7 1 3 8	8 9 5 4	5 8 6 8	5 4 5 6	5 6 4 0	6 9 7 7	8 5 7
5 8 4 0	0 5 4 8	4 6 3 0	1 7 6 4	5 4 7 6	9 6 5 4	7 2 4 3	1 3 5 4	9 2 4 1	6 8 1
3 3 0 7	5 2 1 5	7 6 7 3	3 4 4 6	2 8 6 1	1 8 6 3	6 3 6 3	4 4 8 4	4 6 8 4	6 7 6
1 0 0 1	6 7 7 6	0 2 4 7	5 9 2 9	9 1 2 5	7 3 6 8	3 6 7 9	8 3 5 5	3 8 1 6	2 6 7
4 8 7 7	4 6 1 7	2 2 5 7	0 2 5 6	0 1 3 5	4 2 6 9	2 5 6 7	7 4 1 0	7 3 2 2	8 7 7
5 0 3 2	9 8 0 2	9 8 3 1	6 2 3 0	3 6 3 6	8 8 8 8	2 3 5 4	7 0 9 3	7 2 1 6	7 6 8
5 2 3 0	3 5 3 1	0 6 7 6	9 4 2 7	0 7 0 2	7 5 4 6	5 6 6 4	9 7 5 7	0 3 5 3	1 1 0
3 3 4 2	5 4 4 2	6 1 9 8	6 6 2 1	7 3 8 7	9 6 9 1	1 8 3 3	1 3 8 7	1 7 5 4	5 1 1
2 3 2 7	1 0 8 2	8 1 1 4	4 7 4 0	7 2 1 6	0 5 2 1	7 6 8 1	4 3 4 5	4 0 6 2	8 1 5
6 2 4 6	4 5 5 2	6 2 4 6	1 6 7 3	5 2 4 7	1 4 7 4	3 2 7 8	8 6 2 6	7 5 1 5	7 4 8
5 1 3 8	0 7 2 7	0 4 7 8	8 3 8 4	3 0 1 8	6 6 0 8	4 2 5 0	9 5 5 8	1 8 6 6	1 1 1
6 3 4 4	1 7 3 1	6 3 0 5	5 5 9 3	3 4 3 7	8 2 2 4	9 2 8 9	1 8 8 5	1 1 6 5	3 8 7
4 8 4 0	2 7 7 7	1 1 5 7	3 6 3 3	7 4 2 6	5 5 4 8	2 3 4 7	1 4 4 2	4 0 0 6	4 4 5
5 6 3 1	7 4 5 7	5 4 8 7	2 3 4 2	3 0 0 0	7 4 1 6	6 2 4 5	8 5 4 5	1 7 7 1	2 8 8
2 4 2 8	1 4 8 3	3 5 3 3	2 9 9 1	5 0 6 4	8 5 8 5	5 3 6 2	2 4 3 5	4 7 5 3	7 9 2
0 2 5 2	4 7 3 2	3 8 4 4	7 0 5 1	2 6 4 4	0 5 6 6	2 6 8 2	4 4 9 1	6 7 1 2	6 4 9
4 6 5 5	8 7 9 7	2 0 7 6	9 8 3 3	7 4 5 4	7 0 9 6	5 6 8 8	0 3 3 4	6 6 7 5	5 5 6
0 0 5 2	2 7 7 0	6 4 6 2	5 7 2 8	8 4 2 2	8 1 9 2	9 1 6 1	5 5 2 3	3 3 3 6	9 3 0
1 1 1 9	9 6 6 7	8 0 3 2	3 1 3 8	5 8 5 1	4 6 9 5	2 5 6 5	1 8 9 0	4 8 6 2	0 2 3
1 7 3 9	6 8 1 2	7 3 2 3	1 7 1 9	2 8 9 1	0 7 0 4	5 1 9 1	3 6 1 6	7 2 1 1	8 0 7
1 6 5 6	5 2 5 7	5 2 2 8	4 2 7 8	2 6 7 3	1 7 1 2	5 7 3 0	7 0 5 8	5 6 7 6	8 2 9
8 7 6 7	5 0 3 2	1 4 0 5	1 6 7 8	2 7 3 9	4 0 5 5	8 5 3 3	1 8 4 4	6 1 7 9	6 6 9
5 2 2 2	8 4 2 6	1 6 2 5	5 4 9 3	7 5 3 4	8 7 4 9	0 5 8 4	2 0 8 4	0 0 5 9	7 7 1
4 8 8 4	0 2 1 4	6 7 1 2	1 1 5 0	8 1 5 5	4 7 4 0	7 4 3 4	6 5 8 0	7 6 0 0	5 8 1
5 1 7 0	7 5 6 3	3 7 6 3	1 4 5 6	7 3 4 4	4 8 3 8	5 7 1 7	9 7 3 1	3 3 6 5	4 6 3

Table A.6   Short Table of Random Normal Deviates

				$\mu = 0, \sigma = 1$					
−0.670	0.518	0.387	0.523	0.641	1.243	0.322	−2.607	−1.097	−0.012
−2.912	1.448	1.343	−0.122	0.726	−0.617	0.609	2.319	−0.450	−1.197
−0.028	−0.790	0.057	1.425	1.940	1.161	−0.878	−0.716	−0.244	−1.151
−1.257	0.774	0.003	0.388	1.060	1.028	−0.236	1.172	0.442	−0.157
2.372	−1.376	−1.318	1.236	0.738	0.337	−0.534	0.090	0.886	0.676
−0.970	0.438	−0.672	−0.180	0.667	1.370	−0.481	0.329	0.842	0.449
−1.228	0.129	−0.426	−0.165	0.028	2.696	1.201	−1.351	0.724	−1.017
−0.369	0.310	0.432	0.237	0.884	−1.224	0.539	0.852	0.497	−0.283
1.161	1.219	1.615	0.336	1.100	−0.528	0.161	0.278	0.675	−1.143
−0.284	2.609	0.792	1.825	−0.249	1.654	0.621	0.979	−1.472	−1.173
−0.578	−0.789	0.106	0.832	−0.597	0.496	−0.561	−1.033	−0.578	−0.378
0.074	0.261	−0.766	−1.046	0.361	−0.043	−1.927	1.527	0.605	1.475
0.230	0.046	0.978	−1.901	1.162	−0.545	0.697	1.151	2.033	0.080
2.162	−0.562	1.190	0.925	−1.057	0.015	−1.371	1.067	−1.080	−1.129
−1.020	−1.130	−0.315	0.628	−0.140	2.050	−0.030	−0.629	0.128	−1.221
1.323	−0.836	−0.284	−0.249	−0.768	1.242	−1.879	−0.417	0.013	−0.502
2.329	1.884	0.033	0.598	−0.217	0.260	0.431	−1.914	0.205	1.155
2.761	1.800	−0.562	0.714	−0.407	0.009	−0.724	−1.168	0.247	1.166
−0.232	0.605	−0.023	−0.531	0.542	−0.155	0.697	1.037	−0.316	−0.003
−0.742	0.210	−0.741	−1.099	0.158	2.112	−0.765	−0.319	−0.247	0.345
−1.410	0.413	0.705	1.444	1.057	−0.843	0.043	−0.571	−0.001	0.203
2.272	−0.719	0.679	2.007	−0.180	0.698	−1.137	0.688	−0.571	−0.100
2.832	0.925	−1.350	1.529	−0.260	−1.007	−2.350	−1.501	0.289	1.522
−1.086	−0.558	−0.973	−1.285	−0.021	0.077	0.915	−0.241	−0.249	−0.529
0.134	1.815	0.313	1.571	−0.216	2.261	0.696	−0.130	0.393	0.017
0.783	0.600	−0.745	1.127	−0.684	−0.519	0.125	−0.499	1.543	−0.082
0.174	−0.897	0.575	−0.751	0.694	−2.959	0.529	1.587	0.339	−0.813

(Continued)

Table A.6 (Continued)

				$\mu = 0, \sigma = 1$					
−1.319	0.556	2.963	1.218	1.199	−1.746	1.611	0.467	−0.490	0.202
1.298	−0.940	−1.143	−1.136	−1.516	0.548	0.629	0.250	−1.087	0.322
−0.676	−1.107	−1.483	0.278	0.493	−0.442	1.078	−0.336	−0.177	−0.057
− 1.287	0.775	−1.095	1.161	−1.877	1.874	1.703	−1.619	−0.725	−1.407
0.260	−0.028	−1.982	0.811	0.999	1.662	0.908	1.476	−1.137	−0.945
0.481	1.060	1.441	0.163	0.720	1.490	−0.026	−0.502	0.427	−0.351
0.794	0.725	1.971	0.384	−0.579	−1.079	−1.440	−0.859	−0.346	0.007
0.584	−0.554	1.460	0.791	−0.426	−0.682	0.430	1.922	−2.099	0.221
−0.114	0.379	−0.698	1.570	−0.511	−0.725	0.680	−0.591	−1.091	0.357
−1.128	−1.707	0.921	−0.859	−1.566	1.523	−0.900	−0.988	0.264	0.282
0.691	0.153	0.076	1.691	0.553	0.457	−1.107	0.322	0.633	0.007
1.115	0.777	−0.738	0.868	1.484	−0.792	0.950	−0.842	−0.192	0.620
−0.389	0.559	0.670	−0.315	1.234	0.475	1.117	1.286	−0.649	−1.880
0.330	0.750	−0.642	0.148	−0.608	0.866	−1.720	0.653	−0.210	−0.959
−0.333	−0.084	1.239	−0.049	−0.095	−0.197	−0.213	−1.420	−0.491	0.102
1.718	1.111	−0.548	−0.653	1.534	−0.456	−0.395	1.614	−0.531	−0.785
−0.182	0.620	1.178	−1.071	0.444	−0.072	−1.001	1.325	−0.302	−1.119
1.260	−1.192	0.182	−0.397	−0.705	−1.085	− 1.492	1.642	0.673	−0.707
−1.204	−1.725	1.695	1.473	0.665	−0.489	0.020	0.267	1.230	0.865
−0.619	0.307	−0.226	−0.096	0.987	−1.195	−1.412	0.433	2.052	0.022
−0.272	−0.096	0.137	−0.361	0.653	−0.156	1.309	−0.480	−0.397	1.302
0.245	−0.690	0.493	−1.123	1.465	0.132	0.582	−0.429	0.225	0.125
0.101	−0.855	0.782	−1.040	2.113	−1.423	−1.010	0.158	0.106	−1.232

GLOSSARY OF TERMS

Accuracy of information Degree to which information reflects reality.

Accuracy in sampling Is affected by nonreponse bias, memory error, misunderstanding of questions, problem of definition of terms, and processing error.

ACNielsen BASES Panel-based research conducted by the marketing research/consulting firm ACNielsen using the Internet for data collection.

Adequate sample A sample that is of sufficient size to provide confidence in the stability of its characteristics.

After-only with control group design A true experiment requiring one treatment and an after measurement of both the experimental and control groups.

All-variable regression Multiple regression with all independent variables included simultaneously.

Alpha error See *Type I error*.

Alternate forms reliability The extent to which measurement scores from equivalent forms of the measure administered to the same sample are the same.

Alternative hypothesis A hypothesis making statement of expected difference.

Ambiguity of questions and responses Errors made in the transmission of information in interpreting written or spoken words or behavior.

Analysis The categorizing, aggregating into constituent parts, and manipulation of data to obtain answers to the research question(s) underlying the research project.

Analysis of variance (ANOVA) A test of the differences in k group means for one or more variables (factors).

Applied research See *Decisional research*.

Area sample A probability sample where the primary sampling is of geographical units.

Arithmetic mean See *Mean*.

ASP model See *Online Application Service Provider*.

Associative variation A measure of the extent to which occurrences of two variables, or changes of two variables, are associated. Also known as concomitant variation.

Attitude measurement Measurement of the person's mental state toward a certain stimuli according to specified sets of dimensions and instructions.

Audimeter An electromechanical device used to record automatically the times a household's television set is turned on and off and the stations that it is tuned to.

Availability of information Availability of information when a decision is being made.

Balanced scale A rating scale with an equal number of response alternatives in opposite directions from some midpoint (e.g., positive and negative alternatives).

Balancing See *Matching*.

Bases for inferring causation The means by which causation can be inferred: (1) associative variation, (2) sequence of events, and (3) absence of other possible causal factors.

Basic research See *Fundamental research*.

Before-after with one control group design A true experimental design with one treatment and with measurements of the experimental and control groups made both before and after the treatment is administered.

Behaviorally anchored rating scale (BARS) A rating scale using behavioral incidents to define each position on the rating scale rather than verbal, graphic, or numeric labels.

Beta error See *Type II error*.

Bias The difference between the true value of that which is being measured and the average value derived from a number of independent measures of it.

Bivariate analysis The analysis of relationships between two variables.

Bounded recall An approach for reducing telescoping by asking questions about events of concern in previous time periods as well as the time period of research interest.

Bulletin board Qualitative research online technology at a website that allows users to register and then participate in unmoderated discussions of topics of interest to participants of the bulletin board.

Canonical correlation analysis A generalization of multiple correlation analysis to two or more criterion variables.

Canonical correlation coefficient In discriminant analysis it is a measure of the association that summarizes how the discriminant function is related to the groups, and in canonical correlation analysis it is a measure of the association between the independent variables and the set of dependent variables.

CATI A computer-aided telephone interview in which the interviewer reads the questions from a computer and enters the responses directly.

Causal study Research design that attempts to determine the causes of what is being predicted (i.e., the reasons why).

Census All members of the population are included for study.

Central tendency error Reluctance of respondents to give extreme scores or to use an extreme position on an individual scale item.

Cheater question A question included in a questionnaire that will disclose a respondent giving fabricated answers.

Chi-square test For a simple tabulation it tests the goodness-of-fit between the observed distribution and the expected distribution of a variable, and for cross tabulation it tests whether the observed association or relationship between the variables is statistically significant.

Classification matrix A cross-tabulation-type table showing the results of discriminant analysis' ability to correctly classify observations into categories of a criterion variable.

Cluster analysis A class of statistical techniques whose objective is to separate objects into groups such that the similarity of objects within each group is maximized while maximizing the difference between groups.

Cluster sampling A probability sample in which a simple random or stratified random sample is selected of all primary sampling units, and then all elements within the selected primary units are sampled.

Codebook/coding manual A manual that shows how the data have been coded for analysis.

Coding The process by which responses are assigned to data categories and symbols (usually numbers) are assigned to identify them with the categories.

Coefficient alpha A measure of internal consistency reliability for a multi-item measure that is a type of mean reliability coefficient for all possible ways to split the items into two groups.

Coefficient of determination (R^2) A measure of the strength of association between variables in regression; it specifies how much of the variation in the dependent variable can be explained by the variation in the independent variable(s).

Coefficient of multiple correlation Correlation coefficient when the number of independent variables is two or more.

Commercial data Data sold in the form of syndicated services. Collected by commercial marketing research firms or industry associations. See *Syndicated services*.

Comparative rating scale Objects are rated in comparison with other objects.

Completely randomized design A statistical design where experimental treatments are assigned to test units on a random basis.

Concept An abstraction formed by generalization about particulars.

Conceptual definition A construct is defined in terms of other constructs. Also known as *Constitutive definition*.

Concept testing How people, without prompting, interpret deliberately a sketchy idea for a new product or service.

Concomitant variation See *Associative variation*.

Concurrent validity See *Criterion validity*.

Confidence interval A range of values with a given probability of covering the true population value (parameter).

Confounding In an experiment, it is the tangling effects of two or more levels of a treatment variable or two or more treatment variables.

Confusion matrix See *Classification matrix.*

Conjoint analysis A technique of research that measures psychological judgments by decomposing a set of overall responses so that the utility of each stimulus attribute and attribute level can be inferred from the respondent's overall evaluations of the stimuli.

Constant sum question A question in which the respondent is asked to allocate a fixed sum of points to options to show the importance (or some other attribute or characteristic) of each option.

Constitutive definition See *Conceptual definition.*

Construct A concept that is the conscious invention of researchers to be used for a special research purpose.

Construct validity A form of external validity that assesses the extent to which generalizations can be made about higher-order constructs from research operations; it is a measurement issue and is concerned with how and why a measurement works.

Content analysis Coding of free responses to open-end questions.

Content validity The extent to which a scale or measurement instrument represents the universe of the property or characteristic being measured.

Continuity correction A correction factor in chi-square analysis that adjusts for the use of a continuous distribution to estimate probability in a discrete distribution. Known as the Yates continuity correction.

Continuous panel A sample of individuals, households, or firms from whom information is obtained at successive time periods.

Controlled experiment A research design in which the investigator intervenes by manipulating at least one assumed causal variable and in which subjects (respondents) are assigned randomly to experimental and control groups.

Convergent validity A type of construct validity concerned with the correspondence in results between measuring the same construct by two or more independent methods.

Convenience sample A nonprobability sample chosen by a convenient process and because elements are easy to obtain.

Conversational interviewing In personal or telephone interviewing the interviewer answers queries from respondents about question meaning and understanding.

Correlation analysis The analysis of the extent to which changes in one variable are related to changes in one or more other variables.

Correlation coefficient A measure of the association between two or more variables.

Correspondence analysis A special case of canonical correlation analysis that examines the relations between the categories of two discrete variables.

Coverage error Occurs when the sample frame or group from which the sample is drawn does not represent the population as a whole. See also *Frame error*.

Criterion validity The extent to which the measurement instrument works in predicting the future (predictive validity) or reflecting the present (concurrent validity). Also known as *Pragmatic validity*.

Criterion variable See *Dependent variable*.

Critical path method (CPM) A network approach in which the component activities are diagrammed in sequence of performance and a time estimate for each activity is presented. See *Program evaluation and review technique (PERT)*.

Cross-over design A statistical experimental design in which different treatments are applied to the same test units in different time periods.

Cross-sectional design A research design where several groups are measured at the same time, with each group exposed to a different level of the treatment variable.

Cross-tabulation The simultaneous counting of the number of observations that occur in each of the data categories of two or more variables.

Cross-validation A procedure in regression analysis and discriminant analysis for examining whether the predictive equations derived hold up beyond the data on which parameters are based.

Cumulative scale A scale constructed of a set of items with which the respondent indicates agreement or disagreement; it is unidimensional, and there is a pattern of item responses that is related to the total score.

Data collection techniques The means by which data are collected by communication or by observation.

Data matrix A rectangular array of data entries where the rows are a respondent's responses and the columns are the variables or data fields for the responses. Also known as the *Basic data matrix*.

Decision model See *Problem-situation model*.

Decisional research Applied research that attempts to use existing knowledge to aid in the solution of some given problem(s).

Dependent variable The effect of interest or outcome in an experiment.

Depth interview An often unstructured interview that is used to explore the underlying predisposition, needs, desires, feelings, and emotions of consumers toward products and services. May consist of direct and/or indirect questions.

Descriptive study Provides information such as describing market characteristics or functions on groups and phenomena that already exist; there is prior formulation of specific research questions. Also known as an observational study.

Determinants of a research project The problem, the researcher, the respondent/subject, and the client.

Deterministic cause Any event that is necessary and sufficient for the subsequent occurrence of another event.

Dichotomous question A multiple-choice question with only two alternative responses.

Differential scale A rating scale, assumed to be interval, in which a respondent is asked to agree with only a subset of items (statements) about an object, with each item having a predetermined scale value (position on the scale), and the items agreed with correspond to the respondent's position on the dimension being measured.

Direct interview An interview in which the purposes of the questions are not purposely disguised.

Direct-judgment rating method A respondent is asked to give a numerical rating to each stimulus with respect to some designated attribute.

Directory-based sampling A directory or other physical listing is used as a sample frame to select sample elements to be called in a telephone survey.

Discriminant analysis A multivariate technique of analysis that examines the ability of predictor variables to discriminate (i.e., to separate) between categories of a criterion (dependent) variable or groups.

Discriminant validity A form of construct validity that assesses the extent to which a measure is unique and not simply a reflection of other variables.

Disk-by-mail A type of survey where the questionnaire is placed on a personal computer diskette and mail is used to send it to a respondent and by the respondent to return it to the research organization.

Disproportionate stratified sampling A stratified sample in which characteristics other than just relative size, such as relative size of stratum variances, are taken into account.

Distance A characteristic of the real number system where the differences between ordered numbers are ordered.

Double opt-in mailing list A list of people with e-mail addresses who have indicated agreement to receive surveys.

Drop-off/pick-up survey A survey where the questionnaire is left with a respondent and a representative of the research organization returns later to pick up the completed questionnaire, or the questionnaire can be returned by mail.

Editing The process of reviewing the data to ensure maximum accuracy and clarity.

Electronic surveying See *Online research.*

E-mail submission form A form used when the researcher builds a HTML online survey, distributes actively to the respondent, and receives the respondent's answers as part of an e-mail message that is directed back to the researcher.

Emic versus etic issue An issue in cross-national/cultural research in which a researcher must decide whether constructs and methods are culture-specific (emic) or culture-free (etic).

E-panel Doing panel research using the Internet for data collection.

Equal-appearing intervals See *Differential scale*.

Ethical behavior Behavior conforming to professional standards of conduct; it is what most people in a given society view as being moral, good, or right.

Ethics Moral principles, quality, or practice.

Ethnography A qualitative approach to research that studies human behavior within a cultural context.

Executive summary That part of a formal research report that reduces the essentials of the study—the why, the what, the how, the conclusions, and the recommendations—to one or two pages.

Experimental error Noncorrespondence of the true (or actual) impact of, and the impact attributed to, the independent variable(s).

Experimentation A research method where there is researcher intervention and control over the factors affecting the response variable of interest, thus allowing for the establishment of causal relationships.

Explicit model A model described verbally, graphically or diagrammatically, mathematically (symbolically), or as a logical sequence of questions (logical flow).

Ex post facto **design** A quasi-experiment in which the test and control groups are not known until after the treatment has been administered.

Exploratory study A study whose purposes include the identification of problems, more precise formulation of problems (including identification of relevant variables), and the formulation of new alternative courses of action.

External secondary information Secondary information that must be obtained from outside sources.

External validity The generalizability of a relationship beyond the circumstances under which it is observed.

Extraneous variable A variable other than the manipulated independent variable that could influence the dependent variable.

Factor A variable or construct that is not directly observable but is developed as a linear combination of observed variables.

Factor analysis A class of statistical techniques whose purpose often is data reduction and summarization, which is accomplished by representing a set of observed variables, persons, or occasions in terms of a smaller number of hypothetical, underlying, and unknown dimensions, which are called factors.

Factorial design A statistical experimental design where there is an equal number of observations made of all combinations involving at least two levels of at least two variables.

False negative error A respondent reports not to have an attitude when he or she really does have one.

False positive error Statements by respondents that appear to be complimentary but really are not, or when respondents appear to have an attitude and they do not.

Field experiment An experiment conducted in a natural environmental setting.

Fixed-size sampling The number of elements to be included in the sample is decided on in advance.

Focus group A group of topic knowledgeable people who jointly participate in an interview that does not use a structured question-and-answer methodology. Usually consists of 8 to 12 people selected purposively.

Formal research report Consists of a number of components that can be organized into three components: prefatory pages, report body, and appended parts.

Four-group, six-study design Combines an after-only with control group design and a before-after with control group design.

Fractionation A rating scale in which the respondent is given two stimuli at a time and is asked to give some numerical estimate of the ratio between them with respect to some attribute.

Frame error Noncorrespondence of the sought sample to the required sample. Occurs when the sample frame is incomplete, has multiple entries for elements, or has elements included that are not in the relevant population.

Framing effects The difference in response to objectively equivalent information depending on the manner in which the information is labeled or framed.

Free answer question A question that has no fixed alternatives to which the answer must conform. Also known as *Open-ended text.*

Frequency distribution See *Simple tabulation.*

Full profile conjoint analysis Conjoint analysis where different stimulus (e.g., a product) descriptions are developed and presented to the respondent for acceptability or preference evaluations.

Fundamental research Seeks to extend the boundaries of knowledge in a given area with no necessary immediate application to existing problems.

Funnel approach An approach to questionnaire design that specifies a sequence of questions where one proceeds from the general to the specific or from the easier questions to those that are more difficult to answer.

Goodness-of-fit test An analysis of whether the data obtained in a research study fit or conform to a model or distribution.

Graphic positioning scale A semantic differential used for multiple object ratings where all objects are evaluated on each scale item.

Graphic rating scale A rating scale in which respondents indicate their ratings of a stimulus on a graphical response item.

Guided imagery A modified TAT where participants are asked to appraise a product or brand by concentrating on creating and experiencing an associated image.

Guttman scalogram analysis See *Cumulative scale*.

History Events outside an experimental design that affect the dependent variable.

Hypothesis An assertion about the state of nature or the relation between things that often, from a practical standpoint, implies a possible course of action with a prediction of the outcome if the course of action is followed.

Implicit model A model that guides a decision but has not been specified in an explicit or formal manner.

Inaccuracy in response Errors made in the formulation of information. May be *concurrent* or *predictive* (e.g., when reported intentions are not carried out).

Independent variable In an experiment, it is a variable whose effect on some other variable the experiment is designed to measure; it is the variable that is manipulated and is also known as the *treatment* variable.

Indexes of agreement Measures of the strength of association between two variables in a cross-tabulation, including the phi correlation coefficient, the contingency coefficient, the lambda-asymmetric coefficient, and the lambda-symmetric coefficient.

Indirect interview An interview that is neither fully structured nor unstructured, and in which the purposes of the questions asked are intentionally disguised.

Information Recorded experience that is useful for decision-making; communicated knowledge that changes the state of knowledge of the person who receives it.

In-store interviewing A type of mall intercept in which the interviews take place in a single store, usually at the point of purchase.

Instrument effect Changes in the measuring instrument or process that may affect the measurement obtained in an experiment.

Intentions Presently planned actions to be taken in a specified future time period.

Interaction The situation in an experiment where the response to changes in the levels of one treatment variable is dependent on the level of some other treatment variable(s).

Interactive interviewing Interviews that are conducted by having a respondent respond on a personal computer. Some software may customize new questions based on responses to previously answered questions.

Intercoder reliability The reliability of coding done by multiple persons.

Internal consistency reliability Reliability within single testing occasions in which the variables are grouped.

Internal secondary information Secondary information that is available from within the company or the organization.

Internal validity Assesses whether the observed effect is due solely to the experimental treatments and not due to some extraneous variable(s).

Interpretation The process of taking the results of analysis, making inferences relevant to the research relationships studied, and drawing managerially useful conclusions about these relationships.

Interval scale A measurement scale that possesses the characteristics of order and distance, and the zero point of the scale is arbitrary.

Interview A form of person-to-person (dyadic) communication between two parties that involves the asking and answering of questions.

Interviewer A person who asks questions in an interview of a respondent.

Judgment sample A nonprobability sample where the elements to be included are selected on the basis of the researcher's sound judgment or expertise and an appropriate strategy.

Kolmogorov-Smirnov one-sample test A goodness-of-fit test of the agreement between an observed distribution of a set of sample values and some specified theoretical distribution.

Kolmogorov-Smirnov two-sample test A test of whether two independent samples come from the same population or from populations with the same distribution.

Kurtosis The shape of a data distribution in terms of height or flatness.

Laboratory experiment An experiment conducted in a controlled laboratory or laboratory-type setting.

Laddering See *Means-end analysis*.

Leniency error occurs when respondents consistently use the extreme positions on a rating scale with relatively little use of intermediate scale positions.

Likert scale A balanced rating scale in which a respondent is asked to indicate extent of agreement with a series of statements, using a set of verbal categories from strongly agree to strongly disagree for response. See also *Summated scale*.

Limited-response category scale A rating scale in which a respondent is limited to choosing from a predetermined set of response categories.

Logit A type of multiple regression analysis where the categorical dependent variable is assumed to follow a logistic distribution.

Mail interview A type of survey where the questionnaire is sent to a respondent by mail and the respondent returns the completed questionnaire by mail.

Make or buy decision The decision by a research client whether the research is to be done in-house (make) or by an outside supplier (buy).

Mall intercept Interviewers are stationed at selected places in a shopping mall or other centralized public place and they request interviews from people who pass by.

Management summary See *Executive summary*.

Mann-Whitney U test A test of whether two independent groups providing data are from the same population and whether there is a relationship between two variables.

Marketing decision support system (MDSS) A coordinated collection of data, systems, tools, and techniques with supporting software and hardware by which an organization gathers and interprets relevant information from the business and the environment and turns it into a basis for marketing action.

Marketing information system (MIS) A formal system within an organization for obtaining, processing, and disseminating decision information. Subsystems are marketing research, internal records, marketing intelligence, and information analysis.

Marketing intelligence A subsystem of an MIS in which a set of procedures and sources are used to provide information about relevant developments in the marketing environment.

Marketing research The systematic and objective search for, and analysis of, information relevant to the identification and solution of any problem in the field of marketing.

Matching A control technique where subjects are equated on the variable(s) to be controlled. Also known as *balancing*.

Maturation Changes that occur with the passage of time in the people involved in an experimental design.

Mean The point on a scale around which the values of a distribution balance; it is the sum of all the values divided by the number of respondents.

Means-end analysis An in-depth one-on-one interviewing technique that identifies the linkages people make between product attributes (means), the benefits derived from those attributes (the consequences), and the values that underlie why the consequences are important (the ends). Also known as *laddering* and *means-end chain*.

Measurement A way of assigning symbols to represent the properties of persons, objects, events, or states; the symbols have the same relevant relationships to each other as do the things represented.

Measurement error The difference between the information obtained and the information wanted by the researcher; it is generated by the measurement process itself.

Median The midpoint of the data in a distribution.

Memory error Inaccuracy in response that occurs when a respondent gives the wrong factual information because of not remembering an event asked about.

Method of choices A procedure for indirectly arriving at paired comparison proportions of the form $p(B > A)$ by asking respondents to choose the one of a set of stimuli that has the most of, is the best, or is preferred, and so on, on the basis of the attribute or characteristic being studied.

Method of inquiry The broad approach to conducting a research project and the philosophy underlying the approach. Methods include objectivist, subjectivist, Bayesian, and phenomenologist.

Metric measurement Direct numerical judgments made by a respondent that are assumed to be either interval- or ratio-scaled.

Metric multidimensional scaling Multidimensional scaling in which the input data are ratio-scaled.

Mind Track A brainwave-to-computer interface developed by Advanced Neurotechnologies, Inc., that measures direct emotional response to most any communication medium.

MIS See *Marketing information system.*

MIS activities Discovery, collection, interpretation, analysis, and intracompany dissemination of information.

Misunderstanding error Inaccuracy in response often due to careless question design.

Mode The typical or most frequently occurring value in a distribution.

Model The linking of propositions together in a way that provides a meaningful explanation for a system or process.

Moderator A person conducting a focus group whose job is to direct the group's discussion to the topics of interest.

Monadic rating scale Each object is rated by itself independently of any other objects being rated.

Multicollinearity A condition in multiple regression analysis where the predictor variables show very high correlation among themselves.

Multidimensional scaling A set of techniques that portray psychological relations among stimuli—either empirically obtained similarities or preferences (or other kinds of orderings)—as geometric relationships among points in a multidimensional space.

Multi-item scale A scale consisting of a number of closely related individual rating scales whose responses are combined into a single index, composite score, or value. See also *Summated scale.*

Multiple-choice question A question that has at least two fixed alternative response categories and the respondents can select *k* out of *n* choices.

Multiple correlation analysis Correlation analysis when the number of independent variables is two or more.

Multiple regression analysis Regression analysis with two or more independent variables.

Multiplicity sample See *Snowball sample.*

Multistage sampling A multilevel probability sample in which a sample is selected of larger areas (or groups), and then a sample is selected from each of the areas (groups) selected at the first level, and so on.

Multitrait multimethod matrix A generalized approach for establishing the validity and reliability of a set of measurements (traits).

Multivariate analysis Statistical procedures that simultaneously analyze measurements of multiple variables on each individual or object under study.

Natural experiment An experiment in which the investigator intervenes only to the extent required for measurement, and there is no manipulation of an assumed causal variable. The variable of interest has occurred in a natural setting, and the investigator looks at what has happened.

Nominal scale A measurement scale that does not possess the characteristics of order, distance, and origin.

Nomogram A graphic instrument for specifying sample size relating allowable error, confidence level, mean or proportion, and standard deviation.

Nomological validity A form of construct validity that attempts to relate measurements to a theoretical model that leads to further deductions, interpretations, and tests.

Nonmetric multidimensional scaling Multidimensional scaling in which input data are rank order data (ordinally scaled) but output is interval-scaled.

Nonparametric statistical methods Distribution-free methods in which inferences are based on a test statistic whose sampling distribution does not depend on the specific distribution of the population from which the sample is drawn.

Nonprobability sample A sample selected based on the judgment of the investigator, convenience, or some other means not involving the use of probabilities.

Nonresponse error Noncorrespondence of the obtained sample to the original sample.

Nonsampling error All errors other than sampling error that are associated with a research project; typically is a systematic error but can have a random component.

Null hypothesis A hypothesis that states no difference.

Numerical comparative scale A semantic differential used for multiple object ratings where all objects are evaluated on each scale item using a verbally anchored numerical scale.

Numerical rating scale A rating scale that uses a series of integers, which may or may not have verbal descriptions, to represent degrees of some property.

Observation technique Information on respondents' behavior is obtained by observing it rather than by asking about it.

One-more-question syndrome The tendency to add an additional question to a survey because the cost is very low to do so.

One-on-one interview See *Depth interview*.

Online application service provider (ASP) Accessed through the Internet, where surveys are built online, requiring no user software, server, or IT support.

Online research Using the Internet as a mode of data collection. Often used in conjunction with e-mail.

Operational definition Assigns meaning to a variable by specifying what is to be measured and how it is to be measured.

Order A characteristic of the real number series in which the numbers are ordered.

Ordered-category sorting A respondent assigns (sorts) a set of stimuli into different categories that are ordered on the basis of some property.

Ordinal scale A measurement scale that possesses only the characteristic of order; it is a ranking scale.

Origin A characteristic of the real number series where there is a unique origin indicated by the number zero.

Paired comparisons The respondent is asked to choose one of a pair of stimuli on the basis of some property of interest.

Pantry audit A data collection technique whereby a field worker takes an inventory of brands, quantities, and package sizes that a consumer has on hand.

Parameter A summary property of a collectivity, such as a population, when that collectivity is not considered to be a sample.

Partially structured indirect interview An interview using a predevised set of words, statements, cartoons, pictures, or other representation to which a person is asked to respond, and the interviewer is allowed considerable freedom in questioning the respondent to ensure a full response.

Personal interview An interviewer asks questions of respondents in a face-to-face situation.

Pictogram A pictorial chart that depicts data with the help of symbols, such as stars, stacks of coins, trees, facial expressions, caricatures of people, and so forth.

Pilot study A small-scale test of what a survey will be, including all activities that will go into the final survey.

Planned information Exists when a manager recognizes a need and he or she makes a request that information be obtained.

Politz-Simmons method A method of estimating both the direction and magnitude of nonresponse error.

Population The totality of all the units or elements (individuals, households, organizations, etc.) possessing one or more particular relevant features or characteristics in common, to which one desires to generalize study results.

Population specification error Noncorrespondence of the required population to the population selected by the researcher.

Popular report A research report that minimizes technical details and emphasizes simplicity.

Postcoding Coding done after the data are collected.

Power of a hypothesis test It is 1 minus the probability of a Type II error $(1-\beta)$.

Practical significance See *Substantive significance*.

Pragmatic validity See *Criterion validity*.

Precision Refers to *sampling error* and the size of the confidence limits placed on an estimate.

Precoding Coding done before the data are collected.

Predictive validity See *Criterion validity*.

Predictor variable See *Independent variable*.

Pre-experimental design A research design with total absence of control.

Pretesting The testing of a questionnaire or measurement instrument before use in a survey or experiment.

Probabilistic cause Any event that is necessary, but not sufficient, for the subsequent occurrence of another event.

Probability sampling Every element in the population has a known nonzero probability (chance) of being selected for inclusion in a study.

Probit A type of multiple regression analysis where the categorical dependent variable is assumed to be normally distributed.

Problem formulation A stage in the research process in which a management problem is translated into a research problem.

Problem-situation model A conceptual scheme that specifies a measure of the outcome(s) to be achieved, the relevant variables, and their functional relationship to the outcomes(s).

Program evaluation and review technique (PERT) A probabilistic scheduling approach using three time estimates: optimistic, most likely, and pessimistic. See also *Critical path method (CPM)*.

Projection A research technique whereby a respondent projects his/her personality characteristics and so on to a nonpersonal, ambiguous situation that he/she is asked to describe, expand, or build a structure around it.

Proportionate stratified sampling A stratified sample in which the sample that is drawn from each stratum is proportionate in size to the relative size of the stratum in the population.

Proposition A statement of the relationship between variables, including the form of the relationship.

Protocol A record of a respondent's verbalized thought processes while performing a decision task or while problem solving (concurrent) or just after the task is completed (retrospective).

Psychogalvanometer A device for measuring the extent of a subject's response to a stimulus, such as an advertisement.

Purposive sampling See *Judgment sample*.

Q-sort A scaling technique in which the respondent is asked to sort a number of statements or other stimuli into a predetermined number of categories, formed on the basis of some criterion, with a specified number having to be placed in each category.

Quasi-experimental design A controlled experiment design where there is manipulation of at least one assumed causal variable but there is not random assignment of subjects to experiment and control groups.

Questionnaire An instrument for data collection that requests information from respondents by asking questions.

Quota sample A nonprobability sample in which population subgroups are classified on the basis of researcher judgment and the individual elements are selected by interviewer judgment.

Random-digit-dialing A probability sampling procedure used in telephone surveys where the telephone number to be called is generated by selecting random digits.

Randomized response technique A technique for obtaining information about sensitive information.

Random sampling error See *Sampling error*.

Rank correlation The correlation between variables that are measured by ranking. Measures used are Spearman *rho* and Kendall *tau*.

Ranking Respondents are asked to order stimuli with respect to some designated property.

Rank order question A question where the answer format requires the respondent to assign a rank (order) position for the first, second, and so on, to the *n*th item to be ordered.

Rating A measurement method where a respondent paces that which is being rated along a continuum or in one of an ordered set of categories.

Ratio scale A measurement scale possessing all the characteristics of the real number series: order, distance, and origin.

Reactive effects of experimental situation Effects that may arise from subjects' reacting to the situation surrounding the conduct of an experiment rather than the treatment variable.

Reactive effects of testing The learning or conditioning of the persons involved in an experimental design as a result of knowing that their behavior is being observed and/or that the results are being measured.

Regression analysis The mathematical relationship between a dependent variable and one or more independent variables.

Regression coefficient Represented by *b*, it shows the amount of change that will occur in the dependent variable for a unit change in the independent variable it represents.

Relevancy of information Pertinency and applicability of information to the decision.

Reliability The consistency of test results over groups of individuals or over the same individual at different times.

Repeated measures design A research design where subjects are measured more than once on a dependent variable. See also *Cross-over design*.

Repertory grid A partially structured measurement technique that requires the respondent to compare objects along dimensions that he or she selects.

Representative sample A relatively small piece of the population that mirrors the various patterns and subclasses of the population.

Research design The specification of methods and procedures for acquiring the information needed to structure or to solve problems. The operational design stipulates what information is to be collected, from which sources, and by what procedures.

Research method Experimental or nonexperimental; the major difference between the two lies in the control of extraneous variables and the manipulation of at least one assumed causal variable by the investigator in an experiment.

Research plan A formal written document that serves as the overall master guide for conducting a research project.

Research process A series of interrelated steps that define what a research project is all about, starting with problem formulation and ending with the research report.

Research proposal A shorter and less technical version of a research plan that is used to elicit the project and gain a commitment of funding.

Research question States the purpose of the research, the variables of interest, and the relationships to be examined.

Research report The major vehicle by which researchers communicate by a written statement and/or oral presentation research results, recommendations for strategic and tactical action, and other conclusions to management in the organization or to an outside organization.

Respondent A person who participates in a research project by responding and answering questions verbally, in writing, or by behavior.

Response bias See *Response error*.

Response error The difference between a reported value and the true value of a variable.

Robust statistical technique A technique of analysis whereby if certain assumptions underlying the proper use of the technique are violated, the technique performs okay and can handle such a violation.

Sample A subset of the relevant population selected for inclusion in a research study.

Sample design A statement about a sample that specifies where the sample is to be selected, the process of selection, and the size of the sample; it is the theoretical basis and the practical means by which data are collected so that the characteristics of the population can be inferred with known estimates of error.

Sample frame A means of accounting for the elements in a population, usually a physical listing of the elements, but may be a procedure that produces a result equivalent to a physical listing, from which the sampled elements are selected.

Sampling distribution The probability distribution of a specified sample statistic (e.g., the mean) for all possible random samples of a given size n drawn from the specified population.

Sampling error Variable error resulting from the chance specification of population from elements according to the sampling plan. Often called random sampling error, it is the noncorrespondence of the sample selected by probability means and the representative sample sought by the researcher.

Sampling unit A population element that is actually chosen by the sampling process.

Scaling Generation of a continuum on which measured objects are located.

Scanner data Data on products purchased in retail stores that are obtained by electronic scanning at checkout of the Universal Product Code (UPC); unit and price information are recorded.

Scree chart In factor analysis, it is a discrete line chart that relates the amount of variance accounted for by each factor to the factor number (1 . . . k).

Secondary information Information that has been collected by persons or agencies for purposes other than the solution of the problem at hand and that is available for the project at hand.

Selection error The sampling error for a sample selected by a nonprobability method. It is also a term used for the effect of the selection procedure for the test (treatment) and control groups on the results of an experimental study.

Self-hosted server software Survey building software that requires housing on the researcher's server.

Semantic differential A rating procedure in which the respondent is asked to describe a concept or object by means of ratings on a set of bipolar adjectives or phrases, with the resulting measurements assumed to be intervally scaled.

Sentence completion test A respondent is given a sentence stem (the beginning phrase) and is asked to complete the sentence with the first thought that occurs to him or her.

Sequential sample An approach to selecting a sample size whereby a previously determined decision rule is used to indicate when sampling is to be stopped during the process of data collection.

Simple random sample A probability sample where each sample element has a known and equal probability of selection, and each possible sample of *n* elements has a known and equal probability of being the sample actually selected.

Simple tabulation A count of the number of responses that occur in each of the data categories that comprise a variable. Also known as *Marginal tabulation*.

Simulation A set of techniques for manipulating a model of some real-world process for the purpose of finding numerical solutions that are useful in the real process that is being modeled.

Single-source data Obtaining all data from one research supplier on product purchases and causal factors, such as media exposure, promotional influences, and consumer characteristics, from the same household.

Skewness A measure of a given data distribution's asymmetry.

Snowball sampling A nonprobability sample in which initial respondents are selected randomly but additional respondents are obtained by referrals or by some other information provided by the initial respondents.

Socioeconomic characteristics The social and economic characteristics of respondents, including, for example, income, occupation, education level, age, gender, marital status, and size of family.

Split-half reliability A measure of internal consistency reliability where the items in a multi-item measure are divided into two equivalent groups and the item responses are correlated.

Standard deviation A measure of dispersion (variation) around the sample mean, it is the square root of the variance.

Standard error The standard deviation of the specified sampling distribution of a statistic.

Standard error of the difference The standard deviation of the sampling distribution of the difference between statistics such as means and proportions.

Standardized interviewing In a survey using personal or telephone interviewing the interpretation of questions asked is left up to the respondent as the interviewer is not allowed to answer any query.

Stapel scale An even-numbered balanced nonverbal rating scale that is used in conjunction with single adjectives or phrases.

State of nature An environmental condition.

Static-group comparison A quasi-experimental design in which a group exposed to a treatment is compared to a group that was not exposed.

Statistical conclusion validity Involves the specific question whether the presumed independent and dependent variables are indeed related.

Statistical experimental design After-only designs in which there are at least two treatment levels. Includes completely randomized, factorial, Latin-Square, randomized block, and covariance designs.

Statistical power Ability of a sample to protect against the type II error (beta risk).

Statistical regression The tendency with repeated measures for scores to regress to the population mean of the group.

Stepwise regression Multiple regression analysis in which the independent variable explaining the most variance is sequentially included one at a time.

Story completion A qualitative research technique where a respondent is presented with the beginning of a situational narrative and is asked to complete it.

Stratified sampling A probability sample where the population is broken into different strata or subgroups based on one or more characteristics and then a simple random sample is taken from each stratum of interest in the population.

Structured interview An interview in which a formal questionnaire has been developed and the questions asked in a prearranged order.

Stub-and-banner table A table that presents one dependent variable cross-tabulated by multiple independent variables.

Substantive significance An association that is statistically significant and of sufficient strength.

Sufficiency of information Degree of completeness and/or detail of information to allow a decision to be made.

Summated scale A rating scale constructed by adding scores from responses to a set of Likert scales with the purpose of placing respondents along an attitude continuum of interest. See also *Likert scale* and *Multi-item scale*.

Surrogate information error Noncorrespondence of the information being sought and that required to solve the problem.

Survey A research method in which the information sought is obtained by asking questions of respondents.

Survey tracking and address books Online survey technology that uses imbedded codes to facilitate the identification and tracking of survey respondents and nonrespondents.

Syndicated services Information collected and tabulated on a continuing basis by research organizations for purposes of sale to firms; data are made available to all who wish to subscribe. See *Commercial data.*

Systematic error See *Nonsampling error.*

Systematic sampling A probability sample where the population elements are ordered in some way and then after the first element is selected all others are chosen using a fixed interval.

Tabulation The process of sorting data into previously established categories, making initial counts of responses and using summarizing measures.

Technical report A research report that emphasizes the methods used and underlying assumptions and presents the findings in a detailed manner.

Telephone interview Interviews that are conducted by telephone.

Telescoping A response error that occurs when a respondent reports an event happening at a time when it did not happen. It may be *forward* (report it happening more recently than it did) or *backward* (reporting it happening earlier than it did).

Testing effect The effect of a first measurement on the scores of a second measurement.

Test of independence A test of the significance of observed association involving two or more variables.

Test-retest reliability The stability of response over time.

Thematic apperception test (TAT) A test consisting of one or more pictures or cartoons that depict an ambiguous situation relating to the subject being studied, and research subjects are asked to make up a story about what is happening, or the subject is asked to assume the role of a person in the situation and then describe what is happening and who the others in the scene are.

Third-person technique A projective qualitative research method in which a respondent is indirectly interviewed by asking for his or her view of what a neighbor or some other person would respond to the interview.

Thurstone Case V scaling Based on Thurstone's law of comparative judgment, this method allows the construction of a unidimensional interval scale using responses from ordinal measurement methods, such as paired comparisons.

Time series design Data are obtained from the same sample (or population) at successive points in time.

Total study error Sampling error plus nonsampling error.

Treatment variable See *Independent variable*.

Trend design Data are obtained from statistically matched samples drawn from the same population over time.

True experiment See *Controlled experiment*.

t-**test** A test of the difference in means of two groups of respondents that focuses on sample means and variances.

Type I error The probability that one will incorrectly reject Ho, the null hypothesis of no difference, or any hypothesis.

Type II error The probability that one will incorrectly accept a null hypothesis, or any hypothesis.

Unlimited-response category scale A direct-judgment rating scale where the respondent is free to choose his/her own number or insert a tick mark along some line to represent his/her judgment about the magnitude of the stimulus relative to some reference points.

Unobtrusive measures Nonreactive measures of behavior, past and present.

Unsolicited information Information that may, in fact, exist within and be obtainable within the company but that potential users do not know is available unless they happen to chance upon it.

Unstructured interview An interview in which there is no formal questionnaire and the questions may not be asked in a prearranged order.

Useful information Information that is accurate, current, sufficient, available, and relevant.

Validity of measurement The extent to which one measures what he or she believes is being measured.

VALS A syndicated segmentation scheme known as Values and Lifestyle segmentation that combines demographic, attitudinal, and psychographic data, according to predefined segments.

Variance A measure of dispersion, it is the mean of the squared deviation of individual measurements from the arithmetic mean of the distribution.

Variation in measurement Differences in individual scores within a set of measurements that may be due to the characteristic or property being measured (the true difference) and/or the measurement process itself.

Verbal measures Include spoken and written responses, including responses provided interactively with a personal computer.

Verbal rating scale A rating scale using a series of verbal options for rating an object.

Warranty form of interview A type of mail interview where the questions asked are included on the warranty card to be returned to the manufacturer.

Weighting data Procedures used to adjust the final sample so that the specific respondent subgroups of the sample are found in identical proportions to those found in the population.

Wilcoxon rank sum (T) test A test of the relationship between two sets of measurements from dependent samples in which the data are collected in matched pairs.

Wilks' lambda In discriminant analysis it is a multivariate measure of group differences over discriminating variables.

Word association test A series of stimulus words are presented to a respondent who is asked to answer with the first word that comes to mind after hearing each stimulus word.

Name Index

Subject Index

ABOUT THE AUTHORS

Scott M. Smith is Professor of Marketing in the Marriott School of Management, Brigham Young University, Provo, Utah. His research and publication interests are online survey technologies for marketing research, Internet research and methodology, and computer modeling. He is the founder of Qualtrics, Inc., the parent company of SurveyZ.com, SurveyTime. com, and SurveyPro.com, which are online ASPs offering the most advanced survey research, database, and analysis tools. He is the author of the PC-MDS statistical software programs for conjoint and multidimensional scaling analysis for the personal computer. He has authored 12 books and monographs and more than 60 articles and papers. He has published in *Marketing Research, Journal of Consumer Research, Journal of Business Research, Journal of the Academy of Marketing Science, Journal of Marketing Education* (awarded the year's outstanding article), and *Journal of Business Ethics*. His most recently completed academic books are titled *Internet Marketing, Multidimensional Scaling* (with Paul E. Green and Frank J. Carmone Jr.), and *Computer Assisted Decisions in Marketing* (with William R. Swinyard).

Gerald S. Albaum is Research Professor at the Robert O. Anderson Schools of Management, the University of New Mexico; Professor Emeritus of Marketing, University of Oregon; and Senior Research Fellow, IC2 Institute, University of Texas at Austin. His major teaching areas include international marketing and marketing research methodology. His research interests include measurement and scaling, issues in research methodology, direct selling relationships, management style and decision making, foreign market entry strategy, and international marketing. Much of his more recent research has been cross-cultural/national in nature.

He has written numerous articles published in journals including *Journal of Marketing Research, Journal of the Academy of Marketing Science, Journal of the Market Research Society* (now the *International Journal of Market Research*), *Psychological Reports, Journal of Retailing, Journal of Business, Journal of Business Research*, and *Journal of Personal Selling and Sales Management*. He is the author, coauthor, or editor of 18 books and monographs including *International Marketing and Export Management,* Fifth Edition (with E. Duerr and J. Strandskov), published by Pearson Education Limited (UK), 2005, and *Research for Marketing Decisions,* Fifth Edition (with P. Green and D. Tull), published by Prentice Hall, 1988.